Mass Communication Law

Cases and Comment

Fourth Edition

Mass Communication Law

Cases and Comment

Fourth Edition

DONALD M. GILLMOR
Professor of Journalism and Mass Communication
University of Minnesota

JEROME A. BARRON
Dean and Professor of Law, National Law Center
George Washington University

West Publishing Company
St. Paul—New York—Los Angeles—San Francisco

50 West Kellogg Boulevard
P.O. Box 3526
St. Paul, Minnesota 55165

Printed in the United States of America

Library of Congress Cataloging in Publication Data

Gillmor, Donald M.
Mass communication law.

Includes index.
1. Press law—United States—Cases. 2. Telecommunication—Law and legislation—United States—Cases.
I. Barron, Jerome A. II. Title.
KF2750.A7G5 1984 343.73'0998 83–17042
ISBN 0–314–78005–X 347.303998

For

Sophie, Vivian, and Peter

and for

Myra, Jonathan, David, and Jennifer

Contents

Table of Cases

Principal cases are in italic type. Nonprincipal cases are in roman type. References are to pages.

C

D

E

F

G

Y

Z

Preface

We have learned from the teachers who use this book that they like our practice of letting the courts speak for themselves. We have extended this pattern in the fourth edition of *Mass Communication Law.* Two new and, we hope, helpful features of this edition are that we have tried to include more of the current law review literature than in the past, and we have added *Media Law Reporter* citations to all recent cases. The fourth edition retains the auxiliary portions of previous editions: diagrams of state and federal court systems with applicable changes, an expanded glossary of legal terms, and an outline on legal research are included. These should be of particular use to journalism, broadcast, and advertising students. We have also added the Constitution of the United States.

Changes in the organization of this edition are a response either to developments in the field or to comments and criticisms of colleagues and students who use the book. Thus, the libel chapter, Chapter II, has abandoned the retrospective approach to the *New York Times v. Sullivan—Gertz* case law which was used in the third edition. A straightforward chronological approach beginning with *New York Times* and proceeding to *Gertz* and later developments is used instead.

In place of a separate chapter, we have made obscenity the final section of Chapter VIII, Selected Problems of Law and Journalism. On the other hand, the material on public access to the print media, which comprised a section of the Selected Problems chapter in past editions, has been placed in a separate chapter in response to the comments of our users who find the combination of ethical and First Amendment issues which surround the access question to be a source of lively discussion and interest among their students.

The electronic media chapter, Chapter IX, has been substantially revised to reflect the increasing importance of cable. The deregulation activities of the Reagan-era FCC, in both cable and broadcasting, have been emphasized. Some general information about new technological developments in the electronic media and the problems these developments pose for governance are also discussed. A new section on the "reasonable access" case, *CBS v. FCC,* has also been included in the electronic media chapter.

As in past editions, this book remains a truly collaborative effort. Primary responsibility for authoring and editing the following chapters and sections is as follows—Professor Barron: Chapters I, VII, and IX and three sections of Chapter VIII: The Media and the Labor Laws, Copyright and the Electronic Media and Lobbying and Campaign Regulation; Professor Gillmor: Chapters II, III, IV, V, and VI and six sections of Chapter VIII: The Law and Regulation of Advertising, The Press and the Antitrust Laws, Copyright, Unfair Competition and the Print Media, Lotteries, Students and the First Amendment and Pornography. In this edition, each author critically edited the work of the other in an effort to present fairly and accurately both journalistic and legal views. Much of the book is written from the perspective of the potential media defendant.

The principal aim of the authors of this fourth edition has been to meet the needs of faculties and students in schools and departments of journalism and mass communication. For an undergraduate journalism school, a basic course might begin with a review of the first section of Chapter I, An Introduction To The Study Of The First Amendment.

After that, the following sequence is suggested: Chapter II (libel), Chapter III (privacy), Chapter IV (journalist's privilege), Chapter V (access to legislative and executive branches), Chapter VI (access to judicial process and the range of free press–fair trial problems), Chapter VIII (the sections on antitrust and labor laws and the two copyright sections), the problems of the electronic media dealing with equal time and the fairness doctrine discussed in Chapter IX. Advertising and public relations students ought to be assigned the appropriate sections of Chapter VIII. Advanced courses probably will want to begin with a study of the entire First Amendment chapter (Chapter I), and then move to questions of access to the print media discussed in Chapter VII, antitrust problems and advertising discussed in Chapter VIII and segments of the electronic media chapter, (Chapter IX).

This book can be and is used in law schools as well as in journalism programs. Its authors, a journalist and a lawyer, continue to try to indicate in each chapter the many ways in which law and journalism interact. Dean Barron suggests the following sequence of assignments for a survey course in media law in a law school: Ch. IX (electronic media), Ch. VIII, the section on copyright and the electronic media, Ch. VI (free press and fair trial), Ch. II (libel), Ch. III (privacy and the press), Ch. IV (journalist's privilege), and Ch. VII (public access to the print media). The suggested sequence of chapters is unlikely to repeat subjects found elsewhere in the law school curriculum and at the same time provide a survey of some of the most difficult and important issues in contemporary media law.

Professor Gillmor, ever indebted to former graduate and undergraduate students, wishes to acknowledge the very real contributions of each of the following to particular segments of the manuscript: Everette Dennis (long since a colleague and co-author), legal research and information as property; Richard Kielbowicz and Patrick Parsons, freedom of information; Kent Middleton, advertising and commercial speech; Robert Drechsel, libel, privacy, and freedom of information; Kermit Netteburg, copyright and camera in the courtroom; Herbert Terry and Arlette Soderberg, legal research and broadcast law and regulation; Robert Trager, student press law and free press-fair trial; Charles Whitney, libel; Peter Flanderka, antitrust; and Derek Cathcart for his "dissertation" on pragmatic logic. Most are now colleagues teaching their own courses in mass communication law.

Dean Barron wishes once again to express his thanks to La Mona Rivers, Executive Assistant to the Dean, for wondrous patience, skill, and care in working on the manuscript. He would also like to thank Mark A. Warnquist of the second year class at the National Law Center, George Washington University, for the high quality of his research assistance.

Invaluable to any student of press law are the annual meetings of the Communication Law section of the Practising Law Institute and their comprehensive handbooks, *Communications Law*, the *Media Law Reporter* of the Bureau of National Affairs, a must for schools without law libraries, and the publication of the Reporters Committee for Freedom of the Press, *The News Media and the Law.*

When a casebook proceeds from one edition to another, there is always the danger that the outdated furniture of earlier editions will remain in place in the new edition. We have tied hard to discard much of that old furniture. This edition is a substantial rewrite of its predecessor. Our goal has been not to write an encyclopedia of mass media law but rather to provide a book which will be informative and teachable at the same time. We shall hear from you, our students and colleagues, as to whether or not we have succeeded.

DONALD M. GILLMOR
Minneapolis, Minn.
JEROME A. BARRON
Washington, D. C.
October 1983

The Federal Court System

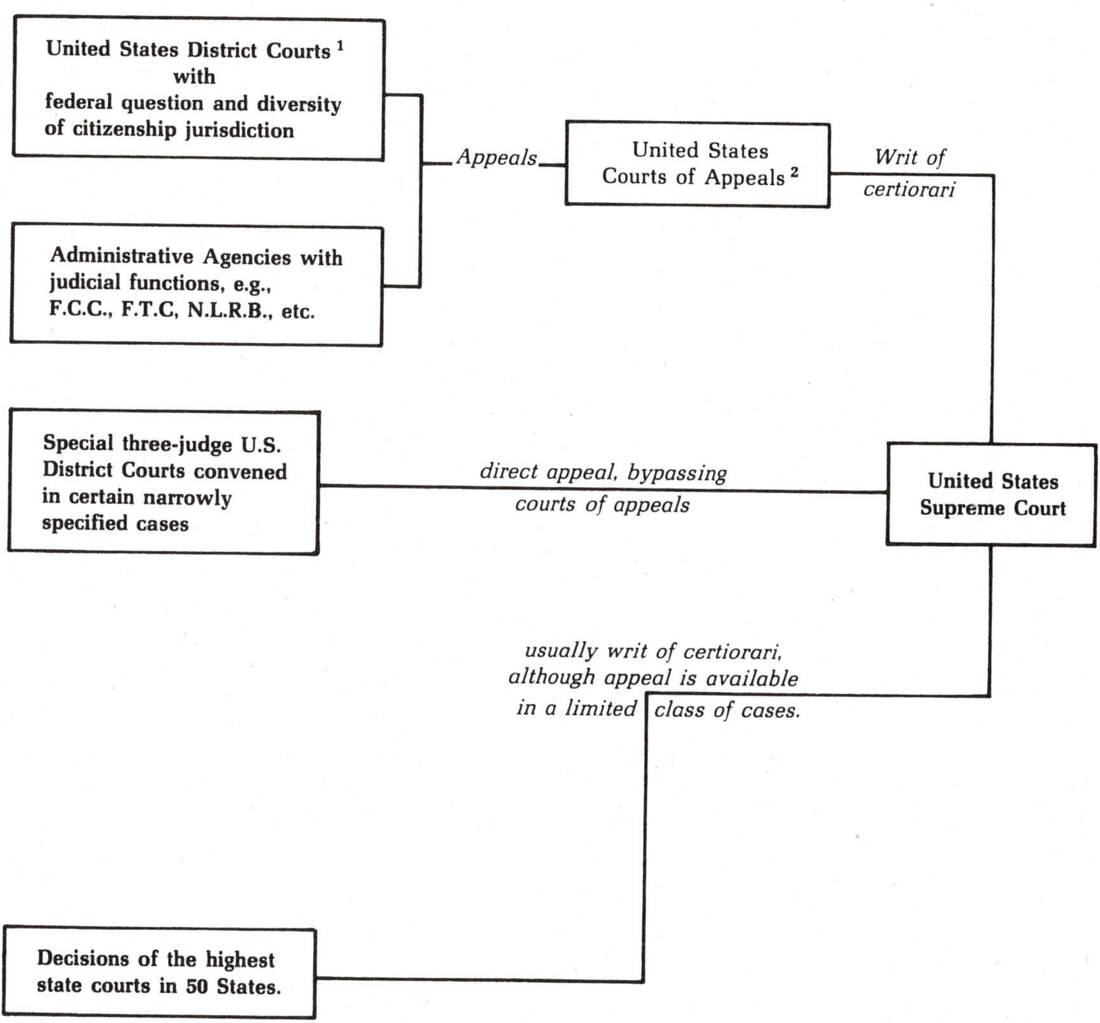

1. There is a least one federal district court in every state.

2. The United States is divided into eleven numbered federal judicial circuits, plus the United States Court of Appeals for the District of Columbia. In addition, there is the United States Courts of Appeals for the Federal Circuit which was established by the Congress in 1982. This court succeeded to the appellate jurisdiction of the United States Court of Claims and the United States Court of Customs and Patent Appeals, both of which were abolished. Another new court, the United States Claims Court, succeeded to the trial jurisdiction of the old United States Court of Claims.

A State Court System

The state court system outlined below is one example of a state court system. It is intended to provide a guide to the state judicial process for the student who is unfamiliar with the organization of state courts. There is substantial variation from state to state. The following figure illustrates the California Court system.

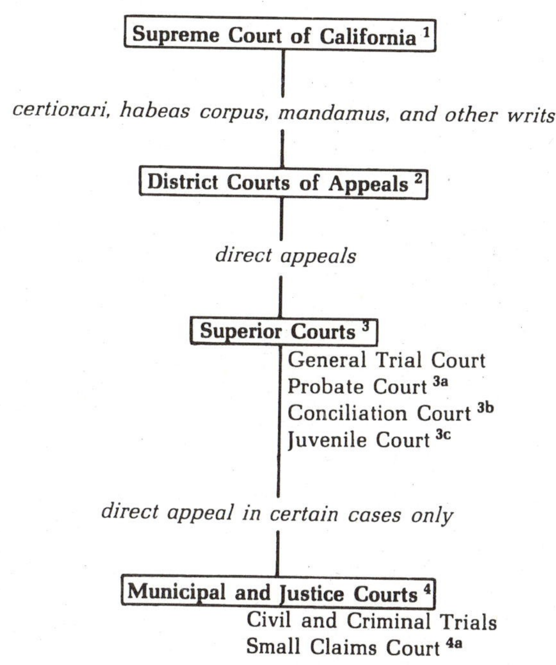

1. Has no obligatory appellate jurisdiction; that is, it reviews cases by granting petitions for writs of certiorari and thus retains complete discretionary control of its jurisdiction.

2. Consequently the great bulk of cases reach final decision in these five District Courts of Appeals.

3. Superior Court, the trial court of general jurisdiction, also has three special divisions: the General Trial Court, Probate Court, Conciliation Court and Juvenile Court.

3a. This court has jurisdiction over the administration of estates, wills, and related matters.

3b. The conciliation court is a rather unique institution that takes jurisdiction over family disputes that could lead to the dissolution of a marriage to the detriment of a minor child.

3c. The juvenile court considers certain types of cases involving persons under 18 years of age.

4. There is one Superior Court in each county. The Municipal and Justice Courts represent subdivisions of each county by population. These courts are trial courts with limited jurisdiction. Their civil jurisdiction is in cases involving generally less than $5000 in controversy. They also have original and exclusive criminal jurisdiction for violations of local ordinances within their districts.

4a. The small claims court is the familiar forum used to settle small disputes, here less than $500, using informal procedure and prohibiting lawyers for the disputing parties.

Note: Superior Court is usually the last state court to which a decision of these lowest courts can be appealed. It is possible that a case from one of these courts could be ineligible for further state review, and could have further review only in the U.S. Supreme Court.

A "Brief" on Legal Research for Journalists

Cases, statutes and constitutions are the primary stuff of the law. If you cannot retrieve and read them, you are forever doomed to secondary sources—someone else will have read and interpreted them for you.

Many campuses will not have law school libraries. There are alternatives. Metropolitan counties often have substantial law libraries in their courthouses or government centers. State capitols usually house law libraries. In addition, general public libraries, political science departments and private law firms may be able to assist you.

A new and invaluable resource for college, school or department is the Bureau of National Affairs *Media Law Reporter* (Med.L.Rptr.). On a weekly basis it reports almost all court cases having a bearing on journalism and communication law. Issues include news notes, occasional bibliographies, Supreme Court schedules or dockets, and special reports (for example, a 1977 report on the federal Freedom of Information Act). The heart of its content is the presentation of complete decisions or substantial case excerpts covering the broadest spectrum of mass communication law. Subscriptions are $358 per year, after an initial $413 first-year charge. The service is a must for schools and departments of journalism.

A more general predecessor is *United States Law Week* (U.S.L.W.) at $349 after an initial $364 first-year charge. It comes in two parts, one providing Supreme Court opinions shortly after they are rendered, the other federal statutes, administrative agency rulings, and significant lower court decisions.

If you have access to a law library, you have at your fingertips an ingenious information retrieval system, much of which is now, or soon will be, computerized and thereby accessible in less laborious ways. Two computer systems now in place are Lexis and Westlaw.

Abbreviations used in the following section are part of a *Uniform System of Citation* 13th ed. (Cambridge, Mass.: Harvard Law Review Ass'n., 1981), used in all legal writing and reporting, and designed for precise communication and for brevity.

Remember that constitutions, legislative enactments, and court decisions of the jurisdiction involved are primary authorities. Treatises, law reviews, the *Restatements* of the American Law Institute, for example, are secondary sources. These sources, however, are frequently cited and accepted as persuasive authority by all levels of courts in various jurisdictions and at the federal level throughout the country. Annotations, encyclopediae, loose-leaf services and dictionaries are primarily used to find references to primary materials such as court reporters, statutes or constitutional provisions. The primary materials may after thorough examination then be cited as actual authority for a legal proposition or definition. Digests, citators and indexes are used principally to lead a researcher to primary materials.

A first step in legal research might be to find the words, the legal vocabulary of your problem. Any one of a number of law dictionaries would serve this purpose (*Black's, Ballentine's Gifis', or Oran's Law Dictionary for Non-Lawyers*). Assuming some legal knowledge of your topic, you might prefer to begin with a resource that demonstrates how state and federal courts have construed your concept. Such a work is *Words and Phrases*, an alphabetical list of words and phrases followed by abstracts of judicial decisions using them. Pocket parts or supplements inside the back cover keep this and many other legal publications up to date. Don't overlook them.

Legal encyclopediae—notably *Corpus Juris Secundum* (CJS) and *American Jurisprudence 2d* (Am.Jur.2d)—provide yet wider sweeps of legal issues and principles. Use their general index volumes and, again, don't forget the updating pocket supplements. *American Jurisprudence 2d* will reference you to *American Law Reports* (ALR, ALR 2d, ALR 3d, ALR 4th and ALR Fed.) which contains brief essays or annotations on significant legal topics suggested by the approximately 10 per cent of state and federal appellate court decisions this service considers leading cases. A good annotation may discuss all previously reported decisions on your topic. There are topical *Digests* to the first two series and a *Quick Index* for each series. ALR and ALR 2d are updated by a *Blue Book* and a *Later Case Service* respectively, ALR 3d, ALR 4th and ALR Fed. by pocket supplements.

By now you have encountered a good many *case* citations and, in West Publishing Company's *Words and Phrases* and *Corpus Juris Secundum*, Key Numbers.

All reported cases can be found in West's National Reporter System, a description of which follows.

NATIONAL REPORTER SYSTEM

West Publishing Company's National Reporter System reprints decisions of all of the highest state courts, many state appellate courts, the U.S. Supreme Court, U.S. Courts of Appeals and selected decisions of U.S. District Courts.

Decisions of the Federal Court System

Decisions of the United States Supreme Court are found in the Supreme Court Reporter (S.Ct.). A second major unofficial publication of United States Supreme Court decisions is United States Supreme Court Reports (Lawyer's Edition—L.Ed. and L.Ed.2d), which annotates leading cases. The official publication of Supreme Court decision is United States Reports (U.S.). Thus a complete (sometimes called parallel) citation for a United State Supreme Court decision will include both official and unofficial publications and appear as: *New York Times v. Sullivan, 376 U.S. 245, 84 S.Ct. 710, 11 L.Ed.2d 686 (1964).* The first number in a citation refers to a volume number, the second to a page number.

Secondary unofficial publications of Supreme Court decisions are *United States Law Week* and the Commerce Clearing House (CCH) *United States Supreme Court Bulletin*, the first publications to print the full text of Supreme Court decisions, normally within a few days, and the newer *Media Law Reporter.* Begun in 1978, *Landmark Briefs and Arguments of the Supreme Court of the United States: Constitutional Law* (Kurland & Casper, eds.) presents oral arguments and written briefs of landmark Supreme Court cases going back to 1793. Publisher is University Publications of America, Inc., Frederick, Md.

Summaries of lawyers written briefs are found in *L.Ed.2d.* Complete briefs can sometimes be obtained from law libraries or from the law firms on either side of a case. Their addresses can be found in a legal directory called *Martindale Hubbell.* Most large law libraries maintain microforms of U.S. Supreme Court records and briefs.

The Federal Reporter (F. and F.2d) currently prints decisions of the U.S. Courts of Appeals, the U.S. Court of Customs and Patent Appeals, the U.S. Court of Claims, and Temporary Emergency Court of Appeals.

The Federal Supplement (F.Supp.) contains selected decisions of U.S. District Courts and of the U.S. Customs Court, plus rulings of the Judicial Panel on Multidistrict Litigation.

Federal Rules Decisions (F.R.D.) prints U.S. District Court Decisions primarily involving the Federal Rules of Criminal and Civil Procedure, and also contains miscellaneous reports and articles.

West Military Justice Reporter includes cases decided in the United States Court of Military Appeals and selected deicisons of the Courts of Military Review.

Decisions of State Courts

Official reports of each state's highest court and some intermediate courts are usually published by the state. Some states have discontinued such publishing and have designated West as official reporter. West publishes seven regional reporters that contain decisions of the highest state court and selected intermediate appellate court decisions. The New York Supplement (N.Y.S.) contains decisions of all New York state courts including its highest court, the N. Y. Court of Appeals whose opinions are also published in the North Eastern Reporter. The California Reporter (Cal.Rptr.) contains decisions of the California Supreme Court, District Courts of Appeal and Appellate Department of Superior Court. Decisions of the California Supreme Court are also reprinted in the Pacific Reporter. The map below indicates states included in each regional reporter.

Cases, of course, can be cited as persuasive authority. But it is important in reading cases to learn to distinguish between what a court *rules* and what it says in passing (*dicta*), for example, concurring and dissenting opinions. *Dicta*, of course, can influence future decisions.

The next task is to find aids that will lead quickly to all the cases in point. For this purpose we use *Digests, Indexes*, and *Citators*. A Digest is a case finder or an index to the law. One of the best known Digests is West's *American Digest System* which cumulates all reported state and federal cases in 10-year segments or decennials, the most recent being the *Ninth Decennial Digest*, Part I, 1976–1981, cumulating five years of cases. Current cases are found in the *General Digest* and organized around the Key Number System.

Key Numbers represent principles or points of law. Once having found one or more key numbers relating to your problem, you should be able to find all the relevant cases in the *American Digest System*. Digests have been prepared for individual states, such as the Minnesota Digest, groups of neighboring states or regional digest, such as the Pacific Digest, single courts, such as the United States Supreme Court Digest, or for a court system, such as West's Federal Practice Digest, 2nd, which covers decisions of all federal courts including the U. S. Supreme Court. Each digest has a *Descriptive Word Index* to help you get started. A *Cumulative Table of Key Numbers* in the General Digest *Descriptive Word Index* will tell you which volumes of the set have digest material relating to the Key Numbers you have.

One specialized Digest is Lawyers Cooperative's *U.S. Supreme Court Reports Digest*. Volume 16 is an index. A separate index to annotations covers the annotations in *L.Ed.2d* and *ALR Federal*.

Citators trace the life history of a case, a statute, or an administrative ruling. Has it been modified, reversed, affirmed, superseded, criticized, distinguished, explained, limited, overruled or questioned? What have attorneys-general and law review writers said about a case? Is it still good authority? Has a statute been amended, appealed, or declared unconstitutional? How has it been treated by courts and periodical commentators? There are *Shepard's Citations* for every state, each region of West's National Reporter System, for lower federal courts and the U.S. Supreme Court, for federal administrative agencies, for the Code of Federal Regulations for state and federal constitutions, the U.S. and various state codes, municipal ordinances, labor law, and for the law reviews. Now to statutes.

If you know approximately when a federal statute or an amendment to a statute was passed, it can often be located in *U.S. Code, Congressional and Administrative News*. From it one can construct the legislative histories of federal statutes and review congressional committee reports. *United States Code Annotated* (U.S.C.A.) and *United States Code Service* (U.S.C.S.) are the best places to go for federal law. Both are updated by pocket parts and intervening pamphlets. Annotations include summaries of court decisions interpreting the laws, text of the Constitution and their interpretation, opinions of attorneys-general, and, occasionally, citations to law reviews or other secondary sources. There are also indexed, annotated codes for most states. Each compilation has a multi-volume index.

United States Code Congressional and Administrative News publishes the full text of Public Laws enacted, together with a selected legislative history. Of notable interest for some research purposes are the positions of various interest groups in relation to a bill.

The *United States Congressional Record* provides an edited transcript of Congressional debates. It has a *Daily Digest.* See also, the Commerce Clearing House (CCH) *Congressional Index* which provides a summary and the status of each bill, along with much useful information. The *Congressional Information Service* monthly Index and CIS Annual Abstracts provide much of the raw material of the legislative process. Full text is available on microfiche.

Rules and regulations of the federal administrative agencies, organized by subject matter, are found in the *Code of Federal Regulations* supplemented by the daily *Federal Register.* The latter includes official notices of each rulemaking and other proceedings to be conducted by agencies such as the Federal Communications Commission (FCC). In the rulemaking process FCC dockets or files, unfortunately located in Washington, D.C., often contain primary evidence in support of one regulatory position or another.[1]

One of the many loose-leaf services necessary to the study of administrative law is *Pike and Fischer Radio Regulation* (R.R. and R.R.2d). This is the most comprehensive source of FCC decisions and regulations, and statutes and court decisions pertaining to broadcasting and cable television.[2] The key to using *Pike and Fischer* expeditiously is to begin with the volume titled *Finding Aids*, which includes a "Master Index" to the Federal Communications Act paragraph numbers by which all materials are ordered. The *Current Service* volumes—presently six of them—contain up-to-date versions of laws and regulations and any pending proposals for change. The four *Digest* volumes contain subject matter digests of FCC and court actions and decisions, while the *Cases* volumes (now in Vol. 53) contain full texts. Index paragraphs in *Pike and Fischer* are referenced to sections of the amended Federal Communications Act of 1934 and to the Code of Federal Regulations.

If you do not find what you want in the *Federal Register*, the offical *FCC Annual Reports, Broadcasting Yearbook, Television Factbook*, or *Pike and Fischer*, call the FCC's public information officer and specify what you are looking for.

After you have a *Pike and Fischer* or official *FCC Reports* citation, you can use Shepard's *United States Administrative Citations* to find all subsequent citations to that FCC action. *Broadcasting* magazine will keep you posted on pending FCC actions. *Trade Regulation Reporter* (CCH) provides a like service for advertising communication and the work of the Federal Trade Commission (FTC). *Advertising Age* is the most useful counterpart trade publication. *Broadcasting* and *Advertising Age* are indexed in *Business Periodicals Index* and *Broadcasting* has published its own comprehensive indexes for the years 1972–1981. *Editor & Publisher* is the newspaper industry's leading trade journal.

There is a monthly *U.S. Catalog of Government Publications* and a *State Checklist of Government Documents.* The U.S. Catalog is a monthly compilation of all federal executive, legislative and administrative documents open to the public. It has cumulative annual indexes and some cumulative multi-year indexes.

1. Erwin G. Krasnow and G. Gail Crotts, *Inside the FCC: An Information Searchers Guide*, Public Telecommunications Review 5:49–56 (July/August 1975).

2. Don R. LeDuc, *Broadcast Legal Documentation: A Fourth-Dimensional Guide*, 17 Journal of Broadcasting 131–145 (Spring 1973); Joseph M. Foley, *Broadcast Regulation Research: A Primer for Non-Lawyers*, 17 Journal of Broadcasting 147–157 (Spring 1973). See also, Henry Fischer, *Uses of Pike & Fischer*, Broadcast Monographs No. 1, Issues in Broadcast Regulation 134–138 (1974); Russell Eagen, *How a Broadcast Attorney Researches Law*, Broadcast Monographs No. 1, Issues in Broadcast Regulation, 139–143 (1974).

When primary research is completed, it is time to survey the *Index to Legal Periodicals* to see what others have written about your topic. Some advise beginning legal research with the *Index* in order to survey the boundaries of a topic. It is tempting, however, to rely too heavily on these secondary sources at too early a stage. There is also an *Index to Foreign Legal Periodicals* and a new (Jan. 1, 1980) more comprehensive *Legal Resource Index* on microfilm with paper edition counterpart, *Current Law Index.* LRI is much broader in coverage than the older *Index to Legal Periodicals* and includes the *New York Times, Wall Street Journal*, and *Christian Science Monitor.*

Books or textbooks on legal topics are called *treatises* and a library's holdings are indexed in its card catalogue. A *Horn Book* is a single volume summary of a field of law. A *Nutshell* is an even more drastic summary. There are a number of legal bibliographies, among them *Harvard Law School Library* and *Current Publications in Legal and Related Fields.*

The American Law Institute's *Restatements of the Law* are attempts to reorganize, simplify, and move case law toward comprehensible codes. Begin with the *General Index to the Restatement of the Law.*

For legal style and citation forms see *A Uniform System of Citation* published by the Harvard Law Review Association, and sometimes referred to as the Harvard Blue Book. Any standard text on legal research and writing will provide similar information.[3]

3. Cohen, How To Find the Law, 7th ed. (St. Paul: West Publishing Co., 1976); Cohen, Legal Research in a Nutshell, 3d ed. (St. Paul: West Publishing Co., 1978); Jacobstein and Mersky, Fundamentals of Legal Research 2d ed. (Mineola: Foundation Press, 1981); Jacobstein and Mersky, Legal Research Illustrated 2d ed. (Mineola: Foundation Press, 1981); Price, Bitner and Bysiewicz, Effective Legal Research, 4th ed. (Boston: Little, Brown, 1979); Sprowl, Manual for Computer-Assisted Legal Research (Chicago: American Bar Foundation, 1976). The above are intended for lawyers and law students. You may also find it useful to consult textbooks for paralegals, for example, e.g. Statsky, Introduction to Paralegalism: Perspectives, Problems and Skills, 2d ed. (St. Paul: West Publishing Co., 1982).

Mass Communication Law

Cases and Comment

Fourth Edition

The First Amendment Impact on Mass Communication: The Theory, the Practice, and the Problems

AN INTRODUCTION TO THE STUDY OF THE FIRST AMENDMENT

In 1791, the First Amendment to the United States Constitution was enacted:

> Congress shall make no law respecting an establishment of religion, or prohibiting the free exercise thereof; or abridging the freedom of speech, or of the press; or the right of the people peaceably to assemble, and to petition the government for a redress of grievances.

The First Amendment wisely guarantees, but does not define, freedom of speech and press. It should be noted that the specific addressee of First Amendment protection is Congress. Nothing in the original Constitution which was ratified by the states imposed any limitations on state legislatures with regard to freedom of speech or press. Whether postrevolutionary America would follow the darker pages in colonial history and hold newspaper editors guilty of legislative contempt and whether the new state governors would follow the precedent set by the royal colonial governors and seek to have newspaper editors indicted for seditious libel were matters that the First Amendment was basically helpless to resolve. All such issues were governed by state rather than federal constitutions.

There the matter stood until 1925 when, in an otherwise insignificant case involving a now forgotten and ultimately repentant Communist, Benjamin Gitlow, the Supreme Court in Gitlow v. New York, 268 U.S. 652, 666 (1925), in a casual statement not necessary to the decision said:

> For present purposes we may and do assume that freedom of speech and of the press—which are protected by the First Amendment from abridgment by Congress—are among the fundamental personal rights and "liberties" protected by the due process clause of the Fourteenth Amendment from impairment by the states.

The textual justification in the Constitution for guaranteeing constitutional protection to freedom of speech and press under the federal constitution was achieved by interpretation of the due process clause of the Fourteenth Amendment enacted in 1868 by the Reconstruction Congress to assure legal equality to the recently emancipated slaves. The second sentence of Section 1 of the Fourteenth Amendment stated:

> No State shall make or enforce any law which shall abridge the privileges or immunities of citizens of the United States; *nor shall any state deprive any person of life, liberty, or property, without due process of law;* nor deny to any person within its jurisdiction the

equal protection of the laws. [Emphasis added.]

The consequence of saying that freedom of speech and of the press were protected by the due process clause of the Fourteenth Amendment from infringement by the states was an important advance in securing liberty of the press. Although the state constitutions have provisions protecting freedom of expression, often their language offers more comfort to state regulation of the press than is the case with the more protective and encompassing language of the First Amendment. To be sure, it is possible to argue that since freedom of the press on the state level is based on the due process clause of the Fourteenth Amendment rather than on explicit language in the First Amendment, the latitude for state regulation of the press is greater than that allowed the federal government. This two-tiered First Amendment theory was advanced by Justice John Marshall Harlan in a special concurring opinion he wrote in Roth v. United States, 354 U.S. 476 (1957), the case in which the Court held that obscenity was not constitutionally protected speech.

The use of the Fourteenth Amendment to make constitutional limitations such as the guarantee of free speech and press binding on the states as well as the federal government has given that amendment an enormous role in the development of constitutional liberty in the United States. The extension of the constitutional guarantee of freedom of speech and press to the states has been of great significance. For a view that state constitutions themselves gave early nurture to freedom of speech, press and greatly influenced the federal courts, see Blanchard, "Filling in the Void: Speech and Press in State Courts Prior to *Gitlow*," in Chamberlin and Brown (eds.), *The First Amendment Reconsidered* (1982).

The First Amendment has rarely been used to invalidate federal legislation on the ground that the legislation is impermissibly restrictive of freedom of speech and press. Indeed when the most dangerous federal legislation limiting freedom of expression ever to come before the Supreme Court in peacetime, the anti-Communist Smith Act case, Dennis v. United States, 341 U.S. 494 (1951) was reviewed, the Court held the challenged law valid, even though it undoubtedly restricted First Amendment values in the interest of governmental self-preservation.

But as the cases and comment on free speech and freedom of the press in this chapter illustrate, numerous state statutes have been declared invalid as violative of the First Amendment since that Amendment is now binding on the states through the due process clause of the Fourteenth Amendment.

The determination on the part of the Framers of the American Constitution to assure protection for freedom of speech and press did not arise in a vacuum. English and American history prior to the American Revolution had persuaded the drafters of the First Amendment of the need for such assurance. Basic to an understanding of the First Amendment, both in terms of its origins and development, is John Milton's great essay in defense of a free press, *The Areopagitica.*

John Milton (1608–1674) was one of the great English poets. A republican in a monarchical age, the power of Milton's language and thought in his *Areopagitica* has made the essay a formidable obstacle to licensing and restraint of the press through the centuries. *The Areopagitica* was written as a protest to government licensing and censorship of the press; although Milton later was himself to serve as a censor for Oliver Cromwell.

In the middle of the seventeenth century, the Parliament of England passed a law licensing the press. The Order of the Lords and Commons, June 14, 1643, forbade the publication of any book, pamphlet, or paper which was published or imported without registration by the Stationers' Company. The Stationers' Company, formed in 1557, has been described as follows:

> The exclusive privilege of printing and publishing in the English dominions was given to 97 London stationers and their successors by regular apprenticeship. All printing was thus centralised in London under the immediate inspection of the Government. No one could legally print, without special license, who did not belong to the Stationers' Company. The Company had power to search for and to seize publications which infringed their privilege. Jebb. ed., Introduction, Milton, *Areopagitica,* xxiii, (Cambridge University, 1918).

Later the licensing authority was divided between various royal and ecclesiastical authorities. The 1643 law, against which Milton directed his famous 1644 pamphlet in defense of freedom of the press, authorized official searches for unlicensed presses and prohibited the publication of anything unlicensed. The 1643 statute was designed to prevent the "defamation of Religion and Government." In Milton's view, truth in both the spheres of religion and government was more likely to emerge from free discussion than from repression. What follows is the most famous and widely quoted passage from *The Areopagitica:*

> And though all the winds of doctrine were let loose to play upon the earth, so Truth be in the field, we do injuriously by licensing and prohibiting to misdoubt her strength. Let her and Falsehood grapple; who ever knew truth put to the worse, in a free and open encounter? Jebb, supra, p. 58.

This passage marked the beginnings of what has become an underlying theme of First Amendment theory. This is the marketplace of ideas theory which was given fresh life by Justice Oliver Wendell Holmes in a famous dissent after World War I in Abrams v. United States, 250 U.S. 616 (1919). In this view, truth is best secured in the open marketplace of ideas. Therefore any government restraint which tends to distort or chill the free play of ideas and, thus, the quest for truth should not be permitted. The challenge that the idea of liberty of expression makes to the infirmity of the human condition should not be underestimated. Also we should remember that even Milton was not an absolutist with regard to freedom of expression. He did not believe in religious freedom for Roman Catholics. But Milton's hostility to the licensing of the press by government and his evident passion for a higher plateau of freedom of expression has been a powerful influence in the development of freedom of the press in the United States. See Siebert, *Freedom of the Press in England, 1476–1776* (1952).

The licensing system ended in England in 1695, but licensing continued in the American colonies several decades thereafter. Gradually, prosecution for criminal or seditious libel supplanted licensing as the instrument for governmental restraint of the press in America in the period prior to the advent of the American Revolution. The common law crime of seditious libel made criticism of government a matter for criminal prosecution. While such prosecutions were not frequent in colonial America, they did occur.

The most famous such prosecution involved a New York printer, John Peter Zenger, editor of the *New York Weekly Journal.* Zenger's paper was used by politicians as a relentless forum for criticism of the colonial governor of New York, William Cosby. Zenger was arrested in 1734 on a charge of publishing seditious libels and jailed for eight months before trial. In August 1735, a jury, ignoring a judge's instructions, determined that Zenger was not guilty. The case thus became the most celebrated victory for freedom of the press in the pre-Revolutionary period.

It was no mean achievement for Zenger's attorney, Andrew Hamilton, to win the case, since, under the common law of seditious libel, the truth of the utterance was irrelevant.

The judge rather than the jury had the responsibility of deciding whether the publication complained of constituted seditious libel. The role of the jury was simply to ascertain whether the defendant had published the offending article. These features of the law of seditious libel gave freedom of expression little breathing space; and in England in 1792 Fox's Libel Act finally altered the law of seditious libel to make truth a defense and to give the jury rather than the judge the power to determine whether the publication was or was not seditious libel. See Emerson, *The System Of Freedom Of Expression* 99 (1970).

Unfortunately, seditious libel had proponents in the newly independent United States.

Congress in 1798 at the behest of the Federalist Party enacted four acts directed against the subversive activities of foreigners in the United States. These became known as the Alien and Sedition Acts. The Federalist fear of radical sympathizers with France, French agents, and hostility toward Republican journalist critics of the Federalist administration led to the passage of the laws. These Acts were the Naturalization Act, the Act Concerning Aliens, the Act Respecting Enemies, and the Act for the Punishment of Crimes. The last mentioned, known as the Sedition Act, has been of great interest to First Amendment historians. Unlike the common law crime of seditious libel, the new law permitted truth as a defense, proof of malice was required, and the jury was permitted to pass on both questions of law and fact. Punishment was set by the statute. Specifically the Act provided that the publishing or printing of any false, scandalous, or malicious writings to bring the government, Congress, or the president into contempt or disrepute, excite popular hostility to them, incite resistance to the law of the United States, or encourage hostile designs against the United States was a misdemeanor. Republicans led by Jefferson and Madison held the law to be a violation of the First Amendment, and among those convicted of violating the law were some of the leading Republican journalists. The Republicans contended that the law was being interpreted to punish and silence Republican critics of the Federalist Administration.

Federalists defended the statute as necessary to the right of government to self-preservation. The question of the constitutionality of the Act was never brought before the Supreme Court, although constitutional historians contend that it would have been upheld by the justices who sat on the Court during John Adams's presidency.

For those who viewed the First Amendment as a rejection of the English law of seditious libel, the enactment of the Sedition Act was obviously unconstitutional. For those who viewed the First Amendment as not promising an absolute protection of speech, the passing of the Act so soon after the Revolution and ratification of the Constitution was proof that not all governmental restraint of expression was prohibited by the First Amendment.

The question of whether the Sedition Act could be consistent with the First Amendment was not directly resolved because the issue of its validity never came to the Court. The Sedition Act expired on March 3, 1801.

One noted American constitutional scholar, Leonard Levy, has argued that the First Amendment was designed to prohibit only prior restraint of the press (administrative censorship, such as licensing), not seditious libel. See Levy, *The Legacy Of Suppression* 247–248 (1960).

The question of the constitutional status of the Alien and Sedition Acts was finally put to rest in the famous case of New York Times v. Sullivan, 376 U.S. 254 (1964), in which the Supreme Court narrowly contracted the scope of libel law. In *Sullivan,* Justice William Brennan, speaking for the Court, declared: "Although the Sedition Act was never tested in this Court, the attack upon its validity has carried the day in the court of history." 376 U.S. 254 at 276.

For one commentator, the *New York Times v. Sullivan* statement on seditious libel was a crucial step in the continuous reinterpretation the First Amendment receives from the Supreme Court. The distinguished First Amendment scholar Professor Harry Kalven considered the crime of seditious libel incompatible with freedom of expression:

> The concept of seditious libel strikes at the very heart of democracy. Political freedom ends when government can use its powers and its courts to silence the critics. See Kalven, *The New York Times Cases: A Note On 'The Central Meaning of the First Amendment',* Supreme Court Review 191 at 205 (1964).

Professor Kalven believed the repudiation of seditious libel had furnished a new key to understanding the meaning of First Amendment protection:

> The Court did not simply, in the face of an awkward history, definitively put to rest the status of the Sedition Act. More important, it found in the controversy over seditious libel the clue "to the central meaning of the First Amendment." The choice of language was unusually apt.
>
> * * *
>
> The central meaning of the Amendment is that seditious libel cannot be made the subject of government sanction. * * * It is now not only the citizen's privilege to criticize his government, it is his duty. At this point in its rhetoric and sweep, the opinion almost literally incorporated the citizen as ruler, Alexander Meiklejohn's thesis that in a democracy the citizen as ruler is our most important public official. Kalven, *supra*, pp. 208–209.

In *New York Times v. Sullivan,* the Court cited John Stuart Mill as well as Milton for its view that even a false statement, so long as it is not calculated falsehood, merits First Amendment protection when the communication at issue involves criticism of elected government officials. The Court's citation to the work of John Stuart Mill is not surprising. Mill, along with Milton, has been one of the vital influences in First Amendment thought.

One of the great influences on modern First Amendment law was this English political philosopher and economist who lived long after the enactment of the First Amendment. John Stuart Mill (1806–1873), wrote widely on philosophy and economics, but it has been justly said that his essay, *On Liberty Of Thought And Discussion* (1859) was his "most lasting contribution to political thought." For Mill, "freedom of thought and investigation, freedom of discussion, and the freedom of self-controlled moral judgment were goods in their own right."

Actually, it is not surprising that Mill, like Milton, should be cited frequently in the vast literature that has arisen interpreting the meaning of freedom of speech and press, much of it in the form of the decisions of the justices of the United States Supreme Court. Modern First Amendment law did not get any extended or serious attention from the Supreme Court until cases involving a clash between governmental censorship and freedom of expression came about in the period after American involvement in World War I.

Constitutional scholars have more or less agreed with Professor Zechariah Chafee's observation that the Framers of the Constitution had no very clear idea of what they intended the guarantee of freedom of speech and press to mean. Chafee, *Free Speech in the United States* (1954). For thoughtful justices, like Justice Holmes, it became important to try to develop a rationale for constitutional protection of freedom of speech and press. In cases like Abrams v. United States, 250 U.S. 616, (1919), Justice Holmes used the marketplace of ideas metaphor to give theoretical underpinning to the First Amendment. The similarity between the Holmesian marketplace of ideas concept of freedom of expression and Mill's rationale for liberty of thought and discussion is striking. It should be noted also that even when justices serving after Holmes returned to the marketplace of ideas theory, words used to describe the theory are very close to the language used by Mill.

Thus, Justice William O. Douglas wrote, dissenting in the Supreme Court decision validating the anti-Communist prosecutions of the fifties, Dennis v. United States, 341 U.S. 494 at 584 (1951):

> When ideas compete in the market for acceptance, full and free discussion expires the false and they gain few adherents. Full and free discussion even of ideas we hate encourages the testing of our own prejudices and preconceptions. Full and free discussion keeps a society from becoming stagnant and unprepared for the stresses and strains that work to tear all civilizations apart.

Mill had defended freedom of expression for very similar reasons nearly a century before in *On Liberty Of Thought And Discussion:*

> But the peculiar evil of silencing the expression of an opinion is, that it is robbing the human race; posterity as well as the existing generation; those who dissent from the opinion, still more than those who hold it. If the opinion is right, they are deprived of the opportunity of exchanging error for truth; if wrong, they lose, what is almost as great a benefit, the clearer perception and livelier impression of truth, produced by its collision with error. See Lindsay, ed., *Mill, Utilitarianism, Liberty and Representative Government* 104 (1951).

The marketplace of ideas theory of freedom of speech, with its traditional aversion to governmental intervention, has been crucially and controversially altered in the case of the electronic media. See text, Chapter IX. But even in that area of First Amendment concern, the continuing impact and resiliency of Mill's thought is demonstrated by the Supreme Court's citation of Mill in 1969 when the Court sustained the FCC's fairness doctrine and personal attack rules against a claim of invalidity under the First Amendment. Red Lion Broadcasting Co. v. FCC, 395 U.S. 367 (1969). In *Red Lion,* Mill was cited by the Court in support of the governmental regulatory doctrines as follows:

> The expression of views opposing those which broadcasters permit to be aired in the first place need not be confined solely to the broadcasters themselves as proxies. "Nor is it enough that he should hear the arguments of his own adversaries from his own teachers, presented as they state them, and accompanied by what they offer as refutations. That is not the way to do justice to the arguments, or bring them into real contact with his own mind. He must be able to hear them from persons who actually believe them; who defend them in earnest, and do their very utmost for them." J. S. Mill, *On Liberty* 32 (R. McCallum ed. 1947).

For some the citation of Mill to support any kind of governmental interference with the press will seem heretical. For others, it will be seen as entirely consistent with Mill's passion for liberty of discussion and hostility to censorship, whether that censorship is public or private.

Despite the emphasis which the foregoing discussion has given the principle of unfettered free discussion as advocated by thinkers such as Mill and Milton, it should not be thought there is any unanimity with regard to the principle of free discussion as an ultimate value.

Thus, the New Left political philosopher, Herbert Marcuse, believed Mill's writings assumed that rational beings participate in free discussion, while in reality most of contemporary humanity are not rational but are manipulated beings, manipulated by media for commercial purposes and by government for political ones. Thus, the glorious concept of tolerance for all ideas, advocated by Milton and Mill, is for Marcuse a repressive tolerance. Marcuse was hostile to the marketplace of ideas. He thought traditional tools for elaborating the proper claims of freedom of expression against the claims of the state for curtailment of expression in the interest of security, such as the clear and present danger doctrine, were unusable. Marcuse wanted to substitute "precensorship" for "the more or less hidden censorship that permeates the free media." See Marcuse, *Repressive Tolerance in Wolff, Moore, and Marcuse, a Critique of Pure Tolerance* (1965).

For still others the wisest course for the future would be to cleave to the following distillation of First Amendment experience as described by Justice Douglas:

> What kind of First Amendment would best serve our needs as we approach the 21st century may be an open question. But the old fashioned First Amendment that we have is the Court's only guideline; and one hard and fast principle has served us through days of calm and eras of strife and I would abide by it until a new First Amendment is adopted. That means, as I view it, that TV and radio, as well as the more conventional methods for disseminating news, are all included in the concept of "press" as used in the First Amendment and therefore are entitled to live under the laissez faire regime which the First Amendment sanctions. Columbia Broadcasting System v. Democratic National Committee, 412 U.S. 94 (1973).

The Supreme Court like most of the American bar, as the subsequent cases in this chapter will illustrate, has engaged in a long-standing practice of making interchangeable use of free speech cases in freedom of the press cases and vice versa.

Although the interchangeable use of the freedom of speech and freedom of the press clauses may have characterized constitutional adjudication in the past, new attention has now been directed to the question of whether the free speech and free press clauses have distinct missions. In 1975, Justice Potter Stewart gave a lecture at Yale Law School in what can now be seen in retrospect as a most significant launching of a new conception of the free press clause. Justice Stewart declared that alone among constitutional guarantees "the Free Press Clause extends protection to an institution." Justice Stewart observed: "The publishing business is, in short, the only organized private business that is given explicit constitutional protection." See Stewart, *"Or of the Press,"* 26 Hastings L.J. 631, 633–34 (1975).

In the Stewart thesis, the freedom of the press clause is designed to protect the press *qua* press. In a sense, it is the antithesis of Justice Felix Frankfurter's conception of freedom of the press as reflected in his concurring opinion in Pennekamp v. Florida, 328 U.S. 331 (1946): "Freedom of the press, however, is not an end in itself but a means to the end of a free society." In the Stewart thesis, direct protection of the press is the function of the press clause. Justice Stewart interprets the freedom of the press clause as follows: "[The] primary purpose of the constitutional guarantee of a free press was * * * to create a fourth institution outside the Government as an additional check on the three official branches." Reactions to the ramifications of the Stewart conception of the press clause permeate recent First Amendment litigation. In the editorial privilege amendment to the *New York Times v. Sullivan* rule fashioned by the United States Court of Appeals for the Second Circuit in Herbert v. Lando, 568 F.2d 974 (2d Cir. 1977), reversed 441 U.S. 153 (1979), text, p. 289, Justice Stewart's idea that the press clause has a distinctive protective mission played a large role. The contention in *Lando* that the free press clause extends special First Amendment protection to editorial decision making to the point that journalists and editors may be deemed excused from some of the customary demands of civil discovery was rejected in the decision by six of the nine justices who passed on the issue.

The issue of whether the free press clause gave a special status to the press arose again to some extent in the so-called corporate speech case, First National Bank of Boston v. Bellotti, 435 U.S. 765 (1978). In that case, the Supreme Court held that Massachusetts could not limit free speech because of the corporate identity of the speaker by attempting through a statutory prohibition against corporate efforts to influence voting in a state referendum on matters of public importance not affecting the property, business, or assets of the corporation. In what was possibly an oblique slap at the thesis that the press clause accords the press a special First Amendment status, Justice Lewis Powell observed for the Court that the inherent value of speech is not affected by the status of the speaker. Although the Court conceded that recent press cases had accorded the press a special "and constitutionally recognized role," Powell nevertheless observed: "But the press does not have a monopoly on either the First Amendment or the ability to enlighten." Chief Justice Warren Burger, in a concurring opinion in the corporate speech case, declared that the Supreme Court had not definitively decided the question of whether the press clause has a separate function distinct from that of the speech clause. However, the Chief Justice appeared to enter the lists against a view of the press clause of First Amendment protection which would accord the press a uniquely privileged status: "In short, the First Amendment does not 'belong' to any definable category of persons or entities: it belongs to all who exercise its freedoms."

What the student of the law of mass communications must recognize at the outset, however, is that the constitutional protection given to freedom of speech and press covers the whole spectrum of the means of communication. The First Amendment has been extended from its specific eighteenth-century addressees mentioned in the constitution itself—free speech and free press—to new media of communication undreamed of in the eighteenth century, such as the sound truck, radio, television, and the movies. Occasionally, the Supreme Court has tried to deal with each medium in terms of its own problems. For example Justice Tom Clark in Joseph Burstyn, Inc. v. Wilson, 343 U.S. 495 '(1952), observed that "To hold that liberty of expression by means of motion pictures is guaranteed by the First and Fourteenth Amendments, however, is not the end of our problem. * * * Each method [of expression] tends to present its own peculiar problems." 343 U.S. 495 at 502–503 (1952). Justice Robert Jackson in Kovacs v. Cooper, 336 U.S. 77 (1949), urged that each medium be considered a law unto itself. Justice Hugo Black rejected this kind of "favoritism." Justice Brennan has urged an approach which would recognize that there are two distinct First Amendment models—the "structural" model and the "speech" model—which do not and need not receive the same degree of protection. See text, p. 149.

On the whole, the Supreme Court and lesser courts in the American judicial system have approached problems of free speech and press rather broadly in terms of the conflicting social values working for and against a governmental restraint on a means of communication in a particular case.

Some commentators have tried to impose order on the Supreme Court's work in the First Amendment area. Professor Laurence Tribe identified two categories for First Amendment claims: "Track one" involves "government regulation" which is "aimed at the communication impact of an act." Regulations which fall into "track one" are unconstitutional unless government can meet the demands of doctrines to which the fact patterns of a case may be relevant, such as the clear and present danger doctrine or the public law of libel.

"Track two" is designed to cope with regulation which "is aimed at the noncommunicative impact of an act." Regulations which are exercised under "track two" will be valid even when applied "to expressive conduct so long as it does not unduly constrict the flow of information and ideas." Under "track two," a "balance" is struck "between the values of freedom of expression and the government's regulatory interests * * * on a case by case basis." See Tribe, *American Constitutional Law,* 582 (1978).

In this First Amendment chapter, as well as in other chapters, one confronts a continuous philosophical debate on the meaning of freedom of speech and press. Through concepts like "clear and present danger," "balancing," "symbolic speech," and "freedom from prior restraint," one begins to learn the constitutional law vocabulary of freedom of speech and press. Sometimes these doctrines disguise the sources of decision rather than illuminate them. It is also true that sometimes a Supreme Court decision owes more to the death or retirement of an old justice and the appointment of a new one than it does to the demands of any particular doctrine.

Nevertheless, the free speech and press doctrines collected in this chapter, in all their variety and contradiction, do reflect the considerable travail of Supreme Court justices in trying to discern the meaning of the First Amendment.

THE DEVELOPMENT OF THE LAW OF FREEDOM OF SPEECH AND PRESS IN THE SUPREME COURT

The Rise of the Clear and Present Danger Doctrine

The First Amendment to the U.S. Constitution must be the necessary starting point for any discussion of the extent and content of legal control of the press. The language of the amendment which has spawned innumerable cases, laws, books, and articles is remarkably stark, direct, and concise. See text, p. 1.

The words which attract our attention are the phrases "freedom of speech, or of the press." Because of the dynamic way in which this constitutional language has been interpreted by the courts, particularly the United States Supreme Court, the press has been held to mean all media of mass communication and not just newspapers. Whether this means that the First Amendment must be applied to all the media in exactly the same way is a question which will particularly concern us in the materials on legal control of broadcasting. But the basic point is that in American law the means of communication enjoy a protected status. The assumptions on which such protection is based and a critical examination of their functional validity is our first task if we are to understand the fundamental role played in the American communications process by the political, legal, and communications theories that have been spun around the First Amendment.

The American law of freedom of speech and press, as enunciated by the opinions of the United States Supreme Court, is in the main a post-World War I phenomenon. The introduction of conscription in the United States in World War I for the first time since the Civil War, the opposition of radical groups to participation in that struggle, and the anti-radical "red scare" of the early nineteen twenties combined to produce a collision between authority and libertarian values. That collision provoked the first significant efforts to develop some guidelines for the problem of reconciling majoritarian impatience, as expressed in an assortment of repressive laws, with constitutional guarantees. The purpose, of course, of a constitution is in a sense to confound a legislative majority. What a constitution does is to remove certain matters from the reach of legislation.

The following case arose out of socialist hostility to the draft and to American participation in World War I. The clash of a federal antiespionage statute with the political protest of the socialists provided a vehicle for an opinion by Justice Oliver Wendell Holmes.

Holmes became one of the principal architects of American free speech and free press theory. In Schenck v. United States, 249 U.S. 47 (1919), Holmes launched a famous doctrine, the clear and present danger doctrine. As you read the opinion, ask yourself what function Holmes expected his clear and present danger doctrine to serve?

SCHENCK v. UNITED STATES

249 U.S. 47, 39 S.CT. 247, 63 L.ED. 470 (1919).

Justice HOLMES delivered the opinion of the Court.

This is an indictment in three counts. The first charges a conspiracy to violate the espionage act of June 15, 1917, by causing and attempting to cause insubordination, &c., in the military and naval forces of the United States, and to obstruct the recruiting and enlistment service of the United States, when the United States was at war with the German Empire, to-wit, that the defendant wilfully conspired to have printed and circulated to men who had been called and accepted for military service under the Act of May 18, 1917, a document set forth and alleged to be calculated to cause such insubordination and obstruction. The count alleges overt acts in pursuance of the conspiracy, ending in the distribution of the document set forth. The second count alleges a conspiracy to commit an offense against the United States, to-wit, to use the mails for the transmission of matter declared to be non-mailable by title 12, § 2, of the act of June 15, 1917, to-wit the above mentioned document, with an averment of the same overt acts. The third count charges an unlawful use of the mails for the transmission of the same matter and otherwise as above. The defendants were found guilty on all the counts. They set up the First Amendment to the Constitution forbidding Congress to make any law abridging the freedom of speech, or of the press, and bringing the case here on that ground have argued some other points also of which we must dispose.

It is argued that the evidence, if admissible, was not sufficient to prove that the defendant Schenck was concerned in sending the documents. According to the testimony Schenck said he was general secretary of the Socialist party and had charge of the Socialist headquarters from which the documents were sent. He identified a book found there as the minutes of the Executive committee of the party. The book showed a resolution of August 13, 1917, that 15,000 leaflets should be printed on the other side of one of them in use, to be mailed to men who had passed exemption boards, and for distribution. Schenck personally attended to the printing. On August 20 the general secretary's report said "Obtained new leaflets from printer and started work addressing envelopes" &c.; and there was a resolve that Comrade Schenck be allowed $125 for sending leaflets through the mail. He said that he had about fifteen or sixteen thousand printed. There were files of the circular in question in the inner office which he said were printed on the other side of the one sided circular and were there for distribution. Other copies were proved to have been sent through the mails to drafted men. Without going into confirmatory details that were proved, no reasonable man could doubt that the defendant Schenck was largely instrumental in sending the circulars about. * * *

* * *

The document in question upon its first printed side recited the first section of the Thirteenth Amendment, said that the idea embodied in it was violated by the conscription act and that a conscript is little better than a convict. In impassioned language it intimated that conscription was despotism in its worst form and a monstrous wrong against humanity in the interest of Wall Street's chosen few. It said, "Do not submit to intimidation," but in form at least confined itself to peaceful measures such as a petition for the repeal of the act. The other and later printed side of the sheet was headed "Assert Your Rights." It stated reasons for alleging that any one violated the Constitution when he refused to recognize "your right to assert your opposition to the draft," and went on, "If you do not assert and support your rights, you are helping to deny or disparage rights which it is the solemn duty of all citizens and residents of the United States to retain." It described the arguments on the other side as coming from cunning politicians and a mercenary capitalist press, and even silent consent to the conscription law as helping to support an infamous conspiracy. It denied the power to send our citizens away to foreign shores to shoot up the people of other lands, and added that words could not express the condemnation such cold-blooded ruthlessness deserves, &c., &c., winding up, "You must do your share to maintain, support and uphold the rights of the people of this country." Of course the document would not have been sent unless it had been intended to have some effect, and we do not see what effect it could be expected to have upon persons subject to the draft except to influence them to obstruct the carrying of it out. The defendants do not deny that the jury might find against them on this point.

But it is said, suppose that that was the tendency of this circular, it is protected by the First Amendment to the Constitution. Two of the strongest expressions are said to be quoted respectively from well-known public men. It well may be that the prohibition of laws abridging the freedom of speech is not confined to previous restraints, although to prevent them may have been the main purpose, as intimated in Patterson v. Colorado, 205 U.S. 454, 462. We admit that in many places and in ordinary times the defendants in saying all that was said in the circular would have been within their constitutional rights. But the character of every act depends upon the circumstances in which it is done. The most stringent protection of free speech would not protect a man in falsely shouting fire in a theatre and causing a panic. It does not even protect a man from an injunction against uttering words that may have all the effect of force. *The question in every case is whether the words used are used in such circumstances and are of such a nature as to create a clear and present danger that they will bring about the substantive evils that Congress has a right to prevent.* [Emphasis added.] It is a question of proximity and degree. When a nation is at war many things that might be said in time of peace are such a hindrance to its effort that their utterance will not be endured so long as men fight and that no Court could regard them as protected by any constitutional right. It seems to be admitted that if an actual obstruction of the recruiting service were proved, liability for words that produced that effect might be enforced. The statute of 1917 * * * punishes conspiracies to obstruct as well as actual obstruction. If the act, (speaking, or circulating a paper,) its tendency and the intent with which it is done are the same, we perceive no ground for saying that success alone warrants making the act a crime. * * *

Judgments affirmed.

COMMENT

1. The most striking observation about the American law of freedom of speech and press is that the abridgment of these freedoms by Congress is not quite as unrestricted as a literal reading of the First Amendment might lead one to suppose. The *Schenck* case is an illustration of Congressional power over political freedom. After all, Schenck was convicted for disseminating a pamphlet urging resistance to the draft and the Supreme Court, in an opinion by one of its most libertarian judges, affirmed. In a companion case to *Schenck*, Justice Holmes remarked that "the First Amendment while prohibiting legislation against free speech as such cannot have been, and obviously was not, intended to give immunity for every possible use of language." Frohwerk v. United States, 249 U.S. 204 at 206 (1919). Justice Holmes made a similar observation in *Schenck* when he said that "free speech would not protect a man in falsely shouting fire in a theatre and causing a panic." In other words, there is no absolute freedom of expression, but rather the scope of protection for such freedom is a question of degree. Holmes authored the clear and present danger doctrine as a guide to indicate the boundaries of protection and nonprotection. Under the rubric of the clear and present danger doctrine, political expression can be punished if circumstances exist to "create a clear and present danger" that the communication in controversy would "bring about the substantive evils that Congress has a right to prevent."

2. Does Holmes indicate in *Schenck* whether the determination of circumstances which would present a "clear and present" danger is a legislative or a judicial responsibility?

3. Since the pamphlet issued by a minor group of socialists was found sufficiently objectionable to place its distributors in jail, should we conclude that the clear and present danger doctrine operates to give relatively little protection to unpopular communications? Or is there a special feature of the *Schenck* case which makes its holding of somewhat limited application?

ABRAMS v. UNITED STATES

250 U.S. 616, 40 S.CT. 17, 63 L.ED. 1173 (1919).

[EDITORIAL NOTE

Abrams and others were accused of publishing and disseminating pamphlets attacking the American expeditionary force sent to Russia by President Woodrow Wilson to defeat the Bolsheviks. The pamphlets also called for a general strike of munitions workers. The majority of the Supreme Court, per Justice John Clarke, held that the publishing and distribution of the pamphlets during the war were not protected expression within the meaning of the First Amendment. Justice Clarke's opinion for the majority failed to make much impact on the law. But the dissent of Justice Holmes, in which he was joined by Justice Louis Brandeis, became one of the significant documents in the literature of the law of free expression.]

Justice HOLMES, dissenting.

This indictment is founded wholly upon the publication of two leaflets. * * * The first count charges a conspiracy pending the war with Germany to publish abusive language about the form of government of the United States, laying the preparation and publishing of the first leaflet as overt acts. The second count charges a conspiracy pending the war to publish language intended to bring the form of government into contempt, laying the preparation and publishing of the two leaflets as overt acts. The third count alleges a conspiracy to encourage resistance to the United States in the same war and to attempt to effectuate the purpose by publishing the same leaflets. The fourth count lays a conspiracy to incite curtailment of production of things necessary to the prosecution of the war and to attempt to accomplish it by publishing the second leaflet to which I have referred.

The first of these leaflets says that the President's cowardly silence about the intervention in Russia reveals the hypocrisy of the plutocratic gang in Washington. * *

The other leaflet, headed "Workers—Wake Up," with abusive language says that America together with the Allies will march for Russia to help the Czecko-Slovaks [sic] in their struggle against the Bolsheviki, and that this time the hypocrites shall not fool the Russian emigrants and friends of Russia in America. It tells the Russian emigrants that they now must spit in the face of the false military propaganda by which their sympathy and help to the prosecution of the war have been called forth and says that with the money they have lent or are going to lend "they will make bullets not only for the Germans but also for the Workers Soviets of Russia," and further, "Workers in the ammunition factories, you are producing bullets, bayonets, cannon to murder not only the Germans, but also your dearest, best, who are in Russia fighting for freedom." It then appeals to the same Russian emigrants at some length not to consent to the "inquisitionary expedition in Russia," and says that the destruction of the Russian revolution is "the politics of the march on Russia," The leaflet winds up by saying "Workers, our reply to this barbaric intervention has to be a general strike!" and after a few words on the spirit of revolution, exhortations not to be afraid, and some usual tall talk ends "Woe unto those who will be in the way of progress. Let solidarity live! The Rebels."

No argument seems to be necessary to show that these pronunciamentos in no way attack the form of government of the United States, or that they do not support either of the first two counts. What little I have to say about the third count may be postponed until I have considered the fourth. With regard to that it seems too plain to be denied that the suggestion to workers in the ammunition factories that they are producing bullets to murder their dearest, and the further advocacy of a general strike, both in the second leaflet, do urge curtailment of production of things necessary to the prosecution of the war within the meaning of the act of May 16, 1918, amending section 3 of the earlier act of 1917. But to make the conduct criminal that statute requires that it should be "within intent by such curtailment to cripple or hinder the United States in the prosecution of the war." It seems to me that no such intent is proved.

* * *

I never have seen any reason to doubt that the questions of law that alone were before this Court in the cases of Schenck, Frohwerk and Debs were rightly decided. I do not doubt for a moment that by the same reasoning that would justify punishing persuasion to murder, the United States constitutionally may punish speech that produces or is intended to produce a clear and imminent danger that it will bring about forthwith certain substantive evils that the United States constitutionally may seek to prevent. The power undoubtedly is greater in time of war than in time of peace because war opens dangers that do not exist at other times.

But as against dangers peculiar to war, as against others, the principle of the right to free speech is always the same. *It is only the present danger of immediate evil or an intent to bring it about that warrants Congress in setting a limit to the expression of opinion where private rights are not concerned.* [Emphasis added.] Congress certainly cannot forbid all effort to change the mind of the country. Now nobody can suppose that the surreptitious publishing of a silly leaflet by an unknown man, without more, would present any immediate danger that its opinions would hinder the success of the government arms or have any appreciable tendency to do so.

* * *

In this case sentences of twenty years imprisonment have been imposed for the publishing of two leaflets that I believe the defendants had as much right to publish as the Government has to publish the Constitution of the United States now vainly invoked by them. Even if I am technically wrong and enough can be squeezed from these poor and puny anonymities to turn the color of legal litmus paper; I will add, even if what I think the necessary intent were shown; the most nominal punishment seems to me all that possibly could be inflicted, unless the defendants are to be made to suffer not for what the indictment alleges but for the creed that they avow—a creed that I believe to be the creed of ignorance and immaturity when honestly held, as I see no reason to doubt that it was held here but which, although made the subject of examination at the trial, no one has a right even to consider in dealing with the charges before the Court.

Persecution for the expression of opinions seems to me perfectly logical. If you have no doubt of your premises or your power and want a certain result with all your heart you naturally express your wishes in law and sweep away all opposition. To allow opposition by speech seems to indicate that you think the speech impotent, as when a man says that he has squared the circle, or that you do not care whole heartedly for the result, or that you doubt either your power or your premises. But when men have realized that time has upset many fighting faiths, they may come to believe even more than they believe the very foundations of their own conduct that the ultimate good desired is better reached by free trade in ideas—that the best test of truth is the power of the thought to get itself accepted in the competition of the market, and that truth is the only ground upon which their wishes safely can be carried out. That at any rate is the theory of our Constitution. It is an experiment, as all life is an experiment. Every year if not every day we have to wager our salvation upon some prophecy based upon imperfect knowledge. While that experiment is part of our system I think that we should be eternally vigilant against attempts to check the expression of opinions that we loathe and believe to be fraught with death, unless they so imminently threaten immediate interference with the lawful and pressing purposes of the law that an immediate check is required to save the country. I wholly disagree with the argument of the Government that the First Amendment left the common law as to seditious libel in force. History seems to me against the notion. I had conceived that the United States through many years had shown its repentance for the Sedition Act of 1798 (act July 14, 1798, c. 73, 1 Stat. 596), by repaying fines that it imposed. Only the emergency that makes it immediately dangerous to leave the correction of evil counsels to time warrants making any exception to the sweeping command, "Congress shall make no law abridging the freedom of speech." Of course I am speaking only of expressions of opinion and exhortations, which were all that were uttered here, but I regret that I cannot put into more impressive words my belief that in their conviction upon this indictment the defendants were deprived of their rights under the Constitution of the United States.

Justice Brandeis concurs with the foregoing opinion.

The Marketplace of Ideas Theory

1. The reader should note that Holmes's theory of freedom of expression is basical-

ly a *laissez-faire* idea. The clash of political ideas is in this view a self-correcting and self-sustaining process. Under the marketplace of ideas theory the responsibility of government is neither to suppress nor to influence the process. This approach is reconciled with the clear and present danger test on the assumption that in a less than ideal world the application of the clear and present danger test permits only a minimum of governmental intervention into the opinion-making process. Holmes's *Abrams* dissent is a classic statement of the "marketplace of ideas" approach to First Amendment theory. In view of the rise of the electronic media, the information explosion, and the concentration of ownership in the mass media, what difficulties are presented in trying to make contemporary applications of statements such as "the best test of truth is the power of the thought to get itself accepted in the competition of the market?" The "market" Holmes is talking about is basically what we call today the mass media and their mass audiences. Is "free trade in ideas" the distinguishing characteristic of these media? If it is not, what deficiencies do you see in the "marketplace of ideas" theory?

2. For a view that a First Amendment model which posits a self-correcting marketplace of ideas is a romantic and unrealistic description of the opinion process in late twentieth-century America, see Barron, *Access to the Press—A New First Amendment Right,* 80 Harv.L.Rev. 1641 (1967).

> There is inequality in the power to communicate ideas just as there is inequality in economic bargaining power; to recognize the latter and deny the former is quixotic. The "marketplace of ideas" has rested on the assumption that protecting the right of expression is equivalent to providing for it. But changes in the communications industry have destroyed the equilibrium in that marketplace. * * * A realistic view of the first amendment requires recognition that a right of expression is somewhat thin if it can be exercised only at the sufferance of the managers of mass communications.

In classic marketplace of ideas theory the role of government is nonintervention. The marketplace of ideas functions on a basis similar to the Darwinian theory of evolution. The assumption is that the best ideas will emerge, after combat, triumphant. But the unstated assumption from the quotation from Professor Barron is that if the marketplace of ideas is to be something more than a metaphor, some government intervention is required. See *Red Lion v. FCC,* text, p. 845.

3. Herbert Marcuse submitted the traditional marketplace of ideas concept of freedom of expression to the following Marxist critique:

> The tolerance which was the great achievement of the liberal era is still professed and (with strong qualifications) practiced, while the economic and political process is subjected to an ubiquitous and effective administration in accordance with predominant interests. The result is an objective contradiction between the economic and political structure on the one side, and the theory and practice of toleration on the other. See Marcuse, *Repressive Tolerance in Wolff, Moore, and Marcuse, A Critique Of Pure Tolerance* 110 (1965).

Marcuse's evident wish to have an intellectual elite direct the media for predetermined social ends will not seem to many an improvement over the present situation. Yet there is disquiet as to whether a marketplace of ideas theory is meaningful when the marketplace is increasingly characterized by concentration of ownership and similarity of viewpoint.

4. Professor Edwin Baker rejects both the classic marketplace of ideas theory and what he calls the market failure model of the First Amendment. Advocates of the latter theory seek governmental intervention in the opinion process in order to correct the actual deficiencies or imba-

lances which they perceive in the actual workings of the communications marketplace (marketplace of ideas). Professor Baker argues: "If provision of adequate access is the goal, the lack of criteria for 'adequacy' undermines the legitimacy of government regulation. For the government to determine what access is adequate involves the government implicitly judging what is the correct resolution of the marketplace debates." See Baker, *Scope of the First Amendment Freedom of Speech*, 25 U.C.L.A. L.Rev. 964 at 986 (1978).

Professor Baker calls for adoption of a liberty model as the appropriate First Amendment model: "On the liberty theory, the purpose of the first amendment is not to guarantee adequate information. * * Speech is protected because without disrespecting the autonomy of other persons, it promotes both the speaker's self-fulfillment and the speaker's ability to participate in change." The liberty model transcends the speech/action dichotomy and would protect "self-chosen, nonverbal conduct" from certain governmental prohibitions as well as speech. See Baker, *supra*, p. 1039.

5. Professor Thomas M. Scanlon, Jr., advocates a positive role for government in the effort to achieve freedom of expression. Professor Scanlon says there may be reasonable disagreement on how best to "refine the right" of freedom of expression. See Scanlon *Freedom of Expression and Categories of Expression*, 40 U. of Pittsburgh L.Rev. 519 (1979). What is this disagreement about?

> But as new threats arise—from, for example, changes in the form of ownership of dominant means of communication—it may be unclear, and a matter subject to reasonable disagreement, how best to refine the right in order to provide the relevant kinds of protection at a tolerable cost. This disagreement is partly empirical—a disagreement about what is likely to happen if certain powers are or are not granted to governments. It is also in part a disagreement at the foundational level over the nature and importance of audience and participant interests and, especially, over what constitutes a sufficiently equal distribution of the means to their satisfaction. The main role of a philosophical theory of freedom of expression, in addition to clarifying what it is we are arguing about, is to attempt to resolve these foundational issues.

GITLOW v. PEOPLE OF STATE OF NEW YORK

268 U.S. 652, 45 S.CT. 625, 69 L.ED. 1138 (1925).

[EDITORIAL NOTE

Benjamin Gitlow, a member of the leftwing section of the Socialist Party, the revolutionary segment of the party, was indicted for the publication of a radical "manifesto" under the criminal anarchy statute of New York. Sixteen thousand copies of THE REVOLUTIONARY AGE, the house organ of the revolutionary section of the party which published the Manifesto, were printed. Some were sold; some were mailed. The New York Criminal Anarchy statute forbade the publication or distribution of material advocating, advising, or "teaching the duty, necessity or propriety of overthrowing or overturning organized government by force or violence." The Manifesto had urged mass strikes by the proletariat and repudiated the policy of the moderate Socialists of "introducing Socialism by means of legislative measures on the basis of the bourgeois state." The New York trial court convicted Gitlow under the Criminal Anarchy statute, and the state appellate courts affirmed. The United States Supreme Court also affirmed. The Court utilized as the measure of constitutionality the question of whether there was a reasonable basis for the legislature to have enacted the statute.]

The Court said, per Justice SANFORD:

* * *

For present purposes we may and do assume that freedom of speech and of the press—which are protected by the First Amendment from abridgment by Congress—are among the fundamental personal rights and "liberties" protected by the due process clause of the Fourteenth Amendment from impairment by the States. [Emphasis added.] We do not regard the incidental statement in Prudential Ins. Co. v. Cheek, 259 U.S. 530, 543, that the Fourteenth Amendment imposes no restrictions on the States concerning freedom of speech, as determinative of this question.

* * *

We cannot hold that the present statute is an arbitrary or unreasonable exercise of the police power of the State unwarrantably infringing the freedom of speech or press; and we must and do sustain its constitutionality.

This being so it may be applied to every utterance—not too trivial to be beneath the notice of the law—which is of such a character and used with such intent and purpose as to bring it within the prohibition of the statute. * * * In other words, when the legislative body has determined generally, in the constitutional exercise of its discretion, that utterances of a certain kind involve such danger of substantive evil that they may be punished, the question whether any specific utterance coming within the prohibited class is likely, in and of itself, to bring about the substantive evil, is not open to consideration. It is sufficient that the statute itself be constitutional and that the use of the language comes within its prohibition.

It is clear that the question in such cases is entirely different from that involved in those cases where the statute merely prohibits certain acts involving the danger of substantive evil, without any reference to language itself, and it is sought to apply its provisions to language used by the defendant for the purpose of bringing about the prohibited results. There, if it be contended that the statute cannot be applied to the language used by the defendant because of its protection by the freedom of speech or press, it must necessarily be found, as an original question, without any previous determination by the legislative body, whether the specific language used involved such likelihood of bringing about the substantive evil as to deprive it of the constitutional protection. In such case it has been held that the general provisions of the statute may be constitutionally applied to the specific utterance of the defendant if its natural tendency and probable effect was to bring about the substantive evil which the legislative body might prevent. Schenck v. United States [249 U.S. 47]; Debs v. United States [249 U.S. 211]. And the general statement in the Schenck Case, [249 U.S. 47] that the "question in every case is whether the words used are used in such circumstances and are of such a nature as to create a clear and present danger that they will bring about the substantive evils,"—upon which great reliance is placed in the defendant's argument—was manifestly intended, as shown by the context, to apply only in cases of this class, and has no application to those like the present, where the legislative body itself has previously determined the danger of substantive evil arising from utterances of a specified character.

* * *

And finding, for the reasons stated that the statute is not in itself unconstitutional, and that it has not been applied in the present case in derogation of any constitutional right, the judgment of the Court of Appeals is affirmed.

Justice HOLMES (dissenting).

Justice Brandeis and I are of opinion that this judgment should be reversed. The general principle of free speech, it seems to me, must be taken to be included in the Fourteenth Amendment, in view of the scope that has been given to the word "liberty" as there used, although perhaps it may be accepted with a somewhat larger latitude of interpretation than is allowed to Congress by the sweeping language that governs or ought to govern the laws of the United States. If I am right then I think that the criterion sanctioned by the full Court in Schenck v. United States, applies:

"The question in every case is whether the words used are used in such circumstances and are of such a nature as to create a clear and present danger that they will bring about the substantive evils that [the State] has a right to prevent."

It is true that in my opinion this criterion was departed from in Abrams v. United States, but the convictions that I expressed in that case are too deep for it to be possible for me as yet to believe that it * * * has settled the law. If what I think the correct test is applied it is manifest that there was no present danger of an attempt to overthrow the government by force on the part of the admittedly small minority who shared the defendant's views. It is said that this manifesto was more than a theory, that it was an incitement. *Every idea is an incitement.* It offers itself for belief and if believed it is acted on unless some other belief outweighs it or some failure of energy stifles the movement at its birth. The only difference between the expression of an opinion and an incitement in the narrower sense is the speaker's enthusiasm for the result. Eloquence may set fire to reason. But whatever may be thought of the redundant discourse before us it had no chance of starting a present conflagration. If in the long run the beliefs expressed in a proletarian dictatorship are destined to be accepted by the dominant forces of the community, the only meaning of free speech is that they should be given their chance and have their way.

If the publication of this document had been laid as an attempt to induce an uprising against government at once and not at some indefinite time in the future it would have presented a different question. The object would have been one with which the law might deal, subject to the doubt whether there was any danger that the publication could produce any result, or in other words, whether it was not futile and too remote from possible consequences. But the indictment alleges the publication and nothing more. * * *

COMMENT

The Court, it should be observed, refused to apply the clear and present danger doctrine to the facts of the *Gitlow* case. The opinion apparently distinguishes the use of the clear and present danger doctrine in cases like *Schenck* and *Abrams* as espionage act cases. The Court asserts that a test of "reasonableness" of the legislative judgment will be used when the legislature itself has determined that certain utterances create a danger of a substantive evil. Such a circumstance, the Court says, differs from the situation in which the legislature has not specified certain utterances as forbidden. In the absence of such legislative specificity, the clear and present danger doctrine may be applied. Justice Brandeis's subsequent definition of the clear and present danger doctrine in his famous concurrence in Whitney v. California, 274 U.S. 357 (1927), infra, p. 22, stated a formulation of the clear and present danger doctrine which yields a far greater protection for freedom of expression than that afforded by Sanford's narrower view of the doctrine in *Gitlow.*

Under Justice Sanford's interpretation of clear and present danger, how could a legislature, determined to suppress a particular political heresy, effectively avoid application of the clear and present danger doctrine?

If the best measure of the constitutional tests of statutes alleged to offend freedom of expression is the latitude a test yields for freedom of expression, how does the "reasonableness" test compare to 1) the clear and present danger doctrine as understood by Sanford, and 2) as understood by Holmes in his dissent in *Gitlow?*

As Holmes discusses the clear and present danger doctrine in *Gitlow,* what would you say appears to be the heart of the doctrine as far as he is concerned?

The portions of the *Gitlow* opinion concerning appropriate tests for legislation affecting freedom of expression are at this point no longer authoritative. It is Brandeis's subsequent formulation of the clear and present danger doctrine rather than Sanford's which has prevailed. What has proved durable in the opinion were some *dicta*, or statements not actually necessary to the result reached by the Court, where Justice Sanford offhandedly extended the limitations on legislation curtailing freedom of expression binding on the federal government by reason of the First Amendment to the states by reason of the due process clause of the Fourteenth Amendment.

Previous *dicta* had indicated that the states were not bound by a federal constitutional guarantee of freedom of speech and press. Justice Sanford's statement to the contrary in *Gitlow* was, therefore, of great importance. As a constitutional matter it is not an exaggeration to say that freedom of speech and press in regard to the states is a judicial creation just sixty years old.

Were it not for his *Gitlow dictum*, Justice Sanford would be largely unremembered. However, the substance of his *Gitlow* opinion has found a champion. Professor Robert Bork argues that the opinion which should be praised in *Gitlow* is not the one authored by Justice Holmes, but the one authored by Justice Sanford. Why?

Professor (now Judge) Bork responds:

> Speech advocating violent overthrow is * * * not "political speech." It is not political speech because it violates constitutional truths about processes and because it is not aimed at a new definition of political truth by a legislative majority. Violent overthrow of government breaks the premises of our system concerning the ways in which truth is defined, and yet those premises are the only reasons for protecting political speech. It follows that there is no constitutional reason to protect speech advocating forcible overthrow. See Bork, *Neutral Principles and Some First Amendment Problems*, 47 Ind. L.J. 1, 20 (1971).

For many, there will be concern whenever political freedom is limited to those who believe in "constitutional truth." The fear is that those not in control of government may make too narrow a definition of what constitutes "constitutional truth." Compare the views of Herbert Marcuse, text, p. 15, with those of Professor Bork. Are there any points of similarity? Any differences?

The Meiklejohn Theory of The First Amendment

The political philosopher, Alexander Meiklejohn, was a severe critic of the views articulated by Justice Holmes. Holmes's clear and present danger test sometimes permitted that which, in Meiklejohn's judgment, the First Amendment prohibited: congressional legislation abridging freedom of expression. See A. Meiklejohn, *Free Speech and Its Relation to Self-Government* 29 (1948). For Meiklejohn, the clear and present danger test was merely a verbal dodge for permitting restriction of free speech and press whenever the Congress was disposed to do so.

Did Professor Meiklejohn believe then that no manner of expression could be restricted by government—even "counselling to murder" or falsely shouting fire in a crowded theatre? Meiklejohn did not go this far either. What he urged was that it is necessary to distinguish between two kinds of expression, one of which has absolute protection and one of which does not. Expression with regard to issues which concern political self-government was in Meiklejohn's judgment absolutely protected by the language of the First Amendment, i.e., "Congress shall make no law abridging * * * freedom of speech, or of the press." But private discussion, discussion which is nonpolitical in character, i.e., falsely shouting fire in a crowded theatre, was not within the ambit of the First Amendment at all but rather within the ambit of the more flexible, and less restrictive, due process clause of the Fifth Amendment, i.e., " * * * nor shall any person * * * be deprived of life, liberty or property, without due process of law."

The rationale of the absolute protection for freedom of speech in Meiklejohn's judgment was to assure that the general citizenry would have the necessary information to make the informed judgments on which a self-governing society is dependent. Speech unrelated to that end was therefore not public speech, and not within the scope of the First Amendment, and so within the regulatory power of legislatures.

Did Meiklejohn underestimate the influence of nonpolitical forms of speech on the process of self-government?

Meiklejohn and the Blasi Critique: The "Checking Value"

The heart of the Meiklejohn thesis was that the First Amendment should be interpreted to safeguard and protect individual self-governance in a free and democratic society. It is precisely this thesis which has recently been exposed to a comprehensive critique. See Blasi, *The Checking Value in First Amendment Theory,* 1977 American Bar Foundation Research Journal 523 at 561. Professor Vincent Blasi believes that the view that the First Amendment is designed essentially to protect individual democratic decision making is outmoded.

"[T]he Meiklejohn thesis vision of active, continued involvement by citizens fails to describe not only the reality but also the shared ideal of American politics."

Blasi instead suggests that the First Amendment should be viewed as a kind of counterpoise to government. The function of the press is to serve as the watchdog of government, and the purpose of the First Amendment is to provide the press with protection in its role of keeping government responsive and accountable. This checking function value in the First Amendment is described by Professor Blasi as follows:

> The central premise of the checking value is that abuse of government is an especially serious evil—more serious than the abuse of private power, even by institutions such as large corporations which can affect the lives of millions of people.

The shift in emphasis on the ultimate purpose of First Amendment protection reflected between Meiklejohn's analysis as compared with that of Blasi is very clear. Protection of the media, rather than protection of the citizenry for purposes of self-expression and democratic decision making, becomes the fundamental First Amendment objective. The press becomes the focal point of First Amendment theory because the press and not the citizenry is seen as the essential "check" on government excess. The Blasi theory makes enduring constitutional interpretation out of the press role in Watergate.

The "checking value" sees the function of citizens in a regime ordered by the First Amendment in a very different light than Professor Meiklejohn perceived it. Professor Blasi acknowledges this difference in perspective and defends it:

> The checking value is premised upon a different vision—one in which the government is structured in such a way that built-in counterforces make it possible for citizens in most, but not all, periods to have the luxury to concern themselves almost exclusively with private pursuits.

In the Meiklejohn theory, the individual is at the heart of First Amendment theory. In the Blasi theory, the media occupy that role. But is this a required substitution? First Amendment theory should be rich enough to give the media adequate protection and yet to continue to grant the citizen the pivotal role which Meiklejohn assigned him. The "checking value" theory quite properly recognizes the almost quasi-constitutional checking role the press plays *vis-à-vis* government. Yet the theory is perhaps somewhat defeatist since it posits the individual citizen as remote and helpless, at least when compared to the two major protagonists, government and the media.

Meiklejohn and Holmes: The Chafee View

Meiklejohn's theory had the advantage of attempting to deal textually with the perplexing latitude of the First Amendment. The dilemma of First Amendment interpretation is that the more generously its language is interpreted, oddly enough, the less protection it renders. This is due to the fact that as a practical and a political matter, legislative majorities are too often unwilling to tolerate unlimited expression. Both Meiklejohn and Holmes, then, were attempting to provide a guide for indicating that which is protected expression and that which is not. Meiklejohn criticized Holmes because Holmes did not segregate the most important aspect of expression, from a political view and immunize it from legislative assault.

Professor Zechariah Chafee subsequently criticized Meiklejohn on the ground that his attempt to immunize political speech—quite beyond the fact that separating that which is public and that which is private speech is no easy matter—was hopelessly unrealistic from a pragmatic point of view, and historically invalid as well.

Professor Chafee's basic point was that the question is not, ideally, how much speech ought to be protected but rather, politically and practically, how much expression can be protected by a court which is asked to defy "legislators and prosecutors." For Chafee, the merit of the clear and present danger doctrine was that it allowed the Congress some room to legislate in the area of public discussion but in such a way that the scope for such legislation was very restricted. For Chafee, the alternative to the Holmesian interpretation of the First Amendment was not Meiklejohn's absolute immunity for public discussion but rather no "immunity at all in the face of legislation." See Chafee, Book Review, 62 Harv.L.Rev. 891 at 898 (1949). It was obvious to Chafee that some concessions must be made to popular intolerance in periods of stress in the form of legislation. It was apparently very clear to him that, if some concessions were not made, the consequences for free expression in any time of turmoil and anxiety would necessarily be worse than if some relaxation of the absolute language of the First Amendment was not permitted.

For Professor Meiklejohn it was a matter of great significance that the First Amendment prohibited the abridgment of "freedom of speech" rather than "speech itself." This for him was the clue that the Framers intended to give absolute protection to public or political speech. That the historical background of the First Amendment by no means implies that the Framers contemplated that absolute freedom of expression championed by Professor Meiklejohn is suggested in Levy, *Legacy of*

Suppression (1960). Even though Professor Levy's study suggests that the Framers had no experience with the broad-gauged theories of absolute freedom of expression, developed in different ways by Professor Meiklejohn, and Justice Black, he suggests that this does not mean that we should be bound by the Framers' understanding of the document which they authored. See Levy, supra, 309. A similar view was voiced by the distinguished political scientist Professor Harold Lasswell:

> Suppose that historical research does succeed in disclosing the perspectives that prevailed in the eighteenth century, and which have been greatly modified since. What of it? * * * In the perspective of a comprehensive value oriented jurisprudence * * * the historical facts about the perspectives of the founding fathers, so briefly adhered to, are not binding on us.

See Lasswell's review of Crosskey, *Politics and The Constitution in the History of The United States*, 22 Geo.Wash.L.Rev. 383 (1953).

What are the comparative advantages and disadvantages for society and for those who work in the mass media of (1) the historical approach to the First Amendment, (2) the Meiklejohn approach, and (3) the Lasswellian approach?

The Clear and Present Danger Test Refined: The Authorized Brandeis Version

WHITNEY v. CALIFORNIA

274 U.S. 357, 47 S.CT. 641, 71 L.ED. 1095 (1927).

[EDITORIAL NOTE

Ms Anita Whitney participated in the convention which set up the Communist Labor Party of California and was elected an alternate member of its state executive committee. Ms Whitney was convicted under the California Criminal Syndicalism Act on the ground that the Communist Labor Party was formed to teach criminal syndicalism and, as a member of the party, she participated in the crime. The state Criminal Syndicalism Act defined criminal syndicalism "as any doctrine or precept advocating, teaching or aiding and abetting the commission of crime, sabotage * * * or unlawful methods of terrorism as a means of accomplishing a change in industrial ownership or control, or effecting any political change."

Ms Whitney insisted, on review to the U.S. Supreme Court, that she had not intended to have the Communist Labor Party of California serve as an instrument of terrorism or violence. Ms Whitney argued that as the convention progressed it developed that the majority of the delegates entertained opinions about violence which she did not share. She asserted she should not be required to have foreseen that development and that her mere presence at the convention should not be considered to constitute a crime under the statute. The Court, per Justice Sanford, said that what Ms Whitney was really doing was asking the Supreme Court to review questions of fact which had already been determined against her in the courts below and that questions of fact were not open to review in the Supreme Court. The Supreme Court upheld Whitney's conviction on the ground that concerted action involved a greater threat to the public order than isolated utterances and acts of individuals.

But it was the concurrence of Justice Brandeis, joined by Justice Holmes, rather than Justice Sanford's opinion for the majority, which shaped the future development of the constitutional law of freedom of expression. Brandeis attempted to do two things in his concurrence in *Whitney*. First, he sought to clarify the clear and present danger doctrine in a sufficiently meaningful way so that the responsibilities of the judiciary and the legislature would be clearly outlined at the same time that the greatest possible protection was provided for freedom of expression. Second, Brandeis sought to analyze the rationale of constitutional protection for freedom of expression.

The student should read the Brandeis opinion in *Whitney* in an effort to state and analyze the conclusions Brandeis reached in trying to serve these two goals.]

Justice BRANDEIS (concurring). Ms Whitney was convicted of the felony of assisting in organizing, in the year 1919, the Communist Labor Party of California, of being a member of it, and of assembling with it. These acts are held to constitute a crime, because the party was formed to teach criminal syndicalism. The statute which made these acts a crime restricted the right of free speech and of assembly theretofore existing. The claim is that the statute, as applied, denied to Ms Whitney the liberty guaranteed by the Fourteenth Amendment.

The felony which the statute created is a crime very unlike the old felony of conspiracy or the old misdemeanor of unlawful assembly. The mere act of assisting in forming a society for teaching syndicalism, of becoming a member of it, or assembling with others for that purpose is given the dynamic quality of crime. There is guilt although the society may not contemplate immediate promulgation of the doctrine. Thus the accused is to be punished, not for attempt, incitement or conspiracy, but for a step in preparation, which, if it threatens the public order at all, does so only remotely. The novelty in the prohibition introduced is that the statute aims, not at the practice of criminal syndicalism, nor even directly at the preaching of it, but at association with those who propose to preach it.

Despite arguments to the contrary which had seemed to me persuasive, it is settled that the due process clause of the Fourteenth Amendment applies to matters of substantive law as well as to matters of procedure. Thus all fundamental rights comprised within the term liberty are protected by the federal Constitution from invasion by the states. The right of free speech, the right to teach and the right of assembly are, of course, fundamental rights. These may not be denied or abridged. But, although the rights of free speech and assembly are fundamental, they are not in their nature absolute. Their exercise is subject to restriction, if the particular restriction proposed is required in order to protect the state from destruction or from serious injury, political, economic or moral. That the necessity which is essential to a valid restriction does not exist unless speech would produce, or is intended to produce, a clear and imminent danger of some substantive evil which the state constitutionally may seek to prevent has been settled. See Schenck v. United States, 249 U.S. 47, 52.

It is said to be the function of the Legislature to determine whether at a particular time and under the particular circumstances the formation of, or assembly with, a society organized to advocate criminal syndicalism constitutes a clear and present danger of substantive evil; and that by enacting the law here in question the Legislature of California determined that question in the affirmative. Compare Gitlow v. New York, 268 U.S. 652, 668, 671. The Legislature must obviously decide, in the first instance, whether a danger exists which calls for a particular protective measure. But where a statute is valid only in case certain conditions exist, the enactment of the statute cannot alone establish the facts which are essential to its validity. Prohibitory legislation has repeatedly been held invalid, because unnecessary, where the denial of liberty involved was that of engaging in a particular business. The powers of the courts to strike down an offending law are no less when the interests involved are not property rights, but the fundamental personal rights of free speech and assembly.

This court has not yet fixed the standard by which to determine when a danger shall be deemed clear; how remote the danger may be and yet be deemed present; and what degree of evil shall be deemed sufficiently substantial to justify resort to abridgment of free speech and assembly as the means of protection. To reach sound conclusions on these matters, we must bear in mind why a state is, ordinarily, denied the power to prohibit dissemination of social, economic and political doctrine which a vast majority of its citizens believes to be false and fraught with evil consequence.

Those who won our independence believed that the final end of the state was to make men free to develop their faculties, and that in its government the deliberative forces should prevail over the arbitrary. They valued liberty both as an end and as a means. They believed liberty to be the secret of happiness and courage to be the secret of liberty. They believed that freedom to think as you will and to speak as you think are means indispensable to the discovery and spread of political truth; that without free speech and assembly discussion would be futile; that with them, discussion affords ordinarily adequate protection against the dissemination of noxious doctrine; that the greatest menace to freedom is an inert people; that public discussion is a political duty; and that this should be a fundamental principle of the American government. They recognized the risks to which all human institutions are subject. But they knew that order cannot be secured merely through fear of punishment for its infraction; that it is hazardous to discourage thought, hope and imagination; that fear breeds repression; that repression breeds hate; that hate menaces stable government; that the path of safety lies in the opportunity to discuss freely supposed grievances and proposed remedies; and that the fitting remedy for evil counsels is good ones. Believing in the power of reason as applied through public discussion, they eschewed silence coerced by law—the argument of force in its worst form. Recognizing the occasional tyrannies of governing majorities, they amended the Constitution so that free speech and assembly should be guaranteed.

Fear of serious injury cannot alone justify suppression of free speech and assembly. Men feared witches and burnt women. It is the function of speech to free men from the bondage of irrational fears. To justify suppression of free speech there must be reasonable ground to fear that serious evil will result if free speech is practiced. There must be reasonable ground to believe that the danger apprehended is imminent. There must be reasonable ground to believe that the evil to be prevented is a serious one. Every denunciation of existing law tends in some measure to increase the probability that there will be violation of it. Condonation of a breach enhances the probability. Expressions of approval add to the probability. Propagation of the criminal state of mind by teaching syndicalism increases it. Advocacy of lawbreaking heightens it still further. But even advocacy of violation, however reprehensible morally, is not a justification for denying free speech where the advocacy falls short of incitement and there is nothing to indicate that the advocacy would be immediately acted on. The wide difference between advocacy and incitement, between preparation and attempt, between assembling and conspiracy, must be borne in mind. In order to support a finding of clear and present danger it must be shown either that immediate serious violence was to be expected or was advocated, or that the past conduct furnished reason to believe that such advocacy was then contemplated.

Those who won our independence by revolution were not cowards. They did not fear political change. They did not exalt order at the cost of liberty. To courageous, self-reliant men, with confi-

dence in the power of free and fearless reasoning applied through the processes of popular government, no danger flowing from speech can be deemed clear and present, unless the incidence of the evil apprehended is so imminent that it may befall before there is opportunity for full discussion. If there be time to expose through discussion the falsehood and fallacies, to avert the evil by the processes of education, the remedy to be applied is more speech, not enforced silence. [Emphasis added.] Only an emergency can justify repression. Such must be the rule if authority is to be reconciled with freedom. Such, in my opinion, is the command of the Constitution. It is therefore always open to Americans to challenge a law abridging free speech and assembly by showing that there was no emergency justifying it.

Moreover, even imminent danger cannot justify resort to prohibition of these functions essential to effective democracy, unless the evil apprehended is relatively serious. Prohibition of free speech and assembly is a measure so stringent that it would be inappropriate as the means for averting a relatively trivial harm to society. A police measure may be unconstitutional merely because the remedy, although effective as means of protection, is unduly harsh or oppressive. Thus, a state might, in the exercise of its police power, make any trespass upon the land of another a crime regardless of the results or of the intent or purpose of the trespasser. It might, also, punish an attempt, a conspiracy, or an incitement to commit the trespass. But it is hardly conceivable that this court would hold constitutional a statute which punished as a felony the mere voluntary assembly with a society formed to teach that pedestrians had the moral right to cross uninclosed, unposted, waste lands and to advocate their doing so, even if there was imminent danger that advocacy would lead to a trespass. The fact that speech is likely to result in some violence or in destruction of property is not enough to justify its suppression. There must be the probability of serious injury to the State. Among free men, the deterrents ordinarily to be applied to prevent crime are education and punishment for violations of the law, not abridgment of the rights of free speech and assembly.

* * * Whenever the fundamental rights of free speech and assembly are alleged to have been invaded, it must remain open to a defendant to present the issue whether there actually did exist at the time a clear danger, whether the danger, if any, was imminent, and whether the evil apprehended was one so substantial as to justify the stringent restriction interposed by the Legislature. The legislative declaration, like the fact that the statute was passed and was sustained by the highest court of the State, creates merely a rebuttable presumption that these conditions have been satisfied.

Whether in 1919, when Ms Whitney did the things complained of, there was in California such clear and present danger of serious evil, might have been made the important issue in the case. She might have required that the issue be determined either by the court or the jury. She claimed below that the statute as applied to her violated the federal Constitution; but she did not claim that it was void because there was no clear and present danger of serious evil, nor did she request that the existence of these conditions of a valid measure thus restricting the rights of free speech and assembly be passed upon by the court or a jury. On the other hand, there was evidence on which the court or jury might have found that such danger existed. I am unable to assent to the suggestion in the opinion of the court that assembling with a political party, formed to advocate the desirability of a proletarian revolution by mass action at some date necessarily far in the future, is not a right within the protection of the Fourteenth Amendment. In the present case, however, there was other testimony which tended to establish the existence of a conspiracy, on the part of members of the International Workers of the World, to commit present serious crimes, and likewise to show that such a conspiracy would be furthered by the activity of the society of which Ms Whitney was a member. Under these circumstances the judgment of the State court cannot be disturbed.

* * *

Justice Holmes joins in this opinion.

COMMENT ON THE BRANDEIS OPINION IN WHITNEY

1. It should be noted that Justice Brandeis only reluctantly agreed that the due process clause of the Fourteenth Amendment applied to matters of substantive law, i.e., imposed a freedom of speech and press limitation on state power. Law and journalism students should observe how the modern American law of speech and press rests on judicial interpretation and creativity and how relatively small a role is played by the formal text, the actual language of the constitutional document.

2. In his discussion of the clear and present danger doctrine, Brandeis stressed that the crucial factor is the immediacy of the danger legislated against. As he puts it, "Only an emergency can justify repression." The corrective for communications objectionable to the state is expression to the contrary. It is only when the "evil apprehended is so imminent that it may befall before there is opportunity for full discussion" that the legislature may act. Brandeis makes it very clear, however, that a legislative judgment that the danger is too immediate and too grave to justify reliance on corrective discussion is not conclusive. As he says, the "enactment of the statute alone cannot alone establish the facts which are essential to its validity." There must be a reasonable basis for the legislative conclusion or for the state's conclusion that a particular repressive statute should be applied because of the imminent danger of the occurrence of a prohibited substantive evil.

This insistence that the courts have the last word in analyzing whether the clear and present danger doctrine should be applied is of the utmost importance. Otherwise, all the legislature would have to do to comply formally with the clear and present danger doctrine would be to merely recite, as the California legislature did in its Criminal Syndicalism Act, that it is concerned with the "immediate preservation of the public peace and safety." By such a formalism, the supposed protection of a constitutional guarantee of freedom of speech and press would be effectively destroyed.

3. The Brandeis opinion in *Whitney,* as we have seen, was the charter for a revised clear and present danger doctrine. Yet, in the end, and despite the eloquence of Brandeis, the conviction of Anita Whitney was affirmed, a result which, it should be noted, was joined in by Justice Holmes.[1]

Functionally, how useful has the clear and present danger doctrine actually proven to be? Dean Robert McKay, in a study of the First Amendment, answered the question very pragmatically. Counting cases from 1919 to 1937, Professor McKay concluded: "In its first eighteen years the clear and present danger test amounted only to this: one majority opinion (upholding the conviction claimed to abridge the freedom of speech), one concurrence, and

---

1. A very similar criminal syndicalism Ohio statute was invalidated by the Supreme Court in Brandenburg v. Ohio, 395 U.S. 444 (1969). *Brandenburg* also reversed the decision of the Court in *Whitney:* "The contrary teaching of Whitney v. California, cannot be supported, and that decision is therefore overruled." See *Brandenburg v. Ohio,* this text, p. 74.

five dissents." See McKay, *The Preference for Freedom*, 34 N.Y.U.L.Rev. 1182 at 1207 (1959).

The Preferred Position Theory

Courts have often declared that they grant a presumption of constitutionality to challenged legislation. In United States v. Carolene Products Co., 304 U.S. 144 (1938), in which the issue was a federal statute concerning economic regulation, Chief Justice Harlan Stone, writing for the Court, voiced the familiar view that the legislative judgment should be accorded a presumption of constitutionality. But in a famous footnote Stone stated that he would exempt a certain class of legislation from the scope of such a presumption. 304 U.S. 144 at 152–153, fn. 4:

> There may be narrower scope for operation of the presumption of constitutionality when legislation appears on its face to be within a specific prohibition of the Constitution, such as those of the first ten amendments, which are deemed equally specific when held to be embraced within the Fourteenth.
>
> It is unnecessary to consider now whether legislation which restricts those political processes which can ordinarily be expected to bring about repeal of undesirable legislation, is to be subjected to more exacting judicial scrutiny under the general prohibitions of the Fourteenth Amendment than are most other types of legislation. On restrictions upon the right to vote, see Nixon v. Condon, 286 U.S. 73; on restraints upon the dissemination of information, see Near v. Minnesota ex rel. Olson, 283 U.S. 697, 713–714, 718–720, 722; Grosjean v. American Press Co., 297 U.S. 233; on interferences with political organizations, see *Whitney v. California, 274 U.S. 357, 373–378; and see Holmes, J., in Gitlow v. New York, 268 U.S. 652, 673;* as to prohibition of peaceable assembly, see De Jonge v. Oregon, 299 U.S. 353, 365.
>
> Nor need we inquire whether similar considerations enter into the review of statutes directed at particular religious, Pierce v. Society of Sisters, 368 U.S. 510, or national, Meyer v. Nebraska, 262 U.S. 390, or racial minorities; *Nixon v. Condon, supra*: whether prejudice against discrete and insular minorities may be a special condition, which tends seriously to curtail the operation of those political processes ordinarily to be relied upon to protect minorities, and which may call for a correspondingly more searching judicial inquiry.

The essence of the preferred position theory stated in *Carolene Products* is that legislation restricting the political freedoms should be exposed to a more searching and exacting judicial review than other legislative challenges. Stone said there is a judicial responsibility to protect political freedom particularly. Restriction of political freedom, unlike other legislative restrictions, endangers the health of the political process. One of the reasons for affording considerable latitude to legislation in constitutional questions is because broad participation in decision making is a value of high dimension in a democratic society. Generally, the legislative process rather than the judicial process is considered more capable of demonstrating and providing such participation. But, if the legislature disenfranchises a segment of the electorate, or restrains freedom of expression so that the electorate is not sufficiently informed to be able to engage rationally in decision making, then the reason for extending the benefit of the doubt to contested legislation is removed. This theory, the "preferred position" or "preferred freedoms" theory of the First Amendment, declares that legislation concerning the political freedoms protected by the First Amendment shall not be able to claim the normal presumption of constitutionality afforded to legislation in general.

In appraising the preferred position along with the other First Amendment doctrines explored in this chapter, it should be noted that the clear and present danger doctrine and the preferred position theory have been thought to be "clearly related." Both theories, it has been said, give judges an active role in First Amendment interpretation and, though they do not provide the certainty of the absolutist approach, they do "in contrast to the pseudo-standards of the reasonableness and balancing doctrines" offer "positive and workable standards to guide judicial judgment." See Pritchett, *The American Constitution,* p. 429 (2d ed. 1968).

Professor C. H. Pritchett's preference for the clear and present danger and preferred position over balancing and reasonableness is that the latter tests offer no definition or presumption to make them applicable or meaningful. If competing interests are to be balanced, how do we know which interest is to be given what weight?

Professor Thomas Emerson has accurately referred to the Burger Court's "neglect of the preferred position doctrine." However, his criticism is directed to the fact that the Court has not yet applied the preferred position theory in a principled across-the-board fashion: "[W]here it feels inclined to defer to legislative judgment, or when it prefers another social interest, it does not feel bound by the preferred position doctrine." See Emerson, *First Amendment Doctrine and the Burger Court*, 68 Calif.L.Rev. 422 at 443 (1980). Although the preferred position doctrine is not to be found by name in the opinions of the Burger Court, its legacy is occasionally visible when the Court applies a more searching standard of review in a First Amendment case than it would otherwise. See discussion of balancing and standards of review, text, p. 82.

The "Fighting Words" Doctrine

Despite the popularity of the phrase "clear and present danger," it has never served as the exclusive judicial method by which to adjudicate First Amendment problems. First Amendment doctrine is rich and various. The abundance of First Amendment approaches is due primarily to the different contexts in which First Amendment problems arise. Thus, "the fighting words" doctrine is really a common sense response to one of the most fundamental of free speech problems: the situation where the exercise of free speech so endangers the public order as to transform protected speech into the illegal action of a riot.

CHAPLINSKY v. NEW HAMPSHIRE

315 U.S. 568, 62 S.CT. 766, 86 L.ED. 1031 (1942).

[EDITORIAL NOTE
The "fighting words" doctrine was born in that frequent spawning ground of First Amendment litigation, the activities of the Jehovah's Witnesses.]

Justice Frank MURPHY stated the facts of the case for a unanimous court as follows: "Chaplinsky was distributing the literature of his sect on the streets of Rochester [New Hampshire] on a busy afternoon. Members of the local citizenry complained to the City Marshal * * * that Chaplinsky was denouncing all religion as a 'racket'. The Marshal told them that Chaplinsky was lawfully engaged, and then warned Chaplinsky that the crowd was getting restless."

The complaint charged that Chaplinsky made the following remarks to the Marshal outside City Hall: "You are a God-damned racketeer and a damned Fascist and the whole government of Rochester are Fascists or agents of Fascists."

Chaplinsky for his part said that he asked the Marshal to arrest those responsible for the disturbance. But the Marshal, according to Chaplinsky, instead cursed him and told Chaplinsky to come along with him. Chaplinsky was prosecuted under a New Hampshire statute, part of which forbade "addressing any offensive, derisive or annoying word to any other person who is lawfully in any street or other public place." The statute also forbade calling such a person "by any offensive or derisive name. * * * "

The state supreme court put a gloss on the statute saying no words were forbidden except such as had a "direct tendency to cause acts of violence by the persons to whom, individually, the remark is addressed," and that launched the "fighting words" concept as a First Amendment doctrine. The United States Supreme Court quoted the New Hampshire Supreme Court with approval: "The word 'offensive' is not to be defined in terms of what a particular addressee thinks. * * * The test is what men of common intelligence would understand to be words likely to cause an average addressee to fight. * * The English language has a number of words and expressions which by general consent are 'fighting words' when said without a disarming smile. * * * Such words, as ordinary men know, are likely to cause a fight. * * *

"The statute, as construed, does no more than prohibit the *face-to-face words* plainly likely to cause a breach of the peace by the speaker—including 'classical fighting words', words in current use less 'classical' but equally likely to cause violence, and other disorderly words, including profanity, obscenity and threats." [Emphasis added.]

The Supreme Court said that as limited the New Hampshire statute did not violate the constitutional right of free expression. The Court said "[a] statute punishing *verbal acts*, carefully drawn so as not unlikely to impair liberty of expression is not too vague for a criminal law." And it added: "Argument is unnecessary to demonstrate that the appellations 'damned racketeer' and 'damned Fascist' are epithets likely to provoke the average person to retaliation, and thereby cause a breach of the peace." [Emphasis added.]

COMMENT

1. The "fighting words" doctrine is very close to the "speech plus" doctrine. Speech plus is the phrase used in First Amendment law to describe the situation where speech or expression is intertwined with action as in the case of picketing, demonstrating, and parading. The admixture of action with expression renders reasonable state regulation permissible; where pure speech alone is involved, the First Amendment intervenes. Of course, the language Chaplinsky spoke to the Marshal was "pure" speech. But it was speech, in the Court's analysis, that was bound to provoke a physical reaction. In other words, "fighting words" are words which are on the verge of action. Speech plus is expression combined with action.

On the other hand, it is not clear that Chaplinsky himself was at a cross-over point to action when he made the controversial utterance to the Marshal. The anticipated reaction to so-called "fighting words" is on the part of the listener and the audience. Why should the audience be exempted from obeying the law, i.e., refraining from violence, when pure speech is engaged in by someone like Chaplinsky? By punishing Chaplinsky, doesn't the law sanction civil disobedience by arresting Chaplinsky rather than those whom the law assumes, because of their short tempers, will resort to violence? The *Chaplinsky* case is an unusual context for the birth of the "fighting words" doctrine. After all, the law should not presume that a police officer like the Marshal could ever be provoked to violence by mere words.

2. Overbreadth problems can arise in "fighting words" cases. Some prosecutions for "fighting words" have been struck down when the ordinance or statute is overbroad and punishes both "fighting words" as well as words which do not by their very utterance inflict damage or tend

to incite an immediate breach of the peace. Thus a Georgia statute and a New Orleans ordinance punishing the use of "opprobrious language" were respectively invalidated by the Supreme Court on the ground that such language is, unless limited, unconstitutionally overbroad. Gooding v. Wilson, 405 U.S. 518 (1972); Lewis v. City of New Orleans, 408 U.S. 913 (1972) (*Lewis I*); Lewis v. City of New Orleans, 415 U.S. 130 (1974), (*Lewis II*).

3. In summary, although the "fighting words" exception to First Amendment protection is still paid formal homage in the Supreme Court, rigorous use of the overbreadth doctrine has diminished the importance of this exception. Indeed, in *Lewis II*, Justice Harry Blackmun, joined by Chief Justice Burger and Justice William Rehnquist, dissented and objected to the use of the overbreadth doctrine as a means of limiting the application of the "fighting words" doctrine:

> Overbreadth and vagueness in the field of speech, as the present case and *Gooding* indicate, have become result-oriented rubber stamps attuned to the easy and imagined self-assurance that "one man's vulgarity is another's lyric." * * * The speech uttered by Mrs. Lewis to the arresting officer "plainly" was profane, "plainly" it was insulting, and "plainly" it was fighting. It therefore is within the reach of the ordinance, as narrowed by Louisiana's highest court. * * * The suggestion that the ordinance is open to selective enforcement is no reason to strike it down. Courts are capable of stemming abusive application of statutes.

The Swastika in Skokie: "Fighting Words"?

In the considerable litigation which was spawned from a planned march of the American Nazi Party through Skokie, Illinois, a predominantly Jewish suburb of Chicago, opponents of the march in one case attempted to take refuge in the "fighting words" doctrine. The Illinois Supreme Court held that the planned display of the swastika in a community containing thousands of concentration camp survivors did not constitute "fighting words." The Illinois Supreme Court overturned a lower court injunction against the display of the swastika on the ground that the display was protected symbolic political speech. Village of Skokie v. National Socialist Party, 373 N.E.2d 21 (Ill.1978). Enjoining such a display was deemed to be an unconstitutional prior restraint on the right to free speech of the American Nazi Party:

> Plaintiff urges, and the appellate court has held, that the exhibition of the Nazi symbol, the swastika, addresses to ordinary citizens a message which is tantamount to fighting words. Plaintiff further asks this court to extend *Chaplinsky*, which upheld a statute punishing the use of such words, and hold that the fighting-words doctrine permits a prior restraint on defendants' symbolic speech. In our judgment we are precluded from doing so.
>
> * * *
>
> The display of the swastika, as offensive to the principles of a free nation as the memories it recalls may be, is symbolic political speech intended to convey to the public the beliefs of those who display it. It does not, in our opinion, fall within the definition of "fighting words," and that doctrine cannot be used here to overcome the heavy presumption against the constitutional validity of a prior restraint.
>
> Nor can we find that the swastika, while not representing fighting words, is nevertheless so offensive and peace threatening to the public that its display can be enjoined. We do not doubt that the sight of this symbol is abhorrent to the Jewish citizens of Skokie, and that the survivors of the Nazi persecutions, tormented by their recollections, may have strong feelings regarding its display. Yet it is entirely clear that this factor does not justify enjoining defendants' speech.
>
> * * *

> In summary, as we read the controlling Supreme Court opinions, use of the swastika is a symbolic form of free speech entitled to first amendment protections. Its display on uniforms or banners by those engaged in peaceful demonstrations cannot be totally precluded solely because that display may provoke a violent reaction by those who view it. Particularly is this true where, as here, there has been advance notice by the demonstrators of their plans so that they have become, as the complaint alleges, "common knowledge" and those to whom sight of the swastika banner or uniforms would be offensive are forewarned and need not view them. A speaker who gives prior notice of his message has not compelled a confrontation with those who voluntarily listen.

The Hostile Audience Problem

In Feiner v. New York, 340 U.S. 315 (1951), a controversial speaker was interrupted in mid-sentence by a policeman who demanded that he step down from his soap box because the street corner audience appeared to be getting restless. When Feiner refused to step down, he was arrested for disturbing the peace. The Supreme Court per Chief Justice Fred Vinson upheld his conviction against a contention by Feiner that his arrest violated his First Amendment rights of free speech. Justice Felix Frankfurter, concurring in *Feiner*, thought that interruption of speech by the police was not unconstitutional when in the best judgment of the police the speech threatened to precipitate disorder:

> It is true that breach-of-peace statutes, like most tools of government, may be misused. Enforcement of these statutes calls for public tolerance and intelligent police administration. These, in the long run, must give substance to whatever this Court may say about free speech.

Feiner raises the so-called "hostile audience" problem. If the audience menaces the speaker to the point where the physical safety of the speaker is at stake or a general melee is threatened, are the police ever justified in arresting the speaker even though the speaker is not intentionally inciting to violence? One way of resolving the problem would be to compare the size of the audience with the number of police. Presumably, if the latter were far out numbered by potentially dangerous audience members and there was a possibility some of them were armed, simple logistics would dictate carting away the speaker rather than the audience. Would such an analysis be a permissible use of the balancing test?

Whom should the police protect? The speaker or the hostile audience.[2] In dissent in *Feiner*, Justice Black's answer was clear: the speaker should be protected.

The case for arresting the speaker in a situation where the speaker is using "fighting words," i.e., words which can be expected to enrage the audience and lead it to physical violence, is stronger than the situation where the speaker's words, on a reasonable analysis, ought not to engender hostility leading to physical violence. Would Justice Black have supported arresting the speaker in this variation of the hostile audience problem?

Justice Frankfurter's approach in *Feiner* was not unlike the logistics approach to the hostile audience problem discussed above. If speech threatens to precipitate disorder, then the police, acting on a nondiscriminatory basis, might be justified in stopping the speech.

Justice Frankfurter's views were directly challenged by Justice Jackson in a dissenting opinion in a companion case, Kunz v. New York, 340 U.S. 290 (1951). Kunz had obtained a street-speaking permit in

2. See generally *Note, Hostile Audience Confrontations: Police Conduct and First Amendment Rights*, 75 Mich.L.Rev. 180 (1976).

New York City, but it was later revoked after many of his speeches aroused complaints and threats of violence from passers-by. His subsequent attempts to obtain a new permit were denied on the basis of the earlier revocation. The Supreme Court held that the denial of a new permit violated Kunz's First Amendment rights. In dissent, Justice Jackson pointed out the irony of the Court's position and especially that of Justice Frankfurter. Of what value, he said, is a rule against prior restraint if the Court is willing, as in *Feiner*, to sanction on-the-street arrests of volatile speakers while they are exercising their First Amendment rights? A fairly administered permit system, said Justice Jackson, "better protects freedom of speech than to let everyone speak without leave, but subject to surveillance and to being ordered to stop in the discretion of the police."

At least a permit system enables a potential speaker to present evidence on his own behalf and to appeal an administrative decision to a higher official. But in *Feiner*, the speaker's right to speak his mind was violated *ex parte* by a police officer who unilaterally decided that enough was enough. Which system, asked Justice Jackson, is more protective of First Amendment liberty?

Justice Frankfurter's analysis of free speech interests, prior restraint, and punishment after-the-fact was disputed by Justices Black, Douglas, and Sherman Minton, who dissented in *Feiner*. Even if Feiner's speech was arousing potential violence among the listening crowd, said Justice Black, the duty of the police was to protect Feiner's right to speak by arresting menacing hecklers, if necessary. In this view, silencing Feiner at the behest of the audience or because of the policeman's own personal prejudice against the speaker's views was not an appropriate alternative. Justice Black agreed with Justice Jackson's analysis of the effect of on-the-spot arrest upon the "freedom" guaranteed by rules against prior restraint. Feiner had criticized President Harry S. Truman.

The overbreadth doctrine has loomed large in hostile audience cases as it has in "fighting words" cases. Terminiello v. Chicago, 337 U.S. 1 (1949), involved a speaker who by using racially discriminatory language angered a largely black crowd standing outside the hall where the speech took place. The speaker was convicted under a law prohibiting speech that "stirs the public to anger, invites dispute or brings about a condition of unrest." The Supreme Court overturned the conviction and declared that the statute was overbroad in that it punished expression which had not been shown to present a clear and present danger. In a famous sentence in his opinion for the Court, Justice Douglas observed: "[A] function of free speech under our system of government is to invite dispute." At least inferentially, *Terminiello* suggests that a hostile audience is no justification for taking away the agitator who arouses the audience—at least unless the exacting standards of the clear and present danger test can be met. Which speech situation seemed the more volatile, *Feiner* or *Terminiello*?

Suppose a prior restraint is based on the probability of a hostile crowd reaction? When American Nazis proposed a professedly peaceful march through Skokie, the Village of Skokie enacted ordinances designed to block parades such as that contemplated by the Nazis. In the federal case which dramatically divided the membership of the American Civil Liberties Union, the ACLU provided legal counsel to the Nazis who brought suit to challenge the ordinances. Counsel for Skokie argued that the prospect of swastikas carried by marching Nazis were the equivalent of "fighting" words to a community many of whose members were former inmates of Nazi concentration camps. Furthermore, it was again argued that the specter of Nazi insignia being displayed in public in such a community was bound to provoke a hostile reaction. The federal district court declared the ordinances to be unconstitutional, and the federal court of appeals affirmed. Collin v. Smith, 578 F.2d 1197 (7th Cir. 1978).

Speaking for the court of appeals, Judge Pell said:

> It would be grossly insensitive to deny, as we do not, that the proposed demonstration would seriously disturb, emotionally and mentally, at least some, and probably many of the Village's residents. The problem with engrafting an exception on the First Amendment for such situations is that they are indistinguishable in principle from speech that invite[s] dispute * * * induces a condition of unrest, creates dissatisfaction with conditions as they are, or even stirs people to anger." Terminiello v. Chicago, * * * Yet these are among the "high" purposes of the First Amendment.
>
> * * *
>
> This case does not involve intrusion into people's homes. There *need* be no captive audience, as Village residents may, if they wish, simply avoid the Village Hall for thirty minutes on a Sunday afternoon, which no doubt would be their normal course of conduct on a day when the Village Hall was not open in the regular course of business. Absent such intrusion or captivity, there is no justifiable substantial privacy interest to save [the ordinance under consideration] from constitutional infirmity, when it attempts, by fiat, to declare the entire Village, at all times, a privacy zone that may be sanitized from the offensiveness of Nazi ideology and symbols.

In short, the federal court of appeals held that protected First Amendment activity could not be proscribed because of an anticipated hostile audience reaction particularly in circumstances where the audience involved could easily avoid the viewing of unwanted activity and where the audience was in no sense captive.[3] In such circumstances, the fact that a hostile audience reaction could be predicted as a result of the exercise of particular protected First Amendment activity could not authorize a prior restraint in the form of an ordinance prohibiting the parade in controversy: "Our decision that [the ordinance under consideration] cannot constitutionally be applied to the proposed march means that a permit for the march may not be denied on the basis of anticipated violations thereof." The decision of the federal court of appeals in the *Collin* case indicates that a heavy burden will have to be met by the state before a prior restraint on protected First Amendment expression is authorized out of fear that a hostile crowd will engage in disruptive activity as a result of permitting the expression in controversy.

The First Amendment and State Regulation of Pamphleteering, Solicitation, Parades, and Demonstrations

Alma Lovell, a Jehovah's Witness, was arrested in the town of Griffin, Georgia,

3. See Village of Skokie v. National Socialist Party, 373 N.E.2d 21 (Ill.1978), this text, p. 30, where a hostile audience to a Nazi parade was predicted but the Illinois Supreme Court, nonetheless, held that, in the circumstances, a prior restraint on the parade was not permissible:

> Similarly, the Court of Appeals for the Seventh Circuit, in reversing the denial of defendant Collin's application for a permit to speak in Chicago's Marquette Park, noted that courts have consistently refused to ban speech because of the possibility of unlawful conduct by those opposed to the speaker's philosophy.
>
> Starting with Terminiello v. City of Chicago, 337 U.S. 1 (1949), and continuing to Gregory v. City of Chicago, 394 U.S. 111 (1969), it has become patent that a hostile audience is not a basis for restraining otherwise legal First Amendment activity. As with many of the cases cited herein, if the actual behavior is not sufficient to sustain a conviction under a statute, then certainly the anticipation of such events cannot sustain the burden necessary to justify a prior restraint. Collin v. Chicago Park District, 460 F.2d 746, 754 (7th Cir. 1972).

For a discussion of the foregoing case in terms of the "fighting words" doctrine, see text, p. 30.

for violation of a city ordinance which banned any pamphleteering or leafletting without prior written permission from the Griffin city manager. She never sought permission from the Griffin city manager. She appealed her conviction under this ordinance and urged that it violated the First Amendment.

In a unanimous decision in Lovell v. Griffin, 303 U.S. 444 (1938), delivered by Chief Justice Charles Evans Hughes, the United States Supreme Court found the Griffin ordinance invalid on its face as a violation of freedom of speech and freedom of the press.

The Chief Justice pointed out that the ordinance "prohibits the distribution of literature of any kind, at any time, at any place, and in any manner without a permit from the city manager." The Griffin ordinance made no distinctions but covered all "literature" in all circumstances. Again this First Amendment infirmity is called *overbreadth.*

If the town was concerned about a particular problem, such as litter, or scurrilous libels, it ought to have drafted the ordinance to meet that problem rather than embracing all forms of pamphleteering. Secondly, the ordinance as drafted created a one-man censorship board in the person of the city manager with no guidelines to direct decisions prohibiting or permitting circulation of a particular leaflet. The city manager of Griffin had total unquestioned discretion to regulate the flow of printed communication in the town. Under the doctrine of *Lovell v. Griffin*, the officials who administer a permit system must have their authority specified and articulated in the legislation creating the system.

In *dictum* in *Lovell v. Griffin*, Chief Justice Hughes noted that the First Amendment is not confined to protection of newspapers and magazines, but includes pamphlets and leaflets as well. "The press," he wrote, "in its historic connotation comprehends every sort of publication which affords a vehicle of information and opinion." Furthermore, freedom to distribute and circulate press materials is as protected under the First Amendment as freedom to publish in the first place.

In *Lovell*, the Court spoke in strong terms of the threat to a free press posed by a licensing scheme. If a statute or regulation is narrowly drawn and contains procedural safeguards (unlike the pamphleteering ordinance in *Lovell*), would it be upheld despite overtones of "licensing"? Would noncompliance with the statute then be justified if someone had doubts about the validity of the statute?

Since the ordinance in *Lovell* was found "void on its face," the Court held that it was not necessary for Alma Lovell "to seek a permit under it." The Court held that she was "entitled to contest its validity in answer to the charge against her."

Isn't the usual view that a court rather than an individual should decide the constitutionality of legislation? Why then didn't the Court insist that Alma Lovell first apply for a permit and show that she had been denied it before determining that the ordinance was invalid? See *Walker v. Birmingham*, this text p. 45.

State Regulation of Solicitation

Cantwell v. Connecticut, 310 U.S. 296 (1940), was yet another case involving the imposition of state criminal penalties on Jehovah's Witnesses. The Cantwells, a father and two sons, were arrested in New Haven, Connecticut, for conducting door-to-door religious solicitation in a predominantly Catholic neighborhood of the city. They were charged with violating a Connecticut statute which provided in part that: "No person shall solicit money * * for any alleged religious * * * cause * * unless * * * approved by the [county] secretary of * * * public welfare." Any person seeking to solicit for a religious cause was required under the statute to file an application with the welfare secretary, who was empowered to decide whether the cause was "a bona fide object of charity" and whether it conformed to "reasonable standards of efficiency and integrity." The penalty for violating the statute was a $100 fine or thirty days' imprisonment or both.

The Cantwells' convictions were affirmed by the state courts of Connecticut. But the United States Supreme Court unanimously, per Justice Owen Roberts, declared the statute unconstitutional as applied to the Cantwells and other Jehovah's Witnesses.

The Cantwells argued that the Connecticut state statute was not regulatory but prohibitory, since it allowed a state official to ban religious solicitation from the streets of Connecticut entirely. Once a certificate of approval was issued by the state welfare secretary, solicitation could proceed without any restriction at all under the Connecticut statute. And once a certificate was denied, solicitation was banned.

The Supreme Court ruled that the Connecticut statute in effect established a prior restraint on First Amendment freedoms which was not alleviated by the availability of judicial review after the fact.

The Supreme Court also pointed out that if the state wished to protect its citizens against door-to-door solicitation for *fraudulent* "religious" or "charity" causes, it had the constitutional power to enact a regulation aimed at that problem. The present law, however, was not such a statute. The Court also noted that it is within the police power of the state to set regulatory limits on religious solicitation (as on other sorts of solicitation), such as the time of day or the right of a householder to terminate the solicitation by demanding that the visitor remove himself from the premises. The state may not, however, force people to submit to licensing of religious speech.

On the breach of the peace conviction, the Supreme Court held that the broad sweep of the common law offense was an infringement of First Amendment rights.

The state had argued that because the Cantwells' solicitation technique had been provocative, it tended to produce violence on the part of their listeners and, therefore, was an appropriate matter for sanction under the common law offense of disturbing the peace.

In the Court's view in *Cantwell*, if the state had defined what is considered to be a clear and present danger to the state in a precisely drawn breach of the peace statute, this might have presented a sufficiently substantial interest to make it appropriate to convict Cantwell under such a statute. But since the breach of the peace offense was an imprecise common law offense rather than an offense set forth in a tightly drawn statute, the Court set aside the breach of the peace conviction. Justice Roberts made the following observations in *Cantwell*:

> When clear and present danger of riot, disorder, interference with traffic upon the public streets, or other immediate threat to public safety, peace, or order, appears, the power of the State to prevent or punish is obvious. Equally obvious is it that a State may not unduly suppress free communication of views, religious or other, under the guise of conserving desirable conditions.

Solicitation and Time, Place, and Manner Controls

VILLAGE OF SCHAUMBURG v. CITIZENS FOR A BETTER ENVIRONMENT

444 U.S. 620, 100 S.CT. 826, 63 L.ED.2D 73 (1980).

Justice WHITE delivered the opinion of the Court.

The issue in this case is the validity under the First and Fourteenth Amendments of a municipal ordinance prohibiting the solicitation of contributions by charitable organizations that do not use at least 75 percent of their receipts for "charitable purposes," those purposes being defined to exclude solicitation expenses, salaries, overhead and other administrative expenses. The Court of Appeals held the ordinance unconstitutional. We affirm that judgment.

Respondent Citizens for a Better Environment (CBE) is an Illinois not-for-profit corporation organized for the purpose of promoting "the protection of the environment." CBE is registered with the Illinois Attorney General's Charitable Trust Division pursuant to Illinois law, and has been afforded tax-exempt status by the United States Internal Revenue Service, and gifts to it are deductible for federal income tax purposes. CBE requested permission to solicit contributions in the Village of Schaumburg, but the Village denied CBE a permit because CBE could not demonstrate that 75 percent of its receipts would be used for "charitable purposes" as required by § 22–20(g) of the Village Code. CBE then sued the Village in the United States District Court for the Northern District of Illinois, charging that the 75 percent requirement of § 22–20(g) violated the First and Fourteenth Amendments. Declaratory and injunctive relief were sought.

The Village's answer to the complaint acknowledged that CBE employed "canvassers" to solicit funds, but alleged that "CBE is primarily raising funds for the benefit and salary of its employees and that its charitable purposes are negligible as compared with the primary objective of raising funds." The Village also alleged "that more than 60% of the funds collected [by CBE] have been spent for benefits of employees and not for any charitable purposes."

The District Court awarded summary judgment to CBE. The court recognized that although the "government may regulate solicitation in order to protect the community from fraud, [a]ny action impinging upon the freedom of expression and discussion must be minimal, and intimately related to an articulated, substantial government interest." The court concluded that the 75 percent requirement of § 22–20(g) of the Village Code on its face was "a form of censorship" prohibited by the First and Fourteenth Amendments. Section 22–20(g) was declared void on its face, its enforcement was enjoined, and the Village was ordered to issue a charitable solicitation permit to CBE.

The Court of Appeals for the Seventh Circuit affirmed.

It is urged that the ordinance should be sustained because it deals only with solicitation and because any charity is free to propagate its views from door to door in the Village without a permit as long as it refrains from soliciting money. But this represents a far too limited view of our prior cases relevant to canvassing and soliciting by religious and charitable organizations.

* * * This Court set aside the convictions [in *Cantwell*]. * * * Although *Cantwell* turned on the free exercise clause the Court has subsequently understood *Cantwell* to have implied that soliciting funds involves interests protected by the First Amendment's guarantee of freedom of speech. *Virginia Pharmacy Board v. Virginia Consumer Council; Bates v. State Bar of Arizona.* * * *

Prior authorities, therefore, clearly establish that charitable appeals for funds, on the street or door to door, involve a variety of speech interests—communication of information, the dissemination and propagation of views and ideas, and the advocacy of causes—that are within the protection of the First Amendment. Soliciting financial support is undoubtedly subject to reasonable regulation but the latter must be undertaken with due regard for the reality that solicitation is characteristically intertwined with informative and perhaps persuasive speech seeking support for particular causes or for particular views on economic, political or social issues, and for the reality that without solicitation the flow of such information and advocacy would likely cease. Canvassers in such contexts are necessarily more than solicitors for money. Furthermore, because charitable solicitation does more than inform private economic decisions and is not primarily concerned with providing information about the characteristics and costs of goods and services, it has not been dealt with in our cases as a variety of purely commercial speech.

The issue before us, then, is not whether charitable solicitations in residential neighborhoods are within the protections of the First Amendment. It is clear that they are.

The issue is whether the Village has exercised its power to regulate solicitation in such a manner as not unduly to intrude upon the rights of free speech. In pursuing this question we must first deal with the claim of the Village that summary judgment was improper because there was an unresolved factual dispute concerning the true character of CBE's organization.

We agree with the Court of Appeals that CBE was entitled to its judgment of facial invalidity if the ordinance purported to prohibit canvassing by a substantial category of charities to which the 75-percent limitation could not be applied consistently with the First and Fourteenth Amendments, even if there was no demonstration that CBE itself was one of these organizations. Given a case or controversy, a litigant whose own activities are unprotected, may nevertheless challenge a statute by showing that it substantially abridges the First Amendment rights of other parties not before the court. In these First Amendment contexts, the courts are inclined to disregard the normal rule against permitting one whose conduct may validly be prohibited to challenge the proscription as it applies to others because of the possibility that protected speech or associative activities may be inhibited by the overly broad reach of the statute.

We have declared the overbreadth doctrine to be inapplicable in certain commercial speech cases, but that limitation does not concern us here. The Court of Appeals was thus free to inquire whether § 22–20(g) was overbroad, a question of law that involved no dispute about the characteristics of CBE. On this basis, proceeding to rule on the merits of the summary judgment was proper. As we have indicated, we also agree with the Court of Appeals' ruling on the motion.

We agree with the Court of Appeals that the 75-percent limitation is a direct and substantial limitation on protected activity that cannot be sustained unless it serves a sufficiently strong, subordinating interest that the Village is entitled to protect. We also agree that the Village's proffered justifications are inadequate and that the ordinance cannot survive scrutiny under the First Amendment.

The Village urges that the 75-percent requirement is intimately related to substantial governmental interests "in protecting the public from fraud, crime and undue annoyance." These interests are indeed substantial, but they are only peripherally promoted by the 75-percent requirement and could be sufficiently served by measures less destructive of First Amendment interests.

Prevention of fraud is the Village's principal justification for prohibiting solicitation by charities that spend more than one-quarter of their receipts on salaries and administrative expenses. The submission is that any organization using more than 25% of its receipts on fundraising, salaries and overhead is not a charitable, but a commercial, for profit enterprise and that to permit it to represent itself as a charity is fraudulent. But, as the Court of

Appeals recognized, this cannot be true of those organizations that are primarily engaged in research, advocacy or public education and that use their own paid staff to carry out these functions as well as to solicit financial support. The Village, consistently with the First Amendment, may not label such groups "fraudulent" and bar them from canvassing on the streets and house to house. Nor may the Village lump such organizations with those that in fact are using the charitable label as a cloak for profit-making and refuse to employ more precise measures to separate one kind from the other. The Village may serve its legitimate interest, but it must do so by narrowly drawn regulations designed to serve those interests without unnecessarily interfering with First Amendment freedoms.

The Village's legitimate interest in preventing fraud can be better served by measures less intrusive than a direct prohibition on solicitation. Fraudulent misrepresentations can be prohibited and the penal laws used to punish such conduct directly. Efforts to promote disclosure of the finances of charitable organizations also may assist in preventing fraud by informing the public of the ways in which their contributions will be employed. Such measures may help make contribution decisions more informed, while leaving to individual choice the decision whether to contribute to organizations that spend large amounts on salaries and administrative expenses.

We also fail to perceive any substantial relationship between the 75-percent requirement and the protection of public safety or of residential privacy. There is no indication that organizations devoting more than one-quarter of their funds to salaries and administrative expenses are any more likely to employ solicitors who would be a threat to public safety than are other charitable organizations.

The 75-percent requirement is related to the protection of privacy only in the most indirect of ways. As the Village concedes, householders are equally disturbed by solicitation on behalf of organizations satisfying the 75-percent requirements as they are by solicitation on behalf of other organizations. The 75-percent requirement protects privacy only by reducing the total number of solicitors, as would any prohibition on solicitation. The ordinance is not directed to the unique privacy interests of persons residing in their homes because it applies not only to door-to-door solicitation, but also to solicitation on "public streets and public ways." Code § 22–20. Other provisions of the ordinance, which are not challenged here, such as the provision permitting homeowners to bar solicitors from their property by posting signs reading "No Solicitors or Peddlers Invited," Code § 22–24, suggest the availability of less intrusive and more effective measures to protect privacy. We find no reason to disagree with the Court of Appeals' conclusion that § 22–20(g) is unconstitutionally overbroad. Its judgment is therefore affirmed.

Justice Rehnquist, dissenting.

The central weakness of the Court's decision, I believe, is its failure to recognize, let alone confront, the two most important issues in this case: how does one define a "charitable" organization, and to which authority in our federal system is application of that definition confided? I would uphold Schaumburg's ordinance as applied to CBE because that ordinance, while perhaps too strict to suit some tastes, affects only door-to-door solicitation for financial contributions, leaves little or no discretion in the hands of municipal authorities to "censor" unpopular speech, and is rationally related to the community's collective desire to bestow its largess upon organizations that are truly "charitable." I therefore dissent.

COMMENT

In his dissent in *Schaumburg*, Justice Rehnquist says that the Court's precedents striking down regulations covering door-to-door solicitation activity turned upon factors not involved in *Schaumburg.* For example, he cited *Cantwell* for the proposition that where the discretion conferred by a regulation on a municipal official to grant or deny a permit was "on the basis of vague or even non-existent criteria," the regulation was invalid.

Furthermore, he pointed out that prior cases established a line between solicitations involving the dissemination of information and solicitations concerned with obtaining money. See Martin v. Struthers, 319 U.S. 141 (1943) with Breard v. Alexandria, 341 U.S. 622 (1951).

Rehnquist says that *Schaumburg* holds that municipalities cannot prohibit door-to-door solicitation for contributions by organizations "primarily engaged in research, advocacy, or public education and that use their own paid staff to carry out these functions as well as to solicit financial support." Such a standard, he adds, has three defects: 1) It reverses the unprotected status for commercial speech rejected by *Virginia Pharmacy.* See text, p. 159. 2) The standard provides no guidance to municipalities on how to identify organizations "whose primary purpose is * * * to * * * disseminate information * * * on matters of public concern." 3) The Court overestimates the constitutional value of door-to-door solicitation for financial contributions. "* * * [A] simple request for money lies far from the core protection of the First Amendment as heretofore interpreted." Is Justice Rehnquist just asking for a return to the pre-*Virginia Pharmacy* status of commercial speech?

In the *Schaumburg* case, an ordinance protecting door-to-door or street solicitation of contributions by charitable organizations not using at least 75 percent of their receipts for "charitable purposes" was held unconstitutional. The doctrine which was the basis of the holding in *Schaumburg* was the overbreadth doctrine.

However, a regulation on solicitation can also be supported by other First Amendment doctrines. "While protection of public, or political protest lies at the very core of the First Amendment, some regulation is permissible with respect to the regulation of the time, place, and manner of such protest." See Barron and Dienes, *Handbook of Free Speech and Free Press* 93 (1979).

Grayned v. City of Rockford, 408 U.S. 104 (1972) provides a helpful guide to permissible time, place, and manner regulation:

> The nature of the place, "the pattern of its normal activities, dictates the kinds of regulations of time, place and manner that are reasonable." Although a silent vigil may not unduly interfere with a public library, making a speech in the reading room almost certainly would. That same speech should be perfectly appropriate in a park. The crucial question is whether the manner of expression is basically compatible with the normal activity of a particular place at a particular time. Our cases make clear that in assessing the reasonableness of regulation, we must weigh heavily the fact that communication is involved; the regulation must be narrowly tailored to further the State's legitimate interest. "Access to [public places] for the purpose of exercising [First Amendment rights] cannot constitutionally be denied broadly." Free expression must not, in the guise of regulation, be abridged or denied.

The *Heffron* case which follows is an illustrative example of permissible time, place, or manner regulation.

HEFFRON v. INTERNATIONAL SOCIETY FOR KRISHNA CONSCIOUSNESS

452 U.S. 640, 101 S.CT. 2559, 69 L.ED.2D 298 (1981).

[The Minnesota Agricultural Society conducts an annual state fair on a 125-acre tract of state land which attracts about 115,000 persons on weekdays and 160,000 on weekends. Pursuant to state law, the Society issued rules, including Rule 6.05 which requires that all persons or groups seeking to sell, exhibit, or distribute materials at the fair must do so only from fixed locations on the fairgrounds. While the rules do not bar walking around and communicating, all sales, distributions, and fund solicitations must be conducted from a booth rented from the fair authorities on a first-come, first-served basis.

[The International Society for Krishna Consciousness, Inc. (ISKCON) brought suit seeking to enjoin application of Rule 6.05 against the religion and its members. It was alleged that the Rule violated the First Amendment by suppressing ISKCON's religious practice of Sankirtan, a ritual requiring members to go into public places to distribute material and solicit donations for the Krishna religion.

[The trial court upheld the constitutionality of Rule 6.05. The Minnesota Supreme Court reversed, holding Rule 6.05 unconstitutionally restricted the Krishnas' religious practice of Sankirtan.]

Justice WHITE delivered the opinion of the Court.

The State does not dispute that the oral and written dissemination of the Krishnas' religious views and doctrines is protected by the First Amendment. Nor does it claim that this protection is lost because the written materials sought to be distributed are sold rather than given away or because contributions or gifts are solicited in the course of propagating the faith.

It is also common ground, however, that the First Amendment does not guarantee the right to communicate one's views at all times and places or in any manner that may be desired. *Adderley v. Florida.* As the Minnesota Supreme Court recognized, the activities of ISKCON, like those of others protected by the First Amendment, are subject to reasonable time, place, and manner restrictions. "We have often approved restrictions of that kind provided that they are justified without reference to the content of the regulated speech, that they serve a significant governmental interest, and that in doing so they leave open ample alternative channels for communication of the information." *Virginia State Board of Pharmacy v. Virginia Citizens Consumer Council.* The issue here, as it was below, is whether Rule 6.05 is a permissible restriction on the place and manner of communicating the views of the Krishna religion, more specifically, whether the Society may require the members of ISKCON who desire to practice Sankirtan at the State Fair to confine their distribution, sales, and solicitation activities to a fixed location.

A major criterion for a valid time, place, and manner restriction is that the restriction "may not be based upon either the content or subject matter of the speech." *Consolidated Edison Co. v. Public Service Commission* [p. 59]. Rule 6.05 qualifies in this respect, since, as the Supreme Court of Minnesota observed, the rule applies even-handedly to all who wish to distribute and sell written materials or to solicit funds. No person or organization, whether commercial or charitable is permitted to engage in such activities except from a booth rented for those purposes.

Nor does Rule 6.05 suffer from the more covert forms of discrimination that may result when arbitrary discretion is vested in some governmental authority. The method of allocating space is a straightforward first-come, first-served system. The rule is not open to the kind of arbitrary application that this Court has condemned as inherently inconsistent with a valid time, place, and manner regulation because such discretion has the potential for becoming a means of suppressing a particular point of view. See *Shuttlesworth v. Birmingham.*

A valid time, place, and manner regulation must also "serve a significant governmental interest." Here, the principal justification asserted by the state in support of Rule 6.05 is the need to maintain the orderly movement of the crowd given the large number of exhibitors and persons attending the fair.

As a general matter, it is clear that a state's interest in protecting the "safety and convenience" of persons using a public forum is a valid governmental objective. Furthermore, consideration of a forum's special attributes is relevant to the constitutionality of a regulation since the significance of the governmental interest must be assessed in light of the characteristic nature and function of the particular forum involved. This observation bears particular import in the present case since respondents make a number of analogies between the fairgrounds and city streets, which have "immemorially been held in trust for the use of the public and have been used for purposes of assembly, communicating thoughts between citizens, and discussing public questions." But it is clear that there are significant differences between a street and the fairgrounds. A street is continually open, often uncongested, and constitutes not only a necessary conduit in the daily affairs of a locality's citizens, but also a place where people may enjoy the open air of the company of friends and neighbors in a relaxed environment. The Minnesota Fair is a temporary event attracting great numbers of visitors who come to the event for a short period to see and experience the host of exhibits and attractions at the fair. The flow of the crowd and demands of safety are more pressing in the context of the fair. As such, any comparisons to public streets are necessarily inexact.

The justification for the Rule should not be measured by the disorder that would result from granting an exemption solely to ISKCON. That organization and its ritual of Sankirtan have no special claim to First Amendment protection as compared to that of other religions who also distribute literature and solicit funds. None of our cases suggest that the inclusion of peripatetic solicitation as part of a church ritual entitles church members to solicitation rights in a public forum superior to those of members of other religious groups that raise money but do not purport to ritualize the process. Nor for present purposes do religious organizations enjoy rights to communicate, distribute, and solicit on the fairgrounds superior to those of other organizations having social, political, or other ideological messages to proselytize. The nonreligious organizations seeking support for their activities are entitled to rights equal to those of religious groups to enter a public forum and spread their views, whether by soliciting funds or by distributing literature.

ISKCON desires to proselytize at the fair because it believes it can successfully communicate and raise funds. In its view, this can be done only by intercepting fair patrons as they move about, and if success is achieved, stopping them momentarily or for longer periods as money is given or exchanged for literature. This consequence would be multiplied many times over if Rule 6.05 could not be applied to confine such transactions by ISKCON and others to fixed locations. Indeed, the court below agreed that without Rule 6.05 there would be widespread disorder at the fairgrounds. The court also recognized that some disorder would inevitably result from exempting the Krishnas from the rule. Obviously, there would be a much larger threat to the State's interest in crowd control if all other religious, nonreligious, and noncommercial organizations could likewise move freely about the fairgrounds distributing and selling literature and soliciting funds at will.

Given these considerations, we hold that the State's interest in confining distribution, selling, and fund solicitation activities to fixed locations is sufficient to satisfy the requirement that a place or manner restriction must serve a substantial state interest.

For similar reasons, we cannot agree with the Minnesota Supreme Court that Rule 6.05 is an unnecessary regulation because the State could avoid the threat to its interest posed by ISKCON by less restrictive means, such as penalizing disorder or disruption, limiting the number of solicitors, or putting more narrowly drawn restrictions on the location and movement of ISKCON's representatives. As we have indicated, the inquiry must involve not only ISKCON, but also all other organizations that would be entitled to distribute, sell or solicit if the booth rule may not be enforced with respect to ISKCON. Looked at in this way, it is quite improbable that the alternative means suggested by the Minnesota Supreme Court would deal adequately with the problems posed by the much larger number of distributors and solicitors that would be present on the fairgrounds if the judgment below were affirmed.

For Rule 6.05 to be valid as a place and manner restriction, it must also be sufficiently clear that alternative forums for the expression of respondents' protected speech exist despite the effects of the rule. Rule 6.05 is not vulnerable on this ground. First, the Rule does not prevent ISKCON from practicing Sankirtan anywhere outside the fairgrounds. More importantly, the rule has not been shown to deny access within the forum in question. Here, the rule does not exclude ISKCON from the fairgrounds, nor does it deny that organization the right to conduct any desired activity at some point within the forum. Its members may mingle with the crowd and orally propagate their views. The organization may also arrange for a booth and distribute and sell literature and solicit funds from that location on the fairgrounds itself. The Minnesota State Fair is a limited public forum in that it exists to provide a means for a great number of exhibitors temporarily to present their products or views, be they commercial, religious, or political, to a large number of people in an efficient fashion. Considering the limited functions of the fair and the combined area within which it operates, we are unwilling to say that Rule 6.05 does not provide ISKCON and other organizations with an adequate means to sell and solicit on the fairgrounds.

[Reversed.]

Justice BRENNAN, with whom Justice Marshall and Justice Stevens join, concurring in part and dissenting in part.

As the Court recognizes, the issue in this case is whether Minnesota State Fair Rule 6.05 constitutes a reasonable time, place, and manner restriction on respondents' exercise of protected First Amendment rights. In deciding this issue, the Court considers, *inter alia*, whether the regulation serves a significant governmental interest and whether that interest can be served by a less intrusive restriction. The Court errs, however, in failing to apply its analysis separately to each of the protected First Amendment activities restricted by Rule 6.05. Thus, the Court fails to recognize that some of the state's restrictions may be reasonable while others may not.

Rule 6.05 restricts three types of protected First Amendment activity: distribution of literature, sale of literature, and solicitation of funds.

I quite agree with the Court that the state has a significant interest in maintaining crowd control on its fairgrounds. I also have no doubt that the State has a significant interest in protecting its fairgoers from fraudulent or deceptive solicitation practices. Indeed, because I believe on this record that this latter interest is substantially furthered by a rule that restricts sales and solicitation activities to fixed booth locations, where the State will have the greatest opportunity to police and prevent possible deceptive practices, I would hold that Rule 6.05's restriction on those particular forms of First Amendment expression is justified as an antifraud measure. Accordingly, I join the judgment of the Court as far as it upholds rule 6.05's restriction on sales and solicitations. However, because I believe that the booth rule is an overly intrusive means of achieving the state's interest in crowd control, and because I cannot accept the validity of the state's third asserted justification [*i.e.*, protection of fairgoers from annoyance and harassment], I dissent from the Court's approval of Rule 6.05's restriction on the distribution of literature.

As our cases have long noted, once a governmental regulation is shown to impinge upon basic First Amendment rights, the burden falls on the government to show the validity of its asserted interest and the absence of less intrusive alternatives. The challenged "regulation must be narrowly tailored to further the State's legitimate interest." Minnesota's Rule 6.05 does not meet this test.

[E]ach and every fairgoer, whether political candidate, concerned citizen, or member of a religious group, is free to give speeches, engage in face-to-face advocacy, campaign, or proselytize. No restrictions are placed on any fairgoer's right to speak at any time, at any place, or to any person. Thus, if on a given day 5,000 members of ISKCON came to the fair and paid their admission fees, all 5,000 would be permitted to wander throughout the fairgrounds, delivering speeches to whomever they wanted, about whatever they wanted. Moreover, because this right does not rest on Sankirtan or any other religious principle, it can be exercised by every political candidate, partisan advocate, and common citizen who has paid the price of admission. All share the identical right to move peripatetically and speak freely throughout the fairgrounds.

Because of Rule 6.05, however, as soon as a proselytizing member of ISKCON hands out a free copy of the Bhagavad-Gita to an interested listener, or a political candidate distributes his campaign brochure to a potential voter, he becomes subject to arrest and removal from the fairgrounds. This constitutes a significant restriction on First Amendment rights. By prohibiting distribution of literature outside the booths, the fair officials sharply limit the number of fairgoers to whom the proselytizers and candidates can communicate their messages. Only if a fairgoer affirmatively seeks out such information by approaching a booth does Rule 6.05 fully permit potential communicators to exercise their First Amendment rights.

In support of its crowd control justification, the state contends that if fairgoers are permitted to distribute literature, large crowds will gather, blocking traffic lanes and causing safety problems. But the state has failed to provide any support for these assertions. It has made no showing that relaxation of its booth rule would create additional disorder in a fair that is already characterized by the robust and unrestrained participation of hundreds of thousands of wandering fairgoers. If fairgoers can make speeches, engage in face-to-face proselytizing, and buttonhole prospective supporters, they can surely distribute literature to members of their audience without significantly adding to the state's asserted crowd control problem. The record is devoid of any evidence that the 125-acre fairgrounds could not accommodate peripatetic distributors of literature just as easily as it now accommodates peripatetic speechmakers and proselytizers.

Relying on a general, speculative fear of disorder, the State of Minnesota has placed a significant restriction on respondents' ability to exercise core First Amendment rights. This restriction is not narrowly drawn to advance the state's interests, and for that reason is unconstitutional.

Justice BLACKMUN, concurring in part and dissenting in part.

For the reasons stated by Justice Brennan, I believe that Minnesota State Fair

Rule 6.05 is unconstitutional as applied to the distribution of literature. I also agree, however, that the rule is *constitutional* as applied to the sale of literature and the solicitation of funds. I reach this latter conclusion by a different route than does Justice Brennan, for I am not persuaded that, under the Court's precedents, the state's interest in protecting fairgoers from fraudulent solicitation or sales practices justifies Rule 6.05's restrictions of those activities.

In *Village of Schaumburg v. Citizens for a Better Environment*, the Court stressed that a community's interest in preventing fraudulent solicitations must be met by narrowly drawn regulations that do not unnecessarily interfere with First Amendment freedoms. There is nothing in this record to suggest that it is more difficult to police fairgrounds for fraudulent solicitations than it is to police an entire community's streets; just as fraudulent solicitors may "melt into a crowd" at the fair, so also may door-to-door solicitors quickly move on after consummating several transactions in a particular neighborhood. Indeed, since respondents have offered to wear identifying tags, and since the fairgrounds are an enclosed area, it is at least arguable that it is easier to police the fairgrounds than a community's streets.

Nonetheless, I believe that the state's substantial interest in maintaining crowd control and safety on the fairgrounds does justify Rule 6.05's restriction on solicitation and sales activities not conducted from a booth. As the Court points out, "[t]he flow of the crowd and demands of safety are more pressing in the context of the Fair" than in the context of a typical street. While I agree with Justice Brennan that the State's interest in order does not justify restrictions upon distribution of literature, I think that common-sense differences between literature distribution, on the one hand, and solicitation and sales, on the other, suggest that the latter activities present greater crowd control problems than the former.

COMMENT

1. *Heffron* held that the restriction by a state entity on distribution, sales, and solicitation activities to a fixed site was a permissible time, place, and manner regulation. What are the characteristics of a valid time, place, and manner regulation?

Justice White identifies four such characteristics: 1) the restriction cannot be based on either the content or subject matter of the speech. 2) A valid time, place, and manner regulation must serve a significant governmental interest. (What significant governmental interest was served by the regulation in *Heffron*?) 3) A time, place, and manner regulation is not valid if the state could accomplish its purpose by less drastic means. (Were less drastic means open to the Minnesota State Fair?) 4) A time, place, and manner regulation is valid if alternative forums exist for the purpose of communicating the expression which is limited by the regulation in controversy. (Were such alternative forums present in the *Heffron* context?)

2. It should be borne in mind by the student that analysis of whether the characteristics of a valid time, place, and manner regulation will vary from context to context. In a dissent in *Metromedia, Inc. v. City of San Diego*, text, p. 174, Chief Justice Burger observed:

> The uniqueness of the medium, the availability of alternative means of communication, and the public interest the regulation serves are important factors to be weighed; and the balance very well may shift when attention is turned from one medium to another. *Heffron v. International Society for Krishna Consciousness, Inc.* Regulating newspapers, for example, is vastly different from regulating billboards.

Is it likely that the characteristics of a valid time, place, and manner regulation will be found to be present more readily in a newspaper context or a billboard context? See Pittsburgh Press Co. v. Pittsburgh Commission on Human Relations, 413 U.S. 376 (1973), where a municipal regulation prohibiting sex-designated want ad columns in a newspaper was upheld.

Parades and Demonstrations and the Duty to Obey the Void Judicial Order

1. *Walker v. City of Birmingham, 388 U.S. 307 (1967)*, an important First Amendment case, arose out of the black civil rights protest movement of the 1960s. Just before Easter 1963, eight black ministers, including the late Dr. Martin Luther King, were arrested and held in contempt for leading civil rights marches in Birmingham on Easter in defiance of an *ex parte* injunction banning all marches, parades, sit-ins, or other demonstrations in violation of the Birmingham parade ordinance. The petitioners contended that the ordinance required a grant of permission from city administrators who had made it clear no permission would be granted. The state courts held that petitioners could not violate the injunction and later challenge its validity. The Supreme Court, per Justice Potter Stewart, affirmed the conviction, 5–4. Justices Warren, Douglas, Brennan, and Abe Fortas dissented. All but Fortas wrote a separate dissent.

The heart of the holding in *Walker* is that even if both the ordinance and the injunction raised substantial constitutional issues, petitioners could only successfully raise those issues by moving to modify or dissolve the injunction, not by disobeying it and then defending against contempt charges on constitutional grounds.

Justice Stewart pointed out that "this is not a case where the injunction was transparently invalid or had only a frivolous pretense to validity." While the language of the Birmingham ordinance might present substantial First Amendment questions, it could not be held invalid on its face. If petitioners, instead of proceeding without a permit, had sought a judicial decree from the state courts interpreting the parade ordinance, the Court might have offered a narrow, "saving" construction, as had the state courts in *Poulos v. New Hampshire*.

A fundamental reason for the decision in *Walker* appears to be that initial obedience is required of even unconstitutional court decrees, like the injunction in *Walker*, even though the same is not required of an unconstitutional ordinance or statute. Chief Justice Warren observed in caustic dissent in *Walker* that petitioners are "convicted and sent to jail because the patently unconstitutional ordinance was copied into an injunction." Further, the injunction was *ex parte* and unlimited as to time.

We have seen cases where the Court has held that an unconstitutional statute need not be obeyed. This is so, even where an ordinance explicitly requires a permit to engage in some form of communication. See Thomas v. Collins, 323 U.S. 516 (1945), and Lovell v. Griffin, 303 U.S. 444 (1938), text, p. 34.

Justice Douglas, in his dissenting opinion, directly confronted the civil disobedience issue in *Walker*. An unconstitutional court decree, he said, is no less invalid than an unconstitutional statute. "It can and should be flouted in the manner of the ordinance itself." The facts of the *Walker* case, most of which were excluded from evidence during the hearing on contempt charges, indicated that the city officials had no intention of ever granting a permit to petitioners, said Justice Douglas. Not only was the parade ordinance probably invalid on its face, but it was enforced in a discriminatory manner to prevent civil rights advocates from exercising their right, guaranteed by the First Amendment, to assemble peacefully and petition for redress of grievances. Affirmance of contempt convictions in such a case, he concluded, could only undermine respect for law, since "[t]he 'constitutional freedom' of which the Court speaks can be won only if judges honor the Constitution."

Justice Brennan filed the third dissenting opinion in *Walker*. In Justice Brennan's view, the Court was faced with the collision between Alabama's interest in enforcing judicial decrees and the petitioners' First Amendment rights of speech and peaceful assembly. In such a conflict, Brennan said, the Supremacy Clause of the United States Constitution demands that the First Amendment interests be given greater weight. Furthermore, in safeguarding First Amendment rights from invalid prior restraints, the Court ought to be even more suspicious of prior restraints contained in *ex parte* injunctions than in "presumably carefully considered, even if hopelessly invalid," statutes. Instead, he said, the Court in *Walker* abandoned its protective function in the First Amendment area and threw its support to the Alabama court decree, a "devastatingly destructive weapon for suppression of cherished freedoms. * * *"

Justice Brennan also pointed to several weaknesses in the Court's argument. The Alabama decree contained no time limitation whatsoever. It was not really "temporary" at all. Secondly, the Court's insistence that petitioners challenge the injunction in court first and march later was in head-on conflict with the Court's own First Amendment doctrine that where an invalid prior restraint is imposed, freedom of speech can not be served if exercise of that freedom is forcibly deferred pending the outcome of lengthy judicial review. Brennan emphasized the factual context of the *Walker* case: a civil rights campaign was planned which was intended to have its climax in a series of marches on Easter weekend. To require petitioners to drop their organizing efforts and spend weeks, months, or years in state and federal courts was to blink at the realities of their situation.

Notice that despite the strong protests by the dissenting justices, the *Walker* majority refused to consider the parade ordinance invalid on its face. The Court's reliance on Howat v. Kansas, 258 U.S. 181 (1922), seems to indicate that even an injunction invalid on its face must be obeyed pending judicial review. If this is so, how does (or might) the Court answer the claim by the dissenting justices that such a ruling opens the door for local officials to impose prior restraint simply by incorporating unconstitutional ordinances into binding judicial decrees?

The *Walker* decision was 5-to-4. Justice Black, who had dissented in *Poulos*, cast a deciding vote in *Walker* to sustain contempt convictions in the face of the vague, overbroad, limitless injunction. Black may have considered the integrity of the judicial process, even when, as in *Walker*, it may have been greatly abused, to be of such a high importance that it outweighed even First Amendment interests. This point of view is in contrast with Justice Douglas's statement that judges, no less than legislators or administrators, must honor the Constitution.

2. Compare *Walker v. City of Birmingham* with *Thomas v. Collins*. In each case a statute which was arguably invalid formed the basis for an injunction which prohibited the exercise of free speech. In each, a person violated the injunction without first taking steps to have it modified or dissolved and without making a serious effort to comply with the requirements of the ordinance on which the injunction was based. When faced with contempt charges, each person sought to defend on the grounds that the underlying ordinance was unconstitutional. In *Thomas*, that argument succeeded; the Supreme Court held that statute invalid and ruled that the contempt conviction could not stand. In *Walker*, there was an opposite result. Why? The Texas statute chal-

lenged in *Thomas* sought to regulate pure speech, while the Birmingham statute in *Walker* purported to regulate the use of public streets. Would this difference be determinative? The majority opinion in *Walker* did not mention *Thomas v. Collins.*

Walker v. Birmingham raises, in a First Amendment context, the issue of whether an order of a lower court which almost certainly will be reversed on appeal must be obeyed by the parties subject to it until the order is set aside by a higher court. This is an issue of great significance to the journalist. In United States v. Dickinson, 465 F.2d 496 (5th Cir. 1972), cert. den. 414 U.S. 979 (1973), a federal court of appeals upheld a criminal contempt citation for violation of a "gag" rule imposed by a federal district judge despite the appeals court's view that the "gag" was a violation of the First Amendment. The court of appeals relied on *Walker* for its decision that even an unconstitutional court order must be obeyed until it is reversed. See discussion of the *Dickinson* case in this text, p. 499.

3. Two years after it decided *Walker v. City of Birmingham*, the Supreme Court considered a different case arising out of the identical facts. The case was *Shuttlesworth v. City of Birmingham, 394 U.S. 147 (1969).* This time, the question was whether Rev. Walker and Rev. Shuttlesworth, *et al.* could be convicted of violating Birmingham's parade ordinance, a part of the city's general code. Petitioners had knowingly violated the ordinance, but they claimed, as they had in *Walker*, that their action was not punishable because the ordinance itself was invalid on its face and discriminatorily applied to deny First Amendment rights. Nevertheless, they were found guilty of violating the parade ordinance and received stiff jail sentences (Rev. Shuttlesworth, for instance, was sentenced to 138 days at hard labor).

A state appeals court reversed, holding that the parade ordinance was an unconstitutional prior restraint upon First Amendment rights since it granted city officials unlimited discretion to grant or deny parade permits. However, the Alabama Supreme Court reinstated the convictions by providing a curative gloss to the parade ordinance. The parade ordinance, said the state supreme court, did not confer discretionary powers upon local officials to withhold parade permits on a discriminatory basis. Rather, it directed them merely to regulate use of the public streets consistent with the goal of insuring public access to public throughways.

This, despite the fact that the parade ordinance provided that the city commission could deny a permit whenever it determined that "the public welfare, peace, safety, health, decency, good order, morals or convenience require." The process by which this language was narrowed by the Supreme Court of Alabama to make the parade ordinance a traffic measure received a backhanded compliment from Justice Stewart in his opinion for the Court: "It is true that in affirming the petitioner's conviction in the present case, the Supreme Court of Alabama performed a remarkable job of plastic surgery upon the face of the ordinance."

By transforming the parade ordinance into a traffic-management ordinance, the Alabama court attempted to avert constitutional problems in much the same way that the New Hampshire court had done in Poulos v. New Hampshire, 345 U.S. 395 (1953). The Alabama court also acted on the suggestion of the Court in *Walker v. City of Birmingham* that a narrow interpretation of the parade ordinance might save it from First Amendment attack. However, even the strenuous effort of the Alabama court to rescue the Birmingham ordinance from constitutional infirmity failed to persuade the Supreme Court to uphold the convictions when *Shuttlesworth* came up for review.

Justice Stewart speaking for the Court, in an interesting twist from his opinion in

Walker, first pointed out that the parade ordinance was, as written, invalid on its face. This was precisely the contention which he had rejected in *Walker*. Now, however, Justice Stewart held:

> There can be no doubt that the Birmingham ordinance, as it was written, conferred upon the city commission virtually unbridled and absolute power [to control the issuance of permits for marches or demonstrations in the city]. * * * This ordinance * * * fell squarely within the ambit of the many decisions of this Court over the last 30 years, holding that a law subjecting the exercise of First Amendment freedoms to the prior restraint of a license, without narrow, objective, and definite standards to guide the licensing authority, is unconstitutional.

Justice Stewart next dealt with the state's argument that that standard is not applicable where the regulation under challenge deals with speech plus, i.e., the use of public streets. Although recognizing the state interest in regulating the use of its public ways, the Court ruled that a licensing system implementing that interest must adhere to constitutional standards. An *overbroad, vague* licensing scheme vesting local officials with limitless discretion over the use of city streets does not square with those standards even though speech plus is involved.

The real question, said Stewart, was whether the parade ordinance was to be obeyed in 1963, notwithstanding the gloss which was put upon the ordinance by the state court four years later.

The Court concluded that Birmingham's parade ordinance, as it was implemented and enforced by Birmingham officials in 1963, was invalid and a denial of First Amendment rights. Petitioners were, therefore, entitled to ignore the parade ordinance and could not be criminally prosecuted for that decision. Justice Stewart described the ministers' unsuccessful efforts to obtain a parade permit from adamant city officials.

> The petitioner was clearly given to understand that under no circumstance would he and his group be permitted to demonstrate in Birmingham, not that a demonstration would be approved if a time and place were selected that would minimize traffic problems. * * [I]t is evident that the ordinance was administered so as * * * "to deny or unwarrantedly abridge the right of assembly and the opportunities for the communication of thought * * * immemorially associated with resort to public places."

Because Birmingham city officials interpreted and implemented the parade ordinance in a fashion consistent with its broad discretionary language, Rev. Shuttlesworth was justified in taking them at their word and acting accordingly. Notwithstanding the state supreme court's effort to save the parade ordinance, it was unconstitutional in 1963, and petitioners could not be punished for violating it under those circumstances.

Justice John Marshall Harlan's concurring opinion took issue with what he called the "seeds of mischief" contained in the opinion of the Court.

The important point, said Harlan, was whether the petitioners could have had a prompt judicial remedy under the special circumstances of their civil rights protest. Hearkening back to Justice Frankfurter's concurring opinion in *Poulos*, Justice Harlan noted that here, as contrasted with *Poulos*, a timely remedy to force issuance of the parade permit was probably out of the question. Had petitioners sought a writ of mandamus to require the Birmingham City Commission to issue a parade permit, they could not have succeeded in time for the Easter demonstrations, and under Alabama law there is no provision for expeditious review of such a petition:

> Given the absence of speedy procedures, the Rev. Shuttlesworth and his associates were faced with a serious dilemma. * * * If they attempted to

> exhaust the administrative and judicial remedies provided by Alabama law, it was almost certain that no effective relief could be obtained by Good Friday. * * * With fundamental rights at stake, he was entitled to adopt the more probable meaning of the ordinance and act on his belief that the city's permit regulations were unconstitutional.

It was not enough, Justice Harlan argued, that petitioner should rely merely upon the attitude of a local official and *his* interpretation of the parade ordinance. If a speedy and effective remedy had been available, petitioners would have been obligated to pursue that remedy before breaking the law, Harlan said. But in this case, on these facts, such a course would have blocked the exercise of First Amendment rights with no promise of effective relief. It was therefore excused, and the convictions could not stand.

Unlike Justice Stewart and the rest of the Court, Justice Harlan was not prepared to concede that the principle of cases such as *Lovell v. Griffin*, text, p. 34, involving licensing of pure speech, should be extended to cover ordinances such as the Birmingham parade statute, which regulated speech plus conduct. Regulation of the use of city streets was "a particularly important state interest." Even if such a regulation were deemed invalid on its face or as applied, perhaps citizens should be less free to ignore that regulation entirely than they would be to ignore an ordinance regulating pure speech.

In *Shuttlesworth*, the Supreme Court vindicated at least some of the points advanced by the four dissenters in *Walker*. The Birmingham parade ordinance was unconstitutional on its face and as applied—a decision the Court had refused to make in *Walker* just two years earlier. In reversing the petitioners' convictions for violating the parade ordinance, the Court did precisely what Chief Justice Warren had envisioned: it ruled that punishment for violating the ordinance could not stand, but (because of *Walker*) disobedience to the command of an identical prohibition, in a court decree, could be punished as contempt. In *Shuttlesworth*, Justice Stewart contended in a brief footnote that "[t]he legal and constitutional issues involved in the *Walker* case were quite different from those involved here." How would you support or take issue with that assertion?

In *Walker*, Chief Justice Warren dissented pointing out that the Birmingham ordinance on its face directed local officials to refuse parade permits on any number of broad, discretionary, vague grounds. Thus, a state court could "save" the Birmingham ordinance only "by repealing some of its language." Is this in fact what the Alabama Supreme Court did in *Shuttlesworth*?

Picketing, Handbilling, and State Action: The Collision Points Between Freedom of Expression and Property Rights

---

THORNHILL v. ALABAMA

310 U.S. 88, 60 S.CT. 736, 84 L.ED. 1093 (1940).

[EDITORIAL NOTE

Thornhill was a First Amendment case which arose out of a local labor dispute at an Alabama factory. Thornhill, a union organizer, was arrested and convicted of a misdemeanor for violating a state antipicketing law which made it a crime for:

> * * * any person or persons * * * without a just cause or legal excuse therefore, [to] go near to or loiter about the * * * place of business of any other person, firm, corporation, [etc.] * * * for the purpose, or with the intent of influencing, or inducing other persons not to trade with, buy from, sell to, have business dealings with or be employed by [that business] * * * State Code of 1923, § 3448.

The same section also prohibited picketing under the same circumstances.

Thornhill's conviction was upheld by the Alabama courts. The United States Supreme Court reversed his conviction and held the right to picket protected by the First Amendment. Justice James McReynolds was the lone dissenter.

Thornhill was arrested when, as part of a small picket line, he peacefully advised would-be strikebreakers to go home and not to cross the picket line. The plant where this took place was part of a company town in which most plant employees lived. The picket line was on private property, as was most of the town].

Justice MURPHY delivered the opinion of the Court.

* * *

* * * The existence of such a statute, which readily lends itself to harsh and discriminatory enforcement by local prosecuting officials, against particular groups deemed to merit their displeasure, results in a continuous and pervasive restraint on all freedom of discussion that might reasonably be regarded as within its purview. It is not any less effective or, if the restraint is not permissible, less pernicious than the restraint on freedom of discussion imposed by the threat of censorship. An accused, after arrest and conviction under such a statute, does not have to sustain the burden of demonstrating that the State could not constitutionally have written a different and specific statute covering his activities as disclosed by the charge and the evidence introduced against him. * *

The vague contours of the term "picket" are nowhere delineated. Employees or others, accordingly, may be found to be within the purview of the term and convicted for engaging in activities identical with those proscribed by the first offense. In sum, whatever the means used to publicize the facts of a labor dispute, whether by printed sign, by pamphlet, by word of mouth or otherwise, all such activity without exception is within the inclusive prohibition of the statute so long as it occurs in the vicinity of the scene of the dispute. * * * We think that Section 3448 is invalid on its face.

* * *

In the circumstances of our times the dissemination of information concerning the facts of a labor dispute must be regarded as within that area of free discussion that is guaranteed by the Constitution. * * * Free discussion concerning the conditions in industry and the causes of labor disputes appears to us indispensable to the effective and intelligent use of the processes of popular government to shape the destiny of modern industrial society. * * *

The range of activities proscribed by Section 3448, whether characterized as picketing or loitering or otherwise, embraces nearly every practicable, effective means whereby those interested—including the employees directly affected—may enlighten the public on the nature and causes of a labor dispute. The safeguarding of these means is essential to the securing of an informed and educated public opinion with respect to a matter which is of public concern. It may be that effective exercise of the means of advancing public knowledge may persuade some of those reached to refrain from entering into advantageous relations with the business establishment which is the scene of the dispute. Every expression of opinion on matters that are important has the potentiality of inducing action in the interests of one rather than another group in society. But the group in power at any moment may not impose penal sanctions on peaceful and truthful discussion of matters of public interest merely on a showing that others may thereby be persuaded to take action inconsistent with its interests. Abridgment of the liberty of such discussion can be justified only where the clear danger of substantive evils arises under circumstances affording no opportunity to test the merits of ideas by competition for acceptance in the market of public opinion. We hold that the danger of injury to an industrial concern is neither so serious nor so imminent as to justify the sweeping proscription of freedom of discussion embodied in Section 3448.

* * *

COMMENT

1. If Alabama desired to guard against violent picketing or harassment of potential customers by union threats, the state could under the First Amendment draft a statute designed to meet such situations. The Alabama antipicketing law made no attempt to consider factors which would distinguish the *Thornhill* picket line from other, more dangerous situations, nor did it consider the number of people gathered at the picket line, the potentiality of violence and harm to passersby, the accuracy of the information which the union was imparting to the public, and the nature of the union dispute.

The statute covered all situations indiscriminately. Since some activities covered by the statute were unquestionably examples of peaceful expression, the statute in its broad sweep could not stand. Enforcement of the statute only in special cases could not repair the fatal defect which the statute bore on its face. And selective enforcement with its potential for discrimination poses a special threat to First Amendment freedom.

2. It is a principle of due process adjudication that criminal statutes should be drawn so that the class affected by them are sufficiently apprised of the conduct expected of them in order that they may comply with the statute and avoid its sanction. This principle is sometimes called the "vagueness" doctrine. See generally, Amsterdam, *The Void for Vagueness Doctrine*, 109 U.Pa.L.Rev. 67 (1960).

Thornhill demonstrates the use of a related constitutional principle: the doctrine of overbreadth. A statute is defectively *overbroad* when it reaches and proscribes activities which are constitutionally protected as well as activities which are not. The statute in *Thornhill* is also defectively *vague*. Note that the Court observed that the term "picket" was inadequately defined. Vagueness is a major First Amendment doctrine, but it has its roots in the notice requirements of procedural due process. If people do not know what is expected of them, it is not fair to punish them. Furthermore, if they do not know what is expected of them, they may fear to engage in the vigorous exercise of First Amendment rights. In a sense, the First Amendment concern to prevent restraints which inhibit freedom of expression and the concern for fairness which is implemented by the constitutional doctrine of *procedural due process* coalesce in the vagueness doctrine. A Roman law maxim was "Nulla poena sine lege" (no penalty without a law). Does this ancient legal concept help explain the vagueness doctrine? Is it possible for a statute to be defectively overbroad but not overly vague?

3. The thrust of *Thornhill* was that the antipicketing section of the Alabama Code was overly broad but that a more narrowly drawn statute might pass constitutional muster under the First Amendment:

> We are not now concerned with picketing *en masse* or otherwise conducted which might occasion such imminent and aggravated danger to state interests in preventing breaches of the peace * * * as to justify a statute narrowly drawn to cover the precise situation giving rise to the danger.

But the Alabama antipicketing law made no attempt to balance the First Amendment against any state interest. The valuable contribution of *Thornhill* to First Amendment law was that it made clear, by extending First Amendment protection to picketing, that nonverbal communication merited First Amendment protection, albeit in a nonabsolute form.

Picketing, Private Property, and the Public Forum: The State Action Problem

1. In Amalgamated Food Employees Local 590 v. Logan Valley Plaza, Inc., 391 U.S. 308 (1968), the Supreme Court refused, per Justice Thurgood Marshall, to enjoin informational picketing in a private shopping center. *Logan Valley*, therefore, subjected privately owned property to First Amendment obligation as the Supreme Court had done only once before in Marsh v. Alabama, 326 U.S. 501 (1946). In *Marsh*, the exercise of First Amendment rights had been recognized in a company-owned town where alternative means of communication for the matter to be communicated were not available. Speaking for the Court in *Logan Valley*, Justice Marshall said:

> All we decide here is that because the shopping center serves as the community business block "and is freely accessible and open to the people in the area and those passing through," Marsh v. State of Alabama, 326 U.S., at 508, the state may not delegate the power through the use of its trespass laws, wholly to exclude those members of the public wishing to exercise their First Amendment rights on the premises in a manner and for a purpose generally consonant with the use to which the property is actually put.

The classic idea of American constitutionalism is the view that the constitution runs against *government*. If one relies on the Bill of Rights directly, one encounters the language, for example, of the First Amendment ("Congress shall make no law * * * abridging the freedom of speech, or of the press * * *"). If, on the other hand, one relies on the due process clause of the Fourteenth Amendment, one meets the following language: "* * * nor shall any *State* deprive any person of life, liberty, or property, without due process of law." This introduces the need for "State action" if a Fourteenth Amendment violation is to be found. This also explains the effort of the Supreme Court in both *Marsh* and *Amalgamated* to view the company-town street and the shopping center parking lot as "quasi-public." (Why is the Court reluctant to come right out and say that First Amendment considerations apply to *private* property?)

Private concentrations of power, such as the nationwide chains of daily newspapers (most papers are located in one newspaper towns), and the networks which supply the programming for much of radio and television broadcasting throughout the country are, therefore, in the classic view, immune from constitutional obligation altogether. This idea, as applied to the privately owned media, was given renewed life in CBS v. Democratic National Committee, 412 U.S. 94 (1973). See text, p. 858.

But decisions like *Marsh* and *Amalgamated* suggest that the capacity of "private governments" to elude constitutional obligation to provide freedom of expression is not infinite after all. The *Marsh* case in 1946 was a surprising breakthrough, but, in a sense, it was ahead of its time. It never blossomed forth into an important or pioneering constitutional doctrine in any meaningful way until the decision of the *Amalgamated Food Employees* case in 1968.

2. For Justice Black, the First Amendment is meant to state what government cannot do, not what a private individual or corporation must do. As a matter of history this view is probably accurate. As a matter of making the goals of freedom of expression and community enlightenment a reality, the question is does such an approach any longer have contemporary relevance? See Justice Douglas's concurring opinion in CBS v. Democratic Nation-

al Committee, 412 U.S. 94 (1973). See this text, p. 865.

In Justice Marshall's opinion for the Court in *Amalgamated*, the following observations appear:

> The picketing carried on by petitioners was directed specifically at patrons of the Weis Market located within the shopping center and the message sought to be conveyed to the public concerned the manner in which that particular market was being operated. We are, therefore, not called upon to consider whether respondents' property rights could, consistently with the First Amendment, justify a bar on picketing which was not thus directly related in its purpose to the use to which the shopping center property was being put.

Did the distinction Justice Marshall attempted to draw between protest picketing where the site of the protest is related to the object of the protest and where the site is unrelated to the object of the protest make sense? Note that the Supreme Court in *Amalgamated Food Employees* did not rule on the constitutional significance of this distinction.

3. Lloyd Corp., Limited v. Tanner, 407 U.S. 551 (1972), answered the question which Justice Marshall raised but did not answer in *Amalgamated Food Employees*: Could the owner of a private shopping center prohibit protest in the form of distribution of handbills on his premises when the object of the protest (hostility to the Vietnam War) did not have a direct relationship to the shopping center? The Supreme Court in *Lloyd Corp.* held that there must be a relationship between the object of the protest and the site of the protest before there can be any right to use private property for purposes of free expression.

In *Lloyd Corp.*, the four Nixon appointees to the Supreme Court, Powell, Blackmun, Rehnquist, and Burger, joined with Kennedy appointee, White, to hold that there must be a relationship between object and site of the protest. The *Lloyd Corp.* case marks a retreat from what had previously been a steady extension by the courts of the state action concept to the exercise of First Amendment rights on private property.

4. In *Amalgamated Food Employees*, Justice Marshall, speaking for the Court, had made a fairly radical statement: "[P]roperty that is privately owned may at least, for First Amendment purposes, be treated as though it were publicly held." The *Lloyd Corp.* case took much of the force out of this statement. It is true that *Logan Valley* was not reversed in *Lloyd Corp.*, and that the Court professed allegiance to the doctrine of *Amalgamated Food Employees* insofar as, under its facts, it authorized the exercise of First Amendment rights on private property so long as the exercise of those rights related to the site of the protest. Nevertheless, the concept that First Amendment obligations only run to governmental institutions received new vigor as a result of the *Lloyd Corp.* case. Consider the following analysis of the *Lloyd Corp.* case:

> * * * [F]ree expression is now likely to be considered less important than whether the site chosen (for its exercise) is private or public property. The majority of the Court denied that the property of a large shopping center is "open to the public" in the same way as is the "business district" of a city, and that a member of the public could exercise the same rights of free expression in a shopping mall that he could in "similar public facilities in the streets of a city or town." Barron, *Freedom Of The Press For Whom?* 106 (1973).

5. The *Lloyd* case left the *Logan Valley* case just barely alive. However, in Hudgens v. NLRB, 424 U.S. 507 (1976), the Supreme Court overruled *Logan Valley*.

The *Hudgens* Court buried Justice Marshall's attempted distinction in *Logan Valley* between situations where the object of the protest was related to the site and situations where the object of the protest was unrelated to the site. The key to understanding the decision of the Court in *Hudgens* appears to be that First Amendment obligation does not run to private property. As the *Hudgens* Court conceived it, if the fact that a particular protest was related to the site of protest imposed First Amendment obligations on the owner of the site, then First Amendment determinations were being made on the basis of analyzing the content of the protest. The Court proclaimed that First Amendment adjudication had to be content-neutral.

In *Hudgens*, the Court, in order to maintain a content-neutral approach to the First Amendment, approved a prohibition by the owner of a shopping center against labor union picketing on its premises. Professor Redish has observed that "the equality principle and the values of free expression conflict." Why? Consider the following:

> Those with greater resources and more power will invariably possess greater access to the media, and therefore to the public, than will those less well situated. These factors may be cited as reasons why a seemingly neutral restriction on picketing should in reality be found to discriminate (and, therefore, constitute a violation of the equality principle). Those with greater resources and power do not need to picket to express their views; those lacking such advantages do. But it would be absurd to think that allowing individuals to picket produces anything approaching equality.

See Redish, *The Content Distinction in First Amendment Analysis*, 34 Harv.L.Rev. 113 at 138 (1981).

Do you think *Marsh v. Alabama*, text, p. 52, survives *Hudgens*? Probably, *Marsh* does survive *Hudgens* since the *Hudgens* Court relied on Justice Black's dissent in *Logan Valley*. In *Logan Valley*, Justice Black distinguished *Marsh*, a decision which he had authored, on the ground that in *Marsh*, unlike the shopping center situations, the private property involved was truly quasi public in that there the company town had "taken all the attributes of a town."

In a conflict between property rights and the exercise of First Amendment rights, shouldn't the edge be given to the exercise of First Amendment rights? Does the *Hudgens* decision reflect the new deference shown to property values as against free expression values on the part of the Burger Court—at least as compared to the Warren Court?

A *Logan Valley*-type response to whether private property can be used as a public response still endures in California on the basis of the state constitutional guarantee of freedom of expression. See *PruneYard Shopping Center v. Robins*, text, p. 179.

CAREY v. BROWN

447 U.S. 455, 100 S.CT. 2286, 65 L.ED.2D 263 (1980).

Justice BRENNAN delivered the opinion of the Court.

At issue in this case is the constitutionality under the First and Fourteenth Amendments of a state statute that bars all picketing of residences or dwellings, but exempts from its prohibition "the peaceful picketing of a place of employment involved in a labor dispute."

On September 7, 1977, several of the appellees, all of whom are members of a civil rights organization entitled the Committee Against Racism, participated in a peaceful demonstration on the public sidewalk in front of the home of Michael Bilandic, then Mayor of Chicago, protesting his alleged failure to support the busing of school children to achieve racial integration. They were arrested and charged with Unlawful Residential Picketing in violation of Ill.Rev.Stat., ch. 38, § 21.1–2, which provides:

> It is unlawful to picket before or about the residence or dwelling of any person, except when the residence or dwelling is used as a place of business. However, this article does not apply to a person peacefully picketing his own residence or dwelling and does not prohibit the peaceful picketing of a place of employment involved in a labor dispute or the place of holding a meeting or assembly on premises commonly used to discuss subjects of general public interest.

Appellees pleaded guilty to the charge and were sentenced to periods of supervision ranging from 6 months to a year.

In April 1978, appellees commenced this lawsuit in the United States District Court for the Northern District of Illinois, seeking a declaratory judgment that the Illinois Residential Picketing Statute is unconstitutional on its face and as applied, and an injunction prohibiting appellants—various state, county, and city officials—from enforcing the statute.

* * * (T)his Court has had occasion to consider the constitutionality of an enactment selectively proscribing peaceful picketing on the basis of the placard's message. *Police Department of Chicago v. Mosley* [408 U.S. 92 (1972)], arose out of a challenge to a Chicago ordinance that prohibited picketing in front of any school other than one "involved in a labor dispute." We held that the ordinance violated the Equal Protection Clause because it impermissibly distinguished between labor picketing and all other peaceful picketing without any showing that the latter was "clearly more disruptive" than the former. [W]e find the Illinois Residential Picketing Statute at issue in the present case constitutionally indistinguishable from the ordinance invalidated in *Mosley*.

There can be no doubt that in prohibiting peaceful picketing on the public streets and sidewalks in residential neighborhoods, the Illinois statute regulates expressive conduct that falls within the First Amendment's preserve.

Nor can it be seriously disputed that in exempting from its general prohibition only the "peaceful picketing of a place of employment involved in a labor dispute," the Illinois statute discriminates between lawful and unlawful conduct based upon the content of the demonstrator's communications. On its face, the act accords preferential treatment to the expression of views on one particular subject; information about labor disputes may be freely disseminated, but discussion of all other issues is restricted. The permissibility of residential picketing under the Illinois statute is thus dependent solely on the nature of the message being conveyed.

In these critical respects, then, the Illinois statute is identical to the ordinance in *Mosley*, and it suffers from the same constitutional infirmities. When government regulation discriminates among speech-related activities in a public forum, the Equal Protection Clause mandates that the legislation be finely tailored to serve substantial state interests, and the justifications offered for any distinctions it draws must be carefully scrutinized. Yet here, under the guise of preserving residential privacy, Illinois has flatly prohibited all nonlabor picketing even though it permits labor picketing that is equally likely to intrude on the tranquility of the home.

Moreover, it is the content of the speech that determines whether it is within or without the statute's blunt prohibition. What we said in *Mosley* has equal force in the present case:

> Necessarily, then, under the Equal Protection Clause, not to mention the First Amendment itself, government may not grant the use of a forum to people whose views it finds acceptable, but deny use to those wishing to express less favored or more controversial views. And it may not select which issues are worth discussing or debating in public facilities. There is an "equality of status in the field of ideas," and government must afford all points of view an equal opportunity to be heard.

> Once a forum is opened up to assembly or speaking by some groups, government may not prohibit others from assembling or speaking on the basis of what they intend to say. Selective exclusions from a public forum may not be based on content alone, and may not be justified by reference to content alone.

Appellants nonetheless contend that this case is distinguishable from *Mosley*. They argue that the state interests here are especially compelling and particularly well-served by a statute that accords differential treatment to labor and nonlabor picketing. We explore in turn each of these interests, and the manner in which they are said to be furthered by this statute.

Appellants explain that whereas the Chicago ordinance sought to prevent disruption of the schools, concededly a "substantial" and "legitimate" governmental concern, the Illinois statute was enacted to ensure privacy in the home, a right which appellants view as paramount in our constitutional scheme. For this reason, they contend that the same content-based distinctions held invalid in the *Mosley* context may be upheld in the present case.

We find it unnecessary, however, to consider whether the state's interest in residential privacy outranks its interest in quiet schools in the hierarchy of societal values. For even the most legitimate goal may not be advanced in a constitutionally impermissible manner. And though we might agree that certain state interests may be so compelling that where no adequate alternatives exist a content-based distinction—if narrowly drawn—would be a permissible way of furthering those objectives, this is not such a case.

First, the generalized classification which the statute draws suggests that Illinois itself has determined that residential privacy is not a transcendent objective: While broadly permitting all peaceful labor picketing notwithstanding the disturbances it would undoubtedly engender, the statute makes no attempt to distinguish among various sorts of nonlabor picketing on the basis of the harms they would inflict on the privacy interest. The apparent over- and underinclusiveness of the statute's restriction would seem largely to undermine appellants' claim that the prohibition of all nonlabor picketing can be justified by reference to the state's interest in maintaining domestic tranquility.

More fundamentally, the exclusion for labor picketing cannot be upheld as a means of protecting residential privacy for the simple reason that nothing in the content-based labor-nonlabor distinction has any bearing whatsoever on privacy. Appellants can point to nothing inherent in the nature of peaceful labor picketing that would make it any less disruptive of residential privacy than peaceful picketing on issues of broader social concern. Standing alone, then, the state's asserted interest in promoting the privacy of the home is not sufficient to save the statute.

The second important objective advanced by appellants in support of the statute is the state's interest in providing special protection for labor protests. The central difficulty with this argument is that it forthrightly presupposes that labor picketing is more deserving of First Amendment protection than are public protests over other issues, particularly the important economic, social, and political subjects which these appellees wish to demonstrate. We reject that proposition.

Appellants' final contention is that the statute can be justified by some combination of the preceding objectives. This argument is fashioned on two different levels. In its elemental formulation, it posits simply that a distinction between labor and nonlabor picketing is uniquely suited to furthering the legislative judgment that residential privacy should be preserved to the greatest extent possible without also compromising the special protection owing to labor picketing. In short, the statute is viewed as a reasonable attempt to accommodate the competing rights of the homeowner to enjoy his privacy and the employee to demonstrate over labor disputes. But this attempt to justify the statute hinges on the validity of both of these goals, and we have already concluded that the latter—the desire to favor one form of speech over all others—is illegitimate.

The second and more complex formulation of appellants' position characterizes the statute as a carefully drafted attempt to prohibit that picketing which would impinge on residential privacy while permitting that picketing which would not. In essence, appellants assert that the exception for labor picketing does not contravene the State's interest in preserving residential tranquility because of the unique character of a residence that is a "place of employment." By "inviting" a worker into his home and converting that dwelling into a place of employment, the argument goes, the resident has diluted his entitlement to total privacy.

The flaw in this argument is that it proves too little. Numerous types of peaceful picketing other than labor picketing would have but a negligible impact on privacy interests, and numerous other actions of a homeowner might constitute "nonresidential" uses of his property and would thus serve to vitiate the right to residential privacy.

We therefore conclude the appellants have not successfully distinguished *Mosley*. We are not to be understood to imply, however, that residential picketing is beyond the reach of uniform and nondiscriminatory regulation. For the right to communicate is not limitless.

Preserving the sanctity of the home, the one retreat to which men and women can repair to escape from the tribulations of their daily pursuits, is surely an important value. Our decisions reflect no lack of solicitude for the right of an individual "to be let alone" in the privacy of the home, "sometimes the last citadel of the tired, the weary, and the sick." The State's interest in protecting the well-being, tranquility, and privacy of the home is certainly of the highest order in a free and civilized society. " 'The crucial question, however, is whether [Illinois' statute] advances that objective in a manner consistent with the command of the Equal Protection Clause.' Reed v. Reed, 404 U.S. [71], 76 (1971)." And because the statute discriminates among pickets based on the subject matter of their expression, the answer must be "No."

Justice REHNQUIST, with whom the Chief Justice and Justice Blackmun join, dissenting.

* * *

The complete language of the statute, set out accurately in the text of the Court's opinion, reveals a legislative scheme quite different from that described by the Court in its narrative paraphrasing of the enactment.

The statute provides that residential picketing is prohibited, but goes on to exempt four categories of residences from this general ban. *First*, if the residence is used as a "place of business" all peaceful picketing is allowed. *Second*, if the residence is being used to "hold[] a meeting or assembly on premises commonly used to discuss subjects of general public interest" *all* peaceful picketing is allowed. *Third*, if the residence is also used as a "place of employment" which is involved in a labor dispute, labor-related picketing is allowed. *Finally*, the statute provides that a resident is entitled to picket his own home. Thus it is clear that information about labor disputes may *not* be "freely disseminated" since labor picketing is restricted to a narrow category of residences. And Illinois has *not* "flatly prohibited all nonlabor picketing" since it allows nonlabor picketing at residences used as a place of business, residences used as public meeting places, and at an individual's own residence.

Only through this mischaracterization of the Illinois statute may the Court attempt to fit this case into the *Mosley* rule prohibiting regulation on the basis of "*content alone*." In contrast, the principal determinant of a person's right to picket a residence in Illinois is not content, as the Court suggests, but rather the character of the residence sought to be picketed. Content is relevant only in one of the categories established by the legislature.

The cases appropriate to the analysis therefore are those establishing the limits on a state's authority to impose time, place, and manner restrictions on speech activities. Under this rubric, even taking into account the limited content distinction made by the statute, Illinois has readily satisfied its constitutional obligation to draft statutes in conformity with First Amendment and equal protection principles. In fact, the very statute which the Court today cavalierly invalidates has been hailed by commentators as "an excellent model" of legislation achieving a delicate balance among rights to privacy, free expression, and equal protection. See Kamin, Residential Picketing and the First Amendment, 61 Nw.U.L.Rev. 177, 207 (1966); Comment, 34 U.Chi.L.Rev. 106, 139 (1966). The state legislators of the Nation will undoubtedly greet today's decision with nothing less than exasperation and befuddlement. Time after time, the states have been assured that they may properly promote residential privacy even though free expression must be reduced. To be sure, our decisions have adopted a virtual laundry list of "Don'ts" that must be adhered to in the process. Heading up that list of course is the rule that legislatures must curtail free expression through the "least restrictive means" consistent with the accomplishment of their purpose, and they must avoid standards which are either vague or capable of discretionary application. But somewhere, the Court says in these cases (with a reassuring pat on the head of the legislature) there *is* the constitutional pot of gold at the end of the rainbow of litigation.

Here, whether Illinois has drafted such a statute, avoiding an outright ban on all residential picketing, avoiding reliance on any vague or discretionary standards, and permitting categories of permissible picketing activity at residences where the state has determined the resident's own action have substantially reduced his interest in privacy, the Court in response confronts the state with the Catch-22 that the less-restrictive categories are constitutionally infirm under principles of equal protection. Under the Court's approach today, the state would fare better by adopting *more* restrictive means, a judicial incentive I had thought this Court would hesitate to afford. Either that, or uniform restrictions will be found invalid under the First Amendment and categorical exceptions found invalid under the Equal Protection Clause, with the result that speech and only speech will be entitled to protection. This can only mean that the hymns of praise in prior opinions celebrating carefully drawn statutes are no more than sympathetic clucking, and in fact the state is damned if it does and damned if it doesn't.

COMMENT

1. Is the statute in *Carey* invalid because residential picketing infringes on constitutionally protected privacy values? The statute is invalid, according to the Court, because it exempts from its general ban the peaceful picketing of a place of employment involved in a labor dispute. The Court criticized the preferential treatment by the legislature of a particular subject. Justice Rehnquist in dissent says this is not a content regulation. Why? Is it a subject category regulation?

2. Should a private residence ever be viewed as a public forum when picketing is the mode of expression chosen by the "speakers"?

3. In *Consolidated Edison*, the case which follows, the privacy values of the unwilling recipients—those who received inserts in their billing envelopes from a utility praising nuclear energy—were subordinated to the value of protecting the liberty of the speaker, the regulated utility. Why was the privacy value weighted so much more heavily by the Court in *Carey*? Was it that residential picketing presents a much greater burden on privacy values than does including an insert in a billing envelope?

CONSOLIDATED EDISON CO. v. PUBLIC SERVICE COMMISSION

447 U.S. 530, 100 S.CT. 2326, 65 L.ED.2D 319 (1980).

Justice POWELL delivered the opinion of the Court.

The question in this case is whether the First Amendment, as incorporated by the Fourteenth Amendment, is violated by an order of the Public Service Commission of the State of New York that prohibits the inclusion in monthly electric bills of inserts discussing controversial issues of public policy.

The Consolidated Edison Company of New York, appellant in this case, placed written material entitled "Independence Is Still a Goal, and Nuclear Power Is Needed To Win The Battle" in its January 1976 billing envelope. The bill insert stated Consolidated Edison's views on "the benefits of nuclear power," saying that they "far outweigh any potential risk" and that nuclear power plants are safe, economical, and clean. The utility also contended that increased use of nuclear energy would further this country's independence from foreign energy sources.

In March 1976, the Natural Resources Defense Council, Inc. (NRDC) requested Consolidated Edison to enclose a rebuttal prepared by NRDC in its next billing envelope. When Consolidated Edison refused, NRDC asked the Public Service Commission of the State of New York to open Consolidated Edison's billing envelopes to contrasting views on controversial issues of public importance.

On February 17, 1977, the commission, appellee here, denied NRDC's request but prohibited "utilities from using bill inserts to discuss political matters, including the desirability of future development of nuclear power." The commission explained its decision in a Statement of Policy on Advertising and Promotion Practices of Public Utilities issued on February 25, 1977. The commission concluded that Consolidated Edison customers who receive bills containing inserts are a captive audience of diverse views who should not be subjected to the utility's beliefs. Accordingly, the commission barred utility companies from including bill inserts that express "their opinions or viewpoints on controversial issues of public policy." The commission did not, however, bar utilities from sending bill inserts discussing topics that are not "controversial issues of public policy." The commission later denied petitions for rehearing filed by Consolidated Edison and other utilities.

The [New York] Court of Appeals held that the order did not violate the Constitution because it was a valid time, place, and manner regulation designed to protect the privacy of Consolidated Edison's customers. We noted probable jurisdiction. We reverse. The restriction on bill inserts cannot be upheld on the ground that Consolidated Edison is not entitled to freedom of speech. In *First National Bank of Boston v. Bellotti* we rejected the contention that a state may confine corporate speech to specified issues.

In the mailing that triggered the regulation at issue, Consolidated Edison advocated the use of nuclear power. The commission has limited the means by which Consolidated Edison may participate in the public debate on this question and other controversial issues of national interest and importance. Thus, the commission's prohibition of discussion of controversial issues strikes at the heart of the freedom to speak.

The commission's ban on bill inserts is not, of course, invalid merely because it imposes a limitation upon speech. We must consider whether the state can demonstrate that its regulation is constitutionally permissible. The commission's arguments require us to consider three theories that might justify the state action. We must determine whether the prohibition is (i) a reasonable time, place, or manner restriction, (ii) a permissible subject-matter regulation, or (iii) a narrowly tailored means of serving a compelling state interest.

A restriction that regulates only the time, place or manner of speech may impose so long as it's reasonable. But when regulation is based on the content of speech, governmental action must be scrutinized more carefully to ensure that communication has not been prohibited "merely because public officials disapprove the speaker's views." As a consequence, we have emphasized that time, place, and manner regulations must be "applicable to all speech regardless of content."

The commission does not pretend that its action is unrelated to the content or subject matter of bill inserts. Indeed, it has undertaken to suppress certain bill inserts precisely because they address issues of public policy. The commission allows inserts that present information to consumers on certain subjects, such as energy conservation measures, but it forbids the use of inserts that discuss public controversies. The commission, with commendable candor, justifies its ban on the ground that consumers will benefit from receiving "useful" information, but not from the prohibited information. The commission's own rationale demonstrates that its action cannot be upheld as a content-neutral time, place, or manner regulation.

The commission next argues that its order is acceptable because it applies to all discussion of nuclear power, whether pro or con, in bill inserts. The prohibition, the commission contends, is related to subject matter rather than to the views of a particular speaker. Because the regulation does not favor either side of a political controversy, the commission asserts that it does not unconstitutionally suppress freedom of speech.

The First Amendment's hostility to content-based regulation extends not only to restrictions on particular viewpoints, but also to prohibition of public discussion of an entire topic. To allow a government the choice of permissible subjects for public debate would be to allow that government control over the search for political truth.

Nevertheless, governmental regulation based on subject matter has been approved in narrow circumstances. The court below relied upon two cases in which this Court has recognized that the government may bar from its facilities certain speech that would disrupt the legitimate governmental purpose for which the property has been dedicated. In *Greer v. Spock* [p. 65], we held that the Federal Government could prohibit partisan political speech on a military base even though civilian speakers had been allowed to lecture on other subjects. In *Lehman v. Shaker Heights* [p. 64], a plurality of the Court similarly concluded that a city transit system that rented space in its vehicle for commercial advertising did not have to accept partisan political advertising.

Greer and *Lehman* properly are viewed as narrow exceptions to the general prohibition against subject-matter distinctions. In both cases, the Court was asked to decide whether a public facility was open to all speakers. The plurality in *Lehman* and the Court in *Greer* concluded that partisan political speech would disrupt the operation of governmental facilities even though other forms of speech posed no such danger.

The analysis of *Greer* and *Lehman* is not applicable to the Commission's regulation of bill inserts. In both cases, a private party asserted a right of access to public facilities. Consolidated Edison has not asked to use the offices of the commission as a forum from which to promulgate its views. Rather, it seeks merely to utilize its own billing envelopes to promulgate its views on controversial issues of public policy. The commission asserts that the billing envelope, as a necessary adjunct to the operations of a public utility, is subject to the state's plenary control. To be sure, the state has a legitimate regulatory interest in controlling Consolidated Edison's activities, just as local governments always have been able to use their police powers in the public interest to regulate private behavior. But the commission's attempt to restrict the free expression of a private party cannot be upheld by reliance upon precedent that rests on the special interests of a government in overseeing the use of its property.

Where a government restricts the speech of a private person, the state action may be sustained only if the government can show that the regulation is a precisely drawn means of serving a compelling state interest. The commission argues finally that its prohibition is necessary (i) to avoid forcing Consolidated Edison's views on a captive audience, (ii) to allocate limited resources in the public interest, and (iii) to ensure that rate-payers do not subsidize the cost of the bill inserts.

Even if a short exposure to Consolidated Edison's views may offend the sensibilities of some consumers, the ability of government "to shut off discourse solely to protect others from hearing it [is] dependent upon a showing that substantial privacy interests are being invaded in an essentially intolerable manner. Where a single speaker communicates to many listeners, the First Amendment does not permit the government to prohibit speech as intrusive unless the "captive" audience cannot avoid objectionable speech.

But customers who encounter an objectionable billing insert may "effectively avoid further bombardment of their sensibilities simply by averting their eyes." The customer of Consolidated Edison may escape exposure to objectionable material simply by transferring the bill insert from envelope to wastebasket.

The commission contends that because a billing envelope can accommodate only a limited amount of information, political messages should not be allowed to take the place of inserts that promote energy conservation or safety, or that remind customers of their legal rights. The commission relies upon *Red Lion Broadcasting v. Federal Communications Commission* [p. 845], in which the Court held that the regulation of radio and television broadcast frequencies permit the Federal Government to exercise unusual authority over speech. But billing envelopes differ from broadcast frequencies in two ways. First, a broadcaster communicates through use of a scarce, publicly owned resource. No person can broadcast without a license, whereas all persons are free to send correspondence to private homes through the mails. Thus, it cannot be said that billing envelopes are a limited resource comparable to the broadcast spectrum. Second, the commission has not shown on the record before us that the presence of the bill inserts at issue would preclude the inclusion of other inserts that Consolidated Edison might be ordered lawfully to include in the billing envelope. Unlike radio or television stations broadcasting on a single frequency, multiple bill inserts will not result in a "cacophony of competing voices."

Finally, the commission urges that its prohibition would prevent ratepayers from subsidizing the costs of policy-oriented bill inserts. But the commission did not base its order on an inability to allocate costs between the shareholders of Consolidated Edison and the ratepayers. Rather, the commission stated "that using bill inserts to proclaim a utility's viewpoint on controversial issues (*even when the stockholder pays for it in full*) is tantamount to taking advantage of a captive audience." Accordingly, there is no basis on this record to assume that the commission could not exclude the cost of these bill inserts from the utility's rate base. Mere speculation of harm does not constitute a compelling state interest.

Justice Stevens, concurring in the judgment.

Any student of history who has been reprimanded for talking about the World Series during a class discussion of the First Amendment knows that it is incorrect to state that a "time, place, or manner restriction may not be based upon either the content or subject matter of speech." And every lawyer who has read our rules, or our cases upholding various restrictions on speech with specific reference to subject matter must recognize the hyperbole in the dictum, "But, above all else, the First Amendment means that government has no power to restrict expression because of its message, its ideas, its subject matter or its content." Indeed, if that were the law, there would be no need for the Court's detailed rejection of the justifications put forward by the state for the restriction involved in this case.

There are, in fact, many situations in which the subject matter, or, indeed, even the point of view of the speaker, may provide a justification for a time, place and manner regulation. Perhaps the most obvious example is the regulation of oral argument in this Court; the appellant's lawyer precedes his adversary solely because he seeks reversal of a judgment. As is true of many other aspects of liberty, some forms of orderly regulation actually promote freedom more than would a state of total anarchy.

The only justification for the regulation relied on by the New York Court of Appeals is that the utilities' bill inserts may be "offensive" to some of their customers. But a communication may be offensive in two different ways. Independently of the message the speaker intends to convey, the form of his communication may be offensive—perhaps because it is too loud or too ugly in a particular setting. Other speeches, even though elegantly phrased in dulcet tones, are offensive simply because the listener disagrees with the speaker's message. The fact that the offensive form of some communication may subject it to appropriate regulation surely does not support the conclusion that the offensive character of an idea can justify an attempt to censor its expression. Since the Public Service Commission has candidly put forward this impermissible justification for its censorial regulation, it plainly violates the First Amendment.

Accordingly, I concur in the judgment of the Court.

Justice BLACKMUN, with whom Justice Rehnquist [in part] joins, dissenting.

I cannot agree with the Court that the New York Public Service Commission's ban on the utility bill insert somehow deprives the utility of its First and Fourteenth Amendment rights. Because of Consolidated Edison's monopoly status and its rate structure, the use of the insert amounts to an exaction from the utility's customers by way of forced aid for the utility's speech. And, contrary to the Court's suggestion, an allocation of the insert's cost between the utility's shareholders and the ratepayers would not eliminate this coerced subsidy.

[Justice Rehnquist did not join in the following portion of the dissent.]

I might observe, additionally, that I am hopeful that the Court's decision in this case has not completely tied a state's hands in preventing this type of abuse of monopoly power. The Court's opinion appears to turn on the particular facts of this case, and slight differences in approach might permit a state to achieve its proper goals.

First, it appears that New York and other States might use their power to define property rights so that the billing envelope is the property of the ratepayers and not of the utility's shareholders. If, under state law, the envelope belongs to the customers, I do not see how restricting the utility from using it could possibly be held to deprive the utility of its rights.

Second, the opinion leaves open the issue of cost allocation. The commission could charge the utility's shareholders all the costs of the envelopes and postage and of creating and maintaining the mailing list, and charge the consumers only the cost of printing and inserting the bill and the consumer service insert. Such an allocation would eliminate the most offensive aspects of the forced subsidization of the utility's speech.

Because I agree with the Appellate Division of the New York Supreme Court, that "[i]n the battle of ideas, the utilities are not entitled to require the consumers to help defray their expenses," I respectfully dissent.

COMMENT

1. Suppose the Public Utilities Commission had ordered Consolidated Edison to include a rebuttal prepared by an antinuclear energy group in its future billing envelopes. Suppose Consolidated Edison had challenged such an order on First Amendment grounds. Would the order be valid?

Professor Emerson has argued in favor of the validity, in the context of *Consolidated Edison,* of such an order. See Emerson, *The Affirmative Side of the First Amendment,* 15 Georgia L.Rev. 795 at 827–828 (1981):

> The Court did not have before it, and hence did not decide, the latent affirmative promotion issue involved in the case. * * *
>
> There is much to be said for the proposition that the first amendment rights of the third parties should be given recognition here. As a result of the monopoly granted by the government, the utility possessed a unique facility for communication, namely, a ready-made audience that was forced to open the billing envelope when it arrived in the home or office. Access to that facility, in a manner compatible with the primary function served by the billing apparatus, plainly would advance the discussion of important issues. Granting access to all comers might not be compatible with effective operation of the billing process. But imposition of a fairness doctrine, under which the utility was required to make adequate provision for the presentation of opposing views, surely would be feasible. The use of the first amendment in such a manner would promote significantly the system of freedom of expression.

2. Should the inclusion of inserts in its bills by Consolidated Edison be viewed as a form of impermissible compelled speech on the part of Con Ed's customers? See *Wooley v. Maynard,* text, p. 177. Justices Blackmun and Rehnquist make a similar argument: "Because of Consolidated Edison's monopoly status and its rate structure, the use of the insert amounts to an exaction from the utility's customers by way of forced aid for the utility's speech." Justice Powell makes it clear in *Consolidated Edison* that *Bellotti* protects Consolidated Edison's right to speak: "* * * [A] state may confine corporate speech to specified issues." On the other hand, if Consolidated Edison is not allowed to speak, i.e., include inserts on policy issues in its billing envelope, this, too, would be a form of impermissible compulsion, i.e., enforced silence. In the *Consolidated Edison* situation, therefore, free speech rights are in conflict. To assure the free speech of the corporate speaker, Consolidated Edison, is to compel the speech of some of its thousands of customers who have a desire

to communicate a different message in the same forum. Suppose the billing envelope is made, as Blackmun suggests, the property of the rate payers and not of the utilities shareholders, how would that affect the compelled speech problem? Would such a device make the inclusion of policy issue inserts in the billing envelope dependent on the consent of the utility's rate payers?

3. Suppose the activities of Con Ed had been deemed so involved with governmental sponsorship as to be deemed the equivalent of government action? Could the inserts have been included over the objection of recipients by Con Ed in that event? See Muir v. Alabama Educational Television Commission, 688 F.2d 1033 (5th Cir. 1982), text, p. 1022.

Would the case for rebuttal inserts by antinuclear energy citizen groups have been stronger if the action of Con Ed were seen as governmental or state action? See *Lehman v. City of Shaker Heights,* below and *Greer v. Spock*, text, p. 65.

Public Facilities and the Public Forum

1. What about the exercise of First Amendment rights on public property? To what extent may a public facility be used as a public forum? In a decision which appeared to suggest an unwillingness by the Supreme Court to recognize a general right of nondiscriminatory access to publicly owned media facilities, the Court, 5–4, upheld a lower court decision, Lehman v. City of Shaker Heights, 296 N.E.2d 683 (Ohio 1973), approving a city's right to prohibit political advertising on city buses. Lehman v. City of Shaker Heights, 418 U.S. 298 (1974). In the *Lehman* case, the Court denied access to publicly owned media to a political candidate who wished to display his political messages along with commercial ads on city owned buses in Shaker Heights, Ohio. Justice Blackmun wrote the Court's opinion in *Lehman,* joined by Justices Burger, White, and Rehnquist. These justices declared that a city had a right as the owner of a commercial venture like a public transportation system to accept ads only for "innocuous" commercial advertising and to prohibit political messages on buses.

The Court denied that the car cards in controversy constituted a "public forum" protected by the First Amendment. Similarly, the Court rejected the contention "that there is a guarantee of nondiscriminatory access to such publicly owned and controlled areas of communication regardless of the primary purpose for which the area is dedicated." Although the Court conceded that American constitutional law had been "jealous to preserve access to public places for purposes of free speech," what is dispositive in such cases is "the nature of the forum and the conflicting interests involved. * * *" Under the circumstances, the claim for the exercise of First Amendment expression in *Lehman* would be rejected:

> Here we have no open spaces, no meeting hall, park, street corner, or other public thoroughfare. Indeed, the city is engaged in commerce. * * * [C]ar card space, although incidental to the provision of public transportation, is a part of the commercial venture. In much the same way that a newspaper or periodical, or even a radio or television station, need not accept every proffer of advertising from the general public, a city transit system had discretion to develop and make reasonable choices concerning the type of advertising that may be displayed in its vehicles.
>
> * * *
>
> No First Amendment forum is here to be found. The city consciously has limited access to its transit system advertising space in order to minimize chances of abuse, the appearance of "favoritism" and the risk of imposing upon a captive audience. These are reasonable legislative objectives ad-

vanced by the city in a proprietary capacity.

2. By means of a separate concurring opinion, Justice Douglas supplied the critical fifth vote. He thought that a bus, from a public forum point of view, was more like a newspaper than a park. On the very day the Court decided *Lehman*, it had decided the *Miami Herald* case, text, p. 584. Relying on *Miami Herald*, Douglas appeared to suggest that the owner of a bus (even though it was a public owner) was equivalent to the owner of a private newspaper: "[The] newspaper owner cannot be forced to include in his offerings news or other items which outsiders may desire but which the owner abhors." If the bus or newspaper was turned into a park for purposes of the public forum concept, then public facilities such as publicly owned buses would be "transformed into forums for the dissemination of ideas upon [a] captive audience."

3. Four justices, Brennan, Stewart, Marshall, and Powell, dissented on the ground that the city's actions denying access violated equal protection in that the city had improperly preferred commercial advertising on its buses to the exclusion of political advertising. The dissenters said that Shaker Heights had opened up its advertising space on its buses as a "public forum." Having done so, the dissenters said the city could not exclude the category of political advertising:

> Having opened a forum of communication, the city is barred by the First and Fourteenth Amendments from discriminating among forum users solely on the basis of message content.
>
> * * *
>
> Once a public forum for communication has been established, both free speech and equal protection principles prohibit discrimination based solely upon subject matter or content. * * * [D]iscrimination among entire classes of ideas, rather than among points of view within a particular class, does not render it any less odious. Subject matter or content censorship in any form is forbidden.

Is the *Lehman* case a severe defeat for the whole idea of public property as a public forum? Or is the case merely a holding that the car cards were not a public forum? Note that there is a major difference in the force of a claim for the exercise of free expression rights in public property as compared with such a claim with respect to private property. In the private property area, there is no state action problem. In such a context, the mandate of First Amendment theory that the state act in an ideologically neutral manner combines with equal protection concepts to ensure that a public facility cannot favor one political viewpoint and banish another.

In *Lehman,* all political viewpoints in the form of political ads were banned. Therefore, arguably, there was no equal protection violation; Justice Brennan was of a contrary opinion, however, wasn't he? Why?

4. The necessity that the public facility which is sought to be used for public forum purposes be consistent with the primary purposes of the facility was emphasized once again by the Supreme Court in Greer v. Spock, 424 U.S. 828 (1976). The Court, per Justice Stewart, in *Greer* rejected an attack on military post regulations which prohibited partisan political activity as well as the dissemination of pamphlets without the prior approval of military authorities. The Court denied that "whenever members of the public are permitted freely to visit a place owned or operated by the Government then that place becomes a public forum for the purposes of the First Amendment." Adderley v. Florida, 385 U.S. 39 (1966), a 5–4 Supreme Court decision denying public forum treatment to jailhouse grounds, was relied on by the *Greer* Court for the idea that the First Amendment did not mean that "people who want to propagandize protests or

views have a constitutional right to do so whenever and however and wherever they please." The purpose of military reservations was to "train soldiers, not to provide a public forum." Justice Brennan, joined by Justice Marshall, dissented in *Greer* and expressed grave concern that a narrow approach to whether "the form of expression is compatible with the activities occurring at the locale" might lead to a "rigid characterization" that "a given locale is not a public forum." The result would be that "certain forms of public speech at the locale" would be suppressed even though the expression involved was entirely compatible with the principal purposes of the public facility in question.

5. In United States Postal Service v. Council of Greenburgh Civic Associations, 453 U.S. 114 (1981), the Court, per Justice Rehnquist, upheld a federal statute which prohibited mailboxes belonging to the government and used in the postal system from being used by civic associations without paying postage. Rehnquist rejected the idea "of a letter box as a public forum" and observed "that the First Amendment does not guarantee access to property simply because it is owned or controlled by the government." Rehnquist appeared to suggest, says Professor Emerson, that no new public forums "would be recognized beyond those that had been considered traditionally to be such."

Despite the result in *Greenburgh Civic Associations*, Emerson believes that "the constitutional right to use public facilities [as a public forum] on a compatible basis seems well-established." What merit is there in generally viewing public facilities as broadly hospitable to public forum purposes? Professor Emerson offers this rationale: "It forces the relevant community to listen to the expression of grievances rather than allowing them to be swept under the rug." See Emerson, *The Affirmative Side of the First Amendment*, 15 Georgia L.Rev. 809 (1981).

Justice Rehnquist objected that applying the test for valid time, place, and manner controls to the question of whether a letter box was a public forum would impose a difficult and impractical task on the Postal Service: "[The] authority to impose regulations cannot be made to depend on all of the variations of climate, population, density, and other factors that may vary significantly within a distance of less than 100 miles."

6. The public forum concept received its classic expression in Kalven, *The Concept of the Public Forum*, 1965 Supreme Ct.Rev. 1. The public forum concept became a vehicle for providing First Amendment-based legitimacy to the civil rights protests of the sixties. Is the absence of a similar movement today one of the reasons for the relative decline of the public forum concept?

Preservation of the State: Decline, Death, and Revival of the Clear and Present Danger Doctrine

DENNIS v. UNITED STATES

341 U.S. 494, 71 S.CT. 857, 95 L.ED. 1137 (1951).

Chief Justice Fred VINSON announced the judgment of the Court and an opinion in which Justice Reed, Justice Burton and Justice Minton join.

Petitioners were indicted in July, 1948, for violation of the conspiracy provisions of the Smith Act, 54 Stat. 671, 18 U.S.C.A. § 11, during the period of April, 1945, to July, 1948. * * * A verdict of guilty as to all the petitioners was returned by the jury on October 14, 1949. The Court of Appeals affirmed the convictions. 183 F.2d 201. We granted certiorari, 340 U.S. 863, limited to the following two questions: (1) Whether either § 2 or § 3 of the Smith Act, inherently or as construed and applied in the instant case, violates the First Amendment and other provisions of the

Bill of Rights; (2) whether either § 2 or § 3 of the act, inherently or as construed and applied in the instant case, violates the First and Fifth Amendments because of indefiniteness.

Sections 2 and 3 of the Smith Act, 54 Stat. 671, 18 U.S.C.A. §§ 10, 11 (see present 18 U.S.C.A. § 2385), provide as follows:

"Sec. 2.

"(a) It shall be unlawful for any person—

"(1) to knowingly or willfully advocate, abet, advise, or teach the duty, necessity, desirability, or propriety of overthrowing or destroying any government in the United States by force or violence, or by the assassination of any officer of any such government; * * *

"(3) to organize or help to organize any society, group, or assembly of persons who teach, advocate, or encourage the overthrow or destruction of any government in the United States by force or violence; or to be or become a member of, or affiliate with, any such society, group, or assembly of persons, knowing the purposes thereof.

* * *

"Sec. 3. It shall be unlawful for any person to attempt to commit, or to conspire to commit, any of the acts prohibited by the provisions of * * * this title."

The indictment charged the petitioners with wilfully and knowingly conspiring (1) to organize as the Communist Party of the United States of America a society, group and assembly of persons who teach and advocate the overthrow and destruction of the Government of the United States by force and violence, and (2) knowingly and wilfully to advocate and teach the duty and necessity of overthrowing and destroying the Government of the United States by force and violence. The indictment further alleged that § 2 of the Smith Act proscribes these acts and that any conspiracy to take such action is a violation of § 3 of the act.

* * *

Our limited grant of the writ of certiorari has removed from our consideration any question as to the sufficiency of the evidence to support the jury's determination that petitioners are guilty of the offense charged. Whether on this record petitioners did in fact advocate the overthrow of the Government by force and violence is not before us, and we must base any discussion of this point upon the conclusions stated in the opinion of the Court of Appeals, which treated the issue in great detail. That court held that the record amply supports the necessary finding of the jury that petitioners, the leaders of the Communist Party in this country, * * * intended to initiate a violent revolution whenever the propitious occasion appeared.

* * *

The obvious purpose of the statute is to protect existing government, not from change by peaceable, lawful and constitutional means, but from change by violence, revolution and terrorism. That it is within the *power* of the Congress to protect the government of the United States from armed rebellion is a proposition which requires little discussion. Whatever theoretical merit there may be to the argument that there is a "right" to rebellion against dictatorial governments is without force where the existing structure of the government provides for peaceful and orderly change. We reject any principle of governmental helplessness in the face of preparation for revolution, which principle, carried to its logical conclusion, must lead to anarchy. No one could conceive that it is not within the power of Congress to prohibit acts intended to overthrow the government by force and violence. The question with which we are concerned here is not whether Congress has such *power*, but whether the *means* which it has employed conflict with the First and Fifth Amendments to the Constitution.

One of the bases for the contention that the means which Congress has employed are invalid takes the form of an attack on the face of the statute on the grounds that by its terms it prohibits academic discussion of the merits of Marxism-Leninism, that it stifles ideas and is contrary to all concepts of a free speech and a free press. * * *

The very language of the Smith Act negates the interpretation which petitioners would have us impose on that act. It is directed at advocacy, not discussion. Thus, the trial judge properly charged the jury that they could not convict if they found that petitioners did "no more than pursue peaceful studies and discussions or teaching and advocacy in the realm of ideas." He further charged that it was not unlawful "to conduct in an American college and university a course explaining the philosophical theories set forth in the books which have been placed in evidence." Such a charge is in strict accord with the statutory language, and illustrates the meaning to be placed on those words. Congress did not intend to eradicate the free discussion of political theories, to destroy the traditional rights of Americans to discuss and evaluate ideas without fear of governmental sanction. Rather Congress was concerned with the very kind of activity in which the evidence showed these petitioners engaged.

But although the statute is not directed at the hypothetical cases which petitioners have conjured, its application in this case has resulted in convictions for the teaching and advocacy of the overthrow of the government by force and violence, which, even though coupled with the intent to accomplish that overthrow, contains an element of speech. For this reason, we must pay special heed to the demands of the First Amendment marking out the boundaries of speech. * * *

[T]his Court has recognized the inherent value of free discourse. An analysis of the leading cases in this Court which have involved direct limitations on speech, however, will demonstrate that both the majority of the Court and the dissenters in particular cases have recognized that this is not an unlimited, unqualified right, but that the societal value of speech must, on occasion, be subordinated to other values and considerations.

* * *

The rule we deduce from these cases [following Schenck] is that where an offense is specified by a statute in nonspeech or nonpress terms, a conviction relying upon speech or press as evidence of violation may be sustained only when the speech or publication created a "clear and present danger" of attempting or accomplishing the prohibited crime, e.g., interference with enlistment. The dissents, * * * in emphasizing the value of speech, were addressed to the argument of the sufficiency of the evidence. Speech is not an absolute, above and beyond control by the legislature when its judgment, subject to review here, is that certain kinds of speech are so undesirable as to warrant criminal sanction. * * *

* * *

In this case we are squarely presented with the application of the "clear and present danger" test, and must decide what that phrase imports. We first note that many of the cases in which this Court has reversed convictions by use of this or similar tests have been based on the fact that the interest which the State was attempting to protect was itself too insubstantial to warrant restriction of speech. * * * Overthrow of the Government by force and violence is certainly a substantial enough interest for the Government to limit speech. Indeed this is the ultimate value of any society, for if a society cannot protect its very structure from armed internal attack, it must follow that no subordinate value can be protected. If, then, this interest may be protected, the literal problem which is presented is what has been meant by the use of the phrase "clear and present danger" of the utterances bringing about the evil within the power of Congress to punish.

Obviously, the words cannot mean that before the Government may act, it must wait until the *putsch* is about to be executed, the plans have been laid and the signal is awaited. If Government is aware that a group aiming at its overthrow is attempting to indoctrinate its members and to commit them to a course whereby they will strike when the leaders feel the circumstances permit, action by the Government is required. * * * Certainly an attempt to overthrow the Government by force, even though doomed from the outset because of inadequate numbers or power of the revolutionists, is a sufficient evil for Congress to prevent. The damage which such attempts create both physically and politically to a nation makes it impossible to measure the validity in terms of the probability of success, or the immediacy of a successful attempt. In the instant case the trial judge charged the jury that they could not convict unless they found that petitioners intended to overthrow the Government "as speedily as circumstances would permit." This does not mean, and could not properly mean, that they would not strike until there was certainty of success. What was meant was that the revolutionists would strike when they thought the time was ripe. We must therefore reject the contention that success or probability of success is the criterion.

The situation with which Justices Holmes and Brandeis were concerned in Gitlow was a comparatively isolated event, bearing little relation in their minds to any substantial threat to the safety of the community. * * * They were not confronted with any situation comparable to the instant one—the development of an apparatus designed and dedicated to the overthrow of the Government, in the context of world crisis after crisis.

Chief Judge Learned Hand, writing for the majority below, interpreted the phrase as follows: *"In each case [courts] must ask whether the gravity of the 'evil,' discounted by its improbability, justifies such invasion of free speech as is necessary to avoid the danger."* 183 F.2d at 212. *We adopt this statement of the rule.* [Emphasis added.] As articulated by Chief Judge Hand, it is as succinct and inclusive as any other we might devise at this time. It takes into consideration those factors which we deem relevant, and relates their significances. More we cannot expect from words.

* * *

We hold that §§ 2(a)(1), 2(a)(3) and 3 of the Smith Act, do not inherently, or as construed or applied in the instant case, violate the First Amendment and other provisions of the Bill of Rights, or the First and Fifth Amendments because of indefiniteness. Petitioners intended to overthrow the Government of the United States as speedily as the circumstances would permit. Their conspiracy to organize the Communist Party and to teach and advocate the overthrow of the Government of the United States by force and violence created a "clear and present danger" of an attempt to overthrow the Government by force and violence. They were properly and constitutionally convicted for violation of the Smith Act. The judgments of conviction are affirmed.

Affirmed.

Justice Clark took no part in the consideration or decision of this case.

Justice FRANKFURTER:

* * *

But even the all-embracing power and duty of self-preservation are not absolute. Like the war power, which is indeed an aspect of the power of self-preservation, it is subject to applicable constitutional limitations. See Hamilton v. Kentucky Distilleries Co., 251 U.S. 146, 156. Our Constitution has no provision lifting restrictions upon governmental authority during periods of emergency, although the scope of a restriction may depend on the circumstances in which it is invoked.

The First Amendment is such a restriction. It exacts obedience even during periods of war; it is applicable when war clouds are not figments of the imagination no less than when they are. * * * The right of a man to think what he pleases, to write what he thinks, and to have his thoughts made available for others to hear or read has an engaging ring of universality. The Smith Act and this conviction under it no doubt restrict the exercise of free speech and assembly. Does that, without more, dispose of the matter?

* * *

Absolute rules would inevitably lead to absolute exceptions, and such exceptions would eventually corrode the rules. The demands of free speech in a democratic society as well as the interest in national security are better served by candid and informed weighing of the competing interests, within the confines of the judicial process, than by announcing dogmas too inflexible for the non-Euclidian problems to be solved.

But how are competing interests to be assessed? Since they are not subject to quantitative ascertainment, the issue necessarily resolves itself into asking, who is to make the adjustment?—who is to balance the relevant factors and ascertain which interest is in the circumstances to prevail? Full responsibility for the choice cannot be given to the courts. Courts are not representative bodies. They are not designed to be a good reflex of a democratic society. Their judgment is best informed, and therefore most dependable, within narrow limits. Their essential quality is detachment, founded on independence. History teaches that the independence of the judiciary is jeopardized when courts become embroiled in the passions of the day and assume primary responsibility in choosing between competing political, economic and social pressures.

Primary responsibility for adjusting the interests which compete in the situation before us of necessity belongs to the Congress. The nature of the power to be exercised by this Court has been delineated in decisions not charged with the emotional appeal of situations such as that now before us. We are to set aside the judgment of those whose duty it is to legislate only if there is no reasonable basis for it. We are to determine whether a statute is sufficiently definite to meet the constitutional requirements of due process, and whether it respects the safeguards against undue concentration of authority secured by separation of power. We must assure fairness of procedure, allowing full scope to governmental discretion but mindful of its impact on individuals in the context of the problem involved. And, of course, the proceedings in a particular case before us must have the warrant of substantial proof. Beyond these powers we must not go; we must scrupulously observe the narrow limits of judicial authority even though self-restraint is alone set over us. Above all we must remember that this Court's power of judicial review is not "an exercise of the powers of a super-Legislature."

* * *

In all fairness, the argument cannot be met by reinterpreting the Court's frequent use of "clear" and "present" to mean an entertainable "probability." In giving this meaning to the phrase "clear and present danger," the Court of Appeals was fastidiously confining the rhetoric of opinions to the exact scope of what was decided by them. We have greater responsibility for having given constitutional support, over repeated protests, to uncritical libertarian generalities. * * *

Justice Black, dissenting.

* * *

Justice DOUGLAS, dissenting.

* * *

The vice of treating speech as the equivalent of overt acts of a treasonable or seditious character is emphasized by a concurring opinion, [Justice Jackson] which by invoking the law of conspiracy makes speech do service for deeds which are dangerous to society. The doctrine of conspiracy has served diverse and oppressive purposes and in its broad reach can be made to do great evil. But never until today has anyone seriously thought that the ancient law of conspiracy could constitutionally be used to turn speech into seditious conduct. Yet that is precisely what is suggested. I repeat that we deal here with speech alone, not with speech *plus* acts of sabotage or unlawful conduct. Not a single seditious act is charged in the indictment. To make a lawful speech unlawful because two men conceive it is to raise the law of conspiracy to appalling proportions. That course is to make a radical break with the past and to violate one of the cardinal principles of our constitutional scheme.

Free speech has occupied an exalted position because of the high service it has given our society. Its protection is essential to the very existence of a democracy. The airing of ideas releases pressures which otherwise might become destructive. When ideas compete in the market for acceptance, full and free discussion exposes the false and they gain few adherents. Full and free discussion even of ideas we hate encourages the testing of our own prejudices and preconceptions. Full and free discussion keeps a society from becoming stagnant and unprepared for the stresses and strains that work to tear all civilizations apart.

Full and free discussion has indeed been the first article of our faith. We have founded our political system on it. It has been the safeguard of every religious, political, philosophical, economic, and racial group amongst us. We have counted on it to keep us from embracing what is cheap and false; we have trusted the common sense of our people to choose the doctrine true to our genius and to reject the rest. This has been the one single outstanding tenet that has made our institutions the symbol of freedom and equality. We have deemed it more costly to liberty to suppress a despised minority than to let them vent their spleen. We have above all else feared the political censor. We have wanted a land where our people can be exposed to all the diverse creeds and cultures of the world.

There comes a time when even speech loses its constitutional immunity. Speech innocuous one year may at another time fan such destructive flames that it must be halted in the interests of the safety of the Republic. That is the meaning of the clear and present danger test. When conditions are so critical that there will be no time to avoid the evil that the speech threatens, it is time to call a halt. Otherwise, free speech which is the strength of the Nation will be the cause of its destruction.

* * *

COMMENT

1. Functionally speaking, Vinson really follows the old "reasonableness" test of Justice Sanford in *Gitlow.* Vinson's formulation of the clear and present danger doctrine is hardly the same as that articulated by Brandeis in his concurrence in *Whitney.* Vinson said he endorsed the test employed by Judge Learned Hand which was "whether the gravity of the 'evil,' discounted by its improbability, justifies such invasion of free speech as is necessary to avoid the danger." Vinson said that the clear and present danger test, thus understood, could not mean that the government action is prohibited "until the

putsch is about to be executed." Reasoning that "success or probability of success is not the criterion," Vinson disregarded the factor of time in applying the clear and present danger test.

2. For Brandeis, time was the key factor in determining whether legislation designed to protect the security of the state was constitutional. See Pritchett, *The American Constitution* (2d ed. 1968). In the Brandeis view, the integrity of the public order was strengthened by free discussion. As Brandeis put it in *Whitney:* "the path of safety lies in the opportunity to discuss freely supposed grievances and proposed remedies."

The crucial inquiry, according to Brandeis, was whether the "evil apprehended is so imminent that it may befall before there is opportunity for discussion." But inquiry into the imminence of the danger—the factor of time—is precisely what Vinson excluded from his reformulation of clear and present danger. In *Dennis*, Chief Justice Vinson professedly used the clear and present danger doctrine to assess the constitutionality of the Smith Act, but, in truth, he completely revised it so that it provided far less protection to freedom of expression than the Brandeis conception of clear and present danger. If the imminence of a danger is quite remote, then in the weighing process which constitutional adjudication involves, the value of freedom of expression should not be subordinated to the value of national security. Arguably, under such an approach the Smith Act should be held unconstitutional since the Smith Act had been interpreted by the Justice Department to proscribe "advocacy." But surely advocacy should be protected from federal legislative restriction under the First Amendment in the absence of an imminent danger under the clear and present danger formulation. Vinson changed the clear and present danger doctrine to the "clear danger" or "clear and improbable danger" doctrine. Vinson's "clear danger" rationale, however, merely asked whether a grave threat was posed to the state in the future if not now. Obviously, under such a weighing process the likelihood of a statute's being held violative of the First Amendment was far less likely.

3. Frankfurter's long concurrence in *Dennis* argued for a balancing approach for cases where the values of freedom of expression and national security are in conflict. But Frankfurter intended the balancing to be done by the Congress rather than by the Court. What difference does it make? It is Congress which has passed the law which is under attack as violative of the First Amendment. If the congressional determination is to be upheld on the theory that the congressional balancing decision should be respected, there is no place for judicial review. Unless it can be said Congress engaged in no balancing process whatever, the congressional determination controls. Frankfurter extolled his approach as implementing the popular or democratic will. Further, he said his approach would cause no lasting damage to civil liberties.

4. Did Frankfurter's opinion in *Dennis* overlook the point that majoritarianism and constitutionalism are not necessarily synonymous? The idea of constitutional limitation, after all, is to protect certain values from legislative repression, to limit the majority. Therefore, it is somewhat anomalous to make majoritarianism the dominant value in a consideration of the meaning of a constitutional limitation.

Contrast Chief Justice Stone's differing view on the impermissibility of democratic repression (limitation on basic freedoms enacted by freely elected legislatures) in the famous footnote in United States v. Carolene Products, 304 U.S. 144 at 152, n. 4 (1938). In that opinion, Stone raised but deferred consideration of the question "whether legislation which restricts those political processes which can ordinarily be expected to bring about repeal of undesirable legislation, is to be subjected to more exacting judicial scrutiny under the general prohibitions of the Fourteenth Amendment than are most other types of legislation." According special judicial scrutiny to legislation restricting freedom of expression has been called the "preferred position" theory of freedom of expression. How does this theory differ from Frankfurter's balancing approach in *Dennis?* Frankfurter appeared to be saying that a presumption of validity should be given to the preference of the majority as reflected in an enacted statute, while Stone appeared to be saying that in freedom of expression cases the presumption should be against the legislative judgment.

5. Of the law of conspiracy Justice Jackson, in a concurring opinion, said that "Congress may make it a crime to conspire with others to do what an individual may lawfully do on his own."

What does this statement mean for the law of freedom of expression? Assume that an editor of a radical newspaper had published an editorial stating that the war in Vietnam was unconstitutional and illegal and that draft resisters merited the approval of the people. Such a statement is presumably not unlawful but rather reflects that criticism of government which it is the purpose of the First Amendment to protect. Suppose, however, that the editor had published the editorial as a member of a group united to frustrate the efforts of the government to conduct the war in Vietnam. Arguably it now becomes a conspiracy and what on an individual basis was lawful becomes transformed into unlawful activity.

"The law of conspiracy," Jackson concluded, "has been the chief means at the Government's disposal to deal with the growing problems created by such organizations. I happen to think it is an awkward and inept remedy, but I find no constitutional authority for taking this weapon from the Government. There is no constitutional right to 'gang up' on the Government."

6. Chief Justice Vinson reformulated the clear and present danger doctrine in such a way as to make it an entirely new test. He said that the government can act before the *putsch* is executed, and the Court rejected the "contention that success or probability of success is the criterion." What this approach does is to remove the factor of time from the clear and present danger formula. The danger must be grave (serious), but apparently, under the *Dennis* case, it is no longer necessary that it be immediate (present). However, the function of time or imminence in the clear and present danger doctrine was to justify legislation restricting freedom of expression where there is reason to believe that there was not enough time for normal debate to counteract the dangers feared by the legislature. By removing time from the clear and present danger equation, Vinson removed the most significant protection the doctrine provided for freedom of expression.

Vinson adopted Learned Hand's formulation in the Court of Appeals: "whether the gravity of the evil discounted by its improbability justifies such invasion of free speech as is necessary to avoid the danger." 183 F.2d at 212. Substituting a test of probability for a test of imminence greatly broadened the scope of governmental power over freedom of expression. Such an approach focuses attention on the gravity of the problem (the "evil") with which the legislature is concerned. The Court said the Smith Act, under which the Communist party leaders were prosecuted, was concerned with the "ultimate value of our society." The nature of this ultimate value? The governmental interest in self-preservation.

7. The Vinson view as to what is the ultimate societal value contrasted sharply with that of Justice Black, who in his dissent argued that free speech and press are the preferred values, the ultimate values, in the American constitutional system.

8. As a result of the *Dennis* decision, the government brought many prosecutions under the Smith Act against minor Communist party leaders. The Supreme Court refused to review any of these cases until 1955 when it finally granted *certiorari* in *Yates v. United States, 354 U.S. 298 (1957).* The Court's decision per Justice Harlan, two years later ostensibly clarified the *Dennis* holding. Actually, it contracted the scope of the *Dennis* case, revived the constitutional law of freedom of expression from its low point in *Dennis* six years before, and made it far more difficult for the government to obtain convictions under the Smith Act. Of the fourteen defendants whose convictions were before the Supreme Court in *Yates,* five convictions were reversed, and new trials were ordered for the rest.

The most authoritative portion of the *Yates* case is certainly Justice Harlan's statement that the "essence of the *Dennis* holding" only sanctioned the restriction of "advocacy found to be directed to 'action for the accomplishment of forcible overthrow.' " In his dissent, Justice Tom Clark said, as he read Chief Justice Vinson's opinion in *Dennis,* that he saw no basis for the distinction between advocacy of unlawful action and advocacy of abstract doctrine which Harlan said was the heart of the *Dennis* case. For Justice Clark's point of view at least this much can be said: the two lower federal courts in *Yates* also joined him in "misconceiving" the *Dennis* case. Justice Harlan's "reading" of *Dennis* in *Yates* may have been merely an indirect way of reversing *Dennis.*

How does the distinction between advocacy of abstract doctrine and advocacy of unlawful action expand the area of expression the government may not restrict?

The *Dennis* case was decided in 1951 during the beginning of the red-baiting years that have since been called the "McCarthy" era after Senator Joseph McCarthy of Wisconsin. By 1957, the reaction against "McCarthyism" had set in. What explanation could be used to place *Dennis* and *Yates* in a political perspective? What does such a perspective contribute to the discussion in *Dennis* about whether it is more appropriate for the judiciary or the legislature to make ultimate political choices?

In his dissent Justice Black said that the "First Amendment provides the only kind of security system which can preserve a free government." This remark was designed to rebut Vinson's contention in *Dennis* that self-preservation is the ultimate value of a society and Frankfurter's contention that self-preservation is an independent constitutional value which competes with freedom of expression. What is the nature of Justice Black's argument here?

What was the status of the "clear and present" danger doctrine after *Dennis* and *Yates?* No clear answer to this question was provided by the Supreme Court until 1969 when the Court quietly resurrected the "clear and present danger" doctrine in *Brandenburg v. Ohio.*

BRANDENBURG v. OHIO

395 U.S. 444, 89 S.CT. 1827,
23 L.ED.2D 430 (1969).

PER CURIAM.

The appellant, a leader of a Ku Klux Klan group, was convicted under the Ohio Criminal Syndicalism statute for "advocat[ing] * * * the duty, necessity, or propriety of crime, sabotage, violence, or unlawful methods of terrorism as a means of accomplishing industrial or political reform" and for "voluntarily assembl[ing] with any society, group, or assemblage of persons formed to teach or advocate the doctrines of criminal syndicalism." Ohio Rev.Code Ann. § 2923.13. He was fined $1,000 and sentenced to one to 10 years' imprisonment. The appellant challenged the constitutionality of the criminal syndicalism statute under the First and Fourteenth Amendments to the United States Constitution, but the intermediate appellate court of Ohio affirmed his conviction without opinion. The Supreme Court of Ohio dismissed his appeal, *sua sponte,* "for the reason that no substantial constitutional question exists herein." It did not file an opinion or explain its conclusions. Appeal was taken to this Court, and we noted probable jurisdiction. 393 U.S. 948 (1968). We reverse.

The record shows that a man, identified at trial as the appellant, telephoned an announcer-reporter on the staff of a Cincinnati television station and invited him to come to a Ku Klux Klan "rally" to be held at a farm in Hamilton County. With the cooperation of the organizers, the reporter and a cameraman attended the meeting and filmed the events. Portions of the films were later broadcast on the local station and on a national network.

The prosecution's case rested on the films and on testimony identifying the appellant as the person who communicated with the reporter and who spoke at the rally. The state also introduced into evidence several articles appearing in the film, including a pistol, a rifle, a shotgun, ammunition, a Bible, and a red hood worn by the speaker in the films.

One film showed 12 hooded figures, some of whom carried firearms. They were gathered around a large wooden cross, which they burned. No one was present other than the participants and the newsmen who made the film. Most of the words uttered during the scene were incomprehensible when the film was projected, but scattered phrases could be understood that were derogatory of Negroes and, in one instance, of Jews.[1] Another scene on the same film showed the appellant, in Klan regalia, making a speech. The speech, in full, was as follows:

"This is an organizers' meeting. We have had quite a few members here today which are—we have hundreds, hundreds of members throughout the State of Ohio. I can quote from a newspaper clipping from the Columbus, Ohio Dispatch, five weeks ago Sunday morning. The Klan has more members in the State of Ohio than does any other organization. We're not a revengent organization, but if our President, our Congress, our Supreme Court, continues to suppress the white, Caucasian race, it's possible that there might have to be some revengeance taken.

"We are marching on Congress July the Fourth, four hundred thousand strong. From there we are dividing into two groups, one group to march on St. Augustine, Florida, the other group to march into Mississippi. Thank you."

The second film showed six hooded figures one of whom, later identified as the appellant, repeated a speech very similar to that recorded on the first film. The reference to the possibility of "revengeance" was omitted, and one sentence was added: "Personally, I believe the nigger should be returned to Africa, the Jew returned to Israel." Though some of the figures in the films carried weapons, the speaker did not.

The Ohio Criminal Syndicalism Statute was enacted in 1919. From 1917 to 1920, identical or quite similar laws were adopted by 20 States and two territories. E. Dowell, A History of Criminal Syndicalism Legislation in the United States 21 (1939). * * * [L]ater decisions have fashioned the principle that the constitutional guar-

1. The significant portions that could be understood were:

"How far is the nigger going to—yeah."; "This is what we are going to do to the niggers."; "A dirty nigger."; "Send the Jews back to Israel."; "Let's give them back to the dark garden."; "Save America."; "Let's go back to constitutional betterment."; "Bury the niggers."; "We intend to do our part."; "Give us our state rights."; "Freedom for the whites."; "Nigger will have to fight for every inch he gets from now on."

antees of free speech and free press do not permit a State to forbid or proscribe advocacy of the use of force or of law violation except where such advocacy is directed to inciting or producing imminent lawless action and is likely to incite or produce such actions. * * * A statute which fails to draw this distinction impermissibly intrudes upon the freedoms guaranteed by the First and Fourteenth Amendments. It sweeps within its condemnation speech which our Constitution has immunized from governmental control. * * *

Measured by this test, Ohio's Criminal Syndicalism Act cannot be sustained. The act punishes persons who "advocate or teach the duty, necessity, or propriety" of violence "as a means of accomplishing industrial or political reform"; or who publish or circulate or display any book or paper containing such advocacy; or who "justify" the commission of violent acts "with intent to exemplify, spread or advocate the propriety of the doctrines of criminal syndicalism"; or who "voluntarily assemble" with a group formed "to teach or advocate the doctrines of criminal syndicalism." Neither the indictment nor the trial judge's instructions to the jury in any way refined the statute's bald definition of the crime in terms of mere advocacy not distinguished from incitement to imminent lawless action.

Accordingly, we are here confronted with a statute which, by its own words and as applied, purports to punish mere advocacy and to forbid, on pain of criminal punishment, assembly with others merely to advocate the described type of action. Such a statute falls within the condemnation of the First and Fourteenth Amendments. * * *

Reversed

BRANDENBURG and the Revival of the Danger Doctrine

1. In Brandenburg v. Ohio, 395 U.S. 444 (1969), the Supreme Court held the Ohio criminal syndicalism statute void on its face for failing to distinguish between mere advocacy of ideas and incitement to unlawful conduct. Nearly half a century earlier, a California criminal anarchy statute suffering an identical weakness had been upheld by the Court in the case of Whitney v. California, 274 U.S. 357 (1927). In *Brandenburg,* the Supreme Court turned a corner in its approach to the legislative suppression of politically unpopular speech. *Brandenburg* expressly overruled *Whitney.*

Yet the Court's approach to the *Brandenburg* decision was perfunctory. The Supreme Court issued its *Brandenburg* decision as an anonymous *per curiam* opinion. Further, in purporting to summarize and clarify fifty years of free speech doctrine, the Court in *Brandenburg* issued a relatively short opinion.

2. Consider the following summary of the holding in *Brandenburg:*

> The *per curiam* opinion summarized past decisions by saying that legislative proscription of advocacy is not constitutional *except:* where such advocacy (1) is directed to inciting or producing imminent lawless action, *and* (2) is likely to incite or produce such action. The Court thus established a two-part test: one, the subjection of the speaker; the other, the objective likelihood that the speaker will succeed in carrying out that intent before time for further dialogue, i.e., imminently.

See Barron and Dienes, *Constitutional Law: Principles and Policy* (2d Ed. 1982), p. 734–35.

3. Is the *Brandenburg per curiam* decision an attempt to abandon or revise the clear and present danger doctrine? Does the *Brandenburg* decision even mention the clear and present danger doctrine by name?

Professor Be Vier appears to argue that the *Brandenburg* test is a different test than the clear and present danger test.

> [The *Brandenburg*] rule avoids the institutional limitations of the clear and present danger test by both limiting the range of external circumstances and providing some criteria for judging those circumstances. Subversive speech is protected unless it is likely to produce imminent lawless action. Implicitly irrelevant, now, is the question of the gravity of the threatened evil; implicitly inappropriate is any effort to discount the gravity of the evil by its improbability; implicitly settled is the issue of whether a "remote" danger can ever be "clear"; implicitly dictated is a relatively confined factual finding of the likelihood that the speech would incite imminent lawless action.

See Be Vier, *The First Amendment and Political Speech: An Inquiry Into the Substance and Limits of Principle,* 30 Stan.L. Rev. 299 at 341 (1978).

4. Oregon Supreme Court Justice Hans Linde perceives in the *Brandenburg* test several new and disturbing elements. Linde, *"Clear and Present Danger" Re-examined: Dissonance in the Brandenburg Concerto,* 22 Stan.L.Rev. 1163 (1970). If proscription of free speech is to be judged, as *Brandenburg* suggests, by the actual danger posed by the advocacy, does this not render useless an examination of the statute on its face? Under such a standard of review, Professor Linde is concerned that a criminal anarchy statute "might well be unconstitutional now but might be constitutional in the light of diverse events in 1945, in 1951, in 1957, and in 1961, perhaps not in 1966, but again in 1968." But is such a result necessarily objectionable? If the American system of judicial review amounts to a continuous constitutional convention, isn't the situation Linde describes inevitable?

Note that Brandenburg, a Ku Klux Klan organizer, was tried and convicted under a criminal syndicalism statute which was enacted in the early 1900s to guard against nihilists, anarchists, and wobblies. Ohio was one of many states which passed such laws to meet a particular threat perceived at the time but long since lost in oblivion. Yet the Ohio statute remained on the books, to be resurrected in *Brandenburg* to meet a situation far afield from the subject of its origins. Would a standard of review which required constitutional judgment of a statute on its face improve this situation?

5. Justices Black and Douglas concurred in *Brandenburg,* joining in the decision to overrule *Whitney* and strike down the Ohio criminal syndicalism statute. But they added separate opinions urging abandonment of the "clear and present danger" test for review of laws proscribing speech (as opposed to conduct). They also stressed their long-held belief that *Dennis* was not good law.

Justice Douglas objected to the "clear and present danger" test because he felt the test had, in the crunch, failed to provide sufficient protection to First Amendment interests.

6. While believing that the drift of recent Court decisions appears to toll the "end of the line" for the doctrine of "clear and present danger," Professor Frank Strong urges that before we bid our "tearless farewells" to that doctrine, we consider its potential usefulness in developing a new, more sensitive approach to First Amendment freedoms. *Fifty years of "Clear and Present Danger": From Schenck to Brandenburg—And Beyond,* 1969 Sup.Ct.Rev. 41.

Professor Strong suspects that the emerging test for legislation proscribing freedom of expression is the *definitional balancing* test. Definitional balancing, unlike the *ad hoc* approach espoused by Justices Frankfurter and Harlan, starts with a heavy presumption in favor of First Amendment freedoms. It incorporates, in other words, Justice Black's notion of "preferred freedom." Definitional balancing would impose a heavier burden of proof upon a legislature for laws infringing First Amendment freedoms than for laws regulating commercial activity, for example.

The reason is that the Court regards a First Amendment infringement as more than the infringement of the rights of an individual person; rather, it considers, as did Meiklejohn, the threat to free self-government which any First Amendment infringement entails. We are still balancing, but the scales are weighted in favor of the First Amendment.

In this view, however, adoption of definitional balancing would just be the first step in judicial review of legislation which proscribes freedom of expression. The second step is a determination of whether the law under challenge is sufficiently tailored to meet the specific harm it seeks to avert. Even if the objective of the legislation is constitutionally permissible, its validity is not assured without this second determination.

It is here, in the second stage of definitional balancing, that Professor Strong advocates a role for a revived and revised "clear and present danger" test. How much of a "nexus" must exist between the legitimate governmental purpose and the sweep of the legislative scheme proposed to implement that purpose? If all that is required is a "reasonable" connection, Professor Strong suggests, the test is diluted enough to sanction virtually any governmental incursion into First Amendment freedoms. A tighter "nexus" is required.

Present Uses of the Clear and Present Danger Doctrine

The clear and present danger doctrine has since been relied on in the Supreme Court to resolve a variety of First Amendment issues which arise out of press reporting of judicial proceedings.

In Nebraska Press Association v. Stuart, 427 U.S. 539 (1976), the Supreme Court, per Chief Justice Burger, invalidated a "gag order" prohibiting reporting or commentary on judicial proceedings held in public. See text, p. 505. The Court held that although there was not an absolute prohibition against "gag orders" under the First Amendment, the general presumption against prior restraints, which would include "gag orders," remained intact. An interesting feature of the case is that the Court indicated that the clear and present danger doctrine should be applied to determine whether "gag orders" are warranted in particular situations:

> We turn now to the record in the case to determine whether, as Learned Hand put it, "the gravity of the 'evil,' discounted by its improbability, justifies such invasion of free speech as is necessary to avoid the danger." *Dennis v. United States*. To do so, we must examine the evidence before the trial judge when the order was entered to determine (a) the nature and extent of pretrial news coverage; (b) whether other measures would be likely to mitigate the effects of unrestrained pretrial publicity; (c) how effectively a restraining order would operate to prevent the threatened danger. The precise terms of the restraining order are also important. We must then consider whether the record supports the entry of a prior restraint on publication, one of the most extraordinary remedies known to our jurisprudence.

If the foregoing passage is examined, it will be seen that the formulation of the clear and present danger doctrine used by the Court appears to be a pre-*Yates* formulation, i.e., a formulation giving less protection to the free expression interest. On the other hand, the exact doctrinal formulation of the clear and present danger doctrine made no difference in the *Nebraska Press Association* case. After all, the Court upheld the free press interest and invalidated the "gag order." Barrett Prettyman, press counsel in the *Nebraska Press Association* case, expressed some misgivings about the use of the clear and present danger doctrine in the case. He argued that although the Court used the danger doctrine to enforce the freedom of the press, lower courts may use the clear and present danger doctrine, particularly in its *Dennis* formulation, to validate "gag orders." Do you agree? It may also be argued that if the clear and present danger doctrine is applied to the dramatic facts of the *Nebraska Press Association* case, the "gag order" should have been upheld—rather than invalidated—a consequence which may merely illustrate the unsuitability of the clear and present danger doctrine as a means to resolve free press-fair trial problems.

In a related context, the clear and present danger doctrine also made an appearance in Landmark Communications, Inc. v. Virginia, 435 U.S. 829 (1978). See text, p. 510. In *Landmark*, the Court refused to uphold a criminal prosecution against a publisher who violated a state law making it criminal to breach the confidentiality of proceedings before a state judicial disciplinary commission. A portion of Chief Justice Burger's opinion for the Court dealing with the clear and present danger doctrine follows:

> The Supreme Court of Virginia relied on the clear and present danger test in rejecting Landmark's claim. We question the relevance of that standard here; moreover we cannot accept the mechanical application of the test which led that court to its conclusion. * * * Properly applied, the test requires a court to make its own inquiry into the imminence and magnitude of the danger said to flow from the particular utterance and then to balance the character of the evil as well as its likelihood, against the need for free and unfettered expression. The possibility that other measures will serve the State's interests should also be weighed.
>
> * * * [T]he legislature itself had made the requisite finding "that a clear and present danger to the orderly administration of justice would be created by divulgence of the confidential proceedings of the commission." This legislative declaration coupled with the stipulated fact that Landmark published the disputed article was regarded by the court as sufficient to justify imposition of criminal sanctions. Deference to a legislative finding cannot limit judicial inquiry when First Amendment rights are at stake. * * * A legislature appropriately inquires into and may declare the reasons impelling legislative action but the judicial function commands analysis of whether the specific conduct charged falls within the reach of the statute and if so whether the legislation is consonant with the Constitution. Were it otherwise, the scope of freedom of speech and of the press would be subject to legislative definition and the function of the First Amendment as a check on legislative power would be nullified.
>
> It was thus incumbent upon the Supreme Court of Virginia to go behind the legislative determination and examine for itself "the particular utterance here in question and the circumstances of [its] publication to determine to what extent the substantive evil of unfair administration of justice was a likely consequence, and whether the degree of likelihood was sufficient to justify [subsequent] punishment." *Bridges v. California*. Our precedents leave little doubt as to the proper outcome of such an inquiry.
>
> In a series of cases raising the question of whether the contempt power could be used to punish out of court comments concerning pending cases or grand jury investigations, this Court has consistently rejected the argument that such commentary constituted a clear and present danger to the administration of justice. See Bridges v. California, 314 U.S. 252; Pennekamp v. Florida, 328 U.S. 331; Craig v. Harney, 331 U.S. 367; Wood v. Georgia, 370 U.S. 375. What emerges from these cases is the "working principle that the substantive evil must be extremely serious and the degree of imminence extremely high before utterances can be punished," and that a "solidity of evidence" is necessary to make the requisite showing of imminence. "The danger must not be remote or even probable: it must immediately imperil."
>
> The efforts of the Supreme Court of Virginia to distinguish those cases from this case are unpersuasive. The threat to the administration of justice posed by the speech and publications in prior

> cases was, if anything, more direct and substantial than the threat posed by Landmark's article. If the clear and present danger test could not be satisfied in the more extreme circumstances of those cases, it would seem to follow that the test cannot be met here. It is true that some risk of injury to the judge under inquiry, to the system of justice, or to the operation of the Judicial Inquiry Commission may be posed by premature disclosure, but the test requires that the danger be "clear and present" and in our view the risk here falls far short of that requirement. Moreover, much of the risk can be eliminated through careful internal procedures to protect the confidentiality of commission proceedings.

Why did the Supreme Court say that it questioned "the relevance" of the clear and present danger doctrine? Perhaps this was because in *Landmark*, unlike *Nebraska Press*, there was no free press-fair trial issue. The clear and present danger doctrine has been used, as *Bridges* evidences, in the contempt area where the performance of judges was criticized. The Court might have been referring to the impropriety of using the danger doctrine where there appears to be on the face of the facts no clear and present danger or threat to the administration of criminal justice. The Court may also have been implying that the clear and present danger should be confined to the political and security context where it was born.

The insistence in the *Landmark* case that a court must probe for itself the validity of a legislative "finding" that a particular area presents a "clear and present danger to the administration of justice" shows the continuing wisdom and vitality of Justice Brandeis's insistence on such an approach in his concurring opinion in *Whitney*.

The "Balancing" Approach and Standards of Review

1. A year after the decision in *Yates*, Justice Harlan wrote the decision for the Court in Barenblatt v. United States, 360 U.S. 109 (1959). The United States House of Representatives Committee on Un-American Activities was investigating Communist infiltration in education. Lloyd Barenblatt, who had been a graduate student at the University of Michigan, refused to answer questions as to whether he was or ever had been a member of the Communist party. He refused to answer any inquiry into his political beliefs on the ground of reliance on the First Amendment. For such refusal he was convicted of violation of a federal statute which makes it a misdemeanor for a witness before a congressional committee to refuse to answer any questions pertinent to the matter under inquiry. See 2 U.S.C.A. § 192. On review to the Supreme Court of the United States, Justice Harlan sustained the conviction using the "balancing" test:

> Where First Amendment rights are asserted to bar governmental interrogation, resolution of the issue always involves a balancing by the courts of the competing private and public interests at stake in the particular circumstances shown. 360 U.S. 109 at 126.

Relying on the need of Congress to inform itself in order to enact legislation and on the point that for purposes of national security, the Communist party could not be viewed as an ordinary political party, Harlan concluded for the Court that "the balance must be struck in favor of the latter, and that therefore the provisions of the First Amendment have not been offended." 360 U.S. 109 at 134 (1959). See Watkins v. United States, 354 U.S. 178 (1957).

Justice Black dissented in *Barenblatt* on the ground he had asserted before and since, i.e., speech is absolutely protected by the express words of the First Amendment. But in the course of his dissent, Justice Black, 360 U.S. 109 at 144–145, made a critique of the "balancing" test:

* * *

> But even assuming what I cannot assume, that some balancing is proper in this case, I feel that the Court after stating the test ignores it completely. At most it balances the right of the government to preserve itself, against Barenblatt's right to refrain from revealing Communist affiliations. Such a balance, however, mistakes the factors to be weighed. In the first place,it completely leaves out the real interest in Barenblatt's silence, the interest of the people as a whole in being able to join organizations, advocate causes and make political "mistakes" without later being subjected to governmental penalties for having dared to think for themselves. It is this right, the right to err politically, which keeps us strong as a Nation. For no number of laws against communism can have as much effect as the personal conviction which comes from having heard its arguments and rejected them, or from having once accepted its tenets and later recognized their worthlessness. Instead, the obloquy which results from investigations such as this not only stifles "mistakes" but prevents all but the most courageous from hazarding any views which might at some later time become disfavored. This result, whose importance cannot be overestimated, is doubly crucial when it affects the universities, on which we must largely rely for the experimentation and development of new ideas essential to our country's welfare. It is these interests of society, rather than Barenblatt's own right to silence, which I think the Court should put on the balance against the demands of the government, if any balancing process is to be tolerated. Instead they are not mentioned, while on the other side the demands of the Government are vastly overstated and called "self preservation." It is admitted that this committee can only seek information for the purpose of suggesting laws, and that Congress' power to make laws in the realm of speech and association is quite limited, even on the Court's test. Its interest in making such laws in the field of education, primarily a state function, is clearly narrower still. Yet the Court styles this attenuated interest self-preservation and allows it to overcome the need our country has to let us all think, speak, and associate politically as we like and without fear of reprisal. Such a result reduces "balancing" to a mere play on words and is completely inconsistent with the rules this Court has previously given for applying a "balancing test," where it is proper: "[T]he courts should be *astute* to examine the *effect* of the challenged legislation. Mere *legislative preferences or beliefs* * * * may well support regulation directed at other personal activities, but be insufficient to justify such as diminishes the exercise of rights so vital to the maintenance of democratic institutions."

* * *

2. Justice Black criticized Harlan's use of the "balancing" test on the ground that the wrong things were balanced. This is another way of saying that the result one gets from the "balancing" test will be determined by how one weights the scale. How useful and how objective is such a test? Assuming that *Barenblatt* follows any of the First Amendment approaches outlined in the various opinions in *Dennis*, one would suppose that Harlan's rationale bears the closest possible relationship to Justice Frankfurter's concurrence in *Dennis*. But Frankfurter's "balancing" test and Harlan's were really not quite the same. Harlan said the *courts* must balance "the competing private and public interests at stake." But Frankfurter insisted that the legislature carried the primary responsibility for such "balancing."

3. Justice Black said in dissent in *Barenblatt* that "balancing" was only to be applied to conduct incidentally involving speech, never to speech itself. Further, Justice Black said, the Court had not properly applied the balancing test, even assuming its validity. Black said the Court posed the issue as the government's right of self-preservation against Barenblatt's right to refrain from revealing Communist affiliations. The real issue, said Justice Black, is the government's interest in its security against the constitutionally pro-

tected rights of association and expression. If "balancing" is capable of such different interpretations, is it not fairly useless as a test for constitutional adjudication? Or as Laurent Frantz put it: "How is the judge to convert balancing into something that does not merely give him back whatever answer he feeds into it?" See Frantz, *Is the First Amendment Law?—A Reply to Professor Mendelson*, 51 Calif.L.Rev. 729 (1963).

4. Is balancing still a significant doctrine in First Amendment law? Increasingly, the Supreme Court appears to be saying that legislation implicating First Amendment interests must meet a more exacting standard of review than legislation does generally. There are three standards of review now being applied by the Supreme Court today in equal protection litigation. 1) First is the traditional standard of review where legislation under constitutional attack is examined for the purpose of determining whether there is any rational basis to justify the legislation. If there is such a basis, the legislation stands. 2) Second is the intermediate standard of review whereby legislation will survive constitutional attack only if the legislation serves important governmental objectives and is substantially related to the achievement of these objectives. 3) Third is the strict scrutiny standard of review whereby legislation will survive constitutional attack only if the state can show a compelling state interest for the legislation under review. The highest type of judicial scrutiny is the strict standard of review. The latter two standards are beginning to influence First Amendment litigation.

Is the defect of old-fashioned "balancing" that a court which applies this test usually ends up using the traditional standard of review—a result which usually works to the disadvantage of First Amendment rights? Certainly, a case can be made that this is so. Has the Supreme Court now adopted a higher standard of review for First Amendment cases?

Has balancing been abandoned by the Burger Court? On this issue, the Court, as might be expected, is ambiguous—even explicitly so! In Minneapolis Star & Tribune Co. v. Minnesota Commissioner of Revenue, 103 S.Ct. 1365 at 1372 (1983), text, p. 142, Justice Sandra Day O'Connor says for the Court:

> Differential taxation of the press, then, places such a burden on the interests protected by the First Amendment that we cannot countenance such treatment unless the State asserts a counterbalancing interest of compelling importance that it cannot achieve without differential taxation.

Reading this quotation, a student might properly conclude that the Court is now using the strict scrutiny standard of review in First Amendment litigation. But on the same page that this standard is set forth in the *Minneapolis Star* case, Justice O'Connor says in a footnote that the problem presented is a First Amendment problem in which the balancing test is applied:

> The appropriate method of analysis thus is to balance the burden implicit in singling out the press against the interest asserted by the State. Under a long line of precedent, the regulation can survive only if the governmental interest outweighs the burden and cannot be achieved by means that do not infringe First Amendment rights as significantly.

From the foregoing, it appears that the student should not conclude that "balancing" is dead. But the student should remember, at the same time, that standards of review have become quite important in First Amendment litigation. The strict scrutiny standard and the intermediate standard of review direct courts on the proper weighting to give the interests at stake. In this respect, higher standards of review applied to First Amendment litigation may remedy the deficiencies of the old, open-ended "balancing" test.

The Speech-Action Dichotomy Today and the Problem of "Symbolic" Speech

A distinction which has been advocated as essential to an understanding of the scope of First Amendment protection is the distinction between speech and action. Out of this speech-action dichotomy has arisen the so-called "absolutist" interpretation of the First Amendment. Justice Black was the foremost judicial exponent of the "absolutist" test, and Professor Thomas I. Emerson has been its foremost academic exponent. Professor Emerson has described the test as follows:

> The so-called "absolute" test is somewhat more unsettled in meaning than the other tests proposed, in part because its opponents have seemingly misunderstood it and in part because its supporters are not in full agreement among themselves. * * * The test is not that all words, writing and other communications are, at all times and under all circumstances, protected from all forms of government restraint.
>
> * * *
>
> Actually, the absolute test involves two components:
>
> (1) The command of the first amendment is "absolute" in the sense that "no law" which "abridges" "the freedom of speech" is constitutionally valid. * * * [T]he point being stressed is by no means inconsequential. For it insists on focusing the inquiry upon the definition of "abridge," "the freedom of speech," and if necessary "law," rather than on a general de novo balancing of interests in each case. * * *
>
> (2) The absolute test includes another component. It is intended to bring a broader area of expression within the First Amendment than the other tests do.

Sée Emerson, *Toward A General Theory of the First Amendment,* 72 Yale L.J. 877 at 914–915 (1963). See generally, Emerson, *The System of Freedom of Expression* (1970).

Some scholars have recently attacked the usefulness of the speech-action dichotomy. Professor Baker has written: "Unfortunately, neither identifying protected 'expression' by determining the conduct's contribution to the purposes of the system nor by using common sense to distinguish between expression and action works." See, Baker, *Scope of the First Amendment Freedom of Speech*, 25 U.C.L.A. L.Rev. 964 at 1010 (1978). Professor Emerson has responded in defense as follows:

> The principal objection to the expression-action dichotomy has been that, since the conduct to be protected almost always consists of both speech and action—verbal as well as nonverbal conduct—the category to be protected cannot be defined in terms of one or the other.
>
> * * * The criticism might be justified if the attempt being made were to frame a definition in strictly literal terms of "verbal" as opposed to "nonverbal" conduct, or simply in a loose sense of "expressing" rather than "doing." The expression-action dichotomy is, of course, not that simple. It attempts to formulate a definition of the kind of conduct that merits special protection under the first amendment.

See Emerson, *First Amendment Doctrine and the Burger Court*, 68 Calif. L.Rev. 422 at 478 (1980).

Judicial Reaction to the Speech-Action Distinction

COHEN v. CALIFORNIA

403 U.S. 15, 91 S.CT. 1780, 29 L.ED.2D 284 (1971).

Justice HARLAN delivered the opinion of the Court.

This case may seem at first blush too inconsequential to find its way into our books, but the issue it presents is of no small constitutional significance.

Appellant Paul Robert Cohen was convicted in the Los Angeles Municipal Court of violating that part of California Penal Code § 415 which prohibits "maliciously and willfully disturb[ing] the peace or quiet of any neighborhood or person, * * * by * * * offensive conduct. * * *" He was given 30 days' imprisonment. The facts upon which his conviction rests are detailed in the opinion of the Court of Appeal of California, Second Appellate District, as follows:

"On April 26, 1968 the defendant was observed in the Los Angeles County Courthouse in the corridor outside of Division 20 of the Municipal Court wearing a jacket bearing the words "Fuck the Draft" which were plainly visible. There were women and children present in the corridor. The defendant was arrested. The defendant testified that he wore the jacket as a means of informing the public of the depth of his feelings against the Vietnam War and the draft.

"The defendant did not engage in, nor threaten to engage in, nor did anyone as the result of his conduct in fact commit or threaten to commit any act of violence. The defendant did not make any loud or unusual noise, nor was there any evidence that he uttered any sound prior to his arrest." 1 Cal.App.3d 94, 97–98, 81 Cal. Rptr. 503, 505 (1969).

In affirming the conviction the Court of Appeal held that "offensive conduct" means "behavior which has a tendency to provoke *others* to acts of violence or to in turn disturb the peace," and that the State had proved this element because, on the facts of this case, "[i]t was certainly reasonably foreseeable that such conduct might cause others to rise up to commit a violent act against the person of the defendant or attempt to forceably remove his jacket." 1 Cal.App.3d, at 99–100, 81 Cal. Rptr., at 506. The California Supreme Court declined review by a divided vote. * * * We now reverse.

In order to lay hands on the precise issue which this case involves, it is useful first to canvass various matters which this record does *not* present.

The conviction quite clearly rests upon the asserted offensiveness of the *words* Cohen used to convey his message to the public. The only "conduct" which the state sought to punish is the fact of communication. Thus, we deal here with a conviction resting solely upon "speech," cf. Stromberg v. California, 283 U.S. 359 (1931), not upon any separately identifiable conduct which allegedly was intended by Cohen to be perceived by others as expressive of particular views but which, on its face, does not necessarily convey any message and hence arguably could be regulated without effectively repressing Cohen's ability to express himself. Cf. United States v. O'Brien, 391 U.S. 367 (1968). Further, the state certainly lacks power to punish Cohen for the underlying content of the message the inscription conveyed. At least so long as there is no showing of an intent to incite disobedience to or disruption of the draft, Cohen could not, consistently with the First and Fourteenth Amendments, be punished for asserting the evident position on the inutility or immorality of the draft his jacket reflected. Yates v. United States, 354 U.S. 298 (1957).

Appellant's conviction, then, rests squarely upon his exercise of the "freedom of speech" protected from arbitrary governmental interference by the Constitution and can be justified, if at all, only as a valid regulation of the manner in which he exercised that freedom, not as a permissible prohibition on the substantive message it conveys. This does not end the inquiry, of course, for the First and Fourteenth Amendments have never been thought to give absolute protection to every individual to speak whenever or wherever he pleases or to use any form of address in any circumstances that he chooses. In this vein, too, however, we think it important to note that several issues typically associated with such problems are not presented here.

In the first place, Cohen was tried under a statute applicable throughout the entire state. Any attempt to support this conviction on the ground that the statute seeks to preserve an appropriately decorous atmosphere in the courthouse where Cohen was arrested must fail in the absence of any language in the statute that would have put appellant on notice that certain kinds of otherwise permissible speech or conduct would nevertheless, under California law, not be tolerated in certain places. * * * No fair reading of the phrase "offensive conduct" can be said sufficiently to inform the ordinary person that distinctions between certain locations are thereby created.

In the second place, as it comes to us, this case cannot be said to fall within those relatively few categories of instances where prior decisions have established the power of government to deal more comprehensively with certain forms of individual expression simply upon a showing that such a form was employed. This is not, for example, an obscenity case. Whatever else may be necessary to give rise to the States' broader power to prohibit obscene expression, such expression must be, in some significant way erotic. Roth v. United States, 354 U.S. 476 (1957). It cannot plausibly be maintained that this vulgar allusion to the Selective Service System would conjure up such psychic stimulation in anyone likely to be confronted with Cohen's crudely defaced jacket.

This Court has also held that the States are free to ban the simple use, without a demonstration of additional justifying circumstances, of so-called "fighting words," those personally abusive epithets which, when addressed to the ordinary citizen, are, as a matter of common knowledge, inherently likely to provoke violent reaction. Chaplinsky v. New Hampshire, 315 U.S. 568 (1942). While the four-letter word displayed by Cohen in relation to the draft is not uncommonly employed in a personally provocative fashion, in this instance it was clearly not "directed to the person of the hearer." Cantwell v. Connecticut, 310 U.S. 296, 309 (1940). No individual actually or likely to be present could reasonably have regarded the words on appellant's jacket as a direct personal insult. Nor do we have here an instance of the exercise of the State's police power to prevent a speaker from intentionally provoking a given group to hostile reaction. Cf. Feiner v. New York, 340 U.S. 315 (1951); Terminiello v. Chicago, 337 U.S. 1 (1949). There is, as noted above, no showing that anyone who saw Cohen was in fact violently aroused or that appellant intended such a result.

Finally, in arguments before this Court much has been made of the claim that Cohen's distasteful mode of expression was thrust upon unwilling or unsuspecting viewers, and that the State might therefore legitimately act as it did in order to protect the sensitive from otherwise unavoidable exposure to appellant's crude form of protest. Of course, the mere presumed presence of unwitting listeners or viewers does not serve automatically to justify curtailing all speech capable of giving offense. While this Court has recognized that government may properly act in many situations to prohibit intrusion into the privacy of the home of unwelcome views and ideas which cannot be totally banned from the public dialogue, e.g., Rowan v. United States Post Office Dept., 397 U.S. 728 (1970), we have at the same time consistently stressed that "we are often 'captives' outside the sanctuary of the home and subject to objectionable speech." Id., at 738. The ability of government, consonant with the Constitution, to shut off discourse solely to protect others from hearing it is, in other words, dependent upon a showing that substantial privacy interests are being invaded in an essentially intolerable manner. Any broader view of this authority would effectively empower a majority to silence dissidents simply as a matter of personal predilections.

In this regard, persons confronted with Cohen's jacket were in a quite different posture than, say, those subjected to the raucous emissions of sound trucks blaring outside their residences. Those in the Los Angeles courthouse could effectively avoid further bombardment of their sensibilities simply by averting their eyes. And, while it may be that one has a more substantial claim to a recognizable privacy interest when walking through a courthouse corridor than, for example, strolling through Central Park, surely it is nothing like the interest in being free from unwanted expression in the confines of one's own home. Given the subtlety and complexity of the factors involved, if Cohen's "speech" was otherwise entitled to constitutional protection, we do not think the fact that some unwilling "listeners" in a public building may have been briefly exposed to it can serve to justify this breach of the peace conviction where, as here, there was no evidence that persons powerless to avoid appellant's conduct did in fact object to it, and where that portion of the statute upon which Cohen's conviction rests evinces no concern, either on its face or as construed by the California courts, with the special plight of the captive auditor, but, instead, indiscriminately sweeps within its prohibitions all "offensive conduct" that disturbs "any neighborhood or person."

Against this background, the issue flushed by this case stands out in bold relief. It is whether California can excise, as "offensive conduct," one particular scurrilous epithet from the public discourse, either upon the theory of the court below that its use is inherently likely to cause violent reaction or upon a more general assertion that the states, acting as guardians of public morality, may properly remove this offensive word from the public vocabulary.

The rationale of the California court is plainly untenable. At most it reflects an "undifferentiated fear or apprehension of disturbance [which] is not enough to overcome the right to freedom of expression." Tinker v. Des Moines Indep. Community School Dist., 393 U.S. 503, 508 (1969). We have been shown no evidence that substantial numbers of citizens are standing ready to strike out physically at whoever may assault their sensibilities with execrations like that uttered by Cohen. There may be some persons about with such lawless and violent proclivities, but that is an insufficient base upon which to erect, consistently with constitutional values, a governmental power to force persons who wish to ventilate their dissident views into avoiding particular forms of expression. The argument amounts to little more than the self-defeating proposition that to avoid physical censorship of one who has not sought to provoke such a response by a hypothetical coterie of the violent and lawless, the states may more appropriately effectuate that censorship themselves. * *

Admittedly, it is not so obvious that the First and Fourteenth Amendments must be taken to disable the states from punishing public utterance of this unseemly expletive in order to maintain what they regard as a suitable level of discourse within the body politic. We think, however, that examination and reflection will reveal the shortcomings of a contrary viewpoint.

At the outset, we cannot overemphasize that, in our judgment, most situations where the state has a justifiable interest in regulating speech will fall within one or more of the various established exceptions, discussed above but not applicable here, to the usual rule that governmental bodies may not prescribe the form or content of individual expression. Equally important to our conclusion is the constitutional backdrop against which our decision must be made. The constitutional right of free expression is powerful medicine in a society as diverse and populous as ours. It is designed and intended to remove governmental restraints from the arena of public discussion, putting the decision as to what views shall be voiced largely into the hands of each of us, in the hope that use of such freedom will ultimately produce a more capable citizenry and more perfect polity and in the belief that no other approach would comport with the premise of individual dignity and choice upon which our political system rests.

* * *

Against this perception of the constitutional policies involved, we discern certain more particularized considerations that peculiarly call for reversal of this conviction. First, the principle contended for by the state seems inherently boundless. How is one to distinguish this from any other offensive word? Surely the state has no right to cleanse public debate to the point where it is grammatically palatable to the most squeamish among us. Yet no readily ascertainable general principle exists for stopping short of that result were we to affirm the judgment below. For, while the particular four-letter word being litigated here is perhaps more distasteful than most others of its genre, it is nevertheless often true that one man's vulgarity is another's lyric. Indeed, we think it is largely because governmental officials cannot make principled distinctions in this area that the Constitution leaves matters of taste and style so largely to the individual.

Additionally, we cannot overlook the fact, because it is well illustrated by the episode involved here, that much linguistic expression serves a dual communicative function: it conveys not only ideas capable of relatively precise, detached explication, but otherwise inexpressible emotions as well. In fact, words are often chosen as much for their emotive as their cognitive force. We cannot sanction the view that the Constitution, while solicitous of the cognitive content of individual speech has little or no regard for that emotive function which practically speaking, may often be the more important element of the overall message sought to be communicated. * * *

Finally, and in the same vein, we cannot indulge the facile assumption that one can forbid particular words without also running a substantial risk of suppressing ideas in the process. Indeed, governments might soon seize upon the censorship of particular words as a convenient guise for banning the expression of unpopular views. We have been able, as noted above, to discern little social benefit that might result from running the risk of opening the door to such grave results.

It is, in sum, our judgment that, absent a more particularized and compelling reason for its actions, the state may not, consistently with the First and Fourteenth Amendments, make the simple public display here involved of this single four-letter expletive a criminal offense. Because that is the only arguably sustainable rationale for the conviction here at issue, the judgment below must be reversed.

Reversed.

Justice BLACKMUN, with whom The Chief Justice and Justice Black join.

I dissent, and I do so for two reasons:

Cohen's absurd and immature antic, in my view, was mainly conduct and little speech. * * * The California Court of Appeal appears so to have described it, 1 Cal.App.3d, at 100, 81 Cal.Rptr., at 503, and I cannot characterize it otherwise. Further, the case appears to me to be well within the sphere of Chaplinsky v. New Hampshire, 315 U.S. 568 (1942), where Justice Murphy, a known champion of First Amendment freedoms, wrote for a unanimous bench. As a consequence, this

Court's agonizing over First Amendment values seem misplaced and unnecessary.

* * *

COMMENT

For the civil libertarian, an annoying feature of *Cohen v. California* is that its result is entirely consistent with the view that there should be absolute First Amendment protection for pure speech. Yet the Court deliberately eschewed taking such a view. The slogan Cohen wore on his jacket was treated by the Court as pure speech. The basis of Cohen's conviction was that the wearing of the jacket bearing the slogan in controversy constituted "offensive conduct" prohibited by the California Penal Code. Although the conviction was reversed, it was not reversed on the view endorsed by Justice Black and Professor Emerson that pure speech must receive absolute protection under the First Amendment. Justice Harlan for the Court very carefully rejected any such approach by pointing out that "the First and Fourteenth Amendments have never been thought to give absolute protection."

Symbolic Speech

The speech-action test proceeds on the assumption that speech or communication is entitled to full First Amendment protection. But sometimes action has a communicative or expressive element. In such circumstances, should function or form control? If a particular kind of activity is essentially communicative in character, then perhaps it should be viewed for what it is—symbolic speech. As symbolic speech, such activity is entitled to full First Amendment protection fully as much as if it were as communicative in substance as it is in form.

Embryonic recognition by the Supreme Court that some modes of activity should be treated as symbolic expression is found as early as Stromberg v. California, 283 U.S. 359 (1931), where the Supreme Court struck down on First Amendment grounds a state statute that prohibited "the display of a red flag as a symbol of opposition by peaceful and legal means to organized government." A fuller and more famous statement which contained the roots of the symbolic speech idea may be found in West Virginia State Board of Education v. Barnette, 319 U.S. 624 (1943), where Justice Jackson said:

> There is no doubt that * * * the [compulsory] flag salute is a form of utterance. Symbolism is a primitive but effective way of communicating ideas. The use of an emblem or flag to symbolize some system, idea, institution, or personality is a short cut from mind to mind.

If action is "symbolic," shouldn't it really be treated as "speech" for First Amendment purposes?

Is a speech-action dichotomy too mechanical an approach, or is it a useful way of thinking about and resolving First Amendment problems?

The following case, which arose out of the "draft card" burnings which occurred in different parts of the country during the controversy about the Vietnam war, shows how the symbolic speech doctrine fared before the Supreme Court when its advocates tried to use it literally under fire.

UNITED STATES v. O'BRIEN

391 U.S. 367, 88 S.CT. 1673, 20 L.ED.2D 672 (1968).

Chief Justice WARREN delivered the opinion of the Court.

On the morning of March 31, 1966, David Paul O'Brien and three companions burned their Selective Service registration certificates on the steps of the South Boston Courthouse. * * *

For this act, O'Brien was indicted, tried, convicted, and sentenced in the United States District Court for the District of Massachusetts. He did not contest the fact that he had burned the certificate. He stated in argument to the jury that he burned the certificate publicly to influence others to adopt his antiwar beliefs, as he put it, "so that other people would reevaluate their positions with Selective Service, with the armed forces, and reevaluate their place in the culture of today, to hopefully consider my position."

The indictment upon which he was tried charged that he "wilfully and knowingly did mutilate, destroy, and change by burning * * * [his] Registration Certificate (Selective Service System Form No. 2); in violation of Title 50, App., United States Code, Section 462(b)." Section 462(b) is part of the Universal Military Training and Service Act of 1948. Section 462(b)(3), one of six numbered subdivisions of § 462(b), was amended by Congress in 1965, 79 Stat. 586 (adding the words italicized below), so that at the time O'Brien burned his certificate an offense was committed by any person, "who forges, alters, *knowingly destroys, knowingly mutilates*, or in any manner changes any such certificate. * * *" [Italics supplied.]

* * *

By the 1965 Amendment, Congress added to § 12(b)(3) of the 1948 act the provision here at issue, subjecting to criminal liability not only one who "forges, alters, or in any manner changes" but also one who "knowingly destroys [or] knowingly mutilates" a certificate. We note at the outset that the 1965 Amendment plainly does not abridge free speech on its face, and we do not understand O'Brien to argue otherwise. Amended § 12(b)(3) on its face deals with conduct having no connection with speech. It prohibits the knowing destruction of certificates issued by the Selective Service System, and there is nothing necessarily expressive about such conduct. The Amendment does not distinguish between public and private destruction, and it does not punish only destruction engaged in for the purpose of expressing views. A law prohibiting destruction of Selective Service certificates no more abridges free speech on its face than a motor vehicle law prohibiting the destruction of drivers' licenses, or a tax law prohibiting the destruction of books and records.

O'Brien nonetheless argues that the 1965 Amendment is unconstitutional in its application to him, and is unconstitutional as enacted because what he calls the "purpose" of Congress was "to suppress freedom of speech." We consider these arguments separately.

O'Brien first argues that the 1965 Amendment is unconstitutional as applied to him because his act of burning his registration certificate was protected "symbolic speech" within the First Amendment. His argument is that the freedom of expression which the First Amendment guarantees includes all modes of "communication of ideas by conduct," and that his conduct is within this definition because he did it in "demonstration against the war and against the draft."

We cannot accept the view that an apparently limitless variety of conduct can be labelled "speech" whenever the person engaging in the conduct intends thereby to express an idea. However, even on the assumption that the alleged communicative element in O'Brien's conduct is sufficient to bring into play the First Amendment, it does not necessarily follow that the destruction of a registration certificate is constitutionally protected activity. *This Court has held that when "speech" and "nonspeech" elements are combined in the same course of conduct, a sufficiently important governmental interest in regulating the nonspeech element can justify incidental limitations on First Amendment freedoms.* To characterize the quality of the governmental interest which must appear, the Court has employed a variety of descriptive terms: compelling; substantial; subordinating; paramount; cogent; strong. Whatever imprecision inheres in these terms, we think it clear that a government regulation is sufficiently justified if it is within the constitutional power of the government; if it furthers an important or substantial governmental interest; if the governmental interest is unrelated to the suppression of free expression; and if the incidental restriction on alleged First Amendment freedom is no greater than is essential to the furtherance of that interest. We find that the 1965 Amendment to § 462(b)(3) of the Universal Military Training and Service Act meets all of these requirements, and consequently that O'Brien can be constitutionally convicted for violating it. [Emphasis added.]

* * *

The many functions performed by Selective Service certificates establish beyond doubt that Congress has a legitimate and substantial interest in preventing their wanton and unrestrained destruction and assuring their continuing availability by punishing people who knowingly and wilfully destroy or mutilate them.

* * *

We think it apparent that the continuing availability to each registrant of his Selective Service certificates substantially furthers the smooth and proper functioning of the system that Congress has established to raise armies. We think it also apparent that the Nation has a vital interest in having a system for raising armies that functions with maximum efficiency and is capable of easily and quickly responding to continually changing circumstances. For these reasons, the Government has a substantial interest in assuring the continuing availability of issued Selective Service certificates.

It is equally clear that the 1965 Amendment specifically protects this substantial governmental interest. We perceive no alternative means that would more precisely and narrowly assure the continuing availability of issued Selective Service certificates than a law which prohibits their wilful mutilation or destruction. * * The 1965 Amendment prohibits such conduct and does nothing more. In other words, both the governmental interest and the operation of the 1965 Amendment are limited to the noncommunicative aspect of O'Brien's conduct. The governmental interest and the scope of the 1965 Amendment are limited to preventing a harm to the smooth and efficient functioning of the Selective Service System. When O'Brien deliberately rendered unavailable his registration certificate, he wilfully frustrated this governmental interest. For this noncommunicative impact of his conduct, and for nothing else, he was convicted.

* * *

O'Brien finally argues that the 1965 Amendment is unconstitutional as enacted because what he calls the "purpose" of Congress was "to suppress freedom of speech." We reject this argument because under settled principles the purpose of Congress, as O'Brien uses that term, is not a basis for declaring this legislation unconstitutional.

* * *

Since the 1965 Amendment to § 12(b)(3) of the Universal Military Training and Service Act is constitutional as enacted and as applied, the Court of Appeals should have affirmed the judgment of conviction entered by the District Court. Accordingly, we vacate the judgment of the Court of Appeals, and reinstate the judgment and sentence of the District Court. This disposition makes unnecessary consideration of O'Brien's claim that the Court of Appeals erred in affirming his conviction on the basis of the nonpossession regulation.

It is so ordered.

Justice Marshall took no part in the consideration or decision of these cases.

Justice Harlan, concurred.

[Justice Douglas dissented on the ground that the basic but undecided constitutional issue in the case was whether conscription was unconstitutional in the absence of a declaration of war.]

COMMENT

1. Perhaps *O'Brien* can be viewed as a failure for the speech-action approach to First Amendment problems—a failure because the definition of "speech" employed is too rigid and formalistic. One observer, writing of the 1968 Boston trial which resulted in the conviction of Dr. Benjamin Spock and three others for conspiracy to aid in the violation of the draft law, urged that a distinction be drawn between isolated acts of "draft card" destruction and systematic destruction of Selective Service files. See Sax, *Civil Disobedience—The Law Is Never Blind,* Saturday Review (September 28, 1968), p. 22. But it is this observer's view that the formal legal system failed to make such distinctions. Professor Sax said of the *O'Brien* case, for instance, that the case illustrates this failure, since, in his view, the draft card burning in *O'Brien* was "an act overwhelmingly of protest content, with only the most trivial justification of need for possession of selective service documents by individual registrants."

Professor Sax argued that a "constructive goal" behind constitutionally unprotected conduct should distinguish such activity from behavior which is directed at "active obstruction of a matter adequately settled through some political or legal institution."

2. Did Chief Justice Earl Warren reject the whole symbolic speech concept in *O'Brien?* It appears that Warren's test in *O'Brien* was just another form of the balancing test frequently used in speech plus cases. Warren pointed out that "when 'speech' and 'non-speech' elements are combined in the same course of conduct, a sufficiently important governmental interest in regulating the nonspeech element can justify incidental limitation on First Amendment freedoms." This test, of course, implicitly rejects the symbolic speech defense because the whole point of that defense is to have conduct for purposes of constitutional litigation conceived as speech and, therefore, immune from governmental restriction under the First Amendment.

Note Warren's formulation of the balancing test he used in *O'Brien:*

> We think it clear that a government regulation is sufficiently justified if it is within the constitutional power of the government; if it furthers an important or substantial governmental interest; if the governmental interest is unrelated to the suppression of free expression; and if the incidental restriction on alleged First Amendment freedom is no greater than is the furtherance of that interest.

Is this "balancing" test particularly weighted in favor of the government? Professor Emerson would say that it is.

Wearing Armbands: Pure Speech?

In Tinker v. Des Moines Independent Community School District, 393 U.S. 503 (1969), the Supreme Court reviewed the controversy which ensued when public school children wore black armbands to school to protest the Vietnam war. The Des Moines school system had prohibited the wearing of the armbands in advance. The Court held that wearing the armband was a "symbolic act" protected under the free speech provision of the First Amendment. Since only seven out of 18,000 students actually wore armbands to school, Justice Fortas held that a more positive showing of interference with normal school operations would have to be shown before the prohibition on wearing armbands could be sustained.

TINKER v. DES MOINES INDEPENDENT SCHOOL DISTRICT

393 U.S. 503, 89 S.CT. 733, 21 L.ED.2D 731 (1969).

Justice FORTAS delivered the opinion of the Court

* * *

The District Court recognized that the wearing of an armband for the purpose of expressing certain views is the type of symbolic act that is within the Free Speech Clause of the First Amendment. * * * As we shall discuss, the wearing of armbands in the circumstances of this case was entirely divorced from actually or potentially disruptive conduct by those participating in it. It was closely akin to "pure speech" which, we have repeatedly held, is entitled to comprehensive protection under the First Amendment. * * *

First Amendment rights, applied in light of the special characteristics of the school environment, are available to teachers and students. It can hardly be argued that either students or teachers shed their constitutional rights to freedom of speech or expression at the schoolhouse gate. This has been the unmistakable holding of this Court for almost 50 years. * * *

In West Virginia State Board of Education v. Barnette, this Court held that under the First Amendment, the student in public school may not be compelled to salute the flag.

* * *

On the other hand, the Court has repeatedly emphasized the need for affirming the comprehensive authority of the states and of school officials, consistent with fundamental constitutional safeguards, to prescribe and control conduct in the schools. Our problem lies in the area where students in the exercise of First Amendment rights collide with the rules of the school authorities.

The problem posed by the present case does not relate to regulation of the length of skirts or the type of clothing, to hair style, or deportment. It does not concern aggressive, disruptive action or even group demonstrations. Our problem involves direct, primary First Amendment rights akin to "pure speech."

The school officials banned and sought to punish petitioners for a silent, passive expression of opinion, unaccompanied by any disorder or disturbance on the part of petitioners. There is here no evidence whatever of petitioners' interference, actual or nascent, with the school's work or of collision with the rights of other students to be secure and to be let alone. Accordingly, this case does not concern speech or action that intrudes upon the work of the schools or the rights of other students.

Only a few of the 18,000 students in the school system wore the black armbands. Only five students were suspended for wearing them. There is no indication that the work of the schools or any class was disrupted. Outside the classrooms, a few students made hostile remarks to the children wearing armbands, but there were no threats or acts of violence on school premises.

The District Court concluded that the action of the school authorities was reasonable because it was based upon their fear of a disturbance from the wearing of the armbands. But, in our system, undifferentiated fear or apprehension of disturbance is not enough to overcome the right to freedom of expression. Any departure from absolute regimentation may cause trouble. Any variation from the majority's opinion may inspire fear. Any word spoken, in class, in the lunchroom, or on the campus, that deviates from the views of another person may start an argument or cause a disturbance.

* * *

In order for the state in the person of school officials to justify prohibition of a particular expression of opinion, it must be able to show that its action was caused by something more than a mere desire to avoid the discomfort and unpleasantness that always accompany an unpopular viewpoint. Certainly where there is no finding and no showing that engaging in the forbidden conduct would "materially and substantially interfere with the requirements of appropriate discipline in the operation of the school," the prohibition cannot be sustained.

In the present case, the District Court made no such finding, and our independent examination of the record fails to yield evidence that the school authorities had reason to anticipate that the wearing of the armbands would substantially interfere with the work of the school or impinge upon the rights of other students. Even an official memorandum prepared after the suspension that listed the reasons for the ban on wearing the armbands made no reference to the anticipation of such disruption.

On the contrary, the action of the school authorities appears to have been based upon an urgent wish to avoid the controversy which might result from the expression, even by the silent symbol of armbands, of opposition to this Nation's part in the conflagration in Vietnam. It is revealing, in this respect, that the meeting at which the school principals decided to issue the contested regulation was called in response to a student's statement to the journalism teacher in one of the schools that he wanted to write an article on Vietnam and have it published in the school paper. (The student was dissuaded.)

It is also relevant that the school authorities did not purport to prohibit the wearing of all symbols of political or controversial significance. The record shows that students in some of the schools wore buttons relating to national political campaigns, and some even wore the Iron Cross, traditionally a symbol of Nazism. The order prohibiting the wearing of armbands did not extend to these. Instead, a particular symbol—black armbands worn to exhibit opposition to this Nation's involvement in Vietnam—was singled out for prohibition. Clearly, the prohibition of expression of one particular opinion, at least without evidence that it is necessary to avoid material and substantial interference with schoolwork or discipline, is not constitutionally permissible.

In our system, state-operated schools may not be enclaves of totalitarianism. School officials do not possess absolute authority over their students. Students in school as well as out of school are "persons" under our Constitution. They are possessed of fundamental rights which the state must respect, just as they themselves must respect their obligations to the State. In our system, students may not be regarded as closed-circuit recipients of only that which the state chooses to communicate. They may not be confined to the expression of those sentiments that are officially approved. In the absence of a specific showing of constitutionally valid reasons to regulate their speech, students are entitled to freedom of expression of their views. * * *

* * *

Under our Constitution, free speech is not a right that is given only to be so circumscribed that it exists in principle but not in fact. Freedom of expression would not truly exist if the right could be exercised only in an area that a benevolent government has provided as a safe haven for crackpots. The Constitution says that Congress (and the states) may not abridge the right to free speech. This provision means what it says. We properly read it to permit reasonable regulation of speech-connected activities in carefully restricted circumstances. But we do not confine the permissible exercise of First Amendment rights to a telephone booth or the four corners of a pamphlet, or to supervised and ordained discussion in a school classroom.

If a regulation were adopted by school officials forbidding discussion of the Vietnam conflict, or the expression by any student of opposition to it anywhere on school property except as part of a prescribed classroom exercise, it would be obvious that the regulation would violate the constitutional rights of students, at least if it could not be justified by a showing that the students' activities would materially and substantially disrupt the work and discipline of the school. Cf. Hammond v. South Carolina State College, 272 F.Supp. 947 (D.C.S.C.1967) (orderly protest meeting on state college campus); Dickey v. Alabama State Board of Education, 273 F.Supp. 613 (D.C.M.D.Ala.1967) (expulsion of student editor of college newspaper). In the circumstances of the present case, the prohibition of the silent, passive "witness of the armbands," as one of the children called it, is no less offensive to the constitution's guarantees.

As we have discussed, the record does not demonstrate any facts which might reasonably have led school authorities to forecast substantial disruption of or material interference with school activities, and no disturbances or disorders on the school premises in fact occurred. These petitioners merely went about their ordained rounds in school. Their deviation consisted only in wearing on their sleeve, a band of black cloth, not more than two inches wide. They wore it to exhibit their disapproval of the Vietnam hostilities and their advocacy of a truce, to make their views known, and, by their example, to influence others to adopt them. They neither interrupted school activities nor sought to intrude in the school affairs or the lives of others. They caused discussion outside of the classrooms, but no interference with work and no disorder. In the circumstances, our Constitution does not permit officials of the state to deny their form of expression.

We express no opinion as to the form of relief which should be granted, this being a matter for the lower courts to determine. We reverse and remand for further proceedings consistent with this opinion.

Reversed and remanded.

Justice Stewart, concurring.

* * *

Justice White, concurring.

* * *

Justice BLACK, dissenting.

* * *

* * * The truth is that a teacher of kindergarten, grammar school, or high school pupils no more carries into a school with him a complete right to freedom of speech and expression than an anti-Catholic or anti-Semite carries with him a complete freedom of speech and religion into a Catholic church or Jewish synagogue. Nor does a person carry with him into the United States Senate or House, or into the Supreme Court, or any other court, a complete constitutional right to go into those places contrary to their rules and speak his mind on any subject he pleases. It is a myth to say that any person has a constitutional right to say what he pleases, where he pleases, and when he pleases. Our Court has decided precisely the opposite. * * *

COMMENT

1. Is *Tinker* a symbolic speech case because its facts reveal no disruptive conduct? In Street v. New York, 394 U.S. 576 (1969), a case involving the burning of an American flag on a street corner, there appeared to be no disruptive conduct in the sense that no one in Street's immedi-

ate audience was offended by his action. If anyone was offended, it was presumably the police officer who arrested him.

In *O'Brien,* on the other hand, members of the crowd at the South Boston courthouse attacked O'Brien and his cohorts after O'Brien burned the flag. Under this approach all the cases are in line. *Street* is consistent with *Tinker* at least in result. *Tinker* is consistent with *O'Brien* in that the draft card burning provoked disruptive conduct, making the symbolic act less pure speech than was the case in *Tinker.*

Whether conduct will be adjudicated a punishable criminal act or protected symbolic speech depends in *Tinker* on whether the conduct involved will materially interfere with the operation of the school.

How material is it that flag and draft card burning were both illegal under preexisting statutes, but armband wearing was not illegal until school officials became aware of the plan to protest the war? Only then did school officials issue a regulation prohibiting armband wearing.

The Court in the *Tinker* case did not cite or discuss *O'Brien.* Is this defensible? Explicable?

2. The majority went to great lengths in *Street* to avoid confronting the question whether flag burning is speech. Harlan found Street to have been punished for engaging in speech, i.e., he was punished for his words. Yet Harlan applied a balancing test even to pure speech.

Justice Black believed that flag burning was not constitutionally protected. Does this show the limitation of the speech-action distinction at least as mechanically applied? Flag burning is an act. Therefore, the state may regulate it. But the flag was burned to express and communicate disrespect for the state. Isn't punishing flag burning in these circumstances a form of seditious libel?

3. Professor Emerson believes that expression was the basic element in Street's flag burning and O'Brien's draft card burning. Moreover, it was precisely the element of expression which the law sought to punish. Therefore, as expression (utilizing the speech-action distinction), Emerson argues that the flag burning in *Street* should not be punished but should be defined as expression under the First Amendment. *The System of Freedom of Expression* 88 (1970). Emerson is persuasive on this point.

4. The rationale of the Court in *Cohen v. California* appears to be very close to that taken in *Tinker,* i.e., "absent a more particularized and compelling reason for its actions," the state may not proscribe the wearing of the jacket bearing a "single four-letter expletive."

Why is *Cohen* close to *Tinker? Tinker* makes the key to whether symbolic protest is constitutionally protected depend on whether the protest unduly interferes with other legitimate activity. The wearing of the jacket bearing the crude slogan was even less of an obstacle to the activities of the courthouse, the forum of the protest in *Cohen,* than was the wearing of the black armbands to the activities of the school, the forum of the protest in *Tinker.* If the Court concludes that symbolic protest is no obstacle to the normal activities of school or courthouse, is this equivalent in a balancing approach to a conclusion that the state has provided no "particularized and compelling reason" for proscribing the particular symbolic protest in controversy? See the last paragraph of Justice Harlan's opinion for the Court in *Cohen.*

5. Taking *Street* and *Cohen* together, don't the deficiencies of the speech-action theory become vividly clear? *Street* which seemed to involve the *act* of flag burning was viewed by the majority of the Supreme Court as a prosecution for the utterance of words, i.e., speech. *Cohen,* on the other hand, which appeared to the majority to involve pure speech was seen by Justice Blackmun, Chief Justice Burger, and, of all people, Justice Black as "mainly conduct and little speech."

Is the abiding difficulty with the speech-action distinction that in the crunch there is too little agreement on what constitutes "speech" and what constitutes "action"? Or is it the most sensible First Amendment "theory" so far proposed?

6. In Spence v. Washington, 418 U.S. 405 (1974), the Court, *per curiam,* overturned a conviction under a flag misuse statute. In *Spence,* the accused had affixed a peace symbol to an American flag and then displayed the flag upside down from his window. On the basis of the factual context of this protest activity, the Court concluded that the accused had "engaged in a form of protected expression." In *Spence*, the Court evidenced a willingness to consider action in certain circumstances the equivalent of communication. For the Court to treat action or conduct in such a fashion, however, it is necessary that there be intent on the part of the speaker to make a particular communication. It is likewise necessary that the context of the protest makes it likely that it would be received and comprehended as a message by those to whom it was addressed. Context may be a key point in distinguishing speech and action.

7. Is there an operational symbolic speech doctrine which is operative in contemporary First Amendment law? If one analyzes *O'Brien, Tinker*, and *Spence* on an overall basis, the outlines of a functional symbolic speech doctrine are discernible. Once the Court has determined that a particular mode of activity is in fact communicative, i.e., constitutes symbolic speech, full First Amendment protection should be extended to the activity.[5] If the state regulation in controversy is directed at the message being communicated, then the state interest, absent a clear and present danger, should not be sufficient to withstand the First Amendment interest favoring protection of the communicative activity. If the regulation is designed to effectuate a substantial governmental interest, is not directed toward repressing of the content of the communicative activity involved, and if the governmental interest would be significantly thwarted by the continuance of the activity at issue, then the regulation should be upheld despite the incidental burden on First Amendment interests.

THE LEGAL AND CONSTITUTIONAL MEANING OF FREEDOM OF THE PRESS

The Doctrine of Prior Restraint

NEAR v. MINNESOTA

283 U.S. 697, 51 S.CT. 625, 75 L.ED. 1357 (1931).

The Legal and Factual Background of the NEAR Case

[EDITORIAL NOTE

The previous cases we have examined in studying the constitutional development of freedom of expression as a concept have dealt with what might be called subsequent punishment, i.e., punishing the speaker or the publisher *after* the act of communication because of state objection to the contents of the communication. This kind of legal sanction over communication obviously performs a certain censorship function. But press censorship, in the sense of being required by law to submit copy to a state official before pub-

5. For an example of a case recognizing the symbolic speech concept, see Village of Skokie v. National Socialist Party, 373 N.E.2d 21 (Ill.1978), text, p. 30 where the planned display of the swastika by a group of American Nazis was upheld as protected symbolic speech.

lication is allowed, is another very significant and even more direct method by which freedom of expression can be restricted. At common law this kind of censorship was known as prior restraint. In *Near v. Minnesota,* the Supreme Court of the United States produced a very valuable precedent for the law of the press because the Court dealt with the constitutionality of press censorship and specifically with prior restraint.

As you read the opinion of the Court in *Near,* be careful to note that the Court did not say prior restraints were absolutely forbidden by the constitutional guarantee of freedom of the press, but rather that they were prohibited except in certain areas. According to Chief Justice Hughes, what are the areas of exception where apparently prior restraints are permitted? Do these exceptions merely repeat the law of the "subsequent punishment" cases previously considered in earlier cases in this chapter.

The factual setting of the *Near* case was as follows. A Minnesota statute provided for the abating as a public nuisance of "malicious, scandalous, and defamatory" newspapers or periodicals. The statute provided that all persons guilty of such a nuisance could be enjoined. Mason's Minnesota Statutes, 1927, §§ 10123–1 to 10123–3.

The county attorney of Hennepin County (Minneapolis), later Populist Governor Floyd Olson, brought an action under the statute to enjoin the publication of a "malicious, scandalous, and defamatory newspaper, magazine, or other periodical" known as *The Saturday Press.* The complaint filed by the county attorney asserted that *The Saturday Press* had accused the law enforcement agencies and officials of Minneapolis with failing to expose and punish gambling, bootlegging, and racketeering, which activities, *The Saturday Press* alleged, were in control of a "Jewish gangster."

The state trial court found that the editors of *The Saturday Press* had violated the statute, and the court "perpetually enjoined" the defendants from conducting "said nuisance under the title of *The Saturday Press* or any other name or title." The state supreme court affirmed, and the defendant Near appealed to the Supreme Court of the United States. For an interesting and lively account of the background of the case, See Friendly, *Minnesota Rag* (1981)].

Chief Justice HUGHES delivered the opinion of the Court: * **

This statute, for the suppression as a public nuisance of a newspaper or periodical, is unusual, if not unique, and raises questions of grave importance transcending the local interests involved in the particular action. It is no longer open to doubt that the liberty of the press and of speech is within the liberty safeguarded by the due process clause of the Fourteenth Amendment from invasion by state action. It was found impossible to conclude that this essential personal liberty of the citizen was left unprotected by the general guaranty of fundamental rights of person and property. * * * In maintaining this guaranty, the authority of the state to enact laws to promote the health, safety, morals, and general welfare of its people is necessarily admitted. The limits of this sovereign power must always be determined with appropriate regard to the particular subject of its exercise. * * * Liberty of speech and of the press is also not an absolute right, and the state may punish its abuse. Liberty, in each of its phases, has its history and connotation, and, in the present instance, the inquiry is as to the historic conception of the liberty of the press and whether the statute under review violates the essential attributes of that liberty.

* * *

First. The statute is not aimed at the redress of individual or private wrongs.

Remedies for libel remain available and unaffected. The statute, said the state court (174 Minn. 457, 219 N.W. 770, 772, 58 A.L.R. 607), "is not directed at threatened libel but at an existing business which, generally speaking, involves more than libel." It is aimed at the distribution of scandalous matter as "detrimental to public morals and to the general welfare," tending "to disturb the peace of the community" and "to provoke assaults and the commission of crime." In order to obtain an injunction to suppress the future publication of the newspaper or periodical, it is not necessary to prove the falsity of the charges that have been made in the publication condemned. In the present action there was no allegation that the matter published was not true. It is alleged, and the statute requires the allegation that the publication was "malicious." But, as in prosecutions for libel, there is no requirement of proof by the state of malice in fact as distinguished from malice inferred from the mere publication of the defamatory matter. The judgment in this case proceeded upon the mere proof of publication. The statute permits the defense, not of the truth alone, but only that the truth was published with good motives and for justifiable ends. * * *

Second. The statute is directed not simply at the circulation of scandalous and defamatory statements with regard to private citizens, but at the continued publication by newspapers and periodicals of charges against public officers of corruption, malfeasance in office, or serious neglect of duty. Such charges by their very nature create a public scandal. They are scandalous and defamatory within the meaning of the statute, which has its normal operation in relation to publications dealing prominently and chiefly with the alleged derelictions of public officers.

Third. The object of the statute is not punishment, in the ordinary sense, but suppression of the offending newspaper or periodical. The reason for the enactment, as the state court has said, is that prosecutions to enforce penal statutes for libel do not result in "efficient repression or suppression of the evils of scandal." Describing the business of publication as a public nuisance does not obscure the substance of the proceeding which the statute authorizes. It is the continued publication of scandalous and defamatory matter that constitutes the business and the declared nuisance. In the case of public officers, it is the reiteration of charges of official misconduct, and the fact that the newspaper or periodical is principally devoted to that purpose, that exposes it to suppression. * * *

This suppression is accomplished by enjoining publication, and that restraint is the object and effect of the statute.

Fourth. The statute not only operates to suppress the offending newspaper or periodical, but to put the publisher under an effective censorship. When a newspaper or periodical is found to be "malicious, scandalous and defamatory," and is suppressed as such, resumption of publication is punishable as a contempt of court by fine or imprisonment. Thus, where a newspaper or periodical has been suppressed because of the circulation of charges against public officers of official misconduct, it would seem to be clear that the renewal of the publication of such charges would constitute a contempt, and that the judgment would lay a permanent restraint upon the publisher, to escape which he must satisfy the court as to the character of a new publication. Whether he would be permitted again to publish matter deemed to be derogatory to the same or other public officers would depend upon the court's ruling. In the present instance the judgment restrained the defendants from "publishing, circulating, having in their possession, selling or giving away any publication whatsoever which is a malicious, scandalous or defamatory newspaper, as defined by law." The law gives no definition except that covered by the words "scandalous and defamatory," and publications charging official misconduct are of that class. While the court, answering the objection that the judgment was too broad, saw no reason for construing it as restraining the defendants "from operating a newspaper in harmony with the public welfare to which all must yield," and said that the defendants had not indicated "any desire to conduct their business in the usual and legitimate manner," the manifest inference is that, at least with respect to a new publication directed against official misconduct, the defendant would be held, under penalty of punishment for contempt as provided in the statute, to a manner of publication which the court considered to be "usual and legitimate" and consistent with the public welfare.

If we cut through mere details of procedure, the operation and effect of the statute in substance is that public authorities may bring the owner or publisher of a newspaper or periodical before a judge upon a charge of conducting a business of publishing scandalous and defamatory matter—in particular that the matter consists of charges against public officers of official dereliction—and, unless the owner or publisher is able and disposed to bring competent evidence to satisfy the judge that the charges are true and are published with good motives and for justifiable ends, his newspaper or periodical is suppressed and further publication is made punishable as a contempt. This is of the essence of censorship.

The question is whether a statute authorizing such proceedings in restraint of publication is consistent with the conception of the liberty of the press as historically conceived and guaranteed. In determining the extent of the constitutional protection, it has been generally, if not universally, considered that it is the chief purpose of the guaranty to prevent previous restraints upon publication. The struggle in England, directed against the legislative power of the licenser, resulted in renunciation of the censorship of the press. The liberty deemed to be established was thus described by Blackstone: "The liberty of the press is indeed essential to the nature of a free state; but this consists in laying no *previous* restraints upon publications, and not in freedom from censure for criminal matter when published. Every freeman has an undoubted right to lay what sentiments he pleases before the public; to forbid this, is to destroy the freedom of the press; but if he publishes what is improper, mischievous or illegal, he must take the consequence of his own temerity." 4 Bl.Com. 151, 152. See Story on the Constitution, §§ 1884, 1889. The distinction was early pointed out between the extent of the freedom with respect to censorship under our constitutional system and that enjoyed in England. Here, as Madison said, "the great and essential rights of the people are secured against legislative as well as against executive ambition. They are secured, not by laws paramount to prerogative, but by constitutions paramount to laws. This security of the freedom of the press requires that it should be exempt not only from previous restraint by the Executive, as in Great Britain, but from legislative restraint also." Report on the Virginia Resolutions, Madison's Works, vol. IV, p. 543. This Court said, in Patterson v. Colorado, 205 U.S. 454, 462: "In the first place, the main purpose of such constitutional provisions is 'to prevent all such previous restraints upon publications as had been practiced by other governments,' and they do not prevent the subsequent punishment of such as may be deemed contrary to the public welfare. Commonwealth v. Blanding, 3 Pick. [Mass.] 304, 313, 314 [15 Am. Dec. 214]; Respublica v. Oswald, 1 Dall. 319, 325. The preliminary freedom extends as well to the false as to the true; the subsequent punishment may extend as well to the true as to the false. This was the law of criminal libel apart from statute in most cases, if not in all. Commonwealth v. Blanding, *ubi supra*; 4 Bl.Com. 150."

The criticism upon Blackstone's statement has not been because immunity from previous restraint upon publication has not been regarded as deserving of special emphasis, but chiefly because that immunity cannot be deemed to exhaust the conception of the liberty guaranteed by state and federal Constitutions. The point of criticism has been "that the mere exemption from previous restraints cannot be all that is secured by the constitutional provisions," and that "the liberty of the press might be rendered a mockery and a delusion, and the phrase itself a byword, if, while every man was at liberty to publish what he pleased, the public authorities might nevertheless punish him for harmless publications." 2 Cooley, Const. Lim. (8th Ed.) p. 885. But it is recognized that punishment for the abuse of the liberty accorded to the press is essential to the protection of the public, and that the common-law rules that subject the libeler to responsibility for the public offense, as well as for the private injury, are not abolished by the protection extended in our Constitutions. Id. pp. 883, 884. The law of criminal libel rests upon that secure foundation. There is also the conceded authority of courts to punish for contempt when publications directly tend to prevent the proper discharge of judicial functions. * * * We have no occasion to inquire as to the permissible scope of subsequent punishment. For whatever wrong the appellant has committed or may commit, by his publications, the state appropriately affords both public and private redress by its libel laws. As has been noted, the statute in question does not deal with punishments; it provides for no punishment, except in case of contempt for violation of the court's order, but for suppression and injunction—that is, for restraint upon publication.

The objection has also been made that the principle as to immunity from previous restraint is stated too broadly, if every such restraint is deemed to be prohibited. That is undoubtedly true; the protection even as to previous restraint is not absolutely unlimited. But the limitation has been recognized only in exceptional cases. * * * No one would question but that a government might prevent actual obstruction to its recruiting service or the *publication of the sailing dates of transports or the number and location of troops*. On similar grounds, the primary requirements of decency may be enforced against obscene publications. The security of the community life may be protected against incitements to acts of violence and the overthrow by force of orderly government. * * * These limitations are not applicable here. Nor are we now concerned with questions as to the extent of authority to prevent publications in order to protect private rights according to the principles governing the exercise of the jurisdiction of courts of equity. [Emphasis added.]

The exceptional nature of its limitations places in a strong light the general conception that liberty of the press, historically considered and taken up by the federal Constitution, has meant, principally although not exclusively, immunity from previous restraints or censorship. The conception of the liberty of the press in this country had broadened with the exigencies of the colonial period and with the efforts to secure freedom from oppressive administration. That liberty was especially cherished for the immunity it afforded from previous restraint of the publication of censure of public officers and charges of official misconduct.

* * *

The fact that for approximately one hundred and fifty years there has been almost an entire absence of attempts to impose previous restraints upon publications relating to the malfeasance of public officers is significant of the deep-seated conviction that such restraints would violate constitutional right. Public officers, whose character and conduct remain open to debate and free discussion in the press, find their remedies for false accusations in actions under libel laws not in proceedings to restrain the publication of newspapers and periodicals. The general principle that the constitutional guaranty of the liberty of the press gives immunity from previous restraints has been approved in many decisions under * * * state constitutions.

The importance of this immunity has not lessened. While reckless assaults upon public men, and efforts to bring obloquy upon those who are endeavoring faithfully to discharge official duties, exert a baleful influence and deserve the severest condemnation in public opinion, it cannot be said that this abuse is greater, and it is believed to be less, than that which characterized the period in which our institutions took shape. Meanwhile, the administration of government has become more complex, the opportunities for malfeasance and corruption have multiplied, crime has grown to most serious proportions, and the danger of its protection by unfaithful officials and of the impairment of the fundamental security of life and property by criminal alliances and official neglect, emphasizes the primary need of a vigilant and courageous press, especially in great cities. The fact that the liberty of the press may be abused by miscreant purveyors of scandal does not make any the less necessary the immunity of the press from previous restraint in dealing with official misconduct. Subsequent punishment for such abuses as may exist is the appropriate remedy, consistent with constitutional privilege.

In attempted justification of the statute, it is said that it deals not with publication per se, but with the "business" of publishing defamation. If, however, the publisher has a constitutional right to publish, without previous restraint, an edition of his newspaper charging official derelictions, it cannot be denied that he may publish subsequent editions for the same purpose. He does not lose his right by exercising it. If his right exists, it may be exercised in publishing nine editions, as in this case, as well as in one edition. If previous restraint is permissible, it may be imposed at once; indeed, the wrong may be as serious in one publication as in several. Characterizing the publication as a business, and the business as a nuisance, does not permit an invasion of the constitutional immunity against restraint. Similarly, it does not matter that the newspaper or periodical is found to be "largely" or "chiefly" devoted to the publication of such derelictions. If the publisher has a right, without previous restraint, to publish them, his right cannot be deemed to be dependent upon his publishing something else, more or less, with the matter to which objection is made.

Nor can it be said that the constitutional freedom from previous restraint is lost because charges are made of derelictions which constitute crimes. With the multiplying provisions of penal codes, and of municipal charters and ordinances carrying penal sanctions, the conduct of public officers is very largely within the purview of criminal statutes. The freedom of the press from previous restraint has never been regarded as limited to such animadversions as lay outside the range of penal enactments. Historically, there is no such limitation; it is inconsistent with the reason which underlies the privilege, as the privilege so limited would be of slight value for the purposes for which it came to be established.

The statute in question cannot be justified by reason of the fact that the publisher is permitted to show, before injunction issues, that the matter published is true and is published with good motives and for justifiable ends. If such a statute, authorizing suppression and injunction on such a basis, is constitutionally valid, it would be equally permissible for the Legislature to provide that at any time the publisher of any newspaper could be brought before a court, or even an administrative officer (as the constitutional protection may not be regarded as resting on mere procedural details), and required to produce proof of the truth of his publication, or of what he intended to publish and of his motives, or stand enjoined. If this can be done, the Legislature may provide machinery for determining in the complete exercise of its discretion what are justifiable ends and restrain publication accordingly. And it would be but a step to a complete system of censorship. The recognition of authority to impose previous restraint upon publication in order to protect the community against the circulation of charges of misconduct, and especially of official misconduct, necessarily would carry with it the admission of the authority of the censor against which the constitutional barrier was erected. The preliminary freedom, by virtue of the very reason for its existence, does not depend, as this court has said, on proof of truth.

Equally unavailing is the insistence that the statute is designed to prevent the circulation of scandal which tends to disturb the public peace and to provoke assaults and the commission of crime. Charges of reprehensible conduct, and in particular of official malfeasance, unquestionably create a public scandal, but the theory of the constitutional guaranty is that even a more serious public evil would be caused by authority to prevent publication. "To prohibit the intent to excite those unfavorable sentiments against those who administer the Government, is equivalent to a prohibition of the actual excitement of them; and to prohibit the actual excitement of them is equivalent to a prohibition of discussions having that tendency and effect; which again, is equivalent to a protection of those who administer the Government, if they should at any time deserve the contempt or hatred of the people, against being exposed to it by free animadversions on their characters and conduct." There is nothing new in the fact that charges of reprehensible conduct may create resentment and the disposition to resort to violent means of redress, but this well-understood tendency did not alter the determination to protect the press against censorship and restraint upon publication. * * *

For these reasons we hold the statute, so far as it authorized the proceedings in this action * * * to be an infringement of the liberty of the press guaranteed by the Fourteenth Amendment. We should add that this decision rests upon the operation and effect of the statute, without regard to the question of the truth of the charges contained in the particular periodical. The fact that the public officers named in this case, and those associated with the charges of official dereliction, may be deemed to be impeccable, cannot affect the conclusion that the statute imposes an unconstitutional restraint upon publication.

Judgment reversed.

Justice BUTLER (dissenting).

* * *

The Minnesota statute does not operate as a *previous* restraint on publication within the proper meaning of that phrase. It does not authorize administrative control in advance such as was formerly exercised by the licensers and censors, but prescribes a remedy to be enforced by a suit in equity. In this case there was previous publication made in the course of the business of regularly producing malicious, scandalous, and defamatory periodicals. The business and publications unquestionably constitute an abuse of the right of free press. The statute denounces the things done as a nuisance on the ground, as stated by the State Supreme Court, that they threaten morals, peace, and good order. There is no question of the power of the state to denounce such transgressions. The restraint authorized is only in respect of continuing to do what has been duly adjudged to constitute a nuisance. * * * There is nothing in the statute purporting to prohibit publications that have not been adjudged to constitute a nuisance. It is fanciful to suggest similarity between the granting or enforcement of the decree authorized by this statute to prevent *further* publication of malicious, scandalous, and defamatory articles and the *previous restraint* upon the press by licensers as referred to by Blackstone and described in the history of the times to which he alludes.

* * *

It is well known, as found by the state Supreme Court, that existing libel laws are inadequate effectively to suppress evils resulting from the kind of business and publications that are shown in this case. The doctrine that measures such as the one before us are invalid because they operate as previous restraints to infringe freedom of press exposes the peace and good order of every community and the business and private affairs of every individual to the constant and protracted false and malicious assaults of any insolvent publisher who may have purpose and sufficient capacity to contrive and put into effect a scheme or program for oppression, blackmail or extortion.

The judgment should be affirmed.

Justice Van Devanter, Justice McReynolds, and Justice Sutherland concur in this opinion.

COMMENT

1. Chief Justice Hughes said in *Near* that freedom from prior restraint was the general principle. But he also made it clear that it was not an absolute principle. The areas of exception were apparently three: 1) cases where national security was involved in time of war; 2) cases where the "primary requirements of decency" were involved, i.e., the problem of obscene publications; 3) cases where the public order was endangered by the incitement to violence and overthrow by force of orderly government.

The *Near* case produced a sharp 5–4 division in the Court. The narrow majority supporting the opinion of Chief Justice Hughes was accused by Justice Pierce Butler, a Minnesotan, of reaching out to decide the constitutional status of prior restraints which were not involved in the case at bar. Technically, Justice Butler was right. The prior restraint known at common law empowered administrative officials rather than judges to review in the first instance the material to be published. In *Near, The Saturday Press* had been able to publish what it chose in the first instance. Moreover, no requirement of submitting future copy to a court as a prerequisite to publication was asked of the editors. Yet, more broadly viewed, the court order probably did create a prior restraint.

Prior restraint has not entirely vanished from the American legal scene. However, prior restraints today appear to be more common in the obscenity field than they are in the area of political freedom. An example is Bantam Books, Inc. v. Sullivan, 372 U.S. 58 (1963). In that case the Rhode Island legislature established a state-supported commission to "advise" magazine and book distributors when a publication was obscene. The advisory letter informed the distributor that if a publication was designated by the commission as obscene and was not removed from circulation, the matter would be turned over to law enforcement authorities for criminal prosecution. The commission itself had no law enforcement powers, and it could not require the regular law enforcement authorities to take action. In what ways did this procedure conform to and differ from the prior restraint known to English common law and described in the opinions in the *Near* case? Could it be fairly said of the Rhode Island procedure litigated in *Bantam Books* that its effect might be even more restrictive of press freedom than the classic form of prior restraint? Why?

With regard to this question, it should be noted that the Supreme Court described the Rhode Island procedure as a "form of regulation that creates hazards to press freedom markedly greater than those that attend reliance upon the criminal law." Bantam Books, Inc. v. Sullivan, 372 U.S. 58, 70 (1963).

2. In the landmark case of New York Times v. Sullivan, 376 U.S. 254 (1964), the Supreme Court sharply limited the ability of public officials to successfully sue newspapers for libel. For an extended discussion of the impact of the *Times* case on the law of libel, see Chapter II, text, infra, p. 213. In the *Times* case, the Court cited the statements in *Near* and other cases that the "Constitution does not protect libelous utterances." But the Court pointed out that neither *Near* nor any other case cited for this proposition actually involved use of the libel laws to restrain expression "critical of the official conduct of public officials." 376 U.S. 254 at 268. In a decision of far-reaching scope, the Court proclaimed the latter kind of expression to be protected by the First Amendment. Justice Brennan said for the Court in *New York Times* that the case of a public official suing a newspaper for libel must be considered "against the background of a profound national commitment to the principle that debate on public issues should be uninhibited, robust and wide-open, and that it may well include vehement, caustic, and sometimes unpleasantly sharp attacks on government and public officials." 376 U.S. 254 at 270.

If *The Saturday Press* were to publish in Minneapolis today an attack on the members of the municipal government of that city—an attack, which, let us assume, until the *New York Times* case would have been actionably libelous—would an injunction now be available to restrain further publications of the attack?

Has the *New York Times* case further restricted the already limited range of prior restraints?

3. From the point of view of freedom of the press, the legal concept of prior restraint is of the greatest importance. If, as a constitutional matter, freedom of the press included nothing else than prior restraint, considerable protection would still have been afforded the printed word. This is because freedom from prior restraint allows the material to be disseminated in the first place. Ideas, no matter how disturbing to established authority, are thus given legal protection in their emergent state. This freedom from prior restraint against the printed word contrasts with the legal concept of subsequent punishment which refers to the imposition of legal sanctions on those who authored the offending words. Punishing Gitlow *after* the publication of his revolutionary newspaper is an example of subsequent punishment. Under what set of facts would *Gitlow* have been a prior restraint case?

It is the contribution of Chief Justice Hughes's opinion in *Near v. Minnesota* that it enriched in a formative case the constitutional interpretation of freedom of the press to include *both* freedom from prior restraint and freedom from subsequent punishment. However, as between the two forms of repression of the press, prior restraint and subsequent punishment, which is the more dangerous in damaging the values for which freedom of press exists as a constitutional guarantee? Why?

For an excellent discussion of prior restraint, see generally Emerson, *The Doctrine of Prior Restraint*, 20 Law & Contemp.Prob. 648 (1955); Symposium, *Near v.*

Minnesota, 50th Anniversary, 66 Minn.L. Rev. 1–208 (November 1981).

The PENTAGON PAPERS Case

The Pentagon Papers or the *New York Times* case of the summer of 1971 brought forth suddenly and with no particular warning one of the great First Amendment and one of the most dramatic prior restraint cases in American constitutional history. For students of the law of mass communication the case can be approached under at least three familiar categories: 1) prior restraint, 2) journalists' privilege to protect their sources, and 3) the public's right to know. All the judges who considered the case had to weigh claims of freedom from prior restraint and freedom of information against claims of government interest and security advanced by the Justice Department lawyers. Was Dr. Daniel Ellsberg, one of the thirty-six authors of the Papers, justified, legally or ethically, in taking classified papers to which he had access and turning them over to the *New York Times*?

The sequence of events which created the Pentagon Papers case came about as follows: In June 1971, the *New York Times,* after much soul searching, decided to publish a secret, classified Pentagon Report outlining the process by which America went to war in Vietnam. At the request of the United States government, a temporary restraining order was issued against the *New York Times* by a newly appointed federal judge, Murray Gurfein, of the Federal District Court for the Southern District of New York. A few days later Judge Gurfein in a stirring decision refused to grant the United States government a permanent injunction to restrain the *New York Times* from publishing the Pentagon Papers:

"A cantankerous press, an obstinate press, a ubiquitous press," said the judge, "must be suffered by those in authority in order to preserve the even greater values of freedom of expression and the right of the people to know."

But the United States Court of Appeals for the Second Circuit reversed this decision, holding that the issue of whether the materials should be published should be decided in further hearings where the government could develop and support its position that the publication of the papers presented a threat to the security of the United States. In the interim, the U.S. Court of Appeals for the Second Circuit ruled that the restraints on publication be continued. Meanwhile, the *Washington Post* entered the fray. The government requested an injunction against the *Post* in the United States District Court in the District of Columbia, but Judge Gerhard Gesell denied the government's attempt to restrain publication of the Pentagon Papers by the *Post.* The government appealed, and the United States Court of Appeals for the District of Columbia came down on the side of the press.

The *Washington Post* and *New York Times* were not the only papers to publish the Pentagon Papers. The *Boston Globe* and the *St. Louis Post Dispatch* had each published one article on the Papers. The government sought and obtained a restraining order against the papers in Boston and St. Louis. The *Chicago Sun Times* and the *Los Angeles Times* published stories based on the Pentagon Papers, but these papers were never the subject of lawsuits by the government. Because of the inconsistent actions with regard to the Pentagon Papers in the federal courts of appeals in New York and Washington, the *Washington Post* was free to publish papers, but the *New York Times* was not.

The federal courts of appeals had given judgment on the matter on June 23, 1971. The *New York Times* filed a petition for a writ of certiorari along with a motion for accelerated consideration of the petition on June 24. On June 30, 1971, the great case, a historic confrontation between government and the press, was decided by the Supreme Court . The result was clear—every newspaper in the land was free to publish the Pentagon Papers. The excitement of victory for the press, however, clouded appreciation by the press of the fact that the bitter struggle between freedom of information and national security had hardly been given a clear resolution by the Supreme Court. The Court's actual order merely held that the government had not met the heavy burden which must be met to justify any government prior restraint on the press. As for the myriad issues raised by the momentous case, nine separate opinions (it would have been impossible to have more) reflected the ambiguities, contradictions, and fundamental disagreements among the justices on basic issues concerning the role of the press in American society.

For a detailed account of the events leading to the Supreme Court's action see Ungar, *The Papers & The Papers* (1973).

NEW YORK TIMES v. UNITED STATES

403 U.S. 713, 91 S.CT. 2140, 29 L.ED.2D 822 (1971).

Per Curiam.

We granted certiorari in these cases in which the United States seeks to enjoin the New York Times and the Washington Post from publishing the contents of a classified study entitled "History of U. S. Decision-Making Process on Viet Nam Policy." * * *

"Any system of prior restraints of expression comes to this Court bearing a heavy presumption against its constitutional validity." Bantam Books, Inc. v. Sullivan, 372 U.S. 58, 70 (1963); see also Near v. Minnesota, 283 U.S. 697 (1931). The government "thus carries a heavy burden of showing justification for the enforcement of such a restraint." Organization for a Better Austin v. Keefe, 402 U.S. 415 (1971). The District Court for the Southern District of New York in the *New York Times* case and the District Court for the District of Columbia and the Court of Appeals for the District of Columbia Circuit in the *Washington Post* case held that the government had not met that burden. We agree. [Emphasis added.]

Justice BLACK, with whom Justice Douglas joins, concurring.

* * * I believe that every moment's continuance of the injunctions against these newspapers amounts to a flagrant, indefensible, and continuing violation of the First Amendment. * * * In my view it is unfortunate that some of my Brethren are apparently willing to hold that the publication of news may sometimes be enjoined. Such a holding would make a shambles of the First Amendment.

Our government was launched in 1789 with the adoption of the Constitution. The Bill of Rights, including the First Amendment, followed in 1791. Now, for the first time in the 182 years since the founding of the Republic, the federal courts are asked to hold that the First Amendment does not mean what it says, but rather means that the government can halt the publication of current news of vital importance to the people of this country.

In seeking injunctions against these newspapers and in its presentation to the Court, the executive branch seems to have forgotten the essential purpose and history of the First Amendment. When the Constitution was adopted, many people strongly opposed it because the document contained no Bill of Rights to safeguard certain basic freedoms. They especially feared that the new powers granted to a central government might be interpreted to permit the government to curtail freedom of religion, press, assembly, and speech. In response to an overwhelming public clamor, James Madison offered a series of amendments to satisfy citizens that these great liberties would remain safe and beyond the power of government to abridge. Madison proposed what later became the First Amendment in three parts, two of which are set out below, and one of which proclaimed: "The people shall not be deprived or abridged of their right to speak, to write, or to publish their sentiments; *and the freedom of the press, as one of the great bulwarks of liberty, shall be inviolable.*" The amendments were offered to *curtail* and *restrict* the general powers granted to the executive, legislative, and judicial Branches two years before in the original Constitution. The Bill of Rights changed the original Constitution into a new charter under which no branch of government could abridge the people's freedoms of press, speech, religion, and assembly. Yet the solicitor general argues and some members of the Court appear to agree that the general powers of the government adopted in the original Constitution should be interpreted to limit and restrict the specific and emphatic guarantees of the Bill of Rights adopted later. I can imagine no greater perversion of history. Madison and the other Framers of the First Amendment able men that they were, wrote in language they earnestly believed could never be misunderstood: "Congress shall make no law * * * abridging the freedom of the press. * * *" Both the history and language of the First Amendment support the view that the press must be left free to publish news, whatever the source, without censorship, injunctions, or prior restraints.

In the First Amendment the Founding Fathers gave the free press the protection it must have to fulfill its essential role in our democracy. The press was to serve the governed, not the governors. The government's power to censor the press was abolished so that the press would remain forever free to censure the government. The press was protected so that it could bare the secrets of government and inform the people. Only a free and unrestrained press can effectively expose deception in government. And paramount among the responsibilities of a free press is the duty to prevent any part of the government from deceiving the people and sending them off to distant lands to die of foreign fevers and foreign shot and shell. In my view, far from deserving condemnation for their courageous reporting, the New York Times, the Washington Post, and other newspapers should be commended for serving the purpose that the Founding Fathers saw so clearly. In revealing the workings of government that led to the Viet Nam war, the newspapers nobly did precisely that which the Founders hoped and trusted they would do.

The government's case here is based on premises entirely different from those that guided the Framers of the First Amendment. The solicitor general has carefully and emphatically stated:

"Now, Mr. Justice [Black], your construction of * * * [the First Amendment] is well known, and I certainly respect it. You say that no law means no law, and that should be obvious. I can only say, Mr. Justice that to me it is equally obvious that 'no law' does not mean 'no law', and I would seek to persuade the Court that that is true. * * * [T]here are other parts of the Constitution that grant power and responsibilities to the Executive and * * * the First Amendment was not intended to make it impossible for the Executive to function or to protect the security of the United States."

And the government argues in its brief that in spite of the First Amendment, "[t]he authority of the Executive Department to protect the nation against publication of information whose disclosure would endanger the national security stems from two interrelated sources: the constitutional power of the president over the conduct of foreign affairs and his authority as Commander-in-Chief."

In other words, we are asked to hold that despite the First Amendment's emphatic command, the executive branch, the

Congress, and the Judiciary can make laws enjoining publication of current news and abridging freedom of the press in the name of "national security." The government does not even attempt to rely on any act of Congress. Instead it makes the bold and dangerously far-reaching contention that the courts should take it upon themselves to "make" a law abridging freedom of the press in the name of equity, presidential power and national security, even when the representatives of the people in Congress have adhered to the command of the First Amendment and refused to make such a law. See concurring opinion of Justice Douglas. * * * To find that the president has "inherent power" to halt the publication of news by resort to the courts would wipe out the First Amendment and destroy the fundamental liberty and security of the very people the government hopes to make "secure." No one can read the history of the adoption of the First Amendment without being convinced beyond any doubt that it was injunctions like those sought here that Madison and his collaborators intended to outlaw in this Nation for all time.

The word "security" is a broad, vague generality whose contours should not be invoked to abrogate the fundamental law embodied in the First Amendment. The guarding of military and diplomatic secrets at the expense of informed representative government provides no real security for our Republic. The Framers of the First Amendment, fully aware of both the need to defend a new nation and the abuses of the English and Colonial governments, sought to give this new society strength and security by providing that freedom of speech, press, religion, and assembly should not be abridged.

Justice DOUGLAS, with whom Justice Black joins, concurring.

While I join the opinion of the Court I believe it necessary to express my views more fully.

It should be noted at the outset that the First Amendment provides that "Congress shall make no law * * * abridging the freedom of speech or of the press." That leaves, in my view, no room for governmental restraint on the press.

There is, moreover, no statute barring the publication by the press of the material which the *Times* and *Post* seek to use. 18 U.S.C.A. § 793(e) provides that "whoever having unauthorized possession of, access to, or control over any document, writing, * * * or information relating to the national defense which information the possessor has reason to believe could be used to the injury of the United States or to the advantage of any foreign nation, wilfully communicates * * * the same to any person not entitled to receive it * * * shall be fined not more than $10,000 or imprisoned not more than ten years or both."

The government suggests that the word "communicates" is broad enough to encompass publication.

There are eight sections in the chapter on espionage and censorship, §§ 792–799. In three of those eight "publish" is specifically mentioned: § 794(b) provides "Whoever in time of war, with the intent that the same shall be communicated to the enemy, collects records, *publishes*, or communicates * * * [the disposition of armed forces]."

Section 797 prohibits "reproduces, *publishes,* sells, or gives away" photos of defense installations.

Section 798 relating to cryptography prohibits: "communicates, furnishes, transmits, or otherwise makes available * * * *or publishes.*"

Thus it is apparent that Congress was capable of and did distinguish between publishing and communication in the various sections of the Espionage Act.

The other evidence that § 793 does not apply to the press is a rejected version of § 793. That version read: "During any national emergency resulting from a war to which the U.S. is a party or from threat of such a war, the president may, by proclamation, prohibit the publishing or communicating of, or the attempting to publish or communicate any information relating to the national defense, which in his judgment is of such character that it is or might be useful to the enemy." During the debates in the Senate the First Amendment was specifically cited and that provision was defeated. 55 Cong.Rec. 2166.

Judge Gurfein's holding in the *Times* case that this act does not apply to this case was therefore preeminently sound. Moreover, the Act of September 23, 1950, in amending 18 U.S.C.A. § 793 states in § 1(b) that:

"Nothing in this act shall be construed to authorize, require, or establish military or civilian censorship or in any way to limit or infringe upon freedom of the press or of speech as guaranteed by the Constitution of the United States and no regulation shall be promulgated hereunder having that effect." 64 Stat. 987. Thus Congress has been faithful to the command of the First Amendment in this area.

So any power that the government possesses must come from its "inherent power."

The power to wage war is "the power to wage war successfully." See Hirabayashi v. United States, 320 U.S. 81, 93. But the war power stems from a declaration of war. The Constitution by Article I, § 8, gives Congress, not the president, power "to declare war." Nowhere are presidential wars authorized. We need not decide therefore what leveling effect the war power of Congress might have.

These disclosures may have a serious impact. But that is no basis for sanctioning a previous restraint on the press.

As we stated only the other day in Organization for a Better Austin v. Keefe, 402 U.S. 415, "any prior restraint on expression comes to this Court with a 'heavy presumption' against its constitutional validity."

The government says that it has inherent powers to go into court and obtain an injunction to protect that national interest, which in this case is alleged to be national security.

Near v. Minnesota, 283 U.S. 697, repudiated that expansive doctrine in no uncertain terms.

The dominant purpose of the First Amendment was to prohibit the widespread practice of governmental suppression of embarrassing information. It is common knowledge that the First Amendment was adopted against the widespread use of the common law of seditious libel to punish the dissemination of material that is embarrassing to the powers-that-be. See Emerson, The System of Freedom of Expression, c. V (1970); Chafee, Free Speech in the United States, c. XIII (1941). The present cases will, I think, go down in history as the most dramatic illustration of that principle. A debate of large proportions goes on in the Nation over our posture in Vietnam. That debate antedated the disclosure of the contents of the present documents. The latter are highly relevant to the debate in progress.

Secrecy in government is fundamentally anti-democratic, perpetuating bureaucratic errors. Open debate and discussion of public issues are vital to our national health. On public questions there should be "open and robust debate." New York Times, Inc. v. Sullivan, 376 U.S. 254, 269–270.

I would affirm the judgment of the court of appeals in the *Post* case, vacate the stay of the court of appeals in the *Times* case and direct that it affirm the district court.

The stays in these cases that have been in effect for more than a week constitute a flouting of the principles of the First Amendment as interpreted in Near v. Minnesota.

Justice BRENNAN, concurring.

I write separately in these cases only to emphasize what should be apparent:

that our judgment in the present cases may not be taken to indicate the propriety in the future, of issuing temporary stays and restraining orders to block the publication of material sought to be suppressed by the government. So far as I can determine, never before has the United States sought to enjoin a newspaper from publishing information in its possession. The relative novelty of the questions presented, the necessary haste with which decisions were reached, the magnitude of the interests asserted, and the fact that all the parties have concentrated their arguments upon the question whether permanent restraints were proper may have justified at least some of the restraints heretofore imposed in these cases. Certainly it is difficult to fault the several courts below for seeking to assure that the issues here involved were preserved for ultimate review by this Court. But even if it be assumed that some of the interim restraints were proper in the two cases before us, that assumption has no bearing upon the propriety of similar judicial action in the future. To begin with, there has now been ample time for reflection and judgment; whatever values there may be in the preservation of novel questions for appellate review may not support any restraints in the future. More important, the First Amendment stands as an absolute bar to the imposition of judicial restraints in circumstances of the kind presented by these cases.

The error which has pervaded these cases from the outset was the granting of any injunctive relief whatsoever, interim or otherwise. The entire thrust of the government's claim throughout these cases has been that publication of the material sought to be enjoined "could," or "might," or "may" prejudice the national interest in various ways. But the First Amendment tolerates absolutely no prior judicial restraints of the press predicated upon surmise or conjecture that untoward consequences may result. Our cases, it is true, have indicated that there is a single, extremely narrow class of cases in which the First Amendment's ban on prior judicial restraint may be overridden. Our cases have thus far indicated that such cases may arise only when the Nation "is at war," Schenck v. United States, 249 U.S. 47, 52 (1919), during which times "no one would question but that a government might prevent actual obstruction to its recruiting service or the publication of the sailing dates of transports or the number and location of troops." Near v. Minnesota, 283 U.S. 697, 716 (1931). Even if the present world situation were assumed to be tantamount to a time of war, or if the power of presently available armaments would justify even in peacetime the suppression of information that would set in motion a nuclear holocaust, in neither of these actions has the government presented or even alleged that publication of items from or based upon the material at issue would cause the happening of an event of that nature. "The chief purpose of [the First Amendment's] guarantee [is] to prevent previous restraints upon publication." Near v. Minnesota, supra, at 713. Thus, only governmental allegation and proof that publication must inevitably, directly and immediately cause the occurrence of an event kindred to imperiling the safety of a transport already at sea can support even the issuance of an interim restraining order. In no event may mere conclusions be sufficient: for if the executive branch seeks judicial aid in preventing publication, it must inevitably submit the basis upon which that aid is sought to scrutiny by the judiciary. And therefore, every restraint issued in this case, whatever its form, has violated the First Amendment—and none the less so because that restraint was justified as necessary to afford the court an opportunity to examine the claim more thoroughly. Unless and until the government has clearly made out its case, the First Amendment commands that no injunction may issue.

Justice STEWART, with whom Justice White joins, concurring.

In the governmental structure created by our Constitution, the executive is endowed with enormous power in the two related areas of national defense and international relations. This power, largely unchecked by the legislative and judicial branches, has been pressed to the very hilt since the advent of the nuclear missile age. For better or for worse, the simple fact is that a president of the United States possesses vastly greater constitutional independence in these two vital areas of power than does, say a prime minister of a country with a parliamentary form of government.

In the absence of the governmental checks and balances present in other areas of our national life, the only effective restraint upon executive policy and power in the areas of national defense and international affairs may lie in an enlightened citizenry—in an informed and critical public opinion which alone can here protect the values of democratic government. For this reason, it is perhaps here that a press that is alert, aware, and free most vitally serves the basic purpose of the First Amendment. For without an informed and free press there cannot be an enlightened people.

Yet it is elementary that the successful conduct of international diplomacy and the maintenance of an effective national defense require both confidentiality and secrecy. * * *

I think there can be but one answer to this dilemma, if dilemma it be. The responsibility must be where the power is. If the Constitution gives the executive a large degree of unshared power in the conduct of foreign affairs and the maintenance of our national defense, then under the Constitution the executive must have the largely unshared duty to determine and preserve the degree of internal security necessary to exercise that power successfully. It is an awesome responsibility, requiring judgment and wisdom of a high order. I should suppose that moral, political, and practical considerations would dictate that a very first principle of that wisdom would be an insistence upon avoiding secrecy for its own sake. *For when everything is classified, then nothing is classified,* and the system becomes one to be disregarded by the cynical or the careless, and to be manipulated by those intent on self-protection or self-promotion. I should suppose, in short, that the hallmark of a truly effective internal security system would be the maximum possible disclosure, recognizing that secrecy can best be preserved only when credibility is truly maintained. But be that as it may, it is clear to me that it is the constitutional duty of the executive—as a matter of sovereign prerogative and not as a matter of law as the courts know law—through the promulgation and enforcement of executive regulations, to protect the confidentiality necessary to carry out its responsibilities in the fields of international relations and national defense. [Emphasis added.]

This is not to say that Congress and the courts have no role to play. Undoubtedly Congress has the power to enact specific and appropriate criminal laws to protect government property and preserve government secrets. Congress has passed such laws, and several of them are of very colorable relevance to the apparent circumstances of these cases. And if a criminal prosecution is instituted, it will be the responsibility of the courts to decide the applicability of the criminal law under which the charge is brought. Moreover, if Congress should pass a specific law authorizing civil proceedings in this field, the courts would likewise have the duty to decide the constitutionality of such a law as well as its applicability to the facts proved.

But in the cases before us we are asked neither to construe specific regulations nor to apply specific laws. We are asked, instead, to perform a function that the Constitution gave to the executive, not the judiciary. We are asked, quite simply, to prevent the publication by two newspapers of material that the executive branch insists should not, in the national interest, be published. I am convinced that the executive is correct with respect to some of the documents involved. But I cannot say that disclosure of any of them will surely result in direct, immediate, and irreparable damage to our Nation or its people. That being so, there can under the First Amendment be but one judicial resolution of the issues before us. I join the judgments of the Court.

Justice WHITE, with whom Justice Stewart joins, concurring.

I concur in today's judgments, but only because of the concededly extraordinary protection against prior restraints enjoyed by the press under our constitutional system. I do not say that in no circumstances would the First Amendment permit an injunction against publishing information about government plans or operations. Nor, after examining the materials the government characterizes as the most sensitive and destructive, can I deny that revelation of these documents will do substantial damage to public interests. Indeed, I am confident that their disclosure will have that result. But I nevertheless agree that the United States has not satisfied the very heavy burden which it must meet to warrant an injunction against publication in these cases, at least in the absence of express and appropriately limited congressional authorization for prior restraints in circumstances such as these.

The government's position is simply stated: The responsibility of the executive for the conduct of the foreign affairs and for the security of the Nation is so basic that the president is entitled to an injunction against publication of a newspaper story whenever he can convince a court that the information to be revealed threatens "grave and irreparable" injury to the public interest; and the injunction should issue whether or not the material to be published is classified, whether or not publication would be lawful under relevant criminal statutes enacted by Congress and regardless of the circumstances by which the newspaper came into possession of the information.

At least in the absence of legislation by Congress, based on its own investigations and findings, I am quite unable to agree that the inherent powers of the executive and the courts reach so far as to authorize remedies having such sweeping potential for inhibiting publications by the press. Much of the difficulty inheres in the "grave and irreparable danger" standard suggested by the United States. If the United States were to have judgment under such a standard in these cases, our decision would be of little guidance to other courts in other cases, for the material at issue here would not be available from the Court's opinion or from public records, nor would it be published by the press. Indeed, even today where we hold that the United States has not met its burden, the material remains sealed in court records and it is properly not discussed in today's opinions. Moreover, because the material poses substantial dangers to national interests and because of the hazards of criminal sanctions, a responsible press may choose never to publish the more sensitive materials. To sustain the government in these cases would start the courts down a long and hazardous road that I am not willing to travel at least without congressional guidance and direction.

It is not easy to reject the proposition urged by the United States and to deny relief on its good-faith claims in these cases that publication will work serious damage to the country. But that discomfiture is considerably dispelled by the infrequency of prior restraint cases. Normally, publication will occur and the damage be done before the government has either opportunity or grounds for suppression. So here, publication has already begun and a substantial part of the threatened damage has already occurred. The fact of a massive breakdown in security is known, access to the documents by many unauthorized people is undeniable and the efficacy of equitable relief against these or other newspapers to avert anticipated damage is doubtful at best.

What is more, terminating the ban on publication of the relatively few sensitive documents the government now seeks to suppress does not mean that the law either requires or invites newspapers or others to publish them or that they will be immune from criminal action if they do. Prior restraints require an unusually heavy justification under the First Amendment; but failure by the government to justify prior restraints does not measure its constitutional entitlement to a conviction for criminal publication. That the government mistakenly chose to proceed by injunction does not mean that it could not successfully proceed in another way.

When the Espionage Act was under consideration in 1917, Congress eliminated from the bill a provision that would have given the president broad powers in time of war to proscribe, under threat of criminal penalty, the publication of various categories of information related to the national defense. Congress at that time was unwilling to clothe the president with such far-reaching powers to monitor the press, and those opposed to this part of the legislation assumed that a necessary concomitant of such power was the power to "filter out the news to the people through some man." 55 Cong.Rec. 2008 (1917) [remarks of Senator Ashurst]. However, these same members of Congress appeared to have little doubt that newspapers would be subject to criminal prosecution if they insisted on publishing information of the type Congress had itself determined should not be revealed. Senator Ashurst, for example, was quite sure that the editor of such a newspaper "should be punished if he did publish information as to the movements of the fleet, the troops, the aircraft, the location of powder factories, the location of defense works, and all that sort of thing." 55 Cong.Rec. 1009 (1917).

The criminal code contains numerous provisions potentially relevant to these cases. Section 797 makes it a crime to publish certain photographs or drawings of military installations. Section 798, also in precise language, proscribes knowing and willful publications of any classified information concerning the cryptographic systems or communication intelligence activities of the United States as well as any information obtained from communication intelligence operations. If any of the material here at issue is of this nature, the newspapers are presumably now on full notice of the position of the United States and must face the consequences if they publish. I would have no difficulty in sustaining convictions under these sections on facts that would not justify the intervention of equity and the imposition of a prior restraint.

The same would be true under those sections of the criminal code casting a wider net to protect the national defense. Section 793(e) makes it a criminal act for any unauthorized possessor of a document "relating to national defense" either (1) willfully to communicate or cause to be communicated that document to any person not entitled to receive it or (2) willfully to retain the document and fail to deliver it to an officer of the United States entitled to receive it. The subsection was added in 1950 because pre-existing law provided no penalty for the unauthorized possessor unless demand for the documents was made. "The dangers surrounding the unauthorized possession of such items are self-evident, and it is deemed advisable to require their surrender in such a case, regardless of demand, especially since their unauthorized possession may be unknown to the authorities who would otherwise make the demand." S.Rep.No.2369, 81st Cong., 2d Sess., 9 (1950). Of course, in the cases before us, the unpublished documents have been demanded by the United States and their import has been made known at least to counsel for the newspapers involved. In Gorin v. United States, 312 U.S. 19, 28 (1941), the words "national defense" as used in a predecessor of § 793 were held by a unanimous court to have "a well understood connotation"—a "generic concept of broad connotations, referring to the military and naval establishments and the related activities of national preparedness"—and to be "sufficiently definite to apprise the public of prohibited activities" and to be consonant with due process. 312 U.S., at 28. Also, as construed by the Court in Gorin, information "connected with the national defense" is obviously not limited to that threatening "grave and irreparable" injury to the United States.

It is thus clear that Congress has addressed itself to the problems of protecting the security of the country and the national defense from unauthorized disclosure of potentially damaging information. Cf. Youngstown Sheet & Tube Co. v. Sawyer, 343 U.S. 579, 585–586 (1952); see also id., at 593–628 (Frankfurter, J., concurring). It has not, however, authorized the injunctive remedy against threatened publication. It has apparently been satisfied to rely on criminal sanctions and their deterrent effect on the responsible as well as the irresponsible press. I am not, of course, saying that either of these newspapers has yet committed a crime or that either would commit a crime if they published all the material now in their possession. That matter must await resolution in the context of a criminal proceeding if one is instituted by the United States. In that event, the issue of guilt or innocence would be determined by procedures and standards quite different from those that have purported to govern these injunctive proceedings.

Justice MARSHALL, concurring.

The government contends that the only issue in this case is whether in a suit by the United States, "the First Amendment bars a court from prohibiting a newspaper from publishing material whose disclosure would pose a grave and immediate danger to the security of the United States." Brief of the government, at 6. With all due respect, I believe the ultimate issue in this case is even more basic than the one posed by the solicitor general. The issue is whether this Court or the Congress has the power to make law.

In this case there is no problem concerning the president's power to classify information as "secret" or "top secret." Congress has specifically recognized presidential authority, which has been formally exercised in Executive Order 10501, to classify documents and information. See, e.g., 18 U.S.C.A. § 798; 50 U.S.C.A. § 783. Nor is there any issue here regarding the president's power as chief executive and commander in chief to protect national security by disciplining employees who disclose information and by taking precautions to prevent leaks.

The problem here is whether in this particular case the Executive Branch has authority to invoke the equity jurisdiction of the courts to protect what it believes to be the national interest. See In re Debs, 158 U.S. 564, 584 (1895). The government argues that in addition to the inherent power of any government to protect itself, the president's power to conduct foreign affairs and his position as commander in chief give him authority to impose censorship on the press to protect his ability to deal effectively with foreign nations and to conduct the military affairs of the country. Of course, it is beyond cavil that the president has broad powers by virtue of his primary responsibility for the conduct of our foreign affairs and his position as commander in chief. * * * And in some situations it may be that under whatever inherent powers the government may have, as well as the implicit authority derived from the president's mandate to conduct foreign affairs and to act as commander in chief, there is a basis for the invocation of the equity jurisdiction of this Court as an aid to prevent the publication of material damaging to "national security," however that term may be defined.

It would, however, be utterly inconsistent with the concept of separation of power for this Court to use its power of contempt to prevent behavior that Congress has specifically declined to prohibit. There would be a similar damage to the basic concept of these coequal branches of government if when the executive has adequate authority granted by Congress to protect "national security" it can choose instead to invoke the contempt power of a court to enjoin the threatened conduct. The Constitution provides that Congress shall make laws, the president execute laws, and courts interpret law. Youngstown Sheet & Tube Co. v. Sawyer, 343 U.S. 579 (1952). It did not provide for government by injunction in which the courts and the Executive can "make law" without regard to the action of Congress. It may be more convenient for the executive if it need only convince a judge to prohibit conduct rather than to ask the Congress to pass a law and it may be more convenient to enforce a contempt order than seek a criminal conviction in a jury trial. Moreover, it may be considered politically wise to get a court to share the responsibility for arresting those who the executive has probable cause to believe are violating the law. But convenience and political considerations of the moment do not justify a basic departure from the principles of our system of government.

In this case we are not faced with a situation where Congress has failed to provide the executive with broad power to protect the Nation from disclosure of damaging state secrets. Congress has on several occasions given extensive consideration to the problem of protecting the military and strategic secrets of the United States. This consideration has resulted in the enactment of statutes making it a crime to receive, disclose, communicate, withhold, and publish certain documents, photographs, instruments, appliances, and information. The bulk of these statutes are found in chapter 37 of U.S.C.A. Title 18, entitled Espionage and Censorship. In that chapter, Congress has provided penalties ranging from a $10,000 fine to death for violating the various statutes.

Thus it would seem that in order for this Court to issue an injunction it would require a showing that such an injunction would enhance the already existing power of the government tract. See Bennett v. Laman, 277 N.Y. 368, 14 N.E.2d 439 (1938). It is a traditional axiom of equity that a court of equity will not do a useless thing just as it is a traditional axiom that equity will not enjoin the commission of a crime. Here there has been no attempt to make such a showing. The solicitor general dces not even mention in his brief whether the government considers there to be probable cause to believe a crime has been committed or whether there is a conspiracy to commit future crimes.

If the government had attempted to show that there was no effective remedy under traditional criminal law, it would have had to show that there is no arguably applicable statute. Of course, at this stage this Court could not and cannot determine whether there has been a violation of a particular statute nor decide the constitutionality of any statute. Whether a good-faith prosecution could have been instituted under any statute could, however, be determined. * * *

It is true that Judge Gurfein found that Congress had not made it a crime to publish the items and material specified in § 793(e): He found that the words "communicates, delivers, transmits * * *" did not refer to publication of newspaper stories. And that view has some support in the legislative history and conforms with the past practice of using the statute only to prosecute those charged with ordinary espionage. But see 103 Cong.Rec. 10449 [remarks of Sen. Humphrey]. Judge Gurfein's view of the statute is not, however, the only plausible construction that could be given. See my Brother White's concurring opinion.

Even if it is determined that the government could not in good faith bring criminal prosecutions against the *New York Times* and the *Washington Post*, it is clear that Congress has specifically rejected passing legislation that would have clearly given the president the power he seeks here and made the current activity of the newspapers unlawful. When Congress specifically declines to make conduct unlawful it is not for this Court to redecide those issues—to overrule Congress. See Youngstown Sheet & Tube v. Sawyer, 345 U.S 579 (1952).

On at least two occasions Congress has refused to enact legislation that would have made the conduct engaged in here unlawful and given the president the power that he seeks in this case. In 1917 during the debate over the original Espionage Act, still the basic provisions of § 793, Congress rejected a proposal to give the president in time of war or threat of war authority to directly prohibit by proclamation the publication of information relating to national defense that might be useful to the enemy. * * *

Congress rejected this proposal after war against Germany had been declared even though many believed that there was a grave national emergency and that the threat of security leaks and espionage were serious. The Executive has not gone to Congress and requested that the decision to provide such power be reconsidered. Instead, the executive comes to this Court and asks that it be granted the power Congress refused to give.

* * * Senator Cotton, proposed that "Congress enact legislation making it a crime for any person willfully to disclose without proper authorization, for any purpose whatever, information classified 'secret' or 'top secret,' knowing, or having reasonable grounds to believe, such information to have been so classified." Report of Commission on Government Security 619–620 (1957). After substantial floor discussion on the proposal, it was rejected. See 103 Cong.Rec. 10447–10450. If the proposal that Senator Cotton championed on the floor had been enacted, the publication of the documents involved here would certainly have been a crime. Congress refused, however, to make it a crime. * *

Either the government has the power under statutory grant to use traditional criminal law to protect the country or, if there is no basis for arguing that Congress has made the activity a crime, it is plain that Congress has specifically refused to grant the authority the government seeks from this Court. In either case this Court does not have authority to grant the requested relief. It is not for this Court to fling itself into every breach perceived by some government official nor is it for this Court to take on itself the burden of enacting law, especially law that Congress has refused to pass.

I believe that the judgment of the United States Court of Appeals for the District of Columbia should be affirmed and the judgment of the United States Court of Appeals for the Second Circuit should be reversed insofar as it remands the case for further hearings.

Chief Justice BURGER, dissenting.

So clear are the constitutional limitations on prior restraint against expression, that from the time of Near v. Minnesota, 283 U.S. 697 (1931), until recently in Organization for a Better Austin v. Keefe, 402 U.S. 415 (1971), we have had little occasion to be concerned with cases involving prior restraints against news reporting on matters of public interest. There is, therefore, little variation among the members of the Court in terms of resistance to prior restraints against publication. Adherence to this basic constitutional principle, however, does not make this case a simple one. In this case, the imperative of a free and unfettered press comes into collision with another imperative, the effective functioning of a complex modern government and specifically the effective exercise of certain constitutional powers of the executive. Only those who view the First Amendment as an absolute in all circumstances—a view I respect, but reject—can find such a case as this to be simple or easy.

This case is not simple for another and more immediate reason. We do not know the facts of the case. No district judge knew all the facts. No court of appeals judge knew all the facts. No member of this Court knows all the facts.

Why are we in this posture, in which only those judges to whom the First Amendment is absolute and permits of no restraint in any circumstances or for any reason, are really in a position to act?

I suggest we are in this posture because these cases have been conducted in unseemly haste. Justice Harlan covers the chronology of events demonstrating the hectic pressures under which these cases have been processed and I need not restate them. The prompt setting of these cases reflects our universal abhorrence of prior restraint. But prompt judicial action does not mean unjudicial haste.

Here, moreover, the frenetic haste is due in large part to the manner in which the *Times* proceeded from the date it obtained the purloined documents. It seems reasonably clear now that the haste precluded reasonable and deliberate judicial treatment of these cases and was not warranted. The precipitous action of this Court aborting a trial not yet completed is not the kind of judicial conduct which ought to attend the disposition of a great issue.

The newspapers make a derivative claim under the First Amendment; they denominate this right as the public right-to-know; by implication, the *Times* asserts a sole trusteeship of that right by virtue of its journalist "scoop." The right is asserted as an absolute. Of course, the First Amendment right itself is not an absolute, as Justice Holmes so long ago pointed out in his aphorism concerning the right to shout of fire in a crowded theater. There are other exceptions, some of which Chief Justice Hughes mentioned by way of example in *Near v. Minnesota.* There are no doubt other exceptions no one has had occasion to describe or discuss. Conceivably such exceptions may be lurking in these cases and would have been flushed had they been properly considered in the trial courts, free from unwarranted deadlines and frenetic pressures. A great issue of this kind should be tried in a judicial atmosphere conducive to thoughtful, reflective deliberation, especially when haste, in terms of hours, is unwarranted in light of the long period the *Times,* by its own choice, deferred publication.

It is not disputed that the *Times* has had unauthorized possession of the documents for three to four months, during which it has had its expert analysts studying them, presumably digesting them and preparing the material for publication. During all of this time, the *Times,* presumably in its capacity as trustee of the public's "right to know," has held up publication for purposes it considered proper and thus public knowledge was delayed. No doubt this was for a good reason; the analysis of 7,000 pages of complex material drawn from a vastly greater volume of material would inevitably take time and the writing of good news stories takes time. But why should the United States Government, from whom this information was illegally acquired by someone, along with all the counsel, trial judges, and appellate judges be placed under needless pressure? After these months of deferral, the alleged right-to-know has somehow and suddenly become a right that must be vindicated instanter.

Would it have been unreasonable, since the newspaper could anticipate the government's objections to release of secret material, to give the government an opportunity to review the entire collection and determine whether agreement could be reached on publication? Stolen or not, if security was not in fact jeopardized, much of the material could no doubt have been declassified, since it spans a period ending in 1968. With such an approach—one that great newspapers have in the past practiced and stated editorially to be the duty of an honorable press—the newspapers and government might well have narrowed the area of disagreement as to what was and was not publishable, leaving the remainder to be resolved in orderly litigation if necessary. To me it is hardly believable that a newspaper long regarded as a great institution in American life would fail to perform one of the basic and simple duties of every citizen with respect to the discovery or possession of stolen property or secret government documents. That duty, I had thought—perhaps naively—was to report forthwith, to responsible public officers. This duty rests on taxi drivers, Justices and the New York Times. The course followed by the *Times* whether so calculated or not, removed any possibility of orderly litigation of the issues. If the action of the judges up to now has been correct, that result is sheer happenstance.

Our grant of the writ before final judgment in the *Times* case aborted the trial in the District Court before it had made a complete record pursuant to the mandate of the Court of Appeals, Second Circuit.

The consequence of all this melancholy series of events is that we literally do not know what we are acting on. As I see it we have been forced to deal with litigation concerning rights of great magnitude without an adequate record, and surely without time for adequate treatment either in the prior proceedings or in this Court. It is interesting to note that counsel in oral argument before this Court were frequently unable to respond to questions on factual points. Not surprisingly they pointed out that they had been working literally "around the clock" and simply were unable to review the documents that give rise to these cases and were not familiar with them. This Court is in no better posture. I agree with Justice Harlan and Justice Blackmun but I am not prepared to reach the merits.[2]

I would affirm the Court of Appeals for the Second Circuit and allow the district court to complete the trial aborted by our grant of certiorari meanwhile preserving the *status quo* in the *Post* case. I would direct that the district court on remand give priority to the *Times* case to the exclusion of all other business of that court but I would not set arbitrary deadlines.

I should add that I am in general agreement with much of what Justice White has expressed with respect to penal sanctions concerning communication or retention of documents or information relating to the national defense.

We all crave speedier judicial processes but when judges are pressured as in these cases the result is a parody of the judicial process.

2. With respect to the question of inherent power of the executive to classify papers, records and documents as secret, or otherwise unavailable for public exposure, and to secure aid of the courts for enforcement, there may be an analogy with respect to this Court. No statute gives this Court express power to establish and enforce the utmost security measures for the secrecy of our deliberations and records. Yet I have little doubt as to the inherent power of the Court to protect the confidentiality of its internal operations by whatever judicial measures may be required.

Justice HARLAN, with whom the Chief Justice and Justice Blackmun join, dissenting.

* * *

With all respect, I consider that the Court has been almost irresponsibly feverish in dealing with these cases.

Both the Court of Appeals for the Second Circuit and the Court of Appeals for the District of Columbia Circuit rendered judgment on June 23. The New York Times' petition for certiorari, its motion for accelerated consideration thereof, and its application for interim relief were filed in this Court on June 24 at about 11 a.m. The application of the United States for interim relief in the *Post* case was also filed here on June 24, at about 7:15 p.m. This Court's order setting a hearing before us on June 26 at 11 a.m., a course which I joined only to avoid the possibility of even more peremptory action by the Court, was issued less than 24 hours before. The record in the *Post* case was filed with the Clerk shortly before 1 p.m. on June 25; the record in the *Times* case did not arrive until 7 or 8 o'clock that same night. The briefs of the parties were received less than two hours before argument on June 23.

This frenzied train of events took place in the name of the presumption against prior restraints created by the First Amendment. Due regard for the extraordinarily important and difficult questions involved in these litigations should have led the Court to shun such a precipitate timetable. In order to decide the merits of these cases properly, some or all of the following questions should have been faced:

1. Whether the attorney general is authorized to bring these suits in the name of the United States. Compare In re Debs, 158 U.S. 564 (1895), with Youngstown Sheet & Tube Co. v. Sawyer, 343 U.S. 579 (1952). This question involves as well the construction and validity of a singularly opaque statute—the Espionage Act, 18 U.S.C.A. § 793(e).

2. Whether the First Amendment permits the federal courts to enjoin publication of stories which would present a serious threat to national security. See Near v. Minnesota, 283 U.S. 697, 716 (1931) (dictum).

3. Whether the threat to publish highly secret documents is of itself a sufficient implication of national security to justify an injunction on the theory that regardless of the contents of the documents harm enough results simply from the demonstration of such a breach of secrecy.

4. Whether the unauthorized disclosure of any of these particular documents would seriously impair the national security.

5. What weight should be given to the opinion of high officers in the executive branch of the government with respect to questions 3 and 4.

6. Whether the newspapers are entitled to retain and use the documents notwithstanding the seemingly uncontested facts that the documents, or the originals of which they are duplicates, were purloined from the government's possession and that the newspapers received them with knowledge that they had been feloniously acquired. Cf. Liberty Lobby, Inc. v. Pearson, 390 F.2d 489 (C.A.D.C.1968).

7. Whether the threatened harm to the national security or the government's possessory interest in the documents justifies the issuance of an injunction against publication in light of—

a. The strong First Amendment policy against prior restraints on publication;

b. The doctrine against enjoining conduct in violation of criminal statutes; and

c. The extent to which the materials at issue have apparently already been otherwise disseminated.

These are difficult questions of fact, of law, and of judgment; the potential consequences of erroneous decision are enormous. The time which has been available to us, to the lower courts, and to the parties has been wholly inadequate for giving these cases the kind of consideration they deserve. It is a reflection on the stability of the judicial process that these great issues—as important as any that have arisen during my time on the Court—should have been decided under the pressures engendered by the torrent of publicity that has attended these litigations from their inception.

Forced as I am to reach the merits of these cases, I dissent from the opinion and judgments of the Court. Within the severe limitations imposed by the time constraints under which I have been required to operate, I can only state my reasons in telescoped form, even though in different circumstances I would have felt constrained to deal with the cases in the fuller sweep indicated above.

It is a sufficient basis for affirming the Court of Appeals for the Second Circuit in the *Times* litigation to observe that its order must rest on the conclusion that because of the time elements the government had not been given an adequate opportunity to present its case to the district court. At the least this conclusion was not an abuse of discretion.

In the *Post* litigation the government had more time to prepare; this was apparently the basis for the refusal of the Court of Appeals for the District of Columbia Circuit on rehearing to conform its judgment to that of the second circuit. But I think there is another and more fundamental reason why this judgment cannot stand—a reason which also furnishes an additional ground for not reinstating the judgment of the district court in the *Times* litigation, set aside by the court of appeals. It is plain to me that the scope of the judicial function in passing upon the activities of the executive branch of the government in the field of foreign affairs is very narrowly restricted. This view is, I think, dictated by the concept of separation of powers upon which our constitutional system rests.

In a speech on the floor of the House of Representatives, Chief Justice John Marshall, then a member of that body, stated:

> The president is the sole organ of the nation in its external relations, and its sole representative with foreign nations. Annals, 6th Cong., col. 613 (1800).

* * * From that time, shortly after the founding of the Nation, to this, there has been no substantial challenge to this description of the scope of executive power. * * *

The power to evaluate the "pernicious influence" of premature disclosure is not, however, lodged in the executive alone. I agree that, in performance of its duty to protect the values of the First Amendment against political pressures, the judiciary must review the initial executive determination to the point of satisfying itself that the subject matter of the dispute does lie within the proper compass of the president's foreign relations power. Constitutional considerations forbid "a complete abandonment of judicial control." Cf. United States v. Reynolds, 345 U.S. 1, 8 (1953). Moreover, the judiciary may properly insist that the determination that disclosure of the subject matter would irreparably impair the national security be made by the head of the executive department concerned—here the secretary of state or the secretary of defense—after actual personal consideration by that officer. This safeguard is required in the analogous area of executive claims of privilege for secrets of state. See United States v. Reynolds, supra, at 8 and n. 20; Duncan v. Cammell, Laird & Co., [1942] A.C. 624, 638 (House of Lords).

But in my judgment the judiciary may not properly go beyond these two inquiries and redetermine for itself the probable impact of disclosure on the national security.

* * *

Even if there is some room for the judiciary to override the executive determination, it is plain that the scope of review must be exceedingly narrow. I can see no indication in the opinions of either the district court or the court of appeals in the *Post* litigation that the conclusions of the executive were given even the deference owing to an administrative agency, much less that owing to a coequal branch of the government operating within the field of its constitutional prerogative.

Accordingly, I would vacate the judgment of the Court of Appeals for the District of Columbia Circuit on this ground and remand the case for further proceedings in the district court. Before the commencement of such further proceedings, due opportunity should be afforded the government for procuring from the secretary of state or the secretary of defense or both an expression of their views on the issue of national security. The ensuing review by the district court should be in accordance with the views expressed in this opinion. And for the reasons stated above I would affirm the judgment of the Court of Appeals for the Second Circuit.

Pending further hearings in each case conducted under the appropriate ground rules, I would continue the restraints on publication. I cannot believe that the doctrine prohibiting prior restraints reaches to the point of preventing courts from maintaining the *status quo* long enough to act responsibly in matters of such national importance as those involved here.

Justice BLACKMUN.

I join Justice Harlan in his dissent. I also am in substantial accord with much that Justice White says, by way of admonition, in the latter part of his opinion.

At this point the focus is on *only* the comparatively few documents specified by the government as critical. So far as the other material—vast in amount—is concerned, let it be published and published forthwith if the newspapers, once the strain is gone and the sensationalism is eased, still feel the urge so to do.

But we are concerned here with the few documents specified from the 47 volumes. * * *

The *New York Times* clandestinely devoted a period of three months examining the 47 volumes that came into its unauthorized possession. Once it had begun publication of material from those volumes, the New York case now before us emerged. It immediately assumed, and ever since has maintained, a frenetic pace and character. Seemingly, once publication started, the material could not be made public fast enough. Seemingly, from then on, every deferral or delay, by restraint or otherwise, was abhorrent and was to be deemed violative of the First Amendment and of the public's "right immediately to know." Yet that newspaper stood before us at oral argument and professed criticism of the government for not lodging its protest earlier than by a Monday telegram following the initial Sunday publication.

The District of Columbia case is much the same.

Two federal district courts, two United States courts of appeals, and this Court—within a period of less than three weeks from inception until today—have been pressed into hurried decision of profound constitutional issues on inadequately developed and largely assumed facts without the careful deliberation that hopefully, should characterize the American judicial process. There has been much writing about the law and little knowledge and less digestion of the facts. In the New York case the judges, both trial and appellate, had not yet examined the basic material when the case was brought here. In the District of Columbia case, little more was done, and what was accomplished in this respect was only on required remand, with the *Washington Post*, on the excuse that it was trying to protect its source of information, initially refusing to reveal what material it actually possessed, and with the district court forced to make assumptions as to that possession.

With such respect as may be due to the contrary view, this, in my opinion, is not the way to try a lawsuit of this magnitude and asserted importance. It is not the way for federal courts to adjudicate, and to be required to adjudicate, issues that allegedly concern the Nation's vital welfare. The country would be none the worse off were the cases tried quickly, to be sure, but in the customary and properly deliberative manner. The most recent of the material, it is said, dates no later than 1968, already about three years ago, and the *Times* itself took three months to formulate its plan of procedure and, thus, deprived its public for that period.

The First Amendment, after all, is only one part of an entire Constitution. Article II of the great document vests in the executive branch primary power over the conduct of foreign affairs and places in that branch the responsibility for the Nation's safety. Each provision of the Constitution is important, and I cannot subscribe to a doctrine of unlimited absolutism for the First Amendment at the cost of downgrading other provisions. First Amendment absolutism has never commanded a majority of this Court. See, for example, Near v. Minnesota, 283 U.S. 697, 708 (1931), and Schenck v. United States, 249 U.S. 47, 52 (1919). What is needed here is a weighing, upon properly developed standards, of the broad right of the press to print and of the very narrow right of the Government to prevent. Such standards are not yet developed. The parties here are in disagreement as to what those standards should be. But even the newspapers concede that there are situations where restraint is in order and is constitutional. Justice Holmes gave us a suggestion when he said in *Schenck,*

"It is a question of proximity and degree. When a nation is at war many things that might be said in time of peace are such a hindrance to its effort that their utterance will not be endured so long as men fight and that no Court could regard them as protected by any constitutional right." 249 U.S., at 52.

I therefore would remand these cases to be developed expeditiously, of course, but on a schedule permitting the orderly presentation of evidence from both sides, with the use of discovery, if necessary, as authorized by the rules, and with the preparation of briefs, oral argument and court opinions of a quality better than has been seen to this point. In making this last statement, I criticize no lawyer or judge. I know from past personal experience the agony of time pressure in the preparation of litigation. But these cases and the issues involved and the courts, including this one, deserve better than has been produced thus far.

It may well be that if these cases were allowed to develop as they should be developed, and to be tried as lawyers should try them and as courts should hear them, free of pressure and panic and sensationalism, other light would be shed on the situation and contrary considerations, for me, might prevail. But that is not the present posture of the litigation.

The Court, however, decides the cases today the other way. I therefore add one final comment.

I strongly urge, and sincerely hope, that these two newspapers will be fully aware of their ultimate responsibilities to the United States of America. Judge Wilkey, dissenting in the District of Columbia case, after a review of only the affidavits before his court (the basic papers had not then been made available by either party), concluded that there were a number of examples of documents that if in the possession of the *Post*, and if published, "could clearly result in great harm to the nation," and he defined "harm" to mean "the death of soldiers, the destruction of alliances, the greatly increased difficulty of negotiation with our enemies, the inability of our diplomats to negotiate * * *." I, for one, have now been able to give at least some cursory study not only to the affidavits, but to the material itself. I regret to say that from this examination I fear that Judge Wilkey's statements have possible foundation. I therefore share his concern. I hope that damage already has not been done. If, however, damage has been done, and if, with the Court's action today, these newspapers proceed to publish the critical documents and there results therefrom "the death of soldiers, the destruction of alliances, the greatly increased difficulty of negotiation with our enemies, the inability of our diplomats to negotiate," to which list I might add the factors of prolongation of the war and of further delay in the freeing of United States prisoners, then the Nation's people will know where the responsibility for these sad consequences rests.

The judgment of the Court of Appeals for the District of Columbia Circuit is therefore affirmed. The order of the Court of Appeals for the Second Circuit is reversed and the case is remanded with directions to enter a judgment affirming the judgment of the District Court for the Southern District of New York. The stays entered June 25, 1971, by the Court are vacated. The judgments shall issue forthwith.

So ordered.

COMMENT

1. The doctrine urged by the government was that the president has the right to enjoin publication of a news story when the context of the story threatens "grave and irreparable" injury to the public interest. Justice White denied both the existence and the validity of this doctrine at least in the absence of legislation authorizing the courts to grant injunctions in such circumstances.

Freedom of the press can be viewed as providing two modes of protection. One is freedom from prior restraint. The second is freedom from subsequent punishment. Criminal prosecution of Sulzberger or Graham, publishers respectively of the *New York Times* and the *Washington Post, after* publication of the Pentagon Papers would be an example of subsequent punishment. Apparently Justice White was of the opinion that the "extraordinary protection" granted the press by the First Amendment against prior restraints is to be distinguished from the protection afforded the press by the First Amendment in the case of subsequent punishments. The greater protection from prior restraint presumably is based on the premise that a restraint on publication *prior* to publication deprives society of the benefit of the idea. The punishment of the writer or publisher *subsequent* to publication still has not hindered the dissemination of the idea. Is this a persuasive distinction?

If the publishers of newspapers are free from prior restraint *prior* to publication but know that *after* publication they may go to jail, doesn't this effectively restrain publication in the first place? The lesser protection against subsequent punishment itself may act as a prior restraint. In effect, the lesser freedom from subsequent punishment forces publishers and journalists to become martyrs when they want to publish information the government desires to suppress.

For Justice White, as for Justice Stewart, the case for criminal convictions against those publishing the Pentagon Papers was much stronger than the case for preventing by injunction the publication of the papers: "I would have no difficulty in sustaining convictions under these sections on facts that would not justify the intervention of equity and the imposition of a prior restraint." Why? Apparently because, in White's view, Congress had authorized criminal prosecutions, but it had not authorized the "injunctive remedy against threatened publication." The journalist and the civil libertarian at this point might wonder whether the 1971 *New York Times* case is a victory or a trap for freedom of information and freedom from prior restraint. The newsperson is being told that he or she may publish but will have to put their bodies on the line if they do. Four of the nine justices would seem to condone criminal penalties if indeed United States interests have been gravely injured.

2. Congress had not by statute authorized the injunctions against the press to prevent publication of material posing a danger to the security interests of the nation, even though it had been asked to do so in two world wars. This single fact was determinative for Justice Marshall, as it had been for Justices White and Stewart. The issue, said Justice Marshall, was whether the Court or the Congress should make law. But the Supreme Court has not hesitated to make law before.

3. Perhaps more squarely than any of the other opinions, Burger's dissent raises the issue of accountability: who should make the ultimate decisions about how far the reach of a free press can extend and to what extent should the demands of government for confidentiality in its dealings be honored? Chief Justice Burger was greatly disturbed by the fact that in the haste of decision the Court had neither time to study the documents themselves nor to consider soberly the great issues presented.

Describing the public right to know as a derivative First Amendment claim, Burger protested the *Times'* apparent position that it was the absolute trustee of the public right to know. He argued that the First Amendment itself was not an absolute, much less were any radiations the Amendment might throw off such as the public's right to know.

Burger's reactions to the issues of the *Times* case are at once protective of the information process and sympathetic to the need of government for confidentiality. The Chief Justice says that the government should have been given an opportunity to review the papers in possession of the *Times* in the hope that agreement about publication could have been reached. On the other hand, the fact that the papers were stolen was in Burger's view no bar to declassification of some of them.

Burger thought it was anomalous that the *Times* would not allow the government to examine the Pentagon Papers in the *Times'* possession for fear this might jeopardize the paper's sources. Yet, said Burger, the *Times* denies the government the right to keep the papers secret. But is the government really interested in protecting sources in the same way the *New York Times* was interested in protecting its sources? Certainly, there was a respectable body of opinion in the country which believed that the government was anxious to protect the identity of participants in decisions on the Vietnam involvement as well as the nature of some of the decisions themselves. The *Times*, however, was anxious to protect the sources which made it possible to learn the identity of participants in vital national decisions. In other words, the interest of the *Times* in protecting its sources was procedural in nature. From whom the newspapers receive information is, informationally speaking, much less significant than the information obtained. Secrecy over such sources is designed to protect the *future* of the information flow. The government, on the other hand, was interested in protecting confidentiality to shield *prior* decisions of the highest substantive character. As a First Amendment matter, doesn't this distinction support the *Times* and not the government?

Chief Justice Burger is truly astonished that the *Times* did not report to the government that papers stolen from the government were in its possession. But the responsibilities to government in this regard were surely overshadowed in the *Times'* judgment by its obligations to the information process, a duty which it believed had First Amendment significance. In the last analysis, the question presented was a choice between a newspaper's determination of the legitimate demands of the public's right to know and the executive's conception of what must remain secret. Which determination should prevail?

4. Is a consequence of Justice Black's absolute view of the First Amendment that there is no recourse if the newspapers are not aware of their responsibilities? It is argued that at least the executive is subject to popular election and may be turned out of office if it is faithless to its responsibilities, but the press is not similarly accountable to the people.

5. A majority of the Court appeared to agree with Justice Brennan's observation that the basic error in the entire proceeding was Judge Gurfein's issuance of the temporary restraining order against the *New York Times.* Why then were there so many opinions in the case? In an interview, Chief Justice Burger answered this question by saying that it was decided that if each justice wrote his own opinion that would make it easier to get an expedited decision of the case.

6. Justice Black emphasized the unprecedented character of the judicial restraint on the press. The *Pentagon Papers* case was the first time an American newspaper had been restrained by a court order from publishing articles and documents the content of which could only be surmised by the government and whose damaging properties therefore could only be assumed. Viewed from that perspective, the 6–3 Supreme Court determination that the issuance of a restraining order in such circumstances was unconstitutional was a victory for freedom of information and freedom of the press. In this regard, the victory was more than an abstract vindication of constitutional theory. The decision unquestionably would deprive the whole government classification program of its legitimacy and its mystery, developments which are in the long term interest of opening up the information process.

7. See the material on the Freedom of Information Act set forth in the text at p. 439. How could the Freedom of Information Act have been used to declassify the Pentagon Papers?

8. The *Times* agonized for three months over whether to publish the Pentagon Papers. They chose to publish and thereby invited a bitter conflict with government. Why? Perhaps the *Times* was still feeling the burn it got when it "cooperated" with the Administration prior to the Bay of Pigs fiasco and, therefore, decided never to get caught in that situation again. Five years after the abortive invasion it was disclosed that the *New York Times* had prior knowledge of the project but had declined to publish it, at the request of President John F. Kennedy, because of national security considerations. Clifton Daniel, then managing editor of the paper, combined this disclosure with his conclusion that the Bay of Pigs operation "might well have been canceled, and the country would have been saved enormous embarrassment, if the *New York Times* and other newspapers had been more diligent in the performance of their duty."

Finally, there is a minor but important theme in the whole *Pentagon Papers* case—the issue of whether government ought to be able to imprison history.

9. In the bizarre *Progressive* case, the federal government sought to prevent *The Progressive* magazine from publishing an article on how to make a hydrogen bomb. The article was based on material that was publicly available. At first, the federal district court granted the government's request for a temporary injunction restraining publication of the article by *The*

Progressive on the ground that the article fell "within the narrow area recognized by the court in *Near v. Minnesota* in which a prior restraint on publication is appropriate." Which *Near* exception was the court relying on? The federal district court also cited Justice Stewart's opinion in the *Pentagon Papers* case as support for its view that a temporary injunction should be issued. The Atomic Energy Act contained a provision authorizing the issuance of injunctive relief to prevent disclosure of particular types of information. Assuming that that provision applied to *The Progressive* article, would the existence of such a statutory provision distinguish *The Progressive* case from the *Pentagon Papers* case? Arguably, it would, because the fact that there was no statutory basis for the granting of injunctive relief in the *Pentagon Papers* case was relied on by a number of justices as ground for not granting relief for the government.

Assuming that the statutory provision did apply to the article in *The Progressive* case, would the statutory provision be valid under the First Amendment? This is a matter of speculation since other newspapers began to publish material similar to that contained in *The Progressive* article and the government decided not to go forward in its effort to secure permanent injunctive relief concerning *The Progressive* article. See United States v. Progressive, Inc., 467 F.Supp. 990 (W.D.Wis.1979), appeal dismissed 610 F.2d 819 (7th Cir.).

Progressive editor Erwin Knoll is on record as saying that the greatest moral error of his life was *not* to have published the original article. Disobey a court injunction, University of Michigan law Professor Vincent Blasi has argued in rebuttal, and you escalate the totalitarian dynamic. The government, as has been noted, based its arguments primarily on provisions of the Atomic Energy Act prohibiting communication, transmission, and disclosure of certain categories of information which, the government contended, were either "classified at birth" or of a technical nature not protected by the First Amendment.

Judge Warren in his opinion for the federal district court saw the issue as one between freedom of speech and press and the freedom to live. If our right to live is extinguished, he said, the right to publish becomes moot. His test would have been that of Justices White and Stewart in their *Pentagon Papers* opinions—"immediate, direct, irreparable harm to the interests of the United States * * * to our nation and its people."

Abandonment of the case by the government was another lost opportunity for appellate courts to face the ultimate and still unresolved question of what is to be the constitutional relationship between prior restraints and national security. In answering that question, the courts will eventually have to define both prior restraints and national security, two complex concepts in precarious balance.

NEBRASKA PRESS and the Future of Prior Restraint

A major case involving the issue of the constitutional validity of prior restraints against the press is the so-called "gag order" case, *Nebraska Press Ass'n v. Stuart*, text, p. 505. Although the case is discussed primarily in the free press-fair trial materials, text, Chapter VI, it has authoritative significance on the present status of prior restraints against the press.

1. The decision of the Court in *Nebraska Press Ass'n* stretched the thesis advanced in earlier cases that there is a presumption against prior restraints and that the state must meet a heavy burden before such a restraint can issue. In result, the *Nebraska Press* case reached the same conclusion as had its predecessors—*Near* and the *Pentagon Papers* case. In each case, the Supreme Court refused to issue a prior restraint against the press.

And yet, although the press was victorious on each occasion, the Court appeared determined to keep alive the possibility that in some undescribed circumstances a prior restraint against the press might be permissible. In short, although the Court has erected the strongest possible obstacles to the issuance of a prior restraint in the context of a "gag order" case, it still appeared resolved to reject "the proposition that a prior restraint can never be employed." Justice White, in a concurring opinion, suggested that if the consequence of the Court's *Nebraska Press* decision is to refuse to issue "gag orders" against the press in case after case on the ground that they are invalid prior restraints, then "we should at some point announce a more general rule and avoid the interminable litigation that our failure to do so would necessarily entail."

2. Justice Brennan's passionate distaste for prior restraints against the press is made vividly clear in his concurring opinion in *Nebraska Press.* He comments proudly on "the rarity of prior restraint cases of any type in this Court's jurisprudence." Analyzing the prior case law, he finds only one occasion where the exception to the presumption against prior restraints against the press might be deemed sufficient to authorize suppression before publication, i.e., the so-called military security exception in *Near.* This would be the situation where a newspaper plans to publish the sailing date of a troop ship in war, or its modern counterpart. The "overriding countervailing" interests that justify such suppression in wartime were, in his view, hardly comparable to the case for a prior restraint against the press in the interests of a fair trial.

Does the following state the essence of the Brennan concurrence? Although prior restraints are not always invalid, prior restraints in the form of "gag orders" against the press in the free press-fair trial context are always invalid. Perhaps the difference between Chief Justice Burger and Justice Brennan on this point is that the Burger opinion kept open the possibility, no matter how remote, that some "gag orders" against the press were yet conceivable while the Brennan view would remove that possibility. Brennan would adhere to the military security exception, despite the general freedom he would accord the press from prior restraint, but would not grant a new exception in the interest of fair trial. Yet the latter is a constitutional value, enshrined in the Sixth Amendment, while secrecy in wartime, although it may be a societal value of great importance, is not mentioned in the constitution.

3. On balance, if one compares *Near* and *New York Times* with the decision in *Nebraska Press*, the conclusion appears clear that never in American constitutional history has the barrier posed by the First Amendment to the issuance of prior restraints against the press been higher and more difficult to surmount. See the discussion in the Access to the Judicial Process: Free Press and Fair Trial chapter on new efforts to circumvent these developments, text, p. 511.

Censorship of the Press by Conditioning the Use of the Mails: The Doctrine of Unconstitutional Conditions

UNITED STATES, ex rel., MILWAUKEE SOCIAL DEMOCRACTIC PUBLISHING CO. v. BURLESON

255 U.S. 407, 41 S.CT. 352, 65 L.ED. 704 (1921).

Justice CLARKE delivered the opinion of the Court.

After a hearing on September 22, 1917, by the third assistant postmaster general, of the time and character of which the relator [plaintiff in error] had due notice and at which it was represented by its president, an order was entered, revoking the second-class mail privilege granted to it in 1911 as publisher of the *Milwaukee Leader.* * * *

[The Milwaukee Social Democratic Publishing Company then instituted suit asking for mandamus to command the postmaster general to restore the newspaper's second-class mailing privilege.]

* * *

The grounds upon which the relator relies are, in substance, that to the extent that the Espionage Act confers power upon the postmaster general to make the order entered against it, that act is unconstitutional, because it does not afford relator a trial in a court of competent jurisdiction; that the order deprives relator of the right of free speech, is destructive of the rights of a free press, and deprives it of its property without due process of law.

* * *

The Espionage Act, one of the first of the national defense laws enacted by Congress after the entry of the United States into the World War (approved June 15, 1917, 40 Stat. 217), provided severe punishment for any person who "when the United States is at war" shall willfully make or convey false reports or false statements with intent to interfere with the operation and success of the military or naval forces of the country, or with the intent to promote the success of its enemies, or who shall cause, or attempt to cause insubordination, disloyalty, mutiny or refusal of duty in such forces, or who shall willfully obstruct the recruiting and enlistment service of the United States (section 3, tit. 1 [Comp.St.1918, Comp.St.Ann.Supp.1919, § 10212c]). One entire title of this act (title 12) is devoted to "Use of the Mails," and in the exercise of its practically plenary power over the mails, Congress therein provided that any newspaper published in violation of any of the provisions of the act should be "nonmailable" and should not be "conveyed in the mails or delivered from any post office or by any letter carrier."

* * *

Without further discussion of the articles, we cannot doubt that they conveyed to readers of them false reports and false statements, with intent to promote the success of the enemies of the United States, and that they constituted a willful attempt to cause disloyalty and refusal of duty in the military and naval forces, and to obstruct the recruiting and enlistment service of the United States, in violation of the Espionage Law (Schenck v. United States), and that therefore their publication brought the paper containing them within the express terms of title 12 of that law, declaring that such a publication shall be "nonmailable" and "shall not be conveyed in the mails or delivered from any post office or by any letter carrier." * * * The order of the postmaster general not only finds reasonable support in this record, but is amply justified by it.

* * *

Government is a practical institution, adapted to the practical conduct of public affairs. It would not be possible for the United States to maintain a reader in every newspaper office of the country, to approve in advance each issue before it should be allowed to enter the mails, and when, for more than five months, a paper had contained, almost daily, articles which, under the express terms of the statute, rendered it "nonmailable," it was reasonable to conclude that it would continue its disloyal publications, and it was therefore clearly within the power given to the postmaster general by R.S. § 396, "to execute all laws relating to the postal service," to enter, as was done in this case, an order suspending the privilege until a proper application and showing should be made for its renewal. The order simply withdrew from the relator the second-class privilege, but did not exclude its paper from other classes, as it might have done, and there was nothing in it to prevent reinstatement at any time. It was open to the relator to mend its ways, to publish a paper conforming to the law, and then to apply anew for the second-class mailing privilege. This it did not do, but for reasons not difficult to imagine, it preferred this futile litigation, undertaken upon the theory that a government competent to wage war against its foreign enemies was powerless against its insidious foes at home. Whatever injury the relator suffered was the result of its own choice and the judgment of the court of appeals is affirmed.

Justice Brandeis, dissenting. This case arose during the World War; but it presents no legal question peculiar to war. It is important, because what we decide may determine in large measure whether in times of peace our press shall be free.

* * *

The question presented is: Did Congress confer upon the postmaster general authority to deny second-class postal rates on that ground? The question is one of statutory construction. No such authority is granted in terms in the statutes which declare what matter shall be unmailable. Is there any provision of the postal laws from which the intention of Congress to grant such power may be inferred? The specific reason why the postmaster general deemed these editorials and news items unmailable was that he considered them violative of title 12 of the Espionage Act. But it is not contended that this specific reason is of legal significance. The scope of the postmaster general's alleged authority is confessedly the same whether the reason for the nonmailable quality of the matter inserted in a newspaper is that it violates the Espionage Act, or the copyright laws, or that it is part of a scheme to defraud, or concerns lotteries, or is indecent, or is in any other respect matter which Congress has declared shall not be admitted to the mails.

* * *

It thus appears that the Postmaster General, in the exercise of a supposed discretion, refused to carry at second-class mail rates all future issues of the *Milwaukee Leader*, solely because he believed it had systematically violated the Espionage Act in the past. It further appears that this belief rested partly upon the contents of past issues of the paper filed with the return and partly upon "representations and complaints from sundry good and loyal citizens", whose statements are not incorporated in this record and which do not appear to have been called to the attention of the publisher of the Milwaukee Leader at the hearing or otherwise. It is this general refusal thereafter to accept the paper for transmission at the second-class mail rates which is challenged as being without warrant in law.

In discussing whether Congress conferred upon the postmaster general the authority which he undertook to exercise in this case, I shall consider, first, whether he would have had the power to exclude the paper altogether from all future mail service on the ground alleged; and, second, whether he had power to deny the publisher the second-class rate.

First. Power to exclude from the mails has never been conferred in terms upon the postmaster general. * * *

Until recently, at least, this appears never to have been questioned and the Post Office Department has been authoritatively advised that the power of excluding matter from the mail was limited to such specific matter as upon examination was found to be unmailable and that the postmaster general could not make an exclusion order operative upon future issues of a newspaper.

* * *

If such power were possessed by the postmaster general, he would, in view of the practical finality of his decisions, become the universal censor of publications. For a denial of the use of the mail would be for most of them, tantamount to a denial of the right of circulation. Congress has not granted to the postmaster general power to deny the right of sending matter by mail even to one who has been convicted by a jury and sentenced by a court for unlawful use of the mail and who has been found by the postmaster general to have been habitually using the mail for frauds or lotteries and is likely to do so in the future. It has, in order to protect the public, directed postmasters to return to the sender mail addressed to one found by the postmaster general to be engaged in a scheme to defraud or in a lottery enterprise. But beyond this Congress has never deemed it wise, if, indeed, it has considered it constitutional to interfere with the civil right of using the mail for lawful purposes.

The postmaster general does not claim here the power to issue an order directly denying a newspaper all mail service for the future. Indeed, he asserts that the mail is still open to the *Milwaukee Leader* upon payment of first, third, or fourth class rates. He contends, however, that in regard to second-class rates special provisions of law apply under which he may deny that particular rate at his discretion. This contention will now be considered.
* * *

It is insisted that a citizen uses the mail at second-class rates, not as of right, but by virtue of a privilege or permission, the granting of which rests in the discretion of the postmaster general. Because the payment made for this governmental service is less than it costs, it is assumed that a properly qualified person has not the right to the service so long as it is offered, and may not complain if it is denied to him. The service is called the second-class privilege. The certificate evidencing such freedom is spoken of as a permit. But, in fact, the right to the lawful postal rates is a right independent of the discretion of the postmaster general. The right and conditions of its existence are defined and rest wholly upon mandatory legislation of Congress. It is the duty of the postmaster general to determine whether the conditions prescribed for any rate exist. This determination in the case of the second-class rate may involve more subjects of inquiry, some of them, perhaps, of greater difficulty, than in cases of other rates. But the function of the postmaster general is the same in all cases. In making the determination he must, like a court or a jury, form a judgment whether certain conditions prescribed by Congress exist, on controverted facts or by applying the law. The function is a strictly judicial one, although exercised in administering an executive office. And it is not a function which either involves or permits the exercise of discretionary power.

* * *

It clearly appears that there was no express grant of power to the postmaster general to deny second-class mail rates to future issues of a newspaper because in his opinion it had systematically violated the Espionage Act in the past, and it seems equally clear that there is no basis for the contention that such power is to be implied. In respect to newspapers mailed by a publisher at second-class rates there is clearly no occasion to imply this drastic power. For a publisher must deposit with the local postmaster, before the first mailing of every issue, a copy of the publication which is now examined for matter subject to a higher rate and in order to determine the portion devoted to advertising.

* * *

If there is illegal material in the newspaper, here is ample opportunity to discover it and remove the paper from the mail. Indeed, of the four classes of mail, it is the second alone which affords to the postal official full opportunity of ascertaining, before deposit in the mail, whether that which it is proposed to transmit is mailable matter. * * * [T]he construction urged by the postmaster general would raise not only a grave question, but a "succession of constitutional doubts." * *

It would in practice seriously abridge the freedom of the press. Would it not also violate the First Amendment? It would in practice deprive many publishers of their property without due process of law. Would it not also violate the Fifth Amendment? It would in practice subject publishers to punishment without a hearing by any court. * * *

In conclusion I say again—because it cannot be stressed too strongly—that the power here claimed is not a war power. There is no question of its necessity to protect the country from insidious domestic foes. To that end Congress conferred upon the postmaster general the enormous power contained in the Espionage Act of entirely excluding from the mails any letter, picture or publication which contained matter violating the broad terms of that act. But it did not confer—and the postmaster general concedes that it did not confer—the vague and absolute authority practically to deny circulation to any publication which in his opinion is likely to violate in the future any postal law. * * *

* * *

Justice HOLMES dissenting.

* * *

* * * The United States may give up the post office when it sees fit, but while it carries it on, the use of the mails is almost as much a part of free speech as the right to use our tongues and it would take very strong language to convince me that Congress ever intended to give such a practically despotic power to any one man. There is no pretence that it has done so. Therefore I do not consider the limits of its constitutional power.

To refuse the second-class rate to a newspaper is to make its circulation impossible and has all the effect of the order that I have supposed. I repeat. When I observe that the only powers expressly given to the postmaster general to prevent the carriage of unlawful matter of the present kind are to stop and to return papers already existing and posted, when I notice that the conditions expressly attached to the second-class rate look only to wholly different matters, and when I consider the ease with which the power claimed by the postmaster could be used to interfere with very sacred rights, I am of opinion that the refusal to allow the relator the rate to which it was entitled whenever its newspaper was carried, on the ground that the paper ought not to be carried at all, was unjustified by statute and was a serious attack upon liberties that not even the war induced Congress to infringe.

HANNEGAN v. ESQUIRE, INC.

327 U.S. 146, 66 S.CT. 456, 90 L.ED. 586 (1946).

Justice DOUGLAS delivered the opinion of the Court.

Congress has made obscene material nonmailable, 35 Stat. 1129, 18 U.S.C.A. § 334, and has applied criminal sanctions for the enforcement of that policy. It has divided mailable matter into four classes, periodical publications constituting the second-class. And it has specified four conditions upon which a publication shall be admitted to the second-class. The Fourth condition, which is the only one relevant here,[2] provides:

2. The first three conditions are:

"First. It must regularly be issued at stated intervals as frequently as four times a year, and bear a date of issue, and be numbered consecutively. Second. It must be issued from a known office of publication. Third. It must be formed of printed paper sheets, without board, cloth, leather, or other substantial binding, such as

"Except as otherwise provided by law, the conditions upon which a publication shall be admitted to the second class are as follows * * * Fourth. It must be originated and published for the dissemination of information of a public character, or devoted to literature, the sciences, arts, or some special industry, and having a legitimate list of subscribers. Nothing herein contained shall be so construed as to admit to the second class rate regular publications designed primarily for advertising purposes, or for free circulation, or for circulation at nominal rates."

Respondent is the publisher of Esquire Magazine, a monthly periodical which was granted a second-class permit in 1933. In 1943, pursuant to the Act of March 3, 1901, 31 Stat. 1107, 39 U.S.C.A. § 232, a citation was issued to respondent by the then Postmaster General (for whom the present Postmaster General has now been substituted as petitioner) to show cause why that permit should not be suspended or revoked. A hearing was held before a board designated by the then Postmaster General. The board recommended that the permit not be revoked. Petitioner's predecessor took a different view. He did not find that Esquire Magazine contained obscene material and therefore was nonmailable. He revoked its second-class permit because he found that it did not comply with the Fourth condition. The gist of his holding is contained in the following excerpt from his opinion:

"The plain language of this statute does not assume that a publication must in fact be 'obscene' within the intendment of the postal obscenity statutes before it can be found not to be 'originated and published for the dissemination of information of a public character, or devoted to literature, the sciences, arts, or some special industry.'

* * *

"A publication to enjoy these unique mail privileges and special preferences is bound to do more than refrain from disseminating material which is obscene or bordering on the obscene. It is under a positive duty to contribute to the public good and the public welfare."

* * *

The issues of Esquire Magazine under attack are those for January to November inclusive of 1943. The material complained of embraces in bulk only a small percentage of those issues. Regular features of the magazine (called "The Magazine for Men") include articles on topics of current interest, short stories, sports articles or stories, short articles by men prominent in various fields of activities, articles about men prominent in the news, a book review department headed by the late William Lyon Phelps, a theatrical department headed by George Jean Nathan, a department on the lively arts by Gilbert Seldes, a department devoted to men's clothing, and pictorial features, including war action paintings, color photographs of dogs and water colors or etchings of game birds and reproductions of famous paintings, prints and drawings. There was very little in these features which was challenged. But petitioner's predecessor found that the objectionable items, though a small percentage of the total bulk, were regular recurrent features which gave the magazine its dominant tone or characteristic. These include jokes, cartoons, pictures, articles, and poems. They were said to reflect the smoking-room type of humor, featuring, in the main, sex. Some witnesses found the challenged items highly objectionable, calling them salacious

distinguish printed books for preservation from periodical publications: Provided, That publications produced by the stencil, mimeograph, or hectograph process or in imitation of typewriting shall not be regarded as printed within the meaning of this clause."

and indecent. Others though they were only racy and risque. Some condemned them as being merely in poor taste. Other witnesses could find no objection to them.

An examination of the items makes plain, we think, that the controversy is not whether the magazine publishes "information of a public character" or is devoted to "literature" or to the "arts." It is whether the contents are "good" or "bad." To uphold the order of revocation would, therefore, grant the postmaster general a power of censorship. Such a power is so abhorrent to our traditions that a purpose to grant it should not be easily inferred.

The second-class privilege is a form of subsidy. From the beginning Congress has allowed special rates to certain classes of publications. * * *

The postal laws make a clear-cut division between mailable and nonmailable material. The four classes of mailable matter are generally described by objective standards which refer in part to their contents, but not to the quality of their contents. The more particular descriptions of the first, third, and fourth classes follow the same pattern, as do the first three conditions specified for second-class matter. If, therefore, the fourth condition is read in the context of the postal laws of which it is an integral part, it too, must be taken to supply standards which relate to the format of the publication and to the nature of its contents, but not to their quality, worth, or value. In that view, "literature" or the "arts" mean no more than productions which convey ideas by words, pictures, or drawings.

If the fourth condition is read in that way, it is plain that Congress made no radical or basic change in the type of regulation which it adopted for second-class mail in 1879. The inauguration of even a limited type of censorship would have been such a startling change as to have left some traces in the legislative history. But we find none. Congressman Money, a member of the Postal Committee who defended the bill on the floor of the House, stated that it was "nothing but a simplification of the postal code. There are no new powers granted to the Department by this bill, none whatever." 8 Cong.Rec. 2134. The bill contained registration provisions which were opposed on the ground that they might be the inception of a censorship of the press. These were deleted. It is difficult to imagine that the Congress, having deleted them for fear of censorship, gave the Postmaster General by the Fourth condition discretion to deny periodicals the second-class rate, if in his view they did not contribute to the public good. * * *

* * *

The policy of Congress has been clear. It has been to encourage the distribution of periodicals which disseminated "information of a public character" or which were devoted to "literature, the sciences, arts, or some special industry," because it was thought that those publications as a class contributed to the public good. The standards prescribed in the Fourth condition have been criticized, but not on the ground that they provide for censorship. * * *

* * *

We may assume that Congress has a broad power of classification and need not open second-class mail to publications of all types. The categories of publications entitled to that classification have indeed varied through the years. And the Court held in Ex parte Jackson, 96 U.S. 727, that Congress could constitutionally make it a crime to send fraudulent or obscene material through the mails. But grave constitutional questions are immediately raised once it is said that the use of the mails is a privilege which may be extended or withheld on any grounds whatsoever. See the dissents of Justice Brandeis and Justice Holmes in United States ex rel. Milwaukee Social Democratic Publishing Co. v. Burleson. Under that view the second-class rate could be granted on condition that certain economic or political ideas not be disseminated. The provisions of the fourth condition would have to be far more explicit for us to assume that Congress made such a radical departure from our traditions and undertook to clothe the Postmaster General with the power to supervise the tastes of the reading public of the country.

It is plain, as we have said, that the favorable second-class rates were granted periodicals meeting the requirements of the fourth condition, so that the public good might be served through a dissemination of the class of periodicals described. * * * The validity of the obscenity laws is recognition that the mails may not be used to satisfy all tastes, no matter how perverted. But Congress has left the postmaster general with no power to prescribe standards for the literature or the art which a mailable periodical disseminates.

This is not to say that there is nothing left to the postmaster general under the fourth condition. It is his duty to "execute all laws relative to the Postal Service." Rev.Stat. § 396, 5 U.S.C.A. § 369. For example questions will arise * * * whether the publication which seeks the favorable second-class rate is a periodical as defined in the fourth condition or a book or other type of publication. And it may appear that the information contained in a periodical may not be of a "public character." But the power to determine whether a periodical (which is mailable) contains information of a public character, literature or art does not include the further power to determine whether the contents meet some standard of the public good or welfare.

Affirmed.

COMMENT

1. In the *Hannegan* case, Justice Douglas said in an opinion for the majority that serious constitutional issues were raised if the proposition was accepted that "the use of the mails is a privilege which may be extended or withheld on any grounds whatever." This statement may be taken to mean that the use of the mails may not be subjected to conditions which are themselves unconstitutional, conditions, for example, which would require newspapers to hue to a particular political philosophy if they are to remain eligible for the second-class mail rate. To support the proposition that unconstitutional conditions cannot be imposed on the press which uses the mails, Justice Douglas relied on the dissents of Justice Brandeis and Justice Holmes in Milwaukee Social Democratic Publishing Co. v. Burleson, 255 U.S. 467 (1921). Yet the Court in *Hannegan* does not reverse the majority opinion in the *Milwaukee Social Democratic Publishing Co.* case, although the cases are profoundly inconsistent.

In a dissenting opinion in the famous obscenity case, Roth v. United States, 354 U.S. 476 (1957), Justice Harlan made the following observation on conditioning the use of the mails, p. 731, fn. 5:

> The hoary dogma of Ex Parte Jackson, 96 U.S. 726, and Public Clearing House of Coyne, 194 U.S. 497, that the use of the mails is a privilege on which the government may impose such conditions as it chooses, has long since evaporated. See Brandeis, J., dissenting in Milwaukee Social Democratic Publishing Co. v. Burleson, 255 U.S. 407, 430–433; Holmes, J., dissenting, in Leach v. Carlile, 259 U.S. 138, 140; Cates v. Haderline, 342 U.S. 804, reversing 189 F.2d 369; Door v. Donaldson, 90 U.S.App.D.C. 188, 195 F.2d 764.

In the light of this information, what do you think is the status of the *Milwaukee Social Democratic Publishing Co.* case today?

To what extent under the existing case law can government condition the availability of the second-class mail rate on requirements which have regard to press content?

2. Should government really be as neutral in terms of aiding the press as it is supposed to be with regard to religion? If so, do special mailing rates for the press infringe on such neutrality? If special mailing rates really function as a governmental subsidy of the press, would the withdrawal of this subsidy be free of First Amendment implications? See Grosjean v. American Press, 297 U.S. 233 (1936).

If special mailing rates for the press exist to aid in the dissemination of information in the service of public enlightenment, does this suggest that other affirmative governmental action with similar aims can be considered consistent with the First Amendment?

3. A more recent example of an attempt to use the mails for censorship purposes was the *Lamont* case which follows. In *Lamont*, the Supreme Court invalidated a federal statute which permitted the mail delivery of "communist political propaganda" which originated in a foreign country only if the addressee specifically requested such delivery. The Court unanimously invalidated the statute. But the Court was not unanimous in the rationalization offered for this conclusion. The absolutist First Amendment rationale employed by the Court in *Lamont* demonstrates the lively existence of alternative theories of First Amendment protection. Often, as in *Lamont*, the Court uses these competing First Amendment theories concurrently, using one First Amendment theory to resolve one set of problems and another for a different set of problems. The student will also note that the Court ignored the clear and present danger doctrine as a rationalization in *Lamont*.

LAMONT v. POSTMASTER GENERAL

381 U.S. 301, 85 S.CT. 1493, 14 L.ED.2D 398 (1965).

Justice DOUGLAS delivered the opinion of the Court.

These appeals present the same question: is § 305(a) of the Postal Service and Federal Employees Salary Act of 1962, 76 Stat. 840, constitutional as construed and applied? The statute provides in part:

"Mail matter, except sealed letters, which originates or which is printed or otherwise prepared in a foreign country and which is determined by the secretary of the treasury pursuant to rules and regulations to be promulgated by him to be 'communist political propaganda,' shall be detained by the postmaster general upon its arrival for delivery in the United States, or upon its subsequent deposit in the United States domestic mails, and the addressee shall be notified that such matter has been received and will be delivered only upon the addressee's request, except that such detention shall not be required in the case of any matter which is furnished pursuant to subscription or which is otherwise ascertained by the postmaster general to be desired by the addressee." 39 U.S.C.A. § 4008(a).

The statute defines "communist political propaganda" as political propaganda (as that term is defined in § 1(j) of the Foreign Agents Registration Act of 1938) which is issued by or on behalf of any country with respect to which there is in effect a suspension or withdrawal of tariff concessions or from which foreign assistance is withheld pursuant to certain specified statutes. 39 U.S.C.A. § 4008(b). The statute contains an exemption from its provisions for mail addressed to government agencies and educational institutions, or officials thereof, and for mail sent pursuant to a reciprocal cultural international agreement. 39 U.S.C.A. § 4008(c).

To implement the statute the Post Office maintains 10 or 11 screening points through which is routed all unsealed mail from the designated foreign countries. At these points the nonexempt mail is examined by customs authorities. When it is determined that a piece of mail is "communist political propaganda," the addressee is mailed a notice identifying the mail being detained and advising that it will be destroyed unless the addressee requests delivery by returning an attached reply card within 20 days.

Prior to March 1, 1965, the reply card contained a space in which the addressee could request delivery of any "similar publication" in the future. A list of the persons thus manifesting a desire to receive "communist political propaganda" was maintained by the Post Office. The government in its brief informs us that the keeping of this list was terminated, effective March 15, 1965. Thus, under the new practice, a notice is sent and must be returned for each individual piece of mail desired. The only standing instruction which it is now possible to leave with the Post Office is *not* to deliver any "communist political propaganda." And the solicitor general advises us that the Post Office Department "intends to retain its assumption that those who do not return the card want neither the identified publication nor any similar one arriving subsequently."

[This case] arose out of the Post Office's detention in 1963 of a copy of the *Peking Review #12* addressed to appellant, Dr. Corliss Lamont, who is engaged in the publishing and distributing of pamphlets. Lamont did not respond to the notice of detention which was sent to him but instead instituted this suit to enjoin enforcement of the statute, alleging that it infringed his rights under the First and Fifth Amendments. The Post Office thereupon notified Lamont that it considered his institution of the suit to be an expression of his desire to receive "communist political propaganda" and therefore none of his mail would be detained. Lamont amended his complaint to challenge on constitutional grounds the placement of his name on the list of those desiring to receive "communist political propaganda." The majority of the three-judge district court nonetheless dismissed the complaint as moot, 229 F.Supp. 913, because Lamont would now receive his mail unimpeded. Insofar as the list was concerned, the majority thought that any legally significant harm to Lamont as a result of being listed was merely a speculative possibility, and so on this score the controversy was not yet ripe for adjudication. * * *

Like Lamont, appellee Heilberg, * * * when his mail was detained, refused to return the reply card and instead filed a complaint in the district court for an injunction against enforcement of the statute. The Post Office reacted to this complaint in the same manner as it had to Lamont's complaint, but the district court declined to hold that Heilberg's action was thereby mooted. Instead the district court reached the merits and unanimously held that the statute was unconstitutional under the First Amendment. * * *

There is no longer even a colorable question of mootness in these cases, for the new procedure, as described above, requires the postal authorities to send a separate notice for each item as it is received and the addressee to make a separate request for each item. Under the new system, we are told, there can be no list of persons who have manifested a desire to receive "communist political propaganda" and whose mail will therefore go through relatively unimpeded. The government concedes that the changed procedure entirely precludes any claim of mootness and leaves for our consideration the sole question of the constitutionality of the statute.

We conclude that the act as construed and applied is unconstitutional because it requires an official act (*viz.,* returning the reply card) as a limitation on the unfettered exercise of the addressee's First Amendment rights. As stated by Justice Holmes in Milwaukee Pub. Co. v. Burleson, 255 U.S. 407, 437 (dissenting): "The United States may give up the Post Office when it sees fit, but while it carries it on the use of the mails is almost as much a part of free speech as the right to use our tongues. * * *"

We struck down in Murdock v. Pennsylvania, 319 U.S. 105, a flat license tax on the exercise of First Amendment rights. A registration requirement imposed on a labor union organizer before making a speech met the same fate in Thomas v. Collins, 323 U.S. 516. A municipal licensing system for those distributing literature was held invalid in Lovell v. Griffin, 303 U.S. 444. * * *

* * *

Here the congress—expressly restrained by the First Amendment from "abridging" freedom of speech and of press—is the actor. The act sets administrative officials astride the flow of mail to inspect it, appraise it, write the addressee about it, and await a response before dispatching the mail. Just as the licensing or taxing authorities in the *Lovell, Thomas,* and *Murdock* cases sought to control the flow of ideas to the public, so here federal agencies regulate the flow of mail. We do not have here, any more than we had in Hannegan v. Esquire, Inc., 327 U.S. 146, any question concerning the extent to which Congress may classify the mail and fix the charges for its carriage. Nor do we reach the question whether the standard here applied could pass constitutional muster. Nor do we deal with the right of Customs to inspect material from abroad for contraband. We rest on the narrow ground that the addressee in order to receive his mail must request in writing that it be delivered. This amounts in our judgment to an unconstitutional abridgment of the addressee's First Amendment rights. The addressee carries an affirmative obligation which we do not think the Government may impose on him. This requirement is almost certain to have a deterrent effect, especially as respects those who have sensitive positions. Their livelihood may be dependent on a security clearance. Public officials, like schoolteachers who have no tenure, might think they would invite disaster if they read what the federal government says contains the seeds of treason. Apart from them, any addressee is likely to feel some inhibition in sending for literature which federal officials have condemned as "communist political propaganda." The regime of this act is at war with the "uninhibited, robust, and wide-open" debate and discussion that are contemplated by the First Amendment. New York Times Co. v. Sullivan, 376 U.S. 254, 270.

We reverse the judgment in [*Lamont*] and affirm that in [*Heilberg*].

It is so ordered.

COMMENT

1. Justice Douglas used the so-called absolutist or plain meaning approach to First Amendment interpretation: The statute is a direct restraint by official act of the government on freedom of expression; the First Amendment protects freedom of expression, *ergo*, the statute is invalid.

2. The remarkable extent to which Justice Holmes's dissents have become the law is illustrated by the *Lamont* decision. Thus, Justice Douglas quotes Holmes's dissent in Milwaukee Publishing Co. v. Burleson, 255 U.S. 407 (1921), rather than the majority opinion for the Court in that case. Insofar as there are two lines of cases with regard to the power of Congress to censor the mails, the later liberal *Hannegan* approach was expressly endorsed in *Lamont* in 1965. Perhaps it can be argued that *Milwaukee Pub. Co. v. Burleson* has at least, implicitly, been overruled. On the other hand, *Milwaukee Pub. Co.* arose in the context of war and First Amendment rights. During wartime, First Amendment liberties, like other constitutionally protected civil liberties, have sometimes been subordinated to other governmental interests. It should be remembered that in *Schenck* Justice Holmes, writing the opinion for the Court, used the clear and present danger

doctrine and still affirmed a conviction under the Espionage Act for the distribution of a pamphlet, during wartime, which advocated to drafted soldiers opposition to the war and the draft.

Taxation of the Press and Censorship

GROSJEAN v. AMERICAN PRESS CO.

297 U.S. 233, 56 S.CT. 444, 80 L.ED. 660 (1936).

[Editorial Note
On July 12, 1934, the Louisiana legislature enacted a law which provided in essence that any newspaper selling advertisements, which had a circulation of more than 20,000 copies, would be required to pay a license tax of 2 percent on its gross receipts. The law was passed at the behest of Governor Huey Long and was aimed at the New Orleans *Times-Picayune,* a New Orleans daily which had been critical of the Long regime. Nine newspaper publishers, publishing thirteen newspapers, brought suit to enjoin the enforcement of the statute.]

Justice SUTHERLAND delivered the opinion of the Court.

* * *

The nine publishers who brought the suit publish thirteen newspapers; and these thirteen publications are the only ones within the state of Louisiana having each a circulation of more than 20,000 copies per week, although the lower court finds there are four other daily newspapers each having a circulation of "slightly less than 20,000 copies per week" which are in competition with those published by appellees both as to circulation and as to advertising. In addition, there are 120 weekly newspapers published in the state, also in competition, to a greater or less degree, with the newspapers of appellees. The revenue derived from appellees' newspapers comes almost entirely from regular subscribers or purchasers thereof and from payments received for the insertion of advertisements therein.

The act requires every one subject to the tax to file a sworn report every three months showing the amount and the gross receipts from the business. * * * The resulting tax must be paid when the report is filed. Failure to file the report or pay the tax as thus provided constitutes a misdemeanor and subjects the offender to a fine not exceeding $500, or imprisonment not exceeding six months, or both, for each violation. Any corporation violating the acts subjects itself to the payment of $500 to be recovered by suit. All of the appellees are corporations.

* * *

The validity of the act is assailed as violating the Federal Constitution in two particulars: (1) That it abridges the freedom of the press in contravention of the due process clause contained in section 1 of the Fourteenth Amendment; (2) that it denies appellees the equal protection of the laws in contravention of the same amendment.

1. The first point presents a question of the utmost gravity and importance; for, if well made, it goes to the heart of the natural right of the members of an organized society, united for their common good, to impart and acquire information about their common interests. The First Amendment to the Federal Constitution provides that "Congress shall make no law * * * abridging the freedom of speech, or of the press." While this provision is not a restraint upon the powers of the states, the states are precluded from abridging the freedom of speech or of the press by force of the due process clause of the Fourteenth Amendment. * * *

That freedom of speech and of the press are rights of the same fundamental character, safeguarded by the due process of law clause of the Fourteenth Amendment against abridgment by state legislation, has likewise been settled by a series of decisions of this court beginning with *Gitlow v. People of State of New York*, and ending with *Near v. State of Minnesota*. The word "liberty" contained in that amendment embraces not only the right of a person to be free from physical restraint, but the right to be free in the enjoyment of all his faculties as well.

* * *

The tax imposed is designated a "license tax for the privilege of engaging in such business," that is to say, the business of selling, or making any charge for, advertising. As applied to appellees, it is a tax of 2 percent on the gross receipts derived from advertisements carried in their newspapers when, and only when, the newspapers of each enjoy a circulation of more than 20,000 copies per week. It thus operates as a restraint in a double sense. First, its effect is to curtail the amount of revenue realized from advertising; and, second, its direct tendency is to restrict circulation. This is plain enough when we consider that, if it were increased to a high degree, as it could be if valid, it well might result in destroying both advertising and circulation.

A determination of the question whether the tax is valid in respect of the point now under review requires an examination of the history and circumstances which antedated and attended the adoption of the abridgment clause of the First Amendment, since that clause expresses one of those "fundamental principles of liberty and justice which lie at the base of all our civil and political institutions," and, as such, is embodied in the concept "due process of law" and, therefore, protected against hostile state invasion by the due process clause of the Fourteenth Amendment. * * *

For more than a century prior to the adoption of the amendment—and, indeed, for many years thereafter—history discloses a persistent effort on the part of the British government to prevent or abridge the free expression of any opinion which seemed to criticize or exhibit in an unfavorable light, however truly, the agencies and operations of the government. The struggle between the proponents of measures to that end and those who asserted the right of free expression was continuous and unceasing. As early as 1644, John Milton, in an "Appeal for the Liberty of Unlicensed Printing," assailed an act of Parliament which had just been passed providing for censorship of the press previous to publication. He vigorously defended the right of every man to make public his honest views "without previous censure"; and declared the impossibility of finding any man base enough to accept the office of censor and at the same time good enough to be allowed to perform its duties. Collett, History of the Taxes on Knowledge, vol. I, pp. 4–6. The act expired by its own terms in 1695. It was never renewed; and the liberty of the press thus became, as pointed out by Wickwar (The Struggle for the Freedom of the Press, p. 15), merely "a right or liberty to publish without a license what formerly could be published only with one." But mere exemption from previous censorship was soon recognized as too narrow a view of the liberty of the press.

In 1712, in response to a message from Queen Anne (Hansard's Parliamentary History of England, vol. 6, p. 1063), Parliament imposed a tax upon all newspapers and upon advertisements. Collett, vol. I, pp. 8–10. That the main purpose of these taxes was to suppress the publication of comments and criticisms objectionable to the Crown does not admit of doubt. Stewart, Lennox and the Taxes on Knowledge, 15 Scottish Historical Review, 322–327. There followed more than a century of resistance to, and evasion of, the taxes, and of agitation for their repeal. * * *

Citations of similar import might be multiplied many times; but the foregoing is enough to demonstrate beyond peradventure that in the adoption of the English newspaper stamp tax and the tax on advertisements, revenue was of subordinate concern; and that the dominant and controlling aim was to prevent, or curtail the opportunity for, the acquisition of knowledge by the people in respect of their governmental affairs. It is idle to suppose that so many of the best men of England would for a century of time have waged, as they did, stubborn and often precarious warfare against these taxes if a mere matter of taxation had been involved. The aim of the struggle was not to relieve taxpayers from a burden, but to establish and preserve the right of the English people to full information in respect of the doings or misdoings of their government. Upon the correctness of this conclusion the very characterization of the exactions as "taxes on knowledge" sheds a flood of corroborative light. In the ultimate, an informed and enlightened public opinion was the thing at stake; for, as Erskine, in his great speech in defense of Paine, has said, "The liberty of opinion keeps governments themselves in due subjection to their duties." Erskine's Speeches, High's Ed., vol. I, p. 525. See May's Constitutional History of England (7th Ed.) vol. 2, pp. 238–245.

In 1785, only four years before Congress had proposed the First Amendment, the Massachusetts Legislature, following the English example, imposed a stamp tax on all newspapers and magazines. The following year an advertisement tax was imposed. Both taxes met with such violent opposition that the former was repealed in 1786, and the latter in 1788. Duniway, Freedom of the Press in Massachusetts, pp. 136, 137.

The framers of the First Amendment were familiar with the English struggle, which then had continued for nearly eighty years and was destined to go on for another sixty-five years, at the end of which time it culminated in a lasting abandonment of the obnoxious taxes. The framers were likewise familiar with the then recent Massachusetts episode; and while that occurrence did much to bring about the adoption of the amendment (see Pennsylvania and the Federal Constitution, 1888, p. 181), the predominant influence must have come from the English experience. It is impossible to concede that by the words "freedom of the press" the framers of the amendment intended to adopt merely the narrow view then reflected by the law of England that such freedom consisted only in immunity from previous censorship; for this abuse had then permanently disappeared from English practice. It is equally impossible to believe that it was not intended to bring within the reach of these words such modes of restraint as were embodied in the two forms of taxation already described. Such belief must be rejected in the face of the then well-known purpose of the exactions and the general adverse sentiment of the colonies in respect of them. Undoubtedly, the range of a constitutional provision phrased in terms of the common law sometimes may be fixed by recourse to the applicable rules of that law.

* * *

In the light of all that has now been said, it is evident that the restricted rules of the English law in respect of the freedom of the press in force when the Constitution was adopted were never accepted by the American colonists, and that by the First Amendment it was meant to preclude the national government, and by the Fourteenth Amendment to preclude the states, from adopting any form of previous restraint upon printed publications, or their circulation, including that which had theretofore been effected by these two well-known and odious methods.

This court had occasion in Near v. State of Minnesota, 283 U.S. 697, at pages

713 et seq., to discuss at some length the subject in its general aspect. The conclusion there stated is that the object of the constitutional provisions was to prevent previous restraints on publication; and the court was careful not to limit the protection of the right to any particular way of abridging it. Liberty of the press within the meaning of the constitutional provision, it was broadly said (283 U.S. 697, 716), meant "principally although not exclusively, immunity from previous restraints or [from] censorship."

Judge Cooley has laid down the test to be applied: "The evils to be prevented were not the censorship of the press merely, but any action of the government by means of which it might prevent such free and general discussion of public matters as seems absolutely essential to prepare the people for an intelligent exercise of their rights as citizens." 2 Cooley's Constitutional Limitations (8th Ed.) p. 886.

It is not intended by anything we have said to suggest that the owners of newspapers are immune from any of the ordinary forms of taxation for support of the government. But this is not an ordinary form of tax, but one single in kind, with a long history of hostile misuse against the freedom of the press.

The predominant purpose of the grant of immunity here invoked was to preserve an untrammeled press as a vital source of public information. The newspapers, magazines, and other journals of the country, it is safe to say, have shed and continue to shed, more light on the public and business affairs of the nation than any other instrumentality of publicity; and since informed public opinion is the most potent of all restraints upon misgovernment, the suppression or abridgment of the publicity afforded by a free press cannot be regarded otherwise than with grave concern. The tax here involved is bad not because it takes money from the pockets of the appellees. If that were all, a wholly different question would be presented. It is bad because, in the light of its history and of its present setting, it is seen to be a deliberate and calculated device in the guise of a tax to limit the circulation of information to which the public is entitled in virtue of the constitutional guaranties. A free press stands as one of the great interpreters between the government and the people. To allow it to be fettered is to fetter ourselves.

In view of the persistent search for new subjects of taxation, it is not without significance that, with the single exception of the Louisiana statute, so far as we can discover, no state during the one hundred fifty years of our national existence has undertaken to impose a tax like that now in question.

The form in which the tax is imposed is in itself suspicious. It is not measured or limited by the volume of advertisements. It is measured alone by the extent of the circulation of the publication in which the advertisements are carried, with the plain purpose of penalizing the publishers and curtailing the circulation of a selected group of newspapers. [Emphasis added.]

Having reached the conclusion that the act imposing the tax in question is unconstitutional under the due process of law clause because it abridges the freedom of the press, we deem it unnecessary to consider the further ground assigned, that it also constitutes a denial of the equal protection of the laws.

Decree affirmed.

COMMENT

Grosjean makes clear that stamp taxes on newspapers and taxes on advertisements were similar practices and as such abhorrent to the eighteenth-century American. *Grosjean* illustrates why a larger definition of freedom of the press than one limited merely to freedom from prior restraint was necessary if the objectives of freedom of the press, as outlined by Justice George Sutherland, were to be secured, i.e., ("In the ultimate, an informed and enlightened public opinion was the thing at stake."). Discriminatory taxes, like licensing on the basis of content and prior restraints, were all forbidden by the constitutional guarantee of freedom of the press. But see United States ex rel. Milwaukee Social Democratic Publishing Co. v. Burleson, 255 U.S. 407 (1921).

Note how helpful Hughes's opinion in *Near* proved to the decision of the Court in *Grosjean.* Hughes's willingness to make the prior restraint concept cover various modes of advance governmental press censorship contributed to the general understanding, made clear in the *Hannegan* case in 1946, that the whole panoply of direct restraints on the press was prohibited by the constitutional phrase "freedom of the press."

Which is more destructive of the purposes of freedom of the press: a prior restraint on printed matter itself or a tax on circulation of daily newspapers? How does Sutherland deal with the state defense that newspapers are a business and as a business, the press, like other businesses, has no constitutional immunity from taxation?

Because of the constitutional guarantees of freedom of the press and freedom of speech, does engagement in such pursuits make governmental regulation unconstitutional? *When* freedom of expression is really at stake and when some other governmental interest, which is a matter of valid governmental concern, is at stake is a particularly perplexing problem in First Amendment cases. What kind of expression is protected? Political expression or commercial advertisements as well? See *Virginia Pharmacy,* text, p. 159, with *Lehman v. City of Shaker Heights,* text, p. 64.

MINNEAPOLIS STAR AND TRIBUNE CO. v. MINNESOTA COMMISSIONER OF REVENUE

— U.S. —, 103 S.CT. 1365, 75 L.ED.2D 295 (1983).

Justice O'CONNOR delivered the opinion of the Court.

This case presents the question of a state's power to impose a special tax on the press and, by enacting exemptions, to limit its effect to only a few newspapers.

Since 1967, Minnesota has imposed a sales tax on most sales of goods for a price in excess of a nominal sum. * * * In general, the tax applies only to retail sales. * * * This use tax applies to any nonexempt tangible personal property unless the sales tax was paid on the sales price. * * * Like the classic use tax, this use tax protects the State's sales tax by eliminating the residents' incentive to travel to States with lower sales taxes to buy goods rather than buying them in Minnesota. * * *

The appellant, Minneapolis Star and Tribune Company "Star Tribune", is the publisher of a morning newspaper and an evening newspaper in Minneapolis. From 1967 until 1971, it enjoyed an exemption from the sales and use tax provided by Minnesota for periodic publications. * * In 1971, however, while leaving the exemption from the sales tax in place, the legislature amended the scheme to impose a "use tax" on the cost of paper and ink products consumed in the production of a publication. * * * Ink and paper used in publications became the only items subject to the use tax that were components of goods to be sold at retail. In 1974, the legislature again amended the statute, this time to exempt the first $100,000 worth of ink and paper consumed by a publication in any calendar year, in effect giving each publication an annual tax credit of $4,000. * * * Publications remained exempt from the sales tax. * * *

After the enactment of the $100,000 exemption, 11 publishers, producing 14 of the 388 paid circulation newspapers in the state, incurred a tax liability in 1974. Star Tribune was one of the 11, and, of the $893,355 collected, it paid $608,634, or roughly two-thirds of the total revenue raised by the tax. See 314 N.W.2d 201, 203 and n. 4 (1981). In 1975, 13 publishers, producing 16 out of 374 paid circulation papers, paid a tax. That year, Star Tribune again bore roughly two-thirds of the total receipts from the use tax on ink and paper.

Star Tribune instituted this action to seek a refund of the use taxes it paid from January 1, 1974 to May 31, 1975. It challenged the imposition of the use tax on ink and paper used in publications as a violation of the guarantees of freedom of the press and equal protection in the First and Fourteenth Amendments. The Minnesota Supreme Court upheld the tax against the federal constitutional challenge. * * * We noted probable jurisdiction, —— U.S. ——, 102 S.Ct. 2955, 73 L.Ed.2d 1347 (1982), and we now reverse.

Star Tribune argues that we must strike this tax on the authority of *Grosjean v. American Press Co., Inc.* * * * Although there are similarities between the two cases, we agree with the State that *Grosjean* is not controlling.

In *Grosjean,* the State of Louisiana imposed a license tax of 2% of the gross receipts from the sale of advertising on all newspapers with a weekly circulation above 20,000. Out of at least 124 publishers in the State, only 13 were subject to the tax. * * * All but one of the large papers subject to the tax had "ganged up" on Senator Huey Long, and a circular distributed by Long and the governor to each member of the state legislature described "lying newspapers" as conducting "a vicious campaign" and the tax as "a tax on lying, 2c [*sic*] a lie." Although the Court's opinion did not describe this history, it stated, "[The tax] is bad because, in the light of its history and of its present setting, it is seen to be a deliberate and calculated device in the guise of a tax to limit the circulation of information," * * an explanation that suggests that the motivation of the legislature may have been significant.

Our subsequent cases have not been consistent in their reading of *Grosjean* on this point. Compare United States v. O'Brien, 391 U.S. 367, 384–385 (1968) (stating that legislative purpose was irrelevant in *Grosjean*) with *Houchins v. KQED, Inc.,* * * * (plurality opinion) (suggesting that purpose was relevant in *Grosjean*); Pittsburgh Press Co. v. Pittsburgh Commission on Human Relations, 413 U.S. 376, 383 * * (1973) (same). Commentators have generally viewed *Grosjean* as dependent on the improper censorial goals of the legislature. See T. Emerson, The System of Freedom of Expression 419 (1970); L. Tribe, American Constitutional Law 592 n. 8, 724 n. 10 (1978). We think that the result in *Grosjean* may have been attributable in part to the perception on the part of the Court that the state imposed the tax with an intent to penalize a selected group of newspapers. In the case currently before us, however, there is no legislative history and no indication, apart from the structure of the tax itself, of any impermissible or censorial motive on the part of the legislature. We cannot resolve the case by simple citation to *Grosjean.* Instead, we must analyze the problem anew under the general principles of the First Amendment.

Clearly, the First Amendment does not prohibit all regulation of the press. It is beyond dispute that the states and the federal government can subject newspapers to generally applicable economic regulations without creating constitutional problems. [Citations omitted.] Minnesota, however, has not chosen to apply its general sales and use tax to newspapers. Instead, it has created a special tax that applies only to certain publications protected by the First Amendment. Although the state argues now that the tax on paper and ink is part of the general scheme of taxation, the use tax provision, quoted in note 2, *supra,* is facially discriminatory, singling out publications for treatment that is, to our knowledge, unique in Minnesota tax law.

Minnesota's treatment of publications differs from that of other enterprises in at least two important respects: it imposes a use tax that does not serve the function of protecting the sales tax, and it taxes an intermediate transaction rather than the ultimate retail sale. A use tax ordinarily serves to complement the sales tax by eliminating the incentive to make major purchases in states with lower sales taxes; it requires the resident who shops out-of-state to pay a use tax equal to the sales tax savings. * * * Minnesota designed its overall use tax scheme to serve this function. As the regulations state, "The 'use tax' is a compensatory or complementary tax." * * * Thus, in general, items exempt from the sales tax are not subject to the use tax, for, in the event of a sales tax exemption, there is no "complementary function" for a use tax to serve. * * * But the use tax on ink and paper serves no such complementary function; it applies to all uses, whether or not the taxpayer purchased the ink and paper in-state, and it applies to items exempt from the sales tax.

Further, the ordinary rule in Minnesota, as discussed above, is to tax only the ultimate, or retail, sale rather than the use of components like ink and paper. "The statutory scheme is to devise a unitary tax which exempts intermediate transactions and imposes it only on sales when the finished product is purchased by the ultimate user." * * * Publishers, however, are taxed on their purchase of components, even though they will eventually sell their publications at retail.

By creating this special use tax, which, to our knowledge, is without parallel in the State's tax scheme, *Minnesota has singled out the press for special treatment.* We then must determine whether the First Amendment permits such special taxation. A tax that burdens rights protected by the First Amendment cannot stand unless the burden is necessary to achieve an overriding governmental interest. See, *e.g., United States v. Lee,* 455 U.S. 252 (1982). Any tax that the press must pay, of course, imposes some "burden." But, as we have observed, this Court has long upheld economic regulation of the press. The cases approving such economic regulation, however, emphasized the general applicability of the challenged regulation to all businesses, * * * suggesting that a regulation that singled out the press might place a heavier burden of justification on the state, and we now conclude that the special problems created by differential treatment do indeed impose such a burden. [Emphasis added.]

There is substantial evidence that differential taxation of the press would have troubled the Framers of the First Amendment. The role of the press in mobilizing sentiment in favor of independence was critical to the Revolution. When the Constitution was proposed without an explicit guarantee of freedom of the press, the Antifederalists objected. Proponents of the Constitution, relying on the principle of enumerated powers, responded that such a guarantee was unnecessary because the Constitution granted Congress no power to control the press. The remarks of Richard Henry Lee are typical of the rejoinders of the Antifederalists:

> "I confess I do not see in what cases the congress can, with any pretence of right, make a law to suppress the freedom of the press; though I am not clear, that congress is restrained from laying any duties whatever on printing, and from laying duties particularly heavy on certain pieces printed." R. Lee, Observation Leading to a Fair Examination of the System of Government, Letter IV, reprinted in 1 B. Schwartz, The Bill of Rights: A Documentary History 466, 474 (1971).

See also A Review of the Constitution Proposed by the Late Convention by a Federal Republican, reprinted in 3 H. Storing, The Complete Anti-Federalist 65, 81–82 (1981); M. Smith, Address to the People of New York on the Necessity of Amendments to the Constitution, reprinted in 1 B. Schwartz, *supra*, 566, 575–576; cf. The Federalist No. 84, p. 440 and n. 1 (A. Hamilton) (M. Beloff ed. 1948) (recognizing and attempting to refute the argument). The concerns voiced by the Antifederalists led to the adoption of the Bill of Rights. See 1 B. Schwartz, *supra,* at 527.

The fears of the Antifederalists were well-founded. A power to tax differentially, as opposed to a power to tax generally, gives a government a powerful weapon against the taxpayer selected. When the state imposes a generally applicable tax, there is little cause for concern. We need not fear that a government will destroy a selected group of taxpayers by burdensome taxation if it must impose the same burden on the rest of its constituency. * * When the state singles out the press, though, the political constraints that prevent a legislature from passing crippling taxes of general applicability are weakened, and the threat of burdensome taxes becomes acute. That threat can operate as effectively as a censor to check critical comment by the press, undercutting the basic assumption of our political system that the press will often serve as an important restraint on government. See generally, Stewart, "Or of the Press," 26 Hastings L.J. 631, 634 (1975). "[A]n untrammeled press [is] a vital source of public information," *Grosjean,* * * * and an informed public is the essence of working democracy.

Further, differential treatment, unless justified by some special characteristic of the press, suggests that the goal of the regulation is not unrelated to suppression of expression, and such a goal is presumptively unconstitutional. See, e.g., Police Department of the City of Chicago v. Mosely, 408 U.S. 92, 95–96 (1972); cf. Brown v. Hartlage, 456 U.S. 45 (1982) (First Amendment has its "fullest and most urgent" application in the case of regulation of the content of political speech). Differential taxation of the press, then, places such a burden on the interests protected by the First Amendment that we cannot countenance such treatment unless the state asserts a counterbalancing interest of compelling importance that it cannot achieve without differential taxation.

The main interest asserted by Minnesota in this case is the raising of revenue. Of course that interest is critical to any government. Standing alone, however, it cannot justify the special treatment of the press, for an alternative means of achieving the same interest without raising concerns under the First Amendment is clearly available: the state could raise the revenue by taxing businesses generally, avoiding the censorial threat implicit in a tax that singles out the press.

Addressing the concern with differential treatment, Minnesota invites us to look beyond the form of the tax to its substance. The tax is, according to the state, merely a substitute for the sales tax, which, as a generally applicable tax, would be constitutional as applied to the press. There are two fatal flaws in this reasoning. First, the state has offered no explanation of why it chose to use a substitute for the sales tax rather than the sales tax itself. The court below speculated that the state might have been concerned that collection of a tax on such small transactions would be impractical. 314 N.W.2d, at 207. That suggestion is unpersuasive, for sales of other low-priced goods are not exempt, see note 1, *supra.* If the real goal of this tax is to duplicate the sales tax, it is difficult to see why the state did not achieve that goal by the obvious and effective expedient of applying the sales tax.

Further, even assuming that the legislature did have valid reasons for substituting another tax for the sales tax, we are not persuaded that this tax does serve as a substitute. The state asserts that this scheme actually *favors* the press over other businesses, because the same rate of tax is applied, but, for the press, the rate applies to the cost of components rather than to the sales price. We would be hesitant to fashion a rule that automatically allowed the state to single out the press for a different method of taxation as long as the effective burden was not different from that on other taxpayers or the burden on the press was lighter than that on other businesses. One reason for this reluctance is that the very selection of the press for special treatment threatens the press not only with the current *differential* treatment, but with the possibility of subsequent differentially *more burdensome* treatment. Thus, even without actually imposing an extra burden on the press, the government might be able to achieve censorial effects, for "[t]he threat of sanctions may deter [the] exercise of [First Amendment] rights almost as potently as the actual application of sanctions." NAACP v. Button, 371 U.S. 415, 433 (1963).

A second reason to avoid the proposed rule is that courts as institutions are poorly equipped to evaluate with precision the relative burdens of various methods of taxation. The complexities of factual economic proof always present a certain potential for error, and courts have little familiarity with the process of evaluating the relative economic burden of taxes. In sum, the possibility of error inherent in the proposed rule poses too great a threat to concerns at the heart of the First Amendment, and we cannot tolerate that possibility.[13] Minnesota, therefore, has offered no adequate justification for the special treatment of newspapers.

Minnesota's ink and paper tax violates the First Amendment not only because it singles out the press, but also because it targets a small group of newspapers. The effect of the $100,000 exemption enacted in 1974 is that only a handful of publishers pay any tax at all, and even fewer pay any significant amount of tax.[15] The state explains this exemption as part of a policy favoring an "equitable" tax system, although there are no comparable exemptions for small enterprises outside the press. Again, there is no legislative history supporting the state's view of the purpose of the amendment. Whatever the motive of the legislature in this case, we think that recognizing a power in the state not only to single out the press but also to tailor the tax so that it singles out a few members of the press presents such a potential for abuse that no interest suggested by Minnesota can justify the scheme. It has asserted no interest other than its desire to have an "equitable" tax system. The current system, it explains, promotes equity because it places the burden on large publications that impose more social costs than do smaller publications and that are more likely to be able to bear the burden of the tax. Even if we were willing to accept the premise that large businesses are more profitable and therefore better able to bear the burden of the tax, the state's commitment to this "equity" is questionable, for the concern has not led

13. If a state employed the same *method* of taxation but applied a lower *rate* to the press, so that there could be no doubt that the legislature was not singling out the press to bear a more burdensome tax, we would, of course, be in a position to evaluate the relative burdens. And, given the clarity of the relative burdens, as well as the rule that differential methods of taxation are not automatically permissible if less burdensome, a lower tax rate for the press would not raise the threat that the legislature might later impose an extra burden that would escape detection by the courts, * * *. Thus, our decision does not, as the dissent suggests, require Minnesota to impose a greater tax burden on publications.

15. In 1974, 11 publishers paid the tax. Three paid less than $1,000, and another three paid less than $8,000. Star Tribune, one of only two publishers paying more than $100,000, paid $608,634. In 1975, 13 publishers paid the tax. Again, three paid less than $1,000, and four more paid less than $3,000. For that year, Star Tribune paid $636,113 and was again one of only two publishers incurring a liability greater than $100,000. See 314 N.W.2d, at 203–204 and nn. 4, 5.

the state to grant benefits to small businesses in general. And when the exemption selects such a narrowly defined group to bear the full burden of the tax, the tax begins to resemble more a penalty for a few of the largest newspapers than an attempt to favor struggling smaller enterprises.

We need not and do not impugn the motives of the Minnesota legislature in passing the ink and paper tax. Illicit legislative intent is not the *sine qua non* of a violation of the First Amendment. See NAACP v. Button, 371 U.S. at 439; NAACP v. Alabama, 357 U.S. 449, 461 (1958); Lovell v. Griffin, 303 U.S. 444, 451 (1938). We have long recognized that even regulations aimed at proper governmental concerns can restrict unduly the exercise of rights protected by the First Amendment. E.g., Schneider v. State, 308 U.S. 147 (1939). A tax that singles out the press, or that targets individual publications within the press, places a heavy burden on the State to justify its action. Since Minnesota has offered no satisfactory justification for its tax on the use of ink and paper, the tax violates the First Amendment, and the judgment below is

Reversed.

Justice White, concurring in part and dissenting in part.

* * *

Justice REHNQUIST, dissenting:

Today we learn from the Court that a state runs afoul of the First Amendment proscription of laws "abridging the freedom of speech, or of the press" where the state structures its taxing system to the advantage of newspapers. This seems very much akin to protecting something so overzealously that in the end it is smothered. While the Court purports to rely on the intent of the "Framers of the First Amendment," I believe it safe to assume that in 1791 "abridge" meant the same thing it means today: to diminish or curtail. Not until the Court's decision in this case, nearly two centuries after adoption of the First Amendment has it been read to prohibit activities which in no way diminish or curtail the freedoms it protects.

I agree with the Court that the First Amendment does not *per se* prevent the State of Minnesota from regulating the press even though such regulation imposes an economic burden. It is evident from the numerous cases relied on by the Court, which I need not repeat here, that this principle has been long settled. I further agree with the Court that application of general sales and use taxes to the press would be sanctioned under this line of cases. Therefore, I also agree with the Court to the extent it holds that any constitutional attack on the Minnesota scheme must be aimed at the classifications used in that taxing scheme. But it is at this point that I part company with my colleagues.

The Court recognizes in several parts of its opinion that the State of Minnesota could avoid constitutional problems by imposing on newspapers the 4% sales tax that it imposes on other retailers. Rather than impose such a tax however, the Minnesota legislature decided to provide newspapers with an exemption from the sales tax and impose a 4% use tax on ink and paper; thus, while both taxes are part of one "system of sales and use taxes," 314 N.W.2d 201, 203 (1981), newspapers are classified differently within that system. The problem the Court finds too difficult to deal with is whether this difference in treatment results in a significant burden on newspapers. * * * To state it in terms of the freedoms at issue here, no First Amendment issue is raised unless First Amendment rights have been infringed; for if there has been no infringement, then there has been no "abridgment" of those guaranties. See Branzburg v. Hayes, 408 U.S. 665 (1972).

Today the Court departs from this rule, refusing to look at the record and determine whether the classifications in the

Minnesota use and sales tax statutes significantly burden the First Amendment rights of petitioner and its fellow newspapers. * * *

Wisely not relying solely on inability to weigh the burdens of the Minnesota tax scheme, the Court also says that even if the resultant burden on the press is lighter than on others:

> "[T]he very selection of the press for special treatment threatens the press not only with the current *differential* treatment, but with the possibility of subsequent differentially *more burdensome* treatment. Thus, even without actually imposing an extra burden on the press, the government might be able to achieve censorial effects, for '[t]he threat of sanctions may deter [the] exercise of [First Amendment] rights almost as potently as the actual application of sanctions.' "

Surely the Court does not mean what it seems to say. The Court should be well aware from its discussion of *Grosjean v. American Press Co., Inc.,* 297 U.S. 233 (1936), that this Court is quite capable of dealing with changes in state taxing laws which are intended to penalize newspapers. * * *

* * * In summary, so long as the state can find another way to collect revenue from the newspapers, imposing a sales tax on newspapers would be to no one's advantage; not the newspaper and its distributors who would have to collect the tax, not the state who would have to enforce collection, and not the consumer who would have to pay for the paper in odd amounts. The reasonable alternative Minnesota chose was to impose the use tax on ink and paper. "There is no reason to believe that this legislative choice is insufficiently tailored to achieve the goal of raising revenue or that it burdens the first amendment in any way whatsoever." 314 N.W.2d, at 207. Cf. Minnesota v. Clover Leaf Creamery Co., 449 U.S. 456 (1981).

The court finds in very summary fashion that the exemption newspapers receive for the first $100,000 of ink and paper used also violates the First Amendment because the result is that only a few of the newspapers actually pay a use tax. I cannot agree. As explained by the Minnesota Supreme Court, the exemption is in effect a $4,000 credit which benefits all newspapers. 314 N.W.2d, at 203. Minneapolis Star & Tribune was benefited to the amount of $16,000 in the two years in question; $4,000 each year for its morning paper and $4,000 each year for its evening paper. *Ibid.* Absent any improper motive on the part of the Minnesota legislature in drawing the limits of this exemption, it cannot be construed as violating the First Amendment. * * * There is no reason to conclude that the State, in drafting the $4,000 credit, acted other than reasonably and rationally to fit its sales and use tax scheme to its own local needs and usages.

To collect from newspapers their fair share of taxes under the sales and use tax scheme and at the same time avoid abridging the freedoms of speech and press, the Court holds today that Minnesota must subject newspapers to millions of additional dollars in sales tax liability. Certainly this is a hollow victory for the newspapers and I seriously doubt the Court's conclusion that this result would have been intended by the "Framers of the First Amendment."

For the reasons set forth above, I would affirm the judgment of the Minnesota Supreme Court.

COMMENT

1. Does the rejection of special tax legislation for the press in *Minneapolis Star* constitute a rejection of the Stewart thesis that the freedom of the press clause warrants a special constitutional status for the press? See Stewart, text, p. 7. Perhaps the majority should have faced up to the implications of the *Grosjean* rationale—a rationale which they profess to accept:

Legislation is unconstitutional if the motive of the legislation is to penalize the press. The Court in *Minneapolis Star* professes not to follow *Grosjean* even though its result led to the invalidation of the challenged legislation, as was the case in *Grosjean.*

It may be argued that in a sense the majority in *Minneapolis Star* does in fact follow *Grosjean* but just expands its approach. Thus, reading *Grosjean* and *Minneapolis Star* together, if the motive of legislation is either to hinder or to help the press, then the motive is impermissible. With respect to the press, the motive of the legislature must be neutral or indifferent. In response to this it may be argued that that was not what was held in *Minneapolis Star.* The test the Court referred to a number of times is that a legislative tax that treats the press differently cannot stand, unless the purpose of the legislation is designed to accomplish an overriding governmental interest. In other words, the strict scrutiny approach to legislation involving the press was used. In short, since Minnesota could not advance any overriding governmental reason for the tax in question, its differential aspect as far as the press was concerned required its invalidation, under the strict standard of judicial review now accorded to legislation challenged on First Amendment grounds.

2. Justice Rehnquist, in dissent, criticized a particular sentence in Justice O'Connor's opinion in *Minneapolis Star:* "The very selection of the press for special treatment threatens the press not only with the current differential treatment, but with the possibility of subsequent differentially *more burdensome* treatment." Does this approach have unwelcome ramifications for the First Amendment? The Newspaper Preservation Act exempts newspapers from the antitrust laws in significant respects. See text, p. 647. Newspapers and magazines are allowed to use the mails on a special and economically advantageous basis, at least compared to the mailing rates charged to ordinary individuals. Is the constitutionality of this kind of special favorable legislative treatment for the press now thrown into doubt as a result of *Minneapolis Star?*

3. In October 1979, Justice Brennan gave a provocative speech in which he identified two First Amendment models conveying differing degrees of constitutional protection. In this view, the "structural" model grants less constitutional protection to the press than does the "speech model":

> Under one model—which I call the "speech" model—the press requires and is accorded the absolute protection of the First Amendment. In the other model—I call it the "structural" model—the press' interests may conflict with other societal interests and adjustment of the conflict on occasion favors the competing claim.
>
> The "speech" model is familiar. It is as comfortable as a pair of old shoes, and the press, in its present conflict with the Court, most often slips into the language and rhetorical stance with which this model is associated even when only the "structural" model is at issue. According to this traditional "speech" model, the primary purpose of the First Amendment is more or less absolutely to prohibit any interference with freedom of expression. The "speech" model thus readily lends itself to the heady rhetoric of absolutism.
>
> The "speech" model, however, has its limitations. It is a mistake to suppose that the First Amendment protects *only* self-expression, only the right to speak out. I believe that the First Amendment in addition fosters the values of democratic self-government.
>
> Another way of saying this is that the First Amendment protects the structure of communications necessary for the existence of our democracy. This insight suggests the second model to describe the role of the press in our society. This second model is structural in nature. It focuses on the relationship of the press to the communicative functions required by our democratic be-

> liefs. To the extent the press makes these functions possible, this model requires that it receive the protection of the First Amendment. A good example is the press' role in providing and circulating the information necessary for informed public discussion. To the extent the press, or, for that matter, to the extent that any institution uniquely performs this role, it should receive unique First Amendment protection.
>
> This "structural" model of the press has several important implications. It significantly extends the umbrella of the press' constitutional protections. The press is not only shielded when it speaks out, but when it performs all the myriad tasks necessary for it to gather and disseminate the news. As you can easily see, the stretch of this protection is theoretically endless. Any imposition of any kind on the press will in some measure affect its ability to perform protected functions. Therefore this model requires a Court to weigh the effects of the imposition against the social interests which are served by the imposition. This inquiry is impersonal, almost sociological in nature. But it does not fit comfortably with the absolutist rhetoric associated with the first model of the press I have discussed. For here, I repeat, the Court must weigh the effects of the imposition inhibiting press access against the social interests served by the imposition.

Does the Court apply the "speech" mode or the "structural" model to the facts in the *Minneapolis Star* case? Which model should it have applied?

The Meaning of the Press Clause: A Special Status For The Press?

In First National Bank of Boston v. Bellotti, 435 U.S. 765 (1978), the Supreme Court invalidated a Massachusetts statute prohibiting corporations from attempting to influence the vote on referendum proposals on issues of public importance which materially affect the property, business, or assets of the corporation. The Massachusetts Supreme Judicial Court upheld the statute and accorded corporations seeking to influence elections on matters not directly concerning such corporations less than full First Amendment protection by validating the statute. The Supreme Court, however, reversed the Massachusetts court. See text, p. 151.

The case did not directly answer the question of whether the free speech rights of corporations are protected, but it did hold that speech should be protected without reference to the identity of the speaker. Since *Bellotti* involved the free expression rights of business corporations, the question of whether media corporations, i.e., the institutional press, could make a greater claim to First Amendment protection than ordinary business corporations also arose. Justice Stewart, it will be recalled, had advanced the idea in a 1974 lecture that the press clause of the First Amendment had accorded a special status to the institutional press. See text, p. 7.

Under this theory, it would be possible to argue that media corporations could make a claim for fuller First Amendment protection than could ordinary business corporations. Indeed, in Stewart's 1974 lecture he had observed: "If the free speech clause guarantee meant no more than freedom of expression, it would be a constitutional redundancy." Justice Powell, who wrote the opinion for the Court, agreed that the press had a special and constitutionally recognized role: "The press cases emphasize the special and constitutionally recognized role of that institution in informing and educating the public, offering criticism, and providing a forum for discussion and debate." But Powell was, nonetheless, not disposed to take a hierarchical view of the First Amendment:

> If the speakers here were not corporations, no one would suggest that the state could validate silence of their

> proposed speech. It is the type of speech indispensable to decision-making in a democracy, and this is no less true because the speech comes from a corporation rather than an individual. The inherent worth of the speech in terms of its capacity for informing the public does not depend upon the identity of its source, whether corporation, association, union or individual.

Although Chief Justice Burger agreed with both the opinion and the result reached by the Court in *Bellotti,* he wrote a separate concurring opinion in order to pose some questions which he thought likely to arise in the future. The issue he particularly wished to discuss was "whether the press clause confers upon the 'institutional press' any freedom from governmental restraint not enjoyed by others."

FIRST NATIONAL BANK OF BOSTON v. BELLOTTI

435 U.S. 765, 98 S.CT. 1407, 55 L.ED.2D 707 (1978).

Chief Justice BURGER, concurring.

* * *

A disquieting aspect of Massachusetts' position is that it may carry the risk of impinging on the First Amendment rights of those who employ the corporate form—as most do—to carry on the business of mass communications, particularly the large media conglomerates. This is so because of the difficulty, and perhaps impossibility, of distinguishing, either as a matter of fact or constitutional law, media corporations from corporations such as the appellants in this case.

Making traditional use of the corporate form, some media enterprises have amassed vast wealth and power and conduct many activities, some directly related—and some not—to their publishing and broadcasting activities. See Miami Herald Publishing Co. v. Tornillo. Today, a corporation might own the dominant newspaper in one or more large metropolitan centers, television and radio stations in those same centers and others, a newspaper chain, news magazines with nationwide circulation, national or worldwide wire news services, and substantial interests in book publishing and distribution enterprises. Corporate ownership may extend, vertically, to pulp mills and pulp timber lands to insure an adequate, continuing supply of newsprint and to trucking and steamship lines for the purpose of transporting the newsprint to the presses. Such activities would be logical economic auxiliaries to a publishing conglomerate. Ownership also may extend beyond to business activities unrelated to the task of publishing newspapers and magazines or broadcasting radio and television programs. Obviously, such far-reaching ownership would not be possible without the state-provided corporate form and its "special rules relating to such matters as limited liability, perpetual life, and the accumulation, distribution, and taxation of assets. * * *"

In terms of "unfair advantage in the political process" and "corporate domination of the electoral process," it could be argued that such media conglomerates as I describe pose a much more realistic threat to valid interests than do appellants and similar entities not regularly concerned with shaping popular opinion on public issues. See Miami Herald Publishing Co. v. Tornillo, supra. In Tornillo, for example, we noted the serious contentions advanced that a result of the growth of modern media empires "has been to place in a few hands the power to inform the American people and shape public opinion." 418 U.S., at 250, 94 S.Ct., at 2836.

In terms of Massachusetts' other concern, the interests of minority shareholders, I perceive no basis for saying that the managers and directors of the media conglomerates are more or less sensitive to the views and desires of minority shareholders than are corporate officers generally.[1] Nor can it be said, even if relevant to First Amendment analysis—which it is not—that the former are more virtuous, wise or restrained in the exercise of corporate power than are the latter. Cf. Columbia Broadcasting System v. Democratic National Committee, 14 The Writings of Thomas Jefferson 46 (A. Libscomb ed. 1904) (letter to Walter Jones, Jan. 2, 1814). Thus, no factual distinction has been identified as yet that would justify government restraints on the right of appellants to express their views without, at the same time, opening the door to similar restraints on media conglomerates with their vastly greater influence.

Despite these factual similarities between media and nonmedia corporations, those who view the press clause as somehow conferring special and extraordinary privileges or status on the "institutional press"—which are not extended to those who wish to express ideas other than by publishing a newspaper—might perceive no danger to institutional media corporations flowing from the position asserted by Massachusetts. Under this narrow reading of the press clause, government could perhaps impose on nonmedia corporations restrictions not permissible with respect to "media" enterprises. Cf. Bezanson, The New Free Press Guarantee, 63 Va.L.Rev. 731, 767–770 (1977).[2] The Court has not yet squarely resolved whether the press clause confers upon the "institutional press" any freedom from government restraint not enjoyed by all others.[3]

I perceive two fundamental difficulties with a narrow reading of the press clause. First, although certainty on this point is not possible, the history of the clause does not suggest that the authors contemplated a "special" or "institutional" privilege. See Lange, the Speech and Press Clauses, 23 U.C.L.A.L.Rev. 77, 88–99 (1975). The common 18th century understanding of freedom of the press is suggested by Andrew Bradford, a colonial American newspaperman. In defining the nature of the liberty he did not limit it to a particular group:

> "But, by the Freedom of the Press, I mean a Liberty, within the Bounds of Law, for any Man to communicate to the Public, his sentiments on the Important Points of Religion and Government; of proposing any Laws, which he apprehends may be for the Good of his Country, and of applying for the Repeal of such, as he Judges pernicious. * * *
>
> "This is the Liberty of the Press, the great Palladium of all our other Liberties, which I hope the good People of this Province, will forever enjoy. * *" A. Bradford, Sentiments on the Liberty of the Press, in L. Levy, Freedom of the Press from Zenger to Jefferson 41–42 (1966) [emphasis deleted] [first published in Bradford's The American Weekly Mercury, a Philadelphia newspaper, April 25, 1734].

1. It may be that a nonmedia corporation, because of its nature, is subject to more limitations on political expression than a media corporation whose very existence is aimed at political expression. For example, the charter of a nonmedia corporation may be so framed as to tender such activity or expression *ultra vires;* or its shareholders may be much less inclined to permit expenditure for corporate speech. Moreover, a nonmedia corporation may find it more difficult to characterize its expenditures as ordinary and necessary business expenses for tax purposes.

2. It is open to question whether limitations can be placed on the free expression rights of some without undermining the guarantees of all. Experience with statutory limitations on campaign expenditures on behalf of candidates or parties may shed some light on this issue. Cf. Buckley v. Valeo.

3. Language in some cases perhaps may be read as assuming or suggesting no independent scope to the Press Clause, see Pell v. Procunier, or the contrary, see Bigelow v. Virginia. The Court, however, has not yet focused on the issue. See Lange, The Speech and Press Clauses, 23 U.C.L.A.L.Rev. 77 (1975); Nimmer, Is Freedom of the Press a Redundancy: What Does It Add to Freedom of Speech?, 26 Hastings L.J. 639 (1975); cf. Bezanson, The New Free Press Guarantee, 63 Va.L.Rev. 731 (1977).

Indeed most pre-First Amendment commentators "who employed the term 'freedom of speech' with great frequency, used it synonymously with freedom of the press." L. Levy, Legacy of Suppression: Freedom of Speech and Press in Early American History 174 (1963).

Those interpreting the press clause as extending protection only to, or creating a special role for, the "institutional press" must either (a) assert such an intention on the part of the Framers for which no supporting evidence is available, cf. Lange, supra, at 89–91; (b) argue that events after 1791 somehow operated to "constitutionalize" this interpretation, see Benzanson, The New Free Press Guarantee, 63 Va.L. Rev. 731, 788 (1977); or (c) candidly acknowledging the absence of historical support, suggest that the intent of the Framers is not important today. See Nimmer, Is Freedom of the Press a Redundancy: What Does It Add To Freedom of Speech?, 26 Hastings L.J. 639, 640–641 (1975).

To conclude that the Framers did not intend to limit the freedom of the press to one select group is not necessarily to suggest that the Press Clause is redundant. The speech clause standing alone may be viewed as a protection of the liberty to express ideas and beliefs,[4] while the press clause focuses specifically on the liberty to disseminate expression broadly and "comprehends every sort of publication which affords a vehicle of information and opinion." Lovell v. Griffin.[5] Yet there is no fundamental distinction between expression and dissemination. The liberty encompassed by the press clause, although complementary to and a natural extension of Speech Clause liberty, merited special mention simply because it had been more often the object of official restraints. Soon after the invention of the printing press, English and continental monarchs, fearful of the power implicit in its use and the threat to establishment thought and order—political and religious—devised restraints, such as licensing, censors, indices of prohibited books, and prosecutions for seditious libel, which generally were unknown in the pre-printing press era. Official restrictions were the official response to the new, disquieting idea that this invention would provide a means for mass communication.

The second fundamental difficulty with interpreting the press clause as conferring special status on a limited group is one of definition. See Lange, *supra*. The very task of including some entities within the

4. The simplest explanation of the speech and press clauses might be that the former protects oral communications; the latter, written. But the historical evidence does not strongly support this explanation. The first draft of what became the free expression provisions of the First Amendment, one proposed by Madison on May 5, 1789, as an addition to Art. 1, § 9, read:

"The people shall not be deprived or abridged of their right to speak, to write, or to publish their sentiments; and the freedom of the press, as one of the great bulwarks of liberty, shall be inviolable." I Annals of Cong. 451 (1789) (published as 1 Debates of Congress).

The language was changed to its current form, "freedom of speech, or of the press," by the Committee of Eleven to which Madison's amendments were referred. [There is no explanation for the change and the language was not altered thereafter.] It seems likely that the Committee shortened Madison's language preceding the semi-colon in his draft to "freedom of speech" without intending to diminish the scope of protection contemplated by Madison's phrase; in short, it was a stylistic change.

Cf. Kilbourn v. Thompson, 103 U.S. 168, 26 L.Ed. 377 (1881); Doe v. McMillan, 412 U.S. 306, 93 S.Ct. 2018, 36 L.Ed.2d 912 (1973) [Speech or Debate Clause extends to both spoken and written expressions within the legislative function].

5. It is not strange that "press," the word for what was then the sole means of broad dissemination of ideas and news, would be used to describe the freedom to communicate with a large, unseen audience.

Changes wrought by 20th century technology, of course, have rendered the printing press as it existed in 1791 as obsolete as Watt's copying or letter press. It is the core meaning of "press" as used in the constitutional text which must govern.

"institutional press" while excluding others, whether undertaken by legislature, court or administrative agency, is reminiscent of the abhorred licensing system of Tudor and Stuart England—a system the First Amendment was intended to ban from this country. Lovell v. Griffin. Further, the officials undertaking that task would be required to distinguish the protected from the unprotected on the basis of such variables as content of expression, frequency or fervor of expression, or ownership of the technological means of dissemination. Yet nothing in this Court's opinions supports such a confining approach to the scope of press clause protection.[6] Indeed, the Court has plainly intimated the contrary view:

> "Freedom of the press is a 'fundamental personal right' which 'is not confined to newspapers and periodicals. It necessarily embraces pamphlets and leaflets. * * * The press in its historic connotation comprehends every sort of publication which affords a vehicle of information and opinion.' * * * The information function asserted by representatives of the organized press * * * is also performed by lecturers, political pollsters, novelists, academic researchers, and dramatists. Almost any author may quite accurately assert that he is contributing to the flow of information to the public. * * *" Branzburg v. Hayes, quoting Lovell v. Griffin.

The meaning of the press clause, as a provision separate and apart from the speech clause, is implicated only indirectly by this case. Yet Massachusetts' position poses serious questions. The evolution of traditional newspapers into modern corporate conglomerates in which the daily dissemination of news by print is no longer the major part of the whole enterprise suggests the need for caution in limiting the First Amendment rights of corporations as such. Thus, the tentative probings of this brief inquiry are wholly consistent, I think, with the Court's refusal to sustain § 8's serious and potentially dangerous restriction on the freedom of political speech.

Because the First Amendment was meant to guarantee freedom to express and communicate ideas, I can see no difference between the right of those who seek to disseminate ideas by way of a newspaper and those who give lectures or speeches and seek to enlarge the audience by publication and wide dissemination. "[T]he purpose of the Constitution was not to erect the press into a privileged institution but to protect all persons in their right to print what they will as well as to utter it. '* * * [T]he liberty of the press is no greater and no less * * *' than the liberty of every citizen of the Republic." Pennekamp v. Florida (Frankfurter, J., concurring).

In short, the First Amendment does not "belong" to any definable category of persons or entities: it belongs to all who exercise its freedoms.

COMMENT

1. Did *Bellotti* really deal with whether corporate speech merits full First Amendment protection? That issue really was not considered. Powell, instead, said the issue was whether the corporate identity of the speech should affect its status under the First Amendment. What is Powell's attitude toward inequality in communicating power? From a First Amendment point of view, in Powell's view, all speakers have an equal claim to liberty of expression. In 1975, Professor Karst wrote: " 'Equality of status in the field of ideas' is not merely a first amendment value; it is

---

6. Near v. Minnesota, 283 U.S. 697, 51 S.Ct. 625, 75 L.Ed. 1357 (1931), which examined the meaning of freedom of the press, did not involve a traditional institutionalized newspaper but rather an occasional publication (nine issues) more nearly approximating the product of a pamphleteer than the traditional newspaper.

the heart of the amendment." See Karst, *Equality as a Central Principle in the First Amendment,* 43 U.Chi.L.Rev. 20 at 43 (1975).

2. In footnote 4 of his concurring opinion, Chief Justice Burger provides the historical background for his argument that the Framers, by making specific references to freedom of speech and press, did not intend to give a uniquely privileged constitutional status to the press. On the other hand, the Chief Justice agreed that the explicit mention of freedom of speech followed by the explicit mention of freedom of the press has some significance. The press clause is not redundant. Burger described the matter as follows: "To conclude that the Framers did not intend to limit the freedom of the press to one select group is not necessarily to suggest that the Press Clause is redundant." The fact that the press clause does not create a special First Amendment caste does not mean that the press clause, like the speech clause, cannot have separate purposes. The speech clause protects the freedom to express ideas, and the press clause protects the freedom to disseminate those ideas.

Burger mentioned some of the difficulties in accepting the thesis that the press clause accords a special protective status to the "institutional press" under the First Amendment. Such a theory would involve the courts in the difficult task of identifying who was a journalist and what publications should be deemed part of the "institutional press." Indeed, the Chief Justice pointed out that the *Near* case, one of the landmarks of the American law of free press, did not involve a "traditional institutionalized newspaper but rather an occasional newspaper." Moreover, it will be remembered that in *Branzburg*, the journalist's privilege case, text, p. 379, one of the reasons the Court refused to create a qualified First Amendment-based privilege was because of its aversion to deciding who was a journalist.

3. Burger wanted general business corporations to have First Amendment protection equivalent to that which would be accorded to media corporations alone under a "special status" theory. Was his purpose to provide a countervailing force to media power in the opinion process by arming business corporations with equivalent First Amendment protection? See Chief Justice Burger's opinion for the Court in *Miami Herald Publishing Co. v. Tornillo*, text p. 584. Does the "special status" theory have its origins in the *Tornillo* decision?

THE MEANING OF PROTECTED SPEECH UNDER THE FIRST AMENDMENT

Anonymous Speech

TALLEY v. CALIFORNIA

362 U.S. 60, 80 S.CT. 536, 4 L.ED.2D 559 (1960).

Justice BLACK delivered the opinion of the Court.

The question presented here is whether the provisions of a Los Angeles City ordinance restricting the distribution of handbills "abridge the freedom of speech and of the press secured against state invasion by the Fourteenth Amendment of the Constitution." The ordinance * * * provides:

"No person shall distribute any handbill in any place under any circumstances, which does not have printed on the cover, or the face thereof, the name and address of the following:

"(a) The person who printed, wrote, compiled or manufactured the same.

"(b) The person who caused the same to be distributed; provided, however, that in the case of a fictitious person or club, in addition to such fictitious name, the true names and addresses of the owners, managers or agents of the person sponsoring said hand-bill shall also appear thereon."

The petitioner was arrested and tried in a Los Angeles Municipal Court for violating this ordinance. It was stipulated that the petitioner had distributed handbills in Los Angeles, and two of them were presented in evidence. Each had printed on it the following:

> National Consumers Mobilization
> Box 6533
> Los Angeles 55, Calif.
> PLeasant 9–1576.

The handbills urged readers to help the organization carry on a boycott against certain merchants and businessmen, whose names were given, on the ground that, as one set of handbills said, they carried products of "manufacturers who will not offer equal employment opportunities to Negroes, Mexicans, and Orientals." There also appeared a blank, which, if signed, would request enrollment of the signer as a "member of National Consumers Mobilization," and which was preceded by a statement that "I believe that every man should have an equal opportunity for employment no matter what his race, religion, or place of birth."

The Municipal Court held that the information printed on the handbills did not meet the requirements of the ordinance, found the petitioner guilty as charged, and fined him $10. The Appellate Department of the Superior Court of the County of Los Angeles affirmed the conviction, rejecting petitioner's contention, timely made in both state courts, that the ordinance invaded his freedom of speech and press in violation of the Fourteenth and First Amendments to the Federal Constitution. 172 Cal.App.2d Supp. 797, 332 P.2d 447. Since this was the highest state court available to petitioner, we granted certiorari to consider this constitutional contention. 360 U.S. 928.

The broad ordinance now before us, barring distribution of "any hand-bill in any place under any circumstances," falls precisely under the ban of our prior cases unless this ordinance is saved by the qualification that handbills can be distributed if they have printed on them the names and addresses of the persons who prepared, distributed or sponsored them. * * * [T]he ordinance here is not limited to handbills whose content is "obscene or offensive to public morals or that advocates unlawful conduct." Counsel has urged that this ordinance is aimed at providing a way to identify those responsible for fraud, false advertising and libel. Yet the ordinance is in no manner so limited, nor have we been referred to any legislative history indicating such a purpose. Therefore we do not pass on the validity of an ordinance limited to prevent these or any other supposed evils. This ordinance simply bars all handbills under all circumstances anywhere that do not have the names and addresses printed on them in the place the ordinance requires.

There can be no doubt that such an identification requirement would tend to restrict freedom to distribute information and thereby freedom of expression. "Liberty of circulating is as essential to that freedom as liberty of publishing; indeed, without the circulation, the publication would be of little value." Lovell v. City of Griffin, 303 U.S. at page 452.

Anonymous pamphlets, leaflets, brochures and even books have played an important role in the progress of mankind. Persecuted groups and sects from time to time throughout history have been able to criticize oppressive practices and laws either anonymously or not at all.

* * *

Even the *Federalist Papers*, written in favor of the adoption of our Constitution, were published under fictitious names. It is plain that anonymity has sometimes been assumed for the most constructive purposes.

We have recently had occasion to hold in two cases that there are times and circumstances when states may not compel members of groups engaged in the dissemination of ideas to be publicly identified. The reason for those holdings was that identification and fear of reprisal might deter perfectly peaceful discussions of public matters of importance. This broad Los Angeles ordinance is subject to the same infirmity. We hold that it, like the Griffin, Georgia, ordinance, is void on its face.

The judgment of the Appellate Department of the Superior Court of the State of California is reversed and the cause is remanded to it for further proceedings not inconsistent with this opinion.

It is so ordered.

* * *

Justice Clark, whom Justice Frankfurter and Justice Whittaker join, dissenting.

* * *

COMMENT

1. The *Talley* case reveals the dilemma of reconciling freedom of information (interpreting that term to mean that all information on an issue ought to be put before the public) with a right of privacy (interpreting that term to mean, among many other things, the right to enter the opinion process anonymously). Phrasing the dilemma in this way, does the decision in *Talley* appear less satisfactory to you?

2. Justice Clark in dissent discerned the problems presented by blanket constitutional protection for anonymous speech in view of the requirement of the Federal Regulation of Lobbying Act that lobbyists divulge their identities and in view of the many states which have enacted corrupt practices legislation prohibiting among other matters the distribution of anonymous printed matter concerning political candidates. How can some regulation of anonymous speech be permitted, and, at the same time, how can the political rights of those whom identification would endanger be protected? Justice Clark suggested a means to accomplish these two objectives. He referred to N.A.A.C.P. v. Alabama, 357 U.S. 449 (1958). That was a case where the Court held that the N.A.A.C.P. could not constitutionally be required to divulge its membership lists to the state of Alabama because of the economic reprisal and physical jeopardy that such disclosure might mean for N.A.A.C.P. members. Clark argued that Talley made no showing that similar restraints would befall him. Did Justice Black respond to Clark's argument that anonymity can claim constitutional protection only when it is indispensable to the exercise of political rights? What counterarguments might be made to Clark's position?

3. Would a less broad statute than the one in *Talley* be constitutional? For a case which held that a New York statute making it a crime to distribute anonymous literature in connection with a political election campaign violated the First Amendment, see Zwickler v. Koota, 290 F.Supp. 244 (E.D.N.Y.1968), reversed on other grounds, Golden v. Zwickler, 394 U.S. 103 (1969).

Commercial Speech

VALENTINE v. CHRESTENSEN

316 U.S. 52, 62 S.CT. 920, 86 L.ED. 1262 (1942).

Justice ROBERTS delivered the opinion of the Court.

The respondent, a citizen of Florida, owns a former United States Navy submarine which he exhibits for profit. In 1940 he brought it to New York City and moored it at a state pier in the East River. He prepared and printed a handbill advertising the boat and soliciting visitors for a stated admission fee. On his attempting to distribute the bill in the city streets, he was advised by the petitioner, as police commissioner, that this activity would violate § 318 of the Sanitary Code which forbids distribution in the streets of commercial and business advertising matter, but was told that he might freely distribute handbills solely devoted to "information or a public protest."

Respondent thereupon prepared and showed to the petitioner, in proof form, a double-faced handbill. On one side was a revision of the original, altered by the removal of the statement as to admission fee but consisting only of commercial advertising. On the other side was a protest against the action of the City Dock Department in refusing the respondent wharfage facilities at a city pier for the exhibition of his submarine, but no commercial advertising. The Police Department advised that distribution of a bill containing only the protest would not violate § 318, and would not be restrained, but that distribution of the double-faced bill was prohibited. The respondent, nevertheless, proceeded with the printing of his proposed bill and started to distribute it. He was restrained by the police.

* * *

The question is whether the application of the ordinance to the respondent's activity, was, in the circumstances, an unconstitutional abridgement of the freedom of the press and of speech.

1. This Court has unequivocally held that the streets are proper places for the exercise of the freedom of communicating information and disseminating opinion and that, though the states and municipalities may appropriately regulate the privilege in the public interest, they may not unduly burden or proscribe its employment in these public thoroughfares. *We are equally clear that the Constitution imposes no such restraint on government as respects purely commercial advertising.* [Emphasis added.] Whether, and to what extent, one may promote or pursue a gainful occupation in the streets, to what extent such activity shall be adjudged a derogation of the public right of user, are matters for legislative judgment. The question is not whether the legislative body may interfere with the harmless pursuit of a lawful business, but whether it must permit such pursuit by what it deems an undesirable invasion of, or interference with, the full and free use of the highways by the people in fulfillment of the public use to which streets are dedicated. If the respondent was attempting to use the streets of New York by distributing commercial advertising, the prohibition of the code provision was lawfully invoked against his conduct.

2. The respondent contends that, in truth, he was engaged in the dissemination of matter proper for public information, none the less so because there was inextricably attached to the medium of such dissemination commercial advertising matter. The court below appears to have taken this view since it adverts to the difficulty of apportioning, in a given case, the contents of the communication as between what is of public interest and what is for private profit. We need not indulge nice appraisal based upon subtle distinctions in the present instance nor assume possible cases not now presented. It is enough for the present purpose that the stipulated facts justify the conclusion that the affixing of the protest against official conduct to the advertising circular was with the intent, and for the purpose, of evading the prohibition of the ordinance. If that evasion were successful, every merchant who desires to broadcast advertising leaflets in the streets need only append a civic appeal, or a moral platitude, to achieve immunity from the law's command.

The decree is reversed.

Reversed.

COMMENT

In *Valentine v. Chrestensen*, the Supreme Court held that commercial speech was outside the ambit of First Amendment protection and therefore subject to regulation by government. The Court believed that Chrestensen printed his noncommercial message solely to evade the regulatory provision. Chrestensen's subjective intent, in other words, belied his claim for First Amendment protection because it was merely a ploy to escape a lawful regulation of the City of New York. If Chrestensen were permitted to distribute his flyers, so could every merchant, simply by affixing to his advertising copy some expression of opinion or protest. The streets of New York would be filled with litter, the sanitary code provision to the contrary notwithstanding.

There may be a Keystone Kops air about *Valentine v. Chrestensen,* but the case for a time sowed the seeds of a constitutional doctrine of significance: the theory that the First Amendment does not embrace what Justice Roberts referred to as "purely" commercial speech. This would come to be called the commercial speech doctrine.

2. Note that *Valentine v. Chrestensen* was a unanimous decision. Why do you think Justice Black, for instance, agreed with the decision?

3. Did the *Chrestensen* doctrine establish a hierarchy for expression, i.e., some communications merit a greater claim to constitutional protection than others? Was the core of the *Chrestensen* doctrine that, if there is a "preference" for speech, the speech "preferred" is political rather than commercial speech? Is the process of distinguishing between such categories necessarily one that must be chiefly responsive to motive? If that is the case, doesn't the *Grosjean* (text, supra, p. 138) case forbid such considerations?

The Decline of the Commercial Speech Doctrine

The first in a series of cases which dealt a body blow to the idea that commercial speech is beyond the pale of First Amendment protection occurred in 1975. In Bigelow v. Virginia, 421 U.S. 809 (1975), the Court set aside the conviction of an editor of a weekly newspaper who had violated a Virginia state law by accepting an advertisement which announced placements in hospitals and clinics for low-cost abortions could be obtained in New York. The Virginia state law which forbade the circulation of publications encouraging the procuring of abortions was held unconstitutional.

Bigelow set forth a ground-breaking doctrine. The Court repudiated the idea that a category of commercial speech such as commercial advertising was "stripped of First Amendment protection merely because it appears in that form." The significance of *Bigelow* has been analyzed as follows:

> [I]t was no longer adequate, in dealing with commercial speech, merely to say that any reasonable state regulation would be permissible. With the advent of a new First Amendment status for commercial speech, the interests of the publisher, the reader, and the consumer would be weighed against any arguments advanced in favor of the statute by the state. The statute proscribed activity [abortion] which was now clearly legal, and the state was held to have failed to justify the ban on publication in view of the overriding interests urged by the editor on behalf of the readers. Therefore, in upholding the right of the editor to publish the advertisement in controversy in *Bigelow,* the Court's approach to commercial speech followed a traditional First Amendment balancing test technique.

See Barron and Dienes, *Handbook of Free Speech and Free Press* 168 (1979).

Bigelow was merely the first development in the waning of the commercial speech doctrine set forth in *Valentine v. Chrestensen.* The *coup de grâce* to the traditional doctrine was dealt by Virginia

State Board of Pharmacy v. Virginia Citizens Consumer Council, Inc., 425 U.S. 748 (1976) which follows.

VIRGINIA STATE BOARD OF PHARMACY v. VIRGINIA CITIZENS CONSUMER COUNCIL, INC.

425 U.S. 748, 96 S.CT. 1817, 48 L.ED.2D 346 (1976).

Justice BLACKMUN delivered the opinion of the Court.

The plaintiff-appellees in this case attack, as violative of the First and Fourteenth Amendments, that portion of § 54–524.35 of Va. Code Ann. (1974), which provides that a pharmacist licensed in Virginia is guilty of unprofessional conduct if he "(3) publishes, advertises or promotes, directly or indirectly, in any manner whatsoever, any amount, price, fee, premium, discount, rebate or credit terms for any drugs which may be dispensed only by prescription." The three-judge district court declared the quoted portion of the statute "void and of no effect," and enjoined the defendant-appellants, the Virginia State Board of Pharmacy and the individual members of that Board, from enforcing it.

The plaintiffs are an individual Virginia resident who suffers from diseases that require her to take prescription drugs on a daily basis, and two nonprofit organizations. Their claim is that the First Amendment entitles the user of prescription drugs to receive information, that pharmacists wish to communicate to them through advertising and other promotional means, concerning the prices of such drugs.

Certainly that information may be of value. Drug prices in Virginia, for both prescription and nonprescription items, strikingly vary from outlet to outlet even within the same locality. It is stipulated, for example, that in Richmond "the cost of 40 Achromycin tablets ranges from $2.59 to $6.00, a difference of 140% *[sic]*," and that in the Newport News-Hampton area the cost of tetracycline ranges from $1.20 to $9.00, a difference of 650%.

The question first arises whether, even assuming that First Amendment protection attaches to the flow of drug price information, it is a protection enjoyed by the appellees as recipients of the information, and not solely, if at all, by the advertisers themselves who seek to disseminate that information.

Freedom of speech presupposes a willing speaker. But where a speaker exists, as is the case here, the protection afforded is to the communication, to its source and to its recipients both. This is clear from the decided cases. If there is a right to advertise, there is a reciprocal right to receive the advertising, and it may be asserted by these appellees.

The appellants contend that the advertisement of prescription drug prices is outside the protection of the First Amendment because it is "commercial speech." There can be no question that in past decisions the Court has given some indication that commercial speech is unprotected.

Our question is whether speech which does "no more than propose a commercial transaction," *Pittsburgh Press Co. v. Pittsburgh Comm'n on Human Relations,* is so removed from any "exposition of ideas," *Chaplinsky v. New Hampshire,* and from " 'truth, science, morality, and arts in general, in its diffusion of liberal sentiments on the administration of Government.' " *Roth v. United States,* that it lacks all protection. Our answer is that it is not.

Focusing first on the individual parties to the transaction that is proposed in the commercial advertisement, we may assume that the advertiser's interest is a purely economic one. That hardly disqualifies him for protection under the First Amendment.

As to the particular consumer's interest in the free flow of commercial information, that interest may be as keen, if not keener by far, than his interest in the day's most urgent political debate. Appellees' case in this respect is a convincing one. Those whom the suppression of prescription drug price information hits the hardest are the poor, the sick, and particularly the aged. A disproportionate amount of their income tends to be spent on prescription drugs; yet they are the least able to learn, by shopping from pharmacist to pharmacist, where their scarce dollars are best spent.

Advertising, however tasteless and excessive it sometimes may seem, is nonetheless dissemination of information as to who is producing and selling what product, for what reason, and at what price. So long as we preserve a predominantly free enterprise economy, the allocation of our resources in large measure will be made through numerous private economic decisions. It is a matter of public interest that those decisions, in the aggregate, be intelligent and well informed. To this end, the free flow of commercial information is indispensable. And if it is indispensable to the proper allocation of resources in a free enterprise system, it is also indispensable to the formation of intelligent opinions as to how that system ought to be regulated or altered. Therefore, even if the First Amendment were thought to be primarily an instrument to enlighten public decisionmaking in a democracy, we could not say that the free flow of information does not serve that goal.

Arrayed against these substantial individual and societal interests are a number of justifications for the advertising ban. These have to do principally with maintaining a high degree of professionalism on the part of licensed pharmacists. Indisputably, the state has a strong interest in maintaining that professionalism.

It appears to be feared that if the pharmacist who wishes to provide the low cost, and assertedly low quality, services is permitted to advertise, he will be taken up on his offer by too many unwitting customers. They will choose the low-cost, low-quality service and drive the "professional" pharmacist out of business. They will respond only to costly and excessive advertising, and end up paying the price. They will go from one pharmacist to another, following the discount, and destroy the pharmacist-customer relationship. They will lose respect for the profession because it advertises. All this is not in their best interests, and all this can be avoided if they are not permitted to know who is charging what.

There is, of course, an alternative to this highly paternalistic approach. That alternative is to assume that this information is not in itself harmful, that people will perceive their own best interests if only they are well enough informed, and that the best means to that end is to open the channels of communication rather than to close them. If they are truly open, nothing prevents the "professional" pharmacist from marketing his own assertedly superior product, and contrasting it with that of the low-cost, high-volume prescription drug retailer. But the choice among these alternative approaches is not ours to make or the Virginia General Assembly's. It is precisely this kind of choice, between the dangers of suppressing information, and the dangers of its misuse if it is freely available, that the First Amendment makes for us. Virginia is free to require whatever professional standards it wishes of its pharmacists; it may subsidize them or protect them from competition in other ways. But it may not do so by keeping the public in ignorance of the entirely lawful terms that competing pharmacists are offering. In this sense, the justifications Virginia has offered for suppressing the flow of prescription drug price information, far from persuading us that the flow is not protected by the First Amendment, have re-enforced our view that it is. We so hold.

In concluding that commercial speech, like other varieties, is protected, we of course do not hold that it can never be regulated in any way. Some forms of commercial speech regulation are surely permissible. We mention a few only to make clear that they are not before us and therefore are not foreclosed by this case.

There is no claim, for example, that the prohibition on prescription drug price advertising is a mere time, place, and manner restriction. We have often approved restrictions of that kind provided that they are justified without reference to the content of the regulated speech, that they serve a significant governmental interest, and that in so doing they leave open ample alternative channels for communication of the information. Whatever may be the proper bounds of time, place, and manner restrictions on commercial speech, they are plainly exceeded by this Virginia statute, which singles out speech of a particular content and seeks to prevent its dissemination completely.

Nor is there any claim that prescription drug price advertisements are forbidden because they are false or misleading in any way. Untruthful speech, commercial or otherwise, has never been protected for its own sake. *Gertz v. Robert Welch, Inc.* Obviously, much commercial speech is not provably false, or even wholly false, but only deceptive or misleading. We foresee no obstacle to a State's dealing effectively with this problem.[24] The First Amendment, as we construe it today, does not prohibit the state from insuring that the stream of commercial information flows cleanly as well as freely.

Also, there is no claim that the transactions proposed in the forbidden advertisements are themselves illegal in any way. Cf. *Pittsburgh Press Co. v. Pittsburgh Comm'n on Human Relations.* Finally, the special problems of the electronic broadcast media are likewise not in this case.

What is at issue is whether a state may completely suppress the dissemination of concededly truthful information about entirely lawful activity, fearful of that information's effect upon its disseminators and its recipients. Reserving other questions, we conclude that the answer to this one is in the negative.

The judgment of the district court is affirmed.

Justice Stevens took no part in the consideration or decision of this case.

Justice Stewart, concurring.

The advertiser's access to the truth about his product and its price substantially eliminates any danger that governmental regulation of false or misleading price or product advertising will chill accurate and nondeceptive commercial expression. There is, therefore, little need to sanction "some falsehood in order to protect speech that matters." *Gertz v. Robert Welch, Inc.*

Justice Rehnquist, dissenting.

Under the Court's opinion the way will be open not only for dissemination of price information but for active promotion of prescription drugs, liquor, cigarettes and other products the use of which it has

24. In concluding that commercial speech enjoys First Amendment protection, we have not held that it is wholly undifferentiable from other forms. There are commonsense differences between speech that does "no more than purpose a commercial transaction," and other varieties. Even if the differences do not justify the conclusion that commercial speech is valueless, and thus subject to complete suppression by the state, they nonetheless suggest that a different degree of protection is necessary to insure that the flow of truthful and legitimate commercial information in unimpaired. The truth of commercial speech, for example, may be more easily verifiable by its disseminator than, let us say, news reporting or political commentary, in that ordinarily the advertiser seeks to disseminate information about a specific product or service that he himself provides and presumably knows more about than anyone else. Also, commercial speech may be more durable than other kinds. Since advertising is the *sine qua non* of commercial profits, there is little likelihood of its being chilled by proper regulation and foregone entirely.

Attributes such as these, the greater objectivity and hardiness of commercial speech, may make it less necessary to tolerate inaccurate statements for fear in silencing the speaker. They may also make it appropriate to require that a commercial message appear in such a form, or include such additional information, warnings and disclaimers, as are necessary to prevent it being deceptive.

previously been thought desirable to discourage. Now, however, such promotion is protected by the First Amendment so long as it is not misleading or does not promote an illegal product or enterprise.

There are undoubted difficulties with an effort to draw a bright line between "commercial speech" on the one hand and "protected speech" on the other, and the Court does better to face up to these difficulties than to attempt to hide them under labels. In this case, however, the Court has unfortunately substituted for the wavering line previously thought to exist between commercial speech and protected speech a no more satisfactory line of its own—that between "truthful" commercial speech, on the one hand, and that which is "false and misleading" on the other. The difficulty with this line is not that it waivers, but on the contrary that it is simply too Procrustean to take into account the congeries of factors which I believe could, quite consistently with the First and Fourteenth Amendments, properly influence a legislative decision with respect to commercial advertising.

COMMENT

1. Professor Edwin Baker has argued, based on his individual liberty model of the First Amendment, that "a complete denial of first amendment protection for commercial speech is not only consistent with, but is required by, first amendment theory." See Baker, *Commercial Speech: A Problem In The Theory of Freedom*, 62 Iowa L.Rev. 1 at 3 (1976). Baker provides the following argument against a protected status for commercial speech:

> [I]n our present historical setting, commercial speech is not a manifestation of individual freedom or choice. * * * [P]rofit-motivated or commercial speech lacks the crucial connections with individual liberty and self-realization which exist for speech generally, and which are central to justifications for the constitutional protection of speech, justifications which in turn define the proper scope of protection under the first amendment.

What values emphasized in *Virginia Pharmacy* does this analysis omit? It could be argued, certainly, that an individual with little in the way of economic resources and dependent for life on an expensive prescription drug might well find information as to the price of these drugs central to "self-realization."

2. Although *Virginia Pharmacy* gave new constitutional protection to commercial speech, it was still, to steal a phrase from George Orwell, a little less equal than other kinds of speech. (See fn. 24) and this text, p. 162. Part of the Court's problem was presented by the perceived need to regulate false and misleading advertising. Professor Redish has challenged some of the Court's reasoning for continuing to validate some regulation of commercial advertising. See Redish, *The Value of Free Speech*, 130 U.Pa.L.Rev. 591 at 633 (1982). Professor Redish questioned whether commercial claims are more easily verified than political ones. "[M]any statements made in the course of political debate—particularly by the press—are simply assertions of fact, which are presumably verifiable. * * * [M]any claims about commercial products, are, in reality, assertions of scientific fact. * * *"

Further, commercial and political expression are not easily distinguished in terms of relative "hardihood" in Professor Redish's view on the supposed "inherent profit nature" of commercial expression. But the press would not stop publishing either if it were requested. "Fear of regulation" might deter the press from dealing with controversy, but it would still publish. Similarly, "the possibility of regulation" would not cause the commercial advertiser to stop advertising, "but it might deter him from making controversial claims for his product."

The distinction between commercial and political speech, according to Professor Redish, has another rationale:

> We presumably find such regulation in the political process so abhorrent not because we wish to condone misleading political claims, but rather because of the dangers inherent in allowing the government to regulate on the basis of the misleading nature of assertions made in the political process. The fear is that those in power will use such authority as a weapon with which to intimidate or defeat the political opposition, a result that has been all too common in our political history. * * * In contrast, there is no reason to believe that much regulation of misleading advertising is similarly motivated.

Do you agree?

Another significant development in the line of cases according a higher degree of First Amendment protection to commercial speech is *Bates v. State Bar of Arizona.*

The case arose out of the following facts. Two members of the Arizona bar were charged with violating a state supreme court disciplinary rule which prohibited lawyers from advertising in newspapers as well as other media. The two lawyers, John Bates and Van O'Steen, opened up a "legal clinic" to serve people of moderate means. The clinic limited itself to "routine" legal services. In order to obtain a sufficient volume of business to make low-cost legal services possible, the two lawyers decided to advertise. They took out an ad in the Phoenix daily newspaper, *Arizona Republic*, where they listed the type of services which they could provide and the fees which they would charge, e.g., uncontested divorces–$100, uncontested adoptions–$225 plus a $10 publications fee. The state bar concluded that the two lawyers had violated the disciplinary rule against lawyer advertising, and the Arizona Supreme Court upheld that determination. The United States Supreme Court affirmed in part and reversed in part.

BATES v. STATE BAR OF ARIZONA

433 U.S. 350, 97 S.CT. 2691, 53 L.ED.2D 810 (1977).

Justice BLACKMUN delivered the opinion of the Court.

* * *

[The Court held that the state ban on lawyer advertising did not violate the Sherman Antitrust Act.]

* * *

[T]he conclusion that Arizona's disciplinary rule is violative of the First Amendment might be said to flow *a fortiori* from [the *Virginia Pharmacy* decision]. Like the Virginia statutes, the disciplinary rule serves to inhibit the free flow of commercial information and to keep the public in ignorance. Because of the possibility, however, that the differences among professions might bring different constitutional considerations into play, we specifically reserved judgment as to other professions.

In the instant case we are confronted with the arguments directed explicitly toward the regulation of advertising by licensed attorneys.

The issue presently before us is a narrow one. First, we need not address the peculiar problems associated with advertising claims relating to the *quality* of legal services. Such claims probably are not susceptible to precise measurement or verification and, under some circumstances, might well be deceptive or misleading to the public, or even false. Appellee does not suggest, nor do we perceive, that appellants' advertisement contained claims, extravagant or otherwise, as to the quality of services. Accordingly, we leave that issue for another day. Second, we also need not resolve the problems associated with in-person solicitation of clients—at the hospital room or the accident site, or in any other situation that breeds undue influence—by attorneys or their agents or "runners." Activity of that kind might well pose dangers of over-reaching and misrepresentation not encountered in newspaper announcement advertising. Hence, this issue also is not before us. Third, we note that appellee's criticism of advertising by attorneys does not apply with much force to some of the basic factual content of advertising: information as to the attorney's name, address, and telephone number, office hours, and the like. The American Bar Association itself has a provision in its current Code of Professional Responsibility that would allow the disclosure of such information, and more, in the classified section of the telephone directory. DR2–102(A)(6) (1976). We recognize, however, that an advertising diet limited to such spartan fare would provide scant nourishment.

The heart of the dispute before us today is whether lawyers also may constitutionally advertise the prices at which certain routine services will be performed. Numerous justifications are proffered for the restriction of such price advertising. [The Court considered each of these policy justifications and rejected them.] * * *

* * *

In the usual case involving a restraint on speech, a showing that the challenged rule served unconstitutionally to suppress speech would end our analysis. In the First Amendment context, the Court has permitted attacks on overly broad statutes without requiring that the person making the attack demonstrate that in fact his specific conduct was protected. * * * Having shown that the disciplinary rule interferes with protected speech, appellants ordinarily could expect to benefit regardless of the nature of their acts.

The First Amendment overbreadth doctrine, however, represents a departure from the traditional rule that a person may not challenge a statute on the ground that it might be applied unconstitutionally in circumstances other than those before the court. * * * The reason for the special rule in First Amendment cases is apparent: an overbroad statute might serve to chill protected speech. First Amendment interests are fragile interests, and a person who contemplates protected activity might be discouraged by the *in terrorem* effect of the statute. See NAACP v. Button, 371 U.S. 415, 433 (1963). Indeed, such a person might choose not to speak because of uncertainty whether his claim of privilege would prevail if challenged. The use of overbreadth analysis reflects the conclusion that the possible harm to society from allowing unprotected speech to go unpunished is outweighed by the possibility that protected speech will be muted.

But the justification for the application of overbreadth analysis applies weakly, if at all, in the ordinary commercial context. As was acknowledged in Virginia Pharmacy Board v. Virginia Consumer Council, there are "commonsense differences" between commercial speech and other varieties. Since advertising is linked to commercial well-being it seems unlikely that such speech is particularly susceptible to being crushed by overbroad regulation. Moreover, concerns for uncertainty in determining the scope of protection are reduced; the advertiser seeks to disseminate information about a product or service that he provides, and presumably he can determine more readily than others whether his speech is truthful and protected. Ibid. Since overbreadth has been described by this Court as "strong medicine," which "has been employed * * * sparingly and only as a last resort," we decline to apply it to professional advertising, a context where it is not necessary to further its intended objective.

* * *

We conclude that it has not been demonstrated that the advertisement at issue could be suppressed. [The Court concludes that the advertising in question is not misleading and "hence unprotected."]

In holding that advertising by attorneys may not be subjected to blanket suppression, and that the advertisement at issue is protected, we, of course, do not hold that advertising by attorneys may not be regulated in any way. We mention some of the clearly permissible limitations in advertising not foreclosed by our holding.

Advertising that is false, deceptive, or misleading of course is subject to restraint. See *Virginia Pharmacy Board v. Virginia Citizens Council.* Since the advertiser knows his product and has a commercial interest in its dissemination, we have little worry that regulation to assure truthfulness will discourage protected speech. And any concern that strict requirements for truthfulness will undesirably inhibit spontaneity seems inapplicable because commercial speech generally is calculated. Indeed, the public and private benefits from commercial speech derive from confidence in its accuracy and reliability. Thus, the leeway for untruthful or misleading expression that has been allowed in other contexts has little force in the commercial arena. * * * In fact, because the public lacks sophistication concerning legal services, misstatements that might be overlooked or deemed unimportant in other advertising may be found quite inappropriate in legal advertising. For example, advertising claims as to the quality of services—a matter we do not address today—are not susceptible to measurement or verification; accordingly, such claims may be so likely to be misleading as to warrant restriction. Similar objections might justify restraints on in-person solicitation. We do not foreclose the possibility that some limited supplementation, by way of warning or disclaimer or the like, might be required of even an advertisement of the kind ruled upon today so as to assure that the consumer is not misled. In sum, we recognize that many of the problems in defining the boundary between deceptive and nondeceptive advertising remain to be resolved, and we expect that the bar will have a special role to play in assuring that advertising by attorneys flows both freely and cleanly.

As with other varieties of speech, it follows as well that there may be reasonable restrictions on the time, place, and manner of advertising. See *Virginia Pharmacy Board v. Virginia Consumer Council.* Advertising concerning transactions that are themselves illegal obviously may be suppressed. See *Pittsburgh Press Co. v. Human Relations Comm'n.* And the special problems of advertising on the electronic broadcast media will warrant special consideration. * * *

The constitutional issue in this case is only whether the state may prevent the publication in a newspaper of appellant's truthful advertisement concerning the availability and terms of routine legal services. We rule simply that the flow of such information may not be restrained, and we, therefore hold the present application of the disciplinary rule against appellants to be violative of the First Amendment.

The judgment of the Supreme Court of Arizona is therefore affirmed in part and reversed in part.

It is so ordered.

Chief Justice Burger, concurring in part and dissenting in part.

* * *

Justice POWELL, with whom Justice Stewart joins, concurring in part and dissenting in part.

[T]he Court fails to give appropriate weight to the two fundamental ways in which the advertising of professional services differs from that of tangible products: the vastly increased potential for deception and the enhanced difficulty of effective regulation in the public interest.

* * *

Although I disagree strongly with the Court's holding as to price advertisements of undefined—and I believe undefinable—

routine legal services, there are reservations in its opinion worthy of emphasis since they may serve to narrow its ultimate reach. First, the Court notes that it had not addressed "the peculiar problems associated with advertisements containing claims as to the *quality* of legal services." * * * Nevertheless the Court's reservation in this respect could be a limiting factor.

Second, as in *Virginia Pharmacy*, the Court again notes that there may be reasonable restrictions on the time, place, and manner of commercial price advertising. In my view, such restrictions should have a significantly broader reach with respect to professional services than as to standardized products. This Court long has recognized the important state interests in the regulation of professional advertising. * * * Although the opinion today finds these interests insufficient to justify prohibition of all price advertising, the state interests recognized in these cases should be weighed carefully in any future consideration of time, place and manner restrictions.

Finally, the Court's opinion does not "foreclose the possibility that some limited supplementation, by way of warning or disclaimer or the like, might be required of even an advertisement of the kind ruled upon today so as to assure that the consumer is not misled." I view this as at least some recognition of the potential for deception inherent in fixed price advertising of specific legal services. This recognition, though ambiguous in light of other statements in the opinion, may be viewed as encouragement to those who believe—as I do—that if we are to have price advertisement of legal services, the public interest will require the most particular regulation.

Justice REHNQUIST, dissenting.

* * *

I continue to believe that the First Amendment speech provision, long regarded by this Court as a sanctuary for expressions of public importance or intellectual interest, is demeaned by invocation to protect advertisements of goods and services. I would hold quite simply that the appellants' advertisement, however truthful or reasonable it may be, is not the sort of expression that the Amendment was adopted to protect.

* * * Once the exception of commercial speech from the protection of the First Amendment which had been established by Valentine v. Chrestensen was abandoned, the shift to case-by-case adjudication of First Amendment claims of advertisers was a predictable consequence.

While I agree with my Brother Powell that the effect of today's opinion on the professions is both unfortunate and not required by the First and Fourteenth Amendments, I cannot join the implication in his opinion that some forms of legal advertising may be constitutionally protected. The *Valentine* distinction was constitutionally sound and practically workable, and I am still unwilling to take even one step down the slippery slope away from it.

COMMENT

1. *Bates* made a distinction between "routine" legal advertising which could not be validly prohibited and bans on "quality" advertising, the validity of which the Court postponed for resolution for another day. *Bates* left room for the state to regulate some kinds of professional advertising. Moreover, the Court limited its ruling to the type of advertising involved in *Bates,* e.g., print media advertising. *Bates* suggested that the case for regulation of professional advertising on the electronic media would be stronger than in the case of the print media. Why?

2. Further illustration that the First Amendment status of commercial speech is inferior to that of other forms of protected speech was found in the Court's discus-

sion of the overbreadth doctrine. Ordinarily, if some protected speech had been regulated by an invalid regulation, a person affected would have been free to have taken advantage of the invalidation of the regulation. But in *Bates* the Court still examined whether the advertisements in question were entitled to First Amendment protection.

3. In *Bates,* the Court reiterated that "[a]dvertising that is false, deceptive or misleading of course is subject to restraint." The Court specifically referred to the fact that "some limited supplementation, by way of warning or disclaimer" might be required even with respect to "routine" legal advertising. In Warner-Lambert Co. v. FTC, 562 F.2d 749 (D.C.Cir. 1977), an FTC order requiring the makers of Listerine to purchase future advertising to correct deceptive advertising resulting from its prior advertising was upheld. See this text, p. 594. See Miami Herald Publishing Co. v. Tornillo, 418 U.S. 241 (1974). If publishers cannot be compelled against their will, why can advertisers be compelled to speak against their will? Does the answer lie in the fact that commercial speech still occupies a lesser First Amendment status than does political speech?

In the *Listerine* case, the FTC-imposed remedy of mandatory corrective advertising was deemed to present no First Amendment problem on the ground that absent the corrective advertising "current and future" Listerine ads would "themselves [be] part of a continuing deception of the public." For the text of the decision in the *Warner–Lambert* case, see text, p. 625. The FTC order required Warner-Lambert, manufacturer of Listerine, to assert that Listerine would not help to "prevent colds or sore throats or lessen their severity." Judge J. Skelly Wright presented the issue for the Court in the *Listerine* case as follows: "Advertising which fails to rebut the prior claims as to Listerine's efficacy inevitably builds upon those claims; continued advertising continues the deception, albeit implicitly rather than explicitly."

As a result of *Warner–Lambert,* advertisers are now aware that the FTC may, in Listerine-type circumstances, compel them to include specific disclaimers in future advertising. The First Amendment justification for this, of course, is that false and deceptive advertising is not accorded full First Amendment protection. But won't the fear of mandatory corrective advertising in the future have a chilling effect on fully protected truthful speech? An advertiser may fear to make "true" claims for fear they may be called "false." See discussion of "overbreadth" in the *Bates* case, text, p. 164.

In *Warner–Lambert,* Judge Wright responded to this criticism by asserting that verifying the truth or falsity of commercial messages was easier than was the case with other kinds of expression. If the First Amendment were interpreted to permit the FTC only to force a cessation of further false advertising, advertisers, Judge Wright feared, would not be deterred since the public would already have been misled.

4. Another development in the general overhaul of the commercial speech doctrine which began with the *Bigelow* case was found in Linmark Associates, Inc. v. Township of Willingboro, 431 U.S. 85 (1977). The town of Willingboro, New Jersey had issued an ordinance forbidding the posting of "For Sale" or "Sold" signs. The point of the ordinance was to prevent a so-called "white" flight from a community whose black population was rapidly increasing. The Supreme Court, per Justice Marshall, ruled that the ordinance was unconstitutional.

The *Linmark* case showed that the First Amendment interest in providing both the buyer and society with an unrestricted flow of commercial information was of high dimension. State concern that use of the "For Sale" sign might cause the community to act irrationally would not justify restricting the most effective option for communication of a particular kind of commercial information—the use of the "For Sale" sign in front of the house to communicate a homeowner's desire to sell his house.

Linmark showed that the status of commercial speech is significant. Although commercial speech may not yet have attained the status of noncommercial speech, a case like *Linmark* demonstrates that the marketplace is worthy of inclusion in a constitutionally protected marketplace of ideas.

As a First Amendment matter, even when expression is protected, *time, place, and manner* regulations are, in appropriate circumstances, nevertheless permissible. Was the restriction on "For Sale" signs merely a restriction on the manner of expression? After all, other opportunities for advertising the sale of houses were available such as the classified columns of the newspapers. The Court refused to view the ordinance prohibiting "For Sale" signs as manner restrictions. The ordinance in the Court's opinion was concerned with restricting the content of a particular mode of communication. Since the Willingboro ordinance was not content-neutral and was designed to restrict a class of expression, even though the expression involved was commercial in character, the ordinance violated the First Amendment.

5. In Carey v. Population Services International, 431 U.S. 678 (1977), the Court invalidated a state ban on advertising or display of contraceptives. A justification offered for the ban was to limit illicit sexual behavior among youth. Neither the interest in protection of the young nor the commercial character of the expression regulated were sufficient to warrant validating the restriction in question.

Carey emphasized an important point about the new approach to commercial speech begun in *Virginia Pharmacy*—the invalidity of state efforts to abolish an entire class of advertising: "Just as in [*Virginia Pharmacy*] the statute challenged here seeks to suppress completely any information about the availability and price of contraceptives." [6] The Court recalled that in *Virginia Pharmacy,* it had held that "a state may not 'completely suppress the dissemination of concededly truthful information about entirely lawful activity,' even when that information could be categorized as 'commercial speech'."

The student should also consult the advertising section of this text where some of these cases are discussed from a regulation, instead of a First Amendment, point of view. See text, p. 605.

CENTRAL HUDSON GAS & ELECTRIC CORP. v. PUBLIC SERVICE COMMISSION

447 U.S. 557, 100 S.CT. 2343, 65 L.ED.2D 341 (1980).

Justice POWELL delivered the opinion of the Court.

This case presents the question whether a regulation of the Public Service Commission of the State of New York violates the First and Fourteenth Amendments because it completely bans promotional advertising by an electrical utility.

In December 1973, the commission, appellee here, ordered electric utilities in New York State to cease all advertising that "promot[es] the use of electricity."

6. The *Virginia Pharmacy* and *Bates* decisions should not, however, be thought to have sounded the death knell for all governmental prohibitions directed against entire categories of advertising. The validation of the federal legislation prohibiting all cigarette advertising on television discussed in connection with the *Capital Broadcasting Co.* case, text, p. 857, has survived the new commercial speech decisions. In *Bates,* the Court remarked on the point as follows: "[S]pecial problems of advertising on the electronic broadcast media will warrant special consideration. Cf. Capital Broadcasting Co. v. Mitchell."

The order was based on the commission's finding that "the interconnected utility system in New York State does not have sufficient fuel stocks or sources of supply to continue furnishing all customer demands for the 1973–1974 winter."

Three years later, when the fuel shortage had eased, the commission requested comments from the public on its proposal to continue the ban on promotional advertising. Central Hudson Gas & Electric Corporation, the appellant in this case, opposed the ban on First Amendment grounds. After reviewing the public comments, the commission extended the prohibition in a policy statement issued on February 25, 1977.

The policy statement divided advertising expenses "into two broad categories: promotional—advertising intended to stimulate the purchase of utility services—and institutional and informational, a broad category inclusive of all advertising not clearly intended to promote sales." The commission declared all promotional advertising contrary to the national policy of conserving energy. It acknowledged that the ban is not a perfect vehicle for conserving energy. Still, the commission adopted the restriction because it was deemed likely to "result in some dampening of unnecessary growth" in energy consumption.

The commission's order explicitly permitted "informational" advertising designed to encourage "*shifts* of consumption" from peak demand times to periods of low electricity demand. [Emphasis in original.] Informational advertising would not seek to increase aggregate consumption, but would invite a leveling of demand throughout any given 24-hour period. The agency offered to review "specific proposals by the companies for specifically described [advertising] programs that meet these criteria."

Appellant challenged the order in state court, arguing that the commission had restrained commercial speech in violation of the First and Fourteenth Amendments. The commission's order was upheld by the trial court and at the intermediate appellate level. The New York Court of Appeals affirmed.

The commission's order restricts only commercial speech, that is, expression related solely to the economic interests of the speaker and its audience. In applying the First Amendment to this area, we have rejected the "highly paternalistic" view that government has complete power to suppress or regulate commercial speech. Even when advertising communicates only an incomplete version of the relevant facts, the First Amendment presumes that some accurate information is better than no information at all.

Nevertheless, our decisions have recognized "the 'common-sense' distinction between speech proposing a commercial transaction, which occurs in an era traditionally subject to government regulation, and other varieties of speech." The Constitution therefore accords a lesser protection to commercial speech than to other constitutionally guaranteed expression. The protection available for particular commercial expression turns on the nature both of the expression and of the governmental interests served by its regulation.

The First Amendment's concern for commercial speech is based on the informational function of advertising. Consequently, there can be no constitutional objection to the suppression of commercial messages that do not accurately inform the public about lawful activity. The government may ban forms of communications more likely to deceive the public than to inform it.

If the communication is neither misleading nor related to unlawful activity, the government's power is more circumscribed. The state must assert a substantial interest to be achieved by restrictions on commercial speech. Moreover, the regulatory technique must be in proportion to that interest. The limitation on expression must be designed carefully to achieve the state's goal. Compliance with this requirement may be measured by two criteria. First, the restriction must directly advance the state interest involved: the regulation may not be sustained if it provides only ineffective or remote support for the government's purpose. Second, if the governmental interest could be served as well by a more limited restriction on commercial speech, the excessive restrictions cannot survive.

Under the first criterion, the court has declined to uphold regulations that only indirectly advance the state interest involved.

The second criterion recognizes that the First Amendment mandates that speech restrictions be "narrowly drawn." The regulatory technique may extend only as far as the interest it serves. The state cannot regulate speech that posess no danger to the asserted state interest, nor can it completely suppress information when narrower restrictions on expression would serve its interest as well.

In commercial speech cases, then, a four-part analysis has developed. At the outset, we must determine whether the expression is protected by the First Amendment. For commercial speech to come within that provision, it at least must concern lawful activity and not be misleading. Next, we ask whether the asserted governmental interest is substantial. If both inquiries yield positive answers, we must determine whether the regulation directly advances the governmental interest asserted, and whether it is not more extensive than is necessary to serve that interest.

We now apply this four-step analysis for commercial speech to the commission's arguments in support of its ban on promotional advertising.

The commission does not claim that the expression at issue either is inaccurate or relates to unlawful activity. Yet the New York Court of Appeals questioned whether Central Hudson's advertising is protected commercial speech. Because appellant holds a monopoly over the sale of electricity in its service area, the state court suggested that the commission's order restricts no commercial speech of any worth. The court stated that advertising in a "noncompetitive market" could not improve the decision making of consumers. The court saw no constitutional problem with barring commercial speech that it viewed as conveying little useful information.

We come finally to the critical inquiry in this case: whether the commission's complete suppression of speech ordinarily protected by the First Amendment is no more extensive than necessary to further the state's interest in energy conservation. The commission's order reaches all promotional advertising, regardless of the impact of the touted service on overall energy use. But the energy conservation rationale, as important as it is, cannot justify suppressing information about electric devices or services that would cause no net increase in total energy use. In addition, no showing has been made that a more limited restriction on the content of promotional advertising would not serve adequately the state's interests.

The commission also had not demonstrated that its interest in conservation cannot be protected adequately by more limited regulation of appellant's commercial expression. To further its policy of conservation, the commission could attempt to restrict the format and content of Central Hudson's advertising. It might, for example, require that the advertisements include information about the relative efficiency and expense of the offered service, both under current conditions and for the foreseeable future. In the absence of a showing that more limited speech regulations would be ineffective, we cannot approve the complete suppression of Central Hudson's advertising.

Justice BLACKMUN, with whom Justice Brennan joins concurring.

The Court asserts, that "a four-part analysis has developed" from our decisions concerning commercial speech. Under this four-part test a restraint on commercial "communication [that] is neither misleading nor related to unlawful activity" is subject to an intermediate level of scrutiny, and suppression is permitted whenever it "directly advance[s]" a "substantial" governmental interest and is "not more extensive than is necessary to serve that interest." I agree with the Court that this level of intermediate scrutiny is appropriate for a restraint on commercial speech designed to protect consumers from misleading or coercive speech, or a regulation related to the time, place, or manner of commercial speech. I do not agree, however, that the Court's four-part test is the proper one to be applied when a state seeks to suppress information about a product in order to manipulate a private economic decision that the state cannot or has not regulated or outlawed directly.

It appears that the Court would permit the state to ban all direct advertising of air conditioning, assuming that a more limited restriction on such advertising would not effectively deter the public from cooling its homes. In my view, our cases do not support this type of suppression. If a governmental unit believes that use or overuse of air conditioning is a serious problem, it must attack that problem directly, by prohibiting air conditioning or regulating thermostat levels. Just as the Commonwealth of Virginia may promote professionalism of pharmacists directly, so too New York may *not* promote energy conservation "by keeping the public in ignorance." *Virginia Pharmacy Board.*

Justice STEVENS, with whom Justice Brennan joins, concurring.

Because "commercial speech" is afforded less constitutional protection than other forms of speech, it is important that the commercial speech concept not be defined too broadly lest speech deserving of greater constitutional protection be inadvertently suppressed. The issue in this case is whether New York's prohibition on the promotion of the use of electricity through advertising is a ban on nothing but commercial speech.

In my judgment one of the two definitions the Court uses in addressing that issue is too broad and the other may be somewhat too narrow. The Court first describes commercial speech as "expression related solely to the economic interests of the speaker and its audience." Although it is not entirely clear whether this definition uses the subject matter of the speech or the motivation of the speaker as the limiting factor, it seems clear to me that it encompasses speech that is entitled to the maximum protection afforded by the First Amendment. Neither a labor leader's exhortation to strike, nor an economist's dissertation on the money supply, should receive any lesser protection because the subject matter concerns only the economic interests of the audience. Nor should the economic motivation of a speaker qualify his constitutional protection: even Shakespeare may have been motivated by the prospect of pecuniary reward. Thus, the Court's first definition of commercial speech is unquestionably too broad.

The Court's second definition refers to "speech proposing a commercial transaction." A salesman's solicitation, a broker's offer, and a manufacturer's publication of a price list or the terms of his standard warranty would unquestionably fit within this concept. Whatever the precise contours of the concept, and perhaps it is too early to enunciate an exact formulation, I am persuaded that it should not include the entire range of communication that is embraced within the term "promotional advertising."

This case involves a governmental regulation that completely bans promotional advertising by an electric utility. This ban encompasses a great deal more than mere proposals to engage in certain kinds of commercial transactions. It prohibits all advocacy of the immediate or future use of electricity. It curtails expression by an informed and interested group of persons of their point of view on questions relating to the production and consumption of electrical energy—questions frequently discussed and debated by our political leaders. The breadth of the ban thus exceeds the boundaries of the commercial speech concept, however that concept may be defined.

I concur in the result because I do not consider this to be a "commercial speech" case. Accordingly, I see no need to decide whether the Court's four-part analysis, adequately protects commercial speech—as properly defined—in the face of a blanket ban of the sort involved in this case.

Justice REHNQUIST, dissenting.

The Court's analysis in my view is wrong in several respects. Initially, I disagree with the Court's conclusion that the speech of a state-created monopoly, which is the subject of a comprehensive regulatory scheme, is entitled to protection under the First Amendment. I also think that the Court errs here in failing to recognize that the state law is most accurately viewed as an economic regulation and that the speech involved (if it falls within the scope of the First Amendment at all) occupies a significantly more subordinate position in the hierarchy of First Amendment values than the Court gives it today. Finally, the Court in reaching its decision improperly substitutes its own judgment for that of the state in deciding how a proper ban on promotional advertising should be drafted. With regard to this latter point, the Court adopts as its final part of a four-part test a "no more extensive than necessary" analysis that will unduly impair a state legislature's ability to adopt legislation reasonably designed to promote interests that have always been rightly thought to be of great importance to the state.

I think New York's ban on such advertising falls within the scope of permissible state regulation of an economic activity by an entity that could not exist in corporate form, say nothing of enjoy monopoly status, were it not for the laws of New York.

This Court has previously recognized that although commercial speech may be entitled to First Amendment protection, that protection is not as extensive as that accorded to the advocacy of ideas.

The test adopted by the Court elevates the protection accorded commercial speech that falls within the scope of the First Amendment to a level that is virtually indistinguishable from that of noncommercial speech. I think the Court in so doing has effectively accomplished the "devitalization" of the First Amendment that it counseled against in *Ohralik*. I think it has also by labeling economic regulation of business conduct as a restraint on "free speech" gone far to resurrect the discredited doctrine of cases such as *Lochner*. New York's order here is in my view more akin to an economic regulation to which virtually complete deference should be accorded by this Court.

[I]n a number of instances government may constitutionally decide that societal interests justify the imposition of restrictions on the free flow of information. When the question is whether a given commercial message is protected, I do not think this Court's determination that the information will "assist" consumers justifies judicial invalidation of a reasonable drafted state restriction on such speech when the restriction is designed to promote a concededly substantial state interest. I consequently disagree with the Court's conclusion that the societal interest in the dissemination of commercial information is sufficient to justify a restriction on the State's authority to regulate promotional advertising by utilities; indeed, in the case of a regulated monopoly, it is difficult for me to distinguish "society" from the state legislature and the Public Service Commission. Nor do I think there is any basis for concluding that individual citizens of the state will recognize the need for and act to promote energy conservation to the extent the government deems appropriate, if only the channels of communication are left open. Thus, even if I were to agree that commercial speech is entitled to some First Amendment protection, I would hold here that the state's decision to ban promotional advertising, in light of the substantial state interest at stake, is a constitutionally permissible exercise of its power to adopt regulations designed to promote the interests of its citizens.

The notion that more speech is the remedy to expose falsehood and fallacies is wholly out of place in the commercial bazaar, where if applied logically the remedy of one who was defrauded would be merely a statement, available upon request, reciting the Latin maxim "*caveat emptor.*" But since "fraudulent speech" in this area is to be remediable under *Virginia Board,* the remedy of one defrauded is a lawsuit or an agency proceeding based on common law notions of fraud that are separated by a world of difference from the realm of politics and government. What time, legal decisions, and common sense have so widely severed, I declined to join in *Virginia Board,* and regret now to see the Court reaping the seeds that it there sowed. For in a democracy, the economic is subordinate to the political, a lesson that our ancestors learned long ago, and that our descendants will undoubtedly have to relearn many years hence.

It is [in] my view inappropriate for the Court to invalidate the state's ban on commercial advertising here based on its speculation that in some cases the advertising may result in a net savings in electrical energy use, and in the cases in which it is clear a net energy savings would result from utility advertising the Public Service Commission would apply its ban so as to proscribe such advertising. Even assuming that the Court's speculation is correct, I do not think it follows that facial invalidation of the ban is the appropriate course.

COMMENT

Does *Central Hudson* take the commercial speech doctrine back to the *Valentine v. Chrestensen* era? This probably would be an unjustified conclusion. *Valentine* suggested that a rational basis asserted by the state to support regulation of commercial speech would be valid. The four-part test of *Central Hudson,* after all, does make it possible to regulate some commercial speech. On the other hand, the four-part test of *Central Hudson* limits the state's incursion into commercial speech.

Is *Central Hudson* a departure from the broad protection for commercial speech promised by *Virgina Pharmacy*? Justice Blackmun observed in *Virginia Pharmacy*: "Some forms of commercial speech regulation are surely permissible." Blackmun mentioned as examples time, place, and manner restrictions, false and misleading advertising, or advertising proposing transactions which are illegal. But the *Central Hudson* doctrine cuts deeper into the fabric of commercial speech than do the examples cited by Justice Blackmun. Isn't the teaching of *Central Hudson* that a "narrowly drawn" statute regulating commercial speech is valid against First Amendment attack? In short, if the criteria of the four-part test are met, the state may regulate.

In Metromedia, Inc. v. San Diego, 453 U.S. 490 (1981), a San Diego ordinance barring most types of billboard advertising was invalidated, but no common rationale attracted a majority of the Court. A plurality opinion for the court, written by Justice White and joined by three others, found the constitutional infirmity of the ordinance to be that while on-site commercial billboard advertising was permitted, other commercial billboard advertising, as well as noncommercial advertising (with some exceptions), was not permitted. The ban on noncommercial advertising was deemed impermissible by Justice White:

> "With respect to noncommercial speech, the city may not choose the appropriate subjects for public discourse. Because some noncommercial messages may be conveyed on billboards throughout the commercial and industrial zones, San Diego must similarly allow billboards conveying other noncommercial messages throughout those zones."

What of the distinction San Diego made between on-site commercial billboards which were permitted and off-site commercial advertising which was not? Was the distinction valid? Justice White said that it was:

> As we see it, the city could reasonably conclude that a commercial enterprise—as well as the interested public—has a stronger interest in identifying its place of business and advertising the products or services available there than it has in using or leasing its available space for the purpose of advertising commercial enterprises located elsewhere. It does not follow from the fact that the city has concluded that some commercial interests outweigh its municipal interests in this context that it must give similar weight to all other commercial advertising. Thus, off-site commercial billboards may be prohibited while on-site commercial billboards are permitted.
>
> The constitutional problem in this area requires resolution of the conflict between the city's land-use interests and the commercial interests of those seeking to purvey goods and services within the city. In light of the above analysis, we cannot conclude that the city has drawn an ordinance broader than is necessary to meet its interests, or that it fails directly to advance substantial government interests. In sum, insofar as it regulates commercial speech the San Diego ordinance meets the constitutional requirements of *Central Hudson*.

A majority of the justices did agree, however, that an ordinance which was drawn with sufficient precision to prohibit only commercial billboard advertising could be valid. In a concurring opinion, Justice Brennan disagreed with that conclusion:

> More importantly, I cannot agree with the plurality's view that an ordinance totally banning commercial billboards but allowing noncommercial billboards would be constitutional. For me, such an ordinance raises First Amendment problems at least as serious as those raised by a total ban, for it gives city officials the right—before approving a billboard—to determine whether the proposed message is "commercial" or "noncommercial." Of course the plurality is correct when it observes that "our cases have consistently distinguished between the constitutional protection afforded commercial as opposed to noncommercial speech," but it errs in assuming that a *governmental unit* may be put in the position in the first instance of deciding whether the proposed speech is commercial or noncommercial. In individual cases, this distinction is anything but clear. Because making such determinations would entail a substantial exercise of discretion by city's officials, it presents a real danger of curtailing noncommercial speech in the guise of regulating commercial speech.

In a recent article, Professor Martin Redish has characterized *Metromedia* as an example of a case where the Court confused subject matter categorizations with content regulation. See, Redish, *The Content Distinction in First Amendment Analysis*, 34 Stan.L.Rev. 1 at 128 (1981):

> [I]t is significant that, in response to the Chief Justice's argument (in dissent) that the Court's function should be limited to assuring governmental neutrality in regulating speech (Burger, C.J., dissenting), the Court did not argue

> that even such content-neutral regulations could significantly impair first amendment interests. Rather, Justice White's plurality opinion merely noted that the traditional concern for neutrality "is applicable to the facts of this case" because "San Diego has chosen to favor certain kinds of messages—such as on-site commercial advertising and temporary political campaign advertisements—over others." The dissent failed to explain, Justice White said, "why San Diego should not be held to have violated this concept of First Amendment neutrality." The decision, then, appears to be nothing more than another instance—like *Mosley* [Police Department v. Mosley, 408 U.S. 92 (1972)]—in which the Court aberrationally decides to view subject matter categorization as a form of content regulation and therefore subject to a stricture form of scrutiny.

Why is subject matter categorization less dangerous from a First Amendment point of view than content regulation?

Compelled Speech

In Abood v. Detroit Board of Education, 431 U.S. 209 (1977), in an opinion by Justice Stewart, the Court cautioned that the state in a regime ordered by the First Amendment could not require an individual to express or support an ideology he did not share. The Court was not altogether consistent in its holding in *Abood.* The Court first held that a law imposing service charges, equivalent to union dues, assessed against nonmembers of the union "to finance expenditures by the union for the purposes of collective bargaining, contract administration, and grievance adjustment" was valid. The Court summarized its position on this point as follows:

> To be required to help finance the union as a collective-bargaining agent may well be thought, therefore, to interfere in some way with an employee's freedom to associate for the advancement of ideas, or to refrain from doing so, as he sees fit. But the judgment * * is that such interference as exists is constitutionally justified by the legislative assessment of the important contribution of the union shop to the system of labor relations established by Congress. * * *

In a separate concurrence, Justice Powell, joined by Chief Justice Burger and Justice Blackmun, disagreed with the Court on the foregoing point. See Buckley v. AFTRA, 496 F.2d 305 (2d Cir. 1974), cert. den. 419 U.S. 1093 (1975), text, p. 666.

However, the Court took a different view in the case of compulsory service charges which were to be used for political or ideological purposes not related to the union's role as a collective bargaining representative.

ABOOD v. DETROIT BOARD OF EDUCATION

431 U.S. 209, 97 S.CT. 1782, 52 L.ED.2D 261 (1977).

Justice STEWART delivered the opinion of the Court.

* * * Our decisions establish with unmistakable clarity that the freedom of an individual to associate for the purpose of advancing beliefs and ideas is protected by the First and Fourteenth Amendments. Equally clear is the proposition that a government may not require an individual to relinquish rights guaranteed him by the First Amendment as a condition of public employment. The appellants argue that they fall within the protection of these cases because they have been prohibited not from actively associating, but rather from refusing to associate. They specifically argue that they may constitutionally prevent the Union's spending a part of their required service fees to contribute to political candidates and to express political views unrelated to its duties as exclusive bargaining representative. We have concluded that this argument is a meritorious one.

One of the principles underlying the Court's decision in Buckley v. Valeo, 424 U.S. 1, was that contributing to an organization for the purpose of spreading a political message is protected by the First Amendment. Because "[m]aking a contribution * * * enables like-minded persons to pool their resources in furtherance of common political goals," the Court reasoned that limitations upon the freedom to contribute "implicate fundamental First Amendment interests."

The fact that the appellants are compelled to make, rather than prohibited from making, contributions for political purposes works no less an infringement of their constitutional rights. For at the heart of the First Amendment is the notion that an individual should be free to believe as he will, and that in a free society one's beliefs should be shaped by his mind and his conscience rather than coerced by the State. And the freedom of belief is no incidental or secondary aspect of the First Amendment's protections:

> If there is any fixed star in our constitutional constellation, it is that no official, high or petty, can prescribe what shall be orthodox in politics, nationalism, religion, or other matters of opinion or force citizens to confess by word or act their faith therein." West Virginia Board of Education v. Barnette, 319 U.S. 624.

These principles prohibit a State from compelling any individual to affirm his belief in God, Torcaso v. Watkins, 367 U.S. 488, or to associate with a political party, Elrod v. Burns, 427 U.S. at 363–364, n. 17, 95 S.Ct. at 2685, as a condition of retaining public employment. They are no less applicable to the case at bar, and they thus prohibit the appellees from requiring any of the appellants to contribute to the support of an ideological cause he may oppose as a condition of holding a job as a public school teacher.

We do not hold that a union cannot constitutionally spend funds for the expression of political views, on behalf of political candidates, or towards the advancement of other ideological causes not germane to its duties as collective bargaining representative. Rather, the Constitution requires only that such expenditures be financed from charges, dues, or assessments paid by employees who do not object to advancing those ideas and who are not coerced into doing so against their will by the threat of loss of governmental employment.

There will, of course, be difficult problems in drawing lines between collective bargaining activities, for which contributions may be compelled, and ideological activities unrelated to collective bargaining, for which such compulsion is prohibited.

* * *

WOOLEY v. MAYNARD

430 U.S. 705, 97 S.CT. 1428, 51 L.ED.2D 752 (1977).

[EDITORIAL NOTE

In *Wooley*, the Court encountered the following fact pattern. A married couple, Jehovah's Witnesses, had covered up the state motto "Live Free or Die" on their New Hampshire automobile license plate. The couple had covered up the motto because it was contrary to their religious and moral beliefs. Could New Hampshire constitutionally enforce criminal sanctions against the couple for so doing? The Court held that New Hampshire could not.]

Chief Justice BURGER delivered the opinion of the Court.

* * *

We are thus faced with the question of whether the state may constitutionally require an individual to participate in the dissemination of an ideological message by displaying it on his private property in a manner and for the express purpose that it be observed and read by the public. We hold that the state may not do so.

We begin with the proposition that the right of freedom of thought protected by the First Amendment against state action includes both the right to speak freely and the right to refrain from speaking at all. See West Virginia State Board of Education v. Barnette, 319 U.S. 624, (1943). A system which secures the right to proselytize religious, political, and ideological causes must also guarantee the concomitant right to decline to foster such concepts. The right to speak and the right to refrain from speaking are complementary components of the broader concept of "individual freedom of mind." This is illustrated by the recent case of Miami Herald Publishing Co. v. Tornillo, 418 U.S. 241, (1974), where we held unconstitutional a Florida statute placing an affirmative duty upon newspapers to publish the replies of political candidates whom they had criticized. We concluded that such a requirement deprived a newspaper of the fundamental right to decide what to print or omit. * * * [See text, p. 584.]

The Court in *Barnette, supra*, was faced with a state statute which required public school students to participate in daily public ceremonies by honoring the flag both with words and traditional salute gestures. In overruling its prior decision in Minersville School District v. Gobitis, 310 U.S. 586 (1940), the Court held that "a ceremony so touching matters of opinion and political attitude may [not] be imposed upon the individual by official authority under powers committed to any political organization under our Constitution." Compelling the affirmative act of a flag salute involved a more serious infringement upon personal liberties than the passive act of carrying the state motto on a license plate, but the difference is essentially one of degree. Here, as in *Barnette*, we are faced with a state measure which forces an individual, as part of his daily life—indeed constantly while his automobile is in public view—to be an instrument for fostering public adherence to an ideological point of view he finds unacceptable. In doing so, the state "invades the sphere of intellect and spirit which it is the purpose of the First Amendment to our Constitution to reserve from all official control."

New Hampshire's statute in effect requires that appellees use their private property as a "mobile billboard" for the state's ideological message—or suffer a penalty, as Maynard already has. As a condition to driving an automobile—a virtual necessity for most Americans—the Maynards must display "Live Free or Die" to hundreds of people each day. The fact that most individuals agree with the thrust of New Hampshire's motto is not the test; most Americans also find the flag salute acceptable. The First Amendment protects the right of individuals to hold a point of view different from the majority and to refuse to foster, in the way New Hampshire commands, an idea they find morally objectionable.

Identifying the Maynards' interests as implicating First Amendment protections does not end our inquiry however. We must also determine whether the state's countervailing interest is sufficiently compelling to justify requiring appellees to display the state motto on their license plates. The two interests advanced by the state are that display of the motto (1) facilitates the identification of passenger vehicles, and (2) promotes appreciation of history, individualism and state pride.

The state first points out that only passenger vehicles, but not commercial, trailer, or other vehicles are required to display the state motto. Thus, the argument proceeds, officers of the law are more easily able to determine whether passenger vehicles are carrying the proper plates. However the record here reveals that New Hampshire passenger license plates normally consist of a specific configuration of letters and numbers, which makes them readily distinguishable from other types of plates, even without reference to state motto. Even were we to credit the state's reasons and "even though the governmental purpose be legitimate and substantial, that purpose cannot be pursued by means that broadly stifle fundamental personal liberties when the end can be more narrowly achieved. The breadth of legislative abridgment must be viewed in the light of less drastic means for achieving the same basic purpose." Shelton v. Tucker, 364 U.S. 479 (1960).

The state's second claimed interest is not ideologically neutral. The state is seeking to communicate to others an official view as to proper "appreciation of history, state pride, [and] individualism." Of course, the state may legitimately pursue such interests in any number of ways. However, where the state's interest is to disseminate an ideology, no matter how acceptable to some, such interest cannot outweigh an individual's First Amendment right to avoid becoming the courier for such message.

We conclude that the State of New Hampshire may not require appellees to display the state motto upon their vehicle license plates, and accordingly, we affirm the judgment of the district court.

Affirmed.

COMMENT

1. *Wooley* sets forth an important principle—the right to refrain from speaking or the right not to be compelled to speak. This freedom from compelled speech derives from an assumption the Court makes about the impact of the First Amendment on government. An aspect of that impact is that the state cannot require its citizens to advertise against their will an official view of things. Where ideology is concerned, must the state be neutral?

Does the fact that government may not restrict freedom of belief mean that government cannot add its views to that of others? The view expressed in *Wooley v. Maynard* appeared to suggest that the state must be ideologically neutral. Some commentators contend that government, under the First Amendment, may add its voice to that of others even though it may not compel the speech or expression of others. See Tribe, *American Constitutional Law*, 588–589 (1978).

2. In *Wooley v. Maynard*, the Court found in the First Amendment a source of protection for individuals compelled to speak by the state. In *Abood*, the Court found in the First Amendment a source of protection for individuals compelled unwillingly to make political contributions. The two cases may be seen as aspects of an important objective of First Amendment protection—freedom of belief.

PRUNEYARD SHOPPING CENTER v. ROBBINS

447 U.S. 74, 100 S.CT. 2035, 64 L.ED.2D 741 (1980).

Justice REHNQUIST delivered the opinion of the Court.

We postponed jurisdiction of this appeal from the Supreme Court of California to decide the important federal constitutional questions it presented. Those are whether state constitutional provisions, which permit individuals to exercise free speech and petition rights on the property of a privately owned shopping center to which the public is invited, violate the shopping center owner's property rights under the Fifth and Fourteenth Amendments or his free speech rights under the First and Fourteenth Amendments.

Appellant PruneYard is a privately owned shopping center in the city of Campbell, Cal. It covers approximately 21 acres—five devoted to parking and 16 occupied by walkways, plazas, sidewalks, and buildings that contain more than 65 specialty shops, 10 restaurants, and a movie theater. The PruneYard is open to the public for the purpose of encouraging the patronizing of its commercial establishments. It has a policy not to permit any visitor or tenant to engage in any publicly expressive activity, including the circulation of petitions, that is not directly related to its commercial purposes. This policy has been strictly enforced in a nondiscriminatory fashion. The PruneYard is owned by appellant Fred Sahadi.

Appellees are high school students who sought to solicit support for their opposition to a United Nations resolution against "Zionism." On a Saturday afternoon they set up a card table in a corner of PruneYard's central courtyard. They distributed pamphlets and asked passersby to sign petitions, which were to be sent to the president and members of Congress. Their activity was peaceful and orderly and so far as the record indicates was not objected to by PruneYard's patrons.

Soon after appellees had begun soliciting signatures, a security guard informed them that they would have to leave because their activity violated PruneYard regulations. The guard suggested that they move to the public sidewalk at the PruneYard's perimeter. Appellees immediately left the premises and later filed this lawsuit in the California Superior Court of Santa Clara County. They sought to enjoin appellants from denying them access to the PruneYard for the purpose of circulating their petitions.

The Superior Court held that appellees were not entitled under either the Federal or California Constitution to exercise their asserted rights on the shopping center property. [See Hudgens v. NLRB, p. 424 U.S. 507 (1976).] It concluded that there were "adequate, effective channels of communication for [appellees] other than soliciting on the private property of the [PruneYard]." The California Court of Appeal affirmed.

The California Supreme Court reversed, holding that the California Constitution protects "speech and petitioning, reasonably exercised, in shopping centers even when the centers are privately owned." 23 Cal.3d 899, 910 (1979). It concluded that appellees are entitled to conduct their activity on PruneYard property.[2] Before this Court, appellants contend that their "constitutionally established rights under the Fourteenth Amendment to exclude appellees from adverse use of appellants' property cannot be denied by invocation of a state constitutional provision or by judicial reconstruction of a state's laws of private property."

Appellants first contend that *Lloyd v. Tanner* [407 U.S. 551 (1972)] prevents the state from requiring a private shopping center owner to provide access to persons exercising their state constitutional rights of free speech and petition when adequate alternative avenues of communication are available.

Our reasoning in *Lloyd*, however, does not *ex proprio vigore* limit the authority of the state to exercise its police power or its sovereign right to adopt in its own Constitution individual liberties more expansive than those conferred by the Federal Constitution. In *Lloyd*, there was no state constitutional or statutory provision that had been construed to create rights to the use of private property by strangers, comparable to those found to exist by the California Supreme Court here. It is, of course, well-established that a state in the exercise of its police power may adopt reasonable restrictions on private property so long as the restrictions do not amount

---

2. Art. I, § 2, of the California Constitution provides:

Every person may freely speak, write and publish his or her sentiments on all subjects, being responsible for the abuse of this right. A law may not restrain or abridge liberty of speech or press.

Art. I, § 3, of the California Constitution provides:

[P]eople have the right to petition government for redress of grievances.

to a taking without just compensation or contravene any other federal constitutional provision.

Appellants next contend that a right to exclude others underlies the Fifth Amendment guarantee against the taking of property without just compensation and the Fourteenth Amendment guarantee against the deprivation of property without due process of law.

Here the requirement that appellants permit appellees to exercise state-protected rights of free expression and petition on shopping center property clearly does not amount to an unconstitutional infringement of appellants' property rights under the taking clause. There is nothing to suggest that preventing appellants from prohibiting this sort of activity will unreasonably impair the value or use of their property as a shopping center.

There is also little merit to appellants' argument that they have been denied their property without due process of law. *Nebbia v. New York.*

Appellants finally contend that a private property owner has a First Amendment right not to be forced by the state to use his property as a forum for the speech of others. They state that in *Wooley v. Maynard* this Court concluded that a state may not constitutionally require an individual to participate in the dissemination of an ideological message by displaying it on his private property in a manner and for the express purpose that it be observed and read by the public. This rationale applies here, they argue, because the message of *Wooley* is that the state may not force an individual to display any message at all.

Wooley, however, was a case in which the government itself prescribed the message, required it to be displayed openly on appellee's personal property that was used "as part of his daily life," and refused to permit him to take any measures to cover up the motto even though the Court found that the display of the motto served no important state interest. Here, by contrast, there are a number of distinguishing factors. Most important, the shopping center by choice of its owner is not limited to the personal use of appellants. It is instead a business establishment that is open to the public to come and go as they please. The views expressed by members of the public in passing out pamphlets or seeking signatures for a petition thus will not likely be identified with those of the owner. Second, no specific message is dictated by the state to be displayed on appellants' property. There consequently is no danger of governmental discrimination for or against a particular message. Finally, as far as appears here appellants can expressly disavow any connection with the message by simply posting signs in the area where the speakers or handbillers stand. Such signs, for example, could disclaim any sponsorship of the message and could explain that the persons are communicating their own messages by virtue of state law.

Appellants also argue that their First Amendment rights have been infringed in light of West Virginia State Board of Education v. Barnette, 319 U.S. 624 (1943) and *Miami Herald Publishing Co. v. Tornillo*, [p. 584]. *Barnette* is inapposite because it involved the compelled recitation of a message containing an affirmation of belief. This Court held such compulsion unconstitutional because it "require[d] the individual to communicate by word and sign his acceptance" of government dictated political ideas, whether or not he subscribed to them. Appellants are not similarly being compelled to affirm their belief in any governmentally prescribed position or view, and they are free to publicly dissociate themselves from the views of the speakers or handbillers.

Tornillo struck down a Florida statute requiring a newspaper to publish a political candidate's reply to criticism previously published in that newspaper. It rests on the principle that the state cannot tell a newspaper what it must print. The Florida statute contravened this principle in that it "exact[ed] a penalty on the basis of the content of a newspaper." There also was a danger in *Tornillo* that the statute would "dampen the vigor and limit the variety of public debate" by deterring editors from publishing controversial political statements that might trigger the application of the statute. Thus, the statute was found to be an "intrusion into the function of editors." These concerns obviously are not present here.

We conclude that neither appellants' federally recognized property rights nor their First Amendment rights have been infringed by the California Supreme Court's decision recognizing a right of appellees to exercise state protected rights of expression and petition on appellants' property. The judgment of the Supreme Court of California is therefore

Affirmed.

Justice MARSHALL, concurring.

Appellants' claim in this case amounts to no less than a suggestion that the common law of trespass is not subject to revision by the state, notwithstanding the California Supreme Court's finding that state-created rights of expressive activity would be severely hindered if shopping centers were closed to expressive activities by members of the public. If accepted, that claim would represent a return to the era of *Lochner v. New York*, [198 U.S. 45 (1905)], when common-law rights were also found immune from revision by state or federal government. Such an approach would freeze the common law as it has been constructed by the courts, perhaps at its 19th century state of development. It would allow no room for change in response to changes in circumstance. The due process clause does not require such a result.

On the other hand, I do not understand the Court to suggest that rights of property are to be defined solely by state law, or that there is no federal constitutional barrier to the abrogation of common-law rights by Congress or a state government. The constitutional terms "life, liberty, and property" do not derive their meaning solely from the provisions of positive law. They have a normative dimension as well, establishing a sphere of private autonomy which government is bound to respect. Quite serious constitutional questions might be raised if a legislature attempted to abolish certain categories of common-law rights in some general way. Indeed, our cases demonstrate that there are limits on governmental authority to abolish "core" common-law rights, including rights against trespass, at least without a compelling showing of necessity or a provision for a reasonable alternative remedy.

That "core" has not been approached in this case. The California Supreme Court's decision is limited to shopping centers, which are already open to the general public. The owners are permitted to impose reasonable restrictions on expressive activity. There has been no showing of interference with appellants' normal business operations. The California court has not permitted an invasion of any personal sanctuary. No rights of privacy are implicated. In these circumstances there is no basis for strictly scrutinizing the intrusion authorized by the California Supreme Court.

I join the opinion of the Court.

Justice POWELL with whom Justice White joins, concurring in part and in the judgment.

The selection of material for publication is not generally a concern of shopping centers. But similar speech interests are affected when listeners are likely to identify opinions expressed by members of the public on commercial property as the views of the owner. If a state law mandated public access to the bulletin board of a freestanding store, hotel, office, or small shopping center, customers might well conclude that the messages reflect the view of the proprietor. The same would be true if the public were allowed to solicit or pamphleteer in the entrance area of a store or in the lobby of a private building. The property owner or proprietor would be faced with a choice: he either could permit his customers to receive a mistaken impression or he could disavow the messages. Should he take the first course, he effectively has been compelled to affirm someone else's belief. Should he choose the second, he has been forced to speak when he would prefer to remain silent. In short, he has lost control over his freedom to speak or not to speak on certain issues. The mere fact that he is free to dissociate himself from the views expressed on his property, cannot restore his "right to refrain from speaking at all."

A property owner also may be faced with speakers who wish to use his premises as a platform for views that he finds morally repugnant. Numerous examples come to mind. A minority-owned business confronted with leafleteers from the American Nazi Party or the Ku Klux Klan, a church-operated enterprise asked to host demonstrations in favor of abortion, or a union compelled to supply a forum to right-to-work advocates could be placed in an intolerable position if state law requires it to make its private property available to anyone who wishes to speak. The strong emotions evoked by speech in such situations may virtually compel the proprietor to respond.

One easily can identify other circumstances in which a right of access to commercial property would burden the owner's First and Fourteenth Amendment right to refrain from speaking. But appellants have identified no such circumstance.

Appellants have not alleged that they object to the ideas contained in the appellees' petitions. Nor do they assert that some groups who reasonably might be expected to speak at the PruneYard will express views that are so objectionable as to require a response even when listeners will not mistake their source. The record contains no evidence concerning the numbers or types of interest groups that may seek access to this shopping center, and no testimony showing that the appellants strongly disagree with any of them.

Because appellants have not shown that the limited right of access held to be afforded by the California Constitution burdened their First and Fourteenth Amendment rights in the circumstances presented. I join the judgment of the Court. I do not interpret our decision today as a blanket approval for state efforts to transform privately owned commercial property into public forums. Any such state action would raise substantial federal constitutional questions not present in this case.

COMMENT

The shopping center owner in *PruneYard* sought refuge in the principle of *Wooley*. The state could not require the Jehovah's Witnesses to use their private property to publicize the ideas of the state. In the *Wooley* case, New Hampshire had mandated that motorists carry the state motto on their license plates. In *PruneYard*, the message in question was not being ordered by the state. Moreover, unlike the private automobile in *Wooley*, the shopping center in *PruneYard* was not used by the owners alone.

By definition, the shopping center's very existence constituted an invitation to the public to come and do business. Messages that are publicized by a shopping center are not necessarily to be identified with the owners of the shopping center. First Amendment law as now interpreted by the Supreme court does not require a shopping center owner to permit the dissemination of news to which he is opposed on his property. See Hudgens v. NLRB, 424 U.S. 507 (1976). Justice Marshall, joined by Justice Brennan, dissented in *Hudgens*. The emphasis on property rights by the majority in *Hudgens* arose "from an overly formalistic view of the relationship between the institution of private ownership of property and the First Amendment's guarantee of freedom of expression."

In *Wooley*, protection of a right to be free from compelled speech protected the individual against the state. In *PruneYard*, was the First Amendment analysis equally consistent with maximizing individual self-expression? Protection of the individual property owner's right to be free from compelled speech in that context works to exclude other individuals seeking an audience for their ideas on premises which may be uniquely suitable for the exchange of ideas.

The rights of free speech and petition, if reasonably exercised, of the public who use privately owned shopping centers were also protected under the California state constitutional guarantee of freedom of expression. The California courts, therefore, did not grant absolute priority to the property owner's claim of self-expression as the Supreme Court has done in interpreting the First Amendment in similar circumstances. The *PruneYard* case illustrates that state and federal constitutional law may occasionally yield divergent results on free expression problems. *PruneYard* also illustrates that transposition of the principle of freedom from compelled speech to a corporate context involving modern patterns of land use may yield quite different results than flow from the less complex but classic conflict in *Wooley* between the state and the individual. It has also been suggested that *PruneYard*, consistent with the decentralist tendencies of the Burger Court, is rooted in federalism: a state court may, if it chooses, read its state constitution more expansively than the United States Supreme Court has read the federal Constitution.

Libel and the Journalist

LIBEL DEFINED

1. Libel is essentially a false and defamatory attack in written form on a person's reputation or character. Slander is oral or spoken defamation. Since most courts have come to define broadcast defamation as libel (a written script usually precedes the spoken word), slander is now of less importance to the journalist.

Reputation measures one's standing in the community, the respect and goodwill one has earned from one's peers. Defamation is anything which tends to injure that reputation and good name by generating adverse, derogatory, or unpleasant feelings against a person. If it's written or in the form of a picture, photograph,[1] cartoon, caricature, film, tape, phonograph, sign, symbol, sticker, effigy, or advertisement—the list is not exhaustive—it's libel.

Words, images, or representations, then, "which tend to expose one to public hatred, shame, obloquy, contumely, odium, contempt, ridicule, aversion, ostracism, degradation or disgrace, or to induce an evil opinion of one in the minds of right-thinking persons, and to deprive one of their confidence and friendly intercourse in society." [2]

A direct and obvious libel is a publication falsely charging that a person has committed a crime, especially a felony. Accusations of moral turpitude, although subject to a wider range of possible interpretation, may also be libelous. Imputations of bad character, vicious motives, or antisocial behavior fall in the same category as do publications suggesting incompetency or lack of integrity in one's profession, trade, business, or calling.

In a sentence, libel is essentially a defamatory, false, malicious, and/or negligent publication which tends to hold a person up to hatred, contempt, or ridicule causing him or her to be shunned or avoided.

The problem with these definitions is the room they leave for ambiguity. Ambiguity is usually a problem for a jury to resolve, and jurors differ depending upon time, place, context, and the current state of community attitudes. It would have seemed strange twenty years ago to construe as defamatory one's activities on behalf of the CIA. Yet in 1976 a New York

1. See Burda, *Photographic Libel: An Inquiry Into the Rights of Photographers* (unpublished M.S. thesis, California State University, San Jose, 1973) for a compilation and analysis of nineteen federal cases between 1850 and 1972 where photographs were involved in libel suits.

2. Kimmerle v. New York Evening Journal, 186 N.E. 217 (N.Y.1933). A newspaper article which said a woman was "courted" by a "murderer" was held not to be libelous. "Courting" did not "imply immoral conduct," and the paper didn't say the woman knew precisely who or what her suitor was.

federal judge found it arguable, "given the current political climate and the sensitive nature of plaintiff's employment, that allegations of CIA involvement are defamatory." [3]

The true connotation of words should be cast in our own times, for the harmless word of yesterday may today be one of reproach and odium,[4] or, in the words of Oliver Wendell Holmes, "A word is not a crystal, transparent and unchanged; it is the skin of a living thought and may vary greatly in color and content according to the circumstances and the time in which it is used." [5]

In a Vermont case, a plaintiff was characterized by a political opponent as a "horse's ass," a "jerk," an "idiot," and "paranoid." Words used in the context of a political skirmish between two candidates for mayor, said the court, could not reasonably have been believed in their literal sense or with a willful or malicious intent to denigrate or ridicule the plaintiff in his profession as an accountant. Such words, the court added, may be insulting, abusive, unpleasant, and objectionable, but they are not defamatory in and of themselves, and they reflect more on the character of the user than on the person for whom they are intended.[6]

Vermont and a number of other states obviously condone the use of such epithets on the premise that a certain amount of vulgar name calling, because it is nothing more than that, ought to be tolerated. South Carolina, for example. Although the plaintiff in a slander action there charged that he was called a "bastard" and a "son-of-a-bitch," the court ruled that such words amounted only to vulgar name calling and were understood as merely being uttered in anger.[7]

Libel may lurk in irony, sarcasm, and even in well intentioned humor. "The principle is clear," said a New York court long ago, "that a person shall not be allowed to murder another's reputation in jest. * * *" [8] In 1957 a columnist in a small town newspaper observed with tongue in cheek that George Powers, a local paper mill employee, was a "classic example of typical Yankee thrift": he was building his own casket and would soon be digging a hole for it. Powers objected to being ridiculed and sued the newspaper for libel, testifying that he was neither building his own casket nor digging his own grave. It was true that he had said to someone in a passing conversation that prices were getting so high that a man would soon have to build his own casket. Turning a metaphor into an economic stereotype caused a court to conclude that Powers had stated a claim for libel.[9]

It is not possible to list all typically libelous expressions, nor is it useful to do so. Empathy is one's guide. What words, allegations, charges would you consider a hurtful attack on your reputation and personality? Make your own list and think of

3. Oliver v. The Village Voice, Inc., 417 F.Supp. 235 (S.D.N.Y.1976). The *Village Voice* escaped liability because the "public figure" plaintiff failed to show the requisite "actual malice." See text, pp. 190–191.

4. Munafo v. Helfand, 140 F.Supp. 234 (S.D.N.Y.1956).

5. Towne v. Eisner, 245 U.S. 418, 425 (1918).

6. Blouin v. Anton, 7 Med.L.Rptr. 17141, 431 A.2d 489 (Vt.1981).

7. Smith v. Phoenix Furniture Co., 339 F.Supp. 969 (D.S.C.1972). Some states, Alabama, Mississippi, and Virginia, for example, have passed "insulting words" laws which are meant to punish insults before they reach the level of defamation. See Hanson, *Libel and Related Torts*, Vol. 1, Case and Comment, 1969, § 17.

8. Triggs v. Sun Printing & Publishing Association, 71 N.E. 739 (N.Y.1904). See also Middlebrooks v. Curtis Publishing Co., 413 F.2d 141 (4th Cir. 1969). In *Middlebrooks,* although agreeing that a reputation may be libeled in jest or in fiction, the court rejected a contention that a fictional portrayal in a book was libelous in view of marked dissimilarities between the fictional character and the plaintiff.

9. Powers v. Durgin-Snow Publishing Co., 144 A.2d 294 (Me.1958).

it as comprising the vocabulary which forms the boundaries of a legal mine field.

But remember that supposedly libelous words are to be considered in their ordinary, commonly accepted meanings. Courts consider the effects of language on ordinary readers and average persons among whom they are intended to circulate.[10]

A letter to the editor of a weekly newspaper referred to a campaign manager of candidates for municipal office as being influenced "by a foreign philosophy alien to the American way" and as using "un-American tactics." A New Jersey court ruled that where a substantial number of respectable people in the community concluded from the letter that the campaign manager was a Communist or a Communist sympathizer, the publication was defamatory as a matter of law, even though other segments of public opinion might disagree and reach contrary conclusions.[11]

In 1976 the U.S. Supreme court declined to review a $485,000 libel award in favor of a former state attorney general against *The Arizona Republic.* The paper had charged in an editorial that the state attorney general had Communist sympathies. Ironically the newspaper had appealed an initial $50,000 judgment against it to the state supreme court and had won a retrial. The newspaper lost and appealed again. But this time a nearly tenfold harsher judgment was upheld by an intermediate appeals court, and the state supreme court refused to review.[12]

On the other hand there is precedent to suggest that calling a person a "bigot" or any other name descriptive of political, racial, economic, or social philosophy generally affords no cause for a libel action.[13]

2. A number of states subscribe to what New York calls the *single-instance* rule. Under this rule, "language charging a professional person with ignorance or error on a single occasion only and not accusing that person of general ignorance or lack of skill is not actionable unless special damages are pleaded." [14]

The rule is premised on the notion that sooner or later everyone makes a mistake. The trick is to avoid an implication of general ignorance or lack of skill applicable to past, present, and future.

3. Idiosyncracy in state libel laws creates legal booby traps for the unwary communicator. A first rule is that the reporter discover the peculiarities and perplexities of the libel laws of the state in which he or she works. If there are special hazards in that jurisdiction, be alert to them.

Libel may hinge upon colloquialisms and connotations. But when a plaintiff attaches an unfamiliar or a special meaning to a word or expression, the burden rests on that person to prove its defamatory nature. If the plaintiff succeeds, the defendant then has an opportunity to rebut by showing that the words could not have been taken in a defamatory sense, were not intended to be taken that way, and had their meaning stretched beyond the obvious understanding of readers and listeners.

Some jurisdictions have written the above proposition into a rule known as the *"innocent construction rule."* If language

10. Robert v. Troy Record Co., 294 N.Y.S.2d 723 (1968).

11. Mosler v. Whelan, 138 A.2d 559 (N.J.1958), reversed 147 A.2d 7 (1958).

12. Phoenix Newspapers, Inc. v. Church, 537 P.2d 1345 (Ariz.1975), appeal dismissed 425 U.S. 908 (1976), rehearing denied 425 U.S. 985.

13. Raible v. Newsweek, Inc. 341 F.Supp. 804 (D.C.Pa. 1972). Where a *Newsweek* magazine article concerning the "white majority" ascribed certain views to that group, the plaintiff as a member of that group was deemed not to have been libeled by the article: "* * * the article, if libelous, libels more than half of the people in the United States and not the plaintiff in particular."

14. Brower v. New Republic, 7 Med.L.Rptr. 1605 (N.Y.Sup.Ct. 1981).

is capable of an innocent construction, it should be interpreted that way. Although a statement may lend itself to a neurotic interpretation, courts following the rule are more interested in ordinary, commonly accepted interpretations rather than convoluted, strained, or otherwise unusual meanings.

Illinois has such a rule. A newspaper editorial paraphrasing a village trustee's argument for higher trustee salaries chose to interpret the trustee's remarks as an expression of his belief that good government had to be paid for. The trustee, however, read the editorial as suggesting that he, the trustee, regarded the alternative to adequate salaries to be the illegal practice of taking money under the table. In a subsequent libel suit against a Niles newspaper, the trustee contended that the editorial constituted a published attack on his ability to perform his duties and on his integrity. An Illinois court preferred to attach an innocent construction to the editorial and denied relief to the trustee.[15]

Not capable of an innocent construction, however, was a city clerk's statement, concerning the city's award of a garbage collection contract, that "I think 240 pieces of silver changed hands—30 for each alderman." When an alderman brought suit, the Illinois Supreme Court held the words to be a defamatory statement of fact, not a constitutionally protected expression of opinion.[16]

It is sometimes a fine line. A New York court said, "It is not libelous to assert that a public official was appointed to a high paying but unnecessary public office as a political reward, without consideration of merit or competence. Such charges are commonplace in the political arena. Whether or not they are true, they are not actionable." [17]

Far more assured of punishment was the newspaper article that, by repeated use of words such as "fix, bribe, payoff," and "improper offers," led average readers to conclude that an attorney had solicited a high legal fee from a drug defendant in order to bribe the judge and "fix" the case. Such language was clearly defamatory, said the Kentucky Supreme Court.[18]

Illustrations and headlines may be libelous by innuendo even when nothing false or defamatory is stated. The Boston *Herald-Traveler* printed a picture of a witness before a congressional committee on its front page. Although the witness had testified as to how he had refused to take part in an alleged fraud, his picture appeared under the banner headline—"Settlement Upped $2,000: $400 Kickback Told." Though no reference was made to the witness in an accompanying article, the court said the innuendo was capable of being defamatory and that the plaintiff was entitled to a jury trial to prove that he was defamed.[19]

In a much discussed case a photograph of the plaintiff's home in a story about how a gang of thieves used the basement of one of their homes as a warehouse for stolen property was declared to state a claim for defamation. The case was *Troman v. Wood.*[20] Similarly an article about trucking companies going out of business was illustrated with an auction notice an-

15. Kaplan v. Greater Niles Township Publishing Corp., 278 N.E.2d 437 (Ill.1971). See also, Levinson v. Time, Inc., 6 Med.L.Rptr. 2167, 411 N.E.2d 1118 (Ill.1980).

16. Catalano v. Pechous, 4 Med.L.Rptr. 2094, 387 N.E.2d 714 (Ill.1978), affirmed, 6 Med.L.Rptr. 2511, 419 N.E.2d 350 (Ill.1980).

17. Lerner v. The Village Voice, Inc., (Sup.Ct.N.Y., Co.) (N.Y. Law Journal 8/24/77).

18. McCall v. Courier-Journal and Louisville Times Co., 7 Med.L.Rptr. 2118, 623 S.W.2d 882 (Ky.1981), cert. den. 456 U.S. 975 (1982).

19. Mabardi v. Boston Herald-Traveler Corp., 198 N.E.2d 304 (Mass.1964).

20. 340 N.E.2d 292 (Ill.1975).

nouncing public sale of trucking equipment owned by the plaintiff. Since the trucking company was not going out of business and nothing in the story said it was, use of the firm's name in the context of the illustration was held to state a claim for libel.[21]

Since reporters seldom write headlines for their stories, they don't feel responsible when headline and story are mismatched. Courts, however, sensitive to the fact that often only the headline is read, have upheld libel judgments on the basis of headlines alone. For example, in Sprouse v. Clay Communication, Inc., 1 Med.L.Rptr. 1695, 211 S.E. 2d 674 (W.Va.1975) a state supreme court upheld a $250,000 award in actual damages against a newspaper which had libeled an unsuccessful gubernatorial candidate by what the court called "misleading words in oversized headlines." Said the court:

> Where oversized headlines are published which reasonably lead the average reader to an entirely different conclusion than the facts cited in the body of the story, and where the plaintiff can demonstrate that it was the intent of the publisher to use such misleading headlines to create a false impression on the normal reader, the headline may be considered separately with regard to whether a known falsehood was published.

The United States Supreme Court declined to review that holding, and the successful plaintiff went on to become a justice of the very court that had upheld his claim.

Similarly in McNair v. Hearst Corp., 494 F.2d 1309 (9th Cir. 1974) a federal appeals court said that if a newspaper publisher knew of the false impression which the headline and first two paragraphs of an article would make upon the reader, fifty subsequent paragraphs countering that impression would not keep the headline and first two paragraphs from constituting libel.

On the other hand, courts have held that a headline must be read in context with an entire article before a judgment can be made about libel.[22]

4. What we are noting, then, is that some publications are directly libelous, others indirectly so. Direct libels—for example, referring to someone as a felon, or discrediting a person in his or her business or profession by charging unethical conduct, incompetence, fraud, or bankruptcy—are called libels *per se,* libels on their face.

Indirect libels, libel by innuendo, by implication, by omission, or libel due to extrinsic circumstances over which the writer may have no knowledge or control (the legal term for the latter is *inducement*), have traditionally been called libels *per quod.* They can present troublesome surprises for reporters and editors.

In libel *per quod* the plaintiff has traditionally had the burden of proving the defamatory sense of the publication and, in almost every jurisdiction, special damages and/or actual malice as well,[23] especially where a reasonably prudent publisher had no warning of defamatory potential or the libel *per quod* was newsworthy matter of public interest. Recent developments in libel law, however, have blurred the distinction between libel *per se* and

21. Drotzmanns, Inc. v. McGraw-Hill, Inc., 500 F.2d 830 (8th Cir. 1974).

22. Gambuzza v. Time, Inc., 239 N.Y.S.2d 466 (1963).

23. In his 1974 dissent in *Gertz v. Robert Welch, Inc.* (see text, p. 236), Justice White reported that in the mid-60s all courts except Virginia were in agreement that any libel which is defamatory on its face (libelous *per se*) would be actionable without proof of special damages. Twenty-four jurisdictions held, at that time, that libel not defamatory on its face (libel *per quod*) would require a showing of special damages to be actionable. In 1971, Dean William Prosser, an authority on tort law, earlier identified thirty-five such states. Justice White in 1974 found ten states supporting an older rule that libel *per quod* did not require proof of special damages, and in six jurisdictions it wasn't clear what the rule was.

libel *per quod.*[24] Nevertheless, the peculiar hazards of libel by indirection should be noted.

In 1968 a woman author and television personality brought a libel action against *TV Guide* for its publication of a promotional blurb which said: "From Party Girl to Call Girl. Scheduled Guest: TV Personality Pat Montandon and Author of *How To Be a Party Girl.*" The original promo submitted to the magazine had a considerably different implication. It read: "From Party Girl to Call Girl? How Far Can the Party Girl Go Until She Becomes a Call Girl is Discussed with TV Personality Pat Montandon, Author (*How To Be a Party Girl*) and a Masked-Anonymous Prostitute!"

Witnesses testified that the average reader would conclude from the edited notice that Montandon had progressed from being a woman who liked to give and go to parties to being a call girl or prostitute. The rewrite was found by both jury and appeals court to be libelous, and the plaintiff was awarded $150,000 in compensatory and $1,000 in punitive damages. Montandon v. Triangle Publications, Inc., 120 Cal.Rptr. 186, (1975), cert. den. 423 U.S. 893.

In the preceding case, careless—the court used the word "reckless"—editing was costly to the magazine. Sometimes a story is libelous not for what it says but for what it fails to say. Suppose, for example, that all members of a city council are indicted for graft except Smith, Jones, and Brown and in the morning paper, Brown's name is omitted. This could be libel by omission. A case will illustrate.

The *Village Voice* carried a series of four articles by Jack Newfield highly critical of a New York judge's performance of his official duties. The newspaper then used excerpts from the articles to promote its subscriptions by means of an advertisement in the *New York Times.* The judge sued for invasion of privacy and for libel. A New York court denied a summary judgment (a ruling made only when the facts are undisputed, where the judge decides the case as a matter of law in favor of one or the other parties) to the *Village Voice.* Aside from the risks of the advertising excerpts misrepresenting the original stories, it was argued by the plaintiff-judge that between the date of publication of the original articles and the advertisement, the *Village Voice* received information that its original publication was inaccurate, incomplete, and in many respects totally false. The effect of the omissions on the libel issue, said the court, was a question of fact for a jury.[25] On appeal the omissions question was left open for trial,[26] until New York's highest court, finding that the judge had failed to set forth enough evidence to generate a triable is-

24. In all jurisdictions, slander to be actionable has required a showing of special damages unless the slander was a slander *per se,* that is, one imputing a crime involving moral turpitude, loathsome disease, incompetency or lack of integrity in business, trade, or profession, or unchastity in a woman. It is at this point that the distinction among slander, slander *per se,* libel *per se,* and libel *per quod* become blurred and confusing. Prosser in his *Law of Torts* (4th ed., 1971), 764–66, recommended combining libel and slander into a single tort in which the primary consideration would be the degree of defamation. Widely disseminated defamation (radio, television, newspaper) would be actionable without proof of special damages. Defamation by postcard, private letter, or in conversation, because of its lesser potential for harm, would require proof of special damages.

Gertz v. Robert Welch, Inc., the landmark libel ruling of 1974, does not suggest a merging of slander and libel, but it does, in its outcomes and by implication, combine libel *per se* and libel *per quod.* At least the distinction between them will be less important in the future.

25. Rinaldi v. Village Voice, 365 N.Y.S.2d 199 (1975).

26. Rinaldi v. Holt, Rinehart & Winston, Inc., 2 Med.L.Rptr. 2169, 386 N.Y.S.2d 818 (1976), cert. den. 434 U.S. 969 (1977).

sue of fact as to defendant's actual malice, dismissed the suit.

6. Special damages must also be shown in cases of *trade libel.* Trade libel may be considered a form of unfair competition whereby property, goods, products, or services are disparaged falsely to the financial disadvantage of their owner. Since personal reputation may not be at stake, trade libel or *disparagement* is simply defined as falsity, although the plaintiff must also demonstrate identification and publication. In addition, he or she must also prove either actual or implied common law malice (ill will, spite, or hostility) and special damages in the form of monetary loss.

A federal district court in Bose Corp. v. Consumers Union, 7 Med.L.Rptr. 2481, 529 F.Supp. 357 (D.Mass.1981) defined trade libel:

> The tort of product disparagement, as distinguished from individual or corporate defamation, is a narrow cause of action. The interests protected are not those of the reputation of the corporation or the intangible concerns peculiar to individual reputation such as community standing, privacy and psychic well-being. * * * A cause of action for product disparagement is made out only when the plaintiff has satisfactorily proved that it suffered special damages flowing from a false statement concerning the nature or quality of plaintiff's product. * * * The tort exists to provide redress only for tangible and direct pecuniary loss, a purely economic injury to which society accords a lesser value than reputational interests. * * * In a product disparagement case, the plaintiff must prove that special damages resulted from the publication and that the disparagement was a substantial factor in inducing others not to buy the plaintiff's product.

The First Circuit Court of Appeals, finding no actual malice in *Consumer Report's* criticism of Bose speakers, even though its evaluation may have been "imprecise," reversed the trial court's finding of liability. Bose Corp. v. Consumers Union, 8 Med.L.Rptr. 2391, 692 F.2d 189 (1st Cir. 1982). Bose's petition for review was accepted by the Supreme Court in mid-1983 and major press groups joined to urge the Court to affirm the Court of Appeals holding consistent with *New York Times v. Sullivan* and progeny. Bose sought review on the ground that the scope of appellate review of evidence of actual malice in a public figure libel case should be extremely limited. Bose claimed that independent review by the appellate court of the facts behind the actual malice constructions of the trial court is objectionable. Resolution of this issue by the Supreme Court could be extremely important to the future of libel law. [cert. granted 103 S.Ct. 1872 (1983)]

In National Dynamics Corp. v. Petersen Publishing Co., 185 F.Supp. 573 (S.D.N.Y. 1960) a federal district court said that where a publication states that the construction of a manufacturer's product is not as good as that of a competitor, there is a libel of the product only. No inference can be drawn that the manufacturer is practicing a deceit on the public simply because he is selling a product which is not the best in its field. The court added that, under New York law, disparagement of a product, even to the extent of saying it is completely worthless, is not sufficient to make out a case of libel *per se* of the manufacturer.

On the other hand, when Jerry Lewis said on a television program that a product called "Snooze," a sleep aid, was full of habit-forming drugs, that nothing short of a hospital cure could make one stop taking it, and that one would feel like "a run-down hound dog" and would lose weight under its effects, the New York Court of Appeals ruled that such an aspersion could readily be understood as charging the manufacturer, even though his name was not mentioned, with fraud and deceit in putting unwholesome and dangerous products on the market. The statement was libelous *per se,* and a showing of special damages was unnecessary. Harwood Pharmacal Co. v. National Broadcasting Co., Inc., 214 N.Y.S.2d 725, 174 N.E.2d 602 (1961).

The distinction between an attack on a product and an attack on its producer must be carefully drawn by the publisher who would avoid litigation. See Note, *Corporate Defamation and Product Disparagement: Narrowing the Analogy to Personal Defamation,* 75 Colum.L.Rev. 963 (1975).

7. As has been implied, a corporation may sue for libel damages if its credit or financial soundness is impugned, although courts are divided on whether corporations possess defensible reputations.[27] Similarly union officers may bring suits to preserve their union's reputation. Until 1966, civil suits for libel generated by union activities and governed by the National Labor Relations Act were barred in the interests of a single, uniform federal rule allowing a wide latitude of speech and counterspeech to competing parties.

In 1966 the United States Supreme Court lifted the constraint. The Court noted that unions when vying for membership are prone to denounce one another: "[B]oth labor and management often speak bluntly and recklessly, embellishing their respective positions with imprecatory language."[28] An example of the latter was the successful libel suit brought by a fruit company against a labor union for a false assertion in a film that the company maintained substandard housing for its migrant workers.[29]

Nonprofit organizations, foundations, and special interest groups can likewise attempt libel actions on behalf of their collective membership and their organiza-

27. El Meson Espanol v. NYM Corp., 521 F.2d 737 (2d Cir. 1975); Golden Palace, Inc. v. NBC, 386 F.Supp. 107 (D.D.C.1974), affirmed 530 F.2d 1094 (D.C.Cir.1976); Safarets, Inc. v. Gannett Co., Inc., 361 N.Y.S.2d 276 (1974); Transworld Accounts v. Associated Press, 425 F.Supp. 814 (N.D.Cal.1977). In the latter case the court declared that there is no meaningful distinction between the protectible interest in reputation of corporations and individuals, given the fact that many enterprises which are corporations in form are in economic reality actually conducted as individual proprietorships or partnerships. For purposes of libel the court was prepared to treat corporations as private persons in some circumstances.

A year earlier, another federal district court had held otherwise. In Martin Marietta Corp. v. Evening Star Newspaper, 417 F.Supp. 947, 956 (D.D.C.1976)—a newspaper had alleged that prostitutes were being provided government officials by defense contractors—the federal district court said: "[T]he values considered important enough to merit accommodation with interests protected by the first amendment are associated solely with natural persons, and that corporations, while legal persons for some purposes, possess none of the attributes the (Gertz) Court sought to protect." Martin Marietta, by providing an atmosphere in which, it was also alleged, a naked lady could swing from a stuffed moose head, had become a public figure by thrusting itself into a matter of public controversy. So what would come to be called a public issue or a *Rosenbloom* test was appropriate in trying the libel case.

But then again the Marietta approach was expressly rejected in Reliance Insurance Co. v. Barron's, 3 Med.L.Rptr. 1033, 442 F.Supp. 1341 (S.D.N.Y.1977). So courts must determine on the basis of facts and circumstances whether a corporation is a public or private entity in applying the rules of *Gertz.*. In Bruno & Stillman v. Globe Newspaper, 6 Med.L.Rptr. 2057, 633 F.2d 583 (lst Cir. 1980), for example, a successful corporation not involved in a public controversy was held not to be a public figure.

28. Linn v. United Plant Guard Workers of America, Local 114, 383 U.S. 53 (1966). For earlier cases establishing that unions have reputations which are the common property of their members and which can be damaged by publication, see Daniels v. Sanitarium Association Inc., 30 Cal.Rptr. 828, 381 P.2d 652 (1963); Kelly v. New York Herald Tribune, Inc., 175 N.Y.S.2d 598 (1958); Kirkman v. Westchester Newspapers, Inc., 39 N.E.2d 919 (N.Y.1942).

29. Di Giorgio Fruit Corp. v. AFL–CIO, 30 Cal.Rptr. 350 (1963). See also, Safarets, Inc. v. Gannett Co., Inc., 361 N.Y.S.2d 276 (1974).

tion's reputation,[30] but successful suits in this category are rare.

8. Units of government, political parties, and political interest groups *cannot* sue for libel because the citizen's right to criticize such groups and entities, no matter how abusive the criticism, is held to be of overriding importance. A municipal corporation, furthermore, has been held to have no legal personality capable of being defamed. Similarly, utterances or publications directed against a government or city have been considered absolutely privileged.[31]

In 1920 the City of Chicago sued the *Chicago Tribune* for libeling its credit in the bond market and impairing its functioning as a municipality. The Illinois Supreme Court ruled against the city noting that "no court of last resort in this country has ever held, or even suggested, that prosecutions for libel on government have any place in the American system of jurisprudence; " * * * and * * * "assuming that there was a temporary damage to the city and a resultant increase in taxes, it is better that an occasional individual or newspaper that is so perverted in judgment or so misguided in his or its civic duty should go free than that all of the citizens should be put in jeopardy of imprisonment or economic subjugation if they venture to criticize an inefficient or corrupt government." City of Chicago v. Tribune Co., 139 N.E. 86 (Ill.1923). That sentiment was perhaps ahead of its time.[32]

9. It is not libelous to accuse a person of something that person has a legal right to do. A news report that John Chaloner shot John Gillard "while the latter was abusing his wife * * *" was held to be nondefamatory in 1919.[33] It would probably still be nondefamatory today.

10. Misdemeanors reported in print do not ordinarily constitute actionable libels because no moral turpitude is implied. If surrounding circumstances make a reference unexpectedly damaging and if special damages can be proven, we may have a different, and actionable, case.

11. Carelessness is undoubtedly the greatest enemy of the journalist. Nothing substitutes for accuracy, corroborative sources, and documentation where it might be needed. Sensitivity to language is no less important. The differences between "he said" and "he admitted" and between "she fell" and "she jumped" ought to be obvious, but writers do have mental lapses.

Speaking of mental lapses, imagine, if you can, the consternation of an Indiana newspaper when it discovered after a press run that a young reporter had confused the name of a judge with the name of a defendant in a story of a criminal trial for assault and battery with intent to satisfy sexual desires on a fourteen-year-old girl. The last paragraph of the flawed story reported that the judge was pleading an alibi defense.

Despite prayer, the article came to the attention of the judge who thereupon wrote the following letter to the newspaper:

30. New York Society for the Suppression of Vice v. MacFadden Publications, 221 N.Y.S. 563 (1927), affirmed 226 N.Y.S. 870 (1928); Munhall Homestead Housing v. Messenger Publishing Co., 25 D.&C.2d 1, 109 P.L.J. 225 (Pa.Com.Pl.1961).

31. Johnson City v. Cowles Communications, Inc., 477 S.W.2d 750 (Tenn.1972). Johnson City, Tenn. sued the now vanished *Look* magazine for libel. The state supreme court of Tennessee held that Johnson City, a municipal corporation, was not a "person" within the meaning of the state's libel statute and *Look* could not be sued for defamation. The same court held that any citizen, individual, or corporate body is absolutely privileged ("excepting only treasonable utterances") to make any statements about a city or government.

32. See also State v. Time, Inc., 249 So.2d 328 (La.1971), where it was held that the state of Louisiana could not sue a magazine for libel even if the charges made in the offending article were false and malicious.

33. Washington Post Co. v. Chaloner, 250 U.S. 290 (1919).

> I enclose a Xerox copy from your paper which has just been handed to me. I appreciate the fact that, because of bad circulation, your paper is understaffed and your writers are poorly trained. The subject matter of this article was highly technical and, therefore, the writer of this article could not be expected to get it right the very first time. I, therefore, am going to point out some of the idiom used in court and identify the cast of characters.
>
> First, the judge (that's me) sits up in front of the courtroom on a raised dais with a robe on and scowls at people. Secondly, the defendant is the fellow sitting at counsel table with his lawyer, with an apprehensive look on his face. Thirdly, the prosecutor is the young man sitting at the other counsel table representing truth and justice. The press are those people sitting over at the side of the courtroom with long hair, whiskers, and barefooted.
>
> Now, in criminal proceedings, the judge is not charged with crime. The defendant is charged with crime. The judge does not claim alibi. He is the head honcho.
>
> I am sure that if your writer carefully reviews the above information he may eventually be able to get his article correct.
>
> I wish you to know, in passing, that I am a great admirer of the Fourth Estate, and sometimes get very emotional when I observe their crusade for truth and justice. Therefore, you have my permission to pass these instructions on to other newspapers who are in like situations so that they may benefit from these simple instructions.

Be assured that not all judges[34] have this well developed a sense of humor. His "instructions" were duly disseminated.

The judge, of course, is a public person and, as we shall see, that makes a difference. Where purely private persons are concerned, these kinds of errors can have devastating effects on the press. When the media have been negligent, they will be required to pay damages to those they have libeled.

Supreme Court Justice Wiley Rutledge showed sympathetic understanding of the press when he wrote in a concurring opinion:

> There is perhaps no area of news more inaccurately reported factually, on the whole, though with some notable exceptions, than legal news. Some part of this is due to carelessness, often induced by the haste with which news is gathered and published, a smaller portion to bias or more blameworthy causes. But a great deal of it must be attributed, in candor, to ignorance which frequently is not at all blameworthy. For newspapers are conducted by men who are laymen to the law. With rare exceptions their capacity for misunderstanding the significance of legal events and procedures, not to speak of opinions, is great. But this is neither remarkable nor peculiar to newsmen. For the law, as lawyers best know, is full of perplexities. Pennekamp v. Florida, 328 U.S. 331, 371 (1946).

Libel is unusually full of perplexities. Yet ignorance of the law and carelessness do not keep journalists out of court. Our purpose here is to become more than laymen to the law of mass communication.

Damages

1. In passing we have mentioned three kinds of damages—compensatory, special, and punitive.

Compensatory or *general* damages are intended as a monetary compensation for injury to reputation. Until recently, as we shall see, compensatory damages were presumed in cases of libel *per se.* The jury would fix the amount, the court would review and sometimes reduce excessive awards when they appeared to be out of

34. One study does demonstrate that jurors are less lenient with press defendants than are judges. See Franklin, *Suing Media for Libel: A Litigation Study,* 1981 A.B. Foundation Res.J. 795.

proportion to the injury inflicted. Compensatory damages are based on injured feelings, humiliation, shame or insult, mental and physical anguish, and injury to business or occupation. In reaching a decision on compensatory damages a jury will consider the degree of negligence or fault on the part of the press, the nature of the publication, the character, condition, and status of the parties to the suit, the peculiar circumstances of the case, the breadth of publication, and the intensity of the pain suffered as a consequence.

Special or *actual* damages have traditionally been meant to compensate one for real, tangible monetary loss which is provable, for example the loss of one's income or employment due to a false and defamatory publication. They must also be proven in cases of trade libel and slander. Since the Supreme Court's landmark ruling in the 1974 case Gertz v. Robert Welch, Inc., 418 U.S. 323 (1974), the distinction between general and special damages has become blurred. Part of the problem may be semantic. Actual injury, the Court said in *Gertz,* need not encompass only financial loss, but may include impairment of reputation and standing in the community, personal humiliation, and mental anguish and suffering.

Actual damages as compensation for actual injury seem to have taken the place of the older concept of compensatory or general damages as payment for presumed injury to reputation resulting from libel *per se*, although the idea of *per se* defamation persists in the lexicon of the courts. The following paragraph from a 1981 ruling of the Virginia Supreme Court reflects the confusion which may be attributed to *Gertz:*

> Moore did not allege or prove that he suffered any monetary loss. He did allege, however, that he had been insulted, mortified, held up to ridicule, and humiliated by the statement. We conclude that in libel actions not based upon *per se* defamation, where knowing falsity or reckless disregard for the truth [the *Gertz* rule] is not shown, the compensatory damages should be limited to the actual damages proved to have been sustained, but such damages should not necessarily be restricted to out-of-pocket loss * * * [but based] upon proof of actual injury, including such elements as damage to * * * reputation and standing in the community, embarrassment, humiliation, and mental suffering. "Special damages," which under the common-law rule must be shown as a prerequisite to recovery where the defamatory words are not actionable *per se*, are not to be limited to pecuniary loss.[35]

The key to understanding what the Court intended in *Gertz* may be that no compensation of any kind in a libel suit was envisioned unless the plaintiff could show actual injury. Actual injury warrants actual damages. Therefore actual damages now cover matters which used to be called general or compensatory damages. The significant difference is that mere presumptions about injury to reputation are no longer enough to establish grounds for damages.

For these reasons, it may be helpful to distinguish between special and actual damages, terms that have heretofore been interchangeable, reserving the term special damages for demonstrated financial loss.

Punitive or exemplary damages—what lawyers sometimes call "smart" money because they hurt—are meant to punish and make an example of libelers in order to discourage similar behavior in others. Additional semantic "noise" has resulted from the fact that courts have come to call punitive damages "presumed" damages, a term that has in the past been synonymous with general damages. Use of the word "presumed" may be inappropriate in that no presumed or punitive damages are permitted by *Gertz*, absent a showing by

35. Fleming v. Moore, 7 Med.L.Rptr. 1313, 275 S.E.2d 632 (Va. 1981).

clear and convincing evidence of actual malice, that is, knowing falsehood or reckless disregard for truth. A question of intent of course, may always be somewhat more presumptive than a question of actual injury.

Punitive damages are controversial. However much the Supreme Court in *Gertz* sought to discourage them, New York and other courts have been protective of large punitive awards. California courts, in comparison, guard against excessive punitive damages by requiring that they be reasonably proportionate to the award of actual or general damages.[36] And, if excessive, they will be reduced or fashioned to what an impecunious defendant can afford.[37]

The proper relationship between compensatory and punitive damages will remain an issue of some significance. Justice Harlan provided a guideline in his concurring opinion in Rosenbloom v. Metromedia, 403 U.S. 29, 75, n. 4 (1971):

> A carefully and properly instructed jury should ordinarily be able to arrive at damage awards that are self-validating. * * * [T]o the extent that supervision of jury verdicts would be required * * * defendant's resources, the actual harm suffered by the plaintiff, and the publication's potential for actual harm are all susceptible of more or less objective measurement. * * * I would hold unconstitutional, in a private libel case, jury authority to award punitive damages which is unconfined by the requirement that these awards bear a reasonable and purposeful relationship to the actual harm done.

Justices Marshall and Stewart in dissent thought no such objective measurement possible. In their view, punitive damages would remain a threat to the First Amendment. The Supreme Court may still have to resolve this question.

Nine states including Massachusetts, Oregon, and Washington,[38] prohibit punitive damages under any circumstances. A small number of additional states have laws or rules which discourage punitive damages. Most states, however, will allow juries to go beyond *Gertz* in finding reasons for punitive damages, e.g., an intent to harm or evidence of an insensitive response to a request for retraction. Some state laws allow punitive damages only on proof by plaintiff of a refusal to print a retraction when one has been requested.

Punitive damages greatly concern media lawyers because of their destructive potential. And "chilling effect" arguments may appeal to appellate judges more often than to jurors. In Carol Burnett's libel case against the *National Enquirer,* the court took into consideration the assets and profits of the defendant so as to punish and deter rather than destroy.[39] But, as we shall see, such judicial concern is not always the rule. Eventually the United States Supreme Court may have to consider the connection between publication, bankruptcy, and prior restraint.

Nominal or token damages represent a moral victory (a six cent or one dollar award) where there has been no real, substantial, or serious harm to a plaintiff's reputation or financial standing. Because *Gertz* requires a showing of actual injury

36. Maheu v. Hughes Tool Co., 3 Med.L.Rptr. 1847, 569 F.2d 459, 480 (9th Cir. 1977). Occasionally punitive damages are awarded in the absence of general damages. See, for example, Tunnell v. Edwardsville Intelligencer, Inc., 241 N.E.2d 28 (Ill. 1968).

37. Davis v. Schuchat, 510 F.2d 731 (D.C.Cir. 1975).

38. Stone v. Essex County Newspaper, 330 N.E.2d 161 (Mass.1975); Wheeler v. Green, 593 P.2d 777 (Or.1979); Taskett v. King Broadcasting Co., 1 Med.L.Rptr. 1716, 546 P.2d 81 (Wash.1976).

39. Burnett v. National Enquirer, 7 Med.L.Rptr. 1321 (Cal.Super.Ct.1981). A California Court of Appeal held the initial punitive damages award of $750,000 too high and ordered a new trial on that question unless Burnett would accept a reduced award of $150,000. See 9 Med.L.Rptr. 1921 (1983).

in libel suits, nominal damages may no longer be available.

The Traditional Threshold Elements of Actionable Libel: Defamation, Identification, and Publication

1. No libel action can succeed unless the plaintiff can prove that the *defamatory* meaning discussed in the previous section applies to him or her, that is, that there is specific *identification*. Someone must understand that the reference is to the plaintiff, even though identification is by nickname, pseudonym, or circumstance. One authority elaborates:

> It is sufficient if he is described by his initial letters, or by the first and last letters of his name, or even by asterisks, or blanks, or if he be referred to under the guise of an allegorical, historical, fictitious or fanciful name, or by means of a description of his physical peculiarities, or by the places which he has visited on his travels. Gatley, *Libel and Slander* (4th ed. 1953), 113.

Circumstances may pinpoint identification. An example from the past. In 1906 the borough of Manhattan had four coroners, and each coroner had a deputy who was a qualified physician. One of the coroners was convicted of attempted bribery in the performance of his duties. He would threaten bereaved survivors or commercial establishments, such as hotels, with unnecessary autopsies. A newspaper, in a broad exposé of the entire department, described how the shakedown worked and concluded that corruption pervaded the entire system. The convicted coroner's deputy-physician brought a successful libel action, although he had not been named in the news story.[40]

Note here that the group was small enough to permit individual identification. An article which referred to a "parking lot racket" in Washington, D.C., however, was held to be too broad to permit the operator of one of the lots to sue.[41] And when *Time* magazine charged that western officials of a union were conspiring with Seattle gamblers to control Portland's law enforcement agencies, the Oregon representative of the union was not sufficiently identified with the libel, said a federal court, to warrant his bringing an action.[42]

A radio-television actor named Joe Julian faced the same problem when he brought a libel action against a black-listing "anti-Communist" organization. Its publication, *Red Channels,* correctly reported that the actor had participated in Communist-front meetings in the 40s and in its introduction used words like "Communist dupe, tool, sucker, part of a transmission belt, fellow traveler, and red channel" to describe those of whom it disapproved. There were 151 such persons mentioned in the publication, but no indication as to which category applied to Julian. The actor couldn't overcome the problem of proving that the alleged libelous material was published of and concerning him.[43] A subsequent case—Faulk v. Aware, Inc., 155 N.Y.S.2d 726 (1956)—demonstrated that calling an entertainer a Communist or a pro-Communist could be an expensive indulgence. The case and the events leading up to it were described in detail in John Henry Faulk's book, *Fear on Trial* (1963), and in a subsequent CBS documentary. Attorney Louis Nizer won a $550,000 judgment for his client, although

40. Weston v. Commercial Advertiser Association, 77 N.E. 660 (N.Y.1906).

41. Service Parking Corp. v. Washington Times Co., 92 F.2d 502 (D.C.Cir.1937).

42. Crosby v. Time, Inc., 254 F.2d 927 (7th Cir. 1958).

43. Julian v. American Business Consultants, Inc., 155 N.Y.S.2d 1, 137 N.E.2d 1 (1956).

Faulk was never able to collect from his bankrupt adversaries.

Someone other than the plaintiff or defendant, then, must reasonably infer from the publication that the defamatory reference is to the plaintiff. And that someone may be a single person.[44] But there must be a third party. If a name is not used, the plaintiff must show, by what lawyers call *colloquium,* that the defamatory reference is to him or her.

Mistaken identity can ensnare the press. *Time* magazine found itself in libel litigation when, in an article on the unprofessional conduct of some lawyers, it confused attorney Richard J. Ryder with attorney Richard R. Ryder. The U.S. District Court for the District of Columbia granted *Time's* motion for summary judgment on grounds that the attorney as a public official or public figure appeared not to be able to prove actual malice. Disagreeing that the plaintiff was either a public figure or public official, the D.C. Court of Appeals reversed and remanded. "A modicum of care would have provided the correct identity" in terms of both name and address, said the appeals court. Ryder v. Time, Inc., 2 Med.L.Rptr. 1221, 557 F.2d 824 (D.C.Cir.1976). On remand a U.S. magistrate granted *Time* summary judgment again because the report, though erroneous, dealt with a matter of "public or general concern" and under Virginia law at the time this required a showing of actual malice.

"No one at *Time,* involved in writing, checking, or editing the Essay," said the court, "had ever heard of plaintiff or had any reason to believe that there might be more than one attorney named Richard Ryder in Virginia. * * * *Time* followed its standard procedures in preparing the Essay, and those procedures do not include a requirement for adding middle initials or local addresses." Ryder v. Time, Inc., 3 Med.L.Rptr. 1170 (D.D.C.1977).

Obviously more care with the name and address would have saved *Time* considerable trouble.

2. In libel the real harm is in the *publication,* in throwing the defamation to the four winds. Print media because of their permanence, radio and television because of their reach and impact can convey libels with devastating effect.

For there to be a libel, or a slander, there must be publication to a third person. The third person may be anyone, including a member of the plaintiff's family, although publication to one's spouse, attorney, physician, or priest is generally insufficient, since these are frequently privileged relationships.

In Avery Corp. v. Peterson, 178 F.Supp. 132 (D.Pa.1959), dictation of a defamatory letter to a corporation secretary by an officer of the firm was ruled a publication.

Printing, posting, circulating, or disseminating is the first step in publication; someone reading, viewing, or hearing the message is the second step. The third person, of course, must know to whom the defamatory publication refers for there to be *identification.*

3. Some states, including California, Illinois, and Pennsylvania, either by case law or by adoption of the Uniform Single Publication Act (13 U.L.A. 517), subscribe to what is called the *single publication rule:* an entire edition of a newspaper is treated as a single publication, rather than every single copy constituting a distinct publication and therefore a separate basis for a libel suit. In other words, the initial publication is one libel, one offense, one tort regardless of how many persons read it or how often they read it. The number of readers neither increases the magnitude of the libel nor allows for multiple causes of action, although a plaintiff is permitted

44. Gnapinsky v. Goldyn, 128 A.2d 697 (N.J.1957); Robinson v. Guy Gannett Publishing Co., 297 F.Supp. 722 (D.Me.1969).

to plead and prove extent of circulation as evidence bearing on damages.[45]

The Supreme Court of Georgia said in 1964: "To allow a suit for damages each time a different person sees the newspaper would unreasonably shackle the press and might quickly bankrupt it, thus doing great harm to both the publisher and the readers."[46]

In spite of California's Uniform Single Publication Act, a new libel action based on the paperback edition of a book was permitted, even though identical passages in the original hardcover edition had already been litigated.[47]

In cases of multistate circulation of newspapers or magazines, the single publication rule dictates that a cause of action for libel be absolutely complete at the time of first publication. Later circulation is relevant only in computing damages.[48] The rule obviously protects a publisher from the perpetual harassment of multiple and never-ending libel actions.[49]

A suit may be brought in the place where the defendant resides or does business, and this is frequently the point of publication; or in the place of largest circulation of the offending publication; or where the greatest harm was done the plaintiff—generally the plaintiff's place of residence. What lawyers call long-arm statutes can be applied to publishers of national newspapers without violating due process. So the *Los Angeles Times* and other news media could be sued in Wyoming for a story on organized crime that was researched in Wyoming by three *Times* reporters and had its major impact there. Anselmi v. Denver Post, Inc., 2 Med.L.Rptr. 1530, 552 F.2d 316 (10th Cir. 1977).

Generally, however, a newspaper published in a distant place must have sufficient business and professional impact or activity where the alleged libel has occurred to trigger a long-arm statute.

"[T]o sustain jurisdiction over a nonresident newspaper," said a court of appeals in 1964, "plaintiff must show more than 'mere circulation of a periodical through the mail to subscribers * * * and sporadic news gathering by reporters.'" Buckley v. New York Times Co., 338 F.2d 470, 474 (5th Cir. 1964).

In dismissing a libel suit for want of jurisdiction, a United States district court in Texas concluded that twenty-eight daily copies of the *Detroit Free Press* (.0044 percent of the paper's total daily circulation) were insufficient to constitute the minimum contacts necessary to sustain jurisdiction under the due process clause. Kersh v. Angelosante, 8 Med.L.Rptr. 1282 (N.D.Tex.1982).

Where the single publication rule is in effect, the libel suit may have to be brought in the place here the libel was published or where publication first occurred. Several courts have refused to let the single publication rule cross state lines and have allowed a separate cause of action in each state where publication

45. Rives v. Atlanta Newspapers, Inc., 139 S.E.2d 395 (Ga.1964).

46. Ibid., p. 398. See also Waskow v. Associated Press, 462 F.2d 1173 (D.C.Cir. 1972). Waskow, a "public figure" under the *New York Times v. Sullivan* doctrine, see text, p. 203, had argued that "back issues" of the *Washington Star* were sold subsequent to the date of the appearance of the original item in the *Star* libeling him and that as a result the libel was "republished" under the *New York Times* malice test. In view of the deadline under which metropolitan newspapers operate and the predetermined distribution system that they use once an edition is printed, the court rejected the libel plaintiff's republication theory: "[F]or purposes of the *Times* rule, a daily newspaper is 'published' once only—when it is printed and placed in the distribution system—unless it is redistributed *outside the normal channels* with the specific intent to convey the libelous information."

47. Kanarek v. Bugliosi, 6 Med.L.Rptr. 1864, 166 Cal.Rptr. 526 (1980).

48. Insul v. New York World Telegram Corp., 273 F.2d 166 (7th Cir. 1959).

49. Sorge v. Parade Publications, Inc., 247 N.Y.S.2d 317 (1964).

took place. A Pennsylvania rule recognized one aggregate cause of action for all single publication states plus additional causes of action for libels committed in multiple publication states.[50]

4. As has been noted, the second step in publication is taken when the libel effectively reaches those readers, listeners, viewers for whom publication is intended. In Zuck v. Interstate Publishing Corp., 317 F.2d 727 (2d Cir. 1963), it was decided that mere delivery of bundles of a periodical designed as an insert for a newspaper to a carrier or distributor did not constitute publication. There was no publication until the newspaper went on sale or began to circulate to the great mass of its subscribers. In such cases, the third party to publication is defined as the bulk of readers rather than a small or atypical segment of them.[51]

On the other hand, a number of courts have held that publication is effected when the libelous matter is delivered to common carriers for distribution. See Konigsberg v. Long Island Daily Press Publishing Co., 293 N.Y.S.2d 861 (1968); Novel v. Garrison, 294 F.Supp. 825 (D.Ill.1969). Whatever the rule, there is no necessity to prove that any part of the content of a publication has been read. See Hornby v. Hunter, 385 S.W.2d 473 (Tex.Civ.App. 1964).

Every purposive repetition of a defamation—picking up a libel from another publication, a new edition of a book, a rebroadcast—is a new publication. Identifying the source and leaving room for disbelief by an attribution such as "it is alleged" is no defense,[52] although it could mitigate damages. There is no liability, however, if a libelous article or statement is reprinted or rebroadcast without the original author's participation or consent,[53] or reprinted accidentally, unintentionally, or in a distorted form.[54]

The main point to remember is that for a libel action to proceed three conditions must be met by plaintiff: there must be defamation, identification, and intentional publication. Absent any one of these elements, no successful libel action can be brought.

5. Everyone who takes a conscious part in a publication is theoretically *liable* for damages. Usually the corporation—the party capable of paying hefty damages—is named defendant. A news source who generates a libel and authorizes its publication may also be liable.[55] Innocent coworkers such as carrier boys, vendors, broadcast engineers are generally not liable.[56] Reporters are often named as defendants by angry plaintiffs.

Plaintiffs in a minority of states—including New York and California where a high proportion of publishing takes place—must show actual malice on the part of executives higher up for punitive damages. For example, in Dresbach v. Doubleday Co., 7 Med.L.Rptr. 2105, 518 F.Supp. 1285 (D.D.C.1981), a United States district court held that a book publisher is not responsible for the independent verification of everything a reputable author writes. In most states, however, higher-ups *are* re-

50. Hartmann v. Time, Inc., 166 F.2d 127 (3d Cir. 1948), cert. den. 334 U.S. 838.

51. Osmers v. Parade Publications, Inc., 234 F.Supp. 924 (S.D.N.Y.1964); Fleury v. Harper & Row, 7 Med.L.Rptr. 1795 (D.Cal.1981).

52. Maloof v. Post Publishing Co., 28 N.E.2d 458 (Mass.1940).

53. Di Giorgio Corp. v. Valley Labor Citizen, 67 Cal.Rptr. 82 (1968).

54. Seroff v. Simon & Schuster, Inc., 162 N.Y.S.2d 770 (1957), affirmed 210 N.Y.S.2d 479 (1960). See also, Storch v. Gordon, 197 N.Y.S.2d 309 (1960).

55. Roberts v. Breckon, 52 N.Y.S. 638 (1898); Storch v. Gordon, 197 N.Y.S.2d 309 (1960), reargument 202 N.Y.S.2d 43; Campo v. Paar, 239 N.Y.S.2d 494 (1963).

56. Seroff v. Simon & Schuster, Inc., 162 N.Y.S.2d 770 (1957).

sponsible for libel committed by permanent or free-lance employees. This proposition is known as the *complicity rule.*

Under the *complicity rule,* editors or publishers could deny knowing what their reporters were doing; but this is hardly the mark of a responsible newspaper and could redound to the disadvantage of defendant when a court or jury considers the question of fault. Conversely, in New York or California a plaintiff might argue that a reporter is operating at a managerial level with a full mandate from a publisher. In the *Alton, Illinois* case, which will be referred to subsequently in the context of "megaverdicts," plaintiff could not show that the publisher knew of the defamatory memo sent by *Telegraph* reporters to a federal prosecutor, and, as it turned out, he didn't have to.

It is not a defense to say that the libel came from a regular and usually reliable news service. A Georgia court put it well:

> While the Associated Press no doubt deserves all that is said for it as being a trustworthy, honest, and accurate news gatherer, a newspaper, in publishing Associated Press news reports, cannot justify itself as publishing a privileged communication. * * * [57]

Again, the offense is in the publication, in the spreading of the defamatory falsehood.

COMMON LAW LIBEL AND THE ORIGINS OF THE CONSTITUTIONAL DEFENSE

Strict Liability

Under the common law rule of *strict liability,* libel *per se* was defined as defamatory words published in reference to a plaintiff with obvious and substantial damage to reputation. Falsity as to fact, lack of justification as to opinion, malice on the part of the publisher, and injury to the plaintiff were all presumed. Plaintiff having met the three threshold elements of actionable libel, the burden of proof then shifted to the defendant to present an affirmative defense of truth, privilege, or fair comment and criticism. Since these three common law defenses are still available to defendants, they will be discussed in more detail in later sections.

The problem with the rule of strict liability was that it took no account of a publisher's intent, degree of negligence, or level of professionalism, nor did it consider the extent of injury suffered by plaintiff. Indeed a publisher could be liable even where there was no apparent fault on his or her part. The rule begged timidity and self-censorship, although there is little evidence that such occurred.

Constitutionalizing the Law of Libel

1. Influenced by Alexander Meiklejohn's thesis that speech in the public realm is crucial to self-government and therefore warrants near absolute protection, Justice William Brennan in his 1964 opinion for the Court in *New York Times v. Sullivan* made libel of public officials a constitutional matter. But for the qualification of *actual malice,* Brennan would have reached the Meiklejohnian summit of protection for public speech.[58]

2. The *New York Times* case rose out of the turmoil of the Black Revolution. On March 29, 1960, a full-page editorial advertisement appeared in the *New York Times*

57. Wood v. Constitution Publishing Co., 194 S.E. 760 (Ga.1937).

58. Gillmor, "Justice William Brennan and the Failed "Theory" of Actual Malice," 59 *Journalism Quarterly* 249 (Summer 1982).

under the headline, "Heed Their Rising Voices." The ad copy began by stating that the nonviolent civil rights movement in the South was being met by a wave of terror. The ad concluded with an appeal for funds in support of the student movement, voting rights, and the legal defense of Martin Luther King, Jr. In addition to the signatures of sixty-four prominent Americans, sixteen southern clergymen were purported to have signed the ad. Segments of two paragraphs of the text became the focal points of subsequent litigation:

> In Montgomery, Alabama, after students sang "My Country 'Tis of Thee" on the State Capitol steps, their leaders were expelled from school, and truckloads of police armed with shotguns and tear-gas ringed the Alabama State College Campus. When the entire student body protested to state authorities by refusing to re-register, their dining hall was padlocked in an attempt to starve them into submission. * * *
>
> Again and again the Southern violators have answered Dr. King's peaceful protests with intimidation and violence. They have bombed his home almost killing his wife and child. They have assaulted his person. They have arrested him seven times—for "speeding," "loitering" and similar "offenses." And now they have charged him with "perjury"—a *felony* under which they could imprison him for *ten years.* * *

L. B. Sullivan, one of three elected commissioners of Montgomery, brought a civil libel action against four black Alabama clergymen, whose names had appeared in the ad, and the *Times.* In accordance with Alabama law, Sullivan, before bringing action, demanded in writing a public retraction from the clergymen and the newspaper. The clergymen did not respond on the grounds that use of their names was unauthorized. The *Times* did not publish a retraction but wrote Sullivan asking how the statements in the ad reflected on him. The commissioner filed suit without answering the query.

Although not mentioned by name, Sullivan contended that he represented the "police" referred to in the ad; therefore he was being accused of ringing the campus with police and starving the students into submission. He also claimed that the term "Southern violators" was meant to apply to him; therefore he was being accused of "intimidation and violence," bombing Dr. King's home, assaulting his person, and charging the civil rights leader with perjury. Witnesses testified that they identified the commissioner in the ad.

With the elements of libel thus established, Sullivan proceeded to show that most of the charges could not in fact have applied to him because they referred to incidents which had occurred before his election. Moreover, there were serious inaccuracies in the ad, creating a presumption of general damages under Alabama law.

In its defense, the *Times* pointed out that the ad had come to it from a New York advertising agency representing the signatory committee. A letter from A. Philip Randolph accompanied the ad and certified that the persons whose names appeared in it had given their permission. It was not considered necessary to confirm the accuracy of the ad by the manager of the Advertising Acceptability Department or anyone else at the *Times.* Nor were there any doubts about the authorization of the ad by the individual southern clergymen (they were later absolved of any responsibility because they were unaware of the ad).

The *Times* could not see how any of the language of the ad referred to Sullivan.

The trial judge submitted the case to the jury under instructions that the statements in the ad were libelous *per se* and without privilege. He also left the door open for punitive damages by an imprecise definition of what was required to support them.

The Circuit Court awarded $500,000 to Sullivan. The Supreme Court of Alabama affirmed, and the *Times* appealed to the United States Supreme Court.

At the heart of the brief submitted to the Court on behalf of Sullivan was the argument that "the Constitution has never required that states afford newspapers the privilege of leveling false and defamatory 'facts' at persons simply because they hold public office. The great weight of American authority has rejected such a plea by newspapers." See Brief for the Respondent, 376 United States Supreme Court Records and Briefs 254–314 (Vol. 12), p. 23.

The argument for the *Times* was more provocative and, as it turned out, more persuasive. In part it stated:

> Under the doctrine of *libel per se* applied below a public official is entitled to recover "presumed" and punitive damages for a publication found to be critical of the official conduct of a governmental agency under his general supervision if a jury thinks the publication "tends" to "injure" him "in his reputation" to "bring" him "into public contempt" as an official. The publisher has no defense unless he can persuade the jury that the publication is entirely true in all its factual, material particulars. The doctrine not only dispenses with proof of injury by the complaining official, but presumes malice and falsity as well. Such a rule of liability works an abridgement of the freedom of the press. Brief for the Petitioner, 376 United States Supreme Court Records and Briefs 254–314 (Vol. 12), pp. 28–29.

Attorneys for the *Times* had deftly raised the specter of seditious libel, and the Court responded.

NEW YORK TIMES CO. v. SULLIVAN

376 U.S. 254, 84 S.CT. 710, 11 L.ED.2D 686 (1964).

Justice BRENNAN delivered the Opinion of the Court: * * *

Because of the importance of the constitutional issues involved, we granted the separate petitions for certiorari of the individual petitioners and of the Times. * * * We reverse the judgment. We hold that the rule of law applied by the Alabama courts is constitutionally deficient for failure to provide the safeguards for freedom of speech and of the press that are required by the First and Fourteenth Amendments in a libel action brought by a public official against critics of his official conduct. We further hold that under the proper safeguards the evidence presented in this case is constitutionally insufficient to support the judgment for respondent.

We may dispose at the outset of two grounds asserted to insulate the judgment of the Alabama courts from constitutional scrutiny. The first is the proposition relied on by the State Supreme Court—that "The Fourteenth Amendment is directed against State action and not private action." That proposition has no application to this case. Although this is a civil lawsuit between private parties, the Alabama courts have applied a state rule of law which petitioners claim to impose invalid restrictions on their constitutional freedoms of speech and press. * * *

The second contention is that the constitutional guarantees of freedom of speech and of the press are inapplicable here, at least so far as the Times is concerned, because the allegedly libelous statements were published as part of a paid, "commercial" advertisement. The argument relies on Valentine v. Chrestensen, 316 U.S. 52 (1942), where the Court held that a city ordinance forbidding street distribution of commercial and business advertising matter did not abridge the First Amendment freedoms, even as applied to a handbill having a commercial message on one side but a protest against certain official action on the other. The reliance is wholly misplaced. The Court in Chrestensen reaffirmed the constitutional protection for "the freedom of communicating information and disseminating opinion"; its holding was based upon the factual conclusions that the handbill was "purely commercial advertising" and that the protest against official action had been added only to evade the ordinance.

The publication here was not a "commercial" advertisement in the sense in which the word was used in Chrestensen. It communicated information, expressed opinion, recited grievances, protested claimed abuses, and sought financial support on behalf of a movement whose existence and objectives are matters of the highest public interest and concern. That the *Times* was paid for publishing the advertisement is as immaterial in this connection as is the fact that newspapers and books are sold. Any other conclusion would discourage newspapers from carrying "editorial advertisements" of this type, and so might shut off an important outlet for the promulgation of information and ideas by persons who do not themselves have access to publishing facilities—who wish to exercise their freedom of speech even though they are not members of the press. The effect would be to shackle the First Amendment in its attempt to secure "the widest possible dissemination of information from diverse and antagonistic sources." To avoid placing such a handicap upon the freedoms of expression, we hold that if the allegedly libelous statements would otherwise be constitutionally protected from the present judgment, they do not forfeit that protection because they were published in the form of a paid advertisement.

Under Alabama law as applied in this case, a publication is "libelous per se" if the words "tend to injure a person * * * in his reputation" or to "bring [him] into public contempt"; the trial court stated that the standard was met if the words are such as to "injure him in his public office, or impute misconduct to him in his office, or want of official integrity, or want of fidelity to a public trust * * *." The jury must find that the words were published "of and concerning" the plaintiff, but where the plaintiff is a public official his place in the governmental hierarchy is sufficient evidence to support a finding that his reputation has been affected by statements that reflect upon the agency of which he is in charge. Once "libel per se" has been established, the defendant has no defense as to stated facts unless he can persuade the jury that they were true in all their particulars. * * * His privilege of "fair comment" for expressions of opinion depends on the truth of the facts upon which the comment is based. * * * Unless he can discharge the burden of proving truth, general damages are presumed, and may be awarded without proof of pecuniary injury. A showing of actual malice is apparently a prerequisite to recovery of punitive damages, and the defendant may in any event forestall a punitive award by a retraction meeting the statutory requirements. Good motives and belief in truth do not negate an inference of malice, but are relevant only in mitigation of punitive damages if the jury chooses to accord them weight. * * *

The general proposition that freedom of expression upon public questions is secured by the First Amendment has long been settled by our decisions. The constitutional safeguard, we have said, "was fashioned to assure unfettered interchange of ideas for the bringing about of political and social changes desired by the people." "The maintenance of the opportunity for free political discussion to the end that government may be responsive to the will of the people and that changes may be obtained by lawful means, an opportunity essential to the security of the Republic, is a fundamental principle of our constitutional system." "[I]t is a prized American privilege to speak one's mind, although not always with perfect good taste, on all public institutions," and this opportunity is to be afforded for "vigorous advocacy" no less than "abstract discussion." * * *

The First Amendment, said Judge Learned Hand, "presupposes that right conclusions are more likely to be gathered out of a multitude of tongues, than through any kind of authoritative selection. To many this is, and always will be, folly; but we have staked upon it our all." United States v. Associated Press, 52 F.Supp. 362, 372 (S.D.N.Y.1943).

Thus we consider this case against the background of a profound national commitment to the principle that debate on public issues should be uninhibited, robust, and wide-open, and that it may well include vehement, caustic, and sometimes unpleasantly sharp attacks on government and public officials. [Emphasis added.] The present advertisement, as an expression of grievance and protest on one of the major public issues of our time, would seem clearly to qualify for the constitutional protection. The question is whether it forfeits that protection by the falsity of some of its factual statements and by its alleged defamation of respondent.

Authoritative interpretations of the First Amendment guarantees have consistently refused to recognize an exception for any test of truth—whether administered by judges, juries, or administrative officials—and especially one that puts the burden of proving truth on the speaker. * * *

[E]rroneous statement is inevitable in free debate, and * * * it must be protected if the freedoms of expression are to have the "breathing space" that they "need * * * to survive." * * *

Just as factual error affords no warrant for repressing speech that would otherwise be free, the same is true of injury to official reputation. Where judicial officers are involved, this Court has held that concern for the dignity and reputation of the courts does not justify the punishment as criminal contempt of criticism of the judge or his decision. This is true even though the utterance contains "half-truths" and "misinformation." Such repression can be justified, if at all, only by a clear and present danger of the obstruction of justice. If judges are to be treated as "men of fortitude, able to thrive in a hardy climate," surely the same must be true of other government officials, such as elected city commissioners. Criticism of their official conduct does not lose its constitutional protection merely because it is effective criticism and hence diminishes their official reputations.

If neither factual error nor defamatory content suffices to remove the constitutional shield from criticism of official conduct, the combination of the two elements is no less inadequate. This is the lesson to be drawn from the great controversy over the Sedition Act of 1798, 1 Stat. 596, which first crystallized a national awareness of the central meaning of the First Amendment. See Levy, Legacy of Suppression (1960), at 258 et seq. * * * That statute made it a crime, punishable by a $5,000 fine and five years in prison, "if any person shall write, print, utter or publish * * * any false, scandalous and malicious writing or writings against the government of the United States, or either house of the Congress * * * or the President * * * with intent to defame * * * or to bring them * * * into contempt or disrepute; or to excite against them, or either or any of them, the hatred of the good people of the United States." The Act allowed the defendant the defense of truth, and provided that the jury were to be judges both of the law and the facts. Despite these qualifications, the Act was vigorously condemned as unconstitutional in an attack joined in by Jefferson and Madison. * * * Although the Sedition Act was never tested in this Court, the attack upon its validity has carried the day in the court of history. Fines levied in its prosecution were repaid by Act of Congress on the ground that it was unconstitutional. * * *

What a State may not constitutionally bring about by means of a criminal statute is likewise beyond the reach of its civil law of libel. The fear of damage awards under a rule such as that invoked by the Alabama courts here may be markedly more inhibiting than the fear of prosecution under a criminal statute. * * * Alabama, for example, has a criminal libel law which subjects to prosecution "any person who speaks, writes, or prints of and concerning another any accusation falsely and maliciously importing the commission by such person of a felony, or any other indictable offense involving moral turpitude," and which allows as punishment upon conviction a fine not exceeding $500 and a prison sentence of six months. * * * Presumably a person charged with violation of this statute enjoys ordinary criminal-law safeguards such as the requirements of an indictment and of proof beyond a reasonable doubt. These safeguards are not available to the defendant in a civil action. The judgment awarded in this case—without the need for any proof of actual pecuniary loss—was one thousand times greater than the maximum fine provided by the Alabama criminal statute, and one hundred times greater than that provided by the Sedition Act. And since there is no double-jeopardy limitation applicable to civil lawsuits, this is not the only judgment that may be awarded against petitioners for the same publication.[18] Whether or not a newspaper can survive a succession of such judgments, the pall of fear and timidity imposed upon those who would give voice to public criticism is an atmosphere in which the First Amendment freedoms cannot survive. * *

The state rule of law is not saved by its allowance of the defense of truth. A defense for erroneous statements honestly made is no less essential here than was the requirement of proof of guilty knowledge which, in Smith v. California, we held indispensable to a valid conviction of a bookseller for possessing obscene writings for sale. * * * A rule compelling the critic of official conduct to guarantee the truth of all his factual assertions—and to do so on pain of libel judgments virtually unlimited in amount—leads to a comparable "self-censorship." Allowance of the defense of truth, with the burden of proving it on the defendant, does not mean that only false speech will be deterred. Even courts accepting this defense as an adequate safeguard have recognized the difficulties of adducing legal proofs that the alleged libel was true in all its factual particulars. * * * Under such a rule, would-be critics of official conduct may be deterred from voicing their criticism, even though it is believed to be true and even though it is in fact true, because of doubt whether it can be proved in court or fear of the expense of having to do so. They tend to make only statements which "steer far wider of the unlawful zone." * * * The rule thus dampens the vigor and limits the variety of public debate. It is inconsistent with the First and Fourteenth Amendments.

The constitutional guarantees require, we think, a federal rule that prohibits a public official from recovering damages for a defamatory falsehood relating to his official conduct *unless he proves that the statement was made with "actual malice" —that is, with knowledge that it was false or with reckless disregard of whether it was false or not.* [Emphasis added.] * *

Such a privilege for criticism of official conduct is appropriately analogous to the protection accorded a public official when *he* is sued for libel by a private citizen. *In*

18. The *Times* states that four other libel suits based on the advertisement have been filed against it by others who have served as Montgomery City Commissioners and by the Governor of Alabama; that another $500,000 verdict has been awarded in the only one of these cases that has yet gone to trial; and that the damages sought in the other three total $2,000,000.

Barr v. Matteo, 360 U.S. 564, 575 (1959), this Court held the utterance of a federal official to be absolutely privileged if made "within the outer perimeter" of his duties. [Emphasis added.] The States accord the same immunity to statements of their highest officers, although some differentiate their lesser officials and qualify the privilege they enjoy. But all hold that all officials are protected unless actual malice can be proved. The reason for the official privilege is said to be that the threat of damage suits would otherwise "inhibit the fearless, vigorous, and effective administration of policies of government" and "dampen the ardor of all but the most resolute, or the most irresponsible, in the unflinching discharge of their duties." Barr v. Matteo. Analogous considerations support the privilege for citizen-critic of government. It is as much his duty to criticize as it is the official's duty to administer. As Madison said, "the censorial power is in the people over the Government, and not in the Government over the people." It would give public servants an unjustified preference over the public they serve, if critics of official conduct did not have a fair equivalent of the immunity granted to the officials themselves.

We conclude that such a privilege is required by the First and Fourteenth Amendments.

We hold today that the Constitution delimits a State's power to award damages for libel in actions brought by public officials against critics of their official conduct. Since this is such an action, the rule requiring proof of actual malice is applicable. While Alabama law apparently requires proof of actual malice for an award of punitive damages, where general damages are concerned malice is "presumed." Such a presumption is inconsistent with the federal rule. * * * Since the trial judge did not instruct the jury to differentiate between general and punitive damages, it may be that the verdict was wholly an award of one or the other. But it is impossible to know, in view of the general verdict returned. Because of this uncertainty, the judgment must be reversed and the case remanded. * * *

Since respondent may seek a new trial, we deem that considerations of effective judicial administration require us to review the evidence in the present record to determine whether it could constitutionally support a judgment for respondent. This Court's duty is not limited to the elaboration of constitutional principles; we must also in proper cases review the evidence to make certain that those principles have been constitutionally applied. This is such a case, particularly since the question is one of alleged trespass across "the line between speech unconditionally guaranteed and speech which may legitimately be regulated." In cases where that line must be drawn, the rule is that we "examine for ourselves the statements in issue and the circumstances under which they were made to see * * * whether they are of a character which the principles of the First Amendment, as adopted by the Due Process Clause of the Fourteenth Amendment, protect." * * * We must "make an independent examination of the whole record," * * * so as to assure ourselves that the judgment does not constitute a forbidden intrusion on the field of free expression.

Applying these standards, we consider that the proof presented to show actual malice lacks the *convincing clarity* which the constitutional standard demands, and hence that it would not constitutionally sustain the judgment for respondent under the proper rule of law. The case of the individual petitioners requires little discussion. Even assuming that they could constitutionally be found to have authorized the use of their names on the advertisement, there was no evidence whatever that they were aware of any erroneous statements or were in any way reckless in that regard. The judgment against them is thus without constitutional support. [Emphasis added.]

As to the *Times*, we similarly conclude that the facts do not support a finding of actual malice. The statement by the Times' Secretary that, apart from the padlocking allegation, he thought the advertisement was "substantially correct," affords no constitutional warrant for the Alabama Supreme Court's conclusion that it was a "cavalier ignoring of the falsity of the advertisement [from which], the jury could not have but been impressed with the bad faith of the *Times*, and its maliciousness inferable therefrom." The statement does not indicate malice at the time of the publication; even if the advertisement was not "substantially correct"—although respondent's own proofs tend to show that it was—that opinion was at least a reasonable one, and there was no evidence to impeach the witness' good faith in holding it. The *Times*' failure to retract upon respondent's demand, although it later retracted upon the demand of Governor Patterson, is likewise not adequate evidence of malice for constitutional purposes. Whether or not a failure to retract may ever constitute such evidence, there are two reasons why it does not here. *First,* the letter written by the *Times* reflected a reasonable doubt on its part as to whether the advertisement could reasonably be taken to refer to respondent at all. *Second,* it was not a final refusal, since it asked for an explanation on this point—a request that respondent chose to ignore. * * *

Finally, there is evidence that the *Times* published the advertisement without checking its accuracy against the news stories in the *Times*' own files. The mere presence of the stories in the files does not, of course, establish that the *Times* "knew" the advertisement was false, since the state of mind required for actual malice would have to be brought home to the persons in the *Times*' organization having responsibility for the publication of the advertisement. With respect to the failure of those persons to make the check, the record shows that they relied upon their knowledge of the good reputation of many of those whose names were listed as sponsors of the advertisement, and upon the letter from A. Philip Randolph, known to them as a responsible individual, certifying that the use of the names was authorized. There was testimony that the persons handling the advertisement saw nothing in it that would render it unacceptable under the *Times*' policy of rejecting advertisements containing "attacks of a personal character"; their failure to reject it on this ground was not unreasonable. We think the evidence against the *Times* supports at most a finding of negligence in failing to discover the misstatements, and is constitutionally insufficient to show the recklessness that is required for a finding of actual malice.

We also think the evidence was constitutionally defective in another respect: it was incapable of supporting the jury's finding that the allegedly libelous statements were made "of and concerning" respondent. Respondent relies on the words of the advertisement and the testimony of six witnesses to establish a connection between it and himself. * * * There was no reference to respondent in the advertisement, either by name or official position. A number of the allegedly libelous statements—the charges that the dining hall was padlocked and that Dr. King's home was bombed, his person assaulted, and a perjury prosecution instituted against him—did not even concern the police; despite the ingenuity of the arguments which would attach this significance to the word "They," it is plain that these statements could not reasonably be read as accusing respondent of personal involvement in the acts in question. The statements upon which respondent principally relies as referring to him are the two allegations that did concern the police or police functions: that "truckloads of police

* * * ringed the Alabama State College Campus" after the demonstration on the State Capitol steps, and that Dr. King had been "arrested * * * seven times." These statements were false only in that the police had been "deployed near" the campus but had not actually "ringed" it and had not gone there in connection with the State Capitol demonstration, and in that Dr. King had been arrested only four times. The ruling that these discrepancies between what was true and what was asserted were sufficient to injure respondent's reputation may itself raise constitutional problems, but we need not consider them here. Although the statements may be taken as referring to the police, they did not on their face make even an oblique reference to respondent as an individual. Support for the asserted reference must, therefore, be sought in the testimony of respondent's witnesses. But none of them suggested any basis for the belief that respondent himself was attacked in the advertisement beyond the bare fact that he was in overall charge of the Police Department and thus bore official responsibility for police conduct; to the extent that some of the witnesses thought respondent to have been charged with ordering or approving the conduct or otherwise being personally involved in it, they based this notion not on any statements in the advertisement, and not on any evidence that he had in fact been so involved, but solely on the unsupported assumption that, because of his official position, he must have been. This reliance on the bare fact of respondent's official position was made explicit by the Supreme Court of Alabama. That court, in holding that the trial court "did not err in overruling the demurrer [of the *Times*] in the aspect that the libelous matter was not of and concerning the [plaintiff,]" based its ruling on the proposition that:

"We think it common knowledge that the average person knows that municipal agents, such as police and firemen, and others, are under the control and direction of the city governing body, and more particularly under the direction and control of a single commissioner. In measuring the performance or deficiencies of such groups, praise or criticism is usually attached to the official in complete control of the body."

This proposition has disquieting implications for criticism of governmental conduct. For good reason, "no court of last resort in this country has ever held, or even suggested, that prosecutions for libel on government have any place in the American system of jurisprudence." * * * The present proposition would sidestep this obstacle by transmuting criticism of government, however impersonal it may seem on its face, into personal criticism, and hence potential libel, of the officials of whom the government is composed. There is no legal alchemy by which a *State* may thus create the cause of action that would otherwise be denied for a publication which, as respondent himself said of the advertisement, "reflects not only on me but on the other Commissioners and the community." Raising as it does the possibility that a good-faith critic of government will be penalized for his criticism, the proposition relied on by the Alabama courts strikes at the very center of the constitutionally protected area of free expression. We hold that such a proposition may not constitutionally be utilized to establish that an otherwise impersonal attack on governmental operations was a libel of an official responsible for those operations. Since it was relied on exclusively here, and there was no other evidence to connect the statements with respondent, the evidence was constitutionally insufficient to support a finding that the statements referred to respondent.

The judgment of the Supreme Court of Alabama is reversed and the case is remanded to that court for further proceedings not inconsistent with this opinion.

Reversed and remanded.

Justice BLACK, with whom Justice Douglas joins (concurring).

* * * In reversing, the Court holds that "the Constitution delimits a State's power to award damages for libel in actions brought by public officials against critics of their official conduct." I base my vote to reverse on the belief that the First and Fourteenth Amendments not merely "delimit" a State's power to award damages to "public officials against critics of their official conduct" but completely prohibit a State from exercising such a power. The Court goes on to hold that a State can subject such critics to damages if "actual malice" can be proved against them. "Malice," even as defined by the Court, is an elusive, abstract concept, hard to prove and hard to disprove. The requirement that malice be proved provides at best an evanescent protection for the right critically to discuss public affairs and certainly does not measure up to the sturdy safeguard embodied in the First Amendment. Unlike the Court, therefore, I vote to reverse exclusively on the ground that the *Times* and the individual defendants had an absolute, unconditional constitutional right to publish in the *Times* advertisement their criticisms of the Montgomery agencies and officials. * * *

* * *

Expanding the New York Times Doctrine

1. Later the same year, the Court expanded the *New York Times* doctrine to reach *criminal libel* prosecutions. Historically, criminal libel laws were intended to protect the public peace and good order. Mob violence or other breaches of the peace, it was asserted, would be created by defamations against social groups (religious, racial, family, etc.) or government officials. The distinction between criminal and seditious libels was less than clear.

So the state became plaintiff on behalf of the public. Truth, or truth published with good motives and for justifiable ends, was a defense. Privilege was a defense in some jurisdictions. As a result of Garrison v. Louisiana, 379 U.S. 64 (1964), actual malice had to be proven by the prosecution beyond a reasonable doubt in criminal libel cases.

Because of its closeness to sedition, criminal libel has not found favor in American courts. It reached its high-water mark in 1952 when the United States Supreme Court decided Beauharnais v. Illinois, 343 U.S. 250 (1952).

Beauharnais, a hatemonger who circulated pamphlets designed to pit white against black, was convicted under a 1949 Illinois criminal libel law, a law that would reappear in the *Skokie* cases twenty-five years later. The law made it a crime to exhibit in any public place any publication which "portrays depravity, criminality, unchastity, or lack of virtue of a class of citizens, or any race, color, creed or religion."

Its constitutionality was upheld in a 5–4 decision in which Justice Felix Frankfurter for the Court said no to the question, Is speech devoted to racial hatred so high on the scale of constitutional values that it cannot be abridged by lawmakers?

Frankfurter argued that the importance of protecting groups from harassment and vilification was so important that it justified some limitation on free speech. Furthermore, the Court had held in Chaplinsky v. New Hampshire, 315 U.S. 568 (1942) that "fighting words"—those which by their very utterance inspire violence or tend to incite an immediate breach of the peace—are not constitutionally protected; such expression forms no essential part of the exposition of ideas and has slight social value.

Black and Douglas in dissent contended that free speech is too important a part of the democratic commitment to be sacrificed to the comfort and protection of any single social group. And they advanced a shoe-on-the-other-foot argument: tomorrow, under a criminal libel law, advocacy of rejection of the Ku Klux Klan might be declared illegal.

This confrontation between free speech and social equality remains an interesting one. Which value do we risk? Do some of us need protection from the wrath of the bigot? [59]

Beauharnais has neither been followed nor reversed, but its minority opinions would seem to have carried the day. The fear that criminal libel laws would eventually suppress unpopular expression has prevailed.

For example, a labor organizer was sentenced to six months and fined $3,000 under Kentucky's common law of criminal libel for printing a pamphlet in support of striking miners and defamatory of law enforcement officials and a newspaper publisher.

On appeal, Justice Douglas, writing for the Court, said "that to make an offense of conduct which is 'calculated to create disturbances of the peace' leaves wide open the standard of responsibility. It involves calculations as to the boiling point of a particular person or a particular group, not an appraisal of the nature of the comments *per se.* This kind of criminal libel 'makes a man a criminal simply because his neighbors have no self-control and cannot refrain from violence.' " [60]

It has been suggested that bad motives should never be assumed where public speech is concerned, and rather than limit discussion about minority groups, we should facilitate discussion *by* minority groups.[61]

The *coup de grâce* for criminal libel in the United States may have come when the once notorious District Attorney Jim Garrison took it upon himself to criticize eight New Orleans judges.

GARRISON v. STATE OF LOUISIANA

379 U.S. 64, 85 S.CT. 209, 3 L.ED.2D 125 (1964).

Justice BRENNAN delivered the opinion of the Court.

Appellant is the District Attorney of Orleans Parish, Louisiana. During a dispute with the eight judges of the Criminal District Court of the Parish, he held a press conference at which he issued a statement disparaging their judicial conduct. As a result, he was tried without a jury before a judge from another parish and convicted of criminal defamation under the Louisiana Criminal Defamation Statute. * * * The principal charges alleged to be defamatory were his attribution of a large backlog of pending criminal cases to the inefficiency, laziness, and excessive vacations of the judges, and his accusation that, by refusing to authorize disbursements to cover the expenses of undercover investigations of vice in New Orleans, the judges had hampered his efforts to enforce the vice laws. In impugning their motives, he said:

"The judges have now made it eloquently clear where their sympathies lie in regard to aggressive vice investigations by refusing to authorize use of the DA's funds to pay for the cost of closing down the Canal Street clip joints.

"* * * This raises interesting questions about the racketeer influences on our eight vacation-minded judges."

The Supreme Court of Louisiana affirmed the conviction. * * * The trial

59. David Riesman in *Democracy and Defamation: Control of Group Libel,* 42 Columbia L.Rev. 727 (1942) relates how the Nazis used group defamation to purge their opposition, set up Jewish scapegoats, and prepare the way for the Holocaust.

60. Ashton v. Kentucky, 384 U.S. 195 (1966).

61. Beth, *Group Libel and Free Speech,* 39 Minn.L.Rev. 167 (1955).

court and the State Supreme Court both rejected appellant's contention that the statute unconstitutionally abridged his freedom of expression. * * *

* * * At the outset, we must decide whether, in view of the differing history and purposes of criminal libel, the *New York Times* rule also limits state power to impose criminal sanctions for criticism of the official conduct of public officials. We hold that it does.

Where criticism of public officials is concerned, we see no merit in the argument that criminal libel statutes serve interests distinct from those secured by civil libel laws, and therefore, should not be subject to the same limitations. * * * At common law, truth was no defense to criminal libel. Although the victim of a true but defamatory publication might not have been unjustly damaged in reputation by the libel, the speaker was still punishable since the remedy was designed to avert the possibility that the utterance would provoke an enraged victim to a breach of peace. * * * [P]reference for the civil remedy, which enabled the frustrated victim to trade chivalrous satisfaction for damages, had substantially eroded the breach of the peace justification for criminal libel laws. In fact, in earlier, more violent, times, the civil remedy had virtually pre-empted the field of defamation; except as a weapon against seditious libel, the criminal prosecution fell into virtual desuetude. Changing mores and the virtual disappearance of criminal libel prosecutions lend support to the observation that "* * * under modern conditions, when the rule of law is generally accepted as a substitute for private physical measures, it can hardly be urged that the maintenance of peace requires a criminal prosecution for private defamation."

* * *

* * * In any event, where the criticism is of public officials and their conduct of public business, the interest in private reputation is overborne by the larger public interest, secured by the Constitution, in the dissemination of truth.

* * *

We held in *New York Times* that a public official might be allowed the civil remedy only if he establishes that the utterance was false and that it was made with knowledge of its falsity or in reckless disregard of whether it was false or true. The reasons which led us so to hold in *New York Times* apply with no less force merely because the remedy is criminal. The constitutional guarantees of freedom of expression compel application of the same standard to the criminal remedy. Truth may not be the subject of either civil or criminal sanctions where discussion of public affairs is concerned. And since "* * * erroneous statement is inevitable in free debate, and * * * it must be protected if the freedoms of expression are to have the 'breathing space' that they 'need * * * to survive' * * *," *only those false statements made with the high degree of awareness of their probable falsity demanded by New York Times may be the subject of either civil or criminal sanctions.* [Emphasis added.] For speech concerning public affairs is more than self-expression; it is the essence of self-government.

The use of calculated falsehood, however, would put a different cast on the constitutional question. Although honest utterance, even if inaccurate, may further the fruitful exercise of the right of free speech, it does not follow that the lie, knowingly and deliberately published about a public official, should enjoy a like immunity. At the time the First Amendment was adopted, as today, there were those unscrupulous enough and skillful enough to use the deliberate or reckless falsehood as an effective political tool to unseat the public servant or even topple an administration. * * * That speech is used as a tool for political ends does not automatically bring it under the protective mantle of the Constitution. For the use of the known lie as a tool is at once at odds with the premises of democratic government and with the orderly manner in which economic, social, or political change is to be effected. Calculated falsehood falls into that class of utterances which "are no essential part of any exposition of ideas, and are of such slight social value as a step to truth that any benefit that may be derived from them is clearly outweighed by the social interest in order and morality. * * *" Hence the knowingly false statement and the false statement made with reckless disregard of the truth, do not enjoy constitutional protection.

* * *

We do not think, however, that appellant's statement may be considered as one constituting only a purely private defamation. The accusation concerned the judges' conduct of the business of the Criminal District Court. Of course, any criticism of the manner in which a public official performs his duties will tend to affect his private, as well as his public, reputation. The *New York Times* rule is not rendered inapplicable merely because an official's private reputation, as well as his public reputation, is harmed. The public-official rule protects the paramount public interest in a free flow of information to the people concerning public officials, their servants. *To this end, anything which might touch on an official's fitness for office is relevant.* [Emphasis added.] Few personal attributes are more germane to fitness for office than dishonesty, malfeasance, or improper motivation, even though these characteristics may also affect the official's private character. * *

Applying the principles of the *New York Times* case, we hold that the Louisiana statute, as authoritatively interpreted by the Supreme Court of Louisiana, incorporates constitutionally invalid standards in the context of criticism of the official conduct of public officials. For contrary to the *New York Times* rule, which absolutely prohibits punishment of truthful criticism, the statute directs punishment for true statements made with "actual malice." * * * The statute is also unconstitutional as interpreted to cover false statements against public officials. The *New York Times* standard forbids the punishment of false statements, unless made with knowledge of their falsity or in reckless disregard of whether they are true or false. But the Louisiana statute punishes false statements without regard to that test if made with ill-will; even if ill-will is not established, a false statement concerning public officials can be punished if not made in the reasonable belief of its truth. * * * The reasonable-belief standard applied by the trial judge is not the same as the reckless-disregard-of-truth standard. According to the trial court's opinion, a reasonable belief is one which "an ordinarily prudent man might be able to assign a just and fair reason for"; the suggestion is that under this test the immunity from criminal responsibility in the absence of ill-will disappears on proof that the exercise of ordinary care would have revealed that the statement was false. The test which we laid down in *New York Times* is not keyed to ordinary care; defeasance of the privilege is conditioned, not on mere negligence, but on reckless disregard for the truth.

Reversed.

COMMENT

1. Justice Douglas in a concurring opinion rejected "actual malice" as a constitutional standard, and of criminal libel he said:

> *Beauharnais v. Illinois,* * * * a case decided by the narrowest of margins, should be overruled as a misfit in our constitutional system and as out of line with the dictates of the First Amendment. I think it is time to face the fact

> that the only line drawn by the Constitution is between "speech" on the one side and conduct or overt acts on the other. The two often do blend. I have expressed the idea before: "Freedom of expression can be suppressed if, and to the extent that, it is so closely brigaded with illegal action as to be an inseparable part of it * * *."

Is this essentially the theory of freedom of expression articulated by Thomas I. Emerson in *Toward a General Theory of the First Amendment* (1967) and in *The System of Freedom of Expression* (1970)?

It should be noted that state constitutions may in some cases provide greater protection to free press than the U.S. Constitution, and the U.S. Supreme Court will be reluctant to review state court rulings based on those constitutions.

2. Having extended the *New York Times* rule to criminal libel, the next step in the onward march of the doctrine for the Supreme Court was to define, and by defining to expand, the term "public official."

In Rosenblatt v. Baer, 383 U.S. 75 (1966), Justice Brennan, speaking for the Court, held "that the 'public official' designation applies at the very least to those among the hierarchy of government employees who have, or appear to the public to have, substantial responsibility for government operations * * * lest criticism of government itself be penalized." No matter that plaintiff in the case was a former supervisor of a county recreation area whose policy-making responsibilities were modest.

Within a few years, scores of unsuccessful libel plaintiffs in both state and federal courts learned that a public official could be anyone, past or present, who belonged or had belonged to, a bureaucracy. Officials and quasi officials on the periphery of power were included.[62]

3. There was a prophetic intimation in Justice Douglas's concurring opinion in *Rosenblatt* that the central question in such cases should not be who is a public official but whether a *public issue* is being discussed. The Court would come to that, but there was to be a prior step.

One of the fathers of the atomic bomb and a vocal pacifist, Dr. Linus Pauling, brought unsuccessful suits against the *New York Daily News* and William Buckley's *National Review.* Both had charged him with Communist and pro-Soviet sympathies. A federal court of appeals in the *Daily News* case upheld a district court's characterization of Pauling as a *public figure,* open to the same comment and criticism as a public official. Pauling v. News Syndicate Co., Inc., 335 F.2d 659 (2d Cir. 1964).

Two cases decided together, one involving a football coach and the other a retired army general, brought to fruition the *public figure* test and for a time provided a formula for measuring "reckless disregard of the truth."

The case of the coach began with an article entitled "The Story of a College Football Fix" in the March 23, 1963, issue of the *Saturday Evening Post.* The article reported a telephone conversation between Wally Butts, athletic director at the University of Georgia, and Paul Bryant, then head football coach at the University of Alabama, in which the two allegedly conspired to "fix" a football game between the two schools.

Notes had been taken on the conversation by an insurance salesman of questionable character, who, due to an electronic quirk, cut into the conversation when he

62. For example, Rose v. Koch, 154 N.W.2d 409 (Minn.1967), a former legislator and university professor; News-Journal Co. v. Gallagher, 233 A.2d 166 (Del.1967), a highway department employee; Medina v. Time, Inc., 319 F.Supp. 398 (D.Mass.1970), an army officer; Priestley v. Hastings & Sons Publishing Co. of Lynn, 271 N.E.2d 628 (Mass.1971), a city architect; and Klahr v. Winterble, 418 P.2d 404 (Ariz.1966), a state college student senator.

picked up a telephone receiver at a pay station. Some of his notes appeared in the article, which compared this "fix" to the Chicago "Black Sox" scandal of 1919. The article went on to describe the game, the subsequent presentation of the salesman's notes to Georgia head coach, Johnny Griffith, and Butts's resignation. There was nothing subtle about the *Post's* charges against Butts.

Butts sued for $5 million compensatory and $5 million punitive damages. The *Post* tried to use truth as its defense, but the evidence contradicted its version of what had occurred. Expert witnesses supported Butts by analyzing the salesman's notes and films of the game. The jury returned a verdict of $60,000 in general damages and $3 million in punitive damages.

Soon after the trial, the *New York Times* decision was handed down, and the *Post* sought a new trial under its rules. The motion was rejected by the trial judge. He held *Times* inapplicable because Butts was not a "public official," and he ruled there was ample evidence of "reckless disregard" of the truth in the researching of the article. His judgment was affirmed by the United States Court of Appeals. From there the case went to the Supreme Court.

Justice Harlan who wrote the opinion for the Court focused on the public interest in the circulation of the *Post* and in the activities of Butts. Did Butts, therefore, qualify as a "public figure"? The opinion was a study in the problems presented by the forward motion of *New York Times*, and it defined a separate test for public figures.

CURTIS PUBLISHING CO. v. BUTTS and ASSOCIATED PRESS v. WALKER

388 U.S. 130, 87 S.CT. 1975, 18 L.ED.2D 1094 (1967).

Justice HARLAN delivered the opinion of the Court: * * *

These similarities and differences between libel actions involving persons who are public officials and libel actions involving those circumstanced as were Butts and Walker, viewed in light of the principles of liability which are of general applicability in our society, lead us to the conclusion that libel actions of the present kind cannot be left entirely to state libel laws, unlimited by any overriding constitutional safeguard, but that the rigorous federal requirements of *New York Times* are not the only appropriate accommodation of the conflicting interests at stake. We consider and would hold that a "public figure" who is not a public official may also recover damages for a defamatory falsehood whose substance makes substantial danger to reputation apparent, *on a showing of highly unreasonable conduct constituting an extreme departure from the standards of investigation and reporting ordinarily adhered to by responsible publishers.* [Emphasis added.]

Nothing in this opinion is meant to affect the holdings in *New York Times* and its progeny. * * *

Having set forth the standard by which we believe the constitutionality of the damage awards in these cases must be judged, we turn now, as the Court did in *New York Times*, to the question whether the evidence and findings below meet that standard. * * *

The *Butts* jury was instructed, in considering punitive damages, to assess "the reliability, the nature of the sources of the defendant's information, its acceptance or rejection of the sources, and its care in checking upon assertions." These considerations were said to be relevant to a determination whether defendant had proceeded with "wanton and reckless indifference." In this light we consider that the jury must have decided that the investigation undertaken by the *Saturday Evening Post*, upon which much evidence and argument was centered, was grossly inadequate in the circumstances. * * *

This jury finding was found to be supported by the evidence by the trial judge and the majority in the Fifth Circuit. * *

The evidence showed that the Butts story was in no sense "hot news" and the editors of the magazine recognized the need for a thorough investigation of the serious charges. Elementary precautions were, nevertheless, ignored. The *Saturday Evening Post* knew that Burnett had been placed on probation in connection with bad check charges, but proceeded to publish the story on the basis of his affidavit without substantial independent support. Burnett's notes were not even viewed by any of the magazine's personnel prior to publication. John Carmichael who was supposed to have been with Burnett when the phone call was overheard was not interviewed. No attempt was made to screen the films of the game to see if Burnett's information was accurate, and no attempt was made to find out whether Alabama had adjusted its plans after the alleged divulgence of information.

The *Post* writer assigned to the story was not a football expert and no attempt was made to check the story with someone knowledgeable in the sport. At trial such experts indicated that the information in the Burnett notes was either such that it would be evident to any opposing coach from game films regularly exchanged or valueless. Those assisting the *Post* writer in his investigation were already deeply involved in another libel action, based on a different article, brought against Curtis Publishing Co. by the Alabama coach and unlikely to be the source of a complete and objective investigation. The *Saturday Evening Post* was anxious to change its image by instituting a policy of "sophisticated muckraking," and the pressure to produce a successful exposé might have induced a stretching of standards. In short, the evidence is ample to support a finding of highly unreasonable conduct constituting an extreme departure from the standards of investigation and reporting ordinarily adhered to by responsible publishers.

Affirmed. * * *

COMMENT

Chief Justice Earl Warren concurred in the result but objected to the Court's making a distinction between "public official" and "public figure." Consistent with their absolutist rejection of libel actions against the press, Justices Black and Douglas dissented in *Butts* but concurred in the result in *Walker*.

But four members of the Court—Harlan, Clark, Fortas, and Stewart—adopted a new standard, albeit a shaky one, for public figures. It would come to be known as the *prudent publisher* test, and it would reappear in *Gertz v. Robert Welch, Inc.* in modified form (this text, p. 228).

The *Walker* case did not divide the Court as did *Butts*. General Edwin Walker was clearly an actor in the tumultuous events surrounding the entry of James Meredith into the University of Mississippi. An Associated Press report stated that Walker, who was present on the campus, had taken command of the violent crowd and had personally led a charge against federal marshals. It also described Walker as encouraging rioters to use violence and providing them technical advice on combating the effects of tear gas.

Walker was a private citizen at the time of the riot but, since his resignation from the army, had become a political activist. There was little evidence relating to the preparation of the news dispatch. It was clear, however, that Van Savell, the reporter, was actually present during the events he described and had communicated them almost immediately to the Associated Press office in Atlanta.

Walker sought to collect millions in a chain suit against newspapers and broadcasting stations which had carried the AP reports. The present case began in Texas when a trial court awarded Walker $500,000 in general damages and $300,000 in exemplary or punitive damages. The trial judge, finding no actual malice to support the punitive damages, entered a final judgment of $500,000. The Texas Court of Civil Appeals, agreeing that the defense of fair comment did not apply because the press reports constituted "statements of fact," affirmed the judgment of the trial court. The Texas Supreme Court declined to review the case, and the case went up to the United States Supreme Court. Associated Press v. Walker, 388 U.S. 130 (1967).

Certainly Walker was a public figure, said the Court, for he had cast his personality into the whirlpool of an important public controversy. Moreover, "in contrast to the *Butts* article, the dispatch which concerns us in *Walker* was news which required immediate dissemination. The Associated Press received the information from a correspondent who was present at the scene of the events and gave every indication of being trustworthy and competent. His dispatches in this instance, with one minor exception, were internally consistent and would not have seemed unreasonable to one familiar with General Walker's prior publicized statements on the underlying controversy. Considering the necessity for rapid dissemination, *nothing in this series of events gives the slightest hint of a severe departure from accepted publishing standards.* We therefore conclude that General Walker should not be entitled to damages from the Associated Press." [Emphasis added.]

2. The *public figure* rule was subsequently applied to policemen and firemen seeking election to a public safety council,[63] to a head basketball coach,[64] to a well-known horse trainer,[65] to political party workers and precinct delegates,[66] to letter carriers who, upon refusing to join a union, were called "scabs, traitors, and men of low character and rotten principles," [67] to a suspect in a $1.5 million mail robbery who chose to expose himself publicly by granting interviews and calling press conferences,[68] to a retired professional basketball player,[69] and to an escapee from a federal jail.[70]

3. A further attempt to define "reckless disregard" generated language which has persisted in court opinions. The case is St. Amant v. Thompson, 390 U.S. 727 (1968), and it involved defamatory charges made during the heat of a political campaign.

There Justice Byron White for the Court pointed out that "the defendant in a defamation action brought by a public official cannot * * * automatically insure a favorable verdict by testifying that he published with a belief that the statements were true. The finder of fact must determine whether the publication was indeed made in good faith. Professions of good faith will be unlikely to prove persuasive, for example, where a story is fabricated by the defendant, is the product of his imagination, or is based wholly on an unverified anonymous telephone call. Nor will they be likely to prevail when the publisher's allegations are so inherently

63. Tilton v. Cowles Publishing Co., 459 P.2d 8 (Wash.1969).

64. Grayson v. Curtis Publishing Co., 436 P.2d 756 (Wash.1967).

65. Lloyds v. United Press International, Inc., 311 N.Y.S.2d 373 (1970).

66. Arber v. Stahlin, 159 N.W.2d 154 (Mich.1968).

67. Old Dominion Branch No. 496, National Association of Letter Carriers, AFL–CIO v. Austin, 418 U.S. 264 (1974).

68. Tripoli v. Boston Herald-Traveler Corp., 268 N.E.2d 350 (Mass.1971).

69. Time, Inc. v. Johnston, 448 F.2d 378 (4th Cir. 1971).

70. McFarland v. Hearst Corp., 332 F.Supp. 746 (D.Md.1971).

improbable that only a reckless man would have put them in circulation. Likewise, recklessness may be found where there are obvious reasons to doubt the veracity of the informant or the accuracy of his reports."

Justice White went on to say that "reckless conduct is not measured by whether a reasonably prudent man would have published, or would have investigated before publishing. There must be sufficient evidence to permit the conclusion that the *defendant in fact entertained serious doubts as to the truth of his publication*." [Emphasis added.]

"The occupation of public officeholder," said Justice Abe Fortas in an acerbic dissent, "does not forfeit one's membership in the human race."

4. Public official-public figure designations were to do yeoman service for the press in this period.

The Ocala (Fla.) *Star-Banner* may have come close to the outer limits of permissible comment when it confused a mayor who was a candidate for the office of county tax assessor with his brother and charged falsely that he had been indicted for perjury in a civil rights suit.

A new editor, who had never heard of the mayor's brother, changed the first name when a reporter phoned in the story. A jury awarded the mayor $22,000, but a precise application of the *New York Times* rule of knowing falsehood or reckless disregard of the truth had not been made and the judgment was reversed. Ocala Star-Banner Co. v. Damron, 401 U.S. 295 (1971).

A deputy chief of detectives sued *Time* magazine when it implied in a story about a Civil Rights Commission report that the police officer was guilty of brutality. Although the news magazine had confused a complainant's testimony with the independent findings of the Commission itself, the Supreme Court ruled that in the circumstances of the case the magazine had not engaged in a "falsification" sufficient in itself to sustain a jury finding of "actual malice."

"The author of the *Time* article," said Justice Potter Stewart for the Court, "testified in substance, that the context of the report of the * * * incident indicated to him that the Commission believed that the incident had occurred as described. He therefore denied that he had falsified the report when he omitted the word 'alleged.' The *Time* researcher, who had read the newspaper stories about the incident and two reports from a *Time* reporter in Chicago, as well as the accounts of [the deputy chief's] earlier career, had even more reason to suppose that the Commission took the charges to be true. * * *

"These considerations apply with even greater force to the situation where the *alleged libel consists in the claimed misinterpretation of the gist of a lengthy government document. Where the document reported on is so ambiguous as this one was, it is hard to imagine a test of 'truth' that would not put the publisher virtually at the mercy of the unguided discretion of a jury*." [Emphasis added.] Time, Inc. v. Pape, 401 U.S. 279 (1971).

5. These examples are not meant to suggest that a libel case couldn't be won by a plaintiff in the period following *New York Times v. Sullivan*.

As far back as 1964, a Kentucky court had disallowed application of the *New York Times* rule where it appeared that the published attack was not on the "official" conduct of a policeman.[71] And an Illinois appeals court would not accept the contention that a society columnist's remarks about the marital affairs of a prominent industrial family were privileged because the plaintiffs were "public" people.[72] The Supreme Court of Pennsylvania would

71. Tucker v. Kilgore, 388 S.W.2d 112 (Ky.1964).

72. Lorillard v. Field Enterprises, Inc., 213 N.E.2d 1 (Ill.1965).

not permit application of the rule when a defendant admitted that he knew his defamatory comments were false.[73]

Senator Barry Goldwater, the most notable plaintiff of the period, won a $75,000 judgment against Ralph Ginzburg, publisher of *Fact* magazine. Ginzburg had attempted to put together a "psychobiography" on Goldwater so as to alert the American people to what he perceived to be the potential danger of his presidency. Facts and comments on Goldwater were carefully selected to support Ginzburg's assumptions, including responses from more than 2,000 psychiatrists who had received a manifestly "loaded" questionnaire. The simplistic conclusion from all of this was that Goldwater was mentally ill—his "infantile fantasies of revenge and dreams of total annihilation of his adversaries," his "paralyzing, deep-seated, irrational fear," his "fantasy of a final conflagration" which Ginzburg compared with the "death-fantasy of another paranoiac woven in Berchtesgaden and realized in a Berlin bunker."

At trial Ginzburg was unable to identify a single source for his statements. Nor could he document, in any medical sense, his reports that Goldwater had suffered two nervous breakdowns.

In upholding the judgment, a federal court of appeals relied on the "hot news" premise of the *Butts* and *Walker* cases and the less stringent actual malice definition of *St. Amant.* Goldwater v. Ginzburg, 414 F.2d 324 (2d Cir. 1969).

There were those, nevertheless, who wondered how a candidate for the nation's highest office could argue that any part of his private life, particularly his psyche, be immune from public comment, no matter how willfully distorted and inaccurate.

In dissenting vigorously to a denial of certiorari, Justice Black, joined by Justice Douglas, agreed.

"This suit," wrote Black, "was brought by a man who was then the nominee of his party for the [p]residency of the United States. In our times, the person who holds that high office has an almost unbounded power for good or evil. The public has an unqualified right to have the character and fitness of anyone who aspires to the [p]residency held up for the closest scrutiny. Extravagant, reckless statements and even claims which may not be true seem to me an inevitable and perhaps essential part of the process by which the voting public informs itself of the qualities of a man who would be [p]resident. The decisions of the [d]istrict [c]ourt and the [c]ourt of [a]ppeals in this case can only have the effect of dampening political debate by making fearful and timid those who should under our Constitution feel totally free openly to criticize Presidential candidates. * * *

"Another reason for the particular offensiveness of this case is that the damages awarded Senator Goldwater were, except for $1.00, wholly punitive. Goldwater neither pleaded nor proved any special damages and the jury's verdict of $1.00 nominal compensatory damages establishes that he suffered little if any actual harm. * * * It is bad enough when the First Amendment is violated to compensate a person who has actually suffered a provable injury as a result of libelous statements; it is incomprehensible that a person who has suffered no provable harm can recover libel damages imposed solely to punish a defendant who has exercised his First Amendment rights.

"I would grant certiorari and reverse the [c]ourt of [a]ppeals summarily." Ginzburg v. Goldwater, 396 U.S. 1049 (1970).

In 1970 an equally divided Indiana Supreme Court affirmed a libel judgment in favor of a former sheriff who had been falsely and, said the court, maliciously ac-

73. Fox v. Kahn, 221 A.2d 181 (Pa.1966).

cused by a newspaper of intimidating a grand jury witness and of being an accessory after the fact of murder as a result of a beating in a jail cell. The newspaper, said the court, recklessly failed to check known sources of information and thereby gave evidence of its own doubts as to the truth of the libelous publication.[74]

A physician, a drugstore manager, and a restaurant owner won libel awards when a radio station, which invited the public to call in on an "open-mike" program and used no delay device to edit out defamatory statements, implied the illicit sale and distribution of narcotics. The station was liable, said the court, even though it had no actual knowledge of the falsity of the statements made by an unidentified caller. Liability, however, did not include the unsuspecting sponsor of the program.[75]

A Doctrine Stretched To its Limits: The Public Issue Test

1. Justice Douglas's notion that any matter of legitimate public interest, that is, any public issue, should be the standard for application of the *Times* doctrine was reminiscent of philosopher Alexander Meiklejohn's premise that the people of the United States are both the governors and the governed, and therefore "those activities of thought and communication by which we 'govern' must be free from interference."[76] Speech having social importance, whether of a political nature or not, must be free, said Meiklejohn, not because persons "desire to speak," but because people "need to hear."

That constitutional doctrine was strengthened in 1968 when the United States Court of Appeals for the Ninth Circuit, noting the escalation from *public official* to *public figure* to *public issue* in applications of the *Times* doctrine, ruled against a medical laboratory which had brought a trade libel suit against CBS for a network program exposing faulty laboratory testing and the lack of federal supervision. In part the court said:

> If some analogy were to be looked for here, in caution against an uncertain extension of First Amendment immunity being made, this aspect would exist sufficiently in the elements of the field in which United Labs was engaged being, from the nature and extent of its capacity to affect health, as naturally entitled to public gaze and interest, and as inherently subject to right of public information and discussion. * * *
>
> It is, of course, not possible to say just how far the Court will continue to carry such extensions. But unless all other areas, not merely those of legitimate general interest but also those affecting personal concern to the public, are to be artificially ignored, we are not able to see how the path upon which the Court has been moving can be regarded as having reached an end. United Medical Laboratories, Inc. v. CBS, Inc., 404 F.2d 706, 710, 711 (9th Cir. 1968), cert. den. 394 U.S. 921 (1969).

There was still room for expansion. The Supreme Court held in 1970 that the term "blackmail," when used in characterizing the negotiating position of a real estate developer, was not slander when spoken in the heated public meetings of a city

74. Indianapolis Newspapers, Inc. v. Fields, 259 N.E.2d 651 (Ind.1970).

75. Snowden v. Pearl River Broadcasting Corp., 251 So.2d 405 (La.1971). But see Adams v. Frontier Broadcasting Co., 555 P.2d 556 (Wyo.1976) in which a state supreme court ruled that a radio station's failure to use a tape delay system, resulting in defamation concerning a public figure, did not demonstrate "reckless disregard" within the meaning of *New York Times* since a delay system would reduce "uninhibited, robust, and wide-open" public debate.

76. Meiklejohn, *The First Amendment Is An Absolute*, 1961 Sup.Ct.Rev. 245 at 253–55. See also Meiklejohn, *Political Freedom* (1960).

council and not actionable libel when subsequently reported accurately in newspaper articles.

The plaintiff in the case had entered into agreements with the city for zoning exemptions in the past and was again seeking such favors to expedite the construction of high density housing units. At the same time, the city was trying to obtain from the plaintiff land for the purpose of building a school.

In addition, the trial judge's instructions to the jury, reflecting confusion in his mind as to what the Supreme Court had meant by "actual malice" in earlier cases, was considered by Justice Stewart to be an "error of constitutional magnitude." A trial court judgment against the newspaper was reversed. Greenbelt Co-op Publishing Association v. Bresler, 398 U.S. 6 (1970).

2. Final extension of the *New York Times* doctrine—and it would prove the breaking point—came in 1971 when a badly divided Court upheld a court of appeals reversal of a $275,000 trial court judgment in favor of a magazine distributor. Rosenbloom had been called a "smut distributor" and "girlie-book peddler" in a radio news report, although he was subsequently acquitted of criminal obscenity charges.

ROSENBLOOM v. METROMEDIA

403 U.S. 29, 91 S.CT. 1811, 29 L.ED.2D 296 (1971).

Justice BRENNAN announced the judgment of the Court and an opinion in which The Chief Justice and Justice Blackmun join.

* * * The instant case presents the question whether the *New York Times'* knowing or reckless falsity standard applies in a state civil libel action brought not by a "public official" or a "public figure" but by a private individual for a defamatory falsehood uttered in a news broadcast by a radio station about the individual's involvement in an event of public or general interest. * * *

* * *

Petitioner concedes that the police campaign to enforce the obscenity laws was an issue of public interest, and, therefore, that the constitutional guarantees for freedom of speech and press imposed limits upon Pennsylvania's power to apply its libel laws to compel respondent to compensate him in damages for the alleged defamatory falsehoods broadcast about his involvement. As noted, the narrow question he raises is whether, because he is not a "public official" or a "public figure" but a private individual, those limits required that he prove that the falsehoods resulted from a failure of respondent to exercise reasonable care, or required that he prove that the falsehoods were broadcast with knowledge of their falsity or with reckless disregard of whether they were false or not. That question must be answered against the background of the functions of the constitutional guarantees for freedom of expression.

Self-governance in the United States presupposes far more than knowledge and debate about the strictly official activities of various levels of government. The commitment of the country to the institution of private property, protected by the Due Process and Just Compensation Clauses in the Constitution, places in private hands vast areas of economic and social power that vitally affect the nature and quality of life in the Nation. Our efforts to live and work together in a free society not completely dominated by governmental regulation necessarily encompass far more than politics in a narrow sense. * * *

Although the limitations upon civil libel actions, first held in *New York Times* to be required by the First Amendment, were applied in that case in the context of defamatory falsehoods about the official conduct of a public official, later decisions have disclosed the artificiality, in terms of the public's interest, of a simple distinction between "public" and "private" individuals or institutions. * * *

Moreover, the constitutional protection was not intended to be limited to matters bearing broadly on issues of responsible government. "[T]he Founders * * * felt that a free press would advance 'truth, science, morality, and arts in general' as well as responsible government." * * * *If a matter is a subject of public or general interest, it cannot suddenly become less so merely because a private individual is involved, or because in some sense the individual did not "voluntarily" choose to become involved. The public's primary interest is in the event; the public focus is on the conduct of the participant and the content, effect, and significance of the conduct, not the participant's prior anonymity or notoriety.* [Emphasis added.] The present case illustrates the point. The community has a vital interest in the proper enforcement of its criminal laws, particularly in an area such as obscenity where a number of highly important values are potentially in conflict: the public has an interest both in seeing that the criminal law is adequately enforced and in assuring that the law is not used unconstitutionally to suppress free expression. Whether the person involved is a famous large scale magazine distributor or a "private" businessman running a corner newsstand has no relevance in ascertaining whether the public has an interest in the issue. We honor the commitment to robust debate on public issues, which is embodied in the First Amendment, by extending constitutional protection to all discussion and communication involving matters of public or general concern, without regard to whether the persons involved are famous or anonymous.

* * *

* * * Drawing a distinction between "public" and "private" figures makes no sense in terms of the First Amendment guarantees. The *New York Times* standard was applied to libel of a public official or public figure to give effect to the Amendment's function to encourage ventilation of public issues, not because the public official has any less interest in protecting his reputation than an individual in private life. While the argument that public figures need less protection because they can command media attention to counter criticism may be true for some very prominent people, even then it is the rare case where the denial overtakes the original charge. Denials, retractions, and corrections are not "hot" news, and rarely receive the prominence of the original story. When the public official or public figure is a minor functionary, or has left the position which put him in the public eye, see Rosenblatt v. Baer, the argument loses all of its force. In the vast majority of libels involving public officials or public figures, the ability to respond through the media will depend on the same complex factor on which the ability of a private individual depends: the unpredictable event of the media's continuing interest in the story. Thus the unproven, and highly improbable, generalization that an as yet undefined class of "public figures" involved in matters of public concern will be better able to respond through the media than private individuals also involved in such matters seems too insubstantial a reed on which to rest a constitutional distinction. Furthermore, in First Amendment terms, the cure seems far worse than the disease. If the States fear that private citizens will not be able to respond adequately to publicity involving them, the solution lies in the direction of ensuring their ability to respond, rather than in stifling public discussion of matters of

public concern.[15]

Further reflection over the years since *New York Times* was decided persuades us that the view of the "public official" or "public figure" as assuming the risk of defamation by voluntarily thrusting himself into the public eye bears little relationship either to the values protected by the First Amendment or to the nature of our society. We have recognized that "[e]xposure of the self to others in varying degrees is a concomitant of life in a civilized community." Time, Inc. v. Hill, 385 U.S. 374, 388 (1967). Voluntarily or not, we are all "public" men to some degree. Conversely, some aspects of the lives of even the most public men fall outside the area of matters of public or general concern. * * * Thus, the idea that certain "public" figures have voluntarily exposed their entire lives to public inspection, while private individuals have kept theirs carefully shrouded from public view is, at best, a legal fiction. In any event, such a distinction could easily produce the paradoxical result of dampening discussion of issues of public or general concern because they happen to involve private citizens while extending constitutional encouragement to discussion of aspects of the lives of "public figures" which are not in the area of public or general concern.

* * *

We are aware that the press has, on occasion, grossly abused the freedom it is given by the Constitution. All must deplore such excesses. In an ideal world, the responsibility of the press would match the freedom and public trust given it. But from the earliest days of our history, this free society, dependent as it is for its survival upon a vigorous free press, has tolerated some abuse. * * * We thus hold that a libel action, as here, by a private individual against a licensed radio station for a defamatory falsehood in a newscast relating to his involvement in an event of public or general concern may be sustained only upon clear and convincing proof that the defamatory falsehood was published with knowledge that it was false or with reckless disregard of whether it was false or not. * * *

Petitioner argues finally that *WIP's* failure to communicate with him to learn his side of the case and to obtain a copy of the magazine for examination, sufficed to support a verdict under the *Times* standard. *But our "cases are clear that reckless conduct is not measured by whether a reasonably prudent man would have published, or would have investigated before publishing.* [Emphasis added.] There must be sufficient evidence to permit the conclusion that the defendant in fact entertained serious doubts as to the truth of his publication." St. Amant v. Thompson, 390 U.S., at 731. Respondent here relied on information supplied by police officials. Following petitioner's complaint about the accuracy of the broadcasts, *WIP* checked its last report with the judge who presided in the case. While we may assume that

15. Some States have adopted retraction statutes or right of reply statutes. See Donnelly, The Right of Reply: An Alternative to an Action for Libel, 34 Va.L.Rev. 367 (1948); Note, Vindication of the Reputation of a Public Official, 80 Harv.L.Rev. 1730 (1967). Cf. Red Lion Broadcasting Co. v. FCC, 395 U.S. 367 (1969).

One writer, in arguing that the First Amendment itself should be read to guarantee a right of access to the media not limited to a right to respond to defamatory falsehoods, has suggested several ways the law might encourage public discussion. Barron, Access to the Press—A New First Amendment Right, 80 Harv.L.Rev. 1641, 1666–1678 (1967). [See also, Barron, *Freedom of the Press for whom?* 1973.] It is important to recognize that the private individual often desires press exposure either for himself, his ideas, or his causes. Constitutional adjudication must take into account the individual's interest in access to the press as well as the individual's interest in preserving his reputation, even though libel actions by their nature encourage a narrow view of the individual's interest since they focus only on situations where the individual has been harmed by undesired press attention. A constitutional rule that deters the press from covering the ideas or activities of the private individual thus conceives the individual's interest too narrowly.

the District Court correctly held to be defamatory respondent's characterizations of petitioner's business as "the smut literature racket," and of those engaged in it as "girlie-book peddlers," there is no evidence in the record to support a conclusion that respondent "in fact entertained serious doubts as to the truth" of its reports.

Affirmed.

COMMENT

1. In retrospect it was to be Justice Harlan's dissenting opinion in *Rosenbloom v. Metromedia* which would undo the *public issue* standard.

"It is * * * my judgment," said Harlan, "that the reasonable care standard adequately serves those First Amendment values that must inform the definition of actionable libel and that those special considerations that made even this standard an insufficiently precise technique when applied to plaintiffs who are 'public officials' or 'public figures' do not obtain where the litigant is a purely private individual."

Justice Thurgood Marshall, joined by Justice Stewart in dissent, framed propositions which were also to reappear in *Gertz*. Agreeing with Harlan, he said that the plurality's doctrine would threaten society's interest in protecting private individuals from being thrust into the public eye by the distorting light of defamation.

But beyond that he saw a formidable danger in punitive and presumed damages, and so a proposal:

> The threats to society's interest in freedom of the press that are involved in punitive and presumed damages can largely be eliminated by restricting the award of damages to proven, actual injuries. The jury's wide ranging discretion will largely be eliminated since the award will be based on essentially objective, discernible factors. * * * [S]elf-censorship resulting from the fear of large judgments themselves would be reduced. At the same time society's interest in protecting individuals from defamation will still be fostered.

The Court seemed ready for *Gertz v. Robert Welch, Inc.*

2. In the interim the press enjoyed a respite from libel laws. For a time, organized crime constituted the largest category of cases in which a *Rosenbloom* standard was applied.[77] Of other categories only a few less obvious examples will be cited: the size of an estate left by a church elder;[78] the practice of credit bureaus;[79] the instant minister racket;[80] attendance of a bishop at the night club performance of a singer in his church choir;[81] the quality of a restaurant's food;[82] competence of a trucking firm's president;[83] and the behavior and appearance of American youth living in a cave in Crete.[84]

Yet even under *Rosenbloom* a suit could be won if the plaintiff could demonstrate actual malice. In 1972 a federal district court declared that once a publisher has undertaken an investigation, he should not be permitted to ignore with impunity the fruits of that investigation.

Here the late *Washington Star* had either ignored or overlooked information it had gathered which refuted earlier allega-

77. See, for example, Schwartz v. Time, Inc., 337 N.Y.S.2d 125 (1972); Nigro v. Miami Herald Publishing Co., 262 So.2d 698 (Fla.1972); LaBruzzo v. Associated Press, 353 F.Supp. 979 (D.Mo.1973); Cervantes v. Time, Inc., 330 F.Supp. 936 (E.D.Mo.1971).

78. Gospel Spreading Church v. Johnson Publishing Co., 454 F.2d 1050 (D.C.Cir.1971).

79. Credit Bureau of Dalton, Inc. v. CBS News, 332 F.Supp. 1291 (N.D.Ga.1971).

80. Spern v. Time, Inc., 324 F.Supp. 1201 (D.Pa.1971); Hensley v. Time, Inc., 336 F.Supp. 50 (D.C.Cal.1971).

81. Washington v. New York News, Inc., 322 N.Y.S.2d 896 (1971).

82. Twenty-Five East 40th St. Restaurant Corp. v. Forbes, Inc., 322 N.Y.S.2d 408 (1971).

83. Snead v. Forbes, Inc., 275 N.E.2d 746 (Ill.1971).

84. Goldman v. Time, Inc., 336 F.Supp. 133 (D.C.Cal.1971).

tions that a Washington, D.C. area conference center and its director were financed secretly by the CIA and Pentagon and were, in effect, operating a spy organization.

In a telephone conversation with an editor, the CIA director had emphatically denied any such connection. The story was published anyway.

There was evidence, said the court, that the publisher entertained serious doubts as to the truth of his report and had engaged in the selective reporting of facts. Original jury awards of $418,800 to the Foundation and $100,000 to its director in compensatory damages were said to be excessive and reduced to $50,000 and $10,000 respectively.

To its advantage the *Star* had corrected and apologized for its error and had so advised the major wire services. Airlie Foundation, Inc. v. Evening Star Newspaper Co., 337 F.Supp. 421 (D.D.C.1972). See also Carson v. Allied News Co., 529 F.2d 206 (7th Cir. 1976).

The breadth of application of Justice Brennan's test in *Rosenbloom* was Meiklejohnian. The test itself was not. *Rosenbloom* was Brennan's watershed in libel as *Ginzburg* (see this text, p. 746) had been in obscenity. The Court *was* ready for *Gertz v. Robert Welch, Inc.*

THE PRESENT STATE OF LIBEL: GERTZ AND BEYOND

1. By removing libel from its ancestral home in tort law and putting it under the protection of the Constitution, *New York Times v. Sullivan* was truly a landmark case. Simply put, the Court had decided that in the interests of a vigorous social dialogue public officials would have to surrender their sensitivity to "vehement, caustic, and sometimes unpleasantly sharp" verbal assaults. But the Court left an opening to remedy injury to reputation. If the public official could with convincing clarity [85] prove *actual malice*, that is, that the statement was published *with knowledge that it was false or with reckless disregard of whether it was false or not* a libel suit could still be pursued and won. The major burden of proof, however, was now on the public-person plaintiff, and libel would be governed by a national, First Amendment-based standard of fault. Reviewing courts would make an independent examination of the record to assure that the plaintiff had satisfied the constitutional standard.

Much was made of *New York Times I*, as it would be called, to distinguish it from the *Pentagon Papers* case of 1971. Harry Kalven, Jr. saw it as laying to rest for all time sedition or libel of government—"an impossible notion for a democracy." [86] And Kalven reported Meiklejohn as exclaiming that the ruling was "an occasion for dancing in the streets."

Justices Black, Douglas, and Goldberg, however, had serious reservations, and Black, in a concurring opinion, said of *New York Times*: "The requirement that malice be proved provides at best an evanescent protection for the right critically to

85. "Convincing clarity" is a standard of evidence which falls somewhere between "preponderance of evidence" and "beyond reasonable doubt," the latter the test in criminal cases. Under the standard, proof must be strong, positive, free from doubt, clear, precise, unmistakable, proof that persuades. State court applications of the *Gertz* standard of negligence to private plaintiffs suggest that the "preponderance of evidence" burden of proof will now be sufficient. This is also suggested in the Restatement of Torts (Second) § 580B, Comment i (Tent.Draft No. 21, April 5, 1975). The three standards are discussed by the Massachusetts Supreme Judicial Court in Callahan v. Westinghouse Broadcasting Co. Inc., 2 Med.L.Rptr. 2226, 363 N.E.2d 240 (1977).

86. Kalven, *The New York Times Case: A Note on the Central Meaning of the First Amendment*, 1964 Sup.Ct.Rev. 205.

discuss public affairs and does not measure up to the sturdy safeguard embodied in the First Amendment."

First Amendment theorist Thomas Emerson rejected the ruling for failing to take into account the value of even intentional falsehood in forcing people to defend, justify, and rethink their positions. Emerson referred to Brennan's actual malice test as a "relapse to the two level theory [the idea that certain forms of speech are exempt from First Amendment protection]," and he added:

> [S]uper-refined attempts to separate statements of fact from opinions, to winnow truth out of a mass of conflicting evidence * * * to probe into intents, motives and purposes—all these do not fit into the dynamics of a system of freedom of expression * * * The health and vitality of the system depend more upon untrammeled freedom of discussion, in which all citizens contend vigorously, than in judicial attempts to establish the motives of participants.[87]

Perennial concern is that because of *New York Times* fewer people will choose to participate in public affairs as officeholders. This is based partly on the assumption that public persons have no superior access to publicity,[88] an assumption of doubtful validity.

2. In the decade following *New York Times,* the Court stretched the application of its *actual malice* rule to public figures in *Butts* and *Walker* and finally, in the 1971 *Rosenbloom* case, to private persons caught up in matters of public interest, even though involuntarily.

"We honor the commitment to robust debate on public issues," said Justice Brennan in his plurality opinion for the *Rosenbloom* Court, "* * * by extending constitutional protection to all discussion and communication involving matters of public or general concern, without regard to whether the persons involved are famous or anonymous."

But the Court was bitterly fragmented on the question of how far the First Amendment ought to go in protecting libel. Dissenting Justice John Marshall Harlan, because he preferred a less severe proof than actual malice for private persons in pursuit of libel damages, was to have the last word. But for three years the press enjoyed a near immunity to libel laws. Whatever was published was, at least by an editor's definition, a matter of public interest and therefore subject to the actual malice test.

3. *Gertz v. Robert Welch, Inc.* swung the pendulum back, not all the way to the position of strict liability but to a point of recognizing the private person in libel law. The onward rush of *New York Times* had ended.

The family of a youth shot by a policeman had retained Elmer Gertz, a nationally known attorney and self-defined public person, to represent them in a civil suit for damages against the policeman. The policeman had already been convicted of second-degree murder. Meanwhile, the editor of the John Birch Society magazine *American Opinion* saw as his patriotic duty the publication of an article discrediting Gertz by identifying him with a "conspiracy" to undermine law enforcement in order to effect a Communist takeover of the United States.[89]

In order to heap opprobrium upon Gertz, the article stated falsely that he had a criminal record, that he had planned the 1968 Chicago demonstrations, and that he was a Leninist and Communist-fronter.

What he was in fact was one of Chicago's best-known lawyers, a legal expert on libel, censorship, civil rights, free speech,

87. Emerson, The System of Freedom of Expression. 1970, pp. 530, 531, 538.

88. Schaefer, *Defamation and the First Amendment: The Coen Lecture,* 52 U. of Colorado L.R. 1 (Fall 1980).

89. See, *Frame-up: Richard Nuccio and the War on Police,* American Opinion, April 1969.

the death penalty, and housing. He was also the author of books, pamphlets, magazine articles, book reviews, and radio plays; a professor of law; a civil rights leader; and a founder and member of countless organizations ranging from the Civil War Roundtable to the Henry Miller Literary Society.

Hardly a private person, Gertz was instrumental in writing a new Illinois constitution, having been elected to the post. He was a dedicated theater buff and literary dilettante. He founded the George Bernard Shaw Society. In 1931 he wrote his first book on Frank Harris, the renegade literary-libertine. He won a parole for Nathan Leopold and a death sentence commutation for Jack Ruby.

Poet and historian Carl Sandburg once said that "Elmer Gertz fears no dragons." Probably true. More likely, though, he knew his libel law and had clearly discerned the divided nature of the Court in *Rosenbloom* and the significant changes in its membership since 1971.

Gertz sued *American Opinion* and a sympathetic jury awarded him $50,000. A federal district court disallowed the award, agreeing with the magazine that the *public issue* rule of *Rosenbloom* protected it against that kind of judgment. The court of appeals affirmed, and Gertz sought review in the Supreme Court.

In an imprecise but significant opinion by Justice Lewis Powell the Supreme Court reversed, declaring the very public Mr. Gertz to be a private person in the circumstances of the case. The Court pointed out that Gertz, unknown to the jury, was simply a lawyer serving a client. On the assumption that private persons don't have the same access to the media that public officials and public figures have—although it was doubtful that this was true of Elmer Gertz—the Court essentially rejected the public issue rule of *Rosenbloom* and held that henceforth purely private or nonpublic persons, to succeed as plaintiffs in a libel suit, need only show *negligence* on the part of the defendant, a much lighter burden than actual malice.

The Court said a lot more, however, and not all of it unfavorable to the press. No longer was it enough for a plaintiff to be falsely defamed (the traditional libel *per se* where falsity, malice, and damages are presumed). There now *must* be a showing of *negligence* for, said Powell, there can be "no liability without fault." And the separate states would be allowed "substantial latitude" in determining the standard of care required of publishers.

Moreover, to discourage damages which may be destructive of unpopular ideas and of the press itself, private-person plaintiffs, said Powell, would have to come all the way up to the actual malice standard to claim punitive damages, which too often in the past had been out of all proportion to the harm inflicted by publication. Awards, then, in private person suits would henceforth be restricted to actual damages for demonstrated injury, whether personal humiliation, mental anguish, or whatever. (Note how Powell's notion of actual damages appears to subsume what we referred to earlier as compensatory or general damages.) A jury would assess injury on the basis of relevant testimony. In addition, there would be no punishment for opinions, no matter how pernicious. Under the First Amendment, said the Court, there is no such thing as a false idea. Facts and opinion would be distinguished whenever possible. *Gertz* governs the present law of libel. The plaintiff in April 1981 was awarded $100,000 in compensatory and $300,000 in punitive damages, and that result was affirmed by the Seventh Circuit Court of Appeals on June 16, 1982 (Gertz v. Welch, 8 Med.L.Rptr. 1769, 680 F.2d 527 [7th Cir. 1982].) Gertz had proven actual malice to the satisfaction of the district court jury, although there was some disagreement between trial and appeals courts as to whether quotations from public documents of a time past required such proof. More than a decade of litigation finally ended in early 1983 when the Supreme Court declined to review the seventh circuit holding.

GERTZ v. ROBERT WELCH, INC.

418 U.S. 323, 94 S.CT. 2997, 41 L.ED.2D 789 (1974).

Justice POWELL delivered the opinion of the Court:

* * *

The principal issue in this case is whether a newspaper or broadcaster that publishes defamatory falsehoods about an individual who is neither a public official nor a public figure may claim a constitutional privilege against liability for the injury inflicted by those statements. The Court considered this question on the rather different set of facts presented in Rosenbloom v. Metromedia, Inc., 403 U.S. 29 * * * (1971). Rosenbloom, a distributor of nudist magazines, was arrested for selling allegedly obscene material while making a delivery to a retail dealer. The police obtained a warrant and seized his entire inventory of 3,000 books and magazines. He sought and obtained an injunction prohibiting further police interference with his business. He then sued a local radio station for failing to note in two of its newscasts that the 3,000 items seized were only "reportedly" or "allegedly" obscene and for broadcasting references to "the smut literature racket" and to "girlie-book peddlers" in its coverage of the court proceeding for injunctive relief. He obtained a judgment against the radio station, but the Court of Appeals for the Third Circuit held the *New York Times* privilege applicable to the broadcast and reversed. 415 F.2d 892 (1969).

This Court affirmed the decision below, but no majority could agree on a controlling rationale. The eight Justices who participated in *Rosenbloom* announced their views in five separate opinions, none of which commanded more than three votes. The several statements not only reveal disagreement about the appropriate result in that case, they also reflect divergent traditions of thought about the general problem of reconciling the law of defamation with the First Amendment. One approach has been to extend the *New York Times* test to an expanding variety of situations. Another has been to vary the level of constitutional privilege for defamatory falsehood with the status of the person defamed. And a third view would grant to the press and broadcast media absolute immunity from liability for defamation. To place our holding in the proper context, we preface our discussion of this case with a review of the several *Rosenbloom* opinions and their antecedents.

In affirming the trial court's judgment in the instant case, the Court of Appeals relied on Justice Brennan's conclusion for the *Rosenbloom* plurality that "all discussion and communication involving matters of public or general concern," warrant the protection from liability for defamation accorded by the rule originally enunciated in New York Times Co. v. Sullivan, 376 U.S. 254 * * * (1964). There this Court defined a constitutional privilege intended to free criticism of public officials from the restraints imposed by the common law of defamation. The *Times* ran a political advertisement endorsing civil rights demonstrations by black students in Alabama and impliedly condemning the performance of local law-enforcement officials. A police commissioner established in state court that certain misstatements in the advertisement referred to him and that they constituted libel *per se* under Alabama law. This showing left the *Times* with the single defense of truth, for under Alabama law neither good faith nor reasonable care would protect the newspaper from liability. This Court concluded that a "rule compelling the critic of official conduct to guarantee the truth of all his factual assertions" would deter protected speech, and announced the constitutional privilege designed to counter that effect:

> "The constitutional guarantees require, we think, a federal rule that prohibits a public official from recovering damages for a defamatory falsehood relating to his official conduct unless he proves that the statement was made with 'actual malice'—that is, with knowledge that it was false or with reckless disregard of whether it was false or not." [6]

Three years after *New York Times,* a majority of the Court agreed to extend the constitutional privilege to defamatory criticism of "public figures." This extension was announced in Curtis Publishing Co. v. Butts and its companion, Associated Press v. Walker, 388 U.S. 130 * * * (1967). The first case involved the Saturday Evening Post's charge that Coach Wally Butts of the University of Georgia had conspired with Coach "Bear" Bryant of the University of Alabama to fix a football game between their respective schools. *Walker* involved an erroneous Associated Press account of former Major General Edwin Walker's participation in a University of Mississippi campus riot. Because Butts was paid by a private alumni association and Walker had resigned from the Army, neither could be classified as a "public official" under *New York Times.* Although Justice Harlan announced the result in both cases, a majority of the Court agreed with Mr. Chief Justice Warren's conclusion that the *New York Times* test should apply to criticism of "public figures" as well as "public officials." [7] The

6. *New York Times* and later cases explicated the meaning of the new standard. In *New York Times* the Court held that under the circumstances the newspaper's failure to check the accuracy of the advertisement against news stories in its own files did not establish reckless disregard for the truth. 376 U.S., at 287–288, * *. In St. Amant v. Thompson, 390 U.S. 727, 731 * * * (1968), the Court equated reckless disregard of the truth with subjective awareness of probable falsity: "There must be sufficient evidence to permit the conclusion that the defendant in fact entertained serious doubts as to the truth of his publication." In Beckley Newspapers Corp. v. Hanks, 389 U.S. 81 * * * (1967), the Court emphasized the distinction between the *New York Times* test of knowledge of falsity or reckless disregard of the truth and "actual malice" in the traditional sense of ill-will. Garrison v. Louisiana, 379 U.S. 64, * * * (1964), made plain that the new standard applied to criminal libel laws as well as to civil actions and that it governed criticism directed at "anything which might touch on an official's fitness for office." Id., at 77 85 S.Ct., at 217. Finally, in Rosenblatt v. Baer, 383 U.S. 75, 85 * * * (1966), the Court stated that "the 'public official' designation applies at the very least to those among the hierarchy of government employees who have, or appear to the public to have, substantial responsibility for or control over the conduct of governmental affairs."

In Time, Inc. v. Hill, 385 U.S. 374 * * * (1967), this text, p. 318, the Court applied the *New York Times* standard to actions under an unusual state statute. The statute did not create a cause of action for libel. Rather, it provided a remedy for unwanted publicity. Although the law allowed recovery of damages for harm caused by exposure to public attention rather than by factual inaccuracies, it recognized truth as a complete defense. Thus, nondefamatory factual errors could render a publisher liable for something akin to invasion of privacy. The Court ruled that the defendant in such an action could invoke the *New York Times* privilege regardless of the fame or anonymity of the plaintiff. Speaking for the Court, Justice Brennan declared that this holding was not an extension of *New York Times* but rather a parallel line of reasoning applying that standard to this discrete context: "This is neither a libel action by a private individual nor a statutory action by a public official. Therefore, although the First Amendment principles pronounced in *New York Times* guide our conclusion, we reach that conclusion only by applying these principles in this discrete context. It therefore serves no purpose to distinguish the facts here from those in *New York Times.* Were this a libel action, the distinction which has been suggested between the relative opportunities of the public official and the private individual to rebut defamatory charges might be germane. And the additional state interest in the protection of the individual against damage to his reputation would be involved. * * *"

7. Professor Kalven once introduced a discussion of these cases with the apt heading, "You Can't Tell the Players without a Score Card." Kalven, The Reasonable Man and the First Amendment: Hill, Butts, and Walker, 1967 Sup.Ct.Rev. 267, 275. Only thee other Justices joined Justice Harlan's analysis of the issues involved. In his concurring opinion, Chief Justice Warren stated the principle for which these cases stand—that

Court extended the constitutional privilege announced in that case to protect defamatory criticism of nonpublic persons who "are nevertheless intimately involved in the resolution of important public questions or, by reason of their fame, shape events in areas of concern to society at large."

In his opinion for the plurality in *Rosenbloom v. Metromedia, Inc.*, Justice Brennan took the *New York Times* privilege one step further. He concluded that its protection should extend to defamatory falsehoods relating to private persons if the statements concerned matters of general or public interest. He abjured the suggested distinction between public officials and public figures on the one hand and private individuals on the other. He focused instead on society's interest in learning about certain issues: "If a matter is a subject of public or general interest, it cannot suddenly become less so merely because a private individual is involved, or because in some sense the individual did not 'voluntarily' choose to become involved." Thus, under the plurality opinion, a private citizen involuntarily associated with a matter of general interest has no recourse for injury to his reputation unless he can satisfy the demanding requirements of the *New York Times* test.

Two Members of the Court concurred in the result in *Rosenbloom* but departed from the reasoning of the plurality. Justice Black restated his view, long shared by Justice Douglas, that the First Amendment cloaks the news media with an absolute and indefeasible immunity from liability for defamation. Justice White concurred on a narrower ground. He concluded that "the First Amendment gives the press and the broadcast media a privilege to report and comment upon the official actions of public servants in full detail, with no requirement that the reputation or the privacy of an individual involved in or affected by the official action be spared from public view." He therefore declined to reach the broader questions addressed by the other Justices.

Justice Harlan dissented. Although he had joined the opinion of the Court in *New York Times*, in *Curtis Publishing Co.* he had contested the extension of the privilege to public figures. There he had argued that a public figure who held no governmental office should be allowed to recover damages for defamation "on a showing of highly unreasonable conduct constituting an extreme departure from the standards of investigation and reporting ordinarily adhered to by responsible publishers." In his *Curtis Publishing Co.* opinion Justice Harlan had distinguished *New York Times* primarily on the ground that defamation actions by public officials "lay close to seditious libel. * * *" Recovery of damages by one who held no public office, however, could not "be viewed as a vindication of governmental policy." Additionally, he had intimated that, because most public officials enjoyed absolute immunity from liability for their own defamatory utterances under Barr v. Matteo, 360 U.S. 564 * * * (1959), they lacked a strong claim to the protection of the courts.

In *Rosenbloom* Justice Harlan modified these views. He acquiesced in the application of the privilege to defamation of public figures but argued that a different rule should obtain where defamatory falsehood harmed a private individual. He noted that a private person has less likelihood "of securing access to channels

---

the *New York Times* test reaches both public figures and public officials. Justice Brennan and Justice White agreed with the Chief Justice on that question. Justice Black and Justice Douglas reiterated their view that publishers should have an absolute immunity from liability for defamation, but they acquiesced in the Chief Justice's reasoning in order to enable a majority of the Justices to agree on the question of the appropriate constitutional privilege for defamation of public figures.

of communication sufficient to rebut falsehoods concerning him" than do public officials and public figures, and has not voluntarily placed himself in the public spotlight. Justice Harlan concluded that the States could constitutionally allow private individuals to recover damages for defamation on the basis of any standard of care except liability without fault.

Justice Marshall dissented in *Rosenbloom* in an opinion joined by Justice Stewart. He thought that the plurality's "public or general interest" test for determining the applicability of the *New York Times* privilege would involve the courts in the dangerous business of deciding "what information is relevant to self-government." He also contended that the plurality's position inadequately served "society's interest in protecting private individuals from being thrust into the public eye by the distorting light of defamation." Justice Marshall therefore reached the conclusion, also reached by Justice Harlan, that the States should be "essentially free to continue the evolution of the common law of defamation and to articulate whatever fault standard best suits the State's need," so long as the States did not impose liability without fault. The principal point of disagreement among the three dissenters concerned punitive damages. Whereas Justice Harlan thought that the States could allow punitive damages in amounts bearing "a reasonable and purposeful relationship to the actual harm done * * *." Justice Marshall concluded that the size and unpredictability of jury awards of exemplary damages unnecessarily exacerbated the problems of media self-censorship and that such damages should therefore be forbidden.

We begin with the common ground. *Under the First Amendment there is no such thing as a false idea.* However pernicious an opinion may seem, we depend for its correction not on the conscience of judges and juries but on the competition of other ideas. But there is no constitutional value in false statements of fact. Neither the intentional lie nor the careless error materially advances society's interest in "uninhibited, robust, and wide-open" debate on public issues. New York Times Co. v. Sullivan, 376 U.S., at 270 * * *. They belong to that category of utterances which "are no essential part of any exposition of ideas, and are of such slight social value as a step to truth that any benefit that may be derived from them is clearly outweighed by the social interest in order and morality." Chaplinsky v. New Hampshire, 315 U.S. 568, 572 * * * (1942). [Emphasis added.]

Although the erroneous statement of fact is not worthy of constitutional protection, it is nevertheless inevitable in free debate. As James Madison pointed out in the Report on the Virginia Resolutions of 1798: "Some degree of abuse is inseparable from the proper use of every thing; and in no instance is this more true than in that of the press." 4 J. Elliot, Debates on the Federal Constitution of 1787, p. 571 (1876). And punishment of error runs the risk of inducing a cautious and restrictive exercise of the constitutionally guaranteed freedoms of speech and press. *Our decisions recognize that a rule of strict liability that compels a publisher or broadcaster to guarantee the accuracy of his factual assertions may lead to intolerable self-censorship.* Allowing the media to avoid liability only by proving the truth of all injurious statements does not accord adequate protection to First Amendment liberties. As the Court stated in *New York Times Co. v. Sullivan,* "Allowance of the defense of truth with the burden of proving it on the defendant, does not mean that only false speech will be deterred." The First Amendment requires that we protect some falsehood in order to protect speech that matters. [Emphasis added.]

The need to avoid self-censorship by the news media is, however, not the only societal value at issue. If it were, this Court would have embraced long ago the view that publishers and broadcasters enjoy an unconditional and indefeasible immunity from liability for defamation. Such a rule would, indeed, obviate the fear that the prospect of civil liability for injurious falsehood might dissuade a timorous press from the effective exercise of First Amendment freedoms. Yet absolute protection for the communications media requires a total sacrifice of the competing value served by the law of defamation.

The legitimate state interest underlying the law of libel is the compensation of individuals for the harm inflicted on them by defamatory falsehood. We would not lightly require the State to abandon this purpose, for, as Justice Stewart has reminded us, the individual's right to the protection of his own good name

> "reflects no more than our basic concept of the essential dignity and worth of every human being—a concept at the root of any decent system of ordered liberty. The protection of private personality, like the protection of life itself, is left primarily to the individual States under the Ninth and Tenth Amendments. But this does not mean that the right is entitled to any less recognition by this Court as a basic of our constitutional system." Rosenblatt v. Baer, 383 U.S. 75, 92 (1966) (concurring opinion).

* * *

The *New York Times* standard defines the level of constitutional protection appropriate to the context of defamation of a public person. Those who, by reason of the notoriety of their achievements or the vigor and success with which they seek the public's attention, are properly classed as public figures and those who hold governmental office may recover for injury to reputation only on clear and convincing proof that the defamatory falsehood was made with knowledge of its falsity or with reckless disregard for the truth. This standard administers an extremely powerful antidote to the inducement to media self-censorship of the common-law rule of strict liability for libel and slander. And it exacts a correspondingly high price from the victims of defamatory falsehood. Plainly many deserving plaintiffs, including some intentionally subjected to injury, will be unable to surmount the barrier of the *New York Times* test. Despite this substantial abridgment of the state law right to compensation for wrongful hurt to one's reputation, the Court has concluded that the protection of the *New York Times* privilege should be available to publishers and broadcasters of defamatory falsehood concerning public officials and public figures. We think that these decisions are correct, but we do not find their holdings justified solely by reference to the interest of the press and broadcast media in immunity from liability. Rather, we believe that the *New York Times* rule states an accommodation between this concern and the limited state interest present in the context of libel actions brought by public persons. For the reasons stated below, we conclude that the state interest in compensating injury to the reputation of private individuals requires that a different rule should obtain with respect to them.

* * *

* * * The first remedy of any victim of defamation is self-help—using available opportunities to contradict the lie or correct the error and thereby to minimize its adverse impact on reputation. Public officials and public figures usually enjoy significantly greater access to the channels of effective communication and hence have a more realistic opportunity to counteract false statements than private individuals normally enjoy. Private individuals are therefore more vulnerable to injury, and the state interest in protecting them is correspondingly greater.

More important than the likelihood that private individuals will lack effective opportunities for rebuttal, there is a compelling normative consideration underlying the distinction between public and private defamation plaintiffs. An individual who decides to seek governmental office must accept certain necessary consequences of that involvement in public affairs. He runs the risk of closer public scrutiny than might otherwise be the case. And society's interest in the officers of government is not strictly limited to the formal discharge of official duties. As the Court pointed out in Garrison v. Louisiana, 379 U.S., at 77 * * *, the public's interest extends to "anything which might touch on an official's fitness for office. * * * Few personal attributes are more germane to fitness for office than dishonesty, malfeasance, or improper motivation, even though these characteristics may also affect the official's private character."

Those classed as public figures stand in a similar position. *Hypothetically, it may be possible for someone to become a public figure through no purposeful action of his own, but the instances of truly involuntary public figures must be exceedingly rare.* For the most part those who attain this status have assumed roles of especial prominence in the affairs of society. Some occupy positions of such persuasive power and influence that they are deemed public figures for all purposes. More commonly, those classed as public figures have thrust themselves to the forefront of particular public controversies in order to influence the resolution of the issues involved. In either event, they invite attention and comment. [Emphasis added.]

Even if the foregoing generalities do not obtain in every instance, the communications media are entitled to act on the assumption that public officials and public figures have voluntarily exposed themselves to increased risk of injury from defamatory falsehood concerning them. No such assumption is justified with respect to a private individual. He has not accepted public office or assumed an "influential role in ordering society." He has relinquished no part of his interest in the protection of his own good name, and consequently he has a more compelling call on the courts for redress of injury inflicted by defamatory falsehood. Thus, private individuals are not only more vulnerable to injury than public officials and public figures; they are also more deserving of recovery.

For these reasons we conclude that the States should retain substantial latitude in their efforts to enforce a legal remedy for defamatory falsehood injurious to the reputation of a private individual. The extension of the *New York Times* test proposed by the *Rosenbloom* plurality would abridge this legitimate state interest to a degree that we find unacceptable. And it would occasion the additional difficulty of forcing state and federal judges to decide on an *ad hoc* basis which publications address issues of "general or public interest" and which do not—to determine, in the words of Justice Marshall, "what information is relevant to self-government." Rosenbloom v. Metromedia, Inc., 403 U.S., at 79 * * *. We doubt the wisdom of committing this task to the conscience of judges. Nor does the Constitution require us to draw so thin a line between the drastic alternatives of the *New York Times* privilege and the common law of strict liability for defamatory error. The "public or general interest" test for determining the applicability of the *New York Times* standard to private defamation actions inadequately serves both of the competing values at stake. One the one hand, a private individual whose reputation is injured by defamatory falsehood that does concern an issue of public or general interest has no recourse unless he can meet the rigorous requirements of *New York Times.* This is true despite the factors that distinguish the state interest in compensating private individuals from the analogous interest involved in the context of public persons. On the other hand, a publisher or broadcaster of a defamatory error which a court deems unrelated to an issue of public or general interest may be held liable in damages even if it took every reasonable precaution to ensure the accuracy of its assertions. And liability may far exceed compensation for any actual injury to the plaintiff, for the jury may be permitted to presume damages without proof of loss and even to award punitive damages.

We hold that, so long as they do not impose liability without fault, the states may define for themselves the appropriate standard of liability for a publisher or broadcaster of defamatory falsehood injurious to a private individual. This approach provides a more equitable boundary between the competing concerns involved here. It recognizes the strength of the legitimate state interest in compensating private individuals for wrongful injury to reputation, yet shields the press and broadcast media from the rigors of strict liability for defamation. At least this conclusion obtains where, as here, the substance of the defamatory statement "makes substantial danger to reputation apparent." This phrase places in perspective the conclusion we announce today. Our inquiry would involve considerations somewhat different from those discussed above if a State purported to condition civil liability on a factual misstatement whose content did not warn a reasonably prudent editor or broadcaster of its defamatory potential. Such a case is not now before us, and we intimate no view as to its proper resolution. [Emphasis added.]

Our accommodation of the competing values at stake in defamation suits by private individuals allows the States to impose liability on the publisher or broadcaster of defamatory falsehood on a less demanding showing than that required by *New York Times.* This conclusion is not based on a belief that the considerations which prompted the adoption of the *New York Times* privilege for defamation of public officials and its extension to public figures are wholly inapplicable to the context of private individuals. Rather, we endorse this approach in recognition of the strong and legitimate state interest in compensating private individuals for injury to reputation. *But this countervailing state interest extends no further than compensation for actual injury. For the reasons stated below, we hold that the States may not permit recovery of presumed or punitive damages, at least when liability is not based on a showing of knowledge of falsity or reckless disregard for the truth.* [Emphasis added.]

The common law of defamation is an oddity of tort law, for it allows recovery of purportedly compensatory damages without evidence of actual loss. Under the traditional rules pertaining to actions for libel, the existence of injury is presumed from the fact of publication. Juries may award substantial sums as compensation for supposed damage to reputation without any proof that such harm actually occurred. The largely uncontrolled discretion of juries to award damages where there is no loss unnecessarily compounds the potential of any system of liability for defamatory falsehood to inhibit the vigorous exercise of First Amendment freedoms. Additionally, the doctrine of presumed damages invites juries to punish unpopular opinion rather than to compensate individuals for injury sustained by the publication of a false fact. More to the point, the States have no substantial interest in securing for plaintiffs such as this petitioner gratuitous awards of money damages far in excess of any actual injury.

We would not, of course, invalidate state law simply because we doubt its wisdom, but here we are attempting to reconcile state law with a competing interest grounded in the constitutional command of the First Amendment. It is therefore appropriate to require that state remedies for defamatory falsehood reach no farther than is necessary to protect the legitimate interest involved. *It is necessary to restrict defamation plaintiffs who do not prove knowledge of falsity or reckless disregard for the truth to compensation for actual injury. We need not define "actual injury," as trial courts have wide experience in framing appropriate jury instructions in tort actions. Suffice it to say that actual injury is not limited to out-of-pocket loss.* Indeed, the more customary types of actual harm inflicted by defamatory falsehood include impairment of reputation and standing in the community, personal humiliation, and mental anguish and suffering. Of course, juries must be limited by appropriate instructions, and all awards must be supported by competent evidence concerning the injury, although there need be no evidence which assigns an actual dollar value to the injury. [Emphasis added.]

We also find no justification for allowing awards of punitive damages against publishers and broadcasters held liable under state-defined standards of liability for defamation. In most jurisdictions jury discretion over the amounts awarded is limited only by the gentle rule that they not be excessive. Consequently, juries assess punitive damages in wholly unpredictable amounts bearing no necessary relation to the actual harm caused. And they remain free to use their discretion selectively to punish expressions of unpopular views. *Like the doctrine of presumed damages, jury discretion to award punitive damages unnecessarily exacerbates the danger of media self-censorship, but, unlike the former rule, punitive damages are wholly irrelevant to the state interest that justifies a negligence standard for private defamation actions.* They are not compensation for injury. Instead, they are private fines levied by civil juries to punish reprehensible conduct and to deter its future occurrence. *In short, the private defamation plaintiff who establishes liability under a less demanding standard than that stated by New York Times may recover only such damages as are sufficient to compensate him for actual injury.* [Emphasis added.]

Notwithstanding our refusal to extend the *New York Times* privilege to defamation of private individuals, respondent contends that we should affirm the judgment below on the ground that petitioner is either a public official or a public figure. There is little basis for the former assertion. Several years prior to the present incident, petitioner had served briefly on housing committees appointed by the mayor of Chicago, but at the time of publication he had never held any remunerative governmental position. Respondent admits this but argues that petitioner's appearance at the coroner's inquest rendered him a "de facto public official." Our cases recognized no such concept. Respondent's suggestion would sweep all lawyers under the *New York Times* rule as officers of the court and distort the plain meaning of the "public official" category beyond all recognition. We decline to follow it.

Respondent's characterization of petitioner as a public figure raises a different question. That designation may rest on either of two alternative bases. *In some instances an individual may achieve such pervasive fame or notoriety that he becomes a public figure for all purposes and in all contexts. More commonly, an individual voluntarily injects himself or is drawn into a particular public controversy and thereby becomes a public figure for a limited range of issues.* In either case such persons assume special prominence in the resolution of public questions. [Emphasis added.]

Petitioner has long been active in community and professional affairs. He has served as an officer of local civic groups and of various professional organizations, and he has published several books and articles on legal subjects. Although petitioner was consequently well known in some circles, he had achieved no general fame or notoriety in the community. None of the prospective jurors called at the trial had ever heard of petitioner prior to this litigation, and respondent offered no proof that this response was atypical of the local population. We would not lightly assume that a citizen's participation in community and professional affairs rendered him a public figure for all purposes. *Absent clear evidence of general fame or notoriety in the community, and pervasive involvement in the affairs of society, an individual should not be deemed a public personality for all aspects of his life. It is preferable to reduce the public-figure question to a more meaningful context by looking to the nature and extent of an individual's participation in the particular controversy giving rise to the defamation.* [Emphasis added.]

In this context it is plain that petitioner was not a public figure. He played a minimal role at the coroner's inquest, and his participation related solely to his representation of a private client. He took no part in the criminal prosecution of Officer Nuccio. Moreover, he never discussed either the criminal or civil litigation with the press and was never quoted as having done so. He plainly did not thrust himself into the vortex of this public issue, nor did he engage the public's attention in an attempt to influence its outcome. We are persuaded that the trial court did not err in refusing to characterize petitioner as a public figure for the purpose of this litigation.

We therefore conclude that the *New York Times* standard is inapplicable to this case and that the trial court erred in entering judgment for respondent. Because the jury was allowed to impose liability without fault and was permitted to presume damages without proof of injury, a new trial is necessary. We reverse and remand for further proceedings in accord with this opinion.

It is so ordered.

Reversed and remanded.

COMMENT

1. Justices Brennan and White wrote strong dissenting opinions for different reasons. Brennan, who authored the landmark opinion for the Court in *New York Times v. Sullivan* and the opinion for the plurality in *Rosenbloom v. Metromedia,* did not wish to abandon the *actual malice* standard of those cases. In his view anyone involved in events of public or general interest should have to show knowing or reckless falsity to win a libel judgment.

Matters of public interest, said Brennan, reiterating his opinion for the Court in *Rosenbloom,* do not "suddenly become less so merely because a private individual is involved, or because in some sense the individual did not 'voluntarily' choose to become involved."

Brennan had used his opinion for the Court in the landmark privacy case, Time, Inc. v. Hill, 385 U.S. 374 (1967), this text, p. 318, to argue for a "public issue" or "newsworthiness" test in all libel and privacy cases. Anything less, for example a "reasonable care" standard is "elusive," said Brennan, and would saddle the press with "the intolerable burden of guessing how a jury might assess the reasonableness of steps taken by it to verify the accuracy of every reference to a name, picture or portrait." The result would be self-censorship.

At the other end of the spectrum, Justice White would have moved the Court back to the common law standard of "strict liability." That is, one who publishes a statement that later turns out to be inaccurate can never be "without fault," for one is not compelled to circulate a falsehood.

White, joined by Chief Justice Warren Burger, objected to the scrapping of state libel laws in favor of a newly announced First Amendment mandate which required private plaintiffs to prove actual injury to their reputations and culpability on the part of the defendant. People would now be powerless to protect their reputations. "No longer," said White, "will the plaintiff be able to rest his case with proof of a libel defamatory on its face or proof of a slander historically actionable *per se*." And it was the apparent demise of libel *per se* through a discarding of "history and precedent" that White lamented.

It was also the "severe invasion of the prerogatives of the [s]tates" that exercised Justice White. Whatever the merits of his long and vigorous dissent, he may have been partially correct when he suggested that "judges and juries who must live by these rules [the *Gertz* rules] will find them * * * incomprehensible."

It is for this reason that we now turn to a second Supreme Court case which attempted to clarify the meaning of *Gertz.*

The case is *Time, Inc. v. Firestone,* and it involves the failure of a series of reporters to understand the precise meaning of a court order in a celebrated divorce action. The result was a brief report in *Time* magazine which declared erroneously that Russell Firestone, the scion of a rubber company, was granted a divorce from his wife, Mary Alice Firestone, on grounds of adultery. When the magazine refused to retract, Mrs. Firestone sued and was awarded a $100,000 libel judgment by a Florida Circuit Court. The judgment was later affirmed by the Supreme Court of Florida, and *Time* appealed to the United States Supreme Court.

TIME, INC. v. FIRESTONE

424 U.S. 448, 96 S.CT. 958, 47 L.ED.2D 154 (1976).

Justice REHNQUIST delivered the opinion of the Court.

* * *

Respondent, Mary Alice Firestone, married Russell Firestone, the scion of one of America's wealthier industrial families, in 1961. In 1964, they separated, and respondent filed a complaint for separate maintenance in the Circuit Court of Palm Beach County, Fla. Her husband counterclaimed for divorce on grounds of extreme cruelty and adultery. After a lengthy trial the Circuit Court issued a judgment granting the divorce requested by respondent's husband. In relevant part the court's final judgment read:

> This cause came on for final hearing before the court upon the plaintiff wife's second amended complaint for separate maintenance (alimony unconnected with the causes of divorce), the defendant husband's answer and counterclaim for divorce on grounds of extreme cruelty and adultery, and the wife's answer thereto setting up certain affirmative defenses. * * *
>
> * * *
>
> According to certain testimony in behalf of the defendant, extramarital escapades of the plaintiff were bizarre and of an amatory nature which would have made Dr. Freud's hair curl. Other testimony, in plaintiff's behalf, would indicate that defendant was guilty of bounding from one bedpartner to another with the erotic zest of a satyr. The court is inclined to discount much of this testimony as unreliable. Nevertheless, it is the conclusion and finding of the court that neither party is domesticated, within the meaning of that term as used by the Supreme Court of Florida. * * *
>
> * * *
>
> In the present case, it is abundantly clear from the evidence of marital discord that neither of the parties has shown the least susceptibility to domestication, and that the marriage should be dissolved.
>
> * * *

"The premises considered, it is thereupon

"ORDERED AND ADJUDGED as follows:

> 1. That the equities in this cause are with the defendant; that defendant's counterclaim for divorce be and the same is hereby granted, and the bonds

> of matrimony which have heretofore existed between the parties are hereby forever dissolved.
>
> * * *
>
> 4. That the defendant shall pay unto the plaintiff the sum of $3,000 per month as alimony beginning January 1, 1968, and a like sum on the first day of each and every month thereafter until the death or remarriage of the plaintiff. * * *"

Time's editorial staff, headquartered in New York, was alerted to the fact that a judgment had been rendered in the Firestone divorce proceeding by a wire service report and an account in a New York newspaper. The staff subsequently received further information regarding the Florida decision from *Time's* Miami bureau chief and from a "stringer" working on a special assignment basis in the Palm Beach area. On the basis of these four sources, *Time's* staff composed the following item, which appeared in the magazine's "Milestones" section the following week:

> DIVORCED. By Russell A. Firestone, Jr., 41, heir to the tire fortune: Mary Alice Sullivan Firestone, 32, his third wife; a onetime Palm Beach schoolteacher; on grounds of extreme cruelty and adultery; after six years of marriage, one son; in West Palm Beach, Fla. The 17-month intermittent trial produced enough testimony of extramarital adventures on both sides, said the judge, "to make Dr. Freud's hair curl."

* * *

* * * Petitioner advances several contentions as to why the judgment is contrary to decisions of this Court holding that the First and Fourteenth Amendments of the United States Constitution limit the authority of state courts to impose liability for damages based on defamation.

Petitioner initially contends that it cannot be liable for publishing any falsehood defaming respondent unless it is established that the publication was made "with actual malice," as that term is defined in New York Times Co. v. Sullivan, 376 U.S. 254 * * * (1964). Petitioner advances two arguments in support of this contention: that respondent is a "public figure" within this Court's decisions extending *New York Times* to defamation suits brought by such individuals. See, e.g., Curtis Publishing Co. v. Butts, 388 U.S. 130, * * * (1967); and that the *Time* item constituted a report of a judicial proceeding, a class of subject matter which petitioner claims deserves the protection of the "actual malice" standard even if the story is proven to be defamatorily false or inaccurate. We reject both arguments.

In *Gertz v. Robert Welch, Inc.*, we have recently further defined the meaning of "public figure" for the purposes of the First and Fourteenth Amendments:

> For the most part those who attain this status have assumed roles of especial prominence in the affairs of society. Some occupy positions of such persuasive power and influence that they are deemed public figures for all purposes. More commonly, those classed as public figures have thrust themselves to the forefront of particular public controversies in order to influence the resolution of the issues involved.

Respondent did not assume any role of especial prominence in the affairs of society, other than perhaps Palm Beach society, and she did not thrust herself to the forefront of any particular public controversy in order to influence the resolution of the issues involved in it. [Emphasis added.]

Petitioner contends that because the Firestone divorce was characterized by the Florida Supreme Court as a "cause célèbre," it must have been a public controversy and respondent must be considered a public figure. But in so doing petitioner seeks to equate "public controversy" with all controversies of interest to the public. Were we to accept this reasoning, we would reinstate the doctrine advanced in the plurality opinion in Rosenbloom v. Metromedia, Inc., 403 U.S. 29 * * * (1971), which concluded that the *New York Times* privilege should be extended to falsehoods defamatory of private persons whenever the statements concern matters of general or public interest. In *Gertz,* however, the Court repudiated this position, stating that "extension of the *New York Times* test proposed by the *Rosenbloom* plurality would abridge [a] legitimate state interest to a degree that we find unacceptable."

Dissolution of a marriage through judicial proceedings is not the sort of "public controversy" referred to in *Gertz,* even though the marital difficulties of extremely wealthy individuals may be of interest to some portion of the reading public. Nor did respondent freely choose to publicize issues as to the propriety of her married life. She was compelled to go to court by the state in order to obtain legal release from the bonds of matrimony. *We have said that in such an instance "[r]esort to the judicial process * * * is no more voluntary in a realistic sense than that of the defendant called upon to defend his interests in court."* Her actions, both in instituting the litigation and in its conduct, were quite different from those of General Walker in Curtis Publishing Co. *She assumed no "special prominence in the resolution of public questions."* We hold respondent was not a "public figure" for the purpose of determining the constitutional protection afforded petitioner's report of the factual and legal basis for her divorce. [Emphasis added.]

For similar reasons we likewise reject petitioner's claim for automatic extension of the *New York Times* privilege to all reports of judicial proceedings. It is argued that information concerning proceedings in our Nation's courts may have such importance to all citizens as to justify extending special First Amendment protection to the press when reporting on such events. We have recently accepted a significantly more confined version of this argument by holding that the Constitution precludes States from imposing civil liability based upon the publication of truthful information contained in official court records open to public inspection. Cox Broadcasting Corp. v. Cohn, 420 U.S. 469 * * * (1975).

Petitioner would have us extend the reasoning of *Cox Broadcasting* to safeguard even inaccurate and false statements, at least where "actual malice" has not been established. But its argument proves too much. It may be that all reports of judicial proceedings contain some informational value implicating the First Amendment, but recognizing this is little different from labeling all judicial proceedings matters of "public or general interest," as that phrase was used by the plurality in *Rosenbloom.* Whatever their general validity, use of such subject matter classifications to determine the extent of constitutional protection afforded defamatory falsehoods may too often result in an improper balance between the competing interests in this area. It was our recognition and rejection of this weakness in the *Rosenbloom* test which led us in *Gertz* to eschew a subject matter test for one focusing upon the character of the defamation plaintiff. By confining inquiry to whether a plaintiff is a public officer or a public figure who might be assumed to "have voluntarily exposed themselves to increased risk of injury from defamatory falsehoods," we sought a more appropriate accommodation between the public's interest in an uninhibited press and its equally compelling need for judicial redress of libelous utterances.

Presumptively erecting the *New York Times* barrier against all plaintiffs seeking to recover for injuries from defamatory falsehoods published in what are alleged to be reports of judicial proceedings would effect substantial depreciation of the individual's interest in protection from such harm, without any convincing assurance that such a sacrifice is required under the First Amendment. And in some instances such an undiscriminating approach might achieve results directly at odds with the constitutional balance intended. Indeed, the article upon which the *Gertz* libel action was based purported to be a report on the murder trial of a Chicago police officer. Our decision in that case should make it clear that no such blanket privilege for reports of judicial proceedings is to be found in the Constitution.

It may be argued that there is still room for application of the *New York Times* protections to more narrowly focused reports of what actually transpires in the courtroom. But even so narrowed, the suggested privilege is simply too broad. Imposing upon the law of private defamation the rather drastic limitations worked by *New York Times* cannot be justified by generalized references to the public interest in reports of judicial proceedings. The details of many, if not most, courtroom battles would add almost nothing towards advancing the uninhibited debate on public issues thought to provide principal support for the decision in *New York Times.* And while participants in some litigation may be legitimate "public figures," either generally or for the limited purpose of that litigation, the majority will more likely resemble respondent drawn into a public forum largely against their will in order to attempt to obtain the only redress available to them or to defend themselves against actions brought by the State or by others. There appears little reason why these individuals should substantially forfeit that degree of protection which the law of defamation would otherwise afford them simply by virtue of their being drawn into a courtroom. *The public interest in accurate reports of judicial proceedings is substantially protected by Cox Broadcasting Co., supra. As to inaccurate and defamatory reports of facts, matters deserving no First Amendment protection, we think Gertz provides an adequate safeguard for the constitutionally protected interests of the press and affords it a tolerable margin for error by requiring some type of fault.* [Emphasis added.]

Petitioner has urged throughout this litigation that it could not be held liable for publication of the "Milestones" item because its report of respondent's divorce was factually correct. In its view the *Time* article faithfully reproduced the precise meaning of the divorce judgment. But this issue was submitted to the jury under an instruction intended to implement Florida's limited privilege for accurate reports of judicial proceedings. By returning a verdict for respondent the jury necessarily found that the identity of meaning which petitioner claims does not exist even for laymen. The Supreme Court of Florida upheld this finding on appeal, rejecting petitioner's contention that its report was accurate as a matter of law. Because demonstration that an article was true would seem to preclude finding the publisher at fault, we have examined the predicate for petitioner's contention. We believe the Florida courts properly could have found the "Milestones" item to be false.

For petitioner's report to have been accurate, the divorce granted Russell Firestone must have been based on a finding by the divorce court that his wife had committed extreme cruelty towards him *and* that she had been guilty of adultery. This is indisputably what petitioner reported in its "Milestones" item, but it is equally indisputable that these were not the facts. Russell Firestone alleged in his counterclaim that respondent had been guilty of adultery, but the divorce court never made any such finding. Its judgment provided that Russell Firestone's "counterclaim for divorce be and the same is hereby granted," but did not specify that the basis for the judgment was either of the two grounds alleged in the counterclaim. The Supreme Court of Florida on appeal concluded that the ground actually relied upon by the divorce court was "lack of domestication of the parties," a ground not theretofore recognized by Florida law. The Supreme Court nonetheless affirmed the judgment dissolving the bonds of matrimony because the record contained sufficient evidence to establish the ground of extreme cruelty.

Petitioner may well argue that the meaning of the trial court's decree was unclear, but this does not license it to choose from among several conceivable interpretations the one most damaging to respondent. Having chosen to follow this tack, petitioner must be able to establish not merely that the item reported was a conceivable or plausible interpretation of the decree, but that the item was factually correct. We believe there is ample support for the jury's conclusion, affirmed by the Supreme Court of Florida, that this was not the case. There was, therefore, sufficient basis for imposing liability upon petitioner if the constitutional limitations we announced in *Gertz* have been satisfied. These are a prohibition against imposing liability without fault, and the requirement that compensatory awards "be supported by competent evidence concerning the injury."

As to the latter requirement little difficulty appears. Petitioner has argued that because respondent withdrew her claim for damages to reputation on the eve of trial, there could be no recovery consistent with *Gertz*. Petitioner's theory seems to be that the only compensable injury in a defamation action is that which may be done to one's reputation, and that claims not predicated upon such injury are by definition not actions for defamation. But Florida has obviously decided to permit recovery for other injuries without regard to measuring the effect the falsehood may have had upon a plaintiff's reputation. This does not transform the action into something other than an action for defamation as that term is meant in *Gertz*. *In that opinion we made it clear that [s]tates could base awards on elements other than injury to reputation, specifically listing "personal humiliation, and mental anguish and suffering" as examples of injuries which might be compensated consistently with the Constitution upon a showing a fault.* [Emphasis added.] Because respondent has decided to forgo recovery for injury to her reputation, she is not prevented from obtaining compensation for such other damages that a defamatory falsehood may have caused her.

The trial court charged, consistently with *Gertz*, that the jury should award respondent compensatory damages in "an amount of money that will fairly and adequately compensate her for such damages," and further cautioned that "It is only damages which are a direct and natural result of the alleged libel which may be recovered." There was competent evidence introduced to permit the jury to assess the amount of injury. Several witnesses [6] testified to the extent of respondent's anxiety and concern over *Time* inaccurately reporting that she had been found guilty of adultery, and she herself took the stand to elaborate on her fears that her young son would be adversely affected by this falsehood when he grew older. The jury decided these injuries should be compensated by an award of $100,000. We have no warrant for re-examining this determination.

6. These included respondent's minister, her attorney in the divorce proceedings, plus several friends and neighbors, one of whom was a physician and testified to having to administer a sedative to respondent in an attempt to reduce discomfort wrought by her worrying about the article. [*Editorial Note:* The $100,000 award was premised entirely on the injury of mental pain and anguish. All claims as to injury to reputation were withdrawn prior to trial, and no evidence concerning damage to reputation was presented at trial. Justice Brennan believed this to be in conflict with *Gertz* and a return to the old rule of presumed damages.]

Gertz established, however, that not only must there be evidence to support an award of compensatory damages, there must also be evidence of some fault on the part of a defendant charged with publishing defamatory material. No question of fault was submitted to the jury in this case, because under Florida law the only findings required for determination of liability were whether the article was defamatory, whether it was true, and whether the defamation, if any, caused respondent harm.

The failure to submit the question of fault to the jury does not, of itself establish noncompliance with the constitutional requirements established in *Gertz*, however. Nothing in the Constitution requires that assessment of fault in a civil case tried in a state court be made by a jury, nor is there any prohibition against such a finding being made in the first instance by an appellate, rather than a trial, court. The First and Fourteenth Amendments do not impose upon the States any limitations as to how, within their own judicial systems, factfinding tasks shall be allocated. If we were satisfied that one of the Florida courts which considered this case had supportably ascertained petitioner was at fault, we would be required to affirm the judgment below.

But the only alternative source of such a finding, given that the issue was not submitted to the jury, is the opinion of the Supreme Court of Florida. That opinion appears to proceed generally on the assumption that a showing of fault was not required, but then in the penultimate paragraph it recites:

> Furthermore, this erroneous reporting is clear and convincing evidence of the negligence in certain segments of the news media in gathering the news. Gertz v. Welch, Inc., supra. Pursuant to Florida law in effect at the time of the divorce judgment (Section 61.08, Florida Statutes), a wife found guilty of adultery could not be awarded alimony. Since petitioner had been awarded alimony, she had not been found guilty of adultery nor had the divorce been granted on the ground of adultery. A careful examination of the final decree prior to publication would have clearly demonstrated that the divorce had been granted on the grounds of extreme cruelty, and thus the wife would have been saved the humiliation of being accused of adultery in a nationwide magazine. This is a flagrant example of "journalistic negligence." 305 So.2d, at 178.

It may be argued this is sufficient indication the court found petitioner at fault within the meaning of *Gertz*. Nothing in that decision or in the First or Fourteenth Amendments requires that in a libel action an appellate court treat in detail by written opinion all contentions of the parties, and if the jury or trial judge had found fault in fact, we would be quite willing to read the quoted passage as affirming that conclusion. But without some finding of fault by the judge or jury in the Circuit Court, we would have to attribute to the Supreme Court of Florida from the quoted language not merely an intention to affirm the finding of the lower court, but an intention to find such a fact in the first instance.

Even where a question of fact may have constitutional significance, we normally accord findings of state courts deference in reviewing constitutional claims here. But that deference is predicated on our belief that at some point in the state proceedings some factfinder has made a conscious determination of the existence or nonexistence of the critical fact. Here the record before us affords no basis for such a conclusion.

It may well be that petitioner's account in its "Milestones" section was the product of some fault on its part, and that the libel judgment against it was, therefore, entirely consistent with Gertz. But in the absence of a finding in some element of the state court system that there was fault, we are not inclined to canvass the record to make such a determination in the first instance. [Emphasis added.] Accordingly, the judgment of the Supreme Court of Florida is vacated and the case remanded for further proceedings not inconsistent with this opinion.

So ordered.

COMMENT

Note that Mrs. Firestone, in spite of her social prominence and her propensity for press conferences and clipping services, was classified by the Court as a *private person* who was simply availing herself of the legal process. Therefore *negligence*, a test of fault well below the *New York Times v. Sullivan* standard of actual malice, was all the plaintiff was required to demonstrate. But Justice William Rehnquist, recognizing perhaps that the court order in the divorce suit was unusually subject to misinterpretation, based as it was on "a ground not thereto recognized by Florida law," held that the *Gertz* requirement of fault on the part of the publisher had not been addressed by either the Florida jury or the Florida courts.

Ultimately the case centered on the question of how much care the publication took in reading an admittedly ambiguous court order. Should the magazine have known that Florida law denies alimony to an adulterous wife? At least, said Rehnquist, the court cannot ignore such questions. And so the case was sent back to the trial court.

In passing, Rehnquist said that inaccurate reports taken from judicial documents are not protected from civil liability. In Cox Broadcasting Corp. v. Cohn, 420 U.S. 469 (1975), the Court did say that the Constitution precludes states from imposing liability on *truthful* publication based on official court records open to public inspection. There a father brought a privacy suit following a broadcast identifying his raped and murdered daughter (see this text, p. 337).

The ostensible difference between *Cox* and *Firestone* is that a privilege will extend to the press where its judicial reports are true but not when its judicial reports are false.

By requiring a consideration of the degree of negligence or fault, *Gertz* and *Firestone* sought to shield the press and broadcast media from a rule of strict liability (libel *per se*, where fault, damages, and injury are presumed) that could lead to intolerable self-censorship and at the same time to recognize the legitimate state interest in compensating private individuals for wrongful injury from defamatory falsehoods. The Court sought a middle ground. How well it has succeeded in protecting both these values is still a matter of much speculation.

Of the many questions not answered by *Gertz* and *Firestone* the most perplexing for the press are: how does an editor, or for that matter a lower court, decide how to distinguish between public and private persons? How can the reporter writing a story know whether the judicial records she is reading are true or false? If the publicity-seeking Mrs. Firestone was not a voluntary public figure, then who is? If the erroneous report had only been published locally, would Mrs. Firestone then have been a public figure? In other words, while not a public figure in a national arena, was she a public figure in Miami, or in Florida?

Firestone is also problematical because, borrowing from *Gertz*, it sets injury to reputation aside and permits a libel award based on "personal humiliation, and mental anguish and suffering." It was noted at the outset that libel changes the way other people feel and think about a person. In *Firestone* the Court suggested that the way you come to think about yourself may also support libel damages. Should *Firestone*, then, have been a privacy suit instead of a libel suit?

USING THE CONSTITUTIONAL DEFENSE: QUESTIONS TO CONSIDER

Falsity

Once it is clear that the threshold elements of libel—*defamation, identification,* and *publication*—have been or will be met by plaintiff, a prospective defendant must consider additional elements of the *New York Times* or constitutional defense, as elaborated in *Gertz.*

Both private and public-person plaintiffs in at least half the states have the burden of proving the allegedly libelous statements *false*, since there is no longer a presumption of falsity. The rule with respect to private persons was first stated unequivocally by the Sixth Circuit Court of Appeals in Wilson v. Scripps-Howard Broadcasting Co., 7 Med.L.Rptr. 1169, 642 F.2d 371 (1981). In overturning Tennessee's strict liability rule of presuming falsity, the court used *Firestone* to support its claim that the plaintiff has the burden of proving falsity and "that demonstration that an article was true would seem to preclude finding the publisher at fault." Similarly in *Cox Broadcasting v. Cohn* (this text, p. 337), Justice Lewis Powell, concurring in the Court's opinion that public-person plaintiffs must prove the falsity of a libel with convincing clarity, noted, "It is fair to say that if the statements are true, the standard contemplated by *Gertz* cannot be satisfied."

Falsity, then, is an element of the fault that must be demonstrated in some states to prove publisher liability. In other states the burden remains with defendant.

State Standards of Fault

1. Adding great complexity to the tapestry of libel law was *Gertz's* invitation to the states to define for themselves the appropriate standard of liability for defamation concerning private persons. There would be "no liability without fault," said the Court, and application of this proposition might vary from state to state. A majority of states has adopted the *negligence* rule of *Gertz* in private-person libels. Among them are Arkansas, Arizona, California, the District of Columbia, Hawaii, Illinois, Kansas, Kentucky, Louisiana, Maryland, Massachusetts, Mississippi, New Mexico, Ohio, Oklahoma, Pennsylvania, Puerto Rico, Tennessee, Texas, Utah, Virginia, Washington, and Wisconsin. In half the states the issue remained unsettled in 1983.

2. Those few states retaining an *actual malice* test for private-person plaintiffs when they are involved in matters of public interest—Alaska, Colorado, Florida, Indiana, and Michigan—suggest the sturdiness and inexorable logic of *Rosenbloom's public issue* test. For example, the Michigan Court of Appeals held that a nursing home owner, while neither a public official nor a public figure, was required to show that defendant newspaper and television station had published defamatory reports with actual malice "since defendants have a qualified privilege to report on 'public interest' businesses such as plaintiff's." [90] And a Florida appeals court said that a private plaintiff (lawyer-landlord) whose apartments and rooming houses had been criticized in print would have to show that a newspaper had acted with actual malice because the articles "concerned matters of legitimate public interest." [91]

In an Indiana case, plaintiff, a heating and air conditioning firm, had installed a furnace in a home three weeks before a

90. Bortell v. Citizens for Better Care, 6 Med.L.Rptr. 1797 (Mich.1980).

91. Sobel v. Miami Daily News, 7 Med.L.Rptr. 1100, 395 So.2d 282 (Fla.1981).

fatal electrical fire; defendant newspaper publisher had speculated in news reports about the fire and its cause.

In upholding a summary judgment for the newspaper, the Court of Appeals of Indiana specifically drew its standard of "an issue of general and public concern" from the plurality opinion of the Supreme Court in *Rosenbloom*:

> When a general or public interest is recognized, it becomes unimportant in terms of ascertaining whether the public has a legitimate interest in an issue or even, whether the person involved is a famous, large-scale distributor of heating and air-conditioning equipment or a 'private' businessman operating a similar enterprise in a small community. * * * The key analytic determinant in the application of constitutional protections for speech and press in libel actions by 'private' individuals must be whether the communication involved concerns *an issue of general or public interest* without regard to whether the individual is famous or anonymous.[92] [Emphasis added]

3. New York's somewhat unique private person test, somewhere between negligence and actual malice, echoes the *Butts-Walker* "prudent-publisher" test. A New York public school teacher sued a Utica newspaper for reporting erroneously that he was part of a trio arrested for a serious drug offense involving heroin. A trial court denied the newspaper's motion for summary judgment, but the appellate division reversed and was affirmed by the court of appeals, New York's highest court. The news report was said to fall within a sphere of legitimate public concern. In such circumstances a plaintiff may recover only if it is established by a preponderance of evidence that the publisher acted in a *grossly irresponsible* manner and without due consideration for standards of information gathering and dissemination ordinarily followed by responsible journalists. The offending article was written only after two authoritative sources had been consulted, and it was not published until it had been checked by at least two persons other than the writer. Chapadeau v. Utica Observer-Dispatch, 1 Med.L.Rptr. 1693, 379 N.Y.S.2d 61 (1975). In Greenberg v. CBS, 5 Med.L.Rptr. 1470, 419 N.Y.S.2d 988, 997 (1979), another New York court used a "gross negligence" standard. Yet another in Karaduman v. Newsday, 6 Med. L.Rptr. 2345, 435 N.Y.S.2d 556 (1980) spoke of plaintiffs having to show that an editor acted in a "grossly irresponsible manner."

4. A number of undecided states, among them Alabama, Connecticut, Georgia, Iowa, New Hampshire, and Wyoming, appear to require something less than actual malice but more than negligence for private-libel plaintiffs.

5. *Chapadeau* would suggest that the standard of fault to be followed is that of the profession of journalism, an industry standard, or what is "normal" publishing practice. In a few cases, notably Troman v. Wood, 340 N.E.2d 292 (Ill.1975) and Memphis Publishing Co. v. Nichols, 4 Med. L.Rptr. 1573, 569 S.W.2d 412 (Tenn.1978), courts were unwilling to allow the press to establish its standard as the norm. Where industry standards have prevailed, journalists and journalism educators are frequently asked to give expert testimony in libel cases.[93] For the latter group, the practice has become controversial.

6. Since the plaintiff's attorney will have to demonstrate fault beyond mere falsity, he or she will want to explore the reporter's motives for publication, the

92. AAFCO Heating and Air Conditioning Co. v. Northwest Publication, Inc., 1 Med.L.Rptr. 1683, 321 N.E.2d 580 (Ind.1974). See also, Gay v. Williams, 5 Med.L.Rptr. 1755, 486 F.Supp. 12 (D. Alaska 1979); Walker v. Colorado Springs Sun, 538 P.2d 450 (Colo.1975), cert. den., 423 U.S. 1025.

93. Editor & Publisher, May 29, 1982, p. 28; Columbia Journ. Rev., July/August 1982, p. 16.

kind, quality, and number of sources,[94] the depth and independence of a reporter's investigation, the existence of contrary information or conflicting sources prior to publication,[95] and the nature of material not included in the story.

7. Normally a publication circulating throughout the country should be prepared to meet the *negligence* standard of *Gertz*. Federal courts have followed the case more strictly than state courts,[96] although federal courts will show deference to state libel laws.

Remember that for fault, as frequently for falsity, the burden of proof is on the plaintiff. It is this shifting of the burden from defendant to plaintiff that makes the constitutional defense so much more attractive than the common law defenses. In responding to allegations of either negligence or actual malice, think about your sources and the pains you took to check their information. A single and suspect source will not suffice. Your efforts toward accuracy may determine whether you win a summary judgment or go on to an expensive trial.

"We are not here dealing with the correctness of all of the statements made in the paragraph complained of," said the Fifth Circuit Court of Appeals in approving summary judgment for a magazine. "We are concerned with the means by which (the reporter) obtained the basis for the statements and * * * the efforts he made to check the information." [97]

The crux of the ruling of a federal district judge in the fourth trial of a $12½ million libel suit brought against *Look* magazine by former San Francisco mayor Joseph Alioto is contained in a single paragraph:

> Taking into consideration the nature and substance of the reports, the quality of their source, the passage of time since the original statements were said to have been made, and the complete absence of corroboration from law enforcement agencies who for several reasons would have been expected to have received some information about the meetings [allegedly between Alioto and the Cosa Nostra], the Court is compelled to conclude that there were "obvious reasons to doubt the veracity of the informant [and] the accuracy of his reports."[98]

The verdict of the judge was upheld on appeal.

"A failure to make a reasonable investigation into the truth of the statement is obviously a relevant factor," said the Illinois Supreme Court in discussing the negligence standard.[99] Look out for sources with axes to grind or a financial interest in what you publish.

In the meantime, look to your highest state court for guidance on local application of the *Gertz* rules.

What Is Actual Malice?

1. Since Joseph Alioto was a public person, his burden of proof was actual malice. It was on this question that three

94. With respect to anonymous sources see Holter v. WLCY T.V., Inc., 4 Med.L.Rptr. 2251, 366 So.2d 445 (Fla.1978).

95. Goldwater v. Ginzburg, 414 F.2d 324 (2d Cir. 1969), cert. den., 396 U.S. 1049 (1970), reh. den., 397 U.S. 978 remains a classic case of malice aforethought.

96. Collins and Drushal, *The Reaction of the State Courts to* Gertz, 28 Case Western Reserve L.Rev. 306 (Winter 1978).

97. Time, Inc. v. McLaney, 406 F.2d 565 (5th Cir. 1969).

98. Alioto v. Cowles Communications, Inc., 2 Med.L.Rptr. 1801, 430 F.Supp. 1363 (D.Cal.1977), affirmed, 623 F.2d 616 (9th Cir. 1980), cert. den. 449 U.S. 1102 (1981).

99. Troman v. Wood, 340 N.E.2d 292 (Ill.1975), Kidder v. Anderson, 3 Med.L.Rptr. 1881, 345 So.2d 922 (La.1977).

earlier juries had failed to agree. It has also been argued that "* * * actual malice is a constitutional issue to be determined initially by the trial judge on motion for summary judgment." [100] But what is actual malice?

Actual malice, a concept well established in common law and much discussed in America at least since passage of the Sedition Act of 1798, had long been defined as "well knowing" or "designed" falsity. In *New York Times*, Justice Brennan relied on the influential opinion of Judge Rousseau Burch for the Kansas Supreme Court in a 1908 case, *Coleman v. MacLennan*.[101] Although Burch's thresholds for state interference with freedom of the press are lower than today's courts would allow, he did speak of the need for a plaintiff to show actual malice where matters of public interest were involved. By 1964 and the Supreme Court's landmark ruling, at least six states and a number of legal commentators had adopted, or favored, what had evolved from the nineteenth century as a more liberal but still minority rule of public-person defamation.

A problem remains in distinguishing actual malice from common law malice. "In the context of a libel suit," said a federal district judge in *Reliance Insurance Co. v. Barron's*,[102] " 'actual malice' simply does not mean ill will or spite. Rather, 'malice' must be taken to mean fraudulent, knowing publication of a falsehood or reckless disregard of falsity. And we also note that reckless does not mean grossly negligent, its common use, but rather *intentional disregard*. When the Supreme Court uses a word, it means what the Court wants it to mean."

Ill will, for example, a prior statement of hatred of plaintiff by defendant, may be relevant and admissible as evidence of a state of mind conducive to reckless disregard of falsity,[103] but it is not itself actual malice. Specific evidence does seem to be needed: fabrication, fictionalization, failure to check with available sources or with parties to your investigation, use of anonymous or unverified phone calls, obviously biased sources, or inherently improbable allegations. An Oklahoma reporter, overhearing a telephone conversation in a sheriff's office and without further checking, assumed and reported that a police officer in breaking up a fight between two boys had kidnapped one at gunpoint. The Oklahoma Supreme Court said that was reckless disregard of truth or falsity.[104]

Protection for defendants will be found in agreement among reputable sources as to what was said to reporters and how accurately it was recounted; by headlines that agree with the possibly defamatory portions of a story; and by prompt publication of retractions, although retractions alone are not sufficient to establish lack of malice.[105] With "hot" news, slight inaccuracies may not constitute actual malice.[106]

Actual malice may simply be negligence or common law malice raised to a

---

100. Bon Air Hotel v. Time, Inc., 426 F.2d 858, 867 (5th Cir. 1970).

101. 98 P. 281 (Kan.1908).

102. 3 Med.L.Rptr. 1033, 442 F.Supp. 1341, 1349–50 (D.N.Y.1977).

103. Cochrane v. Indianapolis Newspapers, 3 Med.L.Rptr. 2131, 372 N.E.2d 1211 (Ind.1978).

104. Akins v. Altus Newspapers, Inc., 3 Med.L.Rptr. 1449, 609 P.2d 1263 (Okl.1977). Rinaldi v. Viking Penguin, Inc., 5 Med.L.Rptr. 2506, 422 N.Y.S.2d 552 (1979), affirmed 7 Med.L.Rptr. 1202, 438 N.Y.S.2d 496 (1981) is instructive on the degree to which facts should be checked.

105. Kerwick v. Orange County Publications, 5 Med.L.Rptr. 2502, 422 N.Y.S.2d 179 (1979), reversed 7 Med.L.Rptr. 1152, 438 N.Y.S.2d 778 (1981); DiLorenzo v. New York News, 7 Med.L.Rptr. 1452, 432 N.Y.S.2d 483 (1981).

106. Simonson v. United Press International, Inc., 6 Med.L.Rptr. 2313, 500 F.Supp. 1261 (D.Wis.1980), affirmed 7 Med.L.Rptr. 1737, 654 F.2d 478 (7th Cir. 1981).

higher power. And what a trial judge said about malice in 1898 may still be appropriate:

> The jumble in some modern textbooks on slander and libel concerning malice, actual malice, malice in law, malice in fact, implied malice and express malice (all derived from judicial utterances, it is true), is a striking testimony of the limitations of the human mind.[107]

Public or Private Person?

1. Of all the questions dealt with in this section this is the most vexing and the first that has to be addressed directly and in the first instance by the reporter or editor.

Appellate courts have developed three major categories of libel plaintiff: public officials, public figures, and private persons. The distinctions are seldom clear.

Public Officials. Public officials are elected or appointed government officials, law enforcement officers, public school teachers and administrators, city, town, and municipal employees of responsibility, government attorneys, and county medical examiners. But not all public employees. And not all public school teachers. In these and other categories it would seem that to qualify as a public person a public employee must have some policy-making authority and thus some access to the media.

The Texas Supreme Court reversed a summary judgment in favor of a Laredo newspaper and remanded for trial a libel suit brought by an elected county surveyor whom the paper had implied was responsible for a flooding problem. Amid a welter of tortured distinctions the court decided that the surveyor was indeed a public official in the circumstances of the case, but that the complained of publication may not have related to his "official" conduct. Nor could his "limited participation in the controversy" and his reluctance to "engage the public's attention" make him a public figure. So the elected surveyor pursued his libel suit as a private person under Texas law.[108]

Without drawing any precise boundaries, Chief Justice Burger did suggest in footnote 8 in Hutchinson v. Proxmire, 5 Med.L.Rptr. 1279, 443 U.S. 111 (1979) that not all public employees are public officials. In that case the Court also held that Senator Proxmire, in making his often uninformed Golden Fleece award to a publicly funded research behavioral scientist, was not insulated by the Constitution's speech or debate clause from a libel suit based on a press release sent from his office. The speech or debate clause, Proxmire argued, gave absolute immunity to libel committed in the course of one's legislative duties or, more generally, as part of the "informing function" of the Congress. Has the Court overruled, without citing it, *Barr v. Matteo* (see this text, p. 207) in which it held the "utterance of a federal official to be absolutely privileged if made 'within the outer perimeter' of his duties?" Senator Proxmire retracted erroneous statements contained in his newsletter and paid Dr. Hutchinson $10,000 in a settlement. The United States Senate paid $125,000 out of public funds for Proxmire's defense.

Nor has the Court drawn boundaries between the public and private lives of public officials. Can the two be separated? What aspects of one's private life bear on one's fitness or capacity for public office? Does a stormy marriage negatively affect the decision-making capabilities of a head of state? Does a record of psychiatric treatment disqualify a person for the vice-presidency of the United States?

107. Ullrich v. New York Press Co., 50 N.Y.S. 788 (1898).

108. Foster v. Laredo Newspapers, Inc., 530 S.W.2d 611 (Tex.1976).

Does a state investment board chairman's assignations with a notorious prostitute threaten the public interest?

Public Figures. These may be divided into at least three subcategories:

Pervasive or All Purpose. Public figures of this type are the very famous, the stars of stage and screen and the sports world, the Frank Sinatras and the Mohammed Alis. Those whose positions in the public spotlight are secure.

Vortex or Limited Purpose. Public figures in this category are those who, standing in the wings or sitting in the audience may, voluntarily or involuntarily, make brief appearances on the stage of life. Here today but gone tomorrow.

Gertz defined vortex public figures as those who have "thrust themselves to the forefront of particular public controversies in order to influence the resolution of the issues involved." In *Firestone* the Court noted, "A person who engages in criminal conduct does not automatically become a public figure for purposes of comment on a limited range of issues relating to his conviction." To hold otherwise would create an "open season" for all who sought to defame persons convicted of crime.

In a companion case to *Hutchinson* —Wolston v. Reader's Digest Association, Inc., 5 Med.L.Rptr. 1273, 443 U.S. 157 (1979) —a plaintiff who twenty years earlier had pleaded guilty to criminal contempt of court charges during grand jury investigations into spy charges was said not to be a public figure. Although Wolston at a point in time past had consciously and half voluntarily chosen not to appear before a grand jury, he had long since returned to private life and had made no effort at any time to inject himself into a public controversy in order to change its course.

"A private individual," wrote Justice William Rehnquist for the Court, "is not automatically transformed into a public figure by becoming involved in or associated with a matter that attracts public attention. To accept such reasoning would in effect re-establish the doctrine advanced by the plurality opinion in *Rosenbloom v. Metromedia.*"

An older rule—once a public figure always a public figure—was suggested by the Sixth Circuit Court of Appeals in Street v. National Broadcasting Co., 7 Med.L.Rptr. 1001, 645 F.2d 1227 (6th Cir. 1981). The plaintiff, whom NBC had assumed to be dead, had been a witness forty years before in the rape prosecutions of the nine young and black Scottsboro Boys. NBC's docudrama depicted a judge setting aside a guilty verdict because he did not believe Street's testimony. The Sixth Circuit held that once a person becomes a public figure in connection with a particular public controversy, that person remains a public figure for purposes of later commentary on the same controversy. Street had given press conferences at the time of the trial. She therefore had access to the media. If she had been raped in 1931, however, her involvement in the case from that point forward could never have been *a priori* voluntary.

NBC chose to settle out of court before the Supreme Court could hear arguments, leaving only partly resolved the question of whether a public figure can retreat into anonymity and whether the factual accuracy of the broadcast would affect the issue of voluntariness. In other words, what effort was made by the plaintiff to attract public attention during the original episode? The key question seems to be: Can there be any such category as *involuntary public figure?* Can the media foist public figure status on an unwilling person? If the courts say no, are they making editorial judgments about public figures and public issues? What about potentially newsworthy people—criminals, for example—who take great pains to remain anonymous and behind the scene, or mask their involvement, but nevertheless contribute mightily to the passing parade?

In the meantime, the major question for the journalist in distinguishing public and private people is how intensively and consciously involved in the event reported was the subject of the news story? This and other questions relevant to journalistic procedures are discussed in the case that follows.

REBOZO v. WASHINGTON POST

673 F.2D 375 (5TH CIR. 1981), CERT. DEN. 454 U.S. 964.

RONEY, Circuit Judge:

This is an appeal from a summary judgment entered for the defendant newspaper in a defamation suit. The district court found that plaintiff was a public figure and that no genuine issue of material fact existed as to whether defendant acted with actual malice. We affirm the court's finding that plaintiff is a public figure. We reverse, however, as to the decision that there was no genuine issue of material fact on the question of whether defendant acted with actual malice in publishing the newspaper article that forms the basis of this suit, and remand for further proceedings.

I. FACTS

Because the case was decided on defendant's motion for summary judgment, we must construe the record most favorably to plaintiff. *Wolston v. Reader's Digest Association, Inc.*, 443 U.S. 157, 162 n. 5, * * (1979); *Time, Inc. v. Ragano*, 427 F.2d 219, 221 (5th Cir. 1970).

In June 1973 Ronald Kessler, a reporter with substantial financial and reporting experience for defendant's newspaper, *The Washington Post*, was assigned by his editor to prepare a series of articles on the finances of then-President Richard M. Nixon. As part of his preparation Kessler became interested in plaintiff Charles G. Rebozo because of his relationship with the former President. Rebozo had been, and continues to be, a close friend and financial adviser of the former President, and serves as chairman of the board and president of the Key Biscayne Bank in Miami.

Newsday, a Long Island, New York, newspaper in 1971 had published a series of articles about Rebozo, one of which described a Miami lawsuit involving allegations that the Key Biscayne Bank had converted 900 shares of stock belonging to E.F. Hutton & Co. Some of the stock had apparently been pledged as collateral for a loan at the Key Biscayne Bank, and was later sold when the loan was called. During the course of his investigation, Kessler reviewed the file in the case, which by that time was pending in this Court on appeal, in order to determine whether it contained any subsequent unreported developments. * * *

Among other things Kessler studied the deposition of George H. Riley, Jr., who had been retained to investigate a claim filed by E.F. Hutton with its surety, the Fidelity and Casualty Company of New York. In his deposition, Riley described a meeting he had with Rebozo in October 1968 as follows:

Q Did you tell Mr. Rebozo at the time that the stock had been stolen or was missing from E.F. Hutton & Co.?

A Yes, sir.

Q Can you recall exactly what you told him?

A As I previously stated, I advised Mr. Rebozo that I was investigating the theft of nine 100-share certificates from the vaults of E.F. Hutton & Co. in New York.

Q Did you advise him of the numbers of the certificates that you were investigating?

A Yes. And the numbers corresponded to the numbers he gave me.

It is undisputed that 300 shares of the stock were sold on November 13, 1968, although the parties differ on whether the stock was sold by the Key Biscayne Bank itself, or on Rebozo's personal account.

After Kessler read the court file in Miami and New Orleans, he called Riley on the telephone because, as Kessler described, "I wanted, somehow to get a feeling from him, at least as to whether he understood the possible significance of his testimony." Kessler recounted a portion of his telephone conversation with Riley as follows on deposition:

Q Did you specifically ask him whether his statement in the deposition concerning his conversation with Mr. Rebozo was accurate?

A No.

Q Why not?

A I attach great significance to testimony given under oath and most newspaper articles, of course, are based on statements that are not made under oath. So, when a reporter obtains statements that are made under oath, it is certainly of more significance than otherwise.

Q It would have been significant, wouldn't it Mr. Kessler, if Mr. Riley told you he had made an error or a misstatement in his sworn testimony?

A Yes.

Q You didn't think it important to find out whether he would say whether he was right or wrong in that statement?

A No.

Q You didn't want to know what he wanted to say on that issue?

[Objection omitted]

Kessler also contacted Rebozo's attorney, who told him Rebozo "flatly denies" that Riley told Rebozo during their October 1968 meeting that the stock was stolen. The attorney followed up the conversation with a letter, repeating that Riley's testimony was false in that respect.

The question whether Rebozo personally, or the Bank, had cashed the stock was the subject of an October 6 internal memorandum from Kessler to his *Post* editor, Harry Rosenfeld, prompted by the telephone conversation between Kessler and Rebozo's attorney. A portion of that memorandum states:

> So who cashed the stock? Neither Rebozo nor other witnesses were asked this question in the depositions. There are no other legal papers in the court file to answer the question.
>
> But there are copies of the bills, receipts, and checks covering the sale transaction. As is clear from the attached, they all bear Rebozo's name.
>
> * * *
>
> The fact that Rebozo's name appears on them, and that the transactions were executed on his personal account, appear to me to be more than sufficient evidence for the purposes of an accurate and fair newspaper account of what appears in the court file that Rebozo technically and substantively cashed the stock.

Kessler and Rosenfeld discussed the content of an article Kessler had prepared on the stock transaction, and reviewed the sources of the information contained in the article.

On October 25, 1973, *The Washington Post* published a front-page article containing the headline, "Bebe Rebozo Said to Cash Stolen Stock," accompanying a photograph of plaintiff, and the following four paragraphs.

> Charles G. (Bebe) Rebozo, President Nixon's close friend, cashed $91,500 in stolen stocks in 1968 after he was told by an insurance investigator it was stolen, the investigator's sworn statement and other records in a Miami court file indicate.

> A lawyer for Rebozo conceded the investigator visited Rebozo but said Rebozo "flatly denies" the investigator told him the stock was stolen.
>
> The $91,500 in securities represented 300 of the 900 shares of International Business Machines Corp. stock that federal prosecutors say was stolen by the Mafia in 1968 from the vaults of E.F. Hutton & Co., a New York stock brokerage firm.
>
> The stock came into Rebozo's possession when it was offered as collateral for a loan from Rebozo's bank, Key Biscayne Bank in Florida.

The story continued for a total of 126 paragraphs, with the balance of the article appearing on pages A14 and A15 of defendant's newspaper. The "main point" of the story, according to Kessler, was contained in the "lead," or first paragraph. Farther along in paragraph number 99, the *Post* article quoted the passage from investigator Riley's deposition, in which Riley was questioned about whether the stock "had been stolen *or was missing.*" [Emphasis added].

Rebozo's complaint contends the article's lead sentence is false in two respects: (1) the investigator did not tell him the stocks were stolen; and (2) the stocks were cashed by the bank, not by him. The question of the article's falsity, however, is not an issue in this appeal.

II. WAS REBOZO A PUBLIC FIGURE?

In *New York Times Co. v. Sullivan,* 376 U.S. 254 * * * (1964), the Supreme Court held that a public official cannot recover damages for defamation relating to official conduct absent a showing of " 'actual malice'—that is, with knowledge that it was false or with reckless disregard of whether it was false or not." * * * Three years later the Court held in *Curtis Publishing Co. v. Butts,* 388 U.S. 130 * * * (1967), that the *New York Times* standard is applicable to "public figures" as well. *See also Associated Press v. Walker,* 388 U.S. 130 * * * (1967). The Court elucidated the applicability of *New York Times* to public figures, but refused to expand the protection afforded by that standard to actions brought by private persons, in *Gertz v. Robert Welch, Inc.,* 418 U.S. 323, 344–47 * * * (1974).

Application of the *New York Times* rule to public figures, the Court observed, is supported by two factors. First, public figures, because they "enjoy significantly greater access to the channels of effective communication and hence have a more realistic opportunity to counteract false statements than private individuals normally enjoy," are less vulnerable to injury from defamatory statements. *Gertz v. Robert Welch, Inc.,* 418 U.S. at 344, * * *; *see Wolston v. Reader's Digest Association, Inc.,* 443 U.S. at 164, * * *. A second consideration, and one that has been given greater weight by the Court, is that public figures, the news media may assume, "have voluntarily exposed themselves to increased risk of injury from defamatory falsehood concerning them." *Gertz v. Robert Welch, Inc.,* 418 U.S. at 345, * * *. The Court went on to describe two ways in which a person may become a public figure for first amendment purposes.

> For the most part those who attain this status have assumed roles of especial prominence in the affairs of society. Some occupy positions of such persuasive power and influence that they are deemed public figures for all purposes. More commonly, those classed as public figures have thrust themselves to the forefront of particular public controversies in order to influence the resolution of the issues involved.

418 U.S. at 345, * * *. *See also Wolston v. Reader's Digest Association, Inc.,* 443 U.S. at 164, * * *; *Time, Inc. v. Firestone,* 424 U.S. 448, 453 * * * (1976). Thus, under the analysis suggested in *Gertz v. Robert Welch, Inc.,* two types of public figures emerge: Those who are pub-

lic figures for all purposes, and those who are public figures for a limited range of issues.

The district court held as a matter of law that plaintiff "had achieved such pervasive fame and notoriety as of * * * the date of publication * * * that he had become a public figure 'for all purposes and in all context' " (quoting Gertz v. Robert Welch, Inc., 418 U.S. at 351 * * *.) Our review of this conclusion requires that we consider, first, whether plaintiff's purported status as a public figure is appropriate for decision on summary judgment and, second, whether the evidence considered in a light most favorable to plaintiff, shows him to be a public figure for the purposes of this litigation.

The Supreme Court has on numerous occasions, treated the public figure and public official questions as matters of law, for the trial court to decide. See, e.g., Time, Inc. v. Firestone, 424 U.S. 448 (1976) * * *; Gertz v. Robert Welch, Inc., 418 U.S. 323 (1974) * * *; Rosenblatt v. Baer, 383 U.S. 75 * * * (1966). This Court has observed in this same context that "where undisputed facts admit to but one conclusion, then, on motion for summary judgment, the court properly decides the issue." Rosanova v. Playboy Enterprises, Inc., 580 F.2d 859, 862 * * * (5th Cir. 1978). Even if summary judgment were improper because of issues of fact that could only be resolved after evidentiary hearing, the trial court, not a jury, must determine whether the evidence showed that plaintiff was a public figure. Brewer v. Memphis Publishing Co., 626 F.2d 1238 * * * (5th Cir. 1980). in the absence of conflicting inferences to be drawn from the record in this case, we conclude the district court was justified in considering the public figure question on summary judgment.

The record in this case contains sufficient undisputed facts to show that Rebozo, at the time of publication, was a public figure. As is well known, Rebozo was President Nixon's closest friend while Nixon was in the White House. While this in and of itself has considerable significance, we need not decide whether a confidential relationship with the President of the United States automatically converts one into a public figure, since the record indicates Rebozo had in other ways voluntarily exposed himself to the risk of close public scrutiny.

Rebozo played a substantial role in the former President's financial affairs, acting as the President's agent in the management of the President's bank accounts at the Key Biscayne Bank, and in the purchase of two homes. Plaintiff also played a role in the purchase and sale of other investments for the former President. In addition Rebozo's relationship with the President was not confined to counseling on business and financial matters. Rebozo freely admitted he offered his opinions to President Nixon on various matters, and transmitted to the former President the views of other important people on certain policy matters. The two discussed the Watergate situation when it began to arise in late 1973.

More significantly for purposes of this case, Rebozo played an active role in the President's 1972 re-election campaign, helping to arrange major contributions for the President's political benefit. The Senate Select Committee on Presidential Campaign Activities, the so-called Watergate Committee, investigated closely Rebozo's role in the 1972 campaign and his involvement in President Nixon's finances, eventually publishing five volumes of data describing Rebozo's connections with the former President and his campaign.

Press coverage of Rebozo has focused both upon his relationship to the President and upon his own business and personal affairs, although the public's interest in his activities has certainly been enhanced by his connections with the former President. The record indicates that during the six months prior to October 25, 1973, the date of the *Washington Post* article, *The New York Times* published 48 articles mentioning Rebozo, while *The Miami Herald* published 76. Prominent stories in 1968 and 1971, in *The New York Times* and *Newsday,* described Rebozo's business and financial dealings in some detail. Rebozo himself recognized, "[W]hen you are traveling in the circles that I have traveled in there are press people all over the place."

In view of the foregoing, Rebozo, met, as a matter of law, both *Gertz v. Robert Welch, Inc.,* public figure considerations. First, he "enjoy[ed] significantly greater access to the channels of effective communication and hence [had] a more realistic opportunity to counteract false statements than private individuals enjoy." 418 U.S. at 344. * * * There is evidence in the record that following publication of the *Post* article, both *The Miami Herald* and a major television network published Rebozo's response.

Second, on the basis of his voluntary activities, "the communications media [were] entitled to act on the assumption" plaintiff "had voluntarily exposed [himself]" to the risk of close public scrutiny. Gertz v. Robert Welch, Inc., 418 U.S. at 345. * * *. Rebozo's activities—including his association with President Nixon, taking part in his financial affairs, and involvement with the re-election effort—made him a prime subject of public comment.

Accordingly, we affirm the district court's conclusion that for the purposes of this litigation plaintiff Rebozo was a public figure at the time this article was published.

III. WAS THE MALICE QUESTION APPROPRIATE FOR RESOLUTION ON SUMMARY JUDGMENT?

The district court, having decided that plaintiff was a public figure, applied the correct standard of liability but held there was no genuine issue of material fact on the question of "actual malice," as defined by New York Times Co. v. Sullivan, 376 U.S. at 279–80, * * * Because we conclude that the facts in this case, taken in a light most favorable to Rebozo, raised such an issue of fact, we reverse the summary judgment entered for defendant.

* * *

On this record we conclude the district court was confronted with a genuine issue of material fact on the details of investigator Riley's conversation with Rebozo, and reporter Kessler's review of it. In investigating the story, even though Kessler went to the trouble of calling Riley, he failed to review with Riley the words in Riley's earlier deposition upon which Kessler eventually based the article's lead. Regardless of whether Riley knew at the time of his conversation with Rebozo whether the pledged stock had in fact been stolen, the seminal question may be what Riley actually told Rebozo before the stock was sold to cover the loan. We note in passing that on the second appeal in the conversion case, the Court found that not until December 1968, nearly two months after the stock sale, did E.F. Hutton learn that the stock involved in this case was among those shares that had been missing from its vault. Fidelity & Casualty Co. v. Key Biscayne Bank, 501 F.2d 1322, 1324 (5th Cir. 1974). Despite Kessler's professed belief in the veracity of Riley's deposition testimony, Kessler's resolution of the obvious ambiguity whether Riley told Rebozo the stock was (a) missing, (b) stolen, or (c) missing or stolen, in favor of the most potentially damaging alternative creates a jury question on whether the publication was indeed made without serious doubt as to its truthfulness. St. Amant v. Thompson, 390 U.S. at 732. * * *

There is, moreover, a material question of fact suggested by Kessler's October 6, 1973 memorandum to his editor, in which the reporter expressed uncertainty about whether the Key Biscayne Bank or Rebozo himself cashed the stock. Kessler stated in that memorandum that if the bank, rather than Rebozo had actually cashed the stock, the article's proposed lead paragraph would have to be modified. This memorandum, plus the fact that Kessler resolved the uncertainty expressed in it in such a way as to cast plaintiff Rebozo in the worst possible light and to make for Kessler a frontpage story of an episode which otherwise might not have commanded any significant attention, when taken in a light most favorable to Rebozo, could amount to evidence of the reporter's reckless disregard for the truth or falsity of the assertion that "Charles G. (Bebe) Rebozo, President Nixon's close friend, cashed $91,500 in stolen stock. * * *" * * Thus we cannot say "the record is devoid of genuine issues of fact as to whether the alleged defamatory statement was published with actual knowledge of its falsity or with reckless disregard of whether it was true or false." Bon Air Hotel, Inc. v. Time, Inc., 426 F.2d at 865. Accordingly, the district court's summary judgment on the question of actual malice is reversed and the case is remanded for further proceedings.

Reversed and remanded.

COMMENT

Rebozo was subsequently settled out of court. Assuming that some agreement is possible on who would qualify as a *pervasive* public figure, let us look at other examples of those the courts have designated *vortex* public figures: an author who became embroiled in a controversy as to how intimate he was with Ernest Hemingway; [109] the sons of Julius and Ethel Rosenberg who publicly asserted the innocence of their parents in speeches and a book; [110] persons who voluntarily involved themselves in the fluoridation controversy; [111] a high school coach who verbally assaulted referees; [112] a civil rights activist; [113] a major corporation making a public stock option; [114] a civic organization member who wrote a letter to a newspaper editor on a public issue; [115] advertisers involved in an intensive advertising campaign; [116] a discharged police officer who had complained to the media; [117] and a student senate president who ran for a school board seat.[118]

Public Personality. This has been suggested as an additional public person category, applying to those who appear to be neither pervasive nor vortex public figures. A belly dancer, although her public spotlight may not be very bright, has at least made a deliberate effort to attract public attention and approval. One dancer's mistake may have been to grant an interview which led to a feature story in a Rochester, New York newspaper. The re-

109. Hotchner v. Castillo-Puche, 404 F.Supp. 1041 (D.N.Y.1975), reversed 2 Med.L.Rptr. 1545, 551 F.2d 910 (2d Cir. 1977) on failure to show actual malice.

110. Meeropol v. Nizer, 381 F.Supp. 29 (D.N.Y.1974), affirmed 2 Med.L.Rptr. 2269, 560 F.2d 1061 (2d Cir. 1977).

111. Exner v. American Medical Association, 529 P.2d 863 (Wash.1974); Yiamouyiannis v. Consumers Union, 6 Med.L.Rptr. 1065, 619 F.2d 932 (2d Cir. 1980).

112. Winter v. Northern Tier Publishing Co., 4 Med.L.Rptr. 1348 (N.Y.1978).

113. Williams v. Trust Co. of Georgia, 230 S.E.2d 45 (Ga.1976).

114. Reliance Insurance Co. v. Barron's, 3 Med.L.Rptr. 1033, 442 F.Supp. 1341 (D.N.Y.1977).

115. Wright v. Haas, 586 P.2d 1093 (Okl.1978).

116. Steaks Unlimited v. Deaner, 6 Med.L.Rptr. 1129, 623 F.2d 264 (3d Cir. 1980).

117. DiLeo v. Koltnow, 6 Med.L.Rptr. 2011, 613 P.2d 318 (Colo.1980).

118. Henderson v. Kaulitz, 6 Med.L.Rptr. 2409, 644 F.2d 885 (6th Cir. 1981). See also, Fitzgerald v. Penthouse, International, 7 Med.L.Rptr. 2385, 525 F.Supp. 585 (D.Md.1981), judgement affirmed in part, reversed in part 691 F.2d 666 (1982), cert. denied 103 S.Ct. 1277, 75 L.Ed.2d 497 (1983).

porter quoted the dancer as saying, "Men is my business." The court placed an innocent construction on that language. The dancer did not. Faced with having to prove actual malice, the dancer contended that the reporter's refusal to permit her to review the article before publication was evidence of reckless disregard for the truth.

Congruent with journalistic norms the court wrote:

> It would hardly be conducive to a free press to impose a requirement that all persons quoted or mentioned in a publication be permitted to review the report prior to publication. * * * [P]republication review, including a review of direct quotations, would, in effect, impose the equivalent of censorship traditionally anathema in our society. * * * Publications establish their own method of verifying information and the fact that the subject of an article was not offered, prior to publication, an opportunity for review and comment, does not, by itself, establish that the publisher acted maliciously or recklessly. Only where the publisher has, or should have had, reasons to doubt the accuracy of the report or its reporter is there a legal duty to make further inquiry. James v. Gannett Co., Inc., * * 386 N.Y.S.2d 871 (1976).

A summary judgment in favor of the newspaper was upheld.

When a newspaper article implied that singer Anita Brewer had tried to revive a faltering career on the back of a romantic relationship with Elvis Presley and reported falsely that she and her husband were divorced, the Brewers sued a Memphis newspaper. After three jury verdicts in their favor, the Brewers lost on the actual malice test in a federal appeals court. Brewer v. Memphis Publishing Co., 6 Med. L.Rptr. 2025, 626 F.2d 1238 (5th Cir. 1980).

In a 1976 case involving *Playboy* magazine and an alleged mobster, a federal district court in Georgia said that "Defining public figures is much like trying to nail a jellyfish to the wall." To rebut *Playboy's* evidence of extensive contacts over a period of years with underworld figures and criminal prosecutions, Louis Rosanova argued that he was not a public figure because he didn't have access to the media to contradict charges against him and because he had not thrust himself voluntarily into the vortex of any public issue. Again the involuntary public figure. But this time in classic form!

The court defined Rosanova somewhat vaguely as a public figure because of "his voluntary contacts and involvements related to the subject matter of the [offending] article." In the absence of clear and convincing proof of actual malice or reckless disregard of truth, the court granted *Playboy* summary judgment. Rosanova v. Playboy Enterprises, Inc., 411 F.Supp. 440 (D.Ga.1976).

In each of these cases plaintiffs were suing for statements unrelated to their participation in any kind of public controversy. But each, in his or her own way, was a public personality, a person always with the potential or higher probability of becoming a vortex public figure. And when they do, they fit, though not always very well, the category of *involuntary public figure*, a category less rare perhaps than the courts have presumed.

Private Persons. Anyone who doesn't fit the categories already discussed may be a private person. For example, a consulting engineer on a public project who had no policy-making authority;[119] an attorney appointed to handle a criminal appeal;[120] a physician who prescribed amphetamines and, beyond publishing scientific articles,

119. Forrest v. Lynch, 3 Med.L.Rptr. 1187, 347 So.2d 1255 (La.1977), cert. den. sub nom. Times-Picayune v. Forrest, 3 Med.L.Rptr. 2232, 435 U.S. 971 (1978).

120. Peisner v. Detroit Free Press, 4 Med.L.Rptr. 1062, 266 N.W.2d 693 (Mich.1978).

sought no media attention;[121] an administrative aide to Spiro Agnew and then political adviser to Senator Orrin Hatch's 1978 campaign, who was called a "bagman" for the former vice-president by then incumbent Senator Frank Moss;[122] a man whose brother was convicted of murdering their parents but who played no part in the event;[123] an historical and archaeological research corporation employed by a county as a scientific fact-finding consultant for the county's water supply;[124] a defendant in a wrongful-death civil action;[125] a former airlines executive whose competence was brought into question;[126] five corporate plaintiffs and two owners of a movie and television production company in a $490 million libel suit against *Penthouse* magazine;[127] and a Gulf + Western personnel director negligently accused of taking kickbacks.[128]

In instructions to the jury in the *Penthouse* case, the trial judge said that corporate plaintiffs would be public figures for all purposes only if they had achieved such pervasive fame or notoriety and were so involved in the affairs of society that they had become public figures for all purposes and in all contexts. Selling one's services to the public, buying advertising, and having access thereby to the media alone does not constitute the thrusting of oneself into a public controversy.

In the foregoing *Gulf + Western* case, a federal district court judge faulted the reporter for using third-hand information and then distorting or misinterpreting what she had. A negligence test was appropriate, said the court, because the plaintiff held no public office, did not have general fame or notoriety in the community, had no pervasive involvement in public affairs, and had not injected himself into a public controversy. All corporate officers were not to be swept under the actual malice rule.

As the public figure definition is narrowed by the courts, it seems more than ever incumbent upon journalists to gauge the *voluntariness* of a newsmaker's involvement in controversial public events. In most cases, the decision on how to categorize a plaintiff will be a question of law for a judge.[129] If a publisher disagrees with that decision, the onus is on him or her to establish that the plaintiff is indeed a public person. Better at the outset to make the correct threshold judgment as to whether the subject of your allegations is a public or private person.

A final question that might be considered is whether the rules of *Gertz* apply to nonmedia defendants. In 1976 the Maryland Court of Appeals held in Jacron Sales Co., Inc. v. Sindorf, 350 A.2d 688 (Md.1976) that they did, arguing that it would be a "bizarre result as a matter of tort law to hold individual defendants liable without fault while the media were

121. Greenberg v. CBS, 5 Med.L.Rptr. 1470 (1979).

122. Lawrence v. Moss, 6 Med.L.Rptr. 2377, 639 F.2d 634 (10th Cir. 1981), cert. den. 451 U.S. 1031. This was a close case. Conversely to Mrs. Firestone, who might have been a public figure in Florida but was not nationally, plaintiff Lawrence, by implication, might have been a public figure in a national arena, but he was not a public figure in Utah where the defamation was first published.

123. Dresbach v. Doubleday & Co., 7 Med.L.Rptr. 2105, 518 F.Supp. 1285 (D.D.C.1981).

124. Arctic Co. Limited v. Loudoun Times-Mirror, 6 Med.L.Rptr. 1433, 624 F.2d 518 (4th Cir. 1980), cert. den., 449 U.S. 1102.

125. Newell v. Field Enterprises, 6 Med.L.Rptr. 2450, 415 N.E.2d 434 (Ill.1980).

126. Dixson v. Newsweek, 3 Med.L.Rptr. 1123, 562 F.2d 626 (10th Cir. 1977).

127. Rancho La Costa, Inc. v. Superior Court, 6 Med.L.Rptr. 1351, 165 Cal.Rptr. 347 (1980).

128. Lawlor v. Gallagher Presidents' Report, Inc., 394 F.Supp. 721 (S.D.N.Y.1975).

129. For an exception—where the decision was said to be an issue of fact for the jury—see McCusker v. Valley News, 428 A.2d 493 (N.H.1981), cert. den. 454 U.S. 1017.

liable only for negligence. * * * Further, an individual's defamatory statement is, on the whole, likely to create a smaller risk of harm than a media publication. * * Finally, the media are more likely to be aware of the risk of liability, and thus more likely to insure against it. * * *" See *The Supreme Court, 1973 Term*, 88 Harvard L.Rev. 41, 148, fn. 52 (1974); Anderson v. Muscatine, 7 Med.L.Rptr. 1726, 304 N.W.2d 239 (Iowa 1981).

Conversely, in Wisconsin, the constitutional protection applicable to a media defendant under *Gertz* does not apply to a nonmedia defendant. In a 1975 case, Calero v. Del Chemical Corp., 228 N.W.2d 737, the Wisconsin Supreme Court said, "This focus on the media and the matter of public concern which the court makes in this passage is the key to the distinction between constitutional and non-constitutional conditional privileges in defamation law." This view is reiterated in Denny v. Mertz, 8 Med.L.Rptr. 1369, 318 N.W.2d 141 (Wis.1982), and must depend upon a constitutional distinction of some kind between speech and press. *Denny* was also an unfortunate case for defendants in that a corporation's former general counsel, who had been active in a stockholder dispute, was categorized as a private person because the stockholder dispute was held not to be a public controversy.

Has the Plaintiff Suffered Actual Injury?

Actual injury must be proven by plaintiff under the rules of *Gertz* and *Firestone*. It may now include personal humiliation and mental anguish as well as injury to reputation. Recall that Mrs. Firestone's physician testified that he had to medicate his patient following the *Time* magazine publication.

Plaintiff's attorney will look for reader reaction to the defamation in letters to his or her client, in letters to editors, and in articles in other publications. Attorneys will also pursue evidence of damage to business or profession and loss of customers, clients, and profits. Perhaps a plaintiff's pattern of association or community activities have been adversely affected.

At the same time, of course, plaintiff's attorney will be looking for material favorable to his or her client: deletions from notes or outtakes and anything else that suggests the reporter might have had doubts about the veracity of sources or the accuracy of subsequent published reports.

Fact or Opinion?

Does the libel comprise comment or opinion rather than a false allegation of fact? Under *Gertz* and the First Amendment "there is no such thing as a false idea." This has been interpreted as meaning no liability for pure statements of opinion—the editorial, the book review, the political cartoon. Opinions may place a publisher in jeopardy, however, if they are clearly based on false statements of fact, either explicit or implicit. Obviously the line between fact and opinion is not always clear. In a 1982 case, the New Jersey Supreme Court attempted to make that line more distinct.

A letter-to-the-editor used the pejorative terms "huge cover-up" and "conspiracy" in criticizing a mayor and a tax collector for not revealing the names of property owners who were delinquent in their payment of property taxes. The writer disclosed the facts upon which his opinions were based. And the words "conspiracy" and "cover-up," said the court, were employed here in a loose, figurative sense and as rhetorical hyperbole, much as was the word "blackmail" in the *Greenbelt* case, 398 U.S. at 14 (see this text, p. 220).

The court relied heavily for its holding on the following useful paragraph from the

Restatement (Second) of Torts, Section 566 (1977):

> "Pure" statement of fact is found when the maker of the comment states the facts on which he bases his opinion of the plaintiff and then states a view as to the plaintiff's conduct, qualification or character. "Pure" expression of opinion occurs also when the maker of the comment does not spell out the alleged facts on which the opinion is based but both parties to the communication know the facts or assume their existence and the statement of opinion is obviously based on those assumed facts as justification for the opinion. The second, or "mixed" type of expression of opinion is one that, while an opinion in form or content, is apparently based on facts about the plaintiff or his conduct that have neither been stated by the defendant nor assumed to exist by the parties to the communication.

Expressions of "pure" opinion on matters of public concern may no longer be the basis of an action for defamation, said the court, and it drew the rule that pejorative statements of opinion are entitled to constitutional protection no matter how extreme, vituperous, or vigorously expressed.

But the court noted that false and defamatory statements of fact are actionable. Language that could reasonably be understood as implying specific criminal acts, though disguised as opinion, would not fall within the *Gertz* protection; outright charges of illegal conduct, if false, would be protected solely by the actual malice test.

In granting summary judgment for both the writer of the letter and the newspaper, the court symbolized the letter-to-editor column as the last remaining forum of public opinion. Kotlikoff v. Community News, 8 Med.L.Rptr. 1549, 444 A.2d 1086 (N.J.1982).

Finally, an illustration in a sociology textbook showing a white police officer prodding a black man with a nightstick to prevent him from falling asleep in a public place, accompanied by a caption asking rhetorically whether the policeman would do the same to a well-dressed, middle-aged white, was said in Cibenko v. Worth Publishers, 7 Med.L.Rptr. 1298, 510 F.Supp. 761 (D.N.J.1981) to be an expression of opinion and therefore not subject to either libel or false light privacy claims.

Since the fact/opinion distinction is the basis of the common law defense of fair comment and criticism, it will be addressed again in a subsequent section.

COMMON LAW OR STATUTORY DEFENSES

Common law defenses against libel—notably truth, qualified privilege, and fair comment and criticism—were the primary defenses prior to *New York Times.* Their lack of attractiveness since 1964 is due to the fact that they place the *burden of proof* on the defendant, whereas the *New York Times* or constitutional defense places it on the plaintiff. This means that a publisher will always look first for a *New York Times* defense.

Although the shifted burden has created conceptual confusion around the traditional defenses, it is safe to say that they have survived. Since a plaintiff must now demonstrate the falsity of a defamatory charge—falsity is no longer presumed—truth remains a central issue and a logical counterclaim for a defendant.

Having established falsity, a plaintiff must in addition demonstrate at least negligence on the defendant's part. Historically a minority of states required of a defendant not only proof of truth but truth with good motives and for justifiable ends, an additional burden no longer imposed on defendants.

Truth alone would now appear to be a complete defense.

Likewise, the traditional defense of fair comment and criticism has meant that a communication medium may go to the utmost lengths of denunciation, satirization, sarcasm, and condemnation in criticizing men, measures, and institutions seeking public approval, if it is done so without malice.

This is essentially the doctrine of *New York Times,* except that the burden of proving malice, or lack of malice, has shifted from defendant to plaintiff.

Although the *New York Times* rule may seem to have subsumed state statutory and common law privileges where media defendants are sued by public persons, the state law privileges—now statutory in most jurisdictions—are still vital in countering a charge of negligent misstatement where the libel plaintiff is a private person.

The Defense of Truth

1. Where *truth* or justification alone is pleaded as a defense, the proof must be at least as broad as the charge. "[I]t is generally agreed," said Prosser, an authority on tort law, "that it is not necessary to prove the literal truth of the accusation in every detail, and that it is sufficient to show that the imputation is substantially true, or, as it is often put, to justify the 'gist,' the 'sting,' or the 'substantial truth' of the defamation." [130]

Where a plaintiff, in testifying before a congressional committee, attacked "political Zionist planners for absolute rule via a one-world government," a newspaper article charging that the plaintiff had attacked Jews was held substantially true and therefore not actionable.[131]

2. It is important for the press to understand that a truth defense requires proof of a defamatory charge, not simply proof that the charge has been made. For example, when a newspaper charging an architectural firm with the faulty design of a school building based its article on a confidential report, it was faced with proving not only that its informant made the statements attributed to him but with proving that those statements were in fact true.[132]

The defense of truth until recently was never satisfied by simply showing that the report was an accurate repetition of a libelous charge. For the journalist, the basic question was whether the facts he or she had stated were probably true, regardless of where they came from.

3. A publication will be considered in its entirety and in relation to its structure, nuances, implications, and connotations. It is not sufficient to take sentences separately and demonstrate their individual accuracy, detached and wrenched out of context. An allegation of crime need not be established beyond a reasonable doubt, but it must be shown by a fair preponderance of evidence.[133]

4. Sometimes the evidence needed to prove the truth is just not available. Until it is, an alleged defamatory statement is presumed to be false under this common law defense.[134] A defendant may need depositions, affidavits, exhibits—difficult to obtain after the fact. Truth can be a costly and hazardous defense.

130. Prosser, *Handbook of the Law of Torts* (4th ed. 1971), 798. See also, Fairbanks Publishing Co. v. Pitka, 445 P.2d 685 (Alaska 1968); Mitchell v. Peoria Journal-Star, Inc., 221 N.E.2d 516 (Ill.1966); Meier v. Meurer, 98 N.W.2d 411 (Wis.1959).

131. Dall v. Pearson, 246 F.Supp. 812 (D.D.C.1963).

132. Miller, Smith & Champagne v. Capital City Press, 142 So.2d 462 (La.1962).

133. Clark v. Pearson, 248 F.Supp. 188 (D.D.C.1965).

134. Medico v. Time, Inc., 6 Med.L.Rptr. 1968, 509 F.Supp. 268 (D.Pa.1980), affirmed 6 Med.L.Rptr. 2529, 643 F.2d 134 (3d Cir. 1981).

When Ben Bagdikian, then a reporter for the *Providence Journal-Bulletin,* charged that Harold Noel Arrowsmith was a "sophisticated fascist" and "a shy, reticent anti-Semite," the truth was proved by cross-examination in the courtroom. It was demonstrated to the jury that Arrowsmith believed Franklin D. Roosevelt to be part of an international Zionist conspiracy, and that Arrowsmith had had a working relationship with American Nazi leader George Lincoln Rockwell in the dissemination of viciously anti-Jewish propaganda.[135]

Few defendants pleading truth are this fortunate, for truth, an elusive concept at best, is generally of more subtle definition. And it will not do to defend a half-truth or to try to prove the unprovable.

5. The strength of one's belief in a defamatory publication does not constitute truth or justification. Truth may be a dangerous defense also because, if it cannot be proven, its very pleading becomes a republication of the libel and may be interpreted as malice. The courts discourage those who would insist upon defending a falsehood.

When attorneys for the news media suspect a defamation is false or that proof of its truth is unlikely, they look for another defense.

Qualified Privilege

1. The theory of qualified or conditional *privilege* is that in some situations the public interest in the full disclosure of public business overrides harm to individual reputation. A news medium may publish with impunity a fair and accurate report of any judicial, quasi-judicial, legislative, executive, or other public and official proceeding at any level of government. Reports and documents relating to such proceedings are also protected. The qualification or condition is an absence of malice.

Qualified privilege—sometimes called the "public record" privilege or the "public eye" doctrine—is statutory in most states, and these laws may differ in detail and interpretation.

In some jurisdictions reports on closed, executive sessions of municipal councils or school boards would be privileged.[136]

Generally the privilege attaches only to fair and accurate republications of statements made in government documents. Gertz v. Welch, 8 Med.L.Rptr. 1769, 680 F.2d 527 (7th Cir. 1982). Statements based on nonofficial records, such as personal interviews, are not privileged. Dresbach v. Doubleday, 8 Med. L.Rptr. 1793, 518 F.Supp. 1285 (D.D.C.1982).

In some states, privilege has been expanded to include reports of all public meetings where public issues are discussed. These might include chamber of commerce forums,[137] public meetings of stockholders, union members, church boards, political parties, and medical or bar associations.

States differ in their willingness to protect the informal statements of officials. For example, when a policeman was quoted as saying that a former Marine had threatened to kill his wife, a New York court ruled that assertions by policemen do not constitute official proceedings.[138]

However, when a plaintiff's picture appeared in the *Topeka Daily Capital* in connection with an article on a grain theft ring, based on an interview with the state attorney general, the Kansas Supreme Court reached a contrary conclusion. The newspaper has a qualified privilege, said

135. Arrowsmith v. United Press International, 205 F.Supp. 56 (D.Vt.1962).

136. Swede v. Passaic Daily News, 153 A.2d 36 (N.J.1959).

137. Phoenix Newspapers v. Choisser, 312 P.2d 150 (Ariz.1957).

138. Kelley v. Hearst Corp., 157 N.Y.S.2d 498 (1956).

the court, to publish in good faith anything involving violations of the law, particularly where the source of information is the highest law enforcement officer of the state. Express malice would have destroyed the privilege.[139] Note, of course, that these are pre-*New York Times* cases. Since 1964 the qualified privilege doctrine—at least with respect to public figures and public officials—has been given First Amendment status in the form of the actual malice doctrine.

A substantially accurate account of a state auditor's report of "questionable ties" between a school board administrator and the suppliers of educational materials was also said to be protected.[140]

But a police log of "hot line" reports was said to represent only informal arrangements between the police and media and, not being an official record, was not privileged. The newspaper falsely reported that a husband had shot his wife.[141]

2. More complex are the rules of qualified privilege relating to judicial proceedings. In most states privilege depends upon some official action having been taken by a judge or some other officer of the court. A pleading or deposition filed in a case, but not yet acted upon, may not be privileged. The assumption is that these documents, containing possibly false, scurrilous, and uncontradicted charges, are addressed to the courts and not to the public at large.

Beginning in 1927 a significant minority of states began extending qualified privilege to all proceedings in a legal action, including pleadings on file, even though no formal judicial action had been initiated.

Under the headline, "Healer and Inventor Face Swindle Charge: Mrs. Elizabeth Nichols Says They Took $16,000 From Her Through Fraud," a story in the *New York Post* quoted Mrs. Nichols, a wealthy widow, as saying that Mrs. Anne McCoy Campbell, a widely known Christian Science practitioner, and a male companion had succeeded in winning control over her mind.

The legal papers in the action had been filed with the clerk of court. But before any judicial action was taken, Mrs. Nichols withdrew her charges and dropped the suit. Mrs. Campbell then brought a libel action against five newspapers: the newspapers pleaded qualified privilege. Mrs. Campbell won in the trial court, but the highest New York court, the court of appeals, turned its back on precedent and in a historic decision wrote:

> In this case it appears that the action against plaintiff was discontinued; that Mrs. Nichols thus got her alleged false and scurrilous charges before the public as news and then dropped her case. It is contended that such acts should not be deemed privileged so as to protect the publisher. The contention is too far reaching. Scandalous matter may come before the public in connection with law suits. Personal malice may thus be given a hearing. A complaint withdrawn may not be the vindication that a decision favorable to the accused would be. But complaints are withdrawn after applications have been made to the courts and suits have been dropped before verdicts. Consistency requires us to go forward or we go back. We cannot go back and exclude the publication of daily reports of trials before a final decision is reached. The present distinction is indefensible. Therefore, we proceed to a logical conclusion and uphold the claim of privilege on the ground that the filing of a pleading is a public and official act in the course of judicial proceedings. Campbell v. New York Evening Post, 157 N.E. 153 (N.Y.1927).

139. Beyl v. Capper Publications, Inc., 305 P.2d 817 (Kan.1957)

140. Hines v. New York News, 6 Med.L.Rptr.1982 (N.Y.Sup.Ct.1980).

141. Phillips v. Evening Star Newspaper Co., 6 Med.L.Rptr. 2191, 424 A.2d 78 (D.C.1980), cert. den. 451 U.S. 989.

The *Campbell* doctrine has been adopted in California, Ohio, and Pennsylvania, for example. Under it a reporter must still be certain that a legal document has been served on the party named as defendant before the contents of that document are divulged; if legal papers are filed in a court clerk's office but the defendant has not been served with process, there is no privilege, for no legal proceeding has begun.

Most states require that some more significant judicial action be taken before privilege can be invoked. See Sanford v. Boston Herald-Traveler Corp., 61 N.E.2d 5 (Mass.1945).

3. In most jurisdictions sealed records and documents withheld from public scrutiny by court order, or affidavits which have not become part of a judicial proceeding, are distinctly not privileged. The woman friend of a convicted robber charged in an affidavit to a district attorney that a police sergeant, searching her home after a robbery, had taken a large sum of money from a clothes closet and had not returned it after her release from arrest. The woman's attorney then passed the document on to a newspaper, and it became part of a general news story. Truth could be the newspaper's only common law defense here, for the affidavit was not part of an official proceeding. The policeman was awarded $1,500 in compensatory damages.[142]

In some states, court rules or statutes provide that papers filed in juvenile, matrimonial, divorce, and morals cases are sealed and are not open to the public generally. Court sessions dealing with such matters, even though closed, may be privileged in the absence of statutory authority for secrecy. A fair and factually accurate report of a judicial proceeding involving a youthful offender not open to the public was nevertheless held privileged by a New York court.[143] But here the terrain is swampy. Ordinarily, the privilege accorded to reports of judicial proceedings relates to judicial proceedings which are public and have retained their public character.

Depositions taken after a suit has begun are privileged in the same way as is evidence in a trial. Even in the absence of the judge and jury, the examination of witnesses is part of the judicial proceeding. And the fact that some of the statements made in such proceedings will not be admissible later in evidence does not bar their use in news stories. If the deposition taking is closed, news stories can be based on the comments of those who were there, but, of course, they must be balanced and fair.

Many statements made from the witness stand in open court are stricken from the record. Generally such testimony was thought not to be privileged, although in rare cases it may have been.

A New York court shed light on this question by declaring that statements made in open court are privileged if they are in any way pertinent to the litigation. In making such a determination the court is not limited to the narrow and technical rules applied to the admissibility of evidence. Nothing that is said in the courtroom may be the subject of a libel suit unless "it is so obviously impertinent as not to admit of discussion, and so needlessly defamatory as to warrant inference of express malice." The court added that "to be outside of privilege, a statement made in open court must be so outrageously out of context as to permit one to conclude, from the mere fact that the statement was uttered, that it was motivated by no other desire than to defame." [144]

142. Lubore v. Pittsburgh Courier Publishing Co., 101 F.Supp. 234 (D.D.C.1951).

143. Gardner v. Poughkeepsie Newspapers, Inc., 326 N.Y.S.2d 913 (1971).

144. Martirano v. Frost, 307 N.Y.S.2d 425 (1969).

4. A California appeals court ruled that the *absolute privilege* accorded to judicial proceedings also attaches to any publication that has any reasonable relation to the judicial proceeding even though the publication is made outside the courtroom and no function of the court or its officers is involved. The court added that the defamatory matter need not be relevant, pertinent, or material to any issue before the court; it need only have some connection or some relation to the judicial proceeding. This absolute privilege accorded to judicial and quasi-judicial proceedings extends to preliminary conversations and interviews between a prospective witness and an attorney if they are in some way related to or connected with a pending or contemplated action.[145] This, of course, is a very liberal construction of the privilege to report judicial proceedings. And note that it is an absolute privilege. The difference between a qualified and an absolute privilege is that malice destroys the qualified privilege but does not affect the absolute privilege.

5. All reports of judicial proceedings must be balanced, fair, and substantially accurate, whether or not they are abridgments. Seldom are they verbatim. Nor do such reports have to be technically accurate in a legal sense. The reporter must avoid mistakes in names, embellishments of news accounts of judicial proceedings with facts from the newspaper's own extra-legal "investigation," [146] reporting what an official document merely stated to be "alleged" as a fact; and, of course, the epitome of malice: reckless disregard of the truth.[147] So as to avoid giving the impression of reporting an official document when it is not official, some courts have held that the source of what is being reported must be included if privilege is to be invoked.[148]

6. It can safely be reported that a crime has been committed and a particular person is being held for questioning. The assumption is that the statement, while not privileged, is provably true. An arrest should not be reported until a suspect is booked, that is, his name has been entered on a police blotter. When a police blotter or log book is an official public record, required by law to be kept, a news story based on the blotter is protected by qualified privilege, if the report is fair and accurate. A Louisiana court ruled in favor of a newspaper whose correspondent, relying on a police log book, reported that the plaintiff had been arrested and charged with possession of narcotics and contributing to the delinquency of a juvenile. There was no presumption of guilt in the news story.

"We feel," said the court, "that since a newspaper may report the fact that a person was arrested and the charge for which he was arrested, it may rely for such a report upon the principal record kept by the arresting authority, which record is a 'public record,' to show accurately whether the arrest was made and the specific charges which were being filed against the arrested person. This is particularly true where there has been nothing to indicate to the publisher that such public record may not be reliable, * * * even though the [l]og [b]ook may have contained an incorrect statement of the charges for which plaintiff was arrested.[149]" Good journalistic practice in such cases is to seek a comment from the defamed person

145. Ascherman v. Natanson, 100 Cal.Rptr. 656 (1972). See also Trans World Accounts, Inc. v. Associated Press, 425 F.Supp. 814 (D.Calif.1977).

146. Purcell v. Westinghouse Broadcasting Co., 191 A.2d 662 (Pa.1963).

147. Hogan v. New York Times Co., 313 F.2d 354 (2d Cir. 1963).

148. Hughes v. Washington Daily News, 193 F.2d 922 (D.C.Cir.1952).

149. Francois v. Capital City Press, 166 So.2d 84 (La.App.1964).

or his spokesman, an attorney, for example, in the interests of a balanced story.

Where a newspaper article concerning a suspected counterfeiter gave not only the details of the arrest but added inaccurate additional language about engraving plates hidden in a false panel of the suspect's truck, the newspaper's qualified privilege was lost.[150]

7. Although some states have by statute extended the protection of privilege to reports of arresting officers, police chiefs, county prosecutors, and coroners, collateral details on investigations and speculation on the evidence from these sources are generally not privileged. A newspaper would print at its peril, for example, a statement by an attorney that the victim of his client's alleged rape had consented to it.[151]

Under common law rules a grand jury indictment could be safely reported after it had been delivered to a judge, if it was reported with reasonable precision. Since grand juries are closed, comment on testimony before them from participants must be handled with great care.[152] But by no means is a reporter confined to coverage of the trial alone.

Preliminary proceedings, such as a hearing or the issuance of an injunction, generally may be covered. Conditional privilege applies to any action of a judge in his official capacity.

8. Given the admonitions above, any fair, impartial, and accurate summary of a judicial or quasi-judicial proceeding, whether in a courtroom or not, is qualifiedly privileged. A news story based on a judicial proceeding may be lively and filled with human interest, if it remains substantially correct.[153]

A news story reporting that the plaintiff, driver of an automobile involved in a fatal accident, was indicted on a charge of criminal negligence and prefaced by the headline, "Driver of Death Car Heads Indictment List," was ruled privileged in view of the fact that it was a fair and accurate report of a judicial proceeding.[154]

Any discussion of qualified privilege with respect to liability for defamation in connection with reporting of judicial proceedings must now reckon with Time, Inc. v. Firestone, 424 U.S. 448 (1976). In *Firestone* the Court said the *New York Times* rule does not automatically extend to all judicial proceedings. The Court said that there was no reason that libel plaintiffs "should substantially forfeit that degree of protection which the law of defamation would otherwise afford them simply by virtue of their being drawn into a courtroom." With respect to defamation suits involving reports of judicial proceedings, the Court held that the *Gertz* rules remained generally applicable. In *Firestone,* the Court said that no *New York Times* -based privilege would attach to aid the libel defendant because the defamation relied on judicial records which were inaccurate. The case was distinguished from Cox Broadcasting Corp. v. Cohn, 420 U.S. 469 (1975) (this text, p. 337), where the Court held that the First Amendment prevented liability on a right of privacy theory for stating the name of a rape victim on television contrary to Georgia law. The name of the rape victim had been obtained from court documents open to the public, i.e., the indictment in the case. The Court in *Firestone* distinguished the *Cohn* case on the ground that the public records relied upon there had been accurate. Would *libel* defendants in cases involving

150. Britt v. Knight Publishing Co., 291 F.Supp. 781 (D.S.C.1968).

151. Kennedy v. Cannon, 182 A.2d 54 (Md.1962).

152. Bridgwood v. Newspaper PM Inc., 93 N.Y.S.2d 613 (1949).

153. Bock v. Plainfield Courier-News, 132 A.2d 523 (N.J.1957).

154. Rouse v. Olean Times Herald Corp., 219 N.Y.S.2d 835 (1961).

inaccurate reports of judicial proceedings be able to claim the benefit of the *New York Times* privilege? What if such reports are ambiguous or unclear?

The refusal of the Court in *Firestone* to extend the *New York Times* rule to all reports of judicial proceedings makes the prior cases discussed in this section very important. As a result of *Firestone,* libel actions involving reports of judicial proceedings will continue to be governed by the relevant state law with respect to qualified privilege.

9. Senator Joseph McCarthy's anti-Communist crusade taught the press that professional ethics dictate that whenever possible a reporter ought to try to get a defamed person's side of the story. It is the reporter's moral duty in every case to weigh the public interest against injury to personal reputation and to be fair and balanced in what is written.

Fair Comment and Criticism

1. Traditionally the defense of *fair comment and criticism,* which Prosser called a special category of qualified privilege, protected honest criticism of men, measures, and public institutions. Governmental bodies, charitable organizations, businesses, unions, educators, coaches, the creators of books, articles, plays, music, art, film, radio and television programs, scientific discoveries, and all who invite public attention or controversy are open to attack.[155]

Obviously the *New York Times* doctrine has incorporated this defense, and its rules now apply.

Since fair comment was a defense for the libelous expression of an opinion or intellectual judgment, a perennial problem in most jurisdictions was to distinguish between opinion and fact and to avoid basing opinions on erroneous facts. When you consider that factual innuendos are implicit in opinions—the editorial or review, for example—the task was not an easy one.

New York Times came to the rescue by extending protection to false facts in the absence of actual malice. And Justice Powell held in *Gertz* that there could be no false ideas [opinions].

The distinction between facts and opinions suggested by Powell, and the lower burden of proof for private-person plaintiffs using a negligence test, means that the distinction is still valid.

A United States court of appeals judge thought the distinction important in a libel suit brought by William F. Buckley, Jr. against an author and Bible scholar.

"Fellow traveler," "Fascist," and "radical right" were terms of opinion, said the judge, but a charge that Buckley had lied about and implicitly libeled several people, who could have taken him to court, was defamatory under both the public and the private law of libel. The most litigious paragraph follows:

> Buckley has been caught out for misquotations [with quotation marks!] and for repeating radical right malice and rumor, but he never admits a mistake or apologizes to the victims. Like Westbrook Pegler, who lied day after day in his column about Quentin Reynolds and goaded him into a lawsuit (see Reynolds v. Pegler, 123 F.Supp. 36 (D.N.Y.1954), affirmed 223 F.2d 429 (2d Cir. 1955), Buckley could be taken to court by any one of several people who

155. The privilege apparently came into the common law in Carr v. Hood, 1 Camp. 355, 170 Eng.Rep. 983 (1808). A classic American case is Cherry v. Des Moines Leader, 86 N.W. 323 (Iowa 1901). See also, Outcault v. New York Herald Co., 102 N.Y.S. 685 (1907); Berg v. Printer's Ink Publishing Co., 54 F.Supp. 795 (D.N.Y.1943); Pearson v. Fairbanks Publishing Co., 413 P.2d 711 (Alaska 1966); Buckley v. Vidal, 327 F.Supp. 1051 (D.N.Y.1971); Keogh v. Pearson, 244 F.Supp. 482 (D.D.C.1965); Steak Bit of Westbury, Inc. v. Newsday, Inc., 334 N.Y.S.2d 325 (1972).

had enough money to hire competent legal counsel and nothing else to do. Reynolds won his suit, of course, but it took all of his time and resources for most of three years, and he died shortly thereafter.

BUCKLEY v. LITTELL

539 F.2D 882 (2D CIR. 1976).

OAKES, Circuit Judge:

* * *

Gertz v. Robert Welch, Inc., made the distinction—crucial to the issue—between "false statements of fact" which receive no constitutional protection, and "ideas" and "opinions" which by definition can never be "false" so as to constitute false statements which are unprotected when made with actual malice. The district court recognized that the "boundary line" between fact and opinion is not a precise one, and acknowledged that "to call someone a fascist fellow traveler is perhaps not as concrete a statement of facts as to say that someone committed a theft. * * *" Nevertheless the court found that

> [W]hen Littell speaks of Buckley as a fellow traveler of fascism, indicating that he sympathizes with and promotes conspiracy and subversion * * * we are surely dealing with questions of fact, and not merely ideas.

We find, to the contrary, that the use of "fascist," "fellow traveler" and "radical right" as political labels in *Wild Tongues* [Littell's book] cannot be regarded as having been proved to be statements of fact, among other reasons, because of the tremendous imprecision of the meaning and usage of these terms in the realm of political debate, an imprecision which is simply echoed in the book. * * * The search for the precisely articulable meaning of the statements about Buckley to the ordinary reader could only be, in a sense, an arbitrary one because of the ambiguous and sometimes even contradictory content of the terminology necessarily utilized in Littell's polemical tract. This is not a case where a person is being accused of being a member of the Communist Party, or a legislative representative of the Communist Party, as in the New York cases relied upon by the district court. * * * Such allegations of membership or well-defined political affiliation are readily perceivable as allegations of fact susceptible to proof or disproof of falsity. They are quite dissimilar to the terms "fellow traveler," "fascism" and "radical right" which, whether as used by Littell or as perceived by a reader, are concepts whose content is so debatable, loose and varying, that they are insusceptible to proof of truth or falsity. The use of these terms in the present context is in short within the realm of protected opinion and idea under *Gertz.*

* * *

We find further that there was nothing libelous in the statement as it appears in *Wild Tongues* that the *National Review* and "On the Right" frequently "print 'news items' and interpretations picked up from the openly fascist journals." The issue of what constitutes an "openly fascist" journal is as much a matter of opinion or idea as is the question what constitutes "fascism" or the "radical right" in *Wild Tongues.* Buckley himself admitted that he or the *National Review* had occasionally printed items and interpretations picked up from openly fascist journals even as he defined them, although "for the purpose of denouncing them." Surely the difference of opinion between Buckley and Littell regarding what is "approval" of what one calls "fascist" and the other calls "radical right" or "denunciation" of the same highly debatable categories cannot give rise to recovery by the one against the other in this case.

We have a different factual context, however, concerned in the third alleged libel. For here appellant's book says, "Like Westbrook Pegler, who lied day after day in his column about Quentin Reynolds and goaded him into a lawsuit, Buckley could be taken to court by any one of several people who had enough money to hire competent legal counsel and nothing else to do." *This is an assertion of fact, namely that Buckley had lied about and implicitly libeled several people who, if they wanted to and could afford it, could take him to court for his lies.* [Emphasis added.] As opposed to the loosely definable, variously interpretable statements of opinion above referred to made inextricably in the contest of political, social or philosophical debate, in this instance appellant's comment makes a factual assertion relating to Buckley's journalistic integrity. Even while *Gertz v. Robert Welch, Inc.,* in effect states that an expression of "pure opinion" may not be the basis of an action for defamation, it also said, that "there is no constitutional value in false statements of fact." Regardless of what other implicit but unelaborated comparisons Littell was attempting to draw between Buckley and Pegler, and regardless of whether he was attempting to say that Buckley lied about individuals precisely in the way that Pegler did, it seems to us that this third remark as it appears on its face states that Buckley was engaging in libelous journalism. Given the proof of falsity which was presented and not successfully rebutted, it is constitutionally as well as tortiously defamatory.

While Littell suggested that he intended in the passage only to criticize Buckley's "goading, hounding and excessive pursuit" of many people, particularly of certain church men and church women Littell had in mind, as well as of Martin Luther King and Robert Kennedy, he also testified that he equated Buckley's frequent literary attacks as "falling within the general category of lying." Although he testified that he did not remember the specifics of the Pegler libels and did not mean to make a direct analogy between Pegler's libels and Buckley, what is critical is that Littell knew, as is evident from the passage itself, that Pegler's lies had been proved (by Reynolds) to be libels. Littell must have known that when he directly compared Buckley's statements with those of a proven libeler, the clear meaning to be inferred was that he considered Buckley to be a libeler like Pegler.

In response to Buckley's proof of the falsity of this accusation of libelous journalism, appellant's only rebutting proof of the truth of his charge was that Buckley had been sued in the past for libel; only one suit, however, had been successful, and that only by way of settlement. As we read Judge Griesa's findings, he found that Littell's statement that Buckley engaged in libelous journalism was made with knowledge of its falsity or in reckless disregard of its truth or falsity, and this is a finding based in part upon credibility and demeanor which we cannot go behind. In this connection we emphasize that Littell's testimony clearly indicated that he could recall no instances of Buckley's lies about people as matters of fact, and that the lies he had in mind were not really "precise detailed lies" but rather lies on "a theoretical level" involving, as the record makes clear, Buckley's political opinions. Although he denied it, Littell also may have had in mind his own experience with Buckley and the latter's item, "Who Are the Totalitarians?", but that exchange hardly gave Littell license to attack Buckley's personal candor by the accusation of being a regular liar in print as to "several people." Furthermore, Littell's publisher was very much concerned about the paragraph in which the Pegler reference occurs, although not specifically about the sentence here found to be libelous; this concern should have been a red flag to Littell.

In short, whatever might be said of a person's political views, any journalist, commentator or analyst is entitled not to be lightly characterized as inaccurate and dishonest or libelous. We cannot disagree with the finding of the court below that it is "crucial" to such a person's career that he or she not be so treated. To call a journalist a libeler and to say that he is so in reference to a number of people is defamatory in the constitutional sense, even if said in the overall context of an attack otherwise directed at his political views.

COMMENT

Buckley had been awarded $1.00 in compensatory damages by the district court. That judgment was upheld, but $7,500 in punitive damages were reduced to $1,000.

Where there are no misstatements of fact, plaintiffs have no assurance of even this modest success. State courts have held that it is not actionable to characterize a public official as inept, incompetent, and indecisive [156] or a school principal as unsuited for his position.[157]

Given that the distinction, or the relationship, between fact and opinion is not always clear, pure comment is a shaky defense for the columnist, reviewer, or editorialist. Nevertheless the rule has emerged that defamatory opinions are actionable only if they are based on the allegation of undisclosed, false, and defamatory facts. If the facts forming the basis for the opinion are accurately set out, the opinion is protected.[158]

Opinions require no justification and are not a matter for judicial scrutiny or control. But accusations of criminal activity cannot be protected as opinions. An editorial saying of a public securities attorney for a city, "No bond buyer would buy a nickel's worth of securities on McHale's opinion," illustrates the precariousness of the distinction. The Louisiana Supreme Curt affirmed that the statement was not an opinion but a false attack on the attorney's competence published with actual malice.[159]

Sometimes communicators are on the receiving end. A letter-to-the-editor asserted that a journalist had conducted the "worst single example of a journalistic smear" in covering the appointment of a college president, and it called him "journalistic scum of the earth." Protected opinion, said the New Hampshire Supreme Court.[160]

Opinion also when a magazine described a newspaper publisher as "near-Neanderthal," as one who has a "stranglehold on the life of an entire state," and whose newspaper is published "by paranoids for paranoids." A federal district court in New York called those remarks rhetorical hyperbole absolutely protected under the First Amendment, a rule of law Publisher William Loeb of Manchester, New Hampshire might have been expected to appreciate.[161]

Finally, magazine statements describing a television announcer as the "worst" sports announcer in Boston and as being "enrolled in a course for remedial speak-

---

156. Palm Beach Newspapers, Inc. v. Early, 334 So.2d 50 (Fla.App.1976). A charge of having "his fingers in the pot," though caustic and pejorative, said the court, had a basis in fact and thus was not a false statement of fact. The court referred to the statements as "rhetorical hyperbole" or "the conventional give and take in our economic and political controversies."

157. Kapiloff v. Dunn, 343 A.2d 251 (Md.1975).

158. Rinaldi v. Holt, Rinehart & Winston, 2 Med.L.Rptr. 2169, 397 N.Y.S.2d 943 (1977), cert. den., 434 U.S. 969; Orr v. Argus Press Co., 4 Med.L.Rptr. 1593, 586 F.2d 1108 (6th Cir. 1978), cert. den., 4 Med.L.Rptr. 2536, 440 U.S. 960 (1979); Sierra Breeze v. Superior Court, 4 Med.L.Rptr. 2141, 149 Cal.Rptr. 914 (1978).

159. McHale v. Lake Charles American Press, 6 Med.L.Rptr. 2478, 390 So.2d 556 (La.1980), cert. den., 452 U.S. 941 (1981). See also, Cianci v. New Times Publishing Co., 6 Med.L.Rptr. 1625, 639 F.2d 54 (2d Cir. 1980); Anton v. St. Louis Suburban Newspapers, 5 Med.L.Rptr. 2601, 598 S.W.2d 493 (Mo.1980).

160. Pease v. Telegraph Publishing, 7 Med.L.Rptr. 1114, 426 A.2d 463 (N.H.1981).

161. Loeb v. New Times Communication Corp., 6 Med.L.Rptr. 1438, 497 F.Supp. 85 (D.N.Y.1980).

ing" were, said the highest court of Massachusetts, protected statements of opinion, especially in the context of a humorous "best and worst" article. Summary judgment was granted the magazine.[162]

It is a question, then, of context and of style and means of delivery. More latitude might be given a heated political debate than a carefully considered newspaper editorial. Leading cases on this point are Gregory v. McDonnell Douglas Corp., 131 Cal.Rptr. 641 (1976); Information Control Corp. v. Genesis One Computer Corp., 611 F.2d 781 (9th Cir. 1980), and Cole v. Westinghouse Broadcasting, 435 N.E.2d 1021 (Mass.1982). Nevertheless the fair comment defense may be fragile.

Dissenting in a denial of certiorari in Miskovsky v. Oklahoma Pub. Co., 7 Med.L. Rptr. 2607, 654 P.2d 587 (Okl.1982), Justices Rehnquist and White rejected the "no false idea" rule of *Gertz*, and *Gertz* itself, opting instead for the old common law rule of strict liability for a publisher.

The "Community of Interests" Privilege

Closely related to the broader defense of qualified privilege is the conditional privilege to publish defamatory matter in defense of one's own reputation or property rights; or to circulate defamation among members of religious, fraternal, labor, corporate, or charitable organizations in pursuit of mutual property, business, or professional interests; among members of one's own family; or in fulfilling one's social obligations to assist in law enforcement.[163] Such activities frequently involve credit agencies, hired investigators, and prospective employers. Seldom does this defense pertain to the press.

A father's letter objecting to the involvement of a suspended policeman in a Boy Scout bus trip in which the father's fifteen-year-old son was a participant was conditionally privileged. The father's complaint was sent to the directors and officers of the corporation planning the trip. The policeman, who was facing trial for burglary, had the burden of showing actual malice on the part of the father in order to win a libel judgment.[164]

Neutral Reportage

1. Court definitions of "reckless disregard" have greatly modified the reporter's liability for simply stating someone else's libelous charges. To have a reliable source and to represent it objectively may be all that is needed.

"While verification of the facts remains an important reporting standard," the Fifth Circuit Court of Appeals said in 1966, "a reporter, without a 'high degree of awareness of their probable falsity,' may rely on statements made by a single source even though they reflect only one side of the story without fear of libel prosecution. * * *"[165]

And the constitutional rule of *Medina v. Time, Inc.* in 1971[166] was that news media reports of statements made by participants in a public controversy are pro-

162. Myers v. Boston Magazine, 403 N.E.2d 376 (Mass.1980).

163. Barr v. Matteo, 360 U.S. 564 (1959). See also, Warfield v. McGraw-Hill, Inc., 108 Cal.Rptr. 652 (1973); Greenya v. George Washington University, 512 F.2d 556 (D.C.Cir.1975); Ward v. Sears, Roebuck & Co., 339 So.2d 1255 (La.App.1976); Trans World Accounts, Inc. v. Associated Press, 425 F.Supp. 814 (D.Calif.1977).

164. Coopersmith v. Williams, 468 P.2d 739 (Colo.1970).

165. New York Times Co. v. Connor, 365 F.2d 567, 576 (5th Cir. 1966). See also, Time, Inc. v. Johnson, 448 F.2d 378 (4th Cir. 1971).

166. 439 F.2d 1129 (1st Cir. 1971). The case involved Captain Medina of My Lai fame. See also, Thuma v. Hearst Corp., 340 F.Supp. 867 (D.Md.1972).

tected, where the fact that one participant levels charges against another is itself a newsworthy event.

The difficult but necessary task is to report such charges dispassionately and not to assert them as your own views. Perhaps courts are willing to concede that newspapers are in no position to guarantee the truth of everything they print.

When the Illinois Crime Investigating Commission director said in a published interview that two men were "lieutenants of * * * [a] Southern Illinois crime syndicate chieftan," one of the men filed suit against the *Chicago Sun-Times.* An appellate court upheld a lower court's granting of a summary judgment to the newspaper and ruled that the news story was an accurate account of a government official's statement and was therefore privileged. Doss v. Field Enterprises, Inc., 332 N.E.2d 497 (Ill.1976). Similarities to the qualified privilege of reporting governmental processes were also noted in Joplin v. WEWS Television Station, 6 Med.L.Rptr. 1331 (Ohio App.1980).

2. The defense of *neutral reportage* came into its own in the framework of a long and heated controversy between opponents and proponents of the use of DDT. While both sides were impugning the honesty of the other, the *New York Times* got in the middle and in 1972 reported that officials of the National Audubon Society were accusing a number of prominent scientists of being "paid to lie" by pesticide companies.

The reporter, however, contacted as many of the maligned scientists as he could and incorporated their angry responses into his story. Three of them nevertheless brought libel suits against the Society and the *New York Times,* and a jury awarded them each $20,000 in damages.

Concluding that the jury believed the reporter "reckless" in failing to investigate further when the scientists warned him of the libel potential of the charges, the trial judge let the verdict stand. The court of appeals reversed, dismissing the complaints.

Relying on a series of cases beginning with *Time, Inc. v. Pape* (see this text, p. 218), as appellant's brief had proposed, Judge Irving R. Kaufman for the United States Court of Appeals for the Second Circuit gave the defense of *neutral reportage* its initial articulation.

EDWARDS v. NATIONAL AUDUBON SOCIETY

556 F.2D 113 (2D CIR. 1977), CERT. DEN. 434 U.S. 1002.

Irving R. KAUFMAN, Chief Judge:

* * *

At stake in this case is a fundamental principle. Succinctly stated, when a responsible, prominent organization like the National Audubon Society makes serious charges against a public figure, the First Amendment protects the accurate and disinterested reporting of those charges, regardless of the reporter's private views regarding their validity. What is newsworthy about such accusations is that they were made. We do not believe that the press may be required under the First Amendment to suppress newsworthy statements merely because it has serious doubts regarding their truth. Nor must the press take up cudgels against dubious charges in order to publish them without fear of liability for defamation. The public interest in being fully informed about controversies that often rage around sensitive issues demands that the press be afforded the freedom to report such charges without assuming responsibility for them.

The contours of the press's right of *neutral reportage* are, of course defined by the principle that gives life to it. Literal accuracy is not a prerequisite: if we are to enjoy the blessings of a robust and unintimidated press, we must provide immunity from defamation suits where the journalist believes, reasonably and in good faith, that his report accurately conveys the charges made. It is equally clear, however, that a publisher who in fact espouses or concurs in the charges made by others, or who deliberately distorts these statements to launch a personal attack of his own on a public figure, cannot rely on a privilege of *neutral reportage.* In such instances he assumes responsibility for the underlying accusations. See Goldwater v. Ginzburg, 414 F.2d 324 (2d Cir. 1969), cert. den., 396 U.S. 1049 (1970). [Emphasis added.]

* * * The *Times* article * * * was the exemplar of fair and dispassionate reporting of an unfortunate but newsworthy contretemps. Accordingly, we hold that it was privileged under the First Amendment.

COMMENT

1. Publication of a "completely fabricated accusation" and "wholly imagined but supposedly precisely quoted conversations" will destroy any privilege of neutral reportage,[167] as will an admission by a defendant that "he did not know whether what he said was true" and that he "did nothing, or almost nothing, to verify his charges." [168] Such behavior also reflects "reckless disregard" for the truth.

Echoes of *Rosenbloom's* public issue test ring in *Edwards.* A newsworthy source, even an irresponsible one, may develop into a libel defense. A year later in Dickey v. CBS, 4 Med.L.Rptr. 1353, 583 F.2d 1221, 1225–6, (3d Cir. 1978), the Third Circuit took pains to repudiate the rule of *Edwards.* But the rule was adopted by an Illinois appeals court in Krauss v. Champaign News Gazette, 3 Med.L.Rptr. 2507, 375 N.E.2d 1362 (Ill.1978), and rejected by another Illinois court in Catalano v. Pechous, 4 Med.L.Rptr. 2094, 387 N.E.2d 714 (1978), affirmed 6 Med.L.Rptr. 2511, 419 N.E.2d 350 (Ill.1980). Kentucky's Supreme Court disavowed the neutral reportage defense in McCall v. Courier Journal & Louisville Times, 7 Med.L.Rptr. 2118, 623 S.W.2d 882 (Ky.1981).

2. Neutral reportage remains a new and half-fashioned common law defense that ought to be approached with caution. Many federal courts—but not the U.S. Supreme Court—have given *Edwards* some credence, although less enthusiastically, or not at all, where the plaintiff is a private person [169] or where the charges are originated by the media.[170] A New York federal district court judge said pointedly in a 1980 ruling that the *Edwards* privilege did not apply to investigative reporting: "Unlike *Edwards,* no controversy raged around the libelous statement before the reporter entered the scene." [171]

There remains substantial disagreement among courts on the constitutional acceptability of the neutral reportage defense. A number of state courts, including those of New York, have said that *Edwards* does not apply in their jurisdictions. For a time the controlling New York case was Hogan v. Herald Co., 8 Med.L.Rptr. 1137, 446 N.Y.S.2d 836 (1982). In 1983, fewer than ten jurisdictions had clearly accepted the defense. Most had not decided.

---

167. Carson v. Allied News Co., 529 F.2d 206 (7th Cir. 1976).

168. Guam Teachers' Local 1581 (AFT) v. Ysrael, 492 F.2d 438 (9th Cir. 1974), cert. den., 419 U.S. 872 (1974).

169. Dixson v. Newsweek, 3 Med.L.Rptr. 1123, 562 F.2d 626 (10th Cir. 1977). In Dresbach v. Doubleday, 8 Med.L.Rptr. 1793, 518 F.Supp. 1285 (D.D.C.1981), the defense was limited to statements made about public figures.

170. Schermerhorn v. Rosenberg, 6 Med.L.Rptr. 1376, 426 N.Y.S.2d 274 (1980).

171. McManus v. Doubleday, 7 Med.L.Rptr. 1475, 513 F.Supp. 1383 (D.N.Y.1981). For a useful review of the defense see Stonecipher, *Neutral Reportage Privilege Faces an Uncertain Future,* 59 Journ.Q. 367 (Autumn 1982).

TECHNICAL DEFENSES

Consent

Consent, especially if it is in written form, may on occasion be a sturdy defense. Most often, however, consent is simply implied. When a reporter asks a person to comment on a charge someone has made against him or her, it is not possible to write about a denial without mentioning the original charge. A denial alone could be meaningless.

Controversy of any kind obligates the reporter to try hard to get both sides and to tell readers he or she has tried. When successful, consent may be implied in what was reported.

A vice chairman of the Democratic National Committee was fired for negotiating a $9 million tungsten contract with the federal government on behalf of a Portuguese corporation. In his own defense he gave the old *New York Herald Tribune* a detailed statement for publication, and he issued a statement to the wire services. One day before the statute of limitations would have run, he brought libel actions against a number of newspapers. In ruling against him a federal appeals court judge, Chief Judge Parker, wrote:

> The only portions of the article of which plaintiffs can complain as not being statements of fact is that portion relating to the Herald-Tribune's terming the case "the biggest five percenter deal ever exposed in Washington" and General Eisenhower's referring to it as the "sort of crookedness that goes on and on in Washington." These, however, cannot be deemed unfair comments when read, as they must be, in connection with the remainder of the article, which sets forth in detail the facts to which the comments relate and carries the statement of Westbrook with regard thereto including his denial that he had used or attempted to use his position to influence the awarding of the contract or that his services were of the "so-called 'five percenter' variety." *In view of the fact that Westbrook gave this statement to the press in an interview to be published, he is hardly in a position to complain of the publication with it of the charge to which it was an answer, even if the latter were otherwise objectionable.* [Emphasis added.] Pulvermann v. A. S. Abell Co., 228 F.2d 797 (4th Cir. 1956).

Similarly, when a Methodist minister and his family were unintentionally libeled in a college humor magazine, the minister found himself without a remedy after granting interviews to two student journalists. Where the plaintiff told the reporters that he wanted publicity, and publicity printed in his own words, and then referred them to his lawyer for legal details, the newspaper publication was absolutely privileged. The Tennessee court of appeals dismissed the minister's libel suit against the college newspaper, and a similar suit against the humor magazine never came to trial. Langford v. Vanderbilt University, 318 S.W.2d 568 (Tenn. 1958).

Similarly, the Rev. Jerry Falwell was unsuccessful in a suit against *Penthouse* magazine following publication of a concededly accurate account of an interview he had granted. Violation of conditions imposed by the minister did not negate his *consent* nor constitute publication with actual malice. Falwell v. Penthouse International, Limited, 7 Med.L.Rptr. 1891, 521 F.Supp. 1204 (D.Va.1981).

Statute of Limitations

Statutes of limitations define the time span within which legal actions can be brought. Their purpose is to protect an alleged wrongdoer against stale claims which he or she may be totally unprepared to meet. The statutes of limitations for libel are one, two, or three years in all jurisdictions. The one-year states are New York, California, New Jersey, Mississippi, and Maryland. Statutes of limitations provide an absolute defense against libel actions.

Parade magazine tried to deny liability in a libel action by arguing that 1,800 advance copies had been sold a month earlier in a particular locale, thus giving the magazine the protection of the statute of limitations. But a federal court said that under such a rule scurrilous articles could be printed without fear of retribution simply by selling a few advance copies and keeping the date secret until a libel action had been brought. This would be particularly easy where the statute is a single year. So the statute starts running, said the court, when the publication goes into general circulation for the first time. Osmers v. Parade Publications, 234 F.Supp. 924 (D.N.Y.1964).

In at least one state, the statute covers an analogous false light invasion of privacy claim. Smith v. Esquire, Inc., 6 Med.L. Rptr., 1825, 494 F.Supp. 967 (D.Md.1980).

Kathy Keeton, associate publisher of *Penthouse,* sued *Hustler* and its publisher, Larry Flynt, in Ohio in 1977 for libel and invasion of privacy. The claims were dismissed because of a statute of limitations defense. Keeton then filed suit in New Hampshire because the statute of limitations there had not expired. The federal court found *Hustler's* contacts with New Hampshire significant, but Keeton's were not. Therefore they dismissed her case. The United State Court of Appeals for the First Circuit affirmed. The issue is whether a publisher should be open to a libel suit "as long as there is any state anywhere with a statute of limitations that has not expired." Keeton v. Hustler, Inc., 682 F.2d 33 (1st Cir. 1982), cert. granted, 103 S.Ct. 813 (1983).

Equal Time in Political Broadcasts

Political Broadcasts. Prior to 1959, radio and television stations granting equal time to political candidates under the provisions of § 315 of the Federal Communications Act of 1934 were liable for any defamation in those broadcasts. At the same time, a station was absolutely prohibited from censoring a political talk:

> (a) If any licensee shall permit any person who is a legally qualified candidate for any public office to use a broadcasting station, he shall afford equal opportunities to all other such candidates for that office in the use of such broadcasting station: *Provided,* That such licensee shall have no power of censorship over the material broadcast under the provisions of this section. No obligation is imposed upon any licensee to allow the use of its station by any such candidate. 47 U.S. C.A. § 315(a).

Surely then, the broadcasting industry had argued for many years, if stations are required to carry libelous speeches and prevented from exerting any editing judgment, they should not be held responsible for damages.

The test case came in North Dakota. On October 29, 1956, A.C. Townley, a colorful remnant of the Progressive movement which had swept the Dakotas like a prairie fire four decades earlier, demanded equal time as an independent candidate for the United States Senate. Equal time was provided, and in a telecast over WDAY–TV, Fargo, a highly reputable station, Townley charged that the North Dakota Farmers Union was Communist controlled. WDAY had warned Townley that it believed his charge was libelous.

It was, and the Farmers Union brought a $100,000 damage suit against Townley and the station. A district court dismissed the complaint against WDAY on the ground that § 315 rendered the station immune from liability. The Farmers Union carried an appeal to the North Dakota Supreme Court, and that court became the first appellate court in the country to consider the question of whether a broadcasting station is liable for defamatory statements made by a political candidate using the station's facilities in accordance with federal law.

Attorneys for the Farmers Union contended that § 315 did not apply in this case because a third party—the Farmers Union—was involved, making the case something more than a heated confrontation between opposing political candidates. They cited a Nebraska case, Sorensen v. Wood, 243 N.W. 82 (Neb.1932), which they interpreted as holding that a station could not willingly join in publication of a libel and that the "no censorship" provision referred only to the political content of the speech.

In a 4–1 decision the North Dakota Supreme Court ruled that radio and television broadcasters are not liable for false or libelous statements made over their facilities by political candidates. Noting that WDAY had advised Townley that his remarks, if false, were libelous, the court said: "We cannot believe that it was the intent of Congress to compel a station to broadcast libelous statements and at the same time subject it to the risk of defending actions for damages." Farmers Educational & Cooperative Union of America, North Dakota Division v. WDAY, 89 N.W.2d 102, 109 (N.D.1958).

The majority felt the attack on the Farmers Union was "in context" with a candidate's criticism of his opponent since "Communism" was a campaign issue. The majority added that the Farmers Union should have brought action against Townley alone. (The problem here was that Townley's income was a mere $98.50 a month—a promise of little satisfaction to an aggrieved party.)

The Farmers Union carried an appeal to the Supreme Court of the United States. The American Civil Liberties Union intervened on the side of WDAY and in support of the North Dakota Supreme Court decision. In its appeal, the Farmers Union posed three questions with constitutional implications:

a. Does § 315 relieve radio and television stations from liability for broadcasting libelous statements by candidates when the statements defame a third party not a competing candidate?

b. Did Congress, when it passed the 1934 act, intend to repeal or annul state laws covering liability?

c. Does § 315 deprive the Farmers Union of its liberty and property, including reputation, without due process of law (in violation of the intent of the 5th and 14th amendments)?

In a surprisingly close 5–4 decision, the U.S. Supreme Court answered "yes" to the first two questions and affirmed the North Dakota decision upholding WDAY.

FARMERS EDUCATIONAL AND COOPERATIVE UNION OF AMERICA v. WDAY INC.

360 U.S. 525, 79 S.CT. 1302, 3 L.ED.2D 1407 (1959).

Justice BLACK delivered the Opinion of the Court:

* * * Petitioner argues that § 315's prohibition against censorship leaves broadcasters free to delete libelous material from candidates' speeches, and that therefore no federal immunity is granted a broadcasting station by that section. The term censorship, however, as commonly understood, connotes *any* examination of thought or expression in order to prevent publication of "objectionable" material. We find no clear expression of legislative intent, nor any other convincing reason to indicate Congress meant to give "censorship" a narrower meaning in § 315. In arriving at this view, we note that petitioner's interpretation has not generally been favored in previous considerations of the section. Although the first, and for years the only judicial decision dealing with the censorship provision did hold that a sta-

tion may remove defamatory statements from political broadcasts, subsequent judicial interpretations of § 315 have with considerable uniformity recognized that an individual licensee has no such power. And while for some years the Federal Communications Commission's views on this matter were not clearly articulated, since 1948 it has continuously held that licensees cannot remove allegedly libelous matter from speeches by candidates. Similarly, the legislative history of the measure both prior to its first enactment in 1927, and subsequently, shows a deep hostility to censorship either by the Commission or by a licensee. More important, it is obvious that permitting a broadcasting station to censor allegedly libelous remarks would undermine the basic purpose for which § 315 was passed—full and unrestricted discussion of political issues by legally qualified candidates. That section dates back to, and was adopted verbatim from, the Radio Act of 1927. In that Act, Congress provided for the first time a comprehensive federal plan for regulating the new and expanding art of radio broadcasting. Recognizing radio's potential importance as a medium of communication of political ideas, Congress sought to foster its broadest possible utilization by encouraging broadcasting stations to make their facilities available to candidates for office without discrimination, and by insuring that these candidates when broadcasting were not to be hampered by censorship of the issues they could discuss. Thus, expressly applying this country's tradition of free expression to the field of radio broadcasting, Congress has from the first emphatically forbidden the Commission to exercise any power of censorship over radio communication. It is in line with this same tradition that the individual licensee has consistently been denied "power of censorship" in the vital area of political broadcasts.

The decision a broadcasting station would have to make in censoring libelous discussion by a candidate is far from easy. Whether a statement is defamatory is rarely clear. Whether such a statement is actionably libelous is an even more complex question, involving as it does, consideration of various legal defenses such as "truth" and the privilege of fair comment. Such issues have always troubled courts. Yet, under petitioner's view of the statute they would have to be resolved by an individual licensee during the stress of a political campaign, often, necessarily, without adequate consideration or basis for decision. Quite possibly, if a station were held responsible for the broadcast of libelous material, all remarks even faintly objectionable would be excluded out of an excess of caution. Moreover, if any censorship were permissible, a station so inclined could intentionally inhibit a candidate's legitimate presentation under the guise of lawful censorship of libelous matter. Because of the time limitation inherent in a political campaign, erroneous decisions by a station could not be corrected by the courts promptly enough to permit the candidate to bring improperly excluded matter before the public. It follows from all this that allowing censorship, even of the attenuated type advocated here, would almost inevitably force a candidate to avoid controversial issues during political debates over radio and television, and hence restrict the coverage of consideration relevant to intelligent political decision. We cannot believe, and we certainly are unwilling to assume, that Congress intended any such result.

Petitioner alternatively argues that § 315 does not grant a station immunity from liability for defamatory statements made during a political broadcast even though the section prohibits the station from censoring allegedly libelous matter. Again, we cannot agree. For under this interpretation, unless a licensee refuses to permit any candidate to talk at all, the section would sanction the unconscionable result of permitting civil and perhaps criminal liability to be imposed for the very conduct the statute demands of the licensee. Accordingly, judicial interpretations reaching the issue have found an immunity implicit in the section. And in all those cases concluding that a licensee had no immunity, § 315 had been construed—improperly as we hold—to permit a station to censor potentially actionable material. In no case has a court even implied that the licensee would not be rendered immune were it denied the power to censor libelous material.

* * * Thus, whatever adverse inference may be drawn from the failure of Congress to legislate an express immunity is offset by its refusal to permit stations to avoid liability by censoring broadcasts. And more than balancing any adverse inferences drawn from congressional failure to legislate an express immunity is the fact that the Federal Communications Commission—the body entrusted with administering the provisions of the Act—has long interpreted § 315 as granting stations an immunity. Not only has this interpretation been adhered to despite many subsequent legislative proposals to modify § 315, but with full knowledge of the Commission's interpretation Congress has since made significant additions to that section without amending it to depart from the Commission's view. In light of this contradictory legislative background we do not feel compelled to reach a result which seems so in conflict with traditional concepts of fairness.

Petitioner nevertheless urges that broadcasters do not need a specific immunity to protect themselves from liability for defamation since they may either insure against any loss, or in the alternative, deny all political candidates use of station facilities. We have no means of knowing to what extent insurance is available to broadcasting stations, or what it would cost them. Moreover, since § 315 expressly prohibits stations from charging political candidates higher rates than they charge for comparable time used for other purposes, any cost of insurance would probably have to be absorbed by the stations themselves. Petitioner's reliance on the stations' freedom from obligation "to allow use of its station by any such candidate," seems equally misplaced. While denying all candidates use of stations would protect broadcasters from liability, it would also effectively withdraw political discussion from the air. Instead the thrust of § 315 is to facilitate political debate over radio and television. Recognizing this, the Communications Commission considers the carrying of political broadcasts a public service criterion to be considered both in license renewal proceedings, and in comparative contests for a radio or television construction permit. Certainly Congress knew the obvious—that if a licensee could protect himself from liability in no other way but by refusing to broadcast candidates' speeches, the necessary effect would be to hamper the congressional plan to develop broadcasting as a political outlet, rather than to foster it. We are aware that causes of action for libel are widely recognized throughout the States. But we have not hesitated to abrogate state law where satisfied that its enforcement would stand "as an obstacle to the accomplishment and execution of the full purposes and objectives of Congress." Here, petitioner is asking us to attribute to § 315 a meaning which would either frustrate the underlying purposes for which it was enacted, or alternatively impose unreasonable burdens on the parties governed by that legislation. In the absence of clear expression by Congress we will not assume that it desired such a result. Agreeing with the state courts of North Dakota that § 315 grants a licensee an immunity from liability for libelous material it broadcasts, we merely read § 315 in accordance with what we believe to be its underlying purpose.

Affirmed.

COMMENT

In a dissent joined by Justices Harlan, Whittaker, and Stewart, Justice Frankfurter appealed broadly for a doctrine of judicial restraint: the Court must not contravene the purpose or play the role of a legislative body. Unable to find evidence that Congress had ever intended immunity for the broadcaster in such situations, Frankfurter gave short shrift to WDAY's dilemma. The state libel laws, he said, merely make political broadcasts potentially less profitable since the station may have to compensate someone libeled during a candidate's broadcast.

Group Libel

1. The question arises as to how small a group must be before a libel against it will permit individual members to sue; or, conversely, how large must a group be before its members become sufficiently anonymous to defy personal identification? Generally speaking, a group must be small enough to permit individual identification of its members. A plaintiff in such circumstances must show that he or she is a member of the defamed group and indicate how the offending words apply to him or her. Journalistic caution is required for groups of less than 100.

2. Jack Lait and Lee Mortimer, authors of *U.S.A. Confidential,* found themselves in a libel suit as a result of the following paragraphs as reported in Neiman-Marcus Co. v. Lait, 13 F.R.D. 311 (D.N.Y.1952):

* * *

* * *

> He [Stanley Marcus, president of plaintiff Neiman-Marcus Company] may not know that some Neiman models are call girls—the top babes in town. The guy who escorts one feels in the same league with the playboys who took out Ziegfeld's glorified. Price, a hundred bucks a night.
>
> The sales girls are good, too—pretty, and often much cheaper—twenty bucks on the average. They're more fun, too, not as snooty as the models. We got this confidential, from a Dallas wolf.
>
> Neiman-Marcus also contributes to the improvement of the local breed when it imports New York models to make a flash at style shows. These girls are the cream of the crop. Oil millionaires toss around thousand-dollar bills for a chance to take them out.
>
> Neiman's was a women's speciality shop until the old biddies who patronized it decided their husbands should get class, too. So Neiman's put in a men's store. Well, you should see what happened. You wonder how all the faggots got to the wild and wooly. You thought those with talent ended up in New York and Hollywood and the plodders got government jobs in Washington. Then you learn the nucleus of the Dallas fairy colony is composed of many Neiman dress and millinery designers, imported from New York and Paris, who sent for their boy friends when the men's store expanded. Now most of the sales staff are fairies, too.

* * *

Houston is faced with a serious homosexual problem. It is not as evident as Dallas', because there are no expensive imported faggots in town like those in the Neiman-Marcus set.

* * *

Nine models, the total number then employed, and fifteen of twenty-five salesmen were allowed to bring suit. But thirty sales girls, acting on behalf of 382, were not, the latter group being too large for individual identification. The case was settled without trial. None of the plaintiffs received compensation, but attorney fees were paid, and the danger signal had flashed. The court in *Neiman-Marcus* did lay down the following rules:

1) Where the group or class libeled is large, none can sue even though the lan-

guage used is inclusive; 2) when the group or class libeled is small and each and every member of the group is referred to, then any individual member can sue; and 3) where there is disagreement whether some or all of a group has been libeled, at least an action can be attempted.

3. Circumstances surrounding a publication may focus an attack on a particular party. For example, when a correspondence school was the object of an attack and it was the only enterprise of that kind in the town in which the newspaper was circulated, the impact of the publication became apparent. Certainly pictorial identification would assist plaintiffs suing as members of a large class.[172]

An AP story identifying a murder and robbery suspect as a member of the Socialist Workers Party did not defame either the party or its chief executive officer, said a New York court.[173]

One of many consequences of the controversial network film, "Death of a Princess," was a libel suit on behalf of "all Muslims." A California federal court would not permit it to proceed in view of the size of the class of allegedly defamed persons. Mansour v. Fanning, 6 Med.L. Rptr. 2055, 506 F.Supp. 186 (D.Calif.1980).

Nor were twenty-four of 325 newspaper employees sufficiently identified to support their libel suit against a larger newspaper. In the same case a federal district court also disallowed three of the newspaper's eight editors from bringing suit. Specificity, however, may be easier to demonstrate in a group as small as eight. Care is recommended. Loeb v. Globe Newspaper, 6 Med.L.Rptr. 1235, 489 F.Supp. 481 (D.Mass.1980).

4. Since group defamation lends itself to the application of criminal libel laws, and criminal libel has been connected to seditious libel, the uncertainty of the *Beauharnais* case (see pp. 210, 213) persists. Is more speech preferable to enforced silence, or do verbally oppressed minorities need a champion in the law? The trend has been toward the "more speech" doctrine, and only a few states retain viable group defamation laws.[174] And certainly the doctrine of *New York Times* runs against the current of group, criminal, or seditious libel statutes.

For a discussion of group libel problems in the broadcast media, see this text, p. 898.

Although not a group libel case per se, the most potentially explosive case of its kind since *Beauharnais* was the *Skokie* case. There the American Nazi Party's display of swastikas during planned demonstrations was said by the Illinois Supreme Court *not* to constitute "fighting words" but symbolic speech entitled to First Amendment protection.

Skokie's large Jewish population, deeply offended and frightened by the Nazi symbols, had gotten an injunction barring their display. Such an injunction was an unconstitutional prior restraint, said the Illinois Supreme Court, on the party's right to freedom of speech. Village of Skokie v. National Socialist Party, 3 Med.L.Rptr. 1704, 373 N.E.2d 21 (Ill.1978).

Though sympathetic with survivors of the Nazi holocaust, the Illinois court found the weight of precedent overwhelming. Relying heavily on Cohen v. California, 403 U.S. 15 (1971), a case in which a defendant's right to wear a jacket bearing the words "Fuck the Draft" in a Los Angeles County courthouse corridor was upheld, the Illinois court found the rationale

172. Lewis, *The Individual Member's Right to Recover for a Defamation Leveled at the Group,* 17 U.Miami L.Rev. 519 (1963).

173. Socialists Workers Party v. Associated Press, 8 Med.L.Rptr. 1554 (N.Y.Sup.Ct.1982).

174. Pemberton, *Can the Law Provide a Remedy for Race Defamation in the United States?* 14 N.Y.L.F. 33 (1968); Note, *Group Libel Laws: Abortive Efforts to Combat Hate Propaganda,* 61 Yale L.J. 252 (1952); Arkes, *Civility and the Restriction of Speech: Rediscovering the Defamation of Groups,* 1974 S.Ct.Rev. 281 (1975).

behind Skokie's injunction "inherently boundless":

> Surely the [s]tate has no right to cleanse public debate to the point where it is grammatically palatable to the most squeamish among us. Yet no readily ascertainable general principle exists for stopping short of that result were we to affirm the judgment below. * * * Indeed, governments might soon seize upon the censorship of particular words (emblems) as a convenient guise for banning the expression of unpopular views.

A hostile audience, the court added, is not a basis for restraining otherwise legal First Amendment activity. Interference would be justified only if the speaker were to incite others to immediate unlawful action.

Quoting a New York appellate court in Rockwell v. Morris, 211 N.Y.S.2d 25 (1961), a case involving former American Nazi leader George Lincoln Rockwell, the Illinois Supreme Court concluded:

> So, the unpopularity of views, their shocking quality, their obnoxiousness, and even their alarming impact is not enough. Otherwise, the preacher of any strange doctrine could be stopped; the anti-racist himself could be suppressed, if he undertakes to speak in 'restricted' areas.

Case law, said the court, directs the citizens of Skokie to avoid the offensive symbol if they can do so without unreasonable inconvenience. See text, p. 30ff.

For subscribing to this "theory" of the First Amendment, the American Civil Liberties Union lost thousands of members in 1977 and 1978.

Libel of the Dead

1. In an effort to avoid assaults on publishers by sensitive survivors and endless chain suits by brothers, sisters, aunts, uncles, and cousins, only a criminal action is permitted for a libel of the dead, the intention being to prevent breaches of the public peace and good order rather than to protect individual reputation. If direct or indirect defamatory references are made to the living, however, a civil action can be brought, but the defamatory implication has to be clear.

When the New York *Daily Mirror* confused the name of a recently deceased person with that of a notorious criminal, the deceased's wife and children, who had been listed in the article, brought an action against the newspaper. See Rose v. Daily Mirror, 31 N.E.2d 182 (N.Y.1940). The court of appeals said:

> Defendant does not deny that the publication complained of was a libel on the memory of the deceased Jack Rose. Plaintiffs make no claim of any right to recover for that wrong. They stand upon the position that the publication—while it did not affect their reputations in respect of any matter of morals—tended to subject them in their own persons to contumely and indignity and was, therefore, a libel upon them. * * In this state, however, it has long been accepted law that a libel or slander upon the memory of a deceased person which makes no direct reflection upon his relatives gives them no cause of action for defamation.

"To libel the dead is not an offence known to our law; the dead have no rights and can suffer no wrongs." Justice Stephen in R. v. Ensor, 3 L.T.R. 366 (1887).[175]

In most states the same rule applies to privacy claims. Hendrickson v. California Newspapers, Inc., 121 Cal.Rptr. 429 (1975).

2. In 1957, Helen C. Frick, daughter and sole survivor of Pennsylvania industrialist Henry Clay Frick, brought a libel suit

---

175. See also Meeropol v. Nizer, 381 F.Supp. 29 (D.N.Y.1974), p. 255 this text; Gonzales v. Times Herald Printing Co., 513 S.W.2d 124 (Tex.1974); Casamasina v. Worcester Telegram & Gazette, Inc., 307 N.E.2d 865 (Mass.1974).

against Dr. Sylvester Stevens, chairman of the Pennsylvania Historical Society and author of a widely acclaimed book, *Pennsylvania: Birthplace of a Nation.* Miss Frick complained that the book misrepresented her father as a stern and autocratic union buster who underpaid and overworked his employees, provided them with minimal safety conditions, pressured them to buy overpriced goods at the company store and to live in shoddy wooden shacks without sanitary facilities at inflated rents. Anything tending to blacken the memory of her father, Miss Frick averred, would tend to lower her in the esteem of the community, for through her philanthropies she had become associated with the memory of her father.

A Pennsylvania county court, embarking upon an historical investigation of its own, found the charges either to be true or nondefamatory. The court implied that Stevens's book was a first-rate historical study, and it added:

> First, no substantial right of the plaintiff will be impaired to a material degree. * * * [N]o rights of the plaintiff are involved here, only the rights of her deceased father, if any. Her name is not mentioned and her reputation is not involved, so that no right of reputation or privacy of hers is involved.
>
> Second, the remedy at law is not inadequate; there has been no wrong done by defendant and plaintiff has suffered no injury so there is nothing to redress in this case. There being no injury, there is no remedy at law or in equity.
>
> * * *
>
> Next, the exercise of previous restraint in a case of this type would impose an impossible burden on the court. It is true the courts are open to redress wrongs, but it would be impossible to exercise previous restraint over the voluminous publications now on the market.
>
> If equity would undertake to decree corrections in a book for every person named therein who sought to obtain corrections satisfactory to his beliefs, a court of equity would be writing the book not the author.
>
> If everyone read a book as plaintiff read this one, by looking into the index for an ancestor's name, and on cursory examination started action to enjoin or correct the book, our bookshelves would either be empty or contain books written only by relatives of the subject. Frick v. Stevens, 43 D. & C.2d 6 (Pa.1964).

For a contrary and decidedly minority view of the rights of deceased persons, see MacDonald v. Time, 9 Med.L.Rptr. 1025 (D.N.J.1983).

A PRACTICAL DEFENSE: INSURANCE

Libel insurance can help restore an editor's flagging courage. Available in one form or another for the past fifty years, it is estimated that only about one-half of publishers and broadcasters carry it. This is probably a mistake. Insurance dims the prospect of devastating losses resulting from frivolous suits and out-of-court settlements.

Leading insurers are Mutual Insurance of Hamilton, Bermuda, organized by the American Newspaper Publishers Association to provide, first, strike insurance in 1939, and then libel insurance in 1963; Continental Casualty, which first specialized in campus publications and is now heavily involved in broadcasting;[176] Fireman's Fund; Employers Reinsurance; Seaboard Surety; Lloyd's of London; and Chubb/Pacific.

Companies are divided on whether and how to cover punitive damages and what exceptions to make for certain kinds of

176. See *Report,* 4: 1 (Winter 1980), Washington, D.C.: The Student Press Law Center.

journalistic behavior. Certainly, coverage of punitive damages is the greatest need, and most policies meet it. Twenty-eight states, however, bar insurance protection against punitive damages if a deliberate intent to harm the plaintiff is shown. New York and California are among them. But gross negligence or reckless disregard for truth does not preclude such coverage in 29 of the 39 states that have addressed the question. Costs of defense (lawyer's fees and court costs) must also be included, and these can become very heavy in the pretrial period. Most policies exclude fines and penalties levied against reporters for criminal offenses such as refusing to identify a source when there are no good statutory or constitutional reasons for doing so, e.g., having been a witness to a crime.

Look for policies also with low premiums and deductibles and with initial coverage of at least $1 million per suit. Be certain also that the insurer leaves you, the editor or publisher, in control of the suit. In the past, insurance companies have often been too eager to settle out of court when principled publishers would have preferred to litigate or appeal adverse judgments. And editors should still be able to choose their own counsel, although insurers may be prepared, indeed must be prepared, to provide expert legal advisers.

Although early policies covered privacy, piracy, and copyright as well as libel, insurance firms are now expanding beyond these to cover, in a separate policy, all forms of First Amendment litigation—closed judicial hearings, prior restraints, access to information, newsroom searches, subpoenas, contempt, and antitrust. Few publications or broadcast stations, if they are to serve public interests aggressively, can afford to be without prepaid legal counsel. Courts have recognized, of course, that libel laws are not intended to provide financial windfalls for ingenious plaintiffs; rather, their purpose is to provide a public forum for vindicating a reputation and for gaining just compensation when reputation has been wantonly damaged. Libel laws are not designed to ruin defendants or destroy their publications,[177] although libel awards in the 80s might cause one to question that proposition. From an insurance claim perspective, dangerous states are California, Oklahoma, Florida, Alabama, South Carolina, Hawaii, Alaska, and, to a lesser extent, Vermont and New Hampshire.

MITIGATING FACTORS

Mitigating factors are the last lines of defense and are intended to demonstrate to a judge and jury good faith and lack of malice on the part of the publisher. They do not get a complaint dismissed or a defendant out of court, but they may make a substantial difference in the amount of damages paid.

Retraction and Correction

1. In more than half the states, retraction statutes limit punitive and general (actual) damages when a retraction is requested and published within the time period specified in the law. Some states allow only special damages when a proper retraction has been made. California's statute is an example:

CALIFORNIA CIVIL CODE § 48a

§ 48a. LIBEL IN NEWSPAPER; SLANDER BY RADIO BROADCAST

Special damages; notice and demand for correction. In any action for damages

177. Clark v. Pearson, 248 F.Supp. 188 (D.D.C.1965).

for the publication of a libel in a newspaper, or of a slander by radio broadcast, plaintiff shall recover no more than special damages unless a correction be demanded and be not published or broadcast, as hereinafter provided. Plaintiff shall serve upon the publisher, at the place of publication or broadcaster at the place of broadcast, a written notice specifying the statements claimed to be libelous and demanding that the same be corrected. Said notice and demand must be served within 20 days after knowledge of the publication or broadcast of the statements claimed to be libelous.

General, special and exemplary damages. If a correction be demanded within said period and be not published or broadcast in substantially as conspicuous a manner in said newspaper or on said broadcasting station as were the statements claimed to be libelous, in a regular issue thereof published or broadcast *within three weeks after such service,* plaintiff, if he pleads and proves such notice, demand and failure to correct, and if his cause of action be maintained, may recover general, special and exemplary damages; provided that no exemplary damages may be recovered unless the plaintiff shall prove that defendant made the publication or broadcast with actual malice and then only in the discretion of the court or jury, and actual malice shall not be inferred or presumed from the publication or broadcast.

Correction prior to demand. A correction published or broadcast in substantially as conspicuous a manner in said newspaper or on said broadcasting station as the statements claimed in the complaint to be libelous, prior to receipt of a demand therefor, shall be of the same force and effect as though such correction had been published or broadcast within three weeks after a demand therefor.

Definitions. As used herein, the terms "general damages," "special damages," "exemplary damages" and "actual malice," are defined as follows:

a "General damages" are damages for loss of reputation, shame, mortification and hurt feelings;

b "Special damages" are all damages which plaintiff alleges and proves that he has suffered in respect to his property, business, trade, profession or occupation, including such amounts of money as the plaintiff alleges and proves he has expended as a result of the alleged libel, and no other;

c "Exemplary damages" are damages which may in the discretion of the court or jury be recovered in addition to general and special damages for the sake of example and by way of punishing a defendant who has made the publication or broadcast with actual malice;

d "Actual malice" is that state of mind arising from hatred or ill will toward the plaintiff; provided, however, that such a state of mind occasioned by a good faith belief on the part of the defendant in the truth of the libelous publication or broadcast at the time it is published or broadcast shall not constitute actual malice. [Added Stats.1931, c. 1018, p. 2034, § 1. As amended Stats.1945, c. 1489, p. 2763, § 5.]

COMMENT

1. Note that California's definition of actual malice in *New York Times v. Sullivan*-type cases would not now pass constitutional muster and that "correction" without apology is sufficient. In some jurisdictions the terms "correction" and "retraction" are not used interchangeably as in the California statute. A "retraction" is more than a "correction." A "correction" may have nothing to do with libel; a "retraction" always does. But both are voluntary, unlike the right-of-reply statute

struck down by the U.S. Supreme Court in *Tornillo* (see this text, p. 584).

Note also that the California statute does not cover magazines. This has proved advantageous to plaintiffs in libel suits, including Carol Burnett in her suit against the *National Enquirer,* 7 Med.L. Rptr. 1321 (1981), see p. 306.

2. Read your own state's retraction statute. It may have unique features and stipulations as to form and timing. See Hanson, *Libel and Related Torts,* Vol. 1, *Case and Comment*, 1969, § 195 for a chart of retraction statutes in the United States and Canada.

It generally makes good sense to be simple, direct, and apologetic in a retraction. Keep a record of what you do from the moment a retraction is requested.

3. Courts have held that failure to retract, even when it is admitted that parts of a defamatory article are false, is not evidence of actual malice in a public plaintiff suit[178] or evidence of negligence in a private plaintiff suit.[179] At the same time, a retraction may have no bearing on the issue of actual malice and may be insufficient to establish lack of actual malice as a matter of law.[180]

4. To be effective in states with traditional retraction statutes, a retraction must be full, fair, unequivocal, without lurking insinuations or hesitant withdrawals. Otherwise it may simply aggravate the original libel or form the basis of a new suit. Generally the retraction should be given the same emphasis and prominence of display as the original libel.

An apology, said a New Jersey court, to constitute a retraction of a defamatory article, must be frank and full, since a guarded and half-hearted apology will only injure the reporter's position. Mere publication of the defamed person's denial of the original story or a news story about the issues relative to the bringing of a libel action do not amount to a retraction. An apology, the court added, must unreservedly withdraw all imputations and express regret for the libel.[181] In other states a correction of facts is sufficient.

Acceptable procedure for a publisher to follow on both legal and ethical grounds is to call the injured party, express regret, and assure him or her that no malice was intended. Apologize and offer to retract, but point out the possibility of further adverse publicity through the retraction itself. If it can be accomplished diplomatically and with finesse, the publisher might also offer a small sum for a legal release.

Publication of a retraction as part of a written or verbal agreement with an injured person that the publication shall constitute a complete accord and satisfaction—also known as a *settlement*—will bar the right of a plaintiff to an action for damages.[182] A legal release, then, precludes future action for defamation in a civil case, although such a waiver is not intended as a license for libel.[183]

Settlements, because they sometimes tempt frivolous plaintiffs to sue, are not attractive to the media. At the same time, an unwillingness to settle may be interpreted as arrogance. Media walk a

178. Samborsky v. Hearst Corp., 2 Med.L.Rptr. 1638 (D.C.Md.1977). See also, New York Times v. Connor, 365 F.2d 567 (5th Cir. 1966); United Medical Laboratories v. CBS, Inc., 404 F.2d 706 (9th Cir. 1968), cert.den., 394 U.S. 921 (1969).

179. Walters v. Sanford Herald, 2 Med.L.Rptr. 1959, 228 S.E.2d 766 (N.C.1977).

180. Post v. Oregonian Publishing Co., 519 P.2d 1258 (Or.1974). Kerwick v. Orange County Publications, 7 Med.L.Rptr. 1152, 438 N.Y.S.2d 778 (1981); DiLorenzo v. New York News, 7 Med.L.Rptr. 1452, 432 N.Y.S.2d 483 (1981).

181. Brogan v. Passaic Daily News, 123 A.2d 473 (1956).

182. Tomol v. Shroyer Publications, Inc., 33 Northumb.L.J. 87 (Pa.Com.Pl.1961).

183. Carlson v. Hillman Periodicals, Inc., 157 N.Y.S.2d 88 (1956).

tightrope. They should be prepared to admit and correct mistakes; they should not cave in to threats or other forms of intimidation.

Once an action has begun, a publisher seeking a settlement should do so only through an attorney so as not to cast aspersions on the righteousness of his or her cause.

5. A libel case once decided by a competent tribunal cannot be revived after a decision on appeal has been made. The doctrine of *res judicata* (things adjudged), applicable in civil litigation generally, establishes the principle of finality in litigation.

6. An offer to retract, whether or not the state has a retraction statute, may also serve to mitigate damages. So will a plaintiff's refusal to accept a retraction offer.

In some states, a written notice to the publisher must precede a libel action, and this may encourage retractions. In other states, failure to give adequate notice may preclude recovery of all but special damages.

7. Courts which have regarded retraction statutes unfavorably have done so because they believe the constitutional protections of life, liberty, and property militate against such laws. They have also argued that the defamed person is denied a speedy recovery for injury to reputation and that retraction statutes represent class legislation favoring the press and denying the equal protection of the laws.

A less philosophical inadequacy of retraction statutes was noted by Justice Brennan in his plurality opinion in *Rosenbloom.* "Denials, retractions, and corrections," he said, "are not 'hot' news, and rarely receive the prominence of the original story." Nevertheless he implied the constitutionality of retraction statutes in his concurring opinion in Miami Herald Publishing Co. v. Tornillo, 418 U.S. 241 (1974), see p. 592 this text. See generally Speranza, *Reply and Retraction In Actions Against the Press for Defamation: The Effect of Tornillo and Gertz,* 43 Fordham L.Rev. 223 (1974).

8. As the ethical standards of the press improve, more and more publishers, short of retraction, are printing or broadcasting corrections and clarifications. In perhaps fifty newspapers, ombudsmen of one kind or another intercede with management in behalf of readers.

Tornillo has invalidated mandatory right-of-reply laws and raised at least a doubt about the constitutionality of retraction statutes. Publication of replies, when they are free of defamation, is becoming a mark of good journalism. But like retractions, their publication must remain voluntary.

With the gradual demise of punitive damages, retractions may be losing some of their appeal. Nevertheless, judges and juries will still consider retraction as evidence of no actual malice. As a general rule it is advisable to use the retraction as a potential mitigating factor in those states that have retraction statutes.

Proof of Previous Bad Reputation

A showing that the character and reputation of the plaintiff are so bad that they cannot be further impaired by a fresh accusation will mitigate damages.

In a case involving a bishop, a U.S. district court said: "On the issue of general damages, the reputation of the plaintiff is a definite issue and the defendant may show the plaintiff's bad reputation in order to mitigate such damages." The court added, however, that bad reputation may not be established by showing misconduct at a time and place far removed from the date and situation of the original injury.[184]

The relationship of the demonstrably bad reputation and the libel must be close. Reference to unrelated acts of misbehavior or crime are no more sufficient in mitigating damages than are general rumors and hearsay.

Reliance on a Usually Reliable Source

Since *New York Times,* reliance on a usually reliable source will contradict a charge of actual malice, but it may only mitigate a charge of negligence. In Time, Inc. v. Pape, 401 U.S. 279 (1971), the Supreme Court said that "Where the source of the news makes bald assertions of fact—such as that a policeman has arrested a certain man on a criminal charge—there may be no difficulty. But where the source itself has engaged in qualifying the information released, complexities ramify. Any departure from full direct quotations of the words of the source, with all its qualifying language, inevitably confronts the publisher with a set of choices."

In this case a Civil Rights Commission report was considered by the Court to be "extravagantly ambiguous," and the reporter's "adoption of one of a number of possible interpretations * * * though arguably reflecting a misconception" was not enough to create liability.

But quotations taken out of context or material selected to fit a publisher's preconceptions, as in Goldwater v. Ginzburg, 414 F.2d 324 (2d Cir. 1969), may not only constitute negligence but actual malice as well. And in *Pape* the Court warned reporters that the word "alleged" may be better than no qualification at all in reports damaging to reputation or those based on less than authoritative sources.

The reporter should try to confirm all potentially libelous information in wire service and other reports about persons in his or her own circulation area. These efforts may at least mitigate damages.

Miscellaneous Mitigating Factors

1. Anything a defendant can do to demonstrate that the harm done was not as great as claimed or to show regret or a lack of malice will help to mitigate damages. The assumption underlying all efforts to find mitigating factors, of course, is that the publisher is at fault. That is not always an acceptable assumption.

Statements uttered in the heat and passion of the moment or provoked by actions of the plaintiff lend themselves to mitigation.[185] Efforts to correct errors by stopping the presses or seeking to retrieve copies of a newspaper containing errors must be considered by the jury in mitigation of damages, said a Maryland court.[186]

Belief in the truth of the facts, a Nevada court observed, even though the evidence has not convinced a jury, should be considered in mitigation.[187] So should evidence that positive items concerning the plaintiff were published before or with the libel or evidence that other responsible publications had carried the same charge. The libel may be an unintended case of mistaken identity. Evidence of partial truth may help, as will evidence of journalistic care and competence in getting the plaintiff's side of the story and, where justified, in giving it adequate space.

184. Nichols v. Philadelphia Tribune Co., 22 F.R.D. 89 (D.Pa.1958). See also, Bausewine v. Norristown Herald, 41 A.2d 736 (Pa.1945); Corabi v. Curtis Publishing Co., 273 A.2d 899 (Pa.1971).

185. Farrell v. Kramer, 193 A.2d 560 (Me.1963).

186. Brush-Moore Newspapers, Inc. v. Pollitt, 151 A.2d 530 (Md.1959).

187. Las Vegas Sun, Inc. v. Franklin, 329 P.2d 867 (Nev.1958).

2. Perhaps the offending statement was published in what the Supreme Court called in Lehman v. City of Shaker Heights, 418 U.S. 298 (1974), a First Amendment forum.

3. Beyond the law, but not divorced from it, are the ethical responsibilities of the journalist. Accuracy, fairness, and a sensitive weighing of private and public needs are the hallmarks of good journalism. Words carry different connotations and meanings. A statement is not necessarily a confession. An indictment is not a finding of guilt.

Anguish and agony photographs do not always serve a public interest. Prior criminal records are not always crucial to a news story. The public in most circumstances may have as much right to know the source of our information as to have the information itself. Bedroom journalism demeans the press; "cheesecake" reflects a sexist preoccupation with stereotyping.

The purpose of this chapter is not to outline what Max Lerner calls a "bottom line" ethic, where minimum attention is paid to minimum standards in order to prevent personal catastrophe. It is instead to arm the reporter with legal guidelines when he or she is right and acting in his or her best perception of the public interest—and that is often!

"To hold a newsperson accountable for his transgressions is not to censor him," said a Louisiana appeals court in upholding a libel judgment in favor of a police chief, "it is merely to make him mindful of the awesome responsibility he has to the public. Accountability is not a clarion call of 'stop the press'; it is but a whisper for respect for the people who make the news." [188]

Should this be the function of the courts? Whatever the case, the journalist will have to write his or her own ethical guidelines.

SEEKING SUMMARY JUDGMENT

1. Once involved in a libel suit, the defendant's primary objective ought to be to secure a favorable summary judgment (see *Rebozo v. Washington Post,* this text, p. 250). Where facts for jury determination are not in dispute, there is no question of identification, and a case raises constitutional questions, courts appear to favor summary judgments. From the media defendant's point of view, the advantage of availing oneself of summary judgment procedure is that, if successful, the expense, delay, and anxiety of trial are avoided. These policies were well stated by Judge J. Skelly Wright in Washington Post Co. v. Keogh, 365 F.2d 965, 968 (D.C.Cir.1966):

* * *

> In the First Amendment area, summary procedures are even more essential. For the stake here, if harassment succeeds, is free debate. One of the purposes of the *Times* principle, in addition to protecting persons from being cast in damages in libel suits filed by public officials, is to prevent persons from being discouraged in the full and free exercise of their First Amendment rights with respect to the conduct of their government. The threat of being put to the defense of a lawsuit brought by a popular public official may be as chilling to the exercise of First Amendment freedoms as fear of the outcome of the lawsuit itself, especially to advocates of unpopular causes. All persons who desire to exercise their right to criticize public officials are not as well equipped financially as the Post to defend against a trial on the merits. Unless persons, including newspapers, desiring to exercise their First Amendment rights are assured freedom from the harassment of lawsuits, they will tend to become self-censors. And to this extent debate on public issues and

188. Kidder v. Anderson, 2 Med.L.Rptr. 1645, 345 So.2d 922 (La.1977).

> the conduct of public officials will become less uninhibited, less robust, and less wide-open, for self-censorship affecting the whole public is "hardly less virulent for being privately administered."

Summary judgment is generally not granted where facts are still at issue. Plaintiff must have an opportunity to challenge defendant's belief in the truth of a statement or to produce evidence of recklessness or intent. That having been done, actual malice becomes "a constitutional issue to be determined initially by the trial judge on motion for summary judgment." [189] "The use of summary judgment to terminate litigation in this fashion prevents all but the strongest libel cases from proceeding to trial, thereby advancing the first amendment policy of shielding the press from harassment." [190] In response to a motion for summary judgment, plaintiff must establish solid evidence, not conjecture, of actual malice to the level of clear and convincing proof. Failure by plaintiff to meet this severe burden of proof with specific evidence will result in dismissal.[191] Statements of opinion generally lend themselves to summary judgment prior to any period of discovery. And summary judgment is more available in some jurisdictions than in others.

2. As troublesome as anything in Hutchinson v. Proxmire, 5 Med.L.Rptr. 1279, 443 U.S. 111 (1979) (this text, p. 248) was footnote 9 in Chief Justice Burger's opinion for the Court. In the body of its opinion the Court noted:

> The [d]istrict [c]ourt relied upon the depositions, affidavits, and pleadings before it to evaluate Hutchinson's claim that respondents had acted with "actual malice." The [d]istrict [c]ourt found that there was no genuine issue of material fact on that issue. It held that neither a failure to investigate nor unfair editing and summarizing could establish "actual malice." It also held that there was nothing in the affidavits or depositions of either Proxmire or Schwartz [the [s]enator's aide] to indicate that they ever entertained any doubts about the truth of their statements. Relying upon cases from other courts, the [d]istrict [c]ourt said that in determining whether a plaintiff had made an adequate showing of "actual malice," summary judgment might well be the rule rather than the exception.

Then in somewhat ominous language, footnote 9 follows:

> Considering the nuances of the issues raised here, we are constrained to express some doubt about the so-called "rule." The proof of "actual malice" calls a defendant's state of mind into question * * * and does not readily lend itself to summary disposition.

Fortunately for the media, footnote 9 has not been followed generally by state and federal appeals courts, and summary judgment in nearly 75 percent of cases remains the rule rather than the exception. See Kotlikoff v. Community News, 8 Med. L.Rptr. 1549, 444 A.2d 1086 (N.J.1982) and Maressa v. New Jersey Monthly, 8 Med.L. Rptr. 1473, 445 A.2d 376 (N.J.1982). The Second Circuit Court of Appeals (possibly for the sake of precedent) and nine or ten states are exceptions. In the Second Circuit case, footnote 9's validity was supported in the statement, "We hold that the same principles applicable to normal summary judgment motions are applicable to such motions when made in a public figure libel suit." [192] In line with that principle, a

189. Bon Air Hotel v. Time, Inc., 426 F.2d 858, 864 (5th Cir. 1970).

190. Martin Marietta Corp. v. Evening Star Newspaper Co., 417 F.Supp. 947, 954 (D.D.C.1976).

191. Mark v. Seattle Times, 7 Med.L.Rptr. 2209, 635 P.2d 1081 (Wash., 1981); National Nutritional Foods Association v. Whelan, 492 F.Supp. 374, 379 (S.D.N.Y.1980).

192. Yiamouyiannis v. Consumers Union, 6 Med.L.Rptr. 1065, 619 F.2d 932, 940 (2d Cir. 1980); see also, Nader v. De Toledano, 6 Med.L.Rptr. 1550, 408 A.2d 31, 50 (D.C.1979).

federal district court added, "The Court thus must disregard the chilling effect on expression protected by the First Amendment and simply examine whether, accepting plaintiff's version of contested facts, 'a reasonable jury could find (actual) malice with convincing clarity'." [193]

3. The latter cases reflect the boomerang quality of *New York Times'* actual malice test, as did Herbert v. Lando, 2 Med.L.Rptr. 1257, 73 F.R.D. 387 (D.N.Y. 1977). In *Herbert* a federal district court held that a public figure who had brought a $45 million libel suit against a "60 Minutes" producer was entitled under the federal rules of civil procedure to undertake pretrial discovery of any documents in the network's files relevant to the broadcast in order to produce evidence of defendant's "slipshod and sketchy investigative techniques."

Plaintiff, a maverick former army colonel, was to be permitted to fathom conclusions reached by CBS reporters during and after their investigations by having access to their informal conversations with one another and with their sources and by plumbing the depths of their states of mind and intentions. A persistent question is how far should the judicial process be allowed to penetrate the editorial process?

"Knowing falsehood" is obviously a state-of-mind question. How else does a plaintiff prove it without enquiry into an editor's state of mind? Will this kind of government intrusion stifle and inhibit the editorial process? In their opinions for the Second Circuit, Judges Kaufman and Oakes, while acknowledging that "knowing falsehood" and its parent concept of malice had always implied the reading of a defendant's mind by hunch, impression, inference, or what Oakes has since called the "inquisition of Galileo," [194] nevertheless closed the door to the kind of judicial probing they found in the record of the case. Exposure of subjective thought processes would chill journalistic endeavor completely.

"A reporter or editor, aware that his thoughts might have to be justified in a court of law," said Kaufman, "would often be discouraged and dissuaded from the creative verbal testing, probing, and discussion of hypotheses and alternatives which are the *sine qua non* of responsible journalism. * * * We cannot permit inquiry into Lando's thoughts, opinions and conclusions to consume the very values which * * * *Sullivan* * * * sought to safeguard."

In his concurring opinion Oakes said that standards for granting summary judgment are "somewhat more relaxed in constitutional libel cases." (fn. 24) Herbert v. Lando, 3 Med.L.Rptr. 1241, 568 F.2d 974 (2d Cir. 1977)

4. Some journalists were distressed at the quantity and kinds of material CBS had already turned over to Colonel Herbert and his attorneys. Lando's deposition required twenty-six sessions and stretched over a year. The nearly 3,000 pages of transcripts and 240 exhibits included reporters' notes, network memoranda, drafts of scripts, unused film, and videotapes of interviews. Plaintiff's depositions were also unusually substantial in size. Journalists were even more distressed when the United States Supreme Court reversed the Second Circuit.

HERBERT v. LANDO ET AL.

441 U.S. 153, 99 S.CT. 1635, 60 L.ED.2D 115 (1979).

Justice WHITE delivered the opinion of the Court.

By virtue of the First and Fourteenth Amendments, neither the Federal nor a

193. Simmons Ford v. Consumers Union, 7 Med.L.Rptr. 1776, 516 F.Supp. 742, 746 (D.N.Y.1981)

194. Oakes, *Actual Malice in Defamation Actions: An Unsolved Dilemma*, 7 Hofstra L.Rev. 655 (Spring 1979).

State Government may make any law "abridging the freedom of speech, or of the press * * *." The question here is whether those Amendments should be construed to provide further protection for the press when sued for defamation than has hitherto been recognized. More specifically, we are urged to hold for the first time that when a member of the press is alleged to have circulated damaging falsehoods and is sued for injury to the plaintiff's reputation, the plaintiff is barred from inquiring into the editorial processes of those responsible for the publication, even though the inquiry would produce evidence material to the proof of a critical element of his cause of action.[2]

* * *

We have concluded that the Court of Appeals misconstrued the First and Fourteenth Amendments and accordingly reverse its judgment.

* * *

* * * *New York Times* and its progeny made it essential to proving liability that plaintiffs focus on the conduct and state of mind of the defendant. To be liable, the alleged defamer of public officials or of public figures must know or have reason to suspect that his publication is false. In other cases proof of some kind of fault, negligence perhaps, is essential to recovery. Inevitably, unless liability is to be completely foreclosed, the thoughts and editorial processes of the alleged defamer would be open to examination.

It is also untenable to conclude from our cases that, although proof of the necessary state of mind could be in the form of objective circumstances from which the ultimate fact could be inferred, plaintiffs may not inquire directly from the defendants whether they knew or had reason to suspect that their damaging publication was in error. In Butts, 388 U.S. 130 (1967), for example, it is evident from the record that the editorial process had been subjected to close examination and that direct as well as indirect evidence was relied on to prove that the defendant magazine had acted with actual malice. The damages verdict was sustained without any suggestion that plaintiff's proof had trenched upon forbidden areas.[6]

2. The Circuit Court summarized the inquiries to which Lando objected as follows:

"1. Lando's conclusions during his research and investigation regarding people or leads to be pursued, or not to be pursued, in connection with the '60 Minutes' segment and the *Atlantic Monthly* article;

"2. Lando's conclusions about facts imparted by interviewees and his state of mind with respect to the veracity of persons interviewed;

"3. The basis for conclusions where Lando testified that he did reach a conclusion concerning the veracity of persons, information or events;

"4. Conversations between Lando and Wallace about matter to be included or excluded from the broadcast publication; and,

"5. Lando's intentions as manifested by his decision to include or exclude certain material."

6. See 388 U.S., at 156–159, where Justice Harlan, writing for the Court, reviewed the record under the standard he preferred to apply to public figures, and upheld the verdict for the plaintiff. Chief Justice Warren independently reviewed the record under the "actual malice" standard of *New York Times* and also concluded in his concurring opinion that the verdict should be upheld. Id., at 168–170. The evidence relied on and summarized in both opinions included substantial amounts of testimony that would fall within the editorial process privilege as defined by respondents. The record before the Court included depositions by the author of the defamatory article, an individual paid to assist the author in preparation, the Sports Editor of *The Saturday Evening Post,* and both its Managing Editor and Editor-in-Chief. These depositions revealed *The Saturday Evening Post*'s motives in publishing the story, sources, conversations among the editors and author concerning the research and development of the article, decisions and reasons relating to who should be interviewed and what should be investigated, conclusions as to the importance and veracity of sources and information presented in the article, and conclusions about the impact that publishing the article would have on the subject. Justice Brennan, writing for himself and Justice White, also thought the evidence of record sufficient to satisfy

Reliance upon such state-of-mind evidence is by no means a recent development arising from *New York Times* and similar cases. Rather, it is deeply rooted in the common-law rule, predating the First Amendment, that a showing of malice on the part of the defendant permitted plaintiffs to recover punitive or enhanced damages. In *Butts,* the Court affirmed the substantial award of punitive damages which in Georgia were conditioned upon a showing of "wanton or reckless indifference or culpable negligence" or "ill will, spite, hatred and an intent to injure * *." 388 U.S., at 165–166. Neither Justice Harlan, id., at 156–162,[8] nor Chief Justice Warren, concurring, id., at 165–168, raised any question as to the propriety of having the award turn on such a showing or as to the propriety of the underlying evidence, which plainly included direct evidence going to the state of mind of the publisher and its responsible agents.

Furthermore, long before *New York Times* was decided, certain qualified privileges had developed to protect a publisher from liability for libel unless the publication was made with malice. Malice was defined in numerous ways, but in general depended upon a showing that the defendant acted with improper motive. This showing in turn hinged upon the intent or purpose with which the publication was made, the belief of the defendant in the truth of his statement, or upon the ill will which the defendant might have borne towards the defendant.

Courts have traditionally admitted any direct or indirect evidence relevant to the state of mind of the defendant and necessary to defeat a conditional privilege or enhance damages. The rules are applicable to the press and to other defendants alike, and it is evident that the courts across the country have long been accepting evidence going to the editorial processes of the media without encountering constitutional objections.

In the face of this history, old and new, the Court of Appeals nevertheless declared that two of this Court's cases had announced unequivocal protection for the editorial process.

In each of these cases, Miami Herald Publishing Co. v. Tornillo, 418 U.S. 241 (1974), and Columbia Broadcasting System v. Democratic National Committee, 412 U.S. 94 (1973), we invalidated governmental efforts to pre-empt editorial decision by requiring the publication of specified material. In *Columbia Broadcasting System,* it was the requirement that a television network air paid political advertisements and in *Tornillo,* a newspaper's obligation to

---

the *New York Times* malice standard. It is quite unlikely that the Court would have arrived at the result it did had it believed that inquiry into the editorial processes was constitutionally forbidden.

The Court engaged in similar analysis of the record in reversing the judgments entered in a companion case to *Butts,* Associated Press v. Walker, 388 U.S., at 158–159; id., at 165 (Warren, C.J., concurring); and in Time v. Hill, 385 U.S 374, 391–394 (1967). In *Hill,* the record included the edited drafts of the allegedly libelous article and an examination and cross-examination of the author. During that examination, the writer explained in detail the preparation of the article, his thoughts, conclusions, and beliefs regarding the material, and a line-by-line analysis of the article with explanations of how and why additions and deletions were made to the various drafts. As in *Butts,* the editorial process was the focus of much of the evidence, and direct inquiry was made into the state of mind of the media defendants. Yet the Court raised no question as to the propriety of the proof.

8. As Justice Harlan noted the jury had been instructed in considering punitive damages to assess "the reliability, the nature of the sources of the plaintiff's information, *its acceptance or rejection of the sources,* its care in checking upon assertions." 388 U.S., at 156 [emphasis added]. The Justice found nothing amiss either with the instruction or the result the jury reached under it. Justice Brennan, dissenting in the *Butts* case, id., at 172–174, analyzed the instructions differently but raised no question as to the constitutionality of turning the award of either compensatory or punitive damages upon direct as well as circumstantial evidence going to the mental state of the defendant.

print a political candidate's reply to press criticism. Insofar as the laws at issue in *Tornillo* and *Columbia Broadcasting System* sought to control in advance the content of the publication, they were deemed as invalid as were prior efforts to enjoin publication of specified materials.

But holdings that neither a State nor the Federal Government may dictate what must or must not be printed neither expressly nor impliedly suggest that the editorial process is immune from any inquiry whatsoever. It is incredible to believe that the Court in *Columbia Broadcasting System* or in *Tornillo* silently effected a substantial contraction of the rights preserved to defamation plaintiffs in *Sullivan, Butts* and like cases.

Tornillo and *Gertz v. Robert Welch, Inc.,* were announced on the same day; and although the Court's opinion in *Gertz* contained an overview of recent developments in the relationship between the First Amendment and the law of libel, there was no hint that a companion case had narrowed the evidence available to a defamation plaintiff. Quite the opposite inference is to be drawn from the *Gertz* opinion, since it, like prior First Amendment libel cases, recited without criticism the facts of record indicating that the state of mind of the editor had been placed at issue. Nor did the *Gertz* opinion, in requiring proof of some degree of fault on the part of the defendant editor and in forbidding punitive damages absent at least reckless disregard of truth or falsity, suggest that the First Amendment also foreclosed direct inquiry into these critical elements.[17]

In sum, contrary to the views of the Court of Appeals, according an absolute privilege to the editorial process of a media defendant in a libel case is not required, authorized or presaged by our prior cases, and would substantially enhance the burden of proving actual malice, contrary to the expectations of *New York Times, Butts* and similar cases.

It is nevertheless urged by respondents that the balance struck in *New York Times* should now be modified to provide further protections for the press when sued for circulating erroneous information damaging to individual reputation. It is not uncommon or improper, of course, to suggest the abandonment, modification or refinement of existing constitutional interpretation, and notable developments in First Amendment jurisprudence have evolved from just such submissions. But in the 15 years since *New York Times,* the doctrine announced by that case, which represented a major development and which was widely perceived as essentially protective of press freedoms, has been repeatedly affirmed as the appropriate First Amendment standard applicable in libel actions brought by public officials and public figures. At the same time, however, the Court has reiterated its conviction—reflected in the laws of defamation of all of the States—that the individual's interest in his reputation is also a basic concern.

We are thus being asked to modify firmly established constitutional doctrine by placing beyond the plaintiff's reach a range of direct evidence relevant to proving knowing or reckless falsehood by the publisher of an alleged libel, elements that are critical to plaintiffs such as Herbert. The case for making this modification is by no means clear and convincing, and we decline to accept it.

---

17. Two years later, in Time, Inc. v. Firestone, 424 U.S. 448 (1976), there was likewise no indication that the plaintiff is subject to substantial evidentiary restrictions in proving the defendant's fault. As Justice Powell and Justice Stewart stated in concurrence, the answer to this question of culpability "depends upon a careful consideration of all the relevant evidence concerning *Time*'s actions prior to the publication of the 'Milestones' article." Id., at 465–466. They suggested that on remand all the evidence of record should be considered, which included evidence going to the beliefs of *Time*'s editorial staff.

In the first place, it is plan enough that the suggested privilege for the editorial process would constitute a substantial interference with the ability of a defamation plaintiff to establish the ingredients of malice as required by *New York Times.* As respondents would have it, the defendant's reckless disregard of the truth, a critical element, could not be shown by direct evidence through inquiry into the thoughts, opinions and conclusions of the publisher but could be proved only by objective evidence from which the ultimate fact could be inferred. It may be that plaintiffs will rarely be successful in proving awareness of falsehood from the mouth of the defendant himself, but the relevance of answers to such inquiries, which the District Court recognized and the Court of Appeals did not deny, can hardly be doubted. To erect an impenetrable barrier to the plaintiff's use of such evidence on his side of the case is a matter of some substance, particularly when defendants themselves are prone to assert their good-faith belief in the truth of their publications, and libel plaintiffs are required to prove knowing or reckless falsehood with "convincing clarity." New York Times v. Sullivan, 376 U.S., at 285–286.

Furthermore, the outer boundaries of the editorial privilege now urged are difficult to perceive. The opinions below did not state, and respondents do not explain, precisely when the editorial process begins and when it ends. Moreover, although we are told that respondent Lando was willing to testify as to what he "knew" and what he had "learned" from his interviews, as opposed to what he "believed," it is not at all clear why the suggested editorial privilege would not cover knowledge as well as belief about the veracity of published reports.[19] It is worth noting here that the privilege as asserted by respondents would also immunize from inquiry the internal communications occurring during the editorial process and thus place beyond reach what the defendant participants learned or knew as the result of such collegiate conversations or exchanges. If damaging admissions to colleagues are to be barred from evidence, would a reporter's admissions made to third parties not participating in the editorial process also be immune from inquiry? We thus have little doubt that Herbert and other defamation plaintiffs have important interests at stake in opposing the creation of the asserted privilege.

Nevertheless, we are urged by respondents to override these important interests because requiring disclosure of editorial conversations and of a reporter's conclusions about the veracity of the material he has gathered will have an intolerable chilling effect on the editorial process and editorial decision-making. But if the claimed inhibition flows from the fear of damages liability for publishing knowing or reckless falsehoods, those effects are precisely what *New York Times* and other cases have held to be consistent with the First Amendment. Spreading false information in and of itself carries no First Amendment credentials. "[T]here is no constitutional value in false statements of fact." Gertz v. Robert Welch, Inc., 418 U.S., at 340.

Realistically, however, some error is inevitable; and the difficulties of separating fact from fiction convinced the Court in *New York Times, Butts, Gertz,* and similar cases to limit liability to instances where some degree of culpability is present in order to eliminate the risk of undue self-censorship and the suppression of truthful material. Those who publish

19. It was also suggested at oral argument that the privilege would cover questions in the "why" form, but not of the "who," "what," "when," and "where" type. But it is evident from Lando's deposition that questions soliciting "why" answers relating to the editorial process were answered, and that he refused to answer others that did not fall into this category.

defamatory falsehoods with the requisite culpability, however, are subject to liability, the aim being not only to compensate for injury but also to deter publication of unprotected material threatening injury to individual reputation. Permitting plaintiffs such as Herbert to prove their cases by direct as well as indirect evidence is consistent with the balance struck by our prior decisions. If such proof results in liability for damages which in turn discourages the publication of erroneous information known to be false or probably false, this is no more than what our cases contemplate and does not abridge either freedom of speech or of the press.

Of course, if inquiry into editorial conclusions threatens the suppression not only of information known or strongly suspected to be unreliable but also of truthful information, the issue would be quite different. But as we have said, our cases necessarily contemplate examination of the editorial process to prove the necessary awareness of probable falsehood, and if indirect proof of this element does not stifle truthful publication and is consistent with the First Amendment, as respondents seem to concede, we do not understand how direct inquiry with respect to the ultimate issue would be substantially more suspect. Perhaps such examination will lead to liability that would not have been found without it, but this does not suggest that the determinations in these instances will be inaccurate and will lead to the suppression of protected information. On the contrary, direct inquiry from the actors, which affords the opportunity to refute inferences that might otherwise be drawn from circumstantial evidence, suggests that more accurate results will be obtained by placing all, rather than part, of the evidence before the decisionmaker. Suppose, for example, that a reporter has two contradictory reports about the plaintiff, one of which is false and damaging, and only the false one is published. In resolving the issue whether the publication was known or suspected to be false, it is only common sense to believe that inquiry from the author, with an opportunity to explain, will contribute to accuracy. If the publication is false but there is an exonerating explanation, the defendant will surely testify to this effect. Why should not the plaintiff be permitted to inquire before trial? On the other hand, if the publisher in fact had serious doubts about accuracy, but published nevertheless, no undue self-censorship will result from permitting the relevant inquiry. Only knowing or reckless error will be discouraged; and unless there is to be an absolute First Amendment privilege to inflict injury by knowing or reckless conduct, which respondents do not suggest, constitutional values will not be threatened.

It is also urged that frank discussion among reporters and editors will be dampened and sound editorial judgment endangered if such exchanges, oral or written, are subject to inquiry by defamation plaintiffs.[22] We do not doubt the direct relationship between consultation and discussion on the one hand and sound decisions on the other; but whether or not there is liability for the injury, the press has an obvious interest in avoiding the infliction of harm by the publication of false information, and it is not unreasonable to expect the media to invoke whatever procedures that may be practicable and useful to that end. Moreover, given exposure to liability when there is knowing or reckless error, there is even more reason to resort to prepublication precautions, such as a frank interchange of fact and opinion. Accordingly, we find it difficult to believe that error-avoiding procedures will be ter-

22. They invoke our observation in United States v. Nixon, 418 U.S. 683, 705 (1974): "[T]hose who expect public dissemination of their remarks may well temper candor with a concern for appearance and for their own interests to the detriment of the decisionmaking process."

minated or stifled simply because there is liability for culpable error and because the editorial process will itself be examined in the tiny percentage of instances in which error is claimed and litigation ensues. Nor is there sound reason to believe that editorial exchanges and the editorial process are so subject to distortion and to such recurring misunderstanding that they should be immune from examination in order to avoid erroneous judgments in defamation suits. The evidentiary burden Herbert must carry to prove at least reckless disregard for the truth is substantial indeed, and we are unconvinced that his chances of winning an undeserved verdict are such that an inquiry into what Lando learned or said during editorial process must be foreclosed.

This is not to say that the editorial discussions or exchanges have no constitutional protection from casual inquiry. There is no law that subjects the editorial process to private or official examination merely to satisfy curiosity or to serve some general end such as the public interest; and if there were, it would not survive constitutional scrutiny as the First Amendment is presently construed. No such problem exists here, however, where there is a specific claim of injury arising from a publication that is alleged to have been knowing or recklessly false.[23]

Evidentiary privileges in litigation are not favored,[24] and even those rooted in the Constitution must give way in proper circumstances. The President, for example, does not have an absolute privilege against disclosure of materials subpoenaed for a judicial proceeding. United States v. Nixon, 418 U.S. 683 (1974). In so holding, we found that although the President has a powerful interest in confidentiality of communications between himself and his advisers, that interest must yield to a demonstrated specific need for evidence. As we stated, in referring to existing limited privileges against disclosure, "[w]hatever their origins, these exceptions to the demand for every man's evidence are not lightly created nor expansively construed, for they are in derogation of the search for truth." Id., at 710.

With these considerations in mind, we conclude that the present construction of the First Amendment should not be modified by creating the evidentiary privilege which the respondents now urge.

Although defamation litigation, including suits against the press, is an ancient phenomenon, it is true that our cases from *New York Times* to *Gertz* have considerably changed the profile of such cases. In years gone by, plaintiffs made out a prima facie case by proving the damaging publication. Truth and privilege were defenses. Intent, motive and malice were not necessarily involved except to counter qualified privilege or to prove exemplary damages. The plaintiff's burden is now considerably expanded. In every or almost every case, the plaintiff must focus on the editorial process and prove a false

23. Justice Brennan would extend more constitutional protection to editorial discussion by excusing answers to relevant questions about in-house conversations until the plaintiff has made a prima facie case of falsity. If this suggestion contemplates a bifurcated trial, first on falsity and then on culpability and injury, we decline to subject libel trials to such burdensome complications and intolerable delay. On the other hand, if, as seems more likely, the prima facie showing does not contemplate a mini-trial on falsity, no resolution of conflicting evidence on this issue, but only a credible assertion by the plaintiff, it smacks of a requirement that could be satisfied by an affidavit or a simple verification of the pleadings. We are reluctant to imbed this formalism in the Constitution.

24. See Elkins v. United States, 364 U.S. 206, 234 (1960) (Frankfurter, J., dissenting): "Limitations are properly placed upon the operation of this general principle [of no testimonial privilege] only to the very limited extent that permitting a refusal to testify or excluding relevant evidence has a public good transcending the normally predominant principle of utilizing all rational means for ascertaining truth." See also 8 J. Wigmore, Evidence § 2192 (McNaughton rev. 1961); 4 The Works of Jeremy Bentham 321 (J. Bowring ed. 1843).

publication attended by some degree of culpability on the part of the publisher. If plaintiffs in consequence now resort to more discovery, it would not be surprising; and it would follow that the costs and other burdens of this kind of litigation have escalated and become much more troublesome for both plaintiffs and defendants. It is suggested that the press needs constitutional protection from these burdens if it is to perform its task,[25] which is indispensable in a system such as ours.

Creating a constitutional privilege foreclosing direct inquiry into the editorial process, however, would not cure this problem for the press. Only complete immunity from liability from defamation would effect this result, and the Court has regularly found this to be an untenable construction of the First Amendment. Furthermore, mushrooming litigation costs, much of it due to pretrial discovery, are not peculiar to the libel and slander area. There have been repeated expressions of concern about undue and uncontrolled discovery, and voices from this Court have joined the chorus. But until and unless there are major changes in the present rules of civil procedure, reliance must be had on what in fact and in law are ample powers of the district judge to prevent abuse.

The Court has more than once declared that the deposition-discovery rules are to be accorded a broad and liberal treatment to effect their purpose of adequately informing the litigants in civil trials. But the discovery provisions, like all of the Federal Rules of Civil Procedure, are subject to the injunction of Rule 1 that they "be construed to secure the just, *speedy,* and *inexpensive* determination of every action." [Emphasis added.] To this end, the requirement of Rule 26(b)(1) that the material sought in discovery be "relevant" should be firmly applied, and the district courts should not neglect their power to restrict discovery where "justice requires [protection for] a party or person from annoyance, embarrassment, oppression, or undue burden or expense. * * *" Fed. Rule Civ.Proc. 26(c). With this authority at hand, judges should not hesitate to exercise appropriate control over the discovery process.

Whether, as a nonconstitutional matter, however, the trial judge properly applied the rules of discovery was not within the boundaries of the question certified under 28 U.S.C.A. § 1292(b) and accordingly is not before us.[27] The judgment of the Court of Appeals is reversed.

So ordered.

Burger, C.J., and Blackmun, Powell, Rehnquist, and Stevens, JJ., joined the opinion of the Court.

Justice POWELL, concurring.

I join the opinion of the Court, and write separately to elaborate. * * * I do not see my observations as being inconsistent with the Court's opinion; rather, I write to emphasize the additional point that, in supervising discovery in a libel suit by a public figure, a district court has a duty to consider First Amendment inter-

25. It is urged that the large costs of defending lawsuits will intimidate the press and lead to self-censorship, particularly where smaller newspapers and broadcasters are involved. It is noted that Lando's deposition alone continued intermittently for over a year, filled 26 volumes containing nearly 3,000 pages and 240 exhibits. As well as out-of-pocket expenses of the deposition, there were substantial legal fees, and Lando and his associates were diverted from news gathering and reporting for a significant amount of time.

27. Justice Stewart would remand to have the trial court rule once again on the relevance of the disputed questions. But the opinion of the trial judge reveals that he correctly understood that *New York Times* and *Gertz* required Herbert to prove either knowing falsehood or reckless disregard for truth. With the proper constitutional elements in mind, the judge went on to rule that the questions at issue were clearly relevant and that no constitutional privilege excused Lando from answering them. We hold that the judge committed no constitutional error but, contrary to Justice Stewart, find it inappropriate to review his rulings on relevancy.

ests as well as the private interests of the plaintiffs.

* * * Whatever standard may be appropriate in other types of cases, when a discovery demand arguably impinges on First Amendment rights a district court should measure the degree of relevance required in light of both the private needs of the parties and the public concerns implicated. On the one hand, as this Court has repeatedly recognized, the solicitude for First Amendment rights evidenced in our opinions reflects concern for the important public interest in a free flow of news and commentary. On the other hand, there also is a significant public interest in according to civil litigants discovery of such matters as may be genuinely relevant to their lawsuit. Although the process of weighing these interests is hardly an exact science, it is a function customarily carried out by judges in this and other areas of the law. In performing this task trial judges—despite the heavy burdens most of them carry—are now increasingly recognizing the "pressing need for judicial supervision."

* * * I join the Court's opinion on my understanding that in heeding these admonitions, the district court must ensure that the values protected by the First Amendment, though entitled to no constitutional privilege in a case of this kind, are weighed carefully in striking a proper balance.

Justice STEWART, dissenting.

It seems to me that both the Court of Appeals and this Court have addressed a question that is not presented by the case before us. As I understand the constitutional rule of New York Times v. Sullivan, 376 U.S. 254 (1964), inquiry into the broad "editorial process" is simply not relevant in a libel suit brought by a public figure against a publisher. And if such an inquiry is not relevant, it is not permissible. Fed.Rule Civ.Proc. 26(b).

Although I joined the Court's opinion in *New York Times,* I have come greatly to regret the use in that opinion of the phrase "actual malice." For the fact of the matter is that "malice" as used in the *New York Times* opinion simply does not mean malice as that word is commonly understood. In common understanding, malice means ill will or hostility, and the most relevant question in determining whether a person's action was motivated by actual malice is to ask "why." As part of the constitutional standard enunciated in the *New York Times* case, however, "actual malice" has nothing to do with hostility or ill will, and the question "why" is totally irrelevant.

Under the constitutional restrictions imposed by *New York Times* and its progeny, a plaintiff who is a public official or public figure can recover from a publisher for a defamatory statement upon convincingly clear proof of the following elements:

1. the statement was published by the defendant.
2. the statement defamed the plaintiff,
3. the defamation was untrue,
4. and the defendant knew the defamatory statement was untrue, or published it in reckless disregard of its truth or falsity.

The gravamen of such a lawsuit thus concerns that which was in fact published. What was *not* published has nothing to do with the case. And liability ultimately depends upon the publisher's state of knowledge of the falsity of what he published, not at all upon his motivation in publishing it—not at all, in other words, upon actual malice as those words are ordinarily understood.

This is not the first time that judges and lawyers have been led astray by the phrase "actual malice" in the *New York Times* opinion. In Greenbelt Cooperative Publishing Association v. Bresler, 398 U.S. 6 (1970), another defamation suit brought by a public figure against a publisher, the trial judge instructed the jury that the plaintiff could recover if the defendant's publication had been made with malice, and that malice means "spite, hostility, or deliberate intention to harm." In reversing the judgment for the plaintiff, we said that this jury instruction constituted "error of constitutional magnitude." 398 U.S., at 10.

In the present case, of course, neither the Court of Appeals nor this Court has overtly committed the egregious error manifested in *Bresler.* Both courts have carefully enunciated the correct *New York Times* test. But each has then followed a false trail, explainable only by an unstated misapprehension of the meaning of *New York Times* "actual malice," to arrive at the issue of "editorial process" privilege. This misapprehension is reflected by numerous phrases in the prevailing Court of Appeals opinions: "a journalist's exercise of editorial control and judgments," "how a journalist formulated his judgments," "the editorial selection process of the press," "the heart of the editorial process," "reasons for the inclusion or exclusion of certain material." See 568 F.2d 974, *passim.* Similar misapprehension is reflected in this Court's opinion by such phrases as "improper motive," "intent or purpose with which the publication is made," "ill will," and by lengthy footnote discussion about the spite or hostility required to constitute malice at common law.

Once our correct bearings are taken, however, and it is firmly recognized that a publisher's motivation in a case such as this is irrelevant, there is clearly no occasion for inquiry into the editorial process as conceptualized in this case. I shall not burden this opinion with a list of the 84 discovery questions at issue.[2] Suffice it to say that few if any of them seem to me to come within even the most liberal construction of Rule 26(b), Fed.Rule Civ.Proc.

* * *

In a system of federal procedure whose prime goal is "the just, speedy, and inexpensive determination of every action," time-consuming and expensive pretrial discovery is burdensome enough, even when within the arguable bounds of Rule 26(b). But totally irrelevant pretrial discovery is intolerable.

Like the Court of Appeals, I would remand this case to the District Court, but with directions to measure each of the proposed questions strictly against the constitutional criteria of *New York Times* and its progeny. Only then can it be determined whether invasion of the editorial process is truly threatened.

Justice MARSHALL, dissenting.

Although professing to maintain the accommodation of interests struck in New York Times Co. v. Sullivan, 376 U.S. 254 (1964), the Court today is unresponsive to the constitutional considerations underlying that opinion. Because I believe that some constraints on pretrial discovery are essential to ensure the "uninhibited [and] robust" debate on public issues which *Sullivan* contemplated, id., at 270, I respectfully dissent.

* * *

---

2. The following are some random samples:

"Did you ever come to a conclusion that it was unnecessary to talk to Capt. Laurence Potter prior to the presentation of the program on February 4th?

"Did you ever come to the conclusion that you did not want to have a filmed interview with Sgt. Carmon for the program?

"When you prepared the final draft of the program to be aired, did you form any conclusion as to whether one of the matters presented by that program was Col. Herbert's view of the treatment of the Vietnamese?

"Do you have any recollection of discussing with anybody at CBS whether that sequence should be excluded from the program as broadcast?

"Prior to the publication of the *Atlantic Monthly* article, Mr. Lando, did you discuss that article or the preparation of that article with any representative of CBS?"

Yet this standard of liability cannot of itself accomplish the ends for which it was conceived. Insulating the press from ultimate liability is unlikely to avert self-censorship so long as any plaintiff with a deep pocket and a facially sufficient complaint is afforded unconstrained discovery of the editorial process. If the substantive balance of interests struck in *Sullivan* is to remain viable, it must be reassessed in light of the procedural realities under which libel actions are conducted.

The potential for abuse of liberal discovery procedures is of particular concern in the defamation context. As members of the bench and bar have increasingly noted, rules designed to facilitate expeditious resolution of civil disputes have too often proved tools for harassment and delay. Capitalizing on this Court's broad mandate in Hickman v. Taylor, 329 U.S. 495, 507 (1947), reaffirmed in Schlagenhauf v. Holder, 379 U.S. 104, 114–115 (1964), that discovery rules be accorded a "broad and liberal" scope, litigants have on occasion transformed Rule 26 devices into tactics of attrition. The possibility of such abuse is enhanced in libel litigation, for many self-perceived victims of defamation are animated by something more than a rational calculus of their chances of recovery.[2] Given the circumstances under which libel actions arise, plaintiffs' pretrial maneuvers may be fashioned more with an eye to deterrence or retaliation than to unearthing germane material.

Not only is the risk of *in terrorem* discovery more pronounced in the defamation context, but the societal consequences attending such abuse are of special magnitude. Rather than submit to the intrusiveness and expense of protracted discovery, even editors confident of their ability to prevail at trial or on a motion for summary judgment may find it prudent to " 'steer far wid[e] of the unlawful zone' thereby keeping protected discussion from public cognizance." Rosenbloom v. Metromedia, Inc., 403 U.S. 29, 53 (1971) [plurality opinion] [citation omitted]. Faced with the prospect of escalating attorney's fees, diversion of time from journalistic endeavors, and exposure of potentially sensitive information, editors may well make publication judgments that reflect less the risk of liability than the expense of vindication.

Although acknowledging a problem of discovery abuse, the Court suggests that the remedy lies elsewhere, in "major changes in the present rules of civil procedure." And somewhat inconsistently, the Court asserts further that district judges already have "in fact and in law * * * ample powers * * * to prevent abuse." I cannot agree. Where First Amendment rights are critically implicated, it is incumbent on this Court to safeguard their effective exercise. By leaving the directives of *Hickman* and *Schlagenhauf* unqualified with respect to libel litigation, the Court has abdicated that responsibility.

In my judgment, the same constitutional concerns that impelled us in *Sullivan* to confine the circumstances under which defamation liability could attach also mandate some constraints on roving discovery. I would hold that the broad discovery principles enunciated in *Hickman* and *Schlagenhauf* are inapposite in defamation cases. More specifically, I would require that district courts superintend pretrial disclosure in such litigation so as to protect the press from unnecessarily protracted or tangential inquiry. To that end, discovery requests should be measured against a strict standard of relevance. Further, because the threat of disclosure may intrude with special force on certain aspects of the editorial process, I believe some additional protection in the form of an evidentiary privilege is warranted.

* * * So long as *Sullivan* makes state of mind dispositive, some inquiry as to the

2. See Anderson, Libel and Press Self-Censorship, 53 Tex.L.Rev. 422, 435 (1975).

manner in which editorial decisions are made is inevitable. And it is simply implausible to suppose that asking a reporter why certain material was or was not included in a given publication will be more likely to stifle incisive journalism than compelling disclosure of other objective evidence regarding that decision.

* * *

External evidence of editorial decision making, however, stands on a different footing. For here the concern is not simply that the ultimate product may be inhibited, but that the process itself will be chilled. Journalists cannot stop forming tentative hypotheses, but they can cease articulating them openly. If pre-publication dialogue is freely discoverable, editors and reporters may well prove reluctant to air their reservations or to explore other means of presenting information and comment. The threat of unchecked discovery may well stifle the collegial discussion essential to sound editorial dynamics. * * * Society's interest in enhancing the accuracy of coverage of public events is ill served by procedures tending to muffle expression of uncertainty. To preserve a climate of free interchange among journalists, the confidentiality of their conversation must be guaranteed.

* * * If full disclosure is available whenever a plaintiff can establish that the press erred in some particular, editorial communication would not be demonstrably less inhibited than under the Court's approach. And by hypothesis, it is precisely those instances in which the risk of error is significant that frank discussion is most valuable.

Accordingly, I would foreclose discovery in defamation cases as to the substance of editorial conversation. Shielding this limited category of evidence from disclosure would be unlikely to preclude recovery by plaintiffs with valid defamation claims. For there are a variety of other means to establish deliberate or reckless disregard for the truth, such as absence of verification, inherent implausibility, obvious reasons to doubt the veracity or accuracy of information, and concessions or inconsistent statements by the defendant. See St. Amant v. Thompson, 390 U.S. 727, 732 (1968). To the extent that such a limited privilege might deny recovery in some marginal cases, it is, in my view, an acceptable price to pay for preserving a climate conducive to considered editorial judgment.

Justice BRENNAN, dissenting in part.

* * * The Court today rejects respondents' claim that an "editorial privilege" shields from discovery information that would reveal respondents' editorial processes. I agree with the Court that no such privilege insulates factual matters that may be sought during discovery, and that such a privilege should not shield respondents' "mental processes." I would hold, however, that the First Amendment requires predecisional communication among editors to be protected by an editorial privilege, but that this privilege must yield if a public figure plaintiff is able to demonstrate to the prima facie satisfaction of a trial judge that the libel in question constitutes defamatory falsehood.

* * * An editorial privilege would thus not be merely personal to respondents, but would shield the press in its function "as an agent of the public at large. * * * The press is the necessary representative of the public's interest in this context and the instrumentality which effects the public's right." Saxbe v. Washington Post Co., 417 U.S. 843, 863–864 (1974) [Powell, J., dissenting].

* * * Through the editorial process expression is composed; to regulate the process is therefore to regulate the expression. The autonomy of the speaker is thereby compromised, whether that speaker is a large urban newspaper or an individual pamphleteer. The print and broadcast media, however, because of their large organizational structure, cannot exist

without some form of editorial process. The protection of the editorial process of these institutions thus becomes a matter of particular First Amendment concern.

* * *

I find compelling these justifications for the existence of an editorial privilege. The values at issue are sufficiently important to justify some incidental sacrifice of evidentiary material. The Court today concedes the accuracy of the underlying rationale for such a privilege, stating that "[w]e do not doubt the direct relationship between consultation and discussion on the one hand and sound decisions on the other * * *." The Court, however, contents itself with the curious observation that "given exposure to liability when there is knowing or reckless error, there is even more reason to resort to prepublication precautions, such as a frank interchange of fact and opinion." Because such "prepublication precautions" will often prove to be extraordinarily damaging evidence in libel actions, I cannot so blithely assume such "precautions" will be instituted, or that such "frank interchange" as now exists is not impaired by its potential exposure in such actions.

I fully concede that my reasoning is essentially paradoxical. For the sake of more accurate information, an editorial privilege would shield from disclosure the possible inaccuracies of the press; in the name of a more responsible press, the privilege would make more difficult of application the legal restraints by which the press is bound. The same paradox, however, inheres in the concept of an executive privilege: so as to enable the government more effectively to implement the will of the people, the people are kept in ignorance of the workings of their government. The paradox is unfortunately intrinsic to our social condition. Judgment is required to evaluate and balance these competing perspectives.

Judgment is also required to accommodate the tension between society's "pervasive and strong interest in preventing and redressing attacks upon reputation," Rosenblatt v. Baer, 383 U.S. 75, 86 (1966), and the First Amendment values that would be served by an editorial privilege. In my view this tension is too fine to be resolved in the abstract. As is the case with executive privilege, there must be a more specific balancing of the particular interests asserted in a given lawsuit. A general claim of executive privilege, for example, will not stand against a "demonstrated, specific need for evidence * * *." United States v. Nixon, 418 U.S. 683, 713 (1974). Conversely, a general statement of need will not prevail over a concrete demonstration of the necessity for executive secrecy. United States v. Reynolds, 345 U.S. 1, 11 (1953). Other evidentiary privileges are similarly dependent upon the particular exigencies demonstrated in a specific lawsuit. Roviaro v. United States, 353 U.S. 53 (1957), for example, held that the existence of an informer's privilege depends "on the particular circumstances of each case, taking into consideration the crime charged, the possible defenses, the possible significance of the informer's testimony, and other relevant factors." Id., at 62. Hickman v. Taylor, 329 U.S. 495 (1947), similarly required ad hoc balancing to determine the existence of an attorneys' work product privilege. The procedures whereby this balancing is achieved, so far from constituting mere "formalism," are in fact the means through which courts have traditionally resolved competing social and individual interests.

In my judgment the existence of a privilege protecting the editorial process must, in an analogous manner, be determined with reference to the circumstances of a particular case. In the area of libel, the balance struck by *New York Times* between the values of the First Amendment and society's interest in preventing and redressing attacks upon reputation must be preserved. This can best be accomplished if the privilege functions to shield the editorial process from general claims of damaged reputation. If, however, a public figure plaintiff is able to establish, to the prima facie satisfaction of a trial judge, that the publication at issue constitutes defamatory falsehood, the claim of damaged reputation becomes specific and demonstrable, and the editorial privilege must yield. Contrary to the suggestion of the Court, an editorial privilege so understood would not create "a substantial interference with the ability of a defamation plaintiff to establish the ingredients of malice as required by *New York Times.*" Requiring a public figure plaintiff to make a prima facie showing of defamatory falsehood will not constitute an undue burden, since he must eventually demonstrate these elements as part of his case-in-chief. And since editorial privilege protects only deliberative and policymaking processes and not factual material, discovery should be adequate to acquire the relevant evidence of falsehood. A public figure plaintiff will thus be able to redress attacks on his reputation, and at the same time the editorial process will be protected in all but the most necessary cases.

Applying these principles to the instant case is most difficult, since the five categories of objectionable discovery inquiries formulated by the Court of Appeals are general, and it is impossible to determine what specific questions are encompassed within each category. It would nevertheless appear that four of the five categories (see fn. 2, Opinion of the Court) concern respondents' mental processes, and thus would not be covered by an editorial privilege. Only the fourth category—"Conversations between Lando and Wallace about matter to be included or excluded from the broadcast publication"—would seem to be protected by a proper editorial privilege. The Court of Appeals noted, however, that respondents had already made available to petitioner in discovery "the contents of pretelecast conversations between Lando and Wallace * * *." 568 F.2d, at 982 [Kaufman, C.J.]. Whether this constitutes waiver of the editorial privilege should be determined in the first instance by the District Court. I would therefore, like the Court of Appeals, remand this case to the District Court, but would require the District Court to determine (a) whether respondents have waived their editorial privilege; (b) if not, whether petitioner Herbert can overcome the privilege through a prima facie showing of defamatory falsehood; and (c) if not, the proper scope and application of the privilege.

COMMENT

Herbert v. Lando got nearly as much attention for its being "leaked" to the press and reported by ABC forty-eight hours before being announced by the Court as it did for its substance.

Some lawyers were quick to note that the ruling did little to disturb the doctrine of *New York Times.* Yet Justice White, consistent with his dissenting opinion in *Gertz,* and in an array of authorities dating back to 1837 (see his fn. 15 in the full text), reiterated his belief in the common law standards of "strict liability," libel *per se,* and broad state definitions of malice.

Justice Powell in a concurring opinion reminded the Court of First Amendment interests, while Justice Stewart, clearly disturbed about White's preferences, especially his flexible definition of actual malice, reminded the Court of what it had done in *New York Times v. Sullivan.*

Justice Thurgood Marshall's dissent best represented the initial fears of the press that investigative reporting of public matters would be discouraged by the ruling and that the status of existing shield laws would be endangered.

Justice William Brennan, dissenting in part, sought a palliative for an actual malice test, a test that didn't seem to be working. The editorial process writ large, said Brennan, that is, predecisional deliberations and interactions in the newsroom, would be privileged in the absence of *prima facie* evidence of defamatory falsehood. Under that rubric, what one says in the newsroom may be better protected than what one thinks. One might have expected that if there had to be probing it would have been of the conscious rather than the unconscious mind.

Brennan is indeed the victim of his own formulation. "[I]t would be anomalous," he said with logical consistency, "to turn substantive liability on a journalist's subjective attitude and at the same time shield from disclosure the most direct evidence of that attitude."

The near hysterical response of the press to *Herbert v. Lando* offended Brennan. It had been a difficult case. It seemed that the press misunderstood the actual malice concept. Brennan, in a speech at Rutgers University, moderately rebuked the press and attempted to rehabilitate the concept.[195] But he remained entangled in it.

Brennan's 1965 invocation of Meiklejohn's theory had largely been in vain. Meiklejohn would have extended, at the very least, an absolute, or near absolute, privilege to all communication bearing on the public behavior of public officials and quite likely to the utterances of public figures involved in controversial issues of public importance as well. Political libel is seditious libel and should not be subject to governmental control.

A final thought on *Lando.* Does *Lando* reflect an aversion on the part of the Supreme Court to creating new First Amendment-based privileges where media liability is concerned? One of the coauthors of this text has stated the issue this way:

> The question for the future is whether *Lando* suggests that when the Supreme Court actually passes on specific lower court holdings recognizing qualified first amendment-based journalist privilege in civil litigation, the Court will reverse the lower court rulings that have moved in this direction and declare that there is no justification for the creation of a first amendment-based qualified journalist's privilege.

See Barron, *The Rise and Fall of a Doctrine of Editorial Privilege: Reflections on Herbert v. Lando,* 47 Geo.Wash.L. Rev. 1002 at 1016 (1979). For more on this issue, see this text, p. 410ff.

SPECULATION ON THE FUTURE OF LIBEL

Many questions addressed in preceding sections remain unanswered. In the meantime, two contrary impressions about libel seem supportable. First, libel suits remain a critical and cost-escalating concern of the media. Second, plaintiffs, generally speaking, have a miserable success rate against the press and lose suits by summary judgment, on motions to dismiss, or on appeal from jury verdicts.[196]

The first impression is supported by those sensational cases that involve ruinous damage awards, labeled "megaverdicts," and large and protracted legal fees. The second is based on evidence compiled by a Stanford University law professor. Both impressions are reflected in the case Rancho La Costa v. Penthouse International Ltd., 8 Med.L.Rptr. 1865 (Cal.1982), still only partly decided in 1983, seven years after plaintiffs filed an initial claim for $630 million and defendant had spent an

195. Brennan, *The Symbiosis Between the Press and the Court,* The National Law Journal (October 29, 1979), p. 15.

196. Franklin, *Suing the Media for Libel: A Litigational Study,* 1981 A.B. Foundation Res.J. 795.

estimated $8 million in court and lawyer costs.

Penthouse had identified a California resort with organized crime. Early stages of the case were taken up with deciding which of nine plaintiffs (four persons and five corporations) were public figures. Two founders of the resort, both of whom had criminal records, were finally so designated. After a five-month trial and fifteen days of deliberation, a jury voted 9–3 against the person-plaintiffs, 10–2 against La Costa and three of its corporate affiliates, and unanimously against its management corporation. 6 Med.L.Rptr. 1351, 165 Cal.Rptr. 347 (1980), cert.den. 450 U.S. 902. But that would not be the end of it.

Amid charges of misbehavior on the part of the jury and defendant's attorneys, the trial judge granted two of the resort owner plaintiffs a new trial. 8 Med.L.Rptr. 1865. Then it was alleged that the same trial judge had been associated with Aladena "Jimmy the Weasel" Fratianno, an admitted Mafia hit man and one of *Penthouse*'s chief witnesses. By 1983 California appellate judges were deciding whether, under those circumstances, the trial judge had jurisdiction to order the rehearing of the case. In seven years there had been eleven appeals in the case, two of them to the United States Supreme Court.

Bad luck may run in streaks. At the same time that a California court was truncating *Penthouse*'s temporary victory, a federal district court in Pennsylvania was awarding a lawyer $30,000 in compensatory and $537,500 in punitive damages for an article entitled, "The Stoning of America," in which *Penthouse* had referred to him as an example of "attorney criminals" trafficking in drugs. Plaintiff, said the court, was a private person who, though he had been indicted by a grand jury on drug charges, had not been tried and found guilty. It was libelous *per se* to presume that he had. Marcone v. Penthouse International, 8 Med.L.Rptr. 1444, 533 F.Supp. 353 (D.Pa.1982).

Meanwhile, *Penthouse* was having serious problems with Kimerli Jayne Pring, a former "Miss Wyoming" to whom a jury had awarded $26 million ($25 million of it in punitive damages) for the magazine's fictitious account of a young woman's quite fantastic and physically impossible sexual exploits. In reducing the judgment to $14 million, the trial judge took the publication's insurance coverage into consideration.[197]

Whether it was proper for the trial judge to do that and whether "Miss Wyoming's" blue costumes and baton-twirling talent constituted sufficient identification were part of the argument heard by the Tenth Circuit Court of Appeals. That court reversed on grounds that what was published was pure fantasy incapable of being applied to any individual or of being believed by a reader. While gross, unpleasant, and crude, said the court, the magazine should not be tried for its moral standards. The First Amendment, after all, is not limited to socially redeeming prose, and it certainly covers parody and satire. Pring v. Penthouse International Limited, 8 Med.L.Rptr. 2409, 695 F.2d 438 (1982).

Also on the brighter side for *Penthouse* was Publisher Robert Guccione's success in persuading a jury to award him $40 million in damages against *Hustler* magazine and its publisher Larry Flynt. *Hustler* had depicted Guccione in a lewd homosexual pose. Although judgment of a trial court was upheld on the issue of liability, the case was remanded for a new trial on the issue of damages.[198]

Although it may have been an atypical case, a libel suit reduced the Alton, Illinois

197. Pring v. Penthouse International, 7 Med.L.Rptr. 1101, 695 F.2d 438 (D.Wyo 1981).

198. Guccione v. Hustler, 7 Med.L.Rptr. 2077 (Ohio Ct.App.1981).

Telegraph to bankruptcy. Information not solid enough for publication was turned over to federal prosecutors by reporters for the newspaper—a questionable practice at best—and that correspondence formed the basis for the suit. In April 1982, an Illinois appellate court dismissed an appeal of jury awards to plaintiff of $6.7 million in compensatory and $2.5 million in punitive damages on grounds that not it but the U.S. Bankruptcy Court had jurisdiction in the case since the *Telegraph* had filed for corporate reorganization under the Bankruptcy Code in order to protect its assets during the appeals process.[199]

Plaintiff, a contractor and real estate developer, complained that he was driven out of business when federal prosecutors, unable to uncover evidence of organized crime connections, in turn passed the memo on to banking officials. A $1.4 million settlement was finally approved by the Bankruptcy Court, but not before plaintiff had attempted to trade control of the newspaper for his dropping the suit.

There is evidence that a good number of cases—perhaps as many as 25 percent—are settled out of court for reasonable sums ranging from $300 to $50,000.[200]

Libel laws, most courts would agree, are meant to punish, not to destroy. "Megaverdicts" invite suits and may encourage a timidity in reporters that fails the public interest. Reporters, editors, and publishers must be able to choose their own ground, to know when there are risks, and to decide when those risks are worth taking. General Westmoreland's $120 million suit against CBS News may have been a case where the risks were worth taking. One can be less certain that benefits outweighed risks in the *Washington Post*'s allegations that William Tavoulareas, president of Mobil Corporation, had set his son up in business.

In its initial stages the case was controversial enough to divide the press on the question of the *Post*'s standards of performance. One damaging piece of evidence against the newspaper was an editor's memo suggesting that the story was impossible to believe. But there was sharp disagreement on how many and how credible were the sources for the story. Even those who thought the *Post* had the law on its side in the case felt that it should have been prepared to admit error rather than ignore a prospective plaintiff for nearly a year.

Tavoulareas, in what was described as a persuasive speech to the 1982 national convention of Sigma Delta Chi in Milwaukee, uncovered a strategic weakness in the *Post*'s case: "In opting for a jury rather than a bench trial, they [the *Post*] apparently were arrogant enough to rely on a public opinion poll which they commissioned and which told them an oil executive would be so unpopular he was unlikely to prevail over the *Post*."

That same jury, misunderstanding the judge's instructions and, according to close observers of the case, an unclear summation by defendant's attorney, confused the truth/falsity dichotomy with the test of actual malice. The result: an award of $250,000 in compensatory damages and $1.8 million in punitive damages to Tavoulareas. See Tavoulareas v. Washington Post, 8 Med.L.Rptr. 2262, 527 F.Supp. 676 (D.D.C.1981).

On May 2, 1983, a federal appeals panel reversed The Tavoulareas judgment on the basis of his not showing clear and convincing evidence of actual malice. Bad reporting, perhaps, but no actual malice. *Tavoulareas v. Washington Post, 9 Med.L.Rptr. 1553 (1983).* Tavoulareas appealed.

199. Green v. Alton Telegraph, 8 Med.L.Rptr. 1345, 438 N.E.2d 203 (Ill.1982).

200. Franklin, *op.cit.*, n. 196.

One lesson of the case may be to avoid juries wherever possible because of the inexplicability of libel concepts, or at least to avoid them in environments that appear hostile to media defendants. See Legal Defense Resource Center *Bulletin,* Spring-Summer, 1983.

While there may continue to be debate on the justifications for the Tavoulareas story, one cannot easily justify *National Enquirer's* treatment of Carol Burnett. Although *Penthouse, Hustler,* and the *Enquirer* are not the standardbearers of American journalism, their travails, because they involve principles of constitutional law common to all publications, can be instructive. Newspeople generally bewailed the outcome of the *Burnett* case. It is not difficult, however, in light of *New York Times, Gertz,* and their progeny, to understand that result. A substantial portion of a Los Angeles County Superior Court's holding follows.

BURNETT v. NATIONAL ENQUIRER

7 MED.L.RPTR. 1321 (1981).

SMITH, J.:

It is not the intention of the court to deal at great length with every issue raised by defendant in its motion for judgment notwithstanding the verdict and motion for new trial, but simply to articulate the reasons for denying defendant's motions, save and except the motion for new trial as it relates to the issue of damages.

Initially, defendant contends that its publication of March 2, 1976 about plaintiff was not libelous per se. It is clear to the court that the average reader, viewing the article in its entirety, would conclude that plaintiff was intoxicated and causing a disturbance. The evidence is undisputed that the article was false. There can be little question that the described conduct of plaintiff holds her up to ridicule within the meaning of California Civil Code section 45.

The *National Enquirer's* protestation that it was not guilty of actual malice borders on absurdity. Not only did plaintiff establish actual malice by clear and convincing evidence, but she proved it beyond a reasonable doubt. At the very minimum Brian Walker, the de facto gossip columnist, had serious doubts as to the truth of the publication. There is a high degree of probability that Walker fabricated part of the publication—certainly that portion relating to plaintiff's row with Henry Kissinger.

Walker received information from Couri Hay, a free lance tipster for the *National Enquirer,* that Carol Burnett had been in the Rive Gauche restaurant, that she ordered a Grand Marnier souffle and that she passed her dessert to other parties in a boisterous or flamboyant manner, that she had been drinking, *but was not drunk.* Hay contends that this was verified through the maitre'd. On the other hand, Hay related to Walker that he had received *unverified* information that Burnett had spilled wine on a customer and the customer had returned the favor by spilling water on her.

Shortly after receiving the information from Hay, Walker called Steve Tinney, the nominal gossip columnist, to see if he had any contacts in Washington who could verify Hay's tip. Walker expressed doubts to Tinney about Hay's trustworthiness. Tinney agreed with Walker's assessment of Hay, but told him he had no contacts in Washington.

Next Walker asked Greg Lyon, defendant's employee, to verify the "incident at the Rive Gauche". Walker told Lyon he had a one hour deadline to meet even though the publication was not due to "hit the streets" for thirteen days.

Lyon was asked to verify the following information: That Carol Burnett had been in a Washington, D.C. restaurant, that she had some sort of interchange with other customers and that an altercation took place with another customer—to wit, "the wine spilling and water throwing incident".

Lyon reported to Walker that he had not been able to verify anything other than the fact that plaintiff had passed dessert to other patrons. Additionally, he told Walker a fact *not* previously disclosed to him by Hay—that Henry Kissinger and plaintiff had carried on a good-natured conversation at the Rive Gauche that same night.

Confronted with this disappointing revelation, Walker expressed concern to Lyon as to whether he should publish the article. He kept pushing Lyon for his opinion. Lyon became angry and told him that he (Walker) was being paid to make those decisions.

At this point, it is fair to infer that Walker decided that there was little news value in the fact that Burnett and Kissinger had a good-natured conversation and that Burnett distributed her dessert to other patrons. A little embellishment was needed to "spice up" the item.

An entire afternoon was devoted to the issue of whether the *National Enquirer* was a newspaper or magazine. The court reaffirms its finding that the defendant does not qualify for the protection of California Civil Code section 48a [California's retraction statute] because, * * * the predominant function of the publication is the conveying of news which is neither timely nor current. Additionally, the defendant has been registered as a magazine with the Audit Bureau of Circulation since 1963, and carries a designation as a magazine or periodical in eight mass media directories.

In *Werner v. Southern California Associated Newspapers*, 216 P.2d 825 (1950) our Supreme Court upheld the constitutionality of California Civil Code section 48a against an attack that it unfairly discriminated in favor of newspaper and radio stations. The court articulated its rationale as follows:

> In view of the complex and far flung activities of the news services upon which newspapers and radio stations must largely rely and the necessity of publishing *news while it's new* [emphasis mine], newspapers and radio stations may in good faith publicize items that are untrue but whose falsity they have neither the time nor the opportunity to ascertain.

Since the defendant rarely deals with "news while it's new", it is not entitled to the protection of Civil Code section 48a.

Defendant has gone to great lengths to blame the adverse jury verdict on prejudicial trial publicity and, in particular, the blast by entertainer Johnny Carson. Some will question the sagacity of Carson's timing, but no one can question his constitutional right to air his grievance with defendant. [Carson defended Burnett against the Enquirer in his nighttime show.] While the defendant had the right to publish an article about Carson, it exercised incredibly poor judgment in publishing the article on the eve of the trial.

The *National Enquirer* successfully challenged two jurors who viewed or heard the Carson tirade. It did not see fit to challenge any others even though the trial could have proceeded with as few as eight jurors. Accordingly, defendant cannot now complain about three other jurors being tainted. The court questioned all jurors individually in chambers in the presence of counsel. Counsel were afforded an opportunity to question the jurors. The court denied the defendant's motion for a mistrial because it was satisfied, without any reservation whatsoever, that the remaining eleven jurors could render a fair trial to defendant.

DAMAGES

Preliminary to the subject of general and punitive damages is the question of whether defendant published an adequate correction since that is an issue relating to the mitigation of damages. In the present case, two critical questions must be answered:

1. Was the correction published with prominence substantially equal to the statement claimed to be libelous?

2. Did the correction without uncertainty and ambiguity, honestly and fully and fairly correct the statement claimed to be libelous?

The answer to both questions is in the negative. Had the defendant published a slightly modified version of Exhibit 154 [plaintiff's request for retraction in copy format, dated 3–15–76] * * * it would not be before the court in its present predicament. The correction would have passed muster even if the reference to defendant's negligence had been deleted. Should the defendant have chosen not to print a headline relating to the retraction, a photo of plaintiff in the gossip column next to the correction would have been sufficient to call attention to the retraction.

Instead, defendant tendered to plaintiff and published a "half hearted" correction that had a tendency to aggravate any reasonable person who had been previously libeled. The correction was buried at the bottom of the gossip column.

One can infer from the evidence that the *National Enquirer*'s failure to publish an adequate correction was primarily motivated by an unwillingness to engage in some form of self deprecation which conceivably might adversely affect its circulation.

Ian Calder, the president of *National Enquirer,* knew shortly after March 2, 1976 that none of the libelous material in the article could be substantiated. Both he and Generoso Pope, the sole stockholder and Chairman of the Board of the defendant, approved the copy of the "correction" that appeared in the April 13, 1976 edition of the National Enquirer.

Despite the fact that Calder knew that none of the libelous material could be substantiated, he insisted on using the words "we understand" as a modifier so that a reader could conclude that even though the defendant had no personal knowledge of the events—that the incident *could have* occurred. It should be noted in passing that the March 2, 1976 gossip column contains an apology to Steve Allen for falsely accusing him of smashing in a glass door of the William Morris Agency. The columnist *unequivocally* observed that Steve Allen is not the window breaking type without prefacing the phrase with the words "we understand."

Calder and Pope's cavalier approach to plaintiff's demand for retraction was simply another manifestation of bad faith and malice.

COMPENSATION DAMAGES

Included within the sum of $300,000 compensatory damages was the sum of $299,750 general damages[1], representing the jury's award for plaintiff's emotional distress. Plaintiff correctly felt that the article portrayed her as being drunk, rude, uncaring and abusive. This portrayal was communicated to approximately sixteen million readers nationally.

Burnett testified, "What really hurts is that I know most people believe what they read." This belief was reinforced when she was taunted by a New York cab driver, whom she never met before, "Hey, Carol, I didn't know you like to get into fights."

Plaintiff is a person who is very sensitive to the problems of alcoholism. Both her parents died at the age of 46 from complications brought about by alcohol abuse. As a result of her tragic experience,

1. Plaintiff claimed special damages of $250.00, a sum expended for attorneys fees in order to obtain a retraction.

Carol Burnett became active in anti-alcohol work. Since the defendant's publication, she has worried about being viewed by the public as a hypocrite if and when she spoke out against alcohol abuse.

While the record is clear that she suffered no actual pecuniary loss as a result of the libelous article, she had every right to suffer anxiety reactions in the immediate aftermath of the March 2, 1976 article and the ineffectual correction. Emotional distress is more difficult to quantify than pain and suffering, but it is no less real. A review of other verdicts for emotional distress is not particularly helpful since the facts of each case vary significantly. The fact that defendant's false publication was communicated to sixteen million readers coupled with an inadequate correction, is of substantial significance in measuring the extent of plaintiff's emotional distress. Finally, the only residual aspect of emotional distress which has lingered with plaintiff since the immediate aftermath of the publication is the fact she occasionally gets a little paranoid about talking too loudly in restaurants.

Defendant points to the fact that Burnett never sought the services of a psychiatrist, psychologist or counselor. Plaintiff acknowledged that she was able to set aside her anxiety to the point where she was able to function in her profession. Miss Burnett should be commended for not seeking the unnecessary services of some "phony build up artist" in order to inflate her damages. She should not be penalized for self-treating.

The court finds that plaintiff was a highly credible witness who did not exaggerate her complaints. Nevertheless, the jury award is clearly excessive and is not supported by substantial evidence. The court finds that the sum of $50,000.00 is a more realistic recompense for plaintiff's emotional distress and special damage.

PUNITIVE DAMAGES

In reviewing the award of $1,300,000 in punitive damages the court must consider the reprehensibility of defendant's acts, the wealth of the defendant and whether punitive damages bear a reasonable relationship to actual damages.

The evidence before the court cries out for a substantial award of punitive damages. The conduct of the defendant was highly reprehensible. The acts of fabrication and reckless disregard by Brian Walker are both clearly proscribed by California Civil Code section 3294. Failure by top management to publish an adequate correction is substantial evidence of malice and bad faith.

The defendant's net worth amounted to approximately $2,600,000 and it had earnings of $1,300,000 after taxes for the last ten month period. The court will not consider any evidence not before the jury, to wit: Mr. Pope's salary and dividends. The function of deterrence will not be served if the wealth of the defendant will allow it to absorb the award with little or no discomfort and by the same token, the function of punitive damages is not served by an award that exceeds the level necessary to properly punish and deter.

This court has the distinct impression, after listening to the testimony of certain officers and employees of the *National Enquirer,* that the defendant has absolutely no remorse for its misdeeds. The only issue defendant has not seriously contested is that the libelous statements were, in fact, false. Couri Hay, the admittedly untrustworthy tipster, whose misinformation started this travesty, was promoted to gossip columnist shortly after the article in question was published—a position he still held during the trial. Brian Walker only recently left the employ of defendant. Haydon Cameron, the spokesman for the defendant, asserts that it is the policy of the *National Enquirer* to publish two or three unflattering articles about celebrities every week.

The defendant engages in a form of legalized pandering designed to appeal to the readers' morbid sense of curiosity. This style of journalism has been enormously profitable to the defendant. While the First Amendment to the United States Constitution permits such journalistic endeavor, it does not immunize the defendant from accountability when the rules are broken in such a flagrant manner.

An award of $1,300,000 will probably not amount to "capital punishment" (bankruptcy), as publicly espoused by defendant's counsel after the jury verdict, because of the defendant's strong cash position. The court finds that it is excessive because it does not bear a reasonable relationship to the compensatory damages that amount to only $50,000. A review of California case law indicates that appellate courts have not sanctioned any particular ratio of general and punitive damages. Each case turns on its own set of facts.

The court finds that there is substantial evidence in the record to support an award of $750,000 in punitive damages, a sum which should be sufficient to deter the defendant from further misconduct.

The motion for judgment notwithstanding the verdict is denied. The motion for new trial is denied because plaintiff accepted the remittitur in open court reducing actual damages to $50,000 and punitive damages to $750,000.

COMMENT

A California appeals court later reduced the punitive damages award to $150,000. See Burnett v. National Enquirer, 9 Med.L.Rptr. 1921 (1983). In response to higher temperatures in the libel area, media, journalists, and insurance companies have organized the Libel Defense Resource Center. Located in New York, the Center provides both research and practical assistance to libel and privacy defendants. An annual state-by-state survey presents useful data in a number of libel and privacy categories.

Privacy and the Press

WHAT IS PRIVACY?

Definitions of privacy are necessarily subjective, abstract, elusive. Invasion of privacy may be by publication of a nondefamatory falsehood or a true but embarrassing personal fact, by intrusion into one's home with a hidden camera or tape recorder, by unauthorized access to a confidential file, or by appropriation of another's name or photograph for commercial gain. Privacy may also be violated by interfering with a person's beliefs [1] or membership preferences.[2] Whatever its form, an invasion of privacy is presumed to have an adverse effect on an identifiable person's psychological well-being.

Unlike defamation, a privacy violation does not depend upon the altered attitudes of other persons toward you. Rather it depends upon how you are made to feel about yourself. It involves your self-esteem, your sense of inviolate personality.

"The injury is to our individuality," says Professor Edward Bloustein, "to our dignity as individuals, and the legal remedy represents a social vindication of the human spirit thus threatened rather than a [dollar and cents] recompense for the loss suffered."[3]

Others are not so sure. Harry Kalven, Jr. thought privacy a petty tort when measured against First Amendment freedoms.[4] Professor Don Pember is concerned about the number of frivolous privacy claims.[5] Clearly, definition remains a problem. In the absence of evidence of an intent to injure or observable symptoms of pain on the part of the victim, one is seldom certain that real damage has been done. How, then, is an invasion of privacy to be measured? There is no clear answer.

Nevertheless there has been in the past two decades an explosion of interest in protecting privacy in its myriad guises against private, governmental, and press encroachments. Privacy is widely recognized in American jurisdictions.

Justice Louis Brandeis, who with a law partner introduced the right to American law, saw it as the "most comprehensive of

1. Schneider v. Smith, 390 U.S. 17, 25 (1968).

2. NAACP v. Alabama, 357 U.S. 449, 462 (1958).

3. Bloustein, *Privacy As An Aspect of Human Dignity*, 39 N.Y.U.L.Rev. 962, at 963, 1003 (1964). Gerety in *Redefining Privacy*, 12 Harvard Civil Rights—Civil Liberties L.Rev. 236 (1977), defines privacy in terms of autonomy, identity, and intimacy.

4. Kalven, "Privacy in Tort Law—Were Warren and Brandeis Wrong"? 31 *Law & Contemporary Problems* 326 (1966).

5. Pember, *Privacy and the Press* (1972).

rights and the right most valued by civilized men."[6] "The right to be let alone," said Justice William O. Douglas, "is indeed the beginning of all freedom."[7] Milton Konvitz, a constitutional scholar, described privacy as "a kind of space that a man may carry with him into his bedroom or into the street."[8]

Alan Westin defined privacy as "the voluntary and temporal withdrawal of a person from the general society through physical or psychological means, either in a state of solitude or small-group intimacy or, when among larger groups, in a condition of anonymity or reserve." Each person, says Westin, must find an acceptable balance between solitude and companionship, intimacy and broader social participation, anonymity and visibility, reserve and disclosure. And a free society will leave these choices to the individual, with only extraordinary exceptions allowed in the general interest of society.[9] It is the extraordinary exceptions that require judicial weighing of privacy claims against freedom of the press.

"It is at least a hypothesis worth testing," said Professor Paul Freund, "that privacy, though in its immediate aspect an individual interest, serves an important socializing function. An unwillingness to suffer disclosure of what has been discreditable in one's life, of one's most intimate thoughts and feelings, reflects an intuitive sense that to share everything would jeopardize the sharing of anything. Complete openness in social life would encounter misunderstandings, inability to forgive, unlimited tolerance for differences. The inner sense of privacy, and mutual respect for it, may be a mechanism that helps to secure the condition for living fraternally in a world where men are not gods, where to know all is not to understand and forgive all." [10]

First Amendment scholar Thomas Emerson defines privacy as a set of rules which cut across any opposing rules of the collectivity and which constitute "a sphere of space that has not been dedicated to public use or control." He would include in that space, at the very least, the privacy of bodily functions—such as procreation and contraception,[11] rights of privacy which have been recognized in recent years by the United States Supreme Court.[12]

Within this concept, privacy would protect the woman in childbirth, the couple privately engaged in sexual intercourse, the sleeper from raucous sound trucks operating in residential neighborhoods in the middle of the night.[13]

The rule would certainly cover the woman in York v. Story, 324 F.2d 450 (9th Cir. 1963) who, when she came to a police station complaining of an assault, was asked to undress and was photographed in the nude; her picture was then circulated among policemen for their amusement. It would also have protected the woman who found herself without a legal remedy when she was photographed in the rest room of Sad Sam's tavern in Delafield,

6. Olmstead v. United States, 277 U.S. 438 (1928).

7. Public Utilities Commission v. Pollak, 343 U.S. 451, 467 (1952) (dissenting opinion). For Justice Black's equivocal views on privacy, see Gillmor, "Black and the Problem of Privacy" in *Justice Hugo Black and the First Amendment,* ed. Dennis, Gillmor, and Grey, (1978).

8. Konvitz, "Privacy and the Law: A Philosophical Prelude", 31 *Law & Contemporary Problems* 272, 279–280 (1966).

9. Westin, *Privacy and Freedom* (1968), pp. 7, 42.

10. Freund, "Privacy: One Concept Or Many" in *Privacy*, ed. Pennock and Chapman (1971) p. 188.

11. Emerson, *The System of Freedom of Expression*, 1970, p. 562.

12. Roe v. Wade, 410 U.S. 113 (1973); Griswold v. Connecticut, 381 U.S. 479 (1965).

13. Kovacs v. Cooper, 336 U.S. 77 (1949).

Wisconsin by the proprietor who used such photos for the entertainment of his male customers;[14] and the parents whose deformed newborn child was photographed in a hospital and the picture published without their consent.[15]

In their separate works on privacy, Westin and Arthur R. Miller[16] were primarily concerned with governmental assaults on privacy for the sake of law enforcement and national security. Computer assisted, government is capable of watching, wiretapping, and data-banking information about the citizenry in a frighteningly Orwellian manner. Everyone—almost—has been reduced to a file.

Electronic snooping by government and business poses a far greater threat to the liberal tradition of individual freedom than vigorous journalism, and, where the press is concerned, courts will continue to be generous in permitting a defense of *newsworthiness* against privacy claims. We shall see, however, that newsworthiness itself is a perplexing idea which frequently gets tangled with notions such as public interest and the public's right to know, notions that are themselves fighting for clarification.[17] Who has ultimate responsibility for defining the term, the editor, the legislator, or the judge? It is not clear. Probing journalism will nevertheless continue to be one of the pressures that wears against privacy.

The distinction, however, between invasions of privacy by government and invasions of one person's privacy by another person or by a nongovernmental entity is important. It is protection against governmental infringements of privacy that has been accorded constitutional status. See *Griswold v. Connecticut*, this text, p. 314. Nongovernmental infringements of privacy, such as those by the press, are still treated, for the most part, as a form of tort or common law injury depending, of course, on the extent to which a particular jurisdiction has recognized privacy as a right.

THE ORIGINS OF PRIVACY

A legal right of privacy was first proposed by Louis Brandeis and Samuel Warren in what was to become a seminal law review article (*The Right to Privacy*, 4 Harv.L. Rev. 193, 1890). The two young Boston lawyers were reacting to what they considered graceless newspaper gossip about the private social affairs of the patrician Warren family. Although there is an aura of "injured gentility" about their rhetoric, Brandeis and Warren were prophetic and perhaps thinking beyond the press of their day when they observed that someday "mechanical devices [would] threaten to make good the prediction that 'what is whispered in the closet shall be proclaimed from the house-tops'."

More important, Brandeis and Warren for the first time wrenched privacy from the domain of property, where it had resided in the common law, and defined it strictly in terms of "inviolate personality."

14. Yoeckel v. Samonig, 75 N.W.2d 925 (Wis.1956). Wisconsin has provided statute protection to privacy since 1977.

15. Bazemore v. Savannah Hospital, 155 S.E. 194 (Ga.1930).

16. Miller, The Assault on Privacy, 1971, *Privacy in the Modern Corporate State*, 25 Admin.L.Rev. 231 (1973), and *The William O. Douglas Lecture: Press v. Privacy*, 16 Gonzaga L.Rev. 843 (1981). See, also, Note, *Privacy and Efficient Government*; *Proposals for a National Data Center*, 82 Harv.L.Rev. 400 (1968); Report, Databanks in a Free Society (Alan Westin, project director), 1972; Rule, Private Lives and Public Surveillance, 1974.

17. Dennis, *The Press and the Public Interest: A Definitional Dilemma*, 23 De Paul L.Rev. 937 (1974); Glasser, *Resolving the Press-Privacy Conflict: Approaches to the Newsworthiness Defense*, Journal of Communication, Spring 1982, p. 23.

They were still prepared to exempt publications of general interest from their law of privacy but, diverging from the rules of libel, would not generally permit truth as a defense in a privacy suit. Again it is important to recognize that privacy originated in the common law and not in constitutional interpretation.

Privacy gained momentum when New York in 1903 passed a law making it a misdemeanor and a tort to use someone's name or picture for trade purposes without authorization (New York Civil Rights Law, §§ 50, 51). The legislature was responding to the plight of a young woman who, finding her portrait on posters advertising flour in stores, warehouse walls, and saloons, could invoke no legal remedy.[18] But the right remained one of property, analogous to a breach of contract or copyright.

Two years later, the Georgia Supreme Court, in a similar case of appropriating one's photograph for trade purposes—this time by an insurance company—became the first court to recognize a personal right of privacy.[19] Under the influence of Brandeis and Warren's arguments, the tort was stretched by courts and commentators to accommodate other kinds of invasions of privacy. The influential Dean William Prosser finally organized the case law into the four categories—appropriation, intrusion, false light, and embarrassing private facts—which today provide a popular framework of analysis. Prosser, *Privacy* 48 Calif.L.Rev. 389 (1960). For a study of the coalescing quality of the four-category typology, see Ellis, *Damages and the Privacy Tort: Sketching a Legal Profile*, 64 Iowa L.Rev. 1111 (1979).

In 1965 some aspects of privacy found protection in the penumbras of the First, Third, Fourth, and Ninth Amendments to the Constitution and in the Bill of Rights' guarantees generally. This "penumbral" right of privacy was set forth in Griswold v. Connecticut, 381 U.S. 479 (1965) when the U.S. Supreme Court struck down a state law making it a crime for even married couples to use contraceptives and, in this case, for the Planned Parenthood League to give advice on such use. Governmental invasions of privacy clearly confront constitutional barriers; private violations do not, even though corporate power has assumed some of the coercive capabilities of government. In *Griswold* the state rather than the press had invaded privacy, and the Court was galled by the prospect of the long arm of government reaching into the marital chamber.

In his opinion for the Court, Justice Douglas began by citing the broad protection afforded speech and press in the First and Fourteenth Amendments.

"[T]he [s]tate may not," he said, "consistently with the spirit of the First Amendment, contract the spectrum of available knowledge. The right of freedom of speech and press includes not only the right to utter or to print, but the right to distribute, the right to receive, the right to read and freedom of inquiry, freedom of thought, and freedom to teach. * * * Without these peripheral rights, the specific rights would be less secure."

"[S]pecific guarantees in the Bill of Rights," Douglas added, "have penumbras, formed by emanations from those guarantees that help give them life and substance. *Various guarantees create zones of privacy*. The right of association contained in the penumbra of the First Amendment is one. * * * The Third Amendment in its prohibition against the quartering of soldiers 'in any house' in time of peace without the consent of the owner is another facet of that privacy. The Fourth Amendment explicitly affirms the 'right of the people to be secure in their persons, houses, papers, and effects,

18. Roberson v. Rochester Folding Box Co., 64 N.E. 442 (N.Y.1902).

19. Pavesich v. New England Life Insurance Co., 50 S.E. 68 (Ga.1905).

against unreasonable searches and seizures.' The Fifth Amendment in its Self Incrimination Clause enables the citizen to create a zone of privacy which government may not force him to surrender to his detriment. The Ninth Amendment provides: 'The enumeration in the Constitution, of certain rights, shall not be construed to deny or disparage others retained by the people.' * * * We have had many controversies over these penumbral rights of 'privacy and repose.' * * * These cases bear witness that the right of privacy which presses for recognition here is a legitimate one." [Emphasis added.]

In a concurring opinion Justice Arthur Goldberg strongly endorsed Douglas's interpretation of the Ninth Amendment. Justices Black and Stewart dissented, Black because here and in earlier cases he could find no language in the Constitution specifically protecting a "broad, abstract and ambiguous" right of privacy.

Some Court watchers viewed the case as a shocking example of judicial improvisation; others saw it as an affirmation of the Doctrine of Judicial Review whereby the Court could invalidate a noxious law which Connecticut representatives dared not repeal.

Justice Harry Blackmun leaned on *Griswold* in his opinion for the Court in its historic 1973 abortion ruling, Roe v. Wade, 410 U.S. 113 (1973). "The Constitution does not explicitly mention any right of privacy," said Blackmun. "In a line of decisions, however, going back perhaps as far as Union Pacific Railway Co. v. Botsford, 141 U.S. 250 (1891), the Court has recognized that a right of personal privacy, or a guarantee of certain areas or zones of privacy, does exist under the Constitution. In varying contexts the Court or individual justices have indeed found at least the roots of that right in the First Amendment; in the Fourth and Fifth Amendments; in the penumbras of the Bill of Rights; in the Ninth Amendment; or in the concept of liberty guaranteed by the first section of the Fourteenth Amendment. These decisions make it clear that only personal rights that can be deemed 'fundamental' or 'implicit in the concept of ordered liberty' are included in this guarantee of personal privacy. They also make it clear that the right has some extension to activities relating to marriage, procreation, contraception, family relationships, and child rearing and education." [case citations are omitted.]

"This right of privacy," Blackmun added, "* * * is broad enough to encompass a woman's decision whether or not to terminate her pregnancy. * * * We therefore conclude that the right of personal privacy includes the abortion decision, but that this right is not unqualified and must be considered against important state interests in regulation."

Most states and the District of Columbia today give common law recognition to some or all of Prosser's four privacy torts. For a state-by-state listing, see *Communications Law 1982* (New York: Practising Law Institute, 1982), Vol. One, pp. 789–819, and subsequent editions. New York, Virginia, Massachusetts, Oklahoma, California, Utah, Florida, Nebraska, and Wisconsin have privacy statutes and by inference, therefore, may not recognize a common law or constitutional right. This view was clearly articulated in Arrington v. New York Times, 6 Med.L.Rptr. 2354, 433 N.Y. S.2d 164 (1980) when a New York appeals court would recognize no common law or constitutional right of privacy, beyond its statute. A false light claim, a category not expressly covered by the New York law, was rejected by the court.

There is no clear authority on the matter in North Dakota and Nevada. Minnesota neither recognizes nor rejects a right of privacy, although it does have one of a few state data privacy laws protecting personal information in official records. Some states recognize one or more of the torts but call them by a different name.

The Federal Privacy Act of 1974 (5 U.S. C.A. § 552a) is designed to safeguard individual privacy from the misuse of federal records and to provide individuals a right of access to data about themselves. In this act, Congress defines privacy as a fundamental constitutional right.

While the older and more general common law right of privacy appears to protect us from one another, the more recently developed constitutional right establishes barriers against violations by government. Infringements by the press generally fall in the first category, although, as we shall see in the next section, one common law category of privacy—"false light"—was constitutionalized in a landmark Supreme Court case.

Still, much of what the press would do to personal privacy is a matter of ethics and good taste rather than of law. Of the agony-and-anguish news photographers, editor Carl Lindstrom once said:

> The picture which creates in the beholder the feeling of intrusion upon grief or private anguish, the feeling of "here I should not be," ought never to be taken.[20]

Press photography is by no means the only journalistic activity that raises ethical questions, but it is a key element in many privacy claims.

Since we cannot deal here with every aspect of what Professor Freund calls the "greedy" concept of privacy, we shall settle on those dimensions of privacy that engage the press. Omitted then are at least the following contexts in which privacy claims arise, claims that are sometimes more urgent and significant than those brought against the press: eavesdropping; surveillance; unreasonable searches and seizures; the reasonable expectation of some privacy in public places or in the public mails against obscenity, inappropriate advertising, or certain forms of picketing; door-to-door solicitation; the privacy of a business office or a college dormitory; bodily privacy, for example, hair length or sexual preference; euthanasia; psychosurgery; self-incrimination; and statutory relational privileges as between husband and wife, doctor and patient, lawyer and client, and priest and penitent.

For a comprehensive review of privacy questions, see The Report of the Privacy Protection Study Commission, *Personal Privacy in an Information Society* (July 1977); and Shattuck, *Rights of Privacy* (ACLU, 1977).

CONSTITUTIONALIZING THE TORT: "FALSE LIGHT" INVASIONS FROM HILL TO GERTZ AND CANTRELL

1. Privacy may be invaded by placing a person in a *false light* through the coincidental use of names, fictionalization, distortion, embellishment, or the misuse of names and pictures in otherwise legitimate news stories. The docudrama has become a troublesome format for broadcasters and their lawyers.

Under the common law, damage awards in false light privacy cases were based, as in libel cases, upon false statements of fact, that is, upon nondefamatory falsehoods.

For example, in 1948 a federal district court granted relief to an honest taxi driver whose photograph had been used by the *Saturday Evening Post* to illustrate a story about crooked cabbies.[21] And an invasion of privacy was acknowledged by

20. Lindstrom, *The Fading American Newspaper* (1960), p. 214. For a comprehensive discussion of press ethics, see Hulteng, *The Messenger's Motives, Ethical Problems of the News Media* (1976).

21. Peay v. Curtis Publishing Co., 78 F.Supp. 305 (D.D.C.1948).

a New York court in 1955 when a law-abiding slum child's photo was used in a story about juvenile delinquents.[22] A more frequently cited case, and one which gave impetus to the false light category of suits, is Leverton v. Curtis Publishing Co., 192 F.2d 974 (3d Cir. 1951). A newspaper photo of a child being helped to her feet after a car ran a stoplight and knocked her down was reprinted twenty months later in the *Saturday Evening Post* under the caption, "They Asked To Be Killed." Although the article was concerned with pedestrian carelessness, it erroneously implied that this particular child pedestrian had been at fault. A trial court judgment of $5,000 was sustained.

The original publication of the photo was not actionable because its legitimate news interest overbalanced any claim to privacy. But the magazine's use of the photo, said the court, exceeded the bounds of privilege and would be offensive to persons of ordinary sensibilities.

Since the *Post* had purchased the photograph from a commercial agency, was it aware of the misleading impression it would create? False light cases today turn on the answers to questions of this kind. How will a publisher know when an unaltered photograph has the capacity of placing someone in a false light, or when something omitted from an article may embarrass? Uncertainty of this magnitude raises First Amendment questions.

2. In 1967 the United States Supreme Court, imbued perhaps with the spirit of *New York Times*, invoked the First Amendment's right of free press to defeat a privacy suit and in doing so tied together false light privacy and defamation with the actual malice test.

The case began in 1952 when James Hill, his wife, and five children were held hostage in their suburban Philadelphia home by three escaped convicts. The Hills were not harmed; in fact they were treated surprisingly well by the intruders. A year later, a novel, *Desperate Hours*, purported to describe the dramatic episode but with the fictionalized addition of captor violence against the father and a son, and a verbal sexual assault on a daughter.

The novel led to a Broadway play and the play to a promotional picture-story review in *Life* magazine. By this time the Hill family had moved to Connecticut, supposedly for the purpose of avoiding any further public attention. Hill's privacy suit, though brought under New York's privacy statute, might have been pursued as a common law false light case.

Hill found particularly offensive to his desire for anonymity *Life's* characterization of the play as "a heart-stopping account of how a family rose to heroism in a crisis." The play was set in the actual house the Hills had occupied in suburban Philadelphia; otherwise there was little resemblance between the docile captivity of the family and the sensationalized story line of the play. The incident inevitably became a Hollywood film starring a commandolike Frederick March as the father and Humphrey Bogart as the convict leader.

Both litigants depended on the New York privacy law. Time, Inc. argued that the family had involuntarily become subjects of public interest. But, said Hill, the portrayal of the family's frightening experience had been flamboyantly inaccurate. Hill won a $75,000 judgment from a jury. The Appellate Division of the New York Supreme Court (which despite its name is the trial court) upheld the verdict for Hill but ordered a new trial on the question of damages. A second jury awarded Hill $30,000 in compensatory damages. That judgment was affirmed by the Court of Appeals, New York's highest court. Time, Inc. appealed to the United States Su-

22. Metzger v. Dell Publishing Co., 136 N.Y.S.2d 888 (1955).

preme Court and argued that the rules pertaining to the standards of newsworthiness had not been measured against guidelines which, since 1964 under *New York Times v. Sullivan*, were required under the First Amendment.

A majority of the Court agreed and applied the *New York Times* rule of actual malice to the *Life* article. Was the publication made with knowledge of its falsity or with reckless disregard as to whether it was false or not? No, said the Court. The judgment of the New York Court of Appeals was reversed and remanded for further proceedings.

TIME, INC. v. HILL

385 U.S. 374, 87 S.CT. 534, 17 L.ED.2D 456 (1967).

Justice BRENNAN delivered the opinion of the Court.

The question in this case is whether appellant, publisher of *Life* Magazine, was denied constitutional protections for speech and press by the application by the New York courts of §§ 50–51 of the New York Civil Rights Law, McKinney's Consol.Laws, c. 6 to award appellee damages on allegations that Life falsely reported that a new play portrayed an experience suffered by appellee and his family.

* * *

Although "Right to Privacy" is the caption of § 51, the term nowhere appears in the text of the statute itself. The text of the statute appears to proscribe only conduct of the kind involved in *Roberson*, that is, the appropriation and use in advertising or to promote the sale of goods, of another's name, portrait or picture without his consent. An application of that limited scope would present different questions of violation of the constitutional protections for speech and press.

The New York courts have, however, construed the statute to operate much more broadly. * * * Specifically, it has been held in some circumstances to authorize a remedy against the press and other communications media which publish the names, pictures, or portraits of people without their consent. Reflecting the fact, however, that such applications may raise serious questions of conflict with the constitutional protections for speech and press, decisions under the statute have tended to limit the statute's application. "[E]ver mindful that the written word or picture is involved, courts have engrafted exceptions and restrictions onto the statute to avoid any conflict with the free dissemination of thoughts, ideas, newsworthy events, and matters of public interest."

In the light of questions that counsel were asked to argue on reargument, it is particularly relevant that the Court of Appeals made crystal clear in the *Spahn* opinion [Spahn v. Julian Messner, Inc., * * 274 N.Y.S.2d 877, 221 N.E.2d 543 (1966), gross fictionalization in an unauthorized biography of a famous baseball player] that truth is a complete defense in actions under the statute based upon reports of newsworthy people or events. * * *

But although the New York statute affords "little protection" to the "privacy" of a newsworthy person, "whether he be such by choice or involuntarily" the statute gives him a right of action when his name, picture, or portrait is the subject of a "fictitious" report or article. *Spahn* points up the distinction. *Spahn* was an action under the statute brought by the well-known professional baseball pitcher, Warren Spahn. He sought an injunction and damages against the unauthorized publication of what purported to be a biography of his life. The trial judge had found that "[t]he record unequivocally establishes that the book publicizes areas of Warren Spahn's personal and private life, albeit inaccurate and distorted, and consists of a host, a preponderant percentage, of factual errors, distortions and fanciful passages. * * *" 250 N.Y.S.2d 529, 542.

The Court of Appeals sustained the holding that in these circumstances the publication was proscribed by § 51 of the Civil Rights Law and was not within the exceptions and restrictions for newsworthy events engrafted on the statute. * * *

The opinion goes on to say that the "establishment of minor errors in an otherwise accurate" report does not prove "fictionalization." Material and substantial falsification is the test. However, it is not clear whether proof of knowledge of the falsity or that the article was prepared with reckless disregard for the truth is also required. In New York Times Co. v. Sullivan, 376 U.S. 254, we held that the Constitution delimits a State's power to award damages for libel in actions brought by public officials against critics of their official conduct. Factual error, content defamatory of official reputation, or both, are insufficient to an award of damages for false statements unless actual malice—knowledge that the statements are false or in reckless disregard of the truth—is alleged and proved. The *Spahn* opinion reveals that the defendant in that case relied on *New York Times* as the basis of an argument that application of the statute to the publication of a substantially fictitious biography would run afoul of the constitutional guarantees. The Court of Appeals held that *New York Times* had no application. The court, after distinguishing the cases on the ground that *Spahn* did not deal with public officials or official conduct, then says, "The free speech which is encouraged and essential to the operation of a healthy government is something quite different from an individual's attempt to enjoin the publication of a fictitious biography of him. No public interest is served by protecting the dissemination of the latter. We perceive no constitutional infirmities in this respect." 274 N.Y. S.2d at 880.

If this is meant to imply that proof of knowing or reckless falsity is not essential to a constitutional application of the statute in these cases, we disagree with the Court of Appeals. *We hold that the constitutional protections for speech and press preclude the application of the New York statute to redress false reports of matters of public interest in the absence of proof that the defendant published the report with knowledge of its falsity or in reckless disregard of the truth.* [Emphasis added.]

The guarantees for speech and press are not the preserve of political expression or comment upon public affairs, essential as those are to healthy government. One need only pick up any newspaper or magazine to comprehend the vast range of published matter which exposes persons to public view, both private citizens and public officials. Exposure of the self to others in varying degrees is a concomitant of life in a civilized community. The risk of this exposure is an essential incident of life in a society which places a primary value on freedom of speech and of press. * * * Erroneous statement is no less inevitable in such case than in the case of comment upon public affairs, and in both, if innocent or merely negligent, " * * * it must be protected if the freedoms of expression are to have the 'breathing space' that they 'need * * * to survive' * *." *New York Times Co. v. Sullivan, supra.* * * * We create grave risk of serious impairment of the indispensable service of a free press in a free society if we saddle the press with the impossible burden of verifying to a certainty the facts associated in news articles with a person's name, picture or portrait, particularly as related to nondefamatory matter. Even negligence would be a most elusive standard, especially when the content of the speech itself affords no warning of prospective harm to another through falsity. A negligence test would place on the press the intolerable burden of guessing how a jury might assess the reasonableness of steps taken by it to verify the accuracy of every reference to a name, picture or portrait.

In this context, sanctions against either innocent or negligent misstatement would present a grave hazard of discouraging the press from exercising the constitutional guarantees. Those guarantees are not for the benefit of the press so much as for the benefit of all of us. A broadly defined freedom of the press assures the maintenance of our political system and an open society. Fear of large verdicts in damage suits for innocent or mere negligent misstatement, even fear of the expense involved in their defense, must inevitably cause publishers to "steer far wider of the unlawful zone." *New York Times Co. v. Sullivan.* * * *

But the constitutional guarantees can tolerate sanctions against *calculated* falsehood without significant impairment of their essential function. We held in *New York Times* that calculated falsehood enjoyed no immunity in the case of alleged defamation of a public official's official conduct. Similarly calculated falsehood should enjoy no immunity in the situation here presented us. * * *

The appellant argues that the statute should be declared unconstitutional on its face if construed by the New York courts to impose liability without proof of knowing or reckless falsity. Such a declaration would not be warranted even if it were entirely clear that this is the view of the New York courts. The New York Court of Appeals, as the *Spahn* opinion demonstrates, has been assiduous to construe the statute to avoid invasion of the constitutional protections for speech and press. We therefore confidently expect that the New York courts will apply the statute consistently with the constitutional command. Any possible difference with us as to the thrust of the constitutional command is narrowly limited in this case to the failure of the trial judge to instruct the jury that a verdict of liability could be predicated only on a finding of knowing or reckless falsity in the publication of the *Life* article.

The judgment of the Court of Appeals is set aside and the case is remanded for further proceedings not inconsistent with this opinion.

It is so ordered.

COMMENT

1. *Time, Inc. v. Hill* required that *actual malice* be proven in all false light privacy cases involving a matter of public interest, no matter whether the plaintiff was a private or public person. Damages might be won in the egregious case. For example, a surviving husband was awarded $5,000 compensatory and $15,000 punitive damages when a *National Enquirer* story under the headline, "Happiest Mother Kills Her Three Children and Herself," was held sufficiently untruthful and offensive to constitute an invasion of privacy. The plaintiff pleaded that he had suffered mental anguish to the extent of requiring psychiatric treatment, unemployment, and the disdain of his friends and acquaintances, the latter offense suggesting the affinity of libel and privacy. The "happiest" mother in reality had been extremely depressed and unstable, and only fictitious dialogue in the story could make her appear otherwise. The actual malice standard of knowing falsehood or reckless disregard of truth or falsity had been met. Varnish v. Best Medium Publishing Co., 405 F.2d 608 (2d Cir. 1968).

For false light claims involving television reporting, see the following, Clark v. ABC, 8 Med.L.Reptr. 2049, 684 F.2d 1208 (6th Cir. 1982) and Cantrell v. ABC, 8 Med. L.Rptr. 1239, 529 F.Supp. 746 (D.Ill.1981). The former involved passers-by in an investigative report on prostitution, the latter a building manager interviewed at the scene of a suspected case of arson.

The Court's plurality in *Rosenbloom*, text, p. 221, would eventually establish the same *public interest* or *public issue* standard for defamation. But *Rosenbloom* was to be superseded by *Gertz* and *Fire-*

stone, two cases which brought the idea of the private person back under the protective cloak of libel law, particularly when the private person's involvement in a matter of public interest was involuntary. What was the effect of the two cases on the law of privacy? Should a negligence test supplant the actual malice test in privacy as it has in libel for private person plaintiffs? Since a public interest test has been rejected as the focal point for the application of the actual malice test of the public law of libel, it is, arguably, illogical to use a newsworthiness test to invoke the actual malice rule in privacy law. In short, shouldn't *Gertz* be read to replace the rule of *Time, Inc. v. Hill* as well as the rule of *Rosenbloom v. Metromedia*?

2. An opportunity either to merge or to distinguish defamation and false light invasions of privacy was provided the Court in an earlier *Cantrell* case, Cantrell v. Forest City Publishing Co., 419 U.S. 245 (1974). In that case a story in the *Cleveland Plain Dealer* Sunday Magazine purported to describe an interview with Margaret Cantrell whose husband had died in a bridge collapse, leaving her and her four children in proud but abject poverty. Mrs. Cantrell, however, had been absent when a reporter and photographer entered the home and talked with one of her children. Inaccuracies and false characterizations such as "She wears the same mask of non-expression she wore at the funeral" were inevitable in the story that followed, and the Court reversed the Court of Appeals for the Sixth Circuit and upheld a district court award of compensatory damages. On these facts alone the case may represent two other categories of privacy—intrusion and true but embarrassing private facts, frequently referred to as *public disclosure*.

Since the actual malice test of *New York Times* had again been met, the Court found "no occasion to consider whether a state may constitutionally impose a more severe standard of liability for a publisher or broadcaster of false statements injurious to a *private individual* under a false-light theory of invasion of privacy, or whether the constitutional standard announced in *Time, Inc. v. Hill* applies to all false-light cases." [Emphasis added.]

"In essence," Justice Potter Stewart wrote, joined by seven of his colleagues, "the theory of the case was that by publishing the false feature story about the Cantrells and thereby making them the objects of pity and ridicule, the respondents damaged Mrs. Cantrell and her son William by causing them to suffer outrage, mental distress, shame and humiliation. * * * These were 'calculated falsehoods,' and the jury was plainly justified in finding that [the reporter] had portrayed the Cantrells in a false light through knowing or reckless untruth." The photographer was exonerated.

3. Margaret Cantrell, though clearly a private person, had no opportunity to charge *negligence* on the part of the *Plain Dealer* because its "calculated falsehoods" had already reached the level of *actual malice* which subsumes *negligence* and makes the lesser standard superfluous. Since *Cantrell*, courts have disagreed on the degree to which *Time, Inc. v. Hill* should track with *Gertz*: a *negligence* test in false light privacy cases for private persons, an *actual malice* test for public persons.

A California appeals court dared resurrect the public interest test of *Rosenbloom* in a 1981 libel and privacy suit.[23] In 1979 an Arkansas court held that a nonpublic, i.e., a private person, must prove *actual malice* in a false light case if the publication is a matter of public concern.[24] An

23. Midwife v. Copley, 7 Med.L.Rptr. 1393 (Cal.1981).

24. Dodrill v. Arkansas Democrat, 5 Med.L.Rptr.1385, 590 S.W.2d 840 (Ark.1979), cert. den., 444 U.S. 1076 (1980).

earlier case, Rinsley v. Brandt, 446 F.Supp. 850 (D.Kan.1977), stood for the rule that *Gertz* limits the *actual malice* standard to false light claims brought by public persons and thus infers that private persons need only show *negligence*. Another federal district court crystallized that inference in Dresbach v. Doubleday, 7 Med.L. Rptr. 2105, 518 F.Supp. 1285 (D.D.C.1981) by applying the District of Columbia's *negligence* standard for libel to false light actions brought by private persons.[25] It is expected that the latter rule, in the interest of legal symmetry, will eventually prevail.[26]

Fictionalization

How can publishers anticipate fictional characters coming to life? There seems to be a proliferation of cases in this transection of the false light category. Newsworthiness or public interest arguments provide the best defense. Sometimes they work; sometimes they don't.

Senator Joseph McCarthy's former aides were portrayed without their consent in a television movie, with their actual names used in advertising and promotion for the program. Their privacy claims were dismissed on public interest grounds.[27] On the other hand, a false light claim was sustained when the real name of an attorney who had represented gangster Lucky Luciano was used in a wholly fictionalized, although nondefamatory, episode in a novel.[28]

Frequently, a prior issue is identification. Did baton-twirling skill and costume color equate Miss Wyoming with the fictitious sex-driven character in the *Penthouse* story? An author was unwise to use the real name and physical description of a casual acquaintance for a fictional transsexual character.[29] Where there is no earlier connection between author and plaintiff the risk may not be as great.[30] In any case, identification if in doubt, will be a question for a jury.

Traditional disclaimers (all characters portrayed in this novel, film, broadcast are wholly fictional, and any resemblance to persons living or dead is purely coincidental.) are useful, but they may not cover every conceivable kind of character. Perhaps disclaimers ought to be more explicit and emphatic. Central characters need to be obscured more fully than bit players. Conversely, the better known a claimant, the potentially stronger the privacy claim. Generally speaking, the rarer a work of imagination, the less vulnerable it will be to false light privacy suits. Composite characters constructed from pseudonymous sources (Janet Cooke's "Jimmy's World", Michael Daly's Northern Irish assassins) have proved damaging to the

25. The same rule was applied in McCall v. Courier Journal, 7 Med.L.Rptr. 2118, 623 S.W.2d 882 (Ky.1981), a case that specifically rejects the public issue test of Midwife v. Copley. For the *Gertz* application, see also Roberts v. Dover, 7 Med.L.Rptr. 2296, 525 F.Supp. 987 (Tenn.1981). Fitzgerald v. Penthouse International, Limited, 7 Med.L.Rptr. 2385, 525 F.Supp. 585 (D.Md.1981) held that a limited purpose public figure must also show actual malice.

26. Hill, *Defamation and Privacy Under the First Amendment,* 76 Colum.L.Rev. 1205, 1274 (Dec.1976).

27. Cohn v. NBC, 4 Med.L.Rptr. 2533, 414 N.Y.S.2d 906 (1979), affirmed 6 Med.L.Rptr. 1398, 430 N.Y.S.2d 265 (1980), cert. den. 449 U.S. 1022. See also, Street v. NBC, 7 Med.L.Rptr. 1001, 645 F.2d 1227 (6th Cir. 1981).

28. Polakoff v. Harcourt Jovanovich, Inc., 3 Med.L.Rptr. 2516 (Sup.Ct.N.Y. 1978), affirmed, 413 N.Y.S.2d 537 (1979).

29. Geisler v. Petrocelli, 6 Med.L.Rptr. 1023, 616 F.2d 636 (2d Cir. 1980).

30. Allen v. Gordon, 6 Med.L.Rptr. 2010 (Sup.Ct.N.Y.1980) 446 N.Y.S.2d 48. A Manhattan psychiatrist said that he was identified by gender, profession, and location in the book, *I'm Dancing As Fast As I Can.* A disclaimer was said not to indicate that all names had been changed. A New York trial court nevertheless thought injunctive relief too drastic a remedy.

credibility of journalism and to the doctrine of journalist's privilege. Reporters owe readers a full report at the outset on what they are doing and why. Disclaimers, therefore, ought to be explicit.

Few fictionalized conversations will be held privileged as fair comment on the life of actual public figures.[31]

In Frosch v. Grosset & Dunlap, 4 Med.L. Rptr. 2307 (N.Y.Sup.Ct.1979), affirmed 6 Med.L.Rptr. 1271, 427 N.Y.S.2d 828 (1980), claims by the executors of Marilyn Monroe's estate against the publisher of Norman Mailer's biography *Marilyn* were dismissed on grounds that false light claims do not survive the death of an individual.

The most ominous example of a case of failed fictionalization and one that exercised the literary world, is Bindrim v. Mitchell, 5 Med.L.Rptr. 1113, 155 Cal.Rptr. 29 (1979), cert. den., 444 U.S. 984, rehearing den. 444 U.S. 1040 (1980). Author Gwen Davis Mitchell not only lost a libel suit (the libel claim here being indistinguishable from a false light claim) to a "nude-encounter" therapist but was also sued by her publisher which, under its contract with her, had a right to recover whatever costs might result from a libel suit. Doubleday had stuck with its author until she finally lost her case. Mitchell, who claimed that she had gone to great pains to change, disguise, and transmute—partly with vulgar dialogue—events at a nude therapy marathon into her novel *Touching,* maintains that there can be no libel in fiction.

The case was complicated by the fact that the plaintiff's appearance and academic credentials had changed to resemble those of the fictional character of "Dr. Herford" between publication and trial. Moreover, Mitchell had signed a contract with the plaintiff not to disclose in any manner what was to take place in the therapy sessions.

Essentially, Mitchell's disguise was inadequate. So again the question of identification. How many persons have to relate the fictional character to an actual person? In *Bindrim,* the California court said that one would suffice. Although technically a libel rather than a false light privacy case, it may be instructive to present here portions of the court's opinion and a dissent from it.

BINDRIM v. MITCHELL

5 MED.L.RPTR. 1113, 92 CAL.APP.2D 61, 155 CAL.RPTR. 29 (1979).

KINGSLEY, J.:

* * *

There is clear and convincing evidence to support the jury's finding that defendant Mitchell entertained actual malice, and that defendant Doubleday had actual malice when it permitted the paperback printing of *Touching,* although there was no actual malice on the part of Doubleday in its original printing of the hardback edition.

Mitchell's reckless disregard for the truth was apparent from her knowledge of the truth of what transpired at the encounter, and the literary portrayals of that encounter.[2] Since she attended sessions there can be no suggestion that she did not know the true facts. Since "actual malice" concentrates solely on defendants' attitude toward the truth or falsity of the material published * * * and not on malicious motives,[3] certainly defendant

31. For an exception to this rule, see Rosemount Enterprises, Inc. v. Random House, 366 F.2d 303 (2d Cir. 1966) where the court said that even the imaginary ramblings of Howard Hughes were of interest to the public.

2. The fact that *Touching* was a novel does not necessarily insulate Mitchell from liability for libel, if all the elements of libel are otherwise present.

3. There is no suggestion that Mitchell was being malicious in the fabrication; her intent may have been to be colorful or dramatic.

Mitchell was in a position to know the truth or falsity of her own material, and the jury was entitled to find that her publication was in reckless disregard of that truth or with actual knowledge of falsity.

However, plaintiff failed to prove by clear and convincing evidence that the original hardback publication by Doubleday was made with knowledge of falsity or in reckless disregard of falsity. McCormick of Doubleday cautioned plaintiff that the characters must be totally fictitious and Mitchell assured McCormick that the characters in *Touching* were incapable of being identified as real persons. McCormick arranged to have the manuscript read by an editor knowledgeable in the field of libel. The cases are clear that reckless conduct is not measured by whether a reasonably prudent person would have published or would have investigated before publishing. There must be sufficient evidence to permit the conclusion that defendant in fact entertained serious doubts as to the truth of his publication, (*St. Amant v. Thompson* (1968) * * * 390 U.S. 727, 731), and there is nothing to suggest that Doubleday entertained such doubts prior to the hardback publication.

Plaintiff suggests that, since the book did not involve "hot news," Doubleday had a duty to investigate the content for truth. Courts have required investigation as to truth or falsity of statements which were not hot news (*Widener v. Pacific Gas & Electric Co.* (1977) * * * 75 Cal. App.3d 445, *Carson v. Allied News Co.* (1976) * * * 529 F.2d 206), but those cases involved factual stories about actual people. In the case at bar, Doubleday had been assured by Mitchell that no actual, identifiable person was involved and that all the characters were fictitious in the novel. Where the publication comes from a known reliable source and there is nothing in the circumstances to suggest inaccuracy, there is no duty to investigate. (See *Baldine v. Sharon Herald Co.* (1968) 391 F.2d 703, 707.) There was nothing in the record to suggest that, prior to the hardback printing defendant Doubleday in fact entertained serious doubts as to the truth or falsity of the publication, and investigatory failure alone is insufficient to find actual malice.

However, prior to the paperback printing there were surrounding circumstances to suggest inaccuracy, such that at that point Doubleday had a duty to investigate. Plaintiff did show that Doubleday sold the rights to the New American Library after receiving a letter from plaintiff's attorney explaining that plaintiff was Herford and the inscription in the paperback said, "This is an authorized edition published by Doubleday and Company." Although, after the receipt of the plaintiff's attorney's letter, Doubleday again inquired of Mitchell as to whether plaintiff was the character in the book, the jury was entitled to find that Mitchell's assurance to Doubleday was not sufficient to insulate Doubleday from liability and that Doubleday had some further duty to investigate. The jury could have inferred that at that point Doubleday either had serious doubts, or should have had serious doubts, as to the possibility that plaintiff was defamed by "Touching" and that at that point Doubleday had some duty to investigate.

* * *

Appellants claim that, even if there are untrue statements, there is no showing that plaintiff was identified as the character, Simon Herford, in the novel *Touching*.

Appellants allege that plaintiff failed to show he was identifiable as Simon Herford, relying on the fact that the character in *Touching* was described in the book as a "fat Santa Claus type with long white hair, white sideburns, a cherubic rosy fact and rosy forearms" and that Bindrim was clean shaven and had short hair. Defendants rely in part on *Wheeler v. Dell Publishing Co.* (1962) 300 F.2d 372, which involved an alleged libel caused by a fictional account of an actual murder trial. The *Wheeler* court said (at p. 376):

> "In our opinion, any reasonable person who read the book and was in a position to identify Hazel Wheeler with Janice Quill would more likely conclude that the author created the latter in an ugly way so that none would identify her with Hazel Wheeler. It is important to note that while the trial and locale might suggest Hazel Wheeler to those who knew the Chenoweth family, suggestion is not identification. In *Levey* [*Levey v. Warner Bros. Pictures* (S.D.N.Y. 1944) 57 F.Supp. 40] the court said those who had seen her act may have been reminded of her by songs and scenes, but would not reasonably identify her."

However, in *Wheeler* the court found that no one who knew the real widow could possibly identify her with the character in the novel. In the case at bar, the only differences between plaintiff and the Herford character in *Touching* were physical appearance and that Herford was a psychiatrist rather than psychologist. Otherwise, the character Simon Herford was very similar to the actual plaintiff. We cannot say, as did the court in *Wheeler*, that no one who knew plaintiff Bindrim could reasonably identify him with the fictional character. Plaintiff was identified as Herford by several witnesses and plaintiff's own tape recordings of the marathon sessions show that the novel was based substantially on plaintiff's conduct in the nude marathon.

Defendant also relies on Middlebrooks v. Curtis Publishing Co. (1969) 413 F.2d 141, where the marked dissimilarities between the fictional character and the plaintiff supported the court's finding against the reasonableness identification. In *Middlebrooks,* there was a difference in age, an absence from the locale at the time of the episode, and a difference in employment of the fictional character and plaintiff; nor did the story parallel the plaintiff's life in any significant manner. In the case at bar, apart from some of those episodes allegedly constituting the libelous matter itself, and apart from the physical difference and the fact that plaintiff had a Ph.D., and not an M.D., the similarities between Herford and Bindrim are clear, and the transcripts of the actual encounter weekend show a close parallel between the narrative of plaintiff's novel and the actual real life events. Here, there were many similarities between the character, Herford, and the plaintiff Bindrim and those few differences do not bring the case under the rule of *Middlebrooks.* (See Fetler v. Houghton Mifflin Co. (1966) 364 F.2d 650.) There is overwhelming evidence that plaintiff and "Herford" were one.

However, even though there was clear and convincing evidence to support the finding of "actual malice," and even though there was support for finding that plaintiff is identified as the character in Mitchell's novel, there still can be no recovery by plaintiff if the statements in *Touching* were not libelous. There can be no libel predicated on an opinion. The publication must contain a false statement of fact. (Gregory v. McDonnell Douglas Corp. (1976) 17 Cal.3d 596.)

Plaintiff alleges that the book as a whole was libelous and that the book contained several false statements of fact. Plaintiff relies in part on [a] conversation between plaintiff and the minister as one libelous statement of fact. Plaintiff also argues that a particular incident in the book is libelous. That incident depicts an encounter group patient as so distressed upon leaving from the weekend therapy that she is killed when her car crashes. Plaintiff also complains of an incident in the book where he is depicted as "pressing," "clutching," and "ripping" a patient's cheeks and "stabbing against a pubic bone." Plaintiff complains, too, of being depicted as having said to a female patient, "Drop it, bitch." There are also other incidents alleged to be libelous.

Our inquiry then, is directed to whether or not any of these incidents can be considered false statements of fact. It is clear from the transcript of the actual encounter weekend proceeding that some of the incidents portrayed by Mitchell are false: i.e., substantially inaccurate description of what actually happened. It is also clear that some of these portrayals cast plaintiff in a disparaging light since they portray his language and conduct as crude, aggressive, and unprofessional.

Defendants here rely on the cases which have considered the difference in published materials between factual statements and matters of mere opinion. While, as we discuss below, we do not feel that those cases necessarily express the rules applicable where, as here, the published material purports to state actual facts concerning the characters in a novel, we proceed, first, to examine the cases on which defendants rely. [Cases discussed are omitted.]

* * *

If viewed as a case involving an issue of "opinion," those cases, and other cases involving that issue, make it clear that, since there was evidence that people had identified plaintiff with the Dr. Herford of the book, the jury's finding against defendants is conclusive on that issue.

However, as we have indicated above, we regard the case at bench as involving a different issue. Defendants contend that the fact that the book was labeled as being a "novel" bars any claim that the writer or publisher could be found to have implied that the characters in the book were factual representations not of the fictional characters but of an actual non-fictional person. That contention, thus broadly stated, is unsupported by the cases. The test is whether a reasonable person, reading the book, would understand that the fictional character therein pictured was, in actual fact, the plaintiff acting as described. (Middlebrooks v. Curtis Publishing Co. (1969) * * * 413 F.2d 141, 143.) Each case must stand on its own facts. In some cases, such as Greenbelt Pub. Assn. v. Bresler (1970) * * 398 U.S. 6, an appellate court can, on examination of the entire work, find that no reasonable person would have regarded the episodes in the book as being other than the fictional imaginings of the author about how the character he had created would have acted. Similarly, in Hicks v. Casablanca Records (D.C.S.D.N.Y.1978) 4 Med.L.Rptr. 1497, 464 F.Supp. 426, a trier of fact was able to find that, considering the work as a whole, no reasonable reader would regard an episode, in a book purporting to be a biography of an actual person, to have been anything more than the author's imaginative explanation of an episode in that person's life about which no actual facts were known. We cannot make any similar determination here. Whether a reader, identifying plaintiff with the "Dr. Herford" of the book, would regard the passages herein complained of as mere fictional embroidering or as reporting actual language and conduct, was for the jury. Its verdict adverse to the defendants cannot be overturned by this court.

Defendants raise the question of whether there is "publication" for libel where the communication is to only one person or a small group of persons rather than to the public at large. Publication for purposes of defamation is sufficient when the publication is to only one person other than the person defamed. (Brauer v. Globe Newspaper Co. (1966) 217 N.E.2d 736, 739.) Therefore, it is irrelevant whether all readers realized plaintiff and Herford were identical.

* * *

FILES, P.J., dissenting:

This novel, which is presented to its readers as a work of fiction, contains a portrayal of nude encounter therapy, and its tragic effect upon an apparently happy and well-adjusted woman who subjected herself to it. Plaintiff is a practitioner of this kind of therapy. His grievance, as described in his testimony and in his briefs on appeal, is provoked by that institutional criticism.[1] Plaintiff's "concession" that he is a public figure appears to be a tactic to enhance his argument that any unflattering portrayal of this kind of therapy defames him.

The decision of the majority upholding a substantial award of damages against the author and publisher poses a grave threat to any future work of fiction which explores the effect of techniques claimed to have curative value.

The majority opinion rests upon a number of misconceptions of the record and the law of libel. I mention a few of them.

Defamation. Libel is a false and unprivileged publication which exposes any person to hatred, contempt, ridicule or obloquy, or which causes him to be shunned or avoided or which has a tendency to injure him in his reputation. (Civ. Code, § 45.) A libel which is defamatory without the necessity of explanatory matter is said to be a libel on its face. Language not libelous on its face is not actionable unless the plaintiff alleges and proves that he has suffered special damage as a result thereof. (Civ. Code, § 45a.)

Whether or not matter is on its face reasonably susceptible of a libelous meaning is a question of law. (McLeod v. Tribune Publishing Co. (1959) 52 Cal.2d 536, 546.)

The complaint in this action quotes verbatim the portions of the defendant's novel which are alleged to be libelous. No explanatory matter or special damages are alleged. The only arguably defamatory matter I can find in that complaint is in the passages which portray the fictitional therapist using coarse, vulgar and insulting language in addressing his patients. Some of the therapeutic techniques described in the quoted passages may seem bizarre, but a court cannot assume that such conduct is so inappropriate that a reputable therapist would be defamed if that technique were imputed to him. The alleged defamation therefore is limited to the imputation of vulgar speech and insulting manners.

The defendants asked the trial court to give an instruction to the jury identifying the matter which it could consider as defamatory. The trial court refused. Instead, the court sent the case to the jury without distinction between actionable defamation and constitutionally protected criticism. In addition, the trial court's instructions authorized the jury to award special damages for loss of income which could have resulted from the lawful expression of opinion.

Identification. Whether or not an allegedly defamatory communication was made "of and concerning the plaintiff" is an issue involving constitutional rights. (New York Times v. Sullivan (1964) 376 U.S. 254, 288 * * * see Rest. Torts, 2d, § 580A Com. (g).) Criticism of an institution, profession or technique is protected by the First Amendment; and such criticism may not be suppressed merely because it may reflect adversely upon someone who cherishes the institution or is a part of it.

Defendants' novel describes a fictitious therapist who is conspicuously different

1. The record demonstrates the essential truth of the author's thesis. A tape recording of an actual encounter session conducted by plaintiff contains this admonition to the departing patients:

"* * * Now, to top that off, you're turned on, that is you're about as turned on as if you've had 50 to 75 gammas of LSD. That's the estimate of the degree of the turn-on is. And it doesn't feel that way, because you're *[sic]* been getting higher a little bit at a time. So don't wait to find out, take my word for it, and drive like you've had three or four martinis. Drive cautiously."

from plaintiff in name, physical appearance, age, personality and profession.

Indeed the fictitious Dr. Herford has none of the characteristics of plaintiff except that Dr. Herford practices nude encounter therapy. Only three witnesses, other than plaintiff himself, testified that they "recognized" plaintiff as the fictitious Dr. Herford. All three of those witnesses had participated in or observed one of plaintiff's nude marathons. The only characteristic mentioned by any of the three witnesses as identifying plaintiff was the therapy practiced.

Plaintiff was cross-examined in detail about what he saw that identified him in the novel. Every answer he gave on this subject referred to how the fictitious Dr. Herford dealt with his patients. * * *

Plaintiff has no monopoly upon the encounter therapy which he calls "nude marathon." Witnesses testified without contradiction that other professionals use something of this kind. There does not appear to be any reason why anyone could not conduct a "marathon" using the style if not the full substance of plaintiff's practices.

Plaintiff's brief discusses the therapeutic practices of the fictitious Dr. Herford in two categories: Those practices which are similar to plaintiff's technique are classified as identifying. Those which are unlike plaintiff's are called libelous because they are false. Plaintiff has thus resurrected the spurious logic which Professor Kalven found in the position of the plaintiff in New York Times v. Sullivan * * * 376 U.S. 254. Kalven wrote: "There is revealed here a new technique by which defamation might be endlessly manufactured. First, it is argued that, contrary to all appearances, a statement referred to the plaintiff; then, that it falsely ascribed to the plaintiff something that he did not do, which should be rather easy to prove about a statement that did not refer to plaintiff in the first place. * * *" Kalven, *The New York Times Case: A Note on "The Central Meaning of the First Amendment,"* 1964 The Supreme Court Review 191, 199.

Even if we accept the plaintiff's thesis that criticism of nude encounter therapy may be interpreted as libel of one practitioner, the evidence does not support a finding in favor of plaintiff.

Whether or not a publication to the general public is defamatory is "whether in the mind of the average reader the publication, considered as a whole, could reasonably be considered as defamatory." [Patton v. Royal Industries, Inc. (1968) 263 Cal.App.2d 760, 765. See Good Government Group of Seal Beach, Inc. v. Superior Court (1978) 22 Cal.3d 672, 682; Rest.Torts, 2d, § 559, comment (e).]

The majority opinion contains this juxtaposition of ideas: "Secondly, defendants' [proposed] instructions that the jury must find that a substantial segment of the public did, in fact, believe the Dr. Simon Herford was, in fact, Paul Bindrim * * * was properly refused. For the tort of defamation, publication to one other person is sufficient, * * *."

The first sentence refers to the question whether the publication was defamatory of plaintiff. The second refers to whether the defamatory matter was published. The former is an issue in this case. The latter is not. Of course, a publication to one person may constitute actionable libel. But this has no bearing on the principle that the allegedly libelous effect of a publication to the public generally is to be tested by the impression made on the average reader.

The jury instruction on identification. The only instruction given the jury on the issue of identification stated that plaintiff had the burden of proving "That a third person read the statement and reasonably understood the defamatory meaning and that the statement applied to plaintiff."

That instruction was erroneous and prejudicial in that it only required proof that one "third person" understood the defamatory meaning.

The word "applied" was most unfortunate in the context of this instruction. The novel was about nude encounter therapy. Plaintiff practiced nude encounter therapy. Of course the novel "applied to plaintiff," particularly insofar as it exposed what may result from such therapy. This instruction invited the jury to find that plaintiff was libeled by criticism of the kind of therapy he practiced. The effect is to mulct the defendants for the exercise of their first amendment right to comment on the nude marathon.

MALICE.

The majority opinion adopts the position that actual malice may be inferred from the fact that the book was "false." That inference is permissible against a defendant who has purported to state the truth. But when the publication purports to be fiction, it is absurd to infer malice because the fiction is false.

As the majority agrees, a public figure may not recover damages for libel unless "actual malice" is shown. Sufficiency of the evidence on this issue is another constitutional issue. (*St. Amant v. Thompson* (1968) 390 U.S. 727, 730.) Actual malice is a state of mind, even though it often can be proven only by circumstantial evidence. The only apparent purpose of the defendants was to write and publish a novel. There is not the slightest evidence of any intent on the part of either to harm plaintiff. No purpose for wanting to harm him has been suggested.

The majority opinion seems to say malice is proved by Doubleday's continuing to publish the novel after receiving a letter from an attorney (not plaintiff's present attorney) which demanded that Doubleday discontinue publication "for the reasons stated in" a letter addressed to Gwen Davis. An examination of the latter demonstrates the fallacy of that inference.

The letter to Davis [Mitchell] asserted that the book violated a confidential relationship, invaded plaintiff's privacy, libelled him and violated a "common law copyright" by "using the unpublished words" of plaintiff. It added "From your said [television] appearances, as well as from the book, it is unmistakable that the 'Simon Herford' mentioned in your book refers to my client."

The letters did not assert that any statement of purported fact in the book was false. The only allegation of falsity was this:

> "In these [television] appearances you stated, directly or indirectly, that nude encounter workshops, similar to the one you attended, are harmful. The truth is that those attending my client's workshops derive substantial benefit from their attendance at such workshops."

These letters gave Doubleday no factual information which would indicate that the book libelled plaintiff.

The letters did not put Doubleday on notice of anything except that plaintiff was distressed by the expression of an opinion unfavorable to nude encounter therapy—an expression protected by the First Amendment. (See Gertz v. Robert Welch, Inc. (1974) 418 U.S. 323, 339 * * *: Gregory v. McDonnel Douglas Corp (1976) 17 Cal.3d 596, 600.]

From an analytical standpoint, the chief vice of the majority opinion is that it brands a novel as libelous because it is "false," i.e., fiction; and infers "actual malice" from the fact that the author and publisher knew it was not a true representation of plaintiff. From a constitutional standpoint the vice is the chilling effect upon the publisher of any novel critical of any occupational practice, inviting litigation on the theory "when you criticize my occupation, you libel me." [Emphasis added.]

I would reverse the judgment.

COMMENT

Although recognizing that rebuttal or retraction, as well as a pleading of truth, would exacerbate an invasion of privacy,[32] Justice Brennan in *Time, Inc. v. Hill* observed that "Many 'right of privacy' cases could in fact have been brought as 'libel per quod' actions * * * all libel cases concern public exposure of false matter, but the primary harm being compensated is damage to reputation. In the 'right of privacy' cases the primary damage is the mental distress from having been exposed to public view, although injury to reputation may be an element bearing upon such damage."

Brennan nevertheless kept libel and privacy distinct, although, as *Rosenbloom* would demonstrate later, their protection would depend on parallel lines of reasoning based on the "public interest" or "public issue" test first suggested by Warren and Brandeis in their *Harvard Law Review* article. Arguably, if determining when a "libel" involves material which affects the "public interest" is an unsuitable task for courts in a regime governed by the First Amendment, it is a similarly unsuitable task for courts to decide when a publication is "newsworthy" in a privacy case since by doing so they interfere with journalistic prerogatives.

Gertz discarded the "public interest" standard for libel, a standard that focused essentially on the subject matter of the defamatory report, in favor of a test based on the *private/public* status of the plaintiff.

Under the rules of *Gertz* there may then be advantages to the press of a future merger of libel and false light privacy. For one, the plaintiff would clearly carry the burden of proving the falsity of the publication. At least one lower court has held that the burden of proof in a false light case is on the defendant.[33] On the other hand, *Cantrell* would permit punitive damages based, not on the *New York Times* definition of actual malice, but on the lesser standard of common law malice, defined frequently as spite or ill will. "In false light cases," Justice Stewart wrote in *Cantrell,* "common-law malice * * * would focus on the defendant's attitude toward the plaintiff's privacy, not toward the truth or falsity of the material published." Since the Cantrells were unable to show that the *Cleveland Plain Dealer* had an intentionally negative attitude toward their privacy, punitive damages were properly disallowed by the district court. But the topsy-turvy effect of making common law malice a more serious breach of duty than the constitutional standard of actual malice was not lost on the press and Court watchers.

Obviously false light invasions do not always carry reputational harm. Baseball pitcher Warren Spahn was given a fictional Bronze Star by his admiring biographer, and the dramatizers of Hill's captivity depicted him as a hero. Humiliation may still follow this kind of fictionalization, although fictionalization seems inevitable in book and documentary treatment of popular heroes and villains.

32. Nimmer in *The Right to Speak from* Times *to* Time: *First Amendment Theory Applied to Libel and Misapplied to Privacy,* 56 Calif.L.Rev. 935 (1968) contends, as have others, that there should be liability for invasions of privacy in spite of the First Amendment. There is an area of intimate privacy to which freedom of the press does not apply, and the "more speech" doctrine of the First Amendment does not provide a remedy for an invasion of privacy. The Court erred conceptually, he believes, in connecting libel and privacy in *Time, Inc. v. Hill.*

33. Corabi v. Curtis Publishing Co., 273 A.2d 899 (Pa.1971). For a discussion of the availability of a privacy action as a substitute for a libel action when success under libel theory seems unlikely, see Greenawalt, *New York's Right of Privacy—The Need for Change,* 42 Brooklyn L.Rev. 159 (1975). A Maryland district court said that its one-year statute of limitations for libel applied also to false light since the claims are "essentially analogous." Smith v. Esquire, 6 Med.L.Rptr. 1825, 494 F.Supp. 967 (D.Md. 1980).

Ordinary people may feel their privacy violated even when accurate information about them is disclosed. Gossip when presented as news can be more objectionable to some than a credit bureau leak; it is also the lifeblood of celebrity, even when that celebrity is fleeting. And there remains the problem here, as in libel, of the involuntary public figure.

Mrs. Firestone, though described as an adulteress, withdrew her claim of injury to reputation and relied solely on a claim of mental pain and anguish. By doing so, she may have brought libel and privacy closer together. In the meantime, the press can only hope that the actual malice bond that joins the two areas of mass communication law will remain sturdy and that, as a corollary, truth will remain a defense against both libel and false light privacy claims.

EMBARRASSING PRIVATE FACTS: "PURE" PRIVACY AND THE DEFENSE OF *NEWSWORTHINESS*

Public disclosure of *embarrassing private facts,* while the purest form of an invasion of privacy, the one which Warren and Brandeis had in mind, and the one to which most current definitions of privacy best apply, is the most difficult for a plaintiff to pursue.

Why? Because the defense of *newsworthiness* intervenes to protect the publisher, a defense so broad that Professor Kalven believed it would virtually "swallow the tort." Newsworthiness, as has been noted, means different things to different people. And for legal purposes, it may not cover everything an editor elects to print. A British parliamentary committee attempted definition—although it came out against a *law* of privacy—when it suggested that a distinction might be made between published material which is *in* the public interest, and that is a concomitant of informed citizenship, and that which is merely *of* public interest, that is an appeal to a general desire for vicarious experience or entertainment.[34]

The problem with such Meiklejohnian interpretations is that they tend to underestimate the significance of nonpolitical and unclassifiable forms of speech. Newsworthiness has been applied to privacy claims with a broad brush anyway, and where plaintiffs have succeeded, they have done so at the cost of additional publicity.

A classic case in point. In 1940, a federal court rejected the privacy claim of William James Sidis, a one-time child prodigy, whose later life as an unknown recluse had been exposed, albeit sympathetically, by a writer for *The New Yorker*[35]. Sidis has been talked about ever since he filed that suit in the late thirties.

The Court of Appeals for the Second Circuit reasoned as follows.

SIDIS v. F–R PUBLISHING CORP.

113 F.2D 806 (2D CIR. 1940).

CLARK, Circuit Judge

* * *

34. Report of the Committee on *Privacy,* Kenneth Younger, Chairman, London, July, 1972, p. 47. See also, Bloustein, Individual and Group Privacy (1978); Bezanson, *Public Disclosures as News: Injunctive Relief and Newsworthiness in Privacy Actions Involving the Press,* 64 Iowa L.Rev. 1073 (1979).

35. Manley, *Where Are They Now? April Fool!* The New Yorker, August 14, 1937. Herbert Strentz, dean of the School of Journalism at Drake University, speculates from evidence contained in James Thurber's *The Years With Ross* that Thurber may have been the author of the Sidis article. April Fool's Day was Sidis's birthdate.

Warren and Brandeis realized that the interest of the individual in privacy must inevitably conflict with the interest of the public in news. Certain public figures, they conceded, such as holders of public office, must sacrifice their privacy and expose at least part of their lives to public scrutiny as the price of the powers they attain. But even public figures were not to be stripped bare. "In general, then, the matters of which the publication should be repressed may be described as those which concern the private life, habits, acts, and relations of an individual, and have no legitimate connection with his fitness for a public office. * * * Some things all men alike are entitled to keep from popular curiosity, whether in public life or not, while others are only private because the persons concerned have not assumed a position which makes their doings legitimate matters of public investigation."

It must be conceded that under the strict standards suggested by these authors plaintiff's right of privacy has been invaded. Sidis today is neither politician, public administrator, nor statesman. Even if he were, some of the personal details revealed were of the sort that Warren and Brandeis believed "all men alike are entitled to keep from popular curiosity."

But despite eminent opinion to the contrary, we are not yet disposed to afford to all of the intimate details of private life an absolute immunity from the prying of the press. Everyone will agree that at some point the public interest in obtaining information becomes dominant over the individual's desire for privacy. Warren and Brandeis were willing to lift the veil somewhat in the case of public officers. We would go further, though we are not yet prepared to say how far. At least we would permit limited scrutiny of the "private" life of any person who has achieved, or has had thrust upon him, the questionable and indefinable status of a "public figure."

William James Sidis was once a public figure. As a child prodigy, he excited both admiration and curiosity. Of him great deeds were expected. In 1910, he was a person about whom the newspapers might display a legitimate intellectual interest, in the sense meant by Warren and Brandeis, as distinguished from a trivial and unseemly curiosity. But the precise motives of the press we regard as unimportant. And even if Sidis had loathed public attention at that time, we think his uncommon achievements and personality would have made the attention permissible. Since then Sidis has cloaked himself in obscurity, but his subsequent history, containing as it did the answer to the question of whether or not he had fulfilled his early promise, was still a matter of public concern. The article in *The New Yorker* sketched the life of an unusual personality, and it possessed considerable popular news interest.

We express no comment on whether or not the newsworthiness of the matter printed will always constitute a complete defense. *Revelations may be so intimate and so unwarranted in view of the victim's position as to outrage the community's notions of decency.* [Emphasis added.] But when focused upon public characters, truthful comments upon dress, speech, habits, and the ordinary aspects of personality will usually not transgress this line. Regrettably or not, the misfortunes and frailties of neighbors and "public figures" are subjects of considerable interest and discussion to the rest of the population. And when such are the mores of the community, it would be unwise for a court to bar their expression in the newspapers, books, and magazines of the day.

Plaintiff in his first "cause of action" charged actual malice in the publication, and now claims that an order of dismissal was improper in the face of such an allegation. We cannot agree. If plaintiff's right of privacy was not invaded by the article, the existence of actual malice in its publication would not change that result. Unless made so by statute, a truthful and therefore non-libelous statement will not become libelous when uttered maliciously. * * *

The second "cause of action" charged invasion of the rights conferred on plaintiff by §§ 50 and 51 of the N.Y. Civil Rights Law. Section 50 states that "A person, firm or corporation that uses for advertising purposes, or for the purposes of trade, the name, portrait or picture of any living person without having first obtained the written consent of such person, or if a minor of his or her parent or guardian, is guilty of a misdemeanor." Section 51 gives the injured person the right to an injunction and to damages.

* * * In this context, it is clear that "for the purposes of trade" does not contemplate the publication of a newspaper, magazine, or book which imparts truthful news or other factual information to the public. Though a publisher sells a commodity, and expects to profit from the sale of his product, he is immune from the interdict of §§ 50 and 51 so long as he confines himself to the unembroidered dissemination of facts. Publishers and motion picture producers have occasionally been held to transgress the statute in New York, but in each case the factual presentation was embellished by some degree of fictionalization. * * *

The case as to the newspaper advertisement announcing the August 14 article is somewhat different, for it was undoubtedly inserted in the World-Telegram "for advertising purposes." But since it was to advertise the article on Sidis, and the article itself was unobjectionable, the advertisement shares the privilege enjoyed by the article. Besides, the advertisement, quoted above, did not use the "name, portrait or picture" of the plaintiff.

* * *

COMMENT

The rule of *Sidis*—that revelations so intimate and so unwarranted in view of the victim's position as to outrage the community's notions of decency are actionable under privacy standards—has stood the test of time. Truthful publication may be punished in some circumstances.

"One who gives publicity to a matter concerning the private life of another is subject to liability to the other for invasion of privacy, if the matter publicized is of a kind that (a) would be highly offensive to a reasonable person and (b) is not of legitimate concern to the public." *Restatement (Second) of Torts* § 652D (1977).

As in libel, where the Supreme Court extended substantial latitude to the states to develop their own standards of fault, the Court in privacy has developed what is essentially a *community standards* test, or what one commentator has called the *unconscionability* rule.[36]

Application of the test is illustrated in a case involving an eccentric body surfer and *Sports Illustrated.* Plaintiff permitted himself to be interviewed but revoked all consent when he learned that the picture-story would include truthful details of what can only be called weird behavior. The article was published anyway and included the following paragraphs:

> He is somewhat of a mystery to most of the regular personnel, partly because he is quiet and withdrawn, usually absent from their get-togethers, and partly because he is considered to be somewhat abnormal.
>
> Virgil's carefree style at the Wedge appears to have emanated from some escapades in his younger days, such as the time at a party when a young lady approached him and asked where she might find an ashtray. "Why, my dear, right here," said Virgil, taking her lighted cigarette and extinguishing it in his

36. Hill, *Defamation and Privacy Under the First Amendment, supra,* n. 26.

> mouth. He also won a small bet one time by burning a hole in a dollar bill that was resting on the back of his hand. In the process he also burned two holes in his wrist.

The article quoted a statement Virgil made to the author about a trip to Mammoth Mountain:

> I quit my job, left home and moved to Mammoth Mountain. At the ski lodge there one night I dove headfirst down a flight of stairs—just because. Because why? Well, there were these chicks all around. I thought it would be groovy. Was I drunk? I think I might have been.

The article quotes Virgil as saying:

> Every summer I'd work construction and dive off billboards to hurt myself or drop loads of lumber on myself to collect unemployment compensation so I could surf at the Wedge. Would I fake injuries? No, I wouldn't fake them. I'd be damn injured. But I would recover. I guess I used to live a pretty reckless life. I think I might have been drunk most of the time.

Again quoting Virgil, the author relates:

> I love tuna fish. Eat it all the time. I do what feels good. That's the way I live my life. If it makes me feel good, whether it's against the law or not, I do it. I'm not sure a lot of the things I've done weren't pure lunacy. Cherilee [plaintiff's wife] says, "Mike also eats spiders and other insects and things."

Virgil was further quoted as saying,

> I've always been determined to find a sport I could be the best in. I was always aggressive as a kid. You know, competitive, mean. Real mean. I bit off the cheek of a Negro in a six-against-30 gang fight. They had tire irons with them. But that was a long time ago. At the Wedge, there are a lot of individualists.

The article notes: "Perhaps because most of his time was spent engaged in such activity, Virgil never learned how to read."

A photo caption reads: "Mike Virgil, the wild man of the Wedge, thinks it possible his brain is being slowly destroyed."

The Ninth Circuit Court of Appeals wrote no brief for the press when it said:

> To hold that privilege extends to all true statements would seem to deny the existence of "private" facts, for if facts be facts—that is, if they be true—they would not (at least to the press) be private, and the press would be free to publicize them to the extent it sees fit. The extent to which areas of privacy continue to exist, then, would appear to be based not on rights bestowed by law but on the taste and discretion of the press. We cannot accept this result.

Nevertheless, the court added that news of legitimate concern to the public is protected by the First Amendment, and "in determining what is a matter of legitimate public interest, account must be taken of the customs and conventions of the community; and in the last analysis what is proper becomes a matter of the community mores. The line is to be drawn when the publicity ceases to be the giving of information of which the public is entitled, and becomes *a morbid and sensational prying into private lives for its own sake, with which a reasonable member of the public, with decent standards, would say that he had no concern.* * * * But if there is room for differing views as to the state of community mores or the manner in which it would operate upon the facts in question, there is room for the jury function." [Emphasis added.] Virgil v. Time, Inc., 1 Med.L.Rptr. 1835, 527 F.2d 1122 (9th Cir. 1975).

The Ninth Circuit in *Virgil* thus concluded that no First Amendment privilege attaches to publication of private facts, even though true, when the facts are not in themselves newsworthy. An order denying summary judgment to Time, Inc. was vacated, and the case was remanded to the district court so that it, applying what at best is a vague and subjective test, could sift private from public facts and decide whether a person of ordinary sensibilities would be offended by the publication of these particular private facts.

The Ninth Circuit had directed the federal district court to consider the case under the "outrageousness" or "unconscionability" standard. The federal district court found that the publication in controversy did not violate that test. Noting that the Ninth Circuit had held that the First Amendment privilege to publish newsworthy information "is controlled by federal rather than state law," the district court granted summary judgment to Time, Inc. and included the following comments of its own:

> The above facts are generally unflattering and perhaps embarrassing, but they are simply not offensive to the degree of morbidity or sensationalism. In fact they connote nearly as strong a positive image as they do a negative one. On the one hand Mr. Virgil can be seen as a juvenile exhibitionist, but on the other hand he also comes across as the tough, aggressive maverick, an archetypal character occupying a respected place in the American consciousness. Given this ambiguity as to whether or not the facts disclosed are offensive at all, no reasonable juror could conclude that they were highly offensive.
>
> Even if the Court had reached the opposite conclusion that the facts disclosed were highly offensive, *Time* would still be entitled to summary judgment. For highly offensive facts, i.e., those having a degree of offensiveness equivalent to "morbid and sensational," to be denied protection as newsworthy, the revelation of them must be "for its own sake." Both parties agree that bodysurfing at the Wedge is a matter of legitimate public interest, and it cannot be doubted that Mike Virgil's unique prowess at the same is also of legitimate public interest. Any reasonable person reading the *Sports Illustrated* article would have to conclude that the personal facts concerning Mike Virgil were included as a legitimate journalistic attempt to explain Virgil's extremely daring and dangerous style of bodysurfing at the Wedge. Virgil v. Sports Illustrated & Time, Inc., 2 Med.L.Rptr. 1271, 424 F.Supp. 1286 (D.Cal.1976).

Iowa's Supreme Court held that a newspaper report of a patient subjected to sterilization was not an invasion of privacy because it was newsworthy and insufficiently intimate to outrage the community's notions of decency, and it was part of a public record. Of the story the court said:

> [I]t offered a personalized frame of reference to which the reader could relate, fostering perception and understanding * * * the editors also had a right to buttress the force of their evidence by naming names. We do not say it was necessary for them to do so, but we are certain they had a right to treat the identity of victims of involuntary sterilization as matters of legitimate public concern. * * * The specificity of the report would strengthen the accuracy of the public perception of the merits of the controversy. Howard v. Des Moines Register and Tribune Co., 5 Med.L.Rptr. 1667, 283 N.W.2d 289 (Ia. 1979), cert. den. 445 U.S. 904 (1980).[37]

When the photo of a formerly fat woman, taken on a beach, was published without consent in an article about obesity, claims of emotional distress and false light were dismissed as insufficiently outrageous to support actions for damages.[38] Nor did a story about a woman's divorce

37. For a close analysis of *Howard* in the context of an effort to delineate the values inherent in both news and privacy, see Bezanson, *Public Disclosures as News: Injunctive Relief and Newsworthiness in Privacy Actions Involving the Press,* 64 Iowa L.Rev. 1061 (1979).

38. McManamon v. Daily Freeman Newspaper, 6 Med.L.Rptr. 2245 (N.Y.Sup.Ct. 1980). See also Sweenek v. Pathe News, 16 F.Supp. 746 (D.N.Y.1936).

from her police officer husband who had been traumatically injured while working on a bomb squad support a private facts claim.[39]

Indeed, successful private facts suits have been difficult to find since *Time, Inc. v. Hill* in 1967. A federal district court thought it had reached the outer boundaries when it denied a prominent Twin Cities television station copies of videotapes that had been shown to a jury in a kidnap-murder trial. The tapes made by defendant, recorded his multiple rape of his former high school teacher and rambling conversations with her while she lay blindfolded and bound on the floor. The victim and her daughter later escaped their captor. A small boy picked up during their abduction was murdered.

"Release of the tapes for public dissemination," said the court, "would impinge upon the precious rights of * * *, the unfortunate victim of the crime and would lend the court's approval to the commercial exploitation of a voice and photographic display catering to prurient interest without proper public purpose or corresponding assurance of public benefit. * * There must be some point where the public's right to information must bow to the dignity of the individual person." In Re Application of KSTP–TV for Video Tapes in the Case of United States v. Ming Sen Shiue, 6 Med.L.Rptr. 2249, 504 F.Supp. 360 (D.Minn.1980).

The ruling appears to be based on the presumption that the television station would broadcast everything the jury had seen submitted in evidence. The issue is what access should the public have to an evidentiary record? Traditionally persons caught up in the criminal justice process, even innocently, have found their privacy in jeopardy. Television news film of a holdup suspect being frisked by police did not support a claim for invasion of privacy, even though plaintiff had not participated in any crime and was released without charge.[40] If an event is newsworthy, even innocent bystanders may lose their right of privacy.[41]

When a temporarily deranged man was arrested at his home by Boise, Idaho police for using a shotgun in a threatening manner, he was framed in his doorway and he was naked. TV cameras filmed the arrest, and for a fraction of a second the man's buttocks and genitals appeared on the evening news. The news editor was fired. The arrested man, claiming embarrassment and humiliation, sued the television station for invasion of privacy, and a jury awarded him $15,000. On appeal to the Supreme Court of Idaho, the judgment was reversed and the case remanded for retrial. The state supreme court went astray, however, by directing the trial court to decide the case on the issue of actual malice, an issue not governing private facts cases but reserved for false light suits.[42]

An outcome similarly disappointing to plaintiff was predictable in the case of the Vietnam veteran who, although confined to a wheelchair, reached out and deflected Sarah Moore's shot at President Gerald Ford. While his heroism was being acclaimed, leaders of San Francisco's gay community identified the veteran as one of them, information which he did not wish to have published and which, he said, exposed him to contempt and ridicule. His $15 million suit against newspapers, magazines, and wire services could not succeed while presidential assassination and homosexuality remain newsworthy

39. Burns v. Denver Post, 5 Med.L.Rptr. 1105 (Colo.1978), affirmed 5 Med.L.Rptr. 2004, 606 P.2d 1310 (1979). See also Winegard v. Larsen, 260 N.W.2d 816 (Iowa 1977).

40. Williams v. KCMO Broadcasting Division, Meredith Corp., 472 S.W.2d 1 (Mo.1971); Johnson v. Evening Star Newspaper Co., 344 F.2d 507 (D.C.Cir. 1965).

41. Cordell v. Detective Publications, Inc., 307 F.Supp. 1212 (D.Tenn.1968), affirmed 419 F.2d 989 (6th Cir.).

42. Taylor v. KTVB, Inc., 525 P.2d 984 (Idaho 1974).

public issues.[43] Editorial sensitivity, taste, and judgment, of course, will determine how cases of this kind are handled.

Even in cases of egregious bad taste and faulty editorial judgment the public interest defense will protect a publisher. A newspaper printed photos of a murdered child's body, wrapped in chains, being pulled from a lake. Additional prints showing the gruesome effects of the crime were sold to the public. But a privacy claim brought by the parents was rejected because, said a Georgia court, the crime, at least until its perpetrator was apprehended, was a matter of urgent public interest. Waters v. Fleetwood, 91 S.E.2d 344 (Ga.1956).

A Cocoa Beach, Florida jury ordered a newspaper to pay $10,000 to a woman who, after being held captive by her estranged husband, was photographed fleeing from her home naked except for a hand towel. The editor thought the published photo "best capsulized the dramatic and tragic event." Plaintiff's lawyer said it simply violated good taste. Cape Publications v. Bridges, 6 Med.L.Rptr. 1884, 387 So.2d 436 (Fla.1980).

Records of the court itself are least vulnerable to private facts suits. In spite of a Georgia statute protecting the identity of rape victims, the privacy claim of a father whose daughter was raped and murdered by six fellow high school students was rejected. A broadcast reporter got the name from a clerk of court since it was included in an official indictment record open to public inspection.

COX BROADCASTING CORP. v. COHN

420 U.S. 469, 95 S.CT. 1029, 43 L.ED.2D 328 (1975).

Justice WHITE delivered the opinion of the Court.

* * *

Georgia stoutly defends both § 26–9901 and the State's common-law privacy action challenged here. Its claims are not without force, for powerful arguments can be made, and have been made, that however it may be ultimately defined, there *is* a zone of privacy surrounding every individual, a zone within which the State may protect him from intrusion by the press, with all its attendant publicity. Indeed, the central thesis of the root article by Warren and Brandeis, "The Right To Privacy", 4 *Harv.L.Rev.* 193, 196 (1980), was that the press was overstepping its prerogatives by publishing essentially private information and that there should be a remedy for the alleged abuses.

More compellingly, the century has experienced a strong tide running in favor of the so-called right of privacy. * * * Nor is it irrelevant here that the right of privacy is no recent arrival in the jurisprudence of Georgia, which has embraced the right in some form since 1905 when the Georgia Supreme Court decided the leading case of Pavesich v. New England Life Insurance Co. * * * 50 S.E. 68 (Ga.1905).

These are impressive credentials for a right of privacy, but we should recognize that we do not have at issue here an action for the invasion of privacy involving the appropriation of one's name or photograph, a physical or other tangible intrusion into a private area, or a publication of otherwise private information that is also false although perhaps not defamatory. The version of the privacy tort now before us—termed in Georgia "the tort of public disclosure,"—is that in which the plaintiff claims the right to be free from unwanted publicity about his private affairs, which, although wholly true, would be offensive to a person of ordinary sensibilities. Because the gravamen of the claimed injury is the publication of infor-

43. Sipple v. Des Moines Register and Tribune Co., 4 Med.L.Rptr. 1041, 147 Cal.Rptr. 59 (1978).

mation, whether true or not, the dissemination of which is embarrassing or otherwise painful to an individual, it is here that claims of privacy most directly confront the constitutional freedoms of speech and press. The face-off is apparent, and the appellants urge upon us the broad holding that the press may not be made criminally or civilly liable for publishing information that is neither false nor misleading but absolutely accurate, however damaging it may be to reputation or individual sensibilities.

It is true that in defamation actions, where the protected interest is personal reputation, the prevailing view is that truth is a defense; and the message of *New York Times Co. v. Sullivan; Garrison v. Louisiana; Curtis Publishing Co. v. Butts,* and like cases is that the defense of truth is constitutionally required where the subject of the publication is a public official or public figure. What is more, the defamed public official or public figure must prove not only that the publication is false but that it was knowingly so or was circulated with reckless disregard for its truth or falsity. Similarly, where the interest at issue is privacy rather than reputation and the right claimed is to be free from the publication of false or misleading information about one's affairs, the target of the publication must prove knowing or reckless falsehood where the materials published, although assertedly private, are "matters of public interest." *Time, Inc. v. Hill.*

The Court has nevertheless carefully left open the question whether the First and Fourteenth Amendments require that truth be recognized as a defense in a defamation action brought by a private person as distinguished from a public official or public figure. [In a concurring opinion, Justice Powell disputes this interpretation of *Gertz:* "It is fair to say that if the statements are true, the standard contemplated by *Gertz* cannot be satisfied. * * * I view that opinion as requiring that the truth be recognized as a complete defense."] *Garrison* held that where criticism is of a public official and his conduct of public business, "the interest in private reputation is overborne by the larger public interest, secured by the Constitution, in the dissemination of truth," but recognized that "different interests may be involved where purely private libels, totally unrelated to public affairs, are concerned; therefore, nothing we say today is to be taken as intimating any views as to the impact of the constitutional guarantees in the discrete area of purely private libels." In similar fashion, *Time, Inc. v. Hill,* expressly saved the question whether truthful publication of very private matters unrelated to public affairs could be constitutionally proscribed.

Those precedents, as well as other considerations, counsel similar caution here. In this sphere of collision between claims of privacy and those of the free press, the interests on both sides are plainly rooted in the traditions and significant concerns of our society. Rather than address the broader question whether truthful publications may ever be subjected to civil or criminal liability consistently with the First and Fourteenth Amendments, or to put it another way, whether the State may ever define and protect an area of privacy free from unwanted publicity in the press, it is appropriate to focus on the narrower interface between press and privacy that this case presents, namely, whether the State may impose sanctions on the accurate publication of the name of a rape victim obtained from public records—more specifically, from judicial records which are maintained in connection with a public prosecution and which themselves are open to public inspection. We are convinced that the State may not do so.

In the first place, in a society in which each individual has but limited time and resources with which to observe at first hand the operations of his government, he relies necessarily upon the press to bring to him in convenient form the facts of those operations. Great responsibility is accordingly placed upon the news media to report fully and accurately the proceedings of government, and official records and documents open to the public are the basic data of governmental operations. Without the information provided by the press most of us and many of our representatives would be unable to vote intelligently or to register opinions on the administration of government generally. With respect to judicial proceedings in particular, the function of the press serves to guarantee the fairness of trials and to bring to bear the beneficial effects of public scrutiny upon the administration of justice. See Sheppard v. Maxwell, 384 U.S. 333 (1966). [This text, p. 492.]

Appellee has claimed in this litigation that the efforts of the press have infringed his right to privacy by broadcasting to the world the fact that his daughter was a rape victim. The commission of crime, prosecutions resulting from it, and judicial proceedings arising from the prosecutions, however, are without question events of legitimate concern to the public and consequently fall within the responsibility of the press to report the operations of government.

* * *

The developing law surrounding the tort of invasion of privacy recognizes a privilege in the press to report the events of judicial proceedings. The Warren and Brandeis article, *supra,* noted that the proposed new right would be limited in the same manner as actions for libel and slander where such a publication was a privileged communication: "the right to privacy is not invaded by any publication made in a court of justice * * * and (at least in many jurisdictions) reports of any such proceedings would in some measure be accorded a like privilege."

The Restatement of Torts, § 867, embraced an action for privacy. Tentative Draft No. 13 of the *Second Restatement of Torts,* §§ 652A–652E, divides the privacy tort into four branches; and with respect to the wrong of giving unwanted publicity about private life, the commentary to § 652D states: "There is no liability when the defendant merely gives further publicity to information about the plaintiff which is already public. Thus there is no liability for giving publicity to facts about the plaintiff's life which are matters of public record. * * *" The same is true of the separate tort of physically or otherwise intruding upon the seclusion or private affairs of another. Section 652B, Comment *c,* provides that "there is no liability for the examination of a public record concerning the plaintiff, or of documents which the plaintiff is required to keep and make available for public inspection." According to this draft, ascertaining and publishing the contents of public records are simply not within the reach of these kinds of privacy actions.

Thus even the prevailing law of invasion of privacy generally recognizes that the interests in privacy fade when the information involved already appears on the public record. The conclusion is compelling when viewed in terms of the First and Fourteenth Amendments and in light of the public interest in a vigorous press. The Georgia cause of action for invasion of privacy through public disclosure of the name of a rape victim imposes sanctions on pure expression—the content of a publication—and not conduct or a combination of speech and nonspeech elements that might otherwise be open to regulation or prohibition. * * *

By placing the information in the public domain on official court records, the State must be presumed to have concluded that the public interest was thereby being served. Public records by their very nature are of interest to those concerned with the administration of government, and a public benefit is performed by the reporting of the true contents of the records by the media. The freedom of the press to publish that information appears to us to be of critical importance to our type of government in which the citizenry is the final judge of the proper conduct of public business. In preserving that form of government the First and Fourteenth Amendments command nothing less than that the States may not impose sanctions on the publication of truthful information contained in official court records open to public inspection.

We are reluctant to embark on a course that would make public records generally available to the media but forbid their publication if offensive to the sensibilities of the supposed reasonable man. Such a rule would make it very difficult for the media to inform citizens about the public business and yet stay within the law. The rule would invite timidity and self-censorship and very likely lead to the suppression of many items that would otherwise be published and that should be made available to the public. At the very least, the First and Fourteenth Amendments will not allow exposing the press to liability for truthfully publishing information released to the public in official court records. If there are privacy interests to be protected in judicial proceedings, the States must respond by means which avoid public documentation or other exposure of private information. Their political institutions must weigh the interests in privacy with the interests of the public to know and of the press to publish.[26] Once true information is disclosed in public court documents open to public inspection, the press cannot be sanctioned for publishing it. In this instance as in others reliance must rest upon the judgment of those who decide what to publish or broadcast.

Appellant Wassell based his televised report upon notes taken during the court proceedings and obtained the name of the victim from the indictments handed to him at his request during a recess in the hearing. Appellee has not contended that the name was obtained in an improper fashion or that it was not on an official court document open to public inspection. Under these circumstances, the protection of freedom of the press provided by the First and Fourteenth Amendments bars the State of Georgia from making appellants' broadcast the basis of civil liability.

Reversed.

COMMENT

1. Is the difference between *Cox* where the First Amendment interest was upheld and *Firestone* where it was not that *Cox* involved the publication of accurate information while *Firestone* did not? See discussion of *Firestone,* text, pp. 239, 243. The High Court has not decided whether truth is an absolute defense.

2. Is the Court suggesting in its footnote 26 that rape trials be closed to the public so as to avoid a public record? If it is, there may be no need for such Draconian measures. In normal circumstances most newspapers will not publish the names of rape victims anyway.

But what about juveniles, drug offenders, morals violators, and all kinds of persons who may have been rehabilitated? Legislators can decide within constitutional limits, what hearings shall be closed and what records purged.

3. In the meantime, what will the Court do if a true and accurate report which invades someone's privacy comes from sources other than public records? The name of a rape victim, for example?

26. We mean to imply nothing about any constitutional questions which might arise from a state policy not allowing access by the public and press to various kinds of official records, such as records of juvenile-court proceedings.

In Campbell v. Seabury Press, 5 Med.L. Rptr. 2612, 614 F.2d 395 (5th Cir. 1980), a federal appeals court seemed to answer that question when it decided that private facts based on references to a former sister-in-law in a civil rights leader's biography were nonactionable. Citing *Cox,* the court extended the public interest or newsworthiness privilege to entirely private persons because of a "logical nexus * * * between the complaining individual and the matter of legitimate public interest." The complainant, who asserted that her virtue had been impugned, would pay for her brother-in-law's notoriety, and he, by inference, would have no private facts claim whatsoever.

In Gilbert v. Medical Economics, 7 Med.L.Rptr. 2372, 665 F.2d 305 (10th Cir. 1981), the subject of an article entitled "Who Let This Doctor in the O.R.?" found no remedy in privacy law because accurate personal facts about the doctor again were closely related to his malpractice suit.

Dresbach v. Doubleday, discussed earlier in a false light context, stretched the *Campbell* rule to the rehabilitation of a criminal and, in the process, summarized a number of important private facts cases. The case involves a book about a son who had murdered his parents twenty years earlier. Plaintiff was the rehabilitated murderer's brother who had played no role in the crime.

DRESBACH v. DOUBLEDAY

518 F.SUPP. 1285 (D.D.C.1981).

GREEN, J.

* * *

Despite the Supreme Court's requirement that not just falsity, but negligent, reckless or intentional falsity, be a defense to a defamation action, the Court has not ruled out a cause of action based upon true statements constituting an unwarranted invasion of privacy. Cox Broadcasting Corp. v. Cohn, 420 U.S. 469, 487–491 (1975); Time, Inc. v. Hill, 382–384 and n. 7; Garrison v. Louisiana, 379 U.S. 64, 70–75 and n. 9 (1964). In order to protect First Amendment values regarding such statements (which would seem more deserving of protection than the false statements which are the subject of defamation actions), the lower courts have given broad latitude to the exception applied to publications which although possibly revealing private information offensive to the ordinary person, are of public or general interest. E.g. Sidis v. F–R Publishing Corp., 113 F.2d 806, 809–810 (2d Cir. 1940), cert. den., 311 U.S. 711; Campbell v. Seabury Press, 614 F.2d 395 (5th Cir.1980). In fact it has been suggested that the exception has swallowed the rule. Kalven, *Privacy in Tort Law-Were Warren and Brandeis Wrong?* 31 Law & Contemporary Problems 326, 335–336 (1966); *Time, Inc. v. Hill,* at n. 7 and cases cited therein.

In our case, plaintiff asserts that there was no public interest in the subject matter of the Book at the time of its publication in 1980, as opposed to the time of the events described, and that the issues of public interest claimed by defendants to be explored in the Book, such as child abuse, violent youth, and the functioning of the criminal justice system, have nothing to do with plaintiff, and do not justify publication of private facts about him. Facts which plaintiff believes cast him in a bad light and are unnecessary to the stated purposes of the Book include the limited number of visits he made to his brother in jail, his "abandonment" of his brother, his failure to render financial assistance to his brother, the fact that he did not share his inheritance from his parents with his brother, and his concealment of his whereabouts from him. In addition, plaintiff objects generally to the inclusion of private facts about his childhood and his life after the murders, as well as to his appearance as a "central character" in the Book.

While plaintiff disputes the accuracy of some of these disclosures, the truth of some, such as the fact that he did not share his inheritance with his brother, is undenied. The cause of action as to true statements will be discussed first, followed by the false light aspect of the claim.

In support of the argument that the passage of time has rendered private subject matter which was admittedly at one time a legitimate subject of public interest, plaintiff cites cases holding that a cause of action may be stated where a publication identifies a rehabilitated criminal with his crime of many years past. Melvin v. Reid, 297 P. 91 (1931); Bernstein v. National Broadcasting Co., 129 F.Supp. 817 (D.D.C. 1955), affirmed 232 F.2d 369 (D.C.Cir.1956), cert. den., 352 U.S. 945; Briscoe v. Readers Digest Association, 93 Cal.Rptr. 866, 483 P.2d 34 (1971). *Melvin v. Reid* involved a movie about a woman who eight years previous had been a prostitute and was tried for murder and acquitted. She had since reformed and become a respectable member of society. Many of her present acquaintances did not know of her past. The Court found that although the republication of events in the public record was not actionable, a cause of action for invasion of privacy was stated based upon the use of plaintiff's correct maiden name in connection with unsavory incidents of her past life. A major reason for allowing such an action, in the eyes of the Court, was society's interest in the "rehabilitation of the fallen and the reformation of the criminal." Melvin v. Reid, *supra,* 297 P. at 93. In *Bernstein,* while finding no privacy cause of action on the facts of that case, the Court stated that there could be a cause of action for unreasonable public identification of a person in his present setting referring to earlier actions which took place at a time when the plaintiff was a legitimate object of public interest. *Briscoe* held that the plaintiff has a cause of action for a publication concerning his involvement in a truck hijacking incident eleven years earlier. Plaintiff alleged that he had been completely rehabilitated since, and that he had many friends, as well as a daughter, who were not previously aware of his involvement in that offense. The Court stated that truthful reports about recent crimes are privileged, as are the facts about past crimes. However, identification of the actors in long past crimes, where the actors had done nothing to reattract public attention, could be found by a jury to be without legitimate public interest and grossly offensive to the average person. The Court believed that a jury could find that the article in question concerning truck hijacking would have lost none of its value by deleting the plaintiff's name. An important factor in the decision was the State's interest in the rehabilitative process.

The State interest in the rehabilitative process was characterized as "most important" in the *Briscoe* case in a recent California Supreme Court case, Forsher v. Bugliosi, 163 Cal.Rptr. 628, 608 P.2d 716 (1980), stating that *Briscoe* was "an exception to the more general rule that 'once a man has become a public figure, or news, he remains a matter of legitimate recall to the public mind to the end of his days." Forsher, 608 P.2d at 726, quoting Prosser, *Privacy,* 48 Cal.L.Rev. 383, 418 (1960).

In our case we must decide whether true matters in the Book were matters of public interest at the time they were published, and whether the inclusion of plaintiff in connection with those matters was legitimate, or whether the countervailing interest in plaintiff's privacy concerning those matters many years after the events renders the publication actionable.

Given the generally broad public interest exception to the right of privacy action, and the fact that the few cases plaintiff has been able to cite in his favor rest strongly upon the plaintiffs' status as rehabilitated criminals, there is no doubt that for the purpose of a privacy action, the subject matter of this Book was of legitimate public interest at the time it was published. (We need not decide whether Wayne Dresbach, as a rehabilitated criminal, could have brought a privacy action concerning this Book, as he has given his consent to its publication). The public has a legitimate interest in the facts about past crimes and their investigation and prosecution, as well as the possible motivating forces in the background of the criminal. Plaintiff cannot prevail on a theory that the subject matter of the Book had become private with the passage of time. He also cannot object to republication of matters which are in the public record of the trial and related proceedings, no matter how private or offensive, as information in the public record is absolutely privileged. Cox Broadcasting Corp. v. Cohn; Harrison v. Washington Post Co., 391 A.2d 781 (D.C. 1978). Nor could the Book have been written, with its implication that the circumstances of Wayne's home life drove him to murder, without including private facts about plaintiff's home life, which obviously was intimately bound up with his brother's. This is even more true here than in the usual case of brothers growing up in the same home, since much of the friction between Wayne and his parents concerned their unfavorable comparison of him with Lee.

Plaintiff's relationship with his brother after the murders and plaintiff's own subsequent history are less obviously integral to the subject matter of the Book. However, we tread on dangerous ground deciding exactly what matters are sufficiently relevant to a subject of legitimate public interest to be privileged. First Amendment values could obviously be threatened by the uncertainty such decisions could create for writers and publishers. "Only in cases of flagrant breach of privacy which has not been waived or obvious exploitation of public curiosity where no legitimate public interest exists should a court substitute its judgment for that of the publisher." Cantrell v. Forest City Publishing Co., 484 F.2d 150 (6th Cir. 1973), reversed on other grounds, 419 U.S. 245 (1974). This is not such a case. The subject matter of Wayne's rehabilitation after his murder conviction, focusing both on prison conditions and the support or lack thereof he received from friends and family, cannot be said to be without legitimate public interest, and facts about Wayne's relationship with his brother are clearly related to that subject. In Campbell v. Seabury Press, 614 F.2d 395 (5th Cir. 1980), the plaintiff was found not to have a cause of action for invasion of privacy for the disclosure of private facts regarding her marriage and home life. The book in question was the autobiography of a man whose brother, plaintiff's former husband, was a religious and civil rights leader. The challenged disclosures were included in the context of plaintiff's relationship with the brother and the impact of that relationship upon the author. The Court held that there is a constitutional privilege to publish news or other matters of public interest, and that the privilege "extends to information concerning interesting phases of human activity and embraces all issues about which information is needed or appropriate so that individuals may cope with the exigencies of their period. * * * [The privilege applies even to] information relating to individuals who have not sought or have attempted to avoid publicity. * * * The privacy of such individuals is protected, however, by requiring that a logical nexus exist between the complaining individual and the matter of legitimate public interest." *Id.* at 397. The Court found that the accounts of the brother's marriage as they impacted upon the author had the requisite logical nexus to fall within the ambit of constitutional protection. Although this Court might not go as far as the *Campbell* court in extinguishing the right to privacy, clearly here, where the important public issues of crime, the criminal justice system, and rehabilitation are concerned, the defendants have shown an adequate nexus between matters of legitimate public interest and the disclosures about the plaintiff to merit constitutional protection.

We are not without compassion for Lee Dresbach's plight. The exercise of defendants' First Amendment rights has imposed a heavy burden upon plaintiff. It is easy to sympathize with his objection to the Book having been written at all, and certainly to his inclusion in it. In his own words in response to the question, "What else do you find objectionable?", he replied, "Me being in the book at all. I asked not to be in the book. I have a right to my own privacy. I can go probably weeks without thinking about seeing two people murdered. Every day since then all I do is think about it." * * * Additionally, a great deal of very sensitive information about plaintiff's past which he has chosen to keep secret is now available to friends, employers, customers, his wife, and in-laws. Yet, there is no doubt that a cause of action based upon truthful material in the Book cannot be permitted consistent with the First Amendment. Clearly, this society has put a higher value on open criminal proceedings and on public discussion of all issues than on the individual's right to privacy. To guard against the possible evils of abuse of power if the criminal justice system were to operate away from the public eye, and of suppression of freedom of thought if writers could not freely explore the causes and handling of past crimes of public interest, the plaintiff's right to bury the past must be sacrificed. Freedom of speech would be crippled if discussions of matters of public interest were narrowly circumscribed in the manner suggested by plaintiff to protect privacy. Summary judgment must be granted in favor of both defendants on plaintiff's privacy claim as to accurate material in the Book.

A cause of action may be stated for a false light invasion of privacy even where the subject matter is of legitimate public interest. * * * Insofar as plaintiff can point to specific passages of the Book which are alleged to be inaccurate, placing him in a false light before the public, which are an offensive invasion of his privacy, and which were written without the exercise of ordinary care to determine their accuracy, a jury issue is created. However, plaintiff has not clearly delineated in his pleadings what portions of the Book he claims meet these requirements. In his deposition testimony, he appears to concede the substantial accuracy of the statements concerning his inheritance, the frequency of his visits to his brother in prison, and his failure to inform his brother of his whereabouts. He does deny the accuracy of some of the incidents described in the Book, such as that regarding Wayne's efforts to borrow money from him to fix his teeth, * * *, and that concerning the will plaintiff made before leaving for Viet Nam, in which according to the Book, he left his brother $5.00. * * * He also denied generally that he was abused by his parents as described in the Book, * * *, and states to the contrary that his father treated him kindly. * * * In order to withstand the motion for summary judgment, plaintiff must make a further submission to the Court delineating precisely which passages in the Book are alleged to invade plaintiff's privacy and place him in a false light, including the manner in which they are claimed to be inaccurate.

* * *

COMMENT

1. Another dimension of the newsworthiness rule, implied in *Sidis* and applied in *Dresbach,* is once a public figure always a public figure, in spite of the Supreme Court's reasoning in *Wolston v. Reader's Digest Association, Inc.* (this text, p. 249) that a public figure's status could dissipate over time. The retention of a newsworthy

image will, it seems, depend upon the significance of the public facts with which the individual was involved. "The public has a legitimate interest in the facts about past crimes and their investigation and prosecution," said the D.C. Circuit Court in *Dresbach,* "as well as the possible motivating forces in the background of the criminal."

In noncriminal cases of notoriety the rule is not as clear and caution is advised, although the Fifth Circuit in *Campbell v. Seabury Press* did note that the privilege to publish news or other matters of public interest "extends to information concerning interesting phases of human activity and embraces all issues about which information is needed or appropriate so that individuals may cope with the exigencies of their period. * * *"

2. As shall be noted in the section on the intrusion category of invasion of privacy, it does make a difference how information is obtained. In Smith v. Daily Mail Publishing Co., 443 U.S. 97 (1979), the Supreme Court said, "[I]f a newspaper lawfully obtains truthful information about a matter of public significance, then state officials may not constitutionally punish publication of the information, absent a need to further a state interest of the highest order." In the cases discussed so far, information was obtained openly.[44]

3. The question that remains only partially answered is what does it take today to outrage a community's sense of decency. Have our sensitivities toward personal privacy diminished? We do know what has outraged some communities and their judicial systems in the past. For example, a woman's disfigured face photographed without her consent while she was semiconscious,[45] a published photograph of an employee's mangled thigh,[46] a photograph of a woman with her skirt blown over her head as she entered a county fair "fun house," [47] and a newspaper piece which contained the words, "Wanna hear a sexy telephone voice? Call * * * and ask for Louise." [48] In the latter case, the court compared the objectionable language of the newspaper with that commonly found on the walls of public lavatories.

Shocking also to the judicial temperament, if not to community mores, was the picture in *Time* magazine of a hospital patient who was photographed against her will, while her attention was diverted, and presented to the world as the "starving glutton," "Insatiable-Eater Barbara," who "eats for ten." Due apparently to a pancreas disorder, the more she ate the more weight she lost.

"Certainly if there is any right of privacy at all," said the Supreme Court of Missouri, "it should include the right to obtain medical treatment at home or in a hospital for an individual personal condition (at least if it is not contagious or dangerous to others) without personal publicity. To enable a physician to treat his patient to advantage, it is often necessary that the patient communicate information which it would be both embarrassing and harmful to have circulated generally through the

44. For example, *Cox Broadcasting v. Cohn* and *Howard v. Des Moines Register.* See also Ayers v. Lee Enterprises, 2 Med.L.Rptr. 1698, 561 P.2d 998 (Or.1977), McCormack v. Oklahoma Publishing, 613 P.2d 737 (Okl.1980), and Ross v. Burns, 5 Med.L.Rptr. 2277, 612 F.2d 271 (6th Cir. 1980). In Griffith v. Rancocas Valley Hospital, 8 Med.L.Rptr. 1760 (1982), a New Jersey court held that publication of the name and address of a sexual assault victim, obtained from police and hospital sources despite victim's request that the information not be released, was not an invasion of privacy. The court relied on *Smith v. Daily Mail* which involved the naming of a juvenile murder suspect.

45. Clayman v. Bernstein, 38 D & C 543 (Pa.1940).

46. Lambert v. Dow Chemical Co., 215 So.2d 673 (La.1968).

47. Daily Times Democrat v. Graham, 162 So.2d 474 (Ala.1964).

48. Harms v. Miami Daily News, Inc., 127 So.2d 715 (Fla.1961).

community." At least her name and photograph could have been omitted from the report. Barber v. Time, Inc., 159 S.W.2d 291 (Mo.1942).

Any iota of voluntariness would seem to invoke the defense of newsworthiness. A news report identifying a twelve-year-old mother, despite her objections, was protected.[49] So was a news review ridiculing an inventor's invention,[50] and a photograph of corpulent women exercising in a gymnasium.[51] A group of young Americans who allowed themselves to be interviewed and photographed living in a communal cave in Crete had no privacy claim.[52] Neither did a casino customer who got caught in a photograph which was later used to dress up an article on gambling and organized crime.[53] The Boston "Strangler's" notoriety and the fact that he had consented to a film portrayal of his life, and had even offered technical advice to the film maker, left him without a privacy claim.[54] A Pennsylvania court held that public figures have no exclusive right to their own biographies and could not claim an invasion of privacy when their life stories were published.[55]

Nathan Leopold was unable to protect his privacy from invasion by a book and motion picture, the fictionalized aspects of which were reasonably true to the record in the celebrated Leopold and Loeb murder case of many years before. Leopold had pleaded guilty, had served a life sentence, and his participation in the murder of Bobby Franks was a matter of public and historical interest, said an Illinois court, even though the plaintiff had since become a useful citizen.[56]

When the photograph of a plaintiff attempting to dissuade a young woman from committing suicide by jumping off a bridge was used two years later, with plaintiff's name, in an article on different forms of suicide, a federal district court in California said the picture was newsworthy and privileged when first published, and the passage of time would not destroy that privilege.[57]

4. Embarrassing facts or public disclosure cases will continue to require a sensitive balancing by the media of competing rights—if not by legal means, then by ethical standards. The courts are especially weak in theory in this area of the law. And if truth is recognized as a defense in this category of privacy, the tort, as Kalven observed, will simply disappear, and any truthful publication will be deemed newsworthy.

Where can a line be drawn between legitimate news and the public's seemingly insatiable appetite for sensational intimacies? Should a line be drawn at all? And, if so, by whom? These questions must await further academic analysis, legislative determination, and case law. In the meantime, there will continue to be uneasiness here, as in other areas of media law, in permitting community norms to determine the application of the broad constitutional principles of freedom of speech and press or to define the boundaries of one's innermost private life.

49. Meetze v. Associated Press, 95 S.E.2d 606 (S.C.1956).

50. Thompson v. Curtis Publishing Co., 193 F.2d 953 (3d Cir. 1952).

51. Sweenek v. Pathe News, 16 F.Supp. 746 (D.N.Y.1936).

52. Goldman v. Time, Inc., 336 F.Supp. 133 (D.Cal.1971).

53. Holmes v. Curtis Publishing Co., 303 F.Supp. 522 (D.S.C.1969).

54. DeSalvo v. Twentieth Century-Fox Film Corp., 300 F.Supp. 742 (D.Mass.1969).

55. Corabi v. Curtis Publishing Co., 273 A.2d 899 (Pa.1971).

56. Leopold v. Levin, 259 N.E.2d 250 (Ill.1970).

57. Samuel v. Curtis Publishing Co., 122 F.Supp. 327 (D.Calif.1954).

INTRUSION: A NEWS–GATHERING OFFENSE

Intrusion upon one's solitude or seclusion is an invasion of privacy likely to occur while news is being gathered but may not result in a lawsuit until the news is published, although publication is not essential to the tort. Surveillance and trespass are forms of intrusion. The *Restatement* includes them both plus a third category.[58] And intrusion may overlap other categories of privacy. In the "Starving Glutton" case, for example, Ms. Barber was photographed against her will in her hospital bed while she was momentarily distracted but her suit was for public disclosure of embarrassing private facts.

Surveillance

A clear case of intrusion occurred when a *Life* magazine reporter and photographer gained access to a "healer's" home by pretending to be the friends of a friend, then surreptitiously took pictures and relayed tape recordings to law enforcement officials waiting outside while the subject of their investigation examined one of them for breast cancer.

Since the district attorney's office and the state department of health were in on the ruse, although they were not totally dependent upon *Life*'s evidence, it did seem that the magazine was acting as an agent of law enforcement.

The "healer," who specialized in clay, minerals, herbs, and gadgetry, was subsequently arrested and charged with practicing medicine without a license. He pleaded *nolo contendere* and was cited for a number of misdemeanors. The basis of a subsequent privacy suit was *Life*'s illustrated article entitled "Crackdown on Quackery."

A federal district court awarded the plaintiff $1,000 for an invasion of his privacy, and *Life* appealed. The judgment was affirmed by a federal appeals court.

DIETEMANN v. TIME, INC.

449 F.2D 245 (9TH CIR. 1971).

HUFSTEDLER, Circuit Judge:

* * *

In jurisdictions other than California in which a common law tort for invasion of privacy is recognized, it has been consistently held that surreptitious electronic recording of a plaintiff's conversation causing him emotional distress is actionable. Despite some variations in the description and the labels applied to the tort, there is agreement that publication is not a necessary element of the tort, that the existence of a technical trespass is immaterial, and that proof of special damages is not required.

Although the issue has not been squarely decided in California, we have little difficulty in concluding that clandestine photography of the plaintiff in his den and the recordation and transmission of his conversation without his consent resulting in his emotional distress warrants recovery for invasion of privacy in California. * * *

Concurrently, with the development of privacy law, California had decided a series of cases according plaintiffs relief from unreasonable penetrations of their mental tranquility based upon the tort of intentional infliction of emotional distress. [Citations omitted.] Although these cases are not direct authority in the privacy

---

58. One who intentionally intrudes, physically or otherwise, upon the solitude or seclusion of another or his private affairs or concerns, is subject to liability to the other for invasion of his privacy, if the intrusion would be highly offensive to a reasonable person. (a) surreptitious surveillance, (b) trespass, (c) consent to enter secluded setting has been exceeded. *Restatement (Second) of Torts* § 652B.

area, they are indicative of the trend of California law to protect interests analogous to those asserted by plaintiff in this case.

We are convinced that California will "approve the extension of the tort of invasion of privacy to instances of intrusion, whether by physical trespass or not, into spheres from which an ordinary man in plaintiff's position could reasonably expect that the particular defendant should be excluded." (Pearson v. Dodd, 410 F.2d at 704.)

Plaintiff's den was a sphere from which he could reasonably expect to exclude eavesdropping newsmen. He invited two of defendant's employees to the den. One who invites another to his home or office takes a risk that the visitor may not be what he seems, and that the visitor may repeat all he hears and observes when he leaves. But he does not and should not be required to take the risk that what is heard and seen will be transmitted by photograph or recording, or in our modern world, in full living color and hi-fi to the public at large or to any segment of it that the visitor may select. A different rule could have a most pernicious effect upon the dignity of man and it would surely lead to guarded conversations and conduct where candor is most valued, e.g., in the case of doctors and lawyers.

The defendant claims that the First Amendment immunizes it from liability for invading plaintiff's den with a hidden camera and its concealed electronic instruments because its employees were gathering news and its instrumentalities "are indispensable tools of investigative reporting." We agree that newsgathering is an integral part of news dissemination. We strongly disagree, however, that the hidden mechanical contrivances are "indispensable tools" of newsgathering. Investigative reporting is an ancient art; its successful practice long antecedes the invention of miniature cameras and electronic devices. *The First Amendment has never been construed to accord newsmen immunity from torts or crimes committed during the course of newsgathering.* [Emphasis added.] The First Amendment is not a license to trespass, to steal, or to intrude by electronic means into the precincts of another's home or office. It does not become such a license simply because the person subjected to the intrusion is reasonably suspected of committing a crime.

Defendant relies upon the line of cases commencing with *New York Times Co. v. Sullivan* and extending through *Rosenbloom v. Metromedia, Inc.* to sustain its contentions that (1) publication of news, however tortiously gathered, insulates defendant from liability for the antecedent tort, and (2) even if it is not thus shielded from liability, those cases prevent consideration of publication as an element in computing damages.

As we previously observed, publication is not an essential element of plaintiff's cause of action. Moreover, it is not the foundation for the invocation of a privilege. Privilege concepts developed in defamation cases and to some extent in privacy actions in which publication is an essential component are not relevant in determining liability for intrusive conduct antedating publication. Nothing in *New York Times* or its progeny suggests anything to the contrary. Indeed, the Court strongly indicates that there is no First Amendment interest in protecting news media from calculated misdeeds. (E.g., Time, Inc. v. Hill, 385 U.S. at 389–390 and 384 n. 9.) [1]

No interest protected by the First Amendment is adversely affected by permitting damages for intrusion to be en-

1. "Nor do we intimate," said Justice Brennan in footnote 9, "any view whether the Constitution limits state power to sanction publication of matter obtained by an intrusion into a protected area, for example, through use of electronic listening devices."

hanced by the fact of later publication of the information that the publisher improperly acquired. Assessing damages for the additional emotional distress suffered by a plaintiff when the wrongfully acquired data are purveyed to the multitude chills intrusive acts. It does not chill freedom of expression guaranteed by the First Amendment. A rule forbidding the use of publication as an ingredient of damages would deny to the injured plaintiff recovery for real harm done to him without any countervailing benefit to the legitimate interest of the public in being informed. The same rule would encourage conduct by news media that grossly offends ordinary men.

The judgment is affirmed.

COMMENT

Dietemann illustrates that in actions for intrusive invasions of privacy a First Amendment defense is very weak. The court failed to consider the news value of the publication itself. Seldom is intrusion as clear-cut as it was when *Life* photographed and "bugged" the about-to-be-convicted quack. What if the plaintiff is a very public person, a celebrity, or a government official suspected of corruption?

The first part of the question was addressed by federal courts in New York in an incredible case involving a peripatetic photographer, said to be America's only *paparazzo,* and Jacqueline Kennedy Onassis. Ronald Galella, a free lance, made a modest living photographing celebrities. But his specialty was Mrs. Onassis. His strategy was aggressive pursuit, described by Jackie as a continual stalking of her, popping up everywhere while emitting a curious "grunting" sound which, she said, terrified her.

Galella argued that his subject was simply a camera-shy and uncooperative public person. When she asked the Secret Service and other police officers to intervene on her behalf, the photographer, claiming that he had been roughed up, brought a $1.3 million damage suit and a plea for an injunction against interference with his making a living. Mrs. Onassis then filed a counterclaim for $1.5 million in compensatory and punitive damages and for injunctive relief. The United States joined her to seek injunctive relief against Galella's interference with the activities of Secret Service agents assigned to protect the former first lady and her children.

The two cases were joined, and a federal district court held that the photographer's antics were not protected by the First Amendment but constituted actionable assault, battery, and harassment, violation of the civil rights statute, and tortious infliction of emotional distress. Both Mrs. Onassis and the government were granted injunctive relief in a ruling in which the court expressed enormous distaste for Galella and rejected his claim along with what it called his perjured testimony. A portion of the ruling follows.

GALELLA v. ONASSIS

353 F.SUPP. 196 (S.D.N.Y.1972).

COOPER, District Judge:

* * * [T]wenty further episodes are summarized in our supplemental findings of fact. These include instances where the children were caused to bang into glass doors, school parents were bumped, passage was blocked, flashbulbs affected vision, telephoto lenses were used to spy, the children were imperilled in the water, a funeral was disturbed, plaintiff pursued defendant into the lobby of a friend's apartment building, plaintiff trailed defendant through the City hour after hour, plaintiff chased defendant by automobile, plaintiff and his assistants surrounded defendant and orbited while shouting, plaintiff snooped into purchases of stockings and shoes, flashbulbs were suddenly fired on lonely black nights—all accompanied

by Galella jumping, shouting and acting wildly. Many of these instances were repeated time after time; all preceded our restraining orders.

He was like a shadow: everywhere she went he followed her and engaged in offensive conduct; nothing was sacred to him whether defendant went to church, funeral services, theatre, school, restaurant, or board a yacht in a foreign land. While plaintiff denied so deporting himself, his admissions clearly spell out his harassment of her and her children.

* * *

Mrs. Onassis' severe emotional distress is evident and reasonable.

When Galella rushed her limousine on September 21, 1969, she was terrified. Galella's pursuit of her and the children at the horse show in Gladstone, New Jersey, caused her concern and anxiety for fear that his activities would frighten the horse and thereby endanger her children. Galella's sudden appearance behind bursting flash bulbs at 2 o'clock in the morning at Oliver Smith's house in Brooklyn Heights stunned and startled her. When Galella crashed about in the tunnel beneath Lincoln Center and tried to push his way through a revolving door with Mrs. Onassis and her children she was frightened that someone would be injured in the door. Galella's antics in the theatre at *40 Carats* so upset Mrs. Onassis that she covered her face with *Playbill.* When Galella cruised around Mrs. Onassis in a power boat as she was swimming off Ischia, he was so close that she was afraid she would be cut by the propeller. Galella's dogging of Mrs. Onassis' footsteps throughout her shopping trip in Capri left her terrified and upset. Galella's taxicab chase with Joyce Smith on October 7, 1971 left Mrs. Onassis a "wreck."

When Galella suddenly jumped from behind the wall in Central Park, frightening John and causing him to lose control of his bicycle, Mrs. Onassis described her state of mind as having been "terrorized." The Santa Claus pursuit in and around the Collegiate School in December 1970 left Mrs. Onassis extremely upset. Galella's outrageous pursuit of Mrs. Onassis on the night of *Two Gentlemen of Verona* terrified her and left her in an "anguished," "humiliated" and "terribly upset" state. Numerous times, and at dangerous speeds, he has followed cars in which the children were passengers, violating the rules of the road, and the Secret Service agents assigned to protect the children have frequently expressed concern for the safety of their principals as a result of Galella's activities.

Additionally, Mrs. Onassis and her children are people who have a very special fear of startling movements, violent activity, crowds and other hostile behavior. It is clear that the assassinations of the first husband of Mrs. Onassis and of her brother-in-law (Senator Robert F. Kennedy) are matters of common knowledge to virtually every citizen. These matters were certainly known to Galella who "specializes" in the affairs of Mrs. Onassis and who chronicled her brother-in-law's funeral. These events make Mrs. Onassis and her children particularly susceptible to Galella's erratic behavior and make his acts all the more outrageous and utterly devoid of any sensitivity whatever for his subjects.

* * *

The proposition that the First Amendment gives the press wide liberty to engage in any sort of conduct, no matter how offensive, in gathering news has been flatly rejected.

* * *

We conclude that the First Amendment does not license Galella to trespass inside private buildings, such as the children's schools, lobbies of friends' apartment buildings and restaurants. Nor does that Amendment command that Galella be permitted to romance maids, bribe employees and maintain surveillance in order to monitor defendant's leaving, entering and living inside her own home.

* * *

In any event, we said at trial, and now repeat, that she is a public figure. Nevertheless, the First Amendment does not immunize all conduct designed to gather information about or photographs of a public figure. There is no general constitutional right to assault, harass, or unceasingly shadow or distress public figures.

* * *

Invasion of privacy. Plaintiff's endless snooping constitutes tortious invasion of privacy.

We venture to suggest that faced with a factual situation comparable to the distressing one before us, with a torrent of almost unrelieved abuse into the privacy of every day activity, the New York Court of Appeals would complete the mission it has already begun of determining what should be actionable under the developing common law right of privacy. Nader v. General Motors Corp., * * * 307 N.Y. S.2d 647, 255 N.E.2d 765 (1970), in which the Court applied District of Columbia law.

First let us reconsider plaintiff's close-shadowing of defendant. Continuously he has had her under surveillance to the point where he is notified of her every movement. He waits outside her residence at all hours. He follows her about irrespective of what she is doing: trailing her up and down the streets of New York, chasing her out of the city to neighboring places and foreign countries when she leaves for recreation or vacation, haunting her at restaurants (recording what she eats), theatres, the opera and other places of entertainment, and pursuing her when she goes shopping, getting close to her at the counter and inquiring of personnel as to her clothing purchases. His surveillance is so overwhelmingly pervasive that he has said he has not married because he has been unable to "get a girl who would be willing to go looking for Mrs. Onassis at odd hours."

He studies her habits, the operations of her household and the procedures of the Secret Service in guarding her children. He has kept her under such close observation for so long a period of time that he has commented at considerable length on her personality, her shopping tastes and habits, and her preferences for entertainment. With evident satisfaction, he referred, while testifying, to his "usual habitual observation." He has intruded into her children's schools, hidden in bushes and behind coat racks in restaurants, sneaked into beauty salons, bribed doormen, hatcheck girls, chauffeurs, fishermen in Greece, hairdressers and schoolboys, and romanced employees. In short, Galella has insinuated himself into the very fabric of Mrs. Onassis' life and the challenge to this Court is to fashion the tool to get him out.

We return now to *Nader.* The Court there sustained the sufficiency of allegations to the effect that plaintiff's "right of privacy" under District of Columbia law had been violated by defendant's activities which consisted of surveillance, shadowing, eavesdropping, and others not here relevant.

Chief Judge Fuld, for the Court, wrote:

> There are * * * allegations that the appellant hired people to shadow the plaintiff and keep him under surveillance. In particular, he claims that, on one occasion, one of its agents followed him into a bank, getting sufficiently close to him to see the denomination of the bills he was withdrawing from his account. From what we have already said, it is manifest that the mere observation of the plaintiff in a public place does not amount to an invasion of his privacy. But, under certain circumstances, surveillance may be so "overzealous" as to render it actionable. * * * A person does not

automatically make public everything he does merely by being in a public place, and the mere fact that Nader was in a bank did not give anyone the right to try to discover the amount of money he was withdrawing.

* * *

As we see it, Galella's conduct falls within the formulation of the right of privacy as expressed in the opinion. The surveillance, close-shadowing and monitoring were clearly "overzealous" and therefore actionable. Moreover, Galella's corruption of doormen, romancing of the personal maid, deceptive intrusions into children's schools, and return visits to restaurants and stores to inquire about purchases were all exclusively for the "purpose of gathering information of a private and confidential nature" which Judge Fuld found to be actionable.

Does the law of New York differ from the law of the District of Columbia as declared by New York's highest court? The dictum in Roberson v. Rochester Folding-Box Co., * * * 64 N.E. 442 (1902), does not support the conclusion that invasion of privacy is not actionable under New York law. * * * *Roberson* involved the commercial appropriation of a likeness, which, Dean Prosser teaches has "almost nothing in common" with intrusion, the gravamen of the case at bar.

* * *

Since the *Roberson* dictum was enunciated, freedom from extensive shadowing and observation has come to be protected in most other jurisdictions.

* * *

The essence of the privacy interest includes a general "right to be left alone," and to define one's circle of intimacy; to shield intimate and personal characteristics and activities from public gaze; to have moments of freedom from the unremitted assault of the world and unfettered will of others in order to achieve some measure of tranquility for contemplation or other purposes, without which life loses its sweetness. The rationale extends to protect against unreasonably intrusive behavior which attempts or succeeds in gathering information, and includes, but is not limited to, such disparate abuses of privacy as the unreasonable seeking, gathering, storing, sharing and disseminating of information by humans and machines.

It has been cogently suggested that the right to privacy proscribes dehumanizing conduct which assaults, "liberty, personality and self-respect." Fried, Privacy, 77 *Yale L.J.* 475, 485 (1960).

* * *

COMMENT

Galella and his agents were enjoined by the district court from approaching within 300 feet of the Onassis and Kennedy homes and the schools attended by the children; they were also required to remain 225 feet from the children and 150 feet from Mrs. Onassis at all other locations. Galella was also prohibited from putting the family under surveillance or trying to communicate with them.

The Court of Appeals for the Second Circuit essentially upheld the lower court decision, noting that the First Amendment does not set up a wall of immunity to protect newsmen from any liability for their conduct while gathering news. Crimes and torts committed in news gathering, said the court, are not protected, and it cited *Branzburg v. Hayes* (this text, p. 379), *Rosenbloom v. Metromedia*, and *Dietemann v. Time, Inc.*

The appeals court did something else. It sharply scaled down the distances Galella was to keep from Mrs. Onassis and her children. It reduced from 150 to 25 feet the distance the photographer must put between himself and Mrs. Onassis; from 225 to 30 feet the distance he must stay from Caroline and John; and it lifted the restriction on Mrs. Onassis's Fifth Avenue home. Galella v. Onassis, 487 F.2d 986 (2d Cir. 1973).

The court of appeals ruling essentially put Galella back in business. But it wasn't until 1982 that the original New York federal district court, more impatient with Galella than ever, held that the photographer's flagrant, deliberate, and persistent violations of federal court orders restricting coverage of Jacqueline Onassis and her children constituted a contempt of court. He had violated the courts' orders on distance-from-subject at least twelve times. Galella v. Onassis, 8 Med.L.Rptr. 1321, 533 F.Supp. 1076, (D.N.Y.1982). The agglutinate Galella had earlier promised a federal district judge following a harassment complaint, never again to take pictures of Onassis or her children "as long as you draw breath." This time Galella would pay his subject $10,000.

Trespass

1. An action for a trespass form of invasion of privacy and for wrongful intentional infliction of emotional distress was brought against Florida news media by a mother whose daughter died in a fire in her home. So badly was she burned that, after removal of the body, a silhouette of her body remained on a bedroom floor. The mother learned of the tragedy by reading a news story and seeing a picture of the silhouette in the *Florida Times-Union*.

Lower courts refused to grant summary judgment to the newspaper's publisher on the trespass count. On appeal the Florida Supreme Court held that where there was an *implied consent by custom and usage* authorizing a news photographer to accompany police and fire marshals into a home, there was no trespass. In fact a fire marshal had requested that the photographer take the "silhouette" picture for his official file.

Television networks, newspapers, wire services, and professional organizations had provided the court with affidavits attesting to the common practice of reporters accompanying officials into homes where there has been crime or tragedy. The court agreed that "as a matter of law an entry, that may otherwise be an actionable trespass, becomes lawful and non-actionable when it is done under common usage, custom and practice."

The court's opinion can be read to imply that had the plaintiff been present and objected to the photographer's entry, she would have had a stronger case. Florida Publishing Co. v. Fletcher, 340 So.2d 914 (Fla.1976), cert. den. 431 U.S. 930 (1977). But see, Prahl v. Brosamle, 295 N.W.2d 768 (Wis.1980).

Support for that conclusion is contained in the holding of a New York trial court that the First Amendment right to gather news did not authorize television reporters and photographers to enter a private home without the consent of the homeowner, even though entry was at the invitation of a humane society investigator who was executing a search warrant. Anderson v. WROC-TV, 7 Med.L.Rptr. 1987, 441 N.Y.S.2d 220 (1981).

Reporters and photographers who entered "Son of Sam's" apartment after his arrest on suspicion of murder were not guilty of criminal trespass, said a New York city court. Although police had earlier entered the apartment with a warrant, they had no "possessory interest." Only Berkowitz himself, or the apartment owner, could have withheld consent from the newsmen. Police, however, could have excluded persons from the premises while a lawful criminal search was being conducted. People v. Berliner, 3 Med.L.Rptr. 1942 (N.Y.City Ct.1978).

2. CBS News was less fortunate when one of its reporters and a camera crew "with cameras rolling" entered a posh French restaurant, Le Mistral, as a follow-up to a New York City Health Service Administra-

tion press release alleging health code violations at several city restaurants. Le Mistral sued for defamation and trespass following a WCBS-TV news report which included film clips of the restaurant's staff attempting to eject the CBS crew.

The trial court judge dismissed the defamation suit on "fair comment" grounds but granted a trial on the trespass count since, he said, "the right to publish does not include the right to break and enter upon and trespass upon the property of these plaintiffs." A year later a jury awarded Le Mistral $250,000 in punitive and $1,200 in compensatory damages for trespass. On CBS's motion the trial court upheld the trespass verdict but set aside the damage awards. "Patronizing a restaurant," said the court, "does not carry with it an obligation to appear on television.

In March 1978 an appeals court reinstated the compensatory damages and directed a new trial solely on the issue of punitive damages. Under New York law, punitive or exemplary damages require a showing of malice (evil or wrongful motive). CBS, the court added, is entitled to explain its motive. One judge, dissenting in part, thought CBS overly aggressive but not malicious in pursuing the story. Le Mistral, Inc. v. CBS, 3 Med.L.Rptr. 1913, 402 N.Y.S.2d 815 (N.Y.1978).

Le Mistral falls somewhere between the news-gathering offenses complained of in *Dietemann* and *Fletcher*.

Should the First Amendment limit liability by media defendants in these circumstances as it does in the law of privacy and the law of libel? Why or why not?

3. A more dramatic form of trespass referred to earlier—that is, where the plaintiff is a public official suspected of corruption—arose in a case involving columnist Drew Pearson and Senator Thomas Dodd. A number of significant questions came into focus in the case.

What is the journalist's liability when he or she receives information "lifted" from the files of a public official? Is receiving information taken without authorization from government files the equivalent of receiving stolen property? In short, how far can the right to gather news be extended?

In the *Pentagon Papers* case, Justices White and Stewart underlined the power of Congress to enact specific criminal laws to protect government property. Justice Marshall also recognized the power of Congress to make criminal the receipt or purchase of certain classifications of official documents. Chief Justice Burger and Justice Blackmun agreed with White that penal sanctions were an appropriate way of protecting government secrets. See text, p. 110ff. In general, the government cannot protect its records by copyright, although it has tried.[59]

In the *Dodd* case, four former employees removed documents from the Senator's office, gave photostats to Drew Pearson and his associate Jack Anderson, then returned the originals to the files. Stories appeared based on the documents, and Dodd sued for libel. A United States district court, invoking the *New York Times* rule, disallowed the libel action.

Dodd's lawyers came back with an invasion of privacy plea and an inventive argument based on the common law tort of trover and conversion—"an unauthorized assumption and exercise of the right of ownership over goods or personal chattels belonging to another, to the alteration of their condition or the exclusion of an owner's rights." [60]

Because of the public interest inherent in the documents, the privacy claim was rejected; but the court granted partial summary judgment to Senator Dodd on the

59. Schnapper, *Constraint By Copyright* (1960).

60. *Corpus Juris Secundum*, Trover and Conversion, § 1, p. 531.

theory of conversion. A portion of the district court opinion follows.

DODD v. PEARSON

279 F.SUPP. 101 (D.D.C.1968) AFF'D IN PART REV'D IN PART 410 F.2D 701.

HOLTZOFF, District Judge. * * *

On the uncontroverted facts, the individuals who without authority entered the plaintiff's office, rifled his files, removed documents and made copies of them, which they turned over to the defendants, would be liable for damages in trespass and conversion. They are not being sued. It is well settled, however, that a person who receives and uses the property of another that has been wrongfully obtained, knowing that it was so obtained, is likewise guilty of conversion and liable for damages. * * *

It would be a work of supererogation to multiply authorities for this proposition of law, which is almost elementary. It is clear, therefore, that on the undisputed facts, the defendants are liable to the plaintiff for damages on the theory of conversion. The mere fact that the defendants received copies of the documents from the trespassers who purloined the originals, instead of the originals themselves, is, of course, immaterial. What the measure of damages should be and whether substantial damages may be recovered under the circumstances, is a matter to be determined at a later stage of this litigation.

Plaintiff's counsel advance an additional alternative theory on which they seek to predicate the plaintiff's right to recover, namely, violation of the right of privacy. The right of privacy has been developed and has gradually gained recognition in the law of torts since the turn of the century. This Court in Peay v. Curtis Pub. Co., D.C., 78 F.Supp. 305, held that it formed a part of the law of the District of Columbia. As this Court stated in the Peay case, the right of privacy has been broadly described as "the right to be let alone." The publication of a photograph of a private individual without his sanction, or depicting events in his personal life that are of no public interest, are illustrative violations of the right of privacy. It is a right to keep the noiseless tenor of one's way along the cool sequestered vale of life without intrusion on the part of the public. There are those who shun publicity and who deplore and even resent any attempt to cast a public gaze on any aspect of their personal life. The law respects this attitude and lends sanction to it by way of an action for damages for its infringement. There are, however, important limitations on the right of privacy. It does not extend to matters of public interest, or to persons properly in the public eye, at least as to matters other than features of their intimate life, Bernstein v. NBC, 129 F.Supp. 817, 828, affirmed * * * 232 F.2d 369.

* * *

The Court concludes that the publication of the material of which the plaintiff complains is not protected by the cloak of the right of privacy, because the publications relate to his activities as a high-ranking public officer, namely, Senator of the United States, in which the public has an interest.

It follows hence that the plaintiff is entitled to recover damages in this case, but only on the theory of a conversion and not on the theory of a violation of a right of privacy. The distinction is not purely theoretical, as a more liberal, flexible and broad measure of damages may perhaps be applicable to actions for invasion of privacy, than govern actions for conversion. * * * In this instance, apparently the plaintiff seeks to recover damages for injury to reputation, personal embarrassment and mental anguish. Whether recovery of such damages may be had in an action for conversion and, in fact, whether on the facts of this case the plaintiff may recover substantial damages at all, must be left for determination at the trial. * *

COMMENT

1. Shouldn't the same First Amendment considerations which made it almost impossible for Dodd to recover from Pearson on either the tort of libel or the tort of invasion of right of privacy make it equally difficult for Dodd to recover from Pearson on a theory of conversion? What, if anything, is there about a conversion theory which makes the First Amendment less compelling?

2. The editors of the Georgetown Law Journal pointed out that allowing an action in conversion to substitute for a libel or right of privacy suit runs counter to the underlying premises of *New York Times v. Sullivan* and *Time, Inc. v. Hill.* The *Dodd* case extended the tort of conversion ("any distinct act of dominion wrongfully exercised over another's property, in denial of or inconsistent with his right") to the delivery by former employees of Senator Dodd of copies of purloined documents to Jack Anderson. See Note, *Conversion As a Remedy for Injurious Publication—New Challenge to the New York Times Doctrine*? 56 Geo.L.J. 1223 at 1224 (1968). The editors noted that Judge Holtzoff observed that " 'Anderson was aware of the manner in which the copies had been obtained.' " Id. at 1224.

The extension by the court of the tort of conversion to information and ideas was criticized on the ground that the court made the liability of the publisher hinge on whether the information in question was known by the publisher to have been wrongfully obtained.

The editors further pointed out that guilty knowledge is not usually a critical factor in imposing liability for conversion and that, unlike *New York Times* and *Hill*, the definition of knowledge revolved around the "source of the speech rather than its content." Note, *supra,* 56 Geo.L.J. 1223 at 1229 (1968). Thus liability was imposed in *Dodd* because of the manner in which the information was obtained rather than because the information was not "newsworthy" or because it was published in "reckless disregard of its truth or falsity."

Is the extension of a conversion theory to these circumstances a completely inconsistent defiance of that vigorous and intense criticism of government which the *New York Times* case was designed to assure?

Should conversion theory never be used in situations like *Dodd v. Pearson*?

The editors of the Georgetown Law Journal made the following compromise suggestion:

> If a columnist actively participates in the commission of a tort, he would obviously be held to have exceeded the bounds of constitutionally protected activity. When the tort directly relates to the publication of information concerning official misconduct, however, the *sine qua non* for liability should be active participation by the publisher in the commission of the tortious act. Such a rule would comport with the policy and spirit underlying similar privileges to other areas, and allow the protection of a well-informed public to outweigh considerations of individual interests.

Does this suggested approach focus on the *content* rather than the *source* of the speech?

From a First Amendment point of view, i.e., vigorous and robust criticism of government, what are the advantages of the suggested approach over that actually used by Judge Holtzoff in *Dodd v. Pearson*?

3. Judge Holtzoff's decision in the district court granting partial summary judgment to Senator Dodd on a theory of conversion and denying partial summary judgment to Senator Dodd on a right of privacy theory were brought by interlocutory ap-

peal to the United States Court of Appeals for the District of Columbia. The Court of Appeals affirmed the district court's ruling on the privacy issue but reversed the same court on its grant of summary judgment for conversion. Pearson v. Dodd, 410 F.2d 701 (D.C.Cir.1969), cert. den. 395 U.S. 947 (1969).

With respect to the privacy point, Dodd's counsel argued that the district court had misunderstood his claim and that his privacy objection was based not on the content of the columns published by Pearson but on the manner in which he obtained the information published. Judge Skelly Wright for the appeals court distinguished intrusion from other invasions of privacy by noting that intrusion does not require the publication of the information obtained. For the tort of intrusion to be accomplished, it is only necessary that the information be obtained "by improperly intrusive means."

Judge Wright concluded that Pearson received the documents from Senator Dodd's files with knowledge that they had been removed from the files without authorization. Should the court hold that Pearson is liable for invasion of privacy since he had received information from an intruder? Judge Wright answered the question in the negative:

> In an untried and developing area of tort law, we are not prepared to go so far. A person approached by an eavesdropper with an offer to share in the information gathered through the eavesdropping would perhaps play the nobler part should he spurn the offer and shut his ears. However, it seems to us that at this point it would place too great a strain on human weakness to hold one liable in damages who merely succumbs to temptation and listens.
>
> Of course, appellants did more than receive and peruse the copies of the documents taken from appellee's [Dodd's] files: they published excerpts from them in the national press. But in analyzing a claimed breach of privacy, injuries from intrusion and injuries from publication should be kept clearly separate. Where there is intrusion, the intruder should generally be liable whatever the content of what he learns. An eavesdropper to the marital bedroom may hear marital intimacies, or he may hear statements of fact or opinion of legitimate interest to the public; for purposes of liability that should make no difference. On the other hand, where the claim is that private information concerning plaintiff has been published, the question of whether that information is genuinely private or is of public interest should not turn on the manner in which it has been obtained. Of course, both forms of invasion may be combined in the same case.
>
> Here we have separately considered the nature of appellant's (Pearson and Anderson) publications concerning appellee, and have found that the matter published was of obvious public interest. The publication was not itself an invasion of privacy. Since we have also concluded that appellant's role in obtaining the information did not make them liable for intrusion to appellee, their subsequent publication, itself no invasion of privacy, cannot reach back to render that role tortious.

4. The Court of Appeals also concluded that Drew Pearson and his colleague Jack Anderson were not guilty of conversion. The court reasoned: "The most significant feature of conversion is the measure of damages, which is the value of the goods converted." Since the documents in Dodd's files were photocopied and the originals returned, the court stated that Dodd was therefore not deprived of his files: "Insofar as the documents' value to appellee resided in their usefulness as records of the business of his office, appellee was clearly not substantially deprived of his use of them." But the court then acknowledged that "documents often have value above and beyond that springing from their physical possession." On the conversion point Judge Wright stated:

> Appellee [Dodd] complains, not of the misappropriation of property bought or created by him, but of the exposure of information either (1) injurious to his reputation or (2) revelatory of matters which he believes he has a right to keep to himself. Injuries of this type are redressed at law by suit for libel and invasion of privacy respectively, where defendants' liability for those torts can be established under the limitations created by common law and by the Constitution.
>
> Because no conversion of the physical contents of appellee's files took place, and because the information copied from the documents in those files has not been shown to be property subject to protection by suit for conversion, the District Court's ruling that appellants are guilty of conversion must be reversed.

Judge Wright's opinion clearly closes the opening wedge of media liability in a Dodd-type fact situation which Judge Holtzoff's opinion in the district court had created. Holtzoff had sketched the outlines of a theory of media liability on a conversion theory even though *Time, Inc. v. Hill* and the *New York Times* doctrine precluded such liability on a right of privacy or libel theory.

5. Do the classifications between injuries from publication and injuries from intrusion separate quite as tidily as Judge Wright suggests? When did the most serious consequence of the intrusion into Dodd's files occur: when the confidential files were removed by the "intruder" or when Pearson published them? What is the real basis for refusal to hold that Pearson's role in the affair was not passive (merely reading and receiving the documents), but active (publishing them)? Is the basic problem that without injury from intrusion there would be no publication and therefore no injury from such publication? But the court wished to separate the intrusion from publication apparently because candid recognition of their interconnection cannot be accomplished without returning to the basic issue of whether an elected public official such as Dodd has any basis for a right of privacy claim against Pearson. In the light of this analysis, note Judge Wright's remark in his Court of Appeals opinion, fn. 6: "Since under common law principles appellants' publication does not amount to an invasion of privacy, we need not reach the serious constitutional questions suggested by Time, Inc. v. Hill, 385 U.S. 374 (1967)."

6. Judge Wright pointed out that files in Dodd's senate office are maintained in an office owned by the United States. Wright noted that this question was not briefed by the parties, but he speculated that it was not entirely clear as to whether the Senator had title to the contents of his files. Assume that Dodd has no "title" to the content of the files. Whose legal position would such an assumption strengthen?

7. Judge Edward Tamm concurred in the result reached by Judge Wright, but he filed a separate concurring opinion:

> Some legal scholars will see in the majority opinion—as distinguished from its actual holding—an ironic aspect. Conduct for which a law enforcement officer would be soundly castigated is, by the phraseology of the majority opinion, found tolerable; conduct which, if engaged in by government agents would lead to the suppression of evidence obtained by these means, is approved when used for the profit of the press. There is an anomaly lurking in this situation: the news media regard themselves as quasi-public institutions yet they demand immunity from the restraints which they vigorously demand be placed on government. That which is regarded as a mortal taint on information secured by any illegal conduct of government would appear from the majority opinion to be permissible as a technique or modus operandi for the journalist. Some will find this confusing, but I am not free to act on my own views under the doctrine of stare decisis which I consider binding upon me.

8. Is it really inconsistent, however, to permit the use of information as evidence (which presumably would be inadmissible in a criminal prosecution) for "profit by the press" in view of the fact that such information as used by the press is also quite damaging to the party against whom it is used? Does Judge Tamm take too great a legal leap when he styles the news media as "quasi-public institutions"? On the other hand, Judge Wright in the majority opinion appeared to take an even greater leap when he suggested that the requirements of the Fourth Amendment should extend to private as well as to governmental conduct: "Just as the Fourth Amendment has expanded to protect citizens from government intrusions where the intrusion is not reasonably expected, so should tort law protect citizens from other citizens."

The Fourth Amendment requires that,

> The right of the people to be secure in their persons, houses, papers, and effects against unreasonable searches and seizures, shall not be violated, and no Warrants shall issue, but upon probable cause, supported by Oath or affirmation, and particularly describing the place to be searched, and the persons or things to be seized.

But how helpful and how basic are Fourth Amendment references in a case permeated with First Amendment considerations? In the light of this conflict between competing constitutional values, reflect on which appears to be the approach which identifies most clearly the fundamental issues involved? Is it the approach of Judge Wright for the majority in the court of appeals or the approach suggested by the editors of the *Georgetown Law Journal?* Why? See Zurcher v. Stanford Daily, 436 U.S. 547 (1978), this text, p. 428. Press objections to unannounced police searches may be weakened when one considers that the public's interest in gaining access to all available evidence of crime, wherever it is to be found, may be equal to the public's interest in knowing about corruption in government. If the press rejects this proposition, is it applying a double standard? Which is more to be feared and which does the Constitution more clearly proscribe: intrusion by the press or intrusion by government?

9. The issue of conversion was raised in another case involving Drew Pearson after he had obtained copies of personal letters from the plaintiff's files. Here the court preferred to ground its ruling on the firmer base of prior restraint. Writing for the United States Court of Appeals for the District of Columbia, then Circuit Court Judge Warren Burger said:

> Upon a proper showing the wide sweep of the First Amendment might conceivably yield to an invasion of privacy and deprivation of rights of property in private manuscripts. But that is not this case; here there is no clear showing as to ownership of the alleged private papers or of an unlawful taking and no showing that Appellees had any part in the removal of these papers or copies from the offices of Appellants or any act other than receiving them from a person with a colorable claim to possession. Liberty Lobby, Inc. v. Pearson, 390 F.2d 489 (D.C.Cir.1968).

Of no advantage to plaintiffs was the fact they were engaged in political lobbying of a highly controversial nature, rendering their affairs a matter of public interest.

What is important about the *Pearson* cases is that they do not preclude the application of conversion theory to First Amendment questions.

10. The second major case involving stolen property arose in California when a reporter for the *Los Angeles Free Press* received and paid for a list of names (with addresses and telephone numbers) of undercover narcotics agents from a young man identifying himself as an employee of the California Attorney General's office.

Two months later in August 1969, to the horror of state officials, the complete list was published under headlines such as "Know Your Local Narc." Publisher Arthur Kunkin and the reporter who had bought the list were indicted by a Los Angeles grand jury on a charge of violating the California Penal Code which places criminal liability on "Every person who buys or receives any property that has been stolen or which has been obtained in any manner constituting theft or extortion, knowing the property to be so stolen or obtained, or who conceals, withholds or aids in concealing or withholding any such property from the owner. * * " Unlike conversion, which Prosser has called the "forgotten tort," receiving stolen property is an active concept in American law.

Convicted in a jury trial, the two newspapermen were fined and placed on probation. The California Court of Appeals affirmed the convictions in a detailed March 1972 ruling. People v. Kunkin, 100 Cal.Rptr. 845 (1972). Citing the United States Supreme Court in Zemel v. Rusk, 381 U.S. 1 (1965), a freedom of travel case, Associate Justice Fleming noted for the California court that "the right to speak and publish does not carry with it the unrestrained right to gather information." Moreover, he was not willing to condone what he called a "Constitutional thieves market"; and he distinguished *Dodd* which, he emphasized, had not held that documents were not property.

"We think a restriction on traffic in stolen documents," said Justice Fleming, "is a valid restriction, even though it may have some impact on news gathering. We think a state is constitutionally warranted in adopting laws against receipt of stolen documents and uniformly enforcing those laws against all persons, including newsmen and publishers, who knowingly receive stolen documents."

The case strengthens the idea of a property right restriction on freedom of the press and reinforces Chief Justice Burger's belief, expressed in his *Pentagon Papers* dissent, that the press has an obligation to report the theft of government papers to the proper authorities, once having verified their origin. The press thus becomes handmaiden to police. Does such an alliance offend the public interest?

"The press as a watchdog on government," says Professor Everette Dennis, "has always depended on disgruntled public officials for leaks and internal memoranda. Such sources of information have often led to the exposure of government corruption and wrongdoing. A mandatory legal verification of all information would quickly close information sources." Dennis, *The Case of the Purloined Papers,* Rights (June/July 1973), p. 11. *Purloined Information as Property: A New First Amendment Challenge*, 50 Journalism Quarterly 456 (Autumn 1973).

In the *Kunkin* case the Supreme Court of California came to the rescue on a technicality. Since the newspaper's informant had not indicated that he was no longer employed by the Attorney General, had insisted that the roster of agents be returned, and had asked to remain anonymous in order to avoid trouble, there was no substantial evidence, said the court, from which the jury could reasonably have inferred that the list was stolen and that the newspapermen therefore had a guilty knowledge. The more substantive question of whether the newspaper has a constitutional right to publish information reaching it through diverse and unorthodox channels was never reached. People v. Kunkin, 107 Cal.Rptr. 184 (1973).

11. Just as a reasonable qualification to a reporter's privilege to protect his sources would be his actual involvement in a crime either as a participant or an observer and thereby an accessory before the fact, a reasonable qualification to permitting the publication of purloined papers might be whether the reporter himself had broken in and rifled personal files. This distinguishes between intrusion and publication and in doing so honors both free-

dom of press and the right of privacy. The distinction is implied in *Pearson v. Dodd*, and it appears to be the theory of Dietemann v. Time, Inc., 449 F.2d 245 (9th Cir. 1971) in which the court would not countenance a physical invasion of privacy by a news reporter whether it be by breaking and entering, theft of personal or professional documents, or surreptitious photography or recording. Intrusion may be the one form of invasion of privacy which the press in the future may clearly not engage in with any sense of constitutional security.

Pearson v. Dodd has generally been followed. There was no intrusion, said a Maryland appeals court, when newspaper reporters received the academic files of University of Maryland basketball players from an unnamed source. The press itself had not sought out, inspected, or solicited the files.[61]

12. Implicit in *Pearson v. Dodd* is the defense of newsworthiness or public interest. It remains a prodigious defense. In spite of the fact that Wayne Williams's parents were practically prisoners in their own home and reporters themselves found the stakeout "gross" and "repellent," close coverage of the murder suspect was not enough to support a privacy claim.[62] Williams was convicted of the murders of two of twenty-eight young blacks slain in Atlanta.

On the other side of the law, a policeman had no privacy claim after being filmed by a television camera through a two-way mirror while investigating a massage parlor. Imagine the policeman's consternation when a door opened and someone suddenly cried, "Channel 7 News" and the camera crew exited filming the scene before them. After making suggestive remarks and physical advances to a "lingerie" model and after she had responded with "sufficient physical contact," the officer arrested her for solicitation.[63] His being a public official served to distinguish this case from *Dietemann* and his homemade gadgetry.

Less dramatic forms of news gathering, especially those involving mundane events, are normally protected by their newsworthiness. A District of Columbia district court rejected a claim against the *Washington Post* for reporting that an undercover police officer had participated in a narcotics therapy program. But it did permit an embarrassing private facts action against another federal officer who had made the information about his colleague-patient available in violation of federal law and the confidentiality of the doctor-patient relationship.[64]

A federal district court dismissed a privacy claim brought by undercover narcotic agents who had been photographed entering a courthouse, but permitted an award of damages for "emotional distress" brought about by their being identified. That award was reversed by the Sixth Circuit which found the publication insufficiently outrageous—"so extreme in degree as to go beyond all possible bounds of decency, and to be regarded as atrocious, and utterly intolerable in a civilized community." [65]

Finally a Washington state appeals court held that filming the interior of a pharmacy from a location open to the public, even though private property, was not

61. Bilney v. Evening Star Newspaper Co., 4 Med.L.Rptr. 1924, 406 A.2d 652 (Md.1979).

62. Williams v. NBC, 7 Med.L.Rptr. 1523 (D.Ga.1981).

63. Cassidy v. ABC, 3 Med.L.Rptr. 2449, 377 N.E.2d 126 (Ill.1978).

64. Logan v. District of Columbia, 3 Med.L.Rptr. 2094, 447 F.Supp. 1328 (D.D.C.1978).

65. Ross v. Burns, 5 Med.L.Rptr. 2277, 612 F.2d 271 (6th Cir. 1980). The language is from the Restatement Commentary, *Restatement (Second) of Torts* § 46, comment d at 73 (1948).

actionable. The story was about medicaid fraud.[66]

It has been suggested that in a *Dietemann* case, or in any other situation where there is criminal activity going on, the press should not be liable for intrusion. Public interest would override physical intrusion. But should the press—except in exceptional circumstances—be given immunity for tortious conduct based on its own conclusions as to guilt or innocence prior to any formal charge? The question is a difficult one. Doesn't the press again assume the role of police or the courts when it argues for such immunity? And government, it should be recalled, is specifically bound by constitutional limitations.

Given the rule that intimate details of the private lives of public figures—whether criminal or not—must bear public scrutiny, the question becomes: what limitations, if any, should be placed on the methods used by reporters to gain access to those details? Do the ends always justify the means? In both the ethical and legal sense the tentative answer must be no! But there will always be cases when an intrusive, irritating, and cantankerous press will be society's last and best defense. And where criminality and official corruption are suspected, intrusion may be worth the risks to both ethical and legal standards. Generally, however, reporters would do well to avoid those techniques of surveillance and information gathering (taping, bugging, peeking, and recording) for which their newspapers have criticized government agencies.

Exceeding Consent by Recording Telephone Conversations

1. Is a reporter liable to wiretap charges when he or she records telephone conversations with sources without their consent? More and more states—there were thirteen at this writing [67]—bar consensual (one-party-consent) recording either of a person or of telephone conversations. Illinois was the first state to do so, but only in Florida has such a law been upheld against a press challenge. There a reporter's tape recording of a caller who was unaware that the conversation was being recorded constituted an illegal wire intercept under Florida's Security of Communication Act, even though the reporter was using the recording only to help her write a news story.[68] The constitutionality of Florida's law requiring that all parties to an interception give prior consent was affirmed by the Florida Supreme Court in Shevin v. Sunbeam Television, 351 So.2d 723 (Fla.1977). The United States Supreme Court declined review. A number of state courts, however, have construed their statutes so as to permit one-party participant recording of telephone conversations.[69]

Journalists have not appreciated finding themselves at the other end of the tape recorder. In 1978 a D.C. Circuit Court panel held that the First Amendment was not violated by law enforcement officials' good faith inspection of the toll-call records of reporters released by the telephone company without prior notice. Any First Amendment news-gathering right, said the court, is subject to those general and incidental burdens that arise from good faith

66. Mark v. KING Broadcasting, 6 Med.L.Rptr. 2224, 618 P.2d 512 (Wash.1980).

67. The states are California, Delaware, Florida, Georgia, Illinois, Massachusetts, Maryland, Michigan, Montana, New Hampshire, Oregon, Pennsylvania, and Washington. For a comprehensive discussion of this issue, see Middleton, *Journalists and Tape Recorders: Does Participant Monitoring Invade Privacy?* 2 Comm/Ent L.Jour. 287 (Winter 1979–80).

68. News-Press v. Florida, 2 Med.L.Rptr. 1240, 345 So.2d 865 (Fla.1977). The Florida statute is Fla.Stat.Ann. § 943.03 (Supp.1978).

69. State v. Birge, 241 S.E.2d 213 (Ga.1978); Rogers v. Ulrich, 125 Cal.Rptr. 306 (1975).

enforcement of valid civil and criminal laws. Reporters Committee for Freedom of the Press v. AT & T, 4 Med.L.Rptr. 1177, 593 F.2d 1030 (D.C.Cir.1978), cert.den. 440 U.S. 949 (1979).

Federal court decisions have interpreted § 2510 of Title III of the Omnibus Crime Control Act of 1968 to mean that if one party to a conversation records it, there is no illegal intercept. United States v. Turk, 526 F.2d 654 (5th Cir. 1976).

2. The FCC, in its supervisory capacity over broadcasting, prohibits the monitoring and divulging of nonpublic radio broadcasts such as police radios, a hallmark of most newsrooms, but it has not enforced the rule. It has admonished broadcasters to respect the rule and has pointed out the danger of attracting crowds to scenes of crime and disaster.[70]

The FCC also prohibits the private use of radio devices to monitor conversations without the consent of all parties (13 Fed. Reg. 3397, 1966); [71] and it requires broadcasters to give advance warning if a recorded telephone conversation is intended for broadcast.[72] This has superseded the earlier "beep-tone" requirement.

Unannounced recording for broadcast purposes is not permitted, but the federal agency has made notable exceptions for reporters investigating crime.

3. Wiretapping and bugging by the media is illegal. Eavesdropping or recording conversations that are within hearing distance in public or quasi-public places is legal for both print and broadcast reporters. A Kentucky court had an opportunity in 1980 to address this question. An indicted drug dealer had given two reporters the impression that a lawyer had agreed to "fix" her case for $10,000. The reporters agreed to provide money to the suspect, if necessary, and asked her to meet with the lawyer in his office and record their conversation with a concealed recording device. When the slightly suspicious lawyer asked her if she was recording, she denied it, and a conversation ensued in which it was clear that the lawyer was not breaking the law or clearly violating his professional code. Nevertheless, part of the recorded conversation was published by the newspaper, and the attorney brought suit. His privacy claims of intrusion by trespass and false light were rejected by the court, as were libel claims. The intrusion portions of the ruling follow.

MCCALL v. COURIER–JOURNAL

6 MED.L.RPTR. 1112 (KY.CT. OF APP.1980).

HOWERTON, Judge. McCall appeals from a summary judgment of the Jefferson Circuit Court dismissing his complaint for damages due to two allegedly libelous newspaper articles appearing in *The Louisville Times,* written by reporters, Krantz and Van Howe. McCall presents two allegations of error; (1) that genuine issues of material fact are yet to be resolved, and (2) that the trial court misconstrued and misapplied the law. Four theories of liability were presented to the trial court, but McCall now relies on only two of these theories, invasion of privacy—intrusion/trespass, and libel.

McCall is an attorney. He counseled with Kristie Frazier concerning two criminal charges. Frazier began spreading insinuations that she could buy her way out of her trouble. The appellees, Krantz and

70. Monitoring of Police and Fire Radio Transmissions by Broadcast Stations, 1 Rad.Reg.2d (P & F) 291 (1963). But see, United States v. Fuller, 202 F.Supp. 356 (D.Cal.1962).

71. 47 C.F.R. §§ 2.701, 15.11 (1978).

72. Broadcast of Telephone Conversations, 23 FCC2d 1, 19 Rad.Reg.2d (P & F) 1504 (codified at 47 C.F.E. § 73.1206 [1978]); Use of Recording Devices in Connection with Telephone Service, 38 FCC2d 579, 26 Rad.Reg.2d (P & F) 40 (1972).

Van Howe, reporters for *The Louisville Times,* met with Frazier. In Frazier's words, McCall told her that "for $10,000.00 he would guarantee me that I'd walk in, but I would turn around and walk back out with him."

Krantz and Van Howe decided to investigate the possibility of bribery in the judiciary and met with Frazier again. They furnished her with a tape recorder and asked her to return to McCall's office. They also instructed her as to what questions to ask. They agreed to provide the $10,000.00 for her, if the dismissal of the criminal charges could be fixed.

On March 10, 1976, Frazier returned to McCall's office with the recorder. She asked the prearranged questions. The attorney told her there would be no "fix" and then inquired a to whether she had a recording device on her person. After Frazier's denial, McCall then stated that if he was able to keep Frazier out of jail, his fee would be $10,000.00, but if not, $9,000.00 would be returned to her. Although McCall's conduct was questionable in relation to the professional code, there was no evidence of bribery in the judicial system. Nevertheless, on March 17, 1976, *The Louisville Times* published and circulated a news article based on these events. On August 19, 1976, the newspaper carried an account of the lawsuit which resulted.

McCall argues that there are disputes regarding several material facts. As to his first meeting with Frazier, he denies her allegations and further contends that the recording of the second meeting confirms this denial. He argues that the articles were unfair since they failed to mention points in the taped conversation favorable to his character and demeanor. It is also argued that the reporters were not justified in suspecting bribery after hearing Frazier's version of the first meeting and that they most certainly should have had doubts as to her credibility. McCall states that Frazier did not return to his office to legitimately discuss employment or her case. In addition, he outlines his own version of what occurred at the taped meeting since he disputes the accuracy of the transcription. Even if we consider all of these facts in a manner most favorable to McCall, this Court must affirm the summary judgment as a matter of law.

The first tort theory argued is labeled by McCall as invasion of privacy—intrusion/trespass. The appellees claim the nonexistence of this tort, stating that McCall created a hybrid cause of action. Prosser labels the tort "intrusion," which consists of "intrusion upon the plaintiff's physical solitude or seclusion, as by invading his home or other quarters * * *." W. Prosser, *Torts* § 117, at 807 (4th ed. 1971). Prosser extends the tort to include eavesdropping upon private conversations through wiretaps or microphones. Necessary elements of the tort include an intrusion in the nature of prying which is offensive or objectionable to a reasonable man. Also, the thing into which there is an intrusion must be private. *Id.* at 808.

In this case, nothing was learned about McCall which was private or personal. The conversation dealt with Frazier and her legal problems and with how McCall proposed to resolve them. McCall spoke to her at his own risk, and Frazier was free to reveal the conversation to anyone. It is well settled that the attorney-client privilege "is not personal to the attorney but for the protection of the client." Carter v. West, * * *, 19 S.W. 592, 593 (1892). Accord, Prichard v. United States, 181 F.2d 326 (6th Cir. 1950), affirmed 339 U.S. 975.

As to the allegation of trespass, we must conclude that neither the conduct of Frazier nor that of the newspaper or its reporters was sufficient under this theory. 75 Am.Jur.2d, *Trespass,* § 14, states:

> The fact that a professional man, merchant, or other person opens an office to transact business with and for the public is a tacit invitation to all persons having business with him, and a

> permission for such persons to enter, unless forbidden. Nevertheless, a person has the right, in his private business, to control it, and may select such persons as he chooses with whom to transact such business. He can prevent whom he pleases from entering his office; and when a person under an implied license has entered, he has the right to request such person to depart, and the latter thereafter has no legal right to remain. *Id.* at 18.

Thus, Frazier cannot be considered a trespasser. When McCall suspected a recorder on her person, he should have asked her to depart. By continuing the conversation, McCall consented to her presence and continued to discuss legal services for a fee. McCall argued that even if Frazier is considered an invitee, the newspaper and its reporters are trespassers. Any person who causes another to trespass is also liable therefor. 75 Am.Jur.2d, *Trespass,* § 32, at 31. However, since Frazier was not a trespasser, this argument must fail.

* * *

The appellees justify their means of investigation by stating that the tape recording was the only way to verify or dispell Ms. Frazier's allegations. Certainly, the public has a right to know if illegality exists in the judicial system. We at least applaud the effort to investigate. However, once it was determined that there was no foundation for the alleged bribery, it appears totally unnecessary for the newspaper to have published the initial article, which cast McCall in a bad, although not false, light. If the appellees sincerely believed a breach of legal ethics or professional conduct had occurred, various remedies were available rather than a public spanking by newspaper.

Undoubtedly, Mr. McCall's professional reputation has been damaged, but the judgment of the Jefferson Circuit must be affirmed.

All concur.

COMMENT

It is important to note that the lower court in *McCall* distinguished *Dietemann* on grounds that no fraud or deception was involved in gaining access to the lawyer's office. As a client, the indicted drug dealer suspect was neither a trespasser nor an intruder. How about the reporters? But were the reporters in *Dietemann* also clients who, at least by implication, had been invited into the "healer's" laboratory? *Dietemann* may be an unusual case, but it does establish one-party (consensual) recording or filming in news gathering as the basis for a tort.

A year later the Kentucky Supreme Court reinstated the lawyer's libel and false light invasion of privacy suits while, at the same time, declining to discuss the intrusion claim. The court seemed to be saying that publication wrongs, i.e., libel and false light privacy violations, were more deserving of a jury's attention than the news-gathering wrong of intrusion. McCall v. Courier-Journal, 7 Med.L.Rptr. 2118, 623 S.W.2d 882 (Ky.1981).

The two parties later reached a settlement and McCall brought a libel suit against the newspaper for its report of the settlement. That suit was dismissed by a circuit court and McCall appealed again seven years after the original publication.

Legislators and judges generally bar tape recorders and other electronic newsgathering devices from their chambers, although, as shall be noted, television cameras and radio microphones are increasingly being admitted to courtrooms.

"APPROPRIATION" AND THE DEFENSE OF CONSENT

1. Appropriation of a name or a picture for commercial purposes without written consent is an offense committed more frequently by advertising and promotion per-

sonnel than by news reporters or news photographers.

In denying summary judgment to a pharmaceutical firm which had used a forty-year-old photo of actress Pola Negri (The Vamp) in a drug ad without her consent, a federal district court held that, although her appearance had changed since 1922, the New York statute was designed to protect "any living person" against the unauthorized use of his or her name or picture for commercial exploitation.

The picture, which appeared in ads in seven medical journals, depicted the actress in a traumatic pose. Friends, fans, and her physician recognized her. Negri claimed severe emotional and mental distress and humiliation, unjust appropriation of her *rights of publicity,* and defendant's enrichment at her expense. The court was sympathetic and said that the drug company was liable for any injuries the jury might decide she had suffered. Negri v. Schering Corp., 333 F.Supp. 101 (D.N.Y. 1971).

The first right of publicity case, Haelan Laboratories, Inc. v. Topps Chewing Gum, Inc., 202 F.2d 866 (2d Cir. 1953), cert. den. 346 U.S. 816, involved bubble gum and baseball cards. Federal courts have since recognized a common law as well as a statutory *right of publicity* in New York.

Had written consent been given for the specific use to which the Negri photo was put, no suit could have ensued. Written consent may be required in states with privacy statutes and is preferable to any kind of oral or implied consent in all jurisdictions.[73]

Many news organizations have standard release forms that may be applicable to any category of privacy. They are particularly important where private persons are the subject of news or promotional activities. Where minors or incompetents are involved, their guardians should be asked to sign the release. A signed release constitutes *consent,* if it truthfully reflects how a fact or a photograph is going to be used.

Major alterations in a photo or its use in a manner not agreed to, of course, would violate an agreement. And since circumstances may alter the disposition of consent, renewed consent should be sought if a picture or a name is to be used for trade purposes after a long period of time has elapsed.

How far beyond the terms of consent a user may go before nullifying consent and whether such misuse is a breach of contract or a tort of appropriation was discussed in Shields v. Gross, 7 Med.L.Rptr. 2349 (Sup.Ct.N.Y.1981), reversed 8 Med.L. Rptr. 1928, 451 N.Y.S.2d 419 (1982).

The first rule is to get permission from celebrities past or present—and from the representatives of deceased celebrities—before using their "personae" in advertising or for any other purely commercial purpose.

But of what benefit to a plaintiff is a claim of nonconsent where the invasion of privacy occurs in the realm of the newsworthy? Newsworthiness may depreciate all categories of privacy. Should it make a difference if the plaintiff is a voluntary news figure? An involuntary news figure? Is the public person/private person distinction of *Gertz* too refined for a defense as broad and formless as newsworthiness? Does it matter if the alleged invasion of privacy casts the plaintiff in an enviable rather than detractive light? Is identification of a person always necessary to convey legitimate news values? Case law has just begun to answer these questions. Although it applies best in cases of misappropriation, *consent* is clearly a defense in

73. See Miller v. Madison Square Garden Corp., 28 N.Y.S.2d 811 (1941) where a New York court explained that under the state statute consent as a complete defense must be in writing. Oral consent would only be a partial defense in mitigation of damages.

embarrassing private facts and intrusion cases as well.

2. Newsworthiness occupies even firmer ground when a publication involves parody, satire, educational, or informative material or biography in books, plays, motion pictures, newspapers, and magazines.[74] Even though all media ultimately depend on a market, their primary purpose may be something other than a purely commercial return. Politics, for example. Use of the photo of a murder suspect in a gubernatorial candidate's campaign commercial was held not to be "for trade purposes" under New York's statute. The First Amendment privilege of political discussion outweighed individual injury.[75]

A shoe-on-the-other-foot situation occurred when a WCBS reporter, who had done a story on home insulation, found herself being used to promote a particular product. She brought a $4.5 million damage suit and asked for an injunction against the unauthorized use of the original news film.

"To be effective," said a New York appellate court in permitting the suit to continue, "a news reporter must maintain an image of absolute integrity and impartiality. The commercial exploitation of an impartial report by the use of a video tape or other reproduction of the name or picture of such reporter, for advertising or trade purposes, will not only tarnish the reporter's reputation for objectivity, but will have a chilling effect on reporters now involved in a field of expanding concern—consumer protection." Reilly v. Rapperswill Corp., 377 N.Y.S.2d 488 (1975).

Isolated references to television news reporters in the book *The Amityville Horror* did not support their invasion-of-privacy claims under New York's law since reports of psychic phenomena were matters of public interest.[76] Following allegations of fraud, they also became matters of public debate.

Joe Namath failed in a suit against *Sports Illustrated* when the magazine used a Super Bowl picture of the football hero it had published in 1969 to promote its subscriptions in other publications. The New York statute permits *incidental* use of once newsworthy photographs for trade purposes but not their direct or *collateral* use. The distinction is sometimes a fine one. But then newsworthiness is a broad and compassing defense. Namath v. Sports Illustrated, 371 N.Y.S.2d 10 (1975), affirmed 386 N.Y.S.2d 397, 352 N.E.2d 584 (1976).

Nor were the book and movie *Dog Day Afternoon* an invasion of the privacy of the unidentified wife and children of the actual bank robber in that real life story. Their pictures were not used in promoting the film and the plaintiffs had chosen to identify themselves. Wojtowicz v. Delacorte Press, 3 Med.L.Rptr. 1992, 395 N.Y. S.2d 205 (1977).

Actress Shirley Booth was denied damages for *Holiday* magazine's incidental use of her photo, taken on a public beach, for its cover, Booth v. Curtis Publishing Co., 223 N.Y.S.2d 737 (1961); and for an imitation of her voice in a television commercial depicting the copyrighted cartoon character "Hazel," portrayed on TV by Booth. Booth v. Colgate-Palmolive Co., 362 F.Supp. 343 (D.N.Y.1973).

---

74. Garner v. Triangle Publications Co., 97 F.Supp. 546 (D.N.Y.1951); Dallesandro v. Henry Holt & Co., 166 N.Y.S.2d 805 (1957); Murray v. New York Magazine, 318 N.Y.S.2d 474 (1971). In Estate of Presley v. Russen, 513 F.Supp. 1339 (D.N.J.1981), "The Big El Show," a theatrical imitation of Presley's work and style, was found "predominantly to commercially exploit the likeness" of Presley without containing any *parody, burlesque, satire, or criticism* of the singer. Since *informational* content was limited, the court found valid a right-of-publicity infringement claim.

75. Davis v. Duryea, 5 Med.L.Rptr. 1937, 417 N.Y.S.2d 624 (1979).

76. Bauman v. Anson, 6 Med.L.Rptr. 1487 (Sup.Ct.N.Y.1980).

But a race car driver was permitted to pursue his case for damages against a tobacco company which had used an obscured but identifiable photograph of his famous car in an advertisement. Clearly, this is an example of *collateral* use of a photograph for advertising purposes. Motschenbacher v. R. J. Reynolds Tobacco Co., 498 F.2d 821 (9th Cir. 1974).

The intricate connections between the defenses of *consent* and *newsworthiness* and an invasion of privacy by appropriation of one's name or picture for commercial purposes were illustrated in what has come to be known as the "human cannonball" case. It was the first case in the misappropriation category to have reached the United States Supreme Court.

Entertainer Hugo Zacchini's act was to shoot himself from a cannon into a net 200 feet away. By all reports it was a dramatic act lasting about fifteen seconds. While performing at an Ohio county fair, Zacchini was approached by a free-lance reporter for a television station who appeared to be going to film the act. Zacchini asked him not to. A day later, on his employer's instructions, the reporter returned, filmed the entire act, and a segment was shown on an evening news program.

Zacchini sued for $25,000 in damages, contending that WEWS–TV, Cleveland, had without consent appropriated his professional property. A trial court granted summary judgment to the television station. An appeals court reversed. Although it recognized Zacchini's "right to the publicity value of his performance," the Supreme Court of Ohio in turn reversed the intermediate court on the grounds of "legitimate public interest." In a fourth judicial step, the United States Supreme Court reversed the Supreme Court of Ohio. Zacchini had won his case. The Court held that, although Ohio might choose under its own law to extend a privilege to the media in a case presenting the facts of Zacchini, Ohio was not obliged to afford the media such a privilege on the basis of the First Amendment.

ZACCHINI v. SCRIPPS-HOWARD

433 U.S. 562, 97 S.CT. 2849, 53 L.ED.2D 965 (1977).

Justice WHITE delivered the opinion of the Court.

* * *

The Ohio Supreme Court held that respondent is constitutionally privileged to include in its newscasts matters of public interest that would otherwise be protected by the right of publicity, absent an intent to injure or to appropriate for some nonprivileged purpose. If under this standard respondent had merely reported that petitioner was performing at the fair and described or commented on his act, with or without showing his picture on television, we would have a very different case. But petitioner is not contending that his appearance at the fair and his performance could not be reported by the press as newsworthy items. His complaint is that respondent filmed his entire act and displayed that film on television for the public to see and enjoy. This, he claimed, was an appropriation of his professional property. The Ohio Supreme Court agreed that petitioner had "a right of publicity" that gave him "personal control over the commercial display and exploitation of his personality and the exercise of his talents." This right of "exclusive control over the publicity given to his performance" was said to be such a "valuable part of the benefit which may be attained by his talents and efforts" that it was entitled to legal protection. It was also observed, or at least expressly assumed, that petitioner had not abandoned his rights by performing under the circumstances present at the Geauga County Fair Grounds.

The Ohio Supreme Court nevertheless held that the challenged invasion was privileged, saying that the press "must be accorded broad latitude in its choice of how much it presents of each story or incident, and of the emphasis to be given to such presentation. No fixed standard which would bar the press from reporting or depicting either an entire occurrence or an entire discrete part of a public performance can be formulated which would not unduly restrict the 'breathing room' in reporting which freedom of the press requires." 351 N.E.2d 454 (1976). Under this view, respondent was thus constitutionally free to film and display petitioner's entire act.

The Ohio Supreme Court relied heavily on Time, Inc. v. Hill, but that case does not mandate a media privilege to televise a performer's entire act without his consent. * * *

Time, Inc. v. Hill, which was hotly contested and decided by a divided court, involved an entirely different tort than the "right of publicity" recognized by the Ohio Supreme Court. * * * It is also abundantly clear that *Time, Inc. v. Hill* did not involve a performer, a person with a name having commercial value, or any claim to a "right of publicity." This discrete kind of "appropriation" case was plainly identified in the literature cited by the Court and had been adjudicated in the reported cases.

The differences between these two torts are important. First, the State's interests in providing a cause of action in each instance are different. "The interest protected" in permitting recovery for placing the plaintiff in a false light "is clearly that of reputation, with the same overtones of mental distress as in defamation." Prosser, 48 Calif.L.Rev., at 400. By contrast, the State's interest in permitting a "right of publicity" is in protecting the proprietary interest of the individual in his act in part to encourage such entertainment. As we later note, the State's interest is closely analogous to the goals of patent and copyright law, focusing on the right of the individual to reap the reward of his endeavors and having little to do with protecting feelings or reputation. Second, the two torts differ in the degree to which they intrude on dissemination of information to the public. In "false light" cases the only way to protect the interests involved is to attempt to minimize publication of the damaging matter, while in "right of publicity" cases the only question is who gets to do the publishing. An entertainer such as petitioner usually has no objection to the widespread publication of his act as long as he gets the commercial benefit of such publication. Indeed, in the present case petitioner did not seek to enjoin the broadcast of his act; he simply sought compensation for the broadcast in the form of damages.

Nor does it appear that our later cases, such as Rosenbloom v. Metromedia, Inc.; Gertz v. Robert Welch, Inc.; and Time, Inc. v. Firestone, require or furnish substantial support for the Ohio court's privilege ruling. These cases, like *New York Times,* emphasize the protection extended to the press by the First Amendment in defamation cases, particularly when suit is brought by a public official or a public figure. None of them involve an alleged appropriation by the press of a right of publicity existing under state law.

Moreover, *Time, Inc. v. Hill, New York Times, Metromedia, Gertz,* and *Firestone* all involved the reporting of events; in none of them was there an attempt to broadcast or publish an entire act for which the performer ordinarily gets paid. It is evident, and there is no claim here to the contrary, that petitioner's state-law right of publicity would not serve to prevent respondent from reporting the newsworthy facts about petitioner's act. Wherever the line in particular situations is to be drawn between media reports that are protected and those that are not, we are quite sure that the First and Fourteenth Amendments do not immunize the media when they broadcast a performer's entire act without his consent. The Constitution no more prevents a State from requiring respondent to compensate petitioner for broadcasting his act on television than it would privilege respondent to film and broadcast a copyrighted dramatic work without liability to the copyright owner. Copyrights Act, Pub.L.No.94–553, 90 Stat. 2541 (1976); or to film and broadcast a prize fight or a baseball game, where the promoters or the participants had other plans for publicizing the event. There are ample reasons for reaching this conclusion.

The broadcast of a film of petitioner's entire act poses a substantial threat to the economic value of that performance. As the Ohio court recognized, this act is the product of petitioner's own talents and energy, the end result of much time, effort and expense. Much of its economic value lies in the "right of exclusive control over the publicity given to his performance"; if the public can see the act for free on television, they will be less willing to pay to see it at the fair. The effect of a public broadcast of the performance is similar to preventing petitioner from charging an admission fee.

"The rationale for [protecting the right of publicity] is the straight-forward one of preventing unjust enrichment by the theft of good will. No social purpose is served by having the defendant get for free some aspect of the plaintiff that would have market value and for which he would normally pay." Kalven, Privacy in Tort Law—Were Warren and Brandeis Wrong?, 31 Law and Contemporary Problems 326, 331 (1966). Moreover, the broadcast of petitioner's entire performance, unlike the unauthorized use of another's name for purposes of trade or the incidental use of a name or picture by the press, goes to the heart of petitioner's ability to earn a living as an entertainer. Thus in this case, Ohio has recognized what may be the strongest case for a "right of publicity"—involving not the appropriation of an entertainer's reputation to enhance the attractiveness of a commercial product, but the appropriation of the very activity by which the entertainer acquired his reputation in the first place.

Of course, Ohio's decision to protect petitioner's right of publicity here rests on more than a desire to compensate the performer for the time and effort invested in his act; the protection provides an economic incentive for him to make the investment required to produce a performance of interest to the public. This same consideration underlies the patent and copyright laws long enforced by this Court. As the Court stated in Mazer v. Stein, 347 U.S. 201, 219 (1954),

> "The economic philosophy behind the clause empowering Congress to grant patents and copyrights is the conviction that encouragement of individual effort by personal gain is the best way to advance public welfare through the talents of authors and inventors in 'Science and useful Arts.' Sacrificial days devoted to such creative activities deserve rewards commensurate with the services rendered."

These laws perhaps regard the "reward to the owner [as] a secondary consideration," United States v. Paramount Pictures, 334 U.S. 131, 158 (1948), but they were "intended definitely to grant valuable, enforceable rights" in order to afford greater encouragement to the production of works of benefit to the public. Washingtonian Publishing Co. v. Pearson, 306 U.S. 30, 36 (1939). The Constitution does not prevent Ohio from making a similar choice here in deciding to protect the entertainer's incentive in order to encourage the production of this type of work.

There is no doubt that entertainment, as well as news, enjoys First Amendment protection. It is also true that entertainment itself can be important news. Time, Inc. v. Hill. But it is important to note that neither the public nor respondent will be deprived of the benefit of petitioner's performance as long as his commercial stake in his act is appropriately recognized. Petitioner does not seek to enjoin the broadcast of his performance; he simply wants to be paid for it. Nor do we think that a state-law damages remedy against respondent would represent a species of liability without fault contrary to the letter or spirit of *Gertz.* Respondent knew exactly that petitioner objected to televising his act, but nevertheless displayed the entire film.

We conclude that although the State of Ohio may as a matter of its own law privilege the press in the circumstances of this case, the First and Fourteenth Amendments do not require it to do so.

Reversed.

COMMENT

1. The Court's opinion is troublesome on a number of counts. Did the news program in fact present *all* of Zacchini's act? It is unlikely that the suspense-building fanfare usually associated with this kind of performance could have been included in the complained about fifteen seconds. So how is the press to be sure in the future whether it is filming all or part of a public performance?

And Zacchini's act was very public. He performed out in the open, and no additional admission charge to see him was levied on fair goers.

Justice Powell, joined by Brennan and Marshall, not infrequently White's antagonists in libel and privacy cases, raised these questions and others in a brief but persuasive dissent. On the question of commercial profit to the broadcaster, Powell wrote:

> * * * I do not view respondent's action as comparable to unauthorized commercial broadcasts of sporting events, theatrical performances, and the like where the broadcaster keeps the profits. There is no suggestion here that respondent made any such use of the film. Instead, it simply reported on what petitioner concedes to be a newsworthy event, in a way hardly surprising for a television station—by means of film coverage. * * * It is a routine example of the press fulfilling the informing function so vital to our system.

With regard to the "appropriation" category of invasion, the commercial purpose of the television station is the key consideration. Could the cannonball film have made any difference to the news program's normal advertising revenue? Might not the fifteen-second film be considered "free" advertising for Zacchini? Is it necessarily true, as the Court states, that once having seen the act free on television, the public would be less willing to pay to see it at the fair? Certainly general admission to the fair promised the public much more than the "human cannonball" show.

Faulting White's mode of analysis, Powell returned to what was essentially the position of the Supreme Court of Ohio:

> When a film is used, as here, for a routine portion of a regular news program, I would hold that the First Amendment protects the station from a "right of publicity" or "appropriation" suit, absent a strong showing by the plaintiff that the news broadcast was a subterfuge or cover for private or commercial exploitation.

Justice White pointed out that the television station ignored Zacchini's objection to having his act filmed. Did the withdrawal of *consent,* followed by WEWS-TV's total disregard of Zacchini's wishes, influence the Court?

Note also how the Court's opinion connects "appropriation" with violations of patent and copyright. Could this simply have been a breach of contract case between Zacchini and the park owners?

The unusual facts of *Zacchini* and the narrow grounds upon which it was decided limit its usefulness. Like *Cox* and *Cantrell* it leaves many interesting privacy questions unanswered. But it does appear that in *Zacchini* the Court found a chink in the armor of *newsworthiness.*

2. Consent may either be implicit or explicit. Actress Ann-Margret claimed privacy violation under the New York statute and a common law right of publicity when a magazine published a partially nude photo taken from one of her movies. Both claims were rejected because she was a public figure and the photo had come from a film already seen by millions.[77]

Without authorization, the *New York Times* published another plaintiff's photo on the cover of its Sunday *Magazine* to illustrate an article about upward mobility in the black middle class. Under the New York statute there was no remedy for the subject of the photo. It was just as well that no false light invasion was asserted because the New York Court of Appeals questioned the very existence of that tort in New York. But plaintiff's allegations that a free-lance photographer and an agency took the pictures without consent and then sold them to the newspaper, again without consent and without knowing that they would be used in a newsworthy context, at least withstood defendant's motion to dismiss. Arrington v. New York Times, 6 Med.L.Rptr. 2354, 433 N.Y. S.2d 164 (N.Y.1980). An amendment to Section 51 would later protect freelance photographers and agencies in the sale and transfer of photographs.

Betty Friedan's husband claimed invasion-of-privacy damages for a twenty-five-year-old family portrait used in articles and advertisements. A New York federal court said that public interest in a leader of the feminist movement overcame the claimed privacy interests. Furthermore, the primary purpose of publication was not commercial, nor was the publication fiction. No consent, therefore, was required. Friedan v. Friedan, 414 F.Supp. 77 (D.N.Y.1976).

Summary judgment was denied *Newsweek* magazine in a privacy suit brought by a man whose photograph had been taken to illustrate what he was told would be a "patriotic article." To his dismay he became part of an October 6, 1969 cover story, "The Troubled American—A Special Report on the White Majority," in which he was represented as a typical "troubled American"—"angry, uncultured, crude, violence prone, hostile to both rich and poor, and racially prejudiced." Only his address was used, and none of these characterizations was attributed directly to him. But a federal district court felt that his friends and neighbors would have no trouble identifying him standing in his front yard by his American flag and that they would presume him to fit the stereotype.

There could be no libel action, said the court, since it is not libelous to call a person a "bigot" or other appropriate names descriptive of political, religious, economic, or sociological philosophies under Pennsylvania law. Anyway such charges might fit half the population. There was a privacy issue, however. It would turn on whether the defendant could show that the plaintiff had consented, and in what sense he had consented, to having his picture taken. And that would be a question for a jury. Raible v. Newsweek, Inc., 341 F.Supp. 804 (D.Pa. 1972).

Massachusetts was able to get an injunction to block general distribution of Frederick Wiseman's critically acclaimed film, *Titicut Follies,* because, contrary to an agreement between Wiseman and state authorities, persons identified in the film had not signed releases giving their consent or else were not competent to do so.

Finding that identifiable inmates of an institution for the criminally insane had been depicted naked or exhibiting the

77. Ann-Margret v. High Society Magazine, Inc., 6 Med.L.Rptr. 1774, 498 F.Supp. 401 (D.N.Y.1980).

painful aspects of mental disease, a trial judge ruled the film an unwarranted intrusion into the right to privacy of each inmate beyond any legitimate public concern. Any releases that may have been obtained would be a nullity, said the judge, and the State had the responsibility to protect persons in its custody from exploitation.

Again the categories of privacy overlap. And in spite of the fact that Massachusetts did not then recognize a legally protected right of privacy, the state's Supreme Judicial Court upheld the trial court on privacy grounds.

Even though the film was originally intended to arouse public interest toward improving mental health facilities, the court would not countenance Wiseman's abuse of the conditional permission granted him and the closeup depiction of individual inmates in degrading situations. The court did, however, permit distribution of the film to specialized audiences, and it eventually made the "film society" circuit around the country. In what could be described as an elitist declaration the court said:

> The effect upon inmates of showing the film to persons with a serious interest in rehabilitation, and with potential capacity to be helpful, is likely to be very different from the effect of its exhibition merely to satisfy general public curiosity. There is a possibility that showings to specialized audiences may be of benefit to the public interest, to the inmates themselves, and to the conduct of an important State institution. Because of the character of such audiences, the likelihood of humiliation, even of identifiable inmates, is greatly reduced. Commonwealth v. Wiseman, 249 N.E.2d 610 (Mass.1969).

Similarly, what a New York court called "commercial exploitation" of a state mental hospital patient in a CBS documentary narrated by Bill Moyers was held to violate both that person's right of privacy and right of publicity (a difficult concept to visualize in these circumstances) under the New York statute. And a signed consent form was void because no conscious consent was possible. Commercial advantage to CBS was said to outweigh its newsworthiness argument. Delan v. CBS, 7 Med.L. Rptr. 2465 (Sup.Ct.N.Y.1981).

Ruling in a different institutional setting, the United States Supreme Court in Saxbe v. Washington Post, 1 Med.L.Rptr. 2314, 417 U.S. 843 (1974) held that prison regulations prohibiting face-to-face interviews by reporters of individually designated inmates did not violate the First Amendment. Prison regulations did not deny press access to sources of information available to the general public. Moreover, information on prison conditions was available elsewhere.

Consistent with *Saxbe,* a federal district court in Utah rejected the *Salt Lake Tribune's* demand for access to the execution of Gary Gilmore and upheld a state law which bans press and public from witnessing executions because of "concerns for institutional discipline and security as well as reasonable deference to the *privacy* of the condemned man."

A few days earlier a federal judge in Dallas held that television reporters *had* a constitutional right to film executions and broadcast them to the public. Private executions, said the court, were unthinkable. On appeal, however, the Fifth Circuit Court of Appeals, citing *Saxbe,* ruled that Texas's policy of allowing news reporters access to executions in state prisons but banning audio or visual recordings of executions did not violate the First Amendment news-gathering rights of a television reporter who sought to film the execution for later broadcast.[78]

First Amendment questions are inescapable in the foregoing cases, especially

78. Garrett v. Estelle, 2 Med.L.Rptr. 2265, 556 F.2d 1274 (5th Cir. 1977).

where injunctive relief is granted to plaintiffs.

A question is whether in light of the emphasis on the First Amendment right of the press to gather information in *Richmond Newspapers,* text, p. 513, *Saxbe* is still the dominant precedent in this area.

4. Recall the *Bindrim* case, used earlier to illustrate fictionalization. Identification of plaintiff was an issue there, and it may also be an issue in appropriation cases.

A New York City psychiatrist, Dr. Emanuel Peterfreund, claimed violation of his statutory right to privacy by the film *Rich Kids,* based on a novel of the same title, in which the stepfather of one of two lead characters is a New York psychiatrist named Simon Peterfreund. The claim was dismissed on grounds that similarity in surnames and profession were insufficient to identify plaintiff with the film character who made only limited appearances in both film and novel.[79]

A New York appeals court dismissed Guy Lombardo's appropriation suit under the New York privacy law because neither his name nor his likeness had been used in a television commercial. It did allow him, however, a common law claim for appropriation of his "public personality" as "Mr. New Year's Eve" which the commercial had depicted.[80]

Portable toilets called "Here's Johnny" were said by a trial court not to exploit entertainer Johnny Carson's "public personality." The Sixth Circuit reversed, however, noting that there was a clearer appropriation here of Carson's persona than if his full proper name had been used.[81]

Descendability

1. A federal district court in the Pola Negri case interpreted the New York statute as protecting the right of publicity of any living person. It did not resolve conflict among New York courts, both state and federal, as to whether 1) misappropriation and the right of publicity are two separate rights, the first, a traditional right to be let alone, the second, a property right, and whether 2) the right of publicity is descendable and assignable, that is, it can be passed on to heirs and beneficiaries.[82]

In a comprehensive review of state law, a New York appellate court held in Brinkley v. Casablancas, 7 Med.L.Rptr. 1457, 438 N.Y.S.2d 1004 (1981) that the two rights were one and the same. But federal courts in New York have found an assignable common law right of publicity apart from the statutory right to be let alone. Factors Etc., Inc. v. Pro Arts, Inc., 4 Med.L. Rptr. 1144, 579 F.2d 215 (2d Cir. 1978), cert. den., 440 U.S. 908 (1979). See also, Price v. Hal Roach Studios, Inc., 400 F.Supp. 836 (D.N.Y.1975), a case involving the images of Laurel and Hardy.

Survivability, in which a right of publicity is recognized, is a matter of state law. In diversity suits, federal courts will be guided by state law. At this writing, the Second and Third Circuit Courts of Appeal and five state laws make the right of publicity assignable to heirs or survivors. Seven state laws and the Sixth Circuit expressly do not. There are other dimensions of the right.

California's Supreme Court held that a right of publicity will survive only for

79. Peterfreund v. United Artists Corp., Bantam Books, et al., 6 Med.L.Rptr. 1754 (Sup.Ct.N.Y.1980). See also, Allen v. Gordon, 6 Med.L.Rptr. 2010 (Sup.Ct.N.Y.1980); Golub v. Warner Communications, 7 Med.L.Rptr. 1647 (Sup.Ct.N.Y.1981).

80. Lombardo v. Doyle, Dane & Bernach, Inc., 2 Med.L.Rptr. 2321, 396 N.Y.S.2d 661 (1977).

81. Carson v. Here's Johnny, 6 Med.L.Rptr. 2112, 498 F.Supp. 71 (D.Mich. 1980), reversed, No. 80–1720 (6th Cir. 1983).

82. Felcher and Rubin, *The Descendability of the Right of Publicity: Is There Commercial Life after Death*? 89 Yale L. J. 1125 (1980); Sims, *Right of Publicity: Survivability Reconsidered.* 49 Ford.L.Rev. 453 (1981).

those opportunities exercised or exploited by a celebrity during his or her lifetime. The case involved Bela Lugosi, the original Hollywood "Count Dracula."[83] On the other hand, a Broadway musical's unauthorized use of the appearance and style of the Marx Brothers act—even in parody—violated the entertainers' common law right of publicity, which they had exploited during their lifetimes so as to create a valuable asset which had survived their deaths.[84] California, less hospitable to descendability than New York, has wondered, in its judicial ruminations, how many generations ought to benefit from what would seem to be a personal right? How is the worth or value of publicity measured at the time of death? Is it a taxable value? Does it apply to public officials? Military heroes? Does the claimant seek economic gain or personal gratification? And does injunctive relief, as provided for in the New York statute, raise litigable First Amendment issues?

Before Tennessee had occasion to recognize a right of publicity, and therefore to rule on its descendability, a good deal of court discussion focused on the publicity rights of survivors of Tennessee-based country singers and of Elvis Presley. For example, when Bluegrass singer Lester Flatt's likeness was used in a Coors beer campaign, a chancery court in Tennessee, citing a Tennessee federal district court in a *Presley* case,[85] held that Flatt had an enforceable right of publicity that was descendable.[86] Subsequently, the Sixth Circuit Court of Appeals had reversed the Tennessee federal district court's ruling, holding that, in the absence of Tennessee's having specifically recognized descendability, the assignment of a right of publicity terminates at death.[87] And the Second Circuit Court of Appeals had reversed a New York District Court's holding which the Tennessee chancery court had found persuasive.[88] The Tennessee chancery court in the *Flatt* case said that it was not bound by the federal circuit court rulings.

Tennessee's belated recognition of descendability in the *Flatt* case had the result of unhinging earlier *Presley* holdings, and that case was reopened on motion of the original *Presley* plaintiffs. The cruel complexities of the case are discussed in a 1982 opinion of the New York federal district court granting a rehearing.[89]

2. Another form of privacy that sometimes conflicts with the information needs of the public is the privacy of data on individual citizens held in government files. State and federal data privacy laws confront state and federal open records or freedom of information laws. This conflict is discussed in a subsequent chapter. And a property right not dissimilar to the right of publicity is discussed in a section on copyright.

---

83. Lugosi v. Universal Pictures, 5 Med.L.Rptr. 2185, 603 P.2d 425 (Cal. 1979).

84. Marx Productions v. Day and Night Co., 7 Med.L.Rptr. 2030, 523 F.Supp. 485 (D.N.Y.1981). Since California law was applicable to the case and California law is unclear as to descendability, the Second Circuit reversed (8 Med.L.Rptr. 2201, 1982).

85. Memphis Development Foundation v. Factors Etc., Inc., 3 Med.L.Rptr. 2012, 441 F.Supp. 1323 (D.Tenn. 1977).

86. Commerce Union Bank v. Coors, 7 Med.L.Rptr. 2204 (1981).

87. Memphis Development Foundation v. Factors, Etc., Inc. 5 Med.L.Rptr. 2521, 616 F.2d 956 (6th Cir. 1980), cert. den. 449 U.S. 953.

88. Factors v. Pro Arts, 7 Med.L.Rptr. 1617, 652 F.2d 278 (2d Cir. 1981).

89. Factors v. Pro Arts, 8 Med.L.Rptr. 1839, 541 F.Supp. 231 (D.N.Y.1982).

IV

Journalist's Privilege

IS THERE A COMMON LAW OR CONSTITUTIONAL PRIVILEGE TO PROTECT NOTES, TAPES, AND THE IDENTITY OF SOURCES?

Traditionally the common law has firmly exempted compelled testimony concerning a lawyer-client relationship; and, in some circumstances, husbands and wives, priests and penitents, and doctors and patients have been accorded a similar privilege. Even government informers have enjoyed anonymity unless their identity goes to the central issue of guilt or innocence.[1] Limited privilege has also been granted against disclosure of religious beliefs, political votes, trade secrets, state secrets, and other categories of official information. Most of the latter are now governed by state and federal statutes.

Similar recognition of the journalist's claim that a privilege to protect the identity of sources and what is contained in unpublished notes, tapes, and photographs will assure the flow of vital information has been slower to emerge.

When Paul Corsetti of the *Boston Herald American* refused in 1982 to testify in court as to what an identified source had told him in a telephone conversation, he was sentenced to three months in jail. He served eight days. The source had implicated himself in a murder. The Supreme Judicial Court of Massachusetts, holding to the common law precept that the state has a right to every person's evidence,[2] found Corsetti guilty of criminal contempt.

Corsetti asserted a constitutional as well as a common law justification for his refusal to testify. In rejecting both common law and constitutional arguments, the Massachusetts court nevertheless implied that in some circumstances it might recognize such a privilege when it said:

> Where the source is disclosed and the testimony sought from the reporter concerns information already made public, the [s]tate's interest in the use of that information overrides the reporter's claim that the use of that information should be restricted. This is not a case where the Commonwealth has used a reporter to obtain an indictment or to do its investigative work.[3]

Even though Massachusetts, claiming a judicial need for full disclosure of the truth, has been more resistant than most states to a privilege for journalists, its highest court reflects the judicial willing-

1. Roviaro v. United States, 353 U.S. 53 (1956).

2. Wigmore, *Evidence* § 2192, at 70 (McNaughton rev. ed. 1961).

3. Massachusetts v. Corsetti, 8 Med.L.Rptr. 2113, 438 N.E.2d 805 (Mass.1982).

ness across the land to balance what the courts perceive as the needs of justice against the reporter's perception of what it takes to serve the public's informational needs.

Indeed, in denying Corsetti's application for a stay of the Massachusetts court's judgment, Justice William Brennan noted that in a close case it may be appropriate to "balance the equities"—to explore the relative harms to applicant and respondent, as well as the interest of the public at large. Brennan doubted that the United States Supreme Court would take the case or find for Corsetti if it did grant certiorari.[4]

On the other hand, flat assertions of either common law or constitutional protection for journalist's privilege have generally been rejected. The Constitution extends no such privilege beyond the Fifth Amendment's provision against self-incrimination.

In 1972, a divided United States Supreme Court in Branzburg v. Hayes, 1 Med.L.Rptr. 2617, 408 U.S. 665 (1972) struck the balance in favor of everyone having a duty—including the president of the United States—to testify in a court of law when called upon to do so. The Court, through Justice Byron White, refused to find either an absolute or a qualified journalist's privilege in the First Amendment.

A minority of four justices, led by Justice Potter Stewart, vigorously pressed divergent views. Stewart modified a position he took in a 1958 case in which Marie Torre, a columnist for the *New York Herald Tribune*, went to jail in spite of her then novel First Amendment justification for refusing to name a source. The source, who remained unidentified, was responsible for a statement that had provoked Judy Garland into bringing a $1 million libel suit against CBS.

Then Second Circuit Judge Stewart held for a unanimous court of appeals that the duty of a witness to testify in a court of law had roots fully as deep in our history as the guarantee of free press. The question asked of Ms. Torre, said the court, *went to the heart of the plaintiff's claim*, and there were no alternate sources. "The right to sue and defend in the courts," said Stewart, "is the alternative of force. In an organized society it is the right conservative of all other rights, and lies at the foundation of orderly government."[5] But, again, the clear suggestion that balancing in these kinds of cases is possible.

Long after *Garland* but before *Branzburg*, Stewart was clearly influenced by the Ninth Circuit Court of Appeals in the *Caldwell* case, a case involving a *New York Times* reporter and his Black Panther sources. A ruling in favor of Caldwell's privilege to protect his sources by not answering the summons of a grand jury on First Amendment grounds would be reversed by the Supreme Court when the case was joined by two others to become the *Branzburg* case.

But the Ninth Circuit had delivered what ultimately would become a key ruling in the realm of journalist's privilege. In reversing a federal district court and recognizing Caldwell's privilege to protect his journalistic integrity and the free flow of information by refusing to appear before the grand jury, the court declared:

> To convert news gatherers into Department of Justice investigators is to invade the autonomy of the press by imposing a governmental function upon them. To do so where the result is to

4. Corsetti v. Massachusetts, 8 Med.L.Rptr. 2117, 438 N.E.2d 805 (Mass.1982), stay denied 103 S.Ct. 3. In Lynch v. Riddell, 8 Med.L.Rptr. 2290 (Mass.1982) disclosure was forced against a TV station in a products liability suit. But the court intimated that it might protect confidential sources and information not shown to be relevant to the defendant's needs.

5. Garland v. Torre, 259 F.2d 545 (2d Cir. 1958), cert.den. 358 U.S. 910.

> diminish their future capacity as news gatherers is destructive of their public function. To accomplish this where it has not been shown to be essential to the Grand Jury inquiry simply cannot be justified in the public interest. Further it is not unreasonable to expect journalists everywhere to temper their reporting so as to reduce the probability that they will be required to submit to interrogation. The First Amendment guards against governmental action that induces self-censorship.[6]

And on the question of Caldwell's attending the grand jury hearing, the circuit court of appeals saw the cost to the public as slight (Caldwell stated in an affidavit that there was nothing to which he could testify beyond what he had already made public) but the cost to the news-gathering process unacceptably high.

The Ninth Circuit did something else. It began to fashion a three-part test to balance these interests which, in the following decade, would permeate the common law of both state and federal courts and find its way directly into the shield laws of Minnesota, New Jersey, and Tennessee. The test of 1) relevance, 2) lack of alternate sources, and 3) a compelling public need would also appear a year later in Alexander Bickel's oral arguments before the Supreme Court on behalf of the *New York Times* in the *Pentagon Papers* case.

Stewart's dissenting opinion in *Branzburg* legitimized the test, or something close to it, so that by the early 80s eight circuit courts of appeal, plus the District of Columbia circuit, recognized a qualified privilege; district courts in the two other circuits recognized it, and it was arguably recognized in a third. At the same time, a three-part test, or some variation of it, had been accepted by the courts of at least twenty-one states, in spite of the fact that half of them had no shield law. In states without shield laws, nearly 75 percent of their courts have applied some or all of Justice Stewart's three-part test of *Branzburg*, and in almost the same percentage of those cases journalist's privilege was upheld.

But first the landmark *Branzburg* decision.

BRANZBURG v. HAYES

408 U.S. 665, 92 S.CT. 2646,
33 L.ED.2D 626 (1972).

[Editorial Note

Certiorari was granted to review judgment of the United States Court of Appeals for the Ninth Circuit, 434 F.2d 1081, upholding refusal of a newsman to appear and testify before a grand jury with respect to confidential sources, and judgments of the Court of Appeals of Kentucky, 461 S.W.2d 345, and the Supreme Judicial Court of Massachusetts, 266 N.E.2d 297, rejecting claimed rights of newsmen to refuse to testify before grand juries with respect to confidential sources. The Supreme Court, per Justice White, held that requiring journalists to appear and testify before state or federal grand juries does not abridge the freedom of speech and press guaranteed by the First Amendment; and that a journalist's agreement to conceal criminal conduct of his news sources, or evidence thereof, does not give rise to any constitutional testimonial privilege with respect thereto.]

* * *

Opinion of the Court by Justice WHITE, announced by The Chief Justice.
* * *

The writ of certiorari in *Branzburg v. Hayes* and *Branzburg v. Meigs*, brings before us two judgments of the Kentucky Court of Appeals, both involving petitioner Branzburg, a staff reporter for the Courier-Journal, a daily newspaper published in Louisville, Jefferson County, Kentucky.

---

6. Caldwell v. United States, 434 F.2d 1081 (9th Cir. 1970).

On November 15, 1969, the Courier-Journal carried a story under petitioner's by-line describing in detail his observations of two young residents of Jefferson County synthesizing hashish from marihuana, (sic) an activity which, they asserted, earned them about $5,000 in three weeks. The article included a photograph of a pair of hands working above a laboratory table on which was a substance identified by the caption as hashish. The article stated that petitioner had promised not to reveal the identity of the two hashish makers. Petitioner was shortly subpoenaed by the Jefferson County grand jury; he appeared, but refused to identify the individuals he had seen possessing marihuana or the persons he had seen making hashish from marihuana. A state trial court judge ordered petitioner to answer these questions and rejected his contention that the Kentucky reporters' privilege statute, Ky.Rev.Stat. 421.100, the First Amendment of the United States Constitution, or §§ 1, 2, and 8 of the Kentucky Constitution authorized his refusal to answer. Petitioner then sought prohibition and mandamus in the Kentucky Court of Appeals on the same grounds that the Court of Appeals denied the petition. It held that petitioner had abandoned his First Amendment argument in a supplemental memorandum he had filed and tacitly rejected his argument based on the Kentucky Constitution. It also construed Ky.Rev.Stat. 421.100 as affording a newsman the privilege of refusing to divulge the identity of an informant who supplied him with information but held that the statute did not permit a reporter to refuse to testify about events he had observed personally, including the identities of those persons he had observed.

The second case involving petitioner Branzburg arose out of his later story published on January 10, 1971, which described in detail the use of drugs in Frankfort, Franklin County, Kentucky. The article reported that in order to provide a comprehensive survey of the "drug scene" in Frankfort, petitioner had "spent two weeks interviewing several dozen drug users in the capital city" and had seen some of them smoking marihuana. A number of conversations with and observations of several unnamed drug users were recounted. Subpoenaed to appear before a Franklin County grand jury "to testify in the matter of violation of statutes, concerning use and sale of drugs," petitioner Branzburg moved to quash the summons; the motion was denied although an order was issued protecting Branzburg from revealing "confidential associations, sources or information" but requiring that he "answer any questions which concern or pertain to any criminal act, the commission of which was actually observed by [him]." Prior to the time he was slated to appear before the grand jury, petitioner sought mandamus and prohibition from the Kentucky Court of Appeals, arguing that if he were forced to go before the grand jury or to answer questions regarding the identity of informants or disclose information given to him in confidence, his effectiveness as a reporter would be greatly damaged. The Court of Appeals once again denied the requested writs, reaffirming its construction of Ky. Rev.Stat. 421.100, and rejecting petitioner's claim of a First Amendment privilege. It distinguished Caldwell v. United States, 434 F.2d 1081 (9th Cir. 1970), and it also announced its "misgivings" about that decision, asserting that it represented "a drastic departure from the generally recognized rule that the sources of information of a newspaper reporter are not privileged under the First Amendment." It characterized petitioner's fear that his ability to obtain news would be destroyed as "so tenuous that it does not, in the opinion of this court, present an abridgement of freedom of the press within the meaning of that term as used in the Constitution of the United States."

Petitioner sought a writ of certiorari to review both judgments of the Kentucky Court of Appeals, and we granted the writ.

In the Matter of Paul Pappas originated when petitioner Pappas, a television newsman-photographer working out of the Providence, Rhode Island, office of a New Bedford, Massachusetts, television station, was called to New Bedford on July 30, 1970, to report on civil disorders there which involved fires and other turmoil. He intended to cover a Black Panther news conference at that group's headquarters in a boarded-up store. Petitioner found the streets around the store barricaded, but he ultimately gained entrance to the area and recorded and photographed a prepared statement read by one of the Black Panther leaders at about 3:00 p.m. He then asked for and received permission to re-enter the area. Returning at about 9:00 p.m. that evening, he was allowed to enter and remain inside Panther headquarters. As a condition of entry, Pappas agreed not to disclose anything he saw or heard inside the store except an anticipated police raid which Pappas, "on his own," was free to photograph and report as he wished. Pappas stayed inside the headquarters for about three hours, but there was no police raid, and petitioner wrote no story and did not otherwise reveal what had transpired in the store while he was there. Two months later, petitioner was summoned before the Bristol County Grand Jury and appeared, answered questions as to his name, address, employment, and what he had seen and heard outside Panther headquarters, but refused to answer any questions about what had taken place inside headquarters while he was there, claiming that the First Amendment afforded him a privilege to protect confidential informants and their information. A second summons was then served upon him, again directing him to appear before the Grand Jury and "to give such evidence as he knows relating to any matters which may be inquired of on behalf of the commonwealth before * * * the Grand Jury." His motion to quash on First Amendment and other grounds was denied by the trial judge who, noting the absence of a statutory newsman's privilege in Massachusetts, ruled that petitioner had no constitutional privilege to refuse to divulge to the Grand Jury what he had seen and heard, including the identity of persons he had observed. The case was reported for decision to the Supreme Judicial Court of Massachusetts. The record there did not include a transcript of the hearing on the motion to quash nor did it reveal the specific questions petitioner had refused to answer, the expected nature of his testimony, the nature of the grand jury investigation, or the likelihood of the grand jury securing the information it sought from petitioner by other means. The Supreme Judicial Court, however, took "judicial notice that in July, 1970, there were serious civil disorders in New Bedford, which involved street barricades, exclusion of the public from certain streets, fires, and similar turmoil. We were told at the arguments that there was gunfire in certain streets. We assume that the grand jury investigation was an appropriate effort to discover and indict those responsible for criminal acts." The Court then reaffirmed prior Massachusetts holdings that testimonial privileges were "exceptional" and "limited," stating that "[t]he principle that the public 'has a right to every man's evidence' " had usually been preferred, in the Commonwealth, to countervailing interests. The Court rejected the holding of the Ninth Circuit in Caldwell v. United States, and "adhere[d] to the view that there exists no constitutional newsman's privilege, either qualified or absolute, to refuse to appear and testify before a court or grand jury." Any adverse effect upon the free dissemination of news by virtue of petitioner's being called to testify was deemed to be only "indirect, theoretical, and uncertain." The court concluded that "The obligation of newsmen * * * is that of every citizen, * * to appear when summoned, with relevant written or other material when required, and to answer relevant and reasonable inquiries." The court nevertheless noted that grand juries were subject to supervision by the presiding judge, who had the duty "to prevent oppressive, unnecessary, irrelevant, and other improper inquiry and investigation," to insure that a witness' Fifth Amendment rights were not infringed, and to assess the propriety, necessity, and pertinence of the probable testimony to the investigation in progress. The burden was deemed to be on the witness to establish the impropriety of the summons or the questions asked. The denial of the motion to quash was affirmed and we granted a writ of certiorari to petitioner Pappas.

United States v. Caldwell arose from subpoenas issued by a federal grand jury in the Northern District of California to respondent Earl Caldwell, a reporter for the New York Times assigned to cover the Black Panther Party and other black militant groups. A subpoena *duces tecum* [a subpoena seeking notes, tapes, documents, or other physical evidence] was served on respondent on February 2, 1970, ordering him to appear before the grand jury to testify and to bring with him notes and tape recordings of interviews given him for publication by officers and spokesmen of the Black Panther Party concerning the aims, purposes, and activities of that organization. Respondent objected to the scope of this subpoena, and an agreement between his counsel and the government attorneys resulted in a continuance. A second subpoena was served on March 16, which omitted the documentary requirement and simply ordered Caldwell "to appear * * * to testify before the Grand Jury." Respondent and his employer, the New York Times, moved to quash on the ground that the unlimited breadth of the subpoenas and the fact that Caldwell would have to appear in secret before the grand jury would destroy his working relationship with the Black Panther Party and "suppress vital First Amendment freedoms * * * by driving a wedge of distrust and silence between the news media and the militants." Respondent argued that "so drastic an incursion upon First Amendment freedoms" should not be permitted "in the absence of a compelling governmental interest—not shown here—in requiring Mr. Caldwell's appearance before the grand jury." The motion was supported by *amicus curiae* memoranda from other publishing concerns and by affidavits from newsmen asserting the unfavorable impact on news sources of requiring reporters to appear before grand juries. The Government filed three memoranda in opposition to the motion to quash, each supported by affidavits. These documents stated that the grand jury was investigating, among other things, possible violations of a number of criminal statutes, including 18 U.S.C.A. § 871 [threats against the President], 18 U.S.C.A. § 1751 [assassination, attempts to assassinate, conspiracy to assassinate the President], 18 U.S.C.A. § 231 [civil disorders], 18 U.S. C.A. § 2101 [interstate travel to incite a riot], and 18 U.S.C.A. § 1341 [mail frauds and swindles]. It was recited that on November 15, 1969, an officer of the Black Panther Party made a publicly televised speech in which he had declared that "We will kill Richard Nixon" and that this threat had been repeated in three subsequent issues of the Party newspaper. Also referred to were various writings by Caldwell about the Black Panther Party, including an article published in the New York Times on December 14, 1969, stating that "[i]n their role as the vanguard in a revolutionary struggle the Panthers have picked up guns" and quoting the Chief of Staff of the Party as declaring that "We advocate the very direct overthrow of the Government by way of force and violence. By picking up guns and moving against it because we recognize it as being oppressive and in recognizing that we know that the only solution to it is armed struggle [*sic*]." The Government also stated that the Chief of Staff of the Party had been indicted by the grand jury on December 3, 1969, for uttering threats against the life of the President in violation of 18 U.S.C.A. § 871 and that various efforts had been made to secure evidence of crimes under investigation through the immunization of persons allegedly associated with the Black Panther Party.

On April 6, the District Court denied the motion to quash, Application of Caldwell, 311 F.Supp. 358 (D.C.Cal.1970), on the ground that "*every person* within the jurisdiction of the government" is bound to testify upon being properly summoned. [Emphasis in original]. Nevertheless, the court accepted respondent's First Amendment arguments to the extent of issuing a protective order providing that although respondent must divulge whatever information had been given to him for publication, he "shall not be required to reveal confidential associations, sources or information received, developed or maintained by him as a professional journalist in the course of his efforts to gather news for dissemination to the public through the press or other news media." The court held that the First Amendment afforded respondent a privilege to refuse disclosure of such confidential information until there had been "a showing by the Government of a compelling and overriding national interest in requiring Mr. Caldwell's testimony which cannot be served by any alternative means." 311 F.Supp. at 362.

Subsequently, the term of the grand jury expired, a new grand jury was convened, and a new subpoena *ad testificandum* [a subpoena seeking direct oral testimony] was issued and served on May 22, 1970. A new motion to quash by respondent and memorandum in opposition by the Government were filed, and by stipulation of the parties, the motion was submitted on the prior record. The court denied the motion to quash, repeating the protective provisions in its prior order but this time directing Caldwell to appear before the grand jury pursuant to the May 22 subpoena. Respondent refused to appear before the grand jury, and the court issued an order to show cause why he should not be held in contempt. Upon his further refusal to go before the grand jury, respondent was ordered committed for contempt until such time as he complied with the court's order or until the expiration of the term of the grand jury.

Respondent Caldwell appealed the contempt order, and the Court of Appeals reversed. Caldwell v. United States, 434 F.2d 1081 (9th Cir. 1970). Viewing the issue before it as whether Caldwell was required to appear before the grand jury at all, rather than the scope of permissible interrogation, the court first determined that the First Amendment provided a qualified testimonial privilege to newsmen; in its view, requiring a reporter like Caldwell to testify would deter his informants from communicating with him in the future and would cause him to censor his writings in an effort to avoid being subpoenaed. Absent compelling reasons for requiring his testimony, he was held privileged to withhold it. The court also held, for similar First Amendment reasons, that absent some special showing of necessity by the Government, attendance by Caldwell at a secret meeting of the grand jury was something he was privileged to refuse because of the potential impact of such an appearance on the flow of news to the public. We granted the United States' petition for certiorari.

Petitioners Branzburg and Pappas and respondent Caldwell press First Amendment Claims that may be simply put: that to gather news it is often necessary to agree either not to identify the source of information published or to publish only part of the facts revealed, or both; that if the reporter is nevertheless forced to reveal these confidences to a grand jury, the source so identified and other confidential sources of other reporters will be measurably deterred from furnishing publishable information, all to the detriment of the free flow of information protected by the First Amendment. Although petitioners do not claim an absolute privilege against official interrogation in all circumstances, they assert that the reporter should not be forced either to appear or to testify before a grand jury or at trial until and unless sufficient grounds are shown for believing that the reporter possesses information relevant to a crime the grand jury is investigating, that the information the reporter has is unavailable from other sources, and that the need for the information is sufficiently compelling to override the claimed invasion of First Amendment interests occasioned by the disclosure. * * *

We do not question the significance of free speech, press or assembly to the country's welfare. Nor is it suggested that news gathering does not qualify for First Amendment protection; without some protection for seeking out the news, freedom of the press could be eviscerated. But this case involves no intrusions upon speech or assembly, no prior restraint or restriction on what the press may publish, and no express or implied command that the press publish what it prefers to withhold. No exaction or tax for the privilege of publishing, and no penalty, civil or criminal, related to the content of published material is at issue here. The use of confidential sources by the press is not forbidden or restricted; reporters remain free to seek news from any source by means within the law. No attempt is made to require the press to publish its sources of information or indiscriminately to disclose them on request.

The sole issue before us is the obligation of reporters to respond to grand jury subpoenas as other citizens do and to answer questions relevant to an investigation into the commission of crime. [Emphasis added.] Citizens generally are not constitutionally immune from grand jury subpoenas; and neither the First Amendment nor other constitutional provision protects the average citizen from disclosing to a grand jury information that he has received in confidence. The claim is, however, that reporters are exempt from these obligations because if forced to respond to subpoenas and identify their sources or disclose other confidences, their informants will refuse or be reluctant to furnish newsworthy information in the future. This asserted burden on news gathering is said to make compelled testimony from newsmen constitutionally suspect and to require a privileged position for them.

It is clear that the First Amendment does not invalidate every incidental burdening of the press that may result from the enforcement of civil or criminal statutes of general applicability. * * *

The prevailing view is that the press is not free with impunity to publish everything and anything it desires to publish. Although it may deter or regulate what is said or published, the press may not circulate knowing or reckless falsehoods damaging to private reputation without subjecting itself to liability for damages, including punitive damages, or even criminal prosecution. See *New York Times Co. v. Sullivan.* * * *

Despite the fact that news gathering may be hampered, the press is regularly excluded from grand jury proceedings, our own conferences, the meetings of other official bodies gathered in executive session, and the meetings of private organizations. Newsmen have no constitutional right of access to the scenes of crime or disaster when the general public is excluded, and they may be prohibited from attending or publishing information about trials if such restrictions are necessary to assure a defendant a fair trial before an impartial tribunal.

* * *

It is thus not surprising that the great weight of authority is that newsmen are not exempt from the normal duty of appearing before a grand jury and answering questions relevant to a criminal investigation. At common law, courts consistently refused to recognize the existence of any privilege authorizing a newsman to refuse to reveal confidential information to a grand jury. * * * These courts have applied the presumption against the existence of an asserted testimonial privilege, and have concluded that the First Amendment interest asserted by the newsman was outweighed by the general obligation of a citizen to appear before a grand jury or at trial, pursuant to a subpoena, and give what information he possesses. * *

The prevailing constitutional view of the newsman's privilege is very much rooted in the ancient role of the grand jury which has the dual function of determining if there is probable cause to believe that a crime has been committed and of protecting citizens against unfounded criminal prosecutions. Grand jury proceedings are constitutionally mandated for the institution of federal criminal prosecutions for capital or other serious crimes, and "its constitutional prerogatives are rooted in long centuries of Anglo-American history." The Fifth Amendment provides that "No person shall be held to answer for a capital, or otherwise infamous crime, unless on a presentment or indictment of a Grand Jury." The adoption of the grand jury "in our Constitution as the sole method for preferring charges in serious criminal cases shows the high place it held as an instrument of justice." Although state systems of criminal procedure differ greatly among themselves, the grand jury is similarly guaranteed by many state constitutions and plays an important role in fair and effective law enforcement in the overwhelming majority of the States. Because its task is to inquire into the existence of possible criminal conduct and to return only well-founded indictments, its investigative powers are necessarily broad. "It is a grand inquest, a body with powers of investigation and inquisition, the scope of whose inquiries is not to be limited narrowly by questions of propriety or forecasts of the probable result of the investigation, or by doubts whether any particular individual will be found properly subject to an accusation of crime." Hence the grand jury's authority to subpoena witnesses is not only historic, but essential to its task. Although the powers of the grand jury are not unlimited and are subject to the supervision of a judge, the long standing principle that "the public has a right to every man's evidence," except for those persons protected by a constitutional, common law, or statutory privilege, 8 J. Wigmore, Evidence § 2192 (McNaughton rev. 1961), is particularly applicable to grand jury proceedings.

A number of States have provided newsmen a statutory privilege of varying breadth, but the majority have not done so, and none has been provided by federal statute. Until now the only testimonial privilege for unofficial witnesses that is rooted in the Federal Constitution is the Fifth Amendment privilege against compelled self-incrimination. We are asked to create another by interpreting the First Amendment to grant newsmen a testimonial privilege that other citizens do not enjoy. This we decline to do. * * *

* * *

Thus, we cannot seriously entertain the notion that the First Amendment protects a newsman's agreement to conceal the criminal conduct of his source, or evidence thereof, on the theory that it is better to write about crime than to do something about it. Insofar as any reporter in these cases undertook not to reveal or testify about the crime he witnessed, his claim of privilege under the First Amendment presents no substantial question. The crimes of news sources are no less reprehensible and threatening to the public interest when witnessed by a reporter than when they are not.

There remain those situations where a source is not engaged in criminal conduct but has information suggesting illegal conduct by others. Newsmen frequently receive information from such sources pursuant to a tacit or express agreement to withhold the source's name and suppress any information that the source wishes not published. Such informants presumably desire anonymity in order to avoid being entangled as a witness in a criminal trial or grand jury investigation. They may fear that disclosure will threaten their job security or personal safety or that it will simply result in dishonor or embarrassment.

The argument that the flow of news will be diminished by compelling reporters to aid the grand jury in a criminal investigation is not irrational, nor are the records before us silent on the matter. But we remain unclear how often and to what extent informers are actually deterred from furnishing information when newsmen are forced to testify before a grand jury. The available data indicates that some newsmen rely a great deal on confidential sources and that some informants are particularly sensitive to the threat of exposure and may be silenced if it is held by this Court that, ordinarily, newsmen must testify pursuant to subpoenas, but the evidence fails to demonstrate that there would be a significant constriction of the flow of news to the public if this Court reaffirms the prior common law and constitutional rule regarding the testimonial obligations of newsmen. Estimates of the inhibiting effect of such subpoenas on the willingness of informants to make disclosures to newsmen are widely divergent and to a great extent speculative. It would be difficult to canvass the views of the informants themselves; surveys of reporters on this topic are chiefly opinions of predicted informant behavior and must be viewed in the light of the professional self-interest of the interviewees. Reliance by the press on confidential informants does not mean that all such sources will in fact dry up because of the later possible appearance of the newsman before a grand jury. The reporter may never be called and if he objects to testifying, the prosecution may not insist. Also, the relationship of many informants to the press is a symbiotic one which is unlikely to be greatly inhibited by the threat of subpoena: quite often, such informants are members of a minority political or cultural group which relies heavily on the media to propagate its views, publicize its aims, and magnify its exposure to the public. Moreover, grand juries characteristically conduct secret proceedings, and law enforcement officers are themselves experienced in dealing with informers and have their own methods for protecting them without interference with the effective administration of justice. There is little before us indicating that informants whose interest in avoiding exposure is that it may threaten job security, personal safety, or peace of mind, would in fact, be in a worse position, or would think they would be, if they risked placing their trust in public officials as well as reporters. We doubt if the informer who prefers anonymity but is sincerely interested in furnishing evidence of crime will always or very often be deterred by the prospect of dealing with those public authorities characteristically charged with the duty to protect the public interest as well as his.

Accepting the fact, however, that an undetermined number of informants not themselves implicated in crime will nevertheless, for whatever reason, refuse to talk to newsmen if they fear identification by a reporter in an official investigation we cannot accept the argument that the public interest in possible future news about crime from undisclosed, unverified sources must take precedence over the public interest in pursuing and prosecuting those crimes reported to the press by informants and in thus deterring the commission of such crimes in the future.

* * *

Of course, the press has the right to abide by its agreement not to publish all the information it has, but the right to withhold news is not equivalent to a First Amendment exemption from the ordinary duty of all other citizens to furnish relevant information to a grand jury performing an important public function. Private restraints on the flow of information are not so favored by the First Amendment that they override all other public interests. As Justice Black declared in another context, "'[f]reedom of the press from governmental interference under the First Amendment does not sanction repression of that freedom by private interests.'' Associated Press v. United States. [See this text, p. 639.]

Neither are we now convinced that a virtually impenetrable constitutional shield, beyond legislative or judicial control, should be forged to protect a private system of informers operated by the press to report on criminal conduct, a system that would be unaccountable to the public, would pose a threat to the citizen's justifiable expectations of privacy, and would equally protect well-intentioned informants and those who pay for or otherwise betray their trust to their employer or associates. The public through its elected and appointed law enforcement officers regularly utilizes informers, and in proper circumstances may assert a privilege against disclosing the identity of these informers. * * * Such informers enjoy no constitutional protection. Their testimony is available to the public when desired by grand juries or at criminal trials; their identity cannot be concealed from the defendant when it is critical to his case. Clearly, this system is not impervious to control by the judiciary and the decision whether to unmask an informer or to continue to profit by his anonymity is in public, not private, hands. We think that it should remain there and that public authorities should retain the options of either insisting on the informer's testimony relevant to the prosecution of crime or of seeking the benefit of further information that his exposure might prevent.

* * *

The requirements of those cases, which hold that a State's interest must be "compelling" or "paramount" to justify even an indirect burden on First Amendment rights, are also met here. As we have indicated, the investigation of crime by the grand jury implements a fundamental governmental role of securing the safety of the person and property of the citizen, and it appears to us that calling reporters to give testimony in the manner and for the reasons that other citizens are called "bears a reasonable relationship to the achievement of the governmental purpose asserted as its justification." If the test is that the Government "convincingly show a substantial relation between the information sought and a subject of overriding and compelling state interest," it is quite apparent (1) that the State has the necessary interest in extirpating the traffic in illegal drugs, in forestalling assassination attempts on the President, and in preventing the community from being disrupted by violent disorders endangering both persons and property; and (2) that, based on the stories Branzburg and Caldwell wrote and Pappas' admitted conduct, the grand jury called these reporters as they would others—because it was likely that they could supply information to help the Government determine whether illegal conduct had occurred, and, if it had, whether there was sufficient evidence to return an indictment.

Similar considerations dispose of the reporters' claims that preliminary to requiring their grand jury appearance, the State must show that a crime has been committed and that they possess relevant information not available from other sources, for only the grand jury itself can make this determination. The role of the grand jury as an important instrument of effective law enforcement necessarily includes an investigatory function with respect to determining whether a crime has been committed and who committed it. To this end it must call witnesses, in the manner best suited to perform its task. "When the grand jury is performing its investigatory function into a general problem area, * * * society's interest is best served by a thorough and extensive investigation." Wood v. Georgia. A grand jury investigation "is not fully carried out until every available clue has been run down and all witnesses examined in every proper way to find if a crime has been committed." Such an investigation may be triggered by tips, rumors, evidence proferred by the prosecutor, or the personal knowledge of the grand jurors. It is only after the grand jury has examined the evidence that a determination of whether the proceeding will result in an indictment can be made. * * * We see no reason to hold that these reporters, any more than other citizens, should be excused from furnishing information that may help the grand jury in arriving at its initial determinations.

The privilege claimed here is conditional, not absolute; given the suggested preliminary showings and compelling need, the reporter would be required to testify. Presumably, such a rule would reduce the instances in which reporters could be required to appear but predicting in advance when and in what circumstances they could be compelled to do so would be difficult. Such a rule would also have implications for the issuance of compulsory process to reporters at civil and criminal trials and at legislative hearings. If newsmen's confidential sources are as sensitive as they are claimed to be, the prospect of being unmasked whenever a judge determines the situation justifies it is hardly a satisfactory solution to the problem. For them, it would appear that only an absolute privilege would suffice.

We are unwilling to embark the judiciary on a long and difficult journey to such an uncertain destination. The administration of a constitutional newsman's privilege would present practical and conceptual difficulties of a high order. Sooner or later, it would be necessary to define those categories of newsmen who qualified for the privilege, a questionable procedure in light of the traditional doctrine that liberty of the press is the right of the lonely pamphleteer who uses carbon paper or a mimeograph just as much as of the large metropolitan publisher who utilizes the latest photocomposition methods. Freedom of the press is a "fundamental personal right" which "is not confined to newspapers and periodicals. It necessarily embraces pamphlets and leaflets * *." The informative function asserted by representatives of the organized press in the present cases is also performed by lecturers, political pollsters, novelists, academic researchers, and dramatists. Almost any author may quite accurately assert that he is contributing to the flow of information to the public, that he relies on confidential sources of information, and that these sources will be silenced if he is forced to make disclosures before a grand jury.

In each instance where a reporter is subpoenaed to testify, the courts would also be embroiled in preliminary factual and legal determinations with respect to whether the proper predicate had been laid for the reporters' appearance: Is there probable cause to believe a crime has been committed? Is it likely that the reporter has useful information gained in confidence? Could the grand jury obtain the information elsewhere? Is the official interest sufficient to outweigh the claimed privilege?

Thus, in the end, by considering whether enforcement of a particular law served a "compelling" governmental interest, the courts would be inextricably involved in distinguishing between the value of enforcing different criminal laws. By requiring testimony from a reporter in investigations involving some crimes but not in others, they would be making a value judgment which a legislature had declined to make, since in each case the criminal law involved would represent a considered legislative judgment, not constitutionally suspect of what conduct is liable to criminal prosecution. The task of judges, like other officials outside the legislative branch is not to make the law but to uphold it in accordance with their oaths.

At the federal level, Congress has freedom to determine whether a statutory newsman's privilege is necessary and desirable and to fashion standards and rules as narrow or broad as deemed necessary to address the evil discerned and, equally important, to re-fashion those rules as experience from time to time may dictate. There is also merit in leaving state legislatures free, within First Amendment limits, to fashion their own standards in light of the conditions and problems with respect to the relations between law enforcement officials and press in their own areas. It goes without saying, of course, that we are powerless to erect any bar to state courts responding in their own way and construing their own constitutions so as to recognize a newsman's privilege, either qualified or absolute. [Emphasis added.]

In addition, there is much force in the pragmatic view that the press has at its disposal powerful mechanisms of communication and is far from helpless to protect itself from harassment or substantial harm. Furthermore, if what the newsmen urged in these cases is true—that law enforcement cannot hope to gain and may suffer from subpoenaing newsmen before grand juries—prosecutors will be loath to risk so much for so little. Thus, at the federal level the Attorney General has already fashioned a set of rules for federal officials in connection with subpoenaing members of the press to testify before grand juries or at criminal trials.[41] These rules are a major step in the direction petitioners desire to move. They may prove wholly sufficient to resolve the bulk of disagreements and controversies between press and federal officials.

Finally, as we have earlier indicated, news gathering is not without its First Amendment protections, and grand jury investigations if instituted or conducted other than in good faith, would pose wholly different issues for resolution under the First Amendment. Official harassment of the press undertaken not for purposes of law enforcement but to disrupt a reporter's relationship with his news sources would have no justification. Grand juries are subject to judicial control and subpoenas to motions to quash. We do not expect courts will forget that grand juries must operate within the limits of the First Amendment as well as the Fifth.

We turn, therefore, to the disposition of the cases before us. From what we have said, it necessarily follows that the decision in *United States v. Caldwell* must be reversed. If there is no First Amendment privilege to refuse to answer the relevant and material questions asked during a good-faith grand jury investigation, then it is *a fortiori* true that there is no privilege to refuse to appear before such a grand jury until the Government demonstrates some "compelling need" for a newsman's testimony. Other issues were urged upon

41. Guidelines for Subpoenas to the News Media were first announced in a speech by the Attorney General on August 10, 1970, and then were expressed in Department of Justice Memo. No. 692 (Sept. 2, 1970), which was sent to all United States Attorneys by the Assistant Attorney General in charge of the Criminal Division. [New guidelines were promulgated in 1980. See Guidelines on News Media Subpoenas, 6 Med.L.Rptr. 2153 (1980)].

us, but since they were not passed upon by the Court of Appeals, we decline to address them in the first instance.

The decisions in *Branzburg v. Hayes* and *Branzburg v. Meigs* must be affirmed. Here, petitioner refused to answer questions that directly related to criminal conduct which he had observed and written about. The Kentucky Court of Appeals noted that marihuana is defined as a narcotic drug by statute, and that unlicensed possession or compounding of it is a felony punishable by both fine and imprisonment. It held that petitioner "saw the commission of the statutory felonies of unlawful possession of marijuana and the unlawful conversion of it into hashish." Petitioner may be presumed to have observed similar violations of the state narcotics laws during the research he did for the story which forms the basis of the subpoena in *Branzburg v. Meigs.* In both cases, if what petitioner wrote was true, he had direct information to provide the grand jury concerning the commission of serious crimes.

The only question presented at the present time in *In the Matter of Paul Pappas* is whether petitioner Pappas must appear before the grand jury to testify pursuant to subpoena. The Massachusetts Supreme Judicial Court characterized the record in this case as "meager," and it is not clear what petitioner will be asked by the grand jury. It is not even clear that he will be asked to divulge information received in confidence. We affirm the decision of the Massachusetts Supreme Judicial Court and hold that petitioner must appear before the grand jury to answer the questions put to him, subject, of course, to the supervision of the presiding judge as to "the propriety, purposes, and scope of the grand jury inquiry and the pertinence of the probable testimony."

So ordered.

Justice POWELL, concurring in the opinion of the Court.

I add this brief statement to emphasize what seems to me to be the limited nature of the Court's holding. The Court does not hold that newsmen, subpoenaed to testify before a grand jury, are without constitutional rights with respect to the gathering of news or in safeguarding their sources. Certainly, we do not hold, as suggested in the dissenting opinion, that state and federal authorities are free to "annex" the news media as "an investigative arm of government." The solicitude repeatedly shown by this Court for First Amendment freedoms should be sufficient assurance against any such effort even if one seriously believed that the media—properly free and untrammeled in the fullest sense of these terms—were not able to protect themselves.

As indicated in the concluding portion of the opinion, the Court states that no harassment of newsmen will be tolerated. If a newsman believes that the grand jury investigation is not being conducted in good faith he is not without remedy. Indeed, if the newsman is called upon to give information bearing only a remote and tenuous relationship to the subject of the investigation, or if he has some other reason to believe that his testimony implicates confidential source relationships without a legitimate need of law enforcement, he will have access to the Court on a motion to quash and an appropriate protective order may be entered. The asserted claim to privilege should be judged on its facts by the striking of a proper balance between freedom of the press and the obligation of all citizens to give relevant testimony with respect to criminal conduct. The balance of these vital constitutional and societal interests on a case-by-case basis accords with the tried and traditional way of adjudicating such questions.

In short, the courts will be available to newsmen under circumstances where legitimate First Amendment interests require protection.

Justice STEWART, with whom Justice Brennan and Justice Marshall join, dissenting.

The Court's crabbed view of the First Amendment reflects a disturbing insensitivity to the critical role of an independent press in our society. The question whether a reporter has a constitutional right to a confidential relationship with his source is of first impression here, but the principles which should guide our decision are as basic as any to be found in the Constitution. While Justice Powell's enigmatic concurring opinion gives some hope of a more flexible view in the future, the Court in these cases holds that a newsman has no First Amendment right to protect his sources when called before a grand jury. The Court thus invites state and federal authorities to undermine the historic independence of the press by attempting to annex the journalistic profession as an investigative arm of government. Not only will this decision impair performance of the press' constitutionally protected functions, but it will, I am convinced, in the long run, harm rather than help the administration of justice.

I respectfully dissent.

The reporter's constitutional right to a confidential relationship with his source stems from the broad societal interest in a full and free flow of information to the public. It is this basic concern that underlies the Constitution's protection of a free press because the guarantee is "not for the benefit of the press so much as for the benefit of all of us."

Enlightened choice by an informed citizenry is the basic ideal upon which an open society is premised, and a free press is thus indispensable to a free society. * * As private and public aggregations of power burgeon in size and the pressures for conformity necessarily mount, there is obviously a continuing need for an independent press to disseminate a robust variety of information and opinion through reportage, investigation and criticism, if we are to preserve our constitutional tradition of maximizing freedom of choice by encouraging diversity of expression.

In keeping with this tradition, we have held that the right to publish is central to the First Amendment and basic to the existence of constitutional democracy.

A corollary of the right to publish must be the right to gather news. The full flow of information to the public protected by the free press guarantee would be severely curtailed if no protection whatever were afforded to the process by which news is assembled and disseminated. We have, therefore, recognized that there is a right to publish without prior governmental approval.

No less important to the news dissemination process is the gathering of information. News must not be unnecessarily cut off at its source, for without freedom to acquire information the right to publish would be impermissibly compromised. Accordingly, a right to gather news, of some dimensions, must exist. * * *

The right to gather news implies, in turn, a right to a confidential relationship between a reporter and his source. This proposition follows as a matter of simple logic once three factual predicates are recognized: (1) newsmen require informants to gather news; (2) confidentiality—the promise or understanding that names or certain aspects of communications will be kept off-the-record—is essential to the creation and maintenance of a news-gathering relationship with informants; and (3) the existence of an unbridled subpoena power—the absence of a constitutional right protecting, in *any* way, a confidential relationship from compulsory process—will either deter sources from divulging information or deter reporters from gathering and publishing information.

It is obvious that informants are necessary to the news-gathering process as we know it today. If it is to perform its constitutional mission, the press must do far more than merely print public statements or publish prepared handouts. Familiarity with the people and circumstances involved in the myriad background activities that result in the final product called "news" is vital to complete and responsible journalism, unless the press is to be a captive mouthpiece of "newsmakers."

It is equally obvious that the promise of confidentiality may be a necessary prerequisite to a productive relationship between a newsman and his informants. An officeholder may fear his superior; a member of the bureaucracy, his associates; a dissident, the scorn of majority opinion. All may have information valuable to the public discourse, yet each may be willing to relate that information only in confidence to a reporter whom he trusts, either because of excessive caution or because of a reasonable fear of reprisals or censure for unorthodox views. The First Amendment concern must not be with the motives of any particular news source, but rather with the conditions in which informants of all shades of the spectrum may make information available through the press to the public. * * *

* * *

Finally, and most important, when governmental officials possess an unchecked power to compel newsmen to disclose information received in confidence, sources will clearly be deterred from giving information, and reporters will clearly be deterred from publishing it, because uncertainty about exercise of the power will lead to "self-censorship." The uncertainty arises, of course, because the judiciary has traditionally imposed virtually no limitations on the grand jury's broad investigatory powers. See Antell, *The Modern Grand Jury: Benighted Supergovernment*, 51 A.B.A.J. (1965).

After today's decision, the potential informant can never be sure that his identity or off-the-record communications will not subsequently be revealed through the compelled testimony of a newsman. A public spirited person inside government, who is not implicated in any crime, will now be fearful of revealing corruption or other governmental wrong-doing, because he will now know he can subsequently be identified by use of compulsory process. The potential source must, therefore, choose between risking exposure by giving information or avoiding the risk by remaining silent.

The reporter must speculate about whether contact with a controversial source or publication of controversial material will lead to a subpoena. In the event of a subpoena, under today's decision, the newsman will know that he must choose between being punished for contempt if he refuses to testify, or violating his profession's ethics and impairing his resourcefulness as a reporter if he discloses confidential information.

Again, the common sense understanding that such deterrence will occur is buttressed by concrete evidence. The existence of deterrent effects through fear and self-censorship was impressively developed in the District Court in *Caldwell.* Individual reporters and commentators have noted such effects. Surveys have verified that an unbridled subpoena power will substantially impair the flow of news to the public, especially in sensitive areas involving governmental officials, financial affairs, political figures, dissidents, or minority groups that require in-depth, investigative reporting. And the Justice Department has recognized that "compulsory process in some circumstances may have a limiting effect on the exercise of First Amendment rights." *No* evidence contradicting the existence of such deterrent effects was offered at the trials or in the briefs here by the petitioners in *Caldwell* or by the respondents in *Branzburg* and *Pappas*.

The impairment of the flow of news cannot, of course, be proven with scientific precision, as the Court seems to demand. Obviously, not every news-gathering relationship requires confidentiality. And it is difficult to pinpoint precisely how many relationships do require a promise or understanding of nondisclosure. But we have never before demanded that First Amendment rights rest on elaborate empirical studies demonstrating beyond any conceivable doubt that deterrent effects exist; we have never before required proof of the exact number of people potentially affected by governmental action, who would actually be dissuaded from engaging in First Amendment activity.

Rather, on the basis of common sense and available information, we have asked, often implicitly, (1) whether there was a rational connection between the cause (the governmental action) and the effect (the deterrence or impairment of First Amendment activity) and (2) whether the effect would occur with some regularity, i.e., would not be *de minimus*. * * * And, in making this determination, we have shown a special solicitude towards the "indispensable liberties" protected by the First Amendment for "freedoms such as these are protected not only against heavy-handed frontal attack, but also from being stifled by more subtle government interference." Once this threshold inquiry has been satisfied, we have then examined the competing interests in determining whether there is an unconstitutional infringement of First Amendment freedoms.

* * *

Thus, we cannot escape the conclusion that when neither the reporter nor his source can rely on the shield of confidentiality against unrestrained use of the grand jury's subpoena power, valuable information will not be published and the public dialogue will inevitably be impoverished.

* * *

Accordingly, when a reporter is asked to appear before a grand jury and reveal confidences, I would hold that the government must (1) show that there is probable cause to believe that the newsman has information which is clearly relevant to a specific probable violation of law; (2) demonstrate that the information sought cannot be obtained by alternative means less destructive of First Amendment rights; and (3) demonstrate a compelling and overriding interest in the information. [Emphasis added.]

This is not to say that a grand jury could not issue a subpoena until such a showing were made, and it is not to say that a newsman would be in any way privileged to ignore any subpoena that was issued. Obviously, before the government's burden to make such a showing were triggered, the reporter would have to move to quash the subpoena, asserting the basis on which he considered the particular relationship a confidential one.

The crux of the Court's rejection of any newsman's privilege is its observation that only "where news sources themselves are implicated in crime or possess information *relevant* to the grand jury's task need they or the reporter be concerned about grand jury subpoenas." But this is a most misleading construct. For it is obviously not true that the only persons about whom reporters will be forced to testify will be those "confidential informants involved in actual criminal conduct" and those having "information suggesting illegal conduct by others." As noted above, given the grand jury's extraordinarily broad investigative powers and the weak standards of relevance and materiality that apply during such inquiries, reporters, if they have no testimonial privilege, will be called to give information about informants who have neither committed crimes nor have information about crime. It is to avoid deterrence of such sources and thus to prevent needless injury to First Amendment values that I think the government must be required to show probable cause that the newsman has information which is clearly relevant to a specific probable violation of criminal law.

Similarly, a reporter may have information from a confidential source which is "related" to the commission of crime, but the government may be able to obtain an indictment or otherwise achieve its purposes by subpoenaing persons other than the reporter. It is an obvious but important truism that when government aims have been fully served, there can be no legitimate reason to disrupt a confidential relationship between a reporter and his source. To do so would not aid the administration of justice and would only impair the flow of information to the public. Thus, it is to avoid deterrence of such sources that I think the government must show that there are no alternative means for the grand jury to obtain the information sought.

Both the "probable cause" and "alternative means" requirements would thus serve the vital function of mediating between the public interest in the administration of justice and the constitutional protection of the full flow of information. These requirements would avoid a direct conflict between these competing concerns, and they would generally provide adequate protection for newsmen. No doubt the courts would be required to make some delicate judgments in working out this accommodation. But that, after all, is the function of courts of law. Better such judgments, however difficult, than the simplistic and stultifying absolutism adopted by the Court in denying any force to the First Amendment in these cases.

The error in the Court's absolute rejection of First Amendment interests in these cases seems to me to be most profound. For in the name of advancing the administration of justice, the Court's decision, I think, will only impair the achievement of that goal. People entrusted with law enforcement responsibility, no less than private citizens, need general information relating to controversial social problems. Obviously, press reports have great value to government, even when the newsman cannot be compelled to testify before a grand jury. The sad paradox of the Court's position is that when a grand jury may exercise an unbridled subpoena power, and sources involved in sensitive matters become fearful of disclosing information, the newsman will not only cease to be a useful grand jury witness; he will cease to investigate and publish information about issues of public import. I cannot subscribe to such an anomalous result, for, in my view, the interests protected by the First Amendment are not antagonistic to the administration of justice. Rather, they can, in the long run, only be complementary, and for that reason must be given great "breathing space."

In deciding what protection should be given to information a reporter receives in confidence from a news source, the Court of Appeals for the Ninth Circuit affirmed the holding of a District Court that the grand jury power of testimonial compulsion must not be exercised in a manner likely to impair First Amendment interests "until there has been a clear showing of a compelling and overriding national interest that cannot be served by alternative means." Caldwell v. United States, 434 F.2d 1081, 1086 (9th Cir. 1970). * * *

I think this decision was correct. On the record before us the United States has not met the burden which I think the appropriate newsman's privilege should require.

* * *

In the *Caldwell* case, the Court of Appeals further found that Caldwell's confidential relationship with the leaders of the Black Panther Party would be impaired if he appeared before the grand jury at all to answer questions, even though not privileged. On the particular facts before it, the Court concluded that the very appearance by Caldwell before the grand jury would jeopardize his relationship with his sources, leading to a severance of the news-gathering relationship and impairment of the flow of news to the public.

* * *

I think this ruling was also correct in light of the particularized circumstances of the *Caldwell* case. Obviously, only in very rare circumstances would a confidential relationship between a reporter and his source be so sensitive that mere appearance before the grand jury by the newsman would substantially impair his news-gathering function. But in this case, the reporter made out a prima facie case that the flow of news to the public would be curtailed. And he stated, without contradiction, that the only nonconfidential material about which he could testify was already printed in his newspaper articles. * * *

Accordingly, I would affirm the judgment of the Court of Appeals in *United States v. Caldwell.* In the other two cases before us, *Branzburg v. Hayes* and *Branzburg v. Meigs,* and *In the Matter of Paul Pappas,* I would vacate the judgments and remand the cases for further proceedings not inconsistent with the views I have expressed in this opinion.

Justice DOUGLAS, dissenting.

* * *

It is my view that there is no "compelling need" that can be shown which qualifies the reporter's immunity from appearing or testifying before a grand jury, unless the reporter himself is implicated in a crime. His immunity in my view is therefore quite complete, for *absent his involvement in a crime*, the First Amendment protects him against an appearance before a grand jury and if he is involved in a crime, the Fifth Amendment stands as a barrier. [Emphasis added.] Since in my view there is no area of inquiry not protected by a privilege, the reporter need not appear for the futile purpose of invoking one to each question. And, since in my view a newsman has an absolute right not to appear before a grand jury it follows for me that a journalist who voluntarily appears before that body may invoke his First Amendment privilege to specific questions. The basic issue is the extent to which the First Amendment * * * must yield to the Government's asserted need to know a reporter's unprinted information.

The starting point for decision pretty well marks the range within which the end result lies. The *New York Times,* whose reporting functions are at issue here, takes the amazing position that First Amendment rights are to be balanced against other needs or conveniences of government. My belief is that all of the "balancing" was done by those who wrote the Bill of Rights. By casting the First Amendment in absolute terms, they repudiated, the timid, watered-down, emasculated versions of the First Amendment which both the Government and the *New York Times* advances in the case.

* * *

A reporter is no better than his source of information. Unless he has a privilege to withhold the identity of his source, he will be the victim of governmental intrigue or aggression. If he can be summoned to testify in secret before a grand jury, his sources will dry up and the attempted exposure, the effort to enlighten the public, will be ended. If what the Court sanctions today becomes settled law, then the reporter's main function in American society will be to pass on to the public the press releases which the various departments of government issue.

The intrusion of government into this domain is symptomatic of the disease of this society. As the years pass the power of government becomes more and more pervasive. It is a power to suffocate both people and causes. Those in power, whatever their politics, want only to perpetuate it. Now that the fences of the law and the tradition that has protected the press are broken down, the people are the victims. The First Amendment, as I read it, was designed precisely to prevent that tragedy.

COMMENT

1. Long before courts ruled in either *Caldwell* or *Branzburg*, journalists had contended that the First Amendment implied at least a qualified or conditional right of confidentiality. For at least 100 years, reporters and editors had argued that testimony compelled to discover the identity of a source would violate their employers' rules and perhaps cause them to lose their jobs, or it would contradict their own professional codes of ethics. Self-incrimination and irrelevancy were also used as arguments to deflect subpoenas.

In the tumultuous political period between the 1968 Democratic Convention in Chicago and the Watergate scandal, a cloudburst of subpoenas hit the press. In a typical case, Will Lewis, manager of station KPFK–FM in Los Angeles, was held in contempt and jailed in 1973 for refusing to turn over to a federal grand jury the originals of a letter and tape recording sent him by two radical groups claiming to have inside information on the Patty Hearst affair.

After sixteen days in solitary confinement at Terminal Island Federal Prison, Lewis was released by Supreme Court Justice William O. Douglas pending appeal. The Ninth Circuit Court of Appeals affirmed the contempt conviction, Lewis appealed, and the U.S. Supreme Court denied review. That left Lewis with the choice of going back to jail or turning over the subpoenaed material to federal prosecutors. Lewis chose the latter.[7] Other reporters have chosen either to remain in or to go back to jail.

William Farr of the *Los Angeles Herald-Examiner*, for example, refused to disclose to a county court judge the names of prosecution attorneys who had supplied him with a copy of a witness's deposition in the gruesome Charles Manson case, this after the judge had forbidden officers of the court to publicize the case. Farr spent two months in jail.[8]

Judges—especially in California it would seem—take umbrage when their direct orders are defied. In the *Rosato* case,[9] bribery-conspiracy indictments had been handed down by a Fresno County grand jury against three accused. A day before the grand jury transcripts would have become public documents, the judge sealed the record for the duration of the trial and issued a restrictive order prohibiting public communications by attorneys, parties, public officials, and witnesses. Stories replete with quotations from the sealed transcript nevertheless appeared in the *Fresno Bee*, and the judge demanded to know where they came from. When he asked reporters to name their sources, he was met with silence. Two reporters, the city editor, and the managing editor of the *Bee* were then cited for contempt.

The court's rationale was that in enforcing its power over its own officers, the concomitant interest of journalists in protecting their sources was irrelevant and the California "shield" law inapplicable. The journalists went to jail. Their sentences were upheld by the California Supreme Court, and the U.S. Supreme Court again denied review. They were released a short time later, however, when the sentencing judge decided that "they had acted

7. In re Lewis, 377 F.Supp. 297 (C.D.Cal.1974), aff'd 501 F.2d 418 (9th Cir.), cert. den. 420 U.S. 913 (1975).

8. Farr v. Superior Court of Los Angeles County, 99 Cal.Rptr. 342 (1971), cert. den. 409 U.S. 1011 (1972).

9. Rosato v. Superior Court, 1 Med.L.Rptr. 2560, 124 Cal.Rptr. 427 (1975), cert. den. 427 U.S. 912 (1976). In spite of subsequent state recognition of a First Amendment privilege, there is no privilege against disclosure of unpublished information. See KSDO v. Riverside Superior Court, 8 Med.L.Rptr. 2360, 186 Cal.Rptr. 211 (1982).

in good faith and continued imprisonment would not cause them to reveal their sources."

Frequently punishment has resulted from refusals to cooperate with grand juries. In a celebrated case of yesteryear, Peter Bridge of the *Newark News* was jailed for three weeks because he would not reveal to a grand jury unpublished details of an interview with a state bureaucrat who alleged she had been offered a bribe. Bridge had forfeited protection under the New Jersey shield law, as it stood in 1972, by naming the source in this article. New Jersey's highest court declined to hear the case, and the U.S. Supreme Court denied a stay of his contempt sentence.[10]

Television news reporter Stewart Dan and cameraman Roland Barnes of WGR–TV, Buffalo, were pressed to tell a grand jury what they had seen and heard inside Attica prison during the 1971 riot. They refused, and later Dan was sentenced to thirty days in jail. Reporter Joe Pennington of KAKZ–TV, Wichita, was sentenced to sixty days for criminal contempt after he refused to turn over information believed by defendant's counsel to be relevant to the issue of guilt or innocence.[11]

The Meaning of *BRANZBURG*

In *Branzburg* the Court held narrowly that the First Amendment, because it is silent on the privilege, does not immunize the journalist from the ordinary duty of any citizen to respond to a grand jury subpoena seeking evidence or testimony in a criminal case. A journalist witnessing a crime, moreover, would clearly have no testimonial privilege.

In Justice White's opinion for the Court an explicit invitation was extended to Congress and the state legislatures to create, within constitutional limits, a statutory privilege. Led by Maryland in 1896, twenty-five state legislatures had done just that—six since the *Branzburg* decision was announced. "At the federal level," said White, "Congress has freedom to determine whether a statutory newsman's privilege is necessary and desirable * * * [and] there is also merit in leaving state legislatures free, within First Amendment limits, to fashion their own standards in light of the relations between law enforcement officials and the press in their own areas."

Pressing the latter point, White added, "It goes without saying, of course, that we are powerless to erect any bar to state courts responding in their own way and construing their constitutions so as to recognize a newsman's privilege, either qualified or absolute."

Aside from legislative resolution, Justice Stewart's arguments in his dissent for a qualified privilege, bulwarked by Justice Powell's equivocal concurrence with the majority, have come to be interpreted by lower courts as a Supreme Court preference for a qualified privilege. At least that is the direction in which the law is moving. But only a qualified privilege. Courts, legislatures, and executive agencies are not prepared to recognize an absolute privilege. In some circumstances journalists will always be required to testify or submit evidence to governmental bodies, or pay the consequences.

As long ago as 1857 a select committee of the United States House of Representatives summoned reporter James Simonton of the *New York Times* to reveal the sources of information for a series of articles about congressmen who appeared

10. In re Bridge, 295 A.2d 3 (N.J.1972), cert. den. 410 U.S. 991 (1973).

11. People by Fischer v. Dan, 342 N.Y.S.2d 731 (App.Div.1973); State v. Sandstrom, 4 Med.L.Rptr. 1333, 581 P.2d 812 (Kan.1978), cert.den. 440 U.S. 929 (1979).

willing to sell their votes. Using arguments with a contemporary ring to them to defend his privilege, Simonton refused to cooperate and spent nineteen days in the custody of the House sergeant at arms.

Note that none of the Court's opinions discusses the constitutional status of notes, tapes, or other raw materials of a reporter's work-a-day world. The single question, Justice White emphasized in a footnote, is "whether a newspaper reporter who has published articles about an organization can, under the First Amendment, properly refuse to appear before a grand jury investigating possible crimes by members of that organization who have been quoted in the published articles." Nor did Justice Stewart believe that a subpoena could simply be ignored.

2. Both leading opinions showed an awareness of the available empirical evidence as to the effect of subpoenas on the flow of news, whatever the quality of that evidence. In a footnote Justice Stewart responding to White's concern about the "speculative nature" of the newsman's claim, elaborated on the relationship between empirical studies and constitutional decision making:

> Empirical studies, after all, can only provide facts. It is the duty of courts to give legal significance to facts; and it is the special duty of this Court to understand the constitutional significance of facts. We must often proceed in a state of less then perfect knowledge, either because the facts are murky or the methodology used in obtaining the facts is open to question. It is then that we must look to the Constitution for the values that inform our presumptions. And the importance to our society of the full flow of information to the public has buttressed this Court's historic presumption in favor of First Amendment values.

3. Justice White said that a subpoena is just another example of the application to the press of valid general laws like tax laws or labor-management laws, but these laws are enforced neutrally and impose no particular burden on First Amendment freedoms. Justice White also observed that prosecutors risk a great deal when they subpoena newsmen. Does the press, as White suggests, have powerful means of protecting itself?

What do reporters actually risk when, having assured their sources that they will go to jail rather than reveal their identities, they ignore subpoenas or refuse to testify? James Reston, perhaps facetiously, sees jail sentences as providing reporters much needed respite from the hurly-burly. But should jail be an occupational hazard of journalism?

4. Does the journalist have a right to gather information beyond that of the ordinary citizen? Justice White said that reporters have no constitutional right of access to scenes of crime or disaster. Can you visualize, as he does, reporters constituting part of a private system of informers, reporting on crime, but really quite unaccountable to the public or anyone else?

5. The greatest puzzle perhaps of the various opinions in *Branzburg* was presented by the dispositive concurring opinion of Justice Powell. Powell, although he joined in the result in *Branzburg,* did not reject a First Amendment-based qualified privilege. Powell suggested that such claims of privilege should be judged on their precise facts "by the striking of a proper balance between freedom of the press and the obligations of all citizens to give relevant testimony with respect to criminal conduct." Powell emphasized that the courts would be open to journalists "under circumstances where legitimate First Amendment interests require protection."

Why didn't Powell join the dissenters? He did not think journalists had a First Amendment right to refuse the summons of a grand jury. In other contexts, would Powell's approach then be the same as that of Justice Stewart? No. Powell's approach differed from that of Stewart. For Powell, the Stewart three-fold test placed too heavy a burden on the government. A balancing approach, on the other hand, placed the clashing and "vital constitutional and societal interests" in a more desirable state of rough equivalence.

6. Do you agree with Justice Powell that a newsman should at least appear before the grand jury and that his rights to confidentiality should be determined after questions have been put to him? In *Caldwell* the court emphasized that a reporter would not always be in as sensitive a relationship with his sources as was Caldwell with the Black Panthers. An interesting sidelight on the *Caldwell* case is the fact that the *New York Times*, although paying legal expenses, did not wholeheartedly support the appeal.

"We are not joining the appeal," said Managing Editor A.M. Rosenthal in a memo to his staff, "because we feel that when a reporter refuses to authenticate his story, the *Times* must, in a formal sense, step aside. Otherwise some doubt may be cast upon the integrity of the *Times* news stories." How does this square with the position of the *Times* in the *Pentagon Papers* case? In the *Farber* case? See text, p. 420ff.

7. Enactment of an unqualified federal shield law seems unlikely, as does the enactment of any federal shield law at all. The great surprise of the *Branzburg* decision was that its most influential feature has not been Justice White's plurality decision but Justice Stewart's dissent advocating a qualified First Amendment-based journalist's privilege. The Stewart approach now governs much of the law of journalist's privilege in the context of civil proceedings. The three-part test of Stewart's *Branzburg* dissent has thus become enormously important. Governmental demands for information from journalists should be based, Stewart said, on the following three-part test: 1) relevance to a specific probable violation of law; 2) that the information cannot be obtained by alternative means less destructive of First Amendment rights; and 3) compelling and overriding interest in the information.

The fact that the Stewart dissent has become so influential is really not that remarkable if a careful count of how the justices actually voted in *Branzburg* is undertaken. The plurality opinion authored by Justice White, refusing to acknowledge the existence of a First Amendment-based privilege, either absolute or qualified, in the context of the criminal grand jury, was supported by three justices in addition to Justice White. Justice Powell, however, filed a concurring opinion which did acknowledge that courts would be "available to newsmen under circumstances where legitimate First Amendment interests require protection." Two justices (Brennan and Marshall) joined Justice Stewart in his dissent in *Branzburg* in support of a qualified First Amendment-based journalist's privilege to be applied according to the three-part test. Justice Douglas, in a separate dissent, advocated even greater First Amendment protection in the way of a First Amendment-based privilege for journalists than that advocated by Justice Stewart. As a result, if a careful count of the justices in *Branzburg* is made it becomes clear that a majority were ready to support some basis in the First Amendment for the establishment of a constitutionally based journalist's privilege. The paradox, then, of *Branzburg*—a happy paradox for journalists—is that far from being the death knell of a First Amendment-based journalist's privilege, *Branzburg*, in retrospect, may be seen as having inaugurated the basis for such privilege, at least on a qualified basis.

8. When a murder defendant sought documents from reporters for the University of New Hampshire student newspaper that would have identified their sources, the state supreme court affirmed a lower court order quashing the subpoena. Even though the state had no shield law, a qual-

ified privilege based on both the First Amendment and the state constitution was held to exist. This qualified privilege could be overcome only by the following showing on the part of the defendant: 1) exhaustion of alternative sources, 2) relevance, and 3) a reasonable probability that information sought would affect the verdict. The third qualification or condition had not been met. New Hampshire v. Siel, 8 Med.L.Rptr. 1265, 444 A.2d 499 (N.H. 1982).

Variations on the three-part test are sometimes semantic. At other times, they either expand or contract the test. Where "information going to the heart of the claim" subsumes "relevance" and "compelling public need," we have a two-part test. Where the information seeker's purpose must be more than "frivolous," we may have a four-part test. In Ohio "relevance" and "exhaustion of alternate sources" are standard parts of the test, but the information seeker also must make an effort to examine a reporter's nonconfidential information first and request an *in camera* inspection of anything confidential. People v. Monica (Ohio Ct. of Appeals, 8th Dist., No. 39950, April 12, 1979). In Florida "less chilling" means of getting information have to be tried, and there has to be a showing that failure to produce the information sought will result in a miscarriage of justice or substantially prejudice a defendant's case. Florida v. Reid, 8 Med. L.Rptr. 1249 (Fla.1982).

Washington state's qualified privilege, said to be part of its common law, at least in civil cases, requires all or part of a five-part test. The privilege can be defeated by showing that the request for information is necessary, there are no alternative sources, the purpose is non-frivolous, the reporter got the information by unacceptable means, and the source had no reasonable expectation of confidentiality. Senear v. Daily Journal-American, 8 Med. L.Rptr. 1151, 641 P.2d 1180 (Wash.1982). Why do some courts rely on a common law-based privilege rather than a constitutional privilege? In West Virginia, the burden may be placed on the reporter to show harm to the news-gathering process in support of a motion to quash. Maurice v. NLRB, 7 Med.L.Rptr. 2221, 691 F.2d 182 (4th Cir.1981).

9. Some of these qualifications have themselves been subject to litigation, and there have been differences of definition and application from jurisdiction to jurisdiction. On the question of the exhaustion of alternative sources, for example, Justice William Brennan granted a stay of a civil contempt conviction because he thought the information could have been obtained by "other—albeit roundabout—methods." He feared that First Amendment interests were being weighed to their detriment against the court's convenience.

The case—In re Roche, 6 Med.L.Rptr. 1551, 448 U.S. 1312 (1980)—had to do with information about a state judge that led to an investigation by the Massachusetts Commission on Judicial Conduct and formal charges. Sixty-five witnesses, including Roche, a television reporter, were identified. Roche refused to identify any of his sources or disclose what they had said to him unless the judge could independently uncover them on the list, for they were on the list. A judge of Massachusetts' Supreme Judicial Court ordered Roche to testify. He refused and the full court upheld a civil contempt citation. But the citation was not based on the journalist's refusal to identify confidential sources. The court saw the central issue as whether a reporter could determine the sequence of discovery and by that means delay the release of information.

Justice Brennan granted the reporter's petition for a stay of enforcement of the Massachusetts judge's order holding him in civil contempt pending petition for writ of certiorari. Brennan described the matter as follows:

> If I am correct, therefore, that a majority of the Court recognizes at least some degree of constitutional protection for newsgatherers' confidences it is reasonably probable that four of my Brothers will vote to grant certiorari, and there is a fair prospect that the Court will reverse the decision below.

Interestingly enough, the Massachusetts Supreme Judicial Court picked up the gauntlet thrown down by Justice Brennan and subsequently upheld the Massachusetts judge's denial of the journalist's motion for a protective order against disclosure. The Massachusetts court said a protective order would only delay the disclosure of sources and thus the danger to the free flow of information was negligible. See In re Roche, 6 Med.L.Rptr. 2121, 411 N.E.2d 466 (Mass.1980).

10. Justice White's opinion for the Court in *Branzburg* does raise at least one problem with shield laws that has not been resolved. Who is a newsman, a journalist, a reporter? Daniel Ellsberg? Underground, minority, and student editors? Pollsters, pamphleteers, book writers, free lancers, researchers? Justice White believes that shield laws require the courts to define categories of qualified, legitimate, or "respectable" newsmen, a process that offends a First Amendment tradition hostile to any form of state certification.

11. The question was put in memorable language in the case of Annette Buchanan, a college editor who on May 24, 1966 wrote a story for the University of Oregon *Daily Emerald* about pot smoking on the campus. The story quoted seven unidentified marijuana users under the unfortunate headline, "Students Condone Marijuana Use." A district attorney subpoenaed Buchanan, and she twice refused to identify her sources before the grand jury. She was cited for contempt, tried, and convicted. Upholding her conviction the Oregon Supreme Court addressed the problem of adjusting the definition of newsman to the implications of the First Amendment:

> Assuming that legislators are free to experiment with such definitions, it would be dangerous business for courts, asserting constitutional grounds, to extend to an employe of a 'respectable' newspaper a privilege which would be denied to an employe of a disreputable newspaper; or to an episodic pamphleteer; or to a free-lance writer seeking a story to sell on the open market; or, indeed, to a shaggy nonconformist who wishes only to write out his message and nail it to a tree. If the claimed privilege is to be found in the Constitution, its benefits cannot be limited to those whose credentials may, from time to time, satisfy the government. State v. Buchanan, 436 P.2d 729 (Or.1968).

12. In September 1977, Karen Silkwood, a nuclear industry worker, died under mysterious circumstances while driving to meet a reporter to whom she apparently was to divulge information alleging unsafe working conditions at a Kerr-McGee nuclear power plant. The administrator of Silkwood's estate brought a civil action against the company claiming violation of her civil rights by conspiring to prevent her from organizing a labor union and from filing complaints against the company under the Atomic Energy Act and by willfully and wantonly contaminating her with plutonium radiation.

The company subpoenaed Arthur Hirsch, a documentarist who, while not a party to the suit, had investigated Silkwood's death and had received confidential information in the course of his filmmaking. The federal district court denied Hirsch's claim of privilege because he was not a newsman regularly engaged in obtaining, editing, or otherwise preparing news.

The Tenth Circuit Court of Appeals concluded that Hirsch was an investigative reporter as far as the film was concerned and noted that the Supreme Court had not limited the privilege to newspaper reporters. "[The Court] has in fact held that the press comprehends different kinds of publications which communicate to the public information and opinion."

The Tenth Circuit remanded the case so that the trial court could reconsider the demand to enforce the subpoena in terms of the nature of the evidence sought, its relevance and significance to the case, and the availability of alternative sources—the three-part test. On remand, Kerr-McGee formally abandoned further discovery of Hirsch and made no additional attempt to enforce its subpoena against him. Silkwood v. Kerr-McGee, 3 Med.L.Rptr. 1087, 563 F.2d 433 (10th Cir.1977).

STATE SHIELD LAWS: THE STATUTORY BASIS FOR JOURNALIST'S PRIVILEGE

In the absence of either black letter common law or constitutional protection of the confidentiality of journalists' sources or the raw materials of their work, twenty-five states have passed laws extending some degree of privilege to reporters and editors. Another eleven states have recognized a common law or qualified privilege.

The shield law states are Alabama, Alaska, Arizona, Arkansas, California, Delaware, Illinois, Kentucky, Louisiana, Maryland,[12] Michigan, Minnesota, Montana, Nebraska, Nevada, New Jersey, New York, North Dakota, Ohio, Oklahoma, Oregon, Pennsylvania, Rhode Island and Tennessee. New Mexico passed a shield law in 1975, but a year later it was declared unconstitutional by the state supreme court as an interference with judicial prerogatives concerning evidence.[13]

States without shield laws that have nevertheless recognized a common law or qualified privilege are Connecticut, Florida, Iowa, Kansas, New Hampshire, Texas, Vermont, Virginia, Washington, West Virginia, and Wisconsin. Wisconsin, for example, in 1971 implied a qualified common law privilege based upon its constitutional guarantees of freedom of speech and press. The case, State v. Knops, 183 N.W.2d 93 (Wis.1971), grew out of a grand jury investigation into the bombing of a research center on the University of Wisconsin-Madison campus in which a young research assistant was killed.

A Madison "underground" newspaper, *Kaleidoscope*, had printed a front page story entitled "The Bombers Tell Why and What Next—Exclusive to the Kaleidoscope." The editor, Mark Knops, was subpoenaed, appeared, asserted his Fifth Amendment right against self-incrimination, was granted immunity, and then pleaded that he had a First Amendment privilege against revealing his confidential informants.

Wisconsin's Supreme Court rejected his claim and upheld a contempt sentence on the ground that the answers sought carried an overriding need of the public to protect itself against attack. Relevance was discussed when the court, comparing the case with *Caldwell*, noted that unlike that case Knops did not face "an unstructured fishing expedition composed of questions which will meander in and out of his private affairs without apparent purpose or direction."

A telling admission was made, however, in Justice Heffernan's dissenting opinion. Could the compelling state interest in obtaining Knop's testimony have been achieved by alternative means? It was a comment on the times that, according to Heffernan, both state and federal

12. Maryland passed the first shield law in 1896. See Gordon, *The 1896 Maryland Shield Law: The American Roots of Evidentiary Privilege for Newsmen.* Journalism Monographs, No. 22 (February 1972).

13. Ammerman v. Hubbard Broadcasting, Inc. 551 P.2d 1354 (N.M.1976).

officials had stated under oath that they knew who had bombed Sterling Hall and that federal warrants had been issued for the arrest of the suspects. Did official action in the case reflect anathema toward editor Knops and his newspaper more than a concern for criminal justice?

Seven years later in Zelenka v. Wisconsin, 4 Med.L.Rptr. 1055, 266 N.W.2d 279 (Wis.1978), the Wisconsin Supreme Court squarely based a qualified privilege on its constitutional guarantee of freedom of speech and press.

Other states citing state and/or federal constitutions as protective of the privilege are Florida,[14] New Hampshire,[15] Texas (at least by implication),[16] Vermont,[17] Virginia (First Amendment only),[18] and Washington (common law only).[19]

State shield laws, a firmer form of protection perhaps, may be written in absolute or conditional terms. But even the most absolutist privilege laws may fall before the Sixth Amendment rights of a defendant.[20] In civil cases absolute privilege applications are more likely to be made.[21] There are complex variations from state to state. One among many proposals for a federal shield law, the News Media Privacy Act of 1982 (HR 6230), would have attempted to establish some uniformity among states.

Some state laws protect unpublished information, even when the source is known.[22] Others do not. Some forbid *in camera* review in civil cases.[23] Others do not. Some states, Florida and Illinois for example, will not protect reporters who are defendants in libel suits. California's law has been amended to prohibit contempt citations against reporters who refuse to disclose privileged information.[24] This is not to suggest that California media and California courts are compatible. They have frequently been at odds, and, like most courts, California's would prefer to construe the state shield law or have it construed, as narrowly as possible. For example, in a case involving old *Look* magazine and a libel action against it by baseball player Orlando Cepeda, the law since amended to include magazines, was interpreted literally.

14. Florida v. Reid, 8 Med.L.Rptr. 1249 (Fla.1982). See also, Coira v. Depoo Hospital, 4 Med.L.Rptr. 1692 (Fla.1978). The Coira court held also that in civil litigation the reporter's privilege not to produce unpublished information is paramount.

15. Opinion of the Justices, 2 Med.L.Rptr. 1083, 373 A.2d 644 (N.H.1977). In Downing v. Monitor Publishing Co., 6 Med.L.Rptr. 1193, 415 A.2d 683 (N.H.1980) the New Hampshire Supreme Court decided that disclosure was required where plaintiff had no other way to demonstrate that a newspaper had reason to doubt its source under the rule of *St. Amant* (see text p. 217). In the absence of disclosure, the court could assume the newspaper had no source. California did the same in Rancho La Costa, Inc. v. Penthouse, 6 Med.L.Rptr. 1249, 165 Cal.Rptr. 347 (1980).

16. Dallas Oil and Gas, Inc. v. Mouer, 533 S.W.2d 70 (Tex.Civ.App.1976).

17. Vermont v. Blais, 6 Med.L.Rptr. 1537 (Vt.1980).

18. Brown v. Commonwealth, 204 S.E.2d 429 (Va.1977), cert. den. 419 U.S. 966 (1974).

19. Senear v. The Daily Journal American, 8 Med.L.Rptr. 1151, 641 P.2d 1180 (Wash.1982).

20. Hammarlay v. Superior Court, 4 Med.L.Rptr. 2055, 89 Cal.App.3d 588 (1979). Oregon v. Knorr, 8 Med.L.Rptr. 2067 (Or.1982).

21. Mazzella v. Philadelphia Newspapers, 5 Med.L.Rptr. 1983, 479 F.Supp. 523 (E.D.N.Y.1979).

22. Aerial Burials v. Minneapolis Star & Tribune, 8 Med.L.Rptr. 1653 (Minn.1982). But see, Lightman v. State, 294 A.2d 149 (Md.1972).

23. Weiss v. Thomson Newspapers, Inc., 8 Med.L.Rptr. 1258 (Ohio 1981). Shield law said to preclude order for *in camera* inspection in civil cases, a privilege yielding only to 6th Amendment rights.

24. West's Ann.Calif.Evid. Code § 1070(a) (1979 Supp.) and Constitution of State of California, Article I, § 2(b), as amended June 3, 1980. See Los Angeles Coliseum Commission v. NFL, 6 Med.L.Rptr. 2380, 89 F.R.D. 489 (C.D.Cal.1981); KSDO v. Riverside Superior Court, 8 Med.L.Rptr. 2360, 186 Cal.Rptr. 211 (1982).

Cepeda's petition asked that the *Look* writer identify San Francisco Giants officials who he alleged had defamed him. California had had a journalist's privilege law since 1965. Cepeda's attorney deftly submitted that the state statute must be strictly construed to include only "persons connected with or employed upon a *newspaper* or by a *press association* or *wire service,"* * * * or "a *radio* or *television news reporter.* * * *" In accepting this narrow interpretation, excluding protection for magazines, the judge observed that only three of the then eleven other states with shield laws had seen fit to include "journals," "periodicals" or "other publications." He also noted that when the California law was amended to include other classes of news media, only "press association or wire service" and "radio or television news reporter" were added. And he concluded:

> In the absence of specific statutory language creating it, (the privilege) should not be extended to cover other situations not specifically included in the actual terminology of the statute. Application of Cepeda, 233 F.Supp. 465 (D.C.N.Y.1964). In New York v. Le Grand, 4 Med.L.Rptr. 2524, 415 N.Y.S.2d 252 (1979), New York's statute was held not to protect book authors.

The *Look* magazine writer's offer to answer the question after "all possible means of eliciting that information from other sources have been exhausted" was rejected. A witness, said the court, may not decide when it will be convenient for him to make a deposition and thereby interfere with the orderly judicial process.

California's shield law did not protect William Farr while he was between newspaper jobs, even though the information he was ordered to produce was gathered while he was employed as a reporter. A New York court ruled that its law did not cover a television cameraman. In 1981, amendments extended that law's protection to freelancers, photographers, book authors, employers of journalists and nonestablishment media. It also protects information not solicited by a reporter, and thereby from nonconfidential sources, and information that may be highly relevant to a judicial proceeding.[25] Minnesota's statute protects all persons communicating with the public. Does it trivialize the privilege to extend it to those on the periphery of public affairs?

Since sources may be inferred from a journalist's work product, the hazard of state laws that protect only sources should be recognized.[26] Some laws require that there be publication and an implied or express agreement of confidentiality between source and reporter for the privilege to be invoked.[27] The privilege may attach to a reporter but not to his or her employer.[28]

Obviously shield laws must be carefully drafted if they are to avoid judicial interpretations that puncture them. Minnesota's statute provides an example of both comprehensiveness, notably in its broad definition of news gatherer and its incorporation of the three-part test, and an economy of language that discourages strained constructions. Note also its exception for libel suits:

MINNESOTA FREE FLOW INFORMATION ACT

MINNESOTA STATUTES 595.021–025, 1973.

Section 1. (Citation.) Sections 1 and 4 may be cited as the Minnesota free flow of information act.

25. People v. Iannaccone, 8 Med.L.Rptr. 1103, 447 N.Y.S.2d 989 (1982).

26. State v. Sheridan, 236 A.2d 18 (Md.1967); Ohio v. Geis, 7 Med.L.Rptr.1675, 441 N.E.2d 803 (Ohio 1981).

27. Lightman v. State, 294 A.2d 149 (Md.1972); Andrews v. Andreoli, 400 N.Y.S.2d 442 (1977).

28. In re Investigative File, No. 40 SPL (Mont.Dist.Ct. 10/2/78).

Sec. 2 (Public Policy.) In order to protect the public interest and the free flow of information, the news media should have the benefit of a substantial privilege not to reveal sources of information or to disclose unpublished information. To this end, the freedom of press requires protection of the confidential relationship between the news gatherer and the source of information. The purpose of this act is to insure and perpetuate, consistent with the public interest, the confidential relationship between the news media and its (sic) sources.

Sec. 3 (Disclosure Prohibited.) No person who is or has been directly engaged in the gathering, procuring, compiling, editing, or publishing of information for the purpose of transmission, dissemination or publication to the public shall be required by any court, grand jury, agency, department or branch of the state, or any of its political sub-divisions or other public body, or by either house of the legislature or any committee, officer, member, or employee thereof, to disclose in any proceeding the person or means from or through which information was obtained, or to disclose any unpublished information procured by him in the course of his work or any of his notes, memoranda, recording tapes, film or other reportorial data which would tend to identify the person or means through which the information was obtained.

Sec. 4 (Exception and Procedure.) Subdivision 1. A person seeking disclosure may apply to the district court of the county where the person employed by or associated with a news media resides, has his principal place of business or where the proceeding in which the information sought is pending.

Subd. 2. The application shall be granted only if the court determines after hearing the parties that the person making application, by clear and convincing evidence, has met all three of the following conditions:

1. that there is probable cause to believe that the source has information clearly relevant to a specific violation of the law other than a misdemeanor,

2. that the information cannot be obtained by any alternative means or remedy less destructive of first amendment rights, and

3. that there is a compelling and overriding interest requiring the disclosure of the information where the disclosure is necessary to prevent injustice.

Subd. 3. The district court shall consider the nature of the proceedings, the merits of the claims and defenses, the adequacies of alternative remedies, the relevancy of the information sought, and the possibility of establishing by other means that which the source is expected or may tend to prove. The court shall make its appropriate order after making findings of fact, which order may be appealed directly to the Supreme Court according to the appropriate rule of appellate procedure. The order is stayed and non-disclosure shall remain in full force and effect during the pendency of the appeal.

Sec. 5 (Defamation.) Subdivision 1. The prohibition of disclosure provided in Section 3 shall not apply in any defamation action where the person seeking disclosure can demonstrate that the identity of the source will lead to relevant evidence on the issue of actual malice.

Subd. 2. Notwithstanding the provisions of Subdivision 1 of this Section, the identity of the source of information shall not be ordered disclosed unless the following conditions are met:

a. that there is probable cause to believe that the source has information clearly relevant to the issue of defamation;

b. that the information cannot be obtained by any alternative means or remedy less destructive of First Amendment rights.

Subd. 3. The court shall make its order on the issue of disclosure after making findings of fact, which order may be appealed directly to the Supreme Court according to the rules of appellate procedure. During the appeal the order is stayed and nondisclosure shall remain in full force and effect.

AN EXCEPTION FOR LIBEL: THE NEW YORK TIMES DOCTRINE v. JOURNALIST'S PRIVILEGE

1. Two of the mighty currents in modern media law flow against each other in that field of litigation where the principles of *New York Times v. Sullivan*, text, p. 203, and the First Amendment philosophy of the Stewart dissent in *Branzburg* collide. In short, how can a *New York Times v. Sullivan*-type libel plaintiff establish "actual malice" if access to the sources and information behind a story is denied because of a journalist's First Amendment-based claim of privilege? What if a plaintiff in a libel suit can make a concrete demonstration that the identity of a news source will lead to persuasive evidence of actual malice on the part of a defendant, a showing that public officials and public figures must make in order to win damages?

Does a risk to the reporter and the news media of an exception for libel suits lie in the fact that suits may be filed primarily for the purpose of discovering the identity of confidential sources and not for compensation for damage to reputation?

These issues were joined in a suit for $2 million general and $10 million punitive damages brought by Mayor Alfonso Cervantes of St. Louis against *Life* magazine. The Mayor sought to identify specific FBI and Department of Justice sources which had provided information for a *Life* story connecting Cervantes with the underworld.

Except for the identity of sources the story was heavily documented. The Mayor took issue with only four of eighty-seven paragraphs comprising the article, but he argued that he could not prove malice if the reporter's sources remained anonymous.

"These arguments in behalf of compulsory disclosure of confidential news sources," said the U.S. Court of Appeals in a narrow ruling, "* * * do not strike us as frivolous. Especially is this so when much of the information supplied by the anonymous informants has been obtained from the private files of Government. Nevertheless, on the facts of the particular case, we believe that in his preoccupation with the identity of *Life's* news sources, the mayor has overlooked the central point involved in this appeal: that the depositions and other evidentiary materials comprising this record establish, without room for substantial argument, facts that entitled both defendants to judgment as a matter of law, *viz.*, that, quite apart from the tactics employed in collecting data for the article, the mayor has wholly failed to demonstrate with convincing clarity that either defendant acted with knowledge (of falsity) or reckless disregard of the truth."

The court added that "to routinely grant motions seeking compulsory disclosure of anonymous news sources without first inquiring into the substance of a libel allegation would utterly emasculate the fundamental principles that underlay the line of cases articulating the constitutional restrictions to be engrafted upon the enforcement of state libel laws.

"Where there is a concrete demonstration that the identity of the defense news source will lead to persuasive evidence on the issue of malice, a [d]istrict [c]ourt should not reach the merits of a defense motion for summary judgment until and unless the plaintiff is first given a meaningful opportunity to cross-examine these sources, whether they be anonymous or known." Cervantes v. Time, Inc., 464 F.2d 986, 992–993 (8th Cir. 1972), cert. den. 409 U.S. 1125 (1973).

The Mayor's dilemma was not dissimilar to that of Mayor Joseph Alioto of San Francisco who sued *Look* magazine for a story also based on anonymous governmental files and charging personal interactions with the West Coast Mafia. See text, p. 246. Both mayors had the burden of showing that the defendants' published assertions were inherently improbable or that they in fact entertained serious doubts as to their truth, whether the sources were identified or not. Alioto would eventually succeed.

Do you consider the *Cervantes* ruling a fair compromise, or does it place an impossible burden upon the plaintiff in a libel suit? How does one decide when the suit is frivolous and brought simply to unearth a source who, in the case of a public official, may be someone close to him or in his employ; or when a suit is a legitimate response to an unfair and irresponsible report which perhaps has no source at all or a notoriously unreliable one?

None of the proposed federal shield statutes would confer immunity on fictitious stories because the reporter still must reveal whether she had a source. Furthermore, a motion for summary judgment filed by a newspaper in a libel suit is usually supported by a set of affidavits showing that the publisher had good reason to believe that the story was true. Where the source is confidential, a newspaper has great difficulty in making such a showing. For this reason newspapers try to avoid relying solely on confidential sources. Moreover such stories are less believable. In *Cervantes, Life* had corroboration for what its confidential sources had said. Under the *New York Times* doctrine plaintiffs would have had little probability of success. In *Alioto*, corroboration was missing.

Is it likely, then, that the identity of a source will be critical to many libel suits? And when the source is identified, the plaintiff must still meet the standard of *New York Times*. On the other hand, does journalist's privilege make a mockery of the "actual malice" requirement of the *New York Times* doctrine?

2. The problems that arose in *Cervantes* have become more critical, and there is now a significant body of case law, as the cases that follow will illustrate, grappling with the claim of journalist's privilege in libel litigation. The courts faced with the problem, have had varying reactions to it. Some have been more concerned about the erosion recognition of journalist's privilege might work on the "actual malice" standard of *New York Times v. Sullivan*. Others have found recognition of a qualified First Amendment-based journalist's privilege—even in public law of libel cases—to be entirely consistent with the First Amendment interest in vigorous robust debate and public criticism which led to the creation of the *Sullivan* doctrine in the first place.

An illustrative and significant case in this area is Carey v. Hume, 492 F.2d 631 (D.C.Cir.1974), where a qualified First Amendment-based journalist's privilege was recognized in a civil libel suit even though, on the facts of the case, the court required Jack Anderson, the journalist who had refused to identify his sources, to make disclosure. The court noted that "there may be discernible degrees of difference in the social interests attaching to the exaction of testimony in the one [civil] field as compared with the other [criminal]." Yet the court concluded "that civil litigation has its entitlements on proper occasion to the pursuit of truth wherever it may be found."

In *Carey,* the union official plaintiff brought an action for libel based on defendant's newspaper column report that union official had removed documents from the union president's office and then complained to the police that burglars had stolen a box full of items from the office. The court of appeals held that the district court did not abuse its discretion in requiring the journalist who wrote the item to reveal the names of eyewitnesses to the alleged removal. The libel plaintiff in *Carey* was bound by the standard of liability set forth in *New York Times v. Sullivan. Carey* gave forceful expression to the conflict which recent cases now increasingly reveal between the application of the "actual malice" standard of the *Sullivan* case and a qualified journalist's privilege based on the First Amendment:

"In the context of an asserted newsman's privilege to protect confidential news sources, the *Sullivan* rule is a source of tension. On the one hand, the Court's concern that the spectre of potential libel actions might have an inhibiting effect on the exercise of press freedom militates against compulsory disclosure of sources. Contrarily, the heavy burden of proof imposed upon the plaintiff in such a case will often make discovery of confidential sources critical to any hope of carrying that burden."

In an interesting passage, Judge McGowan rejected the idea that, with the advent of the *Sullivan* doctrine and its imposition of new burdens on some libel plaintiffs, the journalist's First Amendment interest in nondisclosure was the weightier interest in case of conflict:

> In striking the constitutional balance contemplated in *Garland* [see p. 378ff], it could perhaps be argued that, although the *Sullivan* decision did not eliminate civil libel suits entirely, it has so downgraded their social importance that a plaintiff's interest in pressing such a claim can rarely, if ever, outweigh a newsman's interest in protecting his sources. The tenor of the Court's opinion in *Sullivan* may be thought to reflect an attitude toward libel actions palpably different from its approach to grand jury proceedings in *Branzburg.* There is, however, the matter of the Court's continuing post-*Sullivan* citations of *Garland.* This strongly suggests the continuing vitality of the latter case, and negates any inference that the Court does not consider the interest of the defamed plaintiff an important one.

In a passage that contrasts sharply with the decision of the Idaho Supreme Court in *Caldero,* which follows, the federal court of appeals in *Carey* concluded that a qualified First Amendment-based privilege endured as far as civil litigation was concerned after *Branzburg:*

> *Branzburg,* in language, if not in holding, left intact, insofar as civil litigation is concerned, the approach taken in *Garland.* That approach essentially is that the court will look to the facts on a case-by-case basis in the course of weighing the need for the testimony in question against the claims of the newsman that the public's right to know is impaired.

The court then explained why it thought that on balance the qualified privilege protecting the journalist had to yield under the facts of *Carey:*

> Turning to the facts of the case before us, the information sought appears to go to the heart of appellee's libel action, certainly the most important factor in *Garland.* It would be exceedingly difficult for appellee to introduce evidence beyond his own testimony to prove that he did not at any time of day or night over an indefinite period of several weeks, remove boxfuls of documents from the UMW offices. Even if he did prove that the statements were false, *Sullivan* also requires a showing of malice or reckless disregard of the truth. That further step might be achieved by proof that

> appellant in fact had no reliable sources, that he misrepresented the reports of his sources, or that reliance upon those particular sources was reckless.
>
> Knowledge of the identity of the alleged sources would logically be an initial element in the proof of any of such circumstances. Although it might be possible to submit the question of malice to the jury simply on the basis of the conflicting allegations of the parties, that procedure would seem to provide the plaintiff little prospect of success in view of his heavy burden of proof. Consequently, we find that the identity of appellant's sources is critical to appellee's claim. See also, Zerilli v. Smith, 656 F.2d 705 (D.C.Cir.1981).

3. A case which contrasts sharply with *Carey* is Caldero v. Tribune Publishing Co., 2 Med.L.Rptr. 1490, 562 P.2d 791 (Idaho 1977), cert. den. 434 U.S. 930 (1977). In *Caldero,* the Idaho Supreme Court gave the opinion for the court in *Branzburg* a harsh reading indeed—at least from the point of view of journalist's privilege. The *Caldero* court apparently was of the opinion that recognition of a First Amendment-based journalist's privilege, whether absolute or qualified, was as inadmissible in civil litigation as in the grand jury context.

Michael Caldero brought a libel suit against the publisher of the *Lewiston Morning Tribune.* Caldero alleged that a story about him contained an " 'unfair, false and malicious account' " of an incident involving Caldero while he was employed as an undercover agent for the Idaho Bureau of Narcotic Enforcement. Caldero and another agent were in the process of arresting one Booth who had tried to sell them narcotics. Johnson was a companion of Booth's. While the two agents were struggling with Booth, Johnson tried to flee the scene in an automobile. Caldero fired three shots through the windshield of Johnson's car, two of which struck and injured Johnson. More than a year later an article by reporter Jay Shelledy discussing the matter appeared in the *Tribune.* The article focused on the "professional propriety of Caldero's conduct." A statement in the article which was of critical importance for the fortunes of the libel suit was the following: "One police expert, in an off-the-record interview with the *Tribune,* said Caldero's justification for shooting didn't add up. His reasoning was derived mainly from logistical facts." The "logistical facts" were then described.

Shelledy was deposed by counsel for the plaintiff and asked questions concerning the part of the article dealing with the opinions of the "police expert." Although Shelledy answered some questions concerning his conversation with his police expert source, he refused to identify him, relying for his refusal on the First Amendment and the professional code of ethics. Reporter Shelledy was then judged in contempt and ordered jailed for thirty days. At the end of that time, the court said it would re-examine him as to the identity and source of his information. The execution of that judgment was stayed pending appeal to the Idaho Supreme Court. That Court affirmed the order, judgment, and sentence below. Contrary to the dominant theme of the civil cases dealing with whether a qualified First Amendment-based journalist's privilege had survived *Branzburg,* the Idaho Supreme Court concluded that "our reading of *Branzburg v. Hayes,* is to the effect that no newsman's privilege against disclosure of confidential sources founded on the First Amendment exists in an absolute or qualified version." The harshness of this ruling was perhaps somewhat moderated by the following statement:

> The only restrictions against compelled disclosure appear to be in those cases where it is demonstrably intended to unnecessarily harass members of the news media on a broad scale by means having an unnecessary impact on protected rights of speech, press or association. Caldero v. Tribune Publishing

Co., 2 Med.L.Rptr. 1490, 562 P.2d 791 (Idaho 1977), cert. denied 434 U.S. 930.

In a controversial reading of *Garland v. Torre*, the Idaho Supreme Court appeared to believe that *Garland* had rejected a First Amendment-based privilege, whether qualified or absolute. The Idaho Supreme Court made no distinction between the interest of the state in seeking information from a journalist in a criminal context with a request for disclosure from a journalist where one civil litigant is suing another. Many of the civil cases involving journalist's privilege have recognized a qualified First Amendment-based privilege in the civil area on the ground that *Branzburg* involved the grand jury context. The state interest in the integrity of its system of criminal justice was seen as superior to the journalist's interest in nondisclosure. In civil litigation, the strength of the state interest in requiring disclosure is seen as inferior to the First Amendment interest in nondisclosure by the journalist. The opinion in the *Caldero* case, however, was remarkably insensitive to the First Amendment dimensions of the journalist's interest in nondisclosure. Despite the breadth of the *Caldero* court's rejection of even a qualified First Amendment based journalist's privilege in civil litigation, or at least in a defamation context, the United States Supreme Court refused to review the case.

Close to the trial date the widow of the reporter's source consented to disclosure. The source was Caldero's boss.

Contemporaneous cases took a far less hostile approach to privilege claims in libel cases. For example, in Winegard v. Oxberger, 258 N.W.2d 847 (Iowa 1977), cert. den, 436 U.S. 905 (1978), the Iowa Supreme Court, even though it disallowed journalist's privilege in the particular case, recognized a variation at least of the original three-part test. The information sought, said the court, ought to be crucial, alternative sources should have been exhausted, and the purpose of the information seeker must not be "patently frivolous."

Before *Herbert v. Lando* [29] was decided by the United States Supreme Court, a qualified privilege of confidentiality for reporters and editors was increasingly assumed. That assumption also holds since *Herbert v. Lando*. Confidential sources cannot generally be used to support an argument by the press of "no actual malice." [30] If a newspaper bases its defense on confidential sources, its privilege may be waived.[31] But a showing by the information seeker of some or all of the three-part test will generally be prerequisite to a court order to disclose.

4. Recall *Herbert v. Lando* in the United States Court of Appeals for the Second Circuit.[32] The court's decision there gave renewed legitimacy to a qualified First Amendment-based privilege. And once again a constitutionally based assertion of journalist's privilege collided with a libel plaintiff's attempt to prove "actual malice" under the *New York Times v. Sullivan* standard of liability. The case arose out of an exposure on "60 Minutes" of some infirmities in Colonel Anthony Herbert's campaign to publicize war crimes committed by the American military in Vietnam. "60 Minutes" producer Barry Lando then wrote an article in the *Atlantic Monthly* in which he detailed some of the weaknesses in Herbert's story. Herbert responded by bring a libel suit against Lando for what was then a breathtaking $45 million. Counsel for Herbert undertook truly massive pretrial discovery, and Lando was

29. 441 U.S. 153 (1979).

30. Greenberg v. CBS, Inc., 5 Med.L.Rptr. 1470, 419 N.Y.S.2d 988 (1979).

31. Mazzella v. Philadelphia Newspapers, Inc., 5 Med.L.Rptr. 1983, 479 F.Supp. 523 (E.D.N.Y.1979).

32. 568 F.2d 974 (2d Cir.1977), reversed 441 U.S. 153 (1979).

questioned in no less than twenty-six separate pretrial depositions.

However, Lando refused to answer certain questions put to him on the ground that they impermissibly inquired into his "beliefs, opinions, intent and conclusions in preparing the program." As such, Lando contended the questions trespassed on the editorial function which was entitled to First Amendment protection. The *Lando* case, therefore, raised a novel problem in the collision between libel law and journalist's privilege. Lando was not protecting his sources. Instead, he was seeking to protect his role as editor.

Judge Haight for the federal district court, Herbert v. Lando, 73 F.R.D. 387 (S.D. N.Y.1977), rejected Lando's claim that he had a First Amendment right to refuse disclosure under these circumstances. The lower federal court did not see how a libel plaintiff, already bound by the rigors of the *New York Times v. Sullivan* standard of liability, could prove actual malice without being able to make use of the fullest discovery available to him under the rules of civil procedure. To the extent that a conclusion of whether actual malice existed turned on the defendant's state of mind, the lower federal court thought that discovery could not be thwarted by the assertion of a new qualification to the *New York Times v. Sullivan* standard of liability which would preclude inquiry into actual malice when such inquiry might infringe on a newly created doctrine of editorial privilege.

Chief Judge Kaufman for the Second Circuit Court of Appeals in *Lando* declared that press "freedom to cull information is logically antecedent and necessary to any effective exercise of the right to distribute news." Relying on *Branzburg,* he found that protection had been accorded by the Supreme Court to the news-gathering process. Judge Kaufman then relied on Miami Herald Publishing Co. v. Tornillo, 418 U.S. 241 (1974) and Columbia Broadcasting System v. Democratic National Committee, 412 U.S. 94 (1973), for the proposition that the First Amendment protected the editorial process:

> The unambiguous wisdom of *Tornillo* and *CBS* is that we must encourage, and protect against encroachment, full and candid discussion within the newsroom itself. In the light of these constitutional imperatives, the issue presented by this case is whether, and to what extent, inquiry into the editorial process, conducted during discovery in a *New York Times v. Sullivan* type libel action, impermissibly burdens the work of broadcasters and reporters.

Making clear that in his view First Amendment considerations should impact on civil discovery procedures in libel cases, Judge Kaufman sketched the broad outlines of an editorial rationale for an editorial process privilege for the media defendant in *Sullivan* -type libel cases:

> [W]e must permit only those procedures in libel actions which least conflict with the principle that debate on public issues should be robust and uninhibited. If we were to allow selective disclosure of how a journalist formulated his judgments on what to print or not to print, we would be condoning judicial review of the editor's thought processes. Such an inquiry, which on its face would be virtually boundless, endangers a constitutionally protected realm, and unquestionably puts a freeze on the free interchange of ideas within the newsroom. A reporter or editor, aware that his thoughts might have to be justified in a court of law, would often be discouraged and dissuaded from the creative verbal testing, probing, and discussion of hypotheses and alternatives which are the *sine qua non* of responsible journalism. Indeed, the *ratio decidendi* for *Sullivan's* restraints on libel suits is the concern that the exercise of editorial judgment would be chilled.

Kaufman emphasized the exhaustive discovery that had already taken place: "Of course, [Herbert] has already discovered what Lando knew, saw, said and wrote during his investigation." Judge Kaufman believed that it would still be possible for a libel plaintiff in a case governed by *New York Times v. Sullivan* to "find that Lando acted with actual malice or in reckless disregard of the truth." But a deeper probe by use of discovery into Lando's subjective state of mind could not be permitted: "The answers [Herbert] seeks strike to the heart of the vital human component of the editorial process. Faced with the possibility of such an inquisition, reporters and journalists would be reluctant to express their doubts."

The court concluded that Lando did not have to answer the questions which he considered would impermissibly penetrate his editorial judgment: "We cannot permit inquiry into Lando's thoughts, opinions and conclusions to consume the very values which the *Sullivan* landmark decision sought to safeguard."

The scope of the *Lando* decision was left in doubt since exactly how "editorial privilege" was to be defined was left unclear. Further, the holding of the case was equally murky. Did Judge Kaufman recognize a qualified First Amendment privilege in the *Lando* case? Or did he create an absolute privilege? Since the journalist's judgment about which questions were editorially privileged was upheld, without a requirement of prior scrutiny by the court, the privilege created in *Lando* was, arguably, an absolute one. On the other hand, the *Lando* decision's constant references to the massive discovery that had already taken place may suggest that the editorial process privilege will be allowed to be asserted by a journalist only in a context where the discovery has been so complete that application of the actual malice standard is possible without inquiry into questions which are said to fall under a category of editorial privilege.

In a separate concurring opinion Judge Oakes described three possible solutions to the problem of the *Lando* case. The first option was to view the *New York Times* ruling as having resolved the issue of reconciling the interest of the libel plaintiff, on the one hand, and the First Amendment interest in untrammeled expression on the other. In this view, the "actual malice" standard is seen as reflecting the compromise the Court has already struck. Therefore, the media defendant would have to make any disclosure which the discovery rules permitted and which proof of the "actual malice" standard required. The second alternative would grant the libel plaintiff liberal discovery except where such discovery would unnecessarily impinge on First Amendment values. In other words, discovery would be permitted in this context only where the material sought was not otherwise available and was critical to the case. The third alternative—and the one Judge Oakes opted for—was to engraft a constitutionally based editorial function privilege on the "actual malice" standard and limit the discovery available to a libel plaintiff bound by the rigors of the "actual malice" standard to the limits set by the new privilege. This would mean that a *New York Times v. Sullivan*-type libel plaintiff would have to prove "actual malice" "by evidence other than that obtained through compelled disclosure at the heart of the editorial process."

Judge Oakes's approach appeared to limit the nature of proof of "actual malice" and removed the editor's state of mind from inquiry since such a line of questioning may be said to intrude on editorial judgment and decision-making. In dissent in *Lando*, Judge Meskill complained that the *Sullivan*-type libel plaintiff already had a heavy burden—he must prove "actual malice" on the part of the defendant by clear and convincing evidence. If his burden must still be sustained while inquiry into the media defendant's state of mind is off limits, the basic compromise between free expression and the reputational interest protected by the libel law has been radically revised.

Was the result in the *Lando* case a two-edged sword for the media? Some communication lawyers worried that the result in the case could lead to precluding any inquiry into state of mind in "actual malice" determinations. However, in some libel cases objective evidence may show reckless disregard whereas an inquiry into the journalist's state of mind may conclusively show the opposite. The Supreme Court reversed the Second Circuit. See text, p. 289.

Although the Supreme Court decision in *Lando* was a disappointment to the press, the consequences have not been all that bad for journalist's privilege. While there has been a resurgence in the number of subpoenas issued, in about equal numbers in criminal cases, civil cases generally, and libel cases specifically, the media win more cases than they lose. On appeal, courts are less likely now than in the past to make doctrinaire judgments against the privilege, a consequence of gradual acceptance of the three-part test and its balance of equities.

Under most court interpretations of *Branzburg*, state statutes, or state common law, lower courts will require disclosure in libel suits if the libel suit is valid, especially in terms of its falsity, if other possible sources have been exhausted, and if the information sought is relevant and of critical importance to the information seeker's case and so outweighs any privilege granted to the press. If the trial court is uncertain about these points, it can defer disclosure pending further discovery and the possibility of a summary judgment. It can also require the exhaustion of nonconfidential sources. It can seal notes and documents and forbid attorneys to discuss evidence with their clients. And it can limit attendance at the taking of depositions.

There may come a time when a reporter's string runs out. That person may then have to comply with the court's order or face a contempt citation. Or, if a libel suit, the reporter will be assumed to have had no source [33] and will be prohibited from entering any evidence of the existence of sources. The consequences may be to lose the suit by default.

5. Since the *Washington Post*'s Janet Cooke episode, editors are looking to reporters to share information with them, especially where there is a possibility of libel. This sharing will often include the identity of sources.

Some states remain relatively absolutist in their protection of confidential sources in any legal proceeding, including libel litigation. Pennsylvania is one of them. In applying Pennsylvania's shield law in a libel action, a federal district court noted:

> Pennsylvania's legislative determination to grant almost absolute protection to a reporter from disclosure of his source impinges upon no constitutionally protected right. * * * The legislature's decision then to favor the public's interest in access to information over an individual's [s]tate common law right to vindicate his reputation is a matter over which the [s]tate has almost complete control and in the circumstances of this case has exercised in a manner adverse to plaintiff's interests. Mazzella v. Philadelphia Newspapers, 5 Med.L.Rptr. 1983, 479 F.Supp. 523 (E.D.N.Y.1979).

JOURNALIST'S PRIVILEGE IN THE CRIMINAL CONTEXT

1. Consistent with *Branzburg*, a journalist who witnesses a crime remains highly vulnerable to subpoena. Typically, a trial court in Pankratz v. Colorado District

33. DeRoburt v. Gannett, 6 Med.L.Rptr. 2473, 548 F.Supp. 1370 (D.Haw.1981).

Court, 6 Med.L.Rptr. 1269, 609 P.2d 1101 (Colo.1980), held that there were no state or federal constitutional or common law privileges when a witness observes a crime. While a common law and/or a three-part test may be argued, chances are the reporter will have to comply.

2. Reporters called to testify before grand juries will also rely on the three-part test, on state and federal constitutions, and on state and federal common law in support of motions to quash. In addition they may interpose state shield laws in those states that have passed them, and the state laws may be influential in federal cases. Grand jury subpoenas may also be attacked on grounds of overbreadth, prematurity, duplication, and harassment. The Fifth Amendment right against self-incrimination may be asserted in appropriate cases, although a grant of immunity will negate it.

In federal cases the Justice Department's *Guidelines on News Media Subpoenas*[34] and the *Federal Rules of Evidence* may be added to the list. The *Guidelines* attempt to strike a balance between news flow and justice, between negotiation and demand, especially where a reporter's telephone toll records are being sought.[35] In such cases the express authorization of the attorney general is required. In every case involving the news media, alternative sources are to be pursued. In at least one 1982 case a subpoena was quashed because the guidelines were not followed.[36]

Under rule 403 of the *Federal Rules of Evidence* a trial judge may exclude relevant evidence or quash subpoenas designed to collect that evidence, if it is needlessly cumulative.[37] Rule 501 provides for federal court recognition of state law. It would also permit application of a federal common law journalist's privilege where there is no state law or the state law is weak. It has been held, however, that where the state law provides greater protection for the reporter's privilege than the common law or the First Amendment, *Branzburg* requires that state law govern the case.[38]

Under rule 17(c) of the *Federal Rules of Criminal Procedure* only "evidentiary materials" may be subpoenaed, in other words, material that would be admissible at trial. States may have analogous rules of criminal procedure. The case which follows illustrates the application of rule 17(c) and the impediment that the Sixth Amendment right of "compulsory process for obtaining witnesses" poses to a federal shield law and to the concept of journalist's privilege generally.

The case, known as *Cuthbertson I* and *Cuthbertson II,* involved CBS "60 Minutes" outtakes and transcripts of interviews with trial witnesses which had been subpoenaed by defendants in their criminal fraud and conspiracy trial. What follows is an edited version of *Cuthbertson II.*

U.S. v. CUTHBERTSON

7 MED.L.RPTR. 1377, 651 F.2D 189 (3D CIR.1981), CERT. DEN. 454 U.S. 1056.

ALDISERT, Circuit Judge.

34. *Guidelines on News Media,* 28 C.F.R. § 50.10, 1979, as amended Nov. 12, 1980, 6 Med.L.Rptr. 2153 (Dec. 9, 1980).

35. In Reporters Committee for Freedom of the Press v. American Telephone and Telegraph Co., 4 Med.L.Rptr. 1177, 593 F.2d 1030 (D.C.Cir.1978), *cert. den.,* 440 U.S. 949 (1979), the court rejected the contention that the First and Fourth Amendments required law enforcement officials to notify reporters of such subpoenas.

36. United States v. Blanton, 8 Med.L.Rptr. 1106, 534 F.Supp. 295 (S.D.Fla.1982).

37. United States v. Hubbard, 5 Med.L.Rptr. 1719, 493 F.Supp. 202 (D.D.C.1979); United States v. Burke, 7 Med.L.Rptr. 2019 (E.D.N.Y.1981).

38. Mazzella v. Philadelphia Newspapers, Inc., 5 Med.L.Rptr. 1983, 479 F.Supp. 523 (E.D.N.Y.1979).

Because the facts are detailed in *Cuthbertson I,* we need set forth only a synopsis. On December 3, 1978, CBS presented on its news program "60 Minutes" an investigative report describing fast-food franchising by an organization known as Wild Bill's Family Restaurants. The report was based on interviews with a number of persons, including certain franchisees and former employees of Wild Bill's, and local government officials. On September 5, 1979, a federal grand jury returned an indictment against several principals of Wild Bill's charging them with fraud and conspiracy in the operation of the company. On February 4, 1980, on the eve of trial, the defendants served on CBS a subpoena pursuant to rule 17(c) of the *Federal Rules of Criminal Procedure* demanding production of all reporters' notes, file "out takes," audiotapes, and transcripts of interviews prepared in connection with the "60 Minutes" program. The district court's denial of CBS' motion to quash the subpoena and its subsequent order holding CBS in contempt were before us in the previous appeal.

In *Cuthbertson I,* we held that "journalists possess a qualified privilege not to divulge confidential sources and not to disclose unpublished information in their possession in criminal cases." 630 F.2d at 147. We recognized that "compelled production of a reporter's resource materials can constitute a significant intrusion into the newsgathering and editorial processes." *Id.* We concluded that this qualified privilege may be superseded by "countervailing interests" in particular cases, requiring the district courts to "balance the defendant's need for the material against the interests underlying the privilege ...." *Id.* at 148.

We also established guidelines for the district courts to use in applying rule 17(c) to subpoenas *duces tecum* directed to third parties. Rule 17(c) was not intended to be a broad discovery device, and only materials that are "admissible as evidence" are subject to subpoena under the rule. See Bowman Dairy Co. v. United States, 341 U.S. 214, 221 (1951). To obtain pretrial production and inspection of unprivileged materials from a third party witness, a party must show:

> (1) that the documents are evidentiary and relevant; (2) that they are not otherwise procurable reasonably in advance of trial by exercise of due diligence; (3) that the party cannot properly prepare for trial without such production and inspection in advance of trial and that the failure to obtain such inspection may tend unreasonably to delay the trial; and (4) that the application is made in good faith and is not intended as a general "fishing expedition." 630 F.2d at 145 (quoting United States v. Nixon, 418 U.S. 683, 699–700 (1974). * * *

Because the district court had ordered *in camera* review rather than presentation to the moving party, however, we deemed the second and third elements of this test inapplicable. 630 F.2d at 145.

Defendants had requested previous statements by persons whose names did not appear on the government's witness list as well as statements by persons whose names did appear. They asserted no basis for admissibility of the non-witness statements other than a hope that they would contain some exculpatory material. Accordingly, we held the district court's order to be invalid under rule 17(c) to the extent it sought non-witness material. 630 F.2d at 146. We found, however, that statements of persons on the government's witness list may be inconsistent with trial testimony and admissible for impeachment purposes. 630 F.2d at 144. We recognized that "because such statements ripen into evidentiary material for purposes of impeachment only if and when the witness testifies at trial, impeachment statements, although subject to subpoena under rule 17(c), generally are not subject to production and inspection by the moving party prior to trial." *Id.*

Nevertheless, because *in camera* review would aid the district court's trial preparation, we held that the district court's order to produce statements by witnesses for *in camera* inspection before trial was not an abuse of discretion under rule 17(c). *Id.* at 145.

After remand from this court, CBS submitted to the district court for *in camera* review transcripts and audio tapes of three interviews with two persons whose names appear on the government witness list. After some skirmishing over and a hearing on related matters, the court ruled that the witness statements would materially aid the defendants and therefore would be turned over to them before trial under the rationale of Brady v. Maryland, 373 U.S. 83 (1963).

The present conflict emerged from that decision. This court had approved *in camera* inspection of witness statements for the purpose of deciding whether they would have impeachment value; if so, they could be turned over to the defendants during the trial *after* the particular government witness had testified. On remand, however, the district court determined that these statements could be turned over to the defendants after commencement of trial but *before* the witnesses testified because they qualified as exculpatory evidence. It entered an order on March 24, 1981, directing disclosure of the materials to defendants on March 30, 1981. The district court's ruling is the subject of the appeal at No. 81–1467 and the mandamus petition at No. 81–1470. On March 25, Judge Gibbons granted a stay of the order, and on March 28, a motions panel consisting of Chief Judge Seitz and Judge Adams extended the stay pending a decision on the merits. The other petition for writ of mandamus, at No. 81–1485, challenges the district court's ruling of March 23, 1981, which required CBS to submit certain non-witness material to enhance intelligibility of the witness statements. Although no formal order directing this submission has been filed, CBS filed this second petition for writ of mandamus on March 28.

* * *

[There follows a discussion on the technicalities of appellate jurisdiction and review.] * * *

In *Cuthbertson I,* CBS sustained a contempt citation by refusing to comply with a subpoena. On appeal, we also ordered CBS to submit some documents to the district court for *in camera* review, and the Supreme Court denied defendants' petition for a writ of certiorari. After denial of the petition for writ of certiorari, CBS had no alternative but to comply by submitting the documents. CBS is not challenging, and indeed under the law of the case it is foreclosed from challenging, the order to submit the witness materials to the district court for an *in camera* inspection. Other issues regarding actual disclosure of the materials to the defendants and use of the materials at trial had not yet arisen at the time of the first appeal, and therefore were not before this court.

We conditioned our mandate, however, by limiting *in camera* inspection to examination of the documents to determine their possible value in impeaching government witnesses. Only after the district court had the materials in its possession did it announce its intention to allow the defendants to examine them prior to the witnesses' trial testimony. Because the trial court was already in possession of the materials as a result of the earlier appeal, it was impossible for CBS to generate an appealable order by resisting production and incurring contempt sanctions.

In the absence of the more lenient methods of appealing interlocutory orders available to civil litigants under 28 U.S.C. § 1292(b) and Fed.R.Civ.P. 54(b), a steadfast requirement that CBS incur contempt before appealing would foreclose it from obtaining review of important issues likely to arise after it submits the documents to the district court. Such a rule would be disadvantageous both to CBS and to the development of this uncertain area of the law. In addition, an invariable requirement of a contempt citation as a ticket to appellate review would work at cross purposes with our earlier admonition that "trial courts should be cautious to avoid an unnecessary confrontation between the courts and the press." Riley v. City of Chester, 612 F.2d 708, 718 (3d Cir.1979). * * We therefore conclude that the district court's order releasing these materials to defendants was a final order for purposes of appeal. We now address the merits of the CBS appeal.

CBS contends that the materials do not qualify as exculpatory evidence retrievable under rule 17(c), and that the defendants have not met the standards for compelling disclosure of press materials under our decisions in *Riley, Cuthbertson,* and *Criden* [see this text, p. 533] because they have not demonstrated that this privileged material is the only source of the desired information. We agree on both points.

Rule 17(c) provides:

> A subpoena may also command the person to whom it is directed to produce the books, papers, documents or other objects designated therein. The court on motion made promptly may quash or modify the subpoena if compliance would be unreasonable or oppressive. The court may direct that books, papers, documents or objects designated in the subpoena be produced before the court at a time prior to the trial or prior to the time when they are to be offered in evidence and may upon their production permit the books, papers, documents or objects or portions thereof to be inspected by the parties and their attorneys.

The Supreme Court has determined that a rule 17(c) subpoena reaches only evidentiary materials. "In short, any document or other materials, *admissible as evidence,* obtained by the Government by solicitation or voluntarily from third persons is subject to subpoena." Bowman Dairy Co. v. United States, 341 U.S. at 221 (emphasis added). The Court extended the admissibility requirement of rule 17(c) to materials held by third parties in United States v. Nixon, 418 U.S. at 699–700, 699 n. 12. See also United States v. Iozia, 13 F.R.D. 335, 338, 340–41 (S.D.N.Y.1952). Neither the government nor the defendants have explained how the CBS materials could be admissible as evidence, unless the interviewees testified and made inconsistent statements.

We believe that the basic error of the district court in its discussion of the statements' potential lay in its failure to discriminate between potential exculpatory material in the possession of the prosecution, generally available under the teachings of *Brady v. Maryland,* and exculpatory evidence in the possession of third parties. Only the latter is retrievable under a rule 17(c) subpoena; naked exculpatory material held by third parties that does not rise to the dignity of admissible evidence simply is not within the rule. That is the teaching of *Bowman Dairy* and *Nixon,* and we applied it in *Cuthbertson I.*

The appellees in this case have not demonstrated, nor does our research disclose, any potential use of the present materials as *evidence* in the trial other than for purposes of impeachment. On their face, these materials are simply hearsay. Neither the government nor defendants have asserted a relevant exception to the hearsay rule. See Fed.R.Ev. 802. Only after a witness has testified will his prior inconsistent statement cease to be hearsay, see Fed.R.Ev. 801(c), but we are unable to speculate on the likelihood of that occurrence.

Accordingly, as a matter of law the materials may not be obtained at this time by a rule 17(c) subpoena. Because the district court's *in camera* possession is based on the necessity of evaluating the material against the evidentiary requirement of rule 17(c), it may not release the material to the parties unless that requirement is met. It failed to make such a determination of admissibility in this case, and we therefore reverse its order releasing the materials to the defendants.

We also reverse the district court's order for a separate and independent reason. We are persuaded that the defendants failed to meet the test consistently announced in this court's *Riley-Cuthbertson-Criden* trilogy of fair trial-free press cases. We have held that to overcome the media's federal common law qualified privilege the seeker of the information must demonstrate that his only practical means of access to the information sought is through the media. In our most recent decision in the reporters' privilege context, United States v. Criden, 633 F.2d 346 (3d Cir.1980), cert. denied sub nom. Schaffer v. United States, U.S., 49 U.S.L.W. 3512 (Jan. 20, 1981), we reviewed our prior decisions in *Cuthbertson I* and *Riley* and cited three criteria that must be met before a reporter may be compelled to disclose confidential information:

> First, the movant must demonstrate that he has made an effort to obtain the information from other sources. Second, he must demonstrate that the only access to the information sought is through the journalist and her sources. Finally, the movant must persuade the Court that the information sought is crucial to the claim, 633 F.2d at 358–359.

In this case, the identities of the possible witnesses are available from the witness list. The statements were made by franchisees and potential franchisees, with whom the defendants have had business relationships. Defense counsel have conceded that "[w]e know because of the dealings that the defendants have had with all the franchisees, who all of these people are."

Appellees have not indicated, and we do not perceive, why the defendants may not themselves interview these same interviewees, whose identities they know, to obtain the desired information. In contrast, the defendants in *Criden* had already cross-examined the self-avowed source, and the testimony of the reporter in that case was relevant to the source's credibility. In this case, the sources have not yet testified. If their testimony at trial differs from their statement to CBS, the defendants will have the opportunity to obtain the materials for impeachment purposes. As we have heretofore observed in this respect, prior statements of prospective witnesses are "unique bits of evidence that are frozen at a particular place and time." Cuthbertson I, 630 F.2d at 148.

Accordingly, even if the defendants could have met the requirements under rule 17(c), the materials would not be available to defendants in this case because defendants failed to prove an element necessary to overcome the media's qualified privilege: that the only practical access to the information sought is through the media source.

Our conclusion that the evidentiary potential of the witness statements will arise only when the witnesses testify governs our disposition of the second petition for writ of mandamus, at No. 81-1485. It is our understanding that, at the time the second petition was filed in this court, no formal order on this issue had been entered by the district court. * * * Moreover, the threshold determination giving rise to the appeal and the first petition—that the materials contain exculpatory information to which defendants are entitled—was not made with regard to the non-witness materials. Therefore, the second petition for writ of mandamus is not ripe, and we need not now address it.

Accordingly, in appeal No. 81–1467, the district court's order of March 24, 1981, releasing the witness materials to the defendants, will be reversed and the cause remanded for further proceedings consistent with this opinion. In No. 81–1470, the petition for writ of mandamus will be dismissed as moot; in No. 81–1485, the petition for writ of mandamus will be dismissed as not ripe.

COMMENT

Essentially the Third Circuit reversed the federal district court order that tapes which would materially aid defendants be conveyed to defendants prior to trial because there had been *no* showing that 1) the tapes would be admissible at trial as required by Rule 17(c) and 2) that alternate sources had been exhausted. Clearly the court recognized a qualified journalist's privilege.

An earlier state case running somewhat parallel to *Cuthbertson II* was Brown v. Commonwealth of Virginia, 204 S.W.2d 429, (Va.1974) cert. den. 419 U.S. 966. In *Brown,* it was held that the journalist's claim that a First Amendment privilege protected his confidential sources could be pierced in the following circumstances: If there were reasonable grounds to believe that information in a journalist's possession was "material to proof of a criminal offense, or to proof of the defense asserted by the defendant, or to a reduction in the classification or gradation of the offense charged, or to a mitigation of the penalty attached, [or] the defendant's need to acquire such information is essential to a fair trial; when such information is not otherwise available, the defendant has a due process *right* to compel disclosure of such information and the identity of the source and any privilege of confidentiality claimed by the newsman must, upon pain of contempt, yield to that right."

In *Brown,* the information sought from a journalist by the defense concerned inconsistent statements of a prosecution witness. The state court in *Brown* had required that the information sought be "essential" if the First Amendment-based journalist's privilege was to be put aside. The information sought in *Brown* was held by the court to be nonessential:

> (T)he record fails to show that either the statements made at trial or the prior statements were material to proof of the crime, to proof of Brown's defense, or to a reduction in the classification or penalty of the crime charged. Since the inconsistent statements were collateral and not material, the identity of the source was irrelevant.

As a result, the Virginia Supreme Court ruled that the trial court did not err when it declined to compel disclosure. The *Brown* case has been summarized as follows:

> In *Brown,* the court thus adopted an "essentiality" test based upon (1) a determination whether information sought was material to the disposition of the guilt or innocence of the accused, and (2) whether there were alternative sources available. Again, no specific mention was made of Justice Stewart's additional (or third) requirement that there be a compelling interest for disclosure. Perhaps, this was included in the "materiality" requirement. Perhaps, the Sixth Amendment rights of the accused to all evidence in his favor were simply assumed to satisfy in themselves the compelling interest standard. The court does indicate that the defendant's interests in obtaining evidence in his favor "are rights of no less dignity than the right of the government to prosecute". See Barron and Dienes, *Handbook of Free Speech and Free Press* 447 (1979).

Similarly, in State of Vermont v. St. Peter, 315 A.2d 254 (Vt.1974), a television news reporter was held to be entitled to refuse to answer questions put to him in a deposition proceeding in a criminal case "unless the interrogator can demonstrate to the judicial officer appealed to that there is no other adequately available source for the information and that it is relevant and material on the issue of guilt or innocence." As these cases illustrate, a qualified First Amendment privilege survived *Branzburg,* following the rough outlines of Justice Stewart's *Branzburg* dissent, in spite of the unequivocal dictates of the Sixth Amendment.

3. In jurisdictions less sympathetic to a journalist's privilege—notably California and New York—neither state shield laws nor the First Amendment will protect the privilege in all circumstances. Recall that in the *Rosato* case (this text, p. 396) a judge anxious to learn who had defied his orders not to discuss a case would recognize neither a privilege for unpublished information nor the idea of having first to exhaust alternative sources, although the former is clearly protected by the California statute.

Similarly in CBS v. Superior Court, 4 Med.L.Rptr. 1568, 149 Cal.Rptr. 421 (1978), the California Court of Appeal would not protect "60 Minutes" outtakes showing negotiations for narcotics sales between defendants and undercover agents because the identities of the officers had been revealed at a hearing on a motion to quash the subpoena. This is sometimes called the "exposure to view" theory: reveal part of your confidential information and you reveal it all. The court, balancing First and Sixth Amendment rights, ordered *in camera* inspection.

Sometimes the balance tips the other way. In United States v. Burke, 7 Med.L. Rptr. 2019 (E.D.N.Y.1981), a federal court, under color of state law, thought that the "integrity of [*Sports Illustrated's*] newsgathering and editorial functions" outweighed the defendant's Sixth Amendment right to the "broadest possible opportunity to cross-examine adverse witnesses." The case revolved around a nonconfidential participant in a college sports point-shaving scandal. Defendant failed to meet the three-part test for what the court said was a qualified First Amendment privilege. The magazine reporter was required to testify after his witness-source had testified, but he did not have to submit any of his work product.

In the "Abscam" cases the question of the role played by investigative reporters in bringing indictments against defendants came up again, as it had in the *Farber* case which follows. At an early stage in the investigation, NBC and newspapers in New York and Philadelphia were privy to prosecutorial strategies in the cases. Defendants wanted to know more about the relationship between press and prosecutors and were able to support their requests for subpoenas *ad testificandum* by meeting the conditions of the three-part test. Justice Department employees were subsequently punished for disclosures made to the press, but reporter testimony was held to a minimum. In re Schaffer, 6 Med.L.Rptr. 1554 (E.D.Pa.1980), affirmed sub nom. United States v. Criden, 6 Med.L. Rptr. 1993, 633 F.2d 346 (3d Cir. 1980), cert. den., 449 U.S. 1113 (1981).

The Special Case of New Jersey: In Re Farber

A much publicized case for a time sounded a retreat from the effort to erect a qualified First Amendment privilege on the ashes of the plurality opinion in *Branzburg*. This was the famous *Farber* case.[39] Investigative work of *New York Times* reporter, Myron Farber, led to the indictment and prosecution of Dr. Mario E. Jascalevich for murder. Jascalevich subpoenaed Farber's notes on the ground that this might enable him to establish his innocence. Farber and his employer, the *New York Times*, contended that its subpoena was overbroad and that the material sought was privileged under both the new New Jersey and New York shield laws and the First Amendment. The trial judge ruled that the notes in controversy were "necessary and material." Farber and the *New York Times* requested a

39. Farber, "Somebody is Lying": The Story of Dr. X (1982).

hearing to air their arguments that the material sought was privileged prior to having to produce it. The trial court judge, William Arnold, rejected this request and ordered that the subpoenaed material be produced for *in camera* inspection by the court.

Farber and the *Times* sought unsuccessfully to stay the trial judge's order for *in camera* or private inspection of Farber's notes in the New Jersey state courts. Both Justices White and Marshall separately declined to stay the trial court's order requiring compliance with the subpoena. Judge Trautwein then determined that Judge Arnold's order for *in camera* inspection had been "willfully condemned" and found Farber and the *Times* guilty as charged.

Judge Trautwein imposed a $100,000 fine on the *New York Times* and ordered Myron Farber to serve six months in the Bergen County jail and to pay a fine of $1,000. In addition, a fine of $5,000 for every day that Judge Arnold's production order was disobeyed was imposed on the *Times*. Farber was confined to the Bergen County jail for forty days. The *Times* and Farber then sought and obtained review of the judgments of civil and criminal contempt against them for their contumacy in refusing to comply with the subpoenas issued against them. The New Jersey Supreme Court affirmed the judgments below. See In re Farber, 394 A.2d 330 (N.J. 1978).

The New Jersey Supreme Court, per Justice Fountain, rejected the contention that the *New York Times* and Myron Farber had a "privilege to remain silent with respect to confidential information and the sources of such information by virtue of the First Amendment.

"In our view the Supreme Court of the United States (in *Branzburg*) has clearly rejected this claim and has squarely held that no such First Amendment right exists." At the same time, it was conceded that "despite the holding in *Branzburg*, those who gather and disseminate news are by no means without First Amendment protections." Among these protections was the right to refrain from revealing sources except upon legitimate "demand."

What was illegitimate demand? "Demand is not legitimate when the desired information is patently irrelevant to the needs of the inquirer or his needs are not manifestly compelling." However, among the protections afforded by the First Amendment to the press, "there is not to be found the privilege of refusing to reveal relevant and confidential information and its sources to a grand jury." The New Jersey Supreme Court concluded as follows:

> The important and conclusive point is that five members of the Court [in *Branzburg*] have all reached the conclusion that the First Amendment affords no privilege to a newsman to refuse to appear before a grand jury and testify as to relevant information he possesses, even though in so doing he may divulge confidential sources. The particular path that any Justice may have followed becomes unimportant when once it is seen that a majority has reached the same destination.
>
> Thus, we do no weighing or balancing of societal interests in reaching our determination that the First Amendment does not afford appellants the privilege they claim. The weighing and balancing has been done by a higher court. Our conclusion that appellants cannot derive the protection they seek from the First Amendment rests upon the fact that the ruling in *Branzburg* is binding upon us and we interpret it as appliable to, and clearly including, the particular issue framed here. It follows that the obligation to appear at a criminal trial on behalf of a defendant who is enforcing his Sixth Amendment rights is at least as compelling as the duty to appear before a grand jury.

The New Jersey Supreme Court's decision in *Farber* was hard to evaluate. Unlike the cases discussed earlier, it appeared to take the position that no First

Amendment-based newsman's privilege may ever attach in a grand jury context or where a criminal defendant seeks information from a reporter *relevant* to his case. The New Jersey court stressed that in its view a majority of the United States Supreme Court in *Branzburg* declined to take a balancing approach in the criminal context. In this situation, the New Jersey Supreme Court considered Justices White and Powell to be in agreement.

At the same time, the New Jersey Supreme Court emphasized that the journalist's duty to provide information to a grand jury, spoken of in *Branzburg,* related to "relevant information he possesses." If we speak of "relevant" information, isn't the implication that a privilege would attach to information sought which would not be "relevant?"

A fascinating aspect of the *Farber* case was that it presented a direct clash between the state and federal constitutions and the state shield law. The New Jersey Supreme Court described its shield law, N.J.S.A., 2A:84A–21 and 21A, as one which was "as strongly worded as any in the country." Approached as a matter of statutory construction, the "appellants come fully within the literal language of the enactment." But it was successfully argued in *Farber* that if the shield law was enforced, the Sixth Amendment to the U.S. Constitution as well as Art. I, § 110 of the New Jersey Constitution would be violated:

> Essentially, the argument is this: The Federal and State Constitutions each provide that in all criminal prosecutions the accused shall have the right "to have compulsory process for obtaining witnesses in his favor." Dr. Jascalevich seeks to obtain evidence to use in preparing and presenting his defense in the ongoing criminal trial in which he has been accused of multiple murders. He claims to come within the favor of these constitutional provisions—which he surely does. Finally, when faced with the shield law, he invokes the rather elementary but entirely sound proposition that where Constitution and statute collide, the latter must yield. Subject to what is said below, we find this argument unassailable.

An important part of the decision of the New Jersey Supreme Court involved its rejection of the contention of Farber and the *Times* that permitting *in camera* inspection by the trial court of the information in controversy would be a violation of the shield law. While agreeing with Farber and the *Times* that "they are entitled to a full hearing on the issues of relevance, materiality, and overbreadth of the subpoena," the New Jersey Supreme Court defended preliminary *in camera* inspection of the information "to determine whether, and if so to what extent, the statutory privilege must yield to the defendant's constitutional rights: * * * Judge Arnold refused to give ultimate rulings with respect to relevance and other preliminary matters until he had examined the material. We think he had no other course. It is not rational to ask a judge to ponder the relevance of the unknown."

The appellants had objected that the subpoena was vague and uncertain and that the data sought under it might not be relevant and material. This was all the more reason "for the trial court to inspect *in camera* the subpoenaed items." The court then pivoted in the direction of the appellants by saying that they, and others who might be similarly situated in the future, "were entitled to a preliminary determination by the trial judge *before* they would have to submit subpoenaed materials to the trial judge for inspection."

IN RE FARBER

394 A.2D 330 (N.J.1978)

FOUNTAIN, J.

* * *

While we agree, then, that appellants should be afforded the hearing they are seeking, one procedural aspect of which calls for their compliance with the order for *in camera* inspection, we are also of the view that they, and those who in the future may be similarly situated, are entitled to a preliminary determination before being compelled to submit the subpoenaed materials to a trial judge for such inspection. Our decision in this regard is not, contrary to the suggestion in some of the briefs filed with us, mandated by the First Amendment; for in addition to ruling generally against the representatives of the press in *Branzburg,* the Court particularly and rather vigorously, rejected the claims there asserted that before going before the grand jury, each of the reporters, at the very least, was entitled to a preliminary hearing to establish a number of threshold issues. Rather, our insistence upon such a threshold determination springs from our obligation to give as much effect as possible, within ever-present constitutional limitations, to the very positively expressed legislative intent to protect the confidentiality and secrecy of sources from which the media derive information. To this end such a determination would seem a necessity.

The threshold determination would normally follow the service of a subpoena by a defendant upon a newspaper, a reporter or other representative of the media. The latter foreseeably would respond with a motion to quash. If the status of the movant—newspaper or media representative—were not conceded, then there would follow the taking of proofs leading to a determination that the movant did or did not qualify for the statutory privilege. Assuming qualification, it would then become the obligation of the defense to satisfy the trial judge, by a fair preponderance of the evidence including all reasonable inferences, that there was a reasonable probability or likelihood that the information sought by the subpoena was material and relevant to his defense, that it could not be secured from any less intrusive source, and that the defendant had a legitimate need to see and otherwise use it.

The manner in which the obligation of the defendant is to be discharged in the proceedings leading to this threshold determination will depend largely upon the facts of the particular case. We wish to make it clear, however, that this opinion is not to be taken as a license for a fishing expedition in every criminal case where there has been investigative reporting, nor as permission for an indiscriminate rummaging through newspaper files.

Although in this case the trial judge did not articulate the findings prescribed above, *it is perfectly clear that on the record before him a conclusion of materiality, relevancy, unavailability of another source, as well as need was quite inescapable.* A review of the record in the exercise of our original jurisdiction, reveals that the knowledge possessed by the trial judge and the material before him at the time he made his determination to conduct an *in camera* inspection afforded a more than adequate factual basis upon which to rest a conclusion that the threshold prerequisites set forth above were in fact fully met. We deem it quite unnecessary to remand the case in order to have the judge set forth formally what we find to be abundantly clear. We set forth below our reasons for this conclusion.

As of June 30, 1978, the date of the challenged decision to examine the materials *in camera,* Judge Arnold had been trying the case for about 18 weeks. He had dealt with earlier pretrial motions. His knowledge of the factual background and of the part Farber had played was intimate and pervasive. Perhaps most significant is the trial court's thorough awareness of appellant Farber's close association with the Prosecutor's office since a time preceding the indictment. This glaring fact of their close working relationship may well serve to distinguish this case from the vast majority of others in which defendants seek disclosure from newsmen in the face of the shield law. Two and a half months before his June 30th decision, Judge Arnold observed,

> The facts show that Farber has written articles for the *New York Times* about this matter, commencing in January 1976. According to an article printed in the *New York Times* (hereinafter the *Times*) on January 8, 1976, Farber showed Joseph Woodcock, the Bergen County Prosecutor at that time, a deposition not in the State's file and *provided additional information that convinced the prosecution to reopen an investigation into some deaths that occurred at Riverdell Hospital.* [Emphasis added.] [State v. Jascalevich; In the Matter of the Application of Myron Farber and the New York Times Company re: Sequestration, 158 N.J.Super. 488, 490 (Law Div. 1978).]

And

> The court has examined the news stories in evidence and they demonstrate exceptional quality, a grasp of intricate scientific knowledge, and a style of a fine journalist. *They, also, demonstrate considerable knowledge of the case before the court and deep involvement by Farber,* showing his attributes as a first-rate investigative reporter. [Emphasis added.] However, if a newspaper reporter assumes the duties of an investigator, he must also assume the responsibilities of an investigator and be treated equally under the law, unless he comes under some exception. [Id. at 493–94.]

In the same vein is a letter before the trial court dated January 14, 1977 from Assistant Prosecutor Moses to Judge Robert A. Matthews, sitting as a Presiding Judge in the Appellate Division, undertaking to explain "how the investigation, from which the [Jascalevich] indictment resulted, came to be reopened." In the course of that explanation it is revealed that sometime in the latter part of 1975 "a reporter for the *New York Times* began an investigation into the 1965–66 deaths and circumstances surrounding them. The results of the *New York Times* inquiry were made available to the Prosecutor. *It was thus determined that there were certain items which were not in the file of the Prosecutor.*" [Emphasis added.]

Further support for the determination that there is a reasonable probability that the subpoenaed materials meet the test formulated above appears in the * * * factual circumstances pointed to by the defendant and supported by documents and transcripts of testimony found in the appendix filed by the defendant. * * *

We hasten to add that we need not, and do not, address (much less determine) the truth or falsity of these assertions. The point to be made is that these are the assertions of the criminal defendant supported by testimonial or documentary proof; and based thereon it is perfectly clear that there was more than enough before Judge Arnold to satisfy the tests formulated above. Of course all of this information detailed above has long been known to appellants. Accordingly we find that preliminary requirements for *in camera* inspection have been met.

We have considered appellants' other contentions as to lack of jurisdiction and the like. So far as they are relevant to the matters herein decided we find them to lack merit.

The judgment of conviction of criminal contempt and that in aid of litigant's rights are affirmed. Stays heretofore entered are vacated effective as of 4:00 p.m., Tuesday September 26, 1978.

COMMENT

1. Chief Justice Hughes, concurring, characterized the press claim that *in camera* inspection of the material sought should not be permitted as follows:

> Their claim to a final adjudication without an *in camera* scrutiny by the court upon which to base its decision

> would project the absurd proposition that the press, and not the courts should be the final arbiter of the constitutional mandate.

2. Justice Pashman, in a strong dissent, rejected the New Jersey Supreme Court's "assertion that appellants were indeed accorded a due process hearing prior to an *in camera* hearing. * * *" Pashman contended that "appellants were to be afforded an opportunity to contest the legality of *in camera* disclosure *only after* the materials had been so disclosed." Pashman continued:

> Farber has therefore never received the hearing to which he is constitutionally entitled. I find it totally unimaginable that the majority can even consider allowing a man to be sent to jail without a full and orderly hearing at which to present his defenses. Mr. Farber probably assumed, as did I, that hearings were supposed to be held and findings made *before* a person went to jail and not *afterwards.*

Pashman's dissent also referred to a much publicized aspect of the *Farber* case. Farber was writing a book on the Jascalevich case (see fn. 39) and had received a $75,000 advance from a publisher. Writing is what writers do, said some journalists in Farber's defense. Pashman challenged the majority's intimation that if a reporter could be categorized as an investigator he could lose shield law protection: "To hold therefore that the Shield Law is not applicable to a reporter who is also an investigator is to hold that the Shield Law will never be applicable."

As for the intimation of defense counsel that a reporter "who informs the public by authoring a book is somehow less deserving of Shield Law protection than one who articulates his findings in a newspaper," Pashman responded: "Publishing journalistic books for money is no less an illustrious way to perform the function of the press than is writing newspaper articles for a salary."

The differences in the procedure held appropriate by the majority in the *Farber* case and the procedure that Justice Pashman thought necessary are summed up as follows:

"The majority suggests that a hearing can be dispensed with, or that its outcome will be foreordained, in every case in which a reporter possesses 'considerable knowledge of [a criminal] case.' Such a conclusion nullifies the provisions of the Media Privilege Act. In effect, the majority has ruled that shield law protection will be withdrawn from reporters who perform their jobs competently—that is, those who gain 'considerable knowledge' concerning a criminal case. A hearing as to relevance, materiality and necessity must be conducted in all cases in which the privilege is invoked. Compelled *in camera* disclosure must be prohibited unless and until the defendant has met this his threshold burden in accordance with the procedures to be discussed below."

"First and Fourteenth Amendments afford journalists a qualified privilege to refuse to give testimony or produce documents in civil and criminal actions to which they are not a party," said a federal district court in Florida, unless the party issuing the subpoena has demonstrated a compelling need for the information and exhaustion of alternative sources.[40]

3. Iowa Beef Producers suing union officers were unable to enforce a subpoena *duces tecum* against the *Wall Street Journal* because the information sought did not go to the "heart of the claim" and "alternative sources had not been exhausted." [41]

As in the criminal context, a qualified privilege for communicators is now widely recognized in civil litigation. And in civil

40. Brown v. Okeechobee, 6 Med.L.Rptr. 2579 (S.D.Fla.1981).

41. In re IBP Litigation, 7 Med.L.Rptr. 2127, 491 F.Supp. 1359 (N.D.Iowa 1981).

cases where the reporter is not a party, the chances of not having to comply with a subpoena are very good indeed.

4. The *Farber* case became a *cause célèbre* in communication law. The majority opinion for the New Jersey Supreme Court clearly placed the Sixth Amendment rights of the defendant and his equivalent state constitutional rights above the interests of the journalist in maintaining the confidentiality of sources or materials.

The court also approved an order requiring Farber's compliance with *in camera* inspection by the trial court prior to a hearing on the relevance or importance of the material believed to be in the reporter's possession.

Was the case unique in that investigative reporter Farber had become *the* expert on the case and could be assumed to hold information vital to the defense? That assumption was part of the New Jersey court's holding.

In a fittingly dramatic finale, the jury acquitted Dr. Jascalevich. The need for information was gone, and Farber was released from jail. With heavy fines still outstanding against it, the *New York Times* sought review in the Supreme Court. The Court refused to take the case.

On January 18, 1982, New Jersey Governor Brendan Byrne pardoned the *New York Times* and Myron Farber and returned $101,000 in criminal penalties to the newspaper.

New Jersey must have felt uncomfortable about the *Farber* case for its legislature soon amended its law to provide for a hearing *prior* to an *in camera* inspection when a journalist is subpoenaed in a criminal proceeding. Once the journalist's status is certified, a defendant in New Jersey must now meet a four-part test of 1) relevance, 2) no alternative sources, 3) substantiality to the issue of guilt or innocence, and 4) that the subpoena is not overbroad or unreasonably burdensome.[42] The law has been interpreted to protect both sources and information, as well as eyewitness news-gathering, unless the crime witnessed involves "physical violence or property damage." [43]

While some New Jersey courts have used the word "absolute" in describing the state's amended shield law, it is less than that. Given that *Farber* was a low point in the development of the privilege, it is a vast improvement. But New Jersey still can't make up its mind. In Maressa v. New Jersey Monthly, 8 Med.L.Rptr. 1473, 445 A.2d 376 (N.J.1982), the court held that partial disclosure does not affect the absolute privilege accorded by the state statute—a rejection of the "exposure to view" doctrine. Nor would the assertion by a media defendant in a libel suit of an affirmative defense such as truth, fair comment, or lack of malice void the privilege. The privilege, said the court, could be waived only by voluntary disclosure. At about the same time, another New Jersey court in Central New Jersey Home v. New York Times, 8 Med.L.Rptr. 1456, 444 A.2d 80 (N.J.1982) ruled that neither the state shield law nor New Jersey's constitution protected a newspaper from disclosing preliminary drafts of an allegedly libelous article during pretrial discovery. Nor would they protect the reporter from answering deposition questions about her knowledge and use of state agency reports that might have exonerated plaintiffs of the charges mentioned in her article. So much for "absolute" shield laws.

JOURNALIST'S PRIVILEGE IN THE CIVIL CONTEXT

1. Claims of privilege in civil cases are much easier to sustain, especially where

42. N.J.Stat.Ann. 2A–21–29 (1980).

43. In re Vrazo, 6 Med.L.Rptr. 2410, 423 A.2d 695 (N.J.1980).

the journalist is a third party and not, for example, defendant in a libel suit. There is often a less compelling need for a journalist's information in civil suits and, at the same time, a greater array of alternative sources.

One of the earliest and most influential post-*Branzburg* cases recognizing the existence of a qualified First Amendment-based privilege in civil litigation was Baker v. F. & F. Investment, 339 F.Supp. 942 (S.D.N.Y.1972), affirmed 470 F.2d 778 (2d Cir. 1972), cert. den. 411 U.S. 966 (1973). Black class suitors, alleging racially discriminatory housing practices on the part of the defendant, sought through pretrial discovery proceedings to extract from Alfred Balk, a *Columbia Journalism Review* editor, his source for an article written by him in the July 4, 1962 issue of the *Saturday Evening Post* entitled "Confessions of A Block-Buster." The federal district court refused to compel journalist Balk to reveal his source. The plaintiffs, said the court, had not shown that all other sources of information such as title and mortgage records had been exhausted or that the disclosure of his source by Balk was essential to the protection of the public interest involved.

In a significant passage the court of appeals, which affirmed the decision below, indicated that the interest in protecting the journalist's sources will be weightier in civil litigation than might be the case where the needs of the grand jury, "the investigative arm of the criminal justice system" are not involved. Judge Kaufman emphasized, as had the lower court, that alternative sources of information to determine the identity of the source sought from the journalist had not been exhausted. As a result the material sought from the journalist did not, to use the famous phrase from *Garland v. Torre,* go to the "heart of the claim."

2. Another case where a qualified First Amendment-based privilege was recognized was Democratic National Committee v. McCord, 356 F.Supp. 1394 (D.D.C.1973). On motions to quash the subpoenas by news organizations, Federal District Judge Charles Richey granted their request and refused to enforce the subpoenas. Even though the issue was raised after the Supreme Court decision in *Branzburg* had declined to create a newsman's privilege in grand jury proceedings based on the First Amendment, Judge Richey held that in these circumstances the news people concerned were entitled to a qualified privilege under the First Amendment. The federal district court, reflecting Justice Stewart's dissent in *Branzburg,* stated that absent a showing that alternative sources of evidence had been exhausted and absent a showing of the materiality of the documents sought, an order quashing the subpoenas was warranted. The federal district court appeared to confine *Branzburg* to the grand jury setting. Judge Richey read *Branzburg* as permitting a qualified First Amendment privilege to protect newsman's privilege in the civil litigation area.

McCord involved subpoenas arising out of civil litigation. In what might be called a "fishing expedition," the Committee for the Re-election of the President (Nixon) seemed to be looking for anything that might help them in a number of civil suits against the opposition party.

Judge Richey in quashing the subpoenas noted that the federal district court in Washington was faced with a constitutional issue of the first magnitude, "What is involved," said Richey, "is the right of the press to gather and publish, and that of the public to receive, news from widespread, diverse, and ofttimes confidential sources."

The news media had presented affidavits from prominent reporters asserting that enforcement of the subpoenas would lead to disclosure and subsequent depletion of confidential news sources without which investigative reporting would be severely, if not totally, hampered. The competing consideration, of course, is the right of the parties to procure evidence in civil litigation.

Recognizing the reluctance of other courts in civil and criminal cases, including the Supreme Court, to recognize even a qualified newsman's privilege, Judge Richey distinguished the present case as being not a criminal case but an action for monetary damages. Moreover the media were not parties but were simply being used to produce documents. More important, the parties on whose behalf the subpoenas had been issued had not demonstrated that the testimony represented by the documents would go to the "heart of their claim." Note the recurrence of this concept.

"Without information concerning the workings of the [g]overnment," said the Judge, "the public's confidence in its integrity will inevitably suffer. This is especially true where, as here, strong allegations have been made of corruption within the highest circles of government and in a campaign for the presidency itself. This court cannot blind itself to the possible 'chilling effect' the enforcement of the subpoenas would have on the flow of information to the press and, thus, to the public. This court stands convinced that if it allows the discouragement of investigative reporting into the highest levels of government, no amount of legal theorizing could allay the public's suspicions. * * *"

Richey appeared to be following the recommendation in Justice Powell's concurring opinion in *Branzburg* that a newsman's claim of privilege should be judged "on its facts by the striking of the proper balance between freedom of the press and the obligation of all citizens to give relevant testimony."

3. But seemingly lesser suits have been lost. Although a federal district court in Texas recognized a qualified privilege, it held a reporter in contempt for refusing to testify *in camera* in a civil action brought by a suspended employee against the Dallas school district. The employee alleged that the school district had released incriminating information to the reporter. The reporter wrote a story, and the school district then used that story to justify its suspension. In light of the employee's due process rights and his effort to exhaust alternative sources, the court, rejecting any notion of an absolute privilege for reporters in civil cases, ordered the reporter to testify.[44]

4. Chilling effect "is a paramount consideration," said a federal district court in New York. A drug company sought the identity of a source that had been consulted for evaluation of a drug in a medical newsletter article but had not met the three-part test.[45] United States Steel, however, was successful in getting outtakes from ABC on its coverage of an underground coal mine fire since there were no confidential sources and ABC had already shown outtakes to one of its outside consultants.[46]

THE STANFORD DAILY OR "INNOCENT" SEARCH CASE

1. One response to odds favoring journalists was a circumvention of the subpoena process altogether and the use of search warrants to permit the ransacking of an "innocent" third-party newspaper. Although there were fewer than thirty of these in ten states between the first and most famous *Standard Daily* case in 1978

44. Trautman v. Dallas School District, 8 Med.L.Rptr. 1088 (N.D.Texas 1982).

45. Apicella v. McNeil Laboratories, Inc., 66 F.R.D. 78 (E.D.N.Y.1975).

46. Davis v. United States Steel, Civ. No. 79–3318 (S.D.N.Y. Nov. 13, 1980).

and ameliorating intervention by federal legislation in 1981, they did represent one of the most serious ruptures ever in press-bench relationships.

Student reporters for *The Stanford Daily* at Stanford University had covered a student demonstration at a hospital which had resulted in violence and injuries to police officers. The newspaper published articles and photographs about the demonstration. A municipal court judge at the request of the police issued a warrant authorizing a search of *The Stanford Daily.* He found probable cause to believe that photographs and negatives would be found on the newspaper premises which would help to identify the demonstrators who had assaulted the police officers. The warrant was issued even though the newspaper's personnel were not suspected of having committed a crime or of having participated in any unlawful acts.

The students brought an action in federal district court against the municipal judge and the law enforcement officers on the ground that their rights under the First and Fourth Amendments had been violated. The federal district court agreed with the students and rendered a declaratory judgment. Where the subject of the search is innocent of wrongdoing and First Amendment considerations are present, the court ruled a search warrant could be issued "only in the rare circumstances where there is a clear showing that (1) important materials will be destroyed or removed from the jurisdiction; and (2) a restraining order would be futile." Since these unusual circumstances had not been found to exist in *The Stanford Daily* case, the federal district court ruled that the search of the newspaper's premises was unconstitutional. The United States Court of Appeals for the Ninth Circuit affirmed. The federal district court opinion was one that much of the American press would have supported although even that opinion declined to view the newsroom as a First Amendment sanctuary. But the Supreme Court resolution of the issue left the press angry and disturbed. The Court upheld the search of a newspaper's premises even though no one on the paper's staff was suspected of any crime.

The line-up of the justices was reminiscent of that in *Branzburg.* Justice White wrote the opinion for the Court. He subjected the newsroom to the mandates of the Fourth Amendment with the same egalitarian philosophy he had employed in *Branzburg.* There he had declared that the journalist, like any other witness, could be required to breach his confidences at the request of a grand jury in pursuit of relevant information. Powell, by means of a separate concurring opinion, tried to steer a middle course, as he tried to do in *Branzburg,* and Stewart dissented just as he had in *Branzburg.*

ZURCHER v. THE STANFORD DAILY

436 U.S. 547, 98 S.CT. 1970, 56 L.ED.2D 552 (1978).

Justice WHITE delivered the opinion of the Court.

* * *

But presumptively protected materials are not necessarily immune from seizure under warrant for use at a criminal trial. Not every such seizure, and not even most, will impose a prior restraint. And surely a warrant to search newspaper premises for criminal evidence such as the one issued here for news photographs taken in a public place carries no realistic threat of prior restraint or of any direct restraint whatsoever on the publication of the *Daily* or on its communication of ideas. The hazards of such warrants can be avoided by a neutral magistrate carrying out his responsibilities under the Fourth Amendment, for he has ample tools at his disposal to confine warrants to search within reasonable limits.

* * *

We accordingly reject the reasons given by the District Court and adopted by the Court of Appeals for holding the search for photographs at *The Stanford Daily* to have been unreasonable within the meaning of the Fourth Amendment and in violation of the First Amendment. Nor has anything else presented here persuaded us that the Amendments forbade this search. It follows that the judgment of the Court of Appeals is reversed.

So ordered.

Justice Brennan took no part in the consideration or decision of this case.

Justice POWELL, concurring.

* * *

While there is no justification for the establishment of a separate Fourth Amendment procedure for the press, a magistrate asked to issue a warrant for the search of press offices can and should take cognizance of the independent values protected by the First Amendment—such as those highlighted by Justice Stewart—when he weighs such factors. If the reasonableness and particularity requirements are thus applied, the dangers are likely to be minimal.

In any event, considerations such as these are the province of the Fourth Amendment. There is no authority either in history or in the Constitution itself for exempting certain classes of persons or entities from its reach.

Justice Stewart, with whom Justice Marshall joins, dissenting.

COMMENT

Press commentary on the care was bitter, as it would be later in *Herbert v. Lando.* How would the ruling have affected Watergate and the *Pentagon Papers* case had it been in place then? Suddenly, subpoenas didn't look so bad; at least you could see them coming.

Following *Stanford Daily* a printer's office was searched in Flint, Michigan, a television newsroom in Boise, Idaho, the Associated Press in Butte, Montana, the home of an editor in Albany, Georgia. On October 13, 1980, Congress passed the Privacy Protection Act (18 U.S.C.A. § 793 ff). While media organizations had lobbied Congress to prevent surprise invasions of the newsroom, they had asked for a ban on searches of the premises of all innocent third parties. What they got was legislation specific to them. Many journalists are uncomfortable with these kinds of laws since they permit lawmakers to intrude themselves into the realm of the First Amendment.

Nevertheless the law, which went into effect for federal searches on January 1, 1981 and for state searches on October 14, 1981, made it unlawful for law enforcement officers to search for or seize raw materials (photos, audio and videotapes, interview notes) or work products (drafts of articles and notes) possessed by anyone engaged in the dissemination of news or information to the public through newspapers, books, or electronic broadcasts unless there was probable cause to believe that the person with the material was committing a crime.

Exceptions were threats to national defense, the theft of classified or restricted information, and seizures that would be necessary to prevent death or serious injury. Searches would also be permitted if there was reason to believe that a subpoena would lead to the destruction of material that would serve the needs of justice. Police are expected to request voluntary cooperation from news organizations and scholars or, if that fails, to seek a subpoena before going after a search warrant.

State laws incorporating some or all of these provisions in ways having both more and less impact than the parent federal law have been passed in California, Connecticut, Illinois, Nebraska, New Jersey, Oregon, Texas, Washington, and Wisconsin. And the Department of Justice Guidelines followed in December of 1980.

POSTSCRIPT

Shield laws and the thought of shield laws have provoked much debate among news people. Many prefer a First Amendment stand to legislative enactment, even when the legislature acts with the best of intentions. Others have argued vigorously for no special privileges at all.[47] Surprisingly in light of *Branzburg,* a qualified First Amendment-based journalist's privilege has emerged. Most jurisdictions, both state and federal, recognize a qualified privilege. In addition, half the states have shield laws.

Estimates of from 30 to 50 percent have been made for the amount of news gathered from confidential sources.[48] Many reporters are prepared to go to jail to protect those sources, and the law has evolved toward what reporters in one pre-*Branzburg* survey thought it ought to—a flexible, ad hoc qualified privilege.[49]

However the privilege is applied, it appears to be a privilege for the communicator, narrowly or broadly defined, and not a privilege for the source. In New Jersey v. Boiardo, 6 Med.L.Rptr. 1195, 414 A.2d 14 (N.J.1980), the court held that the privilege could be invoked by a reporter regardless of whether confidentiality had been waived by the sources or whether the source's identity had been discovered by other means. Only the reporter could waive the privilege, said the court, because it belongs to him and him alone. A broken promise by a reporter raises an ethical question but provides no legal cause of action. When the name of a rape victim obtained from a prosecutor was published despite an alleged promise of confidentiality, the court found the publication constitutionally privileged despite the promise and the newspaper's prior policy of withholding the names of victims of sex crimes.[50]

Casual assurances of confidentiality may be dangerous to a reporter.[51] A court may wish to know how confidentiality was established with a source. A reporter, therefore, ought to have some fairly unambiguous method of establishing the relationship before having to testify in court. Employers are not protected under some state laws. The Associated Press was required to produce a tape recording of a reporter's telephone conversation with a suspected kidnapper that contained an admission that he had shot a police officer because Montana law covered only the reporter.[52]

Journalists are most at risk when their refusals to testify or submit evidence before grand juries or petit juries in criminal cases are weighed against the Sixth Amendment rights of defendants. Civil cases carry less risk, especially where the reporter is an innocent third party. The

47. Lapham, *The Temptations of a Sacred Cow,* Harper's, August 1973.

48. Guest and Stanzler, *The Constitutional Argument for Newsmen Concealing Their Sources,* 64 Northwestern L.Rev. 18 (1969).

49. Blasi, *The Newsman's Privilege: An Empirical Study,* 70 Mich.L.Rev. 229 (1971).

50. Poteet v. Roswell Daily Journal, 4 Med.L.Rptr. 1749, 584 P.2d 1310 (N.M.1979). See, Note, *The Rights of Sources—The Critical Element in the Clash Over Reporter's Privilege,* 88 Yale L.Rev. 1202 (May 1979).

51. Bruno & Stillman, Inc. v. Globe Newspaper Co., 6 Med.L.Rptr. 2057, 633 F.2d 583 (1st Cir. 1980).

52. In re Investigative File, No. 40 SPL (Mont.Dist.Ct. 10/2/78), interpreting R.L.M. 1947, Section 93–601–2, Supp. 1977).

one exception is the libel suit in which the plaintiff may carry the heavy burden of proving actual malice and, on occasion, may need the defendant-reporter's help in doing so.

As has been noted, there are many tactics the reporter may adopt in order to deflect subpoenas. As the three-part test continues to permeate the judicial system, the privilege will gain wider recognition, limiting the need for additional state or federal laws.

Zechariah Chafee may have unintentionally set the standard nearly forty years ago when he said:

> This power to make reporters disclose their confidential sources of information should be exercised with great caution. * * * It is * * * desirable to respect the reporter's claim of confidence except in cases of great necessity where he clearly possesses knowledge which is otherwise unobtainable. Chafee, 2 *Government and Mass Communications,* pp. 497–499 (1947).

V

Access to Government: Executive and Legislative Branches

THE RIGHT TO GATHER NEWS

1. *Richmond Newspapers, Inc. v. Virginia*, text p. 513, undoubtedly gave momentum to what might be eventual clarification, if not emergence, of a broad constitutional right to gather news or to have access to places and people where news is being made. There remains, however, a good deal of judicial ambivalence about how far this right ought to be extended beyond the criminal trial courtroom.

It was, after all, only in 1965 that the Court noted in a case upholding the government's refusal to validate passports for reporters traveling to Cuba that "the right to speak and publish does not carry with it the unrestrained right to gather information." [1] And in *Pell* and *Saxbe*, two cases in which the issue was special access for the press to prison inmates, the Court held that "newsmen have no constitutional right of access to prisons or their inmates beyond that afforded the general public." [2]

Even Justice Brennan, who dissented in the prison cases, was not quite sure what ought to be the scope of a right to gather news. "The Constitution does not require all public acts to be done in a town meeting or an assembly of the whole," he said, concurring in a 1977 case. "[T]his Court's 'own conferences [and] meetings of other official bodies gathered in executive session' may be closed to the public without implicating any constitutional rights whatever." [3]

Nor was the Supreme Court to relent in a 1977 ruling in *Houchins v. KQED*.[4] Speaking of press and public, the Ninth Circuit had observed that, "Although both groups have an equal constitutional right of access to jails, because of differing needs and administrative problems, common sense mandates that the implementation of those correlative rights not be identical. * * * As the eyes and ears of the public, newsmen are entitled to see and to hear everything within the institution about which the general public is entitled to be informed. * * * However, it does

1. Zemel v. Rusk, 1 Med.L.Rptr. 2299, 381 U.S. 1 (1965).

2. Pell v. Procunier, 1 Med.L.Rptr. 2379, 417 U.S. 817 (1974); Saxbe v. Washington Post Co., 1 Med.L.Rptr. 2314, 417 U.S. 843 (1974). In the prison access cases the Court relied heavily on the language of Justice White in *Branzburg:* "It has generally been held that the First Amendment does not guarantee the press a constitutional right of special access to information not available to the public generally. * * * Newsmen have no constitutional right of access to the scenes of crime or disaster when the general public is excluded. * * *"

3. City of Madison v. Wisconsin Employment Relations Commission, 429 U.S. 167, 178 (1977).

4. 3 Med.L.Rptr. 2521, 438 U.S. 1 (1978).

not follow that regulations that are reasonable under the circumstances as applied to touring groups of the public are also reasonable as applied to news media personnel."[5] These views stirred something deep in the minds of at least concurring and dissenting Supreme Court justices in *Houchins*.

In a concurrence Justice Stewart, who had written the opinions for the Court in *Pell* and *Saxbe*, spoke of "flexibility" and the "practical distinctions between the press and the general public." Justice Stevens in dissent, joined by Brennan and Powell, spoke of prison conditions and the public's right to know about them and seemed to think some kind of "effective access" ought to be available to the press:

> An official prison policy of concealing such knowledge from the public by arbitrarily cutting off the flow of information at its source abridges the freedom of speech and of the press protected by the First and Fourteenth Amendments to the Constitution.

But the Court in *Houchins*, through Chief Justice Burger, favored a more general proposition: "This Court has never intimated a First Amendment guarantee of a right of access to all sources of information within government control." Relying in part upon the landmark journalist's privilege case, *Branzburg v. Hayes*[6] the Court denied the press any constitutional rights of access not available to the general public.

2. Press passes are tickets to scenes of crimes and disasters. Refusing to "sell" tickets to alternative media can be a way of "certifying" the orthodox, legitimate, or establishment press. For example, the *Los Angeles Free Press* was denied press passes by police and sheriff because eligibility was judged on the "regular gathering and distribution of hard core news generated through police and fireman activities." What law enforcement officers called "sociological" coverage—riots, demonstrations, and assassinations—didn't qualify one for a press pass.[7]

A federal court in Iowa, however, held that denying an "underground newspaper" access to police department records available to other media constituted a denial of equal protection, unless officials could show a compelling governmental interest in such discrimination. Here the government blatantly excluded news media that were not "established" or "legitimate." Access to records depended on a press pass, and, in the absence of any written policies or regulations, passes went to those media who, in the view of the police, were "responsible" because they "cooperated" in publishing what the department believed to be appropriate. The court added a compelling paragraph:

> The history of this nation and particularly of the development of the institutions of our complex federal system of government has been repeatedly jarred and reshaped by the continuing investigation, reporting and advocacy of independent journalists unaffiliated with major institutions and often with no resource except their wit, persistence, and the crudest mechanisms for placing words on paper.[8]

Press passes have been denied where the reporter had a criminal record.[9] But even in the case of admission to the White House, an access situation at the complete discretion of the Secret Service, courts expect evenhandedness in official decisions as to which reporters to admit and which

5. KQED, Inc. v. Houchins, 2 Med.L.Rptr. 1115, 546 F.2d 284 (9th Cir. 1976).

6. 1 Med.L.Rptr. 2617, 408 U.S. 665 (1972).

7. Los Angeles Free Press, Inc. v. City of Los Angeles, 88 Cal.Rptr. 605 (1970).

8. Quad-City Community News Service, Inc. v. Jebens, 334 F.Supp. 8 (D.Iowa 1971).

9. Watson v. Cronin, 384 F.Supp. 652 (D.Colo.1974).

to exclude; and they prefer an established policy and a procedure for giving notice of and reasons for exclusion so an appeal can be carried forward.[10]

When television reporters failed to develop a "pool" coverage plan, the White House Press Office excluded all TV representatives. The three major networks sought and were awarded a preliminary injunction. Even though a post-*Richmond* case, the court could find no more than a "qualified" right of access "subject to limiting considerations such as confidentiality, security, orderly process, spatial limitations, and doubtless many others."[11] Total exclusion of TV, however, did deny public and press their limited right of access to the White House guaranteed by the First Amendment.

For similar reasons, a federal appeals court in Massachusetts rejected a National Transportation Safety Board order that limited press access to an airplane crash site on public property to one hour a day.[12] Balancing tests? Yes, but with increased weight given to press rights of access.

What of access claims to private property? In 1975 a New Jersey Superior Court ordered photographs returned to staffers of the *Daily Princetonian* after they had been confiscated by state police at the request of a farmer on whose land the pictures had been taken. Since the reporter and photographer were covering migrant worker housing conditions, and they did so reasonably, their activities were clothed with a public interest.[13]

A television station, on the other hand, had no right of access to world figure skating championships, even though they were held in a civic center operated by Hartford, Connecticut. Having entered into the commercial marketplace and having made contractual arrangements whereby anyone entering the civic center with a television camera was to refrain from broadcasting the event until ABC, which had exclusive rights to coverage, had concluded its broadcast, the city, said a federal district court, was operating in its proprietary rather than its governmental capacity. Hartford therefore did not violate the plaintiff's First or Fourteenth Amendment rights.[14]

3. Questions of due process and equal protection have also arisen where legislative bodies have capriciously discriminated against certain reporters but not others. For example, exclusion of a particular reporter and his newspaper from the floor of the Tennessee Senate by a Senate resolution was enjoined.[15] And a federal district court in Massachusetts held that access to city council meetings must be granted equally to all reporters.[16] The mayor of Honolulu was enjoined from denying a reporter he didn't like access to city hall press conferences.[17] A federal court in Alabama recognized a limited First Amendment right of reasonable access to news of state government and to public galleries, press rooms, and press conferences when it prevented enforcement of a law requiring state house reporters to file a "statement of economic interest" detailing their employment status and promising

10. Sherrill v. Knight, 3 Med.L.Rptr. 1514, 569 F.2d 124 (D.C.Cir.1978).

11. Cable News Network v. ABC, 7 Med.L.Rptr. 2053, 518 F.Supp. 1238 (D.Ga.1981).

12. Westinghouse Broadcasting v. National Transportation Safety Board, 8 Med.L.Rptr. 1177, 670 F.2d 4 (1st Cir. 1982).

13. Freedman v. New Jersey State Police, 343 A.2d 148 (1975).

14. Post-Newsweek v. Travelers Insurance, 6 Med.L.Rptr. 2540, 510 F.Supp. 81 (D.Conn.1981).

15. Kovach v. Maddux, 1 Med.L.Rptr. 2367, 238 F.Supp. 835 (D.Tenn.1965).

16. Westinghouse Broadcasting Co. v. Dukakis, 409 F.Supp. 895 (D.Mass.1976).

17. Borreca v. Fasi, 1 Med.L.Rptr. 2410, 369 F.Supp. 906 (D.Hawaii 1974).

that they would not work for lobbyists.[18]

Finally, in Freedom of Information Act (FOIA) and common law suits brought against the Department of Justice and Chairman Peter Rodino of the Committee on the Judiciary of the United States House of Representatives, the District of Columbia District Court held that Congress is subject to the common law rule guaranteeing the public's right to inspect and copy public records:

> The historic common law right to inspect and copy public records is recognized in this jurisdiction. The general rule is that all three branches of government, legislative, executive, and judicial, are subject to the common law right. Defendant Rodino has set forth no persuasive reason why Congress should be exempted from the common law rule. It is true that Congress has exempted itself from the requirements of the Freedom of Information Act. That [a]ct, however, is not coextensive with the common law rule under discussion. It applies to *all* matters in [g]overnment files; the common law rule applies only to "public records." Moreover, we can find no inconsistency or conflict between the Freedom of Information Act and the common law rule. Even if there were an inconsistency or conflict, the [a]ct would have to be construed narrowly, favoring application of the common law, because the Freedom of Information Act is in derogation of the common law.
>
> Accordingly, we hold the Congress is subject to the common law rule which guarantees the public a right to inspect and copy public records. Absent a showing that the matters sought by plaintiff are not "public records" within the meaning of the common law rule or that plaintiff does not possess any "interest" required by the rule, we cannot grant defendant Rodino's motion for dismissal.
>
> If Congress wishes to exempt itself from the common law rule or to impose standards for its application, it has the means to do so readily at its disposal. It has, however, not done so and therefore remains subject to the common law rule. Schwartz v. Justice Department, 3 Med.L.Rptr. 1335, 435 F.Supp. 1203 (D.D.C.1977), affirmed 595 F.2d 888 (D.C.Cir.1978). See also, Relyea, *Access to Congressional Records*, Columbia, Mo.: Freedom of Information Center Report No. 428, October 1980.

This is not to say that Congress and the state legislatures don't have a great deal of latitude in determining and enforcing their own rules of access. After all, state legislators write state open meetings and records laws and frequently exempt themselves. The United States Constitution (Art. I, § 5) gives both House and Senate authority to dictate their own levels of secrecy and openness. Floor meetings of both houses have been open to the public almost without exception. Many committee meetings remain closed, but the trend is toward greater openness. The House permits radio and television coverage of its floor proceedings on a restricted basis. Cameras are run by House staff, and they are not permitted to pan the chamber.

The reluctance of courts to interfere with legislative prerogatives was illustrated by the *Consumers Union* case. The Periodical Correspondents' Association led by Neil MacNeil of *Time* magazine voted not to admit correspondents for *Consumer Reports* to the Periodical Press Galleries. An Association rule against nonprofit publications was designed to protect Congress from lobbyists, and *Consumer Reports* technically fit the category.

District of Columbia federal trial Judge Gerhard Gesell was obviously annoyed, and he held the rule of the "regular" reporters violative of Consumers Union's First Amendment right to freedom of the press and its Fifth Amendment right to due process and the equal protection of the laws. Wrote Gesell:

> There should be no glossing over what this record discloses. Under a broad,

18. Lewis v. Baxley, 1 Med.L.Rptr. 2525, 368 F.Supp. 768 (D.Ala.1973).

> generalized congressional delegation, authority has been given certain newsmen to prevent other newsmen from having access to news of vital consequence to the public. As a result, a group of established periodical correspondents have undertaken to implement arbitrary and unnecessary regulations with a view to excluding from news sources representatives of publications whose ownership or ideas they consider objectionable. * * *
>
> The fact that the galleries for newspapermen and radio and television correspondents have operated with much greater liberality and consequent regard for the demands of the First Amendment serve simply to emphasize the arbitrariness of those managing the periodical galleries. All types of news compete and all types of publications are entitled to an equal freedom to hear and publish the official business of the Congress.
>
> The situation disclosed by this undisputed record flaunts the First Amendment. It matters not that elements of the press as well as Congress itself appear to have been the instruments for denial of constitutional rights in this instance, for those rights limit the actions of legislative agents and instrumentalities as surely as those of Congress itself. * * *
>
> A free press is undermined if the access of certain reporters to the facts relating to the public's business is limited merely because they advocate a particular viewpoint. This is a dangerous and self-defeating doctrine. Consumers Union of United States, Inc. v. Periodical Correspondents' Association, 1 Med.L.Rptr. 2534, 365 F.Supp. 18 (D.D.C.1973).

The association appealed, and the D.C. Circuit Court reversed by relying on, among other things, the speech and debate clause. The court of appeals declared that what the Periodical Correspondents had done was "within spheres of legislative power committed to Congress and the legislative immunity granted by the Constitution [under the speech and debate clause]." 515 F.2d 1341 (D.C.Cir.1975). The Supreme Court denied certiorari a year later. 423 U.S. 1051 (1976).

MacNeil remained adamant in his view that Consumers Union and its Washington representatives were lobbyists, though they may not have been of the "pure" variety, and under an internal rule of Congress were properly excluded from the press galleries.

Both houses of the Maryland legislature were upheld in excluding tape recorders from their sessions. While recognizing some First Amendment protection for news gathering, a Maryland court held that the legislative rule did not interfere with the usual pencil-and-pad duties of reporters. The reporters had based their claim on a speed and accuracy argument and had relied on an earlier case, Nevens v. City of Chino, 44 Cal.Rptr. 50 (1965), in which a similar rule had been struck down. The Maryland court said there was no violation of due process in a rule intended to preserve order and decorum, even if at the expense of increased press efficiency. As to equal protection, the court held that the tape recorder ban was against equipment, not a class of persons. Sigma Delta Chi v. Speaker, Maryland House of Delegates, 1 Med.L.Rptr. 2375, 310 A.2d 156 (1973).

After many years of litigation, the Supreme Court in late 1982 rejected all efforts by Richard M. Nixon to block public access to his infamous White House tapes. The decision applied to thousands of hours of Oval Office conversations unrelated to Watergate and the trials that followed.

In United States v. Nixon, 418 U.S. 683 (1974), the Court recognized a constitutionally based privilege of confidentiality for presidential communications to the extent that such a privilege was necessary to the effective discharge of the president's powers. In 1982, the D.C. Circuit Court of Appeals permitted the General Services Administration to segregate private and public material in the tapes and to allow public access to "presidential historical material." Nixon v. Freeman, 8 Med.L. Rptr. 1001, 670 F.2d 346 (D.C.Cir.1982).

4. Since discussion of what levels of access to information ought to be available to public and press proceeds largely in judicial forums, access to the courtroom is obviously crucial. Which is not to depreciate the importance of the everyday business of government. But courts, sitting as final arbiters, will decide both abstract and concrete questions of access to *all* branches of government.

"A popular government without popular information or the means of acquiring it is but a Prologue to a Farce or Tragedy; or perhaps both," said James Madison.[19]

Of late, an interesting dialogue has centered on whether denials of access constitute prior restraint and whether access and publication are of equal constitutional weight. In the landmark prior restraint cases—*Near, Pentagon Papers*, and *Nebraska Press*— the information suppressed by state statute, a court injunction, initiated by the federal government, and a judicial order, respectively, was information already in hand. Access may or may not lead a reporter to publishable material. A denial of access is not necessarily a proscription against publication. Yet when access is regularly or systematically denied, the effects on the communication process are the same.

While academics and judges have identified a right of access or a right to know, whereby government is said to have an affirmative constitutional obligation to furnish information to the populace,[20] courts have been slow to expand the doctrine. Others consider the doctrine dangerous, even pernicious, because it derogates the rights of speakers and invites government censorship: the rights of audiences become paramount, and, if the public has a right to know, by definition there are things that it has *no* right to know.[21] In such cases, courts are in the position of deciding what the public has a right to know or not to know,[22] a function not intended for government.

Communication lawyers, recognizing the complex interface of prior restraint and access rights, also warn against pushing access too far. Hostile courts in denying access may impose prior restraints, either intentionally or unintentionally. The right to gather information is by no means as sweeping as the right to publish information once gathered.[23]

Professor Steven Helle holds that the dichotomy between news gathering and publication is specious. Government has a general obligation to provide unrestricted access to information. It has no right *not* to speak. The press should not have to assert the public's right to know to exercise its own right of expression while the government need cite only its own interests as justification for not speaking. The failure of the government to release information that furthers self-government is contrary to the broad command of the First Amendment.

> It is because analysis of governmental expression, which is subject to different limitations and obligations regarding its dissemination, is beginning to control analysis of nongovernment expression through means of the news-

19. 9 Writings of James Madison 103 (G. Hunt, ed. 1910). See also, Itzhak Galnoor (ed.) *Government Secrecy in Democracies*, 1977.

20. Emerson, *The Affirmative Side of the First Amendment,* 15 Georgia L.Rev. 795, 805, 828 (Summer 1981). Justice Brennan in Richmond Newspapers, Inc. v. Virginia, 6 Med.L.Rptr. 1833, 1846, 448 U.S. 555, 589 (1980). For a contrary view see, O'Brien, *The Public's Right to Know: The Supreme Court and the First Amendment,* 1981.

21. Baldasty and Simpson, *The Deceptive "Right to Know": How Pessimism Rewrote the First Amendment,* 56 Wash.L.Rev. 365, 395 (July 1981).

22. Goodale, *Legal Pitfalls in the Right to Know*, 1976 Wash.U.L.Rev. 29–36 (1976).

23. Abrams, Remarks at Communications Law 1977 program of the Practising Law Institute, New York City, Nov. 10, 11, 1977.

gathering artifice that the libertarian foundations of nongovernment speech are imperiled.

In a word, Helle faults the courts for defining press rights in terms of the public's rights:

> By orienting the analysis in terms of the public right rather than the private right, the Court has eschewed resort to a body of law founded on libertarian principles and has given itself great latitude to substitute the judgment of the [s]tate for that of the individual in deciding the extent to which rights exist.[24]

If it is the natural tendency of government to compile and conceal information, it is the role of the press to dig it out and put it into circulation. The press cannot expect the government to be its handmaiden.

"There is no constitutional right to have access to particular government information, or to require openness from bureaucracy * * *," said Justice Stewart in his Yale Law School address. "The Constitution itself is neither a Freedom of Information Act nor an Official Secrets Act." [25] That has been the view of the courts. While preserving their own autonomy, except where courts have been made aware of violations of due process or equal protection, Congress and the state legislatures have found ways to open up the executive branches to public scrutiny. Congress did it in 1966 with passage of the Freedom of Information Act.

THE FREEDOM OF INFORMATION ACT

1. In 1966, section 3 of the Administrative Procedure Act of 1946 was amended to incorporate the Freedom of Information Act, 5 U.S.C.A. § 552. The act became law on July 4, 1967. FOIA was a major blow to the developing doctrine of "executive privilege," a doctrine nurtured by two world wars, by the continuously agglomerating powers of the presidency, and brought to maturity by burgeoning theories and laws of privacy. However short the act may fall in implementing the public's right to know, federal government agencies are no longer able to withhold information on the arbitrary ground that its release would be contrary to the public interest.

Underlying the act is the premise that executive branch records are by definition open to public inspection, to any person for whatever purpose, unless agencies can give specific reasons why they should be closed. Nine exemptions in the act make the protection against disclosure of some categories of information "discretionary" with agencies or the federal courts—only one circuit court of appeals has said "mandatory." Westinghouse v. Schlesinger, 542 F.2d 1190 (4th Cir. 1976). The act, then, does not forbid disclosure of exempted categories of information. Nor can promises of confidentiality by an agency in and of themselves defeat the public's right to disclosure. Petkas v. Staats, 501 F.2d 887 (D.C. Cir. 1974).

A federal district court expressed well and simply the broad principle of FOIA: Freedom of information is now the rule and secrecy is the exception. Later the United States Supreme Court would say that "these limited exemptions do not obscure the basic policy that disclosure, not secrecy is the dominant objective of the

24. Helle, *The News-Gathering/Publication Dichotomy and Government Expression*, 1982 Duke L.J. 1, 3–4, 39, 53, 57, 59 (1982).

25. Stewart, *Or of the Press*, 26 Hastings L.Rev. 631, 636 (1976).

Act." [26]

2. FOIA has been crucial to the disclosure of huge quantities of information held by federal agencies that might not otherwise have been available. In its first sixteen years, the act was amended at least four times, and nearly 1,000 court decisions construed its provisions.[27] Amendments in 1974, for example, required agencies to promulgate request procedures, expedited appeal guidelines, uniform search and duplicating costs, and to provide detailed indexes of their holdings. Courts could rule that the government pay court costs and attorney fees for successful FOIA plaintiffs. Judges were also empowered to review at their discretion government documents *in camera* to decide whether or not one or more of the nine exemptions to the Act had been properly applied.[28]

Proposals to amend the act most frequently focus on FBI, CIA, and Secret Service records since information about those agencies accounts for about half of the news stories and columns written as a direct consequence of FOIA. Other law enforcement organizations and business institutions would also be the beneficiaries of proposed amendments. Any plan to curtail the scope of the act leaves the public the loser. Of course, amendments to FOIA can be accomplished indirectly by amending other federal statutes such as those having to do with product safety and tax rules, often without public hearings.

Additional amendments would expand time limits on agency response; increase the costs to requesters; "clarify," tighten, and add exemptions; and limit use of FOIA to citizens and resident aliens. (See § 1730 the Freedom of Information Reform Act.) A million requests each year at a cost to the government of perhaps $60 million may not be too high a price for an open society. For a review of the Reagan Administration's activities in this area see Floyd Abrams, *The New Effort to Control Information,* New York Times Magazine, Sept. 25, 1983.

FOIA applies to every agency, department regulatory commission, and government-controlled corporation in the executive branch of the federal government, including cabinet offices such as departments of State, Defense, Transportation, Interior, Treasury, Justice, etc. It would include independent regulatory agencies such as FCC and FTC, the Post Office, NASA, and the Civil Service Commission and executive offices under presidential control such as the Office of Management and Budget. It does *not* apply to the president himself or to his immediate staff.

FOIA deals with "agency records," not information in the abstract or information that might be anticipated from an interview. The law applies to "records which have been in fact obtained," and not to

26. Wellford v. Hardin, 315 F.Supp. 768 (D.D.C.1970); Department of Air Force v. Rose, 1 Med.L.Rptr. 2509, 425 U.S. 352 (1976).

27. Peacock, *Developments Under the Freedom of Information Act—1980,* 1981 Duke L.J. 338 (April 1981). Annual FOIA-developments articles have appeared in the Duke Law Journal since 1970.

28. The *in camera* provision of the 1974 amendments was meant to overcome the effects of the Supreme Court decision in Environmental Protection Agency v. Mink, 1 Med.L.Rptr. 2448, 410 U.S. 73 (1973). There the Court upheld Exemption 1 (national defense) and Exemption 5 (intra- and interagency memos) arguments blocking requests by Congresswoman Patsy Mink and colleagues for release of recommendations and reports of a divided interdepartmental committee considering the advisability of underground nuclear tests on Amchitka Island in the Aleutians. The Court could not find any grounds for discretionary judicial review of classified material in the legislative history of Exemption 1.

See also, Alfred A. Knopf, Inc. v. Colby, 509 F.2d 1362 (4th Cir. 1975), in which the court of appeals permitted the CIA to make 168 deletions in a book by Victor Marchetti and John Marks, *The CIA and the Cult of Intelligence.* The book was published that way on grounds that any part of a classifiable document may be classified, without any need for *in camera* review.

records which merely could have been obtained. In Forsham v. Harris, 5 Med.L. Rptr. 2473, 445 U.S. 169, 185–186 (1980), the Court held that records of a federally funded university research project were *not* records subject to disclosure under FOIA unless they had been taken over by a government agency for its own review or use. Nor does the act require an agency to retrieve or create records (Kissinger v. Reporters Committee for Freedom of the Press, 6 Med.L.Rptr. 1001, 445 U.S. 136, 153, 1980). Both *Forsham* and *Kissinger* support the principle that materials created by or in the physical custody of an agency are not always "records" for purposes of FOIA.

In *Kissinger*, FOIA requests by the Military Audit Project, the Reporters Committee, and *New York Times* columnist William Safire for copies of transcripts of telephone conversations made by Henry Kissinger while he was assistant to the president for national security and secretary of state were turned down on appeal to the State Department.

After Kissinger left office, the transcripts were donated to the Library of Congress on condition that they not be released for a specified period. A federal district court ordered the Library to return transcripts relating to Kissinger's role as Secretary of State to the State Department because they were agency records subject to disclosure and were wrongly removed without permission. In the case of notes prepared in his role as national security adviser to the president, relief was denied. The court of appeals affirmed, and the Supreme Court granted certiorari.

Justice William Rehnquist for the Court found a way to block access to all parties. Courts may devise remedies and enjoin agencies, he said, only if an agency has 1) improperly 2) withheld 3) agency records. Safire sought a presidential adviser's notes, not agency records. MAP and the Reporters Committee sought records that were no longer in the control or custody of the agency, and the agency, in this case the State Department, was not obliged to retrieve documents that had escaped its possession. What Safire sought was in the possession of the State Department but outside of its control as material belonging to the president's immediate personal staff and, therefore, not agency material subject to FOIA. Possession without control was insufficient to make the documents records for purposes of the act.

Brennan and Stevens dissented in part because they disagreed with the majority's definition of "custody or control." Stevens feared that the ruling would encourage outgoing officials to remove damaging information from their files. An agency retains custody over anything it has a legal right to possess.

Others saw in Rehnquist's opinion a reversal of the presumption that the burden under FOIA is on the agency to prove that the withholding of information was justified. It may be very difficult, as a threshold requirement, for an FOIA plaintiff to show that agency records were improperly withheld. And how does a requester prove that records, if indeed they were under agency control in the first place, are subject to the required degree of agency control?

The *Washington Post* was denied access to the secretary of state's "emergency fund" since Congress, in exercising its authority under the Constitution's "statement and account" clause, has expressed its intent to maintain secrecy in expenditure of funds affecting foreign relations. Washington Post v. Department of State, 6 Med.L.Rptr. 2253, 501 F.Supp. 1152 (D.D.C. 1980).

Court records are not subject to the act, even if located in the U.S. attorney's office.[29] Congressional records are also ex-

29. Valenti v. United States Justice Department, 6 Med.L.Rptr. 2331, 503 F.Supp. 230 (D.La.1980).

empt. An example would be CIA records generated in direct response to the specific request of a congressional committee exercising oversight authority and where Congress had expressed a clear intent to retain control.[30]

Records of state and local government are not subject to disclosure under FOIA, although all states now have their own open records laws. Private corporate records become public only when filed with the federal government. Much pressure has been put on Congress to limit or discontinue altogether disclosure of corporate information.

Interpol (International Criminal Police Organization) is not an agency subject to FOIA. The National Center Bureau, America's liaison with Interpol, is an agency under the act.[31]

USING THE FOIA

Records are defined broadly as to form but would not normally include physical objects which cannot be reproduced. Requesters should identify themselves and describe records with as much specificity as possible as to kind and quantity. Avoid blanket requests.

Any person—U. S. citizen or not—may use the act. So may corporations, public interest groups, and media, and no reason for a request need be given. Persons planning to communicate with the public sometimes get priority attention.

Informal requests ought to be the first step. Each agency, bureau, or department will have a public information or press officer who by telephone or certified mail can be notified of a request for information under FOIA. Your letter may be referred to a more knowledgeable FOIA officer. If informal approaches don't work, the next step is to file a formal written FOIA request. The agency now has a legal duty to reply within ten working days. If the denial persists, you may appeal in writing, preferably within thirty days, to the agency head. That person must reply within twenty working days, although continuing efforts are made to lengthen these time periods. Due to the volume of requests, the FBI, CIA, and departments of State and Justice contend that they are unable to meet these deadlines. Another denial, or no response at all, entitles you under the Act to bring suit in the most convenient federal court with the expectation of an expedited hearing. The burden of proof for nondisclosure will rest squarely on government.

Before filing a lawsuit, you may ask the Office of Information Law and Policy of the Department of Justice, a federal agency responsible for overall administration of FOIA, for a review of your case to date. The office could advise the recalcitrant agency to reverse its decision and release the documents you requested.

The Washington-based Reporters Committee for Freedom of the Press, in a valuable handbook[32] prepared jointly with the Society of Professional Journalists, provides sample letters for formal request, appeals, waivers of fee, and a federal district court complaint form. Suggestions are made as to who, besides yourself,

30. Navasky v. CIA, 6 Med.L.Rptr. 1947, 499 F.Supp. 269 (D.N.Y.1980).

31. Smith v. Interpol, 8 Med.L.Rptr. 1289 (D.D.C.1982).

32. FOI Service Center, How to Use the Federal FOI Act, Washington, D. C.: 1125 15th St. N.W. 20005 (1980). The center has a hotline and will provide legal assistance and advice. See also, United States Government Manual on file in most libraries, and the General Services Administration (GSA) regional federal telephone books, available at cost from that agency. See also, Archibald, *Use of the FOIA*, Columbia, Mo.: Freedom of Information Report No. 457, May 1982. Adler & Halperin, *1983 Edition of Litigation under the Federal Freedom of Information Act and Privacy Act.*

ought to get copies of your letters if you have been unable to pinpoint a record holder. Use registered mail, with return receipts, and envelopes marked "FOI Act Request." Even agency addresses and telephone numbers are included in the handbook.

Agencies are authorized to charge reasonable fees for searching and copying and estimates are available. State your pecuniary limits if funds are in short supply. Fee schedules for the various agencies are published in the *Federal Register.* If they are prohibitive for you and you are a journalist, author, or scholar, indicate your publication plans and ask that fees be waived or at least reduced. FOIA recognizes such requests where a public benefit is being served—although you shouldn't expect any uniformity of response across units of government. Possibly, a trip to inspect documents could be less expensive and more expeditious to your needs than having documents copied.

HOW SUCCESSFUL IS FOIA?

Litigation under the Exemptions

FOIA has created new attitudes toward public information in the minds of both record keepers and record seekers. In the beginning, businessmen and their agents and public interest groups, notably those led by Ralph Nader, made more use of the act than individual citizens or the press. That has been changing over the years.

Brief comments on the nine Exemptions and the kinds of cases they have generated, particularly those involving the press, may be the key to understanding the Act and its significance to media access and the public's right to know.

Exemption 1

This exemption is designed to prevent disclosure of properly classified records, the release of which would cause at least some "identifiable damage" to the national security, "(A) specifically authorized under criteria established by an Executive Order to be kept secret in the interest of national defense or foreign policy and (B) are in fact properly classified pursuant to such Executive Order."

An executive order (Exec. Order No. 12356) which took effect August 1, 1982 eliminated the Carter Administration requirement that officials consider the public interest in disclosure when deciding whether to classify.[33]

Under the new order, information may not be classified "unless its disclosure reasonably could be expected to cause damage to national security. * * * If there is reasonable doubt about the need to classify information, it shall be safeguarded as if it were classified" pending a determination within thirty days "by an original classification authority." If there is a "reasonable doubt" about the appropriate level of classification (top secret, secret, or confidential), the document is to be safeguarded at the highest level of classification—"top secret"—pending a decision within thirty days by the original classification authority.

Initial press interpretation of the order was that it would greatly increase the authority of the executive branch to classify documents where there was only the vaguest threat to national security. One might recall Justice Stewart's admonition in the *Pentagon Papers* case that "when everything is classified, then nothing is classified." A sense of what is or what should be truly secret is lost, and leaks replace honest classification.

33. In re National Security Information, 8 Med.L.Rptr. 1306 (1982).

Certainly the order eliminates the standard of "identifiable damage" to the national security and the discretionary "public interest" balancing of the earlier Carter order. It also retards the declassification process.[34]

The order tracks with congressional passage in June 1982 of the Intelligence Identities Protection Act which, although forsaking prior restraints, makes it a crime to reveal the names of U. S. intelligence agents. Broad enough to ensnare unwary journalists, the law does require the showing of a *pattern of activities* "intending to expose covert agents." So keep a paper record of your purpose or intent.

It also tracks with the Supreme Court's holding in *Haig v. Agee*.[35] There the Court upheld the power of the State Department to revoke the passport of a citizen whose travels abroad might damage U. S. policy through exposure of CIA operations and agents. Chief Justice Burger, writing for the Court, placed such information outside the protection of the First Amendment.

"The protection accorded beliefs standing alone," said Burger, "is very different from the protection afforded conduct. Here, beliefs and speech are only part of respondent's campaign, which presents a serious danger to American officials abroad and to the national security."

Theoretically, the 1974 amendment to FOIA, meant to overcome the Court's reflexive deference to a federal agency's classification of information in *EPA v. Mink*,[36] permits federal judges to determine in the first instance (*de novo*) whether information classified under executive order has been done so properly. Under the new order, it can be expected that even greater weight will be accorded agency "expertise" in the realm of national security.[37]

A later presidential directive required prepublication review of all manuscripts written by federal employees and former employees with access to highly classified information. Political opponents denounced the order as "an official secrets act," a move that would prevent publication of information without national security significance but embarrassing to the government.

In Snepp v. United States, 5 Med.L. Rptr. 2409, 444 U.S. 507 (1980) the Supreme Court, without written or oral arguments, had reinstated a federal district court ruling (456 F.Supp. 176 (E.D.Va.1978)) stripping the author of *Decent Interval*, an account of America's undignified flight from Saigon, of all royalties and enjoining further disclosures of his CIA experiences. Snepp, said the Court, had entered into a secrecy agreement with the intelligence agency and had a "fiduciary obligation" to submit his manuscript for prepublication review. There was wide comment on the implications of the case for informed public debate.

Presumptions in favor of government expertise are not hard to find in the case law. Access to full documentation of the secret "Glomar Project," a project jointly financed by the CIA and the late Howard

34. Peterzell, *The Government Shuts Up*, Columbia J.Rev., July/August 1982, p. 31.

35. 453 U.S. 280 (1981), 101 S.Ct. 2766 (1981).

36. 1 Med.L.Rptr. 2448, 410 U.S. 73 (1973). See fn. 28.

37. For example, in Weismann v. CIA, 2 Med.L.Rptr. 1276, 565 F.2d 6792 (D.C.Cir.1977), the court said that when satisfied that an agency's classification is *reasonable* and made in *good faith*, a court "need not go further to test the expertise of the agency. * * *" The court also thought *in camera* inspections burdensome and without benefit of adversary proceedings. Judges, said the court, don't have expertise to make national security determinations. And in Bell v. United States, 3 Med.L.Rptr. 1154, 563 F.2d 484 (1st Cir. 1977), the court held that before *in camera* inspection is ordered Congress intended that an agency be given an opportunity to demonstrate by affidavit or testimony that the documents at issue are clearly exempt from disclosure. The court is expected to accord "substantial weight" to the agency affidavit.

Hughes apparently to raise an outmoded Russian submarine from the floor of the Pacific but presented to the public as a deep sea mining project, was effectively blocked by the D.C. Circuit Court of Appeals.

To justify withholding the requested documents, the government submitted extensive affidavits detailing the nature of the material withheld and the implications for national security should it be released. The district court found the affidavits sufficient to establish the government's right to withhold and granted summary judgment. On the question of *in camera* judicial review, the circuit court said:

> Throughout their briefs, the appellants suggest that affirmance by us of the district court's grant of summary judgment would be tantamount to a subversion of the statutory requirement that courts conduct *de novo* review of agency classification decisions. An affirmance, they claim, would *de facto* substitute the more deferential "reasonable basis" standard rejected by Congress over a presidential veto in 1974 [the 1974 FOIA amendments]. This is simply not so.
>
> It is well established that summary judgment is properly granted in Exemption 1 cases without an *in camera* inspection or discovery by the plaintiffs when the affidavits submitted by the agency are adequate to the task. We agree with the district court that the lengthy detailed affidavits submitted by the defendants in this case satisfy the well-settled requirements for summary judgment. They describe the sensitive documents at issue with reasonably specific detail; the justifications for non-disclosure are detailed and persuasive. * * * Military Audit Report v. Casey, 7 Med.L.Rptr. 1708, 656 F.2d 724 (D.C.Cir.1981).

Apparently the government sought to protect the identity of other corporations involved in the project, their technology, their business abroad, and the safety of their employees.

When Joan Baez was refused part of her Justice Department file, she sued under FOIA and lost. Upholding the government's use of Exemption 1, the D.C. Circuit stated that "if the description in the affidavits demonstrates that the information logically falls within the claimed exemption and if the information is neither controverted by contrary evidence nor agency bad faith, then summary judgment for the government is warranted." Baez was required to pay the court costs of the Justice Department since it was the prevailing party.[38]

And in *Hayden v. National Security Agency*[39] the same court, rejecting the argument that because some sensitive information was public all of it should be, noted that "This is precisely the sort of situation where Congress intended reviewing courts to respect the expertise of an agency; for us to insist that the agency's rationale here is implausible would be to overstep the proper limits of the judicial role in FOIA review."

The *Navasky* case which follows, while it engages Exemptions 3 and 5 as well as the national security exemption, summarizes a good deal of case law and expresses the supportive mood of federal courts toward Exemption 1 claims.

NAVASKY v. CIA

6 MED.L.RPTR. 1947, 521 F.SUPP. 128 (S.D.N.Y.1981).

METZNER, D.J.:

This matter is before the court on defendant's motion for summary judgment.

Plaintiff, a journalist and magazine editor, instituted the action pursuant to the Freedom of Information Act (FOIA), 5 U.S.C. § 552, seeking disclosure of all doc-

38. Baez v. United States Department of Justice, 8 Med.L.Rptr. 2185, 684 F.2d 999 (D.C.Cir.1982).

39. 5 Med.L.Rptr. 1897, 608 F.2d 1381 (D.C.Cir.1979).

uments relating to clandestine book publishing activities of the defendant, Central Intelligence Agency (CIA), throughout the world. Such activity was briefly discussed in the Final Report of the Select Committee to Study Governmental Operations with Respect to Intelligence Activities. S.Rep. No. 94–755, 94th Cong.2d Sess. (1976) (Church Committee Report), vol. 1 at 192–95, 198–99, 453–54.

For the reasons discussed below, partial summary judgment is granted at this time.

In 1977, after plaintiff's initial request for the subject documents had been denied through administrative appeal, plaintiff filed this suit to require production of three categories of documents: (1) "The titles, authors and publishers of the 'well over a thousand books' referred to in Volume I" of the Church Committee report; (2) "All CIA materials made available to the members of the staff of the Church Committee relating to books produced, subsidized or sponsored by the CIA up to the present time;" and (3) "All other CIA materials and files relating to" such books "whether or not made available to the Church Committee."

The CIA in its answer claimed exemption under the statute. Plaintiff then filed a motion for a detailed justification and index of the CIA's claims of exemption pursuant to Vaughn v. Rosen, 484 F.2d 82 (D.C.Cir.1973), cert. denied, 415 U.S. 977 (1974). The CIA responded with an index of 85 documents in answer to the first two categories of plaintiff's request for production. A 20-page affidavit of John H. Stein, Associate Deputy Director of the Directorate of Operations of the CIA, accompanying the index, set forth the justification for withholding the documents. Expurgated copies of 61 of the 85 documents were attached to the index, with all substantive content deleted. On the basis of these submissions, the CIA now moves for summary judgment.

Before turning to the merits of the instant motion, the court will dispose of the question of in camera inspection that has arisen as a result of the order of October 12, 1979. At that time the court ordered production of certain of the indexed documents for in camera inspection. After further consideration, however, it has become clear that in camera inspection would serve no useful purpose at this time.

There is no doubt that, subsequent to the 1974 amendments to the FOIA, a court may order in camera inspection of exemption 1 and 3 materials. See, e.g., Lead Industries Association, Inc. v. Occupational Safety and Health Administration, 610 F.2d 70, 87 (2d Cir.1979); Ray v. Turner, 587 F.2d 1187, 1194, 1195 (D.C.Cir.1978); Weissman v. CIA, 565 F.2d 692, 696 * * * (D.C.Cir.1977); Bell v. United States, 563 F.2d 484, 487 (1st Cir.1977).

> The ultimate criterion is simply this: whether the district judge believes that in camera inspection is needed in order to make a responsible de novo determination on the claims of exemption. Ray v. Turner, *supra* at 1195.

In camera inspection is essential to responsible de novo determination where the agency's public description of the withheld material is insufficient to allow the court to determine whether its nature is such as to justify nondisclosure under the claimed exemption, or where the court, based on the record before it, wishes to satisfy an "uneasiness" or "doubt" that the exemption claim may be overbroad. Ray v. Turner, *supra* at 1195; Lamont v. Department of Justice, 475 F.Supp. 761, 768–69 (D.N.Y.1979).

In the instant case, there is no issue as to the nature of the items deleted by the CIA. Plaintiff's argument is that the materials *as described* by the agency are not properly withheld. Furthermore, for the reasons discussed below, it is premature for the court to determine whether some of the defendant's claims are overbroad and whether nonexempt portions can be segregated. Resolution of these questions demands more complete agency justification of certain of its exemption claims. See Founding Church of Scientology v. National Security Agency, 610 F.2d 824, 833 * * (D.C.Cir.1979). The court therefore withdraws the order for in camera inspection.

Defendant justifies its nondisclosure of the material on the basis of FOIA exemptions 1, 3 and 5. 5 U.S.C. § 552(b)(1), (3) and (5).

Exemption 1 excludes matters that are "(A) specifically authorized under criteria established by an Executive order to be kept secret in the interest of national defense or foreign policy and (B) are in fact properly classified pursuant to such Executive order." 5 U.S.C. § 552(b)(1). The CIA claims that the deleted material is currently and properly classified pursuant to Executive Order 12065, 3 Fed.Reg. 190 (June 28, 1978) (the EO), under which information concerning "intelligence activities, sources or methods" or "foreign relations or foreign activities of the Unites States" may be classified if "an original classification authority * * * determines that its unauthorized disclosure reasonably could be expected to cause at least identifiable damage to the national security." EO 12065 § 1–301(c), (d), § 1–302.

Exemption 3 excludes "matters that are * * * specifically exempted from disclosure by statute * * *." The CIA relies on the final proviso of section 102(d)(3) of the National Security Act of 1947 (sometimes referred to as the CIA charter), 50 U.S.C. § 403(d)(3), which states that "the Director of Central Intelligence shall be responsible for protecting intelligence sources and methods from unauthorized disclosure."

Exemption 5 exempts "inter-agency or intra-agency memorandums or letters which would not be available by law to a party other than an agency in litigation with the agency."

The principal issues raised herein involve the question of whether exempt status should be accorded to the focal item of plaintiff's request, namely, "the list of English language books, published in the United States with secret CIA funds," and more specifically, "the authors and titles of American-made books where the author was unaware of CIA involvement." Plaintiff requested the other materials "only to insure that the request would encompass [his] chief interest * * *" and the issues arising with respect to them do not require extended discussion.

Several general principles guide the court in its review of the CIA's exemption claims herein. First, the court must make a de novo determination, but in doing so it must accord "substantial weight" to agency affidavits. Hayden v. National Security Agency/Central Security Service, 608 F.2d 1381, 1384 (D.C.Cir.1979). * * * Second, the agency has the burden of justifying nondisclosure by establishing the applicability of the exemption to the particular material. 5 U.S.C. § 552(a)(3); Hayden, *supra* at 1386; *Vaughn v. Rosen, supra* at 823. Specifically, "[i]f the exemption is claimed on the basis of national security, the District Court must * * * be satisfied that proper procedures have been followed and that by its sufficient description the contested document logically falls into the category of the exemption indicated." *Ray, supra* at 1195; *Weissman, supra* at 697. *See also, Hayden, supra* at 1387. Third, the FOIA exemptions are to be construed narrowly, "in such a way as to provide the maximum access consonant with the overall purposes of the Act." *Vaughn, supra* at 823. *See also, Hayden, supra* at 1386; Phillippi v. Central Intelligence Agency, 546 F.2d 1009, 1011 n. 2 (D.C.Cir.1976). Finally, "[i]t is well settled in Freedom of Information Act cases as in any others that '[s]ummary judgment may be granted only if the moving party proves that no substantial and material facts are in dispute and that he is entitled to judgment as a matter of law.'" Founding Church of Scientology, 610 F.2d at 836, quoting from National Cable Television

Ass'n v. FCC, 479 F.2d 183, 186 (D.C.Cir. 1973).

With these principles in mind, we turn now to the contentions of the parties.

We will first discuss exemption 3. Plaintiff contends that the activities concerning which he is seeking information were *ultra vires* the CIA charter. The court is aware of four cases in which illegal CIA activity was claimed as the basis for denying the exemption. In Weissman v. CIA, 565 F.2d 692 (D.C.Cir. 1977), the court found that there was no basis for justification under exemption 7 where the action was illegal under the CIA charter. However, that holding was predicated on the limitation in exemption 7 to a "*lawful* national security intelligence investigation * * *." [Emphasis added.] However, the court remanded the matter to the district court to determine whether the same nondisclosures were justified under exemption 3. The inference to be drawn from such action is that illegality is not a bar to an otherwise valid justification under exemption 3.

A similar inference flows from the remand in Marks v. Central Intelligence Agency, 590 F.2d 997 (D.C.Cir.1978).

This position has been confirmed, albeit somewhat cryptically, in the footnote of a recent decision involving an exemption 3 claim by the National Security Agency (NSA). *Founding Church of Scientology, supra* at 829 n. 49. The court, after citing the plaintiff's reliance in that case on the "recent investigation by the Church Committee of gross illegalities on the part of intelligence agencies," noted in passing that:

> Although NSA would have no protectable interest in suppressing information simply because its release might uncloak an illegal operation, it may properly withhold records gathered illegally if divulgence would reveal currently viable information channels. * * *."

The court offered no further discussion of the point. However, it seems clear that it considered the question of illegality irrelevant to the exemption claims, which it found to turn on the sole issue of whether intelligence sources, illegal or legal, would be revealed.

Finally, on a motion to compel answers to interrogatories requesting a specification whether a CIA intelligence source or method was "domestic," one district court has ruled that "[t]o the extent that such a source may be used, unlawfully, in a domestic investigatory or intelligence activity, the clear implication of *Weissman* is that the lawfulness of the activity is not relevant to the CIA's successful invocation of exemption (b)(3)." *Marks v. Turner*, Docket No. 77–1108 (D.D.C. June 6, 1978) at 3.

Consequently, I find that a claim of activities *ultra vires* the CIA charter is irrelevant to an exemption 3 claim.

There still remains under exemption 3, however, the questions of whether the book publishing activities described the Church Committee Report constitute "intelligence methods" and whether the authors and publishers of the books are "intelligence sources" within the meaning of section 403(d)(3). Defendant has flatly asserted that they are, while plaintiff strenuously urges that they are not, without further elaboration.

There is a paucity of information regarding the phrase "intelligence sources and methods." It is not defined in the National Security Act of 1947, and it received very little treatment in the congressional debates. *See* Church Committee Report at 138–139. Nevertheless, defendant bears the burden of justifying nondisclosure, and it has not convinced the court that authors, publishers and books logically fall into the categories of "intelligence sources and methods."

Section 403(d)(3) empowers the CIA "to correlate and evaluate intelligence relating to the national security and provide for the appropriate dissemination of such intelligence within the Government," and provides that the other agencies "shall continue to collect, evaluate, correlate and disseminate departmental intelligence."

The Church Committee defines "intelligence" as "the product resulting from the collection, collation, evaluation, analysis, integration, and interpretation of all collected information." Church Committee Report, vol. 1 at 624.

Indeed, nothing in the legislative history of the Act indicates that covert propaganda activities of the kind involved here were contemplated by Congress. *See* Church Committee Report at 132, 476–492. It is therefore doubtful that the term "intelligence" as used in Section 403(d)(3) was intended to include such activities.

Finally, the National Security Council directive which first authorized the CIA to conduct covert "psychological" (propaganda) operations under the authority of the National Security Act of 1947 justified that authorization as follows: "The similarity of operational methods involved in covert psychological and intelligence activities * * * renders the CIA the logical agency to conduct such operations." NSC–4–A, 12/17/47. Church Committee Report at 490. This directive recognizes that it is dealing with separate and distinct activities related solely by the similarity of methods used in each.

I accept the definition of "intelligence" as formulated by the Church Committee and apply it to the word as used in section 403(d)(3). Essentially it is a product resulting from the original collection of information. The "intelligence sources and methods" language of section 403(d)(3), therefore, cannot be applied to protect authors, publishers and books involved in clandestine propaganda activities from disclosure.

This conclusion is bolstered by the general rule that FOIA exemptions are to be construed narrowly, *Vaughn, supra* at 823; *Hayden, supra* at 1386; *Phillippi, supra* at 1011 n. 2; *Founding Church of Scientology, supra* at 829.

Of course, it may be that, although authors, publishers and books themselves are not intelligence sources and methods, their disclosure in some or all cases could reasonably be expected to lead to disclosure of intelligence sources and methods. Similarly, disclosure may lead to the disclosure of the names of CIA personnel exempted under section 403g. In either case, nondisclosure would be proper. *See, e.g., Phillippi, supra* at 1015 n. 14. However, because defendant has justified nondisclosure on the assumption that authors, publishers and books were intelligence sources and methods, it is impossible for the court, on the basis of the affidavit presently before it, to distinguish the valid from the invalid exemption claims. Therefore, summary judgment is inappropriate at this time on the basis of exemption 3.

Exemption 1 requires separate analysis. Although both section 403(d)(3) and the EO protect "intelligence sources and methods" (EO § 1–301(c)), the EO also permits classification of documents concerning "foreign relations or foreign activities of the United States" (EO § 1–301(d)). For the reasons discussed above in conjunction with exemption 3, Section 1–301(c) does not sustain a claim under exemption 1 on the basis of the affidavit submitted by defendant. However, documents shown to concern foreign relations or activities of the United States could properly be classified if their disclosure "reasonably could be expected to cause at least identifiable damage to the national security." EO § 1–302.

Plaintiff's *ultra vires* challenge based on EO § 1–601 has no relevance for the very same reason that this challenge fails as to exemption 3. Section 1–601 prohibits "classification to conceal violations of law * * *." The only issue to be considered here is whether the withheld document concerns foreign relations or activities of the United States and whether disclosure reasonably could be expected to cause identifiable damage to the national security. See, Bennett v. United States Department of Defense, 419 F.Supp. 663, 666 (D.N.Y.1976). If properly classified under sections 1–301(d) and 1–302, then by definition it has not been classified "to conceal violations of law" as prohibited by section 1–601. Furthermore, any documents properly classified under EO § 1–301(c) as intelligence sources, activities and methods, as "intelligence" has been defined, would be subject to protection under exemption 3, regardless of their *ultra vires* nature.

Plaintiff challenges the exemption 1 claim on the ground that Stein failed to balance the public interest in disclosure against the need for classification. Such balancing, however, is not a requisite of classification. It is used only in reviewing presently classified documents to determine whether the classification should be continued.

When making such review, section 3–303 requires the agency to weigh the public interest in disclosure only when "questions arise" as to whether the interest in disclosure outweighs the further need for classification. The EO does not specify how such questions "arise"; that issue was left to the agencies. * * * The CIA regulation implementing section 3–303 enumerates five circumstances in which a question is deemed to arise as to whether the public interest in disclosure outweighs continued classification. These criteria seem perfectly reasonable. Stein has determined that none of these circumstances exist in the present case and therefore that a balancing is not required here. The court agrees.

We turn then to the question remaining as to whether defendant's "foreign relations and activities" claim has sufficiently set forth a "reasonable basis for finding potential harm from disclosure." *Hayden, supra* at 1387.

This aspect of de novo review, especially in the area of national security, is circumscribed by the congressional mandate that a court accord "substantial weight" to agency affidavits. S.Rep. No. 1200, 93d Cong., 2d Sess. 12 (1974). *The court, in examining the Agency's arguments, is not to substitute its judgment for that of the Agency in this area of agency expertise, for "[f]ew judges have the skill or experience to weigh the repercussions of disclosure" of such information. Weissman, supra* at 697. [Emphasis added.]

After review of the Stein affidavit the court finds that plausible justifications of identifiable damage to the national security have been made with respect to the following: (1) information identifying a foreign country involved; (2) the existence of a liaison with foreign governments or foreign intelligence services; (3) the location of CIA overseas installations; (4) the identities of individuals in foreign countries, disclosure of which would endanger their lives; (5) United States sponsorship of covert operations in foreign countries; (6) information disclosure of which would otherwise subvert foreign covert operations; (7) information disclosure of which would disrupt foreign relations; (8) information regarding intelligence activities, sources and methods, as "intelligence" has been defined herein; (9) information from foreign intelligence services (see EO § 1–303); (10) cryptonyms and pseudonyms.

The court expressly rejects the defendant's claims of identifiable harm based on possible loss of employment, harm to reputation, or embarrassment resulting to those exposed. The EO does not exempt material due to the possibility of such consequences. See EO § 1–601. Such claims are more properly raised under the privacy provisions of exemption 6—a route which defendant has expressly declined to follow.

Plaintiff argues, however, that prior disclosure of several of the titles and operational details of the CIA's book publishing activities in the Church Committee Report and in the media belies the defendant's claim of present threat of identifiable harm required by the EO. Certainly, the fact that titles already have been released, whether officially or unofficially, disposes of defendant's "blueprint" theory, *i.e.*, that the disclosure of one title will allow persons interested in exposing CIA activities to uncover the general modus operandi of such projects. Suppressing information on that theory would frustrate the policies of the FOIA without even arguably advancing countervailing considerations. *See, Founding Church of Scientology, supra* at 832.

However, the CIA also asserts that Agency disclosure would constitute official acknowledgment of its involvement in *foreign* clandestine book publishing activities, and, as such, could have serious foreign relations consequences. This argument appears eminently reasonable; in the area of international diplomacy there is a difference between unofficial speculation and official acknowledgment of government action. Marks v. Central Intelligence Agency, 426 F.Supp. 708, 712 (D.D.C.1976), *aff'd.* 590 F.2d 997 (D.C.Cir. 1978). * * *

Since in this case proper nondisclosure under exemption 1 has been limited to information which would have foreign relations consequences if released (EO § 1–301(d)), plaintiff's attack based on prior disclosure must fail.

The fact that some of the documents pertain to activities over thirteen to thirty years old does not per se divest them of current national security significance. *Bell v. United States,* 563 F.2d at 486. Stein has found that disclosure of the material withheld would pose present national security risks. "This is precisely the sort of situation where Congress intended reviewing courts to respect the expertise of an agency. * * *." *Hayden v. National Security Agency, supra* at 1388. * * * Therefore plaintiff's bald assertion to the contrary cannot defeat defendant's exemption claim.

Plaintiff's reiteration of the arguments of prior disclosure and alleged staleness in the exemption 3 context is clearly improper. A showing of potential harm is generally not required to sustain an exemption 3 claim. *Baker v. Central Intelligence Agency, supra*; *Goland v. Central Intelligence Agency,* 607 F.2d 339 (D.C.Cir.1978); *Marks v. Turner, supra.*

Plaintiff attacks the claims for exemption under 1 and 3 on the ground that the justification submitted by the government is descriptively insufficient. This contention brings the court to a consideration of the requirement in de novo review that "by its sufficient description, [each] contested document logically falls into the category of the exemption indicated." *Ray v. Turner, supra* at 1195; *Weissman, supra* at 697; *Hayden, supra* at 1387.

The agency's affidavit will pass muster in this regard if it (1) shows in nonconclusory and detailed fashion that the deleted material involves an exempted category of material; (2) lists the deletions; (3) makes clear which exemptions are claimed for the deletions; and (4) explains why the deleted material fits in with the exemption claimed. *Goland v. Central Intelligence Agency, supra* at 351–52. Mere recitation of the statutory standards or vague and sweeping claims will not suffice. *Hayden, supra* at 1387; *Founding Church of Scientology, supra* at 830; *Goland, supra* at 351.

The court has already found that, with respect to the ten specific types of deleted material enumerated above, the agency has justified, in sufficiently detailed fashion, its claim of exemption under exemption 1. Thus, for those enumerated justifications, the agency has complied with the first of the four *Goland* criteria.

As to the other three conditions, the court, with certain exceptions noted below, finds sufficient the method adopted by the CIA in its index of keying specific deletions from each of the documents to the categories of deletions justified in the Stein affidavit. This method is sufficiently detailed as to each document because it indicates, on a deletion-by-deletion—rather than a document-by-document—basis the nature of the information from each document that has been withheld. Since nondisclosure of each category of deleted information has been justified in the Stein affidavit, the result is a description of how disclosure of each deletion would have untoward national security results, in a way that avoids the risk of overbroad exemption. Cf. Lamont v. Department of Justice, 475 F.Supp. 761 (S.D.N.Y.1979).

Of course, the adequacy of this procedure does not make valid the justifications which the court has rejected. Most importantly, as to the exemption 1 and 3 claims based on the "intelligence sources and methods" language of section 403(d)(3) of the National Security Act of 1947 and section 1–301(c) of the EO, the Agency has not made a sufficient showing. The affidavit must provide additional information from which the court can conclude that release of the withheld material can reasonably be expected to lead to disclosure of intelligence sources and methods. * *

It is impossible for the court to offer further guidance at this stage as to what would constitute a sufficient showing. The court therefore merely refers defendant to the fourth *Goland* criterion listed above. If defendant determines that it cannot offer further public explanation of such claims without risking disclosure of the withheld information, it may submit an affidavit for in camera inspection by the court. The court can then release any information in the affidavit which it finds to be nonsensitive. *Hayden, supra* at 1385; *Founding Church of Scientology, supra* at 833; *Ray, supra* at 1218 n. 81; *Phillippi, supra* at 1013.

In addition to its exemption 1 and 3 claims, defendant has withheld certain documents which were prepared in response to specific questions from the Church Committee as congressional records not subject to FOIA requests under 5 U.S.C. § 551(1)(A), or alternatively under exemption 5, 5 U.S.C. § 552(b)(5). The latter provision exempts "inter-agency or intra-agency memorandums or letters which would not be available by law to a party other than an agency in litigation with the agency."

Plaintiff argues that the documents are not congressional materials and therefore not exempt from FOIA, nor are they "inter-agency memorandums," since the term "agency" is expressly defined to exclude Congress, 5 U.S.C. § 551(1)(A).

The justification for exemption 5 fails because Congress is not an "agency." Insofar as "intra-agency" action is concerned, Congress still controls the documents.

The court in *Goland v. Central Intelligence Agency, supra* at 347, set forth three factors to be considered when an agency withholds a congressionally generated document in its possession: (1) the congressional prerogative to prevent disclosure of its own confidential materials; (2) the danger of inhibiting legislative and judicial branches from making documents available to the executive; and (3) Congress' interest in exchanging documents with agencies as part of its oversight authority. *Goland, supra* at 346, 347 n. 48.

Clearly, the documents at issue here were generated by the Agency, not Congress. But they were generated in direct response to the specific request of the Church Committee as part of its exercise of congressional oversight authority. Moreover, the Committee has expressed its wish that no material prepared for it in response to its express interests or resulting from its specific requests be released unless disclosure is approved by vote of the Committee.

Such a clear indication of congressional intention to retain control over the documents, coupled with the proper judicial deference to the congressional oversight process mandated by *Goland* convinces the court that the documents at issue should be deemed exempt from disclosure under the *Goland* rule.

Of course, portions of documents not generated at the direction of the Church Committee which contain information also appearing in the documents that were so generated are not exempt under the *Goland* rationale.

For the reasons discussed above, summary judgment is granted to defendant with respect to all deletions in the index. * * *

Summary judgment is denied with respect to all deletions under [other] categories * * * without prejudice to a renewal on sufficient showing of exemption. * *

So ordered.

Exemption 2

This provision exempts matters "related solely to the internal personnel rules and practices of an agency."

A public interest test has been promulgated in the major Supreme Court decision involving Exemption 2, Department of the Air Force v. Rose, 1 Med.L.Rptr. 2509, 425 U.S. 352 (1976). The Court was prepared to exempt trivial matters "in which the public could not reasonably be expected to have an interest," and this would relieve an agency from having to maintain unnecessary public files. But where there is "a genuine and significant public interest" (perhaps as reflected in editorial judgments) disclosure is compelled *except* "where disclosure may risk circumvention of agency regulation." That is, material may be exempt if disclosure would reveal investigative or prosecutorial strategies.

Rose involved an attempt by law review editors to compel disclosure of case summaries of honors and ethics hearings at the Air Academy with names and other personal references deleted. The district court without *in camera* inspection granted the Department's motion for summary judgment on the ground that the summaries were "matters * * * related solely to the internal personnel rules and practices of an agency." The court of appeals reversed on the ground that *in camera* inspection must precede either an Exemption 2 or an Exemption 6 (a clearly unwarranted invasion of personal privacy) application.

Circuit courts, as the *Hardy* case below illustrates, are divided on whether those parts of agency staff manuals which reveal investigative or prosecutorial strategies are protected under Exemption 2 because their publication would show people how to circumvent agency regulations or because they could not reasonably be expected to have any legitimate public interest.

HARDY v. BUREAU OF ALCOHOL, TOBACCO AND FIREARMS

6 MED.L.RPTR. 2236, 631 F.2D 653 (9TH CIR. 1980).

FARRIS, Circuit Judge:

The Bureau of Alcohol, Tobacco and Firearms appeals the district court's order requiring it to disclose, pursuant to the Freedom of Information Act, 5 U.S.C. § 552, certain portions of its manual entitled "Raids and Searches (Special Agent Basic Training—Criminal Enforcement)." We reverse and remand.

This suit was brought under the Freedom of Information Act by an attorney, David T. Hardy, who sought disclosure of the manual, "Raids and Searches," allegedly for research purposes. On Hardy's initial request the Bureau had disclosed parts of the manual, but had withheld portions concerning techniques used in making law enforcement raids and in conducting searches. The Bureau submitted a detailed affidavit to the district court outlining the subject of each withheld portion; the affidavit explained how disclosure would enable violators to evade or hinder law enforcement personnel. The Bureau claimed that these portions were exempt under 5 U.S.C. § 552(b)(2). The district court disagreed but used its equitable powers to protect certain of the withheld portions from disclosure on the theory that disclosure would "significantly impede the enforcement process." The court ordered the Bureau to disclose the rest of the withheld portions.

* * *

We base our holding on 5 U.S.C. § 552(b)(2). Under this provision, referred to as "Exemption 2," an agency may refuse to disclose materials "related solely to the internal personnel rules and practices of an agency." From its wording, this exemption would appear to apply to the contested portions of the manual here, were it not for the differing interpretations given by the reports of the two Houses of Congress. See Caplan v. Bureau of Alcohol, Tobacco & Firearms, 587 F.2d 544, 546 * * * (2d Cir. 1978). *But see* 1 K. Davis, Administrative Law Treatise § 5.30 (2d ed. Supp. 1980). * * *

Supreme Court guidance on interpreting this exemption is found in Department of Air Force v. Rose, 425 U.S. 352 * * * (1976). There a student researcher sought disclosure of case summaries of the Air Force Academy's honor and ethics hearings. The Air Force had argued that the summaries were exempt under 5 U.S.C. § 552(b)(2). The Court found that the "primary focus of the House Report was on exemption of disclosures that might enable the regulated to circumvent agency regulation. * * *." 425 U.S. at 366–67. The Court specifically declined to consider whether the exemption would apply where a risk of circumvention existed, and indicated that the Senate report should be followed only when this was not a concern. The Court concluded:

> In sum, we think that, at least where the situation is not one where disclosure may risk circumvention of agency regulation, Exemption 2 is not applicable to matters subject to such a genuine and significant public interest. *Id.* at 369.

Assuming that disclosure of the contested portions of the "Raids and Searches" manual would "risk circumvention of agency regulation," we are squarely presented with the issue that the Supreme Court declined to consider in *Rose.*

While no circuit has considered the specific issue which squarely confronts us, five other circuits have considered whether materials similar to those contested here would be subject to disclosure. They have all indicated that such materials would not be subject to disclosure. See Caplan v. Bureau of Alcohol, Tobacco & Firearms, 587 F.2d 544, 547 (2d Cir. 1978) (discussion of the issue; same holding); Stokes v. Brennan, 476 F.2d 699, 702 (5th Cir. 1973); Hawkes v. Internal Revenue Service, 467 F.2d 787, 795 (6th Cir. 1972); Cox v. United States Dept. of Justice, 601 F.2d 1, 4 * * * (D.C.Cir.1979); Sladek v. Bensinger, 605 F.2d 899, 901 (5th Cir. 1979) (indicating that the question is as yet undecided in the Fifth Circuit). *See also* 1 K. Davis, Administrative Law Treatise § 5.30, at 36 (2d ed. Supp.1980). Although these circuits agree that law enforcement materials like those contested here need not be disclosed, they use three different interpretations of the act to reach this result. After considering the three alternative interpretations, we adopt that of the Second Circuit, which has held that law enforcement materials, the disclosure of which may risk circumvention of agency regulation, are exempt under Exemption 2, 5 U.S.C. § 552(b)(2). Caplan v. Bureau of Alcohol, Tobacco & Firearms, 587 F.2d 544,

547 (2d Cir. 1978).[2] The Supreme Court opinion in *Rose* not only does not preclude but furnishes support for this interpretation. As the House report indicates, the language of Exemption 2 is susceptible of this interpretation. Materials instructing law enforcement agents on how to investigate violations concern internal personnel practices. Further, this interpretation is in keeping with the structure of the statute, requiring everything to be disclosed except that which falls within the specific exemptions of subsection (b). *See* 5 U.S.C. § 552(c); NLRB v. Sears, Roebuck & Co., 421 U.S. 132, 136 * * * (1975).

Our interpretation is buttressed by the 1967 amendment to § 552(b)(7). That amendment exempts investigatory records to the extent that production would "disclose investigatory techniques and procedures." This exemption would be pointless unless the manuals instructing agents in those techniques and procedures were also exempt from disclosure.

In adopting the Second Circuit's interpretation of the act, we necessarily reject those of the District of Columbia and Eighth Circuits. While the District of Columbia Circuit has held that similar materials are exempt under Exemption 2, it based its decision not on the risk of circumvention of agency regulation but on the ground that they are materials "in which the public could not reasonably be expected to have a legitimate interest." Cox v. United States Department of Justice, 601 F.2d 1, 4 * * * (D.C.Cir.1979). This "legitimate interest" test is based on an interpretation of the Senate report's discussion of Exemption 2. See Jordan v. United States Department of Justice, 591 F.2d 753, 771 * * * (D.C.Cir.1978) (*en banc*). *Although this approach may reach the same result as the one we adopt, it places courts in the difficult position of determining when the interest of the public in governmental matters is "legitimate."* [Emphasis added.] * * *

We hold that law enforcement materials, disclosure of which may risk circumvention of agency regulation, are exempt from disclosure. In so ruling we recognize the distinction between "law enforcement" and "administrative" materials. See, e.g., Hawkes v. Internal Revenue Service, 467 F.2d 787, 794–95 (6th Cir.1972). "Law enforcement" materials involve methods of enforcing the laws, however interpreted, and "administrative" materials involve the definition of the violation and the procedures required to prosecute the offense. All administrative materials, even if included in staff manuals that otherwise concern law enforcement, must be disclosed unless they come under one of the other exemptions of the act. Such materials contain the "secret law" which was the primary target of the act's broad disclosure provisions. Cox v. United States Department of Justice, 601 F.2d 1, 5 * * * (D.C.Cir.1979). Further, as the Supreme Court observed in Department of the Air Force v. Rose, 425 U.S. 352, 369 (1976), the thrust of Exemption 2 is not to limit disclosure to "secret law" but to relieve agencies of the burden of disclosing information in which the public does not have a legitimate interest. Materials that solely concern law enforcement are exempt under Exemption 2 if disclosure may risk circumvention of agency regulation.

When an agency believes that materials sought in a Freedom of Information Act suit are within the exempt category of law enforcement materials herein described, it should submit to the district court a detailed affidavit describing how disclosure would risk circumvention of agency regulation. See Cuneo v. Schlesinger, 484 F.2d 1086, 1092 (D.C.Cir.1973), *cert. denied*, 415 U.S. 977 (1974). If the explanation is rea-

2. But see Jordan v. Department of Justice, 591 F.2d 753, 771 * * * (D.C.Cir.1978) (considering the issue and reaching an opposite result).

sonable, the district court should find the materials exempt from disclosure, unless *in camera* examination shows that they contain secret law or that the agency has not fairly described the contents in its affidavit. See Cox v. United States Dept. of Justice, 576 F.2d 1302, 1311–12 (8th Cir. 1978). In such a case, those portions not covered by the affidavit or containing secret law may be ordered disclosed. Whether the agency's explanation is reasonable is a question of law and rulings by other courts concerning the same materials should be given weight.

We remand to the district court for a review of the affidavit of the Bureau and the contested portions of the manual to determine whether they involve law enforcement material, the disclosure of which would risk circumvention of agency regulation. If so, the material is exempt from disclosure.

Reversed and remanded.

COMMENT

A week after *Hardy* was announced, that part of the same Bureau's training manual dealing with surveillance of premises and persons was held by the D. C. Circuit not to be exempt under Exemption 2. Relying on its own *en banc* decision in *Jordan v. United States Department of Justice* [40] (discussed in *Hardy*), the court, basing its decision on the proposition alternative to that applied in *Hardy*, concluded:

> There can be little doubt that citizens have an interest in the manner in which they may be observed by federal agents. * * * Neither exemption (b)(2) nor any other exemption prevents a citizen from satisfying his curiosity on these matters. The contents of this document sought by Crooker [the plaintiff] pertaining to surveillance of the public cannot possibly be assimilated to mere "internal housekeeping" concerns. Crooker v. Bureau of Alcohol, Tobacco and Firearms, 6 Med.L. Rptr. 2327, 670 F.2d 1051 (D.C.Cir.1981).

Exemption 3

Under this exemption, called by the Reporters Committee the "catch-all" exemption and a major access loophole, information need not be disclosed if "specifically exempted from disclosure by statute * * * provided that such statute (A) [clearly] requires that the matters be withheld from the public or (B) establishes particular criteria for [discretionary] withholding or [narrowly specifies] particular types of [informational] matters to be withheld."

The Supreme Court liberally construed Exemption 3 in Administrator, FAA v. Robertson, 1 Med.L.Rptr. 2465, 422 U.S. 255 (1975). There the plaintiff sought FAA reports analyzing the operation and maintenance performance of commercial airlines. Section 1104 of the Federal Aviation Act permitted the administrator to withhold reports if disclosure was not in the public interest and if a person contributing information objected. The Air Transport Association objected, arguing that without confidentiality the performance program would be endangered.

Robertson won at district and appeals court levels, but the Supreme Court reversed. Chief Justice Burger wrote for the Court that the information sought was expressly exempt by statute, and the statute, because it ensured a flow of information to the agency, was not inconsistent with the disclosure policy of FOIA. In a concurring opinion, Justice Stewart said that the only determination "in a district court's *de novo* inquiry is the factual existence of such a statute, regardless of how unwise, self-protective, or inadvertent the enactment might be."

Congress reacted to *Robertson* by amending FOIA in 1976 to narrow the

---

40. 4 Med.L.Rptr. 1785, 591 F.2d 753 (D.C.Cir.1978).

scope of the information it shielded. As amended, Exemption 3 requires that the government show 1) that the requested information falls within the scope of the statute cited, and 2) that the statute either vests no discretion to disclose (that is that it mandates secrecy), or that the information fits criteria delineated to authorize withholding.

Exemption 3's legislative history does specify some of the statutes that can or cannot be used to justify the use of this section of FOIA. Federal agencies have cited approximately 100 statutes to justify withholding. Courts have held records exempt under the Consumer Product Safety Act,[41] the National Security Act,[42] federal laws allowing the CIA to prevent unauthorized disclosure,[43] and federal rules protecting material related to grand jury proceedings.[44] Courts have also upheld Exemption 3 claims in cases involving Census Bureau records, tax returns, patent applications, the Privacy Act, and the Postal Reorganization Act.

In these cases, courts are often faced with the difficult task of weighing one federal law against another and rationalizing their choice.

Exemption 4

Exempted under 4 are "trade secrets and commercial or financial information obtained from a person and privileged or confidential."

Trade secrets would be, for example, secret formulae or customer lists, valuable in day-to-day transactions and not generally known in the trade. Commercial or financial information covered by the Exemption is *confidential* material, the disclosure of which "would be likely to cause substantial harm to the competitive position of the person from whom the information was obtained" or "impair the government's ability to obtain necessary information in the future." National Parks and Conservation Association v. Morton, 498 F.2d 765 (D.C.Cir.1974).

"Specific factual or evidentiary material"[45] must be submitted to sustain the burden of proof under Exemption 4, a burden borne by the federal agency. "Conclusory and generalized allegations are * * * unacceptable as a means of sustaining the burden of nondisclosure under the FOIA, since such allegations necessarily elude the beneficial scrutiny of adversary proceedings, prevent adequate appellate review and generally frustrate the fair assertion of rights under the [a]ct."[46]

Moreover, substantial competitive harm can only be shown by proving that persons from whom documents have been obtained by the government actually face competition.[47]

Before 1979, persons supplying information to the government would frequently sue to block disclosure to third parties. These were called reverse FOIA suits. In Chrysler Corporation v. Brown, 4 Med.L. Rptr. 2441, 441 U.S. 281 (1979), the U. S. Supreme Court held that FOIA does not create a private right of action to enjoin or prevent an agency from releasing documents covered by one of the nine exemp-

41. Consumer Product Safety Commission v. GTE Sylvania, Inc., 6 Med.L.Rptr. 1301, 447 U.S. 102 (1980).

42. Hayden v. National Security Agency, 5 Med.L.Rptr. 1897, 608 F.2d 1381 (D.C.Cir.1979); Founding Church of Scientology of Washington, D. C. v. National Security Agency, 5 Med.L.Rptr. 1850, 610 F.2d 824 (D.C.Cir.1979).

43. Phillippi v. CIA, 7 Med.L.Rptr. 2007, 655 F.2d 1325 (D.C.Cir.1981).

44. Piccolo v. United States Department of Justice, 7 Med.L.Rptr. 1366, 90 F.R.D. 287 (D.C.Cir.1981).

45. Pacific Architects and Engineers, Inc. v. The Renegotiation Board, 505 F.2d 383 (D.C.Cir.1974).

46. National Parks and Conservation Association v. Kleppe, 2 Med.L.Rptr. 1245, 547 F.2d 673 (D.C.Cir.1976). See also, Continental Stock & Transfer Co. v. SEC, 566 F.2d 373 (2d Cir. 1977).

47. Ibid.

tions. Information suppliers could, of course, review an agency's decision to release Exemption 4 documents under Section 10(e) of the Administrative Procedures Act, 5 U.S.C. § 706(2)(A). That section authorizes a court to set aside agency action that is "arbitrary, capricious, an abuse of discretion, or otherwise not in accordance with law."

A decision to assert an FOIA exemption is at the discretion of an agency; it is not mandatory that an agency do so, as a reverse FOIA suit would imply. But it would be an abuse of discretion to release documents covered by the Trade Secrets Act, 18 U.S.C. § 1905. A submitter of confidential business information, such as customer lists, can invoke the Trade Secrets Act to bar disclosure by an agency unless that disclosure is authorized by law or by some agency regulation that is in turn authorized by Congress.

Neither the FOIA nor the Housekeeping Statute, 5 U.S.C. § 301, are congressional grants of authority for an agency to issue regulations exempting materials from the Trade Secrets Act's nondisclosure rule. The Court held essentially that a statute authorizing an agency to collect information is, by definition, authorization to disclose that information.

Justice Rehnquist's opinion for the Court in *Chrysler* is a complex analysis of FOIA's legislative history, especially with reference to Exemption 4, but its essence is probably contained in footnote 12's allusion to a 1965 Senate Report on the bill:

> It is not an easy task to balance the opposing interests [secrecy v. disclosure], but it is not an impossible one either. It is not necessary to conclude that to protect one of the interests, the other, must of necessity, either be abrogated or substantially subordinated. Success lies in providing a workable formula which encompasses, balances, and protects all interests, *yet places emphasis on the fullest possible disclosure.* [Emphasis added.][48]

Section 6(f) of the FTC Act, 15 U.S.C. § 46(f), provides that the Commission has power to make public all information it has obtained, except trade secrets and names of customers. In Interco v. FTC, 478 F.Supp. 103 (D.D.C.1979), both district and circuit courts held that § 6(f) was authorization for the FTC to release materials within the scope of FOIA Exemption 4 unless such materials constitute trade secrets or customer lists. The Trade Secrets Act, therefore, does not prevent the FTC from releasing to the public confidential business information other than trade secrets and business lists.

The FTC has defined trade secrets to mean only information with enduring, intrinsic value, primarily secret product formulae, processes, or other secret technical information. The courts in *Interco* accepted that definition.

It should not be surprising that concerted efforts are continually made to exempt business information from the disclosure requirements of FOIA. In the first four years of the act, corporations were by far its largest users. In the fall of 1980, a House-Senate Conference Committee amended the Federal Trade Commission Act to exempt large areas of FTC documents relating to pricing policies, product safety, and truth-in-advertising. In June 1981, another Conference Committee exempted large areas of documents held by the Consumer Products Safety Commission, including information relating to safety and warranty data. And in July 1981, Congress amended the Omnibus Tax Bill, exempting from disclosure the auditing standards and rules adopted by the Internal Revenue Service.

In December of 1981, the Senate Subcommittee on the Constitution reported on S.1730, the Freedom of Information Reform

48. S.Rep.No.813, 89th Cong., 1st Sess., 3 (1965).

Act which then went before the Senate Judicial Committee. The act sought generalized and comprehensive changes in FOIA.

Exemption 5

This exemption prevents disclosure of "interagency or intra-agency memoranda or letters which would not be available by law to a party other than an agency in litigation with the agency."

As construed in NLRB v. Sears, Roebuck & Co., 1 Med.L.Rptr. 2471, 421 U.S. 132 (1975), Exemption 5 is intended to protect "predecisional communications," but not "communications made after the decision and designed to explain it." The Court reasoned that disclosure of memoranda generated before the deliberative process was complete might diminish the quality of decision making. Advisers might be less candid if their recommendations were subject to public scrutiny.

Renegotiation Board v. Grumman Aircraft Engineering Corp., 1 Med.L.Rptr. 2487, 421 U.S. 168 (1975), also gave the exemption a broad construction. Only the report of an agency vested with the final decisional authority is releasable. Memos, recommendations, opinions, policy statements expressly mentioned in a report may be releasable (barring a legitimate Exemption 7 claim) because they constitute the basis for final decision.

If no memorandum or other document explains the final decision, the agency has no obligation to prepare one under FOIA.

Exemption 5 has been called the "executive privilege" exemption. It protects working papers, studies, and reports circulated among agency personnel prior to the making of a decision. Its purpose is to encourage frank discussion. For example, FOIA requires that university research grant applications and progress reports submitted to the federal government be made public on demand. Letters of evaluation, however, that are part of the peer review process, may be kept secret as intra-agency memoranda.[49] Purely factual information, such as names and addresses of unsuccessful applicants for federal funds, is not exempt from disclosure. Nor are factual portions of predecisional documents generally exempt, unless their disclosure would breach a promise of confidentiality and diminish the agency's ability to obtain similar information in the future or unless a compilation of facts would expose the deliberative process itself.

Federal district courts, *in camera*, may decide whether predecisional policy statements, proposals, and letters between agency officials contain factual material that is not exempt.[50]

The distinction between predecisional and postdecisional material is the key to understanding Exemption 5. A Watergate Special Prosecution Force memorandum, expressly incorporated into the group's required report to Congress recommending that Richard Nixon not be indicted, was held disclosable, Exemption 5 notwithstanding, because it was part of a final opinion. Standing alone, it would have been exempt as a "predecisional intra-agency legal memorandum."[51]

In Bristol-Myers Co. v. FTC, 4 Med.L. Rptr. 1379, 598 F.2d 18 (D.C.Cir.1978) the court of appeals held that the FTC's "Blue Minutes," which included written explanations by commissioners of their decisions not to include certain charges in a complaint or not to proceed by rulemaking, would have to be disclosed.

49. Washington Research Project v. HEW, 504 F.2d 238 (D.C.Cir.1974).

50. Union of Concerned Scientists v. Atomic Energy Commission, 2 Med.L.Rptr. 1458, 499 F.2d 1069 (D.D.C.1974).

51. Niemeier v. Watergate Special Prosecution Force, 3 Med.L.Rptr. 1321, 565 F.2d 967 (7th Cir. 1977).

But Exemption 5 does protect against disclosure the attorney-client privilege—communications between an agency and its attorney or another agency acting as attorney, such as the U.S. Department of Justice—or an attorney's work-product if disclosure would reveal trial strategies.

National Public Radio reporter Barbara Newman found herself blocked by Exemption 5 when she tried to get information from the Department of Justice concerning its investigation into the mysterious death of Karen Silkwood, employee of a plutonium manufacturer. Silkwood, suspected of being contaminated by plutonium, was killed in a car accident while on her way to conduct business on behalf of her labor union and to talk with a *New York Times* reporter. There were suspicions that her car had been forced off the highway, and a file of documents she was carrying was never recovered. (See p. 401.)

Using FOIA, Newman sought access to files marked "death investigation" and "contamination." The former was denied on grounds of Exemption 5, the latter on grounds of Exemption 7.

Portions of the "death investigation" file consisted of the working papers of Department of Justice attorneys, including notes and observations for personal use in analyzing evidence and legal issues, said a federal district court. They were clearly exempt under the *NLRB v. Sears* standard applicable to "memoranda prepared by an attorney in contemplation of litigation which set forth the attorney's theory of the case, his litigation strategy." National Public Radio v. Bell, 2 Med.L.Rptr. 1808, 431 F.Supp. 509 (D.D.C.1977)

When *Rolling Stone* magazine tried to find out why so many major news media could be persuaded by the CIA not to publish information about the "Glomar Project"—Jack Anderson was not and broke the story—it was denied access to the full record on the basis of Exemptions 1, 3, 5, and 6. The material was said to contain information properly classified and therefore within the scope of Exemption 1, an argument similar to that pressed in *Military Audit Report v. Casey* (see p. 445). Because release of the information could reasonably be expected to lead to "disclosure of intelligence sources and methods," protected by separate federal statutes, it was also exempt under FOIA Exemption 3. As to Exemption 5, the court explained as follows.

PHILLIPPI v. CIA

6 MED.L.RPTR. 1673 (D.D.C.1980).

GASCH, J.:

* * *

This exemption is intended to give the government the same privilege in FOIA cases that it would enjoy in the civil discovery context. *NLRB v. Sears, Roebuck & Co.*, 421 U.S. 132, 152 * * * (1975). While Exemption 5 is multi-faceted, the defendants are claiming only the protection of that branch of the privilege which protects the "deliberative process."

This privilege is unique to government and is intended to prevent the fear of subsequent disclosure from inhibiting the frank expression of views among government officials to the detriment of the decisionmaking process. Jordan v. Department of Justice, 591 F.2d 753, 772 * * * (D.C.Cir.1978). To qualify for the privilege, a communication first, must be predecisional and second, contain advice or opinion of a deliberative nature. Coastal States Gas Corp. v. Department of Energy, 644 F.2d 969 (D.C.Cir.1981). Factual matter contained in such communications is not exempt and must be disclosed unless it is inextricably intertwined with the decisionmaking process. EPA v. Mink, 410 U.S. 73, 93 (1973); *Coastal States Gas Corp. v. Department of Energy.* * * *

Documents * * * being withheld in reliance on Exemption 5, are summarized transcripts of conversations between then

CIA Director Colby and other high level government officials concerning the agency's efforts to prevent publication of HGE [Hughes Glomar Explorer] stories. Of these six documents, four relate conversations between Mr. Colby and then Assistant to the President for National Security Affairs, General Brent Scowcroft. Of the remaining two, one reports a conversation with an unidentified official apparently in the Executive branch and the other reports a conversation with a member of Congress. Because the agency's affidavits left some doubt as to whether these documents were wholly exempt from disclosure, the Court has examined these documents *in camera*. See EPA v. Mink, 410 U.S. at 93.

Having examined these documents, the Court has concluded that they are of the type protected by Exemption 5. The disclosure of these documents would reveal the frank exchange of views among high level government officials and would inhibit the candid expression of ideas crucial to the decisionmaking process. Mead Data Central, Inc. v. United States Department of the Air Force, 566 F.2d 242, 256 (D.C.Cir.1977). While some of the information contained in these documents is of a factual nature, the disclosure of any meaningful parts of the documents would impinge upon policymaking processes within the protection of Exemption 5. EPA v. Mink, 410 U.S. at 92. For these reasons, the Court has concluded that documents * * * are being properly withheld pursuant to Exemption 5.

* * *

Exemption 6

Exempted are "personnel and medical files and similar files the disclosure of which would constitute a clearly unwarranted invasion of personal privacy."

In the reports accompanying the original FOIA, Congress explicitly authorized the courts to employ a balancing of interests test. The Supreme Court obliged in *Department of the Air Force v. Rose* where it held that mere storage of information in a personnel or related file did not insulate it. "Rather, Congress sought to construct an exemption that would require a balancing of the individual's right of privacy against the preservation of the basic purpose of the Freedom of Information Act 'to open agency action to the light of public scrutiny.' The device adopted to achieve that balance was the limited exemption, where privacy was threatened—for 'clearly unwarranted' invasions of personal privacy." Not all invasions of privacy are meant to be unlawful under FOIA.

Litigation under this exemption thus devolves upon a *de novo* judicial weighing of the public interest served by disclosure against the private interest served by nondisclosure. Several considerations may tip the balance one way or the other:

a. Some courts gauge public interest by the purpose to which information will be put. For example, disclosure which would further the requester's commercial interests (Wine Hobby U.S.A., Inc. v. IRS, 502 F.2d 133 (3d Cir.1974) has been accorded less weight than disclosure for less materialistic purposes. The Supreme Court did emphasize in *Rose* that FOIA should be applied evenhandedly "to any purpose." The use in *Wine Hobby* of a "properly and directly concerned" test for disclosure is not supported by the legislative history of FOIA, and it blunts the purpose of the act.

b. "Clearly unwarranted invasions of privacy" have been narrowed to protect only "intimate personal details" in personnel, medical, or related files, and the courts may determine *de novo* whether exempt portions can be segregated.

c. That a promise of confidentiality would be breached by disclosure adds weight to a claim of exemption. But the mere fact that a supplier was assured confidentiality is insufficient in itself, Ackerly v. Ley, 420 F.2d 1336 (D.C.Cir.1969). This is also true in Exemption 4 cases where the issue of confidentiality arises more frequently. See also, Kurzon v. Health and Human Services, 7 Med.L.Rptr. 1591, 649 F.2d 65 (1st Cir.1981). Names and addresses of unsuccessful research grant applicants said not exempt as "personnel, medical or similar" files.

A 1982 case expanded the scope of the language "personnel, medical and similar files." State Department records indicating whether or not a person holds a U.S. passport were said to be "similar" files and exempt where a privacy interest would outweigh the public interest in disclosure. The *Washington Post* was trying to establish the citizenship of two former Iranian officials. The government, in invoking Exemption 6, said that it was concerned about the safety of the two men. Department of State v. Washington Post, 8 Med.L.Rptr. 1521, 595 U.S. 456, 102 S.Ct. 1957 (1982).

Small Business Administration records that contain the names of noncorporate recipients of funds under one of its programs and that reveal amounts and balances of noncorporate loans classified as "delinquent," "in liquidation," or "charge off," but are not subject to public legal proceedings, were said *not* to be "similar" files protected against disclosure under Exemption 6. Miami Herald Publishing Co. v. SBA, 8 Med.L.Rptr. 1284, 670 F.2d 610 (5th Cir. 1982).

In an earlier case involving the Small Business Administration, a federal district court awarded attorney's fees to the *Miami Herald* in view of the public benefit derived from publication of the information and the unreasonableness of the government in trying to withhold it.[52]

The overall purpose of Exemption 6 is to protect information of an intimate nature. Sometimes this can be achieved by deleting names or otherwise identifying data before a document is released. Those applying for government contracts, research funds, or other government benefits are deemed to have waived their rights to privacy.

In the Exemption 6 portion of *Rolling Stone*'s effort to get "Glomar Project" information, the D.C. District Court held that CIA documents identifying news media personnel contacted by the agency in order to prevent publication, but that did not reveal any personal details on character or integrity, were not "personnel, medical or similar files" exempt under FOIA. But documents in the same file that ambiguously identified certain persons connected with Glomar and would significantly invade personal privacy were exempt under Exemption 6.

PHILLIPPI v. CIA

6 MED.L.RPTR. 1673 (D.D.C.1980).

* * *

GASCH, J.:

The Court's inquiry in Exemption 6 cases must proceed in two steps. The threshold question is whether the documents in issue are the type contemplated by the exemption's reference to personnel, medical and similar files. *Board of Trade v. CFTC,* No. 77–0560, slip op. at 11 (D.C. Cir.1980); Plain Dealer Publishing Co. v. Department of Labor, 471 F.Supp. 1023, 1026 (D.D.C.1979). While it is a relatively simple task to determine that documents are properly considered personnel or medical files, the reference to "similar files" is slightly more vague. It is, however, fairly clear that Exemption 6 protection is intended for files that implicate the same values as personnel or medical files. That is, the information being withheld must be the type that, if disclosed, would

52. Miami Herald Publishing Co. v. Small Business Administration, 6 Med.L.Rptr. 1686 (D.Fla.1980).

subject individuals to the potential embarrassment or imposition of publicly revealing details about their personal lives. *Board of Trade v. CFTC*, slip op. at 10–11; Ditlow v. Schultz, 517 F.2d 166, 170 (D.C. Cir.1975).

The Court's inquiry does not end with a finding that the documents are "similar files" within the meaning of Exemption 6. The exemption does not protect all such files from disclosure but only such as would "constitute a clearly unwarranted invasion of personal privacy." It is only where the public interest in disclosure is clearly outweighed by the individual's interest in privacy that the former must yield to the latter. This determination necessitates a case by case balancing of the respective interests. Department of the Air Force v. Rose, 425 U.S. 352, 370 * * * (1976); Getman v. NLRB, 450 F.2d 670, 673 (D.C.Cir.1971).

Applying these considerations to the present case, the Court has determined that the documents as they pertain to media personnel, * * * are not the type contemplated by the Exemption 6 reference to "similar files" and must be revealed to the plaintiff. On the other hand, the revelation of the identities of the individuals * * * and withheld pursuant to Exemption 6 would compromise the privacy of those individuals while advancing no identifiable public interest in disclosure. These deletions are being properly withheld pursuant to Exemption 6 of the FOIA.

It is undisputed that [some] deletions represent the names of media personnel which appear in the documents. Each of these deletions is separately designated by a numeral. A total of forty-two names were initially in dispute. One of the documents had made reference to the individual designated "E–14" [the files were designated by letters and numerals] having a "drinking problem" and plaintiff withdrew her request for the identity of that individual. The defendants agreed to contact the remaining forty-one individuals and ask if they had any objection to the revelation of their identities. Of these, thirty responded that they had no objection and their names have been released to the plaintiff. Two, "E–16" and "E–14", responded that they would prefer that their names not be disclosed and plaintiff is no longer seeking these. The remaining nine individuals made no response and disclosure of their identities is now in dispute.

The Court has examined the redacted documents in which these deletions appear. The documents do not reveal any personal details about these individuals. They do not cast suspicion on the character or integrity of these individuals. The documents merely report in unambiguous terms that these individuals had in the course of their own journalistic investigations uncovered the government's involvement with the HGE [Hughes Glomer Experiment] and/or had been contacted by the CIA in its efforts to prevent publication of these stories.

The defendants' position seems to be that revelation of the fact that these individuals suppressed stories at the urging of the CIA would damage their professional reputations. This assertion is belied by the fact that thirty of thirty-two individuals stated that they had no objection to revelation of their identities.

The Court has determined that the identities of these individuals as they appear in the documents are not within the intended scope of Exemption 6 and should be disclosed to the plaintiff. Because the Court has determined that these documents are not "personnel," "medical" or "similar files" within the meaning of Exemption 6, there is no need to inquire further into the relative weight of the interests in disclosure and privacy. *Board of Trade v. CFTC*, slip op. at 13; Plain Dealer Publishing Co. v. Department of Labor, 471 F.Supp. at 1026, n. 4 (D.D.C.1979).

The affidavits indicate that all of the "J" deletions refer to the names of private individuals not related to the HGE project.

Unlike the individuals designated by the "E" deletions, however, the documents are not unambiguous as to the extent that individuals designated by the letter "J" participated with the CIA in the HGE project. The mere mention of an individual in a CIA file may be insufficient to warrant the protection of Exemption 6, Ray v. Turner, 587 F.2d at 1198 (per curiam); Fonda v. CIA, 434 F.Supp. 498, 506 (D.D.C.1977), but the mention of an individual which unfairly leads to the suggestion that the individual participated in a covert intelligence operation with the CIA clearly warrants weighing that individual's interest in privacy against the public interest in disclosure. Cf. Ray v. Turner, 468 F.Supp. 730, 737 (D.D.C.1979) (on remand) (names of individuals found on the person of a narcotics smuggler held exempt from disclosure).

The Court cannot discern any identifiable interest which would be advanced by disclosure of these names. The plaintiff asserts that there is a substantial public interest in the relationship between the CIA and the press and that these deletions detract "from the informative value of these documents." Assuming that this interest exists, it is still impossible to ascertain how the identities of these individuals will make any significant contribution to the public beyond the information already contained in the redacted documents.

The Court has determined that disclosure of the identities of these individuals would be a significant invasion of their personal privacy and would advance no public interest in disclosure. For the reasons stated above, the deletions designated by the letter "J" are being properly withheld pursuant to Exemption 6 of the FOIA.

* * *

COMMENT

The United States Court of Appeals for the District of Columbia upheld the district court on all counts, although its discussion focused almost entirely on Exemption 3, material the disclosure of which would compromise intelligence sources and methods.[53]

Since the "clearly unwarranted invasion of personal privacy" language of Exemption 6 connects it with the Federal Privacy Act of 1974, we shall encounter that ill-defined concept again. It is also part of the language of Exemption 7.

Exemption 7

This exemption protects "investigatory records compiled for law enforcement purposes, but only to the extent that the production of such records would (A) interfere with enforcement proceedings, (B) deprive a person of a right to a fair trial or an impartial adjudication, (C) constitute an unwarranted invasion of personal privacy, (D) disclose the identity of a confidential source and, in the case of a record compiled by a criminal law enforcement authority in the course of a criminal investigation, or by an agency conducting a lawful national security intelligence investigation, confidential information furnished only by the confidential source, (E) disclose investigative techniques and procedures, or (F) endanger the life or physical safety of law enforcement personnel."

More economical language in the original exemption was expanded in the 1974 amendments to FOIA specifically to override increasingly broad interpretations which were bringing more and more information under the protective umbrella of Exemption 7.

To qualify under this exemption, the government must first show that the rec-

53. Phillippi v. CIA, 7 Med.L.Rptr. 2006, 655 F.2d 1325 (D.C.Cir.1981).

ord is both "investigatory" and contained in a file "compiled for law enforcement purposes." Law enforcement embraces civil, criminal, administrative, and judicial proceedings. If the material passes this threshold to qualify as exempt, then it must in addition fall within one of the six enumerated categories causing a specified harm. Clauses (A), (C), and (D) have generated the most litigation.

While most records having to do with current investigations of specific crimes or administrative enforcement proceedings (interviews, affidavits, agency notes) are exempt, rap sheets, arrest and conviction records, department manuals, personnel rosters, and other routine compilations and records are not.

In NLRB v. Robbins Tire & Rubber Co., 3 Med.L.Rptr. 2473, 437 U.S. 214 (1978), the Supreme Court held that copies of witness statements which NLRB rules preclude from discovery prior to unfair labor practices hearings were exempt under FOIA Exemption 7(A).

When a plaintiff in an FTC antitrust suit filed an FOIA request for documents that it had failed to request during discovery, a federal district court, discussing Exemption 7(A) said:

"It is clear that where there is an ongoing administrative enforcement proceeding during which plaintiff has been provided with an opportunity to engage in discovery, plaintiff may not use the FOIA to augment the material produced by discovery." [54] So records on the case in FTC investigatory files were properly exempted from disclosure.

All FBI investigatory records are, for purposes of satisfying FOIA Exemption 7, "compiled for law enforcement purposes." The legality of a particular investigation or the sufficiency of a connection between the investigation and federal law enforcement goals generally do not matter. The FBI, however, must still satisfy Exemption 7's remaining criteria in order to withhold disclosure.[55]

Clause (A) exemptions generally apply only when an enforcement proceeding has actually begun or when it is clear that an ongoing investigation will lead to an enforcement proceeding. When an enforcement proceeding has concluded, for example, after trial, conviction and sentencing, the exemption does not apply.

Clause (C) exemptions are designed to prevent unwarranted invasions of personal privacy through disclosure of investigatory records compiled for law enforcement purposes. But the seriousness of the invasion is to be weighed against the public interest to be served by disclosure.[56] For example, the Sixth Circuit approved the redacting or obliteration of information contained in file material collected during the discovery process in civil cases arising out of the 1970 killings by the National Guard of four Kent State University students. The court balanced First Amendment interests against privacy rights and the interests of the law enforcement agencies involved.[57]

A hard blow against access was struck by the U.S. Supreme Court in May 1982 when it upheld Exemption 7(C) claims by the FBI against requests of an independent journalist that FBI documents on Nixon Administration critics be made public. The D.C. Circuit, reversing the district court, had held that FBI information on certain public personalities, which was prepared at the request of the White House and which had not been shown to have been compiled for law enforcement purposes, even though invasive of privacy,

54. Heublein, Inc. v. FTC, 457 F.Supp. 52, 55 (D.D.C.1978).

55. Abrams v. FBI, 7 Med.L.Rptr. 1289, 511 F.Supp. 758 (D.Ill.1981).

56. Alirez v. NLRB, 8 Med.L.Rptr. 1517, 676 F.2d 423 (10th Cir.1982).

57. Krause v. Rhodes, 8 Med.L.Rptr. 1130, 671 F.2d 212 (6th Cir.1982).

was not exempt from disclosure under 7(C). A divided Supreme Court in turn reversed the court of appeals.

Among those on the "enemies list" were Kenneth Galbraith, Reinhold Niebuhr, Benjamin Spock, and Cesar Chavez. The crux of the Court's holding seemed to be that material originally exempt under 7(C) doesn't lose that exemption simply because it is transmitted to a second agency in slightly different form. And, of course, the Court assumed that the original compilation was for law enforcement purposes. To what extent does the ruling expand Exemption 7 by creating a "born classified" category of information? The Court is also concerned about the flow of essential information to the government being slowed down by the court of appeals' position (see fn. 12).

FBI v. ABRAMSON

456 U.S. 615, 102 S.CT. 2054, 72 L.ED.2D 376 (1982).

Justice WHITE delivered the opinion of the Court.

* * *

As the case comes to us, it is agreed that the information withheld by the Bureau was originally compiled for law enforcement purposes. It is also settled that the name check summaries were developed pursuant to a request from the White House for information about certain public personalities and were not compiled for law enforcement purposes. Finally, it is not disputed that if the threshold requirement of Exemption 7 is met—if the documents were compiled for law enforcement purposes—the disclosure of such information would be an unwarranted invasion of privacy. The sole question for decision is whether information originally compiled for law enforcement purposes loses its Section 7 exemption if summarized in a new document not created for law enforcement purposes.

No express answer is provided by the statutory language or by the legislative history. The Court of Appeals resolved the question in favor of Abramson by construing the threshold requirement of Exemption 7 in the following manner. The cover letter to the White House, along with the accompanying summaries and attachments, constituted a "record". Because that "record" was not compiled for law-enforcement purposes, the material within it could not qualify for the exemption, regardless of the purpose for which that material was originally gathered and recorded and regardless of the impact that disclosure of such information would produce. The Court of Appeals supported its interpretation by distinguishing between documents and information. "The statutory scheme of the FOIA very clearly indicates that exemptions from disclosure apply only to documents, and not to the use of the information contained in such documents." — U.S.App.D.C. —, 658 F.2d at 813. A "record" is a "document" and, for the Court of Appeals, the document must be treated as a unit for purposes of deciding whether it was prepared for law enforcement purposes. The threshold requirement for qualifying under Exemption 7 turns on the purpose for which the document sought to be withheld was prepared, not on the purpose for which the material included in the document was collected. The Court of Appeals would apply this rule even when the information for which the exemption is claimed appears in the requested document in the form essentially identical to the original memorialization.

The Court of Appeals' view is a tenable construction of Exemption 7, but there is another interpretation, equally plausible on the face of the statute, of the requirement that the record sought to be withheld must have been prepared for law enforcement purposes. If a requested document, such as the one sent to the White House in this case, contains or essentially reproduces all or part of a record that was previously compiled for law enforcement reasons, it is reasonably arguable that the law enforcement record does not lose its exemption by its subsequent inclusion in a document created for a non-exempt purpose. The Court of Appeals itself pointed the way to this alternative construction by indicating that Exemption 7 protected attachments to the name check summaries that were duplicates of original records compiled for law enforcement purposes. Those records would not lose their exemption by being included in a later compilation made for political purposes. Although in this case the duplicate law enforcement records were attached to the name check summaries, the result hardly should be different if all or part of the prior record were quoted verbatim in the new document. That document, even though it may be delivered to another agency for a non-exempt purpose, contains a "record" qualifying for consideration under Exemption 7.

The question is whether FOIA permits the same result where the exempt record is not reproduced verbatim but is accurately reflected in summary form. The Court of Appeals would have it that because the FBI summarized the relevant records rather than reproducing them verbatim, the identical information no longer qualifies for the exemption. The originally compiled record and the derivative summary would be treated completely differently although the content of the information is the same and although the reasons for maintaining its confidentiality remain equally strong. We are of the view, however, that the statutory language is reasonably construable to protect that part of an otherwise non-exempt compilation which essentially reproduces and is substantially the equivalent of all or part of an earlier record made for law enforcement uses. Moreover, that construction of the statute rather than the interpretation embraced by the Court of Appeals, more accurately reflects the intention of Congress, is more consistent with the structure of the Act, and more fully serves the purposes of the statute.

FOIA contains no definition of the term "record". Throughout the legislative history of the 1974 amendments, representatives and senators used interchangeably such terms as "documents", "records", "matters", and "information". Furthermore, in determining whether information in a requested record should be released, the Act consistently focuses on the nature of the information and the effects of disclosure. After enumerating the nine exemptions from the FOIA, Congress expressly directed that "any reasonably segregable portion of a record" be "provided to any person requesting such record after deletion of the portions which are exempt. * * *" § 552(b). This provision requires agencies and courts to differentiate among the contents of a document rather than to treat it as an indivisible "record" for FOIA purposes. When a record is requested, it is permissible for an agency to divide the record into parts that are exempt and parts that are not exempt, based on the kind of information contained in the respective parts.

The 1974 amendments modified Exemption 7 in two ways. First, by substituting the word "records" for "files," Congress intended for courts to "consider the nature of the particular document as to which exemption was claimed, in order to avoid the possibility of impermissible 'commingling' by an agency's placing in an investigatory file material that did not legitimately have to be kept confidential." NLRB v. Robins Tire & Rubber Co., 437 U.S. 214, 229–230 (1978). Second, by enumerating six particular objectives of the exemption, the amendments required reviewing courts to "look to the reasons" for allowing withholding of information. Id., at 230. The requirement that one of six types of harm must be demonstrated to prevent production of a record compiled for law enforcement purposes was a reaction to a line of cases decided by the Court of Appeals for the District of Columbia Circuit which read the original Exemption 7 as protecting all law enforcement files.[11] The amendment requires that the government "specify some harm in order to claim the exemption" rather than "affording all law enforcement matters a blanket exemption." * * * The enumeration of these categories of undesirable consequences indicates Congress believed the harm of disclosing this type of information would outweigh its benefits. There is nothing to suggest, and no reason for believing, that Congress would have preferred a different outcome simply because the information is now reproduced in a non-law enforcement record.

The Court of Appeals would protect information compiled in a law enforcement record when transferred in original form to another agency for non-exempt purposes but would withdraw that protection if the same information or record is transmitted in slightly different form. In terms of the statutory objectives, this distinction makes little sense.[12] If the Court of Appeals is correct that this kind of information should be disclosed, its position leaves an obvious means of qualifying for the exemption—transmittal of the law enforcement records intact. Conversely, to the extent that Congress intended information initially gathered in the course of a law enforcement investigation to remain private, the Court of Appeals' decision creates a substantial prospect that this purpose, the very reason for Exemption 7's existence, will no longer be served.

Neither are we persuaded by the several other arguments Abramson submits in support of the decision below.

First, we reject the argument that the legitimate interests in protecting information from disclosure under Exemption 7 are satisfied by other exemptions when a record has been recompiled for a non-law

11. Senator Hart, the sponsor of the 1974 Amendment, stated specifically that the amendment's purpose was to respond to four decisions of the Court of Appeals for the District of Columbia Circuit which cumulatively held that all material found in an investigatory file compiled for law enforcement purposes was exempt, even if an enforcement proceeding were neither imminent nor likely. *Weisberg v. United States Department of Justice,* 489 F.2d 1195, 1198 (D.C.Cir.1973), cert. denied, 416 U.S. 993 (1974); *Aspin v. Department of Defense,* 491 F.2d 24, 30 (D.C.Cir.1973); *Ditlow v. Brinegar,* 494 F.2d 1073 (D.C.Cir.1974); *Center for National Policy Review on Race and Urban Issues v. Weinberger,* 502 F.2d 370 (D.C.Cir.1974). These four cases, in Senator Hart's view, erected a "stone wall" preventing public access to any material in an investigatory file.

12. Information transmitted for a non-law enforcement purpose may well still be used in an ongoing investigation. Moreover, by compromising the confidentiality of information gathered for law enforcement purposes, the Court of Appeals' decision could result in restricting the flow of essential information to the government. Deputy Attorney General Schmults stated before the Second Circuit Judicial Conference (May 9, 1981) that "[t]he risk of disclosure of FBI records has made private persons, nonfederal law enforcement officials, and informants reticent about providing vital information. Many informants have actually stopped cooperating with the FBI, for example, because they feared that their identities would be disclosed under the Act." Quoted in 16 Harv.Civil Rights-Civil Liberties L.Rev., at 315 (1981). See FOIA Update (Dept. of Justice, Sept. 1981) 1 ("[E]xperience of the FBI and DEA indicate that there is a widespread perception among confidential information sources that federal investigators cannot fully guarantee the confidentiality of information because of FOIA") The Drug Enforcement Administration claims that 40% of FOIA requests come from convicted felons, many of whom are seeking information with which to identify the informants who helped to convict them. Freedom of Information Act Oversight Hearings before Subcomm. of Comm. on Govt. Operations, 97th Cong., 1st Sess., 165 (Statement of Jonathan Rose, Dept. of Justice); see also Dept. of Justice, Attorney General's Task Force on Violent Crime, at 32 (1981).

The Court has previously recognized that the purposes of the exemptions do not disappear when information is incorporated in a new document or otherwise put to a different use. See *NLRB v. Sears, Roebuck & Co.,* 421 U.S. 132, 166 (1975) (Document protected by exemption 7 does not become discloseable solely because it is referred to in a final agency opinion; "reasons underlying Congress' decision to protect investigatory files remain applicable.")

enforcement purpose. In particular, Abramson submits that Exemption 6 suffices to protect the privacy interest of individuals. Even if this were so with respect to the particular information requested in this case, the threshold inquiry of what constitutes compilation for law enforcement purposes must be considered with regard for all six of the types of harm stemming from disclosure that Congress sought to prevent. Assuming that Exemption 6 provided fully comparable protection against disclosures which would constitute unwarranted invasions of privacy, a questionable proposition itself, no such companion provision in the FOIA would halt the disclosure of information that might deprive an individual of a fair trial, interrupt a law enforcement investigation, safeguard confidential law enforcement techniques, or even protect the physical well-being of law enforcement personnel. No other provision of FOIA could compensate for the potential disruption in the flow of information to law enforcement agencies by individuals who might be deterred from speaking because of the prospect of disclosure. It is therefore critical that the compiled-for-law-enforcement requirement be construed to avoid the release of information that would produce the undesirable results specified.

For much the same reason, the result we reach today is fully consistent without holding in NLRB v. Sears, Roebuck & Co., 421 U.S. 132, 148–154 (1975), that Exemption 5, § 552(b)(5), an exemption protecting from mandatory disclosure pre-decisional communications within an agency and the other internal documents, does not protect internal advisory communication when incorporated in a final agency decision. The purposes behind Exemption 5, protecting the give-and-take of the decisional process, were not violated by disclosure once an agency chooses expressly to adopt a particular text as its official view. As we have explained above, this cannot be said here. The reasons for a § 7 exemption may well remain intact even though information in a law enforcement record is recompiled in another document for a non-law enforcement function.

The result is also consistent with the oft-repeated caveat that FOIA exemptions are to be narrowly construed, Department of Air Force v. Rose, 425 U.S. at 361. While Congress established that the basic policy of the Act is in favor of disclosure, it recognized the important interests served by the exemptions. We are not asked in this case to expand Exemption 7 to agencies or material not envisioned by Congress: "It is * * * necessary for the very operation of our Government to allow it to keep confidential certain material such as the investigatory files of the Federal Bureau of Investigation." S.Rep.No. 813, 89 Cong. 1st Sess. 3 (1965). Reliance on this principle of narrow construction is particularly unpersuasive in this case where it is conceded that the information as originally compiled is exempt under Exemption 7 and where it is the respondent, not the Government, who urges a formalistic reading of the Act.

We are not persuaded that Congress's undeniable concern with possible misuse of governmental information for partisan political activity is the equivalent of a mandate to release any information which might document such activity. Congress did not differentiate between the purposes for which information was requested. NLRB v. Sears, Roebuck & Co., supra 421 U.S. at 149. Rather, the Act required assessment of the harm produced by disclosure of certain types of information. Once it is established that information was compiled pursuant to a legitimate law enforcement investigation and that disclosure of such information would lead to one of the listed harms, the information is exempt. Congress thus created a scheme of categorical exclusion; it did not invite a judicial weighing of the benefits and evils of disclosure on a case-by-case basis.

We therefore find that the construction adopted by the Court of Appeals, while plausible on the face of the statute, lacks support in the legislative history and would frustrate the purposes of Exemption 7. We hold that information initially contained in a record made for law-enforcement purposes continues to meet the threshold requirements of Exemption 7 where that recorded information is reproduced or summarized in a new document prepared for a non-law-enforcement purpose. Of course, it is the agency's burden to establish that the requested information originated in a record protected by Exemption 7. The Court of Appeals refused to consider such a showing as a sufficient reason for withholding certain information. The judgment of the Court of Appeals is therefore reversed and the case is remanded to that court for further proceedings consistent with this opinion.

So ordered.

COMMENT

Joined by Justices Blackmun, Brennan, and Marshall, Justice Sandra O'Connor dissented and charged the majority with rewriting FOIA's Exemption 7 to conform to its concept of public policy. The Exemption's legislative history, she said, left the Court "no reason for overriding the usual presumption that the plain language of a statute controls its construction." Furthermore, doubts ought to be resolved in favor of full agency disclosure. With her three dissenting colleagues, O'Connor agreed with the district court that the documents in the case had been compiled for political, not "law enforcement," purposes.

Taking umbrage and rejecting the premise that the meaning of the statute was plain, Justice White, in a footnote (fn. 7), called much of Justice O'Connor's dissent "rhetorical and beside the point."

Not all FOIA suits turn out as badly for access rights as *Abramson*. When *Playboy* sued the Justice Department for disclosure of a task force report on Gary Thomas Rowe, an FBI informant within the Ku Klux Klan, the department interposed Exemptions 2, 3, 5, 6, and 7 (A–D). The D.C. District Court found that Exemptions 2 (internal rules and practices of an agency) and 6 (unwarranted invasion of personal privacy) did not apply to any portion of the report. Nor would Exemption 5 block full disclosure since factual and informational portions of the report were reasonably segregable from those portions which contained the task force's advice, conclusions, and recommendations. Similarly, Exemption 3 was said to apply only to that information contained in the report which related solely to a grand jury proceeding and could be excised.

In view of the department's failure to show that the report itself was an investigatory record compiled for law enforcement purposes, Exemption 7 could not be invoked. Confidential information obtained solely from confidential sources, however, could be withheld. Playboy v. United States Justice Department, 7 Med.L. Rptr. 1269, 516 F.Supp. 233 (D.D.C.1981).

Exemption 8

This exemption protects federal agency reports about the condition of banks and other federally regulated financial institutions. Specifically it refers to records "contained in or related to examination, operating or condition reports prepared by, on behalf of, or for the use of an agency responsible for the regulation or supervision of financial institutions."

In part, Exemption 8 affirms the intention of Congress to protect confidential information similar to that protected by Exemption 4. In one of the few reported Exemption 8 cases, the District of Columbia District Court held that a Securities and Exchange Commission study of a broker-dealer trading problem did not fall within Exemption 8.[58] On the other hand, a New York federal district court noted in *dicta* that correspondence between a bank and the Federal Reserve Board would probably fall under the Exemption.[59]

Exemption 9

To inhibit speculation based on information about the location of private oil and gas wells, this Exemption incorporates "geological and geophysical information and data, including maps, concerning wells. * * *" The Federal Power Commission used Exemption 9 to deny Ralph Nader access to FPC and American Gas Association estimates of natural gas reserves. Nader contended that the Exemption only applied to geological data and maps that could benefit a competitor. The FPC countered that estimates of reserves were based on such data and indeed could be useful to competing firms.[60]

In 1972 Congress passed the Federal Advisory Committee Act, 5 U.S.C.App. 1, to provide access to information exchanges between the Executive branch of the federal government and outside interest groups that had proffered advice. Again there are exemptions to public access.[61]

The Family Education Rights and Privacy Act of 1974, 20 U.S.C. 1232g (sometimes referred to as the Buckley Amendments), gives parents and students right of access to their own educational records maintained by institutions which received federal funds.

GOVERNMENT–IN–SUNSHINE: THE FEDERAL OPEN MEETINGS LAW

On March 12, 1977, a Government-In-Sunshine Act requiring some fifty federal agencies, commissions, boards, and councils to hold their deliberative meetings in public became law. Any meeting—formal, regular, or bare quorum—in which business is discussed is presumed to be open. Ex parte communications occurring between interested persons and agency members with decision-making power are to be recorded and made part of the public record. Public notice of a meeting is to be made at least one week in advance, preferably with a meaningful agenda.

Since agencies under the new law were permitted to formulate their own rules for open meetings, some extended that process for as long as possible in order to remain tentative about implementation of the law. Even those agencies which were quick to implement the act soon found it more expedient to conduct business between and without regular meetings.

Closed meetings are permitted under ten exemptions, the first nine of which parallel FOIA's exemptions. A Common Cause study of the first three months of the Sunshine Act revealed that 39 percent of agency meetings were closed, 37 percent fully open, and 24 percent partially open. Those figures have since improved for most agencies, although there is frequent litigation over claimed loopholes. Exemption 10, covering an agency's involvement in litigation or adjudication, is

58. M.A. Schapiro & Co. v. SEC, 339 F.Supp. 467 (D.D.C.1972).

59. Kaye v. Burns, 411 F.Supp. 897 (D.N.Y.1976).

60. House Committee on Government Operations, Hearings on U.S. Government Information Policies and Practices—Administration and Operation of the Freedom of Information Act, 92d Cong., 2d Sess., 1972, pt. 6, at 1970–72. See also, Amerada Hess Corp., 50 FPC 1048, 1050–51 (1973).

61. Food Chemical News, Inc. v. Davis, 378 F.Supp. 1048 (D.D.C.1974); Nader v. Baroody, 396 F.Supp. 1231 (D.D.C.1975).

invoked often to save a case or a reputation.

The case that follows involved an attempt by the Nuclear Regulatory Commission to close its budget preparation process. In deciding for the plaintiff, Common Cause, the D.C. Circuit Court of Appeals noted that, unlike FOIA, the Sunshine Act was designed to open, not close, the predecisional deliberative process. Here the government unit cited a clause of Exemption 9, an exemption generally closing meetings where disclosure would lead to significant financial speculation or endanger the stability of a financial institution or interfere with a proposed agency action. It also cited Exemptions 2 and 6.

COMMON CAUSE v. NUCLEAR REGULATORY COMMISSION

8 MED.L.RPTR. 1190, 674 F.2D 921 (D.C.Cir.1982).

WRIGHT, J.:

* * *

The language of the exemption is not self-explanatory; we therefore turn to the legislative history for guidance. The House and Senate committee reports give four concrete examples of Exemption 9(B) situations. First, an agency might consider imposing an embargo on foreign shipment of certain goods; if this were publicly known, all of the goods might be exported before the agency had time to act, and the effectiveness of the proposed action would be destroyed. * * * Second, an agency might discuss whether to approve a proposed merger; premature public disclosure of the proposal might make it impossible for the two sides to reach agreement. * * * Third, disclosure of an agency's proposed strategy in collective bargaining with its employees might make it impossible to reach an agreement. * * * Fourth, disclosure of an agency's terms and conditions for purchase of real property might make the proposed purchase impossible or drive up the price.

We construe Exemption 9(B) to cover those situations delineated by the narrow general principles which encompass all four legislative examples. In each of these cases, disclosure of the agency's proposals or negotiating position could affect private decisions by parties other than those who manage the federal government —exporters, potential corporate merger partners, government employees, or owners of real property. The private responses of such persons might damage the regulatory or financial interests of the government as a whole, because in each case the agency's proposed action is one for which the agency takes final responsibility as a governmental entity.

The budget process differs substantially from the examples given by the House and Senate reports. Disclosure of the agency's discussions would not affect private parties' decisions concerning regulated activity or dealings with the government. Rather, the Commission contends that opening budget discussions to the public might affect political decisions by the President and OMB [Office of Management and Budget, which has an oversight responsibility for access laws]. In addition, disclosure would not directly affect "agency action" for which the Commission has the ultimate responsibility. Instead, the Commission fears that disclosure of its time-honored strategies of item-shifting, exaggeration, and fallback positions would give it less leverage in its "arm's length" dealings with OMB and the President, who make the final budget decisions within the Executive Branch. The Commission argues that it would thereby be impaired in its competition with other government agencies—which also serve the public and implement federal legislation—for its desired share of budgetary resources. It is not clear, however, whether the interests of the government as a whole, or the public interest, would be adversely affected.

Moreover, in the budget context the public interest in disclosure differs markedly from its interest in the four situations described in the committee reports. In those cases disclosure would permit either financial gain at government expense or circumvention of agency regulation. In contrast, disclosure of budget deliberations would serve the affirmative purposes of the Sunshine Act: to open government deliberations to public scrutiny, to inform the public "what facts and policy considerations the agency found important in reaching its decision, and what alternatives it considered and rejected," and thereby to permit "wider and more informed public debate of the agency's policies * * *." S.Rep. No. 94–354, at 5–6.

The budget deliberation process is of exceptional importance in agency policymaking. The agency heads must review the entire range of agency programs and responsibilities in order to establish priorities. According to the Commission, a budget meeting "candidly consider[s] the merits and efficiencies of on-going or expected regulatory programs or projects" and then "decides upon the level of regulatory activities it proposes to pursue * *." * * * These decisions, the government contends, have a significant impact on "the Commission's ability to marshal regulatory powers in a manner which insures the greatest protection of the public health and safety with the most economical use of its limited resources." * * *

If Congress had wished to exempt these deliberations from the Sunshine Act—to preserve the prior practice of budget confidentiality, to reduce the opportunities for lobbying before the President submits his budget to Congress, or for other reasons—it would have expressly so indicated. Absent any such statement of legislative intent, we will not construe Exemption 9(B) of the Sunshine Act to allow budget deliberations to be hidden from the public view.

Thus, the Sunshine Act contains no express exemption for budget deliberations as a whole. Specific items discussed at budget meetings might, however, be exempt and might justify closing portions of commission meetings on an individual and particularized basis.

* * *

1. EXEMPTION 9(B)

Exemption 9(B), as we have discussed, protects agency discussions of material whose premature disclosure could affect the decisions or actions of third parties acting in a nongovernmental capacity, thus causing a significant adverse effect upon the government's financial or regulatory interests. * * * Budget meetings might include discussions of specific topics within the coverage of the exemption. Premature disclosure of possible elimination of a program involving private contracts might make it difficult for the contractor to retain key personnel, frustrating the Commission's ability to implement the program effectively if it is not ultimately eliminated. * * * Premature disclosure of proposed cutbacks in joint research projects with foreign governments might adversely affect the United States government's position in negotiations concerning the foreign government's commitment. Premature disclosure of collective bargaining negotiation strategies might adversely affect labor negotiations with the Commission's own employees.

Even if a budget meeting is likely to discuss these topics, however, it may not be closed under Exemption 9(B) "in any instance where the agency has already disclosed to the public the content or nature of its proposed action[.]" 5 U.S.C. § 552b(c)(9)(B) (1976). The Senate report explained that the exemption "only applies when an agency feels it must act in secret[.]" S.Rep. No. 94–354, *supra,* at 25. Therefore if the private contractor, foreign government, or labor union has already been informed by the Commission that budget cutbacks are being considered in the programs with which they are concerned, then Exemption 9(B) might no longer apply.

Our *in camera* inspection of the transcripts of the July 27, 1981 and October 15, 1981 Commission meetings leads us to conclude that Exemption 9(B) does not support withholding of any portion of the transcripts.

2. EXEMPTION 2

The Commission also relies on Exemption 2—matters that "relate solely to the internal personnel rules and practices of an agency[,]" 5 U.S.C. § 552b(c)(2) (1976)—to justify closing portions of budget meetings. Under the Commission's interpretation, Exemption 2 includes discussions of allocation of personnel among programs, evaluations of the performance of offices and projects within the Commission, and consideration of more economical schemes of "internal management." * * * This construction is belied by the statutory language and legislative history of Exemption 2.

The language in Exemption 2 to the Government in the Sunshine Act is virtually identical with that in Exemption 2 to the Freedom of Information Act. * * * The conference report on the Sunshine Act expressly adopts the standards of Department of Air Force v. Rose, 425 U.S. 352 * * (1976), the leading Supreme Court decision interpreting Exemption 2 of FOIA. * * * Under this standard, personnel-related discussions at budget meetings fall squarely outside the scope of the exemption.

Budget allocations inevitably impinge on personnel matters, because government cannot implement programs without personnel. Salaries and wages are a sizable proportion of the Commission's budget. But budget decisions regarding personnel cutbacks, and evaluations of the prior performance of offices and programs, do not relate *solely* to "internal personnel rules and procedures." Discussions of possible administrative cost savings through adoption of new "internal management" techniques also fall beyond the narrow confines of Exemption 2, because they deal with the impact of budget cuts on the Commission's ability to carry out its responsibilities.

Throughout this litigation the Commission has emphasized the importance of the budget process. An affidavit submitted by the Commission asserts that budget discussions lead to presidential recommendations reflecting the President's "best judgment of how the nation's fiscal resources should be allocated to meet its future economic and social needs." * * * The affidavit recognizes that "vital policies and billions of dollars [are] at issue every year[.]" The public can reasonably be expected to have an interest in matters of such importance. Exemption 2 does not permit the Commission to close budget discussions relating to personnel cutbacks or performance.

In some budget meetings the exemption might permit the Commission to close specific portions of the discussion relating "solely to internal personnel rules and practices." However, *in camera* inspection shows that Exemption 2 does not apply to any portion of either the July 27, 1981 or the October 15, 1981 meeting.

3. EXEMPTION 6

The government invoked Exemption 6 to justify its decisions to close both meetings at issue; it no longer claims that the exemption protects any of the deliberations at the October 15 meeting. Exemption 6 protects information of a personal nature whose disclosure would constitute "an unwarranted invasion of personal privacy[.]" 5 U.S.C. § 552b(c)(6) (1976). The agency contends that this exemption protects discussion of "an individual manager's particular qualifications, characteristics and professional competence in connection with a budget request for that particular manager's program." * * * This contention is unsupported by the legislative history of the Sunshine Act.

Exemption 6 applies to information of a personal nature, including discussions of a person's health, drinking habits, or financial circumstances. It provides greater protection to private individuals, including applicants for federal grants and officials of regulated private companies, and to low-level government employees, than to government officials with executive responsibilities. * * * S.Rep. No. 94–354, *supra,* at 21–22. It was not intended to shelter substandard performance by government executives. The Senate report expressly noted that "if the discussion centered on the alleged incompetence with which a Government official has carried out his duties it might well be appropriate to keep the meeting open, since in that case the public has a special interest in knowing how well agency employees are carrying out their public responsibilities." Exemption 6, the report added, "must not be used by an agency to shield itself from political controversy involving the agency and its employees about which the public should be informed." *Id.* at 21–22. These policy considerations apply *a fortiori* in the budget process, in which the performance of individual executives may affect the Commission's willingness to allocate budgetary resources to particular regulatory programs.

Given the narrow scope of Exemption 6 as applied to managerial officials, we hold that no portion of the discussion at the July 27, 1981 meeting was covered by Exemption 6. The Commission's discussion of individual performance was limited to managerial officials with executive responsibility.

E. COMPLIANCE WITH THE SUNSHINE ACT

Our *in camera* inspection of the transcripts of the July 27, 1981 and October 15, 1981 Commission meetings does not show that any portion of either meeting may be withheld from the public under any of the asserted exemptions to the Sunshine Act. We therefore order the Commission to release the transcripts to the public. * * * The transcripts shall be made available in a place readily accessible to the public, and copies shall be furnished to any person at the actual cost of duplication.

If in the future the Commission wishes to close all or any portion of a budget meeting, the statute requires it to announce its intention and to give a brief statement of its reasons. If any person objects to closing of the meeting, he may file a civil action in the District Court to compel the Commission to comply with the statute. He may include an application for interlocutory relief in his complaint, if the meeting has not yet been held. The District Court should act promptly on any motion for interim relief to avoid frustration of the purposes of the Sunshine Act through delay. In its decision on the merits the District Court may examine *in camera* the transcripts of closed agency meetings and may issue such relief as it deems appropriate, with due regard for orderly administration and the public interest. * * *

OPEN RECORDS AND MEETINGS IN THE STATES

Open Records

1. In 1982, fifty states, the District of Columbia, and the Virgin Islands had open records (freedom of information) laws of some kind. They vary widely, change rapidly, and are therefore difficult to summarize.[62] State courts may construe them

62. The best such effort is Braverman and Heppler, *A Practical Review of State Open Record Laws,* 49 George Washington L.Rev. 720 (May 1981).

broadly or narrowly. Some are more effective than others. Since it is difficult to generalize about them, journalists must know the law of the state in which they work.

If one were designing a model statute, the following elements and issues would be important to consider:

a. How are public records defined and by whom? The more expansive the definition, the better for information seekers. State law definitions generally depend on two factors—physical form and the origin of the public record. Physical form may be stated in the law or implied. A Minnesota Supreme Court decision held that agency records (state subsidized abortions) stored on computer tapes were public records subject to the law.[63] In an Ohio case, microfilm was similarly defined.[64] As to origin, most state laws and court rulings consider the source of the record and the reason for its being kept. On this point, some laws are expansive,[65] some restrictive, covering, for example, only material "required to be kept by law" [66] or "pursuant to law."[67]

As with FOIA, agencies are not required to create or acquire records in response to a request; they are responsible only for existing, identifiable records in their possession and subject to the law.

Definitions of agencies subject to the law are broad and sometimes tied to public funding, in whole or in part. Nongovernmental agencies receiving public funds may also be included. A state-created agency that is federally funded and performs federal functions could be subject to both state open records laws and FOIA.

A majority of states have separate open records laws for their courts and legislatures, and case law appears to support courts' being defined as public agencies.[68] There is no comparable case law for access to legislatures.

Of all restrictions on access to records, the broadest is a "public interest nondisclosure" provision as found in the laws of California [69] and Colorado.[70] Arizona and New York courts, among others, have held that a common law nondisclosure privilege survives if the law does not speak to it.

Ideally, all records, whether required to be kept or not and for whatever purpose, ought to be included in a definition of records. And they should be defined as to content as well as to source (custodial officer or agency).

b. Who may use the laws and for what purpose? In most states the right applies to "any person," as is the case with FOIA. But some eighteen state laws restrict access to citizens of the state. No state retains the common law requirement that a requester have a "special interest." Corporations, partnerships, firms, citizens groups, and associations are included as requesters in state statutes and in their interpretation by the courts. In three states—Arizona, Rhode Island, and Washington—the requester must have "no commercial purpose." State courts have considered a requester's purpose in determining whether an exemption covers the ma-

63. Minnesota Medical Association v. State, 4 Med.L.Rptr. 1872, 274 N.W.2d 84 (Minn.1978).

64. Lorain County Title Co. v. Essex, 373 N.E.2d 1261 (Ohio 1976).

65. Iowa Code Ann. § 68A.1 (West 1973); Fla.Stat.Ann. § 119.011 (West Supp. 1974–1980.

66. Ohio Rev. Code Ann. § 149.43 (Page 1980).

67. Mo.Ann.Stat. § 109.180 (Vernon 1966).

68. Northwest Publications v. Howard, 259 N.W.2d 254 (Minn.1977). See also, Atchinson Topeka & Santa Fe Railway v. Lopez, 531 P.2d 455 (Kan.1975), Ex parte Farley, 570 S.W.2d 617 (Ky.1978).

69. Cal.Govt. Code § 6255 (Deering 1976).

70. Colo.Rev.Stat. § 24–72–204(6) (1974). Iowa, Maryland, New Jersey and Wyoming may also be added to this list.

terial, but usually the record keeper has no discretion over "purpose."

c. What exemptions ought to be allowed? In all states, prior statutes exempt from disclosure specific kinds of information, but state open records laws rarely specify which earlier laws are overriding. Generally they fall in the categories of welfare, tax, bank, education, medical, unemployment compensation, child placement or abuse, and law enforcement and criminal history records.

The last-named category has been unusually problematical for reporters. When a newspaper requested records under New York's Freedom of Information Law, records having to do with complaints of police harassment and use of force, the information was said to constitute personnel records and was therefore exempt.[71] A Missouri Sunshine Law amendment provided for expungement of certain arrest records. When the *St. Louis Globe Democrat* challenged the amendment on grounds of both the First Amendment and the Missouri constitution, it was turned back. *Richmond Newspapers* was said by a Missouri federal district court not to apply because that decision was based on a "tradition" of public attendance at trials. There was no such "tradition" of public access to arrest records.[72]

Exemptions are often those included in the federal FOIA, and courts are expected to resolve conflicts with the public interest in favor of disclosure. State laws are divided between those which make disclosure mandatory and those which make it discretionary. In the absence of legislative guidance, state courts could follow FOIA's *Chrysler Corp. v. Brown*, making agency disclosure discretionary even though an exemption has been shown to apply.

Some state laws contain myriad exemptions. Michigan's Freedom of Information Act has twenty. Wisconsin, Alabama, and North Dakota laws have none. New York's open records law specifies what records are to be open instead of assuming that all governmental records are open by definition, except those expressly exempted.

The most common exemptions found in state laws are the familiar categories of information made confidential by state or federal law, law enforcement and investigatory files, trade secrets and commercial information, predecisional departmental communications, personal privacy, and information relating to litigation against a public body. Ten states have added tax return data and land value information. A few state laws exempt test and examination scores.

FOIA's requirement that "reasonably segregable" portions of a record be disclosed even if other portions are exempt is followed in only five states. State courts have interpreted state laws, however, to meet the federal requirement, illustrating once again that the well-developed body of federal law provides precedent for state cases.

d. Is agency information indexed, and is there a right to copy government documents? Most state laws would permit an index; a few require them. And all state laws, except Indiana's, provide for copying at specified and reasonable rates. Only South Carolina's law follows FOIA in waiving search and copy costs when it is

71. Gannett Co. v. James, 7 Med.L.Rptr. 1294, 438 N.Y.S.2d 901 (1981). Similar results have occurred in North Carolina, North Dakota, Ohio, Oklahoma, Oregon, Pennsylvania, Rhode Island, South Carolina, South Dakota, Tennessee, Texas, Utah, Vermont, Virgin Islands, Virginia, Washington, West Virginia, Wisconsin, and Wyoming.

72. Herald Company v. McNeal, 7 Med.L.Rptr. 1248, 511 F.Supp. 269 (Mo.1981). Similar results have occurred in Montana, Nebraska, New Hampshire, New Jersey, New Mexico, and New York.

in the "public interest" to do so.[73]

e. What procedures must a citizen, or the press, follow in gaining access to records, and how are state open records laws enforced? Only California's law provides FOIA-type guidance for a requester.[74] Time limits for an agency response to a request for information vary from three days in Kentucky to no limit in most states. Rhode Island and District of Columbia laws specify the consequences of failure to comply within their time limits: this would constitute a denial indicating that the requester has exhausted administrative remedies and may seek judicial review. In other states the requester could seek a writ of mandamus to compel a response or assume that inaction is a denial of a request warranting judicial review.

Some state laws allow courts to grant injunctive relief or to require agencies to show cause why such relief should not be granted. In all but sixteen states the laws specifically provide for judicial review, and most provide for *de novo* review of denials and a right of *in camera* inspection by the courts. Here a court may determine the applicability of a claimed exemption unfettered by any presumption in favor of the legitimacy of the agency determination.

Many state laws provide for action intermediate to an agency decision or a court ruling such as appeal to the agency, to the state attorney general, or a state FOI commission. Some are optional, some mandatory.

As with FOIA, the burden of proof in state open records laws is on the agencies. And as to penalties for noncompliance, eighteen states provide criminal sanctions, eight civil fines, and fifteen no penalties at all. Ten state laws have provisions for reimbursing attorney's fees where there has been improper denial by an agency. Many state access procedures need to be streamlined in terms of expense and delay.

However fluid the foregoing figures may be, and in spite of sanctions in some state laws, there remains a great deal of *de facto* classification and denial of access by state agencies. Reporters, their editors, their organizations, and their attorneys must be watchful of those in government who would close, often capriciously and arbitrarily, public records and meetings to public scrutiny.

Denials of access to records which appear to be illegal should be challenged. The journalist should speak to supervisors, ask for written authority for denial, write down reasons given for denial, and generally do what is necessary to develop a record covering the incident. When exceptions or exemptions are cited, they should be presented with precision.

2. In the 80s, state legislators sought to amend or repeal many state open records laws by introducing a Uniform Information Practices Act, brainchild of the National Association of Uniform Laws Commissions. An omnibus records/privacy statute, its effect would be to complicate easily understood records laws and to give almost unlimited discretion to agency heads as to when and when not to release information.

The stated purpose of the law, of course, was to protect the privacy interests of individuals who, in a complex society, increasingly become the subjects of governmental record-keeping systems.

Open Meetings

1. All states, the District of Columbia, and the Virgin Islands have open meetings

73. S.C. Code § 30–4–30(b) (Cum.Supp.1980).

74. Cal.Govt. Code § 6257 (Derring 1973).

laws or constitutional provisions guaranteeing some degree of access to public meetings. Again there are substantial differences from state to state, and these laws are frequently amended. An ideal and comprehensive open meetings law would contain the following provisions:

a. *Access* would apply to both houses of the legislature and its committees, and to all state agencies, boards, commissions, and other political subdivisions of the state, including county boards and city councils. Some statutes use a "public funds" or "public functions" test.

b. *Executive sessions,* and other evasive techniques involving the transaction of public business, should not be exempted. A rule of reason, however, may attach to *purely* informal or social interactions between members of a public body. A quorum should not be a condition of access. Since preliminary steps in the deliberative process may be important to a final outcome, meetings of advisory committees ought to be included within the law. Minutes ought to be kept, and all votes recorded.

c. *Exemptions* ought to be stated precisely, although many state statutes do not allow them. Where exemptions are not included, state attorneys general and courts have made advisory or judicial determinations that consultations between an agency and its attorney regarding pending litigation, some disciplinary hearings, and public employee collective bargaining sessions are exempt.

d. *Enforcement* procedures must be available to press and public, and they must be expeditious. A few statutes declare null and void any official actions taken in secret sessions. Again, injunction or writ of mandamus is the appropriate recourse, and it should be written into the law.

c. *Sanctions* should be imposed on those officials who violate the law. Most open meeting laws contain a provision making violation of the act a misdemeanor. Others impose a civil fine. Criminal penalties are rare. Minnesota alone makes a third violation of its open meeting law punishable by forfeiture of the right to serve on the public body or in the public agency for a period of time equal to the term of office the person was then serving.

2. Many problems remain. Some open meetings laws lack definitions and penalties for noncompliance. Unannounced, irregular, or informal meetings are not covered. Other laws are riddled with loopholes or specified exemptions. Courts are frequently reluctant to breach the separation of powers doctrine by interpreting open meetings laws to apply to the legislative branch of government, and courts protect their own prerogatives as well.

Nevertheless, the open meetings situation is decidedly better than it was a decade ago, and a survey of state cases indicates that when secret meetings are challenged by press and public—and they must be—, under state laws, plaintiffs prevail in a very high proportion of cases. Of course, many closed-door meetings are never challenged.

When denied attendance, ask for reasons and a vote, and try to get it all recorded in the minutes. Be respectful, but do not leave a meeting until ordered to do so. Know what the exceptions are, of course, in your state.

THE CONFLICT BETWEEN OPENNESS AND DATA PRIVACY

The Federal Privacy Act of 1974

In 1974 Congress passed a comprehensive federal Privacy Act. Although its drafters did express concern about nongovernmental record-keeping, the statute deals only with the vast record-creating and computer storage capabilities of federal agencies. The law seeks to protect individual rights against government misuse of personal data by letting citizens know what kinds of files and record systems are being kept and by allowing individuals a right of access to those files so that they can be corrected or challenged if necessary.[75]

Use the FOI Service Center sample Privacy Act request letter (see fn. 32) in making a request. Unlike FOIA, the Privacy Act does not permit agencies to charge for search time, but you will have to pay for duplication. The agency supervising the administration of the act, the Office of Management and Budget, expects other agencies to acknowledge receipt of your request within ten working days and to provide access, if access is to be granted, within thirty days.

Of special interest is that part of the act which prohibits federal agencies from maintaining any records concerning an exercise of First Amendment rights unless authorized by statute, part of an authorized law enforcement activity, or based upon an individual's own consent. This rule prevented the Internal Revenue Service, for example, from keeping records of its surveillance of speeches made by nuclear war protestors, and all records of that kind already in its keeping had to be expunged.[76] It might be assumed that journalists, authors, scholars, and researchers would be primarily engaged in First Amendment activities. And the rule covers peaceful protesting and pamphleteering.

Unless a record is open to public inspection under FOIA, or under one of the Privacy Act's 11 exemptions, a government agency must have a file subject's written consent before it can disclose that file to a third party. An agency must also notify a file subject if it intends to disclose, and it must keep an accounting of certain kinds of disclosure.

Scores of recommendations have been made for amending the act.[77] While the data-collecting activities of an agency are not limited by the act, failure to comply with its specific provisions on disclosure permits an individual to bring a civil suit in a federal district court. To recover damages, attorney's fees and court costs a plaintiff must show that the agency "acted in a manner which was intentional and willful"—a rather heavy burden.

While FOIA's purpose was to increase *public* access to governmental information, the Privacy Act was designed to provide *individuals* more control over the gathering, dissemination, and accuracy of information kept by government about them. The latter is an FOIA for the individual. Surveillance by the government in the name of the public, or surveillance by public and press for its own sake, inevitably collides with personal privacy. How can the two social values be articulated? Can an informed public tolerate insulated individuals? A newspaper's demand for arrest records may be motivated by a desire to assess the performance of a police department, but the consequences may be exposure of individual third-party transgression. It is important to know when denials of disclosure are based on the long tradition of official secrecy and suppression of information and when they are based on a genuine concern for a legal or constitutional right of personal privacy.

The Privacy Act of 1974, as has been noted, contains eleven exemptions to its general prohibition of disclosure of personal files. These apply to entire systems

75. For the language of the Privacy Act, see 5 U.S.C. 552a.

76. Clarkson v. IRS, 8 Med.L.Rptr. 1933, 678 F.2d 1368 (11th Cir. 1982).

77. Report of the Privacy Protection Study Commission, Personal Privacy in an Information Society, Washington, D.C.: GPO, 1977.

of records rather than to specific requests for particular documents as under FOIA. One of the exemptions, (2), provides that a record may be disclosed without written consent of the person about whom the record is kept if disclosure *"would be * * required under Section 552 of this title."* Section 552 is the Freedom of Information Act.

At the same time, FOIA's Exemption 6 states that FOIA disclosure does not apply to matters that are "personnel and medical files and similar files the disclosure of which would constitute *a clearly unwarranted invasion of personal privacy.*"

If it is required that a document be made public by FOIA, then it cannot be suppressed by the Privacy Act. As Judge David Bazelon of the D.C. Circuit Court of Appeals put it: "We must conclude * * * that section (b)(2) of the Privacy Act represents a Congressional mandate that the Privacy Act *not* be used as a barrier to FOIA access." Greentree v. Customs Service, 8 Med.L.Rptr. 1510, 515 F.Supp. 1145 (D.C.Cir.1981). Privacy defers to openness. Government policy has been to allow individuals access to their own files through both FOIA and the Privacy Act. *Greentree* supported the notion that what is exempt from disclosure to an individual under the Privacy Act is not necessarily exempt from the same person under FOIA.

An agency may not use FOIA exemptions as a technicality to deny citizens access to their own files: the Privacy Act states that "no agency shall rely on any exemption contained [in FOIA] to withhold from an individual any record which is otherwise accessible to such individual under the provisions of this section."

Requests for disclosures to third parties are made under FOIA rather than under the Privacy Act. "When the two Acts are read together," said the Privacy Protection Study Commission, "any disclosure of a record about an individual in a system of records as defined by the Privacy Act to any member of the public other than the individual to whom the record pertains is forbidden if the disclosure would constitute a 'clearly unwarranted invasion of personal privacy.' " The reverse obligation also holds: even though a record is about an individual, it cannot be withheld from any member of the public who requests it if the disclosure would *not* constitute "a clearly unwarranted invasion of personal privacy." [78]

There are critics of the way in which the two social interests have been connected. And there is some truth in the words of one that "conflicts between the confidentiality approach of the Privacy Act and the disclosures requirements of the Freedom of Information Act are resolved entirely in favor of the latter." [79]

Openness and privacy represent an almost natural conflict: add to one and you subtract from the other. Courts will have to decide what constitutes a "clearly unwarranted invasion of personal privacy." So far the advantage has gone to openness. This bias was reflected in the Supreme Court's language in *Cox Broadcasting v. Cohn,* although that case dealt with a category of common law privacy rather than data privacy, and the offending information was held in a judicial record:

> Thus even the prevailing law of invasion of privacy generally recognizes that the interests in privacy fade when the information involved already appears on the public record. * * * The freedom of the press to publish that information appears to be of critical importance to our type of government in which the citizenry is the final judge

78. *Ibid.,* p. 25. See also, Bushkin and Schaen, *The Privacy Act of 1974: A Reference Manual for Compliance,* 1976.

79. Greenwalt, *Legal Protections of Privacy, Final Report to the Office of Telecommunications Policy,* Washington, D.C.: 1975; O'Brien, *Privacy, Law and Public Policy,* 1979.

of the proper conduct of public business.[80]

As has been noted, for file subjects the Privacy Act functions as an FOIA statute. Prior to its passage, access refusals under FOIA Exemption 6 (personnel and medical files) were discretionary, not mandatory. An agency could withhold information the disclosure of which would constitute a "clearly unwarranted invasion of personal privacy," but it was not required to do so. Since passage of the Privacy Act, an agency *must* disclose to a file subject where there is no invasion of personal privacy.

In some circumstances FOIA provides more access to individual files than does the Privacy Act. Because the latter provides blanket exemptions for whole systems of records kept by CIA and other investigative and law enforcement agencies, FOIA may be more useful for gaining access to one's own files. In addition, there is no "relevance" requirement for information sought under FOIA.

It should be noted that what might be exempt from disclosure under the Privacy Act as "specifically exempted from disclosure by statute," would also be exempt for the same reason under FOIA's Exemption 3.

There is still much confusion about the articulation of both state and federal access and privacy laws, the latter often being cited as authority for withholding information when in fact such withholding is improper.

Data Privacy in the States

California's Information Practices Act of 1977 is in effect a privacy act and is called that by officials. This act and others like it suffer the same definitional deficiencies of other records statutes and, as would be expected, clash with state open records laws. Only perfunctory efforts have been made at the state level to synchronize the two kinds of records laws.

Taking a cue from the federal Privacy Act of 1974, at least twenty states led by Minnesota, have since passed data practices or privacy laws. Among the leaders, in addition to California, were Arkansas, Connecticut, Indiana, Massachusetts, Ohio, Utah, and Virginia. These are variably called data practices acts, fair information practices acts, or confidentiality of data acts, but they are all designed to protect particular categories of personal privacy. Since they are frequently amended, public access advocates have to remain alert.

State privacy commission studies preceded passage of the Minnesota, Massachusetts, and Indiana statutes, and similar study groups have been established in other states, including Iowa and New Jersey. By 1980 the National Conference of Commissioners on Uniform State Laws had developed a Uniform Information Practices Code. Although premised on openness of public records except where there is a strong presumption of privacy (employment applications and evaluations, for example), there are serious problems of overbreadth in the proposal. Criminal investigation information, especially arrest records, would fall in the protected category.

All existing data privacy laws do protect from disclosure criminal investigation records, either directly or by implication. They also require that record system descriptions be published, that individually identifiable information be relevant, accurate, timely and complete, and that the use and disclosure of information be restricted. Access and the right to challenge the accuracy of file contents rests only with persons about whom the files are kept. Most state statutes comply with the federal requirement that records kept in con-

80. *Law and Public Policy*, 1979. 420 U.S. 469 (1975), see p. 337 this text.

nection with federally funded assistance programs remain confidential. In Minnesota's law, "confidential" means that neither the person named nor anyone else outside government can get the information; "private" information is available to the file subject or that person's agent.

In Kentucky, openness and data privacy are dealt with in a single statute. Similar efforts made in successive sessions of the Minnesota legislature have created much confusion and threatened public access.

Violations of data privacy resemble the common law privacy offense of intrusion in that both are news-gathering offenses. The difference is that the federal Privacy Act of 1974 and its state counterparts are designed chiefly to protect the "inviolate personality" from the power of government or governmental procedures. One might speculate on the degree to which corporate power, including that of the media, might match the government in jeopardizing personal privacy.

Should defining categories of privacy be a legislative or judicial task? The Minnesota legislature has done it with its categories of public, private, and confidential. At the federal level, the courts will eventually do it by deciding what is meant by "clearly unwarranted invasions of personal privacy."

VI

Access to the Judicial Process: Free Press and Fair Trial

THE PARAMETERS OF THE CONFLICT

1. "I remember one of those sorrowful farces, in Virginia," Mark Twain recounts in *Roughing It,* "which we call a jury trial. A noted desperado killed Mr. B., a good citizen, in the most wanton and cold-blooded way. Of course the papers were full of it, and all men capable of reading read about it. And of course all men not deaf and dumb and idiotic talked about it. A jury list was made out, and Mr. B.L., a prominent banker and a valued citizen, was questioned precisely as he would have been questioned in any court in America:

'Have you heard of this homicide?'

'Yes.'

'Have you held conversations upon the subject?'

'Yes.'

'Have you formed or expressed opinions about it?'

'Yes.'

'Have you read the newspaper accounts of it?'

'Yes.'

'We do not want you.'

"A minister, intelligent, esteemed, and greatly respected; a merchant of high character and known probity; a mining superintendent of intelligence and unblemished reputation; a quartz-mill owner of excellent standing, were all questioned in the same way, and all set aside. Each said the public talk and the newspaper reports had not so biased his mind but that sworn testimony would overthrow his previously formed opinions and enable him to render a verdict without prejudice and in accordance with the facts. But of course such men could not be trusted with the case. Ignoramuses alone could mete out unsullied justice.

"When the peremptory challenges were all exhausted, a jury of twelve men was impaneled—a jury who swore they had neither heard, read, talked about, nor expressed an opinion concerning a murder which the very cattle in the corrals, the Indians in the sage-brush, and the stones in the streets were cognizant of! It was a jury composed of two desperadoes, two low beer-house politicians, three barkeepers, two ranchmen who could not read, and three dull, stupid, human donkeys! It actually came out afterward, that one of these latter thought that incest and arson were the same thing.

"The verdict rendered by this jury was, Not Guilty. What else could one expect?

"The jury system puts a ban upon intelligence and honesty, and a premium upon ignorance, stupidity, and perjury. It is a shame that we must continue to use a worthless system because it *was* good a thousand years ago. In this age, when a gentleman of high social standing, intelligence, and probity, swears that testimony given under solemn oath will outweigh, with him, street talk and newspaper reports based upon mere hearsay, he is worth a hundred jurymen who will swear to their own ignorance and stupidity, and justice would be far safer in his hands than in theirs. Why could not the jury law be so altered as to give men of brains and honesty an *equal chance* with fools and miscreants? Is it right to show the present favoritism to one class of men and inflict a disability on another, in a land whose boast is that all its citizens are free and equal? I am a candidate for the legislature. I desire to tamper with the jury law. I wish to so alter it as to put a premium on intelligence and character, and close the jury-box against idiots, blacklegs, and people who do not read newspapers. But no doubt I shall be defeated—every effort I make to save the country 'misses fire.' "

Twain's seriocomic reference is not intended to foreclose debate on the clash between reporter and suspect interests in free press and fair trial, but rather to focus attention on what is still the central question of a contentious dialogue: what *is* the effect of trial and pretrial information on jury verdicts?

Judge Charles Clark, writing for the Second Circuit Court of Appeals in 1951, might have had Twain's admonition in mind when he said:

> Trial by newspaper may be unfortunate, but it is not new and, unless the court accepts the standard judicial hypothesis that cautioning instructions are effective, criminal trials in the metropolitan centers may well prove impossible.

During trial, a copy of the *New York Times,* containing an inaccurate report, had found its way into the jury room. The trial judge reasoned that, since he had given explicit instructions to the jury to disregard the newspaper and had pointed out how the offenses set forth in the indictment differed from those described in the article, there was no error in allowing the trial to proceed.

In a bristling dissent in the same case, Judge Jerome Frank did invoke Mark Twain. "My colleagues admit that 'trial by newspaper' is unfortunate," he declared. "But they dismiss it as an unavoidable curse of metropolitan living (like, I suppose, crowded subways). They rely on the old 'ritualistic admonition' to purge the record. The futility of that sort of exorcism is notorious. As I have elsewhere observed, it is like the Mark Twain story of the little boy who was told to stand in a corner and not to think of a white elephant."[1]

"The naive assumption," said Justice Robert Jackson of the United States Supreme Court in an earlier case, "that prejudicial effects can be overcome by instructions to the jury, all practicing lawyers know to be unmitigated fiction."[2]

Unwilling to rely on this kind of speculation, social scientists in recent years have attempted to measure by survey and experiment the *real* effects of trial and pretrial publication on jury verdicts. Their findings have been equivocal and contradictory. Their methodologies have been faulted for failing to replicate the actual world of the juror.[3] If a hesitant

1. Leviton v. United States, 193 F.2d 848 (2d Cir. 1951), cert. den. 343 U.S. 946 (1952).

2. Krulewitch v. United States, 336 U.S. 440 (1949).

3. Wilcox and McCombs, *Confession Induces Belief in Guilt: Criminal Record and Evidence Do Not,* ANPA News Research Bulletin 15, July 7, 1966; Kline and Jess, *Prejudicial Publicity: Its Effect on Law School Mock Juries,* 43 Journalism Quarterly 113 (1966); Simon, *Murders, Juries, and the Press* in Simon (ed.) The Sociology of Law, 1968; Tans and Chaffee, *Pretrial Publicity and Juror Prejudice,* 43 Journalism Quarterly 647 (1966); Bush

conclusion might be drawn from these studies, it is that juries or prospective jurors are prejudiced when news that a defendant has confessed or has a criminal record comes to their attention. And even on those questions there is less than perfect agreement.

Social science findings, whatever their value in helping to put juror behavior within the bounds of human comprehension, may be academic anyway. Courts, relying on their own impressions of psychological effects, have decided that where press coverage contributes to what appears to be a deep and bitter pattern of community prejudice, convictions will be reversed or mistrials declared.

2. Early cases to reach the Supreme Court in which the issue was wholly or in part the impartiality of the jury stretch back for at least 130 years. Their compound holding appeared to be that the existence of preconceived notions as to guilt or innocence was not enough if a juror could attest to his or her capability of laying aside a bias and deciding a case on its evidence. Subtle doubts were expressed about the influence of the press on jury verdicts in the first place. The burden of proof was clearly on the defendant to demonstrate essential unfairness.[4]

Not until 1961 did the United States Supreme Court reverse a state criminal conviction solely on the grounds that prejudicial pretrial publicity had made a fair trial before an impartial jury impossible.

On April 8, 1955, Leslie Irvin, a parolee, was arrested by Indiana state police on suspicion of burglary and bad check writing. A few days later Evansville, Indiana police and the county prosecutor issued press releases proclaiming that their burglary suspect, "Mad Dog" Irvin, had confessed to six murders, including the killing of three members of a single family. Irvin went to trial in November, was found guilty, and sentenced to death.

Bothersome was the fact that of 430 prospective jurors questioned by the court before trial, 370 said they believed Irvin guilty.[5] Defense counsel was never satisfied with the level of impartiality of the twelve jurors finally accepted by the court. Theoretically the jury selection process is designed to identify bias-free persons. In fact the selection proceeds on radically

---

(ed.), *Free Press and Fair Trial: Some Dimensions of the Problem,* 1971; Riley, *Pre-Trial Publicity: A Field Study,* 50 Journalism Quarterly 17 (1973); Padawer-Singer and Barton, *The Impact of Pretrial Publicity on Jurors' Verdicts* in Simon (ed.), The Jury System in America, 1975; Nagel, *Free Press-Fair Trial Controversy: Using Empirical Analysis to Strike a Desirable Balance,* 20 St. Louis U.L.Rev. 646 (1976). Simon, *Does the Court's Decision in* Nebraska Press Association *Fit the Research Evidence on the Impact on Jurors of News Coverage?* 29 Stanford Law Review 515 (February 1977). An excellent review of social science findings, from a lawyer's perspective, is found in Schmidt, Nebraska Press Association: *An Expansion of Freedom and Contraction of Theory,* 29 Stanford Law Review 443–455 (February 1977).

4. United States v. Reid, 53 U.S. 361 (1851); Reynolds v. United States, 98 U.S. 145 (1878); Hopt v. Utah, 120 U.S. 430 (1886); Ex parte Spies, 123 U.S. 131 (1887); Mattox v. United States, 146 U.S. 140 (1892); Holt v. United States, 218 U.S. 245 (1910); Shepherd v. Florida, 341 U.S. 50 (1951); Stroble v. California, 343 U.S. 181 (1952); U.S. ex rel. Darcy v. Handy, 351 U.S. 454 (1956); and Marshall v. United States, 360 U.S. 310 (1959).

5. After veniremen are sworn, a defendant is allowed a limited number of challenges to the impartiality of those who will decide his fate in a process called *voir dire* ("to speak the truth"). If there appears to be prejudice in either direction or if for some other reason a prospective juror appears unfit to serve, he or she is excused. Once the jury is sworn, a defendant still has a number of peremptory challenges—usually fifteen to twenty in a criminal case—by means of which a juror may be rejected without cause or for the most intuitive of reasons.

Federal court judges rather than attorneys control the examination of prospective federal court jurors. Empaneling is faster, but the procedure is often less thorough than its counterpart in state courts. Defense attorneys in criminal cases are especially critical of the federal procedure because they believe lawyers are better equipped than judges to elicit answers that accurately reflect a potential juror's opinion. For example, see Garry and Riordan, *Gag Orders: Cui Bono?* 29 Stan.L.Rev. 575, at 583 (1977).

different grounds, each attorney scrupulously dedicated to finding jurors whose biases will favor his client's cause.[6]

The Chicago Jury Project estimated that 60 percent of the lawyers' *voir dire* time was spent in indoctrinating jurors and only 40 percent in asking questions to differentiate partial from impartial jurors.[7] In recent years social scientists have been permitted to help lawyers choose jurors. The Harrisburg 13 trial was an example. And a University of California sociologist conducted a telephone survey to support a change of venue for Angela Davis; black psychologists assisted her lawyers in choosing jurors.[8] In 1972 a federal district court in Puerto Rico took notice of a psychologist's expert testimony on attitude formation and the results of a study on jury influence.[9] In addition, a University of Puerto Rico faculty member learned by questionnaire and interview that 59 percent of prospective jurors in the case were highly prejudiced against persons accused of acts of terrorism (the defendant was charged with violating the Explosives Law of Puerto Rico); the court thought it reasonable to draw jurors from the 41 percent in the survey who were conservatively liberal in their attitudes toward terrorists.

Leslie Irvin didn't have the benefit of sophisticated social science techniques. Nevertheless, after six years of legal maneuvering—and a successful prison break—his case reached the United States Supreme Court for a second time. In a unanimous decision the Court, considering Irvin's constitutional claims in terms of prejudicial news reporting, concluded that he had not been accorded a fair trial before an impartial jury. Moreover he should have been granted a second change of venue, said the Justices, in spite of an Indiana law allowing only a single change in the place of the trial; and it was the duty of the court of appeals to evaluate independently the *voir dire* testimony of the jurors.

IRVIN v. DOWD *

366 U.S. 717, 81 S.CT. 1639,
6 L.ED.2D 751 (1961).

Justice CLARK delivered the opinion of the Court:

* * *

It is not required that jurors be totally ignorant of the facts and issues involved, * * * and scarcely any of those best qualified to serve will not have formed some impression or opinion as to the merits of the case. * * * To hold that the mere existence of any preconceived notions as to the guilt or innocence of an accused, without more, is sufficient to rebut the presumption of a prospective juror's impartiality would be to establish an impossible standard. It is sufficient if the juror can lay aside his impression or opinion and render a verdict based on the evidence presented in court.

* * *

Here the build-up of prejudice is clear and convincing. An examination of the

6. Schur, *Scientific Method and the Criminal Trial,* 25 Social Research 173 (1958).

7. Broeder, *The University of Chicago Jury Project,* 38 Neb.L.Rev. 744 (1959). See generally, Kalven and Zeisel, *The American Jury,* 1966.

8. Schulman, Shaver, Colman, Emrich, and Christie, *Recipe for a Jury,* Psychology Today (May 1973); Fried, Kaplan, and Klein, *Juror Selection: An Analysis of Voir Dire* in Simon (ed.), The Jury System in America, 1975.

9. Martinez v. Commonwealth of Puerto Rico, 343 F.Supp. 897 (D.C.Puerto Rico 1972); Simon and Eimerman, *The Jury Finds Not Guilty: Another Look at Media Influence on the Jury,* Journalism Quarterly (Summer 1971), pp. 343–44.

* Although *Irvin* was the first reversal of a state court conviction, two years earlier in Marshall v. United States, 360 U.S. 310 (1959), the Court for the first time reversed a conviction in a federal court solely on grounds of prejudicial pretrial publicity. Jurors were exposed to newspapers containing defendant's criminal record.

then current community pattern of thought as indicated by the popular news media is singularly revealing. For example, petitioner's first motion for a change of venue from Gibson County alleged that the awaited trial of petitioner had become the *cause célèbre* of this small community—so much so that curbstone opinions, not only as to petitioner's guilt but even as to what punishment he should receive, were solicited and recorded on the public streets by a roving reporter, and later were broadcast over the local stations. A reading of the 46 exhibits which petitioner attached to his motion indicates that a barrage of newspaper headlines, articles, cartoons and pictures was unleashed against him during the six or seven months preceding his trial. The motion further alleged that the newspapers in which the stories appeared were delivered regularly to approximately 95% of the dwellings in Gibson County and that, in addition, the Evansville radio and TV stations, which likewise blanketed that county, also carried extensive newscasts covering the same incidents. These stories revealed the details of his background, including a reference to crimes committed when a juvenile, his convictions for arson almost 20 years previously, for burglary and by a court-martial on AWOL charges during the war. He was accused of being a parole violator. The headlines announced his police line-up identification, that he faced a lie detector test, had been placed at the scene of the crime and that the six murders were solved but petitioner refused to confess. Finally, they announced his confession to the six murders and the fact of his indictment for four of them in Indiana. They reported petitioner's offer to plead guilty if promised a 99-year sentence, but also the determination, on the other hand, of the prosecutor to secure the death penalty, and that petitioner had confessed to 24 burglaries (the *modus operandi* of these robberies was compared to that of the murders and the similarity noted). * * * On the day before the trial the newspapers carried the story that Irvin had orally admitted the murder of Kerr (the victim in this case) as well as "the robbery-murder of Mrs. Mary Holland; the murder of Mrs. Wilhelmina Sailer in Posey County, and the slaughter of three members of the Duncan family in Henderson County, Ky."

It cannot be gainsaid that the force of this continued adverse publicity caused a sustained excitement and fostered a strong prejudice among the people of Gibson County. In fact, on the second day devoted to the selection of the jury, the newspapers reported that "strong feelings, often bitter and angry, rumbled to the surface," and that "the extent to which the multiple murders—three in one family—have aroused feelings throughout the area was emphasized Friday when 27 of the 35 prospective jurors questioned were excused for holding biased pretrial opinions. * *" A few days later the feeling was described as "a pattern of deep and bitter prejudice against the former pipe-fitter." Spectator comments, as printed by the newspapers, were "my mind is made up"; "I think he is guilty"; and "he should be hanged."

Finally, and with remarkable understatement, the headlines reported that "impartial jurors are hard to find." * * * An examination of the 2,783-page *voir dire* record shows that 370 prospective jurors or almost 90% of those examined on the point (10 members of the panel were never asked whether or not they had any opinion) entertained some opinion as to guilt—ranging in intensity from mere suspicion to absolute certainty. A number admitted that, if they were in the accused's place in the dock and he in theirs on the jury with their opinions, they would not want him on a jury.

Here the "pattern of deep and bitter prejudice" shown to be present throughout the community, was clearly reflected in the sum total of the voir dire examination of a majority of the jurors finally placed in the jury box. [Emphasis added.] Eight out of the 12 thought petitioner was guilty. With such an opinion permeating their minds, it would be difficult to say that each could exclude this preconception of guilt from his deliberations. The influence that lurks in an opinion once formed is so persistent that it unconsciously fights detachment from the mental processes of the average man. * * * Where one's life is at stake—and accounting for the frailties of human nature—we can only say that in the light of the circumstances here the finding of impartiality does not meet constitutional standards. Two-thirds of the jurors had an opinion that petitioner was guilty and were familiar with the material facts and circumstances involved, including the fact that other murders were attributed to him, some going so far as to say that it would take evidence to overcome their belief. One said that he "could not * * * give the defendant the benefit of the doubt that he is innocent." Another stated that he had a "somewhat" certain fixed opinion as to petitioner's guilt. No doubt each juror was sincere when he said that he would be fair and impartial to petitioner, but psychological impact requiring such a declaration before one's fellows is often its father. Where so many so many times admitted prejudice, such a statement of impartiality can be given little weight. As one of the jurors put it, "You can't forget what you hear and see." With his life at stake, it is not requiring too much that petitioner be tried in an atmosphere undisturbed by so huge a wave of public passion and by a jury other than one in which two-thirds of the members admit, before hearing any testimony, to possessing a belief in his guilt.

COMMENT

1. Irvin's case was remanded to the district court, and he was retried by Indiana in a less emotional atmosphere. He was found guilty and sentenced to life imprisonment—a sentence for which, he confided to his attorney, he was grateful.

2. Justice Felix Frankfurter, long a proponent of curbing pretrial press reports, helped define the parameters of the conflict between free press and fair trial. In a concurring opinion in *Irvin* he said:

> Not a term passes without this Court being importuned to review convictions, had in [s]tates throughout the country, in which substantial claims are made that a jury trial has been distorted because of inflammatory newspaper accounts—too often, as in this case, with the prosecutor's collaboration—exerting pressure upon potential jurors before trial, thereby making it extremely difficult if not impossible to secure a jury capable of taking in, free of prepossessions, evidence submitted in open court. Indeed such extraneous influences, in violation of the decencies guaranteed by our Constitution, are sometimes so powerful that an accused is forced, as a practical matter, to forego trial by jury.

In the same opinion, Frankfurter said that a *per curiam* reversal of a federal court conviction a week earlier turned on a single article in the *St. Louis Post-Dispatch* linking the defendant in an income tax evasion trial with a local "rackets boss" and describing him as a "former convict." [10]

"The Court has not yet decided," Frankfurter warned the press, "that, while convictions must be reversed and miscar-

10. Janko v. United States, 366 U.S. 716 (1960). See also, Shepherd v. Florida, 341 U.S. 50 (1951), where Justice Jackson for the Court concluded that the press, in the trial of three black defendants, had dictated the verdict through inflammatory news reports including the report of a confession. But in Murphy v. Florida, 1 Med.L.Rptr. 1252, 421 U.S. 794 (1975), the Court concluded that press reports had not caused bias to permeate the community. *Murphy* can be read to reject the idea that bias should be implied from the very fact of publicity which, arguably, *Irvin* and later *Estes* may suggest. Or can *Murphy* be distinguished from *Irvin* on the ground that the *voir dire* in *Irvin* disclosed prejudice while in *Murphy* it did not?

riages of justice result because the minds of jurors or potential jurors were poisoned, the poisoner is constitutionally protected in plying his trade."

THE TRADITION OF CRIME REPORTING

Although the fourth chief justice of the United States, John Marshall, took note in 1807 of extralegal newspaper comment in a reference to the Alexandria, Virginia *Expositor's* coverage of the treason trial of Aaron Burr, crime reporting probably came into its own when London's Bow Street police reporters discovered that crime news, when presented sensationally, had mass appeal.

Benjamin Day's *New York Sun,* the first successful penny press, specialized in news of crime and violence. Day hired George Wisner, a Bow Street veteran, to cover the courts, and within a year Wisner was co-owner of the paper.[11] Charles Dickens was a Bow Street reporter *par excellence,* and in 1846 his own paper, the *Daily News,* carried a series of articles by Dickens on the brutalizing effects of the death penalty.

Crime news contributed to the success of Pulitzer's *World;* and James Gordon Bennett's *Herald* had no equal in sensational, aggressive, and even fictional crime coverage. William Randolph Hearst's *Journal* led America's "yellow" tabloids into the Jazz Age of journalism.

In 1907, Irwin S. Cobb wrote 600,000 words on the dramatic Harry K. Thaw murder trial for the *World.* Twelve years later the renowned stylist William Bolitho shocked the nation with his accounts in the *World* of the Paris trial of Henri Landru, better known as Bluebeard.

Ben Hecht and the *Daily News* were just right for Chicago in the roaring 20s. Bernarr Macfadden's *Graphic,* nicknamed the "pornographic," promoted the execution of Ruth Snyder in its inimitable style:

> Don't fail to read tomorrow's *Graphic.* An installment that thrills and stuns. A story that fairly pierces the heart and reveals Ruth Snyder's last thoughts on earth; that pulses the blood as it discloses her final letters. Think of it! A woman's final thoughts just before she is clutched in the deadly snare that sears and burns and FRIES AND KILLS! Her very last words! Exclusively in tomorrow's *Graphic.*[12]

Journalistic history was made when a *New York Daily News* photographer strapped a tiny camera to his leg, smuggled it into Sing Sing's execution chamber, and took a picture of Snyder straining at the thongs of the electric chair moments after the current had been turned on. The picture was a front-page sensation. It sold 250,000 extra copies of the paper.

No wonder Damon Runyon compared the big murder trial with a sporting event. "The trial," he wrote, "is a sort of game, the players on the one side the attorneys for the defense, and on the other side the attorneys for the State. The defendant figures in it merely as the prize."[13]

With the Lindbergh kidnaping trial, American crime reporting perhaps reached its zenith. As many as 800 newspersons and photographers joined by the great figures of stage and screen, United States senators, crooners, social celebrities, and 20,000 curious nobodies turned the little town of Flemington, New Jersey into a midsummer Mardi Gras. The small courtroom became a twenty-four hour propaganda bureau spewing out headlines such as "Bruno Guilty, But Has Aids, Verdict of

11. Emery and Emery, *The Press and America,* 4th ed. 1978, p. 120. A useful historical survey of the free press-fair trial conflict is Lofton, *Justice and the Press,* 1966.

12. Hughes, *News and the Human Interest Story* (1940), p. 235.

13. Frank, *Courts on Trial* (1949), p. 92.

Man in Street," and story references to Bruno Hauptmann as "a thing lacking human characteristics." One report had it that the jury was seriously considering an offer to go into vaudeville.

From Hauptmann's trial to the present, America has never for very long lacked a case *cause célèbre.* Lawyers and police officers remain the surest sources of information about pending cases, and reporters and editors rush into print, sometimes without even a passing thought for the presumption of innocence. The trial of Dr. Samuel Sheppard was such a case. After he had spent twelve years in prison, Sheppard's attorneys were able to get his case heard before the United States Supreme Court. He was given a new trial and acquitted. He died of undetermined causes a short time later.

There had long been agreement among parties on both sides of the case that the responsibility for preventing "trial by newspaper" and the resultant contamination of jurors rested in the first instance on judges, prosecutors, and policemen and not on the press. For the second reversal of a state court conviction on due process grounds, the Supreme Court in *Sheppard v. Maxwell* affirmed that judgment. A suspenseful, detailed story, in which Cleveland newspapers played a voracious part, was retold by the court in the *Sheppard* case which follows.

SHEPPARD v. MAXWELL

384 U.S. 333, 86 S.CT. 1507,
16 L.ED.2D 600 (1966).

Justice CLARK delivered the opinion of the Court:

* * *

The principle that justice cannot survive behind walls of silence has long been reflected in the "Anglo-American distrust for secret trials." In re Oliver, 333 U.S. 257, 268 (1948). A responsible press has always been regarded as the handmaiden of effective judicial administration, especially in the criminal field. Its function in this regard is documented by an impressive record of service over several centuries. The press does not simply publish information about trials but guards against the miscarriage of justice by subjecting the police, prosecutors, and judicial processes to extensive public scrutiny and criticism. This Court has, therefore, been unwilling to place any direct limitations on the freedom traditionally exercised by the news media for "[w]hat transpires in the court room is public property." Craig v. Harney, 331 U.S. 367 (1947). * * * But the Court has also pointed out that "[l]egal trials are not like elections, to be won through the use of the meeting-hall, the radio, and the newspaper." Bridges v. State of California, 314 U.S. at 271 (1941). * * * And we cited with approval the language of Justice Black for the Court in In re Murchison, 349 U.S. 133, 136 (1955), that "our system of law has always endeavored to prevent even the probability of unfairness."

It is clear that the totality of circumstances in this case also warrant such an approach. * * * Sheppard was not granted a change of venue to a locale away from where the publicity originated; nor was his jury sequestered. * * * [T]he Sheppard jurors were subjected to newspaper, radio and television coverage of the trial while not taking part in the proceedings. They were allowed to go their separate ways outside of the courtroom, without adequate directions not to read or listen to anything concerning the case. * * * At intervals during the trial, the judge simply repeated his "suggestions" and "requests" that the jury not expose themselves to comment upon the case. Moreover, the jurors were thrust into the role of celebrities by the judge's failure to insulate them from reporters and photographers. The numerous pictures of the jurors, with their addresses, which appeared in the newspapers before and during the trial itself exposed them to expressions of opinion from both cranks and friends. The fact that anonymous letters had been received by prospective jurors should have made the judge aware that this publicity seriously threatened the jurors' privacy. * * * Sheppard stood indicted for the murder of his wife; the State was demanding the death penalty. For months the virulent publicity about Sheppard and the murder had made the case notorious. Charges and countercharges were aired in the news media besides those for which Sheppard was called to trial. In addition, only three months before trial, Sheppard was examined for more than five hours without counsel during a three-day inquest which ended in a public brawl. The inquest was televised live from a high school gymnasium seating hundreds of people. Furthermore, the trial began two weeks before a hotly contested election at which both Chief Prosecutor Mahon and Judge Blythin were candidates for judgeships.

While we cannot say that Sheppard was denied due process by the judge's refusal to take precautions against the influence of pretrial publicity alone, the court's later rulings must be considered against the setting in which the trial was held. In light of this background, we believe that the arrangements made by the judge with the news media caused Sheppard to be deprived of that "judicial serenity and calm to which [he] was entitled." The fact is that bedlam reigned at the courthouse during the trial and newsmen took over practically the entire courtroom, hounding most of the participants in the trial, especially Sheppard. At a temporary table within a few feet of the jury box and counsel table sat some 20 reporters staring at Sheppard and taking notes. The erection of a press table for reporters inside the bar is unprecedented. The bar of the court is reserved for counsel, providing them a safe place in which to keep papers and exhibits, and to confer privately with client and co-counsel. It is designed to protect the witness and the jury from any distractions, intrusions or influences, and to permit bench discussions of the judge's rulings away from the hearing of the public and the jury. Having assigned almost all of the available seats in the courtroom to the news media the judge lost his ability to supervise that environment. The movement of the reporters in and out of the courtroom caused frequent confusion and disruption of the trial. And the record reveals constant commotion within the bar. Moreover, the judge gave the throng of newsmen gathered in the corridors of the courthouse absolute free rein. Participants in the trial, including the jury, were forced to run a gantlet of reporters and photographers each time they entered or left the courtroom. The total lack of consideration for the privacy of the jury was demonstrated by the assignment to a broadcasting station of space next to the jury room on the floor above the courtroom, as well as the fact that jurors were allowed to make telephone calls during their five-day deliberation.

There can be no question about the nature of the publicity which surrounded Sheppard's trial. * * *

* * * Indeed, every court that has considered this case, save the court that tried it, has deplored the manner in which the news media inflamed and prejudiced the public.

* * *

Nor is there doubt that this deluge of publicity reached at least some of the jury. On the only occasion that the jury was queried, two jurors admitted in open court to hearing the highly inflammatory charge that a prison inmate claimed Sheppard as the father of her illegitimate child. Despite the extent and nature of the publicity to which the jury was exposed during trial, the judge refused defense counsel's other requests that the jury be asked whether they had read or heard specific prejudicial comment about the case, including the incidents we have previously summarized. In these circumstances, we can assume that some of this material reached members of the jury.

The court's fundamental error is compounded by the holding that it lacked power to control the publicity about the trial. From the very inception of the proceedings the judge announced that neither he nor anyone else could restrict prejudicial news accounts. And he reiterated this view on numerous occasions. Since he viewed the news media as his target, the judge never considered other means that are often utilized to reduce the appearance of prejudicial material and to protect the jury from outside influence. We conclude that these procedures would have been sufficient to guarantee Sheppard a fair trial and so do not consider what sanctions might be available against a recalcitrant press nor the charges of bias now made against the state trial judge. [Emphasis added.]

The carnival atmosphere at trial could easily have been avoided since the courtroom and courthouse premises are subject to the control of the court. * * * Bearing in mind the massive pretrial publicity, the judge should have adopted stricter rules governing the use of the courtroom by newsmen, as Sheppard's counsel requested. The number of reporters in the courtroom itself could have been limited at the first sign that their presence would disrupt the trial. They certainly should not have been placed inside the bar. Furthermore, the judge should have more closely regulated the conduct of newsmen in the courtroom. For instance, the judge belatedly asked them not to handle and photograph trial exhibits laying on the counsel table during recesses.

Secondly, the court should have insulated the witnesses. All of the newspapers and radio stations apparently interviewed prospective witnesses at will, and in many instances disclosed their testimony. A typical example was the publication of numerous statements by Susan Hayes, before her appearance in court, regarding her love affair with Sheppard. Although the witnesses were barred from the courtroom during the trial the full *verbatim* testimony was available to them in the press. This completely nullified the judge's imposition of the rule.

Thirdly, the court should have made some effort to control the release of leads, information, and gossip to the press by police officers, witnesses, and the counsel for both sides. Much of the information thus disclosed was inaccurate leading to groundless rumors and confusion. That the judge was aware of his responsibility in this respect may be seen from his warning to Steve Sheppard, the accused's brother, who had apparently made public statements in an attempt to discredit testimony for the prosecution.

* * *

Defense counsel immediately brought to the court's attention the tremendous amount of publicity in the Cleveland press that "misrepresented entirely the testimony" in the case. Under such circumstances, the judge should have at least warned the newspapers to check the accuracy of their accounts. And it is obvious that the judge should have further sought to alleviate this problem by imposing control over the statements made to the news media by counsel, witnesses, and especially the Coroner and police officers. The prosecution repeatedly made evidence available to the news media which was never offered in the trial. Much of the "evidence" disseminated in this fashion was clearly inadmissible. The exclusion of such evidence in court is rendered meaningless when a news media (sic) makes it available to the public.

* * *

The fact that many of the prejudicial news items can be traced to the prosecution, as well as the defense, aggravates the judge's failure to take any action. Effective control of these sources—concededly within the court's power—might well have prevented the divulgence of inaccurate information, rumors, and accusations that made up much of the inflammatory publicity, at least after Sheppard's indictment.

More specifically, the trial court might well have proscribed extra-judicial statements by any lawyer, party, witness, or court official which divulged prejudicial matters, such as the refusal of Sheppard to submit to interrogation or take any lie detector tests; any statement made by Sheppard to officials; the identity of prospective witnesses or their probable testimony; any belief in guilt or innocence; or like statements concerning the merits of the case. * * * Being advised of the great public interest in the case, the mass coverage of the press, and the potential prejudicial impact of publicity, the court could also have requested the appropriate city and county officials to promulgate a regulation with respect to dissemination of information about the case by their employees. In addition, reporters who wrote or broadcast prejudicial stories, could have been warned as to the impropriety of publishing material not introduced in the proceedings. The judge was put on notice of such events by defense counsel's complaint about the WHK broadcast on the second day of trial. In this manner, Sheppard's right to a trial free from outside interference would have been given added protection without corresponding curtailment of the news media. Had the judge, the other officers of the court, and the police placed the interest of justice first, the news media would have soon learned to be content with the task of reporting the case as it unfolded in the courtroom—not pieced together from extra-judicial statements.

From the cases coming here we note that unfair and prejudicial news comment on pending trials has become increasingly prevalent. Due process requires that the accused receive a trial by an impartial jury free from outside influences. Given the pervasiveness of modern communications and the difficulty of effacing prejudicial publicity from the minds of the jurors, the trial courts must take strong measures to ensure that the balance is never weighed against the accused. And appellate tribunals have the duty to make an independent evaluation of the circumstances. *Of course, there is nothing that proscribes the press from reporting events that transpire in the courtroom.* [Emphasis added.] But where there is a reasonable likelihood that prejudicial news prior to trial will prevent a fair trial, the judge should continue the case until the threat abates or transfer it to another county not so permeated with publicity. In addition, sequestration of the jury was something the judge should have raised *sua sponte* with counsel. If publicity during the proceedings threatens the fairness of the trial, a new trial should be ordered. But we must remember that reversals are but palliatives; the cure lies in those remedial measures that will prevent the prejudice at its inception. *The courts must take such steps by rule and regulation that will protect their processes from prejudicial outside interferences.* [Emphasis added.] Neither prosecutors, counsel for defense, the accused, witnesses, court staff nor enforcement officers coming under the jurisdiction of the court should be permitted to frustrate its function. Collaboration between counsel and the press as to information affecting the fairness of a criminal trial is not only subject to regulation, but is highly censurable and worthy of disciplinary measures.

Since the state trial judge did not fulfill his duty to protect Sheppard from the inherently prejudicial publicity which saturated the community and to control disruptive influences in the courtroom, we must reverse the denial of the habeas petition. The case is remanded to the District Court with instructions to issue the writ and order that Sheppard be released from custody unless the State puts him to its charges again within a reasonable time.

It is so ordered.

Justice Black dissents.

THE REARDON REPORT

1. If Justice Clark spoke sternly to the trial judge in the case, mandating him to be master in his own courtroom and use available remedies to counteract unfairness, he also had something to say to the press. It would require self-delusion not to interpret his painstaking account of press coverage in the case as anything but disgust for journalism's obliviousness to fairness. The case would be parent to hundreds of "gag" orders directed at the press by lower court judges, culminating ten years later in the 1976 case *Nebraska Press Ass'n v. Stuart.*

2. In the interim, and partly as a response to criticism in the Warren Report [14] of how the press had dealt with Lee Harvey Oswald, the American Bar Association established an Advisory Committee on Fair Trial and Free Press under the chairmanship of Paul C. Reardon, then associate justice of the Supreme Judicial Court of Massachusetts.[15] While the Reardon Report, as it came to be called, addressed itself primarily to officers of the court, it recommended that judges use their long discredited power to cite for constructive contempt [16]—that is for contempt committed outside of the courtroom—anyone who disseminated extrajudicial statements willfully designed to influence the outcome of a trial or who violated a valid order not to reveal information from a closed judicial hearing. The report also favored closing pretrial hearings to press and public on defendant's motion if it appeared to the court that fair trial was in jeopardy. Ninety percent of cases are disposed of in the pretrial stage.

Laying down categories of prohibited and publishable information, the controversial report was soon exerting nationwide influence on both press and bar. Prohibited comment was to include prior criminal records, character references, confessions, test results, and out-of-court speculation on guilt or innocence or on the merits of evidence. Publishable information would be the fact and circumstances of an arrest, the identity of the arrested person and the arresting officer or agency, descriptions of physical evidence once in hand, the charge and other facts from public court records, and the next probable steps in the judicial process.

Where there was a threatened interference with the right to a fair trial, the report agreed with Justice Clark in *Sheppard* that motions should be granted for change of venue or venire, severance, continuance, waiver of the right to trial by jury, sequestration, new trial, mistrial, and habeas corpus. Under *voir dire,* jurors could be challenged, and once seated, judges could take pains to instruct them on what and what not to consider.

To be sure, these judicial remedies are useful, but there are some obvious prob-

---

14. Report of the President's Commission on the Assassination of President John F. Kennedy, 1964, pp. 201–242 and *passim.*

15. American Bar Association Legal Advisory Committee on Fair Trial and Free Press, *The Rights of Fair Trial and Free Press,* 1969. See also, Gillmor, *The Reardon Report: A Journalist's Assessment,* 1967 Wisc.L.Rev. 215.

16. For a catalogue of English contempt cases involving the press, see Gillmor, *Free Press and Fair Trial in English Law,* 22 Wash. & Lee L.Rev. 17–42 (1965).

lems. The ubiquity of mass media, especially broadcasting, casts a shadow on the effectiveness of changes of venue and venire. A continuance, or postponement, may lead to the disappearance of witnesses and evidence, and, if unable to raise bail, a defendant remains in jail. A mistrial subjects a defendant to the expense and trauma of a new trial. There is some debate over the usefulness of peremptory challenges to jurors and of challenges for cause, both part of *voir dire* proceedings.[17] Jurors as a rule don't like being sequestered, or locked up, and may react adversely to the party initiating such a motion; moreover they have, in most cases, already been exposed to pretrial publicity.[18] Judicial instructions to ignore inflammatory press reports may not overcome pervasive community prejudice, although the University of Chicago Jury Project found that jurors take the admonitions of a judge very seriously.[19]

One survey reported that judges favored most of the above remedies appropriate to the pretrial period. Once the trial had begun, motion for a new trial on due process grounds was their choice. Most agreed that the reporting of criminal records, confessions, and the results of pretrial tests, such as the lie detector, were the most damaging forms of pretrial coverage.[20]

The Contempt Power

1. While the news media were predictably negative toward broad prohibitions against publication of information in public records (criminal records, for example) and toward being excluded from pretrial hearings, given the fact that only a very small percentage of cases ever get to trial, their most vocal condemnation was reserved for that part of the Reardon Report that seemed to propose revival of the contempt power to punish editors for what appeared in their news columns.

As early as 1788, Americans began having doubts about the summary procedure (the judge acts as complainant, jury, and judge in his or her own case) for punishing contempts by publication.[21] Pennsylvania passed a law limiting its use in 1809, followed by New York in 1829. Congress enacted the Federal Contempt Act of 1831 limiting punishable contempt to disobedience to any judicial process or decree and to misbehavior in the presence of the court, *"or so near thereto as to obstruct the administration of justice."*[22]

In 1918 judges were still disagreeing on whether the "so near thereto" phrase should be given a geographical (in the courtroom) or causal construction.[23] Until 1941 the "immemorial" power of judges to punish summarily out-of-court contempt prevailed. Then in Nye v. United States, 313 U.S. 33 (1941), the United States Supreme Court did a right about face and ruled that "so near thereto" meant physical proximity and should be applied geographically rather than causally. It also rejected the "reasonable tendency" rule as applied in earlier cases as the standard

17. Babcock, *Voir Dire: Preserving "Its Wonderful Power,"*, 27 Stan.L.Rev. 545 (1975).

18. Comment, *Sequestration: A Possible Solution to the Free Press-Fair Trial Dilemma,* 23 Am.U.L.Rev. 923 (1974).

19. Kalven and Zeisel, *The American Jury,* 1966.

20. Bush, Wilcox, Siebert, and Hough, *Free Press and Fair Trial,* 1970.

21. Respublica v. Oswald, 1 Dallas 319 (Pa.1788).

22. 18 U.S.C.A. § 401.

23. Toledo Newspaper Co. v. United States, 247 U.S. 402 (1918). In a strong dissent, Justice Holmes, interpreting the phrase as "geographical," sought to discredit the summary power in favor of firm and steadfast judges not easily deflected from their sworn duty.

against which potentially prejudicial out-of-court statements were to be measured.

That same year in Bridges v. California, 314 U.S. 252 (1941), the power of judges to punish publication was severely limited. The case involved labor leader Harry Bridges and the *Los Angeles Times,* both of whom had admonished and criticized a judge and the judicial process while a case was pending. The Court declared in this and subsequent cases [24] that the contempt power could be used against out-of-court comment only when such comment created a "clear and present danger" that justice would be impaired.

"The assumption that respect for the judiciary can be won by shielding judges from published criticism wrongly appraises the character of American public opinion," Justice Hugo Black said in his opinion for the Court. "For it is a prized American privilege to speak one's mind, although not always with perfect good taste, on all public institutions. And an enforced silence, however limited, solely in the name of preserving the dignity of the bench, would probably engender resentment, suspicion, and contempt much more than it would enhance respect."

As for the judicial process, Black observed that "Legal trials are not like elections, to be won through the use of the meeting-hall, the radio, and the newspaper." "But," he said, "we cannot start with the assumption that publications of the kind here involved actually do threaten to change the nature of legal trials, and that to preserve judicial impartiality, it is necessary for judges to have a contempt power by which they can close all channels of public expression to all matters which touch upon pending cases."

In a dissent concurred in by three of his colleagues, Justice Frankfurter argued in defense of the right of the states to decide by law what protection should be afforded their courts:

> [T]hat the conventional power to punish for contempt is not a censorship in advance but a punishment for past conduct and, as such, like prosecution for a criminal libel, is not offensive either to the First or Fourteenth Amendments, has never been doubted throughout this Court's history.

While these cases rejected the protection of judges from press comment in pending cases, they did not speak to the issue of protecting jurors. Justice Frankfurter was so disturbed when his colleagues denied review to a case in which that issue was paramount [State of Maryland v. Baltimore Radio Show, cert. den. 338 U.S. 912, (1950)] that he wrote a personal memorandum in which he discussed the leading English cases on constructive contempt as if to recommend their doctrine to American courts.

Although unresolved,[25] it is highly probable that use of the contempt power to protect jurors against press comment would invite condemnation on First Amendment grounds. But, as we shall see, contempt has again become an urgent concern of the journalist where what is published is done so in direct violation of

---

24. Pennekamp v. Florida, 328 U.S. 331 (1946). Zechariah Chafee, Jr., an eminent commentator on freedom of speech and press, would have made Justice Frankfurter's concurring opinion in the case required reading in every school of journalism, newspaper office, and broadcasting station. See Chafee, *Government and Mass Communications,* Vol. 2, 1947, p. 433. Frankfurter argued that, ultimately, freedom of the press would depend for its survival on an independent judiciary. "To deny," he said, "that bludgeoning or poisonous comment has power to influence, or at least to disturb, the task of judging is to play make-believe and to assume that men in gowns are angels." And he contended that every right carries with it a concomitant responsibility.

In Craig v. Harney, 331 U.S. 367 (1947), the third in a series of cases denying the contempt power to judges, Justice Douglas said: "Judges are supposed to be men of fortitude, able to thrive in a hardy climate."

25. Wood v. Georgia, 370 U.S. 375 (1962).

a judicial order.[26]

2. The Reardon Report had a positive side. It gave its imprimatur and thus momentum to a developing dialogue among and a set of pretrial guidelines for journalists, lawyers, and judges that by the late 70s had led to bilateral free press-fair trial councils either in place or pending in as many as thirty-four states. A dozen or more of these would become moribund or, as in Arizona, Pennsylvania, and Washington, would be loudly disavowed. In late 1982, guidelines remained somewhat viable in only eighteen states. In spite of these efforts, tension continued between the press and the judicial system with the Reardon Report getting the blame for whatever restrictions judges placed on reporters.

A 1971 Baton Rouge murder-conspiracy case reminded reporters that judges were not helpless when it came to enforcing their orders. At a preliminary hearing designed to determine whether the state had a legitimate motive in prosecuting a VISTA worker on a charge of conspiring to murder the city's mayor or whether its action was based on racial prejudice, a federal district judge prohibited the publication of testimony taken at a public hearing. Two *State-Times* reporters ignored the order, wrote their stories, and were adjudged guilty of criminal contempt of court. The reporters appealed to the Fifth Circuit, and, in what may have been a turning point in press-bar cooperation, that court upheld the principle that even an unconstitutional court order must be obeyed pending appeal. The court refused to make the First Amendment question of prior restraint the dispositive issue in the case. And it relied heavily on a United States Supreme Court ruling, Walker v. Birmingham, 388 U.S. 307 (1967)—see p. 45 this text—which required obedience even to a court order in violation of the First Amendment pending appeal of the order.

Noting that no jury was yet involved in the case and the press had not created a carnival atmosphere, the Fifth Circuit court observed that the public's right to know the facts brought out in the hearing was particularly compelling since the issue being litigated was a charge that elected state officials had trumped up charges against an individual solely because of his race and civil rights activities. The federal district court's cure, said the federal appeals court, was worse than the disease. But it went on to say the following.

UNITED STATES v. DICKINSON

1 MED.L.RPTR. 1338, 465 F.2D 596 (5TH CIR. 1972).

John R. BROWN, Chief Judge:

* * *

The conclusion that the District Court's order was constitutionally invalid does not necessarily end the matter of the validity of the contempt convictions. There remains the very formidable question of whether a person may with impunity knowingly violate an order which turns out to be invalid. We hold that in the circumstances of this case he may not.

We begin with the well-established principle in proceedings for criminal contempt that an injunction duly issuing out of a court having subject matter and personal jurisdiction *must be obeyed,* irrespective of the ultimate validity of the order. Invalidity is no defense to criminal contempt. * * * Walker v. City of Birmingham, 388 U.S. 307 (1967). * * * "People simply cannot have the luxury of knowing that they have a right to contest the correctness of the judge's order in de-

26. For a more comprehensive treatment of the history of the contempt power, see Nelles and King, *Contempt by Publication in the United States,* 28 Colum.L.Rev. 401–431 and 525–562 (1928); Goldfarb, *The Contempt Power* (1963); Gillmor, *Free Press and Fair Trial,* 1966, Chapt. 11, "Contempt and the Constitution."

ciding whether to wilfully disobey it. * * Court orders have to be obeyed until they are reversed or set aside in an orderly fashion."

* * *

The criminal contempt exception requiring compliance with court orders, while invalid non-judicial directives may be disregarded, is not the product of self-protection or arrogance of Judges. Rather it is born of an experience-proved recognition that this rule is essential for the system to work. Judges, after all, are charged with the final responsibility to adjudicate legal disputes. It is the judiciary which is vested with the duty and the power to interpret and apply statutory and constitutional law. Determinations take the form of orders. The problem is unique to the judiciary because of its particular role. Disobedience to a legislative pronouncement in no way interferes with the legislature's ability to discharge its responsibilities (passing laws). The dispute is simply pursued in the judiciary and the legislature is ordinarily free to continue its function unencumbered by any burdens resulting from the disregard of its directives. Similarly, law enforcement is not prevented by failure to convict those who disregard the unconstitutional commands of a policeman.

On the other hand, the deliberate refusal to obey an order of the court without testing its validity through established processes requires further action by the judiciary, and therefore directly affects the judiciary's ability to discharge its duties and responsibilities. Therefore, "while it is sparingly to be used, yet the power of the courts to punish for contempts is a necessary and integral part of the independence of the judiciary, and is absolutely essential to the performance of the duties imposed on them by law. Without it they are mere boards of arbitration whose judgments and decrees would be only advisory."

* * *

[P]articular language in the recent Supreme Court decision of New York Times Co. v. United States, 1971, 403 U.S. 713 suggests that that Court would not sanction disobedience of a court order, even where the injunction unconstitutionally restrains publication of news. In the *Times* case, the lower courts had issued temporary restraining orders prohibiting further publication of the Pentagon Papers pending judicial determination of the merits of the Government's objections. Six of the Justices agreed that these injunctions were violative of the First Amendment. Nevertheless, no one suggested that the injunctions could have been ignored with impunity.

* * *

Where the thing enjoined is publication and the communication is "news," this condition presents some thorny problems. Timeliness of publication is the hallmark of "news" and the difference between "news" and "history" is merely a matter of hours. Thus, where the publishing of news is sought to be restrained, the incontestable inviolability of the order may depend on the immediate accessibility of orderly review. But in the absence of strong indications that the appellate process was being deliberately stalled—certainly not so in this record—violation with impunity does not occur simply because immediate decision is not forthcoming, even though the communication enjoined is "news." Of course the nature of the expression sought to be exercised is a factor to be considered in determining whether First Amendment rights can be effectively protected by orderly review so as to render disobedience to otherwise unconstitutional mandates nevertheless contemptuous. But newsmen are citizens, too. They too may sometimes have to wait. They are not yet wrapped in an immunity or given the absolute right to decide with impunity whether a Judge's order is to be obeyed or whether an appellate court is acting promptly enough.

* * *

* * * As a matter of jurisdiction, the District Court certainly has power to formulate Free Press-Fair Trial orders in cases pending before the court and to enforce those orders against all who have actual and admitted knowledge of its prohibitions. Secondly, as the District Court's findings of fact establish, both the District Court and the Court of Appeals were available and could have been contacted that very day, thereby affording speedy and effective but *orderly* review of the injunction in question swiftly enough to protect the right to publish news while it was still "news." Finally, unlike the compelled testimony situations the District Court's order required that information be withheld—not forcibly surrendered—and accordingly, compliance with the Court's order would not require an irrevocable, irretrievable or irreparable abandonment of constitutional privileges.

Under the circumstances, reporters took a chance. As civil disobedients have done before they ran a risk, the risk being magnified in this case by the law's policy which forecloses their right to assert invalidity of the order as a complete defense to a charge of criminal contempt. Having disobeyed the Court's decree, they must, as civil disobeyers, suffer the consequences for having rebelled at what they deem injustice, but in a manner not authorized by law. They may take comfort in the fact that they, as their many forerunners, have thus established an important constitutional principle—which may be all that was really at stake—but they may not now escape the inescapable legal consequence for their flagrant, intentional disregard of the mandates of a Court.

* * *

[I]t is appropriate to remand the case to the District Court for a determination of whether the judgment of contempt or the punishment therefor would still be deemed appropriate in light of the fact that the order disobeyed was constitutionally infirm.

Vacated and remanded.

COMMENT

1. The case was returned to the district court judge, and again he convicted the two reporters and upheld their $300 fines. The appeals court affirmed for a second time. 476 F.2d 373 (5th Cir. 1973).

Although the court of appeals seemed to appreciate the reporters' need for a *speedy* review, nine months had passed between the initial appeal and the final court ruling.

On October 23, 1973, over the objection of Justice Douglas, the Supreme Court refused to review the case. Dickinson v. United States, cert. den. 414 U.S. 979 (1973). Lawyers for the reporters had argued before the High Court that if the decision were allowed to stand, it would arm courts with the power to authorize patently impermissible prior restraints on the exercise of First Amendment rights through the use of the contempt power and so allow them to accomplish indirectly what the Constitution flatly prohibits them from doing directly.

It may be important to distinguish restrictive orders issued by state courts and those issued by federal courts. Until it is overruled, *Dickinson,* and federal cases upon which it rests, holds that no disobedience to a court order will be permitted, even when the order violates the First Amendment. State law, however, may favor an attack on such orders, particularly where they violate state constitutional guarantees.[27]

---

27. See, for example, State ex rel. Superior Court of Snohomish Co. v. Sperry, 483 P.2d 608 (Wash.1971), cert. den. 404 U.S. 939.

An examination of cases since at least the turn of the century indicates that "gag" orders have generally not found favor with state courts and that contempt convictions based upon them have often been reversed on appeal. Cases supporting this conclusion include orders not to publish open court testimony; [28] the names of grand jurors or witnesses before grand juries; [29] testimony in preliminary hearings; [30] the identity of juvenile offenders; [31] criminal records; [32] a jury verdict; [33] a change of plea; [34] out-of-court comment; [35] the photograph of a defendant; [36] trial statement of a defendant implicating others; [37] and a copy of a judge's charge to a jury in a murder case.[38]

If a reporter must disobey a written federal court order directed specifically to him or her, a move ought to be made toward the appeals process, even though a story's timeliness may be jeopardized. And that effort should be continued right up to press or broadcast deadlines. *Dickinson* implies that such appeals will get speedy review.

2. *Dickinson* nevertheless gave impetus to the issuing of protective or restraining orders—what the press prefers to call "gag" orders—in criminal cases. Court proceedings and court records were closed. Names of jurors and witnesses, criminal records, and arrest records were sealed. Prior restraints were imposed by forbidding publication of information about exhibits, pleas, jury verdicts, and editorial comment on guilt or innocence.

With *Sheppard,* the Reardon Report, and *Dickinson* as a base, restrictive orders were bolstered by *dicta* in the landmark journalist's privilege case, Branzburg v. Hayes, 1 Med.L.Rptr. 2617, 408 U.S. 665 (1972):

> Newsmen have no constitutional right of access to the scenes of crime or disaster when the general public is excluded, and they may be prohibited from attending or publishing information about trials if such restrictions are necessary to assure a defendant a fair trial before an impartial tribunal.

The American Bar Association continued to articulate influential guidelines permitting restrictions on the press, at least in extreme cases.

In 1976, under pressure from the Washington-based Reporters Committee for Freedom of the Press, the ABA agreed that no restraining order should be issued without the media being afforded the basic elements of due process—prior notice, the right to be heard, and an opportunity for speedy appellate review. Direct restraints on the press would generally be avoided, and any kind of restraint would be tailored to the specific circumstances of a criminal case.[39]

---

28. Ex parte Foster, 71 S.W. 593 (Tex.1903).

29. State v. Morrow, 11 N.E.2d 273 (Ohio 1937).

30. Phoenix Newspapers, Inc. v. Superior Court, 418 P.2d 594 (Ariz.1966).

31. Ithaca Journal News, Inc. v. City Court of Ithaca, 294 N.Y.S.2d 558 (1968).

32. Oliver v. Postel, 1 Med.L.Rptr. 2399, 331 N.Y.S.2d 407 (1972); New York Times Co. v. Starkey, 380 N.Y.S.2d 239 (1976).

33. Wood v. Goodson, 485 S.W.2d 213 (Ark.1972).

34. Florida v. Payne (1974), unreported.

35. Younger v. Smith, 106 Cal.Rptr. 225 (1973); State ex rel. Miami Herald Publishing Co. v. Rose, 271 So.2d 483 (Fla.1972).

36. Kansas v. Jaben (1975), unreported.

37. State ex rel. Beacon Journal Publishing Co. v. Kainrad, 2 Med.L.Rptr. 1123, 348 N.E.2d 695 (Ohio 1976).

38. Matter of New York Post Corp. v. Leibowitz, 163 N.Y.S.2d 409 (1957).

39. American Bar Association Legal Advisory Committee on Fair Trial and Free Press, *Preliminary Draft Proposed Court Procedure for Fair Trial-Free Press Judicial Restrictive Orders* (July 1975), revised *Recom-*

In 1978 the ABA's Committee on Fair Trial and Free Press proposed that there be no direct restraints on the news media, that press and public be excluded from hearings, and that records be sealed only on clear evidence of a clear and present danger to jury impartiality and a lack of alternative judicial remedies. The committee further recommended that reporters not be subject to the contempt power unless their potentially prejudicial information was acquired by means of bribery, theft, or fraud. Any judicial order affecting the press, said the committee, ought to be preceded by prior notice, a hearing, and, if the order is issued, an opportunity for prompt appellate review of the validity of the order. In proposing that no person be punished for violating an order later invalidated by an appellate court, the committee, in effect, rejected the Fifth Circuit's holding in *United States v. Dickinson.*

At its annual meeting later that year, the ABA's House of Delegates in large part adopted these proposals. The lawyers would categorically forbid a judge to issue an order prohibiting reporters from publishing information in their possession—"Rather than invite courts to probe the limits of the First Amendment in this area and thereby intensify conflicts with the press, it is preferable to close the door entirely to the alternative of prior restraints."

And the clear and present danger test was recommended for gagging lawyers and for closing pretrial hearings and court records.[40]

It was in this somewhat more conciliatory atmosphere that *Nebraska Press Association v. Stuart* came to the Supreme Court.

NEBRASKA PRESS CASE

1. On October 18, 1975 in the tiny prairie town of Sutherland, Nebraska, Erwin Simants walked across his yard to a neighbor's, raped and fatally shot ten-year-old Florence Kellie, then murdered all possible witnesses—her grandparents, her father, a brother, and a sister.[41]

The thirty-year-old Simants, after spending the night in a corn field, turned himself in to authorities. A terrified community was relieved. At his arraignment on six counts of first degree murder a few days later, County Judge Ronald Ruff, with an eye on the Nebraska Bar-Press Guidelines and without notice to the press, issued a broad order prohibiting publication of anything from public pretrial proceedings. In Nebraska, pretrial hearings must be open to the public. Because of an alleged confession and possibly incriminating medical tests relating to sexual assault, Judge Ruff feared that publicity might affect the fairness of the trial that Simants surely faced.

Within nine days a district court judge in Lincoln County, seeing a clear and present danger to a fair trial, set down essentially the same rules and said he

---

mended Court Procedure to Accommodate Rights of Fair Trial and Free Press (Dec. 2, 1975), adopted by the ABA House of Delegates (August 1976). See also, Landau, *Fair Trial and Free Press: A Due Process Proposal,* 62 ABA J. 55 (January 1976).

40. See *Standing Committee on Association Standards for Criminal Justice, Fair Trial and Free Press,* 2d ed., Tentative Draft (1978). Suggestions for making procedures for formulation and review of such guidelines or protective orders statutory came from the ABA's Legal Advisory Committee on Fair Trial-Free Press, the Twentieth Century Fund Task Force on Justice, Publicity and the First Amendment, *Rights in Conflict* (1976), and from *Fair Trial and Free Expression,* a report to the Subcommittee on Constitutional Rights of the Committee on the Judiciary of the United States Senate (1976).

41. An entire issue of the *Stanford Law Review* (29:3, February 1977) is devoted to a symposium on the case. It presents a wide spectrum of views on the free press-fair trial question.

would screen reporters to determine their "suitability" to be in the courtroom. Judge Hugh Stuart did something else. He incorporated the Nebraska Bar-Press Guidelines—or at least his interpretation of them—in his order and then forbade the press to talk about what he had done. Note how easily "voluntary" guidelines had become mandatory ones.

A by now infuriated press saw this as a "gag on a gag." To the chagrin of those who had called for compromise, "voluntary guidelines" had become part of a formal judicial order. The press of Nebraska rallied, soon to be joined by colleagues across the country. Some reporters boycotted the jury selection process, and much of the evidence presented at the preliminary hearing went unreported.

The Nebraska Press Association, firmly supported by broad elements of the national press, sped to the state supreme court and presented that body with a 120-hour ultimatum for extraordinary relief. But the Nebraska Supreme Court was in no hurry and told the press not to expect a ruling before February. The next step was an appeal to U.S. Supreme Court Justice Harry Blackmun who is the overseeing Circuit Justice for the region which includes Nebraska. On November 13, in an almost unprecedented order, Blackmun told the Nebraska Supreme Court to consider the case "forthwith and without delay," since freedom of the press was being irreparably infringed by each passing day.

The state supreme court, now aware that the press was seeking parallel relief from the High Court, still did not do anything. After a few days, Justice Blackmun, in what is known as a chambers opinion, reassured the state court by postponing a stay sought by the press of the original court order until the state supreme court had had time to act.[42]

The judicial minuet was not over. Five days after Blackmun's opinion was issued, the Nebraska Supreme Court set November 25 to hear arguments. Appalled at how much time was passing, the press filed a reapplication for a stay with Blackmun. On November 20, finding that Nebraska court delays had exceeded "tolerable limits," Justice Blackmun handed down a second chambers opinion in which he granted the press a partial stay of the original trial court order.

Blackmun told Judge Stuart that the language of his order was too vague for First Amendment purposes and that prohibitions on the reporting of details of the crime, the identities of the victims, and the testimony of a pathologist at a public preliminary hearing were unjustified. But the rest of Stuart's order stood.[43] With their numbers swelling, the media now asked the full United States Supreme Court to strike down what was left of Judge Stuart's restrictive order.

Meanwhile the Nebraska Supreme Court had heard arguments in the case on November 25 as scheduled. Still reluctant to exercise concurrent jurisdiction with the High Court, the Nebraska Supreme Court nevertheless upheld crucial parts of the original order in a 5–2 decision. Noting that "under some circumstances prior restraint may be appropriate," the state court concluded that a "clear and present danger" to a fair trial in North Platte, Lincoln, or even Denver overcame "the heavy presumption of unconstitutionality of the prior restraint." Missing in the court's analysis was evidence of how press coverage influences jury verdicts or any consideration of why rumors in this case were better for prospective jurors than facts.[44]

42. Nebraska Press Association v. Stuart, 1 Med.L.Rptr. 1059, 423 U.S. 1319 (1975).

43. Nebraska Press Association v. Stuart, 423 U.S. 1327 (1975).

44. State v. Simants, 236 N.W.2d 794 (Neb.1975).

The state supreme court agreed with Justice Blackmun, however, that voluntary press-bar guidelines were not intended to be contractual or mandatory and could not be enforced as though they were. That part of Judge Stuart's order was overturned. But any information implying guilt or a confession was not to be published. The Nebraska court was obviously influenced by Justice Blackmun's second chambers opinion.

On December 12, 1975, the United States Supreme Court agreed to review the Nebraska court's order, but not with the speed Justices Marshall, Brennan, and Stewart thought necessary. The three would have lifted the Nebraska Supreme Court's order pending final resolution of the issue. Justice Blackmun, on the other hand, seemed to have forgotten his own earlier admonition that with each passing day there is a "separate and cognizable infringement of the First Amendment."

Simants was convicted on six counts of first-degree murder on January 17, 1976 and sentenced to death.

2. Twenty-five newspapers, led by the *Washington Post,* and the ABC network filed an *amicus curiae* brief which was to influence the Court.

"Approval of what the Nebraska courts have done here," said the brief, "would restrict the editorial freedom of the press, and indeed would make judges into editors." Judicial remedies available to the court were not considered. Its orders were unconstitutionally vague and overbroad. The question presented in the case, the brief noted, is whether a second (national security being the first), wholly novel, exception to the prior restraint doctrine should be created to apply to the reporting of crimes and the administration of criminal justice. There should not, the brief concluded.

The Supreme Court was not to go quite so far. On June 30, 1976, in an otherwise unanimous decision striking down the Nebraska court's gag order in the Simants case, six justices held that in exceptional circumstances prior restraints might be constitutional in a criminal case. Surprisingly the Chief Justice, speaking for the Court, used a test for prior restraint which had become symbolic of the repression of First Amendment rights: whether "the gravity of the 'evil,' discounted by its improbability, justifies such invasion of free speech as is necessary to avoid the danger." The language is Federal District Court Judge Learned Hand's reformulation of the clear and present danger test which was applied by the Supreme Court in Dennis v. United States, 341 U.S. 494 (1951), the landmark, and since discredited, Communist conspiracy case.

It is also worth noting that every justice writing an opinion in *Nebraska* makes his own intuitive estimate of the effects of reporting on the fairness of a trial. The empirical literature is ignored.

After reviewing the leading free press-fair trial and prior restraint cases and emphasizing the responsibility of the trial judge in applying, short of prior restraint, the "strong measures" outlined in *Sheppard* to protect the defendant, the Court announced the decision below.

NEBRASKA PRESS ASSOCIATION v. STUART

1 MED.L.RPTR. 1059, 427 U.S. 539, 96 S.CT. 2791, 49 L.ED.2D 683 (1976).

Chief Justice BURGER delivered the opinion of the Court:

* * *

The thread running through all these cases is that prior restraints on speech and publication are the most serious and the least tolerable infringement on First Amendment rights. A criminal penalty or a judgment in a defamation case is subject to the whole panoply of protections afforded by deferring the impact of the judgment until all avenues of appellate review have been exhausted. Only after judgment has become final, correct or otherwise, does the law's sanction become fully operative.

A prior restraint, by contrast and by definition, has an immediate and irreversible sanction. If it can be said that a threat of criminal or civil sanctions after publication "chills" speech, prior restraint "freezes" it at least for the time.

The damage can be particularly great when the prior restraint falls upon the communication of news and commentary on current events. Truthful reports of public judicial proceedings have been afforded special protection against subsequent punishment. For the same reasons the protection against prior restraint should have particular force as applied to reporting of criminal proceedings, whether the crime in question is a single isolated act or a pattern of criminal conduct.

* * *

The extraordinary protections afforded by the First Amendment carry with them something in the nature of a fiduciary duty to exercise the protected rights responsibly—a duty widely acknowledged but not always observed by editors and publishers. It is not asking too much to suggest that those who exercise First Amendment rights in newspapers or broadcasting enterprises direct some effort to protect the rights of an accused to a fair trial by unbiased jurors.

Of course, the order at issue—like the order requested in *New York Times*—does not prohibit but only postpones publication. Some news can be delayed and most commentary can even more readily be delayed without serious injury, and there often is a self-imposed delay when responsible editors call for verification of information. But such delays are normally slight and they are self-imposed. Delays imposed by governmental authority are a different matter. * * * As a practical matter, moreover, the element of time is not unimportant if press coverage is to fulfill its traditional function of bringing news to the public promptly.

* * *

The Nebraska courts in this case enjoined the publication of certain kinds of information about the Simants case. There are, as we suggested earlier, marked differences in setting and purpose between the order entered here and the orders in *Near, Keefe,* and *New York Times,* but as to the underlying issue—the right of the press to be free from *prior* restraints on publication—those cases form the backdrop against which we must decide this case.

We turn now to the record in this case to determine whether, as Learned Hand put it, *"the gravity of the 'evil,' discounted by its improbability, justifies such invasion of free speech as is necessary to avoid the danger."* [Emphasis added.] United States v. Dennis, 183 F.2d 201, 212 (1950), aff'd, 341 U.S. 494 (1951); see also L. Hand, The Bill of Rights 58–61 (1958). To do so, we must examine the evidence before the trial judge when the order was entered to determine (a) the nature and extent of pretrial news coverage; (b) whether other measures would be likely to mitigate the effects of unrestrained pretrial publicity; (c) how effectively a restraining order would operate to prevent the threatened danger. The precise terms of the restraining order are also important. We must then consider whether the record supports the entry of a prior restraint on publication, one of the most extraordinary remedies known to our jurisprudence.

In assessing the probable extent of publicity, the trial judge had before him newspapers demonstrating that the crime had already drawn intensive news coverage, and the testimony of the County Judge, who had entered the initial restraining order based on the local and national attention the case had attracted. The District Judge was required to assess the probable publicity that would be given these shocking crimes prior to the time a jury was selected and sequestered. He then had to examine the probable nature of the publicity and determine how it would affect prospective jurors.

Our review of the pretrial record persuades us that the trial judge was justified in concluding that there would be intense and pervasive pretrial publicity concerning this case. He could also reasonably conclude, based on common human experience, that publicity might impair the defendant's right to a fair trial. He did not purport to say more, for he found only "a clear and present danger that pretrial publicity *could* impinge upon the defendant's right to a fair trial." [Emphasis added.] His conclusion as to the impact of such publicity on prospective jurors was of necessity speculative, dealing as he was with *factors unknown and unknowable.* [Emphasis added.]

We find little in the record that goes to another aspect of our task, determining whether measures short of an order restraining all publication would have insured the defendant a fair trial. Although the entry of the order might be read as a judicial determination that other measures would not suffice, the trial court made no express findings to that effect; the Nebraska Supreme Court referred to the issue only by implication.

* * *

We have therefore examined this record to determine the probable efficacy of the measures short of prior restraint on the press and speech. There is no finding that alternative measures would not have protected Simants' rights, and the Nebraska Supreme Court did no more than imply that such measures might not be adequate. Moreover, the record is lacking in evidence to support such a finding.

* * *

Finally, we note that the events disclosed by the record took place in a community of 850 people. It is reasonable to assume that, without any news accounts being printed or broadcast, rumors would travel swiftly by word of mouth. One can only speculate on the accuracy of such reports, given the generative propensities of rumors; they could well be more damaging than reasonably accurate news accounts. But plainly a whole community cannot be restrained from discussing a subject intimately affecting life within it.

Given these practical problems, it is far from clear that prior restraint on publication would have protected Simants' rights.

Finally, another feature of this case leads us to conclude that the restrictive order entered here is not supportable. At the outset the County Court entered a very broad restrictive order, the terms of which are not before us; it then held a preliminary hearing open to the public and the press. There was testimony concerning at least two incriminating statements made by Simants to private persons; the statement—evidently a confession—that he gave to law enforcement officials was also introduced. The State District Court's later order was entered after this public hearing and, as modified by the Nebraska Supreme Court, enjoined reporting of (1) "[c]onfessions or admissions against interests made by the accused to law enforcement officials"; (2) "[c]onfessions or admissions against interest, oral or written, if any, made by the accused to third parties, excepting any statements, if any, made by the accused to representatives of the news media"; and (3) all "[o]ther information strongly implicative of the accused as the perpetrator of the slayings."

To the extent that this order prohibited the reporting of evidence adduced at the open preliminary hearing, it plainly violated settled principles: "there is nothing that proscribes the press from reporting events that transpire in the courtroom." The County Court could not know that closure of the preliminary hearing was an alternative open to it until the Nebraska

Supreme Court so construed state law; but once a public hearing had been held, what transpired there could not be subject to prior restraint.

The third prohibition of the order was defective in another respect as well. As part of a final order, entered after plenary review, this prohibition regarding "implicative" information is too vague and too broad to survive the scrutiny we have given to restraints on First Amendment rights. The third phase of the order entered falls outside permissible limits.

The record demonstrates, as the Nebraska courts held, that there was indeed a risk that pretrial news accounts, true or false, would have some adverse impact on the attitudes of those who might be called as jurors. But on the record now before us it is not clear that further publicity, unchecked, would so distort the views of potential jurors that 12 could not be found who would, under proper instructions, fulfill their sworn duty to render a just verdict exclusively on the evidence presented in open court. We cannot say on this record that alternatives to a prior restraint on petitioners would not have sufficiently mitigated the adverse effects of pretrial publicity so as to make prior restraint unnecessary. Nor can we conclude that the restraining order actually entered would serve its intended purpose. Reasonable minds can have few doubts about the gravity of the evil pretrial publicity can work, but the probability that it would do so here was not demonstrated with the degree of certainty our cases on prior restraint require.

Of necessity our holding is confined to the record before us. But our conclusion is not simply a result of assessing the adequacy of the showing made in this case; it results in part from the problems inherent in meeting the heavy burden of demonstrating, in advance of trial, that without prior restraint a fair trial will be denied. The practical problems of managing and enforcing restrictive orders will always be present. In this sense, the record now before us is illustrative rather than exceptional. It is significant that when this Court has reversed a state conviction, because of prejudicial publicity, it has carefully noted that some course of action short of prior restraint would have made a critical difference. However difficult it may be, we need not rule out the possibility of showing the kind of threat to fair trial rights that would possess the requisite degree of certainty to justify restraint. This Court has frequently denied that First Amendment rights are absolute and has consistently rejected the proposition that a prior restraint can never be employed.

Our analysis ends as it began, with a confrontation between prior restraint imposed to protect one vital constitutional guarantee and the explicit command of another that the freedom to speak and publish shall not be abridged. *We reaffirm that the guarantees of freedom of expression are not an absolute prohibition under all circumstances, but the barriers to prior restraint remain high and the presumption against its use continues intact.* [Emphasis added.] We hold that, with respect to the order entered in this case prohibiting reporting or commentary on judicial proceedings held in public, the barriers have not been overcome; to the extent that this order restrained publication of such material, it is clearly invalid. To the extent that it prohibited publication based on information gained from other sources, we conclude that the heavy burden imposed as a condition to securing a prior restraint was not met and the judgment of the Nebraska Supreme Court is therefore

Reversed.

COMMENT

1. Prior restraints, the Court seemed to be saying, must be preceded by a clear demonstration of the harmful effects of publicity on the jury, a relationship which the

Chief Justice at the same time considered "unknown and unknowable." There must be a showing that the prior restraint would be effective and that no alternatives, e.g., judicial remedies, less destructive of First Amendment rights, are available. It is difficult to imagine these preliminary barriers ever being hurdled. Trial judges were being asked to make judgments about juror prejudice before jurors were examined on the question.

In *Nebraska Press,* Burger said there was a heavy First Amendment presumption against the validity of "gag orders."

Finally the Court seemed to be saying that the effectiveness of a prior restraint must be assured before such an order is issued. (A media organization could only be bound by a court whose jurisdiction it was in.) Again this is a tall order, given the difficulty of predicting how a restraining order would work to protect fair trial.

For a discussion of the impact of *Nebraska Press* on the doctrine of prior restraint, see this text, p. 126.

2. Burger spoke for a Court which was unanimous with respect to the result. Justice White in a concurring opinion doubted, however, whether the *Nebraska*-type restraining order would ever be justifiable. And if that were so, he thought it might be wiser in the long run simply to declare "gag orders" against the press violative of the First Amendment. Justice Brennan, joined by Stewart and Marshall, flatly declared "gag orders" would never be constitutional if applied to the press. Brennan advocated what is sometimes called a *per se* rule: i.e., "gag orders" are *per se* invalid under the First Amendment.

"Settled case law concerning the impropriety and constitutional invalidity of prior restraints on the press," Brennan said in a comprehensive review of the conflict, "compels the conclusion that there can be no prohibition on the publication by the press of any information pertaining to pending judicial proceedings or the operation of the criminal justice system, no matter how shabby the means by which the information is obtained."

Brennan then spoke to the futility of a prior restraint:

> A judge importuned to issue a prior restraint in the pretrial context will be unable to predict the manner in which the potentially prejudicial information would be published, the frequency with which it would be repeated or the emphasis it would be given, the context in which or purpose for which it would be reported, the scope of the audience that would be exposed to the information, or the impact, evaluated in terms of current standards for assessing juror impartiality, the information would have on that audience. These considerations would render speculative the prospective impact on a fair trial of reporting even an alleged confession or other information "strongly implicative" of the accused. Moreover, we can take judicial notice of the fact that given the prevalence of plea bargaining, few criminal cases proceed to trial, and the judge would thus have to predict what the likelihood was that a jury would even have to be impaneled. Indeed, even in cases that do proceed to trial, the material sought to be suppressed before trial will often be admissible and may be admitted in any event. And, more basically, there are adequate devices for screening from jury duty those individuals who have in fact been exposed to prejudicial pretrial publicity.

Brennan feared that the overemployment of restrictive orders would burden the press and the First Amendment so as to discourage crime and court coverage, especially by economically marginal media that might elect not to contest even blatantly unconstitutional restraints. The argument appeared to be taken from a letter written by the editor and publisher of the Anniston (Ala.) *Star* and included in the media's *amicus* brief to the Court.

Simants's first conviction was overturned on the basis of evidence that a sheriff had lobbied a sequestered jury. On retrial he was found not guilty by reason of insanity, a verdict that did not sit well in some Nebraska circles.

Why didn't Chief Justice Burger support a rule that "gag orders" were *per se* invalid?

The Court bolstered *Nebraska Press* when in Oklahoma Publishing Co. v. District Court, 2 Med.L.Rptr. 1456, 430 U.S. 308 (1977), it held that news media could not be prohibited from publishing the name or picture of a juvenile where the name had been reported in open court proceedings and the photograph taken without objection as the juvenile was being escorted from the courthouse. "Once a public hearing has been held," said the court, "what transpired there could not be subject to prior restraint."

Two terms later in Smith v. Daily Mail Publishing Co., 5 Med.L.Rptr. 1305, 443 U.S. 97 (1979), the Court reached an identical conclusion. The First Amendment was violated, said the Court, by a West Virginia statute that imposed criminal sanctions on a newspaper for truthful publication of a juvenile offender's name that had been lawfully obtained. The state interest in protecting the anonymity of a juvenile was insufficient to justify the encroachment on freedom of press. The Court relied on Landmark Communications, Inc. v. Virginia, 3 Med.L.Rptr. 2153, 435 U.S. 829 (1978). There a state law making it a crime to publish information about confidential proceedings before a legislatively authorized judicial review committee hearing complaints against a judge was struck down.

The First Amendment protects the publication of truthful information, and only the highest form of state interest would condone prior restraints.

3. There is yet another problem. How does a judge in a case that attracts wide attention control media coverage outside of his jurisdiction? Before her trial on a charge of attempting to murder Gerald Ford, Lynette Fromme asked a federal district court to enjoin the showing of a "Manson" film in twenty-six California counties. She argued that her depiction coddling a rifle would deny her right to a fair trial. The court agreed but members of the prospective audience did not, and they fought the order until it was mooted by selection of the jury.

4. Wasn't the court's use of a modified clear and present danger test disingenuous? The Simants facts, objectively, seemed to meet a clear and present danger standard. The fact that the Court thought otherwise only suggests the impropriety of the standard and the wisdom of invalidating "gag orders" against the press *per se.* The difficulty with relying on the clear and present danger test in such circumstances is that it will mislead trial courts into issuing "gag orders" which will not survive on appeal.

5. It should be noted that the opinions of the justices in *Nebraska Press* mentioned without comment two alternatives to "gag orders" against the press: 1) "gag orders" against nonmedia personnel such as lawyers, accused, officers of the court,[45]

45. When a gag order aimed directly at lawyers was appealed, the Seventh Circuit in a significant ruling struck it down because the trial court had used a "reasonable likelihood" test rather than a "clear and present danger" or "clear and imminent danger" test. The court was unconvinced that justice would be served by silenced lawyers, especially those representing the defense, given the fact that public opinion weighs heavily against most defendants after arrest and indictment. While recognizing that restraints on lawyers were sometimes permissible, the court found constitutionally infirm the blanket prohibitions contained in the standing rules recommended by the American Bar Association and the Judicial Conference. Seldom would lawyer comments pose a "clear and present danger" to the administration of justice. Chicago Council of Lawyers v. Bauer, 1 Med.L.Rptr. 1094, 522 F.2d 242 (7th Cir. 1975), cert. den., 427 U.S. 912. See also, State ex rel. Angel v. Woodahl, 555 P.2d 501 (Mont.1976). But see, People v. Dupree, 2 Med.L.Rptr. 2015, 388 N.Y.S.2d 203 (1976) and Hirschkop v. Virginia State Bar, 406 F.Supp. 721 (D.Va.1976) where "reasonable likelihood" tests were preferred.

and 2) exclusionary orders barring the public, including the media, from the courtroom. It is little wonder that with such authoritative encouragement, these techniques became the most commonly reported devices used to circumvent the *Nebraska Press* holding.

CLOSED COURTROOMS

1. Generations of debate have focused on questions of access to the judicial process (hearings, trials, and records) and whether the constitutional guarantee of public trial is meant primarily for the protection of an accused or for the benefit of the public.[46] Nonetheless, courtrooms were routinely closed to press and public. They were closed to preserve order and decorum, to protect witnesses, public morality, trade secrets, the confidentiality of police, national security, the privacy rights of participants, and the fragile psyches of juveniles. Judicial records were sealed when it appeared to the court that there were no alternative means to protect a defendant against prejudice. Access might be argued successfully when it could be demonstrated that alternatives to closure had not been considered, that there was no showing of a serious and imminent threat to the fair administration of justice, that no thought had been given to closing portions of a hearing or redacting parts of a record, and that no hearing had been afforded the press pending an exclusionary order.

To complicate matters, there was wide variation in state rules or statutes on suppression hearings, competency hearings, bail hearings, deposition sessions, general preliminary hearings, *voir dire,* matrimonial and juvenile hearings, trials, and post-trial hearings.

In this atmosphere of uncertainty *Gannett v. DePasquale*[47] came to the Supreme Court. A divided Court, at least for a time, was to resolve doubts in favor of the accused. The Court held that press and public have no Sixth Amendment right of access to pretrial suppression hearings closed by agreement of both prosecution and defense. Guarantee of a public criminal trial was for the defendant's benefit alone, said the Court, and no First and Fourteenth Amendment issues were raised by the closure order of the New York trial court.

"To safeguard the due process rights of the accused," the Court added, "a trial judge has an affirmative constitutional duty to minimize the effects of prejudicial pretrial publicity, and he may take protective measures even though they are not strictly and inescapably necessary. Publicity concerning pretrial suppression hearings pose special risks of unfairness because it may influence public opinion against a defendant and inform potential jurors of inculpatory information wholly inadmissible at the actual trial."

Here the defendant's right to a fair trial outweighed the constitutional rights of

46. E.W. Scripps Co. v. Fulton, 125 N.E.2d 896 (Ohio 1955); Kirstowsky v. Superior Court, 300 P.2d 163 (Cal.1956); United Press Association v. Valente, 123 N.E.2d 777 (N.Y.1954); Geise v. United States, 265 F.2d 659 (9th Cir. 1959); Singer v. United States, 380 U.S. 24 (1964); Phoenix Newspapers, Inc. v. Jennings, 1 Med.L.Rptr. 2404, 490 P.2d 563 (Ariz.1971); Oliver v. Postel, 1 Med.L.Rptr. 2399, 331 N.Y.S.2d 407 (1972); United States v. Clark, 475 F.2d 240 (2d Cir. 1973); Gannett Co. v. Mark, 2 Med.L.Rptr. 1189, 387 N.Y.S.2d 336 (1976); Hearst Corp. v. Cholakis, 2 Med.L.Rptr. 2085, 386 N.Y.S.2d 892 (1976); Commercial Printing v. Lee, 2 Med.L.Rptr. 2352, 553 S.W.2d 270 (Ark.1977); CBS, Inc. v. Young, 1 Med.L.Rptr. 1024, 522 F.2d 234 (6th Cir. 1975); Society of Professional Journalists v. Martin, 2 Med.L.Rptr. 2146, 556 F.2d 706 (4th Cir. 1977); United States v. Gurney, 3 Med.L.Rptr. 1081, 558 F.2d 1202 (5th Cir. 1977); New Jersey v. Allen, 2 Med.L.Rptr. 1737, 373 A.2d 377 (N.J.1977); Illinois v. March, 7 Med.L.Rptr. 1465, 419 N.E.2d 1212 (Ill.1981).

47. 5 Med.L.Rptr. 1337, 443 U.S. 368 (1979).

press and public. But Justice Stewart's opinion for the Court was ambiguous as to whether trials as well as pretrial hearings would be covered by the rule. Chief Justice Burger, in a concurring opinion, sharply differentiated trial and pretrial proceedings but provided no clear constitutional distinction. Justice Rehnquist saw no right of access to either part of the judicial process under First or Sixth Amendments.

Only in Justice Powell's concurring opinion [48] could the press find a ray of hope. Powell wrote that there was a qualified First Amendment right to attend pretrial hearings, although he found no equivalent Sixth Amendment right. And press and public must have an opportunity to be heard on the question of their exclusion.

In a vigorous dissenting opinion in which Justices Brennan, White, and Marshall joined, Justice Blackmun read public access in the Sixth Amendment. He would require an accused to show that there existed a "substantial probability that irreparable damage" to fair trial would result from public proceedings and that alternatives to closure would not suffice.

In the twelve-month period after the ruling, an estimated 270 efforts were made to close various phases of criminal proceedings: 131 closure motions were granted and upheld on appeal; 14 were reversed; and 111 were either denied by the trial court or withdrawn by counsel. Of the total number of motions, 171 sought to close pretrial hearings, 49 to close trials. About half were granted in each category.[49]

In the meantime, the justices themselves seemed to be unsure whether the Court's opinion had meant to ease the closing of trials as well as pretrial hearings. That question would be faced in a landmark case a year later, Richmond Newspapers, Inc. v. Virginia, 6 Med.L.Rptr. 1833, 448 U.S. 555 (1980). There Chief Justice Burger held for the Court that closing of a criminal trial in the absence of an overriding counter interest was invalid under First and Fourteenth Amendments.

In spite of the potential significance of the case and the near unanimity of its vote, the Court remained "badly splintered" [50] and imprecise as to what it would take to overcome the federal constitutional right to attend criminal trials.

A brief summary of the *Richmond* opinions may help in reading substantial excerpts from the case itself.

Justice Stewart, who wrote the opinion for the Court in *Gannett,* joined the judgment of the Court in *Richmond* and wrote a separate concurrence recognizing a First Amendment right to attend trials. Stevens, who had joined Stewart in *Gannett,* agreed and characterized the case as a watershed: "[F]or the first time, the Court unequivocally holds that an arbitrary interference with access to important information is an abridgement of the freedom of speech and of the press protected by the First Amendment."

Blackmun, who dissented in *Gannett,* concurred, recognizing a First Amendment right of access to trials in addition to a Sixth Amendment guarantee of access to all judicial proceedings. Brennan and Marshall, who had also dissented in *Gannett,* concurred only in the judgment of the Court, holding that the First Amendment, applied through the Fourteenth, gives the press a structural role to play in keeping the public informed and the public an independent right of access to trials. And Justice White, the fourth dissenter in *Gan-*

48. Powell's concurrence had originally been a dissent. The switch made Stewart's original dissent the opinion for the Court. This last minute and end-of-term rearrangement accounts for some of the uncertainty in the *Gannett* opinions.

49. *News Media & the Law,* August/September, November/December, 1979, pp. 7–9, 10–23.

50. Archibald Cox, *Freedom of Expression,* 1982.

nett, said that that case should have construed the Sixth Amendment to forbid excluding the public from criminal proceedings except under certain narrowly defined circumstances.

Rehnquist held to his *Gannett* view that First and Sixth Amendments extend no right of access to judicial proceedings. Justice Powell took no part in *Richmond.*

None of the justices explained why a Sixth Amendment analysis was used in *Gannett* and a First Amendment approach in *Richmond.* And there is still little agreement on what ought to be the standards for closure.

While he was reluctant to denote a First Amendment right of access in *Richmond,* Justice Blackmun's standard of "substantial probability of irreparable damage" for closing courtrooms would commend itself to Justices Brennan, Marshall, and White. And all four would likely join White in wanting to be sure that alternatives to closure would not work and, if closure were required, it would be effective. It is not clear, however, how far White would support access beyond judicial situations. Brennan and Marshall on the other hand, have suggested that only national security interests should override the virtue of open judicial hearings.

"A reasonable probability of prejudice" would justify closure for Justice Stevens and the Chief Justice. And Burger appears to be more hospitable to the long tradition of public trials than he is to open pretrial hearings, the use of which may not have been anticipated by the Framers. Nor would he automatically extend access to other institutions of government. Although Justice Powell did not participate in *Richmond,* his rather relaxed "likelihood of prejudice" standard might be what he would apply to a trial closure.

So *Richmond,* leaving *Gannett* intact, presented the press with something less than certainty about its news-gathering rights.

RICHMOND NEWSPAPERS, INC. v. VIRGINIA

6 MED.L.RPTR. 1833, 448 U.S. 555, 100 S.CT. 2814, 65 L.ED.2D 973 (1980).

* * *

Chief Justice BURGER announced the judgment of the Court and delivered an opinion in which Justice White and Justice Stevens joined.

The narrow question presented in this case is whether the right of the public and press to attend criminal trials is guaranteed under the United States Constitution.

I

In March 1976, one Stevenson was indicted for the murder of a hotel manager who had been found stabbed to death on December 2, 1975. Tried promptly in July 1976, Stevenson was convicted of second-degree murder in the Circuit Court of Hanover County, Va. The Virginia Supreme Court reversed the conviction in October 1977, holding that a bloodstained shirt purportedly belonging to Stevenson had been improperly admitted into evidence. * * *

Stevenson was retried in the same court. This second trial ended in a mistrial on May 30, 1978 when a juror asked to be excused after trial had begun and no alternate was available.

A third trial, which began in the same court on June 6, 1978, also ended in a mistrial. It appears that the mistrial may have been declared because a prospective juror had read about Stevenson's previous trials in a newspaper and had told other prospective jurors about the case before the retrial began. * * *

Stevenson was tried in the same court for a fourth time beginning on September 11, 1978. Present in the courtroom when the case was called were appellants Wheeler and McCarthy, reporters for appellant Richmond Newspapers, Inc. Before the trial began, counsel for the defendant moved that it be closed to the public:

> [T]here was this woman that was with the family of the deceased when we were here before. She had sat in the Courtroom. I would like to ask that everybody be excluded from the Courtroom because I don't want any information being shuffled back and forth when we have a recess as to what—who testified to what. * * *

The trial judge, who had presided over two of the three previous trials, asked if the prosecution had any objection to clearing the courtroom. The prosecutor stated he had no objection and would leave it to the discretion of the court. * * * Presumably referring to Virginia Code § 19.2–266, the trial judge then announced: "[T]he statute gives me that power specifically and the defendant has made the motion." He then ordered "that the Courtroom be kept clear of all parties except the witnesses when they testify." * * * [2] The record does not show that any objections to the closure order were made by anyone present at the time, including appellants Wheeler and McCarthy.

Later that same day, however, appellants sought a hearing on a motion to vacate the closure order. The trial judge granted the request and scheduled a hearing to follow the close of the day's proceedings. When the hearing began, the court ruled that the hearing was to be treated as part of the trial; accordingly, he again ordered the reporters to leave the courtroom, and they complied.

At the closed hearing, counsel for appellants observed that no evidentiary findings had been made by the court prior to the entry of its closure order and pointed out that the court had failed to consider any other, less drastic measures within its power to ensure a fair trial. * * * Counsel for appellants argued that constitutional considerations mandated that before ordering closure, the court should first decide that the rights of the defendant could be protected in no other way.

Counsel for defendant Stevenson pointed out that this was the fourth time he was standing trial. He also referred to "difficulty with information between jurors," and stated that he "didn't want information to leak out," be published by the media, perhaps inaccurately, and then be seen by the jurors. Defense counsel argued that these things, plus the fact that "this is a small community," made this a proper case for closure. * * *

The trial judge noted that counsel for the defendant had made similar statements at the morning hearing. The court also stated:

> [O]ne of the other points that we take into consideration in this particular Courtroom is layout of the Courtroom. I think that having people in the Courtroom is distracting to the jury. Now, we have to have certain people in here and maybe that's not a very good reason. When we get into our new Court Building, people can sit in the audience so the jury can't see them. The rule of the Court may be different under those circumstances. * * *

The prosecutor again declined comment, and the court summed up by saying:

> I'm inclined to agree with [defense counsel] that, if I feel that the rights of the defendant are infringed in any way, [when] he makes the motion to do something and it doesn't completely override all rights of everyone else, then I'm inclined to go along with the defendant's motion. * * *

2. Virginia Code § 19.2–266 provides in part: "In the trial of all criminal cases, whether the same be felony or misdemeanor cases, the court may, in its discretion, exclude from the trial any persons whose presence would impair the conduct of a fair trial, provided that the right of the accused to a public trial shall not be violated."

The court denied the motion to vacate and ordered the trial to continue the following morning "with the press and public excluded." * * *

What transpired when the closed trial resumed the next day was disclosed in the following manner by an order of the court entered September 12, 1978:

> [I]n the absence of the jury, the defendant by counsel made a Motion that a mis-trial be declared, which motion was taken under advisement. At the conclusion of the Commonwealth's evidence, the attorney for the defendant moved the Court to strike the Commonwealth's evidence on grounds stated to the record, which Motion was sustained by the Court. And the jury having been excused, the Court doth find the accused NOT GUILTY of Murder, as charged in the Indictment, and he was allowed to depart. * * *

On September 27, 1978 the trial court granted appellants' motion to intervene *nun pro tunc* in the Stevenson case. Appellants then petitioned the Virginia Supreme Court for writs of mandamus and prohibition and filed an appeal from the trial court's closure order. On July 9, 1979, the Virginia Supreme Court dismissed the mandamus and prohibition petitions and, finding no reversible error, denied the petition for appeal. * * *

Appellants then sought review in this Court. * * * [W]e grant the petition.

The criminal trial which appellants sought to attend has long since ended, and there is thus some suggestion that the case is moot. * * * If the underlying dispute is "capable of repetition, yet evading review," * * *, it is not moot.

Since the Virginia Supreme Court declined plenary review, it is reasonably foreseeable that other trials may be closed by other judges without any more showing of need than is presented on this record. More often than not, criminal trials will be of sufficiently short duration that a closure order "will evade review, or at least considered plenary review in this Court." Nebraska Press, 427 U.S., at 547. * * * Accordingly, we turn to the merits.

II

We begin consideration of this case by noting that the precise issue presented here has not previously been before this Court for decision. In Gannett Co., Inc. v. DePasquale, 443 U.S. 368, * * * (1979), the Court was not required to decide whether a right of access to *trials,* as distinguished from hearings on *pre* trial motions, was constitutionally guaranteed. The Court held that the Sixth Amendment's guarantee to the accused of a public trial gave neither the public nor the press an enforceable right of access to a *pre* trial suppression hearing. One concurring opinion specifically emphasized that "a hearing on a motion before trial to suppress evidence is not a *trial* * * *." 433 U.S., at 394, * * * (Burger, C.J., concurring). Moreover, the Court did not decide whether the First and Fourteenth Amendments guarantee a right of the public to attend trials, *id.,* at 392 and n. 24, * * *; nor did the dissenting opinion reach this issue. *Id.,* at 447, 99 S.Ct., at 2940 (Blackmun, J., dissenting).

In prior cases the Court has treated questions involving conflicts between publicity and a defendant's right to a fair trial; as we observed in *Nebraska Press Assn. v. Stuart,* * * *, "[t]he problems presented by this [conflict] are almost as old as the Republic." * * * But here for the first time the Court is asked to decide whether a criminal trial itself may be closed to the public upon the unopposed request of a defendant, without any demonstration that closure is required to protect the defendant's superior right to a fair trial, or that some other overriding consideration requires closure.

A

The origins of the proceeding which has become the modern criminal trial in Anglo-American justice can be traced back beyond reliable historical records. We need not here review all details of its development, but a summary of that history is instructive. What is significant for present purposes is that throughout its evolution, the trial has been open to all who care to observe.

In the days before the Norman Conquest, cases in England were generally brought before moots, such as the local court of the hundred or the county court, which were attended by the freemen of the community. Pollock, English Law Before the Norman Conquest, in 1 Selected Essays in Anglo-American Legal History 89 (1907). Somewhat like modern jury duty, attendance at these early meetings was compulsory on the part of the freemen, who were called upon to render judgment. *Id.,* at 89–90; see also 1 W. Holdsworth, A History of English Law 10, 12 (1927).

With the gradual evolution of the jury system in the years after the Norman Conquest, see, *e.g.,* 1 Holdsworth, *supra,* at 316, the duty of all freemen to attend trials to render judgment was relaxed, but there is no indication that criminal trials did not remain public. When certain groups were excused from compelled attendance, see The Statute of Marleborough, 1267, 52 Hen. 3, c. 10; 1 Holdsworth, *supra,* at 79, and n. 4, the statutory exemption did not prevent them from attending; Lord Coke observed that those excused "are not compellable to come, but left to their own liberty." 2 E. Coke, Institutes of the Laws of England 121 (6th ed. 1681).[6]

Although there appear to be a few contemporary statements on the subject, reports of the Eyre of Kent, a general court held in 1313–1314, evince a recognition of the importance of public attendance apart from the "jury duty" aspect. It was explained that:

> the King's will was that all evil doers should be punished after their deserts, and that justice should be ministered indifferently to rich as to poor; *and for the better accomplishing of this,* he prayed the community of the county *by their attendance* there to lend him their aid in the establishing of a happy and certain peace that should be both for the honour of the realm and for their own welfare. 1 Holdsworth, *supra,* at 268, quoting from the S.S. edition of the Eyre of Kent, vol. i., p. 2 (emphasis added).

From these early times, although great changes in courts and procedures took place, one thing remained constant: the public character of the trial at which guilt or innocence was decided. Sir Thomas Smith, writing in 1565 about "the definitive proceedings in causes criminall," explained that, while the indictment was put in writing as in civil law countries:

> All the rest is done openlie in the presence of the Judges, the Justices, the enquest, the prisoner, *and so manie as will or can come so neare as to heare it,* and all depositions and witnesses given aloude, *that all men may heare from the mouth of the depositors and witnesses what is saide.* T. Smith, *De Republica Anglorum* 101 (Alston ed. 1972) [emphasis added].

Three centuries later, Sir Frederick Pollock was able to state of the "rule of publicity" that, "[h]ere we have one tradition, at any rate, which has persisted through all changes." F. Pollock, The Expansion of the Common Law 31–32 (1904). See also E. Jenks, The Book of English Law 73–74 (6th ed. 1967): "[O]ne of the most conspic-

6. Coke interpreted certain language of an earlier chapter of the same statute as specifically indicating that court proceedings were to be public in nature: "These words [In curia Domini Regis] are of great importance, for all Causes ought to be heard, ordered, and determined before the Judges of the King's Courts *openly* in the King's Courts, *wither all persons may resort.* * * *" 2 E. Coke, Institutes of the Laws of England 103 (6th ed. 1681) [emphasis added].

uous features of English justice, that all judicial trials are held in open court, to which the public have free access, * *," appears to have been the rule in England from time immemorial."

We have found nothing to suggest that the presumptive openness of the trial, which English courts were later to call "one of the essential qualities of a court of justice," Daubney v. Cooper, 10 B. & C. 237, 240, 109 Eng.Rep. 438, 440 (K.B.1829), was not also an attribute of the judicial systems of colonial America. In Virginia, for example, such records as there are of early criminal trials indicate that they were open, and nothing to the contrary has been cited. See A. Scott, Criminal Law in Colonial Virginia 128–129 (1930); Reinsch, The English Common Law in the Early American Colonies, in 1 Selected Essays in Anglo-American Legal History 405 (1907). Indeed, when in the mid-1600's the Virginia Assembly felt that the respect due the courts was "by the clamorous unmannerlynes of the people lost, and order, gravity and decoram which should manifest the authority of a court in the court it selfe neglicted," the response was not to restrict the openness of the trials to the public, but instead to prescribe rules for the conduct of those attending them. See Scott, *supra,* at 132.

In some instances, the openness of trials was explicitly recognized as part of the fundamental law of the colony. The 1677 Concessions and Agreements of West New Jersey, for example, provided:

> That in all publick courts of justice for tryals of causes, civil or criminal, any person or persons, inhabitants of the said Province may freely come into, and attend the said courts, and hear and be present, at all or any such tryals as shall be there had or passed, that justice may not be done in a corner nor in any covert manner. Reprinted in Sources of Our Liberties 188 (R. Perry ed. 1959). See also 1 B. Schwartz, The Bill of Rights: A Documentary History 129 (1971).

The Pennsylvania Frame of Government of 1682 also provided "[t]hat all courts shall be open * * *," Sources of Our Liberties, *supra,* at 217; 1 B. Schwartz, *supra,* at 140, and this declaration was reaffirmed in section 26 of the Constitution adopted by Pennsylvania in 1776. See 1 B. Schwartz, *supra,* at 271. See also §§ 12 and 76 of the Massachusetts Body of Liberties, 1641, reprinted in 1 Schwartz, *supra,* at 73, 80.

Other contemporary writings confirm the recognition that part of the very nature of a criminal trial was its openness to those who wished to attend. Perhaps the best indication of this is found in an address to the inhabitants of Quebec which was drafted by a committee consisting of Thomas Cushing, Richard Henry Lee, and John Dickinson and approved by the First Continental Congress on October 26, 1774. 1 Journals of the Continental Congress, 1774–1789, at 101, 105 (1904). This address, written to explain the position of the colonies and to gain the support of the people of Quebec, is an "exposition of the fundamental rights of the colonists, as they were understood by a representative assembly chosen from all the colonies." 1 Schwartz, *supra,* at 221. Because it was intended for the inhabitants of Quebec, who had been "educated under another form of government" and had only recently become English subjects, it was thought desirable for the Continental Congress to explain "the inestimable advantages of a free English constitution of government, which it is the privilege of all English subjects to enjoy." 1 Journals 106.

> [One] great right is that of trial by jury. This provides, that neither life, liberty nor property, can be taken from the possessor, until twelve of his unexceptionable countrymen and peers of his vicinage, who from that neighbourhood may reasonably be supposed to be acquainted with his character, and the characters of the witnesses, upon a fair trial, and full enquiry, face to face, *in open Court, before as many of the peo-*

> *ple as chuse to attend,* shall pass their sentence upon oath against him. * * * 1 Journals 107 [emphasis added].

B

As we have shown, and as was shown in both the Court's opinion and the dissent in *Gannett,* * * * the historical evidence demonstrates conclusively that at the time when our organic laws were adopted, criminal trials both here and in England had long been presumptively open. This is no quirk of history; rather, it has long been recognized as an indispensible attribute of an Anglo-American trial. Both Hale in the 17th century and Blackstone in the 18th saw the importance of openness to the proper functioning of a trial; it gave assurance that the proceedings were conducted fairly to all concerned, and it discouraged perjury, the misconduct of participants, and decisions based on secret bias or partiality. See, *e.g.,* M. Hale, The History of the Common Law of England 343–345 (6th ed. 1820); 3 W. Blackstone, Commentaries * 372–373. Jeremy Bentham not only recognized the therapeutic value of open justice but regarded it as the keystone:

> Without publicity, all other checks are insufficient: in comparison of publicity, all other checks are of small account. Recordation, appeal, whatever other institutions might present themselves in the character of checks, would be found to operate rather as cloaks than checks; as cloaks in reality, as checks only in appearance. 1 J. Bentham, Rationale of Judicial Evidence 524 (1827).[7]

Panegyrics on the values of openness were by no means confined to self-praise by the English. Foreign observers of English criminal procedure in the 18th and early 19th centuries came away impressed by the very fact that they had been freely admitted to the courts, as many were not in their own homelands. See L. Radzinowicz, A History of English Criminal Law 715, and n. 96 (1948). They marveled that "the whole juridical procedure passes in public," 2 P.J. Grosley, A Tour to London; or New Observations on England 142 (Nugent trans. 1772), quoted in Radzinowicz, *supra,* at 717, and one commentator declared that:

> The main excellence of the English judicature consists in publicity, in the free trial by jury, and in the extraordinary despatch with which business is transacted. The publicity of their proceedings is indeed astonishing. *Free access to the courts is universally granted.* C. Goede, A Foreigner's Opinion of England 214 (Horne trans. 1822). [Emphasis added.]

The nexus between openness, fairness, and the perception of fairness was not lost on them:

> [T]he judge, the counsel, and the jury, are constantly exposed to public animadversion; and this greatly tends to augment the extraordinary confidence, which the English repose in the administration of justice. Goede, *supra,* at 215.

This observation raises the important point that "[t]he publicity of a judicial proceeding is a requirement of much broader bearing than its mere effect on the quality of testimony." 6 J. Wigmore, Evidence § 1834, at p. 435 (Chadbourn rev. 1976).[8] The early history of open trials in part reflects the widespread acknowledgement, long before there were behavioral scientists, that public trials had significant community therapeutic value. Even with-

7. Bentham also emphasized that open proceedings enhanced the performance of all involved, protected the judge from imputations of dishonesty, and served to educate the public. *Id.,* at 522–525.

8. A collateral aspect seen by Wigmore was the possibility that someone in attendance at the trial or who learns of the proceedings through publicity may be able to furnish evidence in chief or contradict "falsifiers." 6 Wigmore, *supra,* at 436. Wigmore gives examples of such occurrences. *Id.,* at 436, and n. 2.

out such experts to frame the concept in words, people sensed from experience and observation that, especially in the administration of criminal justice, the means used to achieve justice must have the support derived from public acceptance of both the process and its results.

When a shocking crime occurs, a community reaction of outrage and public protest often follows. See H. Weihofen, The Urge to Punish 130–131 (1956). Thereafter the open processes of justice serve an important prophylactic purpose, providing an outlet for community concern, hostility, and emotion. Without an awareness that society's responses to criminal conduct are underway, natural human reactions of outrage and protest are frustrated and may manifest themselves in some form of vengeful "self-help," as indeed they did regularly in the activities of vigilante "committees" on our frontiers. "The accusation and conviction or acquittal, as much perhaps as the execution of punishment, operate[ ] to restore the imbalance which was created by the offense or public charge, to reaffirm the temporarily lost feeling of security, and, perhaps, to satisfy that latent 'urge to punish.'" Mueller, Problems Posed by Publicity to Crime and Criminal Proceedings, 110 U.Pa.L.Rev. 1, 6 (1961).

Civilized societies withdraw both from the victim and the vigilante the enforcement of criminal laws, but they cannot erase from people's consciousness the fundamental, natural yearning to see justice done—or even the urge for retribution. The crucial prophylactic aspects of the administration of justice cannot function in the dark; no community catharsis can occur if justice is "done in a corner [or] in any covert manner." * * * It is not enough to say that results alone will satiate the natural community desire for "satisfaction." A result considered untoward may undermine public confidence, and where the trial has been concealed from public view an unexpected outcome can cause a reaction that the system at best has failed and at worst has been corrupted. To work effectively, it is important that society's criminal process "satisfy the appearance of justice," Offutt v. United States, 348 U.S. 11, 14 (1954), and the appearance of justice can best be provided by allowing people to observe it.

Looking back, we see that when the ancient "town meeting" form of trial became too cumbersome, twelve members of the community were delegated to act as its surrogates, but the community did not surrender its right to observe the conduct of trials. The people retained a "right of visitation" which enabled them to satisfy themselves that justice was in fact being done.

People in an open society do not demand infallibility from their institutions, but it is difficult for them to accept what they are prohibited from observing. When a criminal trial is conducted in the open, there is at least an opportunity both for understanding the system in general and its workings in a particular case:

> The educative effect of public attendance is a material advantage. Not only is respect for the law increased and intelligent acquaintance acquired with the methods of government, but a strong confidence in judicial remedies is secured which could never be inspired by a system of secrecy. 6 Wigmore, *supra,* at 438. See also 1 Bentham, *supra,* at 525.

In earlier times, both in England and America, attendance at court was a common mode of "passing the time." See, *e.g.,* 6 Wigmore, *supra,* at 436; Mueller, *supra,* at 6. With the press, cinema, and electronic media now supplying the representations or reality of the real life drama once available only in the courtroom, attendance at court is no longer a widespread pastime. Yet "[i]t is not unrealistic even in this day to believe that public inclusion affords citizens a form of legal education and hopefully promotes confidence in the fair administration of justice." State v. Schmit * * * 139 N.W.2d 800, 807 (1966). Instead of acquiring information about trials by firsthand observation or by word of mouth from those who attended, people now acquire it chiefly through the print and electronic media. In a sense, this validates the media claim of functioning as surrogates for the public. While media representatives enjoy the same right of access as the public, they often are provided special seating and priority of entry so that they may report what people in attendance have seen and heard. This "contribute[s] to public understanding of the rule of law and to comprehension of the functioning of the entire criminal justice system * * *." Nebraska Press Association v. Stuart, 427 U.S. 539, 587, * * * (1976) (Brennan, J., concurring).

C

From this unbroken, uncontradicted history, supported by reasons as valid today as in centuries past, we are bound to conclude that a presumption of openness inheres in the very nature of a criminal trial under our system of justice. This conclusion is hardly novel; without a direct holding on the issue, the Court has voiced its recognition of it in a variety of contexts over the years.[9] Even while holding, in Levine v. United States, 362 U.S. 610 * * * (1960), that a criminal contempt proceeding was not a "criminal prosecution" within the meaning of the Sixth Amendment, the Court was careful to note that more than the Sixth Amendment was involved:

> [W]hile the right to a 'public trial' is explicitly guaranteed by the Sixth Amendment only for 'criminal prosecutions,' that provision is a reflection of the notion, deeply rooted in the common law, that 'justice must satisfy the appearance of justice.' * * * [D]ue process demands appropriate regard for the requirements of a public proceeding in cases of criminal contempt * * * as it does for all adjudications through the exercise of the judicial power, barring narrowly limited categories of exceptions * * *. *Id.,* at 616, [citations omitted].[10]

9. "Of course trials must be public and the public have a deep interest in trials." Pennekamp v. Florida, 328 U.S. 331, 361 * * *, (1946) (Frankfurter, J., concurring).

"A trial is a public event. What transpires in the court room is public property." Craig v. Harney, 331 U.S. 367, 374 * * * (1947) (Douglas, J.).

"[W]e have been unable to find a single instance of a criminal trial conducted in camera in any federal, state, or municipal court during the history of this country. Nor have we found any record of even one such secret criminal trial in England since abolition of the Court of Star Chamber in 1641, and whether that court ever convicted people secretly is in dispute. * * * This nation's accepted practice of guaranteeing a public trial to an accused has its roots in our English common law heritage. The exact date of its origin is obscure, but it likely evolved long before the settlement of our land as an accompaniment of the ancient institution of jury trial." In re Oliver, 333 U.S. 257, 266, * * * (1948) (Black, J.) (footnotes omitted).

"One of the demands of a democratic society is that the public should know what goes on in courts by being told by the press what happens there, to the end that the public may judge whether our system of criminal justice is fair and right." Maryland v. Baltimore Radio Show, Inc., 338 U.S. 912, 920, * * * (1950) (Frankfurter, J., dissenting from denial of cert.).

"It is true that the public has the right to be informed as to what occurs in its courts, * * * reporters of all media, including television, are always present if they wish to be and are plainly free to report whatever occurs in open court * * *." Estes v. Texas, 381 U.S. 532, 541–542 * * * (1965) (Clark, J.); see also *id.,* at 583–584, * * * (Warren, C.J., concurring). (The Court ruled, however, that the televising of the criminal trial over the defendant's objections violated his due process right to a fair trial.)

"The principle that justice cannot survive behind walls of silence has long been reflected in the 'Anglo-American distrust for secret trials'" Sheppard v. Maxwell, 384 U.S. 333, 349 * * * (1966) (Clark, J.).

10. The Court went on to hold that, "on the particular circumstances of the case," 362 U.S., at 616 * * *, the accused could not complain on appeal of the "so-called 'secrecy' of the proceedings," *id.,* at 617 * * *, because, with counsel present, he had failed to object or to request the judge to open the courtroom at the time.

And recently in Gannett Co., Inc. v. DePasquale, 443 U.S. 368 * * * (1979), both the majority, 443 U.S., at 384, 386, n. 15 * * *, and dissenting opinions, 443 U.S., at 423 * * *, agreed that open trials were part of the common law tradition.

Despite the history of criminal trials being presumptively open since long before the Constitution, the State presses its contention that neither the Constitution nor the Bill of Rights contains any provision which by its terms guarantees to the public the right to attend criminal trials. Standing alone, this is correct, but there remains the question whether, absent an explicit provision, the Constitution affords protection against exclusion of the public from criminal trials.

III. A

The First Amendment, in conjunction with the Fourteenth, prohibits governments from "abridging the freedom of speech, or of the press; or the right of the people peaceably to assemble, and to petition the Government for a redress of grievances." These expressly guaranteed freedoms share a common core purpose of assuring freedom of communication on matters relating to the functioning of government. Plainly it would be difficult to single out any aspect of government of higher concern and importance to the people than the manner in which criminal trials are conducted; as we have shown, recognition of this pervades the centuries-old history of open trials and the opinions of this Court. * * *

The Bill of Rights was enacted against the backdrop of the long history of trials being presumptively open. Public access to trials was then regarded as an important aspect of the process itself; the conduct of trials "before as many of the people as chuse to attend" was regarded as one of "the inestimable advantages of a free English constitution of government." 1 Journals of the Continental Congress, * * at 106, 107. In guaranteeing freedoms such as those of speech and press, the First Amendment can be read as protecting the right of everyone to attend trials so as to give meaning to those explicit guarantees. "[T]he First Amendment goes beyond protection of the press and the self-expression of individuals to prohibit government from limiting the stock of information from which members of the public may draw." First National Bank of Boston v. Bellotti, 435 U.S. 765, 783 * * * (1978). Free speech carries with it some freedom to listen. "In a variety of contexts this Court has referred to a First Amendment right to 'receive information and ideas.'" Kleindienst v. Mandel, 408 U.S. 753, 762 * * * (1972). What this means in the context of trials is that the First Amendment guarantees of speech and press, standing alone, prohibit government from summarily closing courtroom doors which had long been open to the public at the time that amendment was adopted. "For the First Amendment does not speak equivocally. * * * It must be taken as a command of the broadest scope that explicit language, read in the context of a liberty-loving society, will allow." Bridges v. California, 314 U.S. 252, 263 * * (1941).

It is not crucial whether we describe this right to attend criminal trials to hear, see, and communicate observations concerning them as a "right of access," cf. Gannett, *supra,* 443 U.S., at 397 * * * (Powell, J., concurring); Saxbe v. Washington Post Co., 417 U.S. 843 * * * (1974); Pell v. Procunier, 417 U.S. 817 * * (1974),[11] or a "right to gather information,"

11. *Procunier* and *Saxbe, supra,* are distinguishable in the sense that they were concerned with penal institutions which, by definition, are not "open" or public places. Penal institutions do not share the long tradition of openness, although traditionally there have been visiting committees of citizens, and there is no doubt that legislative committees could exercise plenary oversight and "visitation rights." *Saxbe, supra,* 417

for we have recognized that "without some protection for seeking out the news, freedom of the press could be eviscerated." Branzburg v. Hayes, 408 U.S. 665, 681 * * * (1972). The explicit, guaranteed rights to speak and to publish concerning what takes place at a trial would lose much meaning if access to observe the trial could, as it was here, be foreclosed arbitrarily.[12]

B

The right of access to places traditionally open to the public, as criminal trials have long been, may be seen as assured by the amalgam of the First Amendment guarantees of speech and press; and their affinity to the right of assembly is not without relevance. From the outset, the right of assembly was regarded not only as an independent right but also as a catalyst to augment the free exercise of the other First Amendment rights with which it was deliberately linked by the draftsmen. "The right of peaceable assembly is a right cognate to those of free speech and free press and is equally fundamental." De Jonge v. Oregon, 299 U.S. 353, 364 * * * (1937). People assemble in public places not only to speak or to take action, but also to listen, observe, and learn; indeed, they may "assembl[e] for any lawful purpose," Hague v. CIO, 307 U.S. 496, 519 * * * (1939) (opinion of Stone, J.). Subject to the traditional time, place, and manner restrictions [see, e.g., Cox v. New Hampshire, 312 U.S. 569, * * * (1941)], * * * a trial courtroom also is a public place where the people generally—and representatives of the media—have a right to be present, and where their presence historically has been thought to enhance the integrity and quality of what takes place.

C

The State argues that the Constitution nowhere spells out a guarantee for the right of the public to attend trials, and that accordingly no such right is protected. The possibility that such a contention could be made did not escape the notice of the Constitution's draftsmen; they were concerned that some important rights might be thought disparaged because not specifically guaranteed. It was even argued that because of this danger no Bill of Rights should be adopted. See, *e.g.*, A. Hamilton, The Federalist no. 84. In a letter to Thomas Jefferson in October of 1788, James Madison explained why he, although "in favor of a bill of rights," had "not viewed it in an important light" up to that time: "I conceive that in a certain degree * * * the rights in question are reserved by the manner in which the federal powers are granted." He went on to state "there is great reason to fear that a positive declaration of some of the most essential rights could not be obtained in the requisite latitude." 5 Writings of James Madison 271 (Hunt ed. 1904).

But arguments such as the State makes have not precluded recognition of important rights not enumerated. Notwithstanding the appropriate caution against reading into the Constitution rights not explicitly defined, the Court has acknowledged that certain unarticulated rights are implicit in enumerated guarantees. For

U.S., at 849, * * * noted that "limitation on visitations is justified by what the Court of Appeals acknowledged as 'the truism that prisons are institutions where public access is generally limited.' * * * [Washington Post Co. v. Kleindienst (D.C.Cir.)] 494 F.2d [994], at 999. See Adderley v. Florida, 385 U.S. 39, 41 * * * (1966) [jails]." See also Greer v. Spock, 424 U.S. 828 * * * (1976) (military bases.)

12. That the right to attend may be exercised by people less frequently today when information as to trials generally reaches them by way of print and electronic media in no way alters the basic right. Instead of relying on personal observation or reports from neighbors as in the past, most people receive information concerning trials through the media whose representatives "are entitled to the same rights [to attend trials] as the general public." Estes v. Texas, supra, 381 U.S., at 540.

example, the rights of association and of privacy, the right to be presumed innocent and the right to be judged by a standard of proof beyond a reasonable doubt in a criminal trial, as well as the right to travel, appear nowhere in the Constitution or Bill of Rights. Yet these important but unarticulated rights have nonetheless been found to share constitutional protection in common with explicit guarantees.[16] The concerns expressed by Madison and others have thus been resolved; fundamental rights, even though not expressly guaranteed, have been recognized by the Court as indispensable to the enjoyment of rights explicitly defined.

We hold that the right to attend criminal trials[17] is implicit in the guarantees of the First Amendment; without the freedom to attend such trials, which people have exercised for centuries, important aspects of freedom of speech and "of the press could be eviscerated." *Branzburg, supra,* 408 U.S., at 681. * * *

D

Having concluded there was a guaranteed right of the public under the First and Fourteenth Amendments to attend the trial of Stevenson's case, we return to the closure order challenged by appellants. The Court in *Gannett* * * * made clear that although the Sixth Amendment guarantees the accused a right to a public trial, it does not give a right to a private trial. 443 U.S., at 382. * * * Despite the fact that this was the fourth trial of the accused, the trial judge made no findings to support closure; no inquiry was made as to whether alternative solutions would have met the need to ensure fairness; there was no recognition of any right under the Constitution for the public or press to attend the trial. In contrast to the pretrial proceeding dealt with in *Gannett,* * * * there exist in the context of the trial itself various tested alternatives to satisfy the constitutional demands of fairness. See, e.g. Nebraska Press Association v. Stuart, 427 U.S., at 563–565, * * * Sheppard v. Maxwell, 384 U.S., at 357–362 * * *. There was no suggestion that any problems with witnesses could not have been dealt with by their exclusion from the courtroom or their sequestration during the trial. See Sheppard v. Maxwell, 384 U.S., at 359. * * Nor is there anything to indicate that sequestration of the jurors would not have guarded against their being subjected to any improper information. All of the alternatives admittedly present difficulties for trial courts, but none of the factors relied on here was beyond the realm of the manageable. Absent an overriding interest articulated in findings, the trial of a criminal case must be open to the public.[18]

16. See, e.g., NAACP v. Alabama, 357 U.S. 449 * * * (1958) (right of association); Griswold v. Connecticut, 381 U.S. 479 * * * (1965), and Stanley v. Georgia, 394 U.S. 557 * * * (1969) (right to privacy); Estelle v. Williams, 425 U.S. 501, 503 * * * (1976), and Taylor v. Kentucky, 436 U.S. 478, 483–486 * * * (1978) (presumption of innocence); In re Winship, 397 U.S. 358 * * * (1970) (standard of proof beyond a reasonable doubt); United States v. Guest, 383 U.S. 745, 757–759 * * * (1966), and Shapiro v. Thompson, 394 U.S. 618, 630 * * * (1969) (right to interstate travel).

17. Whether the public has a right to attend trials of civil cases is a question not raised by this case, but we note that historically both civil and criminal trials have been presumptively open.

18. We have no occasion here to define the circumstances in which all or parts of a criminal trial may be closed to the public, *cf., e.g.,* 6 J. Wigmore, Evidence § 1835 (Chadbourn rev. 1876), but our holding today does not mean that the First Amendment rights of the public and representatives of the press are absolute. Just as a government may impose reasonable time, place, and manner restrictions upon the use of its streets in the interest of such objectives as the free flow of traffic [see, e.g., *Cox v. New Hampshire,* 312 U.S. 569 * * * (1941)], so may a trial judge, in the interest of the fair administration of justice, impose reasonable limitations on access to a trial. "[T]he question in a particular case is whether that control is exerted so as not to deny or unwarrantedly abridge * * * the opportunities for the communication of thought and the discussion of public questions immemorially associated with resort to public places." *Id.,* at 574. * * * It is far more important

Accordingly, the judgment under review is reversed.

Reversed.

* * *

Justice WHITE, concurring.

This case would have been unnecessary had Gannett Co. v. DePasquale, 443 U.S. 368 * * * (1979), construed the Sixth Amendment to forbid excluding the public from criminal proceedings except in narrowly defined circumstances. But the Court there rejected the submission of four of us to this effect, thus requiring that the First Amendment issue involved here be addressed. On this issue, I concur in the opinion of The Chief Justice.

Justice STEVENS, concurring.

* * * Until today the Court has accorded virtually absolute protection to the dissemination of information or ideas, but never before has it squarely held that the acquisition of newsworthy matter is entitled to any constitutional protection whatsoever. An additional word of emphasis is therefore appropriate.

Twice before, the Court has implied that any governmental restriction on access to information, no matter how severe and no matter how unjustified, would be constitutionally acceptable so long as it did not single out the press for special disabilities not applicable to the public at large. In a dissent joined by Justice Brennan and Justice Marshall in Saxbe v. Washington Post Co., 417 U.S. 843, 850 * *, Justice Powell unequivocally rejected the conclusion "that *any* governmental restriction of press access to information, so long as it is nondiscriminatory, falls outside the purview of First Amendment concern." *Id.,* at 857 * * * [emphasis in original]. And in Houchins v. KQED, Inc., 438 U.S. 1, 19–40 * * *, I explained at length why Justice Brennan, Justice Powell, and I were convinced that "[a]n official prison policy of concealing * * * knowledge from the public by arbitrarily cutting off the flow of information at its source abridges the freedom of speech and of the press protected by the First and Fourteenth Amendments to the Constitution." *Id.,* at 38, * * *. Since Justice Marshall and Justice Blackmun were unable to participate in that case, a majority of the Court neither accepted nor rejected that conclusion or the contrary conclusion expressed in the prevailing opinions.[1] Today, however, for the first time, the Court unequivocally holds that an arbitrary interference with access to important information is an abridgment of the freedoms of speech and of the press protected by the First Amendment.

It is somewhat ironic that the Court should find more reason to recognize a right of access today than it did in *Houchins.* For *Houchins* involved the plight of a segment of society least able to protect itself, an attack on a longstanding policy of concealment, and an absence of any legitimate justification for abridging public access to information about how government operates. In this case we are pro-

that trials be conducted in a quiet and orderly setting than it is to preserve that atmosphere on city streets. Compare, e.g., Kovacs v. Cooper, 336 U.S. 77 * * * (1949), with Illinois v. Allen, 397 U.S. 337 * * * (1970), and Estes v. Texas, 381 U.S. 532 * * * (1965). Moreover, since courtrooms have limited capacity, there may be occasions when not every person who wishes to attend can be accommodated. In such situations, reasonable restrictions on general access are traditionally imposed, including preferential seating for media representatives. Cf. *Gannett,* 443 U.S., at 397–398 * * * (Powell, J., concurring); Houchins v. KQED, Inc., 438 U.S. 1, 17 * * * (1978) (Stewart, J., concurring); *id.,* at 32, * * * (Stevens, J., dissenting).

1. "Neither the First Amendment nor the Fourteenth Amendment mandates a right of access to government information or sources of information within the government's control." 438 U.S., at 15, * * * (opinion of Burger, C.J.).

"The First and Fourteenth Amendments do not guarantee the public a right of access to information generated or controlled by government * * *. The Constitution does no more than assure the public and the press equal access once government has opened its doors." *Id.,* at 16, * * * (Stewart, J., concurring).

tecting the interests of the most powerful voices in the community, we are concerned with an almost unique exception to an established tradition of openness in the conduct of criminal trials, and it is likely that the closure order was motivated by the judge's desire to protect the individual defendant from the burden of a fourth criminal trial.[2]

In any event, for the reasons stated in Part II of my *Houchins* opinion, 438 U.S., at 30–38, * * * as well as those stated by The Chief Justice today, I agree that the First Amendment protects the public and the press from abridgment of their rights of access to information about the operation of their government, including the Judicial Branch; given the total absence of any record justification for the closure order entered in this case, that order violated the First Amendment.

Justice BRENNAN, with whom Justice Marshall joins, concurring in the judgment.

Gannett Co. v. DePasquale, 443 U.S. 368 * * * (1979), held that the Sixth Amendment right to a public trial was personal to the accused, conferring no right of access to pretrial proceedings that is separately enforceable by the public or the press. The instant case raises the question whether the First Amendment, of its own force and as applied to the States through the Fourteenth Amendment, secures the public an independent right of access to trial proceedings. Because I believe that the First Amendment—of itself and as applied to the States through the Fourteenth Amendment—secures such a public right of access, I agree with those of my Brethren who hold that, without more, agreement of the trial judge and the parties cannot constitutionally close a trial to the public.[1]

While freedom of expression is made inviolate by the First Amendment, and, with only rare and stringent exceptions, may not be suppressed, * * *, the First Amendment has not been viewed by the Court in all settings as providing an equally categorical assurance of the correlative freedom of access to information. * * * Yet the Court has not ruled out a public access component to the First Amendment in every circumstance. Read with care and in context, our decisions must therefore be understood as holding only that any privilege of access to governmental information is subject to a degree of restraint dictated by the nature of the information and countervailing interests in security or confidentiality. * * * These

2. Neither that likely motivation nor facts showing the risk that a fifth trial would have been necessary without closure of the fourth are disclosed in this record, however. The absence of any articulated reason for the closure order is a sufficient basis for distinguishing this case from Gannett v. DePasquale, 443 U.S. 368. * * The decision today is in no way inconsistent with the perfectly unambiguous holding in *Gannett* that the rights guaranteed by the Sixth Amendment are rights that may be asserted by the accused rather than members of the general public. In my opinion the Framers quite properly identified the party who has the greatest interest in the right to a public trial. The language of the Sixth Amendment is worth emphasizing:

"In all criminal prosecutions, *the accused* shall enjoy the right to a speedy and public trial, by an impartial jury of the State and district wherein the crime shall have been committed, which district shall have been previously ascertained by law, and to be informed of the nature and cause of the accusation; to be confronted with the witnesses against him; to have compulsory process for obtaining witnesses in his favor, and to have the Assistance of Counsel for his defense." U.S. Const.Amdt. VI. (Emphasis added.)

1. Of course, the Sixth Amendment remains the source of the *accused's* own right to insist upon public judicial proceedings. *Gannett Co. v. DePasquale.* * * *

That the Sixth Amendment explicitly establishes a public trial right does not impliedly foreclose the derivation of such a right from other provisions of the Constitution. The Constitution was not framed as a work of carpentry, in which all joints must fit snugly without overlapping. Of necessity, a document that designs a form of government will address central political concerns from a variety of perspectives. Significantly, this Court has recognized the open trial right both as a matter of the Sixth Amendment and as an ingredient in Fifth Amendment due process. * * *

cases neither comprehensively nor absolutely deny that public access to information may at times be implied by the First Amendment and the principles which animate it.

The Court's approach in right of access cases simply reflects the special nature of a claim of First Amendment right to gather information. Customarily, First Amendment guarantees are interposed to protect communication between speaker and listener. When so employed against prior restraints, free speech protections are almost insurmountable. * * *. But the First Amendment embodies more than a commitment to free expression and communicative interchange for their own sakes; it has a *structural* role to play in securing and fostering our republican system of self-government. * * *. Implicit in this structural role is not only "the principle that debate on public issues should be uninhibited, robust, and wide-open," New York Times Co. v. Sullivan, 376 U.S. 254, 270 * * * (1964), but the antecedent assumption that valuable public debate—as well as other civic behavior—must be informed. The structural model links the First Amendment to that process of communication necessary for a democracy to survive, and thus entails solicitude not only for communication itself, but for the indispensable conditions of meaningful communication.

However, because "the stretch of this protection is theoretically endless," * *, it must be invoked with discrimination and temperance. For so far as the participating citizen's need for information is concerned, "[t]here are few restrictions on action which could not be clothed by ingenious argument in the garb of decreased data flow." Zemel v. Rusk, * * *, 381 U.S., at 16–17. * * * An assertion of the prerogative to gather information must accordingly be assayed by considering the information sought and the opposing interests invaded.

This judicial task is as much a matter of sensitivity to practical necessities as it is of abstract reasoning. But at least two helpful principles may be sketched. First, the case for a right of access has special force when drawn from an enduring and vital tradition of public entree to particular proceedings or information. * * * Such a tradition commands respect in part because the Constitution carries the gloss of history. More importantly, a tradition of accessibility implies the favorable judgment of experience. Second, the value of access must be measured in specifics. Analysis is not advanced by rhetorical statements that all information bears upon public issues; what is crucial in individual cases is whether access to a particular government process is important in terms of that very process.

To resolve the case before us, therefore, we must consult historical and current practice with respect to open trials, and weigh the importance of public access to the trial process itself. * * *

Tradition, contemporaneous state practice, and this Court's own decisions manifest a common understanding that "[a] trial is a public event. What transpires in the court room is public property." Craig v. Harney, 331 U.S. 367, 374 * * * (1947). As a matter of law and virtually immemorial custom, public trials have been the essentially unwavering rule in ancestral England and in our own Nation. See In re Oliver, *supra,* 333 U.S., at 266–268 * * *; *Gannett Co. v. DePasquale,* * * *, 443 U.S., at 386, n. 15, * * * at 418–432, and n. 11, * * * (Blackmun, J., concurring and dissenting). Such abiding adherence to the principle of open trials "reflect[s] a profound judgment about the way in which law should be enforced and justice administered." Duncan v. Louisiana, 391 U.S. 145, 155 * * * (1968).

Publicity serves to advance several of the particular purposes of the trial (and, indeed, the judicial) process. Open trials play a fundamental role in furthering the efforts of our judicial system to assure the criminal defendant a fair and accurate adjudication of guilt or innocence. * * * But, as a feature of our governing system of justice, the trial process serves other, broadly political, interests, and public access advances these objectives as well. To that extent, trial access possesses specific structural significance.

The trial is a means of meeting "the notion, deeply rooted in the common law, that 'justice must satisfy the appearance of justice.'" Levine v. United States, 362 U.S. 610, 616, * * * (1960), quoting Offutt v. United States, 348 U.S. 11, 14, * * * (1954); * * *. For a civilization founded upon principles of ordered liberty to survive and flourish, its members must share the conviction that they are governed equitably. That necessity underlies constitutional provisions as diverse as the rule against takings without just compensation * * * and the Equal Protection Clause. It also mandates a system of justice that demonstrates the fairness of the law to our citizens. One major function of the trial, hedged with procedural protections and conducted with conspicuous respect for the rule of law, is to make that demonstration. See In re Oliver, 333 U.S., at 270, n. 24. * * *

Secrecy is profoundly inimical to this demonstrative purpose of the trial process. Open trials assure the public that procedural rights are respected, and that justice is afforded equally. Closed trials breed suspicion of prejudice and arbitrariness, which in turn spawns disrespect for law. Public access is essential, therefore, if trial adjudication is to achieve the objective of maintaining public confidence in the administration of justice. See Gannett, *supra,* 443 U.S. at 428–429 * * * (Blackmun, J., concurring and dissenting).

But the trial is more than a demonstrably just method of adjudicating disputes and protecting rights. It plays a pivotal role in the entire judicial process, and, by extension, in our form of government. Under our system, judges are not mere umpires, but, in their own sphere, lawmakers—a coordinate branch of *government.* While individual cases turn upon the controversies between parties, or involve particular prosecutions, court rulings impose official and practical consequences upon members of society at large. Moreover, judges bear responsibility for the vitally important task of construing and securing constitutional rights. Thus, so far as the trial is the mechanism for judicial factfinding, as well as the initial forum for legal decisionmaking, it is a genuine governmental proceeding.

It follows that the conduct of the trial is preeminently a matter of public interest. * * * More importantly, public access to trials acts as an important check, akin in purpose to the other checks and balances that infuse our system of government.

* * *

Finally, with some limitations, a trial aims at true and accurate factfinding. Of course, proper factfinding is to the benefit of criminal defendants and of the parties in civil proceedings. But other, comparably urgent, interests are also often at stake. A miscarriage of justice that imprisons an innocent accused also leaves a guilty party at large, a continuing threat to society. Also, mistakes of fact in civil litigation may inflict costs upon others than the plaintiff and defendant. Facilitation of the trial factfinding process, therefore, is of concern to the public as well as to the parties.[21]

Publicizing trial proceedings aids accurate factfinding. "Public trials come to the attention of key witnesses unknown to the parties." In re Oliver, *supra,* at 270, n. 24.

21. Further, the interest in insuring that the innocent are not punished may be shared by the general public, in addition to the accused himself.

* * * Shrewd legal observers have averred that

> open examination of witnesses *viva voce,* in the presence of all mankind, is much more conducive to the clearing up of truth, than the private and secret examination * * * where a witness may frequently depose that in private, which he will be ashamed to testify in a public and solemn tribunal. 3 Blackstone, Commentaries, * 373. * * *. And experience has borne out these assertions about the truthfinding role of publicity. * * *

Popular attendance at trials, in sum, substantially furthers the particular public purposes of that critical judicial proceeding.[22] In that sense, public access is an indispensable element of the trial process itself. Trial access, therefore, assumes structural importance in our "government of laws," Marbury v. Madison, 1 Cranch 137, 163, 2 L.Ed. 60 (1803).

As previously noted, resolution of First Amendment public access claims in individual cases must be strongly influenced by the weight of historical practice and by an assessment of the specific structural value of public access in the circumstances. With regard to the case at hand, our ingrained tradition of public trials and the importance of public access to the broader purposes of the trial process, tip the balance strongly toward the rule that trials be open. What countervailing interests might be sufficiently compelling to reverse this presumption of openness need not concern us now,[24] for the statute at stake here authorizes trial closures at the unfettered discretion of the judge and parties.[25] Accordingly, Va.Code 19.2–266 violates the First and Fourteenth Amendments, and the decision of the Virginia Supreme Court to the contrary should be reversed.

Justice STEWART, concurring in the judgment.

In Gannett Co. v. DePasquale, 443 U.S. 368, * * * the Court held that the Sixth Amendment, which guarantees "the accused" the right to a public trial, does not confer upon representatives of the press or members of the general public any right of access to a trial.[1] But the Court explicitly left open the question whether such a right of access may be guaranteed by other provisions of the Constitution, *id.,* at 391–393. * * * Justice Powell expressed the view that the First and Fourteenth Amendments do extend at least a limited right of access even to pretrial suppression hearings in criminal cases, *id.,* at 397–403, * * (concurring opinion). Justice Rehnquist expressed a contrary view, *id.,* at 403–406 * * * (concurring opinion). The remaining members of the Court were silent on the question.

Whatever the ultimate answer to that question may be with respect to pretrial suppression hearings in criminal cases, the

22. In advancing these purposes, the availability of a trial transcript is no substitute for a public presence at the trial itself. As any experienced appellate judge can attest, the "cold" record is a very imperfect reproduction of events that transpire in the courtroom. Indeed, to the extent that publicity serves as a check upon trial officials, "[r]ecordation * * * would be found to operate rather as a cloak[] than check[]; as cloak[] in reality, as check[] only in appearance." *In re Oliver, supra,* 333 U.S., at 271, * * *, quoting 1 Bentham, Rationale of Judicial Evidence 524 (1827); see Bentham, * * * at 577–578.

24. For example, national security concerns about confidentiality may sometimes warrant closures during sensitive portions of trial proceedings, such as testimony about state secrets. Cf. United States v. Nixon, 418 U.S. 683, 714–716 * * * (1974).

25. Significantly, closing a trial lacks even the justification for barring the door to pretrial hearings: the necessity of preventing dissemination of suppressible prejudicial evidence to the public before the jury pool has become, in a practical sense, finite and subject to sequestration.

1. The Court also made clear that the Sixth Amendment does not give the accused the right to a *private* trial. 443 U.S., at 382 * * * Compare Singer v. United States, 380 U.S. 24. * * * (Sixth Amendment right of trial by jury does not include right to be tried without a jury.)

First and Fourteenth Amendments clearly give the press and the public a right of access to trials themselves, civil as well as criminal. As has been abundantly demonstrated in Part II of the opinion of The Chief Justice, in Justice Brennan's concurring opinion, and in Justice Blackmun's dissenting opinion last Term in the *Gannett case,* 443 U.S., at 406, * * *, it has for centuries been a basic presupposition of the Anglo-American legal system that trials shall be public trials. The opinions referred to also convincingly explain the many good reasons why this is so. With us, a trial is by every definition a proceeding open to the press and to the public.

In conspicuous contrast to a military base, Greer v. Spock, 424 U.S. 828; * * * a jail, Adderley v. Florida, 385 U.S. 39; * * or a prison, Pell v. Procunier, 417 U.S. 817, * * * a trial courtroom is a public place. Even more than city streets, sidewalks, and parks as areas of traditional First Amendment activity, e.g., Shuttlesworth v. Birmingham, 394 U.S. 147, * * *, a trial courtroom is a place where representatives of the press and of the public are not only free to be, but where their presence serves to assure the integrity of what goes on.

But this does not mean that the First Amendment right of members of the public and representatives of the press to attend civil and criminal trials is absolute. Just as a legislature may impose reasonable time, place and manner restrictions upon the exercise of First Amendment freedoms, so may a trial judge impose reasonable limitations upon the unrestricted occupation of a courtroom by representatives of the press and members of the public. * *. Much more than a city street, a trial courtroom must be a quiet and orderly place. * * *. Moreover, every courtroom has a finite physical capacity, and there may be occasions when not all who wish to attend a trial may do so.[3] And while there exist many alternative ways to satisfy the constitutional demands of a fair trial,[4] those demands may also sometimes justify limitations upon the unrestricted presence of spectators in the courtroom.[5]

Since in the present case the trial judge appears to have given no recognition to the right of representatives of the press and members of the public to be present at the Virginia murder trial over which he was presiding, the judgment under review must be reversed.

It is upon the basis of these principles that I concur in the judgment.

Justice BLACKMUN, concurring in the judgment.

My opinion and vote in partial dissent last Term in Gannett Co. v. DePasquale, * * *, compels my vote to reverse the judgment of the Supreme Court of Virginia.

The decision in this case is gratifying for me for two reasons:

It is gratifying, first, to see the Court now looking to and relying upon legal history in determining the fundamental public character of the criminal trial. * * * The partial dissent in *Gannett,* * * * took great pains in assembling—I believe adequately—the historical material and in stressing its importance to this area of the law. * * * Although the Court in *Gannett* gave a modicum of lip service to legal history, * * * it denied its obvious application when the defense and the prose-

3. In such situations, representatives of the press must be assured access, Houchins v. KQED, Inc., 438 U.S. 1, 16 * * * (concurring opinion).

4. Such alternatives include sequestration of juries, continuances, and changes of venue.

5. This is not to say that only constitutional considerations can justify such restrictions. The preservation of trade secrets, for example, might justify the exclusion of the public from at least some segments of a civil trial. And the sensibilities of a youthful prosecution witness, for example, might justify similar exclusion in a criminal trial for rape, so long as the defendant's Sixth Amendment right to a public trial were not impaired. See, e.g., Stamicarbon, N.V. v. American Cyanamid Co., 506 F.2d 532, 539–542 (CA2 1974).

cution, with no resistance by the trial judge, agreed that the proceeding should be closed.

The court's return to history is a welcome change in direction.

It is gratifying, second, to see the Court wash away at least some of the graffiti that marred the prevailing opinions in *Gannett.* No less than 12 times in the primary opinion in that case, the Court (albeit in what seems now to have become clear dicta) observed that its Sixth Amendment closure ruling applied to the *trial* itself. The author of the first concurring opinion was fully aware of this and would have restricted the Court's observations and ruling to the suppression hearing. *Id.,* at 394 * * *. Nonetheless, he *joined* the Court's opinion, *ibid.,* with its multiple references to the trial itself; the opinion was not a mere concurrence in the Court's judgment. And Justice Rehnquist, in his separate concurring opinion, quite understandably observed, as a consequence, that the Court was holding "without qualification," that " 'members of the public have no constitutional right under the Sixth and Fourteenth Amendments to attend criminal trials,' " *id.,* at 403, * * * quoting from the primary opinion, *id.,* at 391 * * *. The resulting confusion among commentators [1] and journalists [2] was not surprising.

The Court's ultimate ruling in *Gannett,* with such clarification as is provided by the opinions in this case today, apparently is now to the effect that there is no *Sixth* Amendment right on the part of the public—or the press—to an open hearing on a motion to suppress. I, of course, continue to believe that *Gannett* was in error, both in its interpretation of the Sixth Amendment generally, and in its application to the suppression hearing, for I remain convinced that the right to a public trial is to be found where the Constitution explicitly placed it—in the Sixth Amendment.[3]

Having said all this, and with the Sixth Amendment set to one side in this case, I am driven to conclude, as a secondary position, that the First Amendment must provide some measure of protection for public access to the trial. The opinion in partial dissent in *Gannett* explained that the public has an intense need and a deserved right to know about the administration of justice in general; about the prosecution of local crimes in particular; about the conduct of the judge, the prosecutor, defense counsel, police officers, other public servants, and all the actors in the judicial arena; and about the trial itself. * * It is clear and obvious to me, on the ap-

1. See, *e.g.,* Stephenson, Fair Trial-Free Press: Rights in Continuing Conflict, 46 Brooklyn L.Rev. 39, 63 (1979) ("intended reach of the majority opinion is unclear" [footnote omitted]); The Supreme Court, 1978 Term, 93 Harv.L.Rev. 60, 65 (1979) ("widespread uncertainty over what the Court held"); Note, 51 Colo.L.Rev. 425, 432–433 (1980) ("*Gannett* can be interpreted to sanction the closing of trials"; citing "the uncertainty of the language in *Gannett,*" and its "ambiguous sixth amendment holding"); Note, 11 Tex.Tech.L.Rev. 159, 170–171 (1979) ("perhaps much of the present and imminent confusion lies in the Court's own statement of its holding"); Borow and Kruth, Closed Preliminary Hearings, 55 Calif.State Bar.J. 18, 23 (1980) ("Despite the public disclaimers * * *, the majority holding appears to embrace the right of access to trials as well as pretrial hearings"); Goodale, Gannett Means What it Says; But Who Knows What it Says?, Nat'l Law J., Oct. 15, 1979, at 20; see also Keefe, The Boner Called Gannett, 66 A.B.A.J. 227 (1980).

2. The press—perhaps the segment of society most profoundly affected by *Gannett*—has called the Court's decision "cloudy," *Birmingham Post-Herald,* Aug. 21, 1979, at A4; "confused," *Chicago Sun-Times,* Sept. 20, 1979, at 56 (cartoon); "incoherent," *Baltimore Sun,* Sept. 22, 1979, at A14; "mushy," *Washington Post,* Aug. 10, 1979, at A15; and a "muddle," *Time,* Sept. 17, 1979, at 82, and %Newsweek, *Aug. 27, 1979, at 69.*

3. I shall not again seek to demonstrate the errors of analysis in the Court's opinion in *Gannett.* I note, however, that the very existence of the present case illustrates the utter fallacy of thinking, in this context, that "the public interest is fully protected by the participants in the litigation." Gannett Co. v. DePasquale, 443 U.S. 368, 384 * * * (1979). * * *

proach the Court has chosen to take, that, by closing this criminal trial, the trial judge abridged these First Amendment interests of the public.

I also would reverse, and I join the judgment of the Court.

Justice REHNQUIST, dissenting.

In the Gilbert & Sullivan operetta *Iolanthe,* the Lord Chancellor recites:

> The Law is the true embodiment
> of everything that's excellent,
> It has no kind of fault or flaw,
> And I, my lords, embody the law.

It is difficult not to derive more than a little of this flavor from the various opinions supporting the judgment in this case.

* * *

For the reasons stated in my separate concurrence in Gannett Co., Inc. v. DePasquale, 443 U.S. 368, 403 * * * (1979), I do not believe that either the First or Sixth Amendments, as made applicable to the States by the Fourteenth, require that a State's reasons for denying public access to a trial, where both the prosecuting attorney and the defendant have consented to an order of closure approved by the judge, are subject to any additional constitutional review at our hands. And I most certainly do not believe that the Ninth Amendment confers upon us any such power to review orders of state trial judges closing trials in such situations. * *

We have at present 50 state judicial systems and one federal judicial system in the United States, and our authority to reverse a decision by the highest court of the State is limited to only those occasions when the state decision violates some provision of the United States Constitution. And that authority should be exercised with a full sense that the judges whose decisions we review are making the same effort as we to uphold the Constitution. As said by Justice Jackson, concurring in the result in Brown v. Allen, 344 U.S. 443, 540 * * * "We are not final because we are infallible, but we are infallible only because we are final."

The proper administration of justice in any nation is bound to be a matter of the highest concern to all thinking citizens. But to gradually rein in, as this Court has done over the past generation, all of the ultimate decisionmaking power over how justice shall be administered, not merely in the federal system but in each of the 50 States, is a task that no Court consisting of nine persons, however gifted, is equal to. Nor is it desirable that such authority be exercised by such a tiny numerical fragment of the 220 million people who compose the population of this country. In the same concurrence just quoted, Justice Jackson accurately observed that "[t]he generalities of the Fourteenth Amendment are so indeterminate as to what state actions are forbidden that this Court has found it a ready instrument, in one field or another, to magnify federal, and incidentally its own, authority over the states." *Id.,* at 534. * * *

However, high minded the impulses which originally spawned this trend may have been, and which impulses have been accentuated since the time Justice Jackson wrote, it is basically unhealthy to have so much authority concentrated in a small group of lawyers who have been appointed to the Supreme Court and enjoy virtual life tenure. Nothing in the reasoning of Chief Justice Marshall in Marbury v. Madison, 5 U.S. (1 Cranch) 137, 2 L.Ed. 60 (1803) requires that this Court through ever broadening use of the Supremacy Clause smother a healthy pluralism which would ordinarily exist in a national government embracing 50 States.

* * *

THE POST–*RICHMOND* SCENE

1. While lawyers and courts have interpreted *Richmond Newspapers* as granting

only a qualified news-gathering right, reporters, editors, and publishers, where their professional organizations have spoken for them, interpret the case as a generalized right of access to news.[51] These journalistic surrogates, who may not represent the rank and file in their optimism, are also prepared to balance a broad social value, free press, against the more personal and individual value of fair trial, an approach to balancing that jurists have faulted for its predetermined outcomes at least since Dean Roscoe Pound.[52]

This is not to underestimate journalism's commitment to and the public's need for open governmental processes. Given that more than 90 percent of all criminal prosecutions don't get past their pretrial phases, public attendance would seem to be crucial if indeed the public is to monitor, discuss, evaluate, and scrutinize its judicial institutions. Suppression hearings are decisive in the prosecution of crime.

It is difficult to assess the influence and the authority of *Richmond.* A 1981–82 survey of state standards for dealing with motions to clear the courtroom or seal records in order to avoid potential harm to defendants revealed the following tests in use: substantial probability of irreparable harm, the plurality standard of the Court in *Richmond* (California, Michigan, Missouri, North Dakota, and the Eighth Circuit); reasonable probability (New York); some showing of or likelihood of jeopardy (Washington); finding of facts clearly demonstrating jeopardy to fair trial (D.C. Circuit); substantial likelihood (Connecticut and U.S. Department of Justice Guidelines on Open Judicial Proceedings, Oct. 4, 1980); strong likelihood (New York); extreme likelihood (Florida); serious and imminent threat (Florida and Rhode Island); clear showing of a serious and imminent threat (New Jersey); irreparable injury (Third Circuit); strictly and inescapably necessary (Ninth Circuit); clear likelihood of irreparable damage (West Virginia); magnitude and imminence of threatened harm (First Circuit); clear and present danger (Wyoming, Colorado, and Kansas); and clear and convincing evidence of a clear and present danger (Georgia).[53] The Georgia test is more stringent than that of the Supreme Court and would be the test of choice of the press. But obviously there is no uniformity of standards among or within states, and state appellate courts may find their language in state constitutions, state statutes, and state common law.

The U.S. Judicial Conference's Standing Committee on Rules of Practice and Procedure at one time proposed amendments to the Federal Rules of Criminal Procedure that for purposes of prior restraint and closure would require only a "reasonable likelihood" test. (See *Judicial Conference Guidelines,* 6 Med.L.Rptr. 1897, 1980.) It was later deleted.

News media should never expect any absolute right to attend all portions of trials and pretrial hearings. Judges are still a commanding presence in their courtrooms. Parts of trials have been closed in a number of states since *Richmond,* although it appears easier to defeat closure motions designed to protect trials or posttrial hearings than those aimed at pretrial or suppression on hearings.[54] For the lat-

51. American Society of Newspaper Editors & American Newspaper Publishers Association, *Free Press & Fair Trial,* Washington, D.C., 1982.

52. Pound, *A Survey of Social Interest,* 57 Harv.L.Rev. 2 (1943).

53. Page Corp. v. Lumpkin, 8 Med.L.Rptr. 1824, 292 S.E.2d 815 (Ga.1982).

54. Indiana ex rel. Post-Tribune Publishing Co. v. Porter Superior Court, 6 Med.L.Rptr. 2300, 412 N.E.2d 748 (Ind.1980). Upheld exclusion of press and public from pretrial bail hearing. But see, Ohio ex rel. Beacon Journal v. McMonagle, 8 Med.L.Rptr. 1927 (Ohio 1982) where an Ohio appeals court held that a newspaper cannot be prohibited from publishing names of jurors, nor jurors prevented from discussing a trial.

ter, *Gannett* is still shown considerable respect. New York and California have been particularly discouraging arenas for press appeals against closure motions.

2. The public's right to inspect and copy official court records is well established at common law. Courts are divided, however, on whether the common law right extends to records (tapes included) not produced in evidence. In Nixon v. Warner Communications, Inc., 3 Med.L. Rptr. 2074, 435 U.S. 589 (1978),[55] the Supreme Court rejected claims of a First or Sixth Amendment right, or a common law right, to make copies of Nixon tapes that had been introduced into evidence in the criminal trials of his presidential aides. A common law right was rejected because the common law had been superseded by the Presidential Recordings and Materials Preservation Act. Under that act, reporters and other members of the public could hear the tapes in court, read them from a transcript, or come to where they were stored and listen to them.

In early 1982, General Services Administration regulations were issued pursuant to the act giving archivists authority to edit out personal material that might violate Nixon's Fourth Amendment privacy rights, his First Amendment right of associational privacy, and his presidential privilege of confidentiality. In Nixon v. Freeman, 8 Med.L.Rptr. 1001, 670 F.2d 346 (D.C.Cir. 1982), those regulations were upheld by the D.C. Circuit Court of Appeals. The U.S. Supreme Court declined to review the case.

These rulings cast a shadow on the usefulness of *Richmond* as a device for getting at judicial records. Since *Richmond* made much of the common law right of public scrutiny of judicial processes, the case ought to be construed as mandating more of a common law than a constitutional right of access to judicial records.

In the ABSCAM and BRILAB tapes cases, Second, Third, and D.C. Circuits found strong common law arguments for a right to make aural copies of tapes introduced in evidence. The Fifth Circuit, sticking to a literal interpretation of *Nixon,* upheld a trial judge's denial of access.[56]

In cases involving former Congressmen Myers and Jenrette, the Second Circuit recognized a common law right to copy both video and audio ABSCAM tapes admitted into evidence in open court proceedings. Copying, said the court, would advance the interest in open trials identified in *Richmond.* Only the strongest showing of prejudice would serve to deny.[57]

A federal district court in Pennsylvania denied broadcasters permission to copy ABSCAM audio and video tapes because of a pending appeal of defendant and the pending trials of others. Adhering to *Nixon v. Warner Communications,* the court said that showing the tapes would be tantamount to a televised trial, a practice forbidden in federal courts.[58] The Third Circuit reversed and remanded. The public, said the court, has a right to witness firsthand the impact of evidence, even when that impact extends beyond the trial arena. Media are surrogates of the public. Rejected were arguments that post-trial rebroadcasting of the tapes would constitute enhanced punishment and an invasion of privacy. Libelous and scurrilous statements about third parties could be excised at the discretion of the judge. The risk of prejudicing a retrial was potential not ac-

55. Reversing United States v. Mitchell, 2 Med.L.Rptr. 1027, 551 F.2d 1252 (D.C.Cir. 1976) in which Chief Judge Bazelon made a stirring case for access.

56. Belo Broadcasting Corp. v. Clark, 7 Med.L.Rptr. 1841, 654 F.2d 423 (5th Cir. 1981). See also, McNally v. Pulitzer Publishing Co., 532 F.2d 69 (8th Cir. 1976), cert. den. 429 U.S. 855 (1976).

57. In re Application of NBC (United States v. Myers, 6 Med.L.Rptr. 1961, 635 F.2d 945 (2d Cir. 1980)).

58. United States v. Criden, 6 Med.L.Rptr. 1779, 501 F.Supp. 854 (D.Pa.1980).

tual, said the court, and, as with the trial of codefendants, judicial remedies were available to protect defendants. In re Application of NBC (Criden) 7 Med.L.Rptr. 1153, 648 F.2d 814 (3d Cir. 1981).

Similarly in the *Jenrette* case, the U.S. District Court for the District of Columbia held that, where a defendant had motions pending, damage from disclosure would outweigh any public benefit.[59] In a reversal, the United States Court of Appeals for the District of Columbia ruled that the rights of parties must be weighed against a strong tradition of public access to trial records. The mere possibility of a second trial was insufficient to justify denying a broadcaster's request. Instructions were issued to the trial judge to exercise his discretion in excising specific portions of the tapes which might harm innocent third parties [60] a practice that does not comport with common law traditions.

The rule, then, appears to be that federal appeals courts will expect trial courts to consider remedies other than closure before access is denied and to weigh carefully public as against defendant rights before any decision is made.[61]

Grand jury proceedings, and all proceedings related to them, are not meant to be public, no matter how *Richmond* is interpreted.[62]

Since the Sixth Amendment makes no mention of civil proceedings, only access arguments based on the First Amendment and common law will apply to civil cases. Any many of these, those involving "trade secrets," for example, may be closed by statute. Recall that the Chief Justice in his *Richmond* footnote 17 tells us that "historically both civil and criminal trials have been presumptively open."

One may hazard a guess that Brennan, Marshall, and possibly Stevens would extend the access implied in *Richmond* to nonjudicial settings. But it may be slow in coming.

4. Did *Richmond* intend to govern more limited court closures such as those during testimony of minor rape victims? The Supreme Judicial Court of Massachusetts thought not.[63] The United States Supreme Court said yes, in a case hailed by the press but reflecting continuing deep division in the Court on matters of access.

A Massachusetts trial court, relying on a state statute providing for exclusion of the general public from trials of specified sexual offenses involving victims under eighteen, ordered exclusion of press and public from the courtroom during the trial of a defendant charged with the rape of three minor girls. The *Boston Globe* challenged its exclusion, but the highest state court construed the Massachusetts law as requiring, under all circumstances, exclusion of press and public during the testimony of a minor victim in a sex-offense trial.

---

59. In re Application of NBC, 6 Med.L.Rptr. 2265 (D.D.C.1980).

60. In re Application of NBC, 7 Med.L.Rptr. 1193, 653 F.2d 609 (D.C.Cir. 1981). See also, United States v. Dean, 7 Med.L.Rptr. 1405, 527 F.Supp. 413 (D.Ga.1981) in which a broadcaster's application to copy and telecast audio tapes introduced in evidence in a criminal trial was granted. The court held that defendant had failed to demonstrate that the possible prejudice which broadcasting the tapes might have on a retrial outweighed the public's common law right to copy and inspect judicial records.

And in United States v. Reiter, 7 Med.L.Rptr. 1927 (D.Md.1981), a federal district court held that a newspaper has a right to copy video and audio tapes admitted into evidence in a criminal trial. Likewise in In re Griffin Television, 7 Med.L.Rptr. 1947 (D.Okl.1981) a television station was granted access to all audio and video tapes admitted in evidence in a criminal trial.

61. In re U.S. ex rel. Pulitzer Publishing, 6 Med.L.Rptr. 2232, 635 F.2d 676 (8th Cir. 1980). The case involved the question of attendance by press and public at *voir dire* examination proceedings.

62. In re Antitrust Grand Jury Investigation, 508 F.Supp. 397 (D.Va.1980).

63. Globe Newspaper v. Superior Court, 5 Med.L.Rptr. 2617, 401 N.E.2d 360 (Mass.1980).

A divided (6–3) United States Supreme Court, managing nevertheless to speak with a single majority voice, reversed.

GLOBE NEWSPAPER COMPANY v. SUPERIOR COURT FOR THE COUNTY OF NORFOLK

457 U.S. 596, 102 S.CT. 2613, 73 L.ED.2D 248 (1982).

Justice BRENNAN delivered the opinion of the Court.

Section 16A of Chapter 278 of Massachusetts General Laws, as construed by the Massachusetts Supreme Judicial Court, requires trial judges, at trials for specified sexual offenses involving a victim under the age of 18, to exclude the press and general public from the courtroom during the testimony of that victim. The question presented is whether the statute thus construed violates the First Amendment as applied to the States through the Fourteenth Amendment.

* * *

The Court's recent decision in *Richmond Newspapers* firmly established for the first time that the press and general public have a constitutional right of access to criminal trials. Although there was no opinion of the Court in that case, seven Justices recognized that this right of access is embodied in the First Amendment, and applied to the States through the Fourteenth Amendment.

* * *

The state interests asserted to support § 16A, though articulated in various ways, are reducible to two: the protection of minor victims of sex crimes from further trauma and embarrassment; and the encouragement of such victims to come forward and testify in a truthful and credible manner. We consider these interests in turn.

We agree with respondent that the first interest—safeguarding the physical and psychological well-being of a minor—is a compelling one. But as compelling as that interest is, it does not justify a *mandatory* -closure rule, for it is clear that the circumstances of the particular case may affect the significance of the interest. A trial court can determine on a case-by-case basis whether closure is necessary to protect the welfare of a minor victim. Among the factors to be weighed are the minor victim's age, psychological maturity, and understanding, the nature of the crime, the desires of the victim, and the interests of parents and relatives. Section 16A, in contrast, requires closure even if the victim does not seek the exclusion of the press and general public, and would not suffer injury by their presence. In the case before us, for example, the names of the minor victims were already in the public record,[23] and the record indicates that the victims may have been willing to testify despite the presence of the press. If the trial court had been permitted to exercise its discretion, closure might well have been deemed unnecessary. In short, § 16A cannot be viewed as a narrowly tailored means of accommodating the State's asserted interest: That interest could be served just as well by requiring the trial court to determine on a case-by-case basis whether the State's legitimate concern for the well-being of the minor victim necessitates closure. Such an approach ensures that the constitutional right of the press and public to gain access to criminal trials will not be restricted except where necessary to protect the State's interest.[25]

---

23. The Court has held that the government may not impose sanctions for the publication of the names of rape victims lawfully obtained from the public record. Cox Broadcasting Corp. v. Cohn, 420 U.S. 469 * * * (1975). See also Smith v. Daily Mail Publishing Co., 443 U.S. 97 * * * (1979).

25. Of course, for a case-by-case approach to be meaningful, representatives of the press and general public "must be given an opportunity to be heard on the question of their exclusion." Gannett Co. v. DePasquale, 443

Nor can § 16A be justified on the basis of the Commonwealth's second asserted interest—the encouragement of minor victims of sex crimes to come forward and provide accurate testimony. The Commonwealth has offered no empirical support for the claim that the rule of automatic closure contained in § 16A will lead to an increase in the number of minor sex victims coming forward and cooperating with state authorities. Not only is the claim speculative in empirical terms, but it is also open to serious question as a matter of logic and common sense. Although § 16A bars the press and general public from the courtroom during the testimony of minor sex victims, the press is not denied access to the transcript, court personnel, or any other possible source that could provide an account of the minor victim's testimony. Thus § 16A cannot prevent the press from publicizing the substance of a minor victim's testimony, as well as his or her identity. If the Commonwealth's interest in encouraging minor victims to come forward depends on keeping such matters secret, § 16A hardly advances that interest in an effective manner. And even if § 16A effectively advanced the State's interest, it is doubtful that the interest would be sufficient to overcome the constitutional attack, for that same interest could be relied on to support an array of mandatory-closure rules designed to encourage victims to come forward: Surely it cannot be suggested that minor victims of sex crimes are the *only* crime victims who, because of publicity attendant to criminal trials, are reluctant to come forward and testify. The State's argument based on this interest therefore proves too much, and runs contrary to the very foundation of the right of access recognized in *Richmond Newspapers:* namely, "that a presumption of openness inheres in the very nature of a criminal trial under our system of justice." 448 U.S., at 573 * * * (plurality opinion).

For the foregoing reasons, we hold that § 16A, as construed by the Massachusetts Supreme Judicial Court, violates the First Amendment to the Constitution.[27] Accordingly, the judgment of the Massachusetts Supreme Judicial Court is

Reversed.

Chief Justice BURGER, with whom Justice Rehnquist joins, dissenting.

* * *

The Court has tried to make its holding a narrow one by not disturbing the authority of state legislatures to enact more narrowly drawn statutes giving trial judges the discretion to exclude the public and the press from the courtroom during the minor victim's testimony. * * * I also do not read the Court's opinion as foreclosing a state statute which mandates closure except in cases where the victim agrees to testify in open court. But the Court's decision is nevertheless a gross invasion of state authority and a state's duty to protect its citizens—in this case minor victims

U.S. 368, 401, * * * (1979) (Powell, J., concurring). This does not mean, however, that for purposes of this inquiry the court cannot protect the minor victim by denying these representatives the opportunity to confront or cross-examine the victim, or by denying them access to sensitive details concerning the victim and the victim's future testimony. Such discretion is consistent with the traditional authority of trial judges to conduct in camera conferences. See Richmond Newspapers, Inc. v. Virginia, 448 U.S., at 598, n. 23 * * * (Brennan, J., concurring in the judgment). Without such trial court discretion, a State's interest in safeguarding the welfare of the minor victim determined in an individual case to merit some form of closure, would be defeated before it could ever be brought to bear.

27. We emphasize that our holding is a narrow one: that a rule of mandatory closure respecting the testimony of minor sex victims is constitutionally infirm. In individual cases, and under appropriate circumstances, the First Amendment does not necessarily stand as a bar to the exclusion from the courtroom of the press and general public during the testimony of minor sex-offense victims. But a mandatory rule, requiring no particularized determinations in individual cases, is unconstitutional.

of crime. I cannot agree with the Court's expansive interpretation of our decision in Richmond Newspapers, Inc. v. Virginia, 448 U.S. 555 * * * (1980), or its cavalier rejection of the serious interests supporting Massachusetts' mandatory closure rule. Accordingly, I dissent.

* * *

Today Justice Brennan ignores the weight of historical practice. There is clearly a long history of exclusion of the public from trials involving sexual assaults, particularly those against minors. * * * Several states have longstanding provisions allowing closure of cases involving sexual assaults against minors.

* * *

Neither the purpose of the law nor its effect is primarily to deny the press or public access to information; the verbatim transcript is made available to the public and the media and may be used without limit. We therefore need only examine whether the restrictions imposed are reasonable and whether the interests of the Commonwealth override the very limited incidental effects of the law on First Amendment rights. * * * Our obligation in this case is to balance the competing interests: the interests of the media for instant access, against the interest of the state in protecting child rape victims from the trauma of public testimony. In more than half the states, public testimony will include television coverage.

* * *

The law need not be precisely tailored so long as the state's interest overrides the law's impact on First Amendment rights and the restrictions imposed further that interest. Certainly this law, which excludes the press and public only during the actual testimony of the child victim of a sex crime, rationally serves the Commonwealth's overriding interest in protecting the child from the severe—possibly permanent—psychological damage. It is not disputed that such injury is a reality.[5]

The law also seems a rational response to the undisputed problem of the underreporting of rapes and other sexual offenses. The Court rejects the Commonwealth's argument that § 16A is justified by its interest in encouraging minors to report sex crimes, finding the claim "speculative in empirical terms [and] open to serious question as a matter of logic and common sense." * * * There is no basis whatever for this cavalier disregard of the reality of human experience. It makes no sense to criticize the Commonwealth for its failure to offer empirical data in support of its rule; only by allowing state experimentation may such empirical evidence be produced. "It is one of the happy incidents of the federal system that a State may, if its citizens choose, serve as a laboratory, and try novel social and economic experiments without risk to the rest of the country." New State Ice Co. v. Liebmann, 285 U.S. 262, 311 * * * (1932) (Brandeis, J., dissenting). * * *

The Court also concludes that the Commonwealth's assertion that the law might reduce underreporting of sexual offenses fails "as a matter of logic and common sense." This conclusion is based on a misperception of the Commonwealth's argument and an overly narrow view of the protection the statute seeks to afford young victims. The Court apparently believes that the statute does not prevent any significant trauma, embarrassment or humiliation on the part of the victim simply because the press is not prevented from discovering and publicizing both the identity of the victim and the substance of the victim's testimony. * * * Section

5. For a discussion of the traumatic effect of court proceedings on minor rape victims, see E. Hilberman, *The Rape Victim* 53–54; S. Katz & M. Mazur, *Understanding the Rape Victim: A Synthesis of Research Findings* 198–200 (1979), and studies cited therein.

16A is intended not to preserve confidentiality, but to prevent the risk of severe psychological damage caused by having to relate the details of the crime in front of a crowd which inevitably will include voyeuristic strangers.[6] In most states, that crowd may be expanded to include a live television audience, with reruns on the evening news. That ordeal could be difficult for an adult; to a child, the experience can be devastating and leave permanent scars.[7]

* * *

Justice STEVENS, dissenting.

* * *

The question whether the Court should entertain a facial attack on a statute that bears on the right of access cannot be answered simply by noting that the right has its source in the First Amendment. See, e.g., Bates v. State Bar of Arizona, 433 U.S. 350, 380–381; * * * Young v. American Mini Theatres, Inc., 427 U.S. 50, 61. * * For the right of access is plainly not coextensive with the right of expression that was vindicated in *Nebraska Press Assn.* [1] Because statutes that bear on this right of access do not deter protected activity in the way that other laws sometimes interfere with the right of expression, we should follow the norm of reviewing these statutes as applied rather than on their face.

* * *

COMMENT

1. The Court's rejection of a blanket rule excluding press and public from criminal trials involving youthful victims and defendants may not discourage the enforcement of more narrowly drawn statutes, or the recognition of compelling and overriding state interests—privacy in one of its myriad forms perhaps—in protecting the welfare of minors, when such interests can be documented. While the Court left open the possibility of closed juvenile criminal hearings, it rejected the limitations placed on judicial discretion by a "mandatory" act of the legislature.

Prior to *Globe Newspaper,* some state courts were quick to protect defendants against revelation of prior convictions,[64] or against embarrassment,[65] and to shield juvenile victims or witnesses.[66] Others preferred to keep hearings and records open at all costs on state common law or consti-

---

6. As one commentator put it, "Especially in cases involving minors, the courts stress the serious embarrassment and shame of the victim who is forced to testify to sexual acts or whose intimate life is revealed in detail before a crowd of the idly curious." *Berger, Man's Trial, Woman's Tribulation: Rape Cases in the Courtroom,* 77 Colum.L.Rev. 1, 88 (1977). The victim's interest in avoiding the humiliation of testifying in open court is thus quite separate from any interest in preventing the public from learning of the crime. It is ironic that the Court emphasizes the failure of the Commonwealth to seal the trial transcript and bar disclosure of the victim's identity. The Court implies that a state law more severely encroaching upon the interests of the press and public would be upheld.

7. See E. Hilberman, *supra;* L. Holmstrom & A. Burgess, *The Victim of Rape: Institutional Reactions* 222, 227 (1978); Berger, *supra,* at 88, 92–93; Libai, *The Protection of a Child Victim of a Sexual Offense in the Criminal Justice System,* 15 Wayne L.Rev. 977, 1021 (1969). Holmstrom and Burgess report that nearly half of all *adult* rape victims were disturbed by the public setting of their trials. Certainly the impact on children must be greater.

1. For example, even though a reporter may have no right of access to a judge's side-bar conference, it surely does not follow that the judge could enjoin publication of what a reporter might have learned about such a conference.

64. Capital Newspapers v. Clyne, 7 Med.L.Rptr. 1536, 440 N.Y.S.2d 779 (1981).

65. New York v. Jones, 7 Med.L.Rptr. 2096, 418 N.Y.S.2d 359, cert. den. 444 U.S. 946 (1981).

66. Connecticut v. McCloud, 6 Med.L.Rptr. 1613, 422 A.2d 327 (Conn.1980); North Carolina v. Burney, 7 Med.L.Rptr. 1411, 276 S.E.2d 693 (N.C.1981).

tutional grounds.[67] What is the impact of *Globe Newspaper* on closed divorce proceedings, which are closed in the interests of protecting children or the privacy rights of the parties?

While it will take time to measure the sweep and authority of *Richmond* and *Globe* in improving access to judicial hearings, trials, and records, lower federal courts were the first to take the cue. For example, in *United States v. Brooklier*[68] the Ninth Circuit used Brennan's "structural" argument in *Richmond* to keep *voir dire* hearings open. And in *United States v. Dorfman*[69] the Seventh Circuit used Blackmun's three-part *Gannett* test to assure that all phases of a suppression hearing would be accessible to the public: would access do irreparable damage to fair trial (this is sometimes referred to as the compelling or strict necessity test); would the judicial remedies not protect the defendant and make closure unnecessary; and, if imposed, would closure be effective? The court did hold in *Dorfman* that wiretap material would not be disclosable until admitted into evidence. In other words, for a time at least, privacy would outweigh newsworthiness.

One might infer from that case that courts generally intend trials to be more open than suppression hearings. It would also appear that suppression hearings are more open to public scrutiny than court records.

In the meantime, arguments for access could be based on the First Amendment, on the common law which apparently made no distinction between trial and pretrial hearings, on other historical grounds, on state public policy or state constitution, or on whatever grounds seem appropriate.

The *Swedberg* Case

It will take time for the press to recover from a Washington state case that has dampened twenty years of dialogue by press, bar, and judiciary on the fair and ethical coverage of court proceedings. In late 1981 the Washington Supreme Court held that a trial court order allowing press access to pretrial proceedings only on the promise that reporters would abide by the voluntary bar-bench-press guidelines of Washington state was not a prior restraint but a reasonable limitation designed to accommodate the interests of both press and public. Federated Publications v. Swedberg, 7 Med.L.Rptr. 1865, 633 P.2d 74 (Wash.1981). Justice Rosellini, who wrote the opinion for the court, had played a prominent role in drafting the original state guidelines. Tough-minded opponents of voluntary guidelines, in both press and bar, had warned that voluntary agreements might someday be interpreted as mandatory.

In spite of a major effort by press and broadcast organizations to get Supreme Court review for the case, review was denied on May 17, 1982. The press saw the Washington decision as sanctioning prior restraint, as imposing an unconstitutional condition on courtroom access. Moreover, excluding reporters who had refused to comply with "voluntary guidelines" was not a reasonable limitation on access, comparable to a time, place, and manner restriction. And excluding the press, but not the public, violated the First Amendment. Apparently only Justices Brennan and Marshall, who opposed the denial to grant review, accepted any of these arguments.

---

67. Seattle Times v. Ishikawa, 8 Med.L.Rptr. 1041, 640 P.2d 716 (Wash.1982); Cowles Publishing v. Murphy, 6 Med.L.Rptr. 2308, 637 P.2d 966 (Wash.1981). See also, Lexington Herald Leader v. Tackett, 6 Med.L.Rptr. 1436 (Ky.1980) involving a sodomy prosecution.

68. 685 F.2d 1162 (9th Cir. 1982). See also, United States v. Criden, 8 Med.L.Rptr. 1297, 675 F.2d 550 (3d Cir. 1982).

69. 690 F.2d 1230 (7th Cir. 1982).

The argument of the trial judge and his attorney in support of the Washington Supreme Court holding was that exclusion of the press was preferable to closing the courtroom altogether.

Amid predictions that voluntary guidelines would collapse in all thirty-four states that had adopted them, the ABA/ANPA joint task force on press/bar relations adopted a resolution "deploring the use of such voluntary guidelines to condition access or restrain news reporting."

On the same day, the Court also denied review in Sacramento Bee v. United States District Court, 7 Med.L.Rptr. 1929, 656 F.2d 477 (9th Cir. 1981). There a federal district court order had excluded the press, but not the public, from two evidentiary hearings in a criminal trial. On appeal, the United States Court of Appeals for the Ninth Circuit ruled that the federal district court's failure to consider alternatives to exclusion of the press did not constitute such clear error as to warrant issuance of a writ that would bar the court from issuing similar orders in the future. The federal appeals court was surprised that the press had not pushed hard for alternatives to exclusion. At the same time it recommended that courts favor voluntary agreements with the press about the timing and scope of coverage. Justice Brennan would have granted review in *Sacramento Bee.*

While *Swedberg* is applicable only to Washington state and any agreement made by the press not to publish would be a moral commitment only, legally unenforceable, the press cannot help but feel compromised and betrayed. If voluntary guidelines can be incorporated into court orders, they can be enforced by the contempt power, as *Dickinson* teaches. It has been suggested that perhaps the Washington court was simply testing the sincerity of journalist participation in the voluntary guidelines.

In the opinion in the *Swedberg* case which follows, one finds the ingredients of future tension between press and judiciary. The judge faults the judicial remedies for publicity. He sees no prior restraint in orders conditioning attendance at a public trial on a promise not to publish. He is backed by the Judicial Conference of the United States which would make such orders enforceable by contempt citations (October 1981). He distinguishes *Nebraska Press* and relies on *Gannett.*

FEDERATED PUBLICATIONS v. SWEDBERG

7 MED.L.RPTR. 1865, 633 P.2D 74 (WASH.1981).

ROSELLINI, J.:

* * *

While this court has found a right of the public to attend a pretrial hearing, under the language of Const. art. 1, § 10, that right is qualified by the court's right and duty to see that the defendant has a fair trial. The court may order closure, if the objectors fail to demonstrate the availability of some practical alternative.

Here the court found that the only alternatives which could conceivably be effective in protecting the defendant's rights were to either close the hearing or exact a commitment from the members of the media to abide by the Bench-Bar-Press Guidelines.

The Bench-Bar-Press Guidelines, insofar as they are relevant here, are set forth in the appendix to this opinion. They are, by definition, not a set of rules but rather principles which guide the courts, lawyers and court personnel, as well as the media, in protecting the rights of an accused and other litigants to a fair trial, while at the same time respecting and preserving the freedoms of speech and press guaranteed by the state and federal constitutions. Under their express provisions, they honor the right of the news media to report what occurs in the course of the judicial proceeding.

As was pointed out by Justice Finley in his concurring opinion in State ex rel. Superior Court v. Sperry, * * * 483 P.2d 608 (Wash.1971), responsible exercise of constitutional freedoms, with regard for the constitutional rights of accused persons and other litigants, is the essence of the guidelines.

It is true that these guidelines suggest the exercise of caution in reporting matters which may be damaging to the right of an accused to a fair trial, at a time when that risk is greatest—that is, prior to the trial. Ordinarily, members of the media who have declared their adherence to the guidelines do exercise restraint in such reporting, but it had been the experience of the trial judge here that mere oral commitment had not sufficed to produce that restraint. He recognized that by admitting members of the press to such a sensitive proceeding, even upon their written agreement to be guided by these standards, he was placing the defendant's interests in some jeopardy. Yet he was willing to try this method of securing compliance, as an experiment, to see if it would be effective in protecting the defendant while at the same time allowing the public, including the media, to attend the hearing. As we view this measure, it was a good faith attempt to accommodate the interests of both defendant and press which, hopefully, would prove both practical and effective as an alternative to closure.

The petitioner's objection to the ruling is grounded upon its fear that, should it publish reports of the hearing, it would be subject to contempt proceedings. Whether the contempt power of the court could in other circumstances properly extend to punishment for alleged violation of an agreement to adhere to a set of standards as nonobligatory as these is a question which has not been briefed and which we need not decide. It would, however, be contrary to the spirit and intent of the Bench-Bar-Press Guidelines to invoke such a remedy for their alleged violation, and the comments of the lower court in making its ruling indicate that the court was in agreement with that principle. It issued no orders prohibiting publication, nor did it threaten any sanctions, if a person signing an agreement to abide by the guidelines should thereafter ignore them. Its ruling was simply that any media member not willing to put his moral commitment in writing would be excluded from the hearing.

Inasmuch as the court had the authority, under our holding in Federated Publications, Inc. v. Kurtz, * * * 615 P.2d 440 (Wash.1980), to exclude all of the public, including the media, it had also the included power to impose reasonable conditions upon attendance. The exaction of an agreement to abide by standards which have gained the approval of all of the media of mass communications in this state was not unreasonable, particularly in view of the fact that the commitment is a moral one, even when expressed in writing, and not enforceable in a court of law.

The procedure may not prove effective, and it may be that in cases of this kind the rights of the defendant can be secured only by closing the suppression * * * hearings; but it would be a disservice to the public, as well as the media, to declare that a lesser measure, as innocuous as that employed here, is beyond the reach of a court attempting in good faith to accommodate the rights of all concerned.

That reasonable limitations may be imposed upon attendance at a judicial proceeding was recognized in Richmond Newspapers, Inc. v. Virginia, 448 U.S. 555 * * * (1980) (Justice White, concurring). In a footnote at page 581, he said:

> Just as a government may impose reasonable time, place, and manner restrictions upon the use of its streets in the interest of such objectives as the free flow of traffic, see, e.g., Cox v. New Hampshire, 312 U.S. 569 (1941), so may a trial judge, in the interest of the fair administration of justice, impose

reasonable limitations on access to a trial.

Our conclusion is that the limitation imposed here was a reasonable one, and the petition is accordingly denied.

COMMENT

1. Justice Dolliver, joined by three colleagues, saw the trial court order as a prior restraint and dissented: "A review of the record in *Federated Publications, Inc. v. Kurtz* [cited in the majority opinion] shows that there were extensive and detailed findings of fact, plus attached exhibits which enabled the trial court to engage in the required 'weighing of the competing interests of the defendant and the public'." Here the court had simply concluded that the "likelihood of jeopardy to a fair trial is overwhelmingly established" and that "the usual methods to protect a fair trial such as voir dire, peremptory challenges and others are not adequate safeguards."

"These statements and order by the trial court," the dissent added, "do not even come close to meeting our requirements in *Federated Publications v. Kurtz* for the closure of a courtroom in a suppression hearing. Much less do they meet the standards of the United States Supreme Court for prior restraint as articulated in the *Nebraska Press Assn.* case. This court should not allow the great freedoms of the First Amendment and Const. art. 1, § 10 [Washington Constitution] to be traduced in this manner."

2. Recall that in *Gannett* the Court took note of the fact that no timely objection to closure had been made by reporters present in the courtroom. It should be standard practice that reporters object promptly and strenuously to orders not to print or motions to close any part of the judicial process. Major news organizations have developed procedures and forms to deal with these problems.

THE STATUS OF BROADCAST COVERAGE: CAMERAS IN THE COURTROOM

1. In covering crime and the courts, electronic and photojournalism early became victim to its own youthful brashness, raucous commercialism, and intrusive equipment. Bench and bar tended to equate television's power to attract with its power to prejudice.

Policemen had posed suspects for the cameras and permitted them to announce their guilt to the world. In 1961 a jury reenacted its deliberations, theorized on the guilt or innocence of the defendant, and discussed the death penalty for a videotape rebroadcast the day before sentencing.[70] The Supreme Court finally took note of these practices in the case of Wilbur Rideau.

After his arrest on suspicion of bank robbery and murder, Rideau was interviewed in jail by a film crew. A cooperative sheriff stood by posing his prisoner. He confessed and his confession went out over the airwaves, not once but three times. A change of venue was denied; Rideau was tried, convicted, and sentenced to death.

When the case got to the U.S. Supreme Court, Justice Potter Stewart in his opinion for the Court reversed. "For anyone who has ever watched television," he said, "the conclusion cannot be avoided that this spectacle, to the tens of thousands of people who saw and heard it, in a very real sense was Rideau's trial—at which he pleaded guilty to murder. Any subsequent court proceedings in a community so per-

---

70. United States v. Rees, 193 F.Supp. 864 (D.Md.1961).

vasively exposed to such a spectacle could be but a hollow formality." Rideau v. Louisiana, 373 U.S. 723 (1963).

There is a strong implication in the Court's opinion that no judicial remedies in either trial or pretrial period would have overcome the prejudicial effects of the broadcasts. Presumably the power of the camera outstrips the power of the pen—an assumption that may no longer be safe.[71]

2. The case of Billie Sol Estes came to the Court two years later in 1965. Estes, an erstwhile Texas financier, had come to trial in 1962 on charges of theft, swindling, and embezzlement. Over Estes's objections the trial judge permitted television coverage of the pretrial hearing and portions of the trial. Upon conviction Estes appealed partly on the grounds that the cameras had deprived him of due process of law. By a narrow margin the Supreme Court agreed, and courtroom doors closed to cameras with a clang.

Justice Clark, who dissented in *Rideau* because he could see no "substantial nexus between the televised 'interview' and petitioner's trial," spoke for the Court. After noting that there were twelve cameramen in the courtroom, a great snarl of equipment, and considerable disruption—and, after all, newspaper reporters didn't bring their typewriters and printing presses into the courtroom—Clark tried to come to grips with the issue.

ESTES v. STATE OF TEXAS

1 MED.L.RPTR. 1187, 381 U.S. 532,
85 S.CT. 1628, 14 L.ED.2D 543 (1965).

Justice CLARK delivered the opinion of the Court.

* * *

As has been said, the chief function of our judicial machinery is to ascertain the truth. The use of television, however, cannot be said to contribute materially to this objective. Rather its use amounts to the injection of an irrelevant factor into court proceedings. In addition experience teaches that there are numerous situations in which it might cause actual unfairness—some so subtle as to defy detection by the accused or control by the judge. We enumerate some in summary:

1. The potential impact of television on the jurors is perhaps of the greatest significance. They are the nerve center of the fact-finding process. It is true that in States like Texas where they are required to be sequestered in trials of this nature the jurors will probably not see any of the proceedings as televised from the courtroom. But the inquiry cannot end there. From the moment the trial judge announces that a case will be televised it becomes a *cause célèbre.* The whole community, including prospective jurors, becomes interested in all the morbid details surrounding it. The approaching trial immediately assumes an important status in the public press and the accused is highly publicized along with the offense with which he is charged. Every juror carries with him into the jury box these solemn facts and thus increases the chance of prejudice that is present in every criminal case. And we must remember that realistically it is only the notorious trial which will be broadcast, because of the necessity for paid sponsorship. The conscious or unconscious effect that this may have on the juror's judgment cannot be evaluated, but experience indicates that it is not only possible but highly probable that it will have a direct bearing on his vote as to guilt or innocence. Where pretrial publicity of all kinds has created intense public feeling which is aggravated by the telecasting or picturing of the trial the televised jurors cannot help but feel the pressures of knowing that friends and

71. Shaw and McCombs, *The Agenda-Setting Function of the Press* (1977).

neighbors have their eyes upon them. If the community be hostile to an accused, a televised juror, realizing that he must return to neighbors who saw the trial themselves, may well be led "not to hold the balance nice, clear and true between the State and the accused. * * *"

Moreover, while it is practically impossible to assess the effect of television on jury attentiveness, those of us who know juries realize the problem of jury "distraction." The State argues this is *de minimis* since the physical disturbances have been eliminated. But we know that distractions are not caused solely by the physical presence of the camera and its telltale red lights. It is the awareness of the fact of telecasting that is felt by the juror throughout the trial. We are all self-conscious and uneasy when being televised. Human nature being what it is, not only will a juror's eyes be fixed on the camera, but also his mind will be preoccupied with the telecasting rather than with the testimony.

Furthermore, in many States the jurors serving in the trial may see the broadcasts of the trial proceedings. Admittedly, the Texas sequestration rule would prevent this occurring there. In other States following no such practice jurors would return home and turn on the TV if only to see how they appeared upon it. They would also be subjected to reenactment and emphasis of the selected parts of the proceedings which the requirements of the broadcasters determined would be telecast and would be subconsciously influenced the more by that testimony. Moreover, they would be subjected to the broadest commentary and criticism and perhaps the well-meant advice of friends, relatives and inquiring strangers who recognized them on the streets.

Finally, new trials plainly would be jeopardized in that potential jurors will often have seen and heard the original trial when it was telecast. Yet viewers may later be called upon to sit in the jury box during the new trial. These very dangers are illustrated in this case where the court, due to the defendant's objections, permitted only the State's opening and closing arguments to be broadcast with sound to the public.

2. The quality of the testimony in criminal trials will often be impaired. The impact upon a witness of the knowledge that he is being viewed by a vast audience is simply incalculable. Some may be demoralized and frightened, some cocky and given to overstatement; memories may falter, as with anyone speaking publicly, and accuracy of statement may be severely undermined. Embarrassment may impede the search for the truth, as may a natural tendency toward overdramatization. Furthermore, inquisitive strangers and "cranks" might approach witnesses on the street with jibes, advice or demands for explanation of testimony. There is little wonder that the defendant cannot "prove" the existence of such factors. Yet we all know from experience that they exist.

In addition to invocation of the rule against witnesses is frustrated. In most instances witnesses would be able to go to their homes and view broadcasts of the day's trial proceedings, notwithstanding the fact that they had been admonished not to do so. They could view and hear the testimony of preceding witnesses, and so shape their own testimony as to make its impact crucial. And even in the absence of sound, the influences of such viewing on the attitude of the witness toward testifying, his frame of mind upon taking the stand or his apprehension of withering cross-examination defy objective assessment. Indeed, the mere fact that the trial is to be televised might render witnesses reluctant to appear and thereby impede the trial as well as the discovery of the truth.

While some of the dangers mentioned above are present as well in newspaper coverage of any important trial, the circumstances and extraneous influences intruding upon the solemn decorum of court procedure in the televised trial are far more serious than in cases involving only newspaper coverage.

3. A major aspect of the problem is the additional responsibilities the presence of television places on the trial judge. His job is to make certain that the accused receives a fair trial. This most difficult task requires his undivided attention. Still when television comes into the courtroom he must also supervise it. In this trial, for example, the judge on several different occasions—aside from the two days of pretrial—was obliged to have a hearing or enter an order made necessary solely because of the presence of television. Thus, where telecasting is restricted as it was here, and as even the State concedes it must be, his task is made more difficult and exacting. And, as happened here, such rulings may unfortunately militate against the fairness of the trial. In addition, laying physical interruptions aside, there is the ever-present distraction that the mere awareness of television's presence prompts. Judges are human beings also and are subject to the same psychological reactions as laymen. Telecasting is particularly bad where the judge is elected, as is the case in all save a half dozen of our States. The telecasting of a trial becomes a political weapon, which, along with other distractions inherent in broadcasting, diverts his attention from the task at hand—the fair trial of the accused.

* * *

4. Finally, we cannot ignore the impact of courtroom television on the defendant. Its presence is a form of mental—if not physical—harassment, resembling a police line-up or the third degree. The inevitable close-ups of his gestures and expressions during the ordeal of his trial might well transgress his personal sensibilities, his dignity, and his ability to concentrate on the proceedings before him—sometimes the difference between life and death—dispassionately, freely and without the distraction of wide public surveillance. A defendant on trial for a specific crime is entitled to his day in court, not in a stadium, or a city or nationwide arena. The heightened public clamor resulting from radio and television coverage will inevitably result in prejudice. Trial by television is, therefore, foreign to our system. Furthermore, telecasting may also deprive an accused of effective counsel. The distractions, intrusions into confidential attorney-client relationships and the temptation offered by television to play to the public audience might often have a direct effect not only upon the lawyers, but the judge, the jury and the witnesses. * * * The television camera is a powerful weapon. Intentionally or inadvertently it can destroy an accused and his case in the eyes of the public. While our telecasters are honorable men, they too are human. The necessity for sponsorship weighs heavily in favor of the televising of only notorious cases, such as this one, and invariably focuses the lens upon the unpopular or infamous accused. Such a selection is necessary in order to obtain a sponsor willing to pay a sufficient fee to cover the costs and return a profit. We have already examined the ways in which public sentiment can affect the trial participants. To the extent that television shapes that sentiment, it can strip the accused of a fair trial.

The State would dispose of all these observations with the simple statement that they are for psychologists because they are purely hypothetical. But we cannot afford the luxury of saying that, because these factors are difficult of ascertainment in particular cases, they must be ignored. * * *

The judgment is therefore reversed.

COMMENT

1. Chief Justice Earl Warren, joined by Justices Douglas and Goldberg, wrote an

angry concurrence in which he—ironically—included seven photographs to convey and clarify his arguments. Drawing analogies between Estes's trial and Castro's "stadium trials" and the trial of Francis Gary Powers in the Soviet Union, Warren declared that the evil inherent in television coverage outraged the Sixth Amendment.

Television, said Warren, diverts the trial from its proper purpose in that it has an inevitable impact on all the trial participants; it gives the public the wrong impression about the purpose of trials, thereby detracting from the dignity of court proceedings and lessening the reliability of trials; and it singles out certain defendants and subjects them to trials under prejudicial conditions not experienced by others.

"On entering that hallowed sanctuary [the American courtroom]," Warren added, "where the lives, liberty and property of people are in jeopardy, television representatives have only the rights of the general public, namely to be present, to observe the proceedings, and thereafter, if they choose, to report them."

Four members of the Court dissented—Stewart, White, Brennan, and Black. Said Stewart:

> We deal here with matters subject to continuous and unforeseeable change—the techniques of public communication. In an area where all the variables may be modified tomorrow, I cannot at this time rest my determination on hypothetical possibilities not present in the record of this case. There is no claim here based upon any right guaranteed by the First Amendment. But it is important to remember that we move in an area touching the realm of free communication, and for that reason, if for no other, I would be wary of imposing any *per se* rule which, in the light of future technology, might serve to stifle or abridge true First Amendment rights. * * * The suggestion that there are limits upon the public's right to know what goes on in the courts causes me deep concern. The idea of imposing upon any medium of communications the burden of justifying its presence is contrary to where I had always thought the presumption must lie in the area of First Amendment freedoms. And the proposition that nonparticipants in a trial might get the "wrong impression" from unfettered reporting and commentary contains an invitation to censorship which I cannot accept. * * * I cannot say at this time that it is impossible to have a constitutional trial whenever any part of the proceedings is televised or recorded on television film.

"We know too little of the actual impact to reach a conclusion on the bare bones of the evidence before us," Justice White noted.

And Brennan drew attention to Justice Harlan's concurrence with the majority which, typical of Harlan, would give the states leeway for experimentation. It was Harlan who kept *Estes* from becoming a blanket constitutional prohibition against the televising of state criminal trials.

Although "mischievous potentialities" had been at work in the *Estes* case, "*the day may come,*" said Harlan, "*when television will have become so commonplace an affair in the daily life of the average person as to dissipate all reasonable likelihood that its use in courtrooms may disparage the judicial process.*" [Emphasis added.]

Add to these Justice Clark's own qualification—"When the advances in these arts permit reporting by printing press or by television without their present hazards to a fair trial we will have another case"—and you have almost an invitation for the camera to enter the courtroom.

2. Prior to the trial of Bruno Richard Hauptmann for the kidnaping of the Lindbergh baby, camera coverage depended on the presiding judge. Some welcomed it; some banned it. On balance, photographers acquitted themselves well in covering that notorious case, going so far as to pool their resources. Conventional history

would have it otherwise. The transgressions of a newsreel crew are all that is remembered.[72]

After that confused and sensational case had concluded and the American Bar Association had time to think about it, the organization added Canon 35 to its statement of judicial ethics, recommending prohibition of all photographic and broadcast coverage of courtroom proceedings. In 1963 Canon 35 was amended to include television. In 1972 the Code of Judicial Conduct superseded the Canons of Judicial Ethics and Canon 3A(7) reaffirmed and replaced Canon 35. Rule 53 of the Federal Rules of Criminal Procedure and strong admonitions from the Judicial Conference of the United States have kept cameras out of federal courtrooms since 1946.

In 1978 the ABA Committee on Fair Trial-Free Press proposed revised standards that would permit camera coverage at a trial judge's discretion. Its legislative body, the House of Delegates, turned down the proposal a year later. On August 11, 1982 the same body repealed its stand against broadcast coverage of judicial proceedings and called for adoption of a new Canon 3A(7) allowing broadcast coverage "under rules prescribed by a supervising [state] appellate court or other appropriate authority." There was vocal opposition. Erwin Griswold, former dean of the Harvard Law School, said that most television coverage is provided by a "motley crew" who present their material with an eye toward the spectacular.

Meanwhile the Conference of State Chief Justices, by a vote of 44 to 1, had in 1978 approved a resolution recommending that the highest court of each state promulgate standards and guidelines regulating radio, television, and other electronic coverage of court proceedings.

By 1983, at least forty states were permitting some kind of video or audio coverage on either a permanent or experimental basis. Nearly half of these required the consent of some or all of the parties to the proceeding. Thirty-three states permitted coverage of criminal and/or civil trials. Thirty-eight permitted coverage of appeals courts, and, for a time, eight states allowed coverage only of their appellate and/or supreme courts.

More than two-thirds of the experimenting states have so far adopted rules for permanent coverage. No experimenting state has yet decided to ban photographic coverage altogether, although some, Ohio and Iowa, for example, have adopted more restrictive permanent rules. The rules themselves are diverse as to civil and criminal proceedings, the photographing of juries, witnesses, attorneys, defendants, litigants, the range of discretion of the trial judge, regulations concerning permission or consent, and coverage of conferences outside hearing of the jury.

In the Wayne Williams case, a Georgia superior court denied requests for television coverage in view of the defendant's objections and possible harm to children and families of the murdered youths.[73] Georgia was among the first states to adopt rules for TV coverage.

Still nearly half the states, including those with some provision for coverage, keep trial court proceedings closed to the camera. New York's one-year experiment, which began January 1, 1981, included only civil and appellate court proceedings. Those states that would permit criminal trial coverage often exempt, either by court rule or prior statute, those portions of a case involving child custody, divorce, juvenile crime, police informants, relocated witnesses, undercover agents,

72. Kielbowicz, *The Story Behind the Adoption of the Ban on Courtroom Cameras,* 63 Judicature 14 (June-July 1979).

73. Georgia v. Williams, 7 Med.L.Rptr. 1849 and 1852 (1981).

sex crimes, and motions to suppress evidence.

Utah is one of those states that will not budge to accommodate television cameras. It will permit still photos of judges, witnesses, counsel, spectators, and parties subject to their consent and approval of the judge.[74]

At the other pole, Colorado never adopted Canon 35, and as far back as 1956 permitted audio and film coverage of sensational murder trials—the 1956 case, the trial of an accused commercial airline dynamiter.[75] After the trial, the Colorado Supreme Court reviewed the situation and concluded that there was no reason to ban modern camera equipment from the courtroom.[76] After *Estes,* Colorado modified its rule to require defendant's consent as well as the permission of the trial judge, its stated reason being to avoid retrials. Texas and Oklahoma were also permissive regarding camera coverage until the *Estes* ruling.

With Alabama, Georgia, New Hampshire, Texas, Washington, and Colorado, Florida was among the first states to experiment anew with the camera. Its test run began in July 1977.[77] When the pilot program ended, the Florida Supreme Court received and reviewed briefs, reports, letters of comment, and studies. It conducted its own survey of attorneys, witnesses, jurors, and court personnel. A separate survey of judges was taken. The court studied the experience of other states allowing cameras and concluded that "on balance there [was] more to be gained than lost by permitting electronic media coverage of judicial proceedings subject to standards for such coverage."[78] The judge would be in control in the interests of the fair administration of justice, and limited quantities of equipment would be placed in fixed positions. Florida soon became the arena for testing the constitutionality of camera coverage.

The first challenge came when Jules Briklod, charged with conspiracy and grand larceny, contended that live camera coverage would deny him a fair and impartial jury, effective assistance of counsel, and due process of law under Fifth, Sixth, and Fourteenth Amendments. The state trial court overruled his objections, and he went to a U.S. district court. That court, taking a cue from Justice Harlan's concurring opinion in *Estes,* held that Florida's experiment was not "patently and flagrantly" unconstitutional. Injunctive relief was denied. Briklod v. Rivkind, 2 Med.L.Rptr. 2258 (D.Fla.1977).

Next came the murder trial of fifteen-year-old Ronny Zamora, an unfortunate test case perhaps. Zamora's defense of "television made me do it"—specifically an ultraviolent episode of "Kojak"—attracted more attention from an estimated international audience of 200 million than the televising of the trial. Television itself was on trial. As was the concept of media intoxication.

Similar charges of "incitement by television" were rejected in Olivia N. v. NBC, 7 Med.L.Rptr. 2359, 178 Cal.Rptr. 888 (1981), the "Born Innocent" case, and in DeFilippo v. NBC, 8 Med.L.Rptr. 1872, 446 A.2d 1036 (R.I.1982). In the first case a network program's fictional depiction of a broom-handle rape in a state-run home for girls was said to be responsible for a real-life copy of the crime. In the second case a youth hanged himself attempting to imitate a "hanging trick" he'd seen on the Johnny Carson show. For a discussion of

74. In re Canon 3A(7), 7 Med.L.Rptr. 1449 (Utah 1981).

75. Graham v. People, 302 P.2d 737 (Colo.1956).

76. In re Hearings Concerning Canon 35, 296 P.2d 465 (Colo.1956).

77. Petition of the Post-Newsweek Stations, Florida, Inc., 2 Med.L.Rptr. 1832, 347 So.2d 402 (Fla.1976).

78. Petition of the Post-Newsweek Stations, Florida, Inc., 5 Med.L.Rptr. 1039, 370 So.2d 764 (Fla.1979).

these cases and issues in the context of broadcast law, see text, p. 930.

The media restrained in their coverage of the *Zamora* case, agreed to use one "pool camera." Judge Paul Baker of Florida's Circuit Court was ever alert to reporter compulsions to "jazz it up." Although he had misgivings before trial, the judge thought the experiment a success. Cameras were "slightly distracting" to jurors but did not interfere with jurors' being able to concentrate on the arguments of counsel and the court's instructions. Baker thought that both First Amendment rights and the right of the defendant to a fair trial had been protected and that the problems of *Sheppard* and *Estes* had been avoided.

Judge Baker did suggest that the media be restrained from using cameras and lights in the corridors of the courthouse. "What transpires in the courtroom," said the judge, "is a factual account of the trial which is news, but what is elicited in the corridors takes on the color of editorial comment."

Zamora received a life sentence, twenty-five years of it mandatory, for the killing of an elderly neighbor. His attorney had no complaints about the edited camera coverage and, in fact, took notes on his own television performance. The prosecutor had doubts. Viewers were mostly favorable, for, as broadcast reporter Linda O'Bryon observed, they were looking into the "holy of holies" for the first time. Another observer wrote that the broadcasts would win no awards for technical quality, due largely to the use of a single camera and limited lighting, but a first step had been taken.[79]

Florida's Supreme Court next stipulated that requests to exclude electronic media be supported by evidence that coverage would have substantial and "qualitatively different" effects on the process than other types of coverage.[80] Of course, exclusions could be made where the evidence indicated that an otherwise competent criminal defendant would be rendered incompetent by camera coverage.[81]

But the grand test of constitutionality came when two Miami Beach policemen challenged their convictions on burglary charges because portions of their trials had been televised over their objections.

In a unanimous decision grounded in federalism, the Supreme Court rejected their claim and found no constitutional problem with regulated access for cameras in those states which so chose. But the ruling provided no right of camera access in those states which forbade it or in the federal courts.

The decision did not consider any First or Sixth Amendment issues, so threw no additional light on *Gannett* and *Richmond.* It did, however, vindicate the significance of Justice Harlan's concurrence in *Estes* that kept that case from creating a constitutional ban on camera coverage. Chief Justice Burger—who ironically has vowed that as long as he is in office no cameras will enter the Supreme Court chamber and, by implication, the federal courts generally—distinguished *Estes* in his opinion for the Court. Calling for further experimentation to evaluate the camera's psychological effects, he seemed to be saying that *Chandler* would not be the last word on broadcast coverage. Does this track with his *Richmond* opinion in which he makes no distinction between "print and electronic media"? Probably not.

Justices Stewart and White, who dissented in *Estes,* thought *Chandler* had "overruled," "eviscerated" the earlier case.

79. Knopf, *Camera Coverage on Trial,* Quill, November 1977.

80. Florida v. Palm Beach Newspapers, 7 Med.L.Rptr. 1021, 395 So.2d 544 (Fla.1981).

81. Florida v. Green, 7 Med.L.Rptr. 1025, 395 So.2d 532 (Fla.1981).

To be sure, difficult questions do remain unanswered. How will editing affect the perceptions of the audience? Less than three minutes of the Chandler trial were actually broadcast, all of it the prosecution side. How will commercials be handled? How will courtroom coverage be promoted? Can photojournalists function with quiet dignity? In our review of privacy law it was suggested that frequent lapses occur. How does the ruling affect sketch artists who do what the camera does better? [82]

By demonstrating their cool efficiency, photographers, so often victims of the self-inflicted wound, will wear away at judicial assumptions supporting camera bans. And it may be, as Justice Harlan prophesied in *Estes,* that television *has* become so commonplace an affair in the daily life of the average person as to dissipate all reasonable likelihood that its use in courtrooms may disparage the judicial process. Or the legislative process. Or the executive and administrative processes.

CHANDLER v. FLORIDA

449 U.S. 560, 101 S.CT. 802, 66 L.ED.2D 740 (1981).

Chief Justice BURGER delivered the opinion of the Court:

* * *

At the outset, it is important to note that in promulgating the revised Canon 3A(7), the Florida Supreme Court pointedly rejected any state or federal constitutional right of access on the part of photographers or the broadcast media to televise or electronically record and thereafter disseminate court proceedings. It carefully framed its holding as follows:

> While we have concluded that the due process clause does not prohibit electronic media coverage of judicial proceedings per se, by the same token we reject the argument of the [Post-Newsweek stations] that the first and sixth amendments to the United States Constitution mandate entry of the electronic media into judicial proceedings. Petition of the Post-Newsweek Stations, Florida, Inc., 370 So.2d, at 774.

The Florida court relied on our holding in *Nixon v. Warner Communications, Inc.,* 435 U.S. 589 * * * (1977), where we said:

> In the first place, * * * there is no constitutional right to have [live witness] testimony recorded and broadcast. Second, while the guarantee of a public trial, in the words of Mr. Justice Black, is "a safeguard against any attempt to employ our courts as instruments of persecution," it confers no special benefit on the press. Nor does the Sixth Amendment require that the trial—or any part of it—be broadcast live or on tape to the public. The requirement of a public trial is satisfied by the opportunity of members of the public and the press to attend the trial and report what they have observed. *Id.,* at 610 [citations and footnotes omitted].

The Florida Supreme Court predicated the revised Canon 3A(7) upon its supervisory authority over the Florida courts, and not upon any constitutional imperative. Hence, we have before us only the limited question of the Florida Supreme Court's authority to promulgate the canon for the trial of cases in Florida courts.

This Court has no supervisory jurisdiction over state courts and, in reviewing a state court judgment, we are confined to

---

82. In United States v. CBS, 1 Med.L.Rptr. 1351, 497 F.2d 107 (1974), the Fifth Circuit applied a clear and present danger test to a trial judge's order evicting Aggie Whelan, a CBS artist, from the courtroom where the "Gainesville Eight" were being tried. She made her sketches from memory in the park across the street and was cited for contempt. The total ban, said the court, was overbroad where the sketching was neither "obtrusive" nor "disruptive." That is basically the test all states use in permitting sketching which, it has been claimed, can be more distractive than photography. Something to do with squeaky pens.

evaluating it in relation to the Federal Constitution.

Appellants rely chiefly on Estes v. Texas, 381 U.S. 532 * * * (1964), and Chief Justice Warren's separate concurring opinion in that case. They argue that the televising of criminal trials is inherently a denial of due process, and they read *Estes* as announcing a *per se* constitutional rule to that effect.

* * *

Parsing the six opinions in *Estes,* one is left with a sense of doubt as to precisely how much of Justice Clark's opinion was joined in, and supported by, Justice Harlan. In an area charged with constitutional nuances, perhaps more should not be expected. Nonetheless, it is fair to say that Justice Harlan viewed the holding as limited to the proposition that "*what was done in this case* infringed the fundamental right to a fair trial assured by the Due Process Clause of the Fourteenth Amendment."

* * *

Justice Harlan's opinion, upon which analysis of the constitutional holding of *Estes* turns, must be read as defining the scope of that holding; we conclude that *Estes* is not to be read as announcing a constitutional rule barring still photographic, radio and television coverage in all cases and under all circumstances. It does not stand as an absolute ban on state experimentation with an evolving technology, which, in terms of modes of mass communication, was in its relative infancy in 1964, and is, even now, in a state of continuing change.

Since we are satisfied that *Estes* did not announce a constitutional rule that all photographic or broadcast coverage of criminal trials is inherently a denial of due process, we turn to consideration, as a matter of first impression, of the petitioner's suggestion that we now promulgate such a *per se* rule.

Any criminal case that generates a great deal of publicity presents some risks that the publicity may compromise the right of the defendant to a fair trial. Trial courts must be especially vigilant to guard against any impairment of the defendant's right to a verdict based solely upon the evidence and the relevant law. Over the years, courts have developed a range of curative devices to prevent publicity about a trial from infecting jury deliberations. See, e.g., Nebraska Press Association v. Stuart, 427 U.S. 539, 563–565 * * * (1975).

An absolute constitutional ban on broadcast coverage of trials cannot be justified simply because there is a danger that, in some cases, prejudicial broadcast accounts of pretrial and trial events may impair the ability of jurors to decide the issue of guilt or innocence uninfluenced by extraneous matter. The risk of juror prejudice in some cases does not justify an absolute ban on news coverage of trials by the printed media; so also the risk of such prejudice does not warrant an absolute constitutional ban on all broadcast coverage. A case attracts a high level of public attention because of its intrinsic interest to the public and the manner of reporting the event. The risk of juror prejudice is present in any publication of a trial, but the appropriate safeguard against such prejudice is the defendant's right to demonstrate that the media's coverage of his case—be it printed or broadcast—compromised the ability of the particular jury that heard the case to adjudicate fairly. * * *

As we noted earlier, the concurring opinions in *Estes* expressed concern that the very presence of media cameras and recording devices at a trial inescapably give rise to an adverse psychological impact on the participants in the trial. This kind of general psychological prejudice, allegedly present whenever there is broadcast coverage of a trial, is different from the more particularized problem of prejudicial impact discussed earlier. If it could be demonstrated that the mere presence of photographic and recording equipment and the knowledge that the event would be broadcast invariably and uniformly affected the conduct of participants so as to impair fundamental fairness, our task would be simple; prohibition of broadcast coverage of trials would be required.

In confronting the difficult and sensitive question of the potential psychological prejudice associated with broadcast coverage of trials, we have been aided by *amicus* briefs submitted by various state officers involved in law enforcement, the Conference of Chief Justices, and the Attorney Generals of 17 states in support of continuing experimentation such as that embarked upon by Florida, and by the American Bar Association, the American College of Trial Lawyers, and various members of the defense bar representing essentially the views expressed by the concurring Justices in *Estes.*

Not unimportant to the position asserted by Florida and other states is the change in television technology since 1962, when Estes was tried. It is urged, and some empirical data are presented, that many of the negative factors found in *Estes*—cumbersome equipment, cables, distracting lighting, numerous camera technicians—are less substantial factors today than they were at that time.

It is also significant that safeguards have been built into the experimental programs in state courts, and into the Florida program, to avoid some of the most egregious problems envisioned by the six opinions in the *Estes* case. Florida admonishes its courts to take special pains to protect certain witnesses—for example, children, victims of sex crimes, some informants, and even the very timid witness or party—from the glare of publicity and the tensions of being "on camera." Petition of Post-Newsweek Stations of Florida, Inc., 370 So.2d, at 779.

The Florida guidelines place on trial judges positive obligations to be on guard to protect the fundamental right of the accused to a fair trial. The Florida statute, being one of the few permitting broadcast coverage of criminal trials over the objection of the accused, raises problems not present in the statutes of other states. Inherent in electronic coverage of a trial is the risk that the very awareness by the accused of the coverage and the contemplated broadcast may adversely affect the conduct of the participants and the fairness of the trial, yet leave no evidence of how the conduct or the trial's fairness was affected. Given this danger, it is significant that Florida requires that objections of the accused to coverage be heard and considered on the record by the trial court. See, e.g., Green v. State, 377 So.2d 193, 201 * * * (Fla.1979). In addition to providing a record for appellate review, a pretrial hearing enables a defendant to advance the basis of his objection to broadcast coverage and allows the trial court to define the steps necessary to minimize or eliminate the risks of prejudice to the accused. Experiments such as the one presented here may well increase the number of appeals by adding a new basis for claims to reverse, but this is a risk Florida has chosen to take after preliminary experimentation. Here, the record does not indicate that appellants requested an evidentiary hearing to show adverse impact or injury. Nor does the record reveal anything more than generalized allegations of prejudice.

Nonetheless, it is clear that the general issue of the psychological impact of broadcast coverage upon the participants in a trial, and particularly upon the defendant, is still a subject of sharp debate—as the *Amicus* Briefs of the American Bar Association, the American College of Trial Lawyers, and others of the trial bar in opposition to Florida's experiment demonstrate. These *amici* state the view that the concerns expressed by the concurring opinions in *Estes,* * * * have been borne out by actual experience. Comprehensive empirical data is still not available—at least on some aspects of the problem. For example, the *Amici* Brief of the Attorneys General concedes:

> The defendant's interest in not being harassed and in being able to concentrate on the proceedings and confer effectively with his attorney are crucial aspects of a fair trial. There is not much data on defendant's reactions to televised trials available now, but what there is indicates that it is possible to regulate the media so that their presence does not weigh heavily on the defendant. *Particular attention should be paid to this area of concern as study of televised trials continues.* * *

The experimental status of electronic coverage of trials is also emphasized by the *Amicus* Brief of the Conference of Chief Justices:

> Examination and reexamination by state courts of the in-court presence of the electronic news media, *vel non,* is an exercise of the authority reserved to the states under our federalism.

Whatever may be the "mischievous potentialities [of broadcast coverage] for intruding upon the detached atmosphere which should always surround the judicial process," Estes v. Texas, 381 U.S., at 587, at present no one has been able to present empirical data sufficient to establish that the mere presence of the broadcast media inherently has an adverse effect on that process. * * * The appellants have offered nothing to demonstrate that their trial was subtly tainted by broadcast coverage—let alone that all broadcast trials would be so tainted. * * *

Where, as here, we cannot say that a denial of due process automatically, results from activity authorized by a state, the admonition of Justice Brandeis, dissenting in New State Ice Co. v. Liebmann, 385 U.S. 262, 311 (1932), is relevant:

> To stay experimentation in things social and economic is a grave responsibility. Denial of the right to experiment may be fraught with serious consequences to the Nation. It is one of the happy incidents of the federal system that a single courageous state may, if its citizens choose, serve as a laboratory; and try novel social and economic experiments without risk to the rest of the country. This Court has the power to prevent an experiment. We may strike down the statute which embodies it on the ground that, in our opinion, the measure is arbitrary, capricious, or unreasonable. * * * But in the exercise of this high power, we must be ever on our guard, lest we erect our prejudices into legal principles. If we would guide by the light of reason, we must let our minds be bold.

This concept of federalism, echoed by the states favoring Florida's experiment, must guide our decision. [Emphasis added.]

Amici members of the defense bar vigorously contend that displaying the accused on television is in itself a denial of due process. *Amici* Brief of the Public Defenders. This was a source of concern to Chief Justice Warren and Justice Harlan in *Estes:* that coverage of select cases "singles out certain defendants and subjects them to trials under prejudicial conditions not experienced by others." 381 U.S., at 565 (Warren, C.J., concurring). Selection of which trials, or parts of trials, to broadcast will inevitably be made not by judges but by the media, and will be governed by such factors as the nature of the crime and the status and position of the accused—or of the victim; the effect may be to titillate rather than to educate and inform. The unanswered question is whether electronic coverage will bring public humiliation upon the accused with such randomness that it will evoke due process concerns by being "unusual in the same way that being struck by lightning" is "unusual." Furman v. Georgia, 408 U.S. 238, 309 (1972). (Stewart, J., concurring). Societies and political systems, that, from time to time, have put on "Yankee Stadium" "show trials" tell more about the power of the state than about its concern for the decent administration of justice—with every citizen receiving the same kind of justice.

The concurring opinion of Chief Justice Warren joined by Justices Douglas and Goldberg in *Estes* can fairly be read as viewing the very broadcast of some trials as potentially a form of punishment in itself—a punishment before guilt. This concern is far from trivial. But, whether coverage of a few trials will, in practice, be the equivalent of a "Yankee Stadium" setting—which Justice Harlan likened to the public pillory long abandoned as a barbaric perversion of decent justice—must also await the continuing experimentation.

To say that the appellants have not demonstrated that broadcast coverage is inherently a denial of due process is not to say that the appellants were in fact accorded all of the protections of due process in their trial. As noted earlier, a defendant has the right on review to show that the media's coverage of his case—printed or broadcast—compromised the ability of the jury to judge him fairly. Alternatively, a defendant might show that broadcast coverage of his particular case had an adverse impact on the trial participants sufficient to constitute a denial of due process. Neither showing was made in this case.

To demonstrate prejudice in a specific case a defendant must show something more than juror awareness that the trial is such as to attract the attention of broadcasters. Murphy v. Florida, 421 U.S. 794, 800 (1975). No doubt the very presence of a camera in the courtroom made the jurors aware that the trial was thought to be of sufficient interest to the public to warrant coverage. Jurors, forbidden to watch all broadcasts, would have had no way of knowing that only fleeting seconds of the proceeding would be reproduced. But the appellants have not attempted to show with any specificity that the presence of cameras impaired the ability of the jurors to decide the case on only the evidence before them or that their trial was affected adversely by the impact on any of the participants of the presence of cameras and the prospect of broadcast.

Although not essential to our holding, we note that at *voir dire,* the jurors were asked if the presence of the camera would in any way compromise their ability to consider the case. Each answered that the camera would not prevent him from considering the case solely on the merits. * * * The trial court instructed the jurors not to watch television accounts of the trial, * * * and the appellants do not contend that any juror violated this instruction. The appellants have offered no evidence that any participant in this case was affected by the presence of cameras. In short, there is no showing that the trial was compromised by television coverage, as was the case in *Estes.*

It is not necessary either to ignore or to discount the potential danger to the fairness of a trial in a particular case in order to conclude that Florida may permit the electronic media to cover trials in its state courts. Dangers lurk in this, as in most, experiments, but unless we were to conclude that television coverage under all conditions is prohibited by the Constitution, the states must be free to experiment. We are not empowered by the Constitution to oversee or harness state procedural experimentation; only when the state action infringes fundamental guarantees are we authorized to intervene. We must assume state courts will be alert to any factors that impair the fundamental rights of the accused.

The Florida program is inherently evolutional in nature; the initial project has provided guidance for the new canons which can be changed at will, and application of which is subject to control by the trial judge. The risk of prejudice to particular defendants is ever present and must be examined carefully as cases arise. Nothing of the "Roman circus" or "Yankee

Stadium" atmosphere, as in *Estes,* prevailed here, however, nor have appellants attempted to show that the unsequestered jury was exposed to "sensational" coverage, in the sense of *Estes* or of Sheppard v. Maxwell, 384 U.S. 333 (1966). Absent a showing of prejudice of constitutional dimensions to these defendants, there is no reason for this Court either to endorse or to invalidate Florida's experiment.

In this setting, because this Court has no supervisory authority over state courts, our review is confined to whether there is a constitutional violation. We hold that the Constitution does not prohibit a state from experimenting with the program authorized by revised Canon 3A(7).

Justice STEWART, concurring in the result.

Although concurring in the judgment, I cannot join the opinion of the Court because I do not think the convictions in this case can be affirmed without overruling Estes v. Texas, 381 U.S.532.

* * *

Justice WHITE, concurring in the judgment.

* * *

For the reasons stated by Justice Stewart in his concurrence today, I think *Estes* is fairly read as establishing a *per se* constitutional rule against televising any criminal trial if the defendant objects. So understood, *Estes* must be overruled to affirm the judgment below.

* * *

Although the Court's opinion today contends that it is consistent with *Estes,* I believe that it effectively eviscerates *Estes.* The Florida rule has no exception for the sensational or widely publicized case. Absent a showing of specific prejudice, *any* kind of case may be televised as long as the rule is otherwise complied with. In re Petition of Post-Newsweek, 370 So.2d 764, 774 (Fla.1979). Thus, even if the present case is precisely the kind of case referred to in Justice Harlan's concurrence in *Estes,* the Florida rule overrides the defendant's objections. The majority opinion does not find it necessary to deal with appellants' contention that because their case attracted substantial publicity, specific prejudice need not be shown. By affirming the judgment below, which sustained the rule, the majority indicates that not even the narrower reading of *Estes* will any longer be authoritative.

Moreover, the Court now reads *Estes* as merely announcing that on the facts of that case there had been an unfair trial—*i.e.,* it established no *per se* rule at all. Justice Clark's majority opinion, however, expressly recognized that no "isolatable" or "actual" prejudice had been or need be shown, 381 U.S., at 542–543, and Justice Harlan expressly rejected the necessity of showing "specific" prejudice in cases "like this one." 581 U.S., at 593. It is thus with telling effect that the Court now rules that "absent a showing of prejudice of constitutional dimensions to these defendants," there is no reason to overturn the Florida rule, to reverse the judgment of the Florida Supreme Court or to set aside the conviction of the appellants. * * *

By reducing *Estes* to an admonition to proceed with some caution, the majority does not underestimate or minimize the risks of televising criminal trials over a defendant's objections. I agree that those risks are real and should not be permitted to develop into the reality of an unfair trial. Nor does the decision today, as I understand it, suggest that any state is any less free than it was to avoid this hazard by not permitting a trial to be televised over the objection of the defendant or by forbidding cameras in its court rooms in any criminal case.

Accordingly, I concur in the judgment.

A MODEST PROPOSAL

Because courts may have created a publication/news-gathering dichotomy that may not exist in the real world of practical journalism,[83] journalists will continue to press for First Amendment recognition of access rights. But it is also urgent that reporters and editors attempt to conform to voluntary, nonenforceable, flexible press-bar-bench guidelines. They have been thoughtfully worked out over a long period of time and may be our last best hope for avoiding having to choose between free speech and fair trials—"two of the most cherished policies of our civilization."[84] Journalists should also participate in the development, application, and modification of these voluntary codes when called upon.[85]

When any judge attempts to make voluntary guidelines part of a judicial order, as happened in Nebraska and Washington, vigorous exception must be taken in the first instance by the reporter. Similarly, when a courtroom is closed or a record sealed, reporters should be equipped with objection cards and clear procedures to follow in arguing for a written transcript of the judge's order, postponement of the judicial proceeding, a hearing on the closure order, and, beyond that, opportunity for immediate appeal from an adverse ruling. In the meantime, obey the order even though you think it wrong and expect it to be overturned. Because First Amendment rights are involved, press attorneys may argue for an expedited appeal (see National Socialist Party of America v. Village of Skokie, 3 Med.L.Rptr. 1704, 432 U.S. 43 (1977) and *Richmond Newspapers*). The party petitioning for closure bears the burden of proof.

Beyond the procedures of particular media, reporters and their attorneys may cite state voluntary guidelines, state law, alternatives such as postponing suppression hearings until a jury is empaneled and sequestered, state rules of criminal procedure, closure guidelines of the American Bar Association, the Department of Justice, and the U.S. Judicial Conference.

There are times, of course, when publication ought to be postponed. A federal district judge in Philadelphia asked reporters to suspend for a single day publication of the fact that murder charges were pending against a man being tried for perjury. When the request was ignored, the judge turned it into an oral order that was later held by an appeals court to be procedurally deficient.[86] Was the judge asking too much? Would compliance on the part of the press have shaken the foundations of our constitutional system? The right to publish inevitably carries with it the right to refrain from publishing. In the best of worlds, the press will have full access to all information about crime and the courts, and it will make its own editorial decisions on what to publish in the best interests of an informed public and unimpaired justice. The thoughtful course will sometimes be to postpone publication.

There are empirical questions left to answer. More must be learned about the real effect of publicity and photography on jury verdicts. Can fairness be predicated on juror ignorance, a question Mark Twain's prose raised at the beginning of this chapter? If we cannot trust jurors to be fair, can we cajole or deceive them into reaching fair verdicts? A close reading of the cases in this area suggests that the

83. Helle, *The News-Gathering/Publication Dichotomy and Government Expression*, 1982 Duke L.J. 1 (1982). This article is a most comprehensive examination of the Court's theoretical problems with access questions. It is also an appeal for a return to libertarian precepts.

84. Justice Hugo Black in Bridges v. California, 314 U.S. 252 (1941).

85. See, for example, the statement of the National News Council in Protecting Two Vital Freedoms: Fair Trial and Free Press (1980).

86. United States v. Frederick Schiavo, Philadelphia Newspapers, Inc. 504 F.2d 1 (3d Cir. 1974).

Court may be placing greater emphasis on the findings of the behavioral sciences than has been its custom. And there remains the problem of choosing the proper scales in which to weigh individual against social values.

In the meantime, there is evidence that trilateral cooperation has worked. To ignore the sensible recommendations contained in voluntary press-bar-bench guidelines will in the 1980s be a mark of professional immaturity.

Public Access to The Print Media

A RIGHT OF ACCESS AND REPLY TO THE PRESS?

Access to the Press—A New First Amendment Right

 Jerome A. Barron, 80 Harv.Law Rev. 1641 (1967).

The press, long enshrined among our most highly cherished institutions, was thought a cornerstone of democracy when its name was boldly inscribed in the Bill of Rights. Freed from governmental restraint, initially by the first amendment and later by the fourteenth, the press was to stand majestically as the champion of new ideas and the watch dog against governmental abuse. Professor Barron finds this conception of the first amendment, perhaps realistic in the eighteenth century heyday of political pamphleteering, essentially romantic in an era marked by extraordinary technological developments in the communications industry. To make viable the time-honored "marketplace" theory, he argues for a twentieth century interpretation of the first amendment which will impose an affirmative responsibility on the monopoly newspaper to act as sounding board for new ideas and old grievances.

There is an anomaly in our constitutional law. While we protect expression once it has come to the fore, our law is indifferent to creating opportunities for expression. Our constitutional theory is in the grip of a romantic conception of free expression, a belief that the "marketplace of ideas" is freely accessible. But if ever there were a self-operating marketplace of ideas, it has long ceased to exist. The mass media's development of an antipathy to ideas requires legal intervention if novel and unpopular ideas are to be assured a forum—unorthodox points of view which have no claim on broadcast time and newspaper space as a matter of right are in poor position to compete with those aired as a matter of grace.

The free expression questions which now come before the courts involve individuals who have managed to speak or write in a manner that captures public attention and provokes legal reprisal. The conventional constitutional issue is whether expression already uttered should be given first amendment shelter or whether it may be subjected to sanction as speech beyond the constitutionally protected pale. To those who can obtain access to the media of mass communications first amendment case law furnishes considerable help. But what of those whose ideas are too unacceptable to secure access to the media? To them the mass communications industry replies: The first amendment guarantees our freedom to do as we choose with our media. Thus the constitutional imperative of free expression becomes a rationale for repressing competing ideas. First amendment theory must be reexamined, for only by responding to the present reality of the mass media's repression of ideas can the constitutional guarantee of free speech best serve its original purposes.

I. THE ROMANTIC VIEW OF THE FIRST AMENDMENT: A RATIONALE FOR REPRESSION

* * * [A]n essentially romantic view of first amendment has perpetuated the lack of legal interest in the availability to various interest groups of access to means of communication. Symptomatic of this view is Mr. Justice Douglas' eloquent dissent in *Dennis v. United States:*

> When ideas compete in the market for acceptance, full and free discussion exposes the false and they gain few adherents. Full and free discussion even of ideas we hate encourages the testing of our own prejudices and preconceptions. * * *

The assumption apparent in this excerpt is that, without government intervention, there is a free market mechanism for ideas. Justice Douglas's position expresses the faith that, if government can be kept away from "ideas," the self-operating and self-correcting force of "full and free discussion" will go about its eternal task of keeping us from "embracing what is cheap and false" to the end that victory will go to the doctrine which is "true to our genius."

* * *

The possibility of governmental repression is present so long as government endures, and the first amendment has served as an effective device to protect the flow of ideas from governmental censorship: "Happily government censorship has put down few roots in this country. * * * We have in the United States no counterpart of the Lord Chamberlain who is censor over England's stage." But this is to place laurels before a phantom—our constitutional law has been singularly indifferent to the reality and implications of nongovernmental obstructions to the spread of political truth. This indifference becomes critical when a comparatively few private hands are in a position to determine not only the content of information but its very availability, when the soap box yields to radio and the political pamphlet to the monopoly newspaper.

II. OBSTACLES TO ACCESS: THE CHANGING TECHNOLOGY OF THE COMMUNICATIONS PROCESS

* * * Difficulties in securing access, unknown both to the draftsmen of the first amendment and to the early proponents of its "marketplace" interpretation, have been wrought by the changing technology of mass media.

* * *

Many American cities have become one newspaper towns. * * * The failures of existing media are revealed by the development of new media to convey unorthodox, unpopular, and new ideas. Sit-ins and demonstrations testify to the inadequacy of old media as instruments to afford full and effective hearing for all points of view. Demonstrations, it has been well said, are "the free press of the movement to win justice for Negroes. * *" But, like an inadequate underground press, it is a communications medium by default, a statement of the inability to secure access to the conventional means of reaching and changing public opinion. By the bizarre and unsettling nature of his technique the demonstrator hopes to arrest and divert attention long enough to compel the public to ponder his message. But attention-getting devices so abound in the modern world that new ones soon become tiresome. The dissenter must look for ever more unsettling assaults on the mass mind if he is to have continuing impact. Thus, as critics of protest are eager and in a sense correct to say, the prayer-singing student demonstration is the prelude to Watts. But the difficulty with this criticism is that it wishes to throttle protest rather than to recognize that protest has taken these forms because it has had nowhere else to go.

III. MAKING THE FIRST AMENDMENT WORK

The Justices of the United States Supreme Court are not innocently unaware of these contemporary social realities, but they have nevertheless failed to give the "marketplace of ideas" theory of the first amendment the burial it merits. Perhaps the interment of this theory has been denied for the understandable reason that the Court is at a loss to know with what to supplant it. But to put off inquiry under today's circumstances will only aggravate the need for it under tomorrow's.

There is inequality in the power to communicate ideas just as there is inequality in economic bargaining power; to recognize the latter and deny the former is quixotic. The "marketplace of ideas" view has rested on the assumption that protecting the right of expression is equivalent to providing for it. But changes in the communications industry have destroyed the equilibrium in that marketplace. While it may have been still possible in 1925 to believe with Justice Holmes that every idea is "acted on unless some other belief outweighs it or some failure of energy stifles the movement at its birth," it is impossible to believe that now. Yet the Holmesian theory is not abandoned, even though the advent of radio and television has made even more evident that philosophy's unreality. A realistic view of the first amendment requires recognition that a right of expression is somewhat thin if it can be exercised only at the sufferance of the managers of mass communications.

* * *

A corollary of the romantic view of the first amendment is the Court's unquestioned assumption that the amendment affords "equal" protection to the various media. According to this view new media of communication are assimilated into first amendment analysis without regard to the enormous differences in impact these media have in comparison with the traditional printed word. Radio and television are to be as free as newspapers and magazines, sound trucks as free as radio and television.

This extension of a simplistic egalitarianism to media whose comparative impacts are gravely disproportionate is wholly unrealistic. It results from confusing freedom of media content with freedom of the media to restrict access. The assumption in romantic first amendment analysis that the same postulates apply to different classes of people, situations, and means of communication obscures the fact, noted explicitly by Justice Jackson in Kovacs v. Cooper, that problems of access and impact vary significantly from medium to medium: "The moving picture screen, the radio, the newspaper, the handbill, the sound truck and the street corner orator have differing natures, values, abuses and dangers. Each, in my view, is a law unto itself, and all we are dealing with now is the sound truck."

* * *

An analysis of the first amendment must be tailored to the context in which ideas are or seek to be aired. This contextual approach requires an examination of the purposes served by and the impact of each particular medium. If a group seeking to present a particular side of a public issue is unable to get space in the only newspaper in town, is this inability compensated by the availability of the public park or the sound truck? Competitive media only constitute alternative means of access in a crude manner. If ideas are criticized in one forum the most adequate response is in the same forum since it is most likely to reach the same audience. Further, the various media serve different functions and create different reactions and expectations—criticism of an individual or a governmental policy over television may reach more people but criticism in print is more durable.

The test of a community's opportunities for free expression rests not so much in an abundance of alternative media but rather in an abundance of opportunities to secure expression in media with the largest impact. * * *

The late Professor Meiklejohn, who has articulated a view of the first amendment which assumes its justification to be political self-government, has wisely pointed out that "what is essential is not that everyone shall speak, but that everything worth saying shall be said"—that the point of ultimate interest is not the words of the speakers but the minds of the hearers. Can everything worth saying be effectively said? Constitutional opinions that are particularly solicitous of the interests of mass media—radio, television, and mass circulation newspaper—devote little thought to the difficulties of securing access to those media. If those media are unavailable, can the minds of "hearers" be reached effectively? Creating opportunities for expression is as important as ensuring the right to express ideas without fear of governmental reprisal.

* * *

Today ideas reach the millions largely to the extent they are permitted entry into the great metropolitan dailies, news magazines, and broadcasting networks. The soap box is no longer an adequate forum for public discussion. Only the new media of communication can lay sentiments before the public, and it is they rather than government who can most effectively abridge expression by nullifying the opportunity for an idea to win acceptance. As a constitutional theory for the communication of ideas, laissez faire is manifestly irrelevant.

The constitutional admonition against abridgment of speech and press is at present not applied to the very interests which have real power to effect such abridgment. Indeed, nongoverning minorities in control of the means of communication should perhaps be inhibited from restraining free speech (by the denial of access to their media) even more than governing majorities are restrained by the first amendment—minorities do not have the mandate which a legislative majority enjoys in a polity operating under a theory of representative government. What is required is an interpretation of the first amendment which focuses on the idea that restraining the hand of government is quite useless in assuring free speech if a restraint on access is effectively secured by private groups. A constitutional prohibition against governmental restrictions on expression is effective only if the Constitution ensures an adequate opportunity for discussion. Since this opportunity exists only in the mass media, the interests of those who control the means of communication must be accommodated with the interests of those who seek a forum in which to express their point of view.

IV. NEW WINDS OF CONSTITUTIONAL DOCTRINE: THE IMPLICATIONS FOR A RIGHT TO BE HEARD

* * *

The potential of existing law to support recognition of a right of access has gone largely unnoticed by the Supreme Court. Judicial blindness to the problem of securing access to the press is dramatically illustrated by New York Times Co. v. Sullivan, one of the latest chapters in the romantic and rigid interpretation of the first amendment. * * *

The constitutional armor which *Times* now offers newspapers is predicated on the "principle that debate on public issues should be uninhibited, robust, and wide-open, and that it may well include vehement, caustic, and sometimes unpleasantly sharp attacks on government and public officials." But it is paradoxical that although the libel laws have been emasculated for the benefit of defendant newspapers where the plaintiff is a "public official," the Court shows no corresponding concern as to whether debate will in fact be assured. The irony of *Times* and its progeny lies in the unexamined assumption that reducing newspaper exposure to libel litigation will remove restraints on expression and lead to an "informed society." But in fact the decision creates a new imbalance in the communications process. Purporting to deepen the constitutional guarantee of full expression, the actual effect of the decision is to perpetuate the freedom of a few in a manner adverse to the public interest in uninhibited debate. Unless the *Times* doctrine is deepened to require opportunities for the public figure to reply to a defamatory attack, the *Times* decision will merely serve to equip the press with some new and rather heavy artillery which can crush as well as stimulate debate.

* * *

The law of libel is not the only threat to first amendment values; problems of equal moment are raised by judicial inattention to the fact that the newspaper publisher is not the only addressee of first amendment protection. Supreme Court efforts to remove the press from judicial as well as legislative control do not necessarily stimulate and preserve that "multitude of tongues" on which "we have staked * * our all." What the Court has done is to magnify the power of one of the participants in the communications process with apparently no thought of imposing on newspapers concomitant responsibilities to assure that the new protection will actually enlarge and protect opportunities for expression.

If financial immunization by the Supreme Court is necessary to ensure a courageous press, the public officials who fall prey to such judicially reinforced lions should at least have the right to respond or to demand retraction in the pages of the newspapers which have published charges against them. The opportunity for counterattack ought to be at the very heart of a constitutional theory which supposedly is concerned with providing an outlet for individuals "who wish to exercise their freedom of speech even though they are not members of the press." If no such right is afforded or even considered, it seems meaningless to talk about vigorous public debate.

By severely undercutting a public official's ability to recover damages when he had been defamed, the *Times* decision would seem to reduce the likelihood of retractions since the normal mitigation incentive to retract will be absent. For example, the *Times* failed to print a retraction as requested by Sullivan even though an Alabama statute provided that a retraction eliminates the jury's ability to award punitive damages. On the other hand, *Times* was a special case and the Court explicitly left open the question of a public official's ability to recover damages if there were a refusal to retract:[43]

43. 376 U.S. 254 at 286. Retraction statutes have some bearing on enforcing responsive dialogue. These statutes, common in this country, require the publisher to "take back" what has already been said if damages in a defamation suit are to be mitigated. If false statements have been made, and the complainant can convince the publisher to retract on the basis of correct information, such a procedure certainly serves a cleansing function for the information process. For a discussion of the status of retractions after the *Times* decision, see Note, *Vindication of the Reputation of a Public Official,* 80 Harv.L.Rev. 1730, 1740–43 (1967).

> Whether or not a failure to retract may ever constitute such evidence [of "actual malice"], there are two reasons why it does not here. *First,* the letter written by the Times reflected a reasonable doubt on its part as to whether the advertisement could reasonably be taken to refer to respondent at all. *Second,* it was not a final refusal, since it asked for an explanation on this point—a request that respondent chose to ignore.

Although the Court did not foreclose the possibility of allowing public officials to recover damages for a newspaper's refusal to retract, its failure to impose such a responsibility represents a lost opportunity to work out a more relevant theory of the first amendment. Similarly, the Court's failure to require newspapers to print a public official's reply ignored a device which could further first amendment objectives by making debate meaningful and responsive. Abandonment of the romantic view of the first amendment would highlight the importance of giving constitutional status to these responsibilities of the press.

However, even these devices are no substitute for the development of a general right of access to the press. A group that is not being attacked but merely ignored will find them of little use. Indifference rather than hostility is the bane of new ideas and for that malaise only some device of more general application will suffice. It is true that Justice Brennan, writing for the Court in *Times,* did suggest that a rigorous test for libel in the public criticism area is particularly necessary where the offending publication is an "editorial advertisement," since this is an "important outlet for the promulgation of information and ideas by *persons who do not themselves have access to publishing facilities* —who wish to exercise their freedom of speech *even though they are not members of the press.*" This statement leaves us at the threshold of the question of whether these individuals—the "non-press"—should have a right of access secured by the first amendment: should the newspaper have an obligation to take the editorial advertisement? As Justice Brennan appropriately noted, newspapers are an important outlet for ideas. But currently they are outlets entry to which is granted at the pleasure of their managers. The press having been given the *Times* immunity to promote public debate, there seems little justification for not enforcing coordinate responsibility to allocate space equitably among ideas competing for public attention. And, some quite recent shifts in constitutional doctrine may at last make feasible the articulation of a constitutionally based right of access to the media.

* * *

The *Times* decision operates on the assumption that newspapers are fortresses of vigorous public criticism, that assuring the press freedom over its content is the only prerequisite to open and robust debate. But if the *raison d'être* of the mass media is not to maximize discussion but to maximize profits, inquiry should be directed to the possible effect of such a fact on constitutional theory. The late Professor V.O. Key stressed the consequences which flow from the fact that communications is big business:[46]

> [A]ttention to the economic aspects of the communications industries serves to emphasize the fact that they consist of commercial enterprises, not public service institutions. * * * They sell advertising in one form or another, and they bait it principally with entertainment. Only incidentally do they collect and disseminate political intelligence.
>
> * * *
>
> * * * The networks are in an unenviable economic position. They are not

46. V.O. Key, *Public Opinion and American Democracy,* 378–79, 387 (1961).

> completely free to sell their product—air time. If they make their facilities available to those who advocate causes slightly off color politically, they may antagonize their major customers.

The press suffers from the same pressures —"newspaper publishers are essentially people who sell white space on newsprint to advertisers"; in large part they are only processors of raw materials purchased from others.

Professor Key's conclusion—indifference to content follows from the structure of contemporary mass communications—compares well with Marshall McLuhan's view that the nature of the communications process compels a "strategy of neutrality." For McLuhan it is the technology or form of television itself, rather than the message, which attracts public attention. Hence the media owners are anxious that media content not get enmeshed with unpopular views which will undermine the attraction which the media enjoy by virtue of their form alone:[49]

> Thus the commercial interests who think to render media universally acceptable, invariably settle for "entertainment" as a strategy of neutrality. A more spectacular mode of the ostrich-head-in-sand could not be devised, for it ensures maximum pervasiveness for any medium whatever.

Whether the mass media suffer from an institutional distaste for controversy because of technological or of economic factors, this antipathy to novel ideas must be viewed against a background of industry insistence on constitutional immunity from legally imposed responsibilities. A quiet truth emerges from such a study: industry opposition to legally imposed responsibilities does not represent a flight from censorship but rather a flight from points of view. Points of view suggest disagreement and angry customers are not good customers.

* * *

The mass communications industry should be viewed in constitutional litigation with the same candor with which it has been analyzed by industry members and scholars in communication. * * *

If the mass media are essentially business enterprises and their commercial nature makes it difficult to give a full and effective hearing to a wide spectrum of opinion, a theory of the first amendment is unrealistic if it prevents courts or legislatures from requiring the media to do that which, for commercial reasons, they would be otherwise unlikely to do. Such proposals only require that the opportunity for publication be broadened and do not involve restraint on publication or punishment after publication. * * * Justice Douglas remarked that the vice of censorship lies in the substitution it makes of "majority rule where minority tastes or viewpoints were to be tolerated." But what is suggested here is merely that legal steps be taken to provide for the airing and publication of "minority tastes or viewpoints," not that the mass media be prevented from publishing their views. * * * When commercial considerations dominate, often leading the media to repress ideas, these media should not be allowed to resist controls designed to promote vigorous debate and expression by cynical reliance on the first amendment.

* * *

But can a valid distinction be drawn between newspapers and broadcasting stations, with only the latter subject to regulation? It is commonly said that because the number of possible radio and television licenses is limited, regulation is the natural regimen for broadcasting. Yet the number of daily newspapers is certain-

49. H.M. McLuhan, *Understanding Media,* 305 (1964).

ly not infinite and, in light of the fact that there are now three times as many radio stations as there are newspapers, the relevance of this distinction is dubious. Consolidation is the established pattern of the American press today, and the need to develop means of access to the press is not diminished because the limitation on the number of newspapers is caused by economic rather than technological factors. Nor is the argument that other newspapers can always spring into existence persuasive—the ability of individuals to publish pamphlets should not preclude regulation of mass circulation, monopoly newspapers any more than the availability of sound trucks precludes regulation of broadcasting stations.

If a contextual approach is taken and a purposive view of the first amendment adopted, at some point the newspaper must be viewed as impressed with a public service stamp and hence under an obligation to provide space on a nondiscriminatory basis to representative groups in the community.[66] It is to be hoped that an awareness of the listener's interest in broadcasting will lead to an equivalent concern for the reader's stake in the press, and that first amendment recognition will be given to a right of access for the protection of the reader, the listener, and the viewer.

V. IMPLEMENTING A RIGHT OF ACCESS TO THE PRESS

The foregoing analysis has suggested the necessity of rethinking first amendment theory so that it will not only be effective in preventing governmental abridgment but will also produce meaningful expression despite the present or potential repressive effects of the mass media. If the first amendment can be so invoked, it is necessary to examine what machinery is available to enforce a right of access and what bounds limit that right.

* * *

One alternative is a judicial remedy affording individuals and groups desiring to voice views on public issues a right of nondiscriminatory access to the community newspaper. This right could be rooted most naturally in the letter-to-the-editor column[67] and the advertising section. That pressure to establish such a right exists in our law is suggested by a number of cases in which plaintiffs have contended, albeit unsuccessfully, that in certain circumstances newspaper publishers have a common law duty to publish advertisements. In these cases the advertiser sought nondiscriminatory access, subject to even-handed limitations imposed by rates and space.

Although in none of these cases did the newspaper publisher assert lack of space, the right of access has simply been denied.[68] The drift of the cases is that a

66. This is reminiscent of Professor Chafee's query as to whether the monopoly newspaper ought to be treated like a public utility. Contrary to my position, however, he concluded that a legally enforceable right of access would not be feasible. 2 Chafee, Government and Mass Communications 624–50 (1947).

67. In Wall v. World Publishing Co., 263 P.2d 1010 (Okl.1953), a reader of the *Tulsa World* contended that the newspaper's invitation to its readers to submit letters on matters of public importance was a contract offer from the newspaper which was accepted by submission of the letter. The plaintiff argued that, by refusal to publish, the newspaper had breached its contract. Despite the ingenuity of the argument, the court held for defendant. Note, however, that a first amendment argument was not made to the court.

68. Shuck v. Carrol Daily Herald, 247 N.W. 813 (Iowa 1933); J.J. Gordon, Inc. v. Worcester Telegram Publishing Co., 177 N.E.2d 586 (Mass.1961); Mack v. Costello, 143 N.W. 950 (S.D.1913). These cases do not consider legislative power to compel access to the press. Other cases have denied a common law right but have suggested that the area is a permissible one for legislation. Approved Personnel, Inc. v. Tribune Co., 177 So.2d 704 (Fla.1965); Friedenberg v. Times Publishing Co., 127 So. 345 (La.1930); In re Louis Wohl, Inc., 50 F.2d 254 (E.D.Mich.1931); Poughkeepsie Buying Service, Inc. v. Poughkeepsie Newspapers, Inc., 131 N.Y.S.2d 515 (1954).

newspaper is not a public utility and thus has freedom of action regardless of the objectives of the claimant seeking access. One case has the distinction of being the only American case which has recognized a right of access. In Uhlman v. Sherman[69] an Ohio lower court held that the dependence and interest of the public in the community newspaper, particularly when it is the only one, imposes the reasonable demand that the purchase of advertising should be open to members of the public on the same basis.

But none of these cases mentions first amendment considerations. What is encouraging for the future of an emergent right of access is that it has been resisted by relentless invocation of the freedom of contract notion that a newspaper publisher is as free as any merchant to deal with whom he chooses.[70] But the broad holding of these commercial advertising cases need not be authoritative for political advertisement.

* * *

The courts could provide for a right of access other than by reinterpreting the first amendment to provide for the emergence as well as the protection of expression. A right of access to the pages of a monopoly newspaper might be predicated on Justice Douglas's open-ended "public function" theory which carried a majority of the Court in Evans v. Newton, [382 U.S. 296 (1966).] Such a theory would demand a rather rabid conception of "state action," but if parks in private hands cannot escape the stigma of abiding "public character," it would seem that a newspaper, which is the common journal of printed communication in a community, could not escape the constitutional restrictions which quasi-public status invites. If monopoly newspapers are indeed quasi-public, their refusal of space to particular viewpoints is state action abridging expression in violation of even the romantic view of the first amendment.

* * *

Another, and perhaps more appropriate, approach would be to secure the right of access by legislation. A statute might impose the modest requirement, for example, that denial of access not be arbitrary but rather be based on rational grounds. Although some cases have involved a statutory duty to publish,[76] a constitutional basis for a right of access has never been considered. * * *

* * *

Constitutional power exists for both federal and state legislation in this area. Turning first to the constitutional basis for federal legislation, it has long been held that freedom of expression is protected by the due process clause of the fourteenth amendment. The now celebrated section five of the fourteenth amendment authorizing Congress to "enforce, by appropriate legislation" the provisions of the fourteenth amendment, appears to be as resilient and serviceable a tool for effectuating the freedom of expression guarantee of the fourteenth amendment as for implementing the equal protection guarantee. Professor Cox has noted that our recent experience in constitutional adjudication has revealed an untapped reservoir of federal legislative power to define and promote the constitutional rights of individuals in relation to state government. When the consequence of private conduct is to deny to

69. 22 Ohio N.P. (n.s.) 225, 31 Ohio Dec. 54 (C.P.1919).

70. See, e.g., Shuck v. Carroll Daily Herald, 247 N.W. 813 (Iowa 1933).

76. Belleville Advocate Printing Co., v. St. Clair County, 168 N.E. 312 (Ill.1929); Lake County v. Lake County Publishing & Printing Co., 117 N.E. 452 (Ill.1917) (dictum) (statute setting rates chargeable for official notices imposed no duty to publish); Wooster v. Mahaska County, 98 N.W. 103 (Iowa 1904) (dictum) (newspaper had no duty to publish and legislature could not impose one).

individuals the enjoyment of a right owed by the state, legislation which assures public capacity to perform that duty should be legitimate. Alternatively, legislation implementing responsibility to provide access to the mass media may be justified on a theory that the nature of the communications process imposes quasi-public functions on these quasi-public instrumentalities.[95]

* * * However, it is not necessary to amend the first amendment to attain the goal of greater access to the mass media. I do not think it adventurous to suggest that, if Congress were to pass a federal right of access statute, a sympathetic court would not lack the constitutional text necessary to validate the statute. If the first amendment is read to state affirmative goals, Congress is empowered to realize them. My basic premise in these suggestions is that a provision preventing government from silencing or dominating opinion should not be confused with an absence of governmental power to require that opinion be voiced.

If public order and an informed citizenry are, as the Supreme Court has repeatedly said, the goals of the first amendment, these goals would appear to comport well with state attempts to implement a right of access under the rubric of its traditional police power. If a right of access is not constitutionally proscribed, it would seem well within the powers reserved to the states by the tenth amendment of the Constitution to enact such legislation. Of course, if there were conflict between federal and state legislation, the federal legislation would control. Yet, the whole concept of a right of access is so embryonic that it can scarcely be argued that congressional silence preempts the field.

The right of access might be an appropriate area for experimental, innovative legislation. The right to access problems of a small state dominated by a single city with a monopoly press will vary, for example, from those of a populous state with many cities nourished by many competing media. These differences may be more accurately reflected by state autonomy in this area, resulting in a cultural federalism such as that envisaged by Justice Harlan in the obscenity cases. * * *

Utilization of a contextual approach highlights the importance of the degree to which an idea is suppressed in determining whether the right to access should be enforced in a particular case. If all media in a community are held by the same ownership, the access claim has greater attractiveness. This is true although the various media, even when they do reach the same audience, serve different functions and create different reactions and expectations. The existence of competition within the same medium, on the other hand, probably weakens the access claim though competition within a medium is no assurance that significant opinions will have no difficulty in securing access to newspaper space or broadcast time. It is significant that the right of access cases that have been litigated almost invariably involve a monopoly newspaper in a community.

VI. CONCLUSION

The changing nature of the communications process has made it imperative that the law show concern for the public interest in effective utilization of media for the expression of diverse points of view. Confrontation of ideas, a topic of eloquent affection in contemporary decisions, demands some recognition of a right to be heard as a constitutional principle. It is the writer's position that it is open to the courts to fashion a remedy for a right of

95. Evans v. Newton, 382 U.S. 296 (1966); Marsh v. Alabama, 326 U.S. 501 (1946). Both decisions find that private property may become quasi-public without a statute in extreme cases. The Court should surely defer to a congressional determination in an arguable case.

access, at least in the most arbitrary cases, independently of legislation. If such an innovation is judicially resisted, I suggest that our constitutional law authorizes a carefully framed right of access statute which would forbid an arbitrary denial of space, hence securing an effective forum for the expression of divergent opinions. With the development of private restraints on free expression, the idea of a free marketplace where ideas can compete on their merits has become just as unrealistic in the twentieth century as the economic theory of perfect competition. The world in which an essentially rationalist philosophy of the first amendment was born has vanished and what was rationalism is now romance.

Access and Its Critics

1. Professor Edwin Baker has argued that access theory advocates really posit a "market failure" model of the First Amendment. Access theorists, in this view, basically support a marketplace of ideas rationale for the First Amendment and are really seeking to improve the functioning of that marketplace. As Professor Baker sees it, these marketplace of ideas dissidents are usually asking for government intervention to make the marketplace of ideas work better. Their heresy is not that a marketplace of ideas model for the First Amendment is mistaken, but rather that presently the marketplace of ideas does not work and should be improved. Professor Baker is critical of these melioristic efforts. See generally, Baker, *Scope of the First Amendment Freedom of Speech,* 25 U.C.L.A. L.Rev. 964 at 986–987 (1978):

> The correction of market failures requires criteria to guide the state in its intervention. If provision of *adequate* access is the goal, the lack of criteria for "adequacy" undermines the legitimacy of government regulation. For the government to determine what access is adequate involves the government implicitly judging what is the correct resolution of the marketplace debates—or, more bluntly, allows the government to define truth. If a purpose of the first amendment is to protect unpopular ideas that may eventually triumph over the majority's established dogma, then allowing the government to determine adequacy of access stands the first amendment on its head. (In other versions, where equality of input provides the criterion, the parallel problem will be defining equality.)

Is it possible (or desirable) to have access without having equal access?

2. Recently, a distinction has been made for First Amendment purposes between message composers and media owners. The former, in this view, enjoy a greater measure of protection. This distinction and a consequent novel response to the problem of encouraging access to the media is found in Nadel, *A Unified Theory of the First Amendment: Divorcing the Medium from the Message,* 2 Fordham Urban L. Journ. at 183 (1983):

> Although in its role as a seller of space or time, a media owner is protected only by the fifth amendment, it may assert a derivative first amendment right on behalf of its advertisers or syndicated columnists. Such a right can only be claimed in *support* of these individuals' right to speak, as in the cases of *New York Times v. Sullivan* and *Bigelow v. Virginia.*

Professor Nadel summarizes his thesis as follows:

> The theory of the first amendment discussed above distinguishes between the rights of the two groups comprising our system of communication: "hardware" medium owners and "software" message producers. First amendment rights belong solely to the latter—those who edit software messages which are normally entitled to copyrights. The amendment absolutely protects their thinking and editing (inclusion and ex-

> clusion of messages). If the expression of their message does not conflict with some other constitutional value then the government may not impose unreasonable restrictions on their access to media.
>
> The owners of the media are not entitled to any direct first amendment protection, although they may assert rights of inclusion on behalf of those who use their media. The owner's rights to include and exclude messages are solely economic property rights. These permit them to select which messages will gain access to their media. If, however, their economic power becomes great enough to enable them to censor messages and/or the advantages of permitting them to exercise discretion is minimal, then the government may regulate access and even impose common carrier obligations upon them.

Professor Nadel makes a case for greater protection for the editor of the copyrightable software message. If a newspaper were to publish an editorial reply, the reply would have been copyrightable. Why shouldn't this theory protect the access seeker as well as the editor? Why should there be special protection for editors as compared to other writers or speakers?

3. Some writers on access have been very careful to distinguish between access to the privately owned press, which they do not favor, and access to public facilities or to "privately owned facilities which can be considered quasi public in nature." Professor Thomas I. Emerson has insisted on the need to make distinctions of this nature:

> Obviously, any general requirement that private owners make their facilities available to other persons or groups would curtail drastically the freedom of the owners to communicate, would entail an intolerable degree of governmental regulation, and soon would destroy the entire system of freedom of expression. Thus, as is clear from *Miami Herald Publishing Co. v. Tornillo,* there is no obligation on the part of a newspaper to accord any right to reply to a candidate for election who has been attacked in its columns; indeed, action by a state legislature to compel such access was held to violate the first amendment. On the other hand, if the government allocates scarce facilities or grants a monopoly to private owners, a different issue is presented. See Emerson, *The Affirmative Side of the First Amendment,* 15 Ga.L.Rev. 795 at 810 (1981).

Although Professor Emerson does not favor governmental intervention to establish a right of access to the print media, he is of a different mind with regard to electronic media. Thus, he writes approvingly of the efforts that have been made to establish some rights in those "other than the government's licensees" to use broadcasting's "scarce" facilities. Professor Emerson makes these observations on the features of the Federal Communications Act which provides the right of entry to nonlicensees: "The structure thus established for the use of radio and television facilities would seem to constitute the bare minimum demanded by the affirmative side of the first amendment. It falls far short of meeting the standards of a thriving, successful system of freedom of expression." See Emerson, *The Affirmative Side of the First Amendment,* 15 Ga.L. Rev. 795 at 826 (1981).

4. Other writers believe that the access concept is fundamentally at war with the First Amendment and believe that the defect in the existing law is precisely that it makes distinctions. In this view, *Red Lion* and *Tornillo* are inconsistent from a First Amendment point of view. Furthermore, in this view, the only way this inconsistency can be reconciled is to apply the rationale of the *Tornillo* case to broadcasting as well. In short, proponents of this view would ask the court to reverse *Red Lion.* See *Red Lion v. FCC,* text, p. 845:

> The requirement that a licensee devote *any* portion of his broadcast time to issues or to subjects not of his own

selection perforce restricts his own freedom of speech in a way that cannot be reconciled with *Tornillo.* The additional requirement that he ventilate views that would undermine the force of his own view, or such views as he alone prefers to present on his station, is a similar restriction equally repugnant to *Tornillo.* That he must yield his station for the presentation of such matters at his own expense and that he must also supply a free forum for personal replies by those whom he has permitted to be criticized, is more of the same: they all directly abridge the licensee's "editorial control and judgment," and are inconsistent with *Tornillo.* See Van Alstyne, *The Mobius Strip Of The First Amendment: Perspectives on Red Lion,* 29 S.C.L.Rev. 539 at 560–561 (1978).

Professor Van Alstyne disclaims any intention to say that *Red Lion* was "plainly wrong." But it is his basic theme to suggest that "*Tornillo* is a case that represents a fundamentally different and more confident view of the First Amendment."

5. Increasingly, however, as Professor T.M. Scanlon, Jr., has pointed out, a major task of a "philosophical theory of freedom of expression" is to resolve some "fundamental issues" about which there are basic disagreements. What are these issues? To some extent, they are issues that arise from concentrations of ownership in the media and the consequent impact on the concept of free expression in our society. See Scanlon, *Freedom of Expression and Categories of Expression,* 40 U. of Pittsburgh, L.Rev. 519 (1979).

THE LEGAL STATUS OF ACCESS FOR ADVERTISING TO THE PRIVATELY OWNED DAILY PRESS

1. What is the status of a First Amendment-based right of access to the advertising columns of the privately owned press? Has the *Tornillo* case, text, p. 584, with its emphasis on unfettered editorial decision making, foreclosed all claims of access for advertising? Or is the advertising section of the paper more susceptible to access claims? See Pittsburgh Press Co. v. Pittsburgh Comm. on Human Relations, 413 U.S. 376 (1973), text, p. 579. Moreover, *Tornillo* dealt with a statute compelling a newspaper to publish a reply to editorial attack, i.e., with the essential editorial product of the paper rather than with the traditionally open "advertising" section. The First Amendment-based access for advertising cases which follow illustrate the range of issues which occur in this area. See also Chapter VIII, text, p. 609.

2. What is the significance of discrimination in deciding whether there is any legal duty to accept advertisements? In Bloss v. Federated Publications, 145 N.W.2d 800 (Mich.1966), the plaintiff, a theater owner, wanted the Battle Creek *Enquirer and News,* the only daily newspaper in Battle Creek, Michigan, to publish certain advertisements concerning adult movies in the city. The paper had informed the theater owner that it did not wish to "accept advertising for theaters concerning suggestive or prurient material." Although the Michigan Court of Appeals declared that a newspaper is "a business affected with a public interest," it was held that the plaintiff's case failed to survive a motion for summary judgment because the "essential element of discrimination is lacking."

On appeal to the Supreme Court of Michigan that court affirmed. Bloss v. Federated Publications, 157 N.W.2d 241 (Mich.1968).

The case of Uhlman v. Sherman, 22 Ohio N.P., N.S., 225, 31 Ohio Dec. 54 (1919), was discussed in the *Bloss* litigation. It was heavily relied on by the theater owner since it is the only American case which has recognized a right of access to the press. See Barron, *Access to the Press—A New First Amendment Right,*

80 Harv.Law Rev. 1641 at 1667 (1967), this text, p. 559. *Uhlman* concerned discrimination against one *commercial* advertiser but not against other *commercial* advertisers.

ASSOCIATES & ALDRICH CO., INC. v. TIMES MIRROR CO.

440 F.2D 133 (9TH CIR. 1971).

WRIGHT, Circuit Judge:

This appeal presents the question: May a federal court compel the publisher of a daily newspaper to accept and print advertising in the exact form submitted? The district court, granting a motion to dismiss answered the question in the negative. We affirm.

Appellant, a motion picture producer, sought to enjoin the appellee, publisher of the *Los Angeles Times,* from screening, censoring or otherwise changing appellant's proffered advertising copy. Invoking the jurisdiction of the district court under 28 U.S.C.A. §§ 1331, 1343(3) and 42 U.S.C.A. § 1983, it sought particularly to restrain appellee from altering its advertisements for the motion picture, "The Killing of Sister George."

* * *

* * * Even if state action were present, as in an official publication of a state-supported university, there is still the freedom to exercise subjective editorial discretion in rejecting a proffered article. * * *

Appellant has not convinced us that the courts or any other governmental agency should dictate the contents of a newspaper.

There is no difference between compelling publication of material that the newspaper wishes not to print and prohibiting a newspaper from printing news or other material.

Appellant strongly urges that this case is governed by Red Lion Broadcasting Co. v. Federal Communications Comm., 395 U.S. 367 (1969). * * *

Unlike broadcasting, the publication of a newspaper is not a government conferred privilege. As we have said, the press and the government have had a history of disassociation.

We can find nothing in the United States Constitution, any federal statute, or any controlling precedent that allows us to compel a private newspaper to publish advertisements without editorial control of their content merely because such advertisements are not legally obscene or unlawful.

In evaluating appellant's claim we note that its commercial advertisement was printed by the appellee, save for the deletion of items not essential to appellant's sales message and not altering the fundamental characteristics of appellant's presentation. This type of commercial exploitation is subject to less protection than other types of speech. Valentine v. Chrestensen, 316 U.S. 52 (1942).

Affirmed.

COMMENT

1. Should the Ninth Circuit in *Associates & Aldrich* have distinguished between the exercise of editorial discretion in the news columns of newspapers and the exercise of editorial discretion in an "open" section of the paper such as the advertising columns?

2. See generally Barron, *Freedom of the Press for Whom?* pp. 270–87 (1973).

In the light of the new First Amendment status accorded to commercial advertising, don't "porno" movie houses have a new basis upon which to argue that an entire class of advertising cannot be suppressed? See Virginia State Board of Pharmacy v. Virginia Citizens Council, Inc., 425 U.S. 748 (1976), text, p. 159. Or do private newspapers simply have no First Amendment obligation to open up their advertising columns? In the *Virginia Pharmacy* case, it was the state which had attempted to ban a class of advertising. Here it is private newspapers who wish to ban a class of advertising. In short, the movie exhibitors may get wrecked on the shoals of the state action doctrine.

3. Is there a relationship between obscenity law and a right of access to the press? *Associates & Aldrich Co. v. Times-Mirror* illustrates that the actual significance of legal victories restricting the definition of obscenity in the interests of expanding artistic freedom can be frustrated if a right of access to the press is denied. In such circumstances, the end result may be that censorship by the press is substituted for censorship by the state.

4. Efforts to compel a First Amendment-based right of access to the advertising pages of the privately owned daily press still continue, as the *Wisconsin Association of Nursing Homes* case which follows illustrates:

WISCONSIN ASSOCIATION OF NURSING HOMES, INC. v.THE JOURNAL CO.

285 N.W.2D 891 (WISC.1979).

CANNON, Judge.

* * *

Plaintiffs allege in their complaint that the defendants published a series of "investigative reports" in *The Milwaukee Journal* which dealt with the quality of care and services in several nursing homes. Plaintiffs further characterize the conclusions of the article as being "false and erroneous." As a result, plaintiffs prepared a full page advertisement which purported to respond to, and refute the allegations set out in the abovementioned "reports." The defendant newspaper refused to publish the advertisement in the form presented, and referred the question of possibly libelous matter to the attention of plaintiffs' attorneys. The same advertisement was resubmitted to *The Milwaukee Journal,* and was again rejected. Plaintiffs then commenced an action seeking an order of the court directing and compelling publication.

* * *

The issue before us on appeal is whether a court can compel the publisher of a daily newspaper to accept and print an advertisement in the exact form submitted. The court below, granting the motion to dismiss, answered in the negative. We must affirm. The respondents have a right to expect that the courts will respect and protect their constitutional right to exercise their prerogative in accepting or rejecting proposed advertising material.

The existence of a free press as a condition precedent to a free society has, therefore, been a primary concern of our courts. While there have been many arguments advanced by proponents of enforced access to the press, courts have steadfastly refused to permit any erosion of first amendment privileges. The Court, in Associated Press v. United States, 326 U.S. 1, 20 n. 18, (1945) emphasized this in its holding that it would not compel "AP or its members to permit publication of anything which their 'reason' tells them should not be published." New York Times Co. v. United States, 403 U.S. 713, (1971), clearly established the principle that any government action which acted as prior restraint on freedom of the press was presumptively unconstitutional. The Court in Pittsburgh Press Co. v. Human Rel. Comm'n, 413 U.S. 376, 391, (1973) stated:

> Nor, a *fortiori,* does our decision authorize any restriction whatever, whether of content or layout, on stories or commentary originated by Pittsburgh Press, its columnists, or its contributors. On the contrary, we reaffirm unequivocally the protection afforded to editorial judgment and to the free expression of

> views on these and other issues, however controversial.

Most recently, the Court in Miami Herald Publishing Co. v. Tornillo, 418 U.S. 241, 258 (1974) reaffirmed that:

> A newspaper is more than a passive receptacle or conduit for news, comment, and advertising. The choice of material to go into a newspaper, and the decisions made as to limitations on the size and content of the paper, and treatment of public issues and public officials—whether fair or unfair—constitute the exercise of editorial control and judgment. It has yet to be demonstrated how governmental regulation of this crucial process can be exercised consistent with First Amendment guarantees of a free press as they have evolved to this time.

Thus, the clear weight of authority has not sanctioned any enforceable right of access to the press. In sum, a court can no more dictate what a privately owned newspaper can print than what it cannot print. * * *

Absent contractual provisions, then, first amendment protections do not embody any obligation on the part of a privately owned newspaper to publish anything which conflicts with its internal policies or the reasoned judgment of its editors. Nor must such a newspaper accept any advertisement in the form presented. The degree of judgmental discretion which a newspaper has with regard to refusing advertisements is not distinguishable, for purposes of first amendment analysis, from the degree of discretion it has as to the content of any other editorial materials submitted for publication. * * *

Plaintiffs argue, however, that defendants have a "monopoly" over all newspapers of general coverage in the Milwaukee metropolitan area, and that without access to defendants' newspapers, plaintiffs are deprived of any right to present their views to the public. Plaintiffs further contend that, as a result of this "monopoly," defendants have assumed the status of a public institution or quasi-public corporation or utility, and thus have a responsibility to their readers, advertisers, and subscribers to print both sides of a story. Finally, plaintiffs claim that defendants should be compelled to print the advertisement at issue on the ground that *New York Times Co. v. Sullivan, supra* will protect the newspaper from liability even if the material engenders a libel action.

Presumably, the characterization of defendants as a quasi-public institution is to subject them to governmental regulation under the guise of state action inasmuch as fourteenth amendment prohibitions apply only to state actions, and do not affect private enterprise. Burton v. Wilmington Pkg. Auth., 365 U.S. 715, 721 (1961).

In support of their contention, plaintiffs rely primarily on one case, Uhlman v. Sherman, 22 Ohio N.P., N.S. 225, 31 Ohio Dec. 54 (1919). * * *

Plaintiffs' arguments must fail, however, for several reasons:

Uhlman represents the minority rule, and stands alone in its holding that newspapers are amenable to governmental regulation.[1] We decline to accept it as controlling in this instance. We also note the qualifying language employed by the court in *Uhlman* which follows that quoted by plaintiffs:

---

1. It should be noted that a later unpublished Ohio case, Sky High Theatre, Inc. v. Garemer Publishing Co., No. 22820 of the Common Pleas Court of Champaign County, which was reported in Bloss v. Federated Publications, Inc., 5 Mich.App. 74, 83, 145 N.W.2d 800, 804 (1966) later refused to follow *Uhlman:*

> Under the circumstances, is this court bound by the decision in the *Uhlman* Case? The judgment of the circuit court of one district is not conclusive authority upon the judges of another district though the view obtains that the decisions by one court should be followed in other circuits unless it clearly appears to the courts in the latter circuits that the decision is wrong. * * * *It should be followed unless it clearly appears to this court that the decision is wrong—which is the case.* (Emphasis supplied.) [Emphasis in original.]

> We do not intend to hold that a newspaper company may not reject some class or classes of advertising entirely, or that it may not use reasonable discretion in determining whether or not an advertisement presented is a proper one.

Several courts have had occasion to rule on the issue of newspapers as quasi-public institutions. Our conclusion that defendants' conduct cannot be considered state action is in accord with these decisions. Associates & Aldrich Company v. Times Mirror Co., 440 F.2d 133 (9th Cir. 1971); Resident Participation of Denver, Inc. v. Love, 322 F.Supp. 1100 (D.Colo. 1971); Chicago Joint Bd., Amal. Cloth. Wkrs. v. Chicago Tribune Co., 435 F.2d 470 (7th Cir. 1970). In Chicago Tribune, a union sought injunctive relief to compel newspapers to publish an editorial advertisement. The Seventh Circuit Court of Appeals affirmed the district court's determination that there was no state involvement in the conduct of the newspaper's business. The court of appeals quoted from the district court's memorandum opinion at 474:

> Rather than regarded as an extension of the state exercising delegated powers of a governmental nature, the press has long and consistently been recognized as an independent check on governmental power. * * *
>
> In sum, the function of the press from the days the Constitution was written to the present time has never been conceived as anything but a private enterprise, free and independent of government control and supervision. Rather than state power and participation pervading the operation of the press, the news media and the government have had a history of disassociation.

The issue of state control was raised by appellants in *Times Mirror, supra.* There the court at 136 noted:

> Unlike broadcasting, the publication of a newspaper is not a government conferred privilege. As we have said, the press and the government have had a history of disassociation.
>
> We can find nothing in the United States Constitution, any federal statute, or any controlling precedent that allows us to compel a private newspaper to publish advertisements without editorial control of their content merely because such advertisements are not legally obscene or unlawful.

Finally Justice White, in his concurring opinion in *Tornillo, supra,* 418 U.S. at 259, stated that: "A newspaper or magazine is not a public utility subject to 'reasonable' governmental regulation in matters affecting the exercise of journalistic judgment as to what shall be printed."

Plaintiffs' argument that defendants' "monopolistic" control over newspapers in the Milwaukee area is a sufficient basis for the injunctive relief sought is similarly misplaced. While the United States Supreme Court has qualified the right of a publisher to refuse advertising in certain instances involving a claim of monopoly, such a rule is not applicable under the instant fact situation.

In Lorain Journal Co. v. United States, 342 U.S. 143 (1951), a newspaper withheld the right to advertise from a subscriber who also utilized a competitor's radio station for advertising. The Court found that the publisher's conduct amounted to an attempt to use first amendment protections to destroy competition and reestablish a monopoly. Under these circumstances, the Court held the refusal of advertising to be illegal monopolization of interstate commerce. In arriving at its decision, the Court balanced the congressional policy of preventing monopoly against the right of publishers to refuse advertising, and determined that the right of refusal had to yield to the potential for violations of the Sherman Act.

Plaintiffs' allegations of defendants' business practices as a monopoly are, therefore, not pertinent to this appeal.

The complaint is devoid of any allegations which would establish the existence of any contracts, combinations or conspiracies in restraint of trade on the part of defendants. * * * Plaintiffs reaffirmed this in their brief: "Again, we do not allege an effective monopoly of the newspaper field in Milwaukee to establish an action for damages, based upon such monopoly, or combination in restraint of trade." Finally, at oral argument, plaintiffs conceded that this was not a cause of action based on monopoly *per se.*

Plaintiffs' argument that defendants have a duty and obligation to print both sides of an issue to their readers must also fail. They urge that the right of the newspaper to reject advertising must be balanced against the public's right to be aware of all the facts surrounding an issue. In *Chicago Tribune Co., supra,* at 478 the same arguments were raised by *amicus curiae* and rejected by the court:

> It is urged that the privilege of First Amendment protection afforded a newspaper carries with it a reciprocal obligation to serve as a public forum, and if a newspaper accepts any editorial advertising it must publish all lawful editorial advertisements tendered to it for publication at its established rates. We do not understand this to be the concept of freedom of the press recognized in the First Amendment. The First Amendment guarantees of free expression, oral or printed, exist for all—they need not be purchased at the price *amici* would exact. The Union's right to free speech does not give it the right to make use of the defendants' printing presses and distribution systems without defendants' consent.

Plaintiffs cite Fitzgerald v. National Rifle Ass'n of America, 383 F.Supp. 162 (D.N.J.1974) in support of their claim. While it is true that *Fitzgerald* balanced the fiduciary obligations of the National Rifle Association of America against a publisher's right to refuse advertising, the holding is inapplicable here. *Fitzgerald* dealt with an action by a member of a private organization to force publication of an advertisement regarding his candidacy for the association's board of directors. The publication involved was a private journal, and the court found that it was closer in form to a corporate newsletter than to a traditionally commercial publication. The court held that to allow the newspaper to refuse to print the advertisement created the potential for violation of a corporate trust.

Plaintiffs here cannot rely on any fiduciary obligation or corporate trust in their request for a mandatory injunction. We again reaffirm that there is no duty on the part of a private newspaper to print what it otherwise "chooses to leave on the newsroom floor." Tornillo, *supra,* 418 U.S. at 261.

The journalistic discretion utilized by defendants in rejecting plaintiffs' advertisement because it contained possibly libelous material must also be sustained. Editorial policy should not be the subject of judicial interference notwithstanding plaintiffs' contention that defendants are protected by the rule set out in *New York Times Co. v. Sullivan, supra.* Plaintiffs argue that defendants would sustain no liability for publication of the allegedly libelous statement unless it is proved that the statement was made with actual malice. We reject this argument as the basis on which to compel publication of plaintiffs' advertisement. Such an argument begs the question and clouds the real issue. The question before us is not whether plaintiffs' advertisement is libelous, but whether they can compel its publication. It is well established that they cannot.

Order and judgment affirmed.

COMMENT

1. The overwhelming weight of authority is that there is no right of access to newspaper advertising space. Nevertheless, as *Wisconsin Nursing Homes* conceded,

some cases have recognized a right of access to the press. One old chestnut, Uhlman v. Sherman, 22 Ohio N.P., N.S. 225, 31 Ohio, Dec. 54 (1919), a creaking pre-*Tornillo* precedent, is not very authoritative because it contained no discussion of the First Amendment implications of a right of access to the press.

Fitzgerald v. National Rifle Association, 383 F.Supp. 162 (D.N.J.1974), distinguished in *Wisconsin Nursing Homes,* is more significant. Fitzgerald, a candidate for the Board of Directors of the National Rifle Association, submitted an advertisement urging his candidacy to *The American Rifleman,* official journal of the National Rifle Association. Proper payment for the advertisement was proffered and was tendered. But the NRA refused to publish. The NRA states on its advertising rate card that it "reserves the right to reject or discontinue any advertisement and to edit all copy." Although recognizing the "general right of a newspaper or magazine to decide what advertisements it will and will not accept," the court cautioned that the rule was not "absolute in all circumstances," as prior cases demonstrated. For example, the publisher's right to refuse advertisement had been subordinated to the policies of the antitrust laws in Lorain Journal Co. v. United States, 342 U.S. 143 (1951), text, pp. 575, 660. Judge Whipple summarized *Lorain Journal* in *Fitzgerald* as follows: "The Court concluded that when balanced against the Congressional policy of preventing monopoly, the right of publishers to refuse advertisements must yield." See also Hodgson v. United Mine Workers of America, 344 F.Supp. 17 (D.D.C.1972).

The *Fitzgerald* case did not view the right not to publish as absolute. A familiar need to balance competing interests was the tack advocated in *Fitzgerald:*

"In the instant case, this Court must decide whether the publisher's right must give way when balanced against the fiduciary duty of corporate directors to insure fair and open corporate elections. This duty of course extends only to the association membership."

The American Rifleman, neither published nor circulated to the general public, was deemed a vital part of the electoral process of the National Rifle Association. The Nominating Committee's list of candidates for office is published in *The Rifleman:* "This special relationship between the NRA and *The American Rifleman* is closer in form to a corporate newsletter than to a traditionally commercial publication, such as *Time* or *Newsweek.*"

In the light of these special facts, the extent to which *Fitzgerald* should be viewed as a precedent which requires a publisher to publish against his will is unclear: "Indeed, in the instant case, traditional distinctions between a publisher and an advertiser become blurred, since the plaintiffs may justifiably claim an ownership interest in the *American Rifleman.* Plaintiffs are members in good standing of the association which publishes the magazine and their dues go in part to meet the magazine's printing costs."

Does *Fitzgerald* resemble a quarrel among the publishers of a newspaper more closely than it does a quarrel between the publisher and a reader or member of the public seeking access? The court said the management of the NRA was bound to follow the mandates of New York's Not-For-Profit Corporation Law, § 101 (McKinney's Consol. Laws, c. 35, 1970) requiring "directors and officers" to "discharge the duties of their respective positions in good faith."

In *Fitzgerald,* it was held that "the traditional right of a magazine to refuse publication of an advertisement" had to yield for two reasons: 1) the equitable requirements of decency and fair dealing imposed on the NRA by state law, and 2) the unique relationship between *The American Rifleman* and the election process of the NRA. In short, the court ordered *The*

American Rifleman to publish the advertisement originally submitted by the plaintiffs.

The fact that *Fitzgerald* involves a controversy between members of the same association rather than a controversy between the publisher or editor of a mass circulation newspaper and a member of the public is, of course, very important. The duty to publish in *Fitzgerald* is found in the state's nonprofit corporate laws rather than in a statute requiring the daily press to open their columns to those whom they would not otherwise publish. In *Fitzgerald,* the court observed: "Corporate elections become hollow mockeries if candidates are unable to bring their candidacies and platforms to the attention of the stockholders at large."

The right of access of a political candidate to a newspaper to reply to an editorial attack during a political campaign was the precise factual setting of *Tornillo.* It may be asked: Don't political elections particularly in cities or states dominated by one newspaper also become mockeries if candidates cannot reach the voters because coverage is denied them? The question is not far-fetched. Just such an argument by a political candidate was involved in Miami Herald Publishing Co. v. Tornillo, 418 U.S. 241 (1974). Is the *Fitzgerald* decision in conflict with *Tornillo?* The *Fitzgerald* court's first response to this question is that the *Tornillo* facts were different: "This Court is not convinced that the *Tornillo* case is applicable whereas here a commercial advertisement, rather than a political editorial or article, is involved."

Tornillo can perhaps be distinguished from the *Fitzgerald* case on the ground it dealt with political speech. The subject matter of *Fitzgerald* was more akin to commercial speech, what the Supreme Court has described as possessing a greater hardihood. In other words, commercial speech is more susceptible to governmental regulation. See Virginia State Board of Pharmacy v. Virginia Citizens Consumer Council, Inc., 425 U.S. 748 (1976), fn. 24. See Central Hudson Gas & Electric v. Public Service Commission, 447 U.S. 557 (1980). Political speech, on the other hand, is particularly fragile, and therefore attempts by government to regulate are particularly suspect.

Even if *Tornillo* was deemed to apply to commercial advertisements as well as political advertisements, it still was not considered to be a bar by the court to an order requiring publication of the proffered ad. Absolute First Amendment protection for the right to publish was rejected. The balancing test was employed. The obligations imposed on the NRA by the state's corporate law were found to be weightier than an untrammeled right to publish or not to publish, particularly where for the people involved the *Rifleman* was the only forum for reaching the NRA membership.

2. In *Tornillo,* it was argued by the losing side that the First Amendment, because of its interest in "vigorous and robust debate," see New York Times Co. v. Sullivan, 376 U.S. 254 (1964), authorized the enactment of right of reply legislation. *Tornillo* rejected that contention. Paradoxically, the antitrust laws rather than the First Amendment may turn out to be the breeding ground for a right of access to the press. In *Wisconsin Nursing Homes,* the court, referring to Lorain Journal Co. v. United States, 342 U.S. 143 (1951), observed that "the United States Supreme Court has qualified the right of a publisher to refuse advertising in certain instances involving a claim of monopoly." Similar comments were made in *Fitzgerald.* In the *Fitzgerald* case, the possibility that the antitrust laws might require a duty to publish advertising in some circumstances was also mentioned. Illustrative of this principle is Home Placement Service v. Providence Journal, 8 Med.L.Rptr. 1881, 682 F.2d 274 (1st Cir. 1982), see text, pp. 611, 661, which held that the refusal of a newspaper to accept classified advertising from

a rental referral service which charges a fee violates the antitrust laws. Such conduct constituted "strangulation of a competitor."

Currently, a not newspaper is free not to publish advertisements. But a newspaper was not free not to publish in circumstances where the rental referral business which seeks to place an ad is in competition with the newspaper. The newspaper's action was in violation of the Sherman Act. The newspaper was unlawfully using its control of the newspaper advertising market to preclude competition of the market seeking information about housing facts. The court of appeals in *Home Placement Service* remanded the case to the United States District Court for the District of Rhode Island for a determination of whether injunctive relief was appropriate and for an award of damages and attorney's fees.

Does the reward suggest some reluctance by the court of appeals to order a newspaper to accept an ad? Is the suggestion that the appropriate relief in lieu of an order to publish is monetary damages?

Home Placement Service should be contrasted with Homefinders of America v. Providence Journal, 6 Med.L.Rptr. 1018, 621 F.2d 441 (1st Cir. 1980), see text, pp. 611, 661, where the First Circuit held that the Sherman Act was not violated by refusing to publish false and misleading advertisements which had been submitted by a rental referral firm which charged fees to prospective renters. Judge Aldrich said for the First Circuit in *Homefinders*:

> Even when it might lack proof of actual fraud, we would hesitate long before holding that a newspaper, monopoly or not, armed with both the First Amendment and a reasonable business justification, can be ordered to publish advertising against its will. * * * In the present case, we see no question. The antitrust laws are not a shield for deceptive advertising.

Homefinders was distinguished from *Home Placement Service* on the ground that in *Homefinders* the advertisements were deceptive and misleading and, therefore, the refusal to publish them was reasonable. The contention by the newspaper in *Home Placement Service* that the public should not have to pay to find rental housing was rejected by the court as an unacceptable "paternal judgment."

3. Compulsory publication where the newspaper is directed by the state to publish is a form of compelled entry into newspapers which perhaps should be distinguished from compulsory publication when it is sought by members of the public. An example of such state-directed compulsory publication is found in Memphis Publishing Co. v. Leech, 539 F.Supp. 405 (W.D.1982), where a Tennessee statute required certain newspapers in the state to include a warning in alcoholic beverage advertisements setting forth the illegality and potential consequences of transporting alcoholic beverages into the state without a permit from the state Alcoholic Beverage Commission.

The Tennessee statute was ruled invalid because it intruded "impermissibly into the editorial discretion involved in accepting and preparing the copy for commercial advertising." In *Memphis Publishing,* as in other access-to-advertising cases, the party seeking to compel the publication of an advertisement sought to distinguish *Tornillo* by contending that its precedential force did not "extend to decisions regarding the acceptance of commercial advertising." As authority that newspaper advertising may be regulated, Pittsburgh Press Co. v. Pittburgh Commission on Human Relations, 413 U.S. 376 (1973), was relied upon by the Attorney General of Tennessee. In *Pittsburgh Press,* a city ordinance, prohibiting newspapers from using sex-designated advertising columns for job opportunities, was upheld. Should we conclude from recent lower court cases and from *Pittsburgh Press,* text, p. 579, that *Tornillo* in fact has no force in access for advertising cases?

The Chicago Newspaper Case: A Union's Fight for Access to the Daily Press

A union was involved in a dispute with the large Chicago department store, Marshall Field and Company. The union objected to the sale by Marshall Field of imported clothing on the ground that the sale of imported clothing jeopardized the jobs of American clothing workers. The union said it would protest such sales until the countries of origin agreed to voluntary quotas on the amount of clothing to be sent into the United States. The union sought to place an ad explaining its position in each of the then four Chicago daily newspapers. None of the Chicago dailies would publish the ad. The union, the Chicago Joint Board, Amalgamated Clothing Workers of America, AFL–CIO, sued the papers on an access theory to enjoin them to publish the ads and to pay compensatory and exemplary damages.

These were the circumstances in which the first major access case, based squarely on an affirmative view of the First Amendment, was born. The Chicago papers moved for summary judgment on the ground that newspapers had a right to reject advertisements and that the newspapers had not violated the First Amendment since that Amendment applied only to government. The latter argument, that there was no state action, in this situation was the winning argument for the press. Federal Judge Abraham Marovitz granted the newspaper defendants motion for summary judgment. Chicago Joint Board, Amalgamated Clothing Workers of America, AFL–CIO v. Chicago Tribune Co., 307 F.Supp. 422 (N.D.Ill.1969).

In Judge Marovitz's view the First Amendment is sort of the obverse of the Eighteenth Amendment. Just as the Eighteenth Amendment tried to destroy the liquor industry forever in the United States, so the First Amendment is a constitutional attempt to protect permanently the newspaper industry. Justice Stewart, in an influential lecture, has given new force to a similar thesis. See text, pp. 150, 439.

If the plaintiffs had dwelled on the fact that some of the newspapers involved in the *Chicago Joint Board* case also owned television stations, might that have helped the plaintiffs to hurdle the state action barrier? Why?

The union appealed the district court determination only to stumble again on a familiar obstacle, the state action problem. The appeals decision reveals the efforts of the union to show the interdependence between the Chicago daily newspapers and government in the hope that newspaper restraints on expression would be seen as quasi public. Among the fascinating examples of state involvement in the Chicago daily press unearthed by union lawyers—particularly with regard to the newspaper defendants in the *Chicago Joint Board* case—was a Chicago ordinance which restricted newsstands on public streets to the sale of daily newspapers printed and published in the city of Chicago. Also, counsel for the union argued that legal imposition of a duty to publish was not the foreign conception represented by newspaper lawyers, since Illinois, like most states, requires newspaper publication of certain legal notices by the press. It was all to no avail; the appeals court affirmed the district court. The decision of the court of appeals, per Judge Castle, in *Chicago Joint Board,* unlike the celebrated *Red Lion* decision, text, p. 845, was a victory for the view that freedom of the press has as its primary focus the freedom of the publisher. See Chicago Joint Board, Amalgamated Clothing Workers of America, AFL–CIO v. Chicago Tribune Co., 435 F.2d 470 (7th Cir. 1970).

Judge Castle in the *Chicago Joint Board* decision rejected the union argument that "monopoly power in an area of vital public concern" is the equivalent of governmental action: the Chicago daily newspaper market was not a monopoly. This, of course, is true, but wasn't the union position really that in access terms the Chicago newspapers were functionally monopolistic? Since none of the papers would print the union's ad, for First Amendment purposes it was irrelevant that there was more than one daily newspaper in Chicago.

The court of appeals decision in *Chicago Joint Board* is a good statement of the traditional *laissez-faire* approach to freedom of expression which has long dominated American law. Under this view, is the possession of property rights a precondition to the exercise of freedom of the press? Judge Castle states the *laissez-faire* view as follows:

> The union's right to free speech does not give it the right to make use of the defendants' printing presses and distribution systems without defendants' consent.

The Seventh Circuit also decided one other important access case in 1970. In *Lee v. Board of Regents, infra,* text, p. 597, the court decided that spokesmen for differing political and social viewpoints on the campus of the Wisconsin State University at Whitewater had a right of access to the advertising pages of the campus newspaper the *Royal Purple.* The difference between the two cases? The Chicago newspapers are privately owned and therefore are not bound by a constitutional duty not to restrain expression. Wisconsin State University, on the other hand, is a public, tax-supported institution which is bound by constitutional limitations.

A RIGHT OF REPLY TO THE PRESS: A STUDY OF THE *TORNILLO* CASE

1. On June 7, 1971, the Supreme Court, in a further extension of the *New York Times* doctrine in Rosenbloom v. Metromedia, Inc., 403 U.S. 29 (1971), discussed in connection with the libel materials in this text, p. 221, justified further increasing the significant protection against libel newspapers already enjoyed by urging the establishment by the states of a right of access to the press. Justice William Brennan, speaking for the Court, said in an opinion joined by Chief Justice Burger and Justice Blackmun:

> If the States fear that private citizens will not be able to respond adequately to publicity involving them, the solution lies in the direction of ensuring their ability to respond, rather than in a stifling public discussion of matters of public concern.

The Court, in footnote 15 of its opinion, accompanied this remark with a sympathetic discussion of the argument for the creation of a right of access to the press:

> Some States have adopted retraction statutes or right of reply statutes. See Donnelly, *The Right of Reply: An Alternative to an Action for Libel,* 34 Va.L.Rev. 867 (1948); Note, *Vindication of the Reputation of a Public Official,* 80 Harv.L.Rev. 1730 (1967). Cf. Red Lion Broadcasting Co. v. FCC, 395 U.S. 367 (1969).
>
> One writer, in arguing that the First Amendment itself should be read to guarantee a right of access to the media not limited to a right to respond to defamatory falsehoods, has suggested several ways the law might encourage public discussion. Barron, *Access to the Press—A New First Amendment Right,* 80 Harv.L.Rev. 1641, 1666–1678 (1967). It is important to recognize that the private individual often desires press exposure either for himself, his ideas, or his causes. Constitutional adjudication must take into account the individual's interest in access to the press as well as the individual's interest in preserving his reputation, even though libel actions by their nature encourage a narrow view of the individu-

> al's interest since they focus only on situations where the individual has been harmed by undesired press attention. A constitutional rule that deters the press from covering the ideas or activities of the private individual thus conceives the individual's interest too narrowly.

The Court's observations on access in *Rosenbloom* raised some intriguing questions. The Court said "constitutional adjudication" should take account of the individual's interest in access to the press. Was this an intimation that a right of access can be established initially as a matter of First Amendment interpretation contrary to *Chicago Joint Board?*

The Court's remarks in *Rosenbloom* appeared to *assume* the constitutionality of right to reply legislation which would have a much wider scope than merely to provide a response to defamation. Finally, the state action problem which has loomed so large in the lower courts is not mentioned at all.

In May 1973 in CBS v. Democratic National Committee, 412 U.S. 94 (1973), the Supreme Court dealt a blow to the view that the force of the First Amendment was sufficient in itself to require the broadcast networks to abandon their policy of refusing to sell time to political groups and parties for the dissemination of views about ideas. See text, Chapter IX, p. 858. The Supreme Court took the position that so long as the FCC neither forbade nor required the networks to take any particular position with regard to the sale of political time, what the networks did was private action and therefore removed from the realm of constitutional obligation. Although the *CBS* case squarely endorsed the fairness doctrine and to that extent took an affirmative view of the First Amendment, the opinion was a defeat for the view that the First Amendment could support an access theory.

In the much-publicized *Tornillo* case the tantalizing question was squarely presented for consideration: Was it consistent, under the First Amendment, for a state to provide by statute in certain specified circumstances for compelled publication by a daily newspaper of general circulation?

A provision of the Florida Election Code, F.S. 104.38, enacted in 1913, provided that where the publisher of a newspaper assails the personal character of any political candidate or charges him with malfeasance or misfeasance in office, such newspaper shall upon request of the political candidate immediately publish free of cost any reply he may make thereto in as conspicuous a place and in the same kind of type as the matter that calls for the reply:

> F.S.§ 104.38—Newspaper assailing candidate in an election; space for reply. If any newspaper in its columns assails the personal character of any candidate for nomination or for election in any election, or charges said candidate with malfeasance or misfeasance in office, or otherwise attacks his official record, or gives to another free space for such purpose, such newspaper shall upon request of such candidate immediately publish free of cost any reply he may make thereto in as conspicuous a place and in the same kind of type as the matter that calls for such reply, provided such reply does not take up more space than the matter replied to. Any person or firm failing to comply with the provisions of this section shall be guilty of a misdemeanor of the first degree, punishable as provided in § 775.082 or § 775.083.

The statute had been slumbering in the Florida sun for more than half a century. The rise of the idea that the First Amendment might suggest positive duties for the press as well as new immunities had breathed new life into the statute in the late sixties, and at least three law suits involving this little-known provision of the Florida Election Code had been brought.

The most controversial came to involve a lawsuit by one Pat Tornillo, leader of the Dade County Classroom Teachers Association. In 1972, Tornillo ran as Democratic candidate for the Florida legislature.

In 1968, the Dade County Classroom Teachers Association had gone on strike. Under Florida law at the time, a strike by public school teachers was illegal. Tornillo had led the strike in Miami.

The *Miami Herald* on September 20, 1972, published an editorial calling Tornillo a "czar" and a law breaker. The *Herald* said in an editorial that "it would be inexcusable of the voters if they sent Pat Tornillo to the legislature."

Tornillo demanded an opportunity to reply to both these attacks under the Florida right of reply statute. The *Herald* refused to print the reply, and Tornillo filed a suit against the *Herald* and sought, on the strength of the statute, a mandatory injunction requiring the printing of his replies.

The *Tornillo* case required a direct judicial consideration of the validity of affirmative implementation of First Amendment values.

The Florida lower court in the *Tornillo* case held that the right of reply statute was unconstitutional. But the Supreme Court of Florida in a 6–1 decision reversed that court and, in the first test of the validity under the First Amendment of a newspaper right of reply statute, held it to be constitutional. Tornillo v. Miami Herald, 287 So.2d 78 (Fla.1973).

2. An enforceable right of reply in the press, although of relatively long standing in Germany and France, has been a fairly unusual phenomenon in the statutory patterns of American states. See Donnelly, *The Right of Reply: An Alternative to An Action for Libel,* 34 Va.L.Rev. 867 (1948). Yet interest in right of reply statutes had been considerable. It was generated by the increasingly noncompetitive and chain-dominated press and the Supreme Court's ground-breaking decision in New York Times v. Sullivan, 376 U.S. 245 (1964), which so radically revised the American law of libel and provided a measure of relief from libel judgments hitherto unknown in American law.

3. The Supreme Court of Florida strongly relied on the endorsement of right of reply legislation contained in the opinion for the Court in *Rosenbloom,* see text, p. 221. The idea expressed in *Rosenbloom* and the state supreme court decision in *Tornillo* may be outlined as follows: If damages are not to be a remedy for libel, perhaps a right of reply can perform that task. Damages won in a libel action are perhaps a burden on the information process. But a right of reply statute aids the information process in the sense that it provides for access for the person attacked.

4. The circuit court for Dade County had held that the Florida right of reply statute was subject to the constitutional infirmity of vagueness. The lower court complained that no editor could know in advance exactly what words would offend the statute or the scope of the reply required.

The same vagueness charge was made concerning broadcasting's personal attack rules which provide for a right of reply "when during the presentation of views on a controversial issue of public importance, an attack is made upon the honesty, character, integrity, or like personal qualities of an identified *person* or group. * * *" The validity of the personal attack rules was upheld in Red Lion Broadcasting Co. v. FCC, 395 U.S. 367 (1969), where Justice Byron White dismissed the vagueness argument on the ground that the regulations were sufficiently precise. The Florida Supreme Court upheld the vagueness challenge to the Florida right of reply statute on the basis of the *Red Lion* decision.

5. The Florida right of reply law deprives a newspaper publisher, the *Miami Herald* argued, of property without compensation or due process of law in violation of § 9, Art. I of the Florida Constitution and the Fourteenth Amendment of the United States Constitution.

The newspaper argued that the Florida right of reply statute unconstitutionally takes property from the defendant newspaper and gives it to a plaintiff. In Red Lion Broadcasting Co. v. FCC, 395 U.S. 367 (1969), one of the issues that propelled that case to the Supreme Court was whether a person attacked by a radio station should be given *free* time to reply under the FCC's personal attack rules.

Yet the Supreme Court's opinion in *Red Lion* requiring such free reply time did suggest that the provision of free time under either the fairness doctrine or the personal attack rules was an invalid "taking."

Is a free space requirement less of a burden for a newspaper like the *Miami Herald* than the free time requirement was for a broadcaster like the Red Lion Broadcasting Co.? Broadcast time, unlike newspaper space, is finite. Is a newspaper expandable? If advertising business is up, can the paper always put out a larger edition? What of newsprint? A grant of free time appears to be a more costly matter to the station manager in broadcasting than is a grant of free space to the newspaper publisher. Yet the Court of Appeals in *Red Lion* considered the free time requirement as a reasonable burden.

6. After the decision of the Supreme Court of Florida was announced in the *Tornillo* case, the *Miami Herald,* joined by many other newspapers who filed amicus curiae briefs, filed a petition for rehearing with the Supreme Court of Florida. Appellant contended in its petition for rehearing that § 104.38 was a criminal statute and as such that it failed to meet the constitutional standards of precision required of such statutes. The *Miami Herald* argued on rehearing that the Supreme Court of Florida lacked constitutional power to furnish a saving gloss to a criminal statute. The Supreme Court of Florida denied the petition and pointed out that "no criminal penalty" was sought by Tornillo and that "the validity *vel non* of the criminal penalty is not here involved." Pat L. Tornillo, Jr. v. The Miami Herald Publishing Co., 287 So.2d 78 (Fla.1973).

The Supreme Court of Florida denied the *Miami Herald's* petition for rehearing. See Tornillo v. The Miami Herald Publishing Co., 287 So.2d 78, 89 (Fla.1973).

The *Miami Herald* then appealed the decision of the Florida Supreme Court in *Tornillo* to the Supreme Court of the United States. On June 25, 1974, the Court unanimously reversed the Florida Supreme Court.

MIAMI HERALD PUB. CO. v. TORNILLO

418 U.S. 241, 94 S.CT. 2831, 41 L.ED.2D 730 (1974).

Chief Justice BURGER delivered the opinion of the Court.

The issue in this case is whether a state statute granting a political candidate a right to equal space to reply to criticism and attacks on his record by a newspaper, violates the guarantees of a free press.

In the fall of 1972, appellee, Executive Director of the Classroom Teachers Association, apparently a teachers' collective-bargaining agent, was a candidate for the Florida House of Representatives. On September 20, 1972, and again on September 29, 1972, appellant printed editorials critical of appellee's candidacy. In response to these editorials appellee demanded that appellant print verbatim his replies, defending the role of the Classroom Teachers Association and the organization's accomplishments for the citizens of Dade County. Appellant declined to print the appellee's replies, and appellee brought suit in Circuit Court, Dade County, seeking declaratory and injunctive relief and actual and punitive damages in excess of $5,000. The action was premised on Florida Statute § 104.38, a "right of reply" statute which provides that if a candidate for nomination or election is assailed regarding his personal character or official record by any newspaper, the candidate has the right to demand that the newspaper print, free of cost to the candidate, any reply the candidate may make to the newspaper's charges. The reply must appear in as conspicuous a place and in the same kind of type as the charges which prompted the reply, provided it does not take up more space than the charges. Failure to comply with the statute constitutes a first-degree misdemeanor.

Appellant sought a declaration that § 104.38 was unconstitutional. After an emergency hearing requested by the appellee, the Circuit Court denied injunctive relief because, absent special circumstances, no injunction could properly issue against the commission of a crime, and held that § 104.38 was unconstitutional as an infringement on the freedom of the press under the First and Fourteenth Amendments to the Constitution. Tornillo v. Miami Herald Pub. Co., 38 Fla.Supp. 80 (1972). The Circuit Court concluded that dictating what a newspaper must print was no different from dictating what it must not print. The Circuit Judge viewed the statute's vagueness as serving "to restrict and stifle protected expression." 38 Fla.Supp., at 83. Appellee's cause was dismissed with prejudice.

On direct appeal, the Florida Supreme Court reversed holding that § 104.38 did not violate constitutional guarantees. Tornillo v. Miami Herald Pub. Co., 287 So.2d 78 (1973).[3] It held that free speech was enhanced and not abridged by the Florida right of reply statute, which in that court's view, furthered the "broad societal interest in the free flow of information to the public." 287 So.2d, at 82. It also held that the statute was not impermissibly vague; the statute informs "those who are subject to it as to what conduct on their part will render them liable to its penalties." 287 So.2d, at 85.[4] Civil remedies, including damages, were held to be available under this statute; the case was remanded to the trial court for further proceedings not inconsistent with the Florida Supreme Court's opinion.

We postponed consideration of the question of jurisdiction to the hearing of the case on the merits. 414 U.S. 1142 (1974).

* * *

The challenged statute creates a right to reply to press criticism of a candidate for nomination or election. The statute was enacted in 1913 and this is only the second recorded case decided under its provisions.[7]

Appellant contends the statute is void on its face because it purports to regulate the content of a newspaper in violation of the First Amendment. Alternatively it is urged that the statute is void for vagueness since no editor could know exactly what words would call the statute into operation. It is also contended that the statute fails to distinguish between critical comment which is and is not defamatory.

The appellee and supporting advocates of an enforceable right of access to the press vigorously argue that Government has an obligation to ensure that a wide

3. The Supreme Court did not disturb the Circuit Court's holding that injunctive relief was not proper in this case even if the statute were constitutional. According to the Supreme Court neither side took issue with that part of the Circuit Court's decision. 287 So.2d, at 85.

4. The Supreme Court placed the following limiting construction on the statute:

"[W]e hold that the mandate of the statute refers to 'any reply' which is wholly responsive to the charge made in the editorial or other article in a newspaper being replied to and further that such reply will be neither libelous nor slanderous of the publication nor anyone else, nor vulgar nor profane." 287 So.2d, at 86.

7. In its first court test the statute was declared unconstitutional. State v. News-Journal Corp., 36 Fla.Supp. 164 (Volusia County J, Ct., Fla.1972). In neither of the two suits, the instant action and the 1972 action, has the Florida Attorney General defended the statute's constitutionality.

variety of views reach the public.[8] The contentions of access proponents will be set out in some detail.[9] It is urged that at the time the First Amendment to the Constitution was enacted in 1791 as part of our Bill of Rights the press was broadly representative of the people it was serving. While many of the newspapers were intensely partisan and narrow in their views, the press collectively presented a broad range of opinions to readers. Entry into publishing was inexpensive; pamphlets and books provided meaningful alternatives to the organized press for the expression of unpopular ideas and often treated events and expressed views not covered by conventional newspapers. A true marketplace of ideas existed in which there was relatively easy access to the channels of communication.

Access advocates submit that although newspapers of the present are superficially similar to those of 1791 the press of today is in reality very different from that known in the early years of our national existence. In the past half century a communications revolution has seen the introduction of radio and television into our lives, the promise of a global community through the use of communications satellites, and the spectre of a "wired" nation by means of an expanding cable television network with two-way capabilities. The printed press, it is said, has not escaped the effects of this revolution. Newspapers have become big business and there are far fewer of them to serve a larger literate population. Chains of newspapers, national newspapers, national wire and news services, and one-newspaper towns, are the dominant features of a press that has become noncompetitive and enormously powerful and influential in its capacity to manipulate popular opinion and change the course of events. Major metropolitan newspapers have collaborated to establish news services national in scope. Such national news organizations provide syndicated "interpretative reporting" as well as syndicated features and commentary, all of which can serve as part of the new school of "advocacy journalism."

The elimination of competing newspapers in most of our large cities, and the concentration of control of media that results from the only newspaper being owned by the same interests which own a television station and a radio station, are important components of this trend toward concentration of control of outlets to inform the public.

The result of these vast changes has been to place in a few hands the power to inform the American people and shape public opinion.[15] Much of the editorial opinion and commentary that is printed is that of syndicated columnists distributed nationwide and, as a result, we are told, on national and world issues there tends to be a homogeneity of editorial opinion, commentary, and interpretative analysis. The abuses of bias and manipulative reportage are, likewise, said to be the result of the vast accumulations of unreviewable power in the modern media empires. In effect, it is claimed, the public has lost any ability to respond or to contribute in a meaningful way to the debate on issues. The monopoly of the means of communi-

8. See generally Barron, *Access to the Press—A New First Amendment Right,* 80 Harv.L.Rev. 1641 (1967).

9. For a good overview of the position of access advocates see Lange, *The Role of the Access Doctrine in the Regulation of the Mass Media: A Critical Review and Assessment,* 52 N.C.L.Rev. 1, 8–9 (1973) (hereinafter "Lange").

15. "Local monopoly in printed news raises serious questions of diversity of information and opinion. What a local newspaper does not print about local affairs does not see general print at all. And, having the power to take initiative in reporting and enunciation of opinions, it has extraordinary power to set the atmosphere and determine the terms of local consideration of public issues." B. Bagdikian, *The Information Machines* 127 (1971).

cation allows for little or no critical analysis of the media except in professional journals of very limited readership.

> This concentration of nationwide news organizations—like other large institutions—has grown increasingly remote from and unresponsive to the popular constituencies on which they depend and which depend on them. Report of the Task Force, *The Twentieth Century Fund Task Force Report for a National News Council, A Free and Responsive Press* 4 (1973).

Appellees cite the report of the Commission on Freedom of the Press, chaired by Robert M. Hutchins, in which it was stated, as long ago as 1947, that "The right of free public expression has * * * lost its earlier reality." Commission on Freedom of the Press, *A Free and Responsible Press* 15.

The obvious solution, which was available to dissidents at an earlier time when entry into publishing was relatively inexpensive, today would be to have additional newspapers. But the same economic factors which have caused the disappearance of vast numbers of metropolitan newspapers,[16] have made entry into the marketplace of ideas served by the print media almost impossible. It is urged that the claim of newspapers to be "surrogates for the public" carries with it a concomitant fiduciary obligation to account for that stewardship.[17] From this premise it is reasoned that the only effective way to insure fairness and accuracy and to provide for some accountability is for government to take affirmative action. The First Amendment interest of the public in being informed is said to be in peril because the "marketplace of ideas" is today a monopoly controlled by the owners of the market.

Proponents of enforced access to the press take comfort from language in several of this Court's decisions which suggests that the First Amendment acts as a sword as well as a shield, that it imposes obligations on the owners of the press in addition to protecting the press from government regulation. In Associated Press v. United States, 326 U.S. 1, 20 (1945), the Court, in rejecting the argument that the press is immune from the antitrust laws by virtue of the First Amendment, stated:

> The First Amendment, far from providing an argument against application of the Sherman Act, here provides powerful reasons to the contrary. That amendment rests on the assumption that the widest possible dissemination of information from diverse and antagonistic sources is essential to the welfare of the public, that a free press is a condition of a free society. Surely a command that the government itself shall not impede the free flow of ideas does not afford non-governmental combinations a refuge if they impose restraints upon that constitutionally guaranteed freedom. Freedom to publish means freedom for all and not for some. Freedom to publish is guaranteed by the Constitution, but freedom to combine to keep others from publishing is not. Freedom of the press from governmental interference under the First Amendment does not sanction repression of that freedom by private interests. [Footnote omitted.]

In New York Times Co. v. Sullivan, 376 U.S. 254, 270 (1964), the Court spoke of "a profound national commitment to the principle that debate on public issues should be uninhibited, robust, and wide-open." It

16. The newspapers have persuaded Congress to grant them immunity from the antitrust laws in the case of "failing" newspapers for joint operations. 15 U.S.C.A. § 1801 et seq.

17. "Freedom of the press is a right belonging, like all rights in a democracy, to all the people. As a practical matter, however, it can be exercised only by those who have effective access to the press. Where the financial, economic, and technological conditions limit such access to a small minority, the exercise of that right by that minority takes on fiduciary or quasi-fiduciary characteristics." A. MacLeish in W. Hocking, *Freedom of the Press,* 99 n. 4 (1947).

is argued that the "uninhibited, robust" debate is not "wide-open" but open only to a monopoly in control of the press. Appellee cites the plurality opinion in Rosenbloom v. Metromedia, Inc., 403 U.S. 29, 47 & n. 15 (1971), which he suggests seemed to invite experimentation by the States in right to access regulation of the press.

Access advocates note that Justice Douglas a decade ago expressed his deep concern regarding the effects of newspaper monopolies:

> Where one paper has a monopoly in an area, it seldom presents two sides of an issue. It too often hammers away on one ideological or political line using its monopoly position not to educate people, not to promote debate, but to inculcate its readers with one philosophy, one attitude—and to make money. * * * The newspapers that give a variety of views and news that is not slanted or contrived are few indeed. And the problem promises to get worse. * * * *The Great Right* (Ed. by E. Cahn) 124–125, 127 (1963).

They also claim the qualified support of Professor Thomas I. Emerson, who has written that "[a] limited right of access to the press can be safely enforced," although he believes that "[g]overnment measures to encourage a multiplicity of outlets, rather than compelling a few outlets to represent everybody, seems a preferable course of action." T. Emerson, The System of Freedom of Expression 671 (1970).

However much validity may be found in these arguments, at each point the implementation of a remedy such as an enforceable right of access necessarily calls for some mechanism, either governmental or consensual.[19] If it is governmental coercion, this at once brings about a confrontation with the express provisions of the First Amendment and the judicial gloss on that amendment developed over the years.[20]

The Court foresaw the problems relating to government enforced access as early as its decision in Associated Press v. United States, *supra.* There it carefully contrasted the private "compulsion to print" called for by the Association's By-laws with the provisions of the District Court decree against appellants which "does not compel AP or its members to permit publication of anything which their 'reason' tells them should not be published." 326 U.S., at 20 n. 18. In Branzburg v. Hayes, 408 U.S. 665, 681 (1972), we emphasized that the cases then before us "involve no intrusions upon speech and assembly, no prior restraint or restriction on what the press may publish, and no express or implied command that the press publish what it prefers to withhold." In Columbia Broadcasting System, Inc. v. Democratic Nat. Comm., 412 U.S. 94, 117 (1973), the plurality opinion noted:

> The power of a privately owned newspaper to advance its own political, social, and economic views is bounded by only two factors: first, the acceptance of a sufficient number of readers—and hence advertisers—to assure financial success; and, second, the journalistic integrity of its editors and publishers.

An attitude strongly adverse to any attempt to extend a right of access to news-

19. The National News Council, an independent and voluntary body concerned with press fairness, was created in 1973 to provide a means for neutral examination of claims of press inaccuracy. The Council was created following the publication of the Twentieth Century Fund's Task Force Report for a National News Council, A Free and Responsive Press. The Background Paper attached to the Report dealt in some detail with the British Press Council, seen by the author of the paper as having the most interest to the United States of the European press councils.

20. Because we hold that § 104.38 violates the First Amendment's guarantee of a free press we have no occasion to consider appellant's further argument that the statute is unconstitutionally vague.

papers was echoed by several Members of this Court in their separate opinions in that case. 412 U.S., at 145 (Stewart, J., concurring); 412 U.S. at 182 n. 12 (Brennan, J., dissenting). Recently, while approving a bar against employment advertising specifying "male" or "female" preference, the Court's opinion in Pittsburgh Press Co. v. Pittsburgh Comm. on Human Relations, 413 U.S. 376, 391 (1973), took pains to limit its holding within narrow bounds:

> Nor, *a fortiori,* does our decision authorize any restriction whatever, whether of content or layout, on stories or commentary originated by Pittsburgh Press, its columnists, or its contributors. On the contrary, we reaffirm unequivocally the protection afforded to editorial judgment and to the free expression of views on these and other issues, however controversial.

Dissenting in *Pittsburgh Press,* Justice Stewart joined by Justice Douglas expressed the view that no "government agency—local, state or federal—can tell a newspaper in advance what it can print and what it cannot." Id., at 400. See Associates & Aldrich Co. v. Times Mirror Co., 440 F.2d 133, 135 (9th Cir. 1971).

We see that beginning with *Associated Press,* supra, the Court has expressed sensitivity as to whether a restriction or requirement constituted the compulsion exerted by government on a newspaper to print that which it would not otherwise print. The clear implication has been that any such a compulsion to publish that which " 'reason' tells them should not be published" is unconstitutional. A responsible press is an undoubtedly desirable goal, but press responsibility is not mandated by the Constitution and like many other virtues it cannot be legislated.

Appellee's argument that the Florida statute does not amount to a restriction of appellant's right to speak because "the statute in question here has not prevented the *Miami Herald* from saying anything it wished" begs the core question. Compelling editors or publishers to publish that which " 'reason' tells them should not be published" is what is at issue in this case. The Florida statute operates as a command in the same sense as a statute or regulation forbidding appellant from publishing specified matter. Governmental restraint on publishing need not fall into familiar or traditional patterns to be subject to constitutional limitations on governmental powers. Grosjean v. American Press Co., 297 U.S. 233, 244–245 (1936). The Florida statute exacts a penalty on the basis of the content of a newspaper. The first phase of the penalty resulting from the compelled printing of a reply is exacted in terms of the cost in printing and composing time and materials and in taking up space that could be devoted to other material the newspaper may have preferred to print. It is correct, as appellee contends, that a newspaper is not subject to the finite technological limitations of time that confront a broadcaster but it is not correct to say that, as an economic reality, a newspaper can proceed to infinite expansion of its column space to accommodate the replies that a government agency determines or a statute commands the readers should have available.[22]

22. "However, since the amount of a space a newspaper can devote to 'live news' is finite,[39] if a newspaper is forced to publish a particular item, it must as a practical matter, omit something else.

39. "The number of column inches available for news is predetermined by a number of financial and physical factors, including circulation, the amount of advertising, and, increasingly, the availability of newsprint. * * *"

Note, 48 Tulane L.Rev.433, 438 (1974) [footnote omitted].

Another factor operating against the "solution" of adding more pages to accommodate the access matter is that "increasingly subscribers complain of bulky, unwieldly papers." Bagdikian, Fat Newspapers and Slim Coverage, Columbia Journalism Review, Sept./Oct., 1973, at 19.

Faced with the penalties that would accrue to any newspaper that published news or commentary arguably within the reach of the right of access statute, editors might well conclude that the safe course is to avoid controversy and that, under the operation of the Florida statute, political and electoral coverage would be blunted or reduced.[23] Government enforced right of access inescapably "dampens the vigor and limits the variety of public debate," New York Times Co. v. Sullivan, *supra,* 376 U.S., at 279. The Court, in Mills v. Alabama, 384 U.S. 214, 218 (1966), stated that

> there is practically universal agreement that a major purpose of [the First] Amendment was to protect the free discussion of governmental affairs. This of course includes discussion of candidates. * * *

Even if a newspaper would face no additional costs to comply with a compulsory access law and would not be forced to forego publication of news or opinion by the inclusion of a reply, the Florida statute fails to clear the barriers of the First Amendment because of its intrusion into the function of editors. A newspaper is more than a passive receptacle or conduit for news, comment, and advertising.[24] The choice of material to go into a newspaper, and the decisions made as to limitations on the size of the paper, and content, and treatment of public issues and public officials—whether fair or unfair—constitutes the exercise of editorial control and judgment. It has yet to be demonstrated how governmental regulation of this crucial process can be exercised consistent with First Amendment guarantees of a free press as they have evolved to this time. Accordingly, the judgment of the Supreme Court of Florida is reversed.

It is so ordered.

Justice WHITE, concurring.

The Court today holds that the First Amendment bars a State from requiring a newspaper to print the reply of a candidate for public office whose personal character has been criticized by that newspaper's editorials. According to our accepted jurisprudence, the First Amendment erects a virtually insurmountable barrier between government and the print media so far as government tampering, in advance of publication, with news and editorial content is concerned. New York Times Co. v. United States, 403 U.S. 713 (1971). A newspaper or magazine is not a public utility subject to "reasonable" governmental regulation in matters affecting the exercise of journalistic judgment as to what shall be printed. Cf. Mills v. Alabama, 384 U.S. 214, 220 (1966). We have learned, and continue to learn, from what we view as the unhappy experiences of other nations where government has been allowed to meddle in the internal editorial affairs of newspapers. Regardless of how beneficent-sounding the purposes of controlling the press might be, we prefer "the power of reason as applied through public discussion" and remain intensely skeptical about those measures that would allow government to insinuate itself into the editorial rooms of this Nation's press.

* * *

Of course, the press is not always accurate, or even responsible, and may not

23. See the description of the likely effect of the Florida statute on publishers, in Lange, 52 N.C.L.Rev., at 70–71.

24. "[L]iberty of the press is in peril as soon as the government tries to compel what is to go into a newspaper. A journal does not merely print observed facts the way a cow is photographed through a plate glass window. As soon as the facts are set in their context, you have interpretation and you have selection, and editorial selection opens the way to editorial suppression. Then how can the state force abstention from discrimination in the news without dictating selection?" 2 Z. Chafee, Jr., Government and Mass Communications 633 (1947).

present full and fair debate on important public issues. But the balance struck by the First Amendment with respect to the press is that society must take the risk that occasionally debate on vital matters will not be comprehensive and that all viewpoints may not be expressed. The press would be unlicensed because, in Jefferson's words, "[w]here the press is free, and every man able to read, all is safe."[2] Any other accommodation—any other system that would supplant private control of the press with the heavy hand of government intrusion—would make the government the censor of what the people may read and know.

To justify this statute, Florida advances a concededly important interest of ensuring free and fair elections by means of an electorate informed about the issues. But prior compulsion by government in matters going to the very nerve center of a newspaper—the decision as to what copy will or will not be included in any given edition—collides with the First Amendment. Woven into the fabric of the First Amendment is the unexceptionable, but nonetheless timeless, sentiment that "liberty of the press is in peril as soon as the government tries to compel what is to go into a newspaper." 2 Z. Chafee, Jr., Government and Mass Communications 633 (1947).

The constitutionally obnoxious feature of § 104.38 is not that the Florida legislature may also have placed a high premium on the protection of individual reputational interests; for, government, certainly has "a pervasive and strong interest in preventing and redressing attacks upon reputation." Rosenblatt v. Baer, 383 U.S. 75, 86 (1966). Quite the contrary, this law runs afoul of the elementary First Amendment proposition that government may not force a newspaper to print copy which, in its journalistic discretion, it chooses to leave on the newsroom floor. Whatever power may reside in government to influence the publishing of certain narrowly circumscribed categories of material, see e.g., Pittsburgh Press Co. v. Pittsburgh Comm. on Human Relations, 413 U.S. 376 (1973); New York Times Co. v. United States, *supra,* at 730 (concurring opinion), we have never thought that the First Amendment permitted public officials to dictate to the press the contents of its news columns or the slant of its editorials.

But though a newspaper may publish without government censorship, it has never been entirely free from liability for what it chooses to print. See New York Times Co. v. United States, *supra,* at 730 (concurring opinion). Among other things, the press has not been wholly at liberty to publish falsehoods damaging to individual reputation. At least until today, we have cherished the average citizen's reputation interest enough to afford him a fair chance to vindicate himself in an action for libel characteristically provided by state law. He has been unable to force the press to tell his side of the story or to print a retraction, but he has had at least the opportunity to win a judgment if he can prove the falsity of the damaging publication, as well as a fair chance to recover reasonable damages for his injury.

Reaffirming the rule that the press cannot be forced to print an answer to a personal attack made by it, however, throws into stark relief the consequences of the new balance forged by the Court in the companion case also announced today. Gertz v. Robert Welch, Inc., ante, goes far towards eviscerating the effectiveness of the ordinary libel action, which has long been the only potent response available to the private citizen libeled by the press. Under *Gertz,* the burden of proving liability is immeasurably increased, proving damages is made exceedingly more difficult, and vindicating repu-

2. Letter to Col. Charles Yancey, in XIV The Writings of Thomas Jefferson 384 (Lipscomb ed. 1904).

tation by merely proving falsehood and winning a judgment to that effect are wholly foreclosed. Needlessly, in my view, the Court trivializes and denigrates the interest in reputation by removing virtually all the protection the law has always afforded.

Of course, these two decisions do not mean that because government may not dictate what the press is to print, neither can it afford a remedy for libel in any form. *Gertz* itself leaves a putative remedy for libel intact, albeit in severely emaciated form; and the press certainly remains liable for knowing or reckless falsehoods under *New York Times* and its progeny, however improper an injunction against publication might be.

One need not think less of the First Amendment to sustain reasonable methods for allowing the average citizen to redeem a falsely tarnished reputation. Nor does one have to doubt the genuine decency, integrity and good sense of the vast majority of professional journalists to support the right of any individual to have his day in court when he has been falsely maligned in the public press. The press is the servant, not the master, of the citizenry, and its freedom does not carry with it an unrestricted hunting license to prey on the ordinary citizen.

> In plain English, freedom carries with it responsibility even for the press; freedom of the press is not a freedom from responsibility for its exercise. * * *
>
> * * * Without * * * a lively sense of responsibility a free press may readily become a powerful instrument of injustice. Pennekamp v. Florida, 328 U.S. 331, 356, 365 (1946) (Frankfurter, J., concurring).

To me it is a near absurdity to so deprecate individual dignity, as the Court does in *Gertz,* and to leave the people at the complete mercy of the press, at least in this stage of our history when the press, as the majority in this case so well documents, is steadily becoming more powerful and much less likely to be deterred by threats of libel suits.

Justice BRENNAN, with whom Justice Rehnquist joins, concurring.

I join the Court's opinion which, as I understand it, addresses only "right of reply" statutes and implies no view upon the constitutionality of "retraction" statutes affording plaintiffs able to prove defamatory falsehoods a statutory action to require publication of a retraction. See generally Note, Vindication of the Reputation of a Public Official, 80 Harv.L.Rev. 1730, 1739–1747 (1967).

COMMENT

1. In the context of the public law of libel in *Rosenbloom v. Metromedia,* text, p. 221, Justice Brennan had expressed sympathy for the enactment of right to reply legislation. Yet he had joined in the opinion for the Court in *Tornillo.* Furthermore, in *Gertz v. Welch,* text, p. 236, decided the same day as *Tornillo,* Brennan dissented from the court's rejection of the *Rosenbloom* "public issue" approach to the public law of libel. If the *Gertz* Court was concerned that the "public issue" standard would make it too difficult for a libel plaintiff to vindicate his reputation by securing a judgment that the publication was false, Justice Brennan had just the remedy: "the possible enactment of statutes, not requiring proof of fault, which provide for an action for retraction or for publication of a court's determination of falsity if the plaintiff is able to demonstrate that false statements have been published concerning his activities."

But after the *Tornillo* decision, can a newspaper be compelled to publish a retraction against its will? Suppose a statute required a paper to publish the fact that a libel plaintiff had been vindicated in a suit against the paper in that the offending publication had been adjudicated as false? Wouldn't the newspaper challenge the statute and rely on the *Tornillo* case for the proposition that the "choice of material to go into the newspaper" is an editorial and not a legislative decision. Note that in *Tornillo,* Justice Brennan wrote a special concurrence to point out that the question of the constitutional validity of retraction statutes is not addressed by the decision of the Court in *Tornillo.* From a First Amendment point of view, how can the retraction statute be distinguished from the right of reply statute? Is it relevant that in the retraction situation the content of the retraction is composed by the newspaper, while in the reply situation it is the person attacked who dictates the contents of the reply?

2. Would a carefully drafted and limited state statute which provided a right of reply as a remedy for a proven defamatory falsehood be constitutional? Some advocates of the latter type of statute have not favored the more general right of reply statute considered in *Tornillo.* Thus, Justice Brennan appeared to endorse right of reply statutes in a libel context but not generally, as his concurrences in *Rosenbloom* and *Tornillo* illustrate. First Amendment scholar, Thomas I. Emerson, appears to take a similar position. In the *Tornillo* case, counsel for both Pat Tornillo and for the *Miami Herald* quoted Professor Emerson in their briefs to the United States Supreme Court as authority for their respective positions. Thus, counsel for the *Miami Herald* quoted Professor Emerson as follows:

> [A]ny effort to solve the broadest problems of a monopoly press by forcing newspaper to cover all "newsworthy" events and print all viewpoints, under the watchful eyes of petty officials, is likely to undermine such independence as the press now shows without achieving any real diversity. See brief for appellant, *Miami Herald Pub. Co. v. Tornillo,* Supreme Court of the United States, No. 73–797, p. 13 quoting Emerson, *The System of Free Expression* 671 (1970).

In the same treatise, Professor Emerson wrote that a right of reply "would strengthen and vitalize" freedom of expression:

> It is sufficient to note that a right of reply could be made available in most situations in which an individual claims that false assertions (and other forms of attack on him) have been made. It is particularly applicable in the case of the press, where abandonment of the libel action would be felt the most. Such a procedure is the most appropriate and probably the most effective way to deal with the problem. The person attacked would have an opportunity to get his position and his evidence quickly before the public. He would have a forum in which to continue the dialogue, rather than being forced to withdraw to the artificial arena of the courtroom. The discussion would thus be kept going in the marketplace, and the issues left up to the public, which must make the final decision anyway.

Furthermore, Professor Emerson assumes that the appropriate procedure for "allowing a right of reply would probably have to be established by legislation rather than judicial decision." Id. at 539.

Counsel for the appellee, Pat Tornillo, quoted from the above passage in their brief. See Brief for appellee, *Miami Herald Publishing Co. v. Tornillo,* No. 73–797, October Term, p. 11.

3. The *Tornillo* decision has been criticized for setting forth the access arguments but not really answering them. One commentator, in an influential work on access, suggested what might have proved to be a more reasoned and discriminating approach to the problem of access. See Schmidt, *Freedom of the Press v. Public Access* (1976).

Professor Schmidt said the access problem arises out of a conflict between a First Amendment historical tradition of editorial autonomy and an interpretation of the First Amendment which conceives as its function achievement of "the utilitarian goal of diversity of expression." Schmidt thought resolution of the access problem should involve reconciliation of the "values of autonomy and diversity."

How would such a resolution proceed? Professor Schmidt outlines the following mode of analysis:

> The aim of analysis would be to determine which "publishers" should be protected from access so that the values of autonomy can be best preserved. And, conversely, analysis would have to determine which other "publishers" should be made accessible to serve the goals of diversity. Rights of access would have to be allocated to particular publishing units in such a way that the aim of diversity would be served to the maximum, but jeopardy to the values of autonomy would be kept to a minimum. See Schmidt, *supra*, p. 36.

For a more appreciative response to the *Tornillo* case, see Abrams, *In Defense of Tornillo,* 86 Yale L.J. 361 (1976). For a more critical commentary, see *The Supreme Court, 1973 Term,* 88 Harv.L.Rev. 174, 177 (1974).

4. For some, the declaration in *Tornillo* that mandating the press to print something is the same thing as mandating that the press not print something remains unconvincing: "Viewed from the vantage of the public, a 'right of reply' gives John Citizen two sides of a question while suppression or prohibitions give him none." See Lewin, *What's Happening to Free Speech?* The New Republic, July 27, 1974, p. 13.

5. From a legal point of view, the most remarkable aspect of the *Tornillo* decision is that it is innocent of any reference to the *Red Lion* decision. Is this a defensible omission? Perhaps the Court was reluctant to have to say that editorial decision-making was less protected in the electronic media than in the print media, and yet, at the same time, it was unwilling to alter the *Red Lion* decision.

6. On the whole, the reaction by the courts to the access concept has been unsympathetic. The Supreme Court invalidated the FCC's mandatory public access rules for cable. See FCC v. Midwest Video, 440 U.S. 689 (1979), text, p. 991. (It should be noted that the Court decided *Midwest Video* on statutory grounds and specifically refused to comment on the suggestion of the court that the FCC's public access rules "might violate the First Amendment rights of cable operators a-la-Tornillo.") Nevertheless, the *Midwest Video* case was a defeat for access in the cable field. On the other hand, *Warner-Lambert v. FTC,* text, p. 625, where the federal court of appeals approved an FTC mandatory corrective advertising order, illustrates that compelling expression by advertisers is permissible even though, under the *Tornillo* decision, compelling publication by publishers is not.

In Barron *Public Rights and the Private Press* (1981), the status of the access concept eight years after *Tornillo* is described. A major thesis of the book is that the *Tornillo* case did not foreclose access for advertising as distinguished from access for editorial replies. Warner-Lambert Co. v. FTC, 562 F.2d 749 (D.C. Cir. 1977), certiorari denied 435 U.S. 950 (1978), is relied on for this position: "If corrective information by advertisers is imperative for the protection of commercial consumers, such corrective information may be equally necessary in politics for political consumers, the voters. See, Barron, supra, p. 109. Professor Barton Carter, in a review of the book, 50 Geo.Wash.L.Rev. 501 at 507 (1982), observed that the Supreme Court is not likely to be persuaded by this argument:

> Although it has accorded commercial speech some first amendment protection, the Court is far from equating commercial and political speech for the purpose of first amendment analysis. The Court views commercial speech as hardier and thus less likely to be inhibited by governmental restrictions. The fact that a limitation on commercial

speech is held constitutional is far from a guarantee that the same limitation on political speech will be upheld.

7. In Chatzky and Robinson, *A Constitutional Right of Access to Newspapers: Is There Life After Tornillo?,* 16 Santa Clara L.Rev. 453 at 491 (1976), the suggestion is made that a narrowly circumscribed right of access to the press statute might be permissible even after *Tornillo:*

> Congress may well conclude that the "scarcity of frequencies" consideration which prompted enactment of the Radio Act and the Communications Act are paralleled in the modern newspaper industry. Where the Newspaper Preservation Act has "licensed" the merger of publishing resources by exempting certain newspapers from federal antitrust laws, Congress may decide that at least these "licensees" should conform to some standard of public trusteeship. See generally, text, p. 647ff.

8. An important illustration that the access concept was not dead was evidenced by CBS v. FCC, 453 U.S. 367 (1981), text, p. 815. In that case, Chief Justice Burger made some very significant remarks with respect to the impact of *Tornillo* on the future of the access concept. Burger read *Tornillo* as constituting a disapproval of a general right of access to the media. However, the following observations of the Chief Justice for the Court in *CBS v. FCC* appear to imply that the limited rights of access are not foreclosed by *Tornillo:*

> Petitioners are correct that the Court has never approved a *general* right of access to the media. See, e.g., FCC v. Midwest Video Corp., 440 U.S. 689 (1979); Miami Herald Publishing Co. v. Tornillo, 418 U.S. 241, (1974); CBS, Inc. v. Democratic National Committee, *supra.* Nor do we do so today. Section 312(a)(7) created a *limited* right to "reasonable" access that pertains only to legally qualified federal candidates and may be invoked by them only for the purpose of advancing their candidacies once a campaign has commenced.

9. In a recent comment, the decision in *CBS v. FCC* is interpreted to provide a basis for the enactment of a statutory right of access to the newspaper press despite the *Tornillo* precedent. See, Shelledy, Note, *Access to the Press: A Teleological Analysis of a Constitutional Double Standard,* 50 Geo.Wash.L.Rev. 430 at 458–459 (1982):

> The right of reply statute in *Tornillo* established a contingent right, limited to expression in response to an editorial attack on a candidate's character or official record. The right created by section 312(a)(7) is broader in its affirmative character: programmers cannot avoid causing the right of access to arise by refraining from editorializing on political candidates.
>
> This distinction demonstrates that an affirmative right of access to the printed press can withstand a first amendment challenge stemming from *Tornillo.* The chilling effect that the Court found offensive in *Tornillo* is not present with an affirmative right of access to newspapers. An affirmative right is unlikely to blunt or reduce political and electoral coverage, as the *Tornillo* court feared the Florida right of reply might. Indeed, it is even less likely than section 312(a)(7) to impair editorial discretion since a newspaper can more easily expand its format to accommodate those seeking access while maintaining its planned coverage.

Is the difficulty with this proposed noncontingent access to the press statute that, although it may be less vulnerable to chilling effect objections, it poses an even greater danger to editorial autonomy since the degree to which parts of the paper would be subject to access obligations would be necessarily so imprecise? The George Washington Law Review Note also relies on PruneYard Shopping Center v. Robins, 447 U.S. 74 (1980), text, p. 179, as a basis for an affirmative statutory right of access to the newspaper press:

PruneYard lends logical and perhaps precedential support to applying a right of access to the print media. Even if publishers have a property right to exclude others' views from the columns of a newspaper, a reasonable restriction of that right would not violate either the taking clause or the due process clause of the fifth amendment. Like a right of access to shopping centers, reasonable access to newspapers is substantially related to the recognized state objective of expanding opportunities for expression and will not impair the value of newspapers.

A RIGHT OF ACCESS TO THE PUBLIC PRESS—THE CASE OF THE STATE-SUPPORTED CAMPUS PRESS

1. In Avins v. Rutgers, State University of New Jersey, 385 F.2d 151 (3d Cir. 1967), the plaintiff, Alfred Avins, alleged that he had submitted to the *Rutgers Law Review* an article which reviewed the legislative history of the Civil Rights Act of 1975 insofar as it was intended to affect school desegregation. The articles editor of the *Rutgers Law Review* rejected the article and stated that "approaching the problem from the point of view of legislative history alone is insufficient." Avins contended that a law review published by a state-supported university is a public instrumentality in whose columns all must be allowed to present their ideas: The editors are without discretion to reject an article because in their judgment its nature or ideological approach is not suitable for publication.

The federal district court had dismissed the suit, and the federal court of appeals affirmed. Judge Maris, for the court of appeals, rejected plaintiff's contentions:

> [O]ne who claims that his constitutional right to freedom of speech has been abridged must show that he has a right to use the particular medium through which he seeks to speak. This the plaintiff has wholly failed to do. He says that he has published articles in other law reviews and will sooner or later be able to publish in a law review the article here involved. This is doubtless true. Also, no one doubts that he may freely at his own expense print his article and distribute it to all who wish to read it. However, he does not have the right, constitutional or otherwise, to commandeer the press and columns of the *Rutgers Law Review* for the publication of his article, at the expense of the subscribers to the *Review* and the New Jersey taxpayers, to the exclusion of other articles deemed by the editors to be more suitable for publication. On the contrary, the acceptance or rejection of articles submitted for publication in a law school law review necessarily involves the exercise of editorial judgment and this is in no wise lessened by the fact that the law review is supported, at least in part by the [s]tate.

2. Suppose that there were only two or three law journals in the whole country and that the professor in the *Avins* case had filed his court complaint with letters of rejection attached to each of the journals and further that each of these journals rejected plaintiff professor's articles on ideological rather than scholarly grounds? Same result?

Should it make a difference that the journals in question were published by state rather than privately sponsored universities?

3. The struggle for access to the press has met with the most success in the high school and college press, and for a reason: the party denying access was acting pursuant to public authority, and therefore a public restraint on expression was involved. The Wisconsin State University case, which follows, nevertheless, is significant for access theory generally because it recognizes, almost without comment,

that which was formerly not recognized in American law at all: the First Amendment demands opportunity for expression. Prohibition against censorship does not, therefore, exhaust the meaning of the First Amendment; the Amendment has an affirmative dimension.

A ground-breaking case at the high school level was Zucker v. Panitz, 299 F.Supp. 102 (S.D.N.Y.1969), see text, p. 617ff, which upheld the right of high school students to publish a paid ad in their high school newspaper which opposed the war in Vietnam.

A similar case having to do with paid advertisements in college papers was decided in 1969 in a federal district court in Wisconsin. Lee v. Board of Regents of State Colleges, 306 F.Supp. 1097 (1969).

The United States Court of Appeals affirmed the lower court determination that the Board of Regents of the Wisconsin State Colleges had denied the freedom of speech of the plaintiffs who sought to publish editorial advertisements in the *Royal Purple.* Notice that the Seventh Circuit expressly avoided deciding "whether there is a constitutional right of access to the privately-owned press."

LEE v. BOARD OF REGENTS OF STATE COLLEGES

441 F.2D 1257 (7TH CIR. 1971).

FAIRCHILD, Circuit Judge.

It is conceded that the campus newspaper is a state facility. Thus the appeal does not present the question of whether there is a constitutional right of access to press under private ownership.

The substantive question is whether the defendants, having opened the campus newspaper to commercial and certain other types of advertising, could constitutionally reject plaintiffs' advertisements because of their editorial character. The case does not pose the question whether defendants could have excluded all advertising nor whether there are other conceivable limitations on advertising which could be properly imposed.

The student publications board had adopted the following policy:

> "Types of Advertising Accepted
>
> *"The Royal Purple* will accept advertising which has as its main objective the advertising of
>
> 1. A Commercial Product.
>
> 2. A Commercial Service.
>
> 3. A Meeting. The pitch of an advertisement of this type must clearly be 'come to the meeting'. The topic may be announced, but may not be the main feature of the ad.
>
> 4. A Political Candidate whose name will appear on a local ballot. Political advertising must deal solely with the platform of the advertised person. Such copy cannot attack directly opponents or incumbents. Such advertising must contain the following: This advertisement authorized and paid for by (*name of person or organization.*)
>
> 5. A Public Service. Advertising of a public service nature will be accepted if it is general in nature, in good taste, and does not attack specific groups, institutions, products, or persons.
>
> *"The Royal Purple* has the right to refuse to publish any advertisement which it may deem objectionable."

Plaintiff Riley submitted an advertisement describing the purposes of a university employees' union and announcing a meeting on safety regulations. It was rejected under the policy because part of it dealt with the business of the meeting.

Plaintiff Scharmach's advertisement was entitled "An Appeal to Conscience." It was signed by nine ministers and proclaimed the immorality of discrimination on account of color or creed.

Plaintiff Lee submitted an advertisement to be signed by himself and stating as follows:

> " 'You shall love your neighbor as yourself.' (*Matthew 19:19*)
>
> "This verse should mean something to us all who are concerned with race relations and the Vietnam War."

The rejection stated in part, "Your ad could possibly come under the public service ad, but it deals with political issues, and is therefore not a public service."

Decisions cited by the district court support the proposition that a state public body which disseminates paid advertising of a commercial type may not reject other paid advertising on the basis that it is editorial in character. Other decisions condemn other facets of discrimination in affording the use of newspaper and other means of expression on public campuses.

* * *

Defendants point out that the campus newspaper is a facility of an educational institution and itself provides an academic exercise. They suggest that the advertising policy is a reasonable means of protecting the university from embarrassment and the staff from the difficulty of exercising judgment as to material which may be obscene, libelous, or subversive. In *Tinker,* the Supreme Court, albeit in a somewhat different context, balanced the right of free expression against legitimate considerations of school administration. *Tinker* demonstrates how palpable a threat must be present to outweigh the right to expression. The Court said, in part, "But, in our system, undifferentiated fear or apprehension of disturbance is not enough to overcome the right to freedom of expression." * * *

The problems which defendants foresee fall far short of fulfilling the *Tinker* standard.

* * *

The judgment is affirmed.

COMMENT

1. The Wisconsin State University case involved state-financed print media. Does this case and others like it have any significance for the privately owned mass circulation daily newspaper?

Denial of a right of access for political advertising to public facilities has been upheld. See *Lehman v. City of Shaker Heights*, text, p. 64.

2. Some major themes of successful access to the public press cases were gathered together in a case brought by the Radical Lawyers Caucus, an association whose members were also members of the Texas State Bar. The Radical Lawyers Caucus asked the *Texas Bar Journal* to accept an advertisement publicizing a caucus to be held during the annual bar convention. The *Bar Journal* contended that the *Journal* was an instrumentality of the state of Texas and therefore could not take political advertising. Ironically, that argument was the *Texas Bar Journal's* undoing.

In Radical Lawyers Caucus v. Pool, 324 F.Supp. 268 (W.D.Tex.1970), the federal district court held that since the official journal of the Texas state bar association, an agency of the state, had accepted commercial ads and published editorials and passed resolutions on political subjects, the journal could not decline to publish the advertisement submitted by an association of radical lawyers. Such a denial, the court ruled, constituted a denial of free speech and violated equal protection of the laws.

Suppose the *Texas Bar Journal* had not been a state instrumentality but a privately operated journal of a group of lawyers whose organization received no state support? Same result?

The *Radical Lawyers Caucus* case is one of the rare access-to-print-media cases which deals with a magazine. Suppose the Radical Lawyers Caucus had sought to place the same advertisement in magazines such as *Newsweek* or the *National Review?* Were there special circumstances, beside the fact that the bar journal was a state agency, which made access to the *Texas Bar Journal* for the Radical Lawyers Caucus imperative?

The *Mississippi Gay Alliance* Case—Access to the Public Press After *Tornillo*

The foregoing cases dealing with access to the tax-supported, state university campus press or with some form of public press involve the only area where a right of access has been recognized. What is the status of cases like *Zucker* and *Lee v. Board of Regents* in light of the Supreme Court decision in *Miami Herald Publishing Co. v. Tornillo?* A case arising after *Tornillo* and raising this issue is Mississippi Gay Alliance v. Goudelock, 536 F.2d 1073 (5th Cir. 1976). The controversy occurred when the chairwoman of the Mississippi Gay Alliance (MGA) submitted an ad to *The Reflector,* the student newspaper at Mississippi State University (MSU). The contents of the ad were as follows:

> Gay Center—open 6:00 to 9:00 Monday, Wednesday and Friday nights.
>
> We offer—counselling, *Legal aid,* and a library of homosexual literature.
>
> Write to—The Mississippi Gay Alliance, P.O. Box 1328, Mississippi State University, Ms. 39762.

The editor of *The Reflector* refused to publish the ad even though it was a paid advertisement. MGA, alleging a First Amendment violation, then brought suit to compel the editor to publish the ad. The federal district court refused to order publication. The federal court of appeals affirmed and distinguished cases like *Lee v. Board of Regents* and *Zucker* by contending that in the *MGA* case there was no state action since university officials did not control publishing decisions. A student editor rather than a state university official had declined to publish the ad.

The court of appeals speculated that if a state university official had ordered the newspaper not to publish such an order it would still have been constitutionally impermissible. The reason for this conclusion, however, did not derive from the premise of *Lee v. Board of Regents* and *Zucker* that a state-sponsored press could not favor one idea and disfavor another. This conclusion derived instead from an idea purportedly set forth in *Miami Herald Publishing Co. v. Tornillo* —the inviolability of editorial autonomy. Courts could not review editorial decision making undertaken under either private or public auspices. Protection of editorial autonomy, however, was only one component of the rationale of the decision in *MGA.* Since state law made sodomy a crime, the student editor was obliged not to publish an ad which had a connection, albeit peripheral, with such activity. Or as the court put it gingerly: "[S]pecial reasons were present for holding that there was no abuse of discretion by the editor of *The Reflector.*"

In a long and thoughtful dissent, Judge Goldberg denied that a state-sponsored newspaper could, for example, refuse to print a statement on the ground that "it expressed a political view contrary to that of the Governor." Judge Goldberg hypostatized the following example:

> [W]e might posit a newspaper paid for and published by the state—call it the "Open Forum"—in which all citizens are invited to express their views on any issue subject only to reasonable space limitations and a small fee to help offset printing costs. Could the "Open Forum" refuse to print a tendered statement on the ground that it expressed a political view contrary to that of the Governor, or on no state ground at all? Surely not. Conceivably, the state could place many non-content oriented restrictions on the form of the messages, but the state could not refuse tendered statements otherwise similar in form to those regu-

larly accepted solely because the proffered ads were disagreeable in content.

Furthermore, Goldberg thought the principle of equal access to state student publications received implicit support from *CBS v. Democratic National Commission,* text, p. 858:

> The Supreme Court has never passed on a claim of equal access to a state publication. The suggestion that the Court would recognize the rights found in Lee, Zucker, and Radical Lawyers is not undermined by, and indeed receives implicit support from Columbia Broadcasting System v. Democratic National Commission. * * *

Judge Goldberg reasoned that since a "state" newspaper could not publish ads on one side of a public issue and reject ads taking the opposite point of view, it should also be assumed that it would be unconstitutional for a state newspaper to take advertisements dealing with public issues generally but arbitrarily and selectively to exclude advertisements on certain public issues.

If *The Reflector* were "clearly a paper run by and for the state" and MGA's allegations that the "paper regularly accepted paid and unpaid messages and announcements from local groups" were true, then the conclusion followed that the "state would have denied the MGA equal access to a public forum." Judge Goldberg then stated:

> If *The Reflector* were purely a private newspaper, there presumably would exist no such right of access. * * * See *Miami Herald Publishing Co. v. Tornillo* * * * Clearly, then a federal court would have no power, under statutes requiring "state action," to prohibit a non-state newspaper from exercising selective content discrimination in its publication of advertisements.

The issue then became whether *"The Reflector* can be characterized as the state." The issue had been different in *Lee* and *Zucker* since in those cases it had been clear that "officials, not students, exercised ultimate responsibility for the censorship decision." In *MGA,* university officials argued that they could not reverse "specific editorial decisions of the student editor" and, therefore, that "the 'state action' required to trigger the public forum doctrine was lacking." Judge Goldberg contended, however, that the absence of "affirmative involvement by university officials" did not end the state action inquiry:

> The stipulation included the fact that funds supporting *The Reflector* were derived from a non-waivable student fee charged to students at MSU.
>
> *The Reflector's* funding is thus derived from what is in effect a tax charged by the state to the students. The allegations suggest that the imprimatur of the state is clearly stamped on the paper. In these circumstances, I have little doubt that this court would review a decision by the students to exclude blacks from participation on the newspaper staff as a decision imbued with state action. To my mind, the pure "state action" question should be the same in the First Amendment context.

Then Judge Goldberg turned to what he considered "the most significant question in this case: does the Constitution permit student editors at a state university to pursue a general policy of accepting from local groups advertisements dealing with matters of public interest, but at the same time to exclude, because of its content, a certain advertisement proffered by a similarly situated group?"

The trial judge in *MGA* had concluded "that the student editor of *The Reflector* was protected in his decision to reject the MGA advertisement by the same protections which, in *Tornillo,* shielded the *Miami Herald's* decision not to run a reply to its editorial." Relying on Bazaar v. Fortune, 476 F.2d 570 (5th Cir. 1973), affirmed as modified, 489 F.2d 225, (en banc) (5th Cir. 1974) and Joyner v. Whiting, 477 F.2d

456 (4th Cir. 1973), Judge Goldberg reached the following conclusions:

> [S]tate school officials, having provided a forum for free expression by students, cannot censor the content of the messages that the students seek to disseminate. That rule, on its face, would not be inconsistent with a requirement that the columns of the state-sponsored paper be open to anyone with anything to say.

For Goldberg, student editorial autonomy, a student right to edit even a state-sponsored press had to be recognized. At the same time the principle of nondiscriminatory access to state publications also had to be recognized. Judge Goldberg suggested the following accommodation between the two competing interests involved:

> In my opinion, however, a requirement of wide-open access to the pages of a student newspaper would sweep much too broadly. To the extent that the right of student editors to free expression is to be protected, that right must include the right to edit. * * *
>
> I fully support the result in the *Rutgers* case and the implication it bears for a general right to edit on the part of student editors of state-supported publications. * * *
>
> I think that the two interests discussed above can be accommodated through a doctrine which permits student editors of state newspapers unfettered discretion over what might be termed the "editorial product" of the newspaper, yet requires that when the newspaper devotes space to unedited advertisements or announcements from individuals outside the newspaper staff, access to such space must be made available to other similarly situated individuals on a nondiscriminatory basis.
>
> As to the sections of the newspaper which would be subject to the requirement of nondiscriminatory access, I take the two sections of *The Reflector* at issue in this suit to be paradigmatic. According to the allegations of the MGA, the sections of *The Reflector* to which access was sought were regularly available to local organizations for announcements and messages of social, political and informative natures. * * *
>
> I want to emphasize that the right of equal access I would invoke could for the purposes of this case, be carefully circumscribed. For example, the newspaper could perhaps provide access only to students or other members of the university community and not be guilty of content discrimination. * * *
>
> Conceivably, other limitations on the envisioned right of equal access could arise in response to logistics and costs. A state newspaper which had provided a public forum for the publication of any message from anyone could in one week receive thousands of proposed messages on the same subject. * * * If the "public forum" is to remain that, some content neutral means of selection would become necessary—e.g., requiring payment of a reasonable fee, printing the first however many submissions, or selecting statements at random. Again, we need not reach these questions to decide this case. There is no indication that any other advertisements, or announcements in the "briefs" section had ever been refused by the newspaper, or that any other consideration of space limitations was relevant in the decision to exclude the MGA ad.
>
> I mention these possible limitations on the right of equal access to a state student newspaper to illustrate how narrowly a decision in the instant case could be written and how careful a court should be in delineating the scope of such a right.
>
> * * * I would hold that there exists in some situations a right to nondiscriminatory access to the advertising and announcement sections of state-supported newspapers. * * *
>
> One reason for extreme caution in suggesting the sort of rules I have envisioned in my dissent is the danger that the state may provide "nondiscriminatory access" by providing no access, at least through the student newspapers under consideration here. * * * I am not so cynical as to suppose that state

> school officials and student editors of state school publications would uniformly choose to permit no outside views to be expressed in their publications rather than to permit, in a designated section of the publication, a free and open discussion of public issues.
>
> * * *
>
> The key to the reconciliation here is an emphasis in each situation of the powerful interests of speakers and listeners in free expression. In each context—officials attempting to censor students, and students attempting selectively to censor certain messages from the public on the basis of content—the court must balance the competing interest, but always with its thumb on the side of full and open discussion of public issues.

COMMENT

1. The "open" parts of the newspaper—the announcements, the briefs and unedited advertising sections—were not involved in *Tornillo.* Is it correct to conclude that *Tornillo's* recognition of a "right to edit" is not appropriate in these sections of a state-sponsored press? Others beside Judge Goldberg have made the same distinction between the propriety of a claim for access to the advertising section but not to the news and editorial columns of a public press. See Canby, *The First Amendment and the State as Editor: Implications for Public Broadcasting,* 52 Tex.L.Rev. 1123 at 1133–1134 (1974). A difficulty with Judge Goldberg's distinction between the "news and editorial columns" and advertising columns, for example, is that the distinction is not as precise as it should be if it is to be workable. Where would a tendered reply to an "editorial advertisement" fit in Judge Goldberg's scheme if the paper involved didn't wish to publish the reply?

2. The Supreme Court denied review in the *MGA* case. See Mississippi Gay Alliance v. Goudelock, 430 U.S. 982 (1977). As a result, the question of the Supreme Court's reaction to claims for a right of access to the advertising columns of the state-supported press remains an open one. What is the impact of *Tornillo* on the pre-existing cases recognizing a right of access to the public student press? It would appear that these cases are still intact and are unaffected by the *Tornillo* decision. In other words, in *Zucker, Lee,* and *Radical Lawyers Caucus,* state action was present, and, therefore, unlike the *Miami Herald* in *Tornillo,* the papers in the state publication cases were bound by the constitutional principle of equal access. The *MGA* case can be distinguished from these earlier public press cases because state action was not present as it was in the *Lee* case because in *MGA* a student editor and not a university official had rejected the tendered ad.

3. Whether or not the opinion for the court in *MGA* can be distinguished from the older access to the state campus press cases, the philosophy of the court in *MGA* clearly reflects the impact of the *Tornillo* decision. The implicit theme of the *MGA* decision—even though the court of appeals is careful to say that state action is not present—is that when an editor's decision not to publish comes into a conflict with a claim for entry from outside the publication, the claims of unfettered editorial decision making have First Amendment primacy even in a public or state-supported press. The case, in fact, suggests a final question: if editorial decision making is to be considered judicially unreviewable, isn't the presence or absence of state action irrelevant?

4. Besides *MGA,* a print media case, a significant case, *Muir v. AETC,* text, p. 1022ff, involving a public broadcasting station, has also taken the position that publicly owned media do and should engage in editorial decision making. Such editorial decision making is not impermissible censorship. In *Muir,* Judge Hill, speaking for the court, said, citing *Avins v. Rutgers University,* text, p. 596, "* * * the First

Amendment does not preclude the government from exercising editorial control over its own medium of expression."

5. In discussing *Mississippi Gay Alliance,* Professor Nadel has emphasized the special facts of the case: "In upholding the refusal of the paper to print the Gay Alliance advertisement, however, the court may well have treated the restriction as a valid restriction of scope (or 'type') prohibiting advertisements of *illegal* activities." See Nadel, *A Unified Theory of the First Amendment: Divorcing The Medium From The Message,* 11 Fordham Urban Law Journal 163 at 203 (1983).

The implication in the above, perhaps, is that because of its facts, no large First Amendment generalization should be drawn from the *MGA* case. Nadel observed with respect to the publicly supported campus press: "It appears that courts can require editors to abide by the same standards of reasonable conduct (i.e., 'fairness doctrine') that presently govern the conduct of librarians and other school officials."

Further, he suggested, relying on Professor Karst's, *Equality As A Central Principle in the First Amendment,* 43 U. of Chicago L.Rev. 20, 43–52 (1975), that " 'fair' access could be provided to all by forbidding the editor from excluding viewpoints in violation of the equal protection clause."

Selected Problems of Law and Journalism

THE LAW AND REGULATION OF ADVERTISING

Advertising and the First Amendment

1. Second-class status for commercial advertising under the First Amendment may have been given its first and firmest designation by a single sentence in a 1941 Judge Jerome Frank dissent. "Such men as Thomas Paine, John Milton and Thomas Jefferson," he said, "were not fighting for the right to peddle commercial advertising." [1]

That sentiment, to be affirmed in what has been called a "casual, almost offhand" [2] ruling when the case reached the United States Supreme Court, gave birth to the *commercial speech doctrine:* speech touting goods and services is less deserving of constitutional protection than speech promoting other ideas, especially those having political connotation. Valentine v. Chrestensen, 316 U.S. 52 (1942).

Dissenting in a case in which the Court had upheld an ordinance banning door-to-door solicitation of magazine subscriptions, Justice Black said that, while it protected the press, the First Amendment did not apply to a "merchant" who goes from door-to-door "selling" pots.[3] And the Court in *Pittsburgh Press,*[4] a case marking the zenith of the commercial speech doctrine, upheld a city ordinance prohibiting sex-designated columns in help-wanted classifieds. In *Hood v. Dun and Bradstreet*[5] the Fifth Circuit Court of Appeals said flatly that commercial reports lack the "general public interest" necessary for First Amendment protection. No protec-

1. Valentine v. Chrestensen, 122 F.2d 511 (2d Cir. 1941). Edited reports of *Valentine* and later commercial speech cases appear in Chapter I, text, p. 157ff, where the "commercial speech" doctrine is presented in a chapter which attempts to provide an overview of First Amendment theory.

2. The language is Justice Douglas's concurring in Cammarano v. United States, 358 U.S. 498, 514 (1959).

3. Breard v. City of Alexandria, 341 U.S. 622, 650 (1951).

4. Pittsburgh Press v. Pittsburgh Commission on Human Relations, 1 Med.L.Rptr. 1908, 413 U.S. 376 (1973). See Publication Guidelines for Compliance with Title VIII of the Civil Rights Act of 1968, 37 Fed.Reg. 6700 (April 1, 1972). Now part of federal regulations, 45 Fed.Reg. 57102 (1980). Federal law governs real estate advertising. State and local laws sometimes prohibit discriminatory help-wanted ads. Federal laws do not.

5. 486 F.2d 25 (5th Cir. 1973). See also Deltec, Inc. v. Dun and Bradstreet, Inc., 187 F.Supp. 788 (D.Ohio 1960); Securities and Exchange Commission v. Wall St. Transcript, Corp., 422 F.2d 1371 (2d Cir. 1970); and Kansas Electric Supply Co. v. Dun and Bradstreet, Inc., 448 F.2d 647 (10th Cir. 1971), all supporting the proposition that commercial newspapers providing specialized information to selective audiences do not have full First Amendment protection.

tion, of course, extends to false advertising.[6] A city transportation official was able to deny advertising space in public vehicles to candidates for public office.[7] Ads for newspaper subscriptions may not be protected.[8]

In Bigelow v. Virginia, 1 Med.L.Rptr. 1919, 421 U.S. 809 (1975), the commercial speech doctrine began to totter. The Court overturned, on First Amendment grounds, conviction of an editor for running an ad for a New York abortion referral agency at a time when abortions were illegal in Virginia. Virginians have a First Amendment right to receive information, a right to hear, declared Justice Blackmun for the Court. The state had not demonstrated any countervailing interest in prohibiting the ad. Speech, said Blackmun, is not to be stripped of First Amendment protection merely because it appears in commercial form. *Pittsburgh Press* was distinguished: there a particular form of advertising had been made illegal by a city ordinance; the New York abortion service was not illegal in New York at the time of the ad—although it was made so shortly thereafter. The Court may have been influenced by the fact that Bigelow was an editor first, an advertiser second.

While *Bigelow* was pending, the landmark abortion case, *Roe v. Wade,*[9] was decided, Justice Blackmun delivering the opinion of the Court.

It was again Blackmun speaking for the Court when in 1976 the commercial speech doctrine came to near collapse in a case involving the direct price advertising of prescription drugs. On the authority of that case, the New York City ordinance upheld by the Court in *Valentine v. Chrestensen* thirty-five years earlier was to be declared unconstitutional.[10]

At this point Virginia State Board of Pharmacy v. Virginia Citizens Consumers Council, Inc., 1 Med.L.Rptr. 1930, 425 U.S. 748 (1976), because it is a focal case, ought to be reexamined in Chapter I, text, p. 159, or read in its entirety. Mark especially footnote 24 in which the Court declares that the greater hardihood of commercial speech makes it more durable and amenable to state regulation than other forms of speech.

Virginia State Board and the Public's Right to Receive Information. Some commentators would go far beyond Justice Blackmun in *Virginia Pharmacy* and the Court in protecting commercial speech. They consider his approval of state regulation of even false, misleading, and deceptive advertising a serious encroachment on First Amendment terrain.

"The determination by a government agency that a statement is false," says R.H. Coase of the University of Chicago Law School, "is completely alien to the doctrine of free speech and of freedom of the press. * * * The contrast between the philosophy which supports the First Amendment and that which gives authority to the Federal Trade Commission is even more striking when it has to decide, not whether a statement is false but whether it is misleading. This means that the commission has to enquire into the way in which information will be used before deciding whether it will allow it to be disseminated, the very kind of activity which the First Amendment is supposed to

6. Carpets by the Carload, Inc. v. Warren, 368 F.Supp. 1075 (D.Wis.1973).

7. Lehman v. City of Shaker Heights, 418 U.S. 298 (1974). See text, p. 64, for a discussion of the impact of Lehman on the public forum doctrine.

8. Rinaldi v. Village Voice, Inc., 365 N.Y.S.2d 199 (1975).

9. 410 U.S. 113 (1973).

10. People of New York v. Remeny, 387 N.Y.S.2d 415 (1976). The case involved distribution of handbills for a concert.

discourage the government from undertaking." [11]

Conversely there are those who believe that pure product advertising ought to be regulated, not as speech, but as part of commerce, property, or contract. Ads with a meaning beyond a mere sales pitch—corporate image ads, ads promoting periodicals, lectures, concerts, and all kinds of social, cultural, and political policies, opinions, and activities—merit First Amendment protection, says Professor Kent Middleton.[12]

C. Edwin Baker of the University of Oregon Law School provides an example of this distinction by observing that "[w]hatever the personal views of employees, management, or owners about the hazards of cigarette smoking, the threat of bankruptcy forces cigarette companies to choose speech that sells cigarettes. Commercial speech thus lacks the individual liberty and self-realization aspects of speech that justify its constitutional protection. * * *" Here then a clear constitutional distinction between the regulation of property rights and the imposition of limits on personal liberties. Baker, *Press Rights and Government Power to Structure the Press,* 34 U. of Miami L.Rev. 785, 822 (July 1980). See also, Emerson, *Comments* in Proceedings of the Symposium on Media Concentration 193, 194 (FTC 1978); *First Amendment and the Burger Court,* 68 Calif.L.Rev. 422, 458–61 (1980).

The Third Circuit Court of Appeals ruled correctly, in Middleton's view, that a publisher could not be barred from distributing pamphlets—no matter how outlandish—claiming that aluminum cookware caused cancer.[13] But when a cookware competitor engaged in the same practice the Sixth Circuit upheld an FTC cease-and-desist order because the information was now part of trade, a competitive sales appeal.[14]

Middleton's concern is that Justice Blackmun's "half-hearted" First Amendment defense of commercial speech (see fn. 24 in *Virginia Pharmacy,* p. 162 this text) may eventually spill over to political, literary, and social speech. Governmental authority to deny protection to "false" advertising or false speech of any kind is contrary to the First Amendment doctrine of *New York Times* that protects at least the ignorantly false with the true:

> Bringing advertising under the first amendment with an understanding that it does merit the same protections given to political and social expression establishes precedent for routine government review of truth and falsity of constitutionally protected speech that could have undesirable consequences in other more important areas of protected expression.[15]

11. Coase, *Advertising and Free Speech* (unpublished manuscript, 1976), pp. 43–45. See also, Coase, *Advertising and Free Speech,* 6 J.Legal Stud. 1 (1977); Reich, *Consumer Protection and the First Amendment: A Dilemma for the FTC?* 61 Minn.L.Rev. 705 (May 1977).

12. Middleton, *Commercial Speech and the First Amendment* (unpublished doctoral dissertation, University of Minnesota, December 1977). See also, Elman, *Advertising and the First Amendment,* 33 Food Drug Cosmetic L.J. 12 (January 1978).

A slightly more complex view is that of Daniel Farber: Advertising functions as part of the contractual arrangement between buyer and seller. Of course, in addition to serving this contractual function, ads also serve an informative function to which the First Amendment applies. "The critical factor seems to be whether a state rule is based on the informative function or the contractual function of the language." False ads are unfulfilled contractual promises. Farber, *Commercial Speech and First Amendment Theory,* 74 NW.U.L.Rev. 372, 387 (1979).

13. Scientific Manufacturing Co. v. FTC, 124 F.2d 640 (3d Cir. 1941).

14. Perma-Maid Co. v. FTC, 121 F.2d 282 (6th Cir. 1941).

15. Middleton, *op.cit.*, p. 253.

While Coase would put bubble gum ads in the same protected category as an ad for a Picasso exhibit, Middleton would prefer to make a trade/speech distinction between them and in doing so embark upon a journey into that uncertain territory where the social value of or the public interest in a communication may have vague and subjective contours.

The Court's reluctance to go all the way with commercial speech was again demonstrated in the 1978 case Ohralik v. Ohio State Bar Association, 436 U.S. 447 (1978). There a lawyer who was suspended from the practice of law for "ambulance chasing" claimed that his in-person solicitation, which he had surreptitiously recorded, was protected speech. The Court, adhering to the qualifications of *Virginia Pharmacy's* footnote 24, disagreed. Commercial speech, said Justice Powell, has "a limited measure of protection, commensurate with its subordinate position in the scale of First Amendment values."

A year later in Friedman v. Rogers, 4 Med.L.Rptr. 2213, 440 U.S. 1 (1979) the Court continued its post-*Virginia Pharmacy* tendency to show substantial deference to the judgment of legislatures and administrative agencies in balancing the regulation of commercial speech against First Amendment values. There it upheld provisions of the Texas Optometry Act prohibiting practice of that profession under an assumed, trade, or corporate name.

"Because of the special character of commercial speech and the relative novelty of First Amendment protection for such speech," said the Court in footnote 9 of that case, "we act with caution in confronting First Amendment challenges to economic regulation that serves legitimate regulatory interests. Our decision dealing with more traditional First Amendment problems do not extend automatically to this as yet uncharted area."

The uncharted state of commercial speech was reflected in Metromedia, Inc. v. San Diego, 453 U.S. 490 (1981). The Court presented five opinions in striking down a city ordinance forbidding, with specified exceptions, all outdoor or billboard advertising. Justice William Rehnquist called the opinions "a virtual Tower of Babel," out of which no principles could be drawn. A fragmented Court might mean diminished protection for commercial speech.

Justice Rehnquist also dissented in the 1980 case upon which *Metromedia* had depended for its momentum. In Central Hudson Gas & Electric Corp. v. Public Service Commission, 6 Med.L.Rptr. 1497, 447 U.S. 557 (1980), the Court invalidated a state regulation prohibiting advertising to promote the sale of electricity. Justice Powell for the Court suggested a four-part test, based in part upon earlier cases:

1. The commercial speech much concern a lawful activity, *Pittsburgh Press* (see also, Village of Hoffman Estates v. Flipside, Hoffman Estates, 452 U.S. 904 (1982), where the illegal activity advertised was drug use);

2. it must not be misleading (*Warner-Lambert*);

3. the state interest posed against advertising must be substantial and well beyond the mere proprieties of a profession (*Virginia State Board, Bates v. Arizona*); and

4. the state regulation applied must advance the governmental interest claimed and be no more extensive than necessary.

Conservation, the state interest claimed in *Central Hudson,* could have been achieved in other ways, short of an outright ban on advertising. The fourth part of the test had not been met by the New York regulation. Although the four-part test clearly implies a lower level of constitutional protection for commercial speech than for other forms, Rehnquist would have gone the Court one better in banning the speech of a state-created monopoly.

A mechanical application of the four-part test may be hazardous to the free flow of information because the first two steps in the test could get a court's analysis off the First Amendment track. An effort to rectify this was made in In re R.M.J., 455 U.S. 191 (1982). There the Court held that potentially misleading professional advertising might deserve some level of First Amendment protection after all.

Virginia Pharmacy's footnote 24 had also been cited by a New York court in upholding the principle that the First Amendment did not bar an injunction restraining an insurance company from advertising that personal injury awards were "assuming astronomical proportions, often unrelated to the actual extent of injury. * * *" Although the injunction was denied for other reasons, the court went so far as to suggest that footnote 24 language attesting to the "greater objectivity and hardihood of commercial speech" might also permit prior restraints. Quinn v. Aetna Life & Casualty Co., 4 Med.L.Rptr. 1049, 409 N.Y.S.2d 473 (1978). Although unresolved, state Blue Sky laws governing the advertising of securities probably do not offend the First Amendment.

And the Illinois Supreme Court in Talsky v. Department of Registration and Education, 3 Med.L.Rptr. 1315, 370 N.E.2d 173 (Ill.1977), held that while a blanket statutory prohibition of advertising and solicitation by health care professionals "may operate in some cases to suppress commercial speech in violation of the First Amendment," a chiropractor's newspaper ad for "free chicken, free refreshments, and free spinal X-rays" was not protected under *Virginia Pharmacy.* Two dissenting justices objected to the decision's turning on the content of the ad.

Certainly these later cases can be interpreted as a return to at least a qualified commercial speech doctrine. Footnote 24 teaches that advertising is a "hardy" form of speech not easily discouraged or chilled by prior restraints or by overbroad statutes. See generally, Metromedia, Inc. v. San Diego, 435 U.S. 490 (1981).

Media Rights to Refuse and Control the Conditions of Advertising. Following *Virginia Pharmacy,* new forms of commercial speech nevertheless gained constitutional protection. An ordinance designed to prevent panic selling by prohibiting "for sale" signs on residential lawns was struck down in Linmark Associates, Inc. v. Township of Willingboro, 431 U.S. 85 (1977), although *Metromedia* may have overruled *Linmark.* Professional advertising by lawyers,[16] doctors,[17] and opticians[18] has received expanding constitutional approval under particular conditions. Contraceptive advertising,[19] the advertising of

16. Bates v. State Bar of Arizona, 2 Med.L.Rptr. 2097, 433 U.S. 350 (1977). See text, p. 164. See also, Consumers Union of United States, Inc. v. American Bar Association, 427 F.Supp. 506 (D.Va.1976); Jacoby v. The State Bar of California, 138 Cal.Rptr. 77, 562 P.2d 1326 (1977).

17. Health Systems Agency of Northern Virginia v. Virginia State Board of Medicine, 2 Med.L.Rptr. 1107, 424 F.Supp. 267 (D.Va.1976). In 1979 the commission voted to require the American Medical Association to cease restricting physician advertising beyond "reasonable-ethical guidelines" applicable to deceptive advertising including unsubstantiated claims and solicitation of vulnerable patients. The commission was upheld with minor modifications. American Medical Association v. FTC, 638 F.2d 443 (2d Cir. 1980). A law prohibiting the advertising of prescription eyeglasses was held "patently unconstitutional," Wall & Ochs, Inc. v. Hicks, 469 F.Supp. 873 (D.N.C.1979). A city ordinance banning advertising by clinical laboratories was struck down in Metpath, Inc. v. Imperato, 3 Med.L.Rptr. 2284, 450 F.Supp. 115 (D.N.Y.1978) and Metpath, Inc. v. Meyers, 4 Med.L.Rptr. 1884, 462 F.Supp. 1104 (D.Cal.1978).

18. Horner-Rausch Optical Co. v. Ashley, 547 S.W.2d 577 (Tenn.1976).

19. Carey v. Population Services International, 2 Med.L.Rptr. 1935, 431 U.S. 678 (1977).

proprietary drugs on television,[20] and the advertising of saccharin products[21] have withstood legal challenges.

In spite of First Amendment victories for commercial speech, the media have compromised none of their rights of control over access and display of advertising. They may refuse advertising and dictate the conditions of its sale.

In 1965 a Florida appeals court held that, "in the absence of any statutory provisions to the contrary, the law seems to be uniformly settled by the great weight of authority throughout the United States that the newspaper publishing business is a private enterprise and is neither a public utility nor affected with the public interest. The decisions appear to hold that even though a particular newspaper may enjoy a virtual monopoly in the area of its publication, this fact is neither unusual nor of important significance. The courts have consistently held that in the absence of statutory regulation on the subject, a newspaper may publish or reject commercial advertising tendered to it as its judgment best dictates without incurring liability for advertisements rejected by it." Approved Personnel, Inc. v. Tribune Co., 177 So.2d 704 (Fla.1965).[22]

An exception to the rule may be newspapers or periodicals which, because they can be defined as publicly supported channels, raise the issue of "state action." See Zucker v. Panitz, 299 F.Supp. 102 (D.N.Y.1969). Portland Women's Health Center v. Portland Community College, ___ F.Supp. ___ (D.Or.1981). Lee v. Board of Regents of State Colleges, 306 F.Supp. 1097 (Wisc.1969), affirmed 1 Med.L.Rptr. 1947, 441 F.2d 1257 (7th Cir. 1971). See also, Radical Lawyers Caucus v. Pool, 324 F.Supp. 268 (D.Tex.1970). But see Mississippi Gay Alliance v. Goudelock, 536 F.2d 1073 (5th Cir. 1976), cert. den. 430 U.S. 982 (1977). The foregoing cases are discussed in the materials on access to the public press, text, p. 596.

Tornillo, text, p. 584, was relied on when a plaintiff whose "tombstone advertisements" announcing an offer of shares in a pending lawsuit were rejected by a newspaper and he was denied an injunction which would have required the newspaper either to publish the ad or to refrain from publishing all such ads in the future. Such a restraint, said the court, "runs squarely against the wall of freedom of the press. * * * That commercial advertising is involved makes no difference. * * [A]ny such compulsion to publish that which 'reason' tells [a newspaper] should not be published" is unconstitutional. Person v. New York Post, 2 Med.L.Rptr. 1666, 427 F.Supp. 1297 (D.N.Y.1977), affirmed without opinion, 3 Med.L.Rptr. 1784, 573 F.2d 1294 (1977).

Newspapers may allocate their advertising space as they see fit,[23] and statutory requirements to the contrary will have dif-

20. FCC memorandum and order (Dec. 8, 1976). Courts are divided on the constitutionality of laws restricting the advertising of drug paraphernalia. See Record Revolution No. Six, Inc. v. City of Parma, 638 F.2d 916 (6th Cir. 1980), cert. den., 451 U.S. 1013 (1981) and High Ol' Times, Inc. v. Busbee, 4 Med.L.Rptr. 1721, 456 F.Supp. 1035 (D.Ga.1978), affirmed 6 Med.L.Rptr. 1617, 621 F.2d 141 (5th Cir. 1980), Cf. Gasser v. Morgan, 498 F.Supp. 1154 (D.Ala.1980).

21. The Senate Commerce Committee struck a provision from the Saccharin Study Labeling and Advertising Act (S. 1750) on July 26, 1977 which would have prohibited broadcast advertising of saccharin and saccharin products during an eighteen-month study period.

22. The court relied on earlier rulings: Shuck v. Carroll Daily Herald, 247 N.W. 813 (Iowa 1933); Poughkeepsie Buying Service, Inc. v. Poughkeepsie Newspapers, Inc., 131 N.Y.S.2d 515 (1954); and Gordon v. Worcester Telegram Publishing Co., 177 N.E.2d 586 (Mass.1961). See also, Chicago Joint Boards, Amalgamated Clothing Workers of America, AFL–CIO v. Chicago Tribune Co., 307 F.Supp. 422 (D.Ill.1969), affirmed 435 F.2d 470 (7th Cir. 1970), this text, p. 508.

23. National Tire Wholesale v. Washington Post, 3 Med.L.Rptr. 1520, 441 F.Supp. 81 (D.D.C.1977).

ficulty passing constitutional muster. The Fifth Circuit affirmed a federal district court ruling in Florida that the First Amendment was violated by a provision of Florida's campaign financing law requiring newspapers to offer advertising to political candidates at the lowest available rate.[24]

And a Florida law that restricted candidates for public office from making any use of advertising media except in a specified "political season" was held by the Florida Supreme Court to violate the First Amendment since it was primarily designed to limit the quantity of political speech.[25]

If a refusal to accept advertising is in breach of contract or an attempt to monopolize interstate commerce, an injunction may issue. In Lorain Journal Co. v. United States, 342 U.S. 143 (1951), this text, p. 660, a publisher was prohibited from refusing to accept local advertisements from anyone who advertised in a competitive radio station.

The Sherman Act was not violated, the Second Circuit held in Homefinders v. Providence Journal, 6 Med.L.Rptr. 1018, 621 F.2d 441 (1st Cir. 1980), by a newspaper's refusal to publish false and misleading advertisements submitted by a rental referral firm. Where the advertising was honest and aboveboard and the metropolitan daily, the only newspaper of its kind in town, was in direct competition with the advertiser, the result could be a Sherman Act violation. Home Placement Service, Inc. v. Providence Journal Co., 8 Med.L.Rptr. 1881, 682 F.2d 274 (1st Cir. 1982).

But once a newspaper signs a contract to publish an ad, it has given up the right not to publish unless that right is specifically reserved in the contract or some other equitable defense is available to it. Herald-Telephone v. Fatouros, 8 Med.L. Rptr. 1230, 431 N.E.2d 171 (Ind.1982).

By the same token, advertisers may not conspire to withdraw advertising from a newspaper by waging an advertising boycott without violating federal antitrust laws. Mims v. Kemp, Civil Action No. 72–627 (D.S.C.1977). A conglomerate corporation under single ownership, however, may withdraw all its advertising from a newspaper, as Howard Hughes did with the *Las Vegas Sun,* without violating federal law.[26]

But a newspaper may not conspire with a segment of its advertisers to refuse space to a competitive advertiser.[27]

Generally courts have recognized that newspapers have a strong economic self-interest in limiting the kinds of advertising they will accept, since "in the minds of readers, a newspaper's advertising may be every bit as reflective of the policy of a newspaper as its editorial page." Adult Film Association of America v. Times Mirror Co., 5 Med.L.Rptr. 1865, 158 Cal.Rptr. 547 (1979).

Although the broadcast media are under much more direct and stringent governmental supervision than other media, the U.S. Supreme Court in CBS v. Democratic National Committee, 1 Med.L.Rptr. 1855, 412 U.S. 94 (1973), was unwilling to grant a First Amendment right of access to editorial advertising on network television. A second group, Business Executives' Move for Vietnam Peace, had also been denied the opportunity to buy broadcast time.

"There is substantial risk," said Chief Justice Burger writing for the Court, "that such a system [a guaranteed right of ac-

24. Gore Newspapers v. Shevin, 2 Med.L.Rptr. 181, 397 F.Supp. 1253 (D.Fla.1975), affirmed 2 Med.L.Rptr. 1818, 550 F.2d 1057 (5th Cir. 1977).

25. Sadowski v. Shevin, 2 Med.L.Rptr. 1822, 345 So.2d 330 (Fla.1977).

26. Las Vegas Sun v. Summa Corp., 5 Med.L.Rptr. 2073, 610 F.2d 614 (9th Cir. 1979).

27. Greenspun v. McCarran, 105 F.Supp. 662 (D.Nev.1952).

cess] would be monopolized by those who could and would pay the costs, that the effective operation of the Fairness Doctrine itself would be undermined, and that the public accountability which now rests with the broadcaster would be diluted."

Moreover, case-by-case determination by the FCC of who should be heard and when, the Court added, would enlarge the involvement of the government in broadcasting and limit journalistic discretion.

Ironically, it may be too late to worry about the network broadcast system's being monopolized by those able to pay the costs since at least 75 percent of all broadcast advertising is purchased by fewer than 100 firms, and no more than ten large firms account for a quarter of the total.

Commercial advertisers, Brennan argued, who seek to peddle their goods and services to the public—beer, soap, toothpaste—have instantaneous access in whatever format or time period they choose; but individuals seeking to discuss war, peace, pollution, or the suffering of the poor are denied a similar right to speak and instead are compelled to rely on the beneficence of a corporate "trustee" appointed by the government to argue their case for them. For a fuller discussion of the case, see p. 858, this text.

A year after *CBS v. DNC* the FCC issued its *1974 Fairness Report* in which it divided advertising into three categories: editorial, institutional, and product. While continuing to allow the first two categories under some conditions to invoke fairness doctrine claims, the Commission in effect repudiated its *Banzhaf* ruling (WCBS–TV, 8 FCC 2d 381, 1967) which had permitted negative or counter replies to cigarette advertising.

"We believe," said the commission, "that standard product commercials, such as the old cigarette ads, make no meaningful contribution toward informing the public on any side of any issue." The proposition is, of course, eminently debatable. For a discussion of the *Fairness Report* and related matters, see text, p. 867.

Taxes on Advertising. At least since the landmark case, Grosjean v. American Press Co., 297 U.S. 233 (1936), see pp. 138–141 this text, discriminatory or punitive taxes on advertising have been constitutionally impermissible. Newspapers, and by implication other media, do not lose First Amendment protection because they are published for profit. Because general business taxes, if they are levied evenhandedly, can be imposed on the press, state legislatures frequently entertain bills that would tax advertising.

While most states exempt newspapers from sales or use taxes, the question has arisen whether advertising supplements inserted into newspapers enjoy similar exemption. In line with recent modifications in the commercial speech doctrine, the Supreme Judicial Court of Massachusetts made a First Amendment argument in favor of Sears's advertising supplements being exempt from state sales and use taxes. Sears, Roebuck & Co. v. State Tax Commission, 345 N.E.2d 893 (Mass.1976).

A year later, however, the Tennessee Supreme Court held that an advertising "give away" or shopper that resembled a tabloid newspaper in form but devoted itself entirely to ads and announcements of local social and sports events, was not a newspaper and did not qualify for tax exemptions normally granted to newspapers. "The tax in question," said the court, "is not upon the privilege of disseminating information to the public. It is a general tax applying to all persons, whatever their business, who fabricate tangible personal property." Shoppers Guide Publishing Co. v. Woods, 2 Med.L.Rptr. 1825, 547 S.W.2d 561 (Tenn.1977). See also, Memphis Shoppers News, Inc. v. Woods, 5 Med.L.Rptr. 1445, 584 S.W.2d 196 (Tenn. 1979).

The Regulation of Advertising

1. The regulation of advertising grew out of a general assault at the turn of the century on the excesses of *laissez-faire* capitalism and the cynical doctrine of *caveat emptor* (let the buyer beware). Stimulated by the writing of the muckrakers, notably Samuel Hopkins Adams's 1906 *Colliers* series on patent medicines, "The Great American Fraud," the regulatory movement took root in passage of the Pure Food and Drug Act in 1906 and the creation in 1914 of the Federal Trade Commission.

Congress in 1914 was primarily concerned with reinforcing the antitrust provisions of the Sherman and Clayton Acts. The FTC Act declared unfair methods of competition in commerce unlawful. Its purpose was to promote "the preservation of an environment which would foster the liberty to compete." In its early years the act was used by the courts to protect competitors against false and deceptive advertising; the protection of consumers was incidental.

In 1922, for example, Justice Louis Brandeis, in an opinion for the United States Supreme Court, upheld the FTC in a ruling against a manufacturer who had mislabeled underwear as wool when in fact it contained as little as 10 percent wool.

Although Brandeis did recognize a public interest in prohibiting mislabeling, his main argument was that "the practice constitutes an unfair method of competition as against manufacturers of all wool knit underwear and as against those manufacturers of mixed wool and cotton underwear who brand their product truthfully. For when misbranded goods attract customers by means of the fraud which they perpetrate, trade is diverted from the producer of truthfully marked goods. * * *" FTC v. Winsted Hosiery Co., 258 U.S. 483 (1922). See also, FTC v. Beech-Nut, 257 U.S. 441 (1921).

In a similar case ten years later, Justice Benjamin Cardozo in an opinion for the Court upheld an FTC ruling ordering lumber dealers to discontinue selling "Western Yellow Pine" under the trade name of "California White Pine," the latter being a distinct and superior product.

Again the incidental right of the consumer to get what was ordered was acknowledged. But the Court emphasized that "Dealers and manufacturers are prejudiced when orders that would have come to them if the lumber had been rightly named are diverted to others whose methods are less scrupulous. * * *" FTC v. Algoma Lumber Co., 291 U.S. 67 (1933).

That consumer rights in this period were peripheral to the welfare of competitors is best illustrated by the 1931 Supreme Court ruling in the *Raladam* case. Here the Court declared flatly through Justice George Sutherland that the FTC Act would not protect consumers against the phony advertising of an "obesity cure" unless competitive businesses were being hurt. FTC v. Raladam Co., 283 U.S. 643 (1931).

Three years later, however, the Court repudiated *Raladam* in a case involving the deceptive use of a lottery in marketing candy to children (FTC v. R.F. Keppel & Brother, Inc., 291 U.S. 304, 1934); and after *Keppel* unfair competitive practices were not limited to those violative of the antitrust laws. In 1937 Justice Hugo Black overruled an opinion by district court Judge Learned Hand which had struck down an FTC order against deceptive sales practices in selling encyclopediae. Black wrote, for the Court:

> The fact that a false statement may be obviously false to those who are trained and experienced does not change its character nor take away its power to deceive others less experienced. There is no duty resting upon a citizen to suspect the honesty of those with whom he transacts business. Laws are made to protect the trusting as well as the suspicious. The best

element of business has long since decided that honesty should govern competitive enterprises, and that the rule of *caveat emptor* should not be relied upon to reward fraud and deception. FTC v. Standard Education Society, 302 U.S. 112 (1937).

2. Congress legitimized this golden rule in 1938 by adding Section 5(b) to the FTC Act: "Unfair methods of competition in commerce, and unfair or deceptive acts or practices in commerce, are declared unlawful." 15 U.S.C.A. § 45. And to Section 12 was added language that declares false advertising of food, drugs, cosmetics, or devices to be an unfair or deceptive act and, as such, a violation of law.

Known as the Wheeler-Lea Amendments, these changes in the act made "false" and "deceptive" advertising the keystones of the FTC's authority to protect consumers as well as competitors.

"This amendment," said a House report on the legislation, "makes the consumer, who may be injured by an unfair trade practice, of equal concern before the law, with the merchant or manufacturer injured by the unfair methods of a dishonest competitor." [28]

3. There was disagreement in the late 70s as to the effect *Virginia Pharmacy* would have on the FTC's regulatory activities. Robert Pitofsky, a former director of the Commission's Bureau of Consumer Protection, doubted that the case would "appreciably circumscribe FTC regulation of advertising." [29] On the other hand, Robert Reich, then director of the agency's Office of Planning and Evaluation, believed that the case would cause the courts to assume they must scrutinize FTC actions more strictly to prevent unnecessary interference with constitutionally protected speech.[30]

In Beneficial Corp. v. FTC, 542 F.2d 611 (3d Cir. 1976), for example, the court, relying on *Virginia Pharmacy,* refused to enforce an FTC order on the ground that the First Amendment requires the commission to bear the burden of proof and to use the least restrictive remedy available. The court then recommended substitute language for an advertisement confusing an ordinary loan with a federal tax refund in lieu of litigation.

The goals of regulation remain fairness and efficiency in the marketplace and a lessening of competitor and consumer injury depending, in part, upon an increase in the flow of truthful information to the public. The goal of fairness, as shall be noted, came under a cloud in the early 80s.

The commission will issue formal opinions where there is a substantial question of law and no clear precedent, a proposed merger or acquisition is involved, or a matter of significant public interest is before it.

False, Deceptive, and Unfair Advertising. Public and private agencies since at least the early 1960s [31] have shown a resolute interest in consumer rights. Ralph Nader's incalculable contributions to the consumer movement have been accompanied by state and federal laws and regulations protecting buyers in such marketplaces as packaging and labeling, credit, land purchases, warranties, insulation, and a broad range of product safety areas including cigarettes and hair implantation processes.

28. H.R.Rep. No. 1613, 75th Cong., 1st Sess., 3 (1937).

29. Pitofsky, *Beyond Nader: Consumer Protection and the Regulation of Advertising,* 90 Harvard L.Rev. 661, 672 (Feb.1977).

30. Reich, *Consumer Protection and the First Amendment,* 61 Minn.L.Rev. 705, 706 (May 1977).

31. Cox, Fellmuth and Schulz, *The Nader Report on the Federal Trade Commission,* 1969; *The Report of the American Bar Association Committee to Study the Federal Trade Commission,* 1969; Howard and Hulbert, *Advertising and the Public Interest, A Staff Report to the Federal Trade Commission,* 1973.

False and deceptive advertising is regulated under Sections 5 and 12 of the Federal Trade Commission Act [32] and Section 43(a) of the Lanham Trademark Act.[33] The Federal Trade Commission also enforces ten or more consumer protection laws. Each permits consumers to sue for civil damages and attorney's fees.[34]

Congressional support of the FTC appears to by cyclical. Congressional action in the 80s has sought to make the agency, a creature of Congress, more sensitive to business and political trends and to the economic consequences of its rulings. Some businessmen would have the FTC avoid regulating low-cost consumer products and concentrate instead upon validated deception in health and safety fields. And, since the 1934 *Keppel* case, sellers and advertisers have thought the unfairness standard vague and amorphous. Much debate has focused on its meaning.

Unfair methods of competition, even when they do not violate antitrust laws directly and are not deceptive, were condemned in FTC v. The Sperry & Hutchinson Co., 405 U.S. 233 (1972).

"[L]egislative and judicial authorities alike convince us," said Justice Byron White for the Court, "that the Federal Trade Commission does not arrogate excessive power to itself if, in measuring a practice against the elusive but congressionally mandated standard of fairness, it, like a court of equity, considers public values beyond simply those enshrined in the letter or encompassed in the spirit of the antitrust laws."

In broadening the authority of the commission the Court spoke of practices which "offend public policy" because they are "immoral, unethical, oppressive or unscrupulous" and cause "substantial injury to consumers or competitors or other businessmen." The language is from "Statement of Basis and Purpose of Trade Regulation Rule 408, Unfair or Deceptive Advertising and Labeling of Cigarettes in Relation to the Health Hazards of Smoking," 29 Fed.Reg. 8355 (1964).

In 1978, the FTC extended the unfairness doctrine to include a cost-benefit analysis of social and economic factors to be considered in a rulemaking proceeding. See "Advertising and Ophthalmic Goods and Services, Statement of Basis and Purpose," 43 Fed.Reg. 23992, 24000–01 (1978).

Several FTC Magnuson-Moss rulemaking proceedings in the early 80s, for example, used car sales, insurance, and funeral home practices, were criticized by business as attempts to stretch the meaning of unfairness beyond the unconscionability limits of public policy. Perhaps the best example of this alleged overreach was the "Kid-Vid" rulemaking proceedings which examined, under the promise of a trade regulation rule, the effects of television advertising on presumably vulnerable chil-

32. 15 U.S.C. § 45; 15 U.S.C. § 52. Under Section 5(a)(1) it is unfair or deceptive to fail to disclose any safety risk in the use of a product for the purpose for which it is sold, which would not be immediately apparent to a casual purchaser or user. Particularly it is an unfair or deceptive act or practice to fail to disclose latent safety hazards relating to flammability. Where human safety is involved and the buyer must rely on a manufacturer's technical knowledge to assure the validity of its claims, it is an unfair and deceptive act or practice to make a specific advertising claim without supporting data from scientific tests. A scientific test is one in which persons with skill and expertise in the field conduct the test and evaluate its results in a disinterested manner using testing procedures generally accepted in the profession and which best insure accurate results. See Firestone Tire and Rubber Co., 81 F.T.C. 398, 451, 463 (1972), affirmed 481 F.2d 246 (6th Cir. 1973), cert. den. 414 U.S. 1112. Disclosures are to be made in ways that arrest the eye or attract the attention of an average purchaser or user of the product.

33. 15 U.S.C. § 1125(a).

34. For example, Truth in Lending Act, 15 U.S.C. §§ 1601–1667e; Fair Credit Reporting Act, 15 U.S.C. § 1681–1681t; Magnuson-Moss Warranty Act, 15 U.S.C. §§ 2301–2312; Energy Policy and Conservation Act, 42 U.S.C. §§ 6201–6422; Hobby Protection Act, 15 U.S.C. §§ 2101–2106.

dren,[35] notably the advertising of sugared cereals and toys. The proceedings were abruptly terminated on September 30, 1981, and for two years Congress temporarily withdrew from the commission authority to base trade regulation rules on *unfair* as opposed to false and deceptive advertising, pending reauthorization hearings before the Senate Commerce Committee. In May 1982 that Committee voted 13–2 to support legislation forbidding the FTC to regulate unfair advertising.

This action had been preceded by the 1980 FTC Improvements Act (Public Law 96–252) which required the agency to drop its "Kid-Vid" concerns and give business and industry advance notice of contemplated rulemaking, and thereby an opportunity to lean on regulators.

A former FTC chairman saw this development as a naked political sortie by affected industries to evade public accountability for commercial abuse and consumer injury. "This," he added, "from the Congress which, for more than a decade, had consistently urged the commission to undertake these very same initiatives, and in general had flogged the commission for its attention to trivia and lack of responsiveness to consumer interests." [36] The 1980 act also required the FTC to submit all final rules to Congress. Rules can be vetoed by concurrent resolutions of both Houses of Congress if they act within ninety days. Under these conditions does the FTC remain an *independent* regulatory agency?

It is well established that under FTCA Section 5 the commission can challenge practices that violate the Sherman and Clayton Acts. This has been construed as giving the agency unrestrained authority to define "unfair methods of competition" and to condemn any conduct believed to be potentially anticompetitive or economically objectionable. Recommendations have therefore been made to limit the FTC's remedial rulemaking and adjudicative powers in the antitrust field as well and to remind Congress of its oversight role.[37]

First Amendment issues are inherent in the regulatory process. Should the FTC apply a "reasonable" or "ignorant" person standard in evaluating advertising claims? In the absence of evidence of intentional deception, the "reasonable person" standard comports with the common law and tends to discourage broad assaults on the First Amendment. It also legitimizes *puffery:* the exaggerated use of superlatives and hyperbole to describe goods and services, a form of expression defying objective measurement. Courts and commission have held words like "stupendous" to be romantic characterizations not to be read literally. So while a toothpaste may be said to "beautify the smile," [38] a ciga-

35. 46 FR 48710.1. See *Summary and Recommendation: Federal Trade Commission Staff Report on TV Advertising to Children,* summarized in Advertising Age, Feb. 27, 1978. The commission subsequently said that it could not resolve the factual issues and the remedies to be applied on legal and policy grounds in the "Kid-Vid" proceedings without an inordinate commitment of its resources.

36. Pertschuk, *The FTC,* Advertising Age, Dec. 14, 1981.

37. *Report of the Section of Antitrust Law, American Bar Association, Concerning Federal Trade Commission Structure, Powers and Procedure* (February 7, 1980); and *Federal Trade Regulation Rulemaking Procedures Pursuant to the Magnuson-Moss Act* (February 7, 1980).

38. Bristol-Meyers Co., 46 FTC 162 (1949), affirmed 185 F.2d 58 (4th Cir. 1950). But in Aronberg v. FTC, 132 F.2d 165, 167 (7th Cir. 1942), the court interpreted the commission's function as considering what impression an ad would make on the general public, including the "ignorant, the unthinking and the credulous, who in making purchases do not stop to analyze but too often are governed by appearances and general impression." And when an ad is subject to two possible interpretations, one of which is false, the advertisement is found deceptive and misleading (United States v. 95 Barrels of Vinegar, 265 U.S. 438 (1924)).

In Kirchner, 63 F.T.C. 1282 (1963) the commission based a finding of harmless hyperbole on the proposition that *puffery* can be harmless when the consumer does not expect documentation.

rette manufacturer may not safely say that his product is "less irritating." [39]

In Carlay v. FTC, 153 F.2d 493 (7th Cir. 1946), the court noted:

> What was said [Ayds candy mints will make weight reducing easy] was clearly justifiable * * * under those cases recognizing that such words as "easy," "perfect," "amazing," "prime," "wonderful," "excellent," are regarded in law as mere puffing or dealer's talk upon which no charge of misrepresentation can be based.

The trick seems to be to avoid factual or material claims or misrepresentation, but the distinction is often vague and subjective. Puffery therefore has its articulate enemies.[40]

Neither the FTC Act nor its legislative history defines "unfair," "false," or "deceptive." Courts generally defer to the experience and expertise of the FTC. The commission requires no proof of actual deception; a capacity or tendency to deceive an average person, the general "buying public," or a significant percentage of that public may be sufficient, with the burden of proof on the government. Double digit percentages are generally too high. But the FTC will consider the consequences of the deception and the number of persons involved. If the general impression of an ad is, directly or by innuendo, to deceive or mislead so as to result in injury or prejudice to the public or to the irrationality of its buying decisions, the FTC may intervene.

Higher standards may be set for advertising to children (especially nutritional and toy performance claims) [41] and to other vulnerable groups.[42]

Courts and commission have been sensitive to misleading demonstrations, testimonials, and endorsements. The classic case began in 1959 when Colgate Palmolive and its advertising agency Ted Bates presented TV ads suggesting by means of a mock-up that a shaving cream product could shave sandpaper. Seeing its case as having preventive as well as punitive purposes, the FTC stuck by its claim that viewers would be misled into thinking they were seeing an actual experiment all the way to the U.S. Supreme Court. There, in an opinion written for the Court by Chief Justice Warren, it was upheld:

> We agree with the [c]ommission that the undisclosed use of plexiglass in the present commercials, was a material deceptive practice, independent and separate from the other misrepresentation found. We find unpersuasive respondents' other objections to this conclusion. Respondents claim that it will be impractical to inform the viewing public that it is not seeing an actual test, experiment or demonstration, but we think it inconceivable that the ingenious advertising world will be unable, if it so desires, to conform to the [c]ommission's insistence that the public be not misinformed. If, however, it becomes impossible or impractical to show simulated demonstrations on television in a truthful manner, this indicates that television is not a medium that lends itself to this type of commercial, not that the commercial must survive at all costs. FTC v. Colgate-Palmolive Co., 380 U.S. 374 (1965).

Libbey-Owens-Ford Glass Co. and General Motors fared no better when they claimed minimum distortion for safety plate glass used in GM cars with pictures shot through an automobile window from which the glass had been removed. Lib-

39. Liggett & Myers Tobacco Co., 55 F.T.C. 354 (1958).

40. Preston, *The Great American Blow-Up: Puffery in Advertising and Selling*, 1975.

41. Topper, FTC C–2073, and Mattel, FTC C–2071, 1973 CCH Transfer Binder ¶ 19,735 (1971); Hudson Pharmaceutical Corp., 3 CCH Trade Reg.Rptr. ¶ 21,191 (1976), the "Spider Man" vitamins case.

42. Doris Savitch, 50 F.T.C. 828 (1954), Savitch v. FTC, affirmed per curiam 218 F.2d 817 (2d Cir. 1955), women who fear they may be pregnant; S.S.S. Co. v. FTC, 416 F.2d 226 (6th Cir. 1969), poor people.

bey-Owens-Ford Glass Co. v. FTC, 352 F.2d 415 (6th Cir. 1965).

There have been few mock-up complaints since *Colgate-Palmolive,* and the commission has indicated that it will not go after smaller priced items unless public health or safety is involved. In Bristol-Meyers Co., CCH 1973–76, Transfer Binder, ¶ 20,900, the 1975 "Dry Ban" case, the commission was perceived as being unwilling to pursue such supertechnical and inconsequential cases.

In United States v. Reader's Digest, 4 Med.L.Rptr. 2258, 464 F.Supp. 1037 (D.Del. 1978), the court proscribed "simulated checks" as a promotional device and found the governmental interest in preventing deception outweighing *Reader's Digest's* free speech rights because regulation affected only the form of the message, not its content. The court imposed a civil penalty of $1,750,000 on *Reader's Digest.* The Third Circuit affirmed in 7 Med.L.Rptr. 1921, 662 F.2d 955 (3d Cir.1981) and the Supreme Court let it stand, cert. den. 455 U.S. 908.

Claims of uniqueness have run afoul of the agency. When Wonder Bread implied in its advertising that it could cause dramatic growth in children, its makers were challenged. ITT Continental Baking, 3 Trade Reg.Rptr. 20,464 (1973).

Merck & Co. and its advertising agency were ordered to discontinue false germ-killing and pain-relieving claims for Sucrets in 1966. "A false impression can be made by words and sentences which are literally and technically true but framed in such a setting as to mislead or deceive," said the Sixth Circuit Court of Appeals in affirming the commission's order, "and as one writer has pointed out 'The skillful advertiser can mislead the consumer without misstating a single fact. The shrewd use of exaggeration, innuendo, ambiguity and half-truth is more efficacious from the advertiser's standpoint than factual assertions.' " The court would not permit the advertising agency to pass the buck to Merck because, said the court, "This is an area in which the agency has expertise. Its responsibility for creating deceptive advertising cannot be shifted to the principal who is liable in any event." Merck & Co. v. FTC, 392 F.2d 921 (6th Cir. 1968).

Nearly ten years later in December 1977 the FTC had to file a civil penalty suit against Merck for violating its 1966 order. Regulators seemed unable to cope with misrepresentation, although this time the commission would ask the court for a permanent injunction against future violations.

The commission had *Sperry & Hutchinson* in mind when it decided its landmark *substantiation* case. Involved were advertisements for an ointment purporting to anesthetize nerves in sunburned skin on the basis of systematic scientific research, claims which were unsubstantiated. Affirming the decision of a hearing examiner that the commission's staff counsel had failed to establish with conclusive evidence that a cease-and-desist order should issue, FTC Chairman Miles Kirkpatrick nevertheless set the ground rules for future substantiation requirements:

> Given the imbalance of knowledge and resources between a business enterprise and each of its customers, economically it is more rational and imposes far less cost on society, to require a manufacturer to confirm his affirmative product claims rather than impose a burden upon each individual consumer to test, investigate, or experiment for himself. The manufacturer has the ability, the knowhow, the equipment, the time and the resources to undertake such information by testing or otherwise—the consumer usually does not. * * * Absent a reasonable basis for a vendor's affirmative product claims, a consumer's ability to make an economically rational product choice, and a competitor's ability to compete on the basis of price, quality, service or convenience are materially impaired

and impeded. * * * The consumer is entitled, as a matter of marketplace fairness, to rely upon the manufacturer to have a "reasonable basis" for making performance claims. A consumer should not be compelled to enter into an economic gamble to determine whether a product will or will not perform as represented. * * * A sale made as a result of unsupported advertising claims deprives competitors of the opportunity to have made that sale for themselves. Pfizer, Inc., 81 FTC 23 (1972). This ruling remains the regulatory standard in substantiation cases. The court held in Jay Norris, Inc. v. FTC, 598 F.2d 1244 (2d Cir. 1979), cert. den. 444 U.S. 980 (1979), that substantiation was "a reasonable remedy for past violations of the Act" and not an unconstitutional prior restraint. Affirmative disclosure remains central to FTC initiatives in rule making, although some regulators express a preference for self-regulation over affirmative disclosure and substantiation.

"Substantial scientific test data," then, are required to support a claim that "involves a matter of human safety * * * which consumers themselves cannot verify since they have neither the equipment nor the knowledge to undertake the complicated * * * tests required [and therefore] must rely on the technical expertise of the manufacturers to assure the validity of its claims." Firestone Tire & Rubber Co. v. FTC, 81 FTC 398, 451 (1972), affirmed 481 F.2d 246 (6th Cir. 1972), cert. den., 414 U.S. 1112 (1973).

A 1974 FTC order required not only competent scientific tests, but tests that would support an advertising claim of superior product performance at not less than the 95 percent confidence level. That is, nineteen of twenty copies of an advertised product would have to perform at the promised level. In re K Mart Enterprises, Inc., 3 Trade Reg.Rptr. ¶ 20,661 (1974). This expectation may be more urgent where a health claim is made. P. Lorrillard Co. v. FTC, 186 F.2d 52 (4th Cir. 1950).

The FTC obviously has broad powers to remedy false, misleading, and deceptive acts and practices, and the federal courts, deferring to its expertise, will usually sustain its orders. During the Reagan Administration those powers were questioned, and, as part of a program to make regulatory agencies more sensitive to business and political perspectives, Congress reined in its offspring and attempted to remove the presumption of validity of an agency's interpretation of the law when cases came before the federal courts.

The Regulatory Process. *Rulemaking.* Federal Trade Commission consumer protection rules are promulgated under Section 18 of the FTC Act (15 U.S.C. 57a), as amended by the Magnuson-Moss Warranty—FTC Improvement Act of 1975, authorizing the commission to issue rules which "define with specificity" unfair or deceptive acts or practices proscribed by the Act.

In a pre-rulemaking investigative phase, the FTC staff gathers data to assess the seriousness of the problem. A proposal to move on to a formal investigation which may lead to a rulemaking proceeding must be approved by an evaluation committee of the Bureau of Consumer Protection and by that Bureau's director. The investigation then fans out to seek information from industry, state and local government officials, and knowledgeable persons generally. The FTC's Bureau of Economics is consulted. Subpoenas, with commission approval, and investigatory hearings are available in this stage, but voluntary information is preferred.

These efforts result in an initial staff report which includes findings and recommendations concerning the form of any proposed rule. This must be accompanied by a cost projection, an environmental impact assessment where needed, and a proposed initial notice of rulemaking—all approved by the Bureau of Economics—before forwarding to the commission.[43]

An Initial Notice of proposed rulemaking includes (1) the terms or substance of the proposal or a description of the subjects and issues involved, (2) the legal authority under which the rule is proposed, (3) particular reasons for the rule, and (4) an invitation to all interested persons to propose issues within the framework of the proposal. A rulemaking proceeding begins with this invitation for comments and potential issues of disputed facts. These must be submitted within sixty days of the Initial Notice, and written comments are accepted until forty-five days before an informal hearing takes place.

A hearing officer then designates the disputed issues in a final notice, together with the hearing schedule, and deadlines for filing written comments and indications of interest to engage in examination, cross-examination, and rebuttal of witnesses. Ten days after publication of the final notice, interested persons may petition the commission for addition to, deletion, or modification of a designated issue. An additional ten days are set aside for more submissions.

Hearings are held. A final staff report and a report by the presiding officer, who may be an administrative law judge, and who has broad powers to make findings and conclusions, are forwarded to the commission. Both are open to public comment for a period of sixty days. After digesting these public comments, the commission may hold an open meeting at which interested parties are given a final limited opportunity to make oral presentations to the commission. Beyond this, the staff may add specialized memoranda, and counter proposals could come from the Bureau of Consumer Protection. The commission then deliberates and decides whether or not a rule shall issue. Both House and Senate Commerce Committees now review FTC rules before they are promulgated, providing Congress with what in effect is a legislative veto.

It should be noted that the United States Supreme Court in Immigration and Naturalization Service v. Chadha, 103 S.Ct. 2764 (1983) declared a resolution by one House of Congress invalidating an executive branch decision to be an unconstitutional legislative act. The Constitution requires legislation to be passed by both Houses of Congress and presented to the president. The single House legislative veto did apply to the FTC Improvement Act of 1980 (15 U.S.C. 57a–1), but FTC rules generally could only be disapproved by concurrent resolution.

Rule Violations. Federal Trade Commission actions against rule violations begin either with complaints from members of the public or, more frequently, out of a commission investigation. The agency has broad investigatory powers and authority to enforce its own subpoenas. At an early point, the FTC may waive its right to bring a court action against a violator in return for consumer redress provisions in a *consent agreement,* provisions that could go beyond the statutory authority of the courts. The commission has noted that voluntary compliance through a *consent agreement* does not constitute an admission by respondents that they have violated the law. When issued by the commission on a final basis, a consent order carries the force of law with respect to future actions. It has the same effect as an FTC adjudication. Violation of such an order could result in a civil penalty of up to $10,000 per violation per day. Each broadcast of an advertisement may constitute a separate violation.

Adverse publicity and high litigation costs assure that more than 75 percent of cases will end this way. Since 1977, how-

43. Problems with this procedure are discussed in the ABA Report on the FTC. See fn. 37.

ever, the FTC has had the power to ask an advertiser or his agency, during the sixty-day comment period, for documentary material related to the published consent order if releasable under the Freedom of Information Act. This may make consent agreements less attractive to advertisers in the future.

Consent Agreements. Consent agreements, incorporating refunds or other forms of equitable relief, are a major enforcement result of the Magnuson-Moss Act. Under the act, consumer protection rules can be vigorously enforced. Formerly, if the commission had reason to believe that the FTC Act or another federal consumer statute had been violated, a complaint would initiate a *cease-and-desist* order. The order might require of an advertiser an *affirmative disclosure* of what had been omitted from a prior claim.[44]

A respondent then had the right to appear before an administrative law judge and show cause why such an order should not be made. If unsuccessful, that party would have sixty days to challenge a commission order in a federal court of appeals. A *cease-and-desist* order would not become effective until all avenues of opinion had been exhausted. This could take a long time. It took the commission sixteen years to get the "Liver" out of Carter's Little Pills,[45] and in 1959, the year that case was concluded, the FTC began an investigation of Geritol. A complaint was issued in 1962, a cease-and-desist order in 1964; the Sixth Circuit Court of Appeals upheld the commission in 1967,[46] but two years later, finding the company in noncompliance, the commission turned the case over to the Department of Justice. Justice filed a $1 million suit against the company and in 1973 fined it and its advertising agency $812,000. In the intervening fourteen years Geritol had spent an estimated $60 million on television advertising.

Under Magnuson-Moss, consumer protection rules can be more vigorously enforced. In lieu of *cease-and-desist* orders, rules are now directly enforceable in a United States district court with civil penalties of up to $10,000 per day per violation, and consumer redress. Industry-wide Trade Regulation Rules may be enforced in the same manner. Dishonest or fraudulent trade practices—more serious than those unfair or deceptive but less serious than those constituting criminal fraud—seem to require administrative proceedings leading to a final *cease-and-desist* order prior to court action. As well as consumers, persons, partnerships, and corporations may seek redress; individuals as well as companies may be required to give it. For this reason, the line between anticompetitive and consumer protection issues is not always distinct. Culpability depends on a showing that "a reasonable and prudent man under the circumstances would have known of the existence of the rule and that the act or practice was in violation of its provisions."

Violations of *cease-and-desist* orders or other final orders of the commission empower district courts to grant temporary restraining orders or preliminary injunctions. An administrative complaint must follow within twenty days. In some cases the commission may seek and, after proof, a court may issue a permanent injunction. Injunctions are more common in antitrust cases than in consumer protection cases.

Congress amended Section 13 of the FTC Act in 1973 [47] to permit courts to grant

44. Keele Hair & Scalp Specialists, Inc. v. FTC, 275 F.2d 18 (5th Cir. 1960).

45. Carter Products, Inc. v. FTC, 268 F.2d 461 (9th Cir. 1959), cert. den. 361 U.S. 884.

46. J.B. Williams Co., Inc. v. FTC, 381 F.2d 884 (6th Cir. 1967).

47. The amendment to Section 13 was adopted as Section 408(f) of the Trans-Alaska Pipeline Authorization Act of 1973, 15 U.S.C.A. § 53(b).

temporary *injunctions* only "upon proper showing" by the commission that an action against an advertiser would be in the public interest and that the commission would likely succeed in such an undertaking. That standard for invoking the injunctive power was challenged in a federal district court in 1974. *FTC v. National Commission on Egg Nutrition*[48] held that advertising stating that "there is no evidence that eating eggs, even in quantity, increases the risk of heart attacks or heart disease" could continue during a cease-and-desist proceeding and that an injunction would restrict useful public debate on the cholesterol issue and damage the financial interests of respondents.

On the basis of an earlier ruling, FTC v. Rhodes Pharmacal Co., 191 F.2d 744 (7th Cir. 1951), a case approving the lesser standard of "reason to believe" that an ad is false or misleading, the court of appeals in *Egg Nutrition* reversed the district court and permitted the injunction to stand. (517 F.2d 485 (7th Cir. 1975)).

Two years later the same court decided that the advertisement's no-harm statement concerning cholesterol was a misrepresentation affecting the contract of sale, a breach of express warranty, and therefore regulatable commercial speech. The same statement made at a Food and Drug Administration hearing would not be commercial speech at all since contractual promises would be involved.

The Ninth Circuit, however, also citing an earlier case—FTC v. National Health Aids, Inc., 108 F.Supp. 340 (D.Md.1952)—but one requiring the higher standard of "falsity" in the exercise of the extraordinary remedy of injunction, affirmed the denial of an injunction in FTC v. Simeon Management Corp., 391 F.Supp. 697 (D.Cal. 1975), affirmed 532 F.2d 708 (9th Cir. 1976).

Clearly, appeals courts are divided on what Congress intended in amending Section 13. Is it the lesser standard of "reason to believe" or a higher standard requiring the court to make an independent judgment that the public interest demands an injunction against false advertising? While the former test may be more sensitive to the public interest, the latter may be more responsive to the First Amendment. The issue will remain open.

Both tests have their advocates.[49]

Injunctions and other FTC actions are more likely to be triggered when foods, drugs, medical devices, and cosmetics are involved and where a violation is clear and immediately harmful. The Food and Drug Administration has authority over the labeling of these kinds of products under the *Food, Drug and Cosmetic Act of 1938 (21 U.S.C.A. 301–392).*

In all, some twenty federal agencies regulate advertising in specifically defined areas. These include the Securities and Exchange Commission, the Alcohol and Tobacco Tax Division of the Internal Revenue Service, the Civil Aeronautics Board, the Interstate Commerce Commission, and the Federal Power Commission.

State Regulation. All states except Alabama and the District of Columbia, Guam, Puerto Rico, and the U.S. Virgin Islands have "Little FTC" acts, paralleling to some degree the federal statute's Section 5 proscription against unfair or deceptive trade practices. Some are as broad as Section 5 itself. Others reach unfair or deceptive acts or practices but not unfair methods of

48. 1975–1 Trade Cas. ¶ 60,246 (N.D.Ill.1974). See National Commission on Egg Nutrition v. FTC, 3 Med.L.Rptr. 2196, 570 F.2d 157 (7th Cir. 1977), cert. den., 439 U.S. 821 (1978).

49. See, for example, *The FTC's Injunctive Authority Against False Advertising of Food and Drugs,* 75 Michigan L.Rev. 745 (March 1977), and *Yes, FTC, There is a Virginia: The Impact of* Virginia State Board of Pharmacy v. Virginia Citizens Consumer Council *on the FTC's Regulation of Misleading Advertising,* 57 Boston U.L.Rev. 833 (1977).

competition. Still others reach only a specific list of prohibited practices.

Remedies vary also. A number of states grant rulemaking power to a state official, often the attorney general, who may bring suit to stop violations of the state law. By this route, consumers may gain restitution in forty-nine jurisdictions, the state additional civil penalties in thirty-four.

The laws of fifty-three of these jurisdictions authorize the use of subpoenas in civil investigations and the use of cease-and-desist orders or court injunctions to halt anticompetitive, unfair, unconscionable, or deceptive practices. Class actions are permitted in seventeen jurisdictions, *private actions by consumers* in forty-four.

Private actions are generally not allowed under FTCA's Section 5. They nevertheless should be attempted as a complement to FTC actions and will undoubtedly be more frequent in federal litigation as FTC powers are curtailed. Most state laws have been influenced by federal law, and the demise of the "unfairness doctrine" in federal law will probably be reflected in state laws. In the meantime, the paucity of state court interpretations of these relatively recent state statutes insure that guidance will be sought from administrative and judicial decisions under the federal act. Twenty-one state laws specifically encourage this. For example, the intent to deceive is not a necessary element of proof under some state laws. Nor does a plaintiff actually have to have been deceived. It is enough that a defendant's conduct would have a capacity or a tendency to deceive. Together with the possibility of double or treble actual damages, punitive damages, and some attorney's fees and costs, there is an incentive to litigate under state laws. Expectations are that state courts will eventually adopt the standards of the FTC Trade Practice Rules, the Trade Regulation Rules, and the concepts of other federal protection statutes enforced by the FTC. At least thirty-five states use federal standards in enforcing state food and drug laws.[50]

Media are not liable for unlawful advertisements or injuries resulting from defective products,[51] and they have no duty to investigate each advertiser, even when placed on notice as to potential danger.[52] There can be a problem if a publication plays an active role in a false and deceptive ad or specifically endorses a product.[53] Indemnification clauses are now common in rate cards and advertising contracts, especially with regard to errors or omissions in ads, but they probably wouldn't protect a publication in the negligent preparation of an ad.

Corrective Advertising. *Corrective advertising,* a powerful regulatory device, first came to the attention of the FTC in May 1970 when a group called SOUP (Students Opposing Unfair Practices) intervened in an action against the Campbell Soup Company in a situation reminiscent of the *Colgate-Palmolive* sandpaper case. Campbell had used marbles in its video advertising to make its soup appear thicker than it was. No order requiring corrective advertising was issued for lack of a significant public interest, but the commission made its point. Campbell Soup, 3

50. Federal Trade Commission Fact Sheet, State Legislation to Combat Unfair Trade Practices (September 1979, Rev.), and Paul R. Peterson, "The Use of FTC Programs as a Basis for Suit Under State FTC Acts," (April 1, 1980), both reprinted, with a complete list of "Little FTC" state laws in Christopher Smith and Christian S. White, cochairmen, *FTC Consumer Protection Law Institute,* Vol. II, New York: Practising Law Institute, 1980.

51. Goldstein v. Garlick, 318 N.Y.S.2d 370 (1971); Suarez v. Underwood, 426 N.Y.S.2d 208 (1980).

52. Hernandez v. Underwood, 7 Med.L.Rptr. 1535 (N.Y.Sup.Ct.1981); Pressler v. Dow Jones & Co., Inc., 8 Med.L.Rptr. 1680, 450 N.Y.S.2d 884 (1982).

53. Hanberry v. Hearst Corp., 81 Cal.Rptr. 519 (1969).

Trade Reg.Rptr. ¶ 19,261 (FTC May 25, 1970).

The FTC first sought corrective advertising in late 1970 in actions charging Coca-Cola with misrepresenting the nutritional value of Hi-C and Standard Oil of California with falsely claiming that its gasoline reduced air pollution.[54] Both complaints were later dropped.

In August 1971 the FTC issued its first final corrective advertising order against Profile Bread which was promoted as having fewer calories per slice. It did, but only because it was sliced thinner. The order required that ITT Continental Baking Co. and its advertising agency Ted Bates cease and desist for a period of one year from disseminating any advertisements for the product "unless not less than 25 percent of the expenditure (excluding production costs) for each medium in each market be devoted to advertising in a manner approved by authorized representatives of the Federal Trade Commission that Profile is not effective for weight reduction, contrary to possible interpretations of prior advertising." ITT Continental Baking Co., 1973 CCH Transfer Binder, ¶ 19,681 (1971).

The company agreed to devote 25 percent of its advertising expenditure for one year to FTC-approved corrective ads. Its only alternative was not to advertise the product at all.

The difference between a traditional order for affirmative disclosure and one for corrective advertising is that the corrective ad order refers to past rather than current advertising and is designed to dispel misconceptions the consumer may have gained from earlier ads. Although the commission may not impose criminal penalties or award compensatory damages for past acts, it does have a mandate to prevent illegal practices in the future.[55] A corrective order may remind consumers that a particular advertiser is a hard-core offender. Estimates of residual effects on consumers of past advertising require expert testimony.[56]

Profile corrective ads, read by actress Julia Mead, were so well received by the public that the company contemplated spending more than the required 25 percent of its ad budget on their presentation. But the ads, ignoring the fact that the FTC had found deception in earlier ads, gave the company a credibility it didn't deserve. Later corrective orders specified the wording more precisely.

Less than two weeks after the enforcement of its first corrective order against Profile, the FTC ordered seven of the largest foreign and domestic automobile manufacturers to submit to the Commission documentation to support advertising claims concerning the safety, performance, quality, and comparative prices of their advertised products. The order followed a June 1971 resolution requiring all advertisers to submit on demand documentation to support unique advertising claims.[57]

In a case involving a false claim that a brand of Firestone tires was capable of stopping a car 25 percent faster, the FTC staff asserted its authority to require corrective advertising, but the commission refused to issue the order because: 1) there had been a considerable time lapse since the ad had appeared; 2) the tires advertised with the unsubstantiated claim

54. Coca-Cola Co., 3 Trade Reg.Rptr. ¶ 19,351 (FTC 1970); Standard Oil Co. of California, 3 Trade Reg.Rptr. ¶ 19,352 (FTC 1970).

55. FTC v. Ruberoid Co., 343 U.S. 470 (1952).

56. See Notes, *Corrective Advertising—the New Response to Consumer Deception,* 72 Columbia L.Rev. 415 (February 1972); *Corrective Advertising and the FTC,* 70 Michigan L.Rev. 374 (December 1971).

57. Resolution Requiring Submission of Special Reports Relating to Advertising Claims and Disclosure Thereof by the Commission in Connection with a Public Investigation Adopted by the FTC on June 9, 1971, as amended July 7, 1971, 2 CCH Trade Reg.Rptr. 7573 (FTC 1971).

would by now be so old that no owner would believe them safe; 3) the residual effect of the advertising would have been slight by the end of the year; and 4) competitors making the same claim had avoided cease-and-desist orders. Firestone Tire and Rubber Co., 3 Trade Reg.Rptr. ¶ 19,773 (FTC 1971).

In a corrective advertising action against the Sun Oil Co., which had claimed that "cars will operate at maximum power and performance only with Sunoco gasolines," the company had to counter empirical evidence of the effects of its advertising on a sample of the mass audience.

After a flurry of cases a hiatus occurred in corrective advertising partly because the somewhat ponderous process could not keep up with the fluid and ingenious advertising industry: ads would be challenged long after they had served the purposes of advertisers. Then in 1975 an administrative law judge, in the first litigated corrective advertising case, was upheld by the full commission in forbidding Warner-Lambert, the makers of Listerine, to advertise unless each ad included the following language: "Contrary to prior advertising, Listerine will not help prevent colds or sore throats or lessen their severity." Warner-Lambert Co., 86 F.T.C. 1938 (1975). The corrective advertising was to continue until the company had spent $10 million on Listerine advertising, an amount roughly equal to the annual Listerine budget for 1962 to 1974. The D.C. Circuit Court of Appeals affirmed the commission decision in the opinion which follows with the words "contrary to prior advertising" deleted.

WARNER–LAMBERT CO. v. FEDERAL TRADE COMMISSION

562 F.2D 749 (D.C.CIR. 1977), CERT. DEN. 435 U.S. 950 (1978).

J. Skelly WRIGHT, Circuit Judge:

* * *

The first issue on appeal is whether the Commission's conclusion that Listerine is not beneficial for colds or sore throats is supported by the evidence. The Commission's findings must be sustained if they are supported by substantial evidence on the record viewed as a whole. We conclude that they are.

Both the ALJ [Administrative Law Judge] and the Commission carefully analyzed the evidence. They gave full consideration to the studies submitted by petitioner. The ultimate conclusion that Listerine is not an effective cold remedy was based on six specific findings of fact.

* * *

Petitioner contends that even if its advertising claims in the past were false, the portion of the Commission's order requiring "corrective advertising" exceeds the Commission's statutory power. The argument is based upon a literal reading of Section 5 of the Federal Trade Commission Act, which authorizes the Commission to issue "cease and desist" orders against violators and does not expressly mention any other remedies. The Commission's position, on the other hand, is that the affirmative disclosure that Listerine will not prevent colds or lessen their severity is absolutely necessary to give effect to the prospective cease and desist order; a hundred years of false cold claims have built up a large reservoir of erroneous consumer belief which would persist, unless corrected, long after petitioner ceased making the claims.

The need for the corrective advertising remedy and its appropriateness in this case are important issues which we will explore. But the threshold question is whether the Commission has the authority to issue such an order. We hold that it does.

Petitioner's narrow reading of Section 5 was at one time shared by the Supreme Court. In FTC v. Eastman Kodak Co., 274

U.S. 619, 623 (1927), the Court held that the Commission's authority did not exceed that expressly conferred by statute. The Commission has not, the Court said, "been delegated the authority of a court of equity."

But the modern view is very different. In 1963 the Court ruled that the Civil Aeronautics Board has authority to order divestiture in addition to ordering cessation of unfair methods of competition by air carriers. Pan American World Airways, Inc. v. United States, 371 U.S. 296 (1963). The CAB statute, like Section 5, spoke only of the authority to issue cease and desist orders, but the Court said, "We do not read the Act so restrictively. * * * [W]here the problem lies within the purview of the Board, * * * Congress must have intended to give it authority that was ample to deal with the evil at hand." The Court continued, "Authority to mold administrative decrees is indeed like the authority of courts to frame injunctive decrees. * * * [The] power to order divestiture need not be explicitly included in the powers of an administrative agency to be part of its arsenal of authority. * * *"

Later, in FTC v. Dean Foods Co., 384 U.S. 597 (1966), the Court applied *Pan American* to the Federal Trade Commission. In upholding the Commission's power to seek a preliminary injunction against a proposed merger, the Court held that it was not necessary to find express statutory authority for the power. Rather, the Court concluded, "It would stultify congressional purpose to say that the Commission did not have the * * * power * * *. * * * Such ancillary powers have always been treated as essential to the effective discharge of the Commission's responsibilities."

Thus it is clear that the Commission has the power to shape remedies which go beyond the simple cease and desist order. Our next inquiry must be whether a corrective advertising order is for any reason outside the range of permissible remedies. Petitioner and *amici curiae* argue that it is because (1) legislative history precludes it, (2) it impinges on the First Amendment, and (3) it has never been approved by any court.

A. LEGISLATIVE HISTORY

Petitioner relies on the legislative history of the 1914 Federal Trade Commission Act and the Wheeler-Lea amendments to it in 1938 for the proposition that corrective advertising was not contemplated. In 1914 and in 1938 Congress chose not to authorize such remedies as criminal penalties, treble damages, or civil penalties, but that fact does not dispose of the question of corrective advertising.[33]

Petitioner's reliance on the legislative history of the 1975 amendments to the Act[34] is also misplaced. The amendments added a new Section 19 to the Act authorizing the Commission to bring suits in federal District Courts to redress injury to consumers resulting from a deceptive practice. The section authorizes the court to grant such relief as it "finds necessary to redress injury to consumers or other

33. It is true that one Court of Appeals has relied on this history in concluding that the Commission does not have power to order restitution of ill-gotten monies to the injured consumers. Heater v. FTC, 503 F.2d 321 (9th Cir. 1974). But restitution is not corrective advertising. Ordering refunds to *past* consumers is very different from ordering affirmative disclosure to correct misconceptions which *future* consumers may hold. Moreover, the *Heater* court itself recognized this distinction and expressly distinguished corrective advertising, which it said the Commission is authorized to order, from restitution. 503 F.2d at 323 n. 7 and 325 n. 13.

34. The Magnuson-Moss Warranty—Federal Trade Commission Improvement Act, 88 Stat. 2183 (1975). *Note:* Under this Act it is the responsibility of one advertiser to know about a cease-and-desist order against another, if it is litigated [FTCA sec. 205]; the requirement does not apply to consent orders. Failure of the FTC to proceed against an advertiser's competitors is not valid ground to have an order against an advertiser set aside. Johnson Products v. FTC, 549 F.2d 35 (7th Cir. 1977).

persons, partnerships, and corporations resulting from the rule violation or the unfair or deceptive act or practice," including, but not limited to,

> rescission or reformation of contracts, the refund of money or return of property, the payment of damages, and public notification respecting the rule violation or the unfair or deceptive act or practice. * * * 15 U.S.C.A. § 576(b).

Petitioner and *amici* contend that this congressional grant *to a court* of power to order public notification of a violation establishes that the Commission by itself does not have that power.

We note first that "public notification" is not synonymous with corrective advertising; public notification is a much broader term and may take any one of many forms.[36] Second, the "public notification" contemplated by the amendment is directed at *past* consumers of the product ("to redress injury"), whereas the type of corrective advertising currently before us is directed at *future* consumers. Third, petitioner's construction of the section runs directly contrary to the congressional intent as expressed in a later subsection: "Nothing in this section shall be construed to affect any authority of the Commission under any other provision of law." Moreover, this intent is amplified by the conference committee's report:

> The section * * * is not intended to modify or limit any existing power the Commission may have to itself issue orders designed to remedying [*sic*] violations of the law. That issue is now before the courts. It is not the intent of the Conferees to influence the outcome in any way.

We conclude that this legislative history cannot be said to remove corrective advertising from the class of permissible remedies.

B. THE FIRST AMENDMENT

Petitioner and *amici* further contend that corrective advertising is not a permissible remedy because it trenches on the First Amendment. *Petitioner is correct that this triggers a special responsibility on the Commission to order corrective advertising only if the restriction inherent in its order is no greater than necessary to serve the interest involved.* [Emphasis added.] But this goes to the appropriateness of the order in this case, an issue we reach [later in] this opinion. *Amici curiae* go further, arguing that, since the Supreme Court has recently extended First Amendment protection to commercial advertising, mandatory corrective advertising is unconstitutional.

A careful reading of Virginia State Bd. of Pharmacy v. Virginia Citizens Consumer Council compels rejection of this argument. For the Supreme Court expressly noted that the First Amendment presents "no obstacle" to government regulation of false or misleading advertising. The First Amendment, the Court said,

> as we construe it today, does not prohibit the State from insuring that the stream of commercial information flow[s] cleanly as well as freely.

In a footnote the Court went on to delineate several differences between commercial speech and other forms which may suggest "that a different degree of protection is necessary. * * *" For example, the Court said, they may

> make it appropriate to require that a commercial message appear in such a form, or include such additional information, warnings, and disclaimers, as

36. For example, it might encompass requiring the defendant to run special advertisements reporting the FTC finding, advertisements advising consumers of the availability of a refund, or the posting of notices in the defendant's place of business.

> are necessary to prevent its being deceptive.

The Supreme Court clearly foresaw the very question before us, and its statement is dispositive of *amici's* contention.

C. PRECEDENTS

According to petitioner, "The first reference to corrective advertising in Commission decisions occurred in 1970, nearly fifty years and untold numbers of false advertising cases after passage of the Act." In petitioner's view, the late emergence of this "newly discovered" remedy is itself evidence that it is beyond the Commission's authority. This argument fails on two counts. First the fact that an agency has not asserted a power over a period of years is not proof that the agency lacks such power. Second, and more importantly, we are not convinced that the corrective advertising remedy is really such an innovation. The label may be newly coined, but the concept is well established. It is simply that under certain circumstances an advertiser may be required to make affirmative disclosure of unfavorable facts.

One such circumstance is when an advertisement that did not contain the disclosure would be misleading. For example, the Commission has ordered the sellers of treatments for baldness to disclose that the vast majority of cases of thinning hair and baldness are attributable to heredity, age, and endocrine balance (so-called "male pattern baldness") and that their treatment would have no effect whatever on this type of baldness. It has ordered the promoters of a device for stopping bedwetting to disclose that the device would not be of value in cases caused by organic defects or diseases. And it has ordered the makers of Geritol, an iron supplement, to disclose that Geritol will relieve symptoms of tiredness only in persons who suffer from iron deficiency anemia, and that the vast majority of people who experience such symptoms do not have such a deficiency.

Each of these orders was approved on appeal over objections that it exceeded the Commission's statutory authority. The decisions reflect a recognition that, as the Supreme Court has stated,

> If the Commission is to attain the objectives Congress envisioned, it cannot be required to confine its road block to the narrow lane the transgressor has traveled; it must be allowed effectively to close all roads to the prohibited goal, so that its order may not be bypassed with impunity. FTC v. Ruberoid Co., 343 U.S. 470, 473 (1952).

Affirmative disclosure has also been required when an advertisement, although not misleading if taken alone, becomes misleading considered in light of past advertisements. For example, for 60 years Royal Baking Powder Co. had stressed in its advertising that its product was superior because it was made with cream of tartar, not phosphate. But, faced with rising costs of cream of tartar, the time came when it changed its ingredients and became a phosphate baking powder. It carefully removed from all labels and advertisements any reference to cream of tartar and corrected the list of ingredients. But the new labels used the familiar arrangement of lettering, coloration, and design, so that they looked exactly like the old ones. A new advertising campaign stressed the new low cost of the product and dropped all reference to cream of tartar. But the advertisements were also silent on the subject of phosphate and did not disclose the change in the product.

The Commission held, and the Second Circuit agreed, that the new advertisements were deceptive, since they did not advise consumers that their reasons for buying the powder in the past no longer applied. The court held that it was proper to require the company to take affirmative steps to advise the public. To continue to sell the new powder

> on the strength of the reputation attained through 60 years of its manufacture and sale and wide advertising of its superior powder, under an impression induced by its advertisements that the product purchased was the same in kind and as superior as that which had been so long manufactured by it, was unfair alike to the public and to the competitors in the baking powder business. Royal Baking Powder Co. v. FTC, 281 F. 744, 753 (2d Cir. 1922).

In another case the Waltham Watch Company of Massachusetts had become renowned for the manufacture of fine clocks since 1849. Soon after it stopped manufacturing clocks in the 1950's, it transferred its trademarks, good will, and the trade name "Waltham" to a successor corporation, which began importing clocks from Europe for resale in the United States. The imported clocks were advertised as "product of Waltham Watch Company since 1850," "a famous 150-year-old company."

The Commission found that the advertisements caused consumers to believe they were buying the same fine Massachusetts clocks of which they had heard for many years. To correct this impression the Commission ordered the company to disclose in all advertisements and on the product that the clock was not made by the old Waltham company and that it was imported. The Seventh Circuit affirmed, relying on "the well-established general principle that the Commission may require affirmative disclosure for the purpose of preventing future deception." Waltham Watch Co. v. FTC, 318 F.2d 28 (7th Cir. 1963), cert. den. 375 U.S. 944.

It appears to us that the orders in *Royal* and *Waltham* were the same kind of remedy the Commission has ordered here. Like Royal and Waltham, Listerine has built up over a period of many years a widespread reputation. When it was ascertained that that reputation no longer applied to the product, it was necessary to take action to correct it. Here, as in *Royal* and *Waltham*, it is the accumulated impact of *past* advertising that necessitates disclosure in *future* advertising. To allow consumers to continue to buy the product on the strength of the impression built up by prior advertising—an impression which is now known to be false—would be unfair and deceptive.

Having established that the Commission does have the power to order corrective advertising in appropriate cases, it remains to consider whether use of the remedy against Listerine is warranted and equitable. We have concluded that part 3 of the order should be modified to delete the phrase "Contrary to prior advertising." With that modification, we approve the order.

Our role in reviewing the remedy is limited. The Supreme Court has set forth the standard:

> The Commission is the expert body to determine what remedy is necessary to eliminate the unfair or deceptive trade practices which have been disclosed. It has wide latitude for judgment and the courts will not interfere except where the remedy selected has no reasonable relation to the unlawful practices found to exist. Jacob Siegel Co. v. FTC, 327 U.S. 608, 612–613 (1946).

The Commission has adopted the following standard for the imposition of corrective advertising:

> [I]f a deceptive advertisement has played a substantial role in creating or reinforcing in the public's mind a false and material belief which lives on after the false advertising ceases, there is clear and continuing injury to competition and to the consuming public as consumers continue to make purchasing decisions based on the false belief. Since this injury cannot be averted by merely requiring respondent to cease disseminating the advertisement, we may appropriately order respondent to take affirmative action designed to terminate the otherwise continuing ill effects of the advertisement.

We think this standard is entirely reasonable. It dictates two factual inquiries: (1) did Listerine's advertisements play a substantial role in creating or reinforcing in the public's mind a false belief about the product? and (2) would this belief linger on after the false advertising ceases? It strikes us that if the answer to both questions is not yes, companies everywhere may be wasting their massive advertising budgets. Indeed, it is more than a little peculiar to hear petitioner assert that its commercials really have no effect on consumer belief.

For these reasons it might be appropriate in some cases to presume the existence of the two factual predicates for corrective advertising. But we need not decide that question, or rely on presumptions here, because the Commission adduced survey evidence to support both propositions. We find that the "Product Q" survey data and the expert testimony interpreting them constitute substantial evidence in support of the need for corrective advertising in this case.

We turn next to the specific disclosure required: "Contrary to prior advertising, Listerine will not help prevent colds or sore throats or lessen their severity." Petitioner is ordered to include this statement in every future advertisement for Listerine for a defined period. In printed advertisements it must be displayed in type size at least as large as that in which the principal portion of the text of the advertisement appears and it must be separated from the text so that it can be readily noticed. In television commercials the disclosure must be presented simultaneously in both audio and visual portions. During the audio portion of the disclosure in television and radio advertisements, no other sounds, including music, may occur.

These specifications are well calculated to assure that the disclosure will reach the public. It will necessarily attract the notice of readers, viewers, and listeners, and be plainly conveyed. Given these safeguards, we believe the preamble "Contrary to prior advertising" is not necessary. It can serve only two purposes: either to attract attention that a correction follows or to humiliate the advertiser. The Commission claims only the first purpose for it, and this we think is obviated by the other terms of the order.[68] The second purpose, if it were intended, might be called for in an egregious case of deliberate deception, but this is not one. While we do not decide whether petitioner proffered its cold claims in good faith or bad, the record compiled could support a finding of good faith. On these facts, the confessional preamble to the disclosure is not warranted.

Finally, petitioner challenges the duration of the disclosure requirement. By its terms it continues until respondent has expended on Listerine advertising a sum equal to the average annual Listerine advertising budget for the period April 1962 to March 1972. That is approximately ten million dollars. Thus if petitioner continues to advertise normally the corrective advertising will be required for about one year. We cannot say that is an unreasonably long time in which to correct a hundred years of cold claims. But, to petitioner's distress, the requirement will not expire by mere passage of time. If petitioner cuts back its Listerine advertising, or ceases it altogether, it can only postpone the duty to disclose. The Commission concluded that correction was required and that a duration of a fixed period of time might not accomplish that task, since petitioner could evade the order by choosing

68. Cf. United States v. National Society of Professional Engineers, 555 F.2d 978 at 984 (D.C.Cir.1977) (order should not be more intrusive than necessary to achieve fulfillment of the governmental interest) [Editorial note: the decision was affirmed in part and remanded in part, 98 S.Ct. 1355 (1978)]; Beneficial Corp. v. FTC, 542 F.2d 611 at 618–620 (3d Cir. 1976), cert. den. 430 U.S. 983 (1977) (same).

not to advertise at all. The formula settled upon by the Commission is reasonably related to the violation it found.

Accordingly, the order, as modified, is Affirmed.

COMMENT

Judge Robb dissented because he believed the FTC had been conferred power only to prevent future deceptions or to impose a prospective remedy. Corrective advertising constituted a retrospective remedy, a remedy for past claims.

1. In a supplemental opinion denying a rehearing, the court of appeals elaborated on the First Amendment issue, focusing on its interpretation of *Virginia Pharmacy.* Since the Supreme Court had held that "untruthful speech, commercial or otherwise, has never been protected for its own sake," the commission was within its authority in viewing the case against a background of more than 100 years in which Listerine has been proclaimed—and purchased—as a remedy for colds.

"When viewed from this perspective," said the court of appeals, "advertising which fails to rebut the prior claims as to Listerine's efficacy inevitably builds upon those claims; continued advertising continues the deception, albeit implicitly rather than explicitly. It will induce people to continue to buy Listerine thinking it will cure colds. Thus the commission found on substantial evidence that the corrective order was necessary to 'dissipate the effects of respondent's deceptive representations.' "

As to a chilling effect on protected truthful speech, the court of appeals noted that the Court in *Virginia Pharmacy* had considered the truth of commercial speech "more easily verifiable by its disseminator" than other forms of speech, and "since advertising is the *sine qua non* of commercial profits, there is little likelihood of its being chilled by proper regulation and forgone entirely." For discussion of *Warner-Lambert* in an access to the media context, see text, p. 594.

2. It has been urged that corrective orders not be confined to obvious cases such as *Warner-Lambert* where the proof presented to the commission of the success of a deceptive campaign is so striking. Noting the long history of a deceptive claim uniquely asserted for Listerine, the absence of consumer confusion as to which mouthwash was said to be effective against colds, and the persuasive evidence that this claim was believed by consumers after the false advertising had ceased, one commentator observed that "comparable proof of deception-perception-memory influence would be virtually impossible in most advertising cases. * * * If the commission is to do an effective job in regulating deceptive advertising, corrective advertising must apply to more than the one-in-a-million type of ad campaign present in *Warner-Lambert.*" [58]

And in a memorandum in support of a petition for rulemaking, the Institute for Public Interest Representation, Georgetown University Law Center, went beyond the court of appeals in *Warner-Lambert* and argued that to require the level of proof justifying corrective advertising in the Listerine case would so tip "the burden of proof in favor of the wrongdoer at the expense of the consuming public as to frustrate the ability of the commission ever to issue such an order." [59] The petitioners foresaw a "war of experts and surveys" in every deceptive advertising litigation.

Given the length of time it takes to reach the day of final judgment in decep-

---

58. Pitofsky, *Beyond Nader: Consumer Protection and the Regulation of Advertising,* 90 Harv.L.Rev. 661, 698 (February 1977).

59. Kramer et al., *Memorandum in Support of Petition for Rulemaking* (March 7, 1977), p. 3.

tive advertising cases, the procedural impossibility of any kind of consumer restitution, and the mammoth task the FTC has in monitoring an industry as large and as powerful as advertising, these evidentiary shortcuts may seem reasonable. On the other hand, where speech is being hindered by an agency of government, the burden of proof is on the agency, and the standard of proof should be high. And careful judicial review must follow. Most theories of the First Amendment permit nothing less. There appears, therefore, to be an opportunity here for the FTC to make better and more frequent use of empirical evidence, a form of evidence which the courts are more and more coming to appreciate.

What evidence establishes whether false claims about product characteristics create persistent misimpressions or other continuing effects and of what strength and duration? And what forms of corrective advertising would correct misimpressions? Answers to these kinds of factual questions should precede legal and policy considerations. Too often they do not.

On April 4, 1978, the United States Supreme Court denied certiorari to *Warner-Lambert Co. v. FTC.*

3. In May 1978 the FTC for the first time was able to get a product endorser to be personally accountable for advertising claims. Using its injunctive, complaint, and consent powers to challenge the alleged unfair or deceptive marketing practices of an acne "treatment," the commission got celebrity Pat Boone to agree to pay part of any restitution to consumers that would be ordered in the case and to make a reasonable inquiry before endorsing products in the future.

"Unless the endorser is an expert on the subject," said Albert Kramer, then director of the FTC Bureau of Consumer Protection, "the endorser must look to independent reliable sources to validate claims, tests or studies supplied by the advertiser. * * * The endorser may profit from a false advertisement just as much as the manufacturer and thus it is not unreasonable to obligate him to ascertain the truthfulness of the claims he is being paid to make." [60]

Counter Advertising. In early 1972 the Federal Trade Commission in a unanimous brief filed with the Federal Communication Commission urged broadcast support for the concept of counter advertising or "counter commercials" as "a suitable approach to some of the present failings of advertising which are beyond the FTC's capacity." FTC Dkt. ¶ 19,260, Jan. 6, 1972.

Commercial time would be available to those who could pay, free to those who could not, to reply to ads 1) asserting performance and other explicit claims raising controversial issues of current public importance, for example, pollution or automobile safety; 2) stressing broad recurrent themes affecting purchasing decisions, for example, nutrition, drug, and detergent claims; 3) resting on controversial "scientific" statements; and 4) ads silent about possibly negative aspects of a product.

The proposal was undoubtedly influenced by the D.C. Circuit's ruling in the *Banzhaf* case which, for the first time, had applied the Fairness Doctrine to broadcast advertising, specifically cigarette advertising. Banzhaf v. FCC, 1 Med.L.Rptr. 2037, 405 F.2d 1082 (D.C.Cir.1968). See text, p. 855.

The FTC felt the counter ad would go well beyond the corrective ad or the affirmative disclosure because it would not be buried in the advertiser's own message but would come from vigorous advocates of converse points of view. It was sug-

60. FTC News Summary, No. 20, May 19, 1978. See FTC Guidelines—Endorsements and Testimonials, 16 C.F.R. 255, and 45 Fed.Reg. 3870 (Jan. 18, 1980).

gested that the FCC would retain substantial discretion in deciding what commercials would raise Fairness Doctrine claims and what time frames would be suitable.

Miles Kirkpatrick, former director of an American Bar Association study of the FTC and later chairman of the Commission, said he was "deeply concerned by the notion that the majority of advertisers are able or willing to play the game only if the rules free them from disagreement. * * Why, in any event should an advertiser have the right to monopolize the consumer's attention by trumpeting the virtues of his product when a consumer who learned of an aspect undesirable to him might not buy it if the attention monopoly were ended. * * * The TV viewer is a member of the advertiser's captive audience. [And antitrust laws prohibit monopoly] of ideas or of goods." [61]

Advertisers, broadcasters, and the Nixon administration came down hard on the FTC proposal, partly on First Amendment grounds.[62] More important, perhaps, they predicted economic chaos, a bankrupt broadcast industry, and a public hopelessly confused by an "incredible babble of claim and counter claim." [63] Some even called the proposal un-American.[64]

Proponents, on the other hand, were surprised to learn that the broadcast industry was so fragile that counter advertising could destroy it, and they argued that public reply to advertising was more sensitive to First Amendment rights than government challenge, litigation, and penalty.[65] *Advertising Age,* a leading trade publication, agreed in its March 13, 1972 issue that counter advertising might curtail the FTC's intervention in advertising, and it saw no reason why ads were less appropriate subjects for discussion on television than other public matters.

The Consumer Federation of America urged the FCC to incorporate counter advertising in the Fairness Doctrine as a deterrent to exaggerated and untrue merchandising claims and as a stimulant to public dialogue on controversial issues. But the Television Bureau of Advertising came back with the argument that the scheme would shrink discussion of controversial public issues because no one would risk counterattack, an argument that has frequently been used to fault the Fairness Doctrine itself. The bureau sought to make *Banzhaf* a narrow precedent resting on legislative action which had made cigarette smoking an "official" health hazard and which eventually banned broadcast advertising of cigarettes altogether.

The D.C. Circuit, however, a year before the FTC proposal was issued, had already refused to extend the *Banzhaf* ruling to product advertising generally because, it said, to do so would undermine the present system which is based on product commercials, many of which have *some* adverse ecological effects. The case, Friends of the Earth v. FCC, 449 F.2d 1164 (D.C.Cir.1971), involved a complaint about the ecological effects of advertising big cars and high-test gasolines. On its facts, however, the case represented an expansion of *Banzhaf.* In remanding, the court declared that controversial issues of public importance might be involved in the commercial and held that the FCC would have to decide whether the licensee had afforded an opportunity for the presentation of contrasting views. See text, p. 855.

61. *Broadcasting,* March 6, 1972.

62. See Clay Whitehead in *Advertising Age,* Feb. 14, 1972, p. 19.

63. Elton Rule, president of ABC, in *Advertising Age,* May 1, 1972, p. 1.

64. Paul Warnke, former assistant secretary of defense and an attorney, in *Advertising Age,* March 6, 1972, p. 62.

65. Robert Pitofsky in *Advertising Age,* March 6, 1972, p. 3.

By 1974 the same court had decided that comparative efficiency of gasoline engines was not a controversial issue of public importance as long as commercials "made no attempt to glorify conduct or products which endangered public health or contributed to pollution." Neckritz v. FCC, 502 F.2d 411 (D.C.Cir.1974).

The demise of counter advertising seemed assured when in July 1974 the FCC rejected the FTC's proposal as "antithetical to this country's tradition of uninhibited dissemination of ideas." [66] At the same time the FCC issued a statement of policy concerning the Fairness Doctrine and advertising which essentially removed product advertising from the requirements of the Fairness Doctrine unless the advertising itself raised an important controversial issue.[67]

CBS v. Democratic Nat. Comm., see p. 858, by implication and Public Interest Research Group v. FCC, 522 F.2d 1060 (1st Cir. 1975), directly affirm this policy. Discretion in deciding how to meet Fairness Doctrine obligations remains with the broadcaster.[68]

Comparative Advertising. If there is anything that consumers deserve under either classical or contemporary theories of the First Amendment, it is fair and truthful comparative advertising.[69] Courts have held it to be "in harmony with the fundamental objectives of free speech and free enterprise in a free society." [70] The Federal Trade Commission has endorsed it.[71] Advertisers, assuming that comparative claims will inevitably become abusive, are not sure that in the long run comparative advertising won't reduce advertising's credibility.

The "aspirin war" is a case in point. Besides providing information of little use to the consumer, comparisons may slip into defamation, disparagement, or unfair competition, and thus into lawsuits.[72] If Tylenol, Anacin, and Bayer are what comparative advertising comes down to, consumers will have to look elsewhere for product information.

Self-Regulation. Spearhead of self-regulation in advertising is the National Advertising Review Board which acts on consumer and industry complaints about truth and accuracy in national advertising. Thirty national advertisers, ten delegates from advertising agencies, and ten representatives of the public comprise the Board's membership. It is sponsored by the American Advertising Federation, the American Association of Advertising Agencies, the Association of National Ad-

66. 671 ATRR A–16, July 9, 1974.

67. 39 Fed.Reg. 26372 (July 18, 1974). For an edited version of the FCC's *1974 Fairness Report* and related discussion, see this text, p. 867.

68. For persuasive arguments in favor of the demise of counter advertising see, Simmons, *Commercial Advertising and the Fairness Doctrine: The New F.C.C. Policy in Perspective,* 75 Columbia L.Rev. 1083 (1975); and Simmons, *The Fairness Doctrine and the Media,* 1978.

69. Defined by Leonard Orkin, Practising Law Institute, Legal and Business Problems of the Advertising Industry 1978, p. 304 as "Advertisements which direct the prospective customer's attention to similarities or differences between the advertised product and one or more competitors either explicitly or implicitly." See also, Sterk, *The Law of Comparative Advertising: How Much Worse is "Better" Than "Great."* 76 Columbia L.Rev. 80 (1976).

70. Triangle Publications v. Knight-Ridder, Newspapers, 3 Med.L.Rptr. 2086, 445 F.Supp. 875 (D.Fla.1978).

71. FTC recommended comparative advertising on Aug. 13, 1979 in 44 Fed.Reg. 4738. Note that Section 43(a) of the Lanham Trademark Act prohibits *false* disparagement of a competitor's product. See also *FTC News Summary,* Aug. 3, 1979.

72. American Home Products Corp. v. Johnson and Johnson, 3 Med.L.Rptr. 1097, 436 F.Supp. 785 (D.N.Y.1977), affirmed 577 F.2d 160 (2d Cir. 1978).

vertisers, and the Council of Better Business Bureaus. Complaints are handled initially by an investigating staff of the BBB Council called the National Advertising Division. A query from NAD can lead major national advertisers to modify or discontinue unsubstantiated advertising claims. NAD monitors and advises and, in unresolved cases, carries appeals to the National Advertising Review Board. If an advertiser remains recalcitrant after an NARB panel reaches an adverse decision, NARB will notify the appropriate government agency.

Efforts at self-regulation are also made by the National Association of Broadcasters through its Television and Radio Codes. The success of these comprehensive statements can only be measured against one's own sensibilities and values. Supplemental guidelines have been issued on advertising to children, nonprescription drug advertising, and advertising substantiation.

Individual newspapers and broadcast stations and the three networks have their own advertising acceptability or broadcast standards departments. Network standards are generally said to be higher than those of the legal regulators.

Courts in the last decade have recommended greater use by the Federal Trade Commission of advisory opinions, binding upon advertisers until revoked or rescinded by the commission. Courts are also in favor of industry-wide Trade Practice Conferences and the use of Industry Guides or broad interpretations of the FTC Act. Conferences sometimes result in the promulgation of Trade Practice Rules for particular products or services. These do not have the force of law, and no penalties attach to their violation. The FTC itself may publish Trade Regulation Rules, formal statements as to what practices are considered unfair or deceptive.

Much of interest and importance to the student of advertising has been omitted from this brief account of some of advertising's legal problems. The Practising Law Institute's 1978 handbook, *Legal and Business Problems of the Advertising Industry,* is an invaluable reference. It includes: 1) Basic Copy Rules (the use of names, photographs, titles, and excerpts from literary materials, trademarks, testimonials, music, sweepstakes, and contests); 2) Industry Codes and Guidelines; 3) articles on "Agency Liability Under FTC Orders," "Advertising of Non-Prescription Drugs," and "Advertising litigation"; 4) application forms for advertisers' libel and slander, copyright, piracy, plagiarism, and privacy insurance policies; 5) endorsement and contract forms; and 6) a discussion of labor and agency operation problems affecting the advertising industry.

See also, Philip A. Garon (ed.), *Advertising Law Anthology,* Vol. III, Arlington, Va.: International Library, 1975; and Smith and White, *FTC Consumer Protection Law Institute.* PLI, 1980, see fn. 50. The FTC itself issues news summaries, an operating manual, and annual reports. *FTC: Watch* is an interesting "insiders' " report.

Legal or Public Notice Advertising

1. The major premise of public notice advertising is that citizens ought to have an opportunity to know what the laws are, to be notified when their rights or property are to be affected, and to be apprised of how the administration of their government is being conducted. State laws define the classifications of information requiring promulgation. These may include statutes and ordinances, governmental proceedings, articles of incorporation, registration of titles, probate matters, notices of election, appropriation of public funds, tax notices, bids for public works, and judicial orders—the list is by no means exhaustive.

State laws also define the qualifications a newspaper must possess to carry public notices and how legally qualified and/or "official" newspapers are to be selected. See New Jersey Suburbanite v. State, 384 A.2d 831 (N.J.1978). Here the state supreme court denied review when a free distribution shopper challenged a state law restricting legal advertising to newspapers with a paid circulation, average news content of 35 percent, and a second-class mailing permit in effect for at least two years. The number of times a public notice is to be published and how publication is to be certified and paid for are generally statutory matters.

"Official" and legally qualified newspapers are usually required to be stable publications of general and paid-for circulation, of general news coverage and general availability, printed in English, appearing frequently and regularly, and meeting specified minimum conditions of technical excellence. Close interpretation of state statutes has led to certain exceptions being made for specialized urban publications known as commercial newspapers designed to deal with the large volume of legal advertising which typical daily newspapers would find unprofitable. These interpretations have not gone unchallenged. See King County v. Superior Court in and for King County, 92 P.2d 694 (Wash.1939); In re Sterling Cleaners & Dyers, Inc., 81 F.2d 596 (7th Cir. 1936).

2. Another justification for the commercial newspaper has been the diversity of its subscribers rather than their number. Eisenberg v. Wabash, 189 N.E. 301 (Ill. 1934); Burak v. Ditson, 229 N.W. 227 (Iowa 1930). Can this also be challenged on the grounds that the law should require wider and more general publicity than can be provided by any newspaper, whatever its form?

In the landmark case, it was held by the United States Supreme Court that notice by publication of a pending settlement proceeding to known beneficiaries of a common trust fund was a denial of due process. Out of this case emerges the doctrine that notice is adequate only if it is reasonably calculated to apprise interested parties of their right to appear and be heard. Mullane v. Central Hanover Bank & Trust Co., Trustee, 339 U.S. 306 (1949).

Since *Mullane,* the Supreme Court has generally held that something more than notice by publication is required. In 1953, Justice Black wrote that notice by publication is a poor and sometimes hopeless substitute for actual service of notice. City of New York v. New York, N.H. & H.R. Co., 344 U.S. 293 (1953). And in 1956, the Court held invalid a condemnation proceeding based upon notice by publication. Walker v. City of Hutchinson, 352 U.S. 112 (1956). "[N]otice by publication," said the Court in 1962, "is not enough with respect to a person whose name and address are known or very easily ascertainable and whose legally protected interests are directly affected by the proceedings in question." Schroeder v. City of New York, 371 U.S. 211 (1962).

3. *Mullane* points out that notice need not be communicated to every possible interested person, but rather that notice is sufficient if it is "reasonably certain to reach most of those interested in objecting." Would this statement sustain publication of notice in a small town newspaper because, in that atmosphere, face-to-face communication may be quite highly developed and the community newspaper closely read? Jones v. Village of Farnam, 119 N.W.2d 157 (Neb.1963), discussed in *Due Process—Sufficiency of Notice—Adequacy of Published Notice When Subsequent Proceeding Is To Be Held,* 49 Iowa L.Rev. 185 (1963). Finally, a newspaper does not have to accept public notice advertising; Wooster v. Mahaska County, 98 N.W. 103 (Iowa 1904); Commonwealth v. Boston Transcript Co., 144 N.E. 400 (1924), but if it does, it must comply with the statutory requirements of publication.

Belleville Advocate Printing Co. v. St. Clair County, 168 N.E. 312 (Ill.1929).

Political Advertising

Political advertising is governed largely by First National Bank of Boston v. Bellotti, 3 Med.L.Rptr. 1157, 435 U.S. 765 (1978) (this text, p. 151).[73] There the corporation was said to be constitutionally justified in engaging directly in political debate. The same right was later extended to indirect participation through donations to political committees.[74]

Campaign advertising is also governed by state and federal law.[75] Political ads in newspapers or other mass media for a federal candidate must state who or what organization paid for the ad and whether or not it was authorized by the candidate. If not authorized by the candidate, the ad should say so. The rate charged must not be higher than that charged for a comparable use of space for other purposes, that is, the highest rate charged for nonpolitical advertising. Of course, a newspaper is free to refuse a political ad. And when it accepts an ad, it can require advance cash payment. By the same token, it can extend credit to a candidate if the terms are substantially similar to those available to nonpolitical persons.

Under the Federal Election Campaign Laws, a newspaper may also sponsor a debate between or among candidates for federal office on condition that at least two candidates be present and that the setting or circumstances of the debate not favor one candidate over another. Fairness and equal time obligations applicable to broadcasters do not apply to newspapers.

State laws vary widely, but most would contain provisions for requiring identification of those paying for the ad and for equitable ad rates. State laws forbidding election-day advertising, corporate advertising, and use of the American flag in a campaign ad probably could no longer pass constitutional muster. It is generally considered unethical, though not illegal, for a newspaper to accommodate last-minute political attacks that leave no time for refutation or rebuttal.

ANTITRUST LAWS AND THE MEDIA

1. Since the beginning of the century there has been a steady decline in the number of cities with competing daily newspapers. An early 1980s' estimate of the number was thirty-three. That decline and trends toward group ownership (a steadily diminishing 541 independent dailies remained in 1983 [76]), cross-media affiliation, and conglomerate absorption present dim prospects for an idealized, diverse pattern of media ownership.

73. See also, Consolidated Edison Co. of New York, Inc. v. Public Service Commission, 6 Med.L.Rptr. 1518, 447 U.S. 530 (1980).

74. Citizens Against Rent Control/Coalition for Fair Housing v. Berkeley, 454 U.S. 290 (1982). See also, C & C Plywood v. Hanson, 4 Med.L.Rptr. 1954, 583 F.2d 421 (9th Cir. 1978); Let's Help Florida v. Smathers, 453 F.Supp. 1003 (D.Fla.1978), affirmed sub.nom. 621 F.2d 195 (1980); Winn-Dixie Stores, Inc. v. State, 408 So.2d 211 (Fla.1981).

75. Notably the Federal Election Campaign Act of 1971, Pub.L. No. 93–225, 86 Stat. 3, as amended, 1974, Pub.L. No. 93–443, 88 Stat. 1263, as construed by the U.S. Supreme Court in Buckley v. Valeo, 424 U.S. 1 (1976).

76. Sources for the above figures are *Morton Newspaper Research Newsletter,* March 31, 1983, p. 3–6; American Newspaper Publishers Association, *'83 Facts About Newspapers; Editor & Publisher,* January 1, 1983, p. 34; and Compaine, *Who Owns the Media? Concentration of Ownership in the Mass Communication Industry,* 1979.

Of approximately 1,710 daily newspapers, 68 percent are chain or group owned, if a group is defined as two or more newspapers under single ownership. That means that more than 76 percent of national daily circulation is group controlled. The four largest of 160 chains alone account for 21 percent of daily circulation; they are, in order of size, Gannett Newspapers, Knight-Ridder Newspapers, Newhouse Newspapers, and Tribune Company. In 1983, Gannett owned 86 dailies, a national newspaper, *USA Today,* and 33 weeklies, semiweeklies, or monthlies, 7 television stations, 14 radio stations, its own news service, and a satellite information network.

On the brighter side, except for the motion picture industry, no segment of the mass media system is so concentrated as to violate existing antitrust laws. The total system remains relatively diverse, competitive, and pluralistic. There is a publication for almost every conceivable interest group. In ten years, the number of Sunday newspapers has increased by 182, and, despite the demise of many P.M. newspapers, the total number of dailies has remained remarkably stable.

But there are danger signs. Owners of independent newspapers seem unable to resist inflated offers from ever-expanding chains. Inheritance tax laws in large part account for the fact that between 1979 and 1982, for example, of 179 dailies that changed hands all but nineteen became part of groups. Book publishers are rapidly being absorbed by newspaper/magazine chains (e.g., Hearst and Newhouse), large entertainment conglomerates (e.g., CBS and Gulf + Western), and defense contractors (e.g., ITT, IBM, and Raytheon). Accelerated conglomeration is taking place among an estimated 6,000 cable systems. Record companies, movie theaters, newsprint plants, retail book stores, and commercial television stations have also been affected.

Three television networks still account for more than half the advertising sales in that field. Co-located newspaper/broadcast combinations remain an antitrust concern since the United States Supreme Court in FCC v. National Citizens Committee for Broadcasting, 436 U.S. 775 (1978), this text, p. 959, reversed a lower court's ruling that all such combinations be broken up. In 1983, it appeared possible that the Associated Press might soon be without competition as a U.S. world wire service.

While patterns of ownership may be changing, the total number of outlets remains fairly constant. Moreover, the figures on concentration are not meant to suggest that a systematic relationship has been established between type of ownership and the "quality" of information. The social and professional effects of media concentration are not understood. If we are to err, however, perhaps it ought to be in the direction of Judge Learned Hand's "multitude of tongues" thesis in his federal district court opinion in United States v. Associated Press, 52 F.Supp. 362 (S.D.N.Y.1943), an argument based on the proposition that the First Amendment does not contemplate monopolies in the realm of ideas and information.

The major weapons of antitrust enforcement are the Sherman and Clayton Acts. The former, enacted in 1890, is essentially an antimonopoly law. It governs contracts, combinations, trusts, or any conspiracies in restraint of trade. The 1914 Clayton Act includes among its categories of illegal activities corporate mergers, interlocking directorates, discriminatory pricing, and tying (the connecting of the sale of one product or service to the purchasing of a second product or service).

Section 7 of the Clayton Act is aimed at mergers:

> No corporation engaged in commerce shall acquire, directly or indirectly, the whole or any part of the stock or other share of capital * * * of another cor-

> poration engaged also in commerce, where, in any line of commerce in any section of the country, the effect of such acquisition may be substantially to lessen competition or to tend to create a monopoly. (15 U.S.C. § 18)

Section 2 of the Sherman Act condemns monopolizing, the power to exclude competition, and can be applied to actions of a single enterprise:

> Every person who shall monopolize, or attempt to monopolize, or combine or conspire with any other person or persons, to monopolize any part of the trade or commerce among the several [s]tates or foreign nations, shall be guilty of a misdemeanor.

Few more than twenty antitrust suits have been brought against newspapers since 1890, most of those between 1940 and 1970. There is a reason. Antitrust laws as they exist are not readily adaptable to newspapers or newspaper groups. Most dailies already occupy a local monopoly position, a "natural monopoly," if you will, so that it is difficult, if not impossible, to demonstrate that chain acquisition of a local monopoly newspaper is going to have any effect on competition. In typical Section 7 litigation, the government defines the product and its geographical market, calculates the percentage of the market to be controlled by the merged firm, and decides whether that figure is sufficient to create a "reasonable probability" of lessened competition. Even a merger as large as that which was proposed between Gannett and Combined Communication fell below the maximum market gain of 2 percent permitted by the Justice Department. Gannett's 4.8 percent share of total daily circulation at that time and Combined Communication's 0.6 percent share would not have violated the rule. When Knight, the third largest chain in 1974, merged with Ridder, the ninth largest, Ridder had a 2.1 percent market share, just over the Antitrust Division's limit. The new firm was asked to divest some of its broadcast properties. Mergers between members of the top ten or so chains are therefore unlikely.

Courts, interpreting Section 7, have narrowly defined geographical markets. Newspapers do not compete strenuously for national advertisers and seldom for national subscribers. Obviously, newspapers within chains do not compete with one another, but chains themselves compete in their desire to add new members. Are Gannett, Newhouse, and Thomson, for example, rather than individual newspapers, "lines of commerce" that could initiate Section 7 actions to protect the owners of independent newspapers or small chains of newspapers? So far the courts have said no.

Arguments have been made that competition among newspapers is interlayer rather than intralayer. That is, similar sized newspapers do not compete, but categories of newspapers do—suburbans with metropolitans, for example. The *Times-Mirror* case, as shall be noted, was that kind of case in that it prevented a newspaper from one layer from acquiring a newspaper from another. But first the more basic question of whether the antitrust laws do indeed infringe upon the First Amendment rights of the press.

The Constitutionality of Antitrust Laws

ASSOCIATED PRESS ET AL. v. UNITED STATES

326 U.S. 1, 65 S.CT. 1416, 89 L.ED. 2013 (1945).

[EDITORIAL NOTE

In the early forties, Marshall Field's *Chicago Sun,* founded to compete with the *Chicago Tribune,* was denied AP membership, a service thought necessary for survival. The government brought suit under the Sherman Act.

Judge Learned Hand, speaking for the district court in this case, United States v. Associated Press, 52 F.Supp. 362 (S.D.N.Y. 1943), stated that the objectives of the antitrust laws and the interests protected by the First Amendment come very close to converging. This is a radical observation that carries with it some rather innovative implications. To begin with, the First Amendment guarantee of freedom of the press is not to be read as creating an immunity from all government regulation. Second, the real addressees of the First Amendment protection may not be the newspaper industry but the American public and its stake in as free a flow of information as possible. Judge Hand treats the AP as performing a quasi-public function and relies on this status to justify government regulation to secure First Amendment objectives. The following passage from the district court opinion has been an oft-quoted source for authority and thought on the law of the American press:

> However, neither exclusively, nor even primarily, are the interests of the newspaper industry conclusive; for that industry serves one of the most vital of all general interests: the dissemination of news from many different sources, with as many different facets and colors as is possible. That interest is closely akin to, if indeed it is not the same as, the interest protected by the First Amendment; *it presupposes that right conclusions are more likely to be gathered out of a multitude of tongues, than any kind of authoritative selection. To many this is, and always will be folly; but we have staked upon it our all.* [Emphasis added.]

What assumptions are made in this passage? One of Hand's major premises appears to be that the more newspapers, the more varied and untrammelled debate will be. But newspapers for all but local news rely heavily on wire services and feature syndicates. If the pressures that operate on editorial and news decisions presumably are the same commercial pressures that are found throughout the nation, does it matter much whether the newspapers are owned by a chain or individually? Whether a community has one newspaper or two or three?

In other words, does it follow that the antitrust policy of a "multitude of tongues" necessarily works toward First Amendment objectives?

There is an implication in Learned Hand's opinion that the government may act to guarantee access to divergent ideas that would otherwise be unexpressed. See Barron, *Access to the Press—A New First Amendment Right,* 80 Harv.L.Rev. 1641 at 1655 (1967). This acknowledgment that such governmental action is consistent with the First Amendment is of great importance.

Reflect on Judge Hand's statement of these issues as you read the opinion of the U.S. Supreme Court which follows.]

Justice BLACK delivered the opinion of the Court.

* * *

The United States filed a bill in a Federal District Court for an injunction against AP and other defendants charging that they had violated the Sherman Anti-Trust Act, 26 Stat. 209, 15 U.S.C.A. §§ 1–7, 15, in that their acts and conduct constituted (1) a combination and conspiracy in restraint of trade and commerce in news among the states, and (2) an attempt to monopolize a part of that trade.

The heart of the government's charge was that appellants had by concerted action set up a system of By-Laws which prohibited all AP members from selling news to non-members, and which granted each member powers to block its nonmember competitors from membership. These By-Laws to which all AP members had assented, were, in the context of the admitted facts charged to be in violation of the Sherman Act. A further charge related to a contract between AP and Canadian Press, (a news agency of Canada, similar to AP) under which the Canadian agency and AP obligated themselves to furnish news exclusively to each other. The District Court, composed of three judges, held that the By-Laws unlawfully restricted admission to AP membership, and violated the Sherman Act insofar as the By-Laws' provisions clothed a member with powers to impose or dispense with conditions upon the admission of his business competitor. Continued observance of these By-Laws was enjoined. The court further held that the Canadian contract was an integral part of the restrictive membership conditions, and enjoined its observance pending abandonment of the membership restrictions.

Member publishers of AP are engaged in business for profit exactly as are other business men who sell food, steel, aluminum, or anything else people need or want. All are alike covered by the Sherman Act. The fact that the publisher handles news while others handle food does not, as we shall later point out, afford the publisher a peculiar constitutional sanctuary in which he can with impunity violate laws regulating his business practices.

Nor is a publisher who engages in business practices made unlawful by the Sherman Act entitled to a partial immunity by reason of the "clear and present danger" doctrine which courts have used to protect freedom to speak, to print, and to worship. That doctrine, as related to this case, provides protection for utterances themselves, so that the printed or spoken word may not be the subject of previous restraint or punishment, unless their expression creates a clear and present danger of bringing about a substantial evil which the government has power to prohibit. Bridges v. California, 314 U.S. 252, 261. Formulated as it was to protect liberty of thought and of expression, it would degrade the clear and present danger doctrine to fashion from it a shield for business publishers who engage in business practices condemned by the Sherman Act. * * *

The District Court found that the By-Laws in and of themselves were contracts in restraint of commerce in that they contained provisions designed to stifle competition in the newspaper publishing field. The court also found that AP's restrictive By-Laws had hindered and impeded the growth of competing newspapers. This latter finding, as to the *past* effect of the restrictions, is challenged. We are inclined to think that it is supported by undisputed evidence, but we do not stop to labor the point. For the court below found, and we think correctly, that the By-Laws on their face, and without regard to their past effect, constitute restraints of trade. Combinations are no less unlawful because they have not as yet resulted in restraint. An agreement or combination to follow a course of conduct which will necessarily restrain or monopolize a part of trade or commerce may violate the Sherman Act, whether it be "wholly nascent or abortive on the one hand, or successful on the other." For these reasons the argument, repeated here in various forms, that AP had not yet achieved a complete monopoly is wholly irrelevant. Undisputed evidence did show, however, that its By-Laws had tied the hands of all of its numerous publishers, to the extent that they could not and did not sell any part of their news so that it could reach any of their non member competitors. In this respect the Court did find, and that finding cannot possibly be challenged, that AP's By-Laws had hindered and restrained the sale of interstate news to nonmembers who competed with members.

Inability to buy news from the largest news agency, or any one of its multitude of members, can have most serious effects on the publication of competitive newspapers, both those presently published and those which but for these restrictions, might be published in the future. This is illustrated by the District Court's finding that in 26 cities of the United States, existing newspapers already have contracts for AP news and the same newspapers have contracts with United Press and International News Service under which new newspapers would be required to pay the contract holders large sums to enter the field. The net effect is seriously to limit the opportunity of any new paper to enter these cities. Trade restraints of this character, aimed at the destruction of competition, tend to block the initiative which brings newcomers into a field of business and to frustrate the free enterprise system which it was the purpose of the Sherman Act to protect.

* * * It is true that the record shows that some competing papers have gotten along without AP news, but morning newspapers, which control 96% of the total circulation in the United States, have AP news service. And the District Court's unchallenged finding was that "AP is a vast, intricately reticulated organization, the largest of its kind, gathering news from all over the world, the chief single source of news for the American press, universally agreed to be of great consequence."

Nevertheless, we are asked to reverse these judgments on the ground that the evidence failed to show that AP reports, which might be attributable to their own "enterprise and sagacity," are clothed "in the robes of indispensability." The absence of "indispensability" is said to have been established under the following chain of reasoning: AP has made its news generally available to the people by supplying it to a limited and select group of publishers in the various cities; therefore, it is said, AP and its member publishers have not deprived the reading public of AP news; all local readers have an "adequate access" to AP news, since all they need to do in any city to get it is to buy, on whatever terms they can in a protected market, the particular newspaper selected for the public by AP and its members. We reject these contentions. The proposed "indispensability" test would fly in the face of the language of the Sherman Act and all of our previous interpretations of it. Moreover, it would make that law a dead letter in all fields of business, a law which Congress has consistently maintained to be an essential safeguard to the kind of private competitive business economy this country has sought to maintain.

* * *

Finally, the argument is made that to apply the Sherman Act to this association of publishers constitutes an abridgment of the freedom of the press guaranteed by the First Amendment. Perhaps it would be a sufficient answer to this contention to refer to the decisions of this Court in Associated Press v. N.L.R.B., and Indiana Farmer's Guide Pub. Co. v. Prairie Farmer Pub. Co., 293 U.S. 268. It would be strange indeed however if the grave concern for freedom of the press which prompted adoption of the First Amendment should be read as a command that the government was without power to protect that freedom. The First Amendment, far from providing an argument against application of the Sherman Act, here provides powerful reasons to the contrary. That Amendment rests on the assumption that the widest possible dissemination of information from diverse and antagonistic sources is essential to the welfare of the public, that a free press is a condition of a free society. *Surely a command that the government itself shall not impede the free flow of ideas does not afford non-governmental combinations a refuge if they impose restraints upon that constitutionally guaranteed freedom. Freedom to publish means freedom for all and not for some. Freedom to publish is guaranteed by the Constitution, but freedom to combine to keep others from publishing is not. Freedom of the press from governmental interference under the First Amendment does not sanction repression of that freedom by private interests.* [Emphasis added.] The First

Amendment affords not the slightest support for the contention that a combination to restrain trade in news and views has any constitutional immunity.

* * *

Affirmed

COMMENT

1. Obviously the most significant aspect of the *Associated Press* case is the Supreme Court's determination that newspapers are subject to the antitrust laws. The newspaper industry relied on the theories that newspapers were not in interstate commerce, and therefore not covered by the Sherman Antitrust Act, and that the First Amendment guarantee of freedom of the press provided a constitutional exemption from the antitrust laws. The interstate commerce argument came rather late since many areas of economic life had been held to be in interstate commerce by 1946. But the argument that government application of the antitrust laws to the press abridged freedom of the press was a more serious one. What was the nature of the AP's argument on this point? How did Justice Black deal with it in his opinion?

2. Both Justice Roberts and Justice Murphy made the point in dissents that news, after all, is not hoarded by the AP, the news is *there* and the AP had the right to go and get it. If others envy their prowess at this endeavor and wish to do the same, they may. A short but still quite accurate statement by way of rebuttal to this position is found in Comment, *Press Associations and Restraint of Trade,* 55 Yale L.J. 428 at 430 (1946):

> Pressures of time render it literally impossible for any newspaper singlehandedly to secure rapid, reliable and efficient coverage and transmission service from all parts of the world. Thus, unless possessed of a sizeable independent fortune an entrepreneur simply will not launch a newspaper without assurance of access to the requisite news-gathering facilities.

3. Note that Justice Black did not base his opinion for the Court in the AP case on the public interest in the news. He declined to view the press as performing the public or quasi-public function which Judge Learned Hand had ascribed to it in the district court. A later rejection of the view that private property should be considered quasipublic for First Amendment purposes was found in Hudgens v. NLRB, 424 U.S. 507 (1976), this text, p. 53.

Justice Frankfurter's concurrence, on the other hand, clearly recognized that the untrammeled flow of news may be frustrated by "private restraints no less than by public censorship." Since Justice Black wrote the opinion for the Court which applies the antitrust laws to the AP, should we conclude that he agreed that private restraints on freedom of expression are as destructive as public ones and as subject to regulatory control? Or is Justice Black's analysis that, absent discriminatory bylaws such as those struck down in AP, private restraints on or by the press are generally not subject to legal control?

As a result of the Supreme Court's directing the AP to frame new rules of admission, the membership of the AP considerably expanded.

Mergers and Concentration of Ownership in the Daily Press

UNITED STATES v. TIMES MIRROR CO.

274 F.SUPP. 606 (C.D.CAL.1967).

[EDITORIAL NOTE

A United States District Court in California held that the acquisition of The Sun Company by the Times Mirror Company was a violation of Section 1 of the Sherman Act and Section 7 of the Clayton Act and issued an order of divestiture requiring the Times to sell The Sun Company. The Court ruled that the determinative issue of liability was whether the effect of the merger was to lessen substantially competition within the relevant geographic and product markets; competition between the two newspapers was not required. As another federal district court said in Union Leader v. Newspapers of New England, Inc., 180 F.Supp. 125 (D.Mass.1954), modified on other grounds, 284 F.2d 582 (1st Cir. 1960), cert. den. 365 U.S. 833 (1961), it is the purpose of the antitrust laws to protect competitors. There is nothing to prevent a publisher from competing, even if that competition leads to monopoly.

The Times Mirror Company publishes the morning *Los Angeles Times,* which has had the largest daily newspaper circulation in California since 1948. In 1964 the Times Mirror purchased The Sun Company, publishers of the morning *Sun,* the evening *Telegram* and the Sunday *Sun-Telegram* located in San Bernardino County which adjoins Los Angeles County to the east. The Sun Company dominated the daily newspaper business in San Bernardino County and was the largest independent publishing company in Southern California.

The U.S. Department of Justice challenged the acquisition in District Court, asserting that it constituted an unlawful control and combination which unreasonably restrains interstate trade and commerce, in violation of Section 1 of the Sherman Act, 15 U.S.C.A. § 1, and that the effect of the acquisition may be substantially to lessen competition in violation of Section 7 of the Clayton Act, 15 U.S.C.A. § 18.]

FERGUSON, District Judge:

* * *

PURPOSE OF SECTION 7

* * *

The Supreme Court, in Brown Shoe Co. v. United States, 370 U.S. 294, (1962), pointed out in setting forth the legislative history of the 1950 amendment to § 7 of the Clayton Act that:

"The dominant theme pervading congressional consideration of the 1950 amendments was a fear of what was considered to be a rising tide of economic concentration in the American economy. * * * Other considerations cited in support of the bill were the desirability of retaining 'local control' over industry and the protection of small businesses. Throughout the recorded discussion may be found examples of Congress' fear not only of accelerated concentration of economic power on economic grounds, but also of the threat to other values a trend toward concentration was thought to pose." 370 U.S. at 315–16.

The Court declared:

1. Congress made it plain that § 7 applied not only to mergers between actual competitors, but also to vertical and conglomerate mergers whose effect may tend to lessen competition in any line of commerce in any section of the country. 370 U.S. at 317.

* * *

THE PRODUCT MARKET

In actions under § 7 of the Clayton Act, a finding of the appropriate "product market" is a necessary predicate to a determination of whether a merger has the requisite anticompetitive effects. In *Brown Shoe Co. v. United States, supra,* it is set forth:

"Thus, as we have previously noted, '[d]etermination of the relevant market is a necessary predicate to a finding of a violation of the Clayton Act. * * *' "

[EDITORIAL NOTE

The argument that the *Times* and the *Sun* did not compete with each other and for that reason there could not be an antitrust violation had lost all its validity since 1950 amendments to the Clayton Act. The fact that two merging companies presently compete or do not compete is not the significant issue. Congress had directed that the courts must look to the effect and impact of the merger. If its effect is anticompetitive, then there is a violation.]

* * *

In some of the services which they provide, daily newspapers compete with other media, such as radio and television, both for news and advertising. This does not mean, however, that all competitors of any service provided by a daily newspaper must be lumped into the same line of commerce with it. * * *

The defendant argues that each daily newspaper is so unique as to occupy a product market of its own. This argument stems more from pride of publication than from commercial reality. The contention is made that if a reader in Southern California wants depth in international, national and regional news, he buys the *Times* and if he wants depth in the local news of his own community, he buys his small local paper. In effect, it is claimed that the *Times* and the surrounding local daily newspapers are complementary toward each other. As set forth previously, the concept of two products being complementary toward each other is not a barrier to § 7 if the effect of the merger may have anticompetitive effects.

It is now firmly established that products need not be identical to be included in a § 7 analysis of the product market. Furthermore, in Union Leader Corp. v. Newspapers of New England, Inc., the court of appeals recognized that numerous papers published all over New England could comprise a relevant daily newspaper market for both Clayton and Sherman Act purposes.

Finally, when a merger such as here results in a share of from 10.6% to 54.8% of total weekday circulation, from 23.9% to 99.5% of total morning circulation and from 20.3% to 64.3% of total Sunday circulation in the relevant geographic market, the acquisition constitutes a prima facie violation of the Clayton Act. As set forth in United States v. Continental Can Co.:

"Where a merger is of such a size as to be inherently suspect, elaborate proof of market structure, market behavior and probable anticompetitive effects may be dispensed with in view of § 7's design to prevent undue concentration." 378 U.S. at 458.

COMPETITION FOR ADVERTISING

The *Times* competed with the *Sun* for advertising. The largest share of the revenue of a daily newspaper comes from its advertisements, and advertising is its lifeblood.

* * *

* * * After the acquisition, the advertising campaign that both papers waged against each other ceased.

THE GEOGRAPHIC MARKET

It is necessary after defining the product market to determine the geographic market (the "section of the country") in order to determine the anticompetitive effect of the merger.

In 1964, the year of the acquisition, the *Times* had a weekday daily circulation of 16,650 and a Sunday circulation of 31,993 within San Bernardino County. This amounted to 10.6% of the total weekday circulation for both morning and evening newspapers, 23.9% of total morning circulation and 20.3% of the total Sunday circulation.

The *Sun* had its entire circulation, except for a very few copies, within the limits of San Bernardino County. The county therefore encompasses virtually the entire area of circulation and home delivery overlap between the *Times* and the *Sun*. * * *

The defendant contends that the County of San Bernardino is not commercially realistic because county boundaries do not define the boundaries of a newspaper market. It claims that counties are political and administrative boundaries, not necessarily market boundaries. This contention may be true as a generalized statement. In each case the geographic market must be determined with sufficient precision to weigh the anticompetitive effects of the merger. The *Times* claims that the largest part of its circulation was in the west part of San Bernardino County, while the largest part of the circulation of the *Sun* was in the east part. However, as stated previously, the newspaper industry has recognized San Bernardino County as a daily newspaper market. Most important of all, the *Times* itself, in evaluating the acquisition, used the daily newspaper business in the entire San Bernardino County as the relevant market.

* * *

At the time of the acquisition, there was already a heavy concentration of daily newspaper ownership in the ten counties of Southern California. * * *

There has been a steady decline of independent ownership of newspapers in Southern California. A newspaper is independently owned when its owners do not publish another newspaper at another locality. In San Bernardino County as of January 1, 1952, six of the seven daily newspapers were independently owned. On December 31, 1966, only three of the eight dailies published there remained independent.

* * *

In the ten-county area of Southern California in the same period of time, the number of daily newspapers increased from 66 to 82, but the number independently owned decreased from 39 to 20. In 1952, 59% of Southern California dailies were independent; in 1966 only 24% were independent.

The acquisition of the Sun by the Times was particularly anticompetitive because it eliminated one of the few independent papers that had been able to operate successfully in the morning and Sunday fields. * * *

The acquisition has raised a barrier to entry of newspapers in the San Bernardino County market that is almost impossible to overcome. The evidence discloses the market has now been closed tight and no publisher will risk the expense of unilaterally starting a new daily newspaper there.

An acquisition which enhances existing barriers to entry in the market or increases the difficulties of smaller firms already in the market is particularly anticompetitive. * * *

The difficulty of entry anyplace within the Southern California daily newspaper market is illustrated best by the recent failure of one of the most powerful publishers in the United States, the New York Times, to successfully establish a West Coast edition.

* * *

CONCLUSION

The acquisition by The Times Mirror Company of The Sun Company on June 25, 1964, resulted in a violation of § 7 of the Clayton Act. It is an acquisition by one corporation (The Times Mirror Company) of all the stock of another corporation (The Sun Company), both corporations being engaged in interstate commerce, whereby in the daily newspaper business (the relevant product market) in San Bernardino County, California (the relevant geographic market), the effect is substantially to lessen competition.

FORM OF RELIEF

The government seeks an order of divestiture and an injunction prohibiting the defendant from acquiring any other daily newspaper in the relevant geographic market.

Divestiture has become the normal form of relief when acquisitions have been found to violate § 7 of the Clayton Act. * * *

Complete divestiture here is the practical solution to correct the § 7 violation.

However, the request for a perpetual injunction must be denied. * * *

While it is recognized that injunctive relief has been granted in antitrust cases, the court is not able to predict the future of the daily newspaper business in San Bernardino County. For example, on May 1, 1967, the Victorville Daily Press, a weekly, became a daily and the government admits "it is a bit early to predict what its fate will be." In the event that it should become a failing paper and the defendant acquired it, a study must be made of the effect of the acquisition. It may be anticompetitive, or it may come within the congressional exemption as expressed in *Brown Shoe.* Based upon the evidence before it, the court cannot prejudge the newspaper business with sufficient certainty to grant the injunction. The dangers that could result from it outweigh any possible advantage that it may have.

* * *

COMMENT

1. The U.S. Supreme Court affirmed the district court's judgment in the *Times Mirror* case, 390 U.S. 712 (1968).

2. The court ordered the Times Mirror Company to divest itself of its stock in such a way that The Sun Company will "continue as a strong and viable company." What does divestiture really mean in this context? Was it clear that the *Sun* would reemerge as an independent newspaper, according to the court's definition of an independent newspaper (one whose owners "do not publish another newspaper at another locality")?

3. When the Pulitzers, owners of the St. Louis *Post-Dispatch,* had earlier offered the owner of the San Bernardino *Sun* $15 million for his newspaper, the Californian decided that he would rather sell to the Chandlers of Los Angeles because both papers shared political views, Norman Chandler was a director of three of the largest corporations in San Bernardino, and the two were close friends.

4. Most cities provide their daily newspapers with a "natural monopoly." This is partly due to the economies of scale: fixed first issue costs diminish as circulation increases, especially for small or medium-sized dailies. This militates against more than one newspaper's serving similar audiences in a single community, unless that community is large enough to provide segmented audiences for both news and advertising—New York City and Chicago for example. Subscriber and advertiser demands are interdependent. When advertising sales drop, circulation drops, and the result is the beginning of what economist James Rosse calls a downward spiral.[77] As the spiral continues, the economies of scale dictate that single issues of the newspaper cost more. This leads to lower profitability which can only be dealt with by higher prices for both advertising space and subscriptions or by cutting back on costs and presumably quality as well. Either course accelerates the downward spiral.

The Newspaper Preservation Act and Joint Operating Agreements

1. Without private subsidy the few existing second daily newspapers are in delicate health in all but our three or four largest cities. One consequence has been

---

77. Rosse, *The Evolution of One Newspaper Cities* (a discussion draft prepared for the FTC Media Symposium, Washington, D.C., Dec. 14 and 15, 1978).

merger in one form or another. In *Union Leader v. Newspapers of New England, Inc.,* text p. 644, federal courts held that a newspaper might legally acquire its competitor if the geographic market could only support one newspaper. Similarly in United States v. Harte-Hanks Newspapers, Inc., 170 F.Supp. 227 (N.D.Tex.1959), a federal court said that it was not illegal to offer to buy out a competitor if there was no apparent intent to monopolize. As has been noted, daily newspapers increasingly appear to be "natural monopolies."

Group acquisition and conglomerate merger are partially protected by the "failing company" defense of the Newspaper Preservation Act of 1970, Pub.L. No. 91–353, 84 Stat. 466 (codified at 15 U.S.C. § 1801–04). The "failing company" doctrine originated with International Shoe Co. v. FTC, 280 U.S. 291 (1930), a holding that exempted firms facing bankruptcy from antitrust requirements.

Rarely do such mergers in the newspaper business threaten competition in a single market. Chains prefer to buy monopoly newspapers. And where there is a "natural monopoly," competitors are not usually lined up to enter that market. So that geographical markets will not overlap, chain management makes certain that newspaper acquisitions are some distance apart. Chain as well as conglomerate mergers raise social and political rather than economic questions given the present condition of the antitrust laws. The fact is that the statistics of concentration cited by media critics do not approach the thresholds of enforcement against vertical and horizontal merger applied to other industries, even though there are profound differences in intrinsic value between information and ideas on the one hand and garbage bags or bleaches on the other.

However ideal the image of two economically viable community newspapers locked in editorial combat, or of that hometown newspaper remaining forever home-and independently owned, the image is an exercise in nostalgia. Economic pressures toward group ownership are almost overwhelming. Tax laws stimulate the investment of accumulated reserves. Undistributed earnings are not taxed as personal or corporate income if used in the acquisition of additional newspaper properties. And those who already own newspapers generally know how to manage new ones. At the same time, estate taxes are such that few publishers can resist the grossly inflated prices offered by newspaper groups.

In addition there are in mergers the advantages of joint venture risk sharing in new technologies, centralized management, pooled editorial services, and higher standing in the financial market.

2. With newspaper competition more and more a rarity, diversity must be sought in cross-channel competition. And when cross-channel patterns of ownership threaten that remaining diversity, group and conglomerate mergers seem, in contrast, more attractive.[78]

The Newspaper Preservation Act assumes that there is social benefit (again the notion of editorial diversity) in permitting competitors in a natural monopoly setting to share rather than duplicate technical and business facilities.[79] A prior assumption is that one of the two competitors, if both remain independent, will fail anyway. A "failing company" defense therefore must demonstrate that 1) the resources of the acquiring or acquired firm are about to be depleted; 2) prospects of rehabilitation are remote; 3) after strenuous efforts have been made, no potential purchaser has come forward; and 4) reor-

78. Sullivan *Handbook of the Law of Antitrust* (1977), p. 598.

79. Bruce Owen in *Economics and Freedom of Expression* (1975) would expand access to production facilities to all prospective competitors, and such facilities would become a public utility.

ganization of the firm would make no difference to its survival. The act was an attempt in part to undo the work of the United States Supreme Court in Citizen Publishing Co. v. United States, 394 U.S. 131 (1969), infra, by allowing the conditions of the "failing company" defense to be circumvented with the written prior consent of the attorney general. Publishers entering into this kind of merger arrangement, a Joint Operating Agreement (JOA), were, in effect, exempted from the antitrust laws.

JOAs began in Albuquerque, New Mexico in 1933, and by 1966 twenty-two cities had them. The Antitrust Division overlooked their Sherman and Clayton Act implications until *Citizen Publishing Co.* was initiated in 1964. While the case was in progress, a Failing Newspaper Act was introduced in Congress in 1967. After the Court's 1969 holding in *Citizen Publishing Co.,* the bill was refashioned and reintroduced as the euphemistic Newspaper Preservation Act. Despite opposition from many quarters, including community newspapers through their national organization, the National Newspaper Association, the bill passed both houses of Congress in 1970 by wide margins. The act grandfathered all existing JOAs.

Citizen Publishing Co. involved two newspapers in Tucson, Arizona that had entered into a JOA in 1940. Under the terms of their agreement, the news and editorial departments of the two newspapers remained separate while a new corporation operated the merged advertising, circulation, and printing departments. Profits were pooled, and it was agreed that the two would not compete in any other publishing venture.

When a buyer appeared for the dominant *Star,* its partner, the *Citizen,* quickly bought it and became publisher of both newspapers through a holding company. At this point the Department of Justice intervened charging that the JOA violated both Clayton and Sherman Acts. In United States v. Citizen Publishing Co., 280 F.Supp. 978 (D.Ariz.1968), a federal district court agreed that the arrangement constituted price fixing, profit pooling, and a market allocation scheme, all illegal *per se* under the Sherman Act. With their news departments again separated, the two newspapers were allowed to continue to share their mechanical and advertising departments.

In *Citizen Publishing Co.* the U.S. Supreme Court affirmed that the kind of agreement entered into here was a violation of the antitrust laws. Moreover, the acquired company had not met the preconditions of the "failing company" defense, i.e., it was not on the brink of collapse. The Newspaper Preservation Act, with strong support from metropolitan publishers, sought to ameliorate the effects of the Supreme Court ruling.

3. A number of questions immediately come to mind. How long will the editorial policies of JOA newspapers remain different or competitive? And, if local competition is economically unfeasible or improbable anyway, are there alternatives to the kind of mergers condemned by the Court in *Citizen Publishing Co.* and condoned by Congress in the Newspaper Preservation Act? Where will buyers for "failing" newspapers be found? Why would a profitable newspaper want to merge with a company that is truly failing? Is a semblance of editorial competition, no matter how it is accomplished, preferable to a single daily newspaper voice in a community?

Twenty-three JOAs were in place in 1983. Three—Anchorage, Cincinnati, and Chattanooga—had been approved since passage of the Newspaper Preservation Act in 1970. The Anchorage Agreement, first to be signed in 1974 under the new act, was dissolved five years later after a three-year lawsuit in which the financially weaker of the two papers charged mismanagement. An earlier Chattanooga agreement was discontinued in 1966 but revived in 1980. The Cincinnati marriage was consummated in 1979. A Bristol, Tennessee—Franklin-Oil City, Pennsylvania merger ended when one paper died.

4. Meanwhile a merger proposal in Seattle had been hotly contested. The Antitrust Division of the Department of Justice and several ad hoc groups, notably the Committee for an Independent *P-I*, opposed the merger on grounds that the parent Hearst Corporation had not made a good faith effort to sell one of two Seattle newspapers, the *Post-Intelligencer*. Comprising the Committee were *P-I* employees, advertisers, and the publishers of smaller newspapers who feared the power of a metropolitan monopoly.

Nevertheless an Administrative Law Judge and the U.S. attorney general approved the merger. The ALJ argued that the financial health of the newspaper could be considered apart from the condition of the chain to which it belonged. In re Seattle Newspapers, 7 Med.L.Rptr. 2173 (1981), 8 Med.L.Rptr. 1080 (1982). The attorney general whose prior consent must be procured for antitrust exemptions, agreed and added that under the Newspaper Preservation Act there was no requirement to prove the absence of qualified buyers before being designated a "failing newspaper." In re Seattle Newspapers, 8 Med.L.Rptr. 1666 (1982).

Rejecting those decisions, the Committee and other groups filed suit against the attorney general, Hearst, and the second daily, the *Seattle Times*. A federal district judge vacated the attorney general's order on grounds that he had overlooked one of the Administrative Law Judge's findings of fact, to wit, the *Post-Intelligencer* had not been offered for sale and purchase inquiries had been rebuffed; the "correct definition of a 'failing newspaper' must include consideration of the existence of willing buyers," and the parent corporation must "carry the burden of demonstrating that none of those buyers could continue to operate the *P-I* as an independent daily."

At the same time, the trial court disagreed with plaintiffs that the Newspaper Preservation Act violated the First Amendment by jeopardizing the future of smaller newspapers in competition with the JOA. Citing City & County of Honolulu v. Hawaii Newspaper Agency, Inc., 7 Med.L.Rptr. 2495 (D.Hawaii 1981) and Bay Guardian Co. v. Chronicle Publishing Co., 344 F.Supp. 1155 (N.D.Cal.1972), the court denied a direct correlation between market structure and freedom of content. The act, said the Hawaii court, can only be said to offend the First Amendment if it in some way restrains the freedom of the press. In the California case, the court observed that, regardless of the economic or social wisdom of the act, it did not violate freedom of the press. Nor was the delegation of authority to the attorney general vague or overbroad. Committee for an Independent P-I v. Smith, 8 Med.L.Rptr. 2162, 549 F.Supp. 985 (W.D.Wash.1982).

All parties sought an expedited appeal before the Ninth Circuit Court of Appeals, and on April 21, 1983 that body reversed the Washington federal district court on the main issue and allowed the Joint Operating Agreement to proceed. The critical question in determining whether a newspaper is "failing," said the appeals court, is whether it is "suffering losses which more than likely cannot be reversed," despite reasonable management by either present or projected staff.

The court rejected Antitrust Division arguments that an "incremental analysis" would show net benefits to the parent Hearst Corporation, despite the *P-I*'s weekly losses of $200,000. A similar challenge to a JOA in Cincinnati occurred when the *Post*, owned by E.W. Scripps, sought to merge with the *Enquirer*. *Post* employees contended that Scripps had purposely "maneuvered the *Cincinnati Post* into its present financial position to profit from the Newspaper Preservation Act." See text, p. 672.

Under the act, the appeals court held in the Seattle case, a JOA applicant should be analyzed as a "free-standing entity," although a "failing newspaper" achieved by "creative bookkeeping" would not be tolerated.

Finally, the appeals court agreed with the district court that no violation of the First Amendment right of smaller newspapers in the Seattle area was found, although the court found the allegation "imaginative."

COMMITTEE FOR AN INDEPENDENT P-I v. HEARST CORP.

9 MED.L.RPTR. 1489, 704 F.2D 467 (9TH CIR. 1983)

ANDERSON, J.:

This action presents issues of first impression concerning the scope and operation of the Newspaper Preservation Act. This act permits competing newspapers that meet certain qualifications to enter into joint arrangements which otherwise would be violative of the antitrust laws. In a memorandum opinion, the district court overturned the Attorney General's action approving a joint operating agreement proposed between the *Seattle Post-Intelligencer* and the *Seattle Times.* We reverse and reinstate the attorney general's decision.

* * *

There are four substantive issues presented by this action. First, what role, if any, is proof of interested third-party purchasers to play in the determination that a newspaper is in probable danger of financial failure? Second, must it be shown that the failing newspaper would probably close if the proposed joint operating agreement is not allowed? Third, must the Attorney General determine that the proposed JOA is not unnecessarily competitive and that it would not impair the editorial voices of smaller newspapers in the affected market? Fourth, is the Newspaper Preservation Act unconstitutional under the first amendment?

* * *

We agree with the district court to the extent it held that alternatives to a JOA are relevant to the determination that a newspaper qualifies under the Act. We find, however, that Hearst met its burden of showing that the alleged alternatives did not offer a solution to the *P-I*'s difficulties.

We do not find the dispute concerning Finding of Fact 158 crucial to our resolution of the buyer issue. On the one hand, we agree with the Attorney General's argument that the evidence did not require him to adopt Finding of Fact 158.[3] While the evidence showed that six individuals or entities inquired into the possible sale of the *P-I,* it did not show that the *P-I* could in all probability be sold to a buyer who would continue its operation as an independent newspaper. The "inquiries" were just that: they were not offers. We recognize that Hearst responded to most of these inquiries with the simple statement that the "*P-I* was not for sale." Hearst's failure to offer the paper for sale and to favorably respond to such inquiries

3. Finding of fact 158 provides:

Considering that the *Post-Intelligencer* is not, and has not been for sale, and that all inquiries regarding possible purchase have been rebuffed by The Hearst Corporation with statements to that effect, and that responsible prospective purchasers nevertheless continue to appear and express an interest in buying the *Post-Intelligencer,* it must be concluded that the *Post-Intelligencer* could in all probability be sold at fair market value to a person or firm who could, and would, continue it in operation as an independent metropolitan daily.

does not, however, compel the conclusion made by the ALJ in Finding of Fact 158.[6]

Our affirmance of the Attorney General on the Finding of Fact 158 issue does not, as he and Hearst seem to argue, end our analysis. The facts are undisputed that purchase inquiries did occur and that Hearst did not cultivate these inquiries. See Findings of Fact 156 and 157. A close reading of the district court's decision shows that it was premised on these underlying facts and not simply on Finding of Fact 158. While we disagree with the district court's conclusion that an attempt to sell the paper is necessary to prove no reasonable alternatives to the JOA exist, we do agree that reasonable alternatives to a JOA are relevant to our analysis.

The starting point for our analysis must begin with the Congressional intent to repudiate *Citizen Publishing's* application of the failing company defense. We believe that Congress intended a total rejection of the failing company defense as used in *Citizen Publishing,* including the requirement that the applicant attempt to sell the newspaper. [Citations omitted.] The Federal Trade Commission opposed the Act because, among other reasons, it did not require the "search for an available purchaser." * * * Holding that there is no per se sale requirement does not mean, however, that proof of interested purchasers is irrelevant.

The district court agreed that Hearst need not have attempted to sell the paper. But the court held that without such an attempt, Hearst had failed to carry its burden of proving that no reasonable alternatives to the JOA were available. The court's determination that reasonable alternatives must be explored was based on the recommended decision of Administrative Law Judge Donald Moore in a prior application under the Newspaper Preservation Act involving the Cincinnati Post. Dept. of Justice Docket No. 4303244 (1979). * * * ALJ Moore recognized that the significance of evidence of prospective buyers was not clearly set forth in the Act's legislative history. * * * He believed, however, that Congress did intend the "probable danger of financial failure standard" to be interpreted with reference to the Bank Merger Act and the gloss put upon it by the Supreme Court in *United States v. Third National Bank,* 390 U.S. 171 (1967). * * *

Based on *Third National Bank,* ALJ Moore fashioned the following test to judge whether a newspaper qualifies as failing under the Act:

> Accordingly, an applicant which has not sought or considered a noncompeting buyer must establish that it would be futile to require attempts to sell, either because of an unavailability of qualified purchasers or because it is unlikely that the paper's condition would be materially improved by the infusion of new ownership and new management.

* * *

Both the Attorney General and Hearst argue against Judge Moore's analysis. Specifically, they maintain that the Act utilizes a purely intrinsic economic test; alternatives in general and the presence of interested purchasers in particular are relevant, if at all, only to the extent they establish the newspaper operation is not probably failing. They contend primarily that ALJ Moore's analysis need not be considered because it was not expressly adopted by then Attorney General Civiletti. It is true that the Civiletti decision adopted only those conclusions of law necessary to the determination that the

6. Our review on this point is narrow: Was it proper to reject Finding of Fact 158? We will discuss in more detail below the ramifications of Hearst's failure to hold the paper up for sale and its rebuff of potential buyers. For now, we should note that the requirement of attempting to sell the financially distressed company was one of the *Citizen Publishing* requirements rejected by the Newspaper Preservation Act.

Cincinnati Post was a failing newspaper. Just what portions of Judge Moore's recommendations were necessary to his approval of the JOA is not easily answered. Nonetheless, Judge Moore presents a reasonable construction of the somewhat nebulous statements in the legislative history. While we do not adopt in whole the test he utilized, we nevertheless find that his analysis of the failing newspaper standard provides a sound foundation for our interpretation of the Act. And, as will be discussed below, our interpretation is not much different, if at all, than that proffered by the Attorney General.

* * *

The act should receive a commonsense construction. The probable danger standard is, by the plain meaning of its words, primarily an economic standard: Is the newspaper suffering losses which more than likely cannot be reversed? The existence of interested buyers may be relevant to this determination. Also, poor management practices such as concerned the Supreme Court in *Third National Bank* may show that, with managerial improvement, the paper's economic problems can be overcome. We noted earlier in this discussion that the Attorney General and Hearst conceded that interested purchasers *may* be relevant to the determination a newspaper is failing. In particular, the Attorney General does not argue strongly against either ALJ Moore's or the district court's analysis. Significantly, the Attorney General's order approving the JOA application stated that "evidence of purchaser offers or negotiations may be pertinent in assessing the financial conditions and prospects of the allegedly failing newspaper." * * * The pertinence of interested purchasers, as the Attorney General apparently concedes, may require a JOA applicant to prove that the "new ownership and management could not convert the [paper] into a profitable enterprise without resort to a joint operating arrangement." * * * The interpretation of the act is not burdensome. Its primary effect is to prevent newspapers from allowing or encouraging financial difficulties in the hope of reaping long-term financial gains through a JOA. A JOA applicant should not be allowed to engage in poor business practices or maintain inept personnel in anticipation that it may later qualify for an antitrust exemption in the future. * * * In this respect, "alternatives" to a JOA are relevant to both the causes of a newspaper's financial decline and its future prospects.

Our discussion is in substantial agreement with the district court's opinion. We do not agree, however, that the facts are insufficient to support the Attorney General's order. The critical question is whether it was shown that the *P-I*'s financial condition was such that the new management might be successful in reversing the *P-I*'s difficulties. There is sufficient evidence in the record supporting a negative answer.

ALJ Hanscom made detailed findings on the condition of the P-I and the Seattle newspaper market. He found the *P-I* had lost over $14,000,000 since 1969, * * * and that the *P-I* was in a "downward spiral." * * * The ALJ also rejected the argument that Hearst had mismanaged the *P-I.* Instead, he found the *P-I* management had acted competently and reasonably in an effort to return the newspaper to profitability. * * * Judge Hanscom also explored numerous positive prospects and possible remedial measures proposed by the intervenors in their effort to show the *P-I* can be returned to profitability. He rejects them as being "ungrounded in reality." * * * Based on these findings, we believe there is ample support in the record for the Attorney General's * * * [view]:

> Although some of the witnesses in this proceeding were critical of the handling of the Post-Intelligencer, the evidence does not establish that new manage-

> ment would be any more successful than Hearst and current management of the Post-Intelligencer in returning it to profitability

Despite [this], the district court held that Hearst had not sustained its burden of proving new management could not succeed in turning the *P-I* around, apparently because Hearst did not respond favorably to purchase inquiries. In light of the existence of substantial evidence in support of [the Attorney General's view] this was in error. In the absence of a showing that there is a likelihood new management would succeed, Hearst's failure to consider purchase inquiries lost importance. We therefore reverse the district court's holding.

* * *

As an alternative ground for overturning the approval of the Post-Intelligencer/Times joint operating agreement, the Committee contends that the Attorney General failed to interpret the Act to require proof the P-I would be closed if the JOA application were disapproved. The district court held for defendants on this issue. It found it sufficient the Attorney General concluded that, but for the ownership of Hearst, the P-I would probably be closed. We agree.

For purposes of this issue, we accept the Committee's assertion that Hearst never considered closing the P-I, even should the joint operating agreement not be allowed. Our focus, however, is on other language in the failing newspaper definition not yet discussed. A newspaper is defined as failing if it is in probable danger of financial failure "regardless of its ownership or affiliations." 15 U.S.C. § 1802(5). This language supports the ALJ's and the Attorney General's conclusion that the financial strength of Hearst need not be considered in determining whether the P-I is failing. We therefore agree with the district court's resolution of this issue: substantial evidence establishes that the P-I is in dire financial trouble and, without the backing of Hearst, it would probably close.

We do not dispute the Committee's assertion that a primary intent of the Newspaper Preservation Act was to promote the diversity of editorial voices among newspapers. Congress was of the opinion that unique economic forces operate in the newspaper industry, forces which caused the decline and closure of numerous newspapers since the turn of the century. * * In order to maintain editorial diversity, it is beyond question that the purpose of the act is to prevent the *closure* of the ailing newspaper. * * * We note, however, that Congress was just as concerned with the loss of an independent editorial voice through a merger, as with an actual closure of a newspaper.

* * *

We do not accept Hearst's argument that requiring proof of probable closure is the same as requiring the paper be on the brink of collapse, an element of the "failing company" defense which was clearly repudiated by the Newspaper Preservation Act. We adhere to our belief that Congress intended the phrase "probable danger of failure" to mean a probability that the paper would be closed and an editorial voice lost. We do not agree, however, with the Committee's assertion that proof of probable closure is a per se rule applicable to all JOA applications. Our conclusion that Congress intended that there be a showing the newspaper will likely close must be interpreted in light of the language that a newspaper's failing status should be determined without regard to its ownership or affiliations.

We believe the intent of the "regardless of ownership" language is quite clear. It means simply that the ailing newspaper should be analyzed as a free-standing entity, as if it were not owned by a corporate parent. The legislative history does not contradict the plain meaning of this language. * * *

[G]enerally, ownership is not to be a factor in considering whether a newspaper is failing; an exception to the general rule is that ownership may be analyzed to ensure the owner has not created a failing company through creative bookkeeping. The Committee apparently does not dispute that the P-I as a separate entity is in financial trouble. It instead asserts that, based on an "incremental analysis," Hearst is receiving net benefits from the P-I's financial problems for tax and other reasons. As the Attorney General held, these arguable benefits to Hearst do not counter that the P-I, as a separate entity, is in severe financial trouble and would likely close if not owned by Hearst. We affirm the district court on this issue.

* * *

The Committee also argues that the order approving the JOA must be overturned because the Attorney General did not consider the potential injury to other newspapers in the market and did not limit the terms of the JOA to the least anticompetitive approach possible. The argument is that these conditions are implied in the requirement that the Attorney General find that the JOA "effectuate[s] the policy and purpose of the Act." The district court held against the Committee on this issue. For the following reasons, we affirm.

The policy of the act is stated in its first section. That policy is to maintain editorial and reportorial independence among newspapers through the preservation of newspaper publication in areas "where a joint operating agreement has been heretofore entered into because of economic distress or is hereafter effected in accordance with the provisions of this chapter." 15 U.S.C. § 1801. This declaration and the legislative history compel the conclusion that the act itself is a policy determination that the preservation of editorial diversity through joint operating agreements outweighs any potentially anticompetitive effects this antitrust exemption might cause. Congress struck the balance in favor of the act notwithstanding opposition that decried the potential harm to smaller, usually suburban newspapers competing in the market area. As stated in the House Report: "Although commercial competition may have been affected to some extent by these arrangements, they have achieved the more important objective of preserving separate editorial voices." * * *

The act itself contains an important safeguard which prevents the parties to a JOA from engaging in any conduct which would violate the antitrust laws if done by a single entity. 15 U.S.C. § 1803(c). As explained in the Senate Report, this section is designed "to protect the competitive position of newspapers which share the market with a joint operating arrangement." * * *

We conclude that the district court correctly rejected the Committee's claims on this issue. Congress recognized that the approval of a JOA may have anticompetitive ramifications. This was a national policy choice Congress was free to make. It believed those possibly harmful effects were outweighed by other considerations and sufficiently alleviated by the requirements of the act. The JOA is not inconsistent with the act.

* * *

The Committee also argues the Newspaper Preservation Act as a whole is invalid by virtue of the first amendment. The challenge is two-pronged: first, that the act is invalid as applied because approval of the JOA would impair the first amendment rights of smaller newspapers in the market; second, that the act is invalid on its face as an overbroad and vague delegation of power in an area affecting first amendment rights. Although these arguments are imaginative, they lack substantial merit.

The district court rejected the claim that the act is unconstitutional as applied, basing its decision largely on two district court decisions dealing with the same argument. *Bay Guardian v. Chronicle Publishing Co.,* 344 F.Supp. 1155 (N.D.Cal. 1972); *City and County of Honolulu v. Hawaii Newspaper Agency, Inc.,* 7 Media L.Rep. 2495 (D.Hawaii 1981). We agree with the district court's rejection of the Committee's assertion that these cases are distinguishable because the plaintiffs there were challenging preexisting joint operating agreements. In either situation, the courts are faced with the claim that this antitrust exemption may cause economic injury to smaller newspapers, which might lessen circulation, which in turn affects the "breadth" of one's freedom of press.

It is obvious that the Newspaper Preservation Act's antitrust exemption will not affect the *content* of speech of these smaller newspapers. The act is an economic regulation which has the intent of promoting and aiding the press. At most, the act *may* affect the number of "readers" a newspaper has. But that the act may have such an effect is not different, in our view, than any other economic regulation of the newspaper industry. *Associated Press v. NLRB,* 301 U.S. 103, * * * (1937); *Mabee v. White Plains Publishing Co.,* 327 U.S. 178, 184 (1946); *Oklahoma Press Publishing Co. v. Walling,* 327 U.S. 186, * * * (1946). *Grosjean v. American Press Co.,* 297 U.S. 233 (1935). * * *

Whether or not the Newspaper Preservation Act's limited antitrust exemption should be considered a license, as the Committee argues, we do not find first amendment rights implicated. While we recognize the importance of the antitrust laws in our economic system, one cannot lose sight that these laws are the creation of Congress. They are not mandated by the first amendment or anywhere else in the Constitution. What Congress has passed, it may repeal. Apparently, the Committee's actual dissatisfaction with the act is based on its belief that certain newspapers are treated differently, i.e., preferentially. But there is no question that other newspapers in the Seattle area, large or small, may participate in a joint operating agreement if they qualify.

Finally, we see no "vague and overbroad" delegation of power to the Attorney General. First of all, as discussed above, we fail to see any clearly defined first amendment injury. Secondly, our interpretation of the Act rejects the argument that it is overly vague. The Attorney General must base his approval of a proposed JOA on the requirements in the act as we have interpreted them in this opinion. Nothing more definite is required. * *

* * *

We agree with the district court to the extent it held that the alternatives to a joint operating agreement, including sale to a capable noncompeting buyer, are relevant to the determination that a newspaper qualifies for an antitrust exemption under the Newspaper Preservation Act. It is evident, however, that the Times Company and Hearst sufficiently negated the possibility that any such alternatives were available in this case. We reverse the district court for that reason.

The other arguments in support of overturning the Attorney General's approval of the Post-Intelligencer's joint operating agreement are better placed before Congress. The Newspaper Preservation Act was not intended to create antitrust immunities for any newspapers which simply allege they are having difficulties. However, neither does it contain an array of implied conditions which in effect would reinstate the *Citizen Publishing* standards. Simply put, we will not emasculate the Act in the guise of narrowly construing it. We therefore affirm the district court on the issues raised by the Committee's cross-appeal.

* * *

The decision of the district court is affirmed in part and reversed in part.

COMMENT

Where mergers are concerned, no market may be too small or inconsequential to escape notice of the Antitrust Division of the Department of Justice. In United States v. Tribune Co., No. 82–260 (M.D.Fla. 1982), the Department sued to block the acquisition of several shoppers and weekly newspapers by owners of the *Orlando Sentinel* because the merger would have reduced competition in the "local print advertising" submarket.

As in the *Times-Mirror* case, the competition in Orlando was between newspapers in different layers: in the above case, metropolitans v. shoppers. It could also be shoppers v. weeklies or suburbans, suburbans v. metropolitans, and in *Times-Mirror,* regionals v. locals. Interlayer competition may be the only kind of newspaper competition left to preserve. In the *Seattle* case the court saw no threat to weekly and suburban newspapers in keeping alive a metropolitan daily that was about to die from natural economic causes. Although courts have traditionally been hostile to mergers between competing newspapers, they may not have discerned as clearly as the Antitrust Division the competition for advertising between interlayer publications.

Local media markets obviously can be defined narrowly in terms of daily newspaper competition, as rare as that is becoming, or in terms of all print media, or broadly to include all modes of communication, newspapers, radio and television, cable, and electronic systems. In the *Bay Guardian* case, *supra,* it was argued that the JOA in San Francisco made it impossible for the competitive newspaper to get advertisers and therefore violated press freedom. The court disagreed, seeing the Newspaper Preservation Act as "a selective repeal of the antitrust laws" designed to preserve a particular daily newspaper voice.

Courts have not yet confronted the broader question of group ownership in a national arena, and it will be difficult for them to do so. Chains exert little influence over national advertisers because something like 85 percent of their advertising is local, and national advertisers have alternative media to go to anyway.

Antitrust Activities in Other Areas of Mass Communication

Motion Pictures

In spite of antitrust assaults on the motion picture business since the twenties, the industry remains highly oligopolistic. What it might have become without antitrust intervention can only be imagined. The Sherman Act was first applied to the movies in Binderup v. Pathe Exchange, Inc., 263 U.S. 291 (1923), in order to free theater owners from having to show pictures foisted on them by a conspiracy of distributors. And in Paramount Famous Lasky Corp. v. United States, 282 U.S. 30 (1930), a take-it-or-get-nothing contract was held anticompetitive.

Over the years, independent exhibitors were protected from various anticompetitive practices of distributors [80] and large theater circuits,[81] whether intentional or not.[82]

---

80. United States v. First National Pictures, Inc., 282 U.S. 44 (1930).

81. Interstate Circuit v. United States, 306 U.S. 208 (1939).

82. United States v. Griffith, 334 U.S. 100 (1948).

United States v. Crescent Amusement Co., 323 U.S. 173 (1944), was an important divestiture case. Crescent, a monopoly theater chain in many towns, pressured distributors to give it monopoly rights in communities where it had competition. The Supreme Court upheld an order to divest and required the company to demonstrate that it would not restrain trade with any of its future acquisitions. Theater chains and distributors were also prohibited from conspiring to concentrate the movie market in Schine Chain Theatres, Inc. v. United States, 334 U.S. 110 (1948). In yet another case, independent exhibitors were unable to show certain producers' films until they had been shown in studio-owned theaters. The Court in Bigelow v. RKO Radio Pictures, Inc., 327 U.S. 251 (1946), condemned such producer-distributor-exhibitor combines.

In a very significant case, United States v. Paramount Pictures, Inc., 334 U.S. 131 (1948), major film studios were required to divest their theaters, "the most significant change in the structure of a mass medium to be achieved to date under the antitrust laws." [83]

Finally in United States v. Loew's, Inc., 371 U.S. 38 (1962), the Court considered the legality of *block booking* copyrighted motion pictures for television use. No conspiracy was alleged among defendants, but the courts challenged the manner in which each defendant had marketed its product. Television stations were required to sign up for potboiler films in order to get the classics. Relying on *Paramount Pictures,* the Supreme Court held this form of tying to be violation of the Sherman Act.

Feature Syndicates

A federal district court in United States v. Chicago Tribune-New York News Syndicate, Inc., 309 F.Supp. 1301 (S.D.N.Y.1970), held "in unreasonable restraint of trade" feature syndicate contracts with newspapers that prohibited other newspapers within an area surrounding the contracting newspaper's city of publication from subscribing to the features.

Cable

Municipalities may be liable under the antitrust laws for their actions in granting cable television (CATV) franchises. In Community Communications Co., Inc. v. City of Boulder, 455 U.S. 40 (1982), the Court held that a Boulder, Colorado ordinance, prohibiting further expansion by an in-place cable company until a model CATV ordinance had been drafted, could not be exempt from antitrust scrutiny "unless it constitutes the action of the State of Colorado itself in its sovereign capacity, or unless it constitutes municipal action in furtherance or implementation of clearly articulated and affirmatively expressed state policy." States enjoy immunity from antitrust citations in the franchising process.

Boulder's "home-rule" status under Colorado law didn't save it. Citing Parker v. Brown, 317 U.S. 341 (1943), the Court characterized the federal system as a "dual system" of government with no place for "sovereign cities." Colorado had not explicitly authorized Boulder to engage in what could be construed as an anticompetitive practice, i.e., the granting of an exclusive franchise at some future time. The *Boulder* case reinforced precedents holding municipalities to be significantly less well protected from antitrust laws than are states.

In Affiliated Capital Corp. v. City of Houston, 519 F.Supp. 991 (S.D.Tex.1981),

83. Lee, *Antitrust Enforcement, Freedom of the Press, and the "Open Market": The Supreme Court on the Structure and Conduct of Mass Media,* 32 Vanderbilt L.Rev. 1249 (1979).

five CATV companies met with the city to agree on territories for which each would bid. Plaintiff was dealt out of what it and a jury saw as a conspiracy. But because the court found no evidence of harm to Affiliated Capital, defendants were granted judgment notwithstanding the jury verdict.

Granting that CATV may be a natural monopoly and that the only competition may occur in the franchising process, the Fifth Circuit Court of Appeals ruled that "the conspiracy charged in this case is the classic horizontal territorial restraint for which the per se rule was designed." (1983–1 Trade Cas. ¶ 65,281.) Since territorial agreements constituted a Sherman Act violation, the appeals court reversed the lower court and reinstated the jury's verdict of $2,100,000 in damages to plaintiff.

In the future, cable systems will have to be alert to tying and price-fixing complaints, requests for access from program and advertising competitors, and to antitrust problems related to program distribution and pricing, especially that of distributors affiliated with multiple system operators.

Vertical integration of program suppliers and cable operators will trigger antitrust action, especially where the local cable company refuses to deal with unaffiliated programmers or suppliers.

When four movie producer/distributors, Columbia, Universal, Paramount, and Twentieth Century-Fox, backed by Getty Oil, and calling themselves "Premiere," proposed a pay movie program service, a federal district court held the plan to be an attempt at price fixing and an unlawful group boycott. Together the four controlled 50 percent of new, yet to be shown on television motion pictures for which they would have granted exclusive CATV rights after their movie theater runs. In the "Premiere" case, as it came to be called, United States v. Columbia Pictures Industries, Inc., 507 F.Supp. 412 (S.D.N.Y. 1980), the court found a reasonable likelihood that the plan would constitute price fixing and an unlawful boycott of other programming services, violations of the Sherman Act. The project was abandoned.

New Technologies

For all new technologies, cable included, market definitions for antitrust purposes are in flux. Geographic lines are particularly vague and flexible with regard to multipoint distribution services (MDS) and direct broadcast satellites (DBS). Michael Botein, writing in the New York Law School *Law Review,* contemplates tying agreements, e.g., DBS operators may attempt to tie use of their facilities to the purchase of their equipment and programs; exclusive dealing agreements, e.g., operators, exploiting a scarcity of channels, might require programmers to buy all of their transmission service from a single DBS source; and monopolist's refusal to deal, e.g., a DBS operator might refuse to sell time to a programmer who may also have purchased time from a subscription television (STV) station. Vertical integration and merger activities will inevitably stimulate Section 7 Clayton Act responses.[84]

Broadcasting

In the fifties, the Federal Communication Commission permitted the exchange of an NBC station in Cleveland for a Westinghouse station in Philadelphia. The Justice Department learned that NBC and its par-

84. Botein, *Jurisdictional and Antitrust Considerations in the Regulation of the New Communication Technologies,* 25 NY Law School L.Rev. 863 (1980).

ent company RCA had conspired to force the exchange in order to upgrade their holdings. When the government sought review, a district court dismissed on grounds that FCC approval precluded government action. On appeal, the U.S. Supreme Court ruled that the FCC did not have authority to decide antitrust issues, although it could consider antitrust behavior relative to antitrust policy when measuring a broadcaster's conformance to the public interest.[85]

Other antitrust questions involving broadcasters are discussed in this text, Chapter IX.

Advertising

1. Forced Combination Rates and Refusals to Deal. A unit advertising rate compelling advertisers to use both a monopoly newspaper and an affiliated broadcast station was held unlawful in Kansas City Star Co. v. United States, 240 F.2d 643 (8th Cir. 1957), cert.den., 354 U.S. 923. Market dominance was blatantly evident in the fact that the *Star,* delivered to 96 percent of all homes in the Kansas City metropolitan area, accounted for 94 percent of all available advertising revenues. The newspaper used its dominance to discourage competition, or what was left of it. In addition to threatening advertisers with rejection of their ads if they advertised in competitive publications, or burying the ads of those who did, the *Star,* for example, threatened to drop news coverage of a baseball player whose partner in a florist shop advertised in a competitive paper. The *Star* owned WDAF–TV, the only television station in the city at that time. Advertisers could not buy television time unless they advertised in the *Star.* See also Syracuse Broadcasting Corp. v. Newhouse, 236 F.2d 522 (2d Cir. 1956).

The holding in the *Star* case was consistent with the Supreme Court's ruling in Lorain Journal Co. v. United States, 342 U.S. 143 (1951). A publisher's practice of refusing to accept advertising from local businesses which advertised in an independent radio station, WEOL, was held by Justice Harold Burton, writing for the Court, to constitute an attempt to monopolize interstate commerce in violation of the Sherman Act. The radio station derived 16 percent of its advertising income from outside of Ohio. The *Lorain Journal,* on the other hand, reached 99 percent of all families in the city and enjoyed a virtual monopoly in mass dissemination of news and advertising. Loss of local advertising jeopardized the very existence of the radio station. The publisher claimed the right as a private business to select its customers and refuse advertising.

"The right claimed by the publisher," said Burton, "is neither absolute nor exempt from regulation. Its exercise as a purposeful means of monopolizing interstate commerce is prohibited by the Sherman Act. The operator of the radio station, equally with the publisher of the newspaper, is entitled to the protection of the act." The antitrust laws did not violate freedom of the press because they applied to all.

Earlier, the *Mansfield Journal,* jointly owned with the *Lorain Journal,* was denied a license to construct AM and FM radio stations in Mansfield, Ohio, because it had engaged in the same illegal practice. The D.C. Circuit Court of Appeals upheld the Federal Communications Commission in Mansfield Journal Co. v. FCC, 180 F.2d 28 (D.C.Cir.1950).

Combination rates for morning and afternoon papers that simply reflect a reduced cost of publication in more than one edition were legally acceptable in The News, Inc. v. Lindsay Newspapers, Inc.,

85. United States v. Radio Corp. of America, 358 U.S. 334 (1959).

1962 Trade Cas. (CCH) ¶ 70,398 (S.D.Fla. 1962).

An agreement between a newspaper and an advertiser not to sell space to that advertiser's competitor is a Sherman Act violation, although proof of such a conspiracy may be difficult.[86]

Unilateral refusals to deal, if they look like an attempt to maintain a monopoly, violate the Sherman Act, as well as Section 5 of the Federal Trade Commission Act, although courts are divided on whether the latter is germane.

In Homefinders of America, Inc. v. Providence Journal Co., 6 Med.L.Rptr. 1018, 621 F.2d 441 (1st Cir.1980), text, pp. 579, 611, a newspaper found it risky to refuse even misleading advertising, although the court concluded that not even a monopoly newspaper could be ordered to publish advertising against its will. And in Newspaper Printing v. Galbreath, 5 Med.L.Rptr. 1065, 580 S.W.2d 777 (Tenn.1979), it was held that a newspaper's refusal to publish an ad that contained abbreviations did not constitute "predatory pricing or practice." Nor did it violate the First Amendment since newspapers, even where they enjoy monopolies in their areas of publication, have a right either to refuse publication of ads or to condition them on compliance with stated company rules.

First Amendment questions were raised, however, when in Home Placement Service, Inc. v. Providence Journal Co., 8 Med.L.Rptr. 1881, 682 F.2d 274 (1st Cir. 1982), a court held that a newspaper could not reject advertising that had not been found deceptive. Was the court dictating a newspaper's content in conflict with *Tornillo,* see text, p. 584?[87] In conflict with the First Amendment? (*Homefinders* and *Home Placement* are discussed from an access point of view in this text, p. 578ff.)

2. Tying. Time-Picayune Publishing Co. v. United States, 345 U.S. 594 (1953), held that a unit ad rate for A.M. (*Times-Picayune*) and P.M. (*States*) newspapers did not constitute an unlawful tying arrangement because morning and afternoon papers were not separate and distinct products. An independent competitive newspaper, the New Orleans *Item,* was later purchased by Times-Picayune. Although that holding has not been expressly overruled, later cases cast doubt on it,[88] and at least one authority has called it defective.[89]

Noncoercive tie-ins are legal if two newspapers are separately available to an advertiser on a basis as favorable as the tie-in arrangement. In United States v. Wichita Eagle Publishing Co., 1959 Trade Cas. (CCH) ¶ 69,400 (D.Kan.1959), a newspaper was allowed to offer substantial discounts, if the combination was voluntary. Cost savings to an advertiser should reflect savings in production costs.

3. Volume Discounts. In Times Mirror Co., FTC Docket No. 9103 (1977), the Commission challenged the validity of annual volume discounts for retail display advertising under the Robinson-Patman Act, 15 U.S.C. § 13 (1976) and Section 5 of the Federal Trade Commission Act, but courts have disagreed on this interpretation.[90] In 1981, however, the *Times-Mirror* and the FTC entered into a provisional consent

86. Oppenheim & Shields, *Newspapers and the Antitrust Laws,* § 38 (1981).

87. See also, Person v. New York Post Corp., 427 F.Supp. 1297 (E.D.N.Y.1977).

88. Paul v. Pulitzer Publishing Co., 1974–1 Trade Cas. (CCH) ¶ 75,116 (E.D.Mo.1974); Buffalo Courier-Express, Inc. v. Buffalo Evening News, Inc., 441 F.Supp. 628 (W.D.N.Y.1977), reversed on other grounds 601 F.2d 48 (2d Cir. 1979).

89. Areeda and Turner, Antitrust Law ¶ 733e, at 260, n. 9 (1978).

90. Times-Mirror Co. v. FTC, 1979–2 Trade Cas. ¶ 62,756 (C.D.Cal.1979).

decree. Small advertisers in public comments said that they were not hurt competitively by the volume discount rates and that they preferred to preserve their own pricing flexibility. On July 8, 1982, the FTC withdrew its provisional consent decree and dismissed complaints against the *Times-Mirror.*

4. Rate Differential for National and Retail Advertising. In Motors, Inc. v. Times-Mirror Co., 162 Cal.Rptr. 543 (1980), such a differential was challenged as an unfair business practice under the California Civil Code. The newspaper was required to justify the higher rate for national advertisers and their wholesalers.

5. Conscious Parallelism. In Ambook Enterprises v. Time, Inc., 612 F.2d 604 (2d Cir. 1979), cert. dismissed 448 U.S. 914 (1980), a court considered the 15 percent discount off the rate card that the media have traditionally allowed ad agencies. The alleged conspiracy appeared to be of no apparent benefit to the media but reflected a reluctance to depart from a tested way of selling advertising. An inference of an unlawful agreement between the *New York Times* and Time, Inc. and their ad agency can be drawn from the case.

6. Zoned Editions. Community newspapers and shoppers have used the antitrust laws to challenge the competitive response of daily newspapers through zoned editions, without definitive guidelines being set down by the courts. The intent of the dominant daily newspaper, however, will be carefully scrutinized, and tying arrangements of any kind ought to be avoided. Ad rates for zoned editions ought to pay the full costs of these special sections and in time show a profit.[91] Predatory pricing and tying must be avoided as well as anything suggesting a desire to damage a suburban competitor. Similarly, shoppers generated by the dominant newspaper ought to show a profit if they are to avoid suspicions of a predatory monopolistic intent. A court said in Greenvile Publishing Co. v. Daily Reflector, Inc., 496 F.2d 391 (4th Cir. 1974): "Proof that the Shopper's Guide is not paying its own way would support an inference that the defendants' pricing policies were designed to drive the Advocate out of the market." [91]

7. Blanketing. Blanketing, or giving free copies to everyone, should not last longer than a good promotional campaign would dictate. Although firm rules have not been established, generally a newspaper with monopoly power may not be permitted to do things that a smaller and weaker competitor might do with impunity. Where the purpose and effect is to drive a weaker competitor out of the market, a dominant newspaper may be in trouble.[92]

A dominant newspaper must be very careful in its narrowly defined market not to show an intent, explicitly or implicitly, to monopolize, especially in the setting of its advertising rates. They must be high enough to deny an inference of anticompetitive pricing. Combination rates must avoid tying and monopolistic effects. Competitive necessities and cost saving should underlie ad rate differentials.

Distribution

Independent distributors who contract with a newspaper normally charge higher subscription prices than the price set by

91. Paul v. Pulitzer Publishing Co., 1974–1 Trade Cas. (CCH) ¶ 75,116 (E.D.Mo.1974).

92. Morning Pioneer, Inc. v. Bismarck Tribune, 342 F.Supp. 1138 (D.N.D.1972), affirmed 493 F.2d 383 (8th Cir. 1974), cert.den. 419 U.S. 836.

the newspaper itself. They operate in semimonopolistic circulation areas and have no newspaper incomes beyond their sales. Newspapers may persuade distributors to lower their prices in order to sustain advertising revenue and increase circulation, but they may not coerce by dictating the price at which independent contractors resell the paper. Such action would be vertical price fixing in violation of the Sherman Act.

In Albrecht v. The Herald Co., 390 U.S. 145 (1968), the Supreme Court held that newspapers could not compel distributors to sell at a suggested maximum resale price. That rule was reinforced in Auburn News Co. v. Providence Journal Co., 659 F.2d 273 (1st Cir. 1981). No threats, surveillance, or economic sanctions would be tolerated.

Newspapers may, however, within reason, impose territories or distribution monopolies on distributors, if, in doing so, they do not exercise control over prices.[93]

In Newberry v. Washington Post Co., 438 F.Supp. 470 (D.D.C.1977), newspaper dealers brought action against the *Post* under the Sherman Act, the Robinson-Patman Act, and the Clayton Act. The court held that: 1) territorial sales restrictions placed on home sales dealers did not violate the antitrust laws; 2) restrictions placed on home sale dealers against sales to single-copy outlets such as hotels, newsstands, and street vending machines did not violate antitrust laws; 3) evidence did not show that dealers were coerced into charging prices established by the *Post;* 4) differences in prices charged by the newspaper to various home sales and street sales dealers did not violate the Robinson-Patman Act; but 5) evidence that, when one dealer raised the price which he charged to his customers, the newspaper raised the price which it charged to that dealer by a corresponding amount did violate the antitrust laws.

Summary

Conrad Shumadine, commenting on his comprehensive review of antitrust law prepared for the Practising Law Institute,[94] noted that juries in antitrust cases seldom understand the issues, so they operate on the principle of "good guys v. bad guys." The question of intent being paramount in antitrust, media managers should avoid putting anything on paper that suggests an intent to monopolize. Zoned editions or shoppers should contain news. Forced combination rates are dangerous. And Antitrust Compliance Rules, that everyone in the organization understands and that will help managers recognize basic antitrust problems, are a business necessity.

Failure to comply with antitrust laws can have grievous consequences even for the small- or medium-sized broadcaster or publisher. Criminal or civil actions may be brought by the Justice Department and civil actions by the Federal Trade Commission. State civil actions under state antitrust laws are also possible.

THE MEDIA AND THE LABOR LAWS

A Free Press and the Journalist's Right to Collective Bargaining

93. See Continental TV v. GTE Sylvania, Inc., 433 U.S. 36 (1977).

94. Shumadine, Ives and Kelley, *Antitrust and the Media,* Communications Law 1982, New York: Practising Law Institute, pp. 287–448.

ASSOCIATED PRESS v. NATIONAL LABOR RELATIONS BOARD

301 U.S. 103, 57 S.CT. 650,
81 L.ED. 953 (1937).

[EDITORIAL NOTE

The Supreme Court held that § 7 of the National Labor Relations Act, which gives employees the right to organize or join a labor organization to bargain collectively on their behalf, as applied to newspaper employees does not violate the First Amendment guarantee of freedom of the press or free speech. The regulation of union activity by the NLRB was found to have no relation to the impartial distribution of the news.

Morris Watson, an editorial writer for Associated Press, was fired for engaging in union activity. The American Newspaper Guild, a labor organization, filed a charge with the Board alleging that Watson's discharge was in violation of § 7 of the National Labor Relations Act (29 U.S.C.A. § 157) and that AP had engaged in unfair labor practices contrary to 29 U.S.C.A. § 158(1, 3).

At the outset the Court considered whether the particular labor dispute was in interstate commerce, permitting the application of federal regulation. The Court reasoned that the jurisdiction of the NLRB reached disputes involving editorial employees on the basis that, "* * * it is obvious that strikes or labor disputes amongst this class of employees would have as direct an effect upon the activities of [AP] as similar disturbances amongst those who operate the teletype machines or as a strike amongst the employees of telegraph lines over which [AP's] messages travel."

AP argued that its function was to report the news without bias and that in order to perform that function "* * * it must have absolute and unrestricted freedom to employ and to discharge those who, like Watson, edit the news, that there must not be the slightest opportunity for bias or prejudice personally entertained by an editorial employee to color or distort what he writes. * * *" And that "* * * any regulation protective of union activities, or the right collectively to bargain on the part of such employees, is necessarily an invalid invasion of the freedom of the press."

In rejecting AP's argument the Court noted that AP "* * * did not assert and does not now claim that he [Watson] had shown bias in the past. It does not claim that by reason of his connection with the union he will be likely, as [AP] honestly believes, to show bias in the future."

The Court, per Justice ROBERTS, went on to fashion a standard for judging an employer's performance under the act.]

* * * The act does not compel [AP] to employ any one; it does not require that [AP] retain in its employ an incompetent editor or one who fails faithfully to edit the news to reflect the facts without bias or prejudice. The act permits a discharge for any reason other than union activity or agitation for collective bargaining with employees. The restoration of Watson to his former position in no sense guarantees his continuance in petitioner's employ. The [AP] is at liberty, whenever occasion may arise, to exercise its undoubted right to sever his relationship for any cause that seems to it proper save only as a punishment for, or discouragement of, such activities as the act declares permissible.

The business of the Associated Press is not immune from regulation because it is an agency of the press. The publisher of a newspaper has no special immunity from the application of general laws. He has no special privilege to invade the rights and liberties of others. He must answer for libel. He may be punished for contempt of court. He is subject to the antitrust laws. Like others he must pay equitable and nondiscriminatory taxes on his business. The regulation here in question has no relation whatever to the impartial distribution of news. The order of the Board in nowise circumscribes the full freedom and liberty of the [AP] to publish the news as it desires it published or to enforce policies of its own choosing with respect to the editing and rewriting of news for publication, and the [AP] is free at any time to discharge Watson or any editorial employee who fails to comply with the policies it might adopt.

Justice SUTHERLAND, dissenting.

Justice Van Devanter, Justice McReynolds, Justice Butler, and I think the judgment below should be reversed.

* * *

For many years there has been contention between labor and capital. * * * Such news is not only of great public interest; but an unbiased version of it is of the utmost public concern. To give a group of employers on the one hand, or a labor organization on the other, power of control over such a service is obviously to endanger the fairness and accuracy of the service. Strong sympathy for or strong prejudice against a given cause or the efforts made to advance it has too often led to suppression or coloration of unwelcome facts. It would seem to be an exercise of only reasonable prudence for an association engaged in part in supplying the public with fair and accurate factual information with respect to the contests between labor and capital, to see that those whose activities include that service are free from either extreme sympathy or extreme prejudice one way or the other.

* * *

COMMENT

1. *AP v. NLRB* is the fountainhead of any understanding of the relationship of labor law to the press. The case makes clear that the press is subject to the labor laws just as it is subject to the antitrust laws. For the Court, this is just a corollary of the major premise that the "publisher of a newspaper has no special immunity from the application of the general laws."

2. The continuing importance of *Associated Press v. NLRB* was stressed in the recent *Minneapolis Star* decision, text, p. 142, which invalidated a special Minnesota use tax imposed on the cost of paper and ink products consumed in the production of newspapers. Justice O'Connor declared that the *AP* decision suggested the following:

> [A] regulation that singled out the press might place a heavier burden of justification on the [s]tate, and we now conclude that the special problems created by differential treatment do indeed impose such a burden.

Read the *Minneapolis Star* decision. Did Justice O'Connor make an appropriate interpretation of the *AP v. NLRB* decision?

3. Apparently it did not occur to the dissenters in *AP v. NLRB* that, while labor union members who work for AP may be partial to the claims of labor, the ownership of the AP might be equally susceptible to the point of view of capital.

The holding of *AP v. NLRB,* that journalists have a right to collective bargaining, has significant implications for the legal status of the press generally. *AP v. NLRB* made clear that freedom of the press is meant to reach other interests and values beyond the freedom of the publisher.

Note that the Court used *AP v. NLRB* for the proposition that the press is subject to regulation with the proviso that the regulation must not affect the impartial dissemination of news or place a special burden on the press. Do the duties of a rewrite editor and those of an editor with influence on editorial policy have a different effect on the impartial dissemination of the news? The Tenth Circuit said yes in Wichita Eagle & Beacon Publishing Co., Inc. v. NLRB, 480 F.2d 52 (10th Cir. 1973), cert.den. 416 U.S. 982 (1974). The court of appeals, reversing the NLRB, held that editorial writers have the essential characteristics of managerial and confidential employees and are properly excluded from the collective bargaining unit of news department employees:

> To hold that a person who was involved in the formulation of editorial content of a newspaper is not aligned with the newspaper's management would come perilously close to infringing upon the newspaper's First Amendment guarantee of freedom of the press.

Referring to *AP v. NLRB,* the court noted that while including editorial writers in a collective bargaining unit "does not have any relation to the impartial distribution of the news, *per se,* nor to the newspaper's ability and freedom to publish the news as it desires it published, it does infringe upon the newspaper's freedom to determine the content of its editorial voice in an atmosphere of free discussion and exchange of ideas."

4. Morris Watson was fired for "incompetency" a short time after this case was decided. Do you think the Court invited that result?

The First Amendment and the Question of Whether a Journalist Can Be Required to Join a Union

1. In Buckley v. American Federation of Television and Radio Artists, 496 F.2d 305 (2d Cir. 1974), the court of appeals held that a union shop agreement requiring television commentators to pay union dues as a condition of employment is not an infringement of their First Amendment right of free speech. The court found that a restraint on the right of free speech was not a violation of the First Amendment where there is a proper governmental purpose for imposing that restraint and where the restraint is imposed so as not unwarrantedly to abridge acts normally comprehended within the First Amendment.

William F. Buckley, Jr., and M. Stanton Evans, television and radio commentators expressing a conservative point of view on public issues, brought suit in federal court for a declaratory judgment challenging the constitutionality of § 8(a)(3) of the National Labor Relations Act [29 U.S.C.A. § 158(a)(3)], as it applied to their relations with the American Federation of Television and Radio Artists (AFTRA). The main thrust of their complaint was that this provision of the act allowed AFTRA to require them to join in AFTRA strikes or work stoppages against the television and radio networks and to subject them to union discipline (fines or cancellation of membership) for continuing to broadcast their commentary in the face of AFTRA's orders to strike.

Both Buckley and Evans had joined AFTRA under protest and asserted that their continued membership under these conditions had a chilling effect on their exercise of the First Amendment rights of free press and free speech as commentators.

Against the constitutional rights asserted by plaintiffs, the Court balanced the legislative purpose underlying the "union shop" provision of the act:

> * * * Nor is there any abridgement of first amendment rights arising from congressional authorization granting a union the power to collect dues from employees in a "union shop." The congressional purpose in authorizing mandatory union dues is surely a permissible one, for Congress was understandably concerned with minimizing industrial strife and thereby insuring the unimpeded flow of commerce. It was the legislative judgment that these goals are most easily realized if a suitable collective bargaining apparatus exists, and so the national labor laws provide for an exclusive bargaining agent to represent each discrete employee bargaining unit. To enable these agents to fulfill their statutory responsibility to represent all the employees while collectively bargaining

> with the employer, the statutes permit the levying of mandatory dues on all employees who will reap the benefits of the union's representation of them in the contract negotiations with the employer. * * *
>
> Moreover, we find that the means adopted to achieve this proper purpose of reducing industrial strife are reasonable and do not "unwarrantedly abridge" free speech. The dues here are not flat fees imposed directly on the exercise of a federal right. To the contrary, assuming *arguendo* that government action is involved here, the dues more logically would constitute the employee's share of the expenses of operating a valid labor regulatory system which serves a substantial public purpose. If there is any burden on [plaintiffs'] free speech it would appear to be no more objectionable than a "nondiscriminatory [form] of general taxation" which can be constitutionally imposed on the communication media.

AFTRA argued that plaintiffs were seeking to be "free riders"—those who enjoy the benefits of the union's negotiating efforts without assuming a corresponding portion of the union's financial burden. The court of appeals specifically rejected AFTRA's reasoning:

> The district judge * * * found that [although] the appellees derived some benefit from their memberships in union pension plans, he regarded this as not being substantial enough. We disagree with the district court. There is no rational basis for distinguishing between the degrees of benefit one enjoys as a result of a union's bargaining efforts on his behalf.

2. Buckley and Evans did not attack on constitutional grounds the general application of the National Labor Relations Act to the broadcast industry. The NLRB assumed jurisdiction over labor disputes in broadcasting at an early date. Los Angeles Broadcasting Co., 4 NLRB 443 (1937). The major problem the NLRB faced was in determining whether local stations were engaged in interstate commerce as defined in the act since the NLRB had no jurisdiction if the labor dispute did not involve interstate commerce. See AP v. NLRB, 301 U.S. 103 (1937).

The history of the NLRB's solutions to this problem reflects the growth and development of the broadcast industry. Early cases relied for their rulings on the fact that local stations were in interstate commerce depending upon electricity purchased out of state, FCC licensing, and the fact that the station's signals could be picked up in other states. *Los Angeles Broadcasting,* supra, KMOX Broadcasting, 10 NLRB 479 (1938). Later the board relied upon such factors as network affiliation subscription to the AP news service, advertising of nationally distributed products, and payment of copyright royalties to ASCAP or Broadcast Music, Inc. (BMI) in New York City or Chicago, all reflecting the national growth of broadcasting with its mostly recorded, rather than live, music. Instead of disputes with performers at the local level, the board was now considering disputes with engineers and technicians. WELL and WELL–FM, 74 NLRB 1054 (1947); Western Gateway Broadcasting, 77 NLRB 49 (1948); WBSR, Inc., 91 NLRB 63 (1950).

What is important to note about this history is that broadcasters fought the NLRB on jurisdictional grounds. Constitutional arguments, like those made in *AP v. NLRB,* were apparently rarely raised.

3. The AFTRA agreement with the networks originally covered only "entertainers and artists." Does this help to explain part of Buckley's and Evans's difficulties with union membership? Have broadcasters always considered themselves part of the press?

Could this case have been brought by the broadcast stations employing Buckley and Evans on a freedom of the press theory? Their argument would be that a news commentator's job is equivalent to that of the editorial writer in *Wichita Eagle.*

Could Buckley and Evans have argued the same theory on their own behalf?

4. The court in *Buckley* distinguished between the levying of mandatory dues which serve a substantial public interest and flat fees imposed directly on the exercise of free speech. See *Abood v. Detroit Board of Education,* text, p. 176. Is this distinction adequate? Is it immediately apparent when dues serve a substantial public interest?

Buckley and Evans found the imposition of union membership a burden, yet the court reasoned that the levying of union dues was not an *unwarranted* abridgement of free speech. Apparently the court is willing to permit a little abridgement of free speech, but what is "little" to the court may be major to Buckley and Evans.

A year later the Supreme Court denied review of *Buckley v. AFTRA.* Justice Douglas dissented from the denial of certiorari:

> There is a substantial question whether the union dues requirement imposed upon these petitioners should be characterized as a prior restraint or inhibition upon their free speech rights. In some respects, the requirement to pay dues under compulsion can be viewed as the functional equivalent of a "license" to speak. 419 U.S. 1093 (1975).

5. AFTRA's disciplinary code allows disciplinary measures against a member who does not conform to orders. If expelled from the union, the employee can no longer be hired by a broadcaster with a union shop agreement. Fulton Lewis III, a radio commentator, asserted that he was threatened with discipline causing him to suspend broadcasts during a strike. The court of appeals of New York did not find an impermissible restraint on free speech since Lewis was free to resign from the union and seek another job where there was no union agreement. Is the court being realistic? Economic and family considerations may make it difficult for a person to change jobs.

The court noted that the union had not retaliated against other members who did not join the strike. Consider the unofficial pressure brought to bear by coworkers and union officials. See Lewis v. AFTRA, 357 N.Y.S.2d 419, 313 N.E.2d 735, cert.den. 419 U.S. 1093 (1974).

6. Isn't the rationale for union representation the need for equality of bargaining power? Do Dan Rather, Barbara Walters, or William F. Buckley, Jr., need a union to reppresent them? Perhaps the question misses the point. The rest of the AFTRA membership needed members like Buckley in order to have equality of bargaining power.

7. Are private labor agreements under the NLRA infused with sufficient "governmental action" to give rise to a cause of action under the First Amendment? Constitutional guarantees of free expression embrace only abridgements by the federal government. See CBS v. Democratic National Committee, 412 U.S. 94 (1973), text, p. 858. Whether union shop agreements like that in *Buckley* actually constitute governmental rather than individual action is a matter of conflicting interpretation. In *Buckley,* the Second Circuit avoided this issue, holding only that "if there were a burden on free speech it would appear to be no more objectionable than a 'nondiscriminatory [form] of general taxation' which can constitutionally be imposed on the communications media." See Jensen v. Farrel Lines, Inc., 625 F.2d 379 (2d Cir. 1980).

A Note on Blacklisting

1. When a labor union forbids its members to accept employment from a specified list of employers, this practice is called "blacklisting," and it constitutes an unfair labor practice.

AFTRA has had some problems with what it calls its "unfair list." AFTRA went to LK Productions, Inc., producer of a syndicated television show in Houston, Texas, and requested that LK sign AFTRA's "letter of adherence" which set forth the terms and conditions for the appearance of artists on the "Larry Kane Show," produced by LK. When LK refused to sign, AFTRA placed it on the Unfair List. This list, explained an AFTRA publication, "represents employers who have refused to sign the AFTRA codes of fair practice. * * * Accepting employment from any producer on the Unfair List is a violation of AFTRA rules * * * and could result in disciplinary action by the local board, which could mean fines or other penalties." AFTRA also informed theatrical agents and recording companies who dealt with AFTRA artists, warning them that they would face AFTRA sanctions if they dealt with LK Productions.

Section 8(b)(4)(ii)(B) of the National Labor Relations Act, 29 U.S.C.A. 158(b)(4)(i)(ii)(B) (1970), states that it is an unfair labor practice for a labor organization or its agents "to threaten or coerce or restrain any person engaged in commerce or in an industry affected by commerce, * * * where the object thereof is—(B) forcing or requiring any person * * * to cease doing business with any other person." Courts have called this a prohibition against "secondary boycotts," action or threatened action taken against a neutral employer with whom the union has no dispute in order to bring pressure on the primary employer. Secondary boycotts are proscribed in order to prohibit pressure tactically directed at a neutral employer in a labor dispute not his own and to restrict the field of combat in labor disputes by declaring "off limits" to union pressure those employers who are powerless to solve the dispute.

An NLRB administrative law judge ruled that AFTRA's unfair list constituted a secondary boycott, in that agents and recording companies were being pressured into not dealing with LK, and that the unfair list was thus a clear violation of the National Labor Relations Act. American Federation of Television and Radio Artists (LK Productions, Inc.), before the NLRB Division of Judges, Judge Lloyd Buchanan, Case No. 23–CC–463, October 31, 1973.

2. One comment suggested that since there has only been one national strike by AFTRA, the national labor policy of allowing union shops has been effective in keeping the channels of electronic communications open; union security devices may thus further First Amendment values in the context of the national media. Do you agree? See *Are Television and Radio Commentators Exempt from Union Membership?,* 53 B.U.L.Rev. 745 (1973).

The Press and the Fair Labor Standards Act

Minimum Wages and Maximum Hours for Newspaper Employees

MABEE v. WHITE PLAINS PUBLISHING CO.

327 U.S. 178, 66 S.CT. 511, 90 L.ED. 607 (1946).

[EDITORIAL NOTE
The Court held that discrimination on the basis of circulation is a permissible method of classification to determine whether a newspaper will be regulated under the Fair Labor Standards Act. A total of forty-five out-of-state subscribers was considered enough to place a newspaper in interstate commerce.

The Fair Labor Standards Act of 1938 established a minimum wage and maximum number of hours for employees engaged in interstate commerce unless specifically exempted. [29 U.S.C.A. § 216(b)]

The act specifically provided that weekly or semiweekly newspapers with circulations of less than 3,000 were not covered. Daily newspapers, no matter how small their out-of-state circulation, were apparently covered under the statute.

White Plains Publishing Co. contended that an out-of-state circulation of forty-five out of 9,000 to 11,000 copies published was too weak a foundation on which to support a conclusion that the newspaper was in interstate commerce. Moreover, White Plains Publishing Co. contended that the statutory exemption for small weekly newspapers was discriminatory. In Grosjean v. American Press, 297 U.S. 233 (1936), the Louisiana legislature, you will recall, text, p. 138, had placed a tax on large circulation papers but not on small circulation newspapers. A duty to comply with the Fair Labor Standards Act likewise was placed on some newspapers but not others. Therefore White Plains Publishing Co. argued that the statutory exemptions for small circulation newspapers (weekly and semiweekly) represented discriminatory regulation.]

Justice DOUGLAS delivered the opinion of the Court.

* * *

* * * Volume of circulation, frequency of issue, and area of distribution are said to be an improper basis of classification. Moreover, it is said that the Act lays a direct burden on the press in violation of the First Amendment. The Grosjean case is not in point here. There the press was singled out for special taxation and the tax was graduated in accordance with volume of circulation. No such vice inheres in this legislation. As the press has business aspects it has no special immunity from laws applicable to business in general. Associated Press v. NLRB, 301 U.S. 103, 132–133. And the exemption of small weeklies and semi-weeklies is not a "deliberate and calculated device" to penalize a certain group of newspapers. Grosjean v. American Press Co. As we have seen, it was inserted to put those papers more on a parity with other small town enterprises. 83 Cong.Rec. 7445. The Fifth Amendment does not require full and uniform exercise of the commerce power. Congress may weigh relative needs and restrict the application of a legislative policy to less than the entire field. * * *

COMMENT

Prior to the decision in *White Plains,* a federal court had already considered the contention that the application of the Fair Labor Standards Act of 1938 to newspaper publishers was unconstitutional because "the press is immune from Congressional regulation by virtue of the terms of the First Amendment. * * *" Sun Publishing Co. v. Walling, 140 F.2d 445 at 447 (6th Cir.1944).

AP v. NLRB had involved the application of the National Labor Relations Act to the news distributing business. But in the *Sun Publishing Co.* case the argument of the publishers was that enforcement of the minimum wage and maximum hour provisions of the Fair Labor Standards Act might drive financially weak newspapers out of business entirely. The United States Court of Appeals for the Sixth Circuit rejected this argument and observed that the guarantee of freedom of the press was not "a guarantee to a publisher of economic security, or a sanction to free him from the business hazards to which others are subject."

OKLAHOMA PRESS PUBLISHING CO. v. WALLING

327 U.S. 186, 66 S.CT. 494, 90 L.ED. 614 (1946).

[EDITORIAL NOTE

The Court here held that provisions of the Fair Labor Standards Act requiring submission of pertinent records pursuant to a court order do not violate the First and Fourth Amendment rights of a newspaper publisher.

In this companion case to *Mabee,* a Department of Labor Administrator sought judicial enforcement of *subpoenas duces tecum* issued in the course of investigations conducted pursuant to § 11(a) of the Fair Labor Standards Act, 29 U.S.C.A. § 211(a). The *subpoenas* sought records to determine whether Oklahoma Press was violating the Fair Labor Standards Act.

The Court quickly rejected the arguments of *Oklahoma Press* that application of the act to the publishing business and the classification method (circulation) used to determine whether a newspaper may be regulated under the act was in violation of its First Amendment rights.

Instead, the Court examined the contention that enforcement of the *subpoenas* would permit a general fishing expedition into the newspaper's records, without a prior charge, in violation of the Fourth Amendment's search and seizure provisions.]

Justice RUTLEDGE:

What petitioners seek is not to prevent an unlawful search and seizure. It is rather a total immunity to the act's provisions, applicable to all others similarly situated, requiring them to submit their pertinent records for the Administrator's inspection under every judicial safeguard, after and only after an order of court made pursuant to and exact compliance with authority granted by Congress. This broad claim of immunity no doubt is induced by petitioners' First Amendment contentions. But beyond them it is rested also upon conceptions of the Fourth Amendment equally lacking in merit.

* * *

The matter of requiring the production of books and records to secure evidence is not as one-sided, in this kind of situation, as the most extreme expressions of either emphasis would indicate. With some obvious exceptions, there has always been a real problem of balancing the public interest against private security.

* * *

* * * Whatever limits there may be to congressional power to provide for the production of corporate or other business records, therefore, they are not to be found, in view of the course of prior decisions, in any such absolute or universal immunity as petitioners seek.

* * *

The only records or documents sought were corporate ones. No possible element of self-incrimination was therefore presented or in fact claimed. All the records sought were relevant to the authorized inquiry, the purpose of which was to determine two issues, whether petitioners were subject to the act and, if so, whether they were violating it. * * * It is not to be doubted that Congress could authorize investigation of these matters. * * *

On the other hand, [*Oklahoma Press's*] view if accepted would stop much if not all investigation in the public interest at the threshold of inquiry and, in the case of the Administrator, is designed avowedly to do so. This would render substantially impossible his effective discharge of the duties of investigation and enforcement which Congress has placed upon him. And if his functions could be thus blocked, so might many others of equal importance. * * *"

COMMENT

1. The Court in *Oklahoma Press Publishing Co.* pointed out that the case did not raise the issue of whether Congress could enforce a regulatory program including the press by excluding from commerce the newspaper circulation of a publisher refusing to conform. Suppose the Fair Labor Standards Act were amended to make

such exclusion the penalty for a publisher who refused to meet the wages and hours requirements of the Fair Labor Standards Act? Would such a penalty be valid?

2. By allowing administrative officials to subpoena the press for records, does a possibility arise that government may use the subpoena power as a means of reprisal against a hostile press? Should this possibility alter the Court's Fourth Amendment analysis? Are there any safeguards in *Oklahoma Press Publishing Co.* against the possibility of abuse of the subpoena power by government against the press?

Recent Problems of Labor-Management Relations in the Newspaper Industry

1. Technological advances in the production of a newspaper raise serious problems for labor unions. One problem has centered around maintaining the total number of jobs. "Setting bogus" and "overmanning" have represented two union attempts to cope with this problem. One study pointed out that the prospect of losing jobs is extremely serious, not because present workers would be put out of work, but because the union's pension funds are built almost entirely on payments from working members. Unions therefore cannot afford to dwindle away and die because their union funds would die with them.

A solution to this problem might be to allow newspaper managements to stop replacing workers as they retire or quit (by "attrition"), upon the condition that management make payments to the union pension fund equivalent to the payments that would have been made by replacements. See generally H. Kelber & C. Schlesinger, *Union Printers and Controlled Automation* (1967).

Technological advances have also posed the problem of union jurisdiction. The jurisdiction of the newspaper union is generally based upon the type of work done by the newspaper employees of fifty years ago when the unions were first organized. The jurisdictional lines of the unions are becoming increasingly anachronistic under the impact of new technologies. See K. Roberts, *Antitrust Problems in the Newspaper Industry,* 82 Harv. L.Rev. 319 at 364, fn. 214 (1968).

2. For a case discussing a newspaper union's concern about the effect of new technology "on the bargaining unit, the extent of potential job displacement, and the result of new unit employees to operate the new equipment," see Newspaper Printing Corp. v. NLRB, 625 F.2d 956 at 959 (10th Cir.1980). The case also discusses the rise of the video display terminal in the newsroom. See Jaske, *Collective Bargaining Issues in Newspapers,* 4 Comm/Ent 595 at 596 (1982). See generally, Ganzglass, *Impact of New Technology on Existing Bargaining Units in the Newspaper Industry,* 4 Comm/Ent 605 (1982).

3. Among causes for the decline in the total number of daily newspapers in the United States are labor problems in the newspaper industry. In 1962 New York City had seven citywide dailies. Today there are three. Strike days between 1948 and 1978 totalled more than 335, with more than 300 led by the Newspaper Guild and some 30 led by the Deliverers' Union. See *History of New York City Strikes,* Editor and Publisher, August 26, 1978, p. 9, and "Newspaper Busting," editorial, September 2, 1978, p. 4. A strike in 1963 resulted in the closing of the *New York Mirror.* The *World Journal Tribune,* the result of a merger of three newspapers, closed after being struck by the Guild for 140 days in 1966.

4. The *Cincinnati Post* arranged to combine operations with the *Cincinnati Enquirer* on the ground that the *Post* was "a failing newspaper" under the provisions of the Newspaper Preservation Act, 15 U.S.C. § 1801 (1976). After the joint operating agreement was approved and the

agreement between the Cincinnati newspapers was deemed to be exempt from the antitrust laws under the act, the *Cincinnati Post* closed its composing room and fired all the printers. However, these printers earlier had been guaranteed that they would be continuously employed for the remainder of their working lives by the *Post.* The *Post,* however, sought, after the approval of the joint operating agreement, to abrogate the lifetime job guarantee. Is the agreement still enforceable? In Heheman v. Scripps, 6 Med.L.Rptr. 2089, 661 F.2d 1115 (6th Cir.1981), Judge Merritt ruled as follows:

> In this case we are called upon to decide what effect should be given to an agreement in the newspaper industry guaranteeing lifetime job security for printers. The newspaper terminated the workers covered by the agreement following a partial reorganization and merger. We reverse the decision of the District Court which declined to give full effect to the job security agreement.

In a recent analysis of the case it was pointed out that the question of whether a lifetime job guarantee specifies "a particular rate of pay" was left unresolved by the court. Could *Scripps,* the publisher of the *Cincinnati Post,* take the position that although it would adhere to its job guarantee, "its wage proposal would be minimum wage or even zero." See, Jaske, *Collective Bargaining Issues in Newspapers,* 4 Comm/Ent 595 at 599 (1982). Jaske, Vice President for Labor Relations of the Gannett Company, made the following general observations about the issues presented by *Scripps:*

> It is not believed that the union's victory in Scripps will necessarily preclude management, which is desperate for relief from overstaffing, from negotiating changes or attempting to eliminate "lifetime" job guarantees. The outcome of such a challenge will undoubtedly turn on the wording of the guarantee. These questions will continue to dominate negotiations between newspapers and the ITU.

5. From 1970 to 1982, more than 200 daily newspapers have disappeared in this country. In the same period, 189 new dailies have begun publication. However, these papers tend to be too small to organize economically. One significant development that is apparent from the recent wave of newspaper closings is the failure of the large afternoon daily. The demise of these papers have causes independent of labor difficulties. The afternoon dailies in particular have suffered from the availability of local TV news and the flight of urban subscribers to the suburbs. The problems of the *Philadelphia Bulletin,* a well-known afternoon daily which finally closed, are illustrative. The *Bulletin* was forced to extend its distribution routes to keep pace with migration to the suburbs. The greater traveling distances and the problems of heavy daytime city traffic caused the *Bulletin* to have earlier press runs which in turn meant that the paper was less capable of reporting late-breaking news. As a result, an increasing number of subscribers turned away from the *Bulletin* and toward the evening TV news to learn more about late developments. The same problems plagued the now-defunct Washington *Star* and are at least partially responsible for its demise. See *New York Times,* August 16, 1981, at 27, Col. 1; *New York Times,* August 17, 1981, at Col. 1.

6. The National Labor Relations Act defines unfair labor practices by union and management which constitute a violation of the act and authorizes the National Labor Relations Board (NLRB) to act as the tribunal of first instance with respect to their resolution. In The Capital Times Co. and Newspaper Guild of Madison, Local 64, 223 NLRB No. 87 (1976), the NLRB found that the newspaper's refusal to bargain over penalty provisions to enforce a code of ethics, designed chiefly to

cut back on favors and freebies its reporters received from news sources and other third persons, constituted an unfair labor practice. However, the unilateral institution by the newspaper of the ethics code itself was not deemed to be a labor violation. The board said that the motivation to institute the code was to enhance the credibility of the newspaper by setting forth a high ethical standard for its employees and thus was not an economic decision which required discussion through the collective bargaining process. On the other hand, the Board considered "penalties to be mandatory bargaining subjects, since they directly affected job security."

7. In Newspaper Guild of Greater Philadelphia, Local 10 v. NLRB, 6 Med.L.Rptr. 2089, 636 F.2d 550 (D.C.Cir.1980), the Pottstown *Mercury* (Pottstown, Pennsylvania) unilaterally instituted a "code of ethics" which operated to discipline or discharge employees whom the newspaper thought might pose a threat to its editorial integrity. The *Mercury's* ethics code restricted its employees from receiving gifts from protected news sources or from participating in certain community or political activities. The code's purpose was to spell out a standard of integrity, objectivity, and fairness for the paper.

The guild objected to the posting of the *Mercury*'s code, claiming that it was a unilateral change in the terms and conditions of employment and that it therefore constituted an unfair labor practice under § 8(a)(5) of the NLRA, 29 U.S.C. § 158(a)(5). The guild requested that the *Mercury* engage in collective bargaining concerning the matter. That request was refused, as the *Mercury* considered its code to be a discretionary management prerogative which was part and parcel of its editorial process. The matter went to the NLRB which held that the newspaper was not required to bargain collectively concerning the substantive rules of the *Mercury*'s ethics code but was obliged to bargain collectively with respect to the code's penalty provisions.

On appeal, Judge Greene said the case posed this question: may a publisher of a newspaper, consistent with the National Labor Relations Act, refuse to bargain collectively regarding a code of ethics he has unilaterally adopted for his employees?

Greene answered the question for the federal court of appeals in Washington, D.C.:

> We agree with the conclusion reached by the [National Labor Relations] Board in this case and in *Capital Times, supra,* that protection of the editorial integrity of a newspaper lies at the core of publishing control. * * * [E]ditorial control and the ability to shield that control from outside influences are within the First Amendment's zone of protection and therefore entitled to special consideration.
>
> In order to preserve these qualities, a news publication must be free to establish, without interference, reasonable rules designed to prevent its employees from engaging in activities which may directly compromise their standing as responsible journalists and that of the publication for which they work as a medium of integrity.
>
> On this basis, we reject the [g]uild's position that collective bargaining is mandatory on all aspects of the Newspaper's Ethics Code and its Office Rules.

On the other hand, Judge Greene's opinion was not entirely adverse to the newspaper guild's position. Although the court thought that "reasonable rules" could be devised which would protect the newspaper's editorial integrity without being subject to mandatory collective bargaining, Greene remanded the case to the NLRB:

> Upon remand, the [b]oard will be expected to make substantive determinations with respect to the various provisions of the Code of Ethics and the Office Rules and come to a decision

> whether, in light of the principles laid down herein, any particular subject matter is or is not within the mandatory bargaining category. To the extent that it is, any penalty attaching to a substantive rule must be regarded as being likewise mandatorily bargainable; to the extent that it is not, the related penalty provisions will also have to be regarded as exempt from the bargaining requirement.

The journalist should note that in the *Newspaper Guild* case, Judge Greene made the following statement about the significance of the *Associated Press v. NLRB* precedent. See text, p. 664.

> The Mercury's reliance on the First Amendment is plainly foreclosed by long-standing precedent. It is firmly established that a newspaper is not immune from the coverage of the National Labor Relations Act merely because it is an agency of the press. *See, e.g., Associated Press v. NLRB.*

However, as we have seen, Judge Greene also observed that "editorial control and the ability to shield that control from outside influences are within the First Amendment's zone of protection and therefore entitled to special consideration." Are these two observations in conflict?

8. Union jurisdictional disputes resulting in labor strife such as strikes and picketing occur in the electronic as well as the print media. Illustrative is American Broadcasting Companies, Inc. v. Writers Guild of America, West, Inc., 437 U.S. 411 (1978), involving three cases decided together by the Supreme Court. Among the antagonists were the Motion Picture and Television Producers, Inc., and the three television networks, NBC, CBS, and ABC versus the Writers Guild.

Some employees perform various tasks which come within the jurisdiction of more than one union. The employee can be caught in a conflict between pressures from different unions and managements. When one union goes on strike, the other labor organizations may require that employees honor no-strike pledges in their contracts, and management may demand that employees perform duties which are not within the jurisdiction of the striking union. *American Broadcasting Companies* involved disciplinary proceedings brought by the writers guild against a union member, who was a supervisory employee with limited writing duties, for crossing the union's picket line during a strike and performing only his regular supervisory duties which included acting as the employer's grievance representative.

The Supreme Court held that union action in issuing rules prohibiting producers, directors, and story editors from performing their supervisory duties during the course of the strike and imposing sanctions on those who did perform such duties was unlawful. The union violated the National Labor Relations Act which prohibits union attempts to coerce employers in the selection of their representatives for grievance adjustment purposes.

Four justices dissented contending that "The Court holds today that a labor union locked in a direct economic confrontation with an employer is powerless to impose sanctions on its own members who choose to pledge their loyalty to the adversary."

Mergers of Newspaper Unions

The larger newspaper unions are considering an industrywide merger which could give reporters and production workers sufficient clout to challenge the growing newspaper chains and conglomerates. This move has been prompted primarily by the acceleration in automated printing, and has been fueled by recent closings of large well-known daily papers. See, *A Push to Unify the News Unions,* Bus.Wk., November 22, 1982, p. 93.

Mergers are expected between the 107,000 member International Printing and Graphic Communications Union and the

105,000 member Graphic Arts International Union. Also, plans are pending for a merger between the 29,000 reporters and other white-collar workers of the Newspaper Guild and the 43,000 printers and mailers of the International Typographical Union. *Business Week* suggests an ultimate marriage of the Guild and ITU with the 600,000 members of the Communications Workers of America.

Industrywide unions could exert substantial bargaining leverage by striking an entire chain of newspapers rather than focusing on a single daily as is presently done. Mergers might end wasteful jurisdictional disputes that have been partially responsible for the failures of several dailies. An end to jurisdictional disputes would conserve scarce union resources. Similar merger discussions are now occurring among unions in the electronic media. See Segal, *Labor and The Media In the Eighties,* 4 Comm/Ent 579 at 587 (1982).

COPYRIGHT, UNFAIR COMPETITION, AND THE PRINT AND FILM MEDIA

Copyright

1. Article 1, Section 8(8) of the United States Constitution stipulates that "The Congress shall have Power * * * To promote the Progress of Science and useful Arts, by securing for limited Times to Authors and Inventors the exclusive Right to their respective Writings and Discoveries. * * *"

Its purpose is akin to that of the First Amendment: protect the property rights of authors in their creations and in the end you will enhance the flow of information to the people.

The first copyright law was enacted in 1790. The most recent became law on January 1, 1978,[95] and it superseded the copyright law of 1909 and its patchwork amendments. In general terms the new law makes the author, the creative person, the focal point of protection.

a. Duration of a copyright is now the author's life plus 50 years. If a copyright is in its first twenty-eight-year term under the old law, it may be renewed in the twenty-eighth year for an additional forty-seven years or a total copyright term of seventy-five years. Works in their second twenty-eight-year term are automatically extended to seventy-five years from date of original copyright. Joint or co-authored works are protected for fifty years after the last author dies. For works made for hire the new term is seventy-five years from publication or 100 years from creation, whichever is shorter. In such cases the employer becomes the "author."

b. A work is now protected from the moment of its creation, in a "fixed" or tangible form, the author being the first owner of all rights of copyright in every case.

c. An author need not sell all of his or her rights to a single publisher in order to obtain a copyright; under the new law any rights not specifically transferred in writing remain with the author. Copyright is now divisible. What may be copyrighted for newspaper or magazine purposes may be recopyrighted for book publishing or movie adaptation purposes.

d. A transfer of rights to a publisher may be terminated and renegotiated after thirty-five years, and the right to terminate may not be waived in advance. Any transfer of an author's rights must be validated by a signed contract. Without a written agreement, copyright remains with the creator.

95. Copyrights, 17 U.S.C.A. § 101 et seq. (Oct. 19, 1976).

A subsisting copyright may be reclaimed and renegotiated after fifty-six years for an additional nineteen years.

e. Magazine publishers, or other publishers of collected works, acquire only first serial and limited reprint rights to articles or photographs. All other rights are retained by the author.

f. Sound recordings, including those played through jukeboxes, are protected, as are nondramatic literary works such as works of nonfiction, works of the performing arts such as musical compositions, television programs, and motion pictures, and works of the visual arts such as photographs and advertisements. Public broadcasters must pay for noncommercial transmissions of published musical and graphic works. Cablecasters must also pay for transmission of copyrighted works. See text, p. 694.

2. To apply for a copyright. One fills out a form supplied by the Copyright Office, Library of Congress, Washington, D.C. 20559. For a nominal ($10) fee and a specified number of copies of each separate work (usually one copy of unpublished and two copies of published works), you receive a certificate of registration valid from the day on which your application, your copies to be deposited, and your fee reach and are found acceptable by the Copyright Office. There are criminal penalties for failing to deposit copies, but no loss of copyright.

A notice of copyright may then confidently be placed on all publicly distributed copies of the work in one of the following forms: the symbol © (the letter c in a circle), or the word "Copyright," or the abbreviation "Copr."; the year of first publication of the work; and the name of the owner of the copyright: for example, © 1984 Peter Reiter. Consult the act for differences in symbolization dictated by the form of the work for which copyright is sought and for other details of the registration procedure. Mistakes made during registration and even an omission of notice can be corrected within time limits. Negligence by author or publisher does not necessarily forfeit copyright, but publication without notice may provide a defense to an innocent infringer. Registration is no longer a condition of copyright protection, nor of placing a notice of copyright on published or unpublished works, but it is prerequisite to a copyright infringement suit seeking damages and attorney fees, and is therefore encouraged. Notice is particularly important for pre-1978 works, and any work without notice may be presumed to have found its way into the public domain.

All works now receive federal statutory protection from the moment of creation (the act of an author), without regard to whether or not they are published. All common law or state copyright protection is preempted by the new uniform federal system,[96] unless the right in intellectual property at stake is not covered by the federal statute. But the new law is not retroactive. Works already in the public domain remain there, including anything published before September 19, 1906.

3. Works made for hire are works created at the behest of an employer. The new Copyright Act specifies two made-for-hire situations:

1. works "prepared by an employee within the scope of his or her employment," and

2. works "specially ordered or commissioned" and agreed to in writing to be works made for hire. In these circumstances the publisher may be considered the "author" and first copyright owner. These rights are nevertheless limited and

96. Ringer, *Finding Your Way Around in the New Copyright Law,* Practising Law Institute, Communications Law 1977, p. 114. And in 22 New York Law School L.Rev. 477–495 (1976).

divisible: an author may transfer part of a copyright to a publisher while retaining other parts.

Under the definition of works made for hire in § 101 of the 1976 act, a newspaper publisher would be "author" of everything copyrightable in each issue of the newspaper; only by special agreement would a news reporter or a columnist retain rights in his or her copyrightable work. A columnist, for example, would have to make an agreement with a publisher in advance that future book publication rights were to remain with the column writer.

When such questions are litigated, courts consider the creative role played by the employer in guiding, supervising, or directing the work of an employee or an independent contractor—writers, filmmakers, translators, text and test makers. A court ruled for example, that a university professor holds copyright to his own lecture notes since the institution employing him played only an indirect role in their creation.[97] Likewise, Admiral Rickover, not the Navy, owned the copyright in his speeches on public education because the Admiral had not "mortgaged all the products of his brain to his employer." [98] And a local merchant, not the newspaper in which his ad appeared, owned the copyright to an advertisement because the merchant had directed what the ad should contain.[99] On the other hand, a pamphlet written by a company chemist was clearly a project within the scope of his employment, and so the copyright remained with the company.[100]

There is a distinction between employees and independent contractors: employers own the work of their employees unless there is a written agreement to the contrary; but the presumption of authorship remains with independent contractors or freelancers because it takes a written contract in the first place to convert their creative output to "works made for hire." Absent a written agreement, copyright generally resides in the person at whose insistence and expense the work is done—the creative initiator. Reason may dictate exceptions. Work related to one's employment but done after business hours and for purposes outside the scope of that employment may be excepted.[101] For independent contractors, such as illustrators, songwriters, free lancers, textbook authors, the fine print of the initial agreement or contract is important.

4. What some have called the "artistic-effort-invested" philosophy of copyright is reflected in cases decided both before and after passage of the 1976 Act. Anything authored, created, performed, or produced and fixed or transcribed in a tangible or permanent way, rather than improvised, with a few exceptions, is copyrightable. Print, videotape, audiotape, film, television when taped at the time of transmission, computer programs, data bases, art works, choreographies, musical compositions, maps, news programs, compilations like annotated bibliographies, newsletters, singly or in single-year groups are included. Sedition, some classifications of pornography, names, titles, slogans, standard symbols and emblems (although these may be protected as trademarks), and official works, both published and unpublished, of the United States and state governments cannot be copyrighted, although the government may protect its "physical" property. On December 31, 2002, archives existing now will go into the public domain.

97. Williams v. Weisser, 78 Cal.Rptr. 542 (1969).

98. Public Affairs Associates v. Rickover, 268 F.Supp. 444 (D.D.C.1967).

99. Brattleboro Publishing Co. v. Winmill Publishing Corp., 369 F.2d 565 (2d Cir.1966).

100. U.S. Ozone Co. v. United States Ozone Co. of America, 62 F.2d 881 (7th Cir.1932).

101. Franklin Mint v. National Wildlife Art Exchange, 3 Med.L.Rptr. 2169, 575 F.2d 62 (3d Cir.1978).

5. There has been an interesting debate for some time as to whether the copyright law ought to have anything to say about content, for example sedition or pornography. The prevailing view appears to be that it should not and does not.

"There is nothing in the Copyright Act," said the Ninth Circuit Court of Appeals in Belcher v. Tarbox, 486 F.2d 1087 (9th Cir.1973), "to suggest that the courts are to pass upon the truth or falsity, the soundness or unsoundness, of the views embodied in a copyrighted work. The gravity and immensity of the problems, theological, philosophical, economic and scientific that would confront a court if this view were adopted are staggering to contemplate."

The Ninth Circuit relied on *Belcher* when in 1982 it held that the obscenity of a copyrighted film was not a valid defense against a claim of copyright infringement. Since *Miller v. California* (this text, p. —) made obscenity a matter of community definition, acceptance of an obscenity defense, said the court in Clancy v. Jartech, 8 Med.L.Rptr. 1404, 666 F.2d 403 (9th Cir. 1982), would fragment copyright enforcement, protecting registered material in a certain community while, in effect, authorizing pirating in another locale.

The *Clancy* court also cited an important Fifth Circuit ruling, involving the same plaintiffs, for the proposition that both old and new copyright laws, using the inclusive language "all writings of an author" and "original works of authorship" respectively, were intended to be content-free. The case, Mitchell Brothers v. Cinema Adult Theater, 5 Med.L.Rptr. 2133, 604 F.2d 852 (5th Cir.1979), cert. den. 445 U.S. 917 (1980), has been called "the most thoughtful and comprehensive analysis of the issue." [102]

By contrast, the Lanham Act prohibits registration of any trademark that "consists of or comprises immoral, deceptive or scandalous matter," 15 U.S.C. § 1052(a), and inventions must be shown to be "useful" before a patent is issued, 35 U.S.C. § 101. No such language occurs in 1909 or 1976 copyright laws.

A score of works that are today held in high esteem were listed by the Fifth Circuit as having been adjudged obscene in earlier times. On the question of the copyrightability of allegedly obscene creations, the court made the following points.

MITCHELL BROTHERS v. CINEMA ADULT THEATER

604 F.2D 852 (5th CIR.1979),
5 MED.L.RPTR. 2133.

GODBOLD, Circuit Judge:

* * *

Some courts have denied legal redress in infringement suits to holders of copyrights on immoral or obscene works by applying judicially-created doctrines. Two of these doctrines are largely vestiges of a bygone era and need be addressed only briefly. The theory that judges should act as conservators of the public morality was succinctly summarized by the court in *Shook v. Daly,* 49 How.Pr. 366, 368 (N.Y.Sup.Ct.1895): "The rights of the writer are secondary to the rights of the public to be protected from what is subversive of good morals." Application of this theory by the English courts in the nineteenth century led to the suppression of works because they were inconsistent with Biblical teachings or because they were seditious. *See* 46 Fordham L.Rev. 1037, 1038–39 (1978); Schneider, [51 Chi.-Kent L.Rev.], at 694–96. Although this theory has been relied on as recently as 1963, *see Dane v. M. & H. Co.,* 136 U.S.P.Q. (BNA) 426, 429 (N.Y.Sup.Ct.1963) (common law copyright protection denied striptease

102. *Nimmer on Copyright* § 2.17, p. 2–194.2, 1980.

because it did not "elevate, cultivate, inform, or improve the moral or intellectual natures of the audience"), it is evident to us that it is inappropriate for a court, in the absence of some guidance or authorization from the legislature, to interpose its moral views between an author and his willing audience.

A second judicially-created doctrine, the theory that a person can have no property in obscene works, merely expresses by means of a legal fiction the underlying judicial moral conclusion that the work is not worthy of protection. The doctrine has not been adopted in this country, * * and should not be. *Cf. Board of Trade v. Christie Grain & Stock Co.,* 198 U.S. 236 * * * (1905): "If, then, the plaintiffs' collection of information is otherwise entitled to protection, it does not cease to be so, even if it is information concerning illegal acts. The statistics of crime are property to the same extent as any other statistics, even if collected by a criminal who furnishes some of the data."

The third judicially created doctrine, that of unclean hands, has seldom been relied upon by courts that have denied copyright to obscene or immoral works. For the most part, only English courts have relied on this theory. *See generally* Chafee, [*Coming into Equity with Clean Hands* 47 Mich.L.Rev. 1065–70 (1947)]. Of the various American cases allowing obscenity as a defense to a copyright infringement action, few even mention the doctrine of unclean hands. * * * Nevertheless, since the district court permitted obscenity to be asserted as a defense through the medium of the unclean hands rubric, the concept of unclean hands requires more extended discussion.

Assuming for the moment that the equitable doctrine of unclean hands has any field of application in this case, it should not be used as a conduit for asserting obscenity as a limit upon copyright protection. Creating a defense of obscenity—in the name of unclean hands or through any other vehicle—adds a defense not authorized by Congress that may, as discussed above, actually frustrate the congressional purpose underlying an all-inclusive copyright statute. It will discourage creativity by freighting it with a requirement of judicial approval. Requiring authors of controversial, unpopular, or new material to go through judicial proceedings to validate the content of their writings is antithetical to the aim of copyrights. If the copyright holder cannot obtain financial protection for his work because of actual or possible judicial objections to the subject matter, the procreativity purpose of the copyright laws will be undercut.

The Supreme Court and this court have held that equitable doctrines should not be applied where their application will defeat the purpose of a statute. * * * Because the private suit of the plaintiff in a copyright infringement action furthers the congressional goal of promoting creativity, the courts should not concern themselves with the moral worth of the plaintiff.

Furthermore, the need for an additional check on obscenity is not apparent. Most if not all states have statutes regulating the dissemination of obscene materials, and there is an array of federal statutes dealing with this subject, as well. * * * As Professor Chafee concluded, the difficulty inherent in formulating a workable obscenity defense to copyright is sufficient reason not to allow such a defense unless the other criminal and civil statutes dealing with the obscenity problem are shown to be plainly ineffective:

> Sometimes the legislature has expressly entrusted questions of obscenity to the courts, as in criminal statutes, and then judges have to do the best they can, but the results have been quite erratic. This should be a warning against rushing into new obscenity jobs which no legislature has told them to undertake.
>
> The penalties for obscenity are defined by statute. Why should the courts add

> a new penalty out of their own heads by denying protection to a registered copyright which complies with every provision of the copyright act? * * * I think that the added penalty is justifiable only if there is a serious need for extra pressure to induce obedience to the criminal law. In the obscenity situation, this need is not obvious. Chafee, *supra,* at 1068–69.

The effectiveness of controlling obscenity by denying copyright protection is open to question. The district court thought that on the whole the long-term discouragement of the creation of obscene works would outweigh the short-term increase in the dissemination of obscene works caused by the refusal of an injunction. This theory, reached without empirical evidence or expert opinion, is at least doubtful. Many commentators disagree and are of the view that denial of injunctions against infringers of obscene materials will only increase the distribution of such works. The existence of this difference of view, which we need not resolve, makes clear that the question of how to deal with the relationship between copyrights and obscenity is not best suited for case-by-case judicial resolution but is instead most appropriately resolved by legislatures. Congress has not chosen to refuse copyrights on obscene materials, and we should be cautious in overriding the legislative judgment on this issue.

Finally, permitting obscenity as a defense would introduce an unmanageable array of issues into routine copyright infringement actions. It was for this reason that the Ninth Circuit rejected the defense of fraudulent content in copyright infringement cases. *See Belcher v. Tarbox,* 486 F.2d 1087, 1088 (CA9, 1973), *accord* 2 M. Nimmer, *On Copyright* § 2.17, at 2–194. *Cf. Coca-Cola Co. v. Howard Johnson Co.,* 386 F.Supp. 330, 337 (D.Ga.1974) * * * (rejecting violation of antitrust law as defense in trademark infringement suit because it would convert courts into "a battleground for extensive antitrust litigation whenever a trademark holder seeks any, totally unrelated, equitable relief").

Now, we turn to examine our momentary assumption that the unclean hands doctrine can be invoked at all in this case. For reasons that we have set out, obscenity is not an appropriate defense in an infringement action, whether piggybacked on the unclean hands rubric or introduced in some other manner. But even if obscenity were not objectionable as a defense, the unclean hands doctrine could not properly be used as the vehicle for that defense.

The maxim of unclean hands is not applied where plaintiff's misconduct is not directly related to the merits of the controversy between the parties, but only where the wrongful acts "in some measure affect the equitable relations between the parties in respect of something brought before the court for adjudication." *Keystone Driller Co. v. General Excavator Co.,* 290 U.S. 240, 245 * * * (1933). The alleged wrongdoing of the plaintiff does not bar relief unless the defendant can show that he has personally been injured by the plaintiff's conduct. *Lawler v. Gillam,* 569 F.2d 1283, 1294 (4th Cir.1978). The doctrine of unclean hands "does not purport to search out or deal with the general moral attributes or standing of a litigant." *NLRB v. Fickett-Brown Mfg. Co.,* 140 F.2d 883, 884 (CA5, 1944). Here it is clear that plaintiffs' alleged wrongful conduct has not changed the equitable relationship between plaintiffs and defendants and has not injured the defendants in any way.

* * *

Reversed and Remanded.

COMMENT

6. The Fifth Circuit Court of Appeals also made it clear in Miller v. Universal City Studies, 7 Med.L.Rptr. 1785, 650 F.2d 1365 (5th Cir.1981), that copyright protection extends only to the expression of

facts or ideas and not to facts themselves or to the research involved in obtaining them. A *Miami Herald* reporter who covered the kidnapping of a wealthy businessman's daughter and her being buried alive and rescued after five days collaborated with the victim to write a book about that terrifying experience. Titled *83 Hours Till Dawn,* the work was copyrighted, as was a condensed version of it in *Reader's Digest* and a serialization in *Ladies Home Journal.* Without the author's agreement, the book was turned into a television script, *The Longest Night,* and sold to ABC. A jury found infringement and awarded the reporter $200,000 in damages and profits.

"Obviously," said the appeals court in reversing and remanding, "a fact does not originate with the author of a book describing the fact. Neither does it originate with one who 'discovers' the fact. 'The discoverer merely finds and records. He may not claim that the facts are "original" with him although there may be originality and hence authorship in the manner of reporting, i.e., the "expression," of the facts.' Nimmer, *Nimmer on Copyright* § 2.03(E), at 2–34 (1980). Thus, since facts do not owe their origin to any individual, they may not be copyrighted and are part of the public domain available to every person." The distinction between facts and copyrightable forms of expressing them is not always as clear as the foregoing statements would suggest.

Nor is historical research copyrightable. In Rosemont Enterprises, Inc. v. Random House, Inc., 366 F.2d 303 (2d Cir.1966), cert. den., 385 U.S. 1009 (1967), the court said that it could not "subscribe to the view that an author is absolutely precluded from saving time and effort by referring to and relying upon prior published material. * * * It is just such wasted effort that the proscription against the copyright of ideas and facts, and to a lesser extent the privilege of fair use, are designed to prevent." Defendant's biography was said to infringe the copyright on a series of *Look* magazine articles about Howard Hughes.

Similar litigation arose over books and films about the mysterious disaster involving the German dirigible Hindenburg with similar results. Interpretations of historical fact were not copyrightable. Nor were specific facts or the personal research behind them.[103] Said the court:

> The copyright provides a financial incentive to those who would add to the corpus of existing knowledge by creating original works. Nevertheless, the protection afforded the copyright holder has never extended to history, be it documented fact or explanatory hypothesis. The rationale for this doctrine is that the cause of knowledge is best served when history is the common property of all, and each generation remains free to draw upon the discoveries and insights of the past. Accordingly, the scope of copyright in historical accounts is narrowed indeed, embracing no more than the author's original expression of particular facts and theories already in the public domain.

7. An allegation that a copyright owner has generally been exploiting his copyright in a manner violative of the antitrust laws does not affect the owner's claim for relief against an infringement.

8. Works that become part of a federal agency's records, however, even though copyrighted by a third person, are public records under the Freedom of Information Act and cannot be withheld simply because they are copyrighted, said the D.C. Circuit in Weisberg v. United States Department of Justice, 6 Med.L.Rptr. 1401, 543 F.2d 308 (D.C.Cir.1980). The case involved photographs in the government's possession that were taken at the scene of the assassination of Dr. Martin Luther King.

103. Hoehling v. Universal City Studios, Inc., 6 Med.L.Rptr. 1053, 618 F.2d 972 (2d Cir.1979).

Time, Inc., the copyright holder, would permit the photos to be viewed but not copied.

9. While authorship and a modicum of originality is assumed, there are no tests of quality or merit for copyright purposes. The owner of a copyright has the exclusive right to reproduce, to develop derivative works from that which is copyrighted, to distribute, to record, to perform, and to display. Limitations on these rights are twofold: 1) only the expression of an idea, for example, a particular pattern of words or prose elements, is copyrightable—the idea itself is not; and 2) copyright is limited by the *doctrine of fair use* or, conversely, by the law of *unfair competition.*

Unfair Competition

1. Fair use is another dimension of the effort to balance the encouragement of creativity with the flow of information to the public. Reproduction of someone else's work for purposes of criticism, comment, news reporting, scholarship, teaching, and research is permitted within limits: a. the purpose of the copier must not be purely commercial (some leeway is allowed educators); b. the amount used (with proper attribution, of course) is limited to 200 words of prose scattered or clustered. Poetry is not included, nor are complete articles of less than 200 words; c. the effect of such use on the potential market of a copyrighted work must be considered. If the copyright owner is hurt financially and can carry the burden of proof, damages may be awarded.

The doctrine of fair use was substantiated by an equally divided Supreme Court in *Williams & Wilkins Co. v. United States,* a case involving the making of unauthorized copies of medical journal articles by HEW and the National Library of Medicine for research purposes. Said the Court of Claims:

> Precisely because a determination that a use is "fair" or "unfair" depends on an evaluation of the complex of individual and varying factors bearing upon a particular use, there has been no exact or detailed definition of the doctrine. The courts, congressional committees, and scholars have had to be content with a general listing of the main considerations—together with the example of specific instances ruled "fair" or "unfair." These overall factors are now said to be: (a) the purpose and character of the use, (b) the nature of the copyrighted work, (c) the amount and substantiality of the material used in relation to the copyrighted work as a whole, and (d) the effect of the use on the copyright owner's potential market for a value of his work. 203 Ct.Cl. 74, 487 F.2d 1345, 1352 (1973), aff'd w/o opinion, 420 U.S. 376 (1975).

What the Court of Claims called a "fair use," the trial judge had termed "wholesale copying" (many thousands of copies had been made). Where the trial judge found that copying practices in this instance had supplanted the need for original journals, thus decreasing the value of copyrighted works, the Court of Claims found that the practices were in lieu of library loan and did not represent a threat to subscription or reprint sales. In addition, the Court of Claims felt that a "flat proscription" on library copying would harm scientific and medical research; the trial judge thought an award of damages would be a small price for protection of the rights of the copyright owner.

Using the basic fair use test of *Williams & Wilkins,* the 1976 statute attempted to deal with the new technology of photocopying by regulating the reproduction of copyrighted material by libraries and archives. Copying is permitted when it does not substitute for purchase of a copyrighted work or provide profit for the copier.

2. Earlier cases elaborated the concept of fair use. It was not fair use for the *Chicago Record-Herald* to reprint an almost identical version of a story on sub-

marine warfare which had appeared in the rival *Chicago Tribune* after turning down an offer to buy it. The *Tribune*'s story bore the mark of individual enterprise and literary style. Giving the *Tribune* a credit line simply compounded the damage by presenting the plaintiff in a false light.[104]

It was not fair use for a school of modeling to benefit from *Vogue* magazine's prestige by using the magazine's covers in its advertising brochures. *Vogue*'s covers were included in its overall copyright protection. "No one," said a federal district court, "is entitled to save time, trouble, and expense by availing himself to another's copyrighted work for the sake of making an unearned profit." [105]

A different result was reached, however, when the *Miami Herald* in promoting a new television supplement used the cover of *TV Guide* in comparative advertising for its new service. Relying on the *Vogue* case and *Nimmer on Copyright* § 14.4 at 62, a federal district court in Florida concluded that the cover of *TV Guide* "was encompassed within the protections afforded by the copyright registered for that magazine." Moreover there was no "fair use" justification in using the plaintiff's cover for promotional purposes. But a First Amendment purpose was being served in light of judicial recognition of increased constitutional protection for commercial speech.

"Such comparative advertising, when undertaken in the serious manner that defendant did herein," said the court, "represents an important source of information for the education of consumers in a free enterprise system." Since *TV Guide* had not demonstrated irreparable injury and since the First Amendment outweighs any act of Congress, the magazine was denied an injunction against the *Herald's* competitive promotional activities.[106]

Similarly, when *Time* magazine refused an author the use of certain frames of its copyrighted Zapruder film for a scholarly book on the Kennedy assassination and the author used sketches of the frames instead, *Time* failed in a copyright suit because, said the court, there was a *public interest* in the subject and the book would be purchased, not alone for its pictures, but for the author's "theories." [107] Balancing First Amendment and copyright values, Judge Kaufman for the Second Circuit chose the public's right to news contained in former President Ford's memoirs. Editor Victor Navasky's excerpt, said the court, was fair use of information of a public nature, i.e., news reporting.[107a]

There was no fair use, however, when a religious group presented what it called a "nonperverted" version of "Jesus Christ Superstar" using, with sanctimonious modification, the plaintiff's original music and libretto. An argument that the presentation served a "critical" function was rejected because 1) the original was copied exactly and was a substitute for the original, 2) it injured the plaintiff financially, 3) it was in competition with the plaintiff, and 4) it did not serve or advance greater *public interest* in the development of news, art, science, or industry.[108]

A case that reflects the "artistic-effort-invested" philosophy of the new act is Gilliam v. American Broadcasting Companies, Inc., 538 F.2d 14 (2d Cir.1976). Interesting in part because it involved the irre-

104. Chicago Record-Herald v. Tribune Association, 275 F. 797 (7th Cir.1921).

105. Conde Nast Publications, Inc. v. Vogue School of Fashion Modeling, Inc., 105 F.Supp. 325 (D.N.Y.1952).

106. Triangle Publications v. Knight-Ridder, Newspapers, 3 Med.L.Rptr. 2086, 445 F.Supp. 875 (D.Fla.1978), affirmed 6 Med.L.Rptr. 1734, 626 F.2d 1171 (5th Cir.1980).

107. Time, Inc. v. Bernard Geis Associates, 293 F.Supp. 130 (D.N.Y.1968).

107a. Harper and Row and Reader's Digest v. The Nation, — F.2d — (2d Cir., Nov. 18, 1983).

108. Robert Stigwood Group Ltd. v. O'Reilly, 346 F.Supp. 376 (D.Conn.1972).

pressible "Monty Python's Flying Circus," the case began when ABC bought from the BBC the right to show six Python episodes, then cut them to fit the commercial television format in an apparently prudish manner. The Pythons sued for copyright infringement and unfair competition, asking for a permanent injunction against ABC.

In what was by all accounts an entertaining trial,[109] a federal district court, while recognizing a plaintiff's right to protect the artistic integrity of his creation (the film here had lost its "iconoclastic verve," said the judge), denied the injunction on grounds that it was not clear who owned the copyright. Also there was a question as to whether the BBC and Time-Life—the latter had purchased the rights—should have been parties to the litigation. Further, ABC might suffer irreparable harm in its relationships with affiliates, public, and government if it were to withdraw the programs.

The trial judge suggested a disclaimer instead: "The members of Monty Python wish to disassociate themselves from this program, which is a compilation of their shows edited by ABC without their approval." ABC thought this distasteful, a dangerous precedent with respect to other artists and technicians, and a violation of its First Amendment rights. The best Monty Python could get was "Edited for Television by ABC."

A Second Circuit Court of Appeals panel subsequently reversed and remanded the lower court's denial of a preliminary injunction. Seeing Monty Python rather than ABC the greater loser, the court held that "unauthorized editing of the underlying work, if proven, would constitute an infringement of copyright in that work similar to any other use of a work that exceeded the license granted by the proprietor of the copyright." Since BBC itself had no right to make unilateral changes in the script, it could not grant such rights to Time-Life or ABC.

"Our resolution of these technical arguments," said the court somewhat in anticipation of the 1976 Copyright Act, "serves to reinforce our initial inclination that the copyright law should be used to recognize the important role of the artist in our society and the need to encourage production and dissemination of artistic works by providing adequate legal protection for one who submits his work to the public. * * * To deform his work is to present him to the public as the creator of a work not his own, and thus makes him subject to criticism for work he has not done. In such a case, it is the writer or performer, rather than the network, who suffers the consequences of the mutilation, for the public will have only the final product by which to evaluate his work."

Sometimes the question is simply how much is too much use of a copyrighted work. When the Board of Cooperative Educational Services began making 10,000 videotapes a year of copyrighted motion pictures, a federal district court said that was too much. Applying *Williams & Wilkins* the court held that, while the purpose was educational and noncommercial, the effect on the copyright holder's market would be devastating. Entire films were reproduced, and the reproductions were interchangeable with the originals. Since this was not a fair use, an injunction against further copying was made permanent.[110]

A second case illustrates the delicate balance between quantity and commercialism. Here a television network had copied only 8 percent of a copyrighted film, but it had done so for purely commer-

109. Hertzberg, *Onward and Upward With the Arts: Naughty Bits,* New Yorker, March 29, 1976, p. 69. See also, *Protection of Artistic Integrity: Gilliam v. American Broadcasting Companies,* 90 Harv.L.Rev. 473 (December 1976).

110. Encyclopedia Britannica v. Crooks, 3 Med.L.Rptr. 1945, 447 F.Supp. 243 (D.N.Y.1978).

cial purposes. Such was not fair use because it foreclosed plaintiff's potential market.[111]

In *Elsmere Music, Inc. v. NBC,*[112] "Saturday Night Live's" use of New York's public relations song "I Love New York" did not violate fair use because it was used as parody.

When *Screw* magazine portrayed the trade characters, "Poppin Fresh" and "Poppie Fresh" in a compromising pose, the Pillsbury Company was understandably upset. A federal district court ruled, however, that the magazine's use of the copyrighted trade characters, while more pornographic than it needed to be, was intended as a social commentary and thereby protected. Since it did not cause significant economic harm to the company, the portrayal was fair use.[113]

3. Copyright protection was first extended to advertising in Bleistein v. Donaldson Lithographing Co., 188 U.S. 239 (1902), a case involving a copyrighted circus poster. In Ansehl v. Puritan Pharmaceutical Co., 61 F.2d 131 (8th Cir. 1932), the court, granting relief to the creator of a cosmetic ad, recognized protected property rights in the particular wording used and in the arrangement of the elements of the advertisement, beyond the more general consideration of artistic value.

"The defendants," said the court, "might appropriate the ideas and express them in their own pictures and in their own language, but they could not appropriate the plaintiff's advertisement by copying his arrangement of material, his illustrations and language, and thereby create substantially the same composition in substantially the same manner without subjecting themselves to liability for infringement."

Advertising created and composed solely by the newspaper or its employees is included in copyright protection for the entire newspaper. Where advertising is created partly by the newspaper and partly by the advertiser or his agent, the newspaper may secure copyright interest by written contract. Otherwise the advertisements remain the property of the advertiser.

4. What is not fair use under copyright, either because something cannot or has not been copyrighted, may be *unfair competition* or misrepresentation under state law or its federal counterpart, the Lanham Act. The protection of news as "quasi property" against unfair competition was recognized in a broad and influential ruling by the United States Supreme Court in 1918. International News Service was alleged to have "pirated" news from the Associated Press for redistribution to its own customers. No direct question of fraud was raised, and the misappropriated material had not been copyrighted. In the absence of statutory protection, AP relied on the common law doctrine of unfair competition.

The Court considered three major legal issues: 1) whether there is any property in news; 2) whether, if there be property in news collected for the purpose of being published, it survives the instant of its publication in the first newspaper to which it is communicated by the news gatherer; and 3) whether INS's admitted course of conduct in appropriating for commercial use material taken from bulletins or earlier editions of Associated Press newspapers constitutes unfair competition in trade. Each question was answered in favor of the Associated Press. Interna-

111. Iowa State Research Foundation, Inc. v. ABC, 463 F.Supp. 902 (D.N.Y.1978), affirmed 6 Med.L.Rptr. 1855, 621 F.2d 57 (2d Cir.1980).

112. 5 Med.L.Rptr. 2455, 482 F.Supp. 741 (D.N.Y.1980), affirmed 6 Med.L.Rptr. 1457, 623 F.2d 252 (2d Cir.1980).

113. The Pillsbury Company v. Milky Way Productions, 8 Med.L.Rptr. 1016 (D.Ga.1981).

tional News Service v. Associated Press, 248 U.S. 215 (1918).[114]

News, being part of the public domain and like ideas "as free as the air," [115] is excluded from specific copyright protection, but the doctrine of *INS v. AP* does apply to news gathering and news presentation activities. Using one's competitor for news "tips" is an acceptable practice, but bodily appropriation of another's news copy is unfair competition subject to injunctive relief.

In Associated Press v. KVOS, 80 F.2d 575 (9th Cir. 1935), reversed on other grounds 299 U.S. 269 (1936), the appeals court ruled that appropriation for broadcast of the AP wire before neighboring AP newspapers could reach their subscribers—while the news was still "hot"—was enjoinable. An injunction was also granted to a Sitka, Alaska newspaper whose AP stories were being read verbatim by a radio station even before the newspaper hit the streets. Instead of joining its member newspaper in the suit, AP sold the offending radio station an associate membership. Still preferring to read the newspaper's edited AP copy, the broadcaster found himself in a second suit. Nominal damages were awarded, and the radio station agreed to cease pirating news.[116]

In an unreported case, a Kentucky circuit court ruled that a defendant, who had without permission used plaintiff's news stories sixteen to eighteen hours before the newspaper could be delivered to all its subscribers, would in future have to wait twenty hours after publication before engaging in his piracy.[117]

In 1963 the Supreme Court of Pennsylvania left no doubt that the broadcasting of news stories from a newspaper in a competitive situation was unfair competition and an invasion of a property right in uncopyrighted news. The court articulated a doctrine that had been expressed in earlier cases:

> Competition in business is jealously protected by the law and the law abhors that which tends to diminish or stifle competition. While a competitor may, subject to patent, copyright and trademark laws, imitate his rival's business practices, process and methods, yet the protection which the law affords to competition does not and should not countenance the usurpation of a competitor's investment and toil. Pottstown Daily News Publishing Co. v. Pottstown Broadcasting Co., 192 A.2d 657, 663 (Pa.1963).

In a 1966 case involving two business publications, defendant had appropriated information from the plaintiff's wire service in order to publish bond market news contemporaneously with his competitor and without expense or effort.

"It is no longer subject to question," said a New York appeals court, "that there is a property in the gathering of news which may not be pirated. Plaintiff's rights do not depend on copyright; they lie rather in the fact that the information has been acquired through an expenditure of labor, skill and money." [118]

Where plaintiff's rights do depend on copyright, there may be a suit for copyright infringement. So there was when a business newspaper appropriated almost verbatim the most creative and original

114. For a discussion of this case and the whole question of news piracy, unfair competition, and misappropriation, see Sullivan, *News Piracy: Unfair Competition and the Misappropriation Doctrine,* 56 Journalism Monographs, May, 1978.

115. Desney v. Wilder, 46 Cal.2d 715, 299 P.2d 257 (1956), a case dealing with the writing of a play from news stories and quoting Justice Brandeis.

116. Veatch v. Wagner, 109 F.Supp. 537 (Alaska 1953) and 116 F.Supp. 904 (Alaska 1953).

117. Madison Publishing Co., Inc. v. Sound Broadcasters, Inc. (unreported 1966). In a 1956 case involving the Toledo Blade and radio station WOHO, the time period was set at twenty-four hours.

118. Bond Buyer v. Dealers Digest Publishing Co., 267 N.Y.2d 944 (1966).

elements of copyrighted research reports on financial and industrial matters. Rejecting defendant's fair use arguments and finding the tantalizing question of whether copyright laws violate the First Amendment[119] absent from the case, the court nevertheless clarified the relationship between copyright and factual news reports:

> But in considering the copyright protections due a report of news events or factual developments, it is important to differentiate between the substance of the information contained in the report, i.e., the event itself, and "the particular form of collocation of words in which the writer has communicated it." [Citing INS v. AP and Chicago Record-Herald.] What is protected is the manner of expression, the author's analysis or interpretation of events, the way he structures his material and marshals facts, his choice of words, and the emphasis he gives to particular developments. Thus, the essence of infringement lies not in taking a general theme or in coverage of the reports as events, but in appropriating the "particular expression through similarities of treatment, details, scenes, events and characterization." [Citing Reyher v. Children's Television Workshop, 533 F.2d 87, 91 (2d Cir. 1976).] In a parallel manner, the essence or purpose of legitimate journalism is the reporting of objective facts or developments, not the appropriation of the form of expression used by the news source. Wainwright Securities Inc. v. Wall Street Transcript Corp., 2 Med.L.Rptr. 2153, 558 F.2d 91, 95–96 (2d Cir.1977).

5. After a period of some uncertainty, *INS v. AP* was reaffirmed by the 1973 ruling of the U.S. Supreme Court in Goldstein v. California, 412 U.S. 546 (1973). The case, involving record piracy, assures the validity of the misappropriation doctrine and the use of state unfair competition laws. "Running a newsroom with scissors and a paste pot, then," says Paul Sullivan, "is not only unimaginative and unethical, but also quite probably illegal. The newsroom is no place for a plagiarist. Based on historical analysis, it appears that news piracy will be punished."[120]

6. A case with important implications for source-reporter relations is Sinatra v. Wilson, 2 Med.L.Rptr. 2008 (D.N.Y.1977). There a federal district court held that what a celebrity says to a columnist in an interview may be protected by common law copyright. Frank Sinatra said that he planned to publish an autobiography, but columnist Earl Wilson "scooped" him with a "boring" and unauthorized biography alleged to contain Sinatra's "private thoughts, statements, impressions and emotions." Action for a false-light invasion of privacy was also permitted on the basis of what plaintiff alleged to be false and fabricated statements. The issues could only be decided, said the court, after discovery and trial. In 1983 Sinatra sought $2 million in damages and an injunction against publication of another unauthorized biography, this one by Kitty Kelly.

7. A newspaper has the protection of common law trademark in its name. But after eight years of nonpublication and in the absence of a trademark registration for its name, a newspaper plaintiff was said to have no business, property, or goodwill interest which could be damaged by another.[121]

Ten years after it folded, the *New York Herald Tribune's* successor corporation failed to block the fledgling and now defunct New York daily, *The Trib*, from using that nameplate in a suit for common law trademark infringement, unfair competition, and misappropriation. The original *Tribune* was denied a preliminary injunc-

119. Nimmer, *Does Copyright Abridge the First Amendment Guarantees of Free Speech and Press?* 17 UCLA L.Rev. 1180 (1970); Patterson, *Private Copyright and Public Communication: Free Speech Endangered*, 28 Vand. L.Rev. 1161 (1975).

120. Sullivan, *op. cit.*, p. 28.

121. Duff v. Kansas City Star Co., 299 F.2d 320 (8th Cir. 1962).

tion absent a showing of irreparable injury. Only 550 copies of the *International Herald Tribune* circulated in New York City, and there appeared to be no direct competition for advertising. There were also doubts as to whether the original trademark represented goods or services still in use in commerce and as to whether the mark had not been abandoned. The court noted that there were 250 "Tribunes" in the United States and at least two—Chicago and Oakland—were commonly referred to as the "Trib." [122]

8. Many difficult questions about the new copyright act will eventually be answered in litigation. In the meantime, arm yourself with a copy of the sixty-one-page statute and the address of the Copyright Office. The latter will furnish information about methods of securing copyright and the procedures for making registration, will attempt to explain the operations and practices of the Copyright Office, and will relinquish facts filed in the public records of the office.

The Copyright Office, however, will not give legal advice or comment upon the merits, status, or ownership of particular works or upon the extent of protection afforded to particular works by the copyright law.

COPYRIGHT AND THE ELECTRONIC MEDIA

The 1976 Cable Television Copyright Legislation

The Background of the Cable Copyright Problem

One of the most significant new extensions of copyright protection is in the area of cable television. Cable television systems pick up broadcasts of programs originated by others and retransmit them to paying subscribers. A minimum cable system consists of a central antenna system, which receives and amplifies television signals, and a network of cable through which the signals are carried to the television sets of individual subscribers.

In its early period, cable television was often known by the acronym *CATV,* which originally referred to "Community Antenna Television," but today the term "cable television" is usually used. At its inception, community antenna television systems facilitated the reception of local television broadcasts which subscribers could not satisfactorily receive directly from the local station because of mountainous terrain, tall buildings, or other physical conditions. Recently, cable television has made use of sophisticated technology to retransmit signals from broadcasters in distant communities by use of microwave relay or space satellite which subscribers could not otherwise receive.

Until January 1, 1978, the liability of cable television operators for the retransmission of copyrighted programs was governed by the 1909 Copyright Act. Section 1(e) of the act indicates that it is an infringement of the owner's copyright "to perform the copyrighted work publicly for profit if it be a musical composition. * * " 17 U.S.C.A. § 1(e).

What was the relationship of the federal copyright statute to cable television? Did CATV as it operated constitute a copyright infringement? These questions were raised and decided in a Supreme Court case, *Fortnightly Corp. v. United Artists.* Prior to *Fortnightly,* a bill had been introduced in the Senate which

122. I.H.T. Corp. v. Saffir Publishing Corp. v. International Herald Tribune, 3 Med.L.Rptr.1907, 444 F.Supp. 185 (D.N.Y.1978).

would have immunized CATV from copyright coverage in some areas and exposed it to coverage in others. Despite the pendency of proposals for congressional legislation, the Court decided to resolve the issue of the copyright statute's applicability to CATV judicially.

The advent of cable technology is not the first occasion where the application of the 1909 Act to the new electronic media had arisen. The question of whether retransmission of a radio broadcast constitutes a "performance" of the copyrighted work had been considered in Buck v. Jewell-LaSalle Realty Co., 283 U.S. 191 (1931). In *Jewell-LaSalle,* the owner of a copyrighted song sued the management of a Kansas City hotel for distributing a program from a central radio to all public and private rooms by means of a wire distribution system. The federal district court dismissed the case, a result which was affirmed by the federal court of appeals. The Supreme Court reversed and held that the hotel was liable under the Copyright Act on a "multiple performance" theory: "[A] single rendition of a copyrighted selection [can result] in more than one public performance for profit."

When broadcasters sought to challenge the cable industry's asserted exemption from copyright liability, broadcasters not surprisingly contended that cable systems were in the same relationship to broadcasters as the hotel had been in the *Jewell-LaSalle* case. Accordingly, broadcasters argued that when cable operators retransmitted their signals without permission, they infringed the Copyright Act.

In Fortnightly Corp. v. United Artists Television, Inc., 392 U.S. 390 (1968), the first Supreme Court case specifically examining the question of copyright liability of cable systems, United Artists Television brought suit against Fortnightly, an owner and operator of cable television systems in two West Virginia towns, for copyright infringement based on the retransmission of several motion pictures to which plaintiff owned the copyrights.[123] The federal district court applied the *Jewell-LaSalle* "multiple performance" doctrine and found the cable systems liable under the Copyright Act. The Court of Appeals for the Second Circuit affirmed.

The Supreme Court reversed and held that the functions of a cable television system did not constitute a "performance" within the meaning of the 1909 Act. The *Fortnightly* decision has been justly described as a "surprisingly unsophisticated analysis of the functions of the cable television system." [124] The Court's analysis turned on the question of whether cable television acted as "broadcasters" or "viewers." At a time when cable systems mainly performed the functions of a community antenna, the Court reasoned as follows: "Essentially, a CATV system no more than enhances the viewer's capacity to receive the broadcaster's signals; it provides a well-located antenna with an efficient connection to the viewer's television set." For the Court the copyright issue was easily resolved: "Broadcasters per-

123. It should be recognized that a considerable measure of protection had been extended to television copyright proprietors prior to the *Fortnightly* case, and this protection was unaffected by the *Fortnightly* case. To be sure, this protection flowed from regulatory action by the FCC rather than by an extended interpretation of the old federal copyright statute. In order to minimize the loss of potential royalties by television copyright holders as a result of CATV operations in "an unexploited market," the FCC in 1966 issued a regulation preventing CATV from extending distant signals in the top hundred television markets. These markets constitute 90 percent of the total television audience. See Note, 36 Geo.Wash.L.Rev. 672 at 677 (1968); Second Report and Order, Community Antenna Television Systems, 2 FCC2d 725 (1966). For more recent developments, see text, pp. 694, 1007.

124. See S.C. Greene, *The Cable Provisions of the Revised Copyright Act,* 27 Cath.Univ.L.Rev. 263 at 270 (1978).

form. Viewers do not perform." The *Jewell-LaSalle* precedent was referred to as "a questionable 35-year-old decision that in actual practice has not been applied outside its own factual context. * * *"

The *Fortnightly* case concerned cable television retransmission of local broadcast signals and left open the question of copyright liability when the cable systems imported distant signals to viewers who could not otherwise have received them.

The question of copyright liability for cable television continued to simmer, and the failure to resolve it satisfactorily for all the parties concerned undoubtedly served to retard the development of the full potential of cable. But the continued exploitation of valuable copyrighted programming properties by cable operators, permitted by *Fortnightly,* provoked a new legal fight to reconsider the copyright question in cable.

In *CBS v. Teleprompter,* the creators and producers of various television programs brought suit in the federal district court for copyright infringement against owners and operators of cable television systems for retransmitting the programs. Relying on *Fortnightly,* the federal district court dismissed. See CBS, Inc. v. Teleprompter, 355 F.Supp. 618 (S.D.N.Y.1972).

On appeal, the federal appeals court discerned two distinct categories of viewers and determined that a cable system that distributes distant signals which are beyond the capabilities of any local antenna should be held to have "performed" the copyrighted works within the meaning of the 1909 Copyright Act, but that *Fortnightly* was controlling with regard to local signals which could be received by either a community antenna or standard rooftop antenna belonging to the owners of the television sets. CBS v. Teleprompter Corp., 476 F.2d 338 (2d Cir.1973), distinguished *Fortnightly* as follows:

> [I]n this case, the new audience is one that would not have been able to view the programs even if there had been available in its community an advanced antenna such as that used by a CATV system. The added factor in such a case is the signal transmitting equipment, such as microwave links, that is used to bring the programs from the community where the system receives them into the community in which the new audience views them.

The Supreme Court rejected this reasoning and held that the distance between the broadcast station and the ultimate viewer is irrelevant to the determination of whether the retransmission is a broadcaster or viewer function. Teleprompter Corp. v. CBS, 415 U.S. 394 (1974).

Speaking for the Court, Justice Stewart declared:

> By importing signals that could not normally be received with current technology in the community it serves, a CATV system does not, for copyright purposes, alter the function it performs for its subscribers. When a television broadcaster transmits a program, it has made public for simultaneous viewing and hearing the contents of that program. The privilege of receiving the broadcast electronic signals and of converting them into the sights and sounds of the program inheres in all members of the public who have the means of doing so. The reception and rechanneling of these signals for simultaneous viewing is essentially a viewer function, irrespective of the distance between the broadcasting station and the ultimate viewer.

In a 6–3 decision, the Supreme Court affirmed in part and reversed in part the judgment of the court of appeals in *Teleprompter.* The Court agreed with the court of appeals that use of new developments in cable such as program origination, sale of commercials, and interconnection, did not convert the entire cable operation, regardless of distance from the broadcasting station, into a "broadcast function." Such new uses of cable did not subject the cable system to copyright infringement liability.

The Supreme Court further held that the court of appeals in *Teleprompter* was incorrect in holding that importation of "distant" signals from one community into another constitutes a "performance" under the Copyright Act. On this latter point, the Court said:

> By importing signals that could not normally be received with current technology in the community it serves, a CATV system does not, for copyright purposes, alter the function it performs for its subscribers. * * * The reception and rechanneling of these signals for simultaneous viewing is essentially a viewer function, irrespective of the distance between the broadcasting station and the ultimate viewer.

Congress began consideration of copyright law revision in 1955, but it was not until 1967 that the first revision bill was introduced. Barbara A. Ringer, Register of Copyrights, told the House Judiciary Committee that the Supreme Court decision in *Teleprompter* gave new impetus to the need for final congressional resolution of the cable television copyright issue:

> Meanwhile, as the 1967 legislative momentum began to slow more and more, it was increasingly apparent that cable television had become the make-or-break issue for copyright revision. * * By 1971, it was apparent that the bill was completely stymied over the CATV issue, and even the issuance of comprehensive FCC rules in 1972, governing the carriage of signals and programing by cable systems, failed to break the impasse. * * * There may have been other reasons, but certainly the most immediate cause of the new momentum for the proposed copyright provision was the Supreme Court's decision in *Teleprompter v. CBS,* in March 1974, holding that under the 1909 statute, cable systems are not liable for copyright infringement when they import distant signals.
>
> The decision was followed quickly by favorable actions in the Senate Judiciary Subcommittee and full committee, and after a brief referral to the Commerce Committee by passage in the Senate on September 9, 1975, by a vote of 70 to 1.[125]

The Copyright Act of 1976

In 1976, after more than twenty years of legislative effort, Congress passed the first complete revision of the federal copyright law since 1909. The new law, which became effective on January 1, 1978, sought to accommodate the technological changes which had taken place since the 1909 act. For the first time, photocopying, computer and information systems, tape and video recording, and cable television systems were brought within the ambit of intellectual property rights afforded protection.

Rather than place cable system owners in the impractical and burdensome position of negotiating with the copyright holder of each retransmitted program, Congress established a "compulsory license" mechanism under which each cable operation could avoid copyright liability by paying royalties set by statute to the Register of Copyrights. 17 U.S.C.A. § 111(c) (d). In addition, a Copyright Royalty Tribunal was established to distribute the royalties, periodically review and adjust the statutory royalty rates, and resolve disputes over the distribution of royalties. 17 U.S.C.A. § 801. Cable system royalties are computed on the basis of specified percentages of the system's gross receipts for each distant signal non-network program. 17 U.S.C.A. § 111(d)(2)(B). A value referred to as a "distant signal equivalent" is assigned to each distant signal television station carried by a cable system. 17 U.S.C.A. § 111(f); House Comm. on the Judiciary, Report on Copyright Law Revision, H.R.

125. Testimony of Hon. Barbara A. Ringer, Register of Copyrights, May 7, 1975, *House Comm. on the Judiciary, Copyright Law Revision,* H.R.Rep.No.2223, 94th Cong., 1st Sess. 105 (1976).

Rep. No. 1476, 94th Cong. 2d Sess. 100 (1976). A value of one is given to each independent (non-network) station, and a value of one-quarter is assigned to each network and noncommercial educational station for any non-network programming retransmitted by the cable system. The number of distant signal equivalents are totaled and multiplied by declining percentages of the cable system's gross receipts during the six-month reporting period to determine the amount due to the Register of Copyrights. 17 U.S.C.A. § 111(d)(2)(B)(i)–(iv). A minimum compulsory license fee is required whether or not distant signal non-network programming is retransmitted. 17 U.S.C.A. § 111(d)(2)(C, D). In order to lighten the burden on small cable systems, a reduced royalty fee is computed. 17 U.S.C.A. § 111(d)(2)(C)(D).

In sum, the relationship between copyright owners and users of copyrighted material has been radically changed by the 1976 Copyright Act. The copyright holder of a retransmitted distant signal non-network program has no control over its use by a cable system or the royalty fee he receives. Material carried on local or network programs can be retransmitted without liability for the most part. In addition, the burden is placed on the copyright holder to apply to the Copyright Royalty Tribunal for the distribution of royalties. 17 U.S.C.A. § 111(d)(4)(5).

The Copyright Royalty Tribunal and the Courts

The Copyright Royalty Tribunal's distributions of cable royalty fees have occasioned some litigation. NAB v. Copyright Royalty Tribunal, 675 F.2d 367, 8 Med.L. Rptr. 1433 (D.C.Cir. 1982), provided a helpful insight into the workings of the new Copyright Royalty Tribunal. Judge Mikva explained the court's decision to affirm the Tribunal's allocation of cable royalty fees:

These consolidated cases present challenges to the first distribution of cable royalty fees under the 1976 Copyright Act, 17 USC 101 et seq. Section 111 of the act requires cable operators to pay royalties to the creators of copyrighted program material that is used by the cable systems. Recognizing the impracticability of requiring every cable operator to negotiate directly with every copyright owner, the act sets up a two step process. First, cable operators are required to obtain a copyright license and periodically pay royalty fees into a central fund. Second, the Copyright Royalty Tribunal distributes those fees among claimants. The tribunal's first royalty distribution concerned royalties paid for 1978. The distribution was broken down into two phases, with phase one determining the allocation of cable royalties to specific groups of claimants, and phase two allocating royalties to individual claimants within each group. Under phase one, the $15 million fund was distributed in the following manner: programs syndicators and movie producers, 75 percent; sports leagues, 12 percent; television broadcasters, 3.25 percent; public television, 5.25 percent; and music claimants, 4.5 percent. Radio claimants were denied any award. The tribunal observed that movies, syndicated programs, and sports events constitute the largest and most profitable segment of programming transmitted by cable systems, and therefore deserved commensurate compensation.

The challenges to the tribunal's distribution seem motivated essentially by each petitioner's feeling that it deserved a larger share of the fund. Such reactions flow naturally from the not insignificant consequences of changing one or two percentage points in the distribution of $15 million, and the size of the fund is expected to grow enormously in future years as cable systems become more widespread. Claims of this sort are generally well beyond the expertise or authority of courts, however, and review is limited to determining whether the tribunal's actions were arbitrary or capricious, and whether they are supported by substantial evidence.

* * *

> It may be observed that agitation over the tribunal's initial apportionment has been somewhat overstated. The allocation of the 1978 fund will not displace the operation of relevant market forces in the future. Now that the tribunal's methods are known, for example, broadcasters will bargain more knowledgeably with sports teams about telecasts of sports events, and representatives of music, programs, and movies may contract accordingly with television broadcasters. In any event, as the size of the fund grows, the dispute over how to slice the pie may be more vigorous but it will also be more structured. The umpire has established precedents on which the players may rely in submitting their claims. The tribunal's decision has achieved an initial allocation of the fund that is well within the metes prescribed by Congress.

Students should note in Judge Mikva's ruling that judicial review of the allocation of cable royalty fees by the Copyright Royalty Tribunal is limited to determining whether "the tribunal's actions were arbitrary or capricious, and whether they are supported by substantial evidence."

This is a somewhat ambiguous statement because in administrative law the "arbitrary and capricious" standard of review and the "substantial evidence" standard are considered to be separate and distinct standards of review. Generally, an administrative agency will have an easier time showing that its action was not arbitrary or capricious than it will have in showing that its findings were supported by substantial evidence.

Amusement and Music Operators v. Copyright Royalty Tribunal, 676 F.2d 1144, 8 Med.L.Rptr. 1435 (7th Cir. 1982), involved a review of the CRT's petition for decision to raise the compulsory licensing fees for the use by jukebox operators of copyrighted music from the initial fee of $8 set forth in the 1976 Copyright Act. The act directed the CRT to determine "commencing in January 1980 whether an adjustment of the fee" was necessary. Judge Cudahy, speaking for the United States Court of Appeals for the Seventh Circuit, in *Amusement and Music Operators* stated that the appropriate standard for judicial review of CRT determinations was the arbitrary and capricious standard of review:

> The tribunal ruled that royalties should be set at a level of $50 per year per jukebox. In order to avoid disruption of the jukebox industry, the tribunal provided for implementation of this fee in two stages, with a $25 fee being imposed for 1982 and 1983, and the full $50 fee being assessed thereafter. The tribunal also determined to subject the royalty fee to a cost-of-living adjustment in 1987. The first issue is what standard of review should be applied to the tribunal's ruling. The tribunal urges that an "arbitrary and capricious" standard applies, but petitioners argue that the proper standard is to require the tribunal's decisions to be supported by substantial evidence. A close reading of the Administrative Procedure Act indicates that the most appropriate standard is the "arbitrary and capricious" standard. Application of this standard to the instant case will not, however, produce a significantly different result than attempting to determine whether there is substantial evidence in the record to support the tribunal's findings.
>
> * * *
>
> Its reliance on the marketplace evidence together with the statutory criteria and the entire record in arriving at the $50 figure is not arbitrary and capricious.
>
> Rate-making is an art, not a science. We believe that the tribunal did not act either unreasonably or unlawfully by establishing a $50 royalty fee which would be implemented in stages and be subject to future inflationary adjustments.

Sanctions in the New Cable Copyright Law

What are the sanctions of the new cable provision of the revised copyright law? If the terms of the compulsory license [126] are violated, the injured local radio and television broadcaster, as well as the copyright holder, may sue offending cable systems. 17 U.S.C.A. §§ 501–505. One commentator has analyzed these provisions as follows:

> The broadcasters need not show direct injury from the cable system's alteration of their signals. Thus, copyright provides a device through which broadcasters can protect themselves and stem illegal importations by acting as "private attorneys general." [127]

The compulsory licensing scheme, it should be emphasized, is only applicable if the programming of television stations which is retransmitted by cable systems has been authorized by the FCC in the first place. See § 111(c)(1). If a cable system undertakes a retransmission which is not authorized by the FCC regulations, the cable system is subject to an action for infringement of copyright. The ability of a broadcaster to invoke the sanctions of the new copyright act against a cable operator who is violating FCC cable regulations thus gives a new enforcement dimension to those regulations.

For a discussion of the relationship between the new cable copyright legislation and the deregulation of cable (in the context of FCC regulations), see this text, pp. 1002ff, 1007. See also Malrite TV v. FCC, 652 F.2d 1140, 7 Med.L.Rptr. 1649 (2d Cir. 1981), text, p. 1003.

Cable System Liability Under § 111

Formerly, under the *Fortnightly* and *Teleprompter* interpretations of the 1909 Copyright Act, cable system operators had usually been able to avoid royalty payments to broadcasters based on cable's retransmission of broadcast signals. The 1976 Copyright Act adopted the reasoning of the federal court of appeals in Columbia Broadcasting System, Inc. v. Teleprompter Corp., 476 F.2d 338 (2d Cir.1973), and generally made cable systems subject to copyright liability for the retransmission of distant signal non-network programming. 17 U.S.C.A. § 111(d)(2)(B). Thus, those who hold local and network program copyrights do not benefit from the royalties which flow from the compulsory licensing features of the new act.

Specifically, it is § 111 of the Copyright Act which focuses on cable system liability for the retransmission of copyrighted works. House Report, *supra,* p. 88. Bear in mind that the pertinent words of art are in § 111 "primary transmission" and "secondary transmission." The "primary" transmitter is the one whose signals are being picked up and further transmitted by a "secondary" transmitter which must be someone engaged in "the further transmitting of a primary transmission simultaneously with the primary transmission." § 111(f); House Report, p. 98. "Under section 111, secondary transmissions may be of three kinds. They may be completely

126. For a helpful explanation of how the new compulsory licensee fees are to be computed, see *Nimmer on Copyright,* 1978 ed., § 8.18, p. 212, et seq.

127. E. Noreika, *Communications Law,* 1977 Annual Survey of American Law 577, at 583 (This material as well as other passages from the article referred to in this section is reprinted with permission of the 1977 Annual Survey of American Law and New York University). 17 U.S.C.A. §§ 501–505; see also House Report, *supra,* p. 159. Injunction, impoundment of illegal copies, actual or statutory damages as well as allowance of costs and reasonable attorney's fees are among the panoply of remedies afforded the legal or beneficial holder of a copyright under the new act. See §§ 502–505. Criminal penalties of a fine of not more than $10,000 or imprisonment for not more than one year, or both, are also provided for a willful act of infringement, whether for purposes of commercial advantage or private financial gain. 17 U.S.C.A. § 506. In addition, any willful alteration of the retransmitted program by a cable system can subject the cable system to being deprived by the court of its compulsory license for one or more distant signals for up to thirty days. 17 U.S.C.A. § 510(b).

exempt from any liability under the copyright law [§ 111(a)], subject to a compulsory license [§ 111(c)(1), (d)] or fully subject to copyright liability [§ 111(b), (c)(2)–(4), (e)(1)(2)] and, in this latter case, if unauthorized by the copyright owner, actionable as an infringement." G. Meyer, *The Feat of Houdini or How the New Act Disentangles the CATV Copyright Knot* 22 N.Y.L.Sch.L.Rev. 545, at 553.

Congress determined that the retransmission of local broadcast signals or network programming does not injure the copyright owner, while the "transmission of distant non-network programing by cable systems causes damage to the copyright owner by distributing the program in an area beyond which it has been licensed." House Report, *supra*, p. 90. The philosophy of the new act in this regard has been very clearly stated by one commentator:

> The basic principle adopted by the statute is that royalties under the compulsory licenses are payable only for the retransmission of distant signals, not for the retransmission of any local signals or any network programs whether local or distant. The retransmissions which give rise to the payment of royalties are therefore those which pertain to the programs of distant independent stations and of non-network programs telecast by distant network affiliated stations which beside network programs also telecast programs originated in their studios.[128]

A "network station" is considered to be "one or more of the television networks in the United States providing nationwide transmissions." 17 U.S.C.A. § 111(f). A network affiliated station which mainly transmits network programming comes within the definition, which is intended to be strictly construed.[129] Since network station broadcasts are nationwide, the copyright holder's royalty fee has already been calculated on a nationwide basis. Therefore, no payment is required for the retransmission of network programs by a cable system. What is the reason for this? The following rationale has been offered:

> Cable retransmission of a purely local signal is similar to the distant network programming. If the cable retransmission is to the same market audience for which the copyright owner is compensated by the primary transmitter, there is no economic injury to the copyright owner. C.S. Greene, 27 Cath.L.R. 263, at 289.[130]

Certain Secondary Transmissions Exempted. Cable television transmissions which do not qualify for the exemptions within § 111(a) are subject to full copyright liability, which can only be avoided by obtaining a compulsory license. For the exemptions to apply, the primary transmission must have been made to be viewed by the general public. § 111(b); House Report, *supra*, p. 92. Clause (1) of subsection (a) exempts from copyright liability an antenna system constructed "by the management of a hotel, apartment house or similar establishment," for the purpose of relaying a transmission to rooms used as living quarters or for private parties, and does not include such meeting places as dining rooms and ballrooms. House Report *supra*, p. 91; See generally *Nimmer on Copyright*, 1978 ed., § 8.18, p. 198 et seq. Although this exemption is inapplicable if the secondary transmission is made by a cable system, or if there is a direct charge for the transmission, this clause is important as it overrules the *Buck v. Jewell-LaSalle* holding insofar as private rooms are concerned.

128. See Meyer, *supra*, at 558.

129. See House Report, p. 98.

130. (This material as well as other passages from the article referred to in this section is reprinted with permission from the Catholic University Law Review). See also Meyer, Note 128, supra, at 558–559, fn. 63.

An exemption for the use of an ordinary radio or television set in a public room is contained in § 110(5). It has been perceptively observed that the "distinction between this exemption [§ 110(5)] and the liability provided in section 111(a)(1) appears to be principally predicated on the sophistication of the receiving equipment. * * * ". Greene, *supra,* at 284.[131] Thus, a retransmission to a public room in a hotel by a cable system or a radio system as described in *Jewell-LaSalle* is still considered an infringing act.

Clause (2) exempts any systematic instructional programing of "a governmental body or a nonprofit educational institution * * * " as described in § 110(2): "On the other hand, the exemption does not cover the secondary transmission of a performance on educational television or radio of a dramatic work or a dramatic musical work such as an opera or musical comedy, or of a motion picture." [132] Clause (3) exempts secondary transmissions made by a passive carrier who has no direct or indirect control over the content or selection of the primary transmission.[133] Clause (4) exempts secondary transmitters which operate on a nonprofit basis.[134]

Exempt Secondary Transmissions and § 111(a)(3)

A case involving a significant interpretation of what constitutes a secondary transmission made by a passive carrier which is exempt from copyright liability under 17 U.S.C. § 111(a)(3) was Eastern Microwave v. Doubleday Sports, 8 Med.L.Rptr. 2353 (2d Cir. 1982). Eastern Microwave, a common carrier, had been retransmitting the original signals of WOR–TV, a New York City television station, to cable television systems outside WOR's service area.

Judge Markey described the retransmission process in his opinion for the Second Circuit:

> Retransmission is accomplished by converting broadcast signals into microwave signals and relaying the microwave signals via satellite or a string of line-of-sight terrestrial microwave repeater stations. Retransmitted signals are delivered by EMI to the headends of the customers of its transmitting services, cable television (CATV) systems, which then reconvert the microwave signals to television signals for distribution to and viewing by the CATV system's subscribers.

Eastern Microwave, Inc. (EMI) exercised no control over content or the selection of the transmissions. Doubleday Sports, Inc., owner of the New York Mets, contracted with WOR–TV to broadcast approximately 100 Mets games each season. The Mets "owns the copyright in the audiovisual work represented by the Mets games."

EMI did not ask permission of Doubleday to retransmit WOR–TV's signals. In March 1981, Doubleday notified EMI that it considered retransmission of WOR–TV Mets game broadcasts to constitute an infringement of Doubleday's copyright. EMI then sought relief in the federal courts for a "declaratory judgment that it was a passive carrier exempt from copyright liability

131. One commentator interprets § 110(5) and 111(a)(1) to mean that " * * * a single television set or even several loudspeakers placed in a lobby, bar or restaurant of a hotel, apartment house or similar establishment would be exempt * * * if they transmit local broadcasts of copyrighted works. * * * " Meyer, *supra,* at 555. But the House Report, p. 87, notes that "The Committee * * * accepts the traditional * * * interpretation of the *Jewell-LaSalle* decision, under which public communication by means other than a home receiving set, or further transmission of a broadcast to the public is considered an infringing act."

132. Meyer, *supra,* at 555–6.

133. House Report, p. 92.

134. See Greene, *supra,* at 285.

under 17 U.S.C. § 111(a)(3)." The United States Court of Appeals for the Second Circuit ruled that "EMI is not in law infringing Doubleday's exclusive right to display its copyrighted work by passively retransmitting the entirety of its customer WOR–TV's broadcast signal to the headends of its customer CATV systems."

Important portions of Judge Markey's opinion in *Eastern Microwave* are set forth below:

> To remain exempt, a carrier-retransmitter must avoid content control by retransmitting exactly what and all of what it receives, as EMI does here. To do otherwise could be perceived as the carrier's making the transmission its own. That EMI serves customers at one end of the communications chain, and telephone companies serve customers at the other, is not controlling, so long as neither injects its own communications into that chain. If WOR–TV had requested and paid EMI to transmit its broadcast signal, for example, the traditional common carrier context would have been created. That EMI serves numerous receiving CATV systems, with the one available set of signals those customers prefer, rather than serving numerous sending broadcasters, is a difference insufficient to deny EMI the statutory carrier exemption on the ground that it is controlling the content or selection of that set of signals.
>
> The second requirement, an absence of direct or indirect control over the particular recipients of its retransmission, is fully satisfied by EMI. It is undisputed that the "particular recipients" of EMI's retransmissions are the many CATV systems which it serves under contract. That it renders its service to certain CATV systems and not others does not itself constitute, however, any control direct or indirect, over particular recipients.
>
> * * *
>
> EMI also meets the third requirement, that it merely provide wires, cables, or other communications channels for the use of others. As above indicated, the "others" here are the receiving CATV systems which cannot afford their own wires, cables, and channels, rather than the originating senders who use (and cannot afford their own) wires, cables, and channels of more traditional common carriers like a telephone company. EMI provides the wires and cables of its repeater stations for use of its CATV customers in acquiring the signals of WOR–TV and those of many other originators. It provides its single satellite transponder for use of its CATV customers in acquiring the signals of necessarily one orginator, i.e., WOR–TV.
>
> * * *
>
> Congress drew a careful balance between the rights of copyright owners and those of CATV systems, providing for payments to the former and a compulsory licensing program to insure that the latter could continue bringing a diversity of broadcasted signals to their subscribers. The public interest thus lies in a continuing supply of varied programming to viewers. Because CATV systems served by intermediate carriers cannot provide their full current programming to their subscribers without the services of those carriers, imposition of individual copyright owner negotiations on intermediate carriers would strangle CATV systems by choking off their lifeline to their supply of programs, would effectively restore the "freeze" on cable growth described above, and, most importantly, would frustrate the congressional intent reflected in the [a]ct by denying CATV systems the opportunity to participate in the compulsory licensing program. After years of consideration and debate, Congress could not have intended that its work be so easily undone by the interposition of copyright owners to block exercise of the licensing program by cable systems.
>
> EMI is, like all common carriers, compensated for its transmission services as such. In accord with its FCC–approved tariff, and as above indicated, EMI is paid by each CATV system in relation to the number of its subscribers up to a maximum of $4,000. The fee does not increase thereafter, regardless of the number of a CATV system's subscribers. In contrast, the roy-

> alty fee paid by each CATV system under the [a]ct is limited to no maximum, but is entirely based on percentages of gross receipts from subscribers to the CATV service in accord with 17 U.S.C. § 111.
>
> It is undisputed that if each CATV system had its own string of microwave repeaters or satellite transponders it would be liable through the Tribunal to a copyright owner for only the one established royalty fee when and if it publicly performed the copyrighted work by making it available to its subscribers; and that such an integrated CATV system would not be liable for a second royalty fee for having itself retransmitted the original broadcast signal to its headend. We are unpersuaded by counsel's urging that a different result should obtain when a separate entity, e.g., EMI, supplies the retransmission service. That EMI is a separate entity supplies no justification for subjecting EMI to copyright liability when those same activities would not result in copyright liability if carried out by the CATV systems served by EMI. In the Act, Congress established a specific scheme for recognition of the rights of copyright owners. Under that scheme those rights are not unlimited. Neither are they rendered superior to the rights of viewers. If this court were to impose here a requirement that intermediate carriers negotiate with and pay all copyright owners for the right to retransmit their works, assuming such requirement were not impossible to meet, such action would produce a result never intended by Congress, namely a substantially increased royalty payment to copyright owners with no increase in number of viewers.[135]

The Compulsory License. Compulsory copyright licensing is the most controversial aspect of the new Copyright Act because the copyright owner loses control over the use and price of his product. While all cable systems which retransmit primary transmissions made by an FCC-licensed broadcast station are subject to compulsory licensing [§ 111(c)], royalties are only paid for distant signal non-network programmming [§ 111(d)(2)(B)].

Transmissions Fully Liable Under the Copyright Act. The compulsory license does not protect the cable system operator in all instances. A cable operator exposes himself to liability for copyright infringement if he retransmits a program originally transmitted to a limited audience rather than the public at large. § 111(b). This provision applies to the retransmission of "MUZAK," closed circuit broadcasts to theaters, pay television or pay-cable. House Report, p. 92. Full copyright liability also results from the "willful or repeated" retransmission of signals not permissible under the rules and regulations of the FCC § 111(c)(2)(A). The House Report points out that the "words 'willful or repeated' are used to prevent a cable system from being subjected to severe penalties for innocent or casual acts." See House Report, *supra*, p. 93.

Further, the cable system is liable if it has not recorded the compulsory license notice, deposited the statement of account or paid the royalty fee. § 111(c)(2)(B). Cable system operators must be careful not to alter the primary transmission in any way in order to avoid copyright liability. Any willful change whatsoever in the program content or commercial advertising messages "significantly alters the basic nature of the cable retransmission service, and makes its function similar to that of a broadcaster." House Report, p. 93; § 111(c)(3).

Copyright, Television, and the Advent of the Home Video Recorder

Just as the emergence of cable has changed the existing structure of commer-

135. For an example of a case where an exemption under § 111(a)(3) was denied, see WGN v. United Video, 685 F.2d 218, 8 Med.L.Rptr. 2170 (7th Cir. 1982).

cial television, so the advent of the home video recorder is changing commercial VHF television and cable television. The average householder can now thwart the scheduling schemes of the wizards of Madison Avenue. With the development of the home video recorder, finely tuned calculations about audience flow may all go for naught. But if a viewer in his home decides to videorecord off his home TV screen, does he violate the copyright laws?

In Universal City Studios v. Sony, 659 F.2d 963, 7 Med.L.Rptr. 2065, (9th Cir. 1981), the United States Court of Appeals for the Ninth Circuit ruled, reversing an earlier federal district court decision, Universal City Studios, Inc. v. Sony Corp. of America, 5 Med.L.Rptr. 1737, 480 F.Supp. 429 (C.D.Calif.1979), that off-the-air copying of copyrighted visual materials by owners of home video recorders was not a fair use but was a copyright infringement for which the manufacturers, distributors, and sellers of home video recorders were liable. (Why weren't the homeowners liable? Did problems of privacy and enforcement make relief against the homeowner with the video recorder impossible or impractical?) The United States Court of Appeals for the Ninth Circuit ruled that the district court was in error in finding an implied video recording exception in the 1976 Copyright Act. Judge Kilkenny observed:

> There is no clear legislative language indicating that home video recording is not within the exclusive rights granted by § 106. The statute itself and the House and Senate Reports accompanying the 1976 Act do not provide for a broad based home use exception. There was never a considered review of the home video recording problem. The statements supporting the district court's conclusion hardly represent—when considered in the context in which they were made and in the context of the 20 year copyright revision process—a firm expression of Congressional intent to carve out a major exception to the copyright scheme.

The Ninth Circuit Court of Appeals also ruled that home video recording for private, noncommercial use was not a fair use.[136]

The Ninth Circuit Court of Appeals then added:

> New technology, which makes possible the mass reproduction of copyrighted material (effectively taking control of access from the author), places a strain upon the fair use doctrine. A court, if it decides that fair use is applicable, is required to weigh—in "balancing the equities"—the "benefit" of an extremely popular increase in access with the "harm" to a plaintiff. The harm to a copyright plaintiff is inherently speculative, and as *Williams & Wilkins Co.* and the district court decision indicate, a plaintiff is faced with the unenviable task of proving the nonexistence of fair use, which has typically been viewed as a defense.
>
> * * *
>
> It is our conviction that the fair use doctrine does not sanction home videorecording. Without a "productive use", *i.e.* when copyrighted material is reproduced for its intrinsic use, the mass copying of the sort involved in

136. In Gordon, *Fair Use As Market Failure: A Structural and Economic Analysis of the Betamax Case and Its Predecessors,* 82 Col.L.Rev. 1600 at 1614 (1982), the "fair use" analysis used by the Ninth Circuit in *Sony* is criticized and rejected. Instead, a three-part test is advocated:

> Fair use should be awarded to the defendant in a copyright infringement action when (1) market failure is present; (2) transfer of the use to defendant is socially desirable; and (3) an award of fair use would not cause substantial injury to the incentives of the plaintiff copyright owner. The first element of this test ensures that market bypass will not be approved without good cause. The second element of the test ensures that the transfer of a license to use from the copyright holder to the unauthorized user effects a net gain in social value. The third element ensures that the grant of fair use will not undermine the incentive-creating purpose of the copyright law.

this case precludes an application of fair use. An analysis of the four factors listed in § 107 does not dictate a contrary result.

A consideration of the first factor—"the purpose and character of the use, including whether such use is of a commercial nature or is for nonprofit educational purposes"—does not aid appellees' case. * * * The district court, however, emphasized the noncommercial and home use of the copyrighted material. The statute does not, however, draw a simple commercial/noncommercial distinction. The statute contrasts commercial and nonprofit educational purposes, and there is no question that the copying of entertainment works for convenience does not fall within the latter category. The fact that the "infringing" activity takes place in the homes does not warrant a blanket exemption from any *liability.* It seems more appropriate to address the privacy concerns raised by the district court in fashioning the appropriate relief. The suggestion that First Amendment concerns support the purpose of Betamax users to increase the access to copyrighted materials is wholly without merit. "The first amendment is not a license to trammel on legally recognized rights in intellectual property." * * *

The second factor—"the nature of the copyrighted work"—does not support a finding of fair use. * * * The courts inquire whether the nature of the material is such that additional access "would serve the public interest in the free dissemination of information." * * If a work is more appropriately characterized as entertainment, it is less likely that a claim of fair use will be accepted. The district court, however, found it significant that "This case involves only that copyrighted material which plaintiffs voluntarily choose to have telecast over public airwaves to individual homes free of charge." 480 F.Supp. at 453. We fail to see how the method by which appellants have chosen to distribute their works is relevant to this factor of the fair use analysis. * * *

The third factor—"the amount and substantiality of the portions used in relation to the copyrighted work as a whole"—clearly weighs against a finding of fair use. The district court acknowledged that "Home use recording off-the-air usually involves copying the entire work," 480 F.Supp. at 454, and that this typically precludes a finding of fair use. The court concluded, however, that the courts have only been concerned about the "substantiality" of the copying when it produced harm, and that "this taking of the whole still constitutes fair use, because there is no accompanying reduction in the market for 'plaintiff's original work.' " We believe that this view of the case law is completely wrong.

In *Walt Disney Productions v. Air Pirates,* [581 F.2d 751, 759 (9th Cir.1978), cert. den., 439 U.S. 1132 (1979)], We stated "While other factors in the fair use calculus may not be sufficient by themselves to preclude the fair use defense, this and other courts have accepted the traditional American rule that excessive copying precludes fair use." *Id.* at 758. In addition, the district court in *Loew's Inc. v. Columbia Broadcasting System,* 131 F.Supp. 165 (S.D.Cal.1955), stated "The mere absence of competition or injurious effect upon the copyrighted work will not make a use fair. The right of a copyright proprietor to exclude others is absolute and if it has been violated the fact that the infringement will not affect the sale or exploitation of the work or pecuniarily damage him is immaterial." * * * These cases clearly did not limit their discussion of "substantiality" to cases in which the plaintiff had been harmed. It seems clear that these cases are based,in part, on the notion that copyright is a property interest and that it is impermissible, in the vast majority of cases, to "appropriate" the copyrighted material without the owner's consent. The copyright laws afford the author the right to control access to his work, and, absent compelling justifications, this right should not be abridged.

* * *

The fourth factor—"the effect of the use upon the potential market for or value of the copyrighted work"—does not support a contrary result. In light of the preceding discussion, we do not believe that it is necessary to address the harm issue with respect to the liability question. We feel compelled, however, to express our disagreement with the district court's approach on this issue.

First, it seems apparent that the district court was much too strict in requiring appellants to establish its degree of harm. * * *

Nimmer has suggested that the central question in the determination of fair use is whether the infringing work tends to diminish or prejudice the potential sale of plaintiff's work." 3 Nimmer, *supra*, § 13.05(E)(4)(c) at 13–84. Under this sort of standard, it seems clear that appellants should have prevailed. Since the copies made by home videorecording are used for the same purpose as the original, a finding of fair use is not justified. The district court seems to recognize, on several occasions, that appellants will have to take affirmative steps to compete with the appropriated versions of their work. That such competition is necessary supports appellants' allegations of harm; at the least, it makes clear that the "infringing" activity *tends* to prejudice the potential sale of appellants' work. It is clear that home users assign economic value to their ability to have control over access to copyrighted works. The copyright laws would seem to require that the copyright owner be given the opportunity to exploit this market.

Second, we do not believe that the district court paid sufficient attention to the fact that it is extremely difficult for a copyright plaintiff to prove harm from the activities of specific defendants. 3 Nimmer, *supra*, § 13.05(E)(4)(c). * * *

The court, in analyzing the fourth fair use factor, did not pay sufficient attention to the *cumulative* effect of mass reproduction of copyrighted works made possible by videorecorders. It seems clear that absent an inquiry which takes into consideration the full scope of the "infringing" practice, copyright plaintiffs, in cases of this sort, would face insuperable obstacles to the protection of their rights. And, where one looks at the full scope of the activity in question, it seems clear that it tends to diminish the *potential* market for appellants' works.

Editorial Note

A very complex issue in the *Sony* or *Betamax* case was the issue of appropriate relief. Assuming off-the-air copyright of copyrighted audiovisual material from the home television screen was a copyright infringement, how could meaningful relief be provided to the copyright owners? The court of appeals responded to this question as follows:

> Because we have found that home videorecording constitutes copyright infringement and that appellees are liable for such use, the district court's judgment must be reversed and the case remanded for a consideration of the appropriate relief. The relief question is exceedingly complex, and the difficulty in fashioning relief may well have influenced the district court's evaluation of the liability issue. The difficulty of fashioning relief cannot, however, dissuade the federal courts from affording appropriate relief to those whose rights have been infringed.
>
> Appellants stated at oral argument that they were seeking a remand to the district court so that the district court could fashion the appropriate relief. This approach makes a good deal of sense; a district court is in a better position to resolve, in an appropriate fashion, the relief question.
>
> There are a number of possibilities that the district court may want to consider. Because of the difficulty of proving the precise nature of the harm to appellants, statutory damages may be appropriate, 17 U.S.C. § 504(c). The district court also has a broad range of equitable remedies from which to choose. Section 502(a) provides that the court "may * * * grant temporary and final injunctions on such terms as it may deem reasonable to prevent or restrain infringement of a copyright." The district court determined that an injunction would not be an appropriate reme-

> dy. 480 F.Supp. 463–69. The court should reconsider this action.
>
> We note that, as a general rule, a copyright plaintiff is entitled to a permanent injunction when liability has been established and there is a threat of continuing violations. * * * In discussing the analogous photocopying area. Nimmer suggests that when great public injury would result from an injunction, a court could award damages or a continuing royalty. This may very well be an acceptable resolution in this context.
>
> In fashioning relief, the district court should not be overly concerned with the prospective harm to appellees. A defendant has no right to expect a return on investment from activities which violate the copyright laws. Once a determination has been made that an infringement is involved, the continued profitability of appellees' businesses is of secondary concern.

The United States Supreme Court agreed to review the decision of the United States Court of Appeals for the Ninth Circuit in the *Sony* case, but it postponed any decision in the case in the 1983 term so as to hear more evidence on this complex question.

LOBBYING AND POLITICAL CAMPAIGN REGULATION

Lobbying: Problems of Definition

1. In United States v. Harriss, 347 U.S. 612 (1954), the Court in a complex interpretation, which the dissenting justices thought was a rewriting of the law, upheld the constitutionality of provisions of the Federal Regulation of Lobbying Act, 60 Stat. 812, 839, 2 U.S.C.A. §§ 261–270, which require designated reports to Congress from every person "receiving any contributions or expending any money" 2 U.S.C.A. § 264 for the purpose of influencing the passage or defeat of any legislation by Congress; and which require any person "who shall engage himself for pay or for any consideration for the purpose of attempting to influence the passage or defeat of any legislation" to register with Congress and to make specified disclosures. 2 U.S.C.A. § 267.

The Court noted in *Harriss* that many states had enacted legislation regulating lobbying. But the most important aspect of the *Harriss* case was that it made clear that some government regulation of lobbying was permissible. See United States v. Rumely, 345 U.S. 41 (1953). As construed, the Federal Regulation of Lobbying Act was constitutional.

Arguably, the guidance which journalists, speakers, publicists, pressure groups, and organizations needed was provided by a very precise definition which the Court gave of what could be regulated under the Federal Regulation of Lobbying Act in *Harriss.*

The effort of the Court in *Harriss* to rewrite the Lobbying Act received academic as well as judicial criticism. For example, the Court in *Harriss* took the position that the Federal Regulation of Lobbying Act did not apply to persons or organizations which spent their own funds to help defeat or support proposed legislation. Similarly, the Court held that the act did not "affect persons soliciting or expending money unless the principal purpose thereof is to influence legislation."

What relationship does removing from the scope of regulation organizations which spend their own funds, or fund expenditures for purposes not principally designed to influence legislation, have to safeguarding the "right to petition"? What difference does it make whether the organization spends its own or other people's funds to support or defeat legislation? See United States v. International Union, United Automobile Aircraft and Agricultural Implement Workers of America, 352 U.S. 567 (1957), where the Court upheld an indictment charging a union with having used union dues to sponsor commercial television broadcasts designed to promote the election of certain candidates. That case involved consideration of the Federal Corrupt Practices Act. See generally, Comment *The Regulation of Union Political Activity: Majority and Minority Rights and Remedies,* 126 U.Pa.L.Rev. 386 (1977).

2. A landmark case holding that lobbying is protected by the First Amendment is Eastern Railroad President's Conference v. Noerr Motor Freight, Inc., 365 U.S. 127 (1961). However, the student should not conclude that because lobbying is protected by the First Amendment, government is obliged to encourage this protected activity. An important case illustrating that Congress may make distinctions among lobbying organizations vis-á-vis subsidies—as long as the distinctions are not ideological in origin—is Regan v. Taxation With Representation of Washington, 103 S.Ct. 1997 (1983). In this case Taxation With Representation (TWR) applied for tax exempt status under 26 U.S.C. § 501(c)(3) of the Internal Revenue Code. The Internal Revenue Service denied the application on the ground that a substantial portion of TWR's activities would involve legislative lobbying—attempting to influence legislation. Such activity is specifically not permitted by § 501(c)(3). TWR contended that the congressional decision reflected in § 501(c)(3) not to "subsidize its lobbying violates the First Amendment." See Speiser v. Randall, 357 U.S. 513 (1958), where the Court observed: "[T]o deny an exemption to claimants who engage in speech is in effect to penalize them for the same speech." The *Regan* Court ruled that § 501(c) did not violate the First Amendment. Justice Rehnquist ruled for the Court:

> The Code does not deny TWR the right to receive deductible contributions to support its non-lobbying activity, nor does it deny TWR any independent benefit on account of its intention to lobby. Congress has merely refused to pay for the lobbying out of public monies. This Court has never held that the Court must grant a benefit such as TWR claims here to a person who wishes to exercise a constitutional right.
>
> This aspect of the case is controlled by *Cammarano v. United States,* 358 U.S. 498 (1959), in which we upheld a Treasury Regulation that denied business expense deductions for lobbying activities. We held that Congress is not required by the First Amendment to subsidize lobbying. *Id.,* at 513. In this case, like in *Cammarano,* Congress has not infringed any First Amendment rights or regulated any First Amendment activity. Congress has simply chosen not to pay for TWR's lobbying. We again reject the "notion that First Amendment rights are somehow not fully realized unless they are subsidized by the [s]tate."

TWR objected that a specific provision of the Internal Revenue Code, § 170(c)(3), permitted taxpayers "to deduct contributions to veterans' organizations that qualify for tax exemption under § 501(c)(19)." TWR argued that it was an equal protection violation to permit veterans' organizations to lobby but to refuse to "subsidize the lobbying of § 501(c)(3) organizations." The Court, per Justice Rehnquist, rejected this contention:

> The case would be different if Congress were to discriminate invidiously in its subsidies in such a way as to "aim[ ] at the suppression of dangerous ideas." *Cammarano, supra,* at 513, quoting *Speiser, supra,* at 519. But the veterans' organizations that qualify under § 501(c)(19) are entitled to receive tax-deductible contributions regardless of the content of any speech they may use, including lobbying. We find no indication that the statute was intended to suppress any ideas or any demonstration that it has had that effect.

The sections of the Internal Revenue Code here at issue do not employ any suspect classification. The distinction between veterans' organizations and other charitable organizations is not at all like distinctions based on race or national origin.

* * *

Congressional selection of particular entities or persons for entitlement to this sort of largesse "is obviously a matter of policy and discretion not open to judicial review unless in circumstances which here we are not able to find."

* * *

We have held in several contexts that a legislature's decision not to subsidize the exercise of a fundamental right does not infringe the right, and thus is not subject to strict scrutiny. *Buckley v. Valeo,* 424 U.S. 1 (1976), upheld a statute that provides federal funds for candidates for public office who enter primary campaigns, but does not provide funds for candidates who do not run in party primaries. We rejected First Amendment and equal protection challenges to this provision without applying strict scrutiny. *Harris v. McRae,* 448 U.S. 297 (1980), and *Maher v. Roe,* 432 U.S. 464 (1977), considered legislative decisions not to subsidize abortions, even though other medical procedures were subsidized. We declined to apply strict scrutiny and rejected equal protection challenges to the statutes.

The reasoning of these decisions is simple: "although government may not place obstacles in the path of a [person's] exercise of * * * freedom of [speech], it need not remove those not of its own creation." *Harris, supra.* Although TWR does not have as much money as it wants, and thus cannot exercise its freedom of speech as much as it would like, the Constitution "does not confer an entitlement to such funds as may be necessary to realize all the advantages of that freedom." *Id.,* at 318. As we said in *Maher,* "[c]onstitutional concerns are greatest when the [s]tate attempts to impose its will by force of law. * * *" Where governmental provision of subsidies is not "aimed at the suppression of dangerous ideas," *Cammarano, supra,* its "power to encourage actions deemed to be in the public interest is necessarily far broader." *Maher supra* at 476.

We have no doubt but that this statute is within Congress' broad power in this area. TWR contends that § 501(c)(3) organizations could better advance their charitable purposes if they were permitted to engage in substantial lobbying. This may well be true. But Congress—not TWR or this Court—has the authority to determine whether the advantage the public would receive from additional lobbying by charities is worth the money the public would pay to subsidize that lobbying, and other disadvantages that might accompany that lobbying. It appears that Congress was concerned that exempt organizations might use tax-deductible contributions to lobby to promote the private interests of their members. See 78 Cong.Rec. 5861 (1934) (remarks of Senator Reed); *Id.,* at 5959 (remarks of Senator La Follette). It is not irrational for Congress to decide that tax exempt charities such as TWR should not further benefit at the expense of taxpayers at large by obtaining a further subsidy for lobbying.

It is also not irrational for Congress to decide that, even though it will not subsidize substantial lobbying by charities generally, it will subsidize lobbying by veterans' organizations. Veterans have "been obliged to drop their own affairs and take up the burdens of the nation * * * subjecting themselves to the mental and physical hazards as well as the economic and family detriments which are peculiar to military service and which do not exist in normal civil life." *Johnson v. Robison,* 415 U.S. 361, 380 (1974). Our country has a long standing policy of compensating veterans for their past contributions by providing them with numerous advantages. This policy has "always been deemed to be legitimate." *Personnel Administrator v. Feeney,* 442 U.S. 256, 279, n. 25 (1979).

The issue in this case is not whether TWR must be permitted to lobby, but whether Congress is required to provide it with public money with which to lobby. For the reasons stated above, we hold that it is not. Accordingly, the judgment of the [c]ourt of [a]ppeals is reversed.

State Regulation of Political Campaigns and the Press

MILLS v. ALABAMA

384 U.S. 214, 86 S.CT. 1434, 16 L.ED.2D 484 (1966).

Justice BLACK delivered the opinion of the Court.

The question squarely presented here is whether a State, consistently with the United States Constitution, can make it a crime for the editor of a daily newspaper to write and publish an editorial *on election day* urging people to vote a certain way on issues submitted to them.

On November 6, 1962, Birmingham, Alabama, held an election for the people to decide whether they preferred to keep their existing city commission form of government or replace it with a mayor-council government. On election day the Birmingham, Post-Herald, a daily newspaper, carried an editorial written by its editor, appellant, James E. Mills, which strongly urged the people to adopt the mayor-council form of government. Mills was later arrested on a complaint charging that by publishing the editorial *on election day* he had violated § 285 of the Alabama Corrupt Practices Act, Ala.Code, 1940, Tit. 17, §§ 268–286, which makes it a crime "to do any electioneering or to solicit any votes * * * in support of or in opposition to any proposition that is being voted on on the day on which the election affecting such candidates or propositions is being held." * * *

We come now to the merits. * * * The question here is whether it abridges freedom of the press for a State to punish a newspaper editor for doing no more than publishing an editorial on election day urging people to vote a particular way in the election. We should point out at once that this question in no way involves the extent of a State's power to regulate conduct in and around the polls in order to maintain peace, order and decorum there. The sole reason for the charge that Mills violated the law is that he wrote and published an editorial on election day urging Birmingham voters to cast their votes in favor of changing their form of government.

Whatever differences may exist about interpretations of the First Amendment there is practically universal agreement that a major purpose of that Amendment was to protect the free discussion of governmental affairs. This of course includes discussions of candidates, structures and forms of government, the manner in which government is operated or should be operated, and all such matters relating to political processes. The Constitution specifically selected the press, which includes not only newspapers, books, and magazines, but also humble leaflets and circulars, see Lovell v. City of Griffin, 303 U.S. 444, to play an important role in the discussion of public affairs. Thus the press serves and was designed to serve as a powerful antidote to any abuses of power by governmental officials and as a constitutionally chosen means for keeping officials elected by the people responsible to all the people whom they were selected to serve. Suppression of the right of the press to praise or criticize governmental agents and to clamor and contend for or against change, which is all that this editorial did, muzzles one of the very agencies the Framers of our Constitution thoughtfully and deliberately selected to improve our society and keep it free. The Alabama Corrupt Practices Act by providing criminal penalties for publishing editorials such as the one here silences the press at a time when it can be most effective. It is difficult to conceive a more obvious and flagrant abridgment of the constitutionally guaranteed freedom of the press.

Admitting that the state law restricted a newspaper editor's freedom to publish editorials on election day, the Alabama Supreme Court nevertheless sustained the constitutionality of the law on the ground that the restrictions on the press were only "reasonable restrictions" or at least "within the field of reasonableness." The court reached this conclusion because it thought the law imposed only a minor limitation on the press—restricting it only on election days—and because the court thought the law served a good purpose. * * * This argument, even if it were relevant to the constitutionality of the law, has a fatal flaw. The state statute leaves people free to hurl their campaign charges up to the last minute of the day before election. The law held valid by the Alabama Supreme Court then goes on to make it a crime to answer those "last-minute" charges on election day, the only time they can be effectively answered. Because the law prevents any adequate reply to these charges, it is wholly ineffective in protecting the electorate "from confusing last-minute charges and countercharges." We hold that no test of reasonableness can save a state law from invalidation as a violation of the First Amendment when that law makes it a crime for a newspaper editor to do no more than urge people to vote one way or another in a publicly held election.

The judgment of the Supreme Court of Alabama is reversed and the case is remanded for further proceedings not inconsistent with this opinion.

It is so ordered.

Judgment reversed and case remanded.

Justice Douglas, with whom Justice Brennan joins, concurring.

* * *

COMMENT

1. Assume that the Alabama Corrupt Practices Act were amended to provide an exception for "last minute charges" made just prior to an election so that charges could be answered in the press even on election day. The purpose of the amendment would be to render the Alabama Corrupt Practices Act a reasonable restriction of the press. Would even Justice Black have acquiesced if the Alabama Corrupt Practices Act provided for a two-week moratorium on electioneering or vote solicitation preceding all state elections?

2. In *Mills,* the Alabama Corrupt Practices Act case, the argument was pressed on the Court which, if accepted, would have deferred decision of First Amendment issues: it was contended that the judgment before the Court was not sufficiently final to be reviewed by the Supreme Court. Justice Douglas concurred in the result in *Mills* and gave emphatic approval to the Court's decision to face the constitutional issues in view of what he considered to be the consequences of lack of resolution by the United States Supreme Court. (The Alabama Corrupt Practices Act provision at issue had been upheld as constitutional by the Alabama Supreme Court.) The "chilling" effect on the Alabama press was described as follows:

"The threat of penal sanctions has, we were told, already taken its toll in Alabama: the Alabama Press Association and the Southern Newspaper Publishers Association, as amicus curiae, tell us that since November 1962 editorial comment on election day has been nonexistent in Alabama."

3. Narrow construction of the term "lobbying" in *Rumely* and *Harriss* minimized the investigative scope of the legislative investigation in *Rumely* and the regulatory scope of the Act in *Harriss.* Would a limited construction technique have sufficed in *Mills?* Suppose electioneering and vote solicitation were read by the Court as simply not meant to apply to the press?

4. See *Mills v. Alabama, supra,* with the decision of the Supreme Court of Florida sustaining a right of reply to political candidates during campaigns, *Miami Her-*

ald Publishing Co. v. Tornillo this text, pp. 581–584.

State Regulation of Corporate "Speech" and the Opinion Process

A case which intersected with problems of law and journalism on a number of critical issues was the 5–4 decision of the Supreme Court in First National Bank of Boston v. Bellotti, 435 U.S. 765 (1978) text, p. 151. Massachusetts had attempted by a criminal statute to prohibit the efforts of banks and business corporations to make expenditures for the purpose of influencing state elections on referendum proposals. The Supreme Court invalidated the Massachusetts statute in an opinion that was widely publicized as extending free speech rights to business corporations. Just as media corporations were able to claim free press rights under the First Amendment, said the Court, so ordinary business corporations should be able to assert free speech rights under the First Amendment as well.

Is the thrust of the *Bellotti* case an effort by the Court to accord equivalent First Amendment clout to business corporations to make them sufficiently effective contenders with media corporations for purposes of influencing the political process?

At least impliedly, the answer to this question appears to be yes. Thus, when Massachusetts argued to the United States Supreme Court that "communication by corporate members of the institutional press is entitled to greater constitutional protection than the same communication" undertaken by the business corporations in *Bellotti,* Justice Powell rejected the argument:

> Certainly there are voters in Massachusetts, concerned with such economic issues as the tax rate, employment opportunities, and the ability to attract new business into the State and to prevent established businesses from leaving, who would be as interested in hearing [the] view [of the business corporations] on a graduated tax as the views of media corporations that might be less knowledgeable on the subject.

Powell's opinion appears to encourage pluralism in the opinion process among various power aggregates but not between individuals and the same power aggregates. Note that the old Warren Court liberals, Marshall and Brennan, were allied in dissent with Justice White.

Professor Bezanson, defending current trends of concentration and monopoly in the media, has argued that these developments equip the media more adequately to contend with government: "Centralization of power may equip the press to scrutinize and counterbalance the increasingly pervasive influence of expanding government." Bezanson added that the "very attributes of monopolistic power and lack of response to competing views * * * may be positive characteristics of the press under the Burger view." See Bezanson, *The New Free Press Guarantee,* 63 Virginia L.Rev. 731 at 774–775 (1977). The Burger view of the press, as expressed in his *Bellotti* concurrence, appears somewhat less enchanted. See the Chief Justice's concurring opinion in *Bellotti,* text, p. 151. The result and rationale reached by Justice Powell for the Court accords a full measure of First Amendment protection to business corporations. Thus, part of the reason for this holding appears to be designed to allow business corporations the same freedom from restrictive state election campaign regulation which media corporations enjoy. See *Mills v. Alabama, supra.*

Justice White attempted to sketch a different kind of First Amendment hierarchy—between individuals and corporations (whether the corporation is a media or nonmedia corporation is irrelevant in this theory). In this hierarchy, ideas that are the product of "individual choice" have the higher claim to First Amendment protection. Justice Powell rejected this hierarchy because "it would apply to newspaper editorials and every other form of speech created under the auspices of a corporate body."

Justice White sympathized with state efforts to make the opinion process more egalitarian. In his view, the Massachusetts legislation was designed to prevent dislocations in the marketplace of ideas engendered by the corporate form. Justice White ascribed the following objective to the Massachusetts legislation under review in *Bellotti:* "preventing institutions which have been permitted to amass wealth as a result of special advantages extended by the state for certain economic purposes from using that wealth to acquire an unfair advantage in the political process."

Federal Regulation of Campaign Financing—Securing Equality in the Opinion Process

1. In the aftermath of Watergate with its disclosures of misbehavior in the financing of political campaigns, new interest was directed to legislative efforts to clean up the whole process of campaign financing. Accordingly, in 1974 Congress enacted some significant amendments to the Federal Election Campaign Act of 1971. The amendments set forth complex provisions requiring the reporting and disclosure of political contributions to Congress. Further, in an innovative step, Congress set up a scheme for allocating subsidies to candidates in presidential elections. Congress also set forth new and stringent limitations on contributions to candidates and on expenditures by or on behalf of candidates.

The new legislation soon became the subject of major constitutional litigation. In 1976, the Supreme Court in *Buckley v. Valeo,* a 200-page *per curiam* decision, took something of a middle road with respect to the massive congressional intervention into the federal election process represented by the new legislation. The Court ruled that the limitations on political contributions to candidates in federal elections were constitutional. But the new legislation's limitations on expenditures by contributors or by groups in behalf of a clearly identified candidate were not valid. The Court said that the legislation's limitation on political contributions could be justified on the basis of its underlying purpose—prevention of the actuality and appearance of corruption which resulted from large individual financial contributions. The governmental interest in the integrity of the political process in this regard justified the incidental infringement on political association which accompanied the limitation on political contributions. The expenditure limitations, however, were deemed to fall into a different category and were hence invalid. The expenditure limitations were held to constitute a direct and substantial infringement on the ability of individuals, candidates, and organizations not under a candidate's control to conduct political activities.

2. In Justice Marshall's dissent in part and concurrence in part in *Buckley,* he commented on the Court's emphasis on "promoting the reality and appearance of equal access to the public arena." Marshall was indignant because, although the Court permits Congress to limit contributions to political candidates, the Court, by invalidating the expenditure provisions, safeguards against the express wish of Congress, "the wealthy candidate's immediate access to substantial sums of money," even though that access may obtain for the affluent candidate a headstart his opponent will be unable to overtake. In the view of the *Buckley* Court, imbalances in the communications process did not constitute First Amendment violations.

On the contrary, the Court remarked that in *Tornillo* the more "modest burden" of printing a reply was deemed to be constitutionally impermissible. The suggestion in *Buckley v. Valeo* appeared to be that government-imposed equality in the opinion process is apparently not ordained by the First Amendment and indeed may be forbidden by it.

3. In a masterful analysis of *Buckley v. Valeo,* Professor Lawrence Tribe argued that if the case is seen in context, it is just another in a series of cases issued by the Supreme Court in the 1970s in which the Court attempts "to secure for the wealthy the advantages of their position" even in the face of legislative efforts "to move in a more egalitarian direction." Professor Tribe commented on the Court's reaction to the expenditure and contribution provisions of the 1974 amendments to the Federal Campaign Election Act of 1971:

> Whether or not one regards government as responsible for the distribution of wealth underlying this distortion, it is hard to deny that the contribution and expenditure limitations redress it and to that extent increase freedom of speech. If the net effect of the legislation is to enhance freedom of speech, the exacting review reserved for abridgements of free speech is inapposite.

See Tribe, *American Constitutional Law* 803–805 (1978).

4. With respect to the disclosure provisions, note that the Court did not give them an indefinite constitutional bill of health. While the Court validated the disclosure requirements for the moment even as to minor parties, it did leave open the possibility that proof of injury by minor parties in a concrete case might cause the invalidation of the disclosure provisions as to them. Here the concern was that disclosure of one's support for an unpopular political party might fatally sap that party's potential for growth. Minor parties are presumably more likely to stand for unpopular causes, and, therefore, compelled exposure of an individual's support for such a party may well raise First Amendment issues of governmental infringement on associational freedom. Similar issues were considered by the Court when it reflected on the issue of whether there was a right to anonymous speech. See *Talley v. California,* text, p. 155.

Disclosure provisions relating to federal elections, although less encompassing than those considered in *Buckley v. Valeo,* had been upheld by the Court when it reviewed the Federal Corrupt Practices Act of 1925 in Burroughs v. United States, 290 U.S. 534 (1934).

5. The Court in *Buckley v. Valeo* upheld legislation providing for funding presidential elections on the ground that these provisions facilitated and enlarged public discussion and participation in the political process and did not abridge or restrict speech. But a governmental apparatus to subsidize candidates would appear to involve enhancing "the relative voice of others" in the sense that such subsidies benefit the less wealthy candidates. The first part of the *Buckley* decision, it will be recalled, had declared that enhancement of the "relative voice of others" is "foreign to the First Amendment."

It was argued to the Court in *Buckley* "by analogy" to the "no-establishment clause" of the First Amendment that "public financing of election campaigns, however meritorious, violates the First Amendment." The Court rejected the analogy and ruled that the subsidy provisions furthered First Amendment values:

> Legislation to enhance these First Amendment values is the rule, not the exception. Our statute books are replete with laws providing financial assistance to the exercise of free speech, such as aid to public broadcasting and other forms of educational media, 47 U.S.C. §§ 390–399, and preferential postal rates and antitrust exemptions

for newspapers, 39 CFR 132.2 (1975); 15 U.S.C. §§ 1801–1804.

6. The subsidy provisions of the Federal Campaign Finance Act withheld public funding from candidates without significant public support. The Court ruled that Congress could legitimately require that a candidate be able to make an initial showing "of a significant modicum of support" as a requirement for eligibility for subsidy. Such a requirement, said the Court, furthers the goal and "serves the important public interest against providing artificial incentives to 'splintered parties and unrestrained factionalism'." How do these remarks affect the question of whether it is a First Amendment mandate that government be careful to maintain ideological neutrality? See *Wooley v. Maynard,* text, p. 177. Do the foregoing remarks of the Court in *Buckley,* with their evident disdain for splinter parties, suggest that a revision of the "equal time" rule allocating broadcast time to a candidate on the basis, say, of the past voting strength of the candidate's party might be constitutional? See text, p. 805ff.

7. In Justice Powell's opinion for the Court in *Bellotti,* he observed that, although it was doubtless true that corporate advertising might influence the outcome of an election, that was no argument for its prohibition: "But the fact that advocacy may persuade the electorate is hardly a reason to suppress it." Justice Powell then buttressed this argument with the quotation from *Buckley v. Valeo* which declares that the notion that government may enhance the voice of some by restricting the voices of others "is wholly foreign to the First Amendment." But restrictions on political contributions constitute, in effect, the enhancement of the voice of some and the restriction on the voice of others. Perhaps, the explanation is that the Court doesn't consider "money" to be speech. In short, speech cannot be regulated in the same way monetary contributions can be. See *Politics and the Constitution: Is Money Speech?* 85 Yale L.J. 1001 (1976).

8. California Medical Association v. Federal Election Commission (CALPAC), 453 U.S. 182 (1981), rejected a constitutional assault on the validity of 2 U.S.C. § 441a(1)(c) which prohibits individuals and unincorporated associations from contributing more than $5,000 per year to any multicandidate political committee. A plurality opinion by Justice Marshall, joined by Justices Brennan, White, and Stevens, accepted the notion that "proxy speech," or speech emanating from a political committee rather than the contributor himself, was different from direct political speech and deserving of less First Amendment protections. The plurality followed the contribution/spending dichotomy of *Buckley* holding that limitations on contributions to multicandidate political committees was a valid exercise of government authority. Justice Blackmun provided the vital fifth vote in *CALPAC.* He disagreed with the "proxy" ruling of the plurality but nonetheless concurred, finding that the contribution provisions satisfied a strict scrutiny test.

Professor Powe has observed: "An individual choice to have a message with which he agrees prepared by professionals is no less speech. Proxy speech is simply a pejorative name for a political commercial. It is still speech." See Powe, *Mass Speech And The Newer First Amendment,* 1982 Sup.Ct.Rev. 243 at 258–259.

9. Citizens Against Rent Control v. Berkeley, 454 U.S. 290 (1982), dealt with a local California ordinance that limited contributions to political referenda committees to $250 while imposing no restrictions on personal spending on the same issue. The ordinance also afforded similar treatment to corporations and individuals. Although the ordinance appeared to be consistent with the mandates of *Buckley* and *Bellotti,* the Court invalidated the ordinance under NAACP v. Alabama, 357 U.S. 449 (1958), as an impermissible re-

straint on the "freedom of association." The Court reasoned that "[t]o place a spartan limit—or indeed any limit—on individuals wishing to band together to advance their views on a ballot measure, while placing none on individuals acting alone, is clearly a restraint on the right of association."

10. Common Cause v. Schmitt, 455 U.S. 129 (1982), involved the legality of expenditures by several conservative groups which were allied to further the election of Ronald Reagan. Under 26 U.S.C. § 9001–13, a candidate who accepts public financing for his campaign may not accept any form of private financing to augment the public monies other than to compensate for any deficiencies in the federal fund. 26 U.S.C. § 9002 requires that any expenditures on behalf of a political candidate must be made through an "authorized committee." To abide by these regulations, the conservative groups in *Common Cause* maintained an arm's length relationship with the campaign committee of Ronald Reagan. But, in doing so, the groups violated another provision of the Presidential Election Campaign Fund Act, 26 U.S.C. § 9012(f). That provision prohibits any unauthorized group from making independent expenditures of over $1,000 if the expenditures would "further the election" of a candidate receiving public financing. To dramatize the issue presented in *Common Cause,* the conservative groups had collectively spent $7.75 million, making § 9012(f)'s $1,000 limit look like petty cash.

A major purpose behind § 9012(f) was to eliminate the actual or apparent *quid pro quo* which results when individuals or interest groups spend vast sums of money to support a candidate.

Another argument in support of § 9012(f) is that the provision only regulates proxy speech. As such, the provision is not regulating the free speech rights of contributors since they are not engaging in communication. This argument rests on *Buckley* and *CALPAC.* (After *Citizens Against Rent Control v. Berkeley,* is this argument outdated? Doesn't § 9012(f) intrude upon the right of association?)

At the district court level, the arguments in *Common Cause* were scrutinized in the light of *Buckley v. Valeo.* The district court found § 9012(f) invalid on the ground that it regulated expenditures and thus fell on the spending side of the spending/contribution dichotomy:

> *[B]uckley* held that governmental interference in cleansing the electoral process of possible corruption was not enough to validate restrictions on expenditures. A "contribution" case, on the other hand, is entitled to less-exacting judicial scrutiny because the "transformation of contributions into political debate involves speech by someone other than the contributor." The case before this court is an "expenditure" case because it is precisely the speech of individual contributors which is hampered by statutory restriction. *Common Cause v. Schmitt,* 512 F.Supp. 489 (1980).

More specifically, the court ruled that:

> [T]he communication sponsored by the political committees is the language of their members and contributors because the contributions are made based on an understanding and community of political interest among all of the political contributors. The contributors do have power over the speech disseminated by the political committees. Political speech like this is possible in the first instance only because the contributors contribute to one particular committee or another. Contributors associate in a particular political committee because the committee will express their own thoughts which benefit thereby from amplitude in numbers and professionalism. If a committee disappoints its membership, contributions will dry up.

Proceeding from this reasoning, it was an easy step to rule as *Buckley* did that the government interest behind expenditure ceilings could not justify this intrusion into political speech.

In summarily affirming the district court's decision with a four to four vote, the Supreme Court in *Common Cause* provided no guidance in dealing with the contribution/expenditure question or any suggestion as to the continued vitality of enhancement.

Professor Powe has made the following critique of the issues in *Common Cause*:

> [I]f one candidate has no (or few) groups spending independently on his behalf while the other has such supporting groups, then the latter will have the potentiality (and in all probability the likelihood) of more media exposure. Since media exposure is deemed an essential element of a successful campaign, and more is typically better, independent expenditures may give an advantage to one side. Because the goal of public financing is to create a fair and equal campaign, the independent expenditures as such detract from the goal. See Powe, *Mass Speech And The Newer First Amendment*, 1982 Sup. Ct.Rev. 243 at 262.

LOTTERIES

1. A *lottery*, or what is sometimes called a gift enterprise, is a scheme in which there is distribution of a *prize* by *chance* for a *consideration* or a "price." All three elements must be present; absent any one, and there is no lottery.

Prize has been defined as anything of value.

Chance is a condition of winning over which the participant has no control, as when winning entries are drawn randomly or contestants must guess the outcome or the sum of the scores of a sports event. Under federal law, chance is present even when the lottery is only partly based on chance, as in word games or "expert" predictions of sports results. Chance is clearly present in raffles, bingo, punch boards, and football pools, for example.

Consideration generally means that an expenditure in time, effort, or money must be made by the participant. Often there is a monetary price: something has to be purchased or done to make one eligible for the prize—a ticket, a box top, registration, or attendance.

Courts have differed on the degree of effort, financial or otherwise, that must be expended to constitute consideration. Submission of a coupon from a newspaper ad may not be consideration. Playing a punch card game at a service station as an adjunct to buying gasoline was sufficient consideration in Missouri[137] at one time but not in Oregon.[138] Oregon's Supreme Court said that consideration had to be pecuniary. Missouri's Supreme Court, representing a traditionally antilottery state, thought schemes "which appear even superficially to constitute a lottery" ought to be banned. One had to go to a Mobil Oil station to play the game, and the station owner was thereby benefitted.

A Washington state court ruled similarly in 1972 that football forecasting contests run by newspapers were prohibited lotteries under both state law and the state constitution. Consideration was found in the time and attention one would have to devote to the game and in the fact that someone would have to purchase at least one copy of the newspaper. Although some skill was involved in assessing the merits of football teams, chance was the dominant factor in picking correct outcomes for fifteen teams against 900 to 1 odds.[139]

137. Mobil Oil Corp. v. Danforth, 455 S.W.2d 505 (Mo.1970).

138. Cudd v. Aschenbrenner, 377 P.2d 150 (Or.1963).

139. Seattle Times Co. v. Tielsch, 495 P.2d 1366 (Wash.1972).

Missouri, in keeping with increasing permissiveness and an air of resignation toward gambling in America, amended its constitution in 1978 and 1980 to liberalize the definition of *consideration* and to allow charities and nonprofit organizations to operate bingo games. There is now about the land a rash of business promotional games, especially pyramid sales schemes, which flourish in spite of their illegality in Missouri and elsewhere. Promotional contests, drawings, and games are now permitted in a majority of states including Alabama, Arizona, California, Colorado, Illinois, Indiana, Maine, Minnesota, Michigan, Montana, New Hampshire, New York, Ohio, Oregon, Rhode Island, and Texas. In the early eighties they were prohibited in Delaware, Florida, Iowa, Nebraska, and Oklahoma, although the "permitted" list of states will continue to grow.

The Supreme Court of Utah, a holdout state, refused in 1979 to include in its interpretation of *consideration* in its state law incidental benefits accruing to a game promoter. The meaning of *consideration* was limited to what the player gives specifically to obtain a chance to win.[140]

At the federal level, games of chance in the retail food and gasoline industries are regulated to prohibit the misrepresentation of the odds of winning and any form of rigging, but they are not prohibited.[141]

Earlier, however, the United States Supreme Court in an important ruling held that consideration was absent from the radio-TV name-the-tune shows in which the only effort required for participation was listening and answering one's telephone in the remote possibility that it should ring. In reversing a ruling by the Federal Communications Commission, the Court noted that, "To be eligible for a prize on the 'give-away' programs involved here ['Stop the Music,' 'What's My Name,' and 'Sing It Again'], not a single home contestant is required to purchase anything or pay an admission price or leave his home to visit the promoter's place of business; the only effort required for participation is listening." FCC v. ABC, NBC and CBS, 347 U.S. 284 (1954). Chance also might have been absent had any of the shows required a listener to recall the name of a tune, although the issue did not arise in this case.

2. The fact of gambling in America has far outdistanced any Puritan proclivities against it. A 1976 federal commission report on gambling concluded that Americans gamble in massive numbers and that "legalized gambling is a healthy recognition of reality." [142] Nevertheless there has been ambivalence from the beginning. While the thirteen original colonies and some of our most renowned universities were largely financed by lotteries and Thomas Jefferson endorsed the lottery as "a salutary instrument wherein the tax is laid on the willing only," [143] the Supreme Court in 1850 saw lotteries as a "widespread pestilence" * * * "infesting the whole community," * * * praying "upon the hard earnings of the poor," plundering "the ignorant and simple." [144]

Today, gambling is considered by most to be less a moral deficiency than a self-inflicted wound, a victimless crime that harms only the participant.

In 1982 there were fifteen state lotteries, if the District of Columbia were included. Parimutuel betting was either op-

---

140. Albertson's Inc. v. Hansen, 600 P.2d 982 (Utah 1979).

141. Marco Sales Co. v. FTC, 453 F.2d 1, 5 (2d Cir. 1971), 16 C.F.R. § 419.1 (1980).

142. "Gambling in America: Final Report of the Commission on the Review of the National Policy Toward Gambling", 1976, discussed in "Gambling Goes Legit", Time (Dec. 6, 1976), pp. 54–64.

143. Ibid., p. 56.

144. Phalen v. Commonwealth of Virginia, 12 L.D. 1030 (1850).

erational or permissible in thirty-two states, and gambling in one form or another was going on in all fifty states. Neal Peirce, a student of state and local government, called state lotteries "one of the most oversold, misguided and morally reprehensible innovations in state policy this century." [145] Eliot Marshall referred to them as "fraud by governments." [146] Many see lotteries as a most regressive and inefficient form of taxation. Moreover, the tremendous odds against winning are never fully communicated to the public.

3. Although the FCC, FTC, and Postal Service have done much over the years to discourage lotteries, the feds have been quite unsuccessful in influencing the states. And federal laws which had stood a great deal of pressure since the late nineteenth century and before began to crumble in the mid-seventies.

Sections 1302–1306 of Title 18 of the U.S.Code, first passed by Congress in 1868, prohibited use of the mails to promote or advertise lotteries. Later statutes prohibited broadcasting of lottery information or advertising. In 1969 the FCC demonstrated its resolve in enforcing these laws by taking a broadcaster challenge to them to the Second Circuit Court of Appeals. Upholding the FCC, the court ruled that broadcast announcements of New York state lottery winners was prohibited by federal law as enforced by the Commission. Exceptions would be "ordinary news reports concerning legislation authorizing the institution of a state lottery, or of public debate on the course state policy should take"—for example, an editorial for or against the continuation of the lottery or a news story specifying the number of schools that had been built with lottery funds. Although such information might "encourage" the conduct of a lottery, it would not promote it directly as would a plea to buy tickets or information on where to buy them.

It must be emphasized that *newsworthiness* has always been a defense against application of antilottery laws, even though the distinction between "news" and "promotion" is sometimes fine. Broadcasting the names of a list of winners would be "promotion," said the court: an interview with an excited winner would be "news." New York State Broadcasters Association v. United States, 414 F.2d 990 (2d Cir. 1969).

When the Third Circuit in New Jersey State Lottery Commission v. United States, 491 F.2d 219 (D.C. Cir. 1974), disagreed that announcing winning numbers in the state lottery in a newscast offended the law, the FCC petitioned the Supreme Court.

Before the Court could act, Congress intervened to rewrite the law. In January 1975 the new law exempted from earlier prohibitions all information concerning a state lottery 1) contained in a newspaper published in that state, and 2) broadcast by a radio or television station licensed in that state or an adjacent state which conducts such a lottery. 18 U.S.C.A. § 1307. The law favored broadcasters because newspapers were permitted to carry lottery information only if they were published in a state conducting a state lottery. The *New York Times*, for example, could not publish the results of the New Jersey or Pennsylvania state lotteries, although it could report the results of the New York state lottery.

In October 1976, § 1307 was amended to allow newspapers, as well as broadcasters, in lottery states to publish information about state lotteries in adjacent states. P.L. 94–525; 90 Stat. 2478. The statute was further amended in 1979 when mailings to foreign countries of lottery information were permitted so long as the foreign countries permitted it. P.L. 96–90, 93 Stat. 698 (1979).

Federal law still prohibits the mailing of information promoting or advertising a

145. Peirce, *State Lotteries: Sport or Consumer Swindle*? Minneapolis Tribune, June 12, 1977.

146. Marshall, *State Lootery*, New Republic (June 24, 1978), p. 20.

lottery, although efforts have been made to exempt lotteries conducted by nonprofit and charitable organizations in accordance with state law. Questions as to the status of the law ought to be addressed to the Office of the General Counsel, Mailability Division, Postal Service, Washington, D.C.

State laws vary, as has been noted, especially on the definition of *consideration*, the element of bargained-for exchange deemed essential to contractual validity. Where a nationwide scheme, for example a magazine sweepstakes, was legal under federal law but illegal under state law ("void where prohibited by law"), a Missouri trial court ruled that federal law prevails. The Missouri Supreme Court reversed under a long-arm statute, on condition that its judgment would have no deleterious effect on the operations of the U.S. Postal Service.

While there was no *consideration* in this case under federal lottery definitions, there was consideration under the then stricter Missouri statute.[147]

State banking commissions, liquor authorities, insurance departments, consumer protection agencies, and other state organs generally supervise sweepstakes, contests, and lotteries in the states.

STUDENTS AND THE FIRST AMENDMENT

1. Black armbands worn by school children on behalf of their parents' opposition to the Vietnam War led in 1969 to a Supreme Court ruling that became the cornerstone of freedom of speech and press on high school and college campuses.

The rule set forth in Tinker v. Des Moines Independent Community School District, 393 U.S. 503 (1969), was that student First Amendment rights may not be abridged unless school authorities can convince the courts that expression would "materially and substantially interfere with the requirements of appropriate discipline in the operation of the school." [148]

"It can hardly be argued," the Court went on to say, "that either students or teachers shed their constitutional rights to freedom of speech or expression at the schoolhouse gate." And, citing a reference to boards of education in the landmark flag salute case, the Court reaffirmed what may be the foundational concept in this line of cases:

"That they are educating the young for citizenship is reason for scrupulous protection of Constitutional freedoms of the individual, if we are not to strangle the free mind at its source and teach youth to discount important principles of our government as mere platitudes." [149]

2. The *Tinker* Court used the words "enclaves of totalitarianism" to characterize the public schools. While overly harsh perhaps, surveys of scholastic journalism do indicate that censorship and punishment for constitutionally protected student expression are not uncommon and that some school administrators are not sensi-

147. State Ex. Inf. Danforth v. Reader's Digest, 527 S.W.2d 355 (Mo.1975).

148. The language is from Burnside v. Byars, 363 F.2d 744 (5th Cir. 1966), a case in which school authorities were enjoined from enforcing a regulation forbidding students to wear "freedom buttons."

A year later, a federal district court in Dickey v. Alabama State Board of Education, 273 F.Supp. 613 (D.Ala.1967), recognized the constitutional rights of the student press when a student editor's suspension for writing an editorial critical of Alabama's governor was reversed. The court relied on the "material and substantial interference" rule of *Burnside v. Byars.*

149. West Virginia State Board of Education v. Barnette, 319 U.S. 624, 637 (1943).

tive to constitutional values.[150] It is not uncommon for college editors to be required to submit copy for review to a faculty adviser. In high schools, administrators are often the censors.

"Censorship is the fundamental cause of the triviality, innocuousness, and uniformity that characterize the high school press," a national study by the Robert F. Kennedy Memorial concluded. "It has created a high school press that in most places is no more than a house organ for the school administration." [151]

Although only a miniscule number of cases of censorship and punitive action reach the courts, even a brief look at Student Press Law Center Reports documents the problem. In Torrance, California, the high school newspaper adviser was required to adhere to the standards of Rotary International rather than the standards of the First Amendment or appropriate state law in passing upon news and editorial and material—assurance of a pollyanna publication. And an adviser who refused to submit articles to the administration for prior review was fired. A Linden, New Jersey principal ordered the entire edition of a high school newspaper burned because he feared the consequences of an innocuous editorial on community affairs. Wisconsin administrators confiscated an entire monthly issue of a student newspaper because it contained a harmless report on a school board meeting.

Little wonder that the Kennedy study could add to its conclusions that "self-censorship, the result of years of unconstitutional administration and faculty censorship, has created passivity among students and made them cynical about the guarantee of free press under the First Amendment."

The Student Press Law Center estimates that at least 300 cases of censorship and constitutionally suspect punishment for publication occur each year on high school and college campuses. Recently they have taken second place to book-banning cases. In Board of Education Island Trees Union Free School District No. 26 v. Pico, 102 S.Ct. 2799 (1982), a divided Supreme Court upheld the Second Circuit Court of Appeals [152] in remanding for trial a lawsuit challenging the right of a school board to remove books from high school libraries. In a plurality opinion for the Court, Justice Brennan, joined by Justices Marshall and Stevens declared that books cannot be removed simply because school authorities object to their philosophical perspectives. The plurality would extend to students a First Amendment right to receive information, especially in the context of a school library. Chief Justice Burger, joined by Justices Powell, Rehnquist, and O'Connor, dissented because they didn't wish to interfere with the authority of school officials. Justice Blackmun concurred in part and concurred in the judgment. Justice White also wrote a concurrence. Although the Court provided no constitutional guidelines for school actions of this kind, the case may have a deterrent effect on book banning. The Island Trees school board chose to drop the case rather than go back to trial.

Illustrative of a portion of the case law is a ruling that the First Amendment was violated by a school board decision to remove all issues of *MS* magazine from a high school library without any showing of

150. Inglehart, *The College and University Student Press*, 1973; Stevens and Webster, *Law and the Student Press*, 1973; Trager, *Student Press Rights*, 1974; Trager and Dickerson, *College Student Press Law*, 1976; Arnold and Krieghbaum, *Handbook for Student Journalists*, 1976; and Nat Hentoff, *The First Freedom*, 1980, chapters 1–4.

151. Jack Nelson ed., *Captive Voices: The Report of the Commission of Inquiry into High School Journalism*, 1974.

152. Pico v. Board of Education, 638 F.2d 404 (2d Cir. 1980).

a countervailing and legitimate governmental interest, except the political and social views of individual board members. Salvail v. Nashua Board of Education, 5 Med.L.Rptr. 1096, 469 F.Supp. 1269 (N.H. 1979). See also, Right to Read Committee v. Chelsea, 4 Med.L.Rptr. 1113, 454 F.Supp. 703 (D.Mass.1978).

But the problem of scholastic press censorship endures. Indeed, after the Seventh Circuit Court of Appeals held that a Chicago public school rule limiting distribution of any publication on school premises without prior approval of the General Superintendent of Schools was unconstitutional,[153] researchers at Southern Illinois University surveyed public schools in the Seventh Circuit: the court ruling, they found, had little effect on the prior-review practices of school administrators.[154]

Circuit courts generally have been willing to permit the regulation of campus speech where there appears to be a clear and present threat of violence or disruption. An example of the latter was the distribution of fraudulent notices announcing the closing of the university.[155]

Where libel, invasion of privacy, obscenity, or fighting words are claimed to have disruptive potential, their existence ought to depend upon constitutionally acceptable definitions. And an extension of any fair procedure for deciding such questions could be delay of publication pending immediate judicial determination. Federal appellate courts, however, will be exceedingly wary of any procedure that condones prior restraint.[156]

Other state and federal court standards have begun to emerge in case law:

a. Where courts have allowed prior restraints or a denial of the use of college facilities, they have insisted upon due process—clear, unequivocal, and publicized rules as to what is restricted and under what conditions of time, manner, and place of distribution. And to whom is material submitted for review, and how long should a review take? In addition, federal appellate courts will look for precise and intelligible definitions of "disruption" and criteria for predicting it, with the burden of proof on school authorities, and for timely opportunities for appeal.

A leading case in this field is Healy v. James, 408 U.S. 169 (1972), in which a unanimous Court saw no facts supporting contentions of a Connecticut college president that "disruption" would be caused by recognizing an SDS (Students for a Democratic Society) chapter on the campus. The First Circuit Court of Appeals relied on *Healy* when it ruled in Gay Students of University of New Hampshire v. Bonner, 509 F.2d 652 (1st Cir. 1974), that although a topic may infuriate the community, it is nevertheless protected by the First Amendment. Even indirect restrictions, said the court, may be constitutionally impermissible if they impinge upon basic First Amendment guarantees. "Freedoms such as these are protected not only against heavy-handed frontal attack, but also from being stifled by more subtle governmental interference."

And specifically on the point was Nitzberg v. Parks, 525 F.2d 378 (4th Cir. 1975), in which the court held that, even after four rewrites, a school board's prior review policy was still vague and overbroad

153. Fujishima v. Board of Education, 460 F.2d 1355 (7th Cir. 1972). Students may be punished after distribution, said the Seventh Circuit, but there shall be no prior restraints.

154. Trager, Dickerson and Jarvis, an article in Student Press Law Center Report, No. 4 (Spring 1977), p. 1.

155. Speake v. Grantham, 317 F.Supp. 1253 (D.Miss.1970), affirmed without opinion, 440 F.2d 1351 (5th Cir. 1971). And in Jones v. State Board of Education, 407 F.2d 834 (6th Cir. 1969), the court upheld the suspension of students for distributing leaflets calling for a boycott of registration and for disrupting of campus meetings. The latter was seen by the court as conduct rather than speech.

156. Nichols, The *Tinker* Case and its Interpretation, 52 Journalism Monographs, 25–29, fn. 8, December 1977.

as to the meaning of "disruption." A prediction of disruption and nothing more is not enough to warrant prior restraint, said the Second Circuit in Trachtman v. Anker, 3 Med.L.Rptr. 1041, 563 F.2d 512 (2d Cir. 1977).

b. In accordance with Justice Stewart's *Tinker* statement that the "First Amendment rights of children are not co-extensive with those of adults," courts have distinguished the First Amendment rights of college and high school students and of higher and lower grades in secondary schools. The Second Circuit upheld school authorities who refused to allow a school newspaper to distribute a sex survey questionnaire to students in grades nine through twelve.[157]

c. If school administrators take away a publication's subsidy or fire or suspend its editor, it must not be for First Amendment reasons. Although a college president may have authority to distribute student fees, he or she is not the ultimate authority of what is printed in the campus newspaper. "We are well beyond the belief," said a federal district court in Antonelli v. Hammond, 308 F.Supp. 1329 (D.Mass.1970), "that any manner of state regulation is permissible simply because it involves an activity which is part of the university structure and is financed with funds controlled by the administration."

"The state is not necessarily the unrestrained master of that which it creates and fosters," said the Fourth Circuit Court of Appeals in Joyner v. Whiting, 477 F.2d 456 (4th Cir. 1973). "It may well be that a college need not establish a campus newspaper, or, if a paper has been established, the college may permanently discontinue publication for reasons wholly unrelated to the First Amendment. But if a college has a student newspaper, its publication cannot be suppressed because college officials dislike its editorial comment. * * * Censorship of constitutionally protected expression cannot be imposed by * * * withdrawing financial support, or asserting any other form of censorial oversight based on the institution's power of the purse."[158]

d. Punitive actions by school administrators against scholastic publications ought to be *content free,* except in those areas such as libel, obscenity, and disruptive speech (fighting words?) where clear and constitutionally acceptable guidelines have been set down. Campuses may be thought of as *speech forums.* "[O]nce having established such a forum," said a New York court, "the authorities may not then place limitations upon its use which infringe upon the right of the students to free expression as protected by the First Amendment unless it can be shown that the restrictions are necessary to avoid material and substantial interference with the requirements of appropriate discipline on the operation of the school."[159] An attack on religion had jeopardized the newspaper's mandatory subscription fee.

And in a case originating on the campus of the University of North Carolina, the *Daily Tar Heel*'s liberal editorial policy was made the basis for an assault on its university subsidy. A federal district court pointed out that the paper served as a forum for the entire academic community and that its subsidy was not intended and had not been used to accommodate

157. Eisner v. Stamford Board of Education, 440 F.2d 803 (2d Cir. 1971); Quarterman v. Byrd, 453 F.2d 54 (4th Cir. 1971).

158. See also, Thomas v. Board of Education, Granville Central School District, 607 F.2d 1043 (2d Cir. 1979). Note that in Harris v. McRae, 448 U.S. 297 (1980) the Court said that refusal to fund a constitutionally protected activity, without more, could not be equated with imposition of a "penalty" on that activity.

159. Panarella v. Birenbaum, 327 N.Y.S.2d 755 (1971). See also Stanley v. Magrath, 9 Med.L.Rptr. 2352 (8th Cir. 1983).

the propagation of a particular point of view.[160]

A denial of or modification in funding aimed at content considered offensive would be unconstitutionally punitive and discriminatory under Grosjean v. American Press Co., 297 U.S. 233 (1936), this text, p. 138.

"Mere dissemination of ideas, no matter how offensive to good taste on a state university campus may not be shut off in the name alone of the 'conventions of decency'." [161]

And in Police Department of City of Chicago v. Mosley, 408 U.S. 92 (1972), the Court warned that regulation which "slip[s] from the *neutrality* of time, place and circumstance into a concern about content * * * is never permitted."

"Government may be deemed to have abridged speech * * *," says Professor Laurence Tribe, "if on its face a governmental action is targeted at ideas or information that government seeks to suppress, or if a governmental action neutral on its face was motivated by (i.e., would not have occurred but for) an intent to single out constitutionally protected speech for control or penalty." [162]

e. All disciplinary proceedings, of course, must comport with the minimum standards of due process,[163] and this includes a mechanism for appeal.

f. "Unofficial" publications and all less conventional forms of expression such as pamphlets, buttons, signs, or surveys enjoy First Amendment protection under the same rules that govern more traditional publications.[164]

g. School officials will be scrutinized when they declare student publications part of the curriculum, mere instructional tools, and therefore exempt from constitutional scrutiny. Courts, as has been noted, prefer to define school newspapers as public forums for at least student expression.[165]

A federal district court in Virginia vindicated this public forum precept vis-á-vis a principal, an advisory board on student expression, a superintendent and a school board all of whom had successfully prohibited publication of what the court called an innocuous article on contraception in the school newspaper. Defendants argued unsuccessfully that the paper was not a public forum entitled to First Amendment protection, but an "in-house" organ of the school system and its student readers a captive audience.[166]

In California, the state supreme court rejected the contention of school officials that because California law exempts "obscene," "libelous," or "slanderous" utterances from students' rights of free expression, these officials were authorized to set up systems of prior restraint. The case involved an off-campus student newspaper which, because it had challenged a statement of the principal having to do with the school's dress code, was denied distribution rights by school authorities. A tenth-grade writer for the paper challenged the action on grounds of legislative intent and constitutionality.

160. Arrington v. Taylor, 380 F.Supp. 1348 (D.N.C.1974), affirmed 526 F.2d 587 (4th Cir. 1975), cert. den. 424 U.S. 913 (1976).

161. Papish v. Board of Curators, University of Missouri, 410 U.S. 667 (1973); Gay Lib v. University of Missouri, 558 F.2d 848 (8th Cir. 1977), cert. den., 437 U.S. 1080 (1978).

162. Tribe, *American Constitutional Law* (1978), pp. 584–85.

163. Dixon v. Alabama State Board of Education, 294 F.2d 150 (5th Cir. 1961), cert. den., 368 U.S. 930.

164. Sullivan v. Houston Independent High School District, 307 F.Supp. 1328 (D.Tex.1969).

165. Trujillo v. Love, 322 F.Supp. 1266 (D.Colo.1971).

166. Gambino v. Fairfax County School Board, 2 Med.L.Rptr. 1442, 429 F.Supp. 731 (D.Va.1977), affirmed 3 Med.L.Rptr. 1238, 564 F.2d 157 (4th Cir. 1977).

Basing its arguments broadly on *Tinker* and specifically on a Fourth Circuit case dealing with an "underground" newspaper,[167] the California court said of the federal case:

> *Baughman* dealt with a challenge to a regulation requiring students to submit any "underground" newspaper to the principal for review and authorizing the principal to bar distribution of the paper if in his opinion it contained libelous language. The court held the regulation unconstitutional on three bases: 1) that it was procedurally defective in that it failed to specify a reasonably short time for the principal's action and to provide for an expeditious review of his decision; 2) that the term "distribution" was unconstitutionally vague, stating that "there may be no prior restraint" unless there is "a *substantial* distribution"; and 3) that "the use of terms of art such as libelous and obscene are not sufficiently precise and understandable by high school students and administrators untutored in the law to be acceptable criteria [in the context of prior restraint]. * * *" Thus, while school authorities may ban obscenity and unprivileged libelous material, there is an intolerable danger, in the context of prior restraint, that under the guise of such vague labels they may unconstitutionally choke off criticism, either of themselves, or of school policies, which they find disrespectful, tasteless, or offensive.[168]

h. In a few cases, courts have held that where campus speech leads to a disturbance, the first duty of administration and law enforcement is to protect the speaker from the audience rather than the audience from the speaker.[169]

i. While public school boards and officials are agents of the state and their rules, regulations, and responses constitute state action under First and Fourteenth Amendments, private school officials do not function under constitutional limitations. Grievances within the confines of a private school do not appear to raise constitutional issues, and remedies for stifled expression have to be sought elsewhere.

A number of commentators have explored the possibility of using contract law to protect the speech and press rights of private school students. The results have not been promising.[170] A more hopeful approach may be the application of state constitutions. The more detailed language of state charter guarantees of freedom of expression allows interpretations more expansive than those permitted by the First Amendment.[171] There are few cases in point, however, and the usefulness of this tactic will depend on future litigation.

j. Who is the publisher of a school newspaper? Who is ultimately responsible for what it contains? Who will be the

167. Baughman v. Freienmuth, 478 F.2d 1345 (4th Cir. 1973).

168. The California case is Bright v. Los Angeles Unified School Dist., 2 Med.L.Rptr. 1175, 134 Cal.Rptr. 639, 556 P.2d 1090 (1976). It is widely recognized, said the court, that school officials cannot use the labels of poor taste or vulgarity to punish views "they find disrespectful, tasteless, or offensive."

169. While not a school case and puzzling in some of its reasoning, the leading precedent is Terminiello v. Chicago, 337 U.S. 1 (1949), a case in which both "fighting words" and "hostile audience" doctrines were in play and a race riot appeared imminent. The rule of *Terminiello* was followed in Jones v. Board of Regents of University of Arizona, 436 F.2d 618 (9th Cir. 1970) and Shanley v. Northeast Independent School District, 462 F.2d 960 (5th Cir. 1972). Riot and disruption were much less a threat in the two lower court cases.

170. Comment, *Wanted: A Strict Contractual Approach to the Private University/Student Relationship*, 68 Ky.L.J. 439 (1979–80); Note, *Contract Law and the Student-University Relationship*, 48 Ind.L.J. 253 (1973); Note, *Legal Relationship Between the Student and the Private College or University*, 7 San Diego L.R. 244 (1970). See, also, Wisch v. Sanford School, Inc., 420 F.Supp. 1310 (D.Del.1976).

171. Stevens, *Contract Law, State Constitutions and Freedom of Expression in Private Schools*, 58 Journal Quarterly, 613 (Winter 1981).

defendant in a libel or privacy suit? Where public school administrators have asserted the rights of commercial publishers, they have been rebuffed by the courts.[172] If a school administrator cannot control content like a private publisher, should that person be liable for damages? There is no sure answer. In some states, under the protective umbrella of "sovereign immunity," the state and its agents cannot be sued.[173] Another problem for plaintiffs in cases involving school publications is that students who may be liable for damages don't have any money. And a democratically oriented principal who encourages editorial freedom may not be aware of an offending article until the damage has been done.

k. Another protection for student expression may be the evolving concept of academic freedom, a freedom assumed to be inherent in academic communities.[174] In the closing words of its opinion in *Shanley*,[175] the Fifth Circuit Court of Appeals gave support to this assumption when it said, "Our eighteen-year-olds can now vote, serve on juries, and be drafted; yet the board fears the 'awakening' of their intellects without reasoned concern for its effect upon school discipline. The First Amendment cannot tolerate such intolerance."

l. Campus newspapers are just beginning to inquire as to whether or not state open meeting and record laws apply to state institutions of learning and their governing bodies. There have been a few modest victories as of this writing in Gainsville, Florida, Huntington, West Virginia, Boston, and Oklahoma.

Increasingly, school board members, administrators, teachers, and advisers must reckon with the constitutional rights of students and student publications.

Assistance in protecting the First Amendment rights of college and high school students may be obtained from the Student Press Law Center in Washington, D.C.

THE PUZZLE OF PORNOGRAPHY

The Making of a Bog

1. Obscenity is not normally a concern of the professional journalist. Its control or prohibition does engage the First Amendment and the constitutional notion of free and open channels of communication. Cultural schizophrenia about sex will inexorably manifest bizarre symptoms in the body politic. Lawmaking and judicial rulings in the realm of sex expression reflect this social malaise.

In Western civilization, morality early came to have sexual significance, and erotic indecencies and indiscretions were interpreted as outrages against religion. When the *Decameron* came under Papal ban in 1559, it was not for its sex but for its spoofing of the clergy. The index of banned books lasted until 1966.

Louis Henkin has argued that obscenity is forbidden not because it incites sexual misconduct but because it offends notions of holiness and moral propriety. Thomas Bowdler expurgated Shakespeare and Gib-

172. Bazaar v. Fortune, 476 F.2d 570 (5th Cir.1973). "[S]peech cannot be stifled by the state merely because it would perhaps draw an adverse reaction from the majority of people * * * " (at 579).

173. *Tort Liability of a University for Libelous Material in Student Publications*, 71 Michigan L.R. 1061 (1973).

174. Trager, *The College President Is Not Eugene C. Pulliam: Student Publications in a New Light*, 14 College Press Rev. 2 (1975).

175. Op. cit., fn. 169 at 978.

bon's History of the Decline and Fall of the Roman Empire to conform to his own peculiar religious convictions. In our own time the Church's National Office for Decent Literature used criteria for objectionable literature so expansive that they constituted a means for the prevention of literature rather than for its discriminating evaluation. Hemingway, Faulkner, Dos Passos, Orwell, O'Hara, Zola, Koestler, Mailer, Farrell, Edmund Wilson, and scores of others fit one or more of NODL's categories of crime, violence, sex, disrespect for authority, suggestive illustration, blasphemy, and ridicule of racial or religious groups.

Community standards of morality have compelled school boards, acting under the imprimatur of the state, to consign the works of Mark Twain, Aldous Huxley, Steinbeck, Salinger, Heller, Vonnegut, Malamud, Harper Lee, James Dickey, Eldridge Cleaver, and Langston Hughes to the tender mercies of high school furnace rooms; and good teachers have lost their jobs.

Henkin is justified in asking whether the state can legislate merely to preserve a traditional or transitory view of private morality based upon untested hypotheses about character and its corruption. Is not morals legislation an establishment of religion in violation of the First and Fourteenth Amendment?[176] Massachusetts failed in 1977 to repeal its 1697 law outlawing blasphemy: profane comments involving God and things divine there can result in a year in jail and a $300 fine.

What resource has government for determining what is impure? And is what is impure also that which is enjoyed, that which evokes joy, liveliness, love, and even the stirring of lustful thoughts and impulses? Are libidinous thoughts destructive of the social order? Are attempts to repress such works as Kazantzakis's *The Last Temptation of Christ* and Baldwin's *Another Country* essentially efforts to preserve the status quo ante of church and state?

Some federal prosecutors seek religiously conservative juries to try their cases against sex publishers. Publisher Al Goldstein faced a federal jury, not in New York where his *Screw* magazine originates, but in Wichita, Kansas. Relevant to the issue of entrapment was the fact that *Screw* had no newsstand sales in Kansas and only fourteen subscribers in the whole state, four of whom turned out to be postal inspectors. Nevertheless the prosecutor pictured Kansas becoming "a Sodom and Gomorrah like Times Square," and the jury bought it. Indeed the grand jury, which returned a thirteen-count indictment against Goldstein, began its deliberations each day with a prayer. Goldstein's chief defense attorney was convinced that religious lampoons in the magazine did more than anything else to damage his client's case before the trial jury.[177]

To be sure, religious convictions alone do not account for sex censorship. Its suppression is pervaded by poorly disguised efforts to regulate human behavior through the political and ideological control of imagery. Educational Research Analysts, an organization certified and supported by the Right, has developed sixty-seven categories under which a textbook may be banned. They include "trash," "books with suggestive titles," and "works of questionable writers."

Groups normally more comfortable on the Left also support censorship, albeit less vociferously. Feminists see *Hustler*, *Penthouse*, and *Playboy* as exuding a pe-

176. Henkin, *Morals and the Constitution: The Sin of Obscenity*, 63 Colum.L.Rev. 402 (1963).

177. Yoakum, *An Obscene, Lewd, Lascivious, Indecent, Filthy, and Vile Tabloid Entitled SCREW*, Colum.J. Rev. (March/April 1977).

culiarly virulent kind of woman hatred [178]; blacks protest their depiction in film, fiction, and history; homosexuals have been sensitive to their portrayal on television; and concerns about violence cut across social strata. Textbook publishers are ever alert to the educational proclamations of the Moral Majority, the Gablers of Texas, Phyllis Schlafly's Eagle Forum, and the rest.[179]

While America may be afflicted with a plague of pornography (obscenity to a higher power), its treatment seems to depend on a conflagration of censorship. Conservatives condone it. Liberals legitimize it. And extremists on both sides demand it for their special causes.

Prodigious problems of definition result. Most attempts to distinguish good erotica from bad pornography have failed, due in large part to the incredible diversity in human response to infinitely replaceable sexual stimuli.[180] There is a neat contradiction in a capitalist economic system depending on sexual exploitation to sell its products at the same time as its governmental orders pass and enforce laws to punish slightly more vulgar versions of identical themes. One is reminded of the proper Victorians who, while considering sex a topic unfit for polite conversation, kept vast repositories of pornography in the libraries of their mansions.[181]

Censors traditionally have never feared for their own moral demise. Only their peers seem vulnerable to corruption. Time makes a fool of the censor. The obscenities of today have a perverse proclivity for becoming the irrelevancies—or the classics—of tomorrow.

2. Obscenity came into the common law in *Curl's* case [182] in eighteenth century-England when a tasteless tract titled, in part, "Venus in the Cloister or the Nun in Her Smock," was held by a court to jeopardize the general morality. The time was ripe. Obscenity, and vice societies bent on stamping it out, were both gaining momentum. By the beginning of the nineteenth century, England was entering its most pornographic period.

In a vain attempt to suppress sexual material, Lord Campbell's Act of 1857 made the sale and distribution of obscene libel a crime. A decade later, an anti-Catholic diatribe, "The Confessional Unmasked * * *," came to the Court of Queen's Bench on appeal in the landmark case R. v. Hicklin, L.R. 3 Q.B. 360 (1868).

Lord Chief Justice Cockburn announced, in deference to the most feeble-minded and susceptible persons in the community, the following influential test for obscenity: "Whether the tendency of the matter charged as obscenity is to deprave and corrupt those whose minds are open to such immoral influence and into whose hands a publication of this sort may fall." The book at issue was held obscene on the basis of the effect isolated passages would have on the most intellectually and emotionally defenseless readers.

178. Feminists are divided on the level of risk that should be taken in qualifying the First Amendment to combat pornography. There is much more agreement on the destructive effects of pornographic material. For example, see Lederer (ed.), Take Back the Night: Women on Pornography, 1980; and Brownmiller, Against Our Will: Men, Women and Rape, 1975. See especially, Kaminer, "Pornography and the First Amendment" in Lederer.

179. Noah, *Censors Left and Right*, The New Republic, Feb. 28, 1981, p. 12. For a more tempered view of book-banners see, Nocera, *The Big Book-Banning Brawl*, The New Republic, Sept. 13, 1982, p. 20. See also, Craig, *Suppressed Books*, 1963.

180. Sontag, See the concept of "The Pornographic Imagination," an excerpt from *Styles of Radical Will* in D.A. Hughes (ed.) *Perspectives On Pornography*, 1970.

181. Marcus, *The Other Victorians*, 1966.

182. 2 Strange 788, 93 Eng.Rep. 849 (K.B.1727).

America imported *Hicklin.* It seemed consistent with the Tariff Act of 1842, our first obscenity law, prohibiting importation into the United States of obscene literature and with other laws that were defining freedom of speech as freedom for "clean" speech only.

America's first reported obscenity case may have involved *John Cleland's Memoirs of a Woman of Pleasure,* better known as *Fanny Hill,* a novel written in England about 1750. The fictitious Fanny Hill would become a constitutional celebrity in 1966.

3. In 1873, a quite peculiar grocer's clerk named Anthony Comstock somehow managed an omnibus anti-obscenity bill through Congress with help from his lobby, the Committee (later Society) for the Suppression of Vice, an offspring of the YMCA. Substantial portions of that federal law are still in effect. State legislatures have mimicked it.

Congress revised the Comstock Act in 1876 to make obscene publications nonmailable. The Post Office, with the grocer's clerk serving as its special agent, gradually developed a system of administrative censorship and confiscation so formidable that the courts seemed reluctant to intervene.

Using the *Hicklin* test, the federal obscenity statute survived constitutional challenge in a number of early cases.[183] Not until 1913 was its validity questioned by Judge Learned Hand in the case of a publisher charged with selling Daniel Goodman's creditable novel of economic blight and social degradation, *Hagar Revelly.*[184] Another crack appeared in *Hicklin* in 1920 when a New York appellate court ruled in favor of a bookstore clerk who had been arrested for selling a copy of *Mademoiselle de Maupin* by Theophile Gautier. The court held that a book must be judged as a whole and that the opinions of qualified critics as to its merits are important in reaching a decision.[185]

But *Hicklin* was still the governing rule in 1929 when a New York City court declared Radclyffe Hall's sophisticated story of lesbian love, *The Well of Loneliness,* obscene.[186] A year later Theodore Dreiser's *An American Tragedy* was banned in Boston under a *Hicklin* test.[187]

There were counter currents. Federal Appeals Judge Augustus Hand wrote an opinion in 1930 reversing the conviction of Mary Ware Dennett for publication of her pamphlet, *The Sex Side of Life,* a sensitive piece written primarily for her own children, not obscene, but a serious presentation of an important topic.[188]

The world hadn't changed much by 1977. In November of that year New York officials were enjoined by a U.S. district court from enforcing the state's new child pornography law against the publisher and sellers of *Show Me,* a book designed for use by parents in educating their children about sex.[189]

4. *Hicklin* finally crumbled in 1933 when Judge John M. Woolsey delivered his elegantly literate decision in United States v. One Book Called "Ulysses", 5 F.Supp. 182 (D.N.Y.1933). A better test than *Hicklin,* said Woolsey, would be the impact or dominant effect of the whole book on the average reader of normal sensual respons-

183. Ex parte Jackson, 96 U.S. 727 (1878); United States v. Bennett, 24 Fed.Cas. 1093 (S.D.N.Y.1879); United States v. Harmon, 45 F. 414 (D.C.Kan.1891), reversed 50 F. 921 (C.C.).

184. United States v. Kennerley, 209 F. 119 (D.N.Y.1913).

185. Halsey v. New York Society for the Suppression of Vice, 180 N.Y.S. 836 (1920).

186. People v. Friede, 233 N.Y.S. 565 (1929).

187. Commonwealth v. Friede, 171 N.E. 472 (Mass.1930).

188. United States v. Dennett, 39 F.2d 564 (2d Cir. 1930).

189. St. Martin's Press v. Carey, 3 Med.L.Rptr. 1598, 440 F.Supp. 1196 (D.N.Y.1977).

es, and an evaluation of the author's intent—which this Judge had taken intellectual pains to determine. Woolsey's opinion, remarkable for its time, was upheld by Augustus Hand in the United States Court of Appeals. 72 F.2d 705 (2d Cir. 1934). By 1936, Judge Learned Hand, cousin of Augustus, could say bluntly in United States v. Levine, 83 F.2d 156 (2d Cir.1936), that *Hicklin* was out and that an accused book must be taken as a whole. If old, its accepted place in the arts must be regarded. If new, the opinions of competent critics must be taken into account. And what matters, said the judge, is the book's effects upon all whom it is likely to reach.

5. The Post Office and Customs Bureau, federal censors since 1865 and 1842 respectively, began applying a *Ulysses* test, or what came to be known as the "community standards" test, to a wide range of books, pamphlets, and photographs. Because they could effectively block the movement of such material, these government officials became the nation's chief censors, the arbiters of community tastes. The expense and time requirements of litigation generally meant that the courts were avoided.

In 1943 Postmaster General Frank C. Walker revoked *Esquire's* second-class mailing privilege—and the privilege of scores of other periodicals—because the magazine did not appear to be making "the special contribution to the public welfare" that the Postmaster presumed Congress intended. The District of Columbia Court of Appeals reversed a district court ruling in favor of Walker in Esquire, Inc. v. Walker, 151 F.2d 49 (D.C. Cir. 1945), and a unanimous Supreme Court affirmed. Justice Douglas wrote for the Court:

> It is plain * * * that the favorable second-class rates were granted periodicals meeting the requirements of the Fourth condition, so that the public good might be served through a dissemination of the class of periodicals described. But that is a far cry from assuming that Congress had any idea that each applicant for the second-class rate must convince the Postmaster General that his publication positively contributes to the public good or public welfare. Under our system of government there is an accommodation for the widest varieties of tastes and ideas. What is good literature, what has educational value, what is refined public information, what is good art, varies with individuals as it does from one generation to another. * * * The validity of the obscenity laws is recognition that the mails may not be used to satisfy all tastes, no matter how perverted. But Congress has left the Postmaster General with no power to prescribe standards for the literature or the art which a mailable periodical disseminates. * * *" Hannegan v. Esquire, Inc., 327 U.S. 146 (1946). See also this text, p. 131.

After *Esquire,* the revocation power was almost abandoned as an anti-obscenity sanction. By 1945 the entire Post Office procedure had been branded illegal by the D.C. Circuit Court of Appeals in a ruling that Dr. Paul Popenoe's booklet, "Preparing for Marriage," was not unmailable obscenity. Judge Thurman Arnold, who had spoken for the appeals court in *Esquire,* condemned summary seizure of mail as an interference with both liberty and property without due process of law as required by the Fifth Amendment. Walker v. Popenoe, 149 F.2d 511 (D.C. Cir. 1945).

The Post Office was prepared to ignore the decision, but a year later, in the Administrative Procedures Act, Congress moved to require a hearing and the use of established legal procedures in all such cases. The courts subsequently held that interim mail blocks prior to a hearing were illegal. The act also prohibited the government from being judge in its own case, that is, a case which it had investigated and prosecuted.

The power of the Post Office to censor the mails in the application of its particular definitions of obscenity would be challenged again. In 1962, for example, Justice

John Marshall Harlan, in an opinion for the Supreme Court, ruled that the Post Office could not bar a magazine from the mails without proof of the publishers's knowledge that the advertisements in it promoted obscene merchandise. The "merchandise" here was pictures of near-nude male models. Manual Enterprises, Inc. v. Day, 370 U.S. 478 (1962).

In spite of procedural improvements, the postmaster general to this day is able to exercise capricious and ill-defined powers with respect to content, and there are ambiguities as to what court procedures are to be followed in particular cases.

The Customs Bureau has been slightly more permissive than the Post Office and once employed Huntington Cairns of the National Gallery of Art to help it make decisions about the esthetic qualities of foreign art. But in theory the bureau exercises plenary power over the right of adult Americans to import foreign publications and films.

It has been suggested that since these federal agencies are not primarily regulatory in function, their assumption of censorship authority has evolved as a result of agency assertions of power confirmed far more by congressional silence than by any express consent.[190] Congress, of course, is not always loathe to assert itself.

In 1968, for example, it passed the Pandering Advertisement Act [191] which permitted individual householders to define obscenity for themselves. If a person swears that he or she has been sexually aroused by unsolicited mail, the Post Office orders the sender to strike the name from his mailing lists. Penalties for not doing so are substantial. The problem is that the Post Office has received as many as 300,000 complaints in a single year based on the sexually stimulating effects of advertisements for the *Christian Herald,* automobile seat covers, and electronic magazines—to suggest only a minute number of the complained about "turn ons."

The constitutionality of the act was upheld in Rowan v. United States Post Office Department, 397 U.S. 728 (1970). Chief Justice Warren Burger, in an opinion for the Court that emphasized privacy as a right to be protected against obscenity, said that "the mailer's right to communicate is circumscribed only by an affirmative act of the addressee giving notice that he wishes no further mailing from that mailer."

"Nothing in the Constitution," Burger added, "compels us to listen to or view any unwanted communication, whatever its merit. * * * Congress provided this sweeping power not only to protect privacy but to avoid possible constitutional questions that might arise from vesting the power to make any discretionary evaluation of the material in a governmental official."

Not all federal laws designed to interfere with the distribution of obscene materials have fared as well with the Supreme court as the Pandering Advertisement Act. Lower federal courts in California and Georgia ruled in 1970 that sections of the Postal Reorganization Act, authorizing the Postmaster General to halt use of the mails for commerce in allegedly obscene materials and permitting detention of incoming mail, were unconstitutional.

The Supreme Court agreed, holding that the administrative censorship scheme created by the act that permitted the Postmaster General, following hearings, to close the mails to postal money orders, to

190. Paul and Schwartz, *Federal Censorship* (1962), p. 317.

191. 39 U.S.C.A. § 3008. Section 3010 of the same title allows one to tell the Post Office that no sexually oriented advertising is wanted. Mailers must buy lists of such names from the Post Office so as to be forewarned. Section 3010 defines sexually oriented material somewhat in line with Court definitions in *Miller.* Its constitutionality was upheld in Pent-R-Books v. United States Postal Service, 328 F.Supp. 297 (D.N.Y.1971).

block distribution, and to detain a defendant's mail with a court order, pending the outcome of proceedings against him, a violation of the First Amendment. The Court saw inadequate safeguards against the undue inhibition of protected expression. The scheme failed to require governmentally initiated judicial participation in the procedure barring materials from the mails, failed to assure prompt judicial review, and failed to provide that any restraint preceding final judicial determination should be limited to preservation of the status quo for the shortest fixed period compatible with sound judicial resolution. Blount v. Rizzi, 400 U.S. 410 (1970).

ROTH: A Landmark Case

ROTH v. UNITED STATES

354 U.S. 476, 77 S.CT. 1304,
1 L.ED.2D 1498 (1957).

[EDITORIAL NOTE

The landmark Supreme Court decision in this vexing area came in 1957 with the *Roth* case. Roth, a purveyor of decidedly distasteful material, had been convicted under federal law. The court of appeals had affirmed. Judge Jerome Frank concurred in a remarkable opinion which asked the Supreme Court to resolve the long-standing confusion. See United States v. Roth, 237 F.2d 796, 801, 804 (2d Cir. 1956). Judge Frank also attempted a summary of relevant socio-psychological data bearing on the relationship between obscenity and antisocial behavior.

Roth came to the Supreme Court supported by four major arguments: 1) the federal obscenity statute (Comstock Act) violated the First Amendment; 2) the statute was too vague to meet the requirements of the due process clause of the Fifth Amendment; 3) it improperly invaded the powers reserved to the states and the people by the First, Ninth, and Tenth Amendments; and 4) it did not consider whether the publications as a whole were obscene.

The Court addressed itself to the first three questions, and in a 5–4 decision upheld the conviction of Roth, but reached a more sensible level of argument in doing so. In upholding the constitutionality of the Comstock Acts for the majority, Justice Brennan enunciated a revised legal test of obscenity based on the American Law Institute's model statute:

> *Whether to the average person, applying contemporary community standards, the dominant theme of the material taken as a whole appeals to prurient interest.* [Emphasis added.]

The test, as Brennan would recognize in a landmark 1973 case,[192] put the Court on the path to the quagmire. But for the moment, at least, sex and obscenity were no longer to be synonymous.

The elusiveness of a term like "prurient interest" was revealed by a Manhattan jury in 1977. It acquitted a wholesaler of films depicting bestiality because his wares were too disgusting to appeal to normal sexual urges. Going back to *Roth* for a definition, the Court said prurient interest meant "lustful thoughts * * * itching * * * longing * * * lascivious desire." So to be obscene, films would have to arouse healthy sexual responses in average ordinary jurors. Since "Man's Best Friend" and "Every Dog Has His Day" didn't do that, they were not obscene. Were normal sex and obscenity again synonymous?[193]

Decided with *Roth* in 1957 was the case of David Alberts who had been convicted by a Beverly Hills judge of selling and promoting obscene and indecent

192. Paris Adult Theatre I v. Slaton, 413 U.S. 49 (1973), dissenting opinion.

193. *Bestiality Found of Little Appeal, Jury Acquits Movie Wholesaler*, New York Times, Dec. 18, 1977.

books, a misdemeanor under the California Penal Code.]

Justice BRENNAN delivered the opinion of the Court.

The dispositive question is whether obscenity is utterance within the area of protected speech and press. Although this is the first time the question has been squarely presented to this Court, either under the First Amendment or under the Fourteenth Amendment, expressions found in numerous opinions indicate that this Court has always assumed that obscenity is not protected by the freedoms of speech and press. * * *

In light of * * * history, it is apparent that the unconditional phrasing of the First Amendment was not intended to protect every utterance. This phrasing did not prevent this Court from concluding that libelous utterances are not within the area of constitutionally protected speech. At the time of the adoption of the First Amendment, obscenity law was not as fully developed as libel law, but there is sufficiently contemporaneous evidence to show that obscenity, too, was outside the protection intended for speech and press.

The protection given speech and press was fashioned to assure unfettered interchange of ideas for the bringing about of political and social changes desired by the people. * * *

All ideas having even the slightest redeeming social importance—unorthodox ideas, controversial ideas, even ideas hateful to the prevailing climate of opinion—have the full protection of the guaranties, unless excludable because they encroach upon the limited area of more important interests. *But implicit in the history of the First Amendment is the rejection of obscenity as utterly without redeeming social importance.* This rejection for that reason is mirrored in the universal judgment that obscenity should be restrained, reflected in the international agreement of over 50 nations, in the obscenity laws of all of the 48 States, and in the 20 obscenity laws enacted by the Congress from 1842 to 1956. * * * *We hold that obscenity is not within the area of constitutionally protected speech or press.* [Emphasis added.]

It is strenuously urged that these obscenity statutes offend the constitutional guaranties because they punish incitation to impure sexual *thoughts*, not shown to be related to any overt antisocial conduct which is or may be incited in the persons stimulated to such *thoughts*. In *Roth*, the trial judge instructed the jury: "The words 'obscene, lewd and lascivious' as used in the law, signify that form of immorality which has relation to sexual impurity and has a tendency to excite lustful *thoughts.*" [Emphasis added.] In *Alberts*, the trial judge applied the test * * * whether the material has "a substantial tendency to deprave or corrupt its readers by inciting lascivious *thoughts* or arousing lustful desires." [Emphasis added.] It is insisted that the constitutional guaranties are violated because convictions may be had without proof either that obscene material will perceptibly create a clear and present danger of antisocial conduct, or will probably induce its recipients to such conduct. But, in light of our holding that obscenity is not protected speech, the complete answer to this argument is in the holding of this Court in Beauharnais v. People of State of Illinois, 343 U.S. at page 266:

"Libelous utterances not being within the area of constitutionally protected speech, it is unnecessary, either for us or for the State courts, to consider the issues behind the phrase 'clear and present danger.' Certainly no one would contend that obscene speech, for example, may be punished only upon a showing of such circumstances. Libel, as we have seen, is in the same class."

However, sex and obscenity are not synonymous. [Emphasis added.] Obscene material is material which deals with sex in a manner appealing to prurient interest. The portrayal of sex, e.g., in art, literature and scientific works, is not itself sufficient reason to deny material the constitutional protection of freedom of speech and press. Sex, a great and mysterious motive force in human life, has indisputably been a subject of absorbing interest to mankind through the ages; it is one of the vital problems of human interest and public concern.

* * *

The fundamental freedoms of speech and press have contributed greatly to the development and well-being of our free society and are indispensable to its continued growth. Ceaseless vigilance is the watchword to prevent their erosion by Congress or by the States. The door barring federal and state intrusion into this area cannot be left ajar; it must be kept tightly closed and opened only the slightest crack necessary to prevent encroachment upon more important interests. It is therefore vital that the standards for judging obscenity safeguard the protection of freedom of speech and press for material which does not treat sex in a manner appealing to prurient interest.

The early leading standard of obscenity allowed material to be judged merely by the effect of an isolated excerpt upon particularly susceptible persons. Regina v. Hicklin, [1868] L.R. 3 Q.B. 360. Some American courts adopted this standard but later decisions have rejected it and substituted this test: whether to the average person, applying contemporary community standards, the dominant theme of the material taken as a whole appeals to prurient interest. The Hicklin test, judging obscenity by the effect of isolated passages upon the most susceptible persons, might well encompass material legitimately treating with sex, and so it must be rejected as unconstitutionally restrictive of the freedoms of speech and press. On the other hand, the substituted standard provides safeguards adequate to withstand the charge of constitutional infirmity.

Both trial courts below sufficiently followed the proper standard. Both courts used the proper definition of obscenity.

* * *

It is argued that the statutes do not provide reasonably ascertainable standards of guilt and therefore violate the constitutional requirements of due process. * * * The federal obscenity statute makes punishable the mailing of material that is "obscene, lewd, lascivious, or filthy * * * or other publication of an indecent character." The California statute makes punishable, *inter alia*, the keeping for sale or advertising material that is "obscene or indecent." The thrust of the argument is that these words are not sufficiently precise because they do not mean the same thing to all people, all the time, everywhere.

Many decisions have recognized that these terms of obscenity statutes are not precise. This Court, however, has consistently held that lack of precision is not itself offensive to the requirements of due process. * * *

In summary, then, we hold that these statutes, applied according to the proper standard for judging obscenity, do not offend constitutional safeguards against convictions based upon protected material, or fail to give men in acting adequate notice of what is prohibited.

* * *

Affirmed.

Chief Justice WARREN, concurring in the result. * * * The line dividing the salacious or pornographic from literature or science is not straight and unwavering. Present laws depend largely upon the effect that the materials may have upon those who receive them. It is manifest that the same object may have a different impact, varying according to the part of the community it reached. But there is more to these cases. *It is not the book that is on trial; it is a person. The conduct of the defendant is the central issue,* *not the obscenity of a book or picture.* [Emphasis added.] The nature of the materials is, of course, relevant as an attribute of the defendant's conduct, but the materials are thus placed in context from which they draw color and character. A wholly different result might be reached in a different setting.

The personal element in these cases is seen most strongly in the requirement of *scienter.* Under the California law, the prohibited activity must be done "wilfully and lewdly." The federal statute limits the crime to acts done "knowingly." In his charge to the jury, the district judge stated that the matter must be "calculated" to corrupt or debauch. The defendants in both these cases were engaged in the business of purveying textual or graphic matter openly advertised to appeal to the erotic interest of their customers. They were plainly engaged in the commercial exploitation of the morbid and shameful craving for materials with prurient effect. I believe that the State and Federal Governments can constitutionally punish such conduct. That is all that these cases present to us, and that is all we need to decide.

I agree with the Court's decision in its rejection of the other contentions raised by these defendants.

Justice HARLAN, concurring in the result in [*Alberts*] and dissenting in [*Roth*]. * * * In short, I do not understand how the Court can resolve the constitutional problems now before it without making its own independent judgment upon the character of the material upon which these convictions were based. I am very much afraid that the broad manner in which the Court has decided these cases will tend to obscure the peculiar responsibilities resting on state and federal courts in this field and encourage them to rely on easy labeling and jury verdicts as a substitute for facing up to the tough individual problems of constitutional judgment involved in every obscenity case.

My second reason for dissatisfaction with the Court's opinion is that the broad strides with which the Court has proceeded has led it to brush aside with perfunctory ease the vital constitutional considerations which, in my opinion, differentiate these two cases. It does not seem to matter to the Court that in one case we balance the power of a State in this field against the restrictions of the Fourteenth Amendment, and in the other the power of the Federal Government against the limitations of the First Amendment.

* * *

I dissent in * * * Roth v. United States.

We are faced here with the question whether the federal obscenity statute, as construed and applied in this case, violates the First Amendment to the Constitution. To me, this question is of quite a different order than one where we are dealing with state legislation under the Fourteenth Amendment. *I do not think it follows that state and federal powers in this area are the same, and that just because the State may suppress a particular utterance, it is automatically permissible for the Federal Government to do the same.* [Emphasis added] * * *

The Constitution differentiates between those areas of human conduct subject to the regulation of the States and those subject to the powers of the Federal Government. The substantive powers of the two governments, in many instances, are distinct. And in every case where we are called upon to balance the interest in free expression against other interests, it seems to me important that we should keep in the forefront the question of whether those other interests are state or federal. Since under our constitutional scheme the two are not necessarily equivalent, the balancing process must needs often produce different results. Whether a particular limitation on speech or press is to be upheld because it subserves a paramount governmental interest must, to a large extent, I think, depend on whether that government has, under the Constitution, a direct substantive interest, that is, the power to act, in the particular area involved.

The Federal Government has, for example, power to restrict seditious speech directed against it, because that Government certainly has the substantive authority to protect itself against revolution. * * But in dealing with obscenity we are faced with the converse situation, for the interests which obscenity statutes purportedly protect are primarily entrusted to the care, not of the Federal Government, but of the States. Congress has no substantive power over sexual morality. Such powers as the Federal Government has in this field are but incidental to its other powers, here the postal power, and are not of the same nature as those possessed by the States, which bear direct responsibility for the protection of the local moral fabric. * * *

Justice DOUGLAS, with whom Justice Black concurs, dissenting.

When we sustain these convictions, we make the legality of a publication turn on the purity of thought which a book or tract instills in the mind of the reader. I do not think we can approve that standard and be faithful to the command of the First Amendment, which by its terms is a restraint on Congress and which by the Fourteenth is a restraint on the States.

* * *

By these standards punishment is inflicted for thoughts provoked, not for overt acts nor antisocial conduct. This test cannot be squared with our decisions under the First Amendment. * * * This issue cannot be avoided by saying that obscenity is not protected by the First Amendment. The question remains, what is the constitutional test of obscenity?

The tests by which these convictions were obtained require only the arousing of sexual thoughts. Yet the arousing of sexual thoughts and desires happens every day in normal life in dozens of ways. Nearly 30 years ago a questionnaire sent to college and normal school women graduates asked what things were most stimulating sexually. Of 409 replies, 9 said "music"; 18 said "pictures"; 29 said "dancing"; 40 said "drama"; 95 said "books"; and 218 said "man." Alpert, Judicial Censorship of Obscene Literature, 52 Harv.L.Rev. 40, 73.

The test of obscenity the Court endorses today gives the censor free range over a vast domain. To allow the State to step in and punish mere speech or publication that the judge or the jury thinks has an *undesirable* impact on thoughts but that is not shown to be a part of unlawful action is drastically to curtail the First Amendment. As recently stated by two of our outstanding authorities on obscenity, "The danger of influencing a change in the current moral standards of the community, or of shocking or offending readers, or of stimulating sex thoughts or desires apart from objective conduct, can never justify the losses to society that result from interference with literary freedom." Lockhart & McClure, Literature, The Law of Obscenity and the Constitution, 38 Minn.L.Rev. 295, 387.

If we were certain that impurity of sexual thoughts impelled to action, we would be on less dangerous ground in punishing the distributors of this sex literature. But it is by no means clear that obscene literature, as so defined, is a significant factor in influencing substantial deviations from the community standards. * * * The absence of dependable information on the effect of obscene literature on human conduct should make us wary. It should put us on the side of protecting society's interest in literature, except and unless it can be said that the particular publication has an impact on action that the government can control.

As noted, the trial judge in the Roth case charged the jury in the alternative that the federal obscenity statute outlaws literature dealing with sex which offends "the common conscience of the community." That standard is, in my view, more inimical still to freedom of expression.

*The standard of what offends "the common conscience of the community" conflicts, in my judgment, with the command of the First Amendment that "Congress shall make no law * * * abridging the freedom of speech, or of the press." Certainly that standard would not be an acceptable one if religion, economics, politics or philosophy were involved. How does it become a constitutional standard when literature treating with sex is concerned*? [Emphasis added.]

COMMENT

1. Justice Brennan would regret his *Roth* opinion. The ambiguities raised by the decision were never resolved. Who is this average person? The contemporary standards of what community? And who will testify to being sexually aroused so that a jury can measure prurient interest? Although these difficult questions were never to be answered satisfactorily, the case would provide the elements of a futile but sometimes stimulating debate for the next twenty years.

Chief Justice Warren was bothered by commercial exploitation or the conduct of the purveyor. Justice Harlan foretold a preoccupation with local community standards. Black and Douglas never wavered from their near absolute protection for speech and press in any form.

2. For its time *Roth* did have some progressive results. A unanimous Court in 1957 struck down a Michigan statute that prohibited distribution to the general reading public of material "containing obscene, immoral, lewd or lascivious language * * tending to incite *minors* to violent or depraved or immoral acts [or] manifestly tending to the corruption of the morals of youth. * * * "

"The incidence of this enactment," said Justice Frankfurter, "is to reduce the adult population of Michigan to reading only what is fit for children." Butler v. Michigan, 352 U.S. 380 (1957).

Also in the 1957 term, the Court in *per curiam* opinions overruled four U.S. Courts of Appeals decisions that had upheld obscenity convictions of a French motion picture,[194] imported collections of student art,[195] a homosexual magazine,[196] and two nudist magazines.[197]

Two years later, in Kingsley International Pictures Corp. v. Regents, 360 U.S. 684 (1959), the Court considered "ideological obscenity"—depictions in conflict with social norms—in a French movie based on D.H. Lawrence's *Lady Chatterley's Lover.* Conviction of the film distributor was reversed because, said the Court, the applicable state statute violated the First Amendment's basic guarantee of freedom to advocate ideas, even ideas as hateful and as immoral to some as adultery.

Guilty knowledge was made a precondition of punishment for the crime of selling obscene books in Smith v. California, 361 U.S. 147 (1959), and for dispensing twenty-five cent pieces for peep-show machines in Commonwealth v. Thureson, 2 Med.L.Rptr. 1351, 357 N.E.2d 750 (Mass. 1977). The Court in *Smith* reasoned that if the bookseller is criminally liable whether or not he knows what is in the books on his shelves, he will restrict the books he sells to those he has inspected, and the public will end up with a limited choice.

---

194. Times Film Corp. v. City of Chicago, 355 U.S. 35 (1957).

195. Mounce v. United States, 355 U.S. 180 (1957).

196. One, Inc. v. Olesen, 355 U.S. 371 (1958).

197. Sunshine Book Co. v. Summerfield, 355 U.S. 372 (1958).

In an important 1962 case, Manual Enterprises, Inc. v. Day, 370 U.S. 478 (1962), referred to earlier, the Court reached for a definition of "hard-core" pornography. "Patent offensiveness," "self-demonstrating indecency," and "obnoxiously debasing portrayals of sex" were the best the Court could do. What was "patently offensive," of course, would by definition appeal to "prurient interest." Although Justice Harlan, in his opinion for the Court found the male-model magazines "dismally unpleasant, uncouth and tawdry" and appealing only "to the unfortunate persons whose patronage they were aimed at capturing," he could not label them "obscene."

Bantam Books v. Sullivan, 372 U.S. 58 (1963), a landmark prior restraint case, came as a result of Rhode Island's creation of a Commission to Encourage Morality in Youth to educate the public on literature tending to corrupt the young. Without public hearings, lists of objectionable books were prepared, and distributors were threatened with prosecution. "Under the Fourteenth Amendment," said the Court, "a state is not free to adopt whatever procedure it pleases for dealing with obscenity * * * without regard to the possible consequences for constitutionally protected speech." Clearly this was a system of prior censorship depending upon extralegal sanctions.

It is important to note that the language of *Bantam Books* formed the central proposition of the ruling of the Court in the *Pentagon Papers* case: "Any system of prior restraints of expression comes to this Court bearing a heavy presumption against its constitutional validity."

An analogous case came to Court in Southeastern Promotions, Limited v. Conrad, 1 Med.L.Rptr. 1140, 420 U.S. 546 (1975). There the Court held that a Chattanooga municipal board's refusal to permit the rock musical "Hair" to use a city auditorium because of what board members had heard about the presentation constituted a prior restraint under a system lacking in constitutionally required minimal procedural safeguards.

3. Laws having substantially the same effects in Kansas [A Quantity of Copies of Books v. Kansas, 378 U.S. 205 (1964)] and in Missouri [Marcus v. Search Warrant, 367 U.S. 717 (1961)] had been struck down for interfering with distribution prior to an adversary hearing on the issue of obscenity.

By 1964 Henry Miller's *Tropic of Cancer*—tame by contemporary standards—had become the most litigated book in the history of literature. It had faced as many as sixty criminal actions in at least nine states. Some courts found it obscene; others did not.[198] In 1964, *Tropic of Cancer* finally found constitutional protection when five members of the United States Supreme Court voted to reverse a Florida's court's conviction of the book. Grove Press v. Gerstein, 378 U.S. 577 (1964).

The Court's grounds for reversal are found in a companion case, Jacobellis v. State of Ohio, 378 U.S. 184 (1964), decided on the same day but involving a motion picture rather than a book. Writing for Court, Justice Brennan expanded upon his *Roth* ruling.

Obscenity is excluded from constitutional protection, said Brennan, only because it is *"utterly* without redeeming social importance." Sex could be portrayed in art, literature, or scientific works without fear of punishment. Whatever the material, Brennan added, it must go "substantially beyond customary limits of candor," that is, "beyond society's standards of decency."

Are the "contemporary community standards" of *Roth,* then, local or national? Relying on Learned Hand's 1913 *Kennerley* ruling (see fn. 184) in which the

198. Hutchison, *Tropic of Cancer on Trial* (1968).

judge spoke of "general notions about what is decent," Brennan concluded in *Jacobellis* that "society at large * * * the public or people in general" would define community standards. The federal Constitution would not permit the concept of obscenity to have a varying meaning from county to county or town to town.

"It would be a hardy person," wrote Brennan, "who would sell a book or exhibit a film anywhere in the land after this Court had sustained the judgment of one 'community' holding it to be outside the constitutional protection. * * * We thus reaffirm the position taken in *Roth* to the effect that the constitutional status of an allegedly obscene work must be determined on the basis of a national standard. *It is, after all, a national Constitution we are expounding.*" [Emphasis added.]

Chief Justice Warren emphatically disagreed, and it is his view that has prevailed. He said:

> It is my belief that when the Court said in *Roth* that obscenity is to be defined by reference to "community standards," it meant community standards—not a national standard, as is sometimes argued. I believe that there is no provable "national standard" and perhaps there should be none. At all events, this Court has not been able to enunciate one, and it would be unreasonable to expect local courts to divine one. It is said that such a "community" approach may well result in material being proscribed as obscene in one community but not in another, and, in all probability, that is true. But communities throughout the (n)ation are in fact diverse, and it must be remembered that, in cases such as this one, the Court is confronted with the task of reconciling conflicting rights of the diverse communities within our society and of individuals.

Jacobellis is also remembered for Justice Stewart's plunge into pragmatic logic. In a concurring opinion, he declared that, although he couldn't define obscenity, "I know it when I see it."

Film Censorship

1. Although no distinctions have been made so far between print and film, it should be noted that not until 1952 was film brought under the protective custody of the First Amendment—and then equivocally. In what came to be known as the *Miracle* case a sensitive and quite respectful Italian film was banned as sacrilegious by the New York Board of Regents, until 1966 the state's censorship agency.

A unanimous United States Supreme Court held that the New York law, under which the ban was permitted, was an unconstitutional abridgement of free speech and press of which film communication was a legitimate part. But it was the vagueness of the term "sacrilegious" that bothered the Court; a clear implication of the Court's ruling was that censorship would be allowable for other reasons. Joseph Burstyn, Inc. v. Wilson, 343 U.S. 495 (1952). See also, de Grazia and Newman, *Banned Films: Movies, Censors and the First Amendment*, 1983.

Many states and local communities have had film censorship boards. By 1965 state agencies had survived only in New York, Virginia, Kansas, and Maryland. Maryland for a time the lone hold out, abolished its film censorship board in 1981. Two dozen communities, including Chicago, Dallas, Detroit, Memphis, and Atlanta, had from time to time, been strict about the distribution of films. Dallas still had a Motion Picture Classification Board in 1983.

A 1965 challenge to Maryland's motion picture censorship statute had left its law intact, but the U.S. Supreme Court set down strict procedural guidelines for film review. That important ruling may have hastened the demise of all state and local film censorship bodies.

FREEDMAN v. STATE OF MARYLAND

380 U.S. 51, 85 S.CT. 734,
13 L.ED.2D 649 (1965).

Justice BRENNAN delivered the opinion of the Court.

Appellant sought to challenge the constitutionality of the Maryland motion picture censorship statute, Md.Ann.Code, 1957, Art. 66A, and exhibited the film "Revenge at Daybreak" at his Baltimore theatre without first submitting the picture to the State Board of Censors. * * * The State concedes that the picture does not violate the statutory standards and would have received a license if properly submitted, but the appellant was convicted of a * * * violation despite his contention that the statute in its entirety unconstitutionality impaired freedom of expression. The Court of Appeals of Maryland affirmed, 197 A.2d 232 (Md.1964). * * * We reverse.

* * *

[A]ppellant argues that [the law] constitutes an invalid prior restraint because, in the context of the remainder of the statute, it presents a danger of unduly suppressing protected expression. He focuses particularly on the procedure for an initial decision by the censorship board, which, without any judicial participation, effectively bars exhibition of any disapproved film, unless and until the exhibitor undertakes a time-consuming appeal to the Maryland courts and succeeds in having the Board's decision reversed. Under the statute, the exhibitor is required to submit the film to the Board for examination, but no time limit is imposed for completion of Board action. If the film is disapproved, or any elimination ordered [the law] provides that "the person submitting such film or view for examination will receive immediate notice of such elimination or disapproval, and if appealed from, such film or view will be promptly reexamined, in the presence of such person by two or more members of the Board, and the same finally approved or disapproved promptly after such re-examination, with the right of appeal from the decision of the Board to the Baltimore City Court of Baltimore City. There shall be a further right of appeal from the decision of the Baltimore City Court to the Court of Appeals of Maryland, subject generally to the time and manner provided for taking appeal to the Court of Appeals."

Thus there is no statutory provision for judicial participation in the procedure which bars a film, nor even assurance of prompt judicial review. Risk of delay is built into the Maryland procedure, as is borne out by experience; in the only reported case indicating the length of time required to complete an appeal, the initial judicial determination has taken four months and final vindication of the film on appellate review, six months.

* * *

Although the Court has said that motion pictures are not "necessarily subject to the precise rules governing any other particular method of expression," *Joseph Burstyn, Inc. v. Wilson,* it is as true here as of other forms of expression that "[a]ny system of prior restraints of expression comes to this Court bearing a heavy presumption against its constitutional validity." *Bantam Books, Inc. v. Sullivan.* " * * * [U]nder the Fourteenth Amendment, a State is not free to adopt whatever procedures it pleases for dealing with obscenity * * * without regard to the possible consequences for constitutionally protected speech." Marcus v. Search Warrant, 367 U.S. 717, 731. The administration of a censorship system for motion pictures presents peculiar dangers to constitutionally protected speech. Unlike a prosecution for obscenity, a censorship proceeding puts the initial burden on the exhibitor or distributor. Because the censor's business is to censor, there inheres the danger that he may well be less responsive than a court—part of an independent branch of government—to the constitutionally protected interests in free expression. And if it is made unduly onerous, by reason of delay or otherwise, to seek judicial review, the censor's determination may in practice be final.

Applying the settled rule of our cases, we hold that a noncriminal process which requires the prior submission of a film to a censor avoids constitutional infirmity only if it takes place under procedural safeguards designed to obviate the dangers of a censorship system. First, the burden of proving that the film is unprotected expression must rest on the censor. As we said in Speiser v. Randall, 357 U.S. 513, 526, "Where the transcendent value of speech is involved, due process certainly requires * * * that the State bear the burden of persuasion to show that the appellants engaged in criminal speech." Second, while the State may require advance submission of all films, in order to proceed effectively to bar all showings of unprotected films, the requirement cannot be administered in a manner which would lend an effect of finality to the censor's determination whether a film constitutes protected expression. The teaching of our cases is that, because only a judicial determination in an adversary proceeding ensures the necessary sensitivity to freedom of expression, only a procedure requiring a judicial determination suffices to impose a valid final restraint. * * * To this end, the exhibitor must be assured, by statute or authoritative judicial construction, that the censor will, within a specified brief period, either issue a license or go to court to restrain showing the film. *Any restraint imposed in advance of a final judicial determination on the merits must similarly be limited to preservation of the status quo for the shortest fixed period compatible with sound judicial resolution.* [Emphasis added.] Moreover, we are well aware that, even after expiration of a temporary restraint, an administrative refusal to license, signifying the censor's view that the film is unprotected, may have a discouraging effect on the exhibitor. Therefore, the procedure must also assure a prompt final judicial decision, to minimize the deterrent effect of an interim and possibly erroneous denial of a license.

* * *

It is readily apparent that the Maryland procedural scheme does not satisfy these criteria. First, once the censor disapproves the film, the exhibitor must assume the burden of instituting judicial proceedings and of persuading the courts that the film is protected expression. Second, once the Board has acted against a film, exhibition is prohibited pending judicial review, however protracted. Under the statute, appellant could have been convicted if he had shown the film after unsuccessfully seeking a license, even though no court had ever ruled on the obscenity of the film. Third, it is abundantly clear that the Maryland statute provides no assurance of prompt judicial determination. We hold, therefore, that appellant's conviction must be reversed. The Maryland scheme fails to provide adequate safeguards against undue inhibition of protected expression, and this renders the requirement of prior submission of films to the Board an invalid previous restraint.

COMMENT

1. Since 1973 [Heller v. New York, 413 U.S. 483 (1973)], police with a warrant signed by a judge who has viewed a film can seize that film. Pending the results of an adversary hearing, the film may be shown, but the exhibitor may have to pay the costs of making a copy.

2. *Freedman's* insistence upon procedural due process was reflected in a 1976 case, McKinney v. Alabama, 1 Med.L.Rptr. 1516, 424 U.S. 669 (1976), in which the Court held that failure to present the jury

with the factual question of obscenity was a denial of due process. The trial court had relied on the *ex parte*, unilateral determination of a state censorship authority. Proscribing distribution, said the High Court, "without any provision for subsequent re-examination of the determination of the censor would be constitutionally infirm." See also Brockett v. Spokane Arcades, 454 U.S. 1022 (1981), affirming 631 F.2d 135 (9th Cir. 1980) and Vance v. Universal Amusement Co., 445 U.S. 308 (1980).

Chicago's censorship ordinance was upheld by the U.S. Supreme Court in the notable 1961 case Times Film Corp. v. City of Chicago, 365 U.S. 43 (1961). That case, according to facts revealed in Chief Justice Warren's dissent, illustrated the tendency of censorship to engulf everything in its spreading ooze. Chicago licensors had banned newsreels of Chicago policeman shooting at labor pickets, films criticizing Nazi Germany, motion pictures containing the words "rape" and "contraceptive," and a scene from Walt Disney's *Vanishing Prairie* depicting the birth of a buffalo.

A member of the Chicago censor board reinforced an earlier contention of this chapter when she explained that she rejected a film because "it was immoral, corrupt, indecent, against my religious principles." A police sergeant attached to the censor board said, "Coarse language or anything that would be derogatory to the government—propaganda" is ruled out of foreign films. "Nothing pink or red is allowed." Chicago's law fell into disuse when it was found to be incompatible with *Freedman.*

For a long time censorship in Memphis was a one-man affair. All of Ingrid Bergman's movies were banned because Lloyd Binford judged her soul "black as the soot of hell." She'd had a child out of wedlock. There as in Dallas, Pennsylvania, Oklahoma, Providence, R.I., Kenosha, Wisc., Milwaukee, North Carolina, Tennessee, Ohio, and Georgia censorship laws and ordinances fizzled out after court challenges. Most censors were simply not prepared to comply with the due process standards of *Freedman.*

3. The Motion Picture Association of America and individual states, cities, and theater owners have over the years developed classification systems to warn adults and to protect children. The X designation has often served as free advertising for the shabby producer whose numbers are now legion.

The grand climax may have been the film *Deep Throat* which provoked a great deal of pseudo-sophisticated legal, scientific, and artistic debate—and at least $20 million for its producers. A New York Criminal Court judge, Joel Tyler, tried to transform the film into words and, in the process, told us more about himself than about the film:

> The camera angle, emphasis and close-up zooms were directed * * * toward a maximum exposure in detail of the genitalia during the gymnastics, gyrations, bobbing, trundling, surging, ebb and flowing, eddying, moaning, groaning and sighing, all with ebullience and gusto. * * * Such concentration upon the acts of fellatio and cunnilingus overlooked the numerous clear, clinical acts of sexual intercourse, anal sodomy, female masturbation, clear depiction of seminal fluid ejaculation and an orgy scene—a Sodom and Gomorrah gone wild before the fire—all of which is enlivened with the now famous "four letter words" and finally with bells ringing and rockets bursting in climactic ecstasy.

Anthony Burgess suggested that the ebullience and gusto lie in the judge and not in the film. "If only 'Deep Throat' were as Rabelaisian as he makes it seem to be," Burgess lamented. "Our aesthetic condemnation of pornography rests on the fact that it is *not* Rabelaisian—that there is no wit, no belly-humor, no learning, no Holy Bottle and no Abbey or Thelema. In other words, no life and no art. The moral question is, of course, a lot of nonsense." [199]

Since *Deep Throat* was, in the judge's words, "unmistakably hard-core pornography * * * with a vengeance," "a nadir of decadence," and "indisputably obscene by any legal measurement," the film's promoters were convicted of a misdemeanor and fined $100,000 according to a formula not to exceed double the corporation's gain from the offence.[200]

4. Courts have shown a determination to protect children from viewing pornography or from being involved in its manufacture. That determination was underscored in a 1968 U.S. Supreme Court decision upholding the constitutionality of a New York statute prohibiting the sale of "girlie" magazines or anything else alleged to be obscene to anyone under seventeen.

Typical of self-conscious obscenity legislation, the New York law prohibited the sale to a minor of any depiction of nudity that included "the showing of * * * female buttocks with less than a full opaque covering, or the showing of the female breast with less than a fully opaque covering of any portion thereof below the top of the nipple. * * * "

Speaking for the Court, Justice Brennan, citing a 1944 case that held that children selling religious pamphlets on street corners violated a state child's labor laws,[201] ruled that the power of the state to control the conduct of children reaches beyond the scope of its authority over adults. There was, moreover, a strong presumption that parents supported the law. Ginsberg v. State of New York, 1 Med.L.Rptr. 1424, 390 U.S. 629 (1968).

Two aspects of *Ginsberg* should be stressed. First, it illustrated the constitutional validity of the concept of variable obscenity since material that would not have been obscene if sold to an adult was held obscene when sold to a juvenile. Second, the case showed that the First Amendment rights of children are more attenuated than those of adults. The state's claims to regulate in the interests of children in the area of obscenity are accorded particular force in the courts. This view still commanded the support of Justice Brennan, as his broad libertarian dissent in *Paris Adult Theatres* in 1973 (this text, p. 757) and his 1982 concurrence in *New York v. Ferber* reflected.

The latter case presented a constitutional dilemma because of its support for an outright ban on the exhibition of films that visually depict sexual conduct by children under sixteen, regardless of whether such presentations are obscene under the *Miller* guidelines (see this text, p. 752). No distinction was made between conduct and publication.

A New York statute [202] defines "sexual performance" as any performance that includes sexual conduct by a child and "sexual conduct" as actual or simulated sexual intercourse, deviate sexual intercourse, sexual bestiality, masturbation, sado-masochistic abuse, or lewd exhibition of the genitals.

Ferber was convicted under the statute, and the Appellate Division of the New York Supreme Court affirmed. The New York Court of Appeals reversed, holding that the statute violated the First Amendment by being both underinclusive and overbroad. The U.S. Supreme Court in effect placed child pornography in a special category outside the complex and imprecise rules that had already been fash-

199. Burgess, *For Permissiveness, With Misgivings*, The New York Times Magazine, July 1, 1973.

200. People v. Mature Enterprises, Inc., 343 N.Y.S.2d 934 (1973).

201. Prince v. Commonwealth of Massachusetts, 321 U.S. 158 (1944).

202. Penal Law, Article 263, § 263.05ff (1977). A similar statute, but applying to children under eighteen (Code § 18.2–374.1), was upheld by Virginia's Supreme Court in Freeman v. Virginia, 8 Med.L.Rptr. 1340, 288 S.E.2d 461 (Va.1982).

ioned for adults, thus removing child pornography from First Amendment protection altogether—at least where the state statute is sufficiently precise.

The Court noted that forty-seven states and the federal government had passed laws specifically directed at child pornography, and at least half of those did not require that the material presented be legally obscene.

While admitting its own struggle with "the intractable obscenity problem," notably the vacillation over a definition of obscenity, the Court remained firm in the position that "the States have a legitimate interest in prohibiting dissemination or exhibition of obscene material when the mode of dissemination carries with it a significant danger of offending the sensibilities of unwilling recipients or of exposure to juveniles." [203] The essentials of the Court's opinion follow.

NEW YORK v. FERBER

___ U.S. ___, 102 S.CT. 3348,
73 L.ED.2D 1113 (1982).

* * *

Justice WHITE delivered the opinion of the Court.

* * *

First. It is evident beyond the need for elaboration that a state's interest in "safeguarding the physical and psychological well being of a minor" is "compelling." Globe Newspapers v. Superior Court, ___ U.S. ___ (1982). "A democratic society rests, for its continuance, upon the healthy well-rounded growth of young people into full maturity as citizens." Prince v. Massachusetts, 321 U.S. 158, 168 (1944). Accordingly, we have sustained legislation aimed at protecting the physical and emotional well-being of youth even when the laws have operated in the sensitive area of constitutionally protected rights. In *Prince v. Massachusetts, supra*, the Court held that a statute prohibiting use of a child to distribute literature on the street was valid notwithstanding the statute's effect on a First Amendment activity. In Ginsberg v. New York, 390 U.S. 629 (1968), we sustained a New York law protecting children from exposure to nonobscene literature. Most recently, we held that the government's interest in the "well-being of its youth" justified special treatment of indecent broadcasting received by adults as well as children. FCC v. Pacifica Foundation, 438 U.S. 726 (1978).

The prevention of sexual exploitation and abuse of children constitutes a government objective of surpassing importance. The legislative findings accompanying passage of the New York laws reflect this concern:

> "There has been a proliferation of children as subjects in sexual performances. The care of children is a sacred trust and should not be abused by those who seek to profit through a commercial network based on the exploitation of children. The public policy of the state demands the protection of children from exploitation through sexual performances." Laws of N.Y., 1977, ch. 910, § 1.

We shall not second-guess this legislative judgment. Respondent has not intimated that we do so. Suffice it to say that virtually all of the States and the United States have passed legislation proscribing the production of or otherwise combatting "child pornography." The legislative judgment, as well as the judgment found in the relevant literature, is that the use of children as subjects of pornographic materials is harmful to the physiological, emotional, and mental health of the child. [There follows a substantial list of social science authority for the foregoing statement.]

---

203. New York v. Ferber, ___ U.S. ___ (1982).

That judgment, we think, easily passes muster under the First Amendment.

Second. The distribution of photographs and films depicting sexual activity by juveniles is intrinsically related to the sexual abuse of children in at least two ways. First, the materials produced are a permanent record of the children's participation and the harm to the child is exacerbated by their circulation. Second, the distribution network for child pornography must be closed if the production of material which requires the sexual exploitation of children is to be effectively controlled. Indeed, there is no serious contention that the legislature was unjustified in believing that it is difficult, if not impossible, to halt the exploitation of children by pursuing only those who produce the photographs and movies. While the production of pornographic materials is a low-profile, clandestine industry, the need to market the resulting products requires a visible apparatus of distribution. The most expeditious if not the only practical method of law enforcement may be to dry up the market for this material by imposing severe criminal penalties on persons selling, advertising, or otherwise promoting the product. Thirty-five States and Congress have concluded that restraints on the distribution of pornographic materials are required in order to effectively combat the problem, and there is a body of literature and testimony to support these legislative conclusions. * * *

Respondent does not contend that the State is unjustified in pursuing those who distribute child pornography. Rather, he argues that it is enough for the State to prohibit the distribution of materials that are legally obscene under the *Miller* test. While some States may find that this approach properly accommodates its interests, it does not follow that the First Amendment prohibits a State from going further. The *Miller* standard, like all general definitions of what may be banned as obscene, does not reflect the State's particular and more compelling interest in prosecuting those who promote the sexual exploitation of children. Thus, the question under the *Miller* test of whether a work, taken as a whole, appeals to the prurient interest of the average person bears no connection to the issue of whether a child has been physically or psychologically harmed in the production of the work. Similarly, a sexually explicit depiction need not be "patently offensive" in order to have required the sexual exploitation of a child for its production. In addition, a work which, taken on the whole, contains serious literary, artistic, political, or scientific value may nevertheless embody the hardest core of child pornography. "It is irrelevant to the child [who has been abused] whether or not the material * * * has a literary, artistic, political, or social value." * * * We therefore cannot conclude that the *Miller* standard is a satisfactory solution to the child pornography problem.

Third. The advertising and selling of child pornography provides an economic motive for and is thus an integral part of the production of such materials, an activity illegal throughout the nation. "It rarely has been suggested that the constitutional freedom for speech and press extends its immunity to speech or writing used as an integral part of conduct in violation of a valid criminal statute." Giboney v. Empire Storage & Ice Co., 336 U.S. 490, 498 (1949). We note that were the statutes outlawing the employment of children in these films and photographs fully effective, and the constitutionality of these laws have not been questioned, the First Amendment implications would be no greater than that presented by laws against distribution: enforceable production laws would leave no child pornography to be marketed.

Fourth. The value of permitting live performances and photographic reproductions of children engaged in lewd sexual conduct is exceedingly modest, if not *de minimis.* We consider it unlikely that visual depictions of children performing sexual acts or lewdly exhibiting their genitals would often constitute an important and necessary part of a literary performance or scientific or educational work. As the trial court in this case observed, if it were necessary for literary or artistic value, a person over the statutory age who perhaps looked younger could be utilized. Simulation outside of the prohibition of the statute could provide another alternative. Nor is there is any question here of censoring a particular literary theme or portrayal of sexual activity. The First Amendment interest is limited to that of rendering the portrayal somewhat more "realistic" by utilizing or photographing children.

Fifth. Recognizing and classifying child pornography as a category of material outside the protection of the First Amendment is not incompatible with our earlier decisions. "The question whether speech is, or is not protected by the First Amendment often depends on the content of the speech. * * * It is the content of an utterance that determines whether it is a protected epithet or an unprotected 'fighting comment.'" *Young v. American Mini Theatres*, [427 U.S. 50,] at 66. * * * Leaving aside the special considerations when public officials are the target, New York Times v. Sullivan, 376 U.S. 254 (1964), a libelous publication is not protected by the Constitution. Beauharnais v. Illinois, 343 U.S. 250 (1952). Thus, it is not rare that a content-based classification of speech has been accepted because it may be appropriately generalized that within the confines of the given classification, the evil to be restricted so overwhelmingly outweighs the expressive interests, if any, at stake, that no process of case-by-case adjudication is required. When a definable class of material, such as that covered by § 263.15, bears so heavily and pervasively on the welfare of children engaged in its production, we think the balance of competing interests is clearly struck and that it is permissible to consider these materials as without the protection of the First Amendment.

* * *

Because § 263.15 is not substantially overbroad, it is unnecessary to consider its application to material that does not depict sexual conduct of a type that New York may restrict consistent with the First Amendment. As applied to Paul Ferber and to others who distribute similar material, the statute does not violate the First Amendment as applied to the States through the Fourteenth. The decision of the New York Court of Appeals is reversed and the case is remanded to that Court for further proceedings not inconsistent with this opinion.

So ordered.

COMMENT

1. Justice Brennan, in a concurrence joined by Justice Marshall, agreed with the Court that the tiny fraction of material of serious artistic, scientific, or educational value that could conceivably fall within the reach of the New York statute was insufficient to justify striking the law on grounds of overbreadth. But on First Amendment grounds Brennan was not so sure. The constitutional value of depictions of children that are in themselves serious contributions to art, literature, or science could be substantial. And he had to assume harm to children to agree with the Court in the case.

In a separate concurrence, Justice Stevens solidified Brennan's reservation: "The question whether a specific act of communication is protected by the First Amendment always requires some consideration of both its content and its context." Nevertheless, while he disagreed with the Court that the speech reached by the statute was totally without First Amendment protection, Stevens did agree that such marginal speech did not warrant the extraordinary protection afforded by the overbreadth doctrine, a doctrine analyzed at length in the Court's opinion but not included in our excerpt.

Was the Court too quick to disqualify a whole category of speech because of what it perceived as a countervailing social value? In Cooper v. Mitchell Brothers, 7 Med.L.Rptr. 2273, 454 U.S. 849 (1981), the Court decided that states need *not* use a strict standard of proof, in this case "beyond a reasonable doubt," in a public nuisance abatement action by a city against adult theaters. The reasoning was that the "beyond a reasonable doubt" standard of proof was not required in civil proceedings. The case was decided without full written briefs and oral arguments. Justices Stevens, Brennan, and Marshall dissented vigorously. See Justice Brennan's concurrence in McKinney v. Alabama, 1 Med.L.Rptr. 1516, 424 U.S. 669 (1976):

"The hazards to First Amendment freedoms inhering in the regulation of obscenity require that even in * * * a civil proceeding, the State comply with the more exacting standard of proof beyond a reasonable doubt."

2. In 1976 an additional complexity had been added to film censorship when the Supreme Court in Young v. American Mini Theatres, Inc., 1 Med.L.Rptr. 1151, 427 U.S. 50 (1976), upholding a Detroit ordinance, called upon lower courts to decide not only which movies are "obscene" under state and local laws but also which are "adult" within the meaning of a local *zoning* ordinance. In Detroit, "adult" was defined as films depicting "specified sexual activities" or "specified anatomical areas." The specifications were listed.

Although the Detroit ordinance failed to meet *Freedman*'s requirements for judicial review, Justice Stevens held for the Court that a relaxation of the standards for determining obscenity would be acceptable where there was no criminal sanction and dissemination of the material was not being prohibited altogether.

The *Young* case illustrated and encouraged the use of a zoning approach to obscenity regulation. Requiring dispersion of "adult" theaters throughout the city was upheld despite the argument that such legislation constituted an impermissible regulation on the basis of content. The Court viewed the zoning regulation as merely a permissible place regulation. Since access to "adult" theaters was not prohibited and the issue was merely where to place them, the Court declared that there was no direct First Amendment infringement.

Since *Young,* the New Mexico Supreme Court has struck down as unconstitutionally vague a municipal ordinance that prohibited location of adult bookstores, movie theaters, or newsracks within 1,000 feet of a "residential area." Harris Books v. Santa Fe, 8 Med.L.Rptr. 1913, 647 P.2d 868 (N.M.1982).

On the other hand, an ordinance prohibiting exhibition or sale of sexually explicit motion pictures within 100 yards of a church, public school, or residential area was said, citing *Young*, not to violate the First Amendment. Avalon Cinema Corp. v. Thompson, 7 Med.L.Rptr. 2059, 658 F.2d 555 (8th Cir. 1981), reversed 667 F.2d 659. The ordinance, however, was later attacked successfully as an unsupported response to the imminent opening of North Little Rock's first "adult" movie theater. No social science evidence for presumed neighborhood deterioration was cited, said the court. As in Schad v. Borough of Mount Ephraim, 7 Med.L.Rptr. 1426, 452 U.S. 61 (1981) and Marco Lounge v. Federal Heights, 7 Med.L.Rptr. 1229, 625 P.2d 982 (Colo.1981), zoning ordinances seeking to ban all sexually explicit entertainment, even that which was not obscene, did not state sufficient countervailing state interest. Mere nudity is not necessarily obscene.[204] Despite its hard core features appealing to prurient interest, the Louisiana Supreme Court held *Penthouse* magazine not to be obscene when taken as a whole.[205] The North Little Rock ordinance, said the Eighth Circuit Court of Appeals, was clearly a content-based regulation of protected speech. It did not limit itself to obscenity. Avalon Cinema Corp. v. Thompson, 7 Med.L.Rptr. 2588, 667 F.2d 659 (8th Cir. 1981).

"Redeeming Social Value": The *Roth-Memoirs* Standard

1. In *Jacobellis*, Justice Brennan made the test—"utterly without redeeming social importance"—the primary standard against which censurable obscenity would be measured. The emergence of this test and its reformulation into a broader and more liberal "social value" rule are recounted in a delightfully literate book by Charles Rembar, the attorney who directed "Fanny Hill" on her long and perilous journey to the United States Supreme Court.[206]

That journey began in 1821 when "Fanny's" conviction in a Massachusetts court may have been America's first obscenity case. Court appearances followed many years later in New York, New Jersey, and again in Massachusetts. In Massachusetts the book itself was put on trial in an equity suit brought by the state's attorney general. Rembar, attorney for publisher G.P. Putnam's Sons, focused his efforts on getting expert witnesses to testify on the "social value" of the work.

Gerald Gardiner had done the same for "Lady Chatterley" in England. Defense witnesses included Dame Rebecca West, the Bishop of Woolwich, Lord Francis Williams, E.M. Forster, C.D. Lewis, Dilys Powell, and Norman St. John-Stevas. "Lady Chatterley" was acquitted.[207]

It was Rembar's intention and his legal strategy to get the Court to substitute "social value" for "social importance." "Social value" would be a less restrictive test. "Importance," Rembar argued, has other meanings—not synonymous with value—that would impose a tougher standard. "Some value" might not be too hard to show; "some importance" could be something else again.

Rembar sought to replace the "prurient interest" test of *Roth* with his more meaningful "social value" standard. "Social value," he explained in his brief to the Court, "provides a criterion that can be objectively applied, and by a process familiar to the law. Judges and jurors are no longer committed to a total reliance on their individual responses. Traditional judicial techniques come into play. There is evidence to be considered." [208]

The measure of Rembar's success is found in Justice BRENNAN'S plurality opinion for the Court in the "Fanny Hill" case.

A BOOK ETC. v. ATTORNEY GENERAL OF COMMONWEALTH OF MASS.

383 U.S. 413, 86 S.CT. 975, 16 L.ED.2D 1 (1966).

* * *

204. Smith v. Indiana, 6 Med.L.Rptr. 2344, 413 N.E.2d 652 (Ind.1980).

205. Louisiana v. Walden Book, 6 Med.L.Rptr. 1696, 386 So.2d 342 (La.1980).

206. Rembar, *The End of Obscenity* (1968).

207. Rolph (ed.), *The Trial of Lady Chatterley: Regina v. Penguin Books Limited* (1961). See also, Note, *The Use of Expert Testimony in Obscenity Litigation*, 1965 Wis.L.Rev. 113.

208. Rembar, op. cit., 440.

* * * At the hearing before a justice of the Superior Court, which was conducted under § 28F, "in accordance with the usual course of proceedings in equity," the court received the book in evidence and also, as allowed by the section, heard the testimony of experts [2] and accepted other evidence, such as book reviews, in order to assess the literary, cultural, or educational character of the book. This constituted the entire evidence, as neither side availed itself of the opportunity provided by the section to introduce evidence "as to the manner and form of its publication, advertisement, and distribution." The trial justice * * * adjudged *Memoirs* obscene and declared that the book "is not entitled to the protection of the First and Fourteenth Amendments. * * * " The Massachusetts Supreme Judicial Court affirmed the decree. * * * We reverse. * * [T]he sole question before the state courts was whether *Memoirs* satisfies the test of obscenity established in Roth v. United States.

We define obscenity in *Roth* in the following terms: "[W]hether to the average person, applying contemporary community standards, the dominant theme of the material taken as a whole appeals to prurient interest." Under this definition, as elaborated in subsequent cases, three elements must coalesce: it must be established that (a) *the dominant theme of the material taken as a whole appeals to a prurient interest in sex*; (b) *the material is patently offensive because it affronts contemporary community standards relating to the description or representation of sexual matters*; and (c) *the material is utterly without redeeming social value.* [Emphasis added.]

The Supreme Judicial Court purported to apply the *Roth* definition of obscenity and held all three criteria satisfied. We need not consider the claim that the court erred in concluding that *Memoirs* satisfied the prurient appeal and patent offensiveness criteria; for reversal is required because the court misinterpreted the social value criterion. * * *

The Supreme Judicial Court erred in holding that a book need not be "unqualifiedly worthless before it can be deemed obscene." A book cannot be proscribed unless it is found to be *utterly* without redeeming social value. This is so even though the book is found to possess the requisite prurient appeal and to be patently offensive. Each of the three federal constitutional criteria is to be applied independently; the social value of the book can neither be weighed against nor canceled by its prurient appeal or patent offensiveness. Hence, even on the view of the court below that *Memoirs* possessed only a modicum of social value, its judgment must be reversed as being founded on an erroneous interpretation of a federal constitutional standard.

It does not necessarily follow from this reversal that a determination that *Memoirs* is obscene in the constitutional sense would be improper under all circumstances. On the premise, which we have no occasion to assess, that *Memoirs* has the

2. One of the witnesses testified in part as follows: "Cleland is part of what I should call this cultural battle that is going on in the 18th century, a battle between a restricted Puritan, moralistic ethic that attempts to suppress freedom of the spirit, freedom of the flesh, and this element is competing with a freer attitude towards life, a more generous attitude towards life, a more wholesome attitude towards life, and this very attitude that is manifested in Fielding's great novel 'Tom Jones' is also evident in Cleland's novel. * * * [Richardson's] 'Pamela' is the story of a young country girl; [his] 'Clarissa' is the story of a woman trapped in a house of prostitution. Obviously, then Cleland takes both these themes, the country girl, her initiation into life and into experience, and the story of a woman in a house of prostitution, and what hc simply does is to take the situation and reverse the moral standards. Richardson believed that chastity was the most important thing in the world; Cleland and Fielding obviously did not and thought there were more important significant moral values."

requisite prurient appeal and is patently offensive, but has only a minimum of social value, the circumstances of production, sale, and publicity are relevant in determining whether or not the publication or distribution of the book is constitutionally protected. Evidence that the book was commercially exploited for the sake of prurient appeal, to the exclusion of all other values, might justify the conclusion that the book was utterly without redeeming social importance. It is not that in such a setting the social value test is relaxed so as to dispense with the requirement that a book be *utterly* devoid of social value, but rather that, as we elaborate in Ginzburg v. United States, where the purveyor's sole emphasis is on the sexually provocative aspects of his publications, a court could accept his evaluation at its face value. In this proceeding, however, the courts were asked to judge the obscenity of *Memoirs* in the abstract, and the declaration of obscenity was neither aided nor limited by a specific set of circumstances of production, sale, and publicity. All possible uses of the book must therefore be considered, and the mere risk that the book might be exploited by panderers because it so pervasively treats sexual matters cannot alter the fact—given the view of the Massachusetts court attributing to *Memoirs* a modicum of literary and historical value—that the book will have redeeming social importance in the hands of those who publish or distribute it on the basis of that value.

Reversed.

COMMENT

1. Justice Brennan's three-element test would hold the tottering edifice of obscenity law in place for the next eight years. But the Court did something else that day: it decided *Ginzburg v. United States*, a case that permitted Brennan to add a fourth element to his three-part test.

The Court in *Ginzburg* upheld a five-year sentence and a $28,000 fine against Ralph Ginzburg, publisher of *Eros*, a glossy, well-designed magazine (now a collector's item) devoted to relatively sophisticated sexual themes. Ginzburg and his attorneys had not paid heed to Chief Justice Warren's admonition in *Roth* that it is the *conduct* of the purveyor that ought to be punished. Ginzburg's publications were not obscene by the Court's own standards, but a majority of the justices thought that he promoted them as if they were; he defined their "social value." If books cannot be punished, said the Court, booksellers can, especially if they display what Brennan referred to as the "leer of the sensualist."

GINZBURG v. UNITED STATES

383 U.S. 463, 86 S.CT. 942, 16 L.ED.2D 31 (1966).

Justice BRENNAN delivered the opinion of the Court. * * * In the cases in which this Court has decided obscenity questions since *Roth*, it has regarded the materials as sufficient in themselves for the determination of the question. In the present case, however, the prosecution charged the offense in the context of the circumstances of production, sale, and publicity and assumed that, standing alone, the publications themselves might not be obscene. We agree that the question of obscenity may include consideration of the setting in which the publications were presented as an aid to determining the question of obscenity, and assume without deciding that the prosecution could not have succeeded otherwise. * * * [W]e view the publications against a background of commercial exploitation of erotica solely for the sake of their prurient appeal. The record in that regard amply supports the decision of the trial judge that the mailing of all three publications offended the statute.

The three publications were *EROS,* a hard-cover magazine of expensive format; *Liaison,* a bi-weekly newsletter; and *The Housewife's Handbook on Selective Promiscuity* (hereinafter the *Handbook*), a short book. The issue of *EROS* specified in the indictment, * * * contains 15 articles and photo-essays on the subject of love, sex, and sexual relations. The specified issue of *Liaison* * * * contains a prefatory "Letter from the Editors" announcing its dedication to "keeping sex an art and preventing it from becoming a science." The remainder of the issue consists of digests of two articles concerning sex and sexual relations which had earlier appeared in professional journals and a report of an interview with a psychotherapist who favors the broadest license in sexual relationships. * * * The *Handbook* purports to be a sexual autobiography detailing with complete candor the author's sexual experiences from age 3 to age 36. The text includes, and prefatory and concluding sections of the book elaborate, her views on such subjects as sex education of children, laws regulating private consensual adult sexual practices, and the equality of women in sexual relationships. It was claimed at trial that women would find the book valuable, for example as a marriage manual or as an aid to the sex education of their children.

Besides testimony as to the merit of the material, there was abundant evidence to show that each of the accused publications was originated or sold as stock in trade of the sordid business of pandering —"the business of purveying textual or graphic matter openly advertised to appeal to the erotic interest of their customers." *EROS* early sought mailing privileges from the postmasters of Intercourse and Blue Ball, Pennsylvania. The trial court found the obvious, that these hamlets were chosen only for the value their names would have in furthering petitioners' efforts to sell their publications on the basis of salacious appeal; the facilities of the post offices were inadequate to handle the anticipated volume of mail, and the privileges were denied. Mailing privileges were then obtained from the postmaster of Middlesex, New Jersey. *EROS* and *Liaison* thereafter mailed several million circulars soliciting subscriptions from that post office; over 5,500 copies of the *Handbook* were mailed.

The "leer of the sensualist" also permeates the advertising for the three publications. The circulars sent for *EROS* and *Liaison* stressed the sexual candor of the respective publications, and openly boasted that the publishers would take full advantage of what they regarded as an unrestricted license allowed by law in the expression of sex and sexual matters. The advertising for the *Handbook*, apparently mailed from New York, consisted almost entirely of a reproduction of the introduction of the book, written by one Dr. Albert Ellis. [*The American Sexual Tragedy,* 1962.] Although he alludes to the book's informational value and its putative therapeutic usefulness, his remarks are preoccupied with the book's sexual imagery. The solicitation was indiscriminate, not limited to those, such as physicians or psychiatrists, who might independently discern the book's therapeutic worth. * * *

This evidence, in our view, was relevant in determining the ultimate question of obscenity and, in the context of this record, serves to resolve all ambiguity and doubt. The deliberate representation of petitioners' publications as erotically arousing, for example, stimulated the reader to accept them as prurient; he looks for titillation, not for saving intellectual content. Similarly, such representation would tend to force public confrontation with the potentially offensive aspects of the work; the brazenness of such an appeal heightens the offensiveness of the publications to those who are offended by such material. And the circumstances of presentation and dissemination of material are equally relevant to determining whether social importance claimed for material in the courtroom was, in the circumstances, pretense or reality—whether it was the basis upon which it was traded in the market place or a spurious claim for litigation purposes. Where the purveyor's sole emphasis is on the sexually provocative aspects of his publications, that fact may be decisive in the determination of obscenity. Certainly in a prosecution which, as here, does not necessarily imply suppression of the materials involved, the fact that they originate or are used as a subject of pandering is relevant to the application of the *Roth* test. * * *

We perceive no threat to First Amendment guarantees in thus holding that in close cases evidence of pandering may be probative with respect to the nature of the material in question and thus satisfy the *Roth* test. No weight is ascribed to the fact that petitioners have profited from the sale of publications which we have assumed but do not hold cannot themselves be adjudged obscene in the abstract; to sanction consideration of this fact might indeed induce self-censorship, and offend the frequently stated principle that commercial activity, in itself, is no justification for narrowing the protection of expression secured by the First Amendment. Rather, the fact that each of these publications was created or exploited entirely on the basis of its appeal to prurient interests strengthens the conclusion that the transactions here were sales of illicit merchandise, not sales of constitutionally protected matter. A conviction for mailing obscene publications, but explained in part by the presence of this element, does not necessarily suppress the materials in question, nor chill their proper distribution for a proper use. Nor should it inhibit the enterprise of others seeking through serious endeavor to advance human knowledge or understanding in science, literature, or art. All that will have been determined is that questionable publications are obscene in a context which brands them as obscene as that term is defined in *Roth*—a use inconsistent with any claim to the shelter of the First Amendment.

* * *

Affirmed.

COMMENT

1. "Prurient interest" obviously was to remain a central element in adjudging obscenity. More important, the act of pandering somehow superseded any consideration of the intrinsic merits of the publication. "[I]f the First Amendment means anything," said Justice Stewart in dissent, "it means that a man cannot be sent to prison merely for distributing publications which offend a judge's esthetic sensibilities, mine or any other's."

There is a Catch-22 quality about *Ginzburg.* His publications were themselves protected by the First Amendment for, whatever they were, they were not "patently offensive," that is, hard core pornography. Ginzburg's crime was advertising them. "Commercial exploitation" and "titillation," longtime givens in American selling, had suddenly become crimes, and crimes for which Ginzburg was not charged.

The Court's affirmation of Ginzburg's five-year sentence (later reduced to three) sent shock waves through the publishing world.[209] Brennan's new test did not seem to meet minimal standards of due process. Justice Harlan called it "an astonishing piece of judicial improvisation." Rembar compared it with the ancient legal notion of *estoppel*, the idea that you ought to be held to what you say. If a publisher implies that his books are obscene, the Supreme Court will take him at his word. If he guarantees that his materials will cata-

---

209. Epstein, *The Obscenity Business* Atlantic, August 1966; Rembar, *The End of Obscenity*, 484–490.

lyze certain glandular juices, then that is in fact what they do.

Ironically the eroticism of the mid-sixties is not the eroticism of the eighties. In retrospect Ginzburg's incarceration seems unjust and ludicrous.

After ten years of appeals and legal maneuvering Ginzburg was committed to a federal prison where he served eight months of his three-year sentence. Through it all, fellow publishers remained frighteningly silent. After his release in October 1972, Ginzburg vowed to gain vindication in the Supreme Court, a Court which he then held in contempt.[210]

2. Between *Roth* and *Ginzburg* the Court was inclined not to uphold convictions for obscenity. *Ginzburg* opened the gates to a torrent of confusion. Some interpreted the ruling as a "frantic effort to rebalance the scales in favor of the censors after a decade of tipping them in favor of free expression."[211] Was the public to be denied its own assessment of artistic value because a publisher's promotional material was vulgar? How would pandering (obscenity *per quod*) affect the intrinsic merits of a book, a magazine, or a photograph?

"Prurient interest" was equally confounding. Do or do not sexually mature persons have prurient interests? The Kinsey Institute had concluded that "the impulse to seek pleasurable sexual visual stimuli is statistically, biologically, and psychologically normal."[212] Censors, as usual, were reserving prurient experiences for themselves—"privileged prurience," Eliot Fremont-Smith called it—or "like their Puritan ancestors they were objecting to bear-baiting not because it gave pain to the bear but because it gave pleasure to the spectators."[213]

And there was no uniform response to the "patent offensiveness" of hard core pornography. Half of the authors, critics, and university dons who engaged in debate in *The Times* literary supplement over the literary merits of Williams Burrough's *Naked Lunch* thought it a masterpiece; the other half considered it arcane trash!

Only the "social value" test seemed useful. If they felt strongly enough about work, reputable "experts" would testify, and courts could be influenced.

"As to whether the book has any redeeming social value," said a Massachusetts court in one of a number of *Naked Lunch* cases, "* * * it appears that a substantial and intelligent group in the community believes the book to be of some literary significance. Although we are not bound by the opinion of others concerning the book, we cannot ignore the serious acceptance of it by so many persons in the literary community."[214]

3. The Court's brief *per curiam* opinion in Redrup v. New York, 386 U.S. 767 (1967), reversing a conviction for selling obscene books and magazines unobtrusively to willing adults, provided a helpful map of the twisted path trod by the Warren Court. *Roth* and its aftermath had generated a Babel of opinions. The *Redrup* map contained the following landmarks.

The *Roth-Memoirs* test, based on the influential 1957 case and the *Fanny Hill* case of 1966, provided a coalescent, three-element definition of obscenity. Absent any one, and there would be no finding of punishable obscenity.

a. The dominant theme of the material taken as a whole must appeal to a prurient interest in sex;

210. Ginzburg, *Castrated: My Eight Months in Prison*, The New York Times Magazine, Dec. 3, 1972.

211. Note, *The Substantive Law of Obscenity: An Adventure in Quicksand*, 13 N.Y.L.F. 124 (1967).

212. Kinsey Institute for Sex Research, *Sex Offenders*, 403, 671, 678 (1965).

213. Freund, 42 F.R.D. 499 (1967).

214. Attorney-General v. A Book Named "Naked Lunch", 218 N.E.2d 571–572 (Mass.1966).

b. The material must be patently offensive because it affronts contemporary community standards relating to the description or representation of sexual matters, and the community standards were to be national rather than local;

c. The material must be utterly without redeeming social value.

The primary test could be overridden if—

a. there were appeals made to children or juveniles (*Ginsberg*);

b. there was pandering or a commercial exploitation of the natural interest in sex (*Ginzburg*); or

c. there was an assault upon personal privacy through the mail or by other public means. (*Rowan*)

Redrup led to scores of *per curiam* reversals of obscenity convictions, and it tidied up some of the mess left by earlier cases.

4. In 1969 the Court decided Stanley v. Georgia, 394 U.S. 557 (1969), a case of freedom "for" rather than freedom "from" obscenity. Federal and state agents had entered Stanley's home with search warrants to look for evidence of bookmaking activity. They found none. But they did find three reels of 8 mm. film in a bedroom dresser drawer, and with Stanley's screen and projector they amused themselves for a few hours. Stanley was then arrested, charged with the possession of obscene matter, and convicted.

A unanimous Supreme Court reversed. "If the First Amendment means anything," said Justice Marshall for the Court, "it means that a [s]tate has no business telling a man, sitting alone in his own house, what books he may read or what films he may watch. Our whole constitutional heritage rebels at the thought of giving government the power to control men's minds." Marshall did not explain, though, how one might legally procure obscene films.[215]

In 1971 the Court backed off from *Stanley*, or at least distinguished it in two cases. In United States v. Reidel, 402 U.S. 351 (1971), the Court through Justice White upheld the constitutionality of a federal obscenity statute prohibiting the commercial mailing of obscene material even to willing adults. *Stanley* differed from other obscenity cases because it involved constitutionally protected privacy—the privacy of the home. No such zone of privacy was involved in *Reidel.* There was no First Amendment right to receive obscene publications as *Stanley* might have implied.

Stanley and *Reidel*, when seen together, produced an odd result. Material once obtained and brought into the home was safe from obscenity prosecution, but the retailer who sold it to the householder would be fair game.

In United States v. Thirty-Seven (37) Photographs, 402 U.S. 363 (1971), the question was whether *Stanley* permitted the government to seize allegedly obscene materials intended for purely private use from the luggage of a returning tourist. After construing the relevant federal law so as to read into it time limits for its application consistent with the Court's fourteen-day requirement in *Freedman v. Maryland*, the majority concluded that *Stanley* did not prevent Congress from removing obscene materials from the channels of incoming foreign commerce. A port of entry, said Justice White, is not a traveler's home.

Capturing the essential absurdity of the situation, Justice Douglas dissented in both cases:

215. The Arkansas Supreme Court held in 1979 that the First Amendment was violated by a state law that imposed criminal penalties for mere private possession of obscene materials. Buck v. Arkansas, 5 Med.L.Rptr. 1030, 578 S.W.2d 579 (Ark.1979).

> It would seem to me that if a citizen had a right to possess "obscene" material in the privacy of his home he should have the right to receive it voluntarily through the mail. Certainly when a man legally purchases such material abroad he should be able to bring it with him through customs to read later in his home. * * *

This construction of *Stanley*, said Douglas, could only apply to a man who writes salacious books in his attic, prints them in his basement, and reads them in his living room.

5. One reason for the fragility of the Warren Court's obscenity doctrine, as enunciated by Justice Brennan, was Justice Harlan's notion in *Roth* that state autonomy in dealing with the question need not necessarily be bound by the federal rule.

By 1969 the composition of the Court had changed, and its new members were being influenced by the wise and aging Harlan. In Hoyt v. Minnesota, 339 U.S. 524 (1969), Justice Harry Blackmun in a dissent in which he was joined by Chief Justice Warren Burger reflected this influence. Said Blackmun:

> I am not persuaded that the First and Fourteenth Amendments necessarily prescribe a national and uniform measure—rather than one capable of some flexibility and resting on concepts of reasonableness—of what each of our several States constitutionally may do to regulate obscene products within its borders. * * * Six of the seven Justices of the Supreme Court of that [s]tate, citing *Redrup v. New York,* and other decisions of this Court, have identified the offending material "for what it is," have described it as dealing "with filth for the sake of filth," and have held it obscene as a matter of law. * * * I cannot agree that the Minnesota trial court and those six justices are so obviously misguided in their holding that they are to be summarily reversed on the authority of *Redrup.* At this still, for me, unsettled state in the development of the state law of obscenity in the federal constitutional context I find myself generally in accord with the views expressed by Mr. Justice Harlan. * * *

The Warren Court edifice, built on the foundation stone of *Roth,* was beginning to crumble.

An Injection of Sanity: The Lockhart Report

1. The single most comprehensive and systematic study of obscenity and its effect is the *1970 Report of the Presidential Commission on Obscenity and Pornography* (New York: Bantam Books), chaired by William B. Lockhart, former dean of the University of Minnesota Law School.

Considering the value of this document, which deserves to be read in its entirety, it is disappointing that it was rejected by a president and a Congress—in the Senate by resolution—and given only scant attention by the U.S. Supreme Court.

Facts developed by the commission did not support widely held assumptions. Although cautious about its conclusions, the commission could find little evidence that obscene books or motion pictures incite youth or adults to criminal conduct, sexual deviance, or emotional disturbances. And it hoped that its own modest pioneering work in empirical research would help to open the way for more extensive and long-term research.

In the context of constitutional law the commission rejected the three elements of the *Roth-Memoirs* definition—prurient interest, patent offensiveness, and redeeming social value—as vague and highly subjective esthetic, psychological, and moral judgments providing no meaningful guidance for law enforcement officials, juries, or courts. In its inconsistent application the test would interfere with constitutionally protected expression. In addition, public opinion would not, in the final analysis, support legal prohibition of adult use of obscene materials.

"Americans," the commission added, "deeply value the right of each individual to determine for himself what books he wishes to read and what pictures or films he wishes to see. Our traditions of free speech and press also value and protect the right of writers, publishers, and booksellers to serve the diverse interests of the public. The spirit and letter of our Constitution tell us that government should not seek to interfere with these rights unless a clear threat of harm makes that course imperative. Moreover, the possibility of the misuse of general obscenity statutes prohibiting distributions of books and films to adults constitutes a continuing threat to the free communication of ideas among Americans—one of the most important foundations of our liberties."

The commission recommended the repeal of all existing federal, state, and local legislation prohibiting or interfering with consensual distribution of obscene materials to adults.

The commission did not reject the secondary tests that had attached themselves to *Roth-Memoirs*—appeals to the young, pandering, and assaults on personal privacy. Statutes protecting children were supported by the commission on the grounds that insufficient research had been done on the effects of exposure of children to sexually explicit stimuli. Also there were strong ethical feelings against experimenting with children in this realm. The commission respected the stated opinions of parents on the issue of obscenity.

Statutory proposals from the commission covered only pictorial material since it could think of no constitutionally safe way to control the distribution of books and other textual materials. Broadcast material would also be exempted because of adequate self-regulation and supervision by the Federal Communications Commission.

Additional support for the secondary tests was found in the commission's endorsement of state and local laws prohibiting public displays of sexually explicit materials and federal laws dealing with the mailing of unsolicited advertising of a sexually explicit nature. The commission was sensitive to unwanted intrusions upon individual privacy, but here again it would exempt written materials and broadcast programming.

Perhaps the most controversial of all its proposals was that of a massive sex education program beginning in the schools.

Ironically, as it was to turn out, the commission advised against the elimination by Congress of federal judicial jurisdiction in the obscenity areas as a response to vocal citizen criticism of the results of that jurisdiction. "Freedom in many vital areas," said the commission, "frequently depends upon the ability of the judiciary to follow the Constitution rather than strong popular sentiment."

Burger Court Revisionism: The *Roth-Miller* Standard

1. The Warren Court obscenity edifice came crashing down on June 21, 1973 when the Nixon appointees joined by Justice Byron White constituted a five-man majority in five cases in which Chief Justice Burger delivered the opinion of the Court.

The cases are Miller v. State of California, 1 Med.L.Rptr. 1441, 413 U.S. 15 (1973) (mass mailing campaign to advertise illustrated "adult" books); Paris Adult Theatre I et al. v. Slaton, 1 Med.L.Rptr. 1454, 413 U.S. 49 (1973) (commercial showing of two "adult" films); United States v. Orito, 413 U.S. 139 (1973) (interstate transportation of lewd, lascivious, and filthy materials); Kaplan v. State of California, 413 U.S. 115 (1973) (proprietor of "adult" bookstore selling unillustrated book containing repetitively descriptive material of an explicitly sexual nature); and United States v. 12

200-Ft. Reels of Super 8mm. Film et al., 413 U.S. 123 (1973) (importation of obscene matter for personal use and possession).

Essentially the cases reject the "utterly without redeeming social value" element of the *Roth-Memoirs* test, substituting the words "does not have serious literary, artistic, political or scientific value." Secondly, the contemporary community standards against which the jury is to measure prurient appeal and patent offensiveness are to be the standards of the *state or local community.* The trend toward permissiveness had been reversed by the first majority agreement on an obscenity definition since *Roth* in 1957. Justices Brennan, Douglas, Marshall, and Stewart dissented in all five cases.

The most important of the opinions are Chief Justice Burger's opinion for the Court in *Miller*, outlining the new standards, and Justice Brennan's masterful review of sixteen years of judicial tribulation in his *Paris Adult Theatre* dissent.

MILLER v. STATE OF CALIFORNIA

413 U.S. 15, 93 S.CT. 2607, 37 L.ED.2D 419 (1973).

Chief Justice BURGER delivered the opinion of the Court.

* * *

This case involves the application of a state's criminal obscenity statute to a situation in which sexually explicit materials have been thrust by aggressive sales action upon unwilling recipients who had in no way indicated any desire to receive such materials. This court has recognized that the states have a legitimate interest in prohibiting dissemination or exhibition of obscene material when the mode of dissemination carries with it a significant danger of offending the sensibilities of unwilling recipients or of exposure to juveniles. It is in this context that we are called on to define the standards which must be used to identify obscene material that a State may regulate without infringing the First Amendment as applicable to the States through the Fourteenth Amendment.

* * *

While *Roth* presumed "obscenity" to be "utterly without redeeming social value," *Memoirs* required that to prove obscenity it must be affirmatively established that the material is "*utterly* without redeeming social value." Thus, even as they repeated the words of *Roth*, the *Memoirs* plurality produced a drastically altered test that called on the prosecution to prove a negative, i.e., that the material was "*utterly* without redeeming social value"—a burden virtually impossible to discharge under our criminal standards of proof. Such considerations caused Justice Harlan to wonder if the "*utterly* without redeeming social value" test had any meaning at all.

* * *

Apart from the initial formulation in the *Roth* case, no majority of the Court has at any given time been able to agree on a standard to determine what constitutes obscene, pornographic material subject to regulation under the States' police power. We have seen "a variety of views among the members of the Court unmatched in any other course of constitutional adjudication." This is not remarkable, for in the area of freedom of speech and press the courts must always remain sensitive to any infringement on genuinely serious literary, artistic, political, or scientific expression. This is an area in which there are few eternal verities.

The case we now review was tried on the theory that California Penal Code § 311 approximately incorporates the three-stage *Memoirs* test, *supra*. But now *the Memoirs test has been abandoned as unworkable by its author*[4] *and no member of the Court today supports the Memoirs formulation.* [Emphasis added.]

This much has been categorically settled by the Court, that obscene material is unprotected by the First Amendment. The First and Fourteenth Amendments have never been treated as absolutes. We acknowledge, however, the inherent dangers of undertaking to regulate any form of expression. State statutes designed to regulate obscene materials must be carefully limited. *As a result, we now confine the permissible scope of such regulation to works which depict or describe sexual conduct. That conduct must be specifically defined by the applicable state law, as written or authoritatively construed. A state offense must also be limited to works which, taken as a whole, appeal to the prurient interest in sex, which portray sexual conduct in a patently offensive way, and which, taken as a whole, do not have serious literary, artistic, political, or scientific value.* [Emphasis added.]

The basic guidelines for the trier of fact must be: (a) whether "the average person, applying contemporary community standards" would find that the work, taken as a whole, appeals to the prurient interest, (b) whether the work depicts or describes, in a patently offensive way, sexual conduct specifically defined by the applicable state law, and (c) whether the work, taken as a whole, lacks serious literary, artistic, political, or scientific value. We do not adopt as a constitutional standard the "*utterly* without redeeming social value" test of *Memoirs v. Massachusetts*; that concept has never commanded the adherence of more than three Justices at one time. If a state law that regulates obscene material is thus limited, as written or construed, the First Amendment values applicable to the States through the Fourteenth Amendment are adequately protected by the ultimate power of appellate courts to conduct an independent review of constitutional claims when necessary.

We emphasize that it is not our function to propose regulatory schemes for the States. That must await their concrete legislative efforts. It is possible, however, to give a few plain examples of what a state statute could define for regulation under the second part (b) of the standard announced in this opinion, supra:

a. Patently offensive representations or descriptions of ultimate sexual acts, normal or perverted, actual or simulated.

b. Patently offensive representation or descriptions of masturbation, excretory functions, and lewd exhibition of the genitals.

Sex and nudity may not be exploited without limit by films or pictures exhibited or sold in places of public accommodation any more than live sex and nudity can be exhibited or sold without limit in such public places. At a minimum, prurient, patently offensive depiction or description of sexual conduct must have serious literary, artistic, political, or scientific value to merit First Amendment protection. For example, medical books for the education of physicians and related personnel necessarily use graphic illustrations and descriptions of human anatomy. In resolving the inevitably sensitive questions of fact and law, we must continue to rely on the jury system, accompanied by the safeguards that judges, rules of evidence, presumption of innocence and other protective features provide, as we do with rape, murder and a host of other offenses against society and its individual members.

* * *

Under the holdings announced today, no one will be subject to prosecution for the sale or exposure of obscene materials

4. See the dissenting opinion of Justice Brennan in Paris Adult Theatre I v. Slaton, 413 U.S. 49 (1973).

unless these materials depict or describe patently offensive "hard core" sexual conduct specifically defined by the regulating state law, as written or construed. We are satisfied that these specific prerequisites will provide fair notice to a dealer in such materials that his public and commercial activities may bring prosecution.

* * *

It is certainly true that the absence, since *Roth,* of a single majority view of this Court as to proper standards for testing obscenity has placed a strain on both state and federal courts. *But today, for the first time since Roth was decided in 1957, a majority of this Court has agreed on concrete guidelines to isolate "hard core" pornography from expression protected by the First Amendment.* Now we may abandon the casual practice of Redrup v. New York, and attempt to provide positive guidance to the federal and state courts alike. [Emphasis added.]

This may not be an easy road, free from difficulty. But no amount of "fatigue" should lead us to adopt a convenient "institutional" rationale—an absolutist, "anything goes" view of the First Amendment—because it will lighten our burdens. "Such an abnegation of judicial supervision in this field would be inconsistent with our duty to uphold the constitutional guarantees." Nor should we remedy "tension between state and federal courts" by arbitrarily depriving the States of a power reserved to them under the Constitution, a power which they have enjoyed and exercised continuously from before the adoption of the First Amendment to this day. "Our duty admits of no 'substitute for facing up to the tough individual problems of constitutional judgment involved in every obscenity case.' "

Under a national Constitution, fundamental First Amendment limitations on the powers of the States do not vary from community to community, but this does not mean that there are, or should or can be, fixed, uniform national standards of precisely what appeals to the "prurient interest" or is "patently offensive." These are essentially questions of fact, and our nation is simply too big and too diverse for this Court to reasonably expect that such standards could be articulated for all 50 States in a single formulation, even assuming the prerequisite consensus exists. When triers of fact are asked to decide whether "the average person, applying contemporary community standards" would consider certain materials "prurient," it would be unrealistic to require that the answer be based on some abstract formulation. The adversary system, with lay jurors as the usual ultimate fact-finders in criminal prosecutions, has historically permitted triers-of-fact to draw on the standards of their community, guided always by limiting instructions on the law. To require a State to structure obscenity proceedings around evidence of a *national* "community standard" would be an exercise in futility.

* * *

We conclude that neither the State's alleged failure to offer evidence of "national standards," nor the trial court's charge that the jury consider state community standards, were constitutional errors.[216] Nothing in the First Amendment requires that a jury must consider hypothetical and unascertainable "national standards" when attempting to determine whether certain materials are obscene as a matter of fact. * * *

It is neither realistic nor constitutionally sound to read the First Amendment as

216. Chief Justice Burger indicates in a footnote that community standards in the *Miller* case were ascertained by a police officer with many years of specialization in obscenity offenses. He had conducted an extensive statewide survey—the Chief Justice says nothing more specific about the survey—and had given expert evidence on twenty-six occasions in the year prior to the Miller trial.

requiring that the people of Maine or Mississippi accept public depiction of conduct found tolerable in Las Vegas or New York City. People in different States vary in their tastes and attitudes, and this diversity is not to be strangled by the absolutism of imposed uniformity. * * * We hold the requirement that the jury evaluate the materials with reference to "contemporary standards of the State of California" serves this protective purpose and is constitutionally adequate.

* * *

In sum we (a) reaffirm the *Roth* holding that obscene material is not protected by the First Amendment, (b) hold that such material can be regulated by the States, subject to the specific safeguards enunciated above, without a showing that the material is "*utterly* without redeeming social value," and (c) hold that obscenity is to be determined by applying "contemporary community standards," * * * not "national standards."

Vacated and remanded for further proceedings.

PARIS ADULT THEATRE I v. SLATON

413 U.S. 49, 93 S.CT. 2628, 37 L.ED.2D 446 (1973).

[EDITORIAL NOTE

Chief Justice Burger in a second opinion for the Court upheld the judgment of the Georgia Supreme Court that two "adult" movies were constitutionally unprotected. He noted that although there had been a full adversary proceeding on the question, there was no error in failing to require "expert" affirmative evidence that the materials were obscene. "The films, obviously," said Burger, "are the best evidence of what they represent." He rejected the consenting adults standard on the grounds that the state had a legitimate interest in regulating the use of obscene material in local commerce and in all places of public accommodation.

Citing the Hill-Link Minority Report of the Commission on Obscenity and Pornography, which found an arguable correlation between obscene material and crime, the Chief Justice nevertheless depreciated the importance of the Court's resolving empirical uncertainties in legislation unless constitutional rights were being infringed. Legislators and judges, he said, could and must act on unprovable assumptions such as the notion that the crass commercial exploitation of sex debases sex in the development of human personality, family life, and community welfare.

Noting that "free will" is not to be a governing concept in human affairs—we don't leave garbage and sewage disposal up to the individual—Burger, with assistance from social commentator Irving Kristol, found an inconsistency in the liberal stance:

> States are told by some that they must await a "laissez faire" market solution to the obscenity-pornography problem, paradoxically "by people who have never otherwise had a kind word to say for laissez faire," particularly in solving urban, commercial and environmental pollution problems.

Privacy, he added, while encompassing the personal intimacies of the home, the family, marriage, motherhood, procreation, and child rearing does not include the right to watch obscene movies in places of public accommodation. The Chief Justice concluded:

> The idea of a "privacy" right and a place of public accommodation are, in this context, mutually exclusive. Conduct or depictions of conduct that the state police power can prohibit on a public street does not become automatically protected by the Constitution merely because the conduct is moved to a bar or a "live" theatre stage, any more than a "live" performance of a man and woman locked in a sexual embrace at high noon in Times Square

is protected by the Constitution because they simultaneously engage in a valid political dialogue. * * * [W]e reject the claim that the State of Georgia is here attempting to control the minds or thoughts of those who patronize theatres. Preventing unlimited display or distribution of obscene material, which by definition lacks any serious literary, artistic, political or scientific value as communication, is distinct from a control of reason and the intellect. Where communication of ideas, protected by the First Amendment, is not involved, nor the particular privacy of the home protected by *Stanley,* nor any of the other "areas or zones" of constitutionally protected privacy, the mere fact that, as a consequence, some human "utterances" or "thoughts" may be incidentally affected does not bar the state from acting to protect legitimate state interests.

Justice Brennan, since *Roth* the Court's leading spokesman on obscenity law, was joined in his dissent by Justices Stewart and Marshall. His opinion provides an excellent review of the Court's work in this troubling area since 1957, an area which, he says, has demanded a substantial commitment of the Court's time, has generated much disharmony of views, and has remained resistant to the formulation of stable and manageable standards. The dissent should be read in its entirety. A segment follows.]

Justice BRENNAN, dissenting:

* * *

I am convinced that the approach initiated 15 years ago in Roth v. United States, 354 U.S. 476 (1957), and culminating in the Court's decision today, cannot bring stability to this area of the law without jeopardizing fundamental First Amendment values, and I have concluded that the time has come to make a significant departure from that approach.

* * *

The decision of the Georgia Supreme Court rested squarely on its conclusion that the State could constitutionally suppress these films even if they were displayed only to persons over the age of 21 who were aware of the nature of their contents and who had consented to viewing them. For the reasons set forth in this opinion, I am convinced of the invalidity of that conclusion of law, and I would therefore vacate the judgment of the Georgia Supreme Court. I have no occasion to consider the extent of state power to regulate the distribution of sexually oriented materials to juveniles or to unconsenting adults. Nor am I required, for the purposes of this appeal, to consider whether or not these petitioners had, in fact, taken precautions to avoid exposure of films to minors or unconsenting adults. * * * The essence of our problem in the obscenity area is that we have been unable to provide "sensitive tools" to separate obscenity from other sexually oriented but constitutionally protected speech, so that efforts to suppress the former do not spill over into the suppression of the latter. * *

To be sure, five members of the Court did agree in *Roth* that obscenity could be determined by asking "whether to the average person, applying contemporary community standards, the dominant theme of the material taken as a whole appeals to prurient interest." But agreement on that test—achieved in the abstract and without reference to the particular material before the Court,—was, to say the least, short lived. By 1967 the following views had emerged: Justice Black and Justice Douglas consistently maintained that government is wholly powerless to regulate any sexually oriented matter on the ground of its obscenity. Justice Harlan, on the other hand, believed that the Federal Government in the exercise of its enumerated powers could control the distribution of "hard-core" pornography, while the States were afforded more latitude to "[ban] any material which, taken as a whole, has been reasonably found in state judicial proceedings to treat with sex in a fundamentally offensive manner, under rationally established criteria for judging such material." Justice Stewart regarded "hard-core" pornography as the limit of both federal and state power.

The view that, until today, enjoyed the most, but not majority, support was an interpretation of *Roth* (and not, as the Court suggests, a veering "sharply away from the *Roth* concept" and the articulation of "a new test of obscenity," adopted by Chief Justice Warren, Justice Fortas, and the author of this opinion in Memoirs v. Massachusetts, 383 U.S. 413 [1966]). We expressed the view that Federal or State Governments could control the distribution of material where "three elements * * * coalesce: it must be established that (a) the dominant theme of the material taken as a whole appeals to a prurient interest in sex; (b) the material is patently offensive because it affronts contemporary community standards relating to the description or representation of sexual matters; and (c) the material is utterly without redeeming social value." Even this formulation, however, concealed differences of opinion. * * * Nor, finally, did it ever command a majority of the Court.

In the face of this divergence of opinion the Court began the practice in 1967 in Redrup v. New York, 386 U.S. 767, of *per curiam* reversals of convictions for the dissemination of materials that at least five members of the Court, applying their separate tests, deemed not to be obscene. This approach capped the attempt in *Roth* to separate all forms of sexually oriented expression into two categories—the one subject to full governmental suppression and the other beyond the reach of governmental regulation to the same extent as any other protected form of speech or press. Today a majority of the Court offers a slightly altered formulation of the basic *Roth* test, while leaving entirely unchanged the underlying approach.

Our experience with the *Roth* approach has certainly taught us that the outright suppression of obscenity cannot be reconciled with the fundamental principles of the First and Fourteenth Amendments. For we have failed to formulate a standard that sharply distinguishes protected from unprotected speech, and out of necessity, we have resorted to the *Redrup* approach, which resolves cases as between the parties, but offers only the most obscure guidance to legislation, adjudication by other courts, and primary conduct. By disposing of cases through summary reversal or denial of certiorari we have deliberately and effectively obscured the rationale underlying the decision. *It comes as no surprise that judicial attempts to follow our lead conscientiously have often ended in hopeless confusion.* [Emphasis added.]

Of course, the vagueness problem would be largely of our own creation if it stemmed primarily from our failure to reach a consensus on any one standard. But after 15 years of experimentation and debate I am reluctantly forced to the conclusion that none of the available formulas, including the one announced today, can reduce the vagueness to a tolerable level while at the same time striking an acceptable balance between the protections of the First and Fourteenth Amendments, on the one hand, and on the other the asserted state interest in regulating the dissemination of certain sexually oriented materials. Any effort to draw a constitutionally acceptable boundary on state power must resort to such indefinite concepts as "prurient interest," "patent offensiveness," "serious literary value," and the like. The meaning of these concepts necessarily varies with the experience, outlook, and even idiosyncracies of the person defining them. * * *

As a result of our failure to define standards with predictable application to any given piece of material, there is no probability of regularity in obscenity decisions by state and lower federal courts.

That is not to say that these courts have performed badly in this area or paid insufficient attention to the principles we have established. The problem is, rather that one cannot say with certainty that material is obscene until at least five members of this Court, applying inevitably obscure standards, have pronounced it so. The number of obscenity cases on our docket gives ample testimony to the burden that has been placed upon this Court.

But the sheer number of the cases does not define the full extent of the institutional problem. For quite apart from the number of cases involved and the need to make a fresh constitutional determination in each case, we are tied to the "absurd business of perusing and viewing the miserable stuff that pours into the Court. * * *" Interstate Circuit, Inc. v. Dallas, 390 U.S. 676, 707 (1968) (Harlan, J., dissenting). While the material may have varying degrees of social importance, it is hardly a source of edification to the members of this Court who are compelled to view it before passing on its obscenity. Cf. Mishkin v. New York, 383 U.S. 502, 516–517 (1966) (Black, J., dissenting).

Moreover, we have managed the burden of deciding scores of obscenity cases by relying on *per curiam* reversals or denials of certiorari—a practice which conceals the rationale of decision and gives at least the appearance of arbitrary action by this Court. More important, no less than the procedural schemes struck down in such cases as Blount v. Rizzi, 400 U.S. 410 (1971), and Freedman v. Maryland, 380 U.S. 51 (1965), the practice effectively censors protected expression by leaving lower court determinations of obscenity intact even though the status of the allegedly obscene material is entirely unsettled until final review here. In addition, the uncertainty of the standards creates a continuing source of tension between state and federal courts, since the need for an independent determination by this Court seems to render superfluous even the most conscientious analysis by state tribunals. And our inability to justify our decisions with a persuasive rationale—or indeed, any rationale at all—necessarily creates the impression that we are merely second-guessing state court judges.

The severe problems arising from the lack of fair notice, from the chill on protected expression, and from the stress imposed on the state and federal judicial machinery persuade me that a significant change in direction is urgently required. I turn, therefore, to the alternatives that are now open.

1. The approach requiring the smallest deviation from our present course would be to draw a new line between protected and unprotected speech, still permitting the States to suppress all material on the unprotected side of the line. In my view, clarity cannot be obtained pursuant to this approach except by drawing a line that resolves all doubts in favor of state power and against the guarantees of the First Amendment. We could hold, for example, that any depiction or description of human sexual organs, irrespective of the manner or purpose of the portrayal, is outside the protection of the First Amendment and therefore open to suppression by the States. That formula would, no doubt, offer much fairer notice of the reach of any state statute drawn at the boundary of the State's constitutional power. And it would also, in all likelihood, give rise to a substantial probability of regularity in most judicial determinations under the standard. But such a standard would be appallingly overbroad, permitting the suppression of a vast range of literary, scientific, and artistic masterpieces. Neither the First Amendment nor any free community could possibly tolerate such a standard. Yet short of that extreme it is hard to see how any choice of words could reduce the vagueness problem to tolerable proportions, so long as we remain committed to the view that some class of materi-

als is subject to outright suppression by the State.

2. The alternative adopted by the Court today recognizes that a prohibition against any depiction or description of human sexual organs could not be reconciled with the guarantees of the First Amendment. But the Court does retain the view that certain sexually oriented material can be considered obscene and therefore unprotected by the First and Fourteenth Amendments. To describe that unprotected class of expression, the Court adopts a restatement of the *Roth-Memoirs* definition of obscenity: "The basic guidelines for the trier of fact must be: (a) whether 'the average person, applying contemporary community standards' would find that the work, taken as a whole, appeals to the prurient interest, * * * (b) whether the work depicts or describes, in a patently offensive way, sexual conduct specifically defined by the applicable state law, and (c) whether the work, taken as a whole, lacks serious literary, artistic, political, or scientific value." California v. Miller, ante. In an apparent illustration of "sexual conduct," as that term is used in the test's second element the Court identifies "(a) patently offensive representations or descriptions of ultimate sexual acts, normal or perverted, actual or simulated," and "(b) patently offensive representations or descriptions of masturbation, excretory functions, and lewd exhibition of genitals."

The differences between this formulation and the three-pronged *Memoirs* test are, for the most part, academic. The first element of the Court's test is virtually identical to the *Memoirs* requirement that "the dominant theme of the material taken as a whole [must appeal] to a prurient interest in sex." Whereas the second prong of the *Memoirs* test demanded that the material be "patently offensive because it affronts contemporary community standards relating to the description or representation of sexual matters," the test adopted today requires that the material describe, "in a patently offensive way, sexual conduct specifically defined by the applicable state law." The third component of the *Memoirs* test is that the material must be "utterly without redeeming social value." The Court's rephrasing requires that the work, taken as a whole, must be proved to lack "serious literary, artistic, political, or scientific value."

The Court evidently recognizes that difficulties with the *Roth* approach necessitate a significant change of direction. But the Court does not describe its understanding of those difficulties, nor does it indicate how the restatement of the *Memoirs* test is in any way responsive to the problems that have arisen. In my view, the restatement leaves unresolved the very difficulties that compel our rejection of the underlying *Roth* approach, while at the same time contributing substantial difficulties of its own. The modification of the *Memoirs* test may prove sufficient to jeopardize the analytic underpinnings of the entire scheme. And today's restatement will likely have the effect, whether or not intended, of permitting far more sweeping suppression of sexually oriented expression, including expression that would almost surely be held protected under our current formulation.

Although the Court's restatement substantially tracks the three-part test announced in Memoirs v. Massachusetts, it does purport to modify the "social value" component of the test. Instead of requiring, as did *Roth* and *Memoirs*, that state suppression be limited to materials utterly lacking in social value, the Court today permits suppression if the government can prove that the materials lack "*serious* literary, artistic, political, or scientific value." But the definition of "obscenity" as expression utterly lacking in social importance is the key to the conceptual basis of *Roth* and our subsequent opinions. In *Roth* we held that certain expression is obscene, and thus outside the protection of the First Amendment, precisely *because* it lacks even the slightest redeeming social value. The Court's approach necessarily assumes that some works will be deemed obscene—even though they clearly have some social value—because the State was able to prove that the value, measured by some unspecified standard, was not sufficiently "serious" to warrant constitutional protection. That result is not merely inconsistent with our holding in *Roth*; it is nothing less than a rejection of the fundamental First Amendment premises and rationale of the *Roth* opinion and an invitation to widespread suppression of sexually oriented speech. Before today, the protections of the First Amendment have never been thought limited to expressions of *serious* literary or political value.

Although the Court concedes that "*Roth* presumed 'obscenity' to be 'utterly without redeeming social value,'" it argues that *Memoirs* produced "a drastically altered test that called on the prosecution to prove a negative, i.e., that the material was 'utterly without redeeming social value'—a burden virtually impossible to discharge under our criminal standards of proof." One should hardly need to point out that under the third component of the Court's test the prosecution is still required to "prove a negative"—i.e., that the material lacks serious literary, artistic, political, or scientific value. Whether it will be easier to prove that material lacks "serious" value than to prove that it lacks any value at all remains, of course, to be seen.

In any case, even if the Court's approach left undamaged the conceptual framework of *Roth*, and even if it clearly barred the suppression of works with at least some social value, I would nevertheless be compelled to reject it. For it is beyond dispute that the approach can have no ameliorative impact on the cluster of problems that grows out of the vagueness of our current standards. Indeed, even the Court makes no argument that the reformulation will provide fairer notice to booksellers, theatre owners, and the reading and viewing public. Nor does the Court contend that the approach will provide clearer guidance to law enforcement officials or reduce the chill on protected expression. Nor, finally, does the Court suggest that the approach will mitigate to the slightest degree the institutional problems that have plagued this Court and the State and Federal Judiciary as a direct result of the uncertainty inherent in any definition of obscenity.

* * * The Court surely demonstrates little sensitivity to our own institutional problems, much less the other vagueness-related difficulties, in establishing a system that requires us to consider whether a description of human genitals is sufficiently "lewd" to deprive it of constitutional protection; whether a sexual act is "ultimate"; whether the conduct depicted in materials before us fits within one of the categories of conduct whose depiction the state or federal governments have attempted to suppress; and a host of equally pointless inquiries. In addition, adoption of such a test does not, presumably, obviate the need for consideration of the nuances of presentation of sexually oriented material, yet it hardly clarifies the application of those opaque but important factors.

If the application of the "physical conduct" test to pictorial material is fraught with difficulty, its application to textual material carries the potential for extraordinary abuse. Surely we have passed the point where the mere written description of sexual conduct is deprived of First Amendment protection. Yet the test offers no guidance to us, or anyone else, in determining which written descriptions of sexual conduct are protected, and which are not.

Ultimately, the reformulation must fail because it still leaves in this Court the responsibility of determining in each case whether the materials are protected by the First Amendment. * * *

3. I have also considered the possibility of reducing our own role, and the role of appellate courts generally, in determining whether particular matter is obscene. Thus, we might conclude that juries are best suited to determine obscenity *vel non* and that jury verdicts in this area should not be set aside except in cases of extreme departure from prevailing standards. Or, more generally, we might adopt the position that where a lower federal or state court has conscientiously applied the constitutional standard, its finding of obscenity will be no more vulnerable to reversal by this Court than any finding of fact. Cf. Interstate Circuit v. Dallas, 390 U.S. 676, 706–707 (1968) [separate opinion of Harlan, J.]. While the point was not clearly resolved prior to our decision in *Redrup v. New York,* it is implicit in that decision that the First Amendment requires an independent review by appellate courts of the constitutional fact of obscenity. That result is required by principles applicable to the obscenity issue no less than to any other area involving free expression, or other constitutional right. In any event, even if the Constitution would permit us to refrain from judging for ourselves the alleged obscenity of particular materials, that approach would solve at best only a small part of our problem. For while it would mitigate the institutional stress produced by the *Roth* approach, it would neither offer nor produce any cure for the other vices of vagueness. Far from providing a clearer guide to permissible primary conduct, the approach would inevitably lead to even greater uncertainty and the consequent due process problems of fair notice. And the approach would expose much protected sexually oriented expression to the vagaries of jury determinations. *Plainly, the institutional gain would be more than offset by the unprecedented infringement of First Amendment rights.* [Emphasis added.]

4. Finally, I have considered the view, urged so forcefully since 1957 by our Brothers Black and Douglas, that the First Amendment bars the suppression of any sexually oriented expression. That position would effect a sharp reduction, although perhaps not a total elimination, of the uncertainty that surrounds our current approach. Nevertheless, I am convinced that it would achieve that desirable goal only by stripping the States of power to an extent that cannot be justified by the commands of the Constitution, at least so long as there is available an alternative approach that strikes a better balance between the guarantee of free expression and the States' legitimate interests.

Our experience since *Roth* requires us not only to abandon the effort to pick out obscene materials on a case-by-case basis, but also to reconsider a fundamental postulate of *Roth*: that there exists a definable class of sexually oriented expression that may be totally suppressed by the Federal and State Governments. Assuming that such a class of expression does in fact exist, I am forced to conclude that the concept of "obscenity" cannot be defined with sufficient specificity and clarity to provide fair notice to persons who create and distribute sexually oriented materials, to prevent substantial erosion of protected speech as a by-product of the attempt to suppress unprotected speech, and to avoid very costly institutional harms. Given these inevitable side-effects of state efforts to suppress what is assumed to be *unprotected* speech, we must scrutinize with care the state interest that is asserted to justify the suppression. For in the absence of some very substantial interest in suppressing such speech, we can hardly condone the ill-effects that seem to flow inevitably from the effort.

* * *

In short, while I cannot say that the interests of the State—apart from the question of juveniles and unconsenting adults—are trivial or nonexistent, I am compelled to conclude that these interests cannot justify the substantial damage to constitutional rights and to this Nation's judicial machinery that inevitably results from state efforts to bar the distribution even of unprotected material to consenting adults. *I would hold, therefore, that at least in the absence of distribution to juveniles or obtrusive exposure to unconsenting adults, the First and Fourteenth Amendments prohibit the state and federal governments from attempting wholly to suppress sexually oriented materials on the basis of their allegedly "obscene" contents. Nothing in this approach precludes those governments from taking action to serve what may be strong and legitimate interests through regulation of the manner of distribution of sexually oriented material.* [Emphasis added.]

COMMENT

1. In his opinion for the Court in *Orito*, Chief Justice Burger reiterated the view that *Stanley* did not protect obscene materials outside of the home or in interstate commerce. And words alone may constitute obscenity, said the Chief Justice, in finding against the proprietor of the Peek-a-Boo Bookstore in *Kaplan*:

> For good or ill, a book has a continuing life. It is passed hand to hand, and we can take note of the tendency of widely circulated books of this category to reach the impressionable young and have a continuing impact. A [s]tate could reasonably regard the "hard core" conduct described by *Suite 69* as capable of encouraging or causing antisocial behavior, especially in its impact on young people. States need not wait until behavioral experts or educators can provide empirical data before enacting controls of commerce in obscene materials unprotected by the First Amendment or by a constitutional right to privacy.

Finally in *12 200-Ft. Reels of Super 8mm. Film*, Burger closed the Customs Bureau door to the importation of obscene matter.

2. Justice Douglas dissented separately and predictably in all five cases. He seemed to take a quiet satisfaction in noting that the Court had worked hard to define obscenity but concededly had failed. The criminal law had become a trap. "To send men to jail," said Douglas, "for violating standards they cannot understand, construe, and apply is a monstrous thing to do in a Nation dedicated to fair trials and due process." "The Court's test," he added, "would make it possible to ban any paper or any journal or magazine in some benighted place. * * * To give the power to the censor, as we do today, is to make a sharp and radical break with the traditions of a free society." For Douglas obscenity is no more than a classification of offensive ideas, and to make that classification unprotected expression would require a constitutional amendment.

3. If Justice Brennan could have commanded a majority of the Court for a case or two more, essential elements of the Lockhart Commission proposals might have begun to shape the law, and society would have been spared the madness of most obscenity prosecutions. Brennan's desire to protect the privacy of unconsenting adults and to limit the dissemination of erotic material to children has long been subscribed to by liberal commentators.[217]

4. The abiding importance of *Freedman v. Maryland* and its standard of procedural due process was reflected in three 1979 cases. Missouri police learned that seizure of 1,000 allegedly obscene films and 13,000 allegedly obscene magazines from a wholesale distributor before a judicial adversary hearing was an unconstitutional prior restraint.[218] The Florida Supreme

---

217. Emerson, *The System of Freedom of Expression*, 497 (1970) and Kuh, *Foolish Figleaves?* (1967).

218. Missouri v. All Star News Agency, 5 Med.L.Rptr. 1076, 580 S.W.2d 245 (Mo.1979).

Court ruled that a permanent injunction barring sales and distribution of printed material before a judicial determination of obscenity was also a prior restraint.[219] The U.S. Supreme Court itself in 1979 unanimously invalidated seizure of 800 magazines, films, and other material from a bookstore under an open-ended search warrant that grew from two to sixteen pages as the six-hour search proceeded. Presence of a town justice making snap judgments as to what was obscene was no substitute, said the Court, for a "neutral" and "detached" judicial officer. Reminiscent of the pre-Revolution general warrant, the whole procedure was said to violate the First, Fourth, and Fourteenth Amendments.[220]

A year later, Wisconsin's obscenity statute imposing felony sanctions against anyone who intentionally "imports, prints, advertises, sells, has in his possession for sale, or publishes, exhibits or transfers any lewd, obscene or indecent written matters, picture, sound recording or film" was struck down by that state's supreme court. As well as being facially vague and overbroad in violation of the First Amendment, it contained no procedural safeguards for reviewing denials of a license.[221]

That part of a Minnesota municipal ordinance that exempted certain schools, museums, churches, physicians, and government agencies from the strictures of obscenity law was said to be a violation of equal protection.[222] Later the same ordinance was held by a federal court to be an unconstitutional prior restraint in requiring operators of adult bookstores to pay an annual $500 fee to administer and enforce a licensing system.[223] And the First Amendment was also violated by a California municipal ordinance requiring businesses which were open to minors to seal, cover, or remove from the reach of minors all sexually explicit, although nonobscene, material or, as an alternative, to exclude minors unless accompanied by parent or guardian.[224]

5. Applying the obscenity standards of *Miller* and defining community standards has not been so easy. In *Ferber* the Court noted that *Miller* has been followed in the statutory schemes of most states. Thirty-seven states and the District of Columbia have either legislatively adopted or judicially incorporated the *Miller* test for obscenity. Four states in 1982 followed the *Roth-Memoirs* [225] test. They were California, Connecticut, Florida, and Illinois. Five states regulated only the distribution of pornographic material to children. They were Maine, Montana, New Mexico, Vermont, and West Virginia. Three state laws did not fall into any of the above categories. Wisconsin's law was struck down in 1980 by the state's supreme court (fn. 221), and apparently hadn't been resuscitated by mid-1982 when the Supreme Court delivered *Ferber*. Mississippi's obscenity standard was declared invalid in *ABC Interstate Theatres, Inc. v. State* [226] in 1976. Alaska in 1982 had no obscenity law.

Although *Miller* has come to be applied more cautiously and narrowly by lower courts, it has by no means solved the puzzle of pornography. The first misapplication of its standard came to the Supreme

219. Ladoga Canning Corp. v. McKenzie, 5 Med.L.Rptr. 1102, 370 So.2d 1137 (Fla.1979).

220. Lo-Ji Sales v. New York, 442 U.S. 319 (1979).

221. Wisconsin v. Princess Cinema, 6 Med.L.Rptr. 1458, 292 N.W.2d 807 (Wis.1980).

222. Duluth v. Sarette, 5 Med.L.Rptr. 1824, 283 N.W.2d 533 (Minn.1979).

223. Wendling v. Duluth, 6 Med.L.Rptr. 1953, 495 F.Supp. 1380 (D.Minn.1980).

224. American Booksellers Association v. Superior Court, 8 Med.L.Rptr. 2014, 181 Cal.Rptr. 33 (1982).

225. Memoirs v. Massachusetts, 1 Med.L.Rptr. 1390, 383 U.S. 413 (1966), this text, p. 744.

226. 325 So.2d 123 (Miss.1976).

Court from Georgia in 1974 and focused on a critically acclaimed movie titled *Carnal Knowledge*. In Jenkins v. Georgia, 418 U.S. 153 (1974) the Court was plunged into the consequences of its own mischief. The Court in *Miller* had hoped to avoid making an independent assessment of whether or not particular material was obscene. It sought a way out of the quagmire. But *Jenkins* showed that no such path was marked by *Miller*. Technically, the Court reversed the state supreme court in *Jenkins* because that court had misinterpreted *Miller*. It had thought that a jury verdict reached pursuant to *Miller*-based instructions precluded further judicial review. Juries, said the Court, did not have "unbridled discretion" to determine "what is 'patently offensive'." Moreover, *Carnal Knowledge* was not "hard core," said Justice Rehnquist, because the camera did not focus on the bodies of the actors during scenes of "ultimate sexual acts" nor were the actors' genitals exhibited during those scenes. *Miller* had held that the jury could use a "local" community standard in order to give meaning to pruriency and patent offensiveness. *Jenkins* demonstrated that these elements of the test would not remain exclusive where the jury's verdict was dispositive.

Jenkins was a state prosecution under *Miller*. What about a federal prosecution? How would the *Miller* criteria apply? In Hamling v. United States, 1 Med. L.Rptr. 1479, 418 U.S. 87 (1974), the Court upheld the federal conviction of the mailer of an obscene brochure advertising what was purported to be an illustrated edition of the Lockhart Commission Report.

"A juror," said Justice Rehnquist, again speaking for the Court, "is entitled to draw on his own knowledge of the views of the average person [not the most prudish or the most tolerant] in the community or vicinage from which he comes from making the required determination, just as he is entitled to draw on his knowledge of the propensities of a 'reasonable' person in other areas of the law. * * * Our holding in *Miller* that California could constitutionally proscribe obscenity in terms of a 'statewide' standard did not mean that any such precise geographical area is required as a matter of constitutional law."

Expert testimony, the Court added, is irrelevant in defining obscenity or community standards, and there is no need for federal statutes to look to national standards of decency, even though the trial judge in *Hamling* had instructed the jury largely in terms of national standards.

An important aspect of *Hamling*, then, is that the Court made it clear that the fact that the federal jury had been instructed to apply a national community standard did not in itself constitute reversible error. But the boundaries of "community" remain fuzzy and flexible.

"National distributors choosing to send their products in interstate travels will be forced," said Justice Brennan in dissent, "to cope with the community standards of every hamlet into which their goods may wander."

Brennan had observed in *Jenkins* that as long as *Miller* remained in effect "one cannot say with certainty that material is obscene until at least five members of this Court, applying inevitably obscure standards, have pronounced it so." The Court, it seemed, would again have to deal with obscenity on a case-by-case basis.

In Smith v. United States, 2 Med.L.Rptr. 1833, 431 U.S. 291 (1977), the Court held that in a federal obscenity prosecution a jury is not necessarily bound by the definition of contemporary community standards found in a state statute. Federal jurors could determine the meaning of pruriency and patent offensiveness in light of their own understanding of local community standards. In addition the Court in *Smith* rejected a vagueness challenge to 18 U.S.C.A. § 1461, the Comstock Law.

The best guidance the Court can provide is that jurors consider the entire community and not simply their own subjective reactions or the reactions of a sensitive or a callous minority. Community standards will determine what appeals to prurient interest or is patently offensive, and this, said the Court, would be a question of fact for the jurors.

One of four dissenters, Justice Stevens thought it obvious that a federal statute defining a criminal offense should prescribe a uniform standard applicable throughout the country—especially where the First Amendment was involved. Stevens thought it inevitable that community standards, whether national or local, would be subjective, a matter of values and not of fact.

"In my judgment," wrote Stevens, "the line between communications which 'offend' and those which do not is too blurred to identify criminal conduct. It is also too blurred to delimit the protections of the First Amendment. * * *

"I am not prepared to rely on either the average citizen's understanding of an amorphous community standard or on my fellow judge's appraisal of what has serious artistic merit as a basis for deciding what one citizen may communicate to another by appropriate means"—and Stevens did think there were inappropriate means: for example, erotic displays in a residential neighborhood.

South Dakota's Supreme Court would allow "expert" testimony on community standards if witnesses could establish their expertise;[227] Massachusetts's Supreme Judicial Court held that expert testimony on what offends the average person in that state was unnecessary.[228] The Ninth Circuit ruled reluctantly that including children in the definition of community was not reversible error.[229] It was reversed by the Supreme Court in Pinkus v. United States, 3 Med.L.Rptr. 2329, 436 U.S. 293 (1978), but it was no error, said the Court, to include "sensitive" persons in the definition and to permit the jury to consider the appeal of material to the prurient interest of "deviant" groups and the degree to which it was pandered.

Litigation in Florida, resulting from the showing of *Deep Throat* in a journalism law class at a state university in Pensacola, sought to explore whether the academic community was part of or apart from the surrounding community.[230]

A federal district court in Geogria held that the appropriate community standard would be that of the county that had threatened plaintiff with prosecution rather than the entire state of Georgia or the applicable federal judicial district.[231] A Texas appeals court said that public opinion survey evidence as to community standards, while not required, was relevant to a determination of a material fact issue.[232]

6. What is *patently offensive* in Illinois may not be in Ohio. The Supreme Court affirmed an Illinois Supreme Court holding that the sale of sado-masochistic materials was prohibited by the state's obscenity statute.[233] A few months later a federal district court in Ohio ruled that state's pandering obscenity law overbroad in part because it included "display or depiction of extreme or bizarre violence, cruelty, or brutality." After all, *Miller* held that only materials showing or describing sexual

227. Sioux Falls v. Mini-Kota Art Theatres, Inc., 2 Med.L.Rptr. 1318, 247 N.W.2d 676 (S.D.1977).

228. District Attorney for Northern District v. Three Way Theatres Corp., 2 Med.L.Rptr. 1257, 357 N.E.2d 747 (Mass.1977).

229. United States v. Pinkus, 2 Med.L.Rptr. 2217, 551 F.2d 1155 (9th Cir. 1977).

230. Correspondence with Professor Churchill Roberts of the University of West Florida, Jan. 6, 1978.

231. Septum v. Keller, 7 Med.L.Rptr. 1664, 614 F.2d 456 (5th Cir. 1981).

232. Carlock v. Texas, 6 Med.L.Rptr. 2275, 609 S.W.2d 787 (Tex.1980).

233. Ward v. Illinois, 2 Med.L.Rptr. 1929, 431 U.S. 767 (1977).

conduct were obscene.[234]

7. *Prurient interest* may be the deepest, darkest mystery of all. A trial jury in Manhattan acquitted a defendant of charges brought under New York's obscenity law because his films, depicting acts of bestiality, were "too disgusting and repulsive" to appeal to the prurient interest of average people. It is the stimulation of normal, healthy, sexual impulses that are punishable, what the U.S. Supreme Court has referred to as itching, longing, lascivioius desire, a shameful or morbid interest in sex. The more revolting, outrageous, sickening, saddening, or violent the material, the less chance it has of being declared obscene. Could it be that sex and obscenity have come full circle and found themselves again?

The film *Caligula*, while patently offensive under Georgia law, did not appeal to prurient interests in sex—at least not to the prurient interests of the federal district judge who viewed it—and when taken as a whole it had serious artistic and political value.[235]

But even nonobscene films may not be pandered. The *Ginzburg* proscription against commercial exploitation was upheld by the Supreme Court in Splawn v. California, 431 U.S. 595 (1977). A minority of four justices thought *Ginzburg* could no longer stand in light of the Court's having extended First Amendment protection to commercial speech in *Virginia Pharmacy*.[236] Information alone about a product, no matter how tempting that product to the "salaciously disposed," should not be obstructed. Well-informed people can make choices in their own best interests. Moreover, the four justices did not think Mr. Splawn deserved jail for telling the truth about his shabby business.

Much discussion has focused on whether the definition of obscenity ought to be variable or constant. That is, does obscenity vary with time, place, audience, and context? If it does, then it is going to be more available to some than to others—perhaps to the sophisticated or those who can afford it, to adults rather than to juveniles, to professional rather than to nonprofessional persons. Shifting definitions may lead to what Justice Stevens, himself a proponent of the contextual approach, called in Marks v. United States, 2 Med.L.Rptr. 1401, 430 U.S. 188 (1977), the grossly disparate treatment of similar offenders in the criminal enforcement of obscenity law. And in broadcast law, "indecency" has been equated with obscenity because of its timing, its random audience, and its supposed impact. See FCC v. Pacifica Foundation, 3 Med.L.Rptr. 2553, 438 U.S. 726 (1978), this text, p. 920.

Constant definitions of obscenity simply exclude a category of speech from First Amendment protection. Its danger is its dogma. There is the small comfort of consistency where its boundaries can be fixed. For example, Erznoznik v. City of Jacksonville, 1 Med.L.Rptr. 1508, 422 U.S. 205 (1975), struck down a law against drive-in theaters showing nude scenes if the films could be seen from public places such as highways. Nudity, without more, is not obscene said the Court, and had been singled out for special treatment while other protected speech which might pose the same hazard to traffic was let alone. Little more can be said in favor of unbending definitions of obscenity.

Some would abandon use of the word obscenity altogether and invest the effort in protecting captive audiences against privacy-violating nuisances and children

234. Sovereign News v. Falk, 3 Med.L.Rptr. 1337, 448 F.Supp. 306 (D.Ohio 1977).

235. Penthouse v. McAuliffe, 7 Med.L.Rptr. 1798 (N.D.Ga.1981). See also Massachusetts v. Saxon Theatre, 6 Med.L.Rptr. 1979 (Mass.1980).

236. Virginia State Board of Pharmacy v. Virginia Citizens Consumer Council, Inc., 1 Med.L.Rptr. 1930, 425 U.S. 748 (1976). See this text, pp. 159–606.

against abuse.[237] In dismissing the constitutional validity of the Court's *Miller v. California* ruling, Justice Brennan made similar suggestions, some of which are based on predictions of the havoc *Miller* would create. The assumptions behind those predictions have been attacked. Survey data demonstrate, for example, that *Miller* has had little inhibiting effect on the output of sexually explicit material. Indeed the volume has increased. There has been no chilling effect.

Since *Miller* may be interpreted as having limited the discretion of appellate courts, the number of appellate cases has predictably declined, and the proportion of reversals on appeal has decreased, belying Brennan's anticipation of a higher volume of appeals.[238] And, mercifully, fewer cases are getting to the Supreme Court. This is good news only if you are prepared to equate sexually explicit materials with pornography.

More useful is an examination of empirical support for the propositions underlying the law of obscenity. One writer could find practically no support in the behavioral literature for assuming that pornography harmed society, aroused prurient interest, was definable within frameworks of local or national standards, led to antisocial conduct, or had adverse effects on the development of children. Granted that the evidence is sometimes fragmentary and that the methodologies used in collecting and analyzing it are sometimes challengeable, should it be ignored as it is in lawyers' briefs, trial records, and oral arguments?

Justices sometimes rationalize their ignoring of social data by pointing to the lack of agreement among investigators. They are not as prepared in judging obscenity as they are in judging other realms of human behavior to be influenced by the preponderance of evidence. Obscenity provides a vehicle for their own personal beliefs and feelings. Brennan may have been the only justice in the *Miller* cases who permitted facts to change his mind.[239]

In the fabric of American custom and law, pornography is still sex. Sometimes it's funny, sometimes it's ugly. It was funny when five movies and four magazines sent to the Supreme Court in early 1982 as part of an Idaho obscenity case disappeared before the case was heard. All the Court could do for Idaho concerning the missing exhibits was to apologize. Pornography can be ugly when it is combined with gratuitous violence.

Is the remedy here, as with other apostasies, more speech rather than enforced silence? Moral philosophy, esthetics, and accurate information about and artistic representations of sex through open channels and from reliable and sensitive sources could take the place of the warped, shallow, and criminal, although we can have no assurances that they will.

Important legal and constitutional questions remain. To what extent are rights jeopardized when government attempts to prohibit or punish what it cannot define? What is obscene to a feminist may not be obscene to a television producer. What is obscene to a fundamentalist may be the laughter of genius to a drama critic.

"The evil of arousing revulsion in adults who are a non-captive audience," said Harry Kalven, Jr., "[may be] simply too trivial a predicate for constitutional

---

237. Rembar, *Obscenity—Forget It,* Atlantic, May, 1977.

238. Riggs, *Miller v. California Revisited: An Empirical Note.* 1981 B.Y.U.L.Rev. 247.

239. Daniels, *The Supreme Court and Obscenity: An Exercise in Empirical Constitutional Policy-Making,* 17 San Diego L.Rev. 757 (July 1980).

regulation." [240] A pox on censors, said Luis Bunuel. "They are like nannies sitting on our shoulders inhibiting calm and destroying our phantoms." [241]

---

240. Kalven, *The Metaphysics of the Law of Obscenity*, 1960 S.Ct.Rev. 40.

241. Quoted in Penelope Gilliatt, *Long Live the Living*, The New Yorker (Dec. 5, 1977), p. 66.

The Regulation of Radio and Television Broadcasting: Some Problems of Law, Technology, and Policy

INTRODUCTION: THE RATIONALE OF BROADCAST REGULATION

One of the startling legal realities of the law of broadcasting as compared with the law of the press is that the legal framework of broadcasting is altogether different from that of the press. As Judge Warren Burger stated in Office of Communication of United Church of Christ v. FCC, 359 F.2d 994 at 1003 (D.C.Cir. 1966):

> A broadcaster seeks and is granted the free and exclusive use of a limited and valuable part of the public domain; when he accepts that franchise it is burdened by enforceable public obligations. A newspaper can be operated at the whim or caprice of its owners; a broadcast station cannot.

The structure of broadcast regulation under the Federal Communications Act of 1934 is rather extensive. Until 1981, licenses for broadcasting stations were granted only for a period of three years under the act. In 1981, § 307(d) of the Act was amended to provide that the license period should be five years for television licenses and seven years for radio licenses (why the distinction?). According to the act, licenses are to be granted by the Federal Communications Commission provided that "the public convenience, interest, or necessity will be served thereby." 47 U.S.C.A. § 307(a). At the expiration of the licensing period, the licensee is required to apply for renewal which may be granted "if the commission finds that public interest, convenience, and necessity would be served thereby." [1] 47 U.S.C.A. § 307(d).

In the light of these and other provisions of the act, a dominant problem in broadcast regulation has been with the definition of the "public interest" standard. What criteria, for example, should govern the "public interest" principle of § 307 of the act?

It was argued in the NBC case below that the FCC's authority was limited solely to removing the technical and engineering impediments which obstruct effective broadcasting. Otherwise, the argument ran, the FCC has no authority to make any particular qualitative demands of broadcast licensees.

Should the FCC's function be limited to traffic control? Or should it be directed instead to determining the composition of the traffic, i.e., the character and quality of broadcast programming?

1. See generally, Tickton, *At Last, Longer Station License Terms*, 4 Communications and the Law 3 (1982).

NBC v. UNITED STATES
CBS v. UNITED STATES

319 U.S. 190, 63 S.CT. 997,
87 L.ED. 1344 (1943).

Justice FRANKFURTER delivered the opinion of the Court.

In view of our dependence upon regulated private enterprise in discharging the far-reaching role which radio plays in our society, a somewhat detailed exposition of the history of the present controversy and the issues which it raises is appropriate.

* * *

On March 18, 1938, the Commission undertook a comprehensive investigation to determine whether special regulations applicable to radio stations engaged in chain broadcasting[1] were required in the "public interest, convenience, or necessity."

* * *

The regulations, * * * are addressed [directly] to station licensees and applicants for station licenses. They provide, in general, that no licenses shall be granted to stations or applicants having specified relationships with networks. Each regulation is directed at a particular practice found by the Commission to be detrimental to the "public interest," and we shall consider them seriatim. * * *

The commission found that at the end of 1938 there were 660 commercial stations in the United States, and that 341 of these were affiliated with national networks. * * It pointed out that the stations affiliated with the national networks utilized more than 97% of the total night-time broadcasting power of all the stations in the country. NBC and CBS together controlled more than 85% of the total night-time wattage, and the broadcast business of the three national network companies amounted to almost half of the total business of all stations in the United States.

The commission recognized that network broadcasting had played and was continuing to play an important part in the development of radio. "The growth and development of chain broadcasting," it stated, "found its impetus in the desire to give widespread coverage to programs which otherwise would not be heard beyond the reception area of a single station. Chain broadcasting makes possible a wider reception for expensive entertainment and cultural programs and also for programs of national or regional significance which would otherwise have coverage only in the locality of origin. Furthermore, the access to greatly enlarged audiences made possible by chain broadcasting has been a strong incentive to advertisers to finance the production of expensive programs. * * * But the fact that the chain broadcasting method brings benefits and advantages to both the listening public and to broadcast station licensees does not mean that the prevailing practices and policies of the networks and their outlets are sound in all respects, or that they should not be altered. The commission's duty under the Communications Act of 1934, 47 U.S.C.A. § 151 et seq., is not only to see that the public receives the advantages and benefits of chain broadcasting, but also, so far as its powers enable it, to see that practices which adversely affect the ability of licensees to operate in the public interest are eliminated."

The commission found * * * [certain] network abuses were amenable to correction within the powers granted it by Congress.

1. Chain broadcasting is defined in § 3(p) of the Communications Act of 1934, 47 U.S.C.A. § 153(p), as the "simultaneous broadcasting of an identical program by two or more connected stations." In actual practice, programs are transmitted by wire, usually leased telephone lines, from their point of origination to each station in the network for simultaneous broadcast over the air.

Regulation 3.101—Exclusive affiliation of station. The commission found that the network affiliation agreements of NBC and CBS customarily contained a provision which prevented the station from broadcasting the programs of any other network. The effect of this provision was to hinder the growth of new networks. * * *

"Restraints having this effect", the commission observed, "are to be condemned as contrary to the public interest irrespective of whether it be assumed that Mutual [another network] programs are of equal, superior, or inferior quality. The important consideration is that station licensees are denied freedom to choose the programs which they believe best suited to their needs; in this manner the duty of a station licensee to operate in the public interest is defeated. * * *"

* * *

Regulation 3.102—Territorial exclusivity. The commission found another type of "exclusivity" provision in network affiliation agreements whereby the network bound itself not to sell programs to any other station in the same area. The effect of this provision, designed to protect the affiliate from the competition of other stations serving the same territory, was to deprive the listening public of many programs that might otherwise be available.

* * *

The Commission concluded that * * * "It is as much against the public interest for a network affiliate to enter into a contractual arrangement which prevents another station from carrying a network program as it would be for it to drown out that program by electrical interference." * * *

Regulation 3.103—Term of affiliation. The standard NBC and CBS affiliation contracts bound the station for a period of five years, with the network having the exclusive right to terminate the contracts upon one year's notice. The commission, relying upon § 307(d) of the Communications Act of 1934, under which no license to operate a broadcast station can be granted for a longer term than three years, found the five-year affiliation term to be contrary to the policy of the act. * * *

The commission concluded that under contracts binding the affiliates for five years, "stations become parties to arrangements which deprive the public of the improved service it might otherwise derive from competition in the network field; and that a station is not operating in the public interest when it so limits its freedom of action." * * *

Regulation 3.104—Option time. The commission found that network affiliation contracts usually contained so-called network optional time clauses. Under these provisions the network could upon 28 days' notice call upon its affiliates to carry a commercial program during any of the hours specified in the agreement as "network optional time." For CBS affiliates "network optional time" meant the entire broadcast day. * * *

In the commission's judgment these optional time provisions, in addition to imposing serious obstacles in the path of new networks, hindered stations in developing a local program service. * * *

Regulation 3.105—Right to reject programs. The commission found that most network affiliation contracts contained a clause defining the right of the station to reject network commercial programs. The NBC contracts provided simply that the station "may reject a network program the broadcasting of which would not be in the public interest, convenience, and necessity." * * *

While seeming in the abstract to be fair, these provisions, according to the commission's finding, did not sufficiently protect the "public interest." As a practical matter, the licensee could not determine in advance whether the broadcasting of any particular network program would or would not be in the public interest. * *

"In practice, if not in theory, stations affiliated with networks have delegated to the networks a large part of their programming functions. In many instances, moreover, the network further delegates the actual production of programs to advertising agencies. These agencies are far more than mere brokers or intermediaries between the network and the advertiser. To an ever increasing extent, these agencies actually exercise the function of program production. Thus it is frequently neither the station nor the network, but rather the advertising agency, which determines what broadcast programs shall contain. Under such circumstances, it is especially important that individual stations, if they are to operate in the public interest, should have the practical opportunity as well as the contractual right to reject network programs. * * *

"It is the station, not the network, which is licensed to serve the public interest. * * *" (Federal Communications Commission, Report on Chain Broadcasting, 1941, pp. 39, 66.)

* * *

Regulation 3.106—Network ownership of stations. The commission found that [the] * * * 18 stations owned by NBC and CBS * * * were among the most powerful and desirable in the country, and were permanently inaccessible to competing networks. * * * The commission concluded that "the licensing of two stations in the same area to a single network organization is basically unsound and contrary to the public interest," and that it was also against the "public interest" for network organizations to own stations in areas where the available facilities were so few or of such unequal coverage that competition would thereby be substantially restricted. * * *

Regulation 3.108—Control by networks of station rates. * * * Under this provision the station could not sell time to a national advertiser for less than it would cost the advertiser if he bought the time from NBC. * * *

The commission concluded that "it is against the public interest for a station licensee to enter into a contract with a network which has the effect of decreasing its ability to compete for national business. We believe that the public interest will best be served and listeners supplied with the best programs if stations bargain freely with national advertisers."

* * *

The appellants attack the validity of these regulations along many fronts. They contend that the commission went beyond the regulatory powers conferred upon it by the Communications Act of 1934; * * * and that, in any event, the regulations abridge the appellants' right of free speech in violation of the First Amendment. We are thus called upon to determine whether Congress has authorized the commission to exercise the power asserted by the Chain Broadcasting Regulations, and if it has, whether the Constitution forbids the exercise of such authority. * * *

The enforcement of the Radio Act of 1912 presented no serious problems prior to the World War. Questions of interference arose only rarely because there were more than enough frequencies for all the stations then in existence. The war accelerated the development of the art, however, and in 1921 the first standard broadcast stations were established. They grew rapidly in number, and by 1923 there were several hundred such stations throughout the country. The act of 1912 had not set aside any particular frequencies for the use of private broadcast stations; consequently, the secretary of commerce selected two frequencies, 750 and 833 kilocycles, and licensed all stations to operate upon one or the other of these channels. The number of stations increased so rapidly, however, and the situation became so chaotic, that the secretary, upon the recommendation of the National Radio Conferences which met in Washington in 1923 and 1924, established a policy of assigning specified frequencies to particular stations. * * * Since there were more stations than available frequencies, the secretary of commerce attempted to find room for everybody by limiting the power and hours of operation of stations in order that several stations might use the same channel. * * *

The secretary of commerce was powerless to deal with the situation. * * * (and) the plea of the secretary went unheeded. From July, 1926, to February 23, 1927, when Congress enacted the Radio Act of 1927, 44 Stat. 1162, almost 200 new stations went on the air. These new stations used any frequencies they desired, regardless of the interference thereby caused to others. Existing stations changed to other frequencies and increased their power and hours of operation at will. The result was confusion and chaos. With everybody on the air, nobody could be heard. The situation became so intolerable that the President in his message of December 7, 1926, appealed to Congress to enact a comprehensive radio law.

* * *

The plight into which radio fell prior to 1927 was attributable to certain basic facts about radio as a means of communication—its facilities are limited; they are not available to all who may wish to use them; the radio spectrum simply is not large enough to accommodate everybody. There is a fixed natural limitation upon the number of stations that can operate without interfering with one another. Regulation of radio was therefore as vital to its development as traffic control was to the development of the automobile. In enacting the Radio Act of 1927, the first comprehensive scheme of control over radio communication, Congress acted upon the knowledge that if the potentialities of radio were not to be wasted, regulation was essential.

The Radio Act of 1927 created the Federal Radio Commission, composed of five members, and endowed the commission with wide licensing and regulatory powers. We do not pause here to enumerate the scope of the Radio Act of 1927 and of the authority entrusted to the Radio Commission, for the basic provisions of that Act are incorporated in the Communications Act of 1934, * * * 47 U.S.C.A. § 151 et seq., * * * the legislation immediately before us. * * *

The criterion governing the exercise of the commission's licensing power is the "public interest, convenience, or necessity." §§ 307(a)(d), 309(a), 310, 312. In addition, § 307(b) directs the commission that "In considering applications for licenses, and modifications and renewals thereof, when and insofar as there is demand for the same, the commission shall make such distribution of licenses, frequencies, hours of operation, and of power among the several States and communities as to provide a fair, efficient, and equitable distribution of radio service to each of the same."

The act itself establishes that the commission's powers are not limited to the engineering and technical aspects of regulation of radio communication. Yet we are asked to regard the commission as a kind of traffic officer, policing the wave lengths to prevent stations from interfering with each other. But the act does not restrict the commission merely to supervision of the traffic. It puts upon the commission the burden of determining the composition of that traffic. The facilities of radio are not large enough to accommodate all who wish to use them. Methods must be devised for choosing from among the many who apply. And since Congress itself could not do this, it committed the task to the commission.

The commission was, however, not left at large in performing this duty. The touchstone provided by Congress was the "public interest, convenience, or necessity," a criterion which "is as concrete as the complicated factors for judgment in such a field of delegated authority permit." Federal Communications Comm. v. Pottsville Broadcasting Co., 309 U.S. 134, 138 (1940). * * *

The "public interest" to be served under the Communications Act is thus the interest of the listening public in "the larger and more effective use of radio." § 303(g). The facilities of radio are limited and therefore precious; they cannot be left to wasteful use without detriment to the public interest. * * * The commission's licensing function cannot be discharged, therefore, merely by finding that there are no technological objections to the granting of a license. If the criterion of "public interest" were limited to such matters, how could the commission choose between two applicants for the same facilities, each of whom is financially and technically qualified to operate a station? Since the very inception of federal regulation by radio, comparative considerations as to the services to be rendered have governed the application of the standard of "public interest, convenience, or necessity." * * *

The avowed aim of the Communications Act of 1934 was to secure the maximum benefits of radio to all the people of the United States. To that end Congress endowed the communications commission with comprehensive powers to promote and realize the vast potentialities of radio. Section 303(g) provides that the commission shall "generally encourage the larger and more effective use of radio in the public interest"; subsection (i) gives the commission specific "authority to make special regulations applicable to radio stations engaged in chain broadcasting"; and subsection (r) empowers it to adopt "such rules and regulations and prescribe such restrictions and conditions, not inconsistent with law, as may be necessary to carry out the provisions of this act."

These provisions, individually and in the aggregate, preclude the notion that the commission is empowered to deal only with technical and engineering impediments to the "larger and more effective use of radio in the public interest." We cannot find in the act any such restriction of the commission's authority. Suppose, for example, that a community can, because of physical limitations, be assigned only two stations. That community might be deprived of effective service in any one of several ways. More powerful stations in nearby cities might blanket out the signals of the local stations so that they could not be heard at all. The stations might interfere with each other so that neither could be clearly heard. One station might dominate the other with the power of its signal. But the community could be deprived of good radio service in ways less crude. One man, financially and technically qualified, might apply for and obtain the licenses of both stations and present a single service over the two stations, thus wasting a frequency otherwise available to the area. The language of the act does not withdraw such a situation from the licensing and regulatory powers of the Commission, and there is no evidence that Congress did not mean its broad language to carry the authority it expresses.

In essence, the Chain Broadcasting Regulations represent a particularization of the Commission's conception of the "public interest" sought to be safeguarded by Congress in enacting the Communications Act of 1934. The basic consideration of policy underlying the Regulations is succinctly stated in its Report: "With the number of radio channels limited by natural factors, the public interest demands that those who are entrusted with the available channels shall make the fullest and most effective use of them. If a licensee enters into a contract with a network organization which limits his ability to make the best use of the radio facility assigned him, he is not serving the public interest. * * * The net effect [of the practices disclosed by the investigation] has been that broadcasting service has been maintained at a level below that possible under a system of free competition. Having so found, we would be remiss in our statutory duty of encouraging 'the larger and more effective use of radio in the public interest' if we were to grant licenses to persons who persist in these practices."

We would be asserting our personal views regarding the effective utilization of radio were we to deny that the commission was entitled to find that the large public aims of the Communications Act of 1934 comprehend the considerations which moved the commission in promulgating the Chain Broadcasting Regulations. True enough, the act does not explicitly say that the commission shall have power to deal with network practices found inimical to the public interest. But Congress was acting in a field of regulation which was both new and dynamic. "Congress moved under the spur of a widespread fear that in the absence of governmental control the public interest might be subordinated to monopolistic domination in the broadcasting field." Federal Communications Comm. v. Pottsville Broadcasting Co., 309 U.S. 134, 137. In the context of the developing problems to which it was directed, the act gave the commission not niggardly but expansive powers. It was given a comprehensive mandate to "encourage the larger and more effective use of radio in the public interest," if need be, by making "special regulations applicable to radio stations engaged in chain broadcasting." § 303(g)(i).

Generalities unrelated to the living problems of radio communication of course cannot justify exercises of power by the commission. Equally so, generalities empty of all concrete considerations of the actual bearing of regulations promulgated by the commission to the subject-matter entrusted to it, cannot strike down exercises of power by the commission. While Congress did not give the commission unfettered discretion to regulate all phases of the radio industry, it did not frustrate the purposes for which the Communications Act of 1934 was brought into being by attempting an itemized catalogue of the specific manifestations of the general problems for the solution of which it was establishing a regulatory agency. That would have stereotyped the powers for the commission to specific details in regulating a field of enterprise the dominant characteristic of which was the rapid pace of its unfolding. And so Congress did what experience had taught it in similar attempts at regulation, even in fields where the subject-matter of regulation was far less fluid and dynamic than radio. The essence of that experience was to define broad areas for regulation and to establish standards for judgment adequately related in their application to the problems to be solved. * * *

We conclude, therefore, that the Communications Act of 1934 authorized the commission to promulgate regulations designed to correct the abuses disclosed by its investigation of chain broadcasting.

* * *

Since there is no basis for any claim that the commission failed to observe procedural safeguards required by law, we reach the contention that the Regulations should be denied enforcement on constitutional grounds. Here, as in New York Cent. Securities Corp. v. United States, 287 U.S. 12, 24, 25, the claim is made that the standard of "public interest" governing the exercise of the powers delegated to the commission by Congress is so vague and indefinite that, if it be construed as comprehensively as words alone permit, the delegation of legislative authority is unconstitutional. But, as we held in that case, "It is a mistaken assumption that this is a mere general reference to public welfare without any standard to guide determinations. The purpose of the act, the requirements it imposes, and the context of the provision in question show the contrary." Id.

We come, finally, to an appeal to the First Amendment. The Regulations, even if valid in all other respects, must fall because they abridge, say the appellants, their right of free speech. If that be so, it would follow that every person whose application for a license to operate a station is denied by the commission is thereby denied his constitutional right of free speech. Freedom of utterance is abridged to many who wish to use the limited facilities of radio. *Unlike other modes of expression, radio inherently is not available to all. That is its unique characteristic, and that is why, unlike other modes of expression, it is subject to governmental regulation. Because it cannot be used by all, some who wish to use it must be denied.* [Emphasis added.] But Congress did not authorize the commission to choose among applicants upon the basis of their political, economic or social views, or upon any other capricious basis. If it did, or if the commission by these regulations proposed a choice among applicants upon some such basis, the issue before us would be wholly different. The question here is simply whether the commission, by announcing that it will refuse licenses to persons who engage in specified network practices (a basis for choice which we hold is comprehended within the statutory criterion of "public interest"), is thereby denying such persons the constitutional right of free speech. The right of free speech does not include, however, the right to use the facilities of radio without a license. The licensing system established by Congress in the Communications Act of 1934 was a proper exercise of its power over commerce. The standard it provided for the licensing of stations was the "public interest, convenience, or necessity." Denial of a station license on that ground, if valid under the Act, is not a denial of free speech. * * *

Affirmed.

Justice MURPHY, dissenting.

* * * Although radio broadcasting, like the press, is generally conducted on a commercial basis, it is not an ordinary business activity, like the selling of securities or the marketing of electrical power. In the dissemination of information and opinion radio has assumed a position of commanding importance, rivaling the press and the pulpit. Owing to its physical characteristics radio, unlike the other methods of conveying information, must be regulated and rationed by the government. Otherwise there would be chaos, and radio's usefulness would be largely destroyed. But because of its vast potentialities as a medium of communication, discussion and propaganda, the character and extent of control that should be exercised over it by the government is a matter of deep and vital concern. Events in Europe show that radio may readily be a weapon of authority and misrepresentation, instead of a means of entertainment and enlightenment. It may even be an instrument of oppression. In pointing out these possibilities I do not mean to intimate in the slightest that they are imminent or probable in this country but they do suggest that the construction of the instant statute should be approached with more than ordinary restraint and caution, to avoid an interpretation that is not clearly justified by the conditions that brought about its enactment, or that would give the commission greater powers than the Congress intended to confer.

* * *

By means of these regulations and the enforcement program, the commission would not only extend its authority over business activities which represent interests and investments of a very substantial character, which have not been put under its jurisdiction by the act, but would greatly enlarge its control over an institution that has now become a rival of the press and pulpit as a purveyor of news and entertainment and a medium of public discussion. To assume a function and responsibility of such wide reach and importance in the life of the nation, as a mere incident of its duty to pass on individual applications for permission to operate a radio station and use a specific wave length, is an assumption of authority to which I am not willing to lend my assent.

* * *

COMMENT

1. Is the limited access medium rationale the only plausible basis for broadcast regulation? Since Justice Murphy points out that radio "may be a weapon of authority and misrepresentation instead of a means of entertainment and enlightenment," why doesn't he wish to uphold the Chain Broadcasting Regulations and thereby limit the concentration of communicating power?

Justice Murphy's dissent offers the basis for a new rationale for government regulation of broadcasting—the social impact rationale. Under this theory, the pervasiveness and the impact of broadcasting justify a greater measure of government regulation than other media. For application of this theory, see *FCC v. Pacifica Foundation*, p. 920ff.

2. The Chain Broadcasting Regulations revealed an attempt by the FCC to do what Congress failed to do in the Federal Communications Act, i.e., bring the networks under the regulatory authority of the FCC. The FCC was concerned with the problem that the station licensees, the parties regulated by the act, were becoming conduits for the networks. As with radio in 1943, at the present time television programming in the evening or "prime time" hours is largely dominated by the networks.

3. Presently, the networks, although not subject directly to regulation under the Federal Communications Act of 1934, are actually responsive to FCC jurisdiction in at least two ways. First, FCC rules and regulations do, of course, bind broadcast licensees. To the extent these licensees are network affiliates, which in large part they are, the networks are affected by FCC policy. Second, although there are limitations on how many broadcasting outlets of each type a single party may own, the networks utilize to the limit the existing rules which permit them to own a limited number of stations of each type. See text, p. 948. Not surprisingly, therefore, their outlets are found in the largest and most important markets. Therefore, with respect to O and O's (stations owned and operated by the networks) the networks are directly regulated by the FCC.

Should networks be placed under direct regulation?

Should lack of licensee control over programming be a negative factor even if there is no competing applicant?

We have been considering the problem of the station owner who is a network affiliate, who does not know what programming his station will be emitting until he flicks the dial with the rest of the audience. However, the same problem can arise with the station which is not a network affiliate.[2]

4. Although the Federal Communications Act of 1934 itself afforded the FCC no specific authority to regulate the contractual relationships between the individual broadcast licensee and the network, the FCC based its authority to issue the

---

2. See Yale Broadcasting Co. v. FCC, 478 F.2d 594 (D.C.Cir.1973), cert.den. 414 U.S. 914 (1973).

chain broadcasting regulations on the act's many references to the power of the FCC to regulate broadcasting in the "public interest." In the proposed "rewrite" of the Federal Communications Act of 1934, the "Communications Act of 1978," authored by the House Subcommittee on Communications chaired by Congressman Lionel Van Deerlin (D. Calif.), major revisions were proposed for broadcast regulation. The proposal still left the networks unregulated. However, the "rewrite" did make a major change by way of deletion. In the entire 217-page text of the proposed "rewrite" not a single reference was made to the "public interest, convenience and necessity." See H.R. 13015, 95th Cong., 2d Sess., June 6, 1978.

Harry Shooshan, chief counsel of the House Communications Subcommittee, explained the omission by observing that Congressman Van Deerlin "felt that much of what's bad in communications regulation can be traced to the FCC's trying to interpret that phrase" and therefore "decided not to invite any further misinterpretation of Congress' intentions." Shooshan also observed that the "rewrite" was "an effort to fulfill the public interest" and thus spoke for itself. See *Broadcasting,* pp. 39–40, June 12, 1978. Would the FCC and the courts still have to import a "public interest" concept to aid them in enforcing and interpreting a new act? Without importing such a standard into the text of a new act, it is hard to see how the flexibility necessary for effective regulation can exist, particularly in the event of the occurrence of unforeseen developments. After all, the Federal Communications Act of 1934 was applied to television and to cable television even though neither was a reality in 1934. Doesn't a regulatory agency with the task of governing an industry which is bound up with an everchanging technology need some language which authorizes it to exercise a wise discretion? How else can one govern new technology in the electronic field? It would seem that the "public interest" standard was designed to facilitate the exercise of such a wise discretion.

5. A more recent study still considered the *NBC* case to be a critical precedent on whether the FCC can regulate network practices even though the Federal Communications Act does not grant specific authority to the FCC to regulate the networks:

> In NBC, the court addressed three points of continuing interest to the issue of the FCC's jurisdiction. First, the court confirmed that the commission's licensing authority over broadcast stations permits it to promulgate regulations involving network practices addressed to broadcast station licensees that are network affiliates. Second, the Court suggested that courts should construe the 1934 act liberally in evaluating the commission's regulatory powers and responsibilities. Stated simply, courts should view the specific responsibilities assigned the commission as exemplary of its larger responsibilities. Third, the court implied by its silence that the commission's overriding responsibility to regulate television broadcasting and its specific power to regulate stations engaged in chain broadcasting authorize it to regulate networks directly.

See, Krattenmaker and Metzger, *FCC Regulatory Authority Over Commercial Television Networks: The Role of Ancillary Jurisdiction*, 77 Northwestern U.L.Rev. 403 at 431–432 (1982).

EMERGING TECHNOLOGIES

Many of the issues in this chapter concern the legal governance of new communications technologies which were not anticipated when the Federal Communications Act was written. This era particularly is characterized by the constant development of new communications technologies. It will be the challenge to the communications specialists of the future to attempt to provide a structure for the orderly governance of these technologies. Should reasoning such as that found in the *NBC* case be used in the future, at least by analogy, to resolve the issues raised by these new technologies? Examples of some of these new technologies follow.

Direct Broadcast Satellites

Direct Broadcast Satellites (DBS) is a new, highly advanced technology which will permit the broadcast of multiple channels of television directly from satellites to individual homes. Individual subscribers will be equipped with a small, affordable receiving disc as well as an electronics unit which will descramble the satellite signal for display on a regular television set. Individual licensees will construct and launch the satellites and will have the option of either broadcasting their own selected programs or operating a common carrier-type service.

The DBS system has the potential to bring enormous benefits to the public. DBS will help meet the growing consumer demand for diversified and specialized television programming. In particular, DBS will bring improved video service to rural and remote areas that have long been underserved. DBS will also stimulate the program production industry by serving as an outlet for programming. Furthermore, DBS will promote competition in the video marketplace and has the potential to erode the current network dominance of national program distribution.

Permanent guidelines regulating the DBS industry awaited the 1983 Regional Administrative Radio Conference (RARC) which was to develop standards of operation for the Western Hemisphere. 86 FCC2d 719 (1981). Prior to the Conference, the FCC had promulgated a series of provisions which subjected DBS Systems to a minimum of regulations during its "experimental phase". 47 Fed.Reg. 31,555 (1982) (to be codified at 47 C.F.R. Pt. 100). This scheme imposed all applicable statutory requirements upon interim DBS Systems. 47 Fed.Reg. 31,568 n. 85 (1982), e.g., 47 U.S.C. § 201 et seq. (common carriers); 47 U.S.C. § 315 (broadcasters). Thus, DBS operators broadcasting their own programming had to comply with the mandates of the fairness doctrine, the equal time/access rules for political candidates, and the personal attack provisions. Moreover, DBS operators functioning as broadcasters were also subject to the same equal employment requirements as were conventional broadcasters. 47 Fed.Reg. 31,575 (1982) (to be codified at 47 C.F.R. § 100.51). In addition, all DBS operators licensed in the experimental phase were required to meet whatever international standards were agreed to at the 1983 RARC. 47 Fed.Reg. 31,558 n. 25 (1982). However, beyond these requirements, the interim provisions placed no restrictions on cross or multiple ownership, 47 Fed. Reg. 31,570 n. 95 (1982); nor were any restrictions placed on program content, service offerings, or methods of financing outside of the express mandates of the Communications Act. 47 Fed.Reg. 31,570 (1982).

An issue of conflict in the FCC interim provisions involved DBS spectrum allocation and the reassignment of territorial fixed service (FS) operations now using the 12.2–12.7 GHz band proposed for use by DBS operators. In 47 Fed.Reg. 31,562 n. 46, the FCC's compromise resolution established a transition period whereby DBS and FS systems would be considered coequal. Thus, existing FS operations will not have to provide protection to DBS systems, and DBS operators desiring to expand into existing FS markets must accommodate the FS operator through agreement or otherwise.

Multipoint Distribution Service

Multipoint Distribution Service (MDS) is a technological alternative to full-service television broadcasting that has the capacity to fill the programming needs of much of the underserved locations throughout the nation. Technically, MDS consists of a microwave transmitter which broadcasts over a microwave frequency to a receiving antenna located within a coverage area of approximately ten to twenty miles. The microwave signal is converted at the receiving antenna to a lower frequency which then passes through a cable to the customer's set to be viewed on a VHF channel which is vacant in the community. 45 Fed.Reg. 29,350 at 24 (1980). In this manner, the MDS system can avoid objectionable interference with full-service stations while retaining the capability of broadcasting over available VHF channels.

A regulatory feature of the MDS system is that it may only operate as a common carrier. 47 C.F.R. § 21.903 (1981). Thus, the licensee cannot exercise any control over the programming presented on the channel. Moreover, as a common carrier, the licensee is not subject to FCC programming standards such as the fairness doctrine, the equal time/access provisions for political candidates, and the personal attack rules. FCC regulation of MDS broadcasting has focused on the technical side of the operation. See 47 C.F.R. §§ 904–908 (1981), relating to transmission power, standards, equipment, and bandwidths.

In 1983, there were only one or two channels available in most communities for MDS use, with the second channel being available only in fifty of the larger metropolitan areas. 47 C.F.R. § 21.90(c). These channels are allocated via the comparative hearing system. The FCC considered using a lottery method to expedite channel allocation and reduce processing expenses to both the applicant and the Commission. Notice of Inquiry and Proposed Rulemaking in CC Docket No. 80–116, 45 Fed.Reg. 29,335 (1980). However, the commission refused to implement the random selection system pursuant to 47 U.S.C. § 309(i) due to the "inevitable succession of administrative and judicial reviews." 89 FCC2d 257, 283 (1982). The FCC was also reviewing the feasibility of allocating additional MDS channels in the top fifty markets. 45 Fed.Reg. 29,335 (1980).

Low Power Television (LPTV)

As an alternative to CATV, MDS, and full-service television systems, the FCC in 1982 inaugurated the first low power television (LPTV) broadcasting service to be considered by the FCC in twenty years. 47 Fed.Reg. 21,468 (1982). The hope was that these new low power stations would bring television service to locations that otherwise are unserved or underserved as well as satisfy a public desire for additional and diversified television programming. 47 Fed.Reg. 21,468, 21,470 (1982). Low power systems may also open up new opportunities for minority ownership and "attract a new breed of * * * broadcast networks." 45 Fed.Reg. 67,168, 69,191 (1980). These hopes arose out of the peculiar nature of low power service, a service which, because of its particularly small and undefined coverage area, must be directly responsive to the interests of local consumers to assure economic viability.

In light of the nature of the low power service, the FCC has opted for a regulatory scheme of minimal government interference. This scheme protects existing full-service television stations by authorizing low power stations to operate only on a secondary spectrum priority and requiring low power stations to eliminate objectionable interference with full-service stations or cease operations. 47 Fed.Reg. 21,497 (1982) (to be codified at 47 C.F.R. §§ 74.-703–7). Program-related regulations such as the statutory prohibitions on the broadcast of obscene material, plugola, payola, and lotteries as well as the fairness doctrine, the equal time/access rules for political candidates, and the personal attack rules also apply to the low power service. 47 Fed.Reg. 21,491 (1982), to be codified at 47 C.F.R. § 74.780).

Beyond these requirements, the specific nature of low power service programming and operation has been left to the discretion of the licensee, based upon the mandates of the marketplace. There are no restrictions on ownership per se. The FCC believes that free entry into and out of the low power industry will best serve potential applicants as well as the public. 47 Fed.Reg. 21,489 (1982). There are no restrictions on the airing of commercials or the carriage of pay television broadcasts. 47 Fed.Reg. 21,486 (1982). LPTV stations also have no community ascertainment obligations or program log requirements, and there is no spectrum set aside for educational broadcasts. 47 Fed.Reg. 21,491 (1982).

The FCC believes that a minimal regulatory posture will best serve the programming needs of discrete community groups without unnecessarily burdening entry into the low power market. Moreover, as low power stations may be constructed and transferred at relatively low expense, this new service naturally lends itself to operation and ownership by minority groups and other entrants that are newcomers to the broadcast industry.

THE PROGRAMMING DISCRETION OF THE LICENSEE AND BROADCASTING IN THE PUBLIC INTEREST

The Problem of Securing Licensee Control and Responsibility Over Programming

The idea that the individual licensee must retain control over his or her programming and may not abdicate that responsibility is deeply embedded in broadcasting law. In an early and well-known case, Simmons v. FCC, 169 F.2d 670 (D.C.Cir.1948), it was held that a broadcaster is a trustee for the public and as such has a duty to retain control over programming. In *Simmons*, the FCC refused to grant an application for a power increase and a change in a station's frequency where the licensee frankly stated the intention to "plug" into the CBS network from 8 A.M. to 11 P.M. Suppose the licensee argued in such circumstances that its right of free expression includes the right to choose to "plug" into CBS from 8 A.M. to 11 P.M.? This argument was basically rejected in *NBC v. United States*, text, p. 770.

Although the *Simmons* case might be viewed as permitting FCC control of programming and therefore as a precedent for control of program content in broadcasting generally, it should be emphasized that what is being evaluated is "the total performance of stations." The Commission does not determine "which *individual* programs best suit the local needs of each community." Note, *FCC Control of Radio Programming*, 2 Vand. L.Rev. 464 at 465 (1949). Does this distinction between total evaluation of the licensee's performance rather than review of "individual" programs satisfy the requirements of § 326 of the Federal Communications Act. § 326 provides:

> Nothing in this act shall be understood or construed to give the commission the power of censorship over the radio communications or signals transmitted by any radio station, and no regulation or condition shall be promulgated or fixed by the commission which shall interfere with the right of free speech by means of radio communciation. Communications Act of 1934, § 326, 48 Stat. 1091, 47 U.S.C.A. § 326 (1958).

A related issue arose in Cosmopolitan Broadcasting Corp., 59 FCC2d 558 (1976)—

should an FCC inquiry into a renewal applicant's past programming be viewed as censorship? The FCC made the inquiry in order to determine whether the renewal applicant had maintained adequate control over its programming in the past. The court, per Judge Bazelon, refused to view the inquiry into past programming as censorship.

In the *Cosmopolitan* case, the FCC itself designated Cosmopolitan's application for license renewal for hearing. No competing applicant was seeking Cosmopolitan's license. See generally Cosmopolitan Broadcasting Corp. v. FCC, 581 F.2d 917 (D.C.Cir.1978). Does the FCC have authority, under the rationale of *NBC v. US*, text, p. 770, to ascertain whether renewal of a sole applicant's license will be in the public interest? The problem arose in Henry v. FCC, 302 F.2d 191 (D.C.Cir. 1962), where a new applicant sought a permit to construct the first commercial FM station in Elizabeth, New Jersey. In support of the application, the applicant submitted programming proposals to support its license application which were identical in its application for an FM facility in Berwyn, Illinois.

In *Henry*, the court upheld the FCC's authority to reject even the sole applicant for a new license:

> Appellants contend that the statutory licensing scheme requires a grant where, as here, it is established that the sole applicants for a frequency are legally, financially and technically qualified. This view reflects an arbitrarily narrow understanding of the statutory words "public convenience, interest, or necessity." It leaves no room for commission consideration of matters relating to programming.

The court concluded that the FCC could require that even a sole applicant for a license must show an "earnest interest in serving a local community by evidencing familiarity with its particular needs and an effort to meet them." The FCC's action in denying the license application in *Henry* was held to involve "no greater interference with a broadcaster's alleged right to choose its programs free from commission control than the interference involved in National Broadcasting Co."

The *Henry* case looks innocent enough. But it actually represents a challenge to the entire existing rationale for broadcast regulation. The theory of the *NBC* case was that broadcasting was a limited access medium. Therefore, the commission was under obligation to play a role in the "composition of the traffic." But if only one applicant seeks a station license, why should the commission play any role at all? The limited access rationale at this point presumably disappears. Does the *Henry* result suggest an alternative theory of broadcast regulation? If so, what is it?

The Concept of "Balanced" Programming

JOHNSTON BROADCASTING CO. v. FCC

175 F.2D 351 (D.C.CIR. 1949).

PRETTYMAN, Circuit Judge. Two applications, one for a permit to construct a new radio broadcasting station and the other for changes in the frequency and power of an existing station, were presented to the commission, one by Johnston Broadcasting Company and the other by Thomas N. Beach. The applications were mutually exclusive, both being for operation on the same frequency. The commission set them for a comparative hearing.

* * *

A choice between two applicants involves more than the bare qualifications of each applicant. It involves a comparison of characteristics. Both A and B may be qualified, but if a choice must be made, the question is which is the better qualified. Both might be ready, able and willing to serve the public interest. But in choosing between them, the inquiry must reveal which would better serve that interest. So the nature of the material, the findings and the bases for conclusion differ when (1) the inquiry is merely whether an applicant is qualified and (2) when the purpose is to make a proper choice between two qualified applicants. To illustrate, local residence may not be an essential to qualification. But as between two applicants otherwise equally able, local residence might be a decisive factor.

In the present case, the commission easily found both applicants to be qualified for a permit. The question then was which should receive it. Comparative qualities and not mere positive characteristics must then be considered. * * *

In sum, we think that there are no established criteria by which a choice between the applicants must be made. In this respect, a comparative determination differs from the determination of each applicant's qualifications for a permit. A choice can properly be made upon those differences advanced by the parties as reasons for the choice. To illustrate, if neither applicant presents as a material factor, the relative financial resources of himself and his adversary, the commission need not require testimony upon the point or make a finding in respect to it, beyond the requisite ability for bare qualification. It may assume that there is no material difference between the applicants upon that point.

* * *

In the case at bar, there were five points of difference urged by the contesting applicants as pertinent to a choice between them, (1) residence, (2) broadcasting experience, (3) proposed participation in the operation of the station, (4) program proposals, and (5) quality of staff.

The basis for the conclusion of the commission is clearly stated. In its Memorandum Opinion and Order, it said succinctly:

"Our opinion to favor the Beach application on its merits over that of the Johnston application was based on our finding that while there were no sharp distinctions between the applicants in terms of residence, broadcasting experience, or proposed participation in the operation of the facilities applied for, there was a sharp distinction in favor of the applicant Beach in matters of program proposals and planned staff operations."

* * *

As to the program proposals, the difference which the commission found is spelled out in detail in its findings. It found nothing in the record to indicate that Johnston had made or would make an affirmative effort to encourage broadcasts on controversial issues or topics of current interest to the community, such as education, labor, and civic enterprises. On the other hand, it found that Beach has had and proposes to have a program of positive action to encourage such broadcasts, and of complete cooperation with civic interests. The commission concluded that Beach would provide greater opportunity for local expression than would Johnston. The findings are based upon evidence in the record, and the conclusion seems to us to be within the permissible bounds of the commission's discretion.

The difference between the staffs of the applicants is succinctly stated. The commission found, as the evidence indicated, that the proposed positions and duties of the Beach staff promise a much more effective provision for program preparation and presentation than do those of the Johnston staff.

As to appellant's contention that the commission's consideration of the proposed programs was a form of censorship, it is true that the commission cannot choose on the basis of political, economic or social views of an applicant. But in a comparative consideration, it is well recognized that comparative service to the listening public is the vital element, and programs are the essence of that service. So, while the commission cannot proscribe any type of program (except for prohibitions against obscenity, profanity, etc.), it can make a comparison on the basis of public interest and, therefore, of public service. Such a comparison of proposals is not a form of censorship within the meaning of the statute. As we read the commission's findings, the nature of the views of the applicants was no part of the consideration. The nature of the programs was.

We cannot say that the commission acted arbitrarily or capriciously in making its conclusive choice between these two applicants.

Reversed and remanded.

COMMENT

1. Although the commission was reversed on grounds that do not concern us, the commission's estimate of the applicants based on a comparative evaluation of their programming proposals *was* upheld.

2. One of the most influential guides to balanced programming was set forth in the famous "Blue Book" where the commission stated that on a renewal application it would make an inquiry to determine whether the station's previous performance had been in the "public interest." The "Blue Book" required licensees to broadcast 1) sustaining programs (unsponsored, noncommercial, public interest programming); 2) local, live programming; 3) programs devoted to the discussion of public issues; and 4) to make an effort to eliminate advertising excesses. FCC, *Public Service Responsibility of Broadcast Licensees* (1946).

Note that the *Johnston* case is not really a renewal case. But it provides a good illustration of the consequences to license *applicants* of failing to propose local service, sustaining and public affairs programming in accordance with "Blue Book" standards. No licensee on renewal, however, has ever been denied a license for failing, during his previous license period, to broadcast the proper balanced programming mix. Why this leniency by the commission on license renewal as opposed to the original license application? Is such leniency defensible?

3. The *Network Programming Inquiry Report and Statement of Policy*, issued by the FCC on July 29, 1960, was a kind of updating of the "Blue Book." The "*Statement*," 44 FCC 2303, at 2314 (1960) declares:

> The major elements usually necessary to meet the public interest, needs and desires of the community in which the station is located as developed by the industry, and recognized by the commission have included: (1) opportunity for local self-expression, (2) the development and use of local talent, (3) programs for children, (4) religious programs, (5) educational programs, (6) public affairs programs, (7) editorializing by licensees, (8) political broadcasts, (9) agricultural programs, (10) news programs, (11) weather and market reports, (12) sports programs, (13) service to minority groups, (14) entertainment programming.

What differences do you discern between the programming guides of the "Blue Book," as set forth above, and those set forth in the 1960 Program Policy Statement?

In Office of Communication of United Church of Christ v. FCC, 707 F.2d 1413 (D.C.Civ.1983) the action of the FCC in Report and Order, Deregulation of Order, 84 FCC 2d 968 (1981) undertaking a massive deregulation of the commercial radio industry was substantially affirmed. In Memorandum and Order, 87 FCC 2d 797 (1981), the FCC, clarifying its deregulation order, defined the "public interest to require programming responsive to community issues." As Judge Wright put it for the Court in *Office of Communication of United Church of Christ, supra*: "Broadcasters need not then, as a commission requirement, provide any specific types of programming such as those listed above." Thus, the court of appeals approved the repudiation of the 1960 Programming Statement. But it pointedly endorsed the FCC's determination to remain "faithful to its statutory mandate to regulate in the public interest."

At the same time, the Court warned that although the FCC has "reoriented its public interest away from categories, the extent and foreseeable consequence of that policy statement should not be overestimated." Judge Wright indicated that a licensee who conformed with the old 1960 Programming Statement would be in compliance with the "new FCC issue-responsive programming". Judge Wright observed on this point: "(W)e are hard-pressed to think of examples of programming categories described in the 1960 Programming Statement where content could not also be described in issue terms and thus still come within the Commission's delineation of public interest programming in each category."

4. One of the most significant FCC policy statements on the factors involved in choosing among qualified applicants for the same broadcast facilities is found in the Policy Statement on Comparative Broadcast Hearings, 1 FCC2d 393 (1965):

> One of the commission's primary responsibilities is to choose among qualified new applicants for the same broadcast facilities. This commonly requires extended hearings into a number of areas of comparison. The hearing and decision process is inherently complex, and the subject does not lend itself to precise categorization or to the clear making of precedent. The various factors cannot be assigned absolute values, some factors may be present in some cases and not in others, and the differences between applicants with respect to each factor are almost infinitely variable.
>
> * * *
>
> We believe that there are two primary objectives toward which the process of comparison should be directed. They are, first, the best practicable service to the public, and, second, a maximum diffusion of control of the media of mass communications. The value of these objectives is clear. Diversification of control is a public good in a free society, and is additionally desirable where a government licensing system limits access by the public to the use of radio and television facilities. Equally basic is a broadcast service which meets the needs of the public in the area to be served, both in terms of those general interests which all areas have in common and those special interests which areas do not share. An important element of such a service is the flexibility to change as local needs and interests change. Since independence and individuality of approach are elements of rendering good program service, the primary goals of good service and diversification of control are also fully compatible.

Diversification of ownership and "meeting the needs of the public in the area to be served" are both emphasized in the Policy Statement. Diversification of ownership is discussed elsewhere in this chapter. See text, p. 948. But the goal of meeting the needs of the public in the area served was FCC policy both before and after the 1965 Policy Statement. We encounter it in the principle that the broadcast station must retain responsibility over its own programming, in the concept of balanced programming, and again in the development of the ascertainment process.

Changes in Program Format and Broadcasting in the Public Interest

A series of cases which dramatize the clash between claims of groups in the community for diversity in programming and the claims of the individual broadcaster to choose his own programming are the program format cases. These cases raise familiar questions. Should the FCC be required to define the "public interest" in such a way as to involve it in programming determinations? Should programming in the public interest compel a broadcaster to serve a minority taste within the community or should such issues be left for resolution in the marketplace?

WEFM–FM in Chicago, operated by the Zenith Radio Corporation, had a classical musical format for more than thirty years. In 1972, Zenith entered into an agreement to sell the station to GCC Communications of Chicago. GCC proposed to change WEFM's format from classical to "contemporary music, later defined to be 'rock music'." A group of Chicago area citizens, the Citizens Committee to Save WEFM, opposed the transfer because of the proposed change of format. The citizens filed a petition to deny the transfer with the FCC and requested a hearing. The FCC denied the petition and granted the assignment of the license. Initially, a panel of the court of appeals, per Judge Bazelon, affirmed. Citizens Committee to Save WEFM v. FCC, 506 F.2d 246 (D.C.Cir. 1974).

Summarizing prior law, Judge Bazelon, speaking for the court in *WEFM* said: "It is only when the format to be discontinued is apparently unique to the area served that a hearing on the public interest must be held." See, Citizens Committee to Preserve the Voice of the Arts in Atlanta v. FCC, 436 F.2d 263 (D.C.Cir.1970). In such situations, "the public interest in diversity may outweigh the dangers of government intrusion into the content of programming." However, the Chicago area *was* served by another classical music station. Therefore, in the case of *WEFM* transfer, there was no need for a hearing on the diversity point. Judge Bazelon observed that "[I]mportant First Amendment rights are at stake when music formats are regulated. * * * Danger lurks in government regulation of what music can be put on the airwaves. Such regulation, ostensibly in the name of diversity, may open the door to withholding approval of transfers if the new format is more controversial than the one to be abandoned."

However, on rehearing en banc, the court of appeals, in an opinion before Judge McGowan found that the Citizens Committee had raised serious and material questions necessitating a hearing before final disposition of the transfer application. The court therefore set aside the FCC orders in the case. Judge McGowan commented:

> The theory underlying the court's decision in *Citizens Committee of Atlanta* is that the FCC does have some responsibility, under its public interest mandate, for programming content. * * * "The commission is not dictating tastes when it seeks to discover what they presently are, and to consider what assignment of channels is feasible and fair in terms of their gratification." (*Citizens Committee of Atlanta*)

In a significant statement, Judge McGowan declared: "Once a proposed format change engenders 'public grumbling of significant proportions,' the causal relationship between format and finance must be established, and if that requires the resolution of substantial factual questions, as it did in that case, then a hearing must be held."

Judge McGowan then summarized the law of the format change cases:

> There is a public interest in a diversity of broadcast entertainment formats. The disappearance of a distinctive format may deprive a significant segment of the public of the benefits of radio, at least at their first-preference level. When faced with a proposed license assignment encompassing a format change, the FCC is obliged to determine whether the format to be lost is unique or otherwise serves a specialized audience that would feel its loss.

> If the endangered format is of this variety, then the FCC must affirmatively consider whether the public interest would be served by approving the proposed assignment, which may, if there are substantial questions of fact or inadequate data in the application or other officially noticeable materials, necessitate conducting a public hearing in order to resolve the factual issues or assist the commission in discerning the public interest. Finally, it is not sufficient justification for approving the application that the assignor has asserted financial losses in providing the special format; those losses must be attributable to the format itself in order logically to support an assignment that occasions a loss of the format.

Judge McGowan concluded:

> We think it axiomatic that preservation of a format [which] would otherwise disappear, although economically and technologically viable and preferred by a significant number of listeners, is generally in the public interest. There may well be situations in which that is not the case for reasons within the discretion of the FCC to consider, but a policy of mechanistic deference to "competition" in entertainment program format will not focus the FCC's attention on the necessity to discern such reasons before allowing diversity, serving the public interest because it serves more of the public, to disappear from the airwaves.

McGowan noted that the *WEFM* case also raised questions as to whether the other so-called classical station in Chicago (WFMT) was "a reasonable substitute for the service previously offered by WEFM." The court in *WEFM* then ordered the FCC to set the issue of transfer for hearing on the issue of whether the programming of the other "classical" station in Chicago was an adequate substitute for the old "classical" format of WEFM. Also, the issue of whether the classical format of WEFM occasioned financial losses was set for hearing.

In response to the *WEFM* case, the FCC began an inquiry into its policies dealing with changes in entertainment format. See Development of Policy Re: Changes In the Entertainment Formats of Broadcast Stations, 57 FCC2d 580 (1976), reconsideration denied 58 FCC2d 617 (1976). The FCC's distaste for intruding into broadcast judgment in connection with program formats was made clear. "For over 40 years, therefore, broadcast applicants have been free to select their own programming formats. * * * In the present controversy, we are being called upon to substitute our judgment for that of the applicant on the most subjective grounds imaginable without any clear danger to the public interest."

In his concurring opinion, in *WEFM*, Judge Bazelon stated his concern—and ours—with the fact that "the court had set a 'broad view of the commission's authority in the delicate area of programming with nary a syllable spoken to the First Amendment implications of its decision.' We believe that this issue warrants a prompt and thorough review and accordingly, such comments are requested. Specifically, would any system of commission intervention in, or selection of, licensee formats violate the First Amendment?"

In a separate dissenting statement, FCC Commissioner Glen Robinson challenged the line of cases in the United States Court of Appeals for the District of Columbia Circuit which began with the *Voice of the Arts,* see text, p. 786 and ended with *WEFM*: The standard for 'uniqueness' or 'diversity'—the diversity that the public wants enough so as to cause it to grumble when it is diminished—is obviously idiosyncratic and subjective. Quite aside from the constitutional objections * * * this subjective element presents intractable difficulties in administration. See 57 FCC2d 580 at 594 (1976).

Despite *WEFM* and its predecessors, the FCC still prefers to let the economic marketplace rather than the FCC determine problems of change of program format. See Changes in the Entertainment

Formats of Broadcast Stations, Memorandum Opinion and Order, 60 FCC2d 858 at 863–866 (1976).

Professor Canby has supported the FCC's noninterventionist approach to the format change problem. Under the *Voice of the Arts* ruling, whether a broadcaster will be required to suit a particular taste will "depend entirely upon what other broadcasters in the same marketplace may do." In order not to be frozen into a particular format, a broadcaster may avoid "specialty formats" and merely mimic the programming of other stations in the same market. Professor Canby concludes: "This coercive effect of thc format decisions not only interferes with the first amendment rights of the broadcaster but also positively disserves any long-run interest of the audience in diversity." See Canby, *Programming In Response to the Community: The Broadcast Consumer and the First Amendment*, 55 Tex.L.Rev. 67 at 95 (1976).

Others have defended the format change cases in the District of Columbia Circuit on the ground that the cases recognize that unity comes not from the lowest common denominator, but from "the interplay among diverse and authentically expressed views." See Barron, *Freedom of the Press for Whom?* at 237, 238 (1973); and Note, *The Public Interest in Balanced Programming Content: The Case for FCC Regulation of Broadcaster's Format Changes*, 40 Geo.Wash.L.Rev. 933 (1972).

FCC v. WNCN LISTENERS GUILD

450 U.S. 582, 101 S.CT. 1266, 67 L.ED.2D 521 (1981)

* * *

Justice WHITE delivered the opinion of the Court.

Sections 309(a) and 310(d) of the Communications Act of 1934, 47 U.S.C. § 151 *et seq.* (act), empower the Federal Communications Commission to grant an application for license transfer or renewal only if it determines that "the public interest, convenience and necessity" will be served thereby. The issue before us is whether there are circumstances in which the commission must review past or anticipated changes in a station's entertainment programming when it rules on an application for renewal or transfer of a radio broadcast license. The commission's present position is that it may rely on market forces to promote diversity in entertainment programming and thus serve the public interest.

This issue arose when, pursuant to its informal rulemaking authority, the commission issued a "policy statement" concluding that the public interest is best served by promoting diversity in entertainment formats through market forces and competition among broadcasters and that a change in entertainment programming is therefore not a material factor that should be considered by the commission in ruling on an application for license renewal or transfer. Respondents, a number of citizen groups interested in fostering and preserving particular entertainment formats, petitioned for review in the court of Appeals for the District of Columbia Circuit. That court held that the commission's policy statement violated the act. We reverse the decision of the court of appeals.

Beginning in 1970, in a series of cases involving license transfers, the Court of Appeals for the District of Columbia Circuit gradually developed a set of criteria for determining when the "public-interest" standard requires the commission to hold a hearing to review proposed changes in entertainment formats. Noting that the aim of the act is "to secure the maximum benefits of radio to all the people of the United States," *National Broadcasting Co. v. United States*, * * * the court of appeals ruled in 1974 that "preservation of a format [that] would otherwise disappear, although economically and technologically viable and preferred by a significant number of listeners, is generally in the public interest." *Citizens Committee to Save WEFM v. FCC* * * *. It concluded that a change in format would not present "substantial and material questions of fact" requiring a hearing if (1) notice of the change had not precipitated "significant public grumbling"; (2) the segment of the population preferring the format was too small to be accommodated by available frequencies; (3) there was an adequate substitute in the service area for the format being abandoned; or (4) the format would be economically unfeasible even if the station were managed efficiently. The court rejected the commission's position that the choice of entertainment formats should be left to the judgment of the licensee, stating that the commission's interpretation of the public-interest standard was contrary to the act.

In January 1976 the commission responded to these decisions by undertaking an inquiry into its role in reviewing format changes. In particular, the commission sought public comment on whether the public interest would be better served by commission scrutiny of entertainment programming or by reliance on the competitive marketplace.

Following public notice and comment, the commission issued a policy statement pursuant to its rulemaking authority under the act. The commission concluded in the policy statement that review of format changes was not compelled by the language or history of the act, would not advance the welfare of the radio-listening public, would pose substantial administrative problems, and would deter innovation in radio programming. In support of its position, the commission quoted from FCC v. Sanders Brothers Radio Station, 309 U.S. 470, 475, * * * (1940): "Congress intended to leave competition in the business of broadcasting where it found it, to permit a licensee * * * to survive or succumb according to his ability to make his programs attractive to the public." The commission also emphasized that a broadcaster is not a common carrier and therefore should not be subjected to a burden similar to the common carrier's obligation to continue to provide service if abandonment of that service would conflict with public convenience or necessity.

The commission also concluded that practical considerations as well as statutory interpretation supported its reluctance to regulate changes in formats. Such regulation would require the commission to categorize the formats of a station's prior and subsequent programming to determine whether a change in format had occurred; to determine whether the prior format was "unique"; and to weigh the public detriment resulting from the abandonment of a unique format against the public benefit resulting from that change. The commission emphasized the difficulty of objectively evaluating the strength of listener preferences, of comparing the desire for diversity within a particular type of programming to the desire for a broader range of program formats and of assessing the financial feasibility of a unique format.

Finally, the commission explained why it believed that market forces were the best available means of producing diversity in entertainment formats. First, in large markets, competition among broadcasters had already produced "an almost bewildering array of diversity" in entertainment formats. Second, format allocation by market forces accommodates listeners' desires for diversity within a given format and also produces a variety of formats. Third, the market is far more flexible than governmental regulation and responds more quickly to changing public tastes. Therefore, the commission concluded that "the market is the allocation mechanism of preference for entertainment formats and * * * commission supervision in this area will not be conducive either to producing program diversity [or] satisfied radio listeners."

The court of appeals, sitting en banc, held that the commission's policy was contrary to the act as construed and applied in the court's prior format decisions. *WNCN Listeners Guild v. FCC,* * * * The court questioned whether the commission had rationally and impartially re-examined its position and particularly criticized the commission's failure to disclose a staff study on the effectiveness of market allocation of formats before it issued the policy statement. The court then responded to the commission's criticisms of the format doctrine. First, although conceding that market forces generally lead to diversification of formats, it concluded that the market only imperfectly reflects listener preferences and that the commission is statutorily obligated to review format changes whenever there is "strong prima facie evidence that the market has in fact broken down." * * * Second, the court stated that the administrative problems posed by the format doctrine were not insurmountable. Hearings would only be required in a small number of cases, and the commission could cope with problems such as classifying radio format by adopting a "rational classification schema." 197 U.S.App.D.C., at 334, 610 F.2d, at 853. Third, the court observed that the commission had not demonstrated that the format doctrine would deter innovative programming. Finally, the court explained that it had not directed the commission to engage in censorship or to impose common carrier obligations on licensees: *WEFM* did not authorize the commission to interfere with licensee programming choices or to force retention of an existing format; it merely stated that the commission had the power to consider a station's format in deciding whether license renewal or transfer would be consistent with the public interest. * * *

Although conceding that it possessed neither the expertise nor the authority to make policy decisions in this area, the court of appeals asserted that the format doctrine was "law," not "policy," and was of the view that the commission had not disproved the factual assumptions underlying the format doctrine. Accordingly, the court declared that the policy statement was "unavailing and of no force and effect."

Rejecting the commission's reliance on market forces to develop diversity in programming as an unreasonable interpretation of the act's public-interest standard, the court of appeals held that in certain circumstances the commission is required to regard a change in entertainment format as a substantial and material fact in deciding whether a license renewal or transfer is in the public interest. With all due respect, however, we are unconvinced that the court of appeals' format doctrine is compelled by the act and that the commission's interpretation of the public-interest standard must therefore be set aside.

It is common ground that the act does not define the term "public interest convenience, and necessity." The court has characterized the public-interest standard of the act as "a supple instrument for the exercise of discretion by the expert body which Congress has charged to carry out its legislative policy." FCC v. Pottsville Broadcasting Co., 309 U.S. 134 (1940). * *

Furthermore, we recognized that the commission's decisions must sometimes rest on judgment and prediction rather than pure factual determinations. In such cases complete factual support for the commission's ultimate conclusions is not required, since " 'a forecast of the direction in which future public interest lies necessarily involves deductions based on the expert knowledge of the agency.' "

The commission has provided a rational explanation for its conclusion that reliance on the market is the best method of promoting diversity in entertainment formats. The court of appeals and the commission agree that in the vast majority of cases market forces provide sufficient diversity. The court of appeals favors government intervention when there is evidence that market forces have deprived the public of a "unique" format, while the commission is content to rely on the market, pointing out that in many cases when a station changes its format, other stations will change their formats to attract listeners who preferred the discontinued format. The court of appeals places great value on preserving diversity among formats, while the commission emphasizes the value of intra-format as well as inter-format diversity. Finally, the court of appeals is convinced that review of format changes would result in a broader range of formats, while the commission believes that government intervention is likely to deter innovative programming.

In making these judgments, the commission has not forsaken its obligation to pursue the public interest. On the contrary, it has assessed the benefits and the harm likely to flow from government review of entertainment programming, and on balance has concluded that its statutory duties are best fulfilled by not attempting to oversee format changes. This decision was in major part based on predictions as to the probable conduct of licensees and the functioning of the broadcasting market and on the commission's assessment of its capacity to make the determinations required by the format doctrine. * * * It did not assert that reliance on the marketplace would achieve a perfect correlation between listener preferences and available entertainment programming. Rather, it recognized that a perfect correlation would never be achieved, and it concluded that the marketplace alone could best accommodate the varied and changing tastes of the listening public. These predictions are within the institutional competence of the commission.

Our opinions have repeatedly emphasized that the commission's judgment regarding how the public interest is best served is entitled to substantial judicial deference. * * * Furthermore, diversity is not the only policy the commission must consider in fulfilling its responsibilities under the act. The commission's implementation of the public-interest standard, when based on a rational weighing of competing policies, is not to be set aside by the court of appeals, for "the weighing of policies under the 'public interest' standard is a task that Congress has delegated to the commission in the first instance." FCC v. National Citizens Committee for Broadcasting, 436 U.S., at 810 * * *. The commission's position on review of format changes reflects a reasonable accommodation of the policy of promoting diversity in programming and the policy of avoiding unnecessary restrictions on licensee discretion. As we see it, the commission's policy statement is in harmony with cases recognizing that the act seeks to preserve journalistic discretion while promoting the interests of the listening public.

The policy statement is also consistent with the legislative history of the act. Although Congress did not consider the precise issue before us, it did consider and reject a proposal to allocate a certain percentage of the stations to particular types of programming.[33] Similarly, one of the bills submitted prior to passage of the Radio Act of 1927 [34] included a provision requiring stations to comply with programming priorities based on subject matter.[35] This provision was eventually deleted

33. Congress rejected a proposal to allocate 25% of all radio stations to educational, religious, agricultural, and similar nonprofit associations. See 78 Cong.Rec. 8843–8846 (1934).

34. 44 Stat. 1162. The Radio Act of 1927 was the predecessor to the Communications Act.

35. This bill would have required the administrative agency created by the Radio Act of 1927 to prescribe "priorities as to subject matter to be observed by each class of licensed stations." H.R. 7357, 68th Cong., 1st Sess. § 1(B) (1924).

since it was considered to border on censorship. Congress subsequently added a section to the Radio Act of 1927 expressly prohibiting censorship and other "interfer[ence] with the right of free speech by means of radio communication." That section was retained in the Communications Act. As we read the legislative history of the act, Congress did not unequivocally express its disfavor of entertainment format review by the commission, but neither is there substantial indication that Congress expected the public-interest standard to *require* format regulation by the commission. The legislative history of the act does not support the court of appeals and provides insufficient basis for invalidating the agency's construction of the act.

In the past we have stated that "the construction of a statute by those charged with its execution should be followed unless there are compelling indications that it is wrong * * *." Prior to 1970, the commission consistently stated that the choice of programming formats should be left to the licensee. In 1971 the commission restated that position but announced that any application for license transfer or renewal involving a substantial change in program format would have to be reviewed in light of the court of appeals' decision in Citizens Committee to Preserve the Voice of the Arts in Atlanta, * * * 436 F.2d 263, 267 (D.C.Cir.1970), in which the court of appeals first articulated the format doctrine. * * * [A]lthough the commission was obliged to modify its policies to conform to the court of appeals' format doctrine, the policy statement reasserted the commission's traditional preference of achieving diversity in entertainment programming through market forces.

* * * Surely, it is argued, there will be some format changes that will be so detrimental to the public interest that inflexible application of the commission's policy statement would be inconsistent with the commission's duties. But radio broadcasters are not required to seek permission to make format changes. The issue of past or contemplated entertainment format changes arises in the courses of renewal and transfer proceedings; if such an application is approved, the commission does not merely assume but affirmatively determines that the requested renewal or transfer will serve the public interest.

Under its present policy, the commission determines whether a renewal or transfer will serve the public interest without reviewing past or proposed changes in entertainment format. This policy is based on the commission's judgment that market forces, although they operate imperfectly, will not only more reliably respond to listener preference than would format oversight by the commission but will also serve the end of increasing diversity in entertainment programming. This court has approved of the commission's goal of promoting diversity in radio programming, *FCC v. Midwest Video Corp.*, 440 U.S. 689 (1979), but the commission is nevertheless vested with broad discretion in determining how much weight should be given to that goal and what policies should be pursued in promoting it. The act itself, of course, does not specify how the commission should make its public interest determinations.

A major underpinning of its policy statement is the commission's conviction, rooted in its experience, that renewal and transfer cases should not turn on the commission presuming to grasp, measure and weigh the elusive and difficult factors involved in determining the acceptability of changes in entertainment format. To assess whether the elimination of a particular "unique" entertainment format would serve the public interest, the commission would have to consider the benefit as well as the detriment that would result from the change. Necessarily, the commission would take into consideration not only the number of listeners who favor the old and the new programming but also the intensity of their preferences. It would also consider the effect of the format change on diversity within formats as well as on diversity among formats. The commission is convinced that its judgments in these respects would be subjective in large measure and would only approximately serve the public interest. It is also convinced that the market, although imperfect, would serve the public interest as well or better by responding quickly to changing preferences and by inviting experimentation with new types of programming. Those who would overturn the commission's policy statement do not take adequate account of these considerations.

It is also contended that since the commission has responded to listener complaints about nonentertainment programming, it should also review challenged changes in entertainment formats. But the difference between the commission's treatment of nonentertainment programming and its treatment of entertainment programming is not as pronounced as it may seem. Even in the area of nonentertainment programming, the commission has afforded licensees broad discretion in selecting programs. Thus, the commission has stated that "a substantial and material question of fact [requiring an evidentiary hearing] is raised only when it appears that the licensee has abused its broad discretion by acting unreasonably or in bad faith." Mississippi Authority for Educational TV, 71 FCC2d 1296, 1308 (1969). Furthermore, we note that the commission has recently re-examined its regulation of commercial radio broadcasting in light of changes in the structure of the radio industry. See Notice of Inquiry and Proposed Rulemaking, In the Matter of Deregulation of Radio, 73 FCC2d 457 (1979). As a result of that re-examination, it has eliminated rules requiring maintenance of comprehensive program logs, guidelines on the amount of nonentertainment programming radio stations must offer, formal requirements governing ascertainment of community needs, and guidelines limiting commercial time. See Report and Order, In the Matter of Deregulation of Radio, 46 Fed.Reg. 13888 (1981).

This case does not require us to consider whether the commission's present or past policies in the area of nonentertainment programming comply with the act. We attach some weight to the fact that the Commission has consistently expressed a preference for promoting diversity in entertainment programming through market forces, but our decision ultimately rests on our conclusion that the commission has provided a reasonable explanation for this preference in its policy statement.

We decline to overturn the commission's policy statement, which prefers reliance on market forces to its own attempt to oversee format changes at the behest of disaffected listeners. Of course, the commission should be alert to the consequences of its policies and should stand ready to alter its rule if necessary to serve the public interest more fully. * * *

Respondents contend that the court of appeals judgment should be affirmed because, even if not violative of the act, the policy statement conflicts with the First Amendment rights of listeners "to receive suitable access to social, political, esthetic, moral, and other ideas and experience." Red Lion Broadcasting Co. v. FCC, 395 U.S. 367 (1969) * * *. *Red Lion* held that the Commission's "fairness doctrine" was consistent with the public-interest standard of the Communications Act and did not violate the First Amendment, but rather enhanced First Amendment values by promoting "the presentation of vigorous debate of controversial issues of importance and concern to the public." * * * Although observing that the interests of the people as a whole were promoted by debate of public issues on the radio, we did not imply that the First Amendment grants individual listeners the right to have the commission review the abandonment of their favorite entertainment programs. The commission seeks to further the interests of the listening public as a whole by relying on market forces to promote diversity in radio entertainment formats and to satisfy the entertainment preferences of radio listeners. This policy does not conflict with the First Amendment.

Contrary to the judgment of the court of appeals, the commission's policy statement is not inconsistent with the act. It is also a constitutionally permissible means of implementing the public-interest standard of the act. Accordingly, the judgment of the court of appeals is reversed and the case is remanded for further proceedings consistent with this opinion.

So ordered.

Justice MARSHALL, with whom Justice Brennan joins, dissenting.

Under §§ 309(a) and 310(d) of the Communications Act of 1934, 47 U.S.C. § 151 *et seq.* (act), the Federal Communications Commission (commission) may not approve an application for a radio license transfer, assignment or renewal unless it finds that such change will serve "the public interest, convenience, and necessity." Any party in interest may petition the commission to deny the application, § 309(d)(1), and the commission must hold a hearing if "a substantial and material question of fact is presented," § 309(d)(2). In my judgment, the court of appeals correctly held that in certain limited circumstances, the commission may be obliged to hold a hearing to consider whether a proposed change in a licensee's entertainment program format is in the "public interest." Accordingly, I would affirm the judgment of the court of appeals insofar as it vacated the commission's "policy statement."

At the outset, I should point out that my understanding of the court of appeals' format cases is very different from the commission's. Both in its policy statement and in its brief before this court, the commission has insisted that the format doctrine espoused by the court of appeals, "favors a system of pervasive governmental regulation," requiring "comprehensive, discriminating, and continuing state surveillance." The commission further contends that enforcement of the format doctrine would impose "common carrier" obligations on broadcasters and substitute for "the imperfect system of free competition * * * a system of broadcast programming by government decree." Were this an accurate description of the format doctrine, I would join the court in reversing the judgment below. However, I agree with the court of appeals that "the actual features of [its format doctrine] are scarcely visible in [the commission's] highly-colored portrait." * * *

* * *

Although the act does not define "public interest, convenience, and necessity," it is difficult to quarrel with the basic premise of the court of appeals' format cases that the term includes "a concern for diverse entertainment programming." * * The commission has concluded that a general policy of relying on market forces is the best method for promoting diversity in entertainment programming formats. As the majority notes, this determination largely rests on the commission's predictions about licensee behavior and the functioning of the radio broadcasting market.

I agree with the majority that predictions of this sort are within the commission's institutional competence. I am also willing to assume that a general policy of disregarding format changes in making the "public interest" determination required by the act is not inconsistent with the commission's statutory obligation to give individualized consideration to each application. The commission has broad rulemaking power under the act, and we have approved efforts by the commission to implement the act's "public interest" requirement through rules and policies of general application. * * *

The problem with the particular policy statement challenged here, however, is that it lacks the flexibility we have required of such general regulations and policies. * * * The act imposes an affirmative duty on the commission to make a particularized "public interest" determination for each application that comes before it. As we explained in National Broadcasting Co. v. FCC, 319 U.S., at 225, * * * the commission must, in each case, "exercise an ultimate judgment whether the grant of a license would serve the 'public interest, convenience or necessity.'" The policy statement completely forecloses any possibility that the commission will re-examine the validity of its general policy on format changes as it applies to particular situations. Thus, even when it can be conclusively demonstrated that a particular radio market does not function in the manner predicted by the commission, the policy statement indicates that the commission will blindly assume that a proposed format change is in the "public interest." This result would occur even where reliance on the market to ensure format diversity is shown to be misplaced, and where it thus appears that action by the commission is necessary to promote the public interest in diversity. This outcome is not consistent with the commission's statutory responsibilities.

Moreover, our cases have indicated that an agency's discretion to proceed in complex areas through general rules is intimately connected to the existence of a "safety valve" procedure that allows the agency to consider applications for exemptions based on special circumstances. * * For example, in *National Broadcasting Co. v. FCC*, we upheld the Commission's Chain Broadcasting Regulations, but we emphasized the need for flexibility in administering the rules. We noted that the "commission provided that 'networks will be given full opportunity, on proper application * * * to call our attention to any reasons why the principle should be modified or held inapplicable.'" * * * Similarly, in upholding the commission's Multiple Ownership Rules in *United States v. Storer Broadcasting Co.*, * * * we noted that the regulations allowed an opportunity for a "full hearing" for applicants "that set out adequate reasons why the Rules should be waived or amended."

This "safety valve" feature is particularly essential where, as here, the agency's decision that a general policy promotes the public interest is based on predictions and forecasts that by definition lack complete factual support. * * *

In my judgment, this requirement of flexibility compels the commission to provide a procedure through which listeners can attempt to show that a particular radio market differs from the commission's paradigm, and thereby persuade the commission to give particularized consideration to a proposed format change. Indeed, until the policy statement was published, the commission had resolved to "take an extra hard look at the reasonableness of any proposal which would deprive a community of its only source of a particular type of programming." As I see it, the court of appeals' format doctrine was merely an attempt by that court to delineate the circumstances in which the commission must temper its general policy in view of special circumstances. Perhaps the court would have been better advised to leave the task of defining these situations to the commission. But one need not endorse every feature of the court of appeals' approach to conclude that the court correctly invalidated the commission's policy statement because of its omission of a "safety valve" procedure.

This omission is not only a departure from legal precedents; it is also a departure from both the commission's consistent policies and its admissions here. For the commission concedes that the radio market is an imperfect reflection of listener preferences, and that listeners have programming interests that may not be reflected in the marketplace. The commission has long recognized its obligation to examine program formats in making the "public interest" determination required by the act. As early as 1929, the commission's predecessor, the Federal Radio Commission, adopted the position that licensees were expected to provide a balanced program schedule designed to serve all substantial groups in their communities. * * * The commission's famous "Blue Book," published in 1946, reaffirmed the emphasis on a well-balanced program structure and declared that the commission has "an affirmative duty, in its public interest determinations, to give full consideration to program service." * * *

* * *

This theme was reiterated in the commission's 1960 *Program Statement*, which set forth 14 specific categories of programming that were deemed "major elements usually necessary to meet the public interest, needs and desires of the community," and which emphasized the necessity of each broadcaster's programming serving the "tastes and needs" of its local community. * * *

* * *

The majority attempts to minimize the inconsistency in the commission's treatment of entertainment and nonentertainment programming by postulating that the difference "is not as pronounced as it may seem." This observation, even if accurate, is simply beside the point. What is germane is the commission's failure to consider listener complaints about entertainment programming to the same extent and in the same manner as it reviews complaints about nonentertainment programming. Thus, whereas the commission will hold an evidentiary hearing to review complaints about nonentertainment programming where " 'it appears that the licensee has * * * act[ed] unreasonably or in bad faith,' " (quoting Mississippi Authority for Educational TV, 71 FCC2d 1296, 1308 (1979)), the commission will not consider an identical complaint about a licensee's change in its entertainment programming. As I have indicated, * * * neither the commission nor the majority is able to offer a satisfactory explanation for this inconsistency.

Nor can the commission find refuge in its claim that "[e]ven after all the relevant facts [h]ad been fully explored in an evidentiary hearing, [the commission] would have no assurance that a decision finally reached by [the commission] would contribute more to listener satisfaction than the result favored by station management." *Policy Statement, supra*, at 865. The same must be true of the decisions the commission makes after reviewing listener complaints about nonentertainment programming, and I do not see why the commission finds this result acceptable in one situation but not in the other. Much the same can be said for the majority's suggestion that the commission should be spared the burden of "presuming to grasp, measure and weigh * * * elusive and difficult factors" such as determining the number of listeners who favor a particular change and measuring the intensity of their preferences. But insofar as the commission confronts these same "elusive and difficult factors" in reviewing nonentertainment programming, it need only apply the expertise it has acquired in dealing with these problems to review of entertainment programming.

Since I agree with the court of appeals that there may be situations in which the commission is obliged to consider format changes in making the "public interest" determination mandated by the act, it seems appropriate to comment briefly on the commission's claim that the " 'acute practical problem[s]' inherent in format regulation render entirely speculative any benefits that such regulation might produce." One of the principal reasons given in the policy statement for rejecting entertainment format regulation is that it would be "administratively a fearful and comprehensive nightmare," that would impose "enormous costs on the participants and the commission alike." * * *

Although it has abandoned the "administrative nightmare" argument before this court, the commission nonetheless finds other "intractable" administrative problems in format regulation. For example, it insists that meaningful classification of radio broadcasts into format types is impractical, and that it is impossible to determine whether a proposed format change is in the public interest because the intensity of listener preferences cannot be measured. Moreover, the commission argues that format regulation will discourage licensee innovation and experimentation with formats, and that its effect on format diversity will therefore be counterproductive.

None of these claims has merit. Broadcasters have operated under the format doctrine during the past 10 years, yet the commission is unable to show that there has been no innovation and experimentation with formats during this period. Indeed, a commission staff study on the effectiveness of market allocation of formats indicates that licensees have been aggressive in developing diverse entertainment formats under the format doctrine regime. This "evidence"—a welcome contrast to the commission's speculation—undermines the commission's claim that format regulation will disserve the "public interest" because it will inhibit format diversity.

The commission's claim that it is impossible to classify formats, is largely overcome by the court of appeals' suggestion that the commission could develop "a format taxonomy which, even if imprecise at the margins, would be sustainable so long as not irrational." * * * Even more telling is the staff study relied on by the commission to show that there is broad format diversity in major radio markets, for the study used a format classification based on industry practice. As the court of appeals noted, it is somewhat ironic that the commission had no trouble "endorsing the validity of a study largely premised on classifications it claims are impossible to make." To be sure, courts do not sit to second-guess the assessments of specialized agencies like the commission. But where, as here, the agency's position rests on speculations that are refuted by the agency's own administrative record, I am not persuaded that deference is due.

The commission's policy statement is defective because it lacks a "safety valve" procedure that would allow the necessary flexibility in the application of the commission's general policy on format changes to particular cases. In my judgment, the court of appeals' format doctrine was a permissible attempt by that court to provide the commission with some guidance regarding the types of situations in which a re-examination of general policy might be necessary. Even if one were to conclude that the court of appeals described these situations too specifically, a view I do not share, I still think that the court of appeals correctly held that the commission's policy statement must be vacated.

I respectfully dissent.

COMMENT

1. In an article in praise of deregulation, FCC Chairman Mark Fowler and his legal assistant Daniel Brenner described the *WNCN* case as a decision where "the Supreme Court expressly sanctioned the commission's discretion to invoke market forces in its regulatory mission." See, Fowler & Brenner, *A Marketplace Approach to Broadcast Regulation*, 60 Texas Law Review 207 (1982). Fowler and Brenner contend that *NBC*, text, p. 770, *Red Lion*, text, p. 845, and *CBS v. FCC*, text, p. 815, did not directly involve a "conflict between the marketplace and trusteeship

approaches to broadcasting" but that in *WNCN* these policies collided. How does the marketplace model of broadcast regulation differ from the trusteeship model? Fowler and Brenner suggest the following distinction:

> This [marketplace] approach differs from a trusteeship model, under which the commission would require broadcasters to air programs—from public affairs shows to responses to station editorials—that might not be aired voluntarily, and that consumers, insofar as they can be heard in the advertiser-supported marketplace, do not demand.
>
> The market perspective diminishes the importance of the commission's past efforts to define affirmatively the elements of operation "in the public interest." It recognizes as valid communications policy, well within commission discretion, reliance on voluntary broadcaster efforts to attract audiences—whether by specialized formats, as in the case of major market radio, or with a mix of programs, as in the case of television—and to provide the best practicable programming service to the public. It concludes that governmental efforts to improve the broadcast market have led to distortions of programming that have merely yielded a different programming mix, not a better one, and that the costs of government intrusion into the marketplace outweigh the benefits. Important first amendment interests support this conclusion as well.

Fowler and Brenner argue that the *WNCN* case diminishes the significance of the *Red Lion* trusteeship approach to broadcast regulation. They suggest that listener rights are best served when broadcasters, responding to the market, react to "perceived listener demand." This is deemed preferable to requirements that broadcasters respond to a government conception of listener demand.

In short, the marketplace can meet the rights of listeners and viewers fully as much as government can, and so long as the need is met, *Red Lion* is satisfied. Is this really true? Fowler and Brenner concede that they may be reading more into *WNCN* for their revisionist view of *Red Lion* than is warranted. They also concede that the new case of *CBS v. FCC*, text, p. 815, serves to diminish rather than to expand the role of broadcast editorial discretion and, therefore, the free play of the marketplace.

However, they distinguished *CBS v. DNC* as dealing with a narrow access statute. They conclude: "Absent an express commission finding that it cannot rely on licensee discretion to carry out its congressional mandate, however, *WNCN* suggests the compatibility of a marketplace approach and *Red Lion's* emphasis on listeners' rights."

For an article supporting the view that administrative choice of program formats presents graver problems than leaving the choice of program format to unfettered licensee discretion, see Spitzer, *Radio Formats By Administrative Choice*, 47 U. of Chi.L.Rev. 647 (1981). The article was written prior to the Supreme Court decision in the program format case.

2. The format doctrine as developed in the federal courts of appeal held that a change in format upon license transfer or renewal presented a substantial and material question of fact requiring a public hearing (under §§ 309(a) and 310(d) of the Federal Communications Act)—if certain specified circumstances were met. See Citizens Committee to Save WEFM v. FCC, 506 F.2d 246 (D.C.Cir.1974) (en banc). Does the format doctrine constitute an obligation to continue certain programming or stop broadcasting altogether? If so, does the format doctrine violate § 3(h) of the Communications Act which prohibits regulating broadcasters as common carriers? See, 47 U.S.C. § 153(h).

3. After the *WEFM* decision, the FCC issued a policy statement on format changes which asserted that the Federal Communications Act did not require that a proposed change in entertainment format should be reviewed by the FCC. See

Memorandum Opinion and Order (policy statement), 60 FCC 2d 858 (1976), reconsideration denied, 66 FCC 2d 78 (1977). Is the implication of the policy statement that the FCC believed that *WEFM* and kindred cases usurped its authority to determine the public interest?

The policy statement effectively gutted the format doctrine decisions. See, WNCN Listeners Guild v. FCC, 610 F.2d 838 (D.C.Cir.1979). The FCC is the appropriate body to resolve matters of communications *policy*; the courts are the appropriate forums for resolving matters of communications *law*. The FCC, the federal court of appeals in *WNCN*, the *WNCN* Supreme Court majority, and the *WNCN* Supreme Court dissent all agree that the "public interest" standard requires diversity in programming. But should the definition of what the "public interest" requires in this instance be considered a matter of policy or one of statutory interpretation, i.e., law? In short, is the basic issue in *WNCN*—the question of how best to achieve diversity—a matter of policy? If diversity is a matter of policy, then, presumably the FCC is the appropriate body to define how it should be achieved? Did the Supreme Court in *WNCN* view the format change issue as "law" or "policy"?

4. In his *WNCN* dissent, Justice Marshall agreed that diversity is the goal and that the FCC has considerable latitude in determining how to achieve it. He condemned the policy statement's failure to provide a safety valve for special circumstances where FCC intervention might be desirable to achieve diversity in the "public interest." A large audience could desire an economically viable format, yet be denied satisfaction when the market does not operate according to the FCC market forces paradigm.

Justice White, for the *WNCN* majority, responded that the act does not require safety valves merely because the court has previously approved of regulations that include them. Furthermore, a new policy statement could always provide the needed emergency procedures if the FCC determines that they are in the public interest.

5. The challenge by Judge Bazelon in *WEFM* to the limitation of the spectrum rationale for radio regulation has served as a justification for the Reagan-era FCC to repeal much of the prior regulatory structure applicable to radio, i.e., formal ascertainment procedures, guidelines regarding the amount of nonentertainment programming, and guidelines limiting commercial time. See, *Report and Order In the Matter of Deregulation of Radio*, 46 Fed.Reg. 1388 (1981).

How does radio deregulation affect the licensee's underlying public interest obligation to provide different types of programs and to know the needs of the audience? Justice White, in *WNCN*, appears to be sympathetic to allowing deregulation based on the FCC's perception of the public interest. Justice Marshall's dissent demonstrates his belief that nonentertainment programming issues remain relevant to FCC consideration of petitions to deny a license grant or renewal. Since the FCC will continue to examine the reasonableness of a broadcaster's nonentertainment programming decisions, licensees must still know what issues interest their communities.

The FCC is reluctant to regulate entertainment programming. It perceives a greater public interest in diverse nonentertainment programming as well as a greater need for regulation. Because nonentertainment programming generates less revenue, it is less likely to generate market acceptance or rejection.

Whether composite logs are still required is unclear. The fourteen types of programming—the ingredients of a concept of "balanced programming"—are no longer mandated. See Office of Communication of United Church of Christ v. FCC, 707 F.2d 1413 (D.C.Cir.1983) and the textual material on "balanced programming," p. 785. Challenges to entertainment programming are now likely to arise in comparative license renewal hearings. Nonentertainment programming remains subject to a greater scrutiny. Intraprogram diversity and balance are sought through the fairness doctrine, which, having been codified, cannot be deregulated through commission action.

BROADCASTING AND POLITICAL DEBATE: § 315 AND THE "EQUAL TIME" REQUIREMENT

The "Equal Time" Concept

1. The most celebrated provision of the Federal Communications Act is certainly § 315, the "equal time" provision. Although disliked by many broadcasters, it has become a vital part of the political process. It prevents broadcasters from favoring one candidate and ignoring all others. The statute operates as a guaranty that broadcasting will be responsive to the dependency of the political process on the mass media.

The statute, 47 U.S.C.A. § 315(a) (1976), states:

> § 315. Candidates for public office; facilities; rules
>
> (a) If any licensee shall permit any person who is a legally qualified candidate for any public office to use a broadcasting station, he shall afford equal opportunities to all other candidates for that office in the use of such broadcasting station: *Provided*, that such licensee shall have no power of censorship over the material broadcast under the provisions of this section. No obligation is imposed under this subsection upon any licensee to allow the use of its station by any such candidate. Appearance by a legally qualified candidate on any—
>
> 1 bona fide newscast,
>
> 2 bona fide news interview,
>
> 3 bona fide news documentary (if the appearance of the candidate is incidental to the presentation of the subjects covered by the news documentary), or
>
> 4 on-the-spot coverage of bona fide news events (including but not limited to political conventions and activities incidental thereto),
>
> shall not be deemed to be use of a broadcasting station within the meaning of this subsection. Nothing in the foregoing sentence shall be construed as relieving broadcasters, in connection with the presentation of newscasts, news interviews, news documentaries, and on the spot coverage of news events, from the obligation imposed upon them under this chapter to operate in the public interest and to afford reasonable opportunity for the discussion of conflicting views on issues of public importance.
>
> (b) The charges made for the use of any broadcasting station for any of the purposes set forth in this section shall not exceed the charges made for comparable use of such station for other purposes.
>
> (c) The Commission shall prescribe appropriate rules and regulations to carry out the provisions of this section.

2. The essence of the statute is in the term "equal opportunities" itself. Section 315 does not in fact require "equal time." "Equal opportunity" is what is required, not *actual* equality of access to broadcasting. If one candidate is sold time and his opponent cannot afford time, the station is not required to allow the impecunious opponent to speak free.

3. Political campaign coverage by public broadcasting stations operated by state broadcasting authorities can also be governed by state law. See McGlynn v. New Jersey Public Broadcasting Authority, 439 A.2d 54 (N.J.1981), text, p. 1029.

Defining a "Legally Qualified" Candidate

1. The simple operational rule of § 315 is that if one candidate is allowed to pur-

chase prime time then all his "legally qualified" opponents must be allowed to purchase prime time. Who is a "legally qualified" candidate is a question which has not always been very flexibly approached in the past by the FCC. An inquiry into the meaning of the phrase is basic to an understanding of the statute. Flory v. FCC, 528 F.2d 124 (7th Cir. 1975), considered the problem. Ishmael Flory was nominated by the state committee of the Communist party to run in the 1974 election for United States senator from Illinois. Since the Communist party had not polled at least 5 percent of the vote in the preceding election, a nominating petition requiring 25,000 signatures was needed for its candidate to appear on the ballot.

Between the time of the nomination and the time when Flory eventually obtained the necessary signatures, he requested equal time in response to debates aired by broadcasters between the Republican and Democratic candidates. The FCC refused to order the broadcasters to give equal time to Flory: Since Flory had not yet secured a place on the ballot, he was not a legally qualified candidate at the time of the prior broadcasts.

The court held that Flory was not precluded from seeking equal time where the candidate involved had indicated that he would run as a write-in candidate if he did not obtain a place on the ballot:

> We cannot agree with the argument of the commission that the rule which provides qualification either by obtaining a place on the ballot or by becoming eligible by being a write-in candidate must be construed as setting up mutually exclusive routes.

However, the court did not vacate the FCC order in the case because Flory should have sought review of the FCC rulings when they were made rather than attempting to obtain makeup time for past erroneous rulings.

2. As a result of the *Flory* case, the FCC amended its rules defining a "legally qualified" candidate. See Amendment of the Commission's Rules Relating to Broadcasts by Legally Qualified Candidates, 60 FCC2d 615 (1976). Under the new rules, a candidate is legally qualified if he:

1. has publicly announced his candidacy,

2. "meets the qualifications prescribed by the applicable laws to hold the office for which he is a candidate," and

3. either:

a. has qualified for a place on the ballot, or

b. "has publicly committed himself to seeking election by the write-in method, and is eligible under the applicable law" to be voted for by write-in or other method and "makes a substantial showing that he is a bona fide candidate for nomination or office."

The FCC has attempted with this definition to clarify the questions left unanswered by *Flory*. The rules require that the candidate publicly commit himself to seeking election by the write-in method in the event that his attempts to get on the ballot fail. But the question remains: Is the candidate's word alone sufficient "public commitment"? The commission's insistence on a "substantial showing" of bona fide candidacy suggests that more than a casual announcement by a candidate is necessary. Perhaps the pattern of continued assurance that the candidate will turn to a write-in candidacy, such as found in *Flory*, will be sufficient. See also Broadcasts and Cablecasts by Legally Qualified Candidates for Public Office, 44 F.R. 32790 (FCC, July 28, 1978).

Cablecasts by Candidates for Public Office. Is cable bound by an "equal time" rule? FCC regulations in 47 CFR (1981) § 76.205 provide that if a cable system permits a "legally qualified" candidate for public office to use the system's cablecasting channel(s) and facilities, the system operator shall afford equal opportunities to all other such candidates for such office. This requirement, however, does not pertain to a cablecast appearance of any legally qualified candidate on any bona fide newscast, news interview, news documentary, or any on-the-spot news coverage of bona fide news events.

In regulating the charges to be assessed to candidates for the use of the cable system, the FCC requires that during the forty-five days preceding a primary or sixty days prior to the date of a general or special election, cable system operators may charge no more than the "lowest unit charge" for the same class and amount of time. At all other times, candidates shall be charged no more than the prevailing rate, including discount privileges offered by the cable system to commercial advertisers.

Section 76.205 also provides that cable system operators shall have no power of censorship over cablecasts by candidates and that operators may not engage in any form of discrimination which would make or give any preference to any candidate or would subject any candidate to prejudice or disadvantage.

Primary Elections and the "Equal Time" Rule

1. Does the equal time rule apply to primary elections? Richard Kay, the unopposed candidate of the American Independent party for the Ohio Senate, requested broadcast time equivalent to that afforded by broadcasters to major party candidates who were engaged in Ohio primary elections. Both the Democratic and Republican primaries were contested, and in each of these major party primaries the opponents matched against each other were well known: Governor Rhodes and Congressman Taft in the Republican primary and Howard Metzenbaum and John Glenn in the Democratic primary. The candidates for these races had been offered broadcast time for appearances. The FCC refused to order the broadcasters to give Kay equal time. The Federal Court upheld the FCC. Kay v. FCC, 443 F.2d 638 (D.C. Cir.1970).

While agreeing that primary elections were covered under § 315, the court ruled that primary elections held by one party are to be considered separately from primary elections of other parties. Equal opportunity need only be afforded candidates for nomination "for the same office in the same party's primary." Section 315 provides for equal opportunities only when candidates are competing against each other. Appearance on the broadcast media, prior to the primary, of candidates of one party does not entitle candidates of another party equal time. Candidates in primary elections are running solely against other candidates from their own party and not against candidates from other parties.

2. The *Kay* case obviously presents some serious obstacles to the candidate of the minority party. Where a candidate, as was the case in *Kay*, is unopposed in his party's primary, the equal time rule provides no assistance. In short, major party candidates in contested primaries may gain great broadcast impact in terms of coverage and publicity before the equal time rule can be invoked. The *Kay* interpretation with respect to the application of the equal time rule to noncontested primaries is therefore particularly damaging to third party candidates who are necessarily dependent on media exposure if they are to popularize and legitimize their parties and candidacies.

Does the *Kay* ruling open the door for potential abuse by broadcasters? The court of appeals answered this question by declaring its acceptance of the FCC's response to the issue:

> The commission brief said: Were a station to afford extensive time to candidates in one primary race and give little or no coverage of other races involving ultimately the same office, or having given extensive coverage to one party's primary race, a station did not cover the general election campaign involving the same race, a serious question would arise under the fairness doctrine as to the licensee's performance as a public trustee. See Office of Communication, Church of Christ v. FCC, 359 F.2d 994 (D.C.Cir. 1966).

Note that if Richard Kay had had an opponent in the American Independent party primary, his opponent would have had rights to equal time if Kay had been given the broadcast time he requested. The FCC recognized that primary elections were covered by § 315 when it stated that "both primary elections, nominating conventions and general elections are comprehended within the terms of Section 315."

"Equal Time" and Presidential Elections

1. The famous John F. Kennedy-Richard M. Nixon television debates of 1960, which many think led to the election of John F. Kennedy, were made possible by an amendment to § 315 which suspended the operation of § 315 during the presidential campaign of 1960. 74 Stat. 554 (1960). Why wouldn't the debate have been possible otherwise? Suppose the presidential candidate of the Vegetarian or the Prohibition party had asked for "equal time" after the Kennedy-Nixon debate and that § 315 was in effect, would the broadcasters have had to provide time?

There is apparent broadcaster willingness to give time to major party candidates but no such willingness with regard to minority party candidates. See Friedenthal and Medalie, *The Impact of Federal Regulation of Political Broadcasting: § 315 of the Communications Act*, 72 Harv. L.Rev. 445 at 449 (1959). Is the way to deal with the problem a statute which simply repeals § 315 for the purpose of those political contests where the minority party candidates have no real popular support and no chance of victory? Does such a technique assure permanent minority status to minority parties?

2. Notice that § 315 excludes from the "equal time" obligation candidates who appear on bona fide newscasts, news interviews, news documentaries, and on-the-spot coverage of bona fide news events. What is the reason for this exclusion? Do you think such an exclusion is to the advantage of dissent and debate? Does it benefit or hinder third-party candidates?

3. In the 1976 presidential election the equal time question, inevitable in presidential elections, arose once again: Could the television networks carry a live television debate between the candidates for the two major parties, Gerald Ford and Jimmy Carter, without incurring obligations to give "equal time" to third party candidates?

On September 30, 1975, in response to petitions filed by CBS and the Aspen Institute, the FCC held, overruling past decisions,[3] that the exemption in § 315(a)(4) for "on-the-spot coverage of bona fide news events" would free from "equal time" obligations broadcast coverage of debates between candidates sponsored by nonbroadcast entities, i.e., nonstudio debates.[4] In re Aspen Institute and CBS, Inc., 55 FCC2d 697 (1975).

---

3. See The Goodwill Industries Station, Inc., 40 FCC 362 (1962) and National Broadcasting Co. (Wyckoff), 40 FCC 370 (1962).

4. In *Petitions of CBS and Aspen Institute*, the FCC also held that presidential press conferences and press conferences of other candidates for political office which are broadcast "live" and in their entirety would qualify for exemption under § 315(a)(4).

The FCC said that its decisions in the overruled cases were based on an incorrect reading of the legislative history of newscast exemptions. Language in a 1959 House Report had suggested that for a candidate's appearance on the broadcast media to be exempt, it would have to be "incidental to" the main coverage of a news event. By definition, a debate could never qualify for exemption. The appearance of the candidates is the central focus of the event.

However, the FCC stated that the "incidental to" language was removed by congressional conference before the amendment to the Communications Act was passed in 1959. Thus, the FCC's former conclusion that a candidate's appearance must be incidental to be exempt was on re-examination held to be unsupported by legislative history. The FCC said that Congress did not intend the FCC "to take an unduly restrictive approach which would discourage news coverage of political activities of candidates." Accordingly, a program which is otherwise exempt does not lose that status because the appearance of a political candidate is central to the presentation. The FCC stressed that the broadcaster has reasonable latitude in making the initial determination of whether an event will be eligible for exemption under § 315. The FCC can overturn the licensee's determination if it was not reasonable or made in good faith.

Shortly after the *Aspen* decision, plans for a debate between Jimmy Carter and Gerald Ford, sponsored by the League of Women Voters, exclusive of any initiation or control by any broadcast media, was announced. The *Aspen* decision had done its work. A televised debate limited to the candidates of the two major parties had become a reality. Although there were numerous additional legally qualified candidates for president, none was invited by the league to take part in the debates. Broadcast networks ABC, CBS, and NBC were then invited by the league to air "live" each of the three scheduled debates before an invited audience. The panelists assigned to question the candidates were to be selected by the league and not by the broadcasters. Broadcasters would not be permitted to show the audience or its reaction.

4. When the networks agreed to air the debates on the basis of *Aspen*, the National Organization for Women ("NOW") and Representative Shirley Chisholm, a legally qualified candidate for president, challenged the FCC ruling and the legality of the planned debates. In Chisholm v. FCC, 538 F.2d 349 (D.C.Cir.1976), the court affirmed the FCC rulings in *Aspen*.

In *Chisholm*, the court upheld the FCC's new interpretation of the equal time rules. The court stressed the necessity for judicial deference to agency interpretation where Congress has assigned the responsibility for dealing with specific situations to the agency. Moreover, an agency could change its mind about the meaning of a statute no matter how long-standing its prior interpretation. As a result of *Chisholm*, therefore, debates between qualified political candidates, which were initiated by nonbroadcast entities, would be exempt under § 315(a)(4) provided that they

---

In so ruling, the FCC overruled Columbia Broadcasting Systems, Inc., 40 FCC 395 (1964), where the FCC refused to exempt presidential news conferences as "bona fide" news events under § 315(a)(4).

In extending the § 315(a)(4) exemption, the FCC used the same test that it used in determining the status of debates: a program which is otherwise exempt does not lose its status because the central focus is on the candidate. Under this analysis, press conferences do not lose their exemption because the candidate is the main figure of the program.

Although it applied § 315(a)(4) to news conferences, the FCC rejected CBS's contention that a press conference constitutes a "bona fide news interview" under § 315(a)(2). A news interview under § 315(a)(2) must be a regularly scheduled program, initiated by the licensee, with recurrent broadcasts, rather than a program which covers an event initiated by the candidate.

were covered "live" and that there was no evidence of broadcast favoritism. Once these requirements were met, the essential factor was that the decision to cover the debate was based on the good faith determination of the broadcast licensee that the debate was a "bona fide news event" worthy of broadcast coverage.

5. How does one explain the fact that Congress in 1960 had to change the law to permit what in 1976 was found to be permissible anyway, i.e., permitting broadcasters to televise a debate limited to the presidential candidates of the two major parties without incurring any equal time obligations? The court of appeals answered this argument in *Chisholm*:

> [T]he 1960 suspension of Section 315 is more properly viewed as an isolated experiment in total repeal of the equal time requirements for presidential and vice presidential candidates, and not as a recognition or limitation of the scope of the news coverage exemption.

6. The theory of the *Aspen Institute* ruling is that a political debate between presidential candidates can qualify for an exemption under § 315(4) if in the good faith exercise of broadcaster judgment an event can reasonably qualify as "on-the-spot-coverage" of a bona fide news event. The actual televised presidential debate between Carter and Ford arranged by the League of Women Voters was the product of long negotiations between the networks and the league, leading to restrictions on broadcaster judgment. In November 1983, the FCC ruled that network sponsored debates be exempt under § 315(a)(4). See *Broadcasting*, November 21, 1983. Does it strain the reference in § 315(a)(4) to "on-the-spot" coverage of a *bona fide* news event to call an event so contrived either "on-the-spot" coverage or a *bona fide* news event?

Interpreting the Exemption in § 315(a) after Chisholm

KENNEDY FOR PRESIDENT COMMITTEE v. FCC

6 MED.L.RPTR. 1722, 636 F.2D 432 (D.C.CIR.1980).

ROBINSON, *Circuit Judge:* This controversy arose when, on February 13, 1980, President Carter held a press conference carried live in prime time by the four major American television networks. On the day following, petitioner Kennedy for President Committee complained to the networks that the President had taken advantage of the occasion for purposes of his candidacy for the 1980 presidential nomination of the Democratic party. Petitioner asked for "an equal opportunity" for its candidate, Senator Edward M. Kennedy, "to respond to * * * calculated and damaging statements" allegedly made by the President "and to provide contrasting viewpoints * * *." Each of the networks responded negatively, whereupon petitioner turned to the Federal Communications Commission for assistance. On March 7, that agency's Broadcast Bureau denied petitioner's request, and on May 6, by the order now under review, the commission sustained the Bureau's ruling.

Petitioner challenges the commission's decision on several grounds. Foremost are contentions that the commission abdicated a duty to apply the equal-opportunity mandate of Section 315(a) of the Communications Act of 1934, and ignored an independent responsibility to accord First Amendment considerations their just due. The commission, on the other hand, insists that its action kept faith with principles of Section 315(a) interpretation formulated in its *Aspen* decision and approved by this court, and that its disposition furthered the common objective of Section 315(a) and the First Amendment by encouraging maximal coverage of events envisioned by the networks as newsworthy. We agree with the commission and affirm.

The press conference precipitating this litigation transpired on the eve of the 1980 presidential primary in New Hampshire. Petitioner charges that the conference was staged as an integral part of President Carter's so-called "Rose Garden" campaign strategy. During the course of the telecast, the President was asked four questions regarding his candidacy for the Democratic presidential nomination and that of Senator Kennedy, his principal rival. In its protest to the networks, petitioner predicated its equal-opportunity demand on allegedly "distorted and inaccurate statements" by the President in response to queries "about Senator Kennedy's views on a number of issues." In turning petitioner down, each network maintained that the telecast of the conference was free of Section 315(a)'s equal-opportunity obligation because it was an activity within that section's Exemption 4 for "[o]n-the-spot coverage of bona fide news events."

Petitioner then urged the commission "to rule that President Carter's News Conference of February 13 constituted a 'use' of television facilities offered by the major networks and to direct the networks to afford equal time[14] to Senator Kennedy * * *." Petitioner claimed that the President had "devoted more than five minutes * * * to a direct attack upon Senator Kennedy," with the consequence that "millions of viewers were misinformed about Senator Kennedy's views on national and international issues critical to voters in the campaign for the presidential nomination."

The commission's Broadcast Bureau denied petitioner's request, primarily in reliance upon the commission's *Aspen* decision, affirmed by this court in *Chisholm v. FCC*. The bureau concluded that the telecast fell within *Aspen*'s holding that press conferences featuring political candidates are exempt from Section 315(a)'s equal-opportunity requirement as "on-the-spot coverage of bona fide news events." The bureau felt that under *Aspen* the regulatory role in equal-opportunity proceedings is confined to determining "whether or not the broadcaster intends to promote the interest of a particular candidate in presenting coverage of a news event." Noting that petitioner had presented no evidence that the networks were not exercising good faith journalistic judgment in appraising the president's press conference as newsworthy, and detecting no indication of a purpose to favor the president's candidacy over the senator's by televising the event, the bureau rejected petitioner's plea for an order providing an opportunity to respond. The bureau acknowledged that an incumbent president "may well have an advantage over his opponent in attracting media coverage," but declared that "absent strong evidence that broadcasters were not exercising their bona fide news judgment, the commission will not interfere with such judgments." "Senator Kennedy was free," the bureau observed, "to hold a press conference the next day or evening to rebut the President's charges."

Four weeks later, on April 2, petitioner sought reexamination of the Bureau's ruling by the commission. On May 6, the commission denied petitioner's application for review. Since we later draw directly and heavily on the commission's opinion, it suffices for now merely to say that es-

14. The phrases "equal time" and "equal opportunity" are often used interchangeably. The latter is employed in the statute, see 47 U.S.C. § 315(a) (1976), and is the more accurate of the two. A broadcaster's obligations under § 315(a) extend beyond an equal amount of time for the use of rival candidates to such things as availability of the responsive broadcast, be made available at an equal rate, and a comparable hour of the day. See The Law of Political Broadcasting and Cablecasting, 69 FCC2d 2209, 2216, 2260–2262 (1978). Though, literally, § 315(a) makes its exaction only for use of a "broadcasting station," the commission has long held that a candidate may demand equal opportunities from a network presenting his opponent instead of looking to each individual station. Senator Eugene J. McCarthy, 11 FCC2d 511 n. 1 (1968). See also CBS v. FCC, [5 Med.L.Rptr. 2649 at 4649] 629 F.2d 1 (1980) (D.C.Cir.1980) (construing 47 U.S.C. § 312(a)(7)(1976)).

sentially the commission tracked the bureau's reasoning, and ultimately adhered pivotally to its *Aspen* holding that "so long as a covered event is considered newsworthy in the good faith judgment of the broadcaster," it is encompassed by one or more of Section 315(a)'s exemptions from the duty to afford equal opportunity. It is the commission's ensuing order that petitioner now brings before us.

Petitioner challenges the commission's decision on the basis of its construction and application of Section 315(a) and on grounds attributed to the First Amendment. Within these broad categories, petitioner argues that there were factual and analytical flaws in the commission's handling of constitutional, statutory and policy aspects of the controversy. We turn first to an examination of Section 315(a) and the commission's treatment of the statutory issues. We then address the First Amendment questions raised by petitioner.

THE SECTION 315(a) CLAIM
A. General Considerations

* * *

"Equal opportunities" is manifestly a comprehensive term, and the commission has given it rather full sway. Four types of programming, however, are statutorily deemed nonuses of a broadcasting station, and thus are exempted from this requirement. One—embraced by Exemption 4—immunizes the "[a]ppearance by a legally qualified candidate on any * * * on-the-spot coverage of bona fide news events (including but not limited to political conventions and activities incidental thereto)." This provision, in the commission's view, relieved the networks of any equal-opportunity obligation consequent upon the telecasts of the president's February 13 press conference.

The question, then, is whether the commission properly extended Exemption 4 to that conference, and in answering we do not write on a completely clean slate. * *

* * *

Aspen marked the commission's recognition that its original understanding—that candidates' press conferences were "uses" of station facilities enabling their opponents to demand broadcast privileges for their own purposes—was not congenial with the underlying purpose of the 1959 amendments. That construction, the commission admitted, had caused an "undue stifling of broadcast coverage of news events involving candidates for public office." Accordingly, the commission adopted the stance it deemed more in keeping with the legislative aims: that broadcasts of press conferences featuring candidates for political office qualified under Exemption 4 as "on-the-spot coverage of bona fide news events."

We upheld the commission's new determination in *Chisholm*. * * * Moreover, we found credible the commission's declaration in *Aspen* that "*any* appearance by a candidate on the broadcast media is designed, to the best of the candidate's ability, to serve his own political ends." We thus held that the commission acted reasonably in rejecting "the degree of control by the candidate, or the degree to which candidates tailor such events to serve their own political advantages," as a criterion for ascertaining whether the equal-opportunity provision of Section 315(a) had been triggered.

Having so concluded, we faced in *Chisholm* the further question whether the broadcaster's good faith judgment on newsworthiness—the element deemed crucial by the commission—provided an acceptable measure of applicability of Section 315(a)'s exemptions. At the outset, we noted that this standard came directly from the legislative history of Section 315(a): the chairman of the House Committee had explained during debate that "[i]t sets up a test which appropriately leaves reasonable latitude for the exercise of good faith news judgment on the part of broadcasters and networks * * * "

Although we did not find sufficient authority either in the reports or the debates to substantiate the proposition that Congress intended this to be the sole factor the commission could utilize in its calculus, we were satisfied that Congress wished to increase broadcaster discretion as a means of maximizing coverage of campaign activity. Through an examination of other passages in the reports and debates on the 1959 amendments, we learned that Congress had expressed a willingness to grant the commission considerable leeway in interpreting the exemptions and to accept some risks with respect to the equal-opportunity philosophy in order to achieve more complete broadcast coverage of newsworthy events. Accordingly, we upheld the commission's revised approach.

B. THE COMMISSION'S ANALYSIS AND APPLICATION OF SECTION

Petitioner raises four principal objections to the commission's handling of the statutory issues generated by this litigation. These include its use of *Aspen* and *Chisholm* as controlling precedents, the deference accorded broadcaster discretion, the burden placed on petitioners to demonstrate the absence of good faith on the part of the networks, and the commission's refusal to consider post hoc "corrective" action.[61] These we now examine in turn.

1. APPLICATION OF ASPEN AND CHISHOLM AS PRECEDENTS

The first contention advanced by petitioner is that the commission "woodenly applied" *Aspen* by improperly treating it as establishing a per se rule. Certainly we did not in *Chisholm* approve a per se exemption of press conferences from the equal-opportunity requirement of Section 315(a), nor do we think the commission attempted to apply *Aspen* in that manner here.

In *Chisholm*, we upheld the commission's specification of three criteria to govern the decision on whether a candidate's press conference is exempt from the equal-opportunity provision. They are (1) whether the conference is broadcast live, (2) whether it is based upon the good faith determination of the broadcaster that it is a bona fide news event, and (3) whether there is evidence of broadcaster favoritism. It is clear enough that the commission examined the president's February 13 press conference in each of these respects, and not in the least are we moved to impugn the conclusions the commission reached.

There is no suggestion that in any instance the press conference was not broadcast live, nor even so much as a whisper of network bias in favor of the president. Both the Broadcast Bureau and the commission thus correctly perceived the only issue to be whether the networks independently had exercised good faith journalistic judgment in concluding that the event was newsworthy. We move to an examination of the accuracy of the commission's analysis of this question, and to the objections raised thereto by petitioner.

2. GOOD FAITH DETERMINATION OF A BONA FIDE NEWS EVENT

Petitioner contends that the commission effectively delegated to the networks its

61. In sum, no balancing of § 312(a)(7) factors is required under § 315(a). Rather, as we held in Chisholm, 176 U.S.App.D.C. at 3, 538 F.2d at 351, and again in United Church of Christ v. FCC, 191 U.S.App.D.C. at 362–363, 590 F.2d at 1064–1065, if no evidence is brought forth to indicate that the broadcaster has exhibited favoritism toward a particular candidate or candidates at the expense of rivals, the commission need look only to the conditions of the broadcast and whether the broadcaster made a good faith estimate that the event was newsworthy before airing it.

responsibility to determine whether a particular appearance of a candidate is a "use" entitling opponents to equal opportunities. This, petitioner says, the commission did by attaching too great a weight to the broadcasters' good faith judgment of newsworthiness. The flaw in this argument is that, as we have noted, this criterion proceeds directly from the legislative history of Section 315(a). In *Chisholm,* we found congressional intent to expand the role of broadcasters under Section 315(a) and to place considerable reliance on the exercise of their journalistic discretion in order to insure attainment of goals viewed as even more important than equal responsive opportunities.

It would be pointless to restate the analysis carefully expounded in *Chisholm.* It is enough to say that in applying the challenged criterion the commission pursued the course approved by this court as consistent with the legislative history and objectives. Thus we cannot agree with petitioner that the commission here engaged in an unauthorized delegation of its statutory functions merely by following *Aspen* and *Chisholm* as the guiding precedents. On the contrary, the commission quite properly honored *Chisholm's* teaching that "absent evidence of broadcaster intent to advance a particular candidacy, the judgment of the newsworthiness of an event is left to the reasonable news judgment of professionals."

3. THE BURDEN OF ESTABLISHING A PRIMA FACIE CASE OF ABSENCE OF GOOD FAITH

Nor do we believe the commission acted improperly in requiring a candidate seeking an order affording equal opportunities to come forward with evidence that the broadcaster involved did not exercise a bona fide judgment on newsworthiness in covering an appearance by his opponent.

Petitioner has never even alleged that any of the networks failed to make or abide a good faith estimate of newsworthiness. Petitioner thus is hardly in position to complain that the evidentiary burden defined by the commission erects an impermissible barrier to complainants attempting to assert rights under Section 315(a). * * * Requiring a complainant to substantiate his allegations at the outset effectuates this congressional purpose by promoting fearless exercise of the discretion Congress intended broadcasters to have.[72]

Petitioner's apparent inability to satisfy the commission's threshold burden—allegation and corroboration of either bad faith or nonexercise of judgment on newsworthiness by the networks—does not demonstrate that the standard on this score is improvident. On the contrary, it seems evident that one having a legitimate claim in this regard will ordinarily be able to point to something tending to support it. And we do not doubt that when a prima facie showing is made the commission, as it has stated, will inquire into the honesty and reasonableness of a broadcaster's professed news judgment.

4. CORRECTIVE ACTION

Finally, on statutory grounds, petitioner urges that the actual content of a candidate's press-conference broadcast should determine whether the equal-opportunity obligation of Section 315(a) is activated. This contention is linked with the further

72. In its brief the commission points out: While the [agency's] order * * * did not address the types of situations where the reasonableness of a broadcaster's judgment might require further scrutiny, several suggest themselves. For example, if the broadcaster has reason to believe in advance that the press conference questions were going to be "rigged" or that the candidate were going to give his routine stump speech and not accept questions, then the broadcaster's treatment of the press conference as a bona fide news event might be called into question. A pre-existing family or business connection between the candidate and the broadcaster might also warrant closer scrutiny of the broadcaster's judgment.

argument that the commission erroneously failed to consider post hoc whether remedial action should be taken to mitigate damage allegedly wrought. It seems much too late to raise these objections, for petitioner never placed a transcript or other recording of the press conference before the commission. In any event, we are convinced that one of the main purposes of Section 315(a) would be frustrated by requiring the commission to make subjective judgments on the political content of a broadcast program.

As we have previously observed, a major goal of the 1959 amendments to Section 315(a) was preservation of broadcasters' journalistic judgment on news programming. Congress then decided that when broadcasters are allowed to exercise good faith discretion in evaluating the newsworthiness of candidates' appearances on the four exempted types of broadcast programs, the benefits to the public outweigh the detriments to either the public or the candidates. We think the commission steers the right course in declining to undertake assessments on the political or nonpolitical nature of a candidate's appearance, even assuming that there really is much of a difference. As the commission aptly stated, "to draw such distinctions would require [it] to make subjective judgments concerning content, context and potential political impact of a candidate's appearance," and "[n]either Congress nor the commission desires to expand governmental oversight of broadcasters' professional journalistic functions."

We find eminently reasonable, too, the commission's reading of Section 315(a) to require broadcasters to appraise newsworthiness prior to broadcast of the questioned event. Were the commission to hinge operation of the equal-opportunity provision on after-the-fact reexamination of the event broadcast, the purposes for which Congress enacted the Section 315(a) exemptions would largely be set for naught. Broadcasters could never be sure that coverage of any given event would not later result in equal-opportunity obligations to all other candidates; resultantly, broadcaster discretion to carry or not to carry would be seriously if not fatally crippled. * * *

We also deem irrelevant petitioner's assertion that the questioned press conference was "orchestrated as a partisan political event designed to gain maximum political advantage in the New Hampsire primary and subsequent elections—a fact recognized here and throughout the country if not at the commission." When we decided *Chisholm*, we fully explained the insignificance of the candidate's motivation in appearing on the broadcast program. We perceive no good reason to reiterate the discussion here.

We thus are unpersuaded by petitioner's statutory arguments. Together they travel several routes, but they all lead to the same destination. In a word, petitioner's objections to the commission's analysis of Section 315(a) do not warrant reversal of the order under review. We proceed, then, to the constitutional claim.

THE FIRST AMENDMENT CLAIM

Petitioner's First Amendment thesis is that "[p]rivate interests cannot be permitted to abridge the presentation and receipt of legitimate First Amendment expression on the basis of their own subjective values of '*bona fide*' news judgment." Taken simply as a general proposition suitable for application in proper context, few if any expectably would disagree. What petitioner thus characterizes, however, is the commission's deference to the journalistic judgment of broadcasters on newsworthiness of statutorily-exempted events involving candidate appearances, absent some indicium of bad faith or favoritism on the broadcaster's part. In our view, petitioner's legal premise does not fit the situation this case summons us to examine.

* * *

We believe petitioner looks at the First Amendment aspect of this litigation from the wrong standpoint, for in the area of broadcasting the interest of the public is the chief concern. "It is the right of the viewers and listeners, not the right of the broadcasters, which is paramount * * *. It is the right of the public to receive suitable access to social, political, esthetic, moral and other ideas and experiences which is crucial here." From its inception more than a half-century ago, federal regulation of broadcasting has largely entrusted protection of that public right to short-term station licensees functioning under commission supervision, and with liberty as well as responsibility to determine who may get on the air and when. The history of this era portrays Congress' consistent refusal to mandate access to the air waves on a non-selective basis and, contrariwise, its decision "to permit private broadcasting to develop with the widest journalistic experience consistent with its public obligations." The commission has honored that policy in a series of rulings establishing that a private right to utilize the broadcaster's facilities exists only when specially conferred. The net of these many years of legislative and administrative oversight of broadcasting is that "[o]nly when the interests of the public are found to outweigh the private journalistic interests of the broadcasters will government power be asserted within the framework of the act."

While Section 315(a) generally exacts for a candidate's use of broadcast facilities an equal opportunity to his opponents, Congress specifically exempted coverage of a number of arguably "political" news events in the belief that an overly-broad statutory right of access would diminish rather than augment the flow of information to the American public. The real question, then, is whether this legislative scheme transgresses the First Amendment interests of a candidate demanding an opportunity to respond to another candidate's statements on an excepted occasion. We think the answer is evident. As the commission states, "Congress has chosen to enforce the public's primary right in having 'the medium function consistently with the ends and purposes of the First Amendment' by relying on broadcasters as public trustees, periodically accountable for their stewardship, to use their discretion in insuring the public's access to conflicting ideas." More importantly, the Supreme Court has emphasized that no "individual member of the public [has a right] to broadcast his own particular views on any matter," rejecting the "view that every potential speaker is 'the best judge' of what the public ought to hear or indeed the best judge of the merits of his or her views."

* * *

Thus we find no merit in petitioner's First Amendment contention. With the absence also of any valid statutory objection, the order under review is

Affirmed

COMMENT

1. *Kennedy v. FCC* illustrates some of the ambiguities that are present when broadcasters have to make decisions about whether the exemptions of § 315(a) apply. In *Kennedy*, three lines of inquiry were set forth for determining when a press conference was a "bona fide news event" and, therefore, exempt:

a. whether the conference is live;

b. whether it is based upon the good faith determination of a broadcaster that the event broadcast is a bona fide news event;

c. whether there is evidence of broadcaster favoritism.

With respect to item *b* above, the Kennedy for President Committee thought the FCC's approach to exemption decisions constituted an improper delegation to the networks of the question as to whether a particular appearance was a "use" entitling opponents to equal opportunities. Do you agree?

How does a complainant meet the burden of establishing a *prima facie* case of absence of good faith? Note that footnote 72 of the court's opinion points out that the FCC brief gave an example of something that might indicate lack of good faith. The example used was the situation where the broadcaster had cause to believe that press conference questions were "going to be 'rigged' or that the candidate was going to give his routine stump speech and not accept questions." It was also suggested by the commission that lack of good faith might exist where there was a "pre-existing family or business connection between the candidate and the broadcaster."

2. What is the basis for the requirement that broadcasters should appraise newsworthiness prior to the broadcast of the questioned event? The court suggests that if the requirement were otherwise, broadcasters would not be able to forecast in advance whether a particular broadcast would trigger equal opportunities obligations. Why should broadcasters be able to forecast in advance? Perhaps the answer is that the requirement to forecast in advance serves to encourage broadcast of newsworthy events. If the rule were otherwise, a political opponent might have some basis for arguing that some part of a candidate's broadcast appearance had political content. In order to avoid the claims for equal opportunities which such retrospective analyses would produce, broadcasters might decide not to carry the events at all. The FCC takes the position that it should not assess the political or nonpolitical nature of a candidate's appearance. From a First Amendment point of view, this is sound, isn't it? Also, from the point of view of the media recognition factor, it is certainly arguable that all appearances by well-known political personalities are, in fact, political.

A Case for Private Actions Under § 315(a)?

Does a gubernatorial candidate who is denied the use of broadcast facilities in violation of § 315(a) have a basis for a private action against the broadcaster? In Belluso v. Turner Communications Corp., 6 Med.L.Rptr. 2357, 633 F.2d 393 (5th Cir. 1980), this question was answered in the negative. The pervasive nature of broadcast regulation was deemed to indicate that "Congress intended the administrative (FCC) remedy to be exclusive."

Belluso, a Georgia gubernatorial candidate who planned to use hypnotic techniques in his political commercial, contended that because of the short span between the time when a person becomes a qualified candidate and the actual time of the election, FCC intervention is insufficient to accomplish the purpose of § 315(a). The court declined to provide a private remedy where Congress had chosen not to do so.

Some First Amendment contentions were also raised in *Belluso*. It was held that the decision not to air Belluso's political commercial did not constitute governmental action under the First Amendment. Furthermore, even if the action of the station were viewed as governmental action for purposes of the First Amendment, it was held that there was no First Amendment right of access to the broadcast media. The court relied for its conclusion on the First Amendment issue on Kuzco v. Western Connecticut Broadcasting Co., 3 Med.L.Rptr. 1209, 566 F.2d 384 (2d Cir. 1977).

In *Kuzco*, a radio station had censored the material of two candidates who had been granted time pursuant to the equal time rule. The FCC found that the station had violated § 315(a). The candidates then brought a private action for damages against the station for violation of their

First Amendment rights. *Kuzco* held that the station's action did not violate the First Amendment since the conduct of the radio station should be viewed as private rather than governmental action. In short, *Kuzco* held that the state action which is necessary to make the First Amendment operative was lacking.

Belluso also relied on CBS v. Democratic National Committee, 412 U.S. 94 (1973) and Miami Herald Publishing Co. v. Tornillo, 418 U.S. 241 (1974). In *Belluso*, plaintiff argued that "although a broadcaster argued in an area in which journalistic discretion may be exercised in engaging in private conduct, when he is acting in an area in which he has no discretion, his action becomes governmental action."

The argument boils down to this: The broadcaster has to accept advertising for one candidate if he accepts any such advertising. The broadcaster cannot censor any material broadcast under § 315(a). Therefore, Belluso argued, a "decision not to air a particular message in violation of Section 315(a) must be considered governmental action for purposes of a First Amendment challenge."

The Court rejected this argument: "Once it is determined that a broadcaster acts as a private person subject to government regulations, his actions cannot be imputed to the government unless they are in some way approved or sanctioned by the government." Is an argument available that the Supreme Court decision in *CBS v. FCC*, text, p. 815, should change the result in *Belluso* on the First Amendment issues? What is it?

The Meaning of § 315(b)

1. The FCC dealt with § 315(b) (see text, p. 800), in Martin-Trigona, 40 R.R.2d 1189 (1977). Station WBBM–TV refused to sell one hour or one-half hour blocks of prime time programming to Anthony Martin-Trigona, a legally qualified candidate for the Democratic nomination for mayor of Chicago. The station offered Martin-Trigona five minute non-prime time segments and spot announcements during prime time.

The most important question raised by the controversy was the following: Does § 315(b) exclusively concern the allowable rates that a broadcaster may charge a political candidate or does it have some bearing on the segments of broadcast time that the political candidate can claim?

In support of his position that § 315(b) gave him a right to buy particular segments of broadcast time, Martin-Trigona argued "a candidate cannot make an intelligent statement of his stand on an issue" in a spot announcement. The complaint in this regard was that broadcaster policy invalidly discriminated between those candidates who wished to use "spots" for their campaigning and those who wished to use larger blocks of time.

Martin-Trigona argued that the lowest "rate per unit of audience reached" occurs in prime time and under § 315(b) the station is obligated to offer the lowest unit charge. This theory led Martin-Trigona to the assertion that § 315(b) not only required a candidate to be on par with the station's most favored advertiser as to rates, but also as to times available. Under this rationale, if the broadcaster sold five-minute time segments to advertisers, he must also make identical time segments available for sale to political candidates.

The FCC pointed out that the licensee had not entirely denied access to a legally qualified candidate. Martin-Trigona's complaint was that he had not been given the specific amount of broadcast time that he desired. The FCC ruled that § 315(b) did not require a broadcaster to sell a political candidate specific time segments such as the half-hour blocks sought by mayoral candidate Martin-Trigona. Section 315, according to FCC rationale, deals only with allowable rates. It simply states that a broadcaster must charge a political candidate the lowest rate that it would charge to any advertiser during the same time period.

The *Martin-Trigona* ruling narrows the effective access of political candidates to the broadcast media by removing any affirmative duty from the broadcaster to provide more than a short "spot" for candidates during prime time.

2. In connection with the problem of being able to buy segments of time of sufficient length to be able to present adequately one's candidacy, consider the following language which was inserted in the Federal Communications Act by a 1972 amendment. The new statutory language enables the FCC to revoke any station license or construction permit "for willful or repeated failure to allow reasonable access to or to permit purchase of reasonable amounts of time for the use of a broadcasting station by a legally qualified candidate for Federal elective office on behalf of his candidacy." See 47 U.S.C.A. § 312(a)(7). See text, p. 815.

Does 47 U.S.C.A. § 312(a) offer any aid to Martin-Trigona? No, because Martin-Trigona was running for mayor of Chicago and § 312(a) applies only to candidates running for *federal* office. If the facts were otherwise and Martin-Trigona had been running for federal office such as, say, the United States Senate from Illinois, would § 312(a) be of any assistance? See text, p. 815.

"Equal Time" and Nonpolitical Broadcasts

1. In Adrian Weiss, 58 FCC2d 342 (1976), the applicability of the equal time doctrine to nonpolitical broadcasts was tested during the 1976 presidential campaign when a broadcast station in California sought a ruling prior to airing old movies starring Ronald Reagan, a legally qualified candidate in the New Hampshire presidential preferential primary. The FCC remarked that attempting to distinguish between political and nonpolitical use of broadcast facilities by candidates would require highly subjective judgments concerning content and would potentially enlarge government interference with broadcasting operations. Therefore the FCC declined to distinguish between political and nonpolitical appearances and ruled that "the broadcast of movies in which Ronald Reagan appears would be 'use' under Section 315 (Equal Time Doctrine) and would entitle opposing candidates to equal opportunities in the use of the broadcasting station."

2. At the time of the *Weiss* decision, Ronald Reagan was no longer engaged in an acting career. But what of an actor who is still performing on television and who is also campaigning for office? Should such an actor be successful in urging that his nonpolitical appearances should not impose "equal opportunities obligations upon broadcast licensees"? In Paulsen v. FCC, 491 F.2d 887 (9th Cir. 1974), the FCC responded in the negative to this question, and the federal court affirmed. The court explained:

> Paulsen's proposed distinction between political and non-political use would, the FCC contends, require it to make highly subjective judgments concerning the content, context, and potential political impact of a candidate's appearance. We agree.

"Equal Time" and the Broadcaster's Obligation

It should be emphasized that the statute, § 315, forbids the station to censor the material broadcast under the provisions of this section. The issue of whether the station licensee will be granted immunity from liability for defamation, since he has no control over the content of the § 315 political broadcast, is dealt with in Chapter II in a discussion of Farmers Educational and Cooperative Union of America,

North Dakota Division v. WDAY, 360 U.S. 525 (1959). See text, p. 274.

The inability of the station licensee to censor the political broadcast is sometimes defended on the ground that the licensee is not required to provide broadcast time to political candidates. It is only when time is extended to one candidate that the "equal time" rule is set in motion. If the station need not, according to the strict language of § 315, give anyone political broadcast time, would a lawyer be giving wise counsel if he advised his broadcaster clients simply to make no political broadcast time available at all? What does an examination of the following excerpt from the *WDAY* case contribute to the resolution of this question? (The facts and opinion of the *WDAY* case are set forth in the text, Chapter II, p. 275.)

FARMERS EDUCATION AND COOPERATIVE UNION OF AMERICA, NORTH DAKOTA DIVISION v. WDAY, INC.

360 U.S. 525, 79 S.CT. 1302, 3 L.ED.2D 1407 (1959).

Justice BLACK delivered the opinion of the Court:

* * *

Petitioner nevertheless urges that broadcasters do not need a specific immunity to protect themselves from liability for defamation since they may either insure against any loss, or in the alternative, deny all political candidates use of station facilities. We have no means of knowing to what extent insurance is available to broadcasting stations, or what it would cost them. Moreover, since § 315 expressly prohibits stations from charging political candidates higher rates than they charge for comparable time used for other purposes, any cost of insurance would probably have to be absorbed by the stations themselves. Petitioner's reliance on the stations' freedom from obligation "to allow use of its station by any such candidate," seems equally misplaced. While denying all candidates use of stations would protect broadcasters from liability, it would also effectively withdraw political discussion from the air. Instead the thrust of § 315 is to facilitate political debate over radio and television. Recognizing this, the Communications Commission considers the carrying of political broadcasts a public service criterion to be considered both in license renewal proceedings, and in comparative contests for a radio or television construction permit. Certainly Congress knew the obvious—that if a licensee could protect himself from liability in no other way but by refusing to broadcast candidates' speeches, the necessary effect would be to hamper the congressional plan to develop broadcasting as a political outlet, rather than to foster it.

* * *

Affirmed.

§ 312(a)(7) AND THE "REASONABLE ACCESS" PROVISION: A LIMITED RIGHT OF ACCESS FOR FEDERAL POLITICAL CANDIDATES?

CBS, INC. v. FCC

7 MED.L.RPTR. 1563, 453 U.S. 367, 101 S.Ct. 2813, 69 L.Ed.2d 706 (1981).

Chief Justice BURGER delivered the opinion of the Court.

We granted certiorari to consider whether the Federal Communications Commission properly construed 47 U.S.C. § 312(a)(7) and determined that petitioners failed to provide "reasonable access to * * the use of a broadcasting station" as required by the statute.

* * *

On October 11, 1979, Gerald M. Rafshoon, President of the Carter-Mondale Presidential Committee, requested each of the three major television networks to provide time for a 30-minute program between 8 p.m. and 10:30 p.m. on either the 4th, 5th, 6th, or 7th of December 1979. The committee intended to present, in conjunction with President Carter's formal announcement of his candidacy, a documentary outlining the record of his administration.

The networks declined to make the requested time available. Petitioner CBS emphasized the large number of candidates for the Republican and Democratic presidential nominations and the potential disruption of regular programming to accommodate requests for equal treatment, but it offered to sell two 5-minute segments to the committee, one at 10:55 p.m. on December 8 and one in the daytime. Petitioner ABC replied that it had not yet decided when it would begin selling political time for the 1980 Presidential campaign, but subsequently indicated that it would allow such sales in January 1980. Petitioner NBC, noting the number of potential requests for time from presidential candidates, stated that it was not prepared to sell time for political programs as early as December 1979.

On October 29, 1979, the Carter-Mondale Presidential Committee filed a complaint with the Federal Communications Commission, charging that the networks had violated their obligation to provide "reasonable access" under § 312(a)(7) of the Communications Act of 1934, as amended. Title 47 U.S.C. § 312(a)(7) states:

> The commission may revoke any station license or construction permit * *
>
> * * *
>
> for willful or repeated failure to allow reasonable access to or to permit purchase of reasonable amounts of time for the use of a broadcasting station by a legally qualified candidate for federal elective office on behalf of his candidacy.

At an open meeting on November 20, 1979, the commission, by a 4–to–3 vote, ruled that the networks had violated § 312(a)(7). In its Memorandum Opinion and Order, the commission concluded that the networks' reasons for refusing to sell the time requested were "deficient" under its standards of reasonableness, and directed the networks to indicate by November 26, 1979, how they intended to fulfill their statutory obligations. 74 FCC2d 631.

Petitioners sought reconsideration of the FCC's decision. The reconsideration petitioners were denied by the same 4–to–3 vote, and, on November 28, 1979, the commission issued a second Memorandum Opinion and Order clarifying its previous decision. It rejected petitioners' arguments that § 312(a)(7) was not intended to create a new right of access to the broadcast media and that the commission had improperly substituted its judgment for that of the networks in evaluating the Carter-Mondale Presidential Committee's request for time. November 29, 1979, was set as the date for the networks to file their plans for compliance with the statute. 74 FCC2d 657.

The networks, pursuant to 47 U.S.C. § 402, then petitioned for review of the commission's orders in the United States Court of Appeals for the District of Columbia Circuit. The court allowed the Committee and the National Association of Broadcasters to intervene, and granted a stay of the Commission's orders pending review.

Following the seizure of American Embassy personnel in Iran, the Carter-Mondale Presidential Committee decided to postpone to early January 1980 the 30-minute program it had planned to broadcast during the period of December 4–7, 1979. However, believing that some time was needed in conjunction with the president's announcement of his candidacy, the committee sought and subsequently obtained from CBS the purchase of five minutes of time on December 4. In addition, the committee sought and obtained from ABC and NBC offers of time for a 30-minute program in January, and the ABC offer eventually was accepted. Throughout these negotiations, the committee and the networks reserved all rights relating to the appeal.

The court of appeals affirmed the commission's orders, 629 F.2d 1 (1980), holding that the statute created a new, affirmative right of access to the broadcast media for individual candidates for federal elective office. As to the implementation of § 312(a)(7), the court concluded that the commission has the authority to independently evaluate whether a campaign has begun for purposes of the statute, and approved the commission's insistence that "broadcasters consider and address all nonfrivolous matters in responding to a candidate's request for time." For example, a broadcaster must weigh such factors as: "(a) the individual needs of the candidate (as expressed by the candidate); (b) the amount of time previously provided to the candidate; (c) potential disruption of regular programming; (d) the number of other candidates likely to invoke equal opportunity rights if the broadcaster grants the request before him; and, (e) the timing of the request." And in reviewing a broadcaster's decision, the commission will confine itself to two questions: "(1) has the broadcaster adverted to the proper standards in deciding whether to grant a request for access, and (2) is the broadcaster's explanation for his decision reasonable in terms of those standards?"

Applying these principles, the court of appeals sustained the commission's determination that the presidential campaign had begun by November 1979, and, accordingly, the obligations imposed by § 312(a)(7) had attached. Further, the court decided that "the record * * * adequately supports the commission's conclusion that the networks failed to apply the proper standards." In particular, the "across-the-board" policies of all three networks failed to address the specific needs asserted by the Carter-Mondale Presidential Committee. From this the court concluded that the commission was correct in holding that the networks had violated the statute's "reasonable access" requirement.

Finally, the court of appeals rejected petitioners' First Amendment challenge to § 312(a)(7) as applied, reasoning that the statute as construed by the commission "is a constitutionally acceptable accommodation between, on the one hand, the public's right to be informed about elections and the right of candidates to speak and, on the other hand, the editorial rights of broadcasters." In a concurring opinion adopted by the majority, Judge Tamm expressed the view that § 312(a)(7) is saved from constitutional infirmity "as long as the [commission] * * * maintains a very limited 'overseer' role consistent with its obligation of careful neutrality * * *."

We consider first the scope of § 312(a)(7). Petitioners CBS and NBC contend that the statute did not impose any additional obligations on broadcasters, but merely codified prior policies developed by the Federal Communications Commission under the public interest standard. The commission, however, argues that § 312(a)(7) created an affirmative, promptly enforceable right of reasonable access to the use of broadcast stations for individual candidates seeking federal elective office.

The Federal Election Campaign Act, of 1971, which Congress enacted in 1972, included as one of its four titles the Campaign Communications Reform Act (Title I). Title I contained the provision that was codified as 47 U.S.C. § 312(a)(7).

We have often observed that the starting point in every case involving statutory construction is "the language employed by

Congress." Reiter v. Sonotone Corp., 442 U.S. 330, 337 * * * (1979). In unambiguous language, § 312(a)(7) authorizes the Commission to revoke a broadcaster's license. * * *

It is clear on the face of the statute that Congress did not prescribe merely a general duty to afford some measure of political programming, which the public interest obligation of broadcasters already provided for. Rather, § 312(a)(7) focuses on the individual "legally qualified candidate" seeking air time to advocate "*his* candidacy," and guarantees him "reasonable access" enforceable by specific governmental sanction. Further, the sanction may be imposed for "willful *or* repeated" failure to afford reasonable access. This suggests that, if a legally qualified candidate for federal office is denied a reasonable amount of broadcast time, license revocation may follow even a single instance of such denial so long as it is willful; where the denial is recurring, the penalty may be imposed in the absence of a showing of willfulness.

The command of § 312(a)(7) differs from the limited duty of broadcasters under the public interest standard. The practice preceding the adoption of § 312(a)(7) has been described by the commission as follows:

> Prior to the enactment of the [statute], we recognized political broadcasting as one of the fourteen basic elements necessary to meet the public interest, needs and desires of the community. No legally qualified candidate had at that time a specific right of access to a broadcasting station. However, stations were required to make reasonable, good faith judgments about the importance and interest of particular races. Based upon those judgments, licensees were to "determine how much time should be made available for candidates in each race on either a paid or unpaid "basis." There was no requirement that such time be made available for specific "uses" of a broadcasting station to which Section 315 "equal opportunities would be applicable." [footnotes omitted.] Commission Policy in Enforcing Section 312(a)(7) of the Communications Act, 68 FCC2d 1079, 1087–1088 (1978) (1978 Report and Order).

Under the pre-1971 public interest requirement, compliance with which was necessary to assure license renewal, some time had to be given to political issues, but an individual candidate could claim no personal right of access unless his opponent used the station and no distinction was drawn between federal, state, and local elections. See Farmers Educational & Cooperative Union v. WDAY, Inc., 360 U.S. 525, 534 * * * (1959). By its terms, however, § 312(a)(7) singles out legally qualified candidates for *federal* elective office and grants them a special right of access on an individual basis, violation of which carries the serious consequence of license revocation. The conclusion is inescapable that the statute did more than simply codify the pre-existing public interest standard.

The legislative history confirms that § 312(a)(7) created a right of access that enlarged the political broadcasting responsibilities of licensees. When the subject of campaign reform was taken up by Congress in 1971, three bills were introduced in the Senate—S. 1, S. 382, and S. 956. All three measures, while differing in approach, were "intended to increase a candidate's accessibility to the media and to reduce the level of spending for its use." * * * The subsequent report of the Senate Commerce Committee stated that one of the primary purposes of the Federal Election Campaign Act of 1971 was to "give candidates for public office *greater access to the media* so that they may better explain their stand on the issues, and thereby more fully and completely inform the voters." S.Rep. No. 92–96, 92d Cong., 1st Sess., 20 (1971) U.S.Code Cong. & Admin.News 1972, pp. 1773, 1774 [Emphasis added]. The report contained neither an explicit interpretation of the provision that became § 312(a)(7) nor a discussion of its intended impact.

* * *

While acknowledging the "general" public interest requirement, the report treated it separately from the specific obligation prescribed by the proposed legislation.

As initially reported in the Senate, § 312(a)(7) applied broadly to "the use of a broadcasting station by a legally qualified candidate on behalf of his candidacy." The Conference Committee confined the provision to candidates seeking *federal* office. * * * During floor debate in the Conference Report in the House attention was called to the substantial impact § 312(a)(7) would have on the broadcasting industry:

* * *

> [U]nder this provision, a broadcaster, whose license is obtained and retained on basis of performance in the public interest, may be charged with being unreasonable and, therefore, fall subject to revocation of his license. 118 Cong.Rec. 326 (1972) (remarks of Rep. Keith).

Such emphasis on the thrust of the statute would seem unnecessary if it did nothing more than reiterate the public interest standard.

Perhaps the most telling evidence of congressional intent, however, is the contemporaneous amendment of § 315(a) of the Communications Act. That amendment was described by the Conference Committee as a "conforming statement" necessitated by the enactment of § 312(a)(7). * * * Prior to the "conforming amendment," the second sentence of 47 U.S.C. § 315(a) (1970 ed.) read: "No obligation is imposed upon any licensee to allow the use of its station by any such candidate." This language made clear that broadcasters were not common carriers as to affirmative, rather than responsive, requests for access. As a result of the amendment, the second sentence now contains an important qualification: "No obligation is imposed *under this subsection* upon any licensee to allow the use of its station by any such candidate." 47 U.S.C. § 315(a) [emphasis added]. Congress retreated from its statement that "no obligation" exists to afford individual access presumably because § 312(a)(7) compels such access in the context of federal elections. If § 312(a)(7) simply reaffirmed the pre-existing public interest requirement with the added sanction of license revocation, no conforming amendment to § 315(a) would have been needed.

Thus, the legislative history supports the plain meaning of the statute that individual candidates for federal elective office have a right of reasonable access to the use of stations for paid political broadcasts on behalf of their candidacies,[8] without reference to whether an opponent has secured time.

We have held that "the construction of a statute by those charged with its execution should be followed unless there are compelling indications that it is wrong, especially when Congress has refused to alter the administrative construction." * *

Since the enactment of § 312(a)(7), the commission has consistently construed the statute as extending beyond the prior public interest policy. In 1972, the commission made clear that § 312(a)(7) "now imposes on the overall obligation to operate in the public interest *the additional specific requirement* [Emphasis added] that reasonable access and purchase of reasonable amounts of time be afforded candidates for Federal office." Use of Broadcast and Cablecast Facilities by Candidates for Public Office, 34 FCC2d 510, 537–

8. No request for access must be honored under § 312(a)(7) unless the candidate is willing to pay for the time sought. See Kennedy for President Comm. v. FCC, 636 F.2d 432, 446–450 (D.C.Cir. 1980).

538 (1972) (1972 policy statement). * * * In its 1978 Report and Order, the commission stated:

> When Congress enacted Section 312(a)(7), it imposed an additional obligation on the general mandate to operate in the public interest. Licensees were specifically required to afford reasonable access to or to permit the purchase of reasonable amounts of broadcast time for the "use" of Federal candidates.
>
> We see no merit to the contention that Section 312(a)(7) was meant merely as a codification of the commission's already existing policy concerning political broadcasts. There was no reason to commit that policy to statute since it was already being enforced by the commission * * *.

The commission has adhered to this view of the statute in its rulings on individual inquiries and complaints. * * *

Congress has been made aware of the commission's interpretation of § 312(a)(7). In 1973, hearings were conducted to review the operation of the Federal Election Campaign Act of 1971. Hearings on S. 372 before the Subcommittee on Communications of the Senate Committee on Commerce, 93d Cong., 1st Sess. (1973). Commission Chairman Dean Burch testified regarding the agency's experience with § 312(a)(7). He noted that the commission's 1972 policy statement was "widely distributed and represented our best judgment as to the requirements of the law and the intent of Congress." Chairman Burch discussed some of the difficult questions implicit in determining whether a station has afforded "reasonable access" to a candidate for federal office, and in conclusion stated: "We have brought our approach to these problems in the form of the 1972 Public Notice to the attention of Congress. If we have erred in some important construction, we would, of course, welcome congressional guidance." Senator Pastore, Chairman of the Communications Subcommittee, replied:

> * * * I think what we did was reasonable enough, and I think what you did was reasonable enough as well.
>
> * * *

The issue was joined when CBS Vice Chairman Frank Stanton also testified at the hearings and objected to the fact that § 312(a)(7) "grants rights to all legally qualified candidates for Federal office * * * ." He strongly urged "repeal" of the statute, but his plea was unsuccessful.[9]

The commission's repeated construction of § 312(a)(7) as affording an affirmative right of reasonable access to individual candidates for federal elective office comports with the statute's language and legislative history and has received congressional review. Therefore, departure from that construction is unwarranted. "Congress' failure to repeal or revise [the statute] in the face of such administrative interpretation [is] persuasive evidence that that interpretation is the one intended by Congress." * * *

In support of their narrow reading of § 312(a)(7) as simply a restatement of the public interest obligation, petitioners cite our decision in CBS, Inc. v. Democratic National Committee, 412 U.S. 94 * * * (1973), which held that neither the First Amendment nor the Communications Act requires broadcasters to accept paid editorial advertisements from citizens at large. The Court in *Democratic National Com-*

9. Broadcasters have continued to register their complaints about § 312(a)(7) with Congress. See Hearing on S. 22 before the Subcommittee on Communications of the Senate Committee on Commerce, Science, and Transportation, 95th Cong., 2d Sess., 67 (1978). And Congress has considered specific proposals to repeal the statute, but has declined to do so. See S. 22, 95th Cong., 1st Sess., § 3 (1977); S. 1178, 94th Cong., 1st Sess., § 2 (1975). Indeed when the Federal Election Campaign Act was amended in 1974, § 312(a)(7) was left undisturbed. See Pub.L. 93–443, 88 Stat. 1272.

mittee observed that "the commission on several occasions has ruled that no private individual or group has a right to command the use of broadcast facilities," and that Congress has not altered that policy even though it has amended the Communications Act several times. * * * In a footnote, on which petitioners here rely, we referred to the then recently enacted § 312(a)(7) as one such amendment, stating that it had "essentially codified the commission's prior interpretation of § 315(a) as requiring broadcasters to make time available to political candidates." * *

However, "the language of an opinion is not always to be parsed as though we were dealing with language of a statute." *Reiter v. Sonotone Corp., supra.* * * * The qualified observation that § 312(a)(7) "essentially codified" existing commission practice was not a conclusion that the statute was in all respects coextensive with that practice and imposed no additional duties on broadcasters. In *Democratic National Committee*, we did not purport to rule on the precise contours of the responsibilities created by § 312(a)(7) since that issue was not before us. Like the general public interest standard and the equal opportunities provision of § 315(a), § 312(a)(7) reflects the importance attached to the use of the public airwaves by political candidates. Yet we now hold that § 312(a)(7) expanded on those predecessor requirements and granted a new right of access to persons seeking election to federal office.[10]

Although Congress provided in § 312(a)(7) for greater use of broadcasting stations by federal candidates, it did not give guidance on how the commission should implement the statute's access requirement. Essentially, Congress adopted a "rule of reason" and charged the commission with its enforcement. Pursuant to 47 U.S.C. § 303(r), which empowers the commission to "[m]ake such rules and regulations and prescribe such restrictions and conditions, not inconsistent with law, as may be necessary to carry out the provisions of [the Communications Act]," the agency has developed standards to effectuate the guarantees of § 312(a)(7). See also 47 U.S.C. § 154(i). The commission has issued some general interpretative statements, but its standards implementing § 312(a)(7) have evolved principally on a case-by-case basis and are not embodied in formalized rules. The relevant criteria broadcasters must employ in evaluating access requests under the statute can be summarized from the commission's 1978 Report and Order and the Memorandum Opinions and Orders in these cases.

Broadcasters are free to deny the sale of air time prior to the commencement of a campaign, but once a campaign has begun, they must give reasonable and good faith attention to access requests from "legally qualified" candidates[11] for federal elective office. Such requests must be considered on an individualized basis, and broadcasters are required to tailor their responses to accommodate, as much as reasonably possible, a candidate's stated purposes in seeking air time. In responding to access requests, however, broadcasters may also give weight to such factors as the amount

10. See generally Note, The Right of "Reasonable Access" for Federal Political Candidates Under Section § 312(a)(7) of the Communications Act, 78 Colum.L.Rev. 1287 (1978).

11. In order to be "legally qualified" under the commission's rules, a candidate must: (a) be eligible under law to hold the office he seeks; (b) announce his candidacy; and (c) qualify for a place on the ballot or be eligible under law for election as a write-in candidate. Persons seeking nomination for the Presidency or Vice Presidency are "legally qualified" in: (a) those states in which they or their proposed delegates have qualified for the primary or Presidential preference ballot; or (b) those states in which they have made a substantial showing of being serious candidates for nomination. Such persons will be considered "legally qualified" in all states if they have qualified in 10 or more states. See 1978 Primer, *supra*, at 2216–2218.

of time previously sold to the candidate, the disruptive impact on regular programming, and the likelihood of requests for time by rival candidates under the equal opportunities provision of § 315(a). These considerations may not be invoked as pretexts for denying access; to justify a negative response, broadcasters must cite a realistic danger of substantial program disruption—perhaps caused by insufficient notice to allow adjustments in the schedule—or of an excessive number of equal time requests. Further, in order to facilitate review by the commission, broadcasters must explain their reasons for refusing time or making a more limited counteroffer. If broadcasters take the appropriate factors into account and act reasonably and in good faith, their decisions will be entitled to deference even if the commission's analysis would have differed in the first instance. But if broadcasters adopt "across-the-board policies" and do not attempt to respond to the individualized situation of a particular candidate, the commission is not compelled to sustain their denial of access. * * * 1978 Report and Order, at 1089–1092, 1094. Petitioners argue that certain of these standards are contrary to the statutory objectives of § 312(a)(7).

The commission has concluded that, as a threshold matter, it will independently determine whether a campaign has begun and the obligations imposed by § 312(a)(7) have attached. * * * Petitioners assert that, in undertaking such a task, the commission becomes improperly involved in the electoral process and seriously impairs broadcaster discretion.

However, petitioners fail to recognize that the commission does not set the starting date for a campaign. Rather, on review of a complaint alleging denial of "reasonable access," it examines objective evidence to find whether the campaign has already commenced, "taking into account the position of the candidate *and the networks* as well as other factors." [Emphasis added]. As the court of appeals noted, the "determination of when the statutory obligations attach does not control the electoral process, * * * the determination is controlled by the process." 629 F.2d at 16. Such a decision is not, and cannot be, purely one of editorial judgment.

Moreover, the commission's approach serves to narrow § 312(a)(7), which might be read as vesting access rights in an individual candidate as soon as he becomes "legally qualified" without regard to the status of the campaign. See n. 11, *supra*. By confining the applicability of the statute to the period after a campaign commences, the commission has limited its impact on broadcasters and given substance to its command of *reasonable* access.

Petitioners also challenge the commission's requirement that broadcasters evaluate and respond to access requests on an individualized basis. In petitioners' view, the agency has attached inordinate significance to candidates' needs, thereby precluding fair assessment of broadcasters' concerns and prohibiting the adoption of uniform policies regarding requests for access.

While admonishing broadcasters not to " 'second guess' the 'political' wisdom or * * * effectiveness" of the particular format sought by a candidate, the commission has clearly acknowledged that "the candidate's * * * request is by no means conclusive of the question of how much time, if any, is appropriate. Other * * * factors, such as the disruption or displacement of regular programming (particularly as affected by a reasonable probability of requests by other candidates), must be considered in the balance." * * Thus, the commission mandates careful consideration of, not blind assent to, candidates' desires for air time.

Petitioners are correct that the commission's standards proscribe blanket rules concerning access; each request must be examined on its own merits. While the adoption of uniform policies might well prove more convenient for broadcasters, such an approach would allow personal campaign strategies and the exigencies of the political process to be ignored. A broadcaster's "evenhanded" response of granting only time spots of a fixed duration to candidates may be "unreasonable" where a particular candidate desires less time for an advertisement or a longer format to discuss substantive issues. In essence, petitioners seek the unilateral right to determine in advance how much time to afford *all* candidates. Yet § 312(a)(7) assures a right of reasonable access to *individual* candidates for federal elective office, and the commission's requirement that their requests be considered on an *individualized* basis is consistent with that guarantee.

* * * As we held in *CBS, Inc. v. Democratic National Committee, supra*, the commission must be allowed to "remain in a posture of flexibility to chart a workable 'middle course' in its quest to preserve a balance between the essential public accountability and the desired private control of the media." Like the court of appeals, we cannot say that the commission's standards are arbitrary and capricious or at odds with the language and purposes of § 312(a)(7). See 5 U.S.C. § 706(2)(A). Indeed, we are satisfied that the commission's action represents a reasoned attempt to effectuate the statute's access requirement, giving broadcasters room to exercise their discretion but demanding that they act in good faith.[12]

There can be no doubt that the commission's standards have achieved greater clarity as a result of the orders in these cases.[13] However laudable that may be, it raises the question whether § 312(a)(7) was properly applied to petitioners.[14] Based upon the commission's prior decisions and 1978 Report and Order, however, we must conclude that petitioners had adequate notice that their conduct in responding to the Carter-Mondale Presidential Committee's request for access would contravene the statute.

In the 1978 Report and Order, the commission stated that it could not establish a precise point at which § 312(a)(7) obligations would attach for all campaigns because each is unique:

> For instance, *a presidential campaign may be in full swing almost a year before an election*; other campaigns may be limited to a short concentrated period. * * *
>
> [W]e expect licensees to afford access at a reasonable time prior to a convention or caucus. We will review a licensee's decisions in this area on a case-by-case basis. [Emphasis added].

In Anthony R. Martin-Trigona, 67 FCC2d 743 (1978), the commission observed:

12. The dissenters place great emphasis on the preservation of broadcaster discretion. However, endowing licensees with a "blank check" to determine what constitutes "reasonable access" would eviscerate § 312(a)(7).

13. In 1978, the commission issued a Notice of Inquiry, which asked whether rulemaking proceedings should be commenced in order to clarify licensee obligations under § 312(a)(7). 43 Fed.Reg. 12938 (March 28, 1978). Petitioners and others in the broadcasting industry expressed strong opposition to the promulgation of specific rules, and none were formulated. 1978 Report and Order, *supra*, at 1079–1081. Petitioners, therefore, must share responsibility for any vagueness and confusion in the commission's standards.

14. Section 312(a) empowers the commission to "revoke any *station* license or construction permit." [Emphasis added.] In the court of appeals, petitioners argued that the statute applies only to licensees, not to networks. However, the court rejected that contention, reasoning that the commission's jurisdiction to "mandate reasonable network access * * * is 'reasonably ancillary' to the effective enforcement of the individual licensee's Section 312(a)(7) obligations. * * * " 629 F.2d, at 25–27. Petitioners do not contest that holding in this Court. See Tr. of Oral Arg. 16–17. In any event, as the commission noted, each petitioner is "a multistation licensee fully reachable [as to its licenses] by [the express] revocation authority" granted under § 312(a)(7). 74 FCC2d, at 640, n. 10.

"[T]he licensee, *and ultimately the Commission*, must look to the circumstances of each particular case to determine when it is reasonable for a candidate's access to begin * * * ." [Emphasis added.] *Id.*, at 746, n. 4. Further, the 1978 Report and Order made clear that "Federal candidates are the intended beneficiary of Section 312(a)(7) and therefore a candidate's desires as to the method of conducting his or her media campaign should be considered by licensees in granting reasonable access." The agency also stated:

> [A]n arbitrary "blanket" ban on the use by a candidate of a particular class or length of time in a particular period cannot be considered reasonable. A federal candidate's decisions as to the best method of pursuing his or her media campaign should be honored as much as possible under the 'reasonable' limits imposed by the licensee.

Here, the Carter-Mondale Presidential Committee sought broadcast time approximately 11 months before the 1980 presidential election and 8 months before the Democratic national convention. In determining that a national campaign was underway at that point, the commission stressed: (a) that 10 candidates formally had announced their intention to seek the Republican nomination, and two candidates had done so for the Democratic nomination; (b) that various states had started the delegate selection process; (c) that candidates were traveling across the country making speeches and attempting to raise funds; (d) that national campaign organizations were established and operating; (e) that the Iowa caucus would be held the following month; (f) that public officials and private groups were making endorsements; and (g) that the national print media had given campaign activities prominent coverage for almost 2 months. * * * The commission's conclusion about the status of the campaign accorded with its announced position on the vesting of § 312(a)(7) rights and was adequately supported by the objective factors on which it relied.

Nevertheless, petitioners ABC and NBC refused to sell the Carter-Mondale Presidential Committee any time in December 1979 on the ground that it was "too early in the political season." * * * These petitioners made no counteroffers, but adopted "blanket" policies refusing access despite the admonition against such an approach in the 1978 Report and Order. * * Likewise, petitioner CBS, while not barring access completely, had an across-the-board policy of selling only 5-minute spots to all candidates, notwithstanding the commission's directive in the 1978 Report and Order that broadcasters consider "a candidate's desires as to the method of conducting his or her media campaign." * * * Petitioner CBS responded with its standard offer of separate 5-minute segments, even though the Carter-Mondale Presidential Committee sought 30 minutes of air time to present a comprehensive statement launching President Carter's reelection campaign. Moreover, the committee's request was made almost 2 months before the intended date of broadcast, was flexible in that it could be satisfied with any prime time slot during a 4-day period, was accompanied by an offer to pay the normal commercial rate, and was not preceded by other requests from President Carter for access. * * * Although petitioners adverted to the disruption of regular programming and the potential equal time requests from rival candidates in their responses to the Carter-Mondale Presidential committee's complaint, the commission rejected these claims as "speculative and unsubstantiated at best." * * *

Under these circumstances, we cannot conclude that the commission abused its discretion in finding that petitioners failed to grant the "reasonable access" required by § 312(a)(7).[15] * * *

Finally, petitioners assert that § 312(a)(7) as implemented by the commission violates the First Amendment rights of broadcasters by unduly circumscribing their editorial discretion. * * * Petitioners argue that the commission's interpretation of § 312(a)(7)'s access requirement disrupts the "delicate balanc[e]" that broadcast regulation must achieve. We disagree.

A licensed broadcaster is "granted the free and exclusive use of a limited and valuable part of the public domain; when he accepts that franchise it is burdened by enforceable public obligations." *Office of Communication of the United Church of Christ v. FCC.* * * * This Court has noted the limits on a broadcast license:

> A license permits broadcasting, but the licensee has no constitutional right to be the one who holds the license or to monopolize a * * * frequency to the exclusion of his fellow citizens. There is nothing in the First Amendment which prevents the Government from requiring a licensee to share his frequency with others * * * . *Red Lion Broadcasting Co. v. FCC, supra.* * * *

See also *FCC v. National Citizens Comm. for Broadcasting.* * * * Although the broadcasting industry is entitled under the First Amendment to exercise "the widest journalistic freedom consistent with its public [duties]," *CBS, Inc. v. Democratic National Committee, supra,* * * * the Court has made clear that:

> *It is the right of the viewers and listeners, not the right of the broadcasters which is paramount.* It is the purpose of the First Amendment to preserve an uninhibited marketplace of ideas in which truth will ultimately prevail, rather than to countenance monopolization of that market. * * *. It is the right of the public to receive suitable access to social, political, esthetic, moral, and other ideas and experience which is crucial here. *Red Lion Broadcasting Co. v. FCC, supra.* * * *

The First Amendment interests of candidates and voters, as well as broadcasters, are implicated by § 312(a)(7). We have recognized that "it is of particular importance that candidates have the * * opportunity to make their views known so that the electorate may intelligently evaluate the candidates' personal qualities and their positions on vital public issues before choosing among them on election day." *Buckley v. Valeo.* * * * Section 312(a)(7) thus makes a significant contribution to freedom of expression by enhancing the ability of candidates to present, and the public to receive, information necessary for the effective operation of the democratic process.

Petitioners are correct that the Court has never approved a *general* right of access to the media. See, *e.g., FCC v. Midwest Video Corp.* * * *; *Miami Herald Publishing Co. v. Tornillo* * * *; *CBS, Inc. v. Democratic National Committee.* Nor do we do so today. Section 312(a)(7) creates a *limited* right to "reasonable" access that pertains only to legally qualified federal candidates and may be invoked by them only for the purpose of advancing their candidacies once a campaign has commenced. The commission has stated that, in enforcing the statute, it will "provide leeway to broadcasters and not mere-

15. As it did here, the commission, with the approval of broadcasters, engages in case-by-case adjudication of § 312(a)(7) complaints rather than awaiting license renewal proceedings. See Tr. of Oral Arg. 11–16. Although the penalty provided by § 312(a)(7) is license revocation, petitioners simply were directed to inform the commission of how they intended to meet their statutory obligations. See 74 FCC2d, at 651; 74 FCC2d, at 676–677. In essence, the commission entered a declaratory order that petitioners' responses to the Carter-Mondale Presidential Committee constituted a denial of "reasonable access." Such a ruling favors broadcasters by allowing an opportunity for curative action before their conduct is found to be "willful or repeated" and subject to the imposition of sanctions.

ly attempt *de novo* to determine the reasonableness of their judgments * * *." * * * If broadcasters have considered the relevant factors in good faith, the commission will uphold their decisions. * * * Further, § 312(a)(7) does not impair the discretion of broadcasters to present their views on any issue or to carry any particular type of programming.

Section 312(a)(7) represents an effort by Congress to assure that an important resource—the airwaves—will be used in the public interest. We hold that the statutory right of access, as defined by the commission and applied in these cases, properly balances the First Amendment rights of federal candidates, the public, and broadcasters.

The judgment of the court of appeals is Affirmed

Justice WHITE, with whom Justice Rehnquist and Justice Stevens join, dissenting.

The Court's opinion is disarmingly simple and seemingly straightforward: in 1972, Congress created a right of reasonable access for candidates for federal office; the Federal Communications Commission, charged with enforcing the statute, has defined that right; as long as the agency's action is within the zone of reasonableness, it should be accepted even though a court would have preferred a different course. This approach, however, conceals the fundamental issue in this case, which is whether Congress intended not only to create a right of reasonable access but also to negate the long-standing statutory policy of deferring to editorial judgments that are not destructive of the goals of the act. In this case, such a policy would require acceptance of network or station decisions on access as long as they are within the range of reasonableness, even if the commission would have preferred different responses by the networks. It is demonstrable that Congress did not intend to set aside this traditional policy, and the commission seriously misconstrued the statute when it assumed that it had been given authority to insist on its own views as to reasonable access even though this entailed rejection of media judgments representing different but nevertheless reasonable reactions to access requests. As this case demonstrates, the result is an administratively created right of access which, in light of the pre-existing statutory policies concerning access, is far broader than Congress could have intended to allow. The Court unfortunately accepts this major departure from the underlying themes of the Communications Act and from the cases that have construed that statute. With all due respect, I dissent.

* * * It is untenable to suggest that the right of access the commission has created is required or even suggested by the plain language of this section. What is "reasonable" access and what are "reasonable" amounts of time that must be sold are matters about which fair minds could easily differ. * * * I think the commission fell into serious error and that its action was arbitrary, capricious, an abuse of discretion and otherwise contrary to law. 5 U.S.C. § 706(2)(A). * * * There are several reasons for my position.

1. The commission seemed to approach this case as though Congress were legislating on a clean slate, without regard for other provisions of the act and the manner in which those provisions had been construed and applied to avoid undue intrusions upon the editorial judgment of broadcasters and without regard for the longstanding statutory policies about access, including the recognized duty imposed on broadcasters to serve the public interest by keeping the citizenry reasonably informed about political candidates.

* * *

The parties agree that prior to the adoption of § 312(a)(7) individuals or organizations had no specific right of access to broadcast facilities. This was the common view of the commission, the courts, and Congress. As we said in *Columbia Broadcasting System, Inc. v. Democratic National Committee,* * * * Congress had "time and again rejected various legislative attempts that would have mandated a variety of forms of individual access." Broadcasters had obligations with respect to their programming, such as the fairness doctrine which obligated them to cover issues of public importance from opposing points of view, but this obligation was enforced with care so as not to unduly infringe on the "journalistic discretion in deciding how best to fulfill the Fairness Doctrine obligations." * * * We also observed that "in the area of discussion of public issues Congress chose to leave broad journalistic discretion with the licensee. Congress specifically dealt with—and firmly rejected—the argument that the broadcast facilities should be open on a nonselective basis to all persons wishing to talk about public issues." * * Similarly, in *FCC v. Midwest Video Corp.,* * * * where we held that the commission had erred in providing for a general system of access to cable television, we noted that the commission's authority with respect to cable television was derived from the provisions of the Communications Act and concluded that the commission should not have ignored "Congress' stern disapproval—evidenced in § 3(h)—of negation of the editorial discretion otherwise enjoyed by broadcasters and cable operators alike." * * * We reaffirmed "the policy of the act to preserve editorial control of programming in the licensee." * * *

Broadcasters, however, had certain statutory obligations with respect to political broadcasting: As the commission has explained, it had "recognized political broadcasting as one of the fourteen basic elements necessary to meet the public interest, needs and desires of the community." 68 FCC2d 1079, at 1087–1088 (1978). * * * The Communications Act had thus long been construed to impose upon the broadcasters a duty to satisfy the public need for information about political campaigns. As this Court observed in *Farmers Educational and Cooperative Union v. WDAY, Inc.,* * * * a broadcaster policy of "denying all candidates use of stations * * * would * * * effectively withdraw political discussion from the air" and that such result would be quite contrary to congressional intent. Furthermore, § 315 had long provided that should a station permit a political candidate to use its broadcasting facilities, it must "afford equal opportunities to all other such candidates for that office. * * *" As that section expressly provided, however, the provision for equal time created no right of initial access.

It is therefore as clear as can be that the regulation of the broadcast media has been and is marked by a clearly defined "legislative desire to preserve values of private journalism." *Columbia Broadcasting System, Inc. v. Democratic National Committee, supra.* * * * The corollary legislative policy has been not to recognize or attempt to require individual rights of access to the broadcast media. These policies have been so clear and are so obviously grounded in constitutional considerations that in the absence of unequivocal legislative intent to the contrary, it should not be assumed that § 312(a)(7) was designed to make the kind of substantial inroads in these basic considerations that the commission has now mandated. Section 312(a)(7) undoubtedly changed the law governing access in some respects, but the language of the section, as the commission itself concedes, does not require the access rights the commission has now created; and the legislative history, far from supporting the commission's actions in this case, has a contrary thrust.

2. The legislative history, most of which the commission ignored, shows that Congress was well aware of the statutory and regulatory background recounted above. It also shows that Congress had

no intention of working the radical change in the roles of the broadcaster and the commission that the commission now insists is consistent with the statutory mandate.

* * *

The legislative history thus reveals that Congress sought to codify what it conceived to be the pre-existing duty of the broadcasters to serve the public interest by presenting political broadcasts. It also negates any suggestion that Congress believed it was creating the extensive, inflexible duty to provide access that the commission has now fastened upon the broadcasters. This is not to say that § 312(a)(7) did not work important changes in the law, for it did put teeth in the obligation of the broadcasters' duty to serve the public interest by providing the remedy of license revocation for willful or repeated refusals to provide a candidate for federal elective office with reasonable access to broadcast time. The need for this remedy arose out of the concern that other provisions of the Federal Election Campaign Reform Act could lead to a misunderstanding regarding the broadcasters' continuing duty to afford reasonable access to federal candidates.

The commission almost totally ignored the legislative history as a possible limitation on the reach of the broadcasters' duty to provide reasonable access or upon the scope of its oversight responsibilities. The commission did note that one of the purposes of the 1971 act had been described as affording candidates a greater access to the broadcast media. But none of these statements indicated that this was the purpose of § 312(a)(7), the provision at issue here. That purpose was served by other provisions of the amendments, such as the provision requiring the sale of broadcast time at the lowest unit charged during specified periods; § 312(a)(7) itself aimed at preventing the charge limitation from reducing access that might otherwise be available.[2]

The commission also noted, and the Court now heavily relies on, the so-called conforming amendment to § 315, the equal time provision, which then provided that "no obligation is imposed upon any licensee to allow the use of its station by any such candidate." But in its original form, this portion of § 315 had provided that "no obligation is hereby imposed"—the word "hereby" being omitted by the codifier of Title 47 of the United States Code. To the extent that § 315 without the conforming amendment, which returned the relevant provision to approximately its original form, suggested that the act in no way required access to political candidates, it also called into the question the commission's public interest policy of requiring stations to give reasonable access to political candidates. That the conforming amendment was made is understandable, but the Court gives it undue significance.

In any event, the Court relies on the conforming amendment for no more than an affirmative indication that Congress intended to give individual candidates a right of reasonable access, a right that did not exist prior to the enactment of § 312(a)(7). This much may be conceded, but nothing in this bit of legislative history, or in any other, furnishes any support for the commission's sweeping decision in this case. On the contrary, the legislative

2. One of the major purposes of the Federal Election Campaign Act was to shorten the length of campaigns thereby reducing campaign costs. See S.Rep.No. 92–96, 92d Cong., 1st Sess., 20–21, 28 (1971). Television advertising was described as "unquestionably the most used media in political campaigns, and it has been the most significant contributor to the spiraling cost of these campaigns." *Id.*, at 30. *U.S.Code Cong. & Admin. News*, 1972, pp. 1783–1784. The majority's interpretation of § 312(a)(7) runs directly contrary to this broad goal. This decision is nothing more than an open invitation to start campaigning early, thus increasing the overall length of the campaign and the overall costs to all the candidates.

history negates the commission's conclusion that it was free to so drastically limit the discretion of the broadcasters and to so radically expand its own oversight authority.

3. The Court relies, as it must, on the authority of the commission to interpret and apply the statute and on the deference that courts should accord to agency views with respect to the legislation it is charged with enforcing. * * *

I find the commission's current radical version not only quite inconsistent with its prior views but also singularly unpersuasive.

* * *

There was no suggestion in 1972 that the "needs" of the requesting candidate shall be paramount. Indeed, the commission embraced its prior practice. Discretion was thought to remain with the broadcaster, not placed in hands of the candidates or subjected to close and exacting oversight by the commission. Clearly, the commission's contemporaneous construction of § 312(a)(7) is inconsistent with the sweeping construction of the section it has now adopted. * * *

Subsequent interpretations of the scope of § 312(a)(7), including the comprehensive Report and Order: Commission Policy in Enforcing Section § 312(a)(7) of the Communications Act, 68 FCC2d 1079 (1978), have consistently refrained from curtailing broadcaster discretion by refusing to impose stringent standards or to second guess the broadcaster's good faith judgments. In the *Report and Order*, the commission explained,

* * *

> We continue to believe that the best method for achieving a balance between the desires of candidates for air time and the commitments of licensees to the broadcast of other types of programming is to rely on the reasonable, good faith discretion of individual licensees. We are convinced that there are no formalized rules which would encompass all the various circumstances possible during an election campaign.* * *

The commission went on to suggest some very broad guidelines it considered essential in effectuating the intent of Congress under § 312(a)(7). For example, candidates generally were to be afforded some access to prime time, and access was to be flexible, including the possibility of program time and "spot" announcements. Candidates were not entitled, however, "to a particular placement of his or her political announcement on a station's broadcast schedule. * * * It is best left to the discretion of a licensee when and on what date a candidate's spot announcement or program should be aired." * * * The commission specifically refused to arrogate to itself the power to determine when the reasonable access duty attached except on a case-by-case basis leaving the initial judgment in the hands of the broadcast licensee. Finally, there is no statement in this report that requires broadcasters to look to the needs of a candidate in the initial determination of reasonable access other than the admonition that broadcasters could not "follow a policy of flatly banning access by a federal candidate to any of the classes and lengths of program or spot time in the same periods which the station offers to commercial advertisers." Like the initial policy statement issued in 1972, this report lends little credence to the new-found power of the commission to oversee with an iron hand the implementation of § 312(a)(7).

In terms of the degree to which broadcaster editorial judgments should be subject to review and reversal by the commission—the most important issue in this case—it is evident that the commission has been quite inconsistent. Its present radical interpretation of § 312(a)(7) plainly rejects its earlier and more contemporaneous pronouncements as to the meaning and scope of the broadcasters' duties and of its own authority under § 312(a)(7).

4. Equally, if not more fundamental, the commission's opinions in this case are singularly unpersuasive. They contain a plethora of admonitions to the broadcast industry, some quite vague and others very specific but often inconsistent. Altogether, in operation and effect, they represent major departures from prior practice, from prior decisions, including those of this court, and from congressionally recognized policies underlying the Federal Communications Act. As I have indicated, we should not endorse them without much clearer congressional direction than is apparent in the actions leading to the adoption of § 312(a)(7). I shall mention my major difficulties with the commission's opinion and judgment.

The commission stated in a footnote that it should not differ with broadcaster decisions with respect to a candidate's access unless "arbitrary, capricious, an abuse of discretion, or otherwise not in accordance with law," an approach reflecting its traditional stance vis-á-vis the broadcasters. 74 FCC2d, at 642, n. 16. The commission had already determined, however, that because § 312(a)(7) was not self-explanatory on its face and because it failed to find explicit guidance to the contrary in the legislative history, it would and should exercise wide discretion in interpreting and enforcing the act. It is therefore not surprising that the commission's assertions of deference to editorial judgment are palpably incredible.[3]

The commission first confounds itself by announcing that the duty to provide access attaches when the campaign begins and that this threshold issue was to be "based on [an] independent evaluation of the status of the campaign taking into account the position of the candidate and the networks as well as other factors." * * This effectively withdrew the issue of timing from the area of broadcaster judgment and transformed it into a question of law to be determined by the commission *de novo.* It was also a major shift in the agency's position, for its Broadcast Bureau just 2 years before had ruled that the assessment of when a campaign is sufficiently underway to warrant the provision of access was to be left to broadcaster discretion: "A licensee's discretion in providing coverage of elections extends not only to the type and amount of time to be made available to candidates, but to the date on which its campaign coverage will commence." 66 FCC2d 968, at 969 (Broadcast Bureau 1977), app. for review denied, 67 FCC2d 33, reconsideration denied, 67 FCC2d 743 (1978). Although I have some difficulty in perceiving why the access obligation should begin when "the campaign" is underway, even if there is such a triggering event, reasonable men could differ as to when that moment has arrived. The commission overstepped its authority in imposing its own answer on the industry and in rejecting the network's reasonable submissions. The commission gave no explanation whatsoever for its action in this respect. In fact, it did not even acknowledge that it was making its own *de novo* determination until it issued its opinion on reconsideration.

The commission ruled that in responding to its obligation to provide reasonable time, a broadcaster should place particular emphasis on the candidates' needs, weigh each request in its own specific context on a particularized basis and tailor its response to the individual candidate. This approach expressly rejects the thesis of § 315 that all candidates be treated equally. If the networks in this case had responded affirmatively to the candidate's

3. Of a similar tenor is the court of appeals' observation that "[t]he interference with editorial discretion" created by the rigid scheme of regulatory oversight it was endorsing "seems no more or less" than had existed under the broad public interest standard. 629 F.2d, at 23, n. 102.

request, § 315 would require that equal time be extended to all other Democratic candidates and would forbid any kind of individualized consideration that would result in giving them less time than had been previously given to their competitor. There is no trace of support in the language of the act or in the legislative history for this unrealistic approach to § 312(a)(7). Nor does the commission offer any tenable explanation why a broadcaster's decision to provide equal time for all candidates is a violation of the obligation to provide reasonable time to each of them. The inference may be drawn from the commission's position that reasonable access may require unequal access, but § 315 requires equal time for all once it is granted to anyone. The commission's rejection of the equality approach as one of the possible ways of complying with § 312(a)(7) is a plain error.

Of course, the individualized-need approach requires a broadcaster to make an assessment with respect to each request for time, and each of these countless assessments will be subject to review by the commission. If the degree of oversight to be exercised by the commission is to be measured by its work in this case, there will be very little deference paid to the judgment and discretion of the broadcaster. The demands of the candidate will be paramount. * * *

Indicative also of the stringent degree of oversight that the commission now intends to exercise is the manner in which it dealt with the networks' suggestions that in responding to the request for time involved here, they were entitled to take into account the fact that a total of 122 persons had filed notices of candidacy for the presidency with the Federal Election Commission. The commission conceded that this was a proper concern and that Republican candidates might have to be treated equally with Democrats. The commission, however, in its political wisdom, concluded that it was "unlikely" that more than a tiny percentage of all candidates would request time, the net effect being that the networks anticipations based on their professional experience were rejected. As petitioner CBS submits on brief: "Broadcasters are not permitted to consider the likelihood of multiple future requests by similarly situated candidates unless the imminence of such requests can be demonstrated to a near certainty. But the likelihood that there will be multiple demands from other candidates is not susceptible to proof in advance. Candidate needs are necessarily shifting in nature, and no candidate can supply a precise prediction of his future plans. Thus, under the commission's approach, broadcasters can give only limited, if any, weight to potential disruption of normal program schedules, or their view that other material would better serve the interests of their audiences." CBS brief, at 38.

The court tells us, "If the broadcasters take the appropriate factors into account and act reasonably and in good faith, their decision will be entitled to deference even if the commission's analysis would have differed in the first instance." But this language can be taken with a grain of salt, since the commission, the court of appeals and the majority give the networks no deference whatsoever. This is so because the "appropriate factors" are designed to eviscerate broadcaster discretion. The abrupt departure from accepted norms and the truly remarkable extent to which the commission will seek to control the programming of political candidates in the future is best demonstrated by its rejection, as being unreasonable, of the submissions filed by the networks in response to the complaints. * * *

* * *

None of these justifications is patently unreasonable. They become so only because of the commission's conclusion, adopted by the majority, that the reasonableness of access is to be considered from the individual candidate's perspective, including that candidate's particular "needs." While both the Court and the commission describe other factors considered relevant such as the number of candidates and disruption in programming, the overarching focus is directed to the perceived needs of the individual candidate. This highly skewed approach is required because, as the Court sees it, the networks "seek the unilateral right to determine in advance how much time to afford *all* candidates." But such a right, reasonably applied, would seem to fall squarely within the traditionally recognized discretion of the broadcaster. Instead of adhering to this traditional approach, the Court has laid the foundation for the unilateral right of candidates to demand and receive any "reasonable" amount of time a candidate determines to be necessary to execute a particular campaign strategy. The concomitant commission involvement is obvious. There is no basis in the statute for this very broad and unworkable scheme of access. * * *

* * *

COMMENT

1. It has been argued that *Red Lion* and *Tornillo* "cannot be reconciled because the distinctions which have been drawn between them are constitutionally insignificant." But it is contended that "unlike *Red Lion, CBS v. FCC* can be reconciled with *Tornillo*." See, Shelledy, *Note, Access to the Press: Teleological Analysis of a Constitutional Double Standard*, Geo. Wash.L.Rev. 430 (1982). How? *CBS v. FCC* distinguished the right of access sought there from the Florida right of reply statute which was considered in *Tornillo.* The "identity of the medium" was not the critical factor. *Tornillo* is often distinguished from *Red Lion* on the ground that in a newspaper case the restraint which can be imposed under the First Amendment is far more severe in nature than that imposed upon the electronic media.

The George Washington note distinguishes *Tornillo* from *CBS v. FCC* as follows:

> Only one of the limiting characteristics of section 312(a)(7), the reasonableness standard, distinguishes it from the Florida right of reply on a level of constitutional significance: an editor's decision not to broadcast another's message is left undisturbed so long as the decision has been reached reasonably. The Florida statute the *Tornillo* Court invalidated constrained editorial discretion far more severely than section 312(a)(7). Once a triggering editorial vested the Florida right of reply, the editor lost all control over the decision of whether to publish a response, what length to allot to the response, and placement and choice of typeset—notwithstanding reasonable alternatives the editor could have chosen. Had the Florida statute been limited by the reasonableness standard, as is Section 312(a)(7), it would not have transgressed the Court's command in *Tornillo* that any "compulsion to publish that which "reason" tells [editors] should not be published is unconstitutional."

Do you agree?

2. In CBS v. Democratic National Committee, 412 U.S. 94 (1973), the Supreme Court held that an "arbitrary" blanket network policy refusing to sell time to political groups for the discussion of social and political issues did not violate the First Amendment. Yet, in *CBS v. FCC*, the Court held that an "arbitrary" blanket ban by the networks on the use by a candidate of a particular length of time in a particular period could not be considered reasonable under § 312(a)(7). A blanket network ban on a certain category of programming was deemed permissible in one instance and impermissible in the other. Why? The difference is that in *CBS v. FCC* a *statute* conferred particular rights on individual political candidates. The FCC's construction of the statute made the

candidate's "desires as to the method of conducting his or her campaign" a matter to be considered by the licensee in determining whether to grant reasonable access under the statute.

In short, the second *CBS* case involved a limited statutorily conferred right, whereas the first *CBS* case would have required a decision by the Supreme Court that the First Amendment itself was a barrier to the exercise of broadcast editorial judgment.

3. In *Comment, Beyond the Public Interest Standard: The Supreme Court Approves a Statutory Right of Access to the Broadcast Media for Federal Candidates in CBS, Inc. v. FCC*, 48 Brooklyn L.Rev. 355 at 388 (1982), it is suggested that the limited holding in *CBS* "leaves undefined the point at which government-created access rights will offend constitutional guarantees." Furthermore, the comment challenges the attempt the Court makes at creating a distinction between *CBS v. FCC* and the earlier cases of *CBS v. Democratic National Committee*, text, p. 858, *Miami Herald Publishing Co. v. Tornillo*, text, p. 584, and *Midwest Video v. FCC*, text, p. 991:

> The Court, however, never suggested that its decisions in these cases were based upon a distinction between general and limited rights of access. In *Tornillo*, the Court made clear that no right of access to the print media would be upheld, and in *Midwest Video* the constitutional issue was not even addressed. As noted earlier, *Democratic National Committee* raised the issue of what access obligations are constitutionally required rather than what are constitutionally permissible. Thus, even if the Court had made a distinction between general and limited rights of access, its effect on the Court's analysis in *CBS* would have been minimal at best.

The comment speculates, quite properly, that the Court might have been attempting to expound a distinction which will be important in access cases in the future. A distinction between a general right of access (arguably impermissible under the First Amendment) and a specific right of access (arguably permissible under the First Amendment) might be defensible. But then the comment asks if creation of such a distinction was the Court's purpose in *CBS v. FCC*, wasn't it "wholly unnecessary for the Court to distinguish *Democratic National Committee, Tornillo*, and *Midwest Video*"?

4. The *Brooklyn Law Review* comment makes the following observation: "Once the Court determined that the statute vested federal candidates with an individual right of access, it would have been absurd to insist that the commission adhere to the deferential good faith standard, since such a policy would have rendered Section 312(a)(7) virtually unenforceable."

The suggestion here is that if the standard were whether the broadcaster made a good faith reasonable judgment, then the grant in § 312(a)(7) of individual rights of access to federal political candidates would have been meaningless. This is because in most controversial situations the broadcasters will have an arguably reasonable basis for a decision not to grant access. In short, it would be nearly impossible to overcome a broadcaster's assertion that a programming decision was a good faith exercise of editorial judgment. The kind of deference to the good faith-reasonable judgment of the broadcasters which was extolled by Judge Leventhal in the *Pensions* case, text, p. 876, in a Fairness Doctrine setting might be particularly inapplicable in a setting where individual rights of access rather than fairness principles are at stake.

5. Did § 312(a)(7) of the Federal Election Campaign Act of 1971 create an affirmative, promptly enforceable right of access? Or did it merely codify prior FCC policies, i.e., the obligation to provide reasonable access to federal political candi-

dates was part of the public interest standard of the Federal Communications Act.

Chief Justice Burger's answer on this is very clear. Section 312(a) of the Federal Election Campaign Act of 1971 created a *new*, affirmative, promptly enforceable right of access. Why? For one thing, the fact that the second sentence of § 312(a) was contemporaneously amended to make it clear that "no obligation is imposed *under this subsection* upon any licensee to allow the use of its station by any such candidate" is seen as quite significant. The amendment was interpreted by the Court in *CBS v. FCC* as evidence of congressional awareness that § 312(a)(7) had imposed upon broadcast licensees an obligation to allow the use of their stations by federal political candidates in a manner which previously had not obtained under either the public interest standard of the act or the prior unamended text of the second sentence of § 315(a).

6. How does § 312(a)(7) differ anyway from the duty to provide access for political candidates which broadcasters had under the public interest standard? See, Farmers Education and Cooperative Union of America, North Dakota Division v. WDAY, 360 U.S. 525 (1959), text, p. 815. One answer to this question is that previous to the enactment of § 312(a)(7), no legislative candidate had a specific right of access to broadcasting. There was a general public interest obligation to give political candidates some time, but no particularized rights were lodged in the candidates. If one candidate was given time, then, of course, under § 315(a) rights to equal opportunities were triggered for that office by broadcasters. If all candidates were denied time, then all the candidates seeking time would have had to rely on would be the general public interest obligation of broadcasters to provide time for political campaigns. This obligation was difficult to enforce since no particular candidate had any specified rights under such an obligation.

7. Do you agree with Justice White that the majority interpretation of § 312(a)(7) is an "open invitation to start campaigning early"? In § 312(a)(7), the FCC refuses to defer to the editorial judgment of the broadcasters about when a campaign may be deemed to have commenced and reserves that issue for itself. As a result, the candidate may be encouraged to show a "need" to campaign early. If his recognition factor is low and his treasury is full, the incentive to seek access for early campaigning is great. Does the majority opinion suggest any means by which such requests may be countered by the FCC? What are they?

Does § 312(a)(7) Require Broadcasters to Make Free Time Available?

KENNEDY FOR PRESIDENT COMMITTEE v. FCC

6 MED.L.RPTR. 1705, 636 F.2D 432 (D.C.CIR. 1980).

ROBINSON, Circuit Judge: On March 14, 1980, the three major commercial television networks broadcast a half-hour speech by President Carter from 4:00 to 4:30 p.m. and a presidential press conference from 9:00 to 9:30 p.m. On each occasion, the principal topic of discussion was the state of the Nation's economy. Each event was presented in its entirety and, with but one exception, was televised live by each network. The president's statements were also reported in the course of the networks' regularly scheduled national and local newscasts.

The Kennedy for President Committee, the petitioner herein, charges that these programs saturated the American public with the president's views on the economy only four days before the 1980 Illinois presidential primary. That, petitioner asserts, diminished the chances of its candidate, Senator Edward M. Kennedy, of winning the Democratic Party's presidential nomination later in the year. Petitioner claims that Section 312(a)(7) of the Communications Act of 1934 and the well-known fairness doctrine separately entitle the senator to time for telecasts of his own ideas and proposals on economic conditions.

The networks denied petitioner's request for responsive time, and the Federal Communications Commission rejected petitioner's bid for an administrative directive therefor. Before us now is a petition for review of the commission's order. We agree with the commission that petitioner's reliance on Section 312(a)(7) is misplaced, and that petitioner failed to establish the elements of a prima facie case under the fairness doctrine. We accordingly affirm.

I. BACKGROUND

Reacting to announcements of plans to televise President Carter's March 14 speech and press conference, petitioner implored the networks to provide Senator Kennedy with an opportunity to speak in prime time to the American people on the economy. Petitioner attached special importance to an airing of the Senator's views on that subject, stating that the economic situation was "one of the major issues that compelled Senator Kennedy to challenge Mr. Carter for the Democratic nomination." Petitioner asked that time be made available for the Senator's use prior to the March 18 Illinois primary.

Independently, the networks refused. In each instance, they construed petitioner's request as an invocation of the equal-opportunity command of Section 315(a) of the Communications Act, and expressed the belief that the telecasts in question were exempt from that requirement as on-the-spot coverage of bona fide news events. Each network reminded petitioner that it had given extensive coverage to the senator's campaign, and to his position on economic issues. Two of the networks emphasized their earlier presentations of wide spectra of economic commentary and analysis encompassing numerous alternatives to the stratagems advanced by the president.

Petitioner then turned to the commission for "redress [of] a pattern of conduct causing an unacceptably imbalanced presentation of important facts." Petitioner specifically identified Section 312(a)(7) of the Communications Act and the long-established fairness doctrine as bases for a commission order to the networks to make time available to the senator. It is noteworthy that petitioner has pointedly disclaimed any reliance on Section 315(a)'s equal-opportunity provision, and has accused the networks of replying to an equal-opportunity demand never made.

At the first level of commission consideration, the Broadcast Bureau denied relief. It first declared that petitioner's dependence on Section 312(a)(7) was faulty; "[g]iven the availability of prime time for purchase," it said, "the networks' failure to furnish free time does not raise a Section 312(a)(7) question." With respect to the fairness doctrine, the bureau concluded that petitioner had not established a prima facie case of violation because it had neither alleged nor substantiated any instance of bad faith on the networks' part, or any failure to present contrasting views on economic issues in their overall programming. The bureau cited petitioner's statement that it had "no doubt that" the networks "acted in good faith," pointed out that under the fairness doctrine no particular individual or group is entitled to present alternative outlooks, and observed that "[e]ven if [petitioner] believes that the controversial issue of public importance in this case is defined as which candidate for the Democratic party's nomination has the soundest economic proposals, there is no evidence presented that this issue was discussed in the broadcast. * * * [T]he networks have indicated that they have presented coverage of Senator Kennedy's economic viewpoints." The bureau readily acknowledged that an incumbent president commands a media advantage over opponents, but deemed that ascendancy inevitable in light of the public interest in informing all Americans of newsworthy presidential appearances. The bureau noted that it was precisely to increase reporting of campaign activity that Congress in 1959 amended Section 315(a) to exempt news coverage from the equal-opportunity requirement.

In essence, then the bureau held that Section 312(a)(7) does not entitle a candidate to free time when time is available for purchase, and that establishment of a prima facie case under the fairness doctrine demands more than a bare conclusory assertion that a broadcaster has not balanced his programming on an important and controversial issue. Without awaiting an application from petitioner, the commission, in the interest of expedition, examined the bureau's decision and affirmed simply on the basis of the bureau's opinion. Then followed the instant petition for review by this court.

II. THE SECTION 312(A)(7) CLAIM

Petitioner's Section 312(a)(7) contention is that it required the networks to allot free time to Senator Kennedy, particularly in consequence of the so-called saturation coverage of President Carter's economic views shortly before the Illinois primary. Two theories are advanced in attempted support of this position. One is that Section 312(a)(7) provides a candidate for federal elective office with a contingent right of access to free time, triggered in this instance by the telecasts of the president's March 14 speech and press conference. The other is that independently of this contingent right, the section confers upon such a candidate direct and unqualified entitlement to use broadcast facilities without charge.

As soon we shall see, Sections 312(a)(7) and 315(a) of the Communications Act work in tandem to govern access to broadcast media by candidates for public office. With the interaction of these two sections at the heart of federal intervention in political broadcasting, we begin our assessment of petitioner's arguments with an analysis of their interrelationship.

A. THE STATUTORY SCHEME

The first part of Section 315(a) is its equal-opportunity provision, frequently referred to as an equal-time grant. In pertinent part it states:

> If any licensee shall permit any person who is a legally qualified candidate for any public office to use a broadcasting station, he shall afford equal opportunities to all other such candidates for that office in the use of such broadcasting station: *Provided*, * * * No obligation is imposed under this subsection upon any licensee to allow the use of its station by any such candidate.

The import of this language is clear: any broadcaster who permits a "use" of station facilities by a legally qualified candidate must provide equal opportunities to that candidate's opponents. As originally enacted, this was the full extent of Section 315(a), but in 1959 Congress amended it to exclude candidate appearances in bona fide newscasts and news interviews, bona fide documentaries in which the appearance is incidental, and on-the-spot coverage of bona fide news events—which no longer constitute a "use" of broadcast facilities, and therefore are unencumbered by the equal-opportunity obligation. Since Section 315(a), as its proviso specifically states, does not impose an unconditional obligation on broadcasters to allow use of their station facilities by any candidate, the equal-opportunity grant has aptly been characterized as a contingent right of access. It does not compel a broadcaster to afford access to any candidate in the first instance, but it does mandate parity for all candidates for a given office once access by one is permitted. The duty is thus no more or less than to accord equal treatment to all legally qualified candidates for the same public office, and "equal opportunity" encompasses such elements as hour of the day, duration and charges.

As we have noted, four categories of news-type programs are expressly exempted from this equal-opportunity mandate. Those programs, like others, however, remain subject to the exigencies of the public interest and the demands of the fairness doctrine. The last sentence of Section 315(a) makes plain that broadcasters are not relieved,

> in connection with the presentation of newscasts, news interviews, news documentaries, and on-the-spot coverage of news events, from the obligation imposed upon them under [the act] to operate in the public interest and to afford reasonable opportunity for the discussion of conflicting views on issues of public importance.

This language, placed in Section 315(a) in 1959 when Congress added the exemptions to the equal-opportunity provision, codifies the fairness doctrine formulated by the commission in 1949. So, while broadcast of an event exempted by Section 315(a) does not enliven the equal-opportunity requirement, it does summon adherence to public-interest and "fairness" considerations. Since we address the ramifications as well as the confines of the fairness doctrine in detail at a later point, we need not dwell upon them now. It is sufficient merely to say that this is another means by which a candidate might gain entree to broadcast facilities for use in his campaign.

The third leaf of the triad governing candidate access to broadcast media is Section 312(a)(7), which authorizes the commission to

> revoke any station license or construction permit * * * for willful or repeated failure to allow reasonable access to or to permit purchase of reasonable amounts of time for the use of a broadcasting station by a legally qualified candidate for federal elective office on behalf of his candidacy.

The import of this passage is the focus of the instant litigation, and it is immediately apparent that its language alone does not dispense with need for inquiry into whether Section 312(a)(7) was intended to serve as an auxiliary to Section 315(a)'s equal-opportunity specification nor whether, when applicable, it assures candidates of some quantum of free time.

This is not the first time that a controversy has arisen over interpretation of Section 312(a)(7). In our recent decision in *CBS* v. *FCC*, we addressed the question whether Section 312(a)(7) was enacted as a new and additional entitlement to broadcast-media access for federal candidates, or whether it merely codified the pre-existing duty of broadcasters to provide time to such candidates pursuant to the general mandate to operate in the public interest. Reading Section 312(a)(7) in light of its legislative history, we concluded that it does indeed "create an affirmative right of access for individual candidates for federal elective office." We did not, however, attempt to define the monetary parameters of that right, for *CBS* involved refusal of requests to *purchase* time. To resolve the issues now before us—whether Section 312(a)(7) augments Section 315(a) as an additional but broader equal-opportunity exaction, and the extent to which it independently grants access on a free basis—we must return to the legislative history and undertake a somewhat broader analysis.

B. THE LEGISLATIVE HISTORY OF SECTION 312(A)(7)

Section 312(a)(7) had its genesis in the Federal Election Campaign Act of 1971. Title I of that legislation, denominated the "Campaign Communications Reform Act," contained three distinct provisions: the reasonable-access requirement now embodied in Section 312(a)(7); the lowest-unit-cost specification which is now Section 315(b)(1); and a spending limitation on use of communications media by candidates for federal elective office, which has since been repealed. Each provision stemmed from serious congressional concern over the ever-mounting expense of modern electioneering.

As in *CBS* we observed, "[t]oday, there can be no doubt that we are in the 'era of television campaigning.'" "Indeed," we said, "since 95 percent of our people operate a television set for an average of over five hours a day, and 60 percent of them rely primarily on television for news, it would be hard to overestimate the importance of television to our political processes." This has not been an overnight phenomenon; nearly a decade ago Congress recognized that in consequence of its increasing public significance television was both boon and bane to the American electoral process. As one member put it, "we have in the technology of television the potential renaissance of the Athenian forum where the public gathers, political contenders debate the issues and enlightened citizen decisions are formed." [59] But to many the exorbitant cost of television campaigning seemed more likely to inspire a rebirth of the oligarchical aspect of the Athenian government than a resurgence of the high level of civic awareness and participation for which Athenian citizens were renowned. Reliance on radio and television programming had become so expensive a necessity for would-be holders of public office that one Congressman was prompted to accuse the "[s]kyrocketing costs of campaigning in this electronic era" of having "increasingly made elective politics the special preserve of the wealthy or of those who have access to the funds of well-healed [*sic*] special interests."

* * *

It would be a mistake, though, to surmise that the legislators were necessarily determined to limit the role of television in election efforts. Instead, as in 1959—when the equal-opportunity provision of Section 315(a) was modified by exemptions—the goal Congress had in mind in 1971 was to make the medium more responsive to civic needs, and to provide better and more complete information to the American public. The debates on the floors of both Houses evince a congressional intent to improve the quality of television campaigning and at the same time to take measures to decrease its cost. It was believed that the informational and educational aspects of political broadcasting could greatly be enhanced by ensuring that more time would be made available to candidates at lower rates. This expectably would encourage less dependence on thirty- to sixty-second "spots"—necessarily little more than slogans—in favor of longer, more illuminating presentations; it would also enable more candidates to afford the television appearances so instrumental to present-day electioneering.

The amendments forged by the Campaign Communications Reform Act thus were inspired principally by concern that the broadcast media were not making enough time available to candidates and that candidates were being charged excessively high rates for the time they were permitted to purchase. But while these problems were clearly enough defined, approaches to their solutions were not. A number of bills were brought before each House proposing amendments to the Communications Act designed to achieve the desired reforms. The three bills of greatest significance in formulation of the Campaign Communications Reform Act were introduced in the Senate, and the focal point of these proposals was the equal-op-

59. 117 Cong.Rec. 272 (1971) (Remarks of Senator Gravel).

portunity provision of Section 315(a) of the act.

* * *

* * * [T]wo principal bills before the Senate were S. 382 and S. 956. These proposals would have abolished Section 315(a)'s equal-opportunity provision with respect to presidential and vice-presidential candidates, a step advocated by many of those present at the hearings as well as by Members on the floor of each chamber. In the course of the hearings, the networks and various others with expertise in the field—including several Senators and Representatives—testified that the equal-opportunity feature of Section 315(a) was itself the major impediment to the complete and accurate coverage necessary to fully inform the public of candidates' positions on major issues. It was perceived that although the 1959 amendments to Section 315(a)—exempting four categories of bona fide news-type broadcasts from its equal-opportunity requirement—had mitigated the problem, the statutory specification of equality for all legally qualified candidates for public office unduly curtailed coverage of principal contenders because broadcasters feared that allotting time to one candidate would inevitably lead to appearances by a string of hopefuls, even those who had no realistic chance of securing a victory or even of gaining substantial support.

Promoters of abridgement of Section 315(a)'s equal-opportunity mandate also emphasized the recognized quality of broadcast coverage of the 1960 presidential campaign, a period during which Congress had temporarily suspended that requirement. Many witnesses and legislators advanced their belief that the famed televised debates between John F. Kennedy and Richard M. Nixon were able to take place only because the equal-opportunity provision was not in effect. The networks indicated their amenability to free time for such events in the future if they were permitted to limit telecasts to appearances of "major" candidates.

To deal with the problem of high rates for campaign broadcasts, and to enable candidates to cut campaign spending in keeping with a basic purpose of the Federal Election Campaign Act, both S. 382 and S. 956 proposed to amend Section 315(b) of the Communications Act, which then prohibited the cost of broadcast time to candidates from exceeding the cost to comparable users. Both bills contained provisions precluding broadcasters from charging candidates amounts in excess of the lowest unit cost available for their slots, though S. 956 limited this requirement to specified periods preceding elections; during all other periods comparable user-rates could remain in effect. This requirement became part of Title I of the Federal Election Campaign Act and is now codified as Section 315(b)(1) of the Communications Act.[97]

The principal differences between S.382 and S.956 involved their approaches to campaign media spending limitations. One other variation, however, is key to our discussion. Unlike S.382, S.956 included a provision designed "to insure that all licensees make available to legally quali-

---

97. Section 315(b)(1), as thus amended, now stipulates rate ceilings for campaign broadcasts as follows:

The charges made for the use of any broadcasting station by any person who is a legally qualified candidate for any public office in connection with his campaign for nomination for election, or election, to such office shall not exceed—

(1) during the forty-five days preceding the date of primary or primary runoff election and during the sixty days preceding the date of a general or special election in which such person is a candidate, the lowest unit charge of the station for the same class and amount of time for the same period; and

(2) at any other time, the charges made for comparable use of such station by other users thereof.

47 U.S.C. § 315(b)(1) (1976).

fied candidates for public office reasonable amounts of time for use of broadcasting station * * *," and broadcasters who failed to comply with this directive could have their licenses revoked by the commission. Although the principal source of the legislation eventuating as the Federal Election Campaign Act was S.382, it was essentially this provision of S. 956 that was enacted as Section 312(a)(7).

The drafters of S.956 said very little about the function of the reasonable-access provision. We held in CBS that it was intended to confer at least an affirmative entitlement to use broadcast facilities; we found "a clear indication [in the legislative history] that candidates in *federal* elections were being singled out for something beyond the amorphous right of access created by the public interest doctrine." Whether the phrase "reasonable access" extends a still broader right, however, is the issue now before us—whether Section 312(a)(7) requires broadcasters to furnish free time upon request of a candidate for federal elective office.

The most straightforward reading of the language of Section 312(a)(7) is that broadcasters may fulfill their obligation thereunder either by allotting free time to a candidate *or* by selling the candidate time at the rates prescribed by Section 315(b). Section 312(a)(7) in terms authorizes license or permit revocation "for willful or repeated failure to allow reasonable access to *or* to permit purchase of reasonable amounts of time for the use of a broadcasting station," and "or" normally connotes the disjunctive. While "or" permissibly may be accepted in the conjunctive sense when that adequately appears to have been the legislative intent, in this instance the disjunctive interpretation is clearly supported.

Each reference to Section 312(a)(7) in the legislative history of the Campaign Communications Reform Act speaks of the *sale* of time. * * *

This consistent characterization of the statutory text as a mandate for sale of a reasonable amount of time supplies firm support for a disjunctive reading. And when the rejection of S.1's free-time provision is recalled, the possibility that Congress intended to demand more than that broadcasters sell reasonable amounts of time seems very remote. Indeed, it would not make sense to read into Section 312(a)(7) an entitlement Congress unmistakably scrapped when it declined to enact S.1 or any of its provisions into the Campaign Communications Reform Act. This conclusion is in harmony with Senator Pastore's declaration, a year after passage of that act, that "there was a great deal of pressure to mandate free time" but that Congress decided "to avoid that" and imposed something different.

Consequently, we discern no right to free time for candidates for federal elective office under Section 312(a)(7) either from a reading of the statutory text or from our analysis of its legislative history. Remaining to be answered, however, is the question whether the "reasonable access" language of Section 312(a)(7) sometimes accomplishes that and by affording a right of access to broadcast facilities auxiliary to the Section 315(a) right to equal opportunities.

An equal-opportunity quality for Section 312(a)(7) is mentioned only fleetingly in the legislative history. The very few references to the section as an equal-opportunity provision all concerned S.956 and the role that Section 312(a)(7) would play upon the anticipated—but ultimately aborted—revocation of the equal-opportunity mandate of Section 315(a) with respect to presidential and vice-presidential candidates. In this context, there was but one notable allusion to Section 312(a)(7) as a guaranty of fair treatment of such candidates by broadcasters. The idea, advanced by Senator Mathias, was that after excluding presidential and vice-presidential candidates from the benefit of Section 315(a)'s equal-opportunity provision, Section 312(a)(7) could serve as a source of authority for requiring broadcasters selling time to one such candidate to do the same for his opponents. This suggestion seems to have contemplated no more, however, than that Section 312(a)(7) could operate as a means of assuring that broadcasters would make sufficient quantities of time for purchase available to candidates for presidential or vice-presidential office.

Even assuming that these references tended somewhat to depict Section 312(a)(7) as something of an equal-opportunity auxiliary, that justification eroded away when the proposed partial suspension of Section 315(a)'s equal-opportunity provision failed to pass. There was warm support for suspension, which we noted earlier, but many legislators were fearful of abolition of that provision. Despite the positive experience of the suspensions of the 1960's grave doubts were raised, and the consequences of resting at the mercy of the broadcasters were viewed by some as too serious, especially by members of the House who were particularly wary of complete revocation. Consequently, the Conference Committee decided to eliminate the portion of the Senate bill proposing elimination of Section 315(a)'s equal-opportunity requirement in presidential and vice-presidential campaigns, and neither the final Conference Report nor the ensuing debate on the floor of either House again referred to Section 312(a)(7) as an equal-opportunity measure.

C. THE ADMINISTRATIVE INTERPRETATION OF SECTION 312

Save for the instant proceeding, the commission has not had occasion to consider whether Section 312(a)(7) grants an automatic right to respond to broadcast material additional to that defined in Section 315(a); and here the denial of petitioner's rather vague argument on that point was unelucidated. The Broadcast Bureau dismissed reliance on Section 312(a)(7) for that purpose as misplaced, stating merely that this "section of the law was intended to insure that broadcasters make available reasonable amounts of time for *use* by federal candidates," and the commission affirmed without opinion of its own. To be sure, this disposition evinces an underlying construction of Section 312(a)(7) not at all inharmonious with its legislative reflections, but it adds nothing to an understanding of why. There is, however, a significant history of administrative interpretation with respect to whether Section 312(a)(7), when it does obtain, grants its right of access on a free or a paid basis.

The commission has consistently read Section 312(a)(7) as giving broadcasters the option of fulfilling their obligation thereunder by offering to candidates either free time or the privilege of purchasing time. The commission first took this position in 1972, shortly after passage of Section 312(a)(7), when it issued a public notice in the form of questions and answers:

> 5. Q. Does the "reasonable access" provision of Section 312(a)(7) require commecial stations to give free time to legally qualified candidates for Federal elective office?
>
> A. No, but the licensee cannot refuse to give free time and also [refuse] to permit the purchase of reasonable amounts of time. If the purchase of reasonable amounts of time is not permitted, then the station is required to give reasonable amounts of free time.
>
> 6. Q. If a commercial station gives reasonable amounts of free time to candidates for federal elective office, must it also permit purchase of reasonable amounts of time?
>
> A. No. A commercial station is required either to provide reasonable amounts of free time or permit purchase of reasonable amounts of time.

It is not required to do both.[124]

The commission brought this public notice to the attention of Congress in 1973, and neither then nor at any time thereafter has Congress expressed disagreement with the commission's interpretation of Section 312(a)(7). To boot, the commission has reiterated its original interpretation on subsequent occasions. In publications designed to furnish guidance to candidates and licensees, the commission has constantly maintained that Section 312(a)(7) imposes upon licensees "the specific responsibility to afford *either* reasonable free access or the opportunity to purchase reasonable amounts of time to legally qualified candidates for federal elective office." [126] In 1976, the commission denied rulemaking petitions requesting a new regulation mandating free time for candidates. And in its most recent political broadcasting primer, the commission instructed:

> The reader should also note that the law does not require a station to provide free time. It says the station either must provide reasonable access free or "permit purchase of reasonable amounts of time." Thus, if a station gives away enough time to a candidate to amount to "reasonable access" under the circumstances of the case, it is not required to sell time to the candidate, and if it sells the candidate "reasonable amounts" it need not provide free time.[128]

We are duty bound to honor the "venerable principle that the construction of a statute by those charged with its execution should be followed unless there are compelling indications that it is wrong * * *." Especially should we do so when the agency's initial interpretation of the statute is substantially contemporaneous with its enactment. And where, as here, the administrative interpretations have maintained consistency undeviatingly, there can be no doubt that the deference they command is considerably heightened.

D. CONCLUSIONS

The Communications Act envisions integration of two of its sections in a relatively uncomplicated scheme of access to broadcast facilities by candidates for public office. Section 312(a)(7) supplies a right of access by requiring broadcasters, on pain of license revocation, to make reasonable amounts of time available for use by legally qualified persons seeking federal elective office. This right is unconditional in the sense that no prior use by any opponent of that candidate is necessary. Irrefutably, reasonable access is for the asking if the candidate is willing to pay, and the amount he can be charged is carefully limited by law. The measure of the right remains constant, however, at "reasonable access."

Section 315(a), in turn, ordains that whenever a broadcaster permits any candidate for any public office—federal, state or local—to "use" broadcast facilities, the broadcaster must afford an equal opportunity to any legally qualified rival of that candidate who seeks it. This right is contingent in nature; it does not come into fruition unless and until an opponent makes some "use" of station facilities, but once that occurs it ripens, and the candidate becomes unconditionally entitled to equal opportunities, though to no more. The Section 315(a) duty arises, however, only with respect to an opponent's "use" of broadcast facilities; and coverage of an event within the purview of the four ex-

124. Use of Broadcast and Cablecast Facilities by Candidates for Public Office, 34 FCC2d 510, 537 (1972).

126. Licensee Responsibility Under Amendments to the Communications Act Made by the Federal Election Campaign Act of 1971, 47 FCC2d 516 (1974) [Emphasis supplied].

128. The Law of Political Broadcasting and Cablecasting, 69 FCC2d 2209, 2288 (1978) [footnote omitted].

emptions to that section is statutorily deemed a nonuse, and therefore does not activate the equal-opportunity requirement.

The statutory language and historical precedents also make plain that this section does not, however, confer the privilege of using the broadcaster's facilities without charge. Rather, we have found that broadcasters may meet the demands of Section 312(a)(7) either by an allotment of free time or by making time available for purchase.

We are satisfied, too, that a candidate cannot secure broadcast time, free or otherwise, through the simple expedient of reading Section 312(a)(7) as just another equal-opportunity provision. Nothing in the history of the section's evolution or its administrative interpretation serves to validate the thesis that it confers a second responsive right to broadcast privileges that may be employed as a supplement to Section 312(a)'s equal-opportunity mandate. And without some clear indication that Congress so intended, we perceive no justification for such a reading. Settled principles of statutory construction militate strongly against that interpretation, for it would engender grave doubt as to the internal consistency of the statutory scheme.

If Section 312(a)(7) were to be viewed as an auxiliary source of entitlement to equal opportunities, the exemptions to Section 315(a) would easily be destroyed. The purpose of these exclusions, it will be recalled, was to free broadcasters who carried any of four types of newsworthy "political" events from the equal-opportunity burden, and thereby to encourage more complete coverage of these events. Should Section 312(a)(7) be construed as automatically entitling a candidate to responsive broadcast access whenever and for whatever reason his opponent has appeared on the air, Section 315(a)'s exemptions would soon become meaningless. Statutes are to be interpreted, if possible, to give operation to all of their parts, and to maintain them in harmonious working relationship. Congress has devised a comprehensive and cohesive plan in which Section 312(a)(7), Section 315(a) and the latter's exemptions all have well-defined missions. No provision may be misused to defeat the effective functioning of another.

Consequently, we do not find in Section 312(a)(7) a right of access that Section 315 denies. Petitioner has not advanced any claim under Section 315(a), nor has it quarreled with the networks' unanimous conclusion that the broadcasts of the President's March 14 speech and press conference were immune from the equal-opportunity command of that section. We hold that petitioner cannot use Section 312(a)(7) to circumvent the explicit exemptions of Section 315(a).

We further hold that petitioner is not in a position to utilize Section 312(a)(7) in the manner in which Congress designed it to function. Petitioner has never claimed that it was denied an opportunity to buy time; rather, it has insisted that the networks violated Section 312(a)(7) simply by refusing to provide free time to Senator Kennedy. We have seen that the section entitles a candidate to free time only if and when a broadcaster refuses to sell a reasonable quantity of time. No showing of that sort has been made, or indeed undertaken.

We thus find petitioner's Section 312(a)(7) arguments unpersuasive. We turn now to a consideration of its contentions under the fairness doctrine. [The portion of this opinion dealing with the fairness doctrine is reported in the text, p. 891.]

* * *

Affirmed.

THE "FAIRNESS" DOCTRINE AND ACCESS TO BROADCASTING

The "Fairness" Doctrine and the RED LION Case —The Background

In November 1964, the Red Lion Broadcasting Co. of Red Lion, Pennsylvania carried a program series entitled *The Christian Crusade.* One of the programs included an attack by Rev. Billy James Hargis on a book entitled *Goldwater—Extremist Of The Right.*

Hargis made the following statements concerning Fred J. Cook, the book's author:

> Now who is Cook? Cook was fired from the New York World-Telegram after he made a false charge publicly on television against an unnamed official of the New York City government. New York publishers and Newsweek magazine for December 7, 1959, showed that Fred Cook and his pal Eugene Gleason had made up the whole story and this confession was made to the District Attorney, Frank Hogan. After losing his job, Cook went to work for the left-wing publication, *The Nation.* * * * Now among other things Fred Cook wrote for *The Nation* was an article absolving Alger Hiss of any wrongdoing * * * there was a 208 page attack on the FBI and J. Edgar Hoover; another attack by Mr. Cook was on the Central Intelligence Agency * * * now this is the man who wrote the book to smear and destroy Barry Goldwater called *Barry Goldwater—Extremist Of The Right.*

The *Red Lion* case concerns the "personal attack" rule, an aspect of the "fairness" doctrine requiring that, when an individual is personally attacked, the station carrying the attack must give him an opportunity to reply. A question which had been unclear under the personal attack rule was whether the station had to furnish broadcast time free if the person attacked could not obtain a sponsor and was himself unable to pay for the time. (What is the "equal time" rule on this point?)

Cook asked the radio station for an opportunity to reply to Hargis. The radio station replied that the "personal attack" aspect of the "fairness" doctrine only required a licensee to make free time for reply available if no paid sponsorship could be secured. The station therefore insisted that Cook had to warrant that no such paid sponsorship could be found. Cook refused and instead complained to the FCC. The FCC took the position that the station had the duty to furnish reply time, paid or not. The FCC declared that it was not necessary for Cook to show that he could neither afford nor find sponsored time before the station's duty to make reply time available went into effect. The FCC ruled that the public interest required that the public be given an opportunity to learn the other side and that this duty remained even where the time had to be sustained by the station. The FCC entered a formal order to that effect, and the station appealed to the United States Court of Appeals.

The United States Court of Appeals for the District of Columbia in the *Red Lion* case held that the fairness doctrine and the personal attack rules were constitutional. Red Lion Broadcasting Co. v. FCC, 381 F.2d 908 (D.C.Cir. 1967). The court, in its decision recited the history of the personal attack rules. On July 1, 1964, the FCC had issued a Public Notice entitled Applicability of the Fairness Doctrine in the Handling of Controversial Issues of Public Importance, 29 Fed.Reg. 19415 (1964). This document, sometimes called the Fairness Primer, states that fairness complaints would continue to be dealt with on an ad hoc basis. The FCC stated further that broadcast licensees would be afforded an opportunity to take action or to comment upon complaints made against them to the FCC prior to action thereon by the FCC. In the same document the personal attack principle was dealt with in detail and the rules implementing this principle were specified. (The text of the personal attack rules is set forth in the Supreme Court's decision in the *Red Lion* case which follows this note.)

With the *Red Lion* decision in the court of appeals, the fairness doctrine prevailed in the first court test of its validity under the First Amendment as did its corollary, the personal attack rules.

The broadcast industry was shocked by the court of appeals decision in the *Red Lion* case. The Radio Television News Directors Association decided to institute suit for judicial review of FCC orders upholding the personal attack rules and reply time for political editorials. Suit was filed in the United States Court of Appeals for the Seventh Circuit in Chicago, a forum which was perhaps selected because it was thought to be less sympathetic to government than the United States Court of Appeals for the District of Columbia in Washington. The United States Court of Appeals for the Seventh Circuit ruled that the personal attack rules and the political editorial rules would violate the First Amendment. Radio Television News Directors Association v. United States, 400 F.2d 1002 (7th Cir. 1968).

The seventh circuit in the *RTNDA* case essentially adopted many of the prior restraint contentions which the District of Columbia Circuit had rejected in the *Red Lion* case. Basically, the *RTNDA* decision took the position that broadcasters might forego controversial commentary if they had to go to the expense of furnishing transcripts of personal attacks to those attacked, and if they had to furnish time free for responses to those who wished to avail themselves of the right of reply furnished by the personal attack rules. Under such circumstances, the *RTNDA* court reasoned, free speech would be unconstitutionally inhibited.

The Supreme Court had granted review in *Red Lion* but decided to defer decision until the Seventh Circuit Court of Appeals had decided the *RTNDA* case. When the FCC appealed the *RTNDA* ruling, the Supreme Court joined the two cases. The world of broadcast journalism eagerly watched to see how the Supreme Court would break the 1–1 score on the fairness doctrine and personal attack rules produced by the split between the two federal courts of appeal.

To the professed amazement of the broadcast industry, the Supreme Court affirmed the *Red Lion* decision and reversed the *RTNDA* decision. The fairness doctrine and the personal attack rules were upheld as consistent with the First Amendment by a unanimous Supreme Court consisting of all the seven justices who participated in the case. Not only did the Court decision speak warmly of fairness, it spoke equally warmly of a newer doctrine, access. The *Red Lion* decision in the Supreme Court opened up a new affirmative approach to First Amendment theory, at least as applied to the broadcast media. See generally, Barron, *Freedom of the Press for Whom? The Right of Access to Mass Media* 137–149 (1973).

RED LION BROADCASTING CO., INC. v. FCC

UNITED STATES v. RADIO TELEVISION NEWS DIRECTORS ASSOCIATION

395 U.S. 367, 89 S.CT. 1794, 23 L.ED.2D 371 (1969).

Justice WHITE delivered the opinion of the Court.

The Federal Communications Commission has for many years imposed on radio and television broadcasters the requirement that discussion of public issues be presented on broadcast stations, and that each side of those issues must be given fair coverage. This is known as the fairness doctrine, which originated very early in the history of broadcasting and has maintained its present outlines for some time. It is an obligation whose content has been defined in a long series of FCC rulings in particular cases, and which is distinct from the statutory requirement of § 315 of the Communications Act that equal time be allotted all qualified candidates for public office. Two aspects of the fairness doctrine, relating to personal attacks in the context of controversial public issues and to political editorializing, were codified more precisely in the form of FCC regulations in 1967. The two cases before us now, which were decided separately below, challenge the constitutional and statutory bases of the doctrine and component rules. *Red Lion* involves the application of the fairness doctrine to a particular broadcast, and *RTNDA* arises as an action to review the FCC's 1967 promulgation of the personal attack and political editorializing regulations, which were laid down after the *Red Lion* litigation had begun.

* * *

Not long after the *Red Lion* litigation was begun, the FCC issued a Notice of Proposed Rule Making, 31 Fed.Reg. 5710, with an eye to making the personal attack aspect of the fairness doctrine more precise and more readily enforceable, and also to specify its rules relating to political editorials. After considering written comments supporting and opposing the rules, the FCC adopted them substantially as proposed, 32 Fed.Reg. 10303. Twice amended, 32 Fed.Reg. 11531, 33 Fed.Reg. 5362, the rules were held unconstitutional in the *RTNDA* litigation by the Court of Appeals for the Seventh Circuit on review of the rule-making proceeding as abridging the freedoms of speech and press. 400 F.2d 1002 (1968).

As they now stand amended, the regulations read as follows:

"Personal attacks; political editorials.

(a) When, during the presentation of views on a controversial issue of public importance, an attack is made upon the honesty, character, integrity or like personal qualities of an identified person or group, the licensee shall, within a reasonable time and in no event later than one week after the attack, transmit to the person or group attacked: (1) notification of the date, time and identification of the broadcast; (2) a script or tape (or an accurate summary if a script or tape is not available) of the attack; and (3) an offer of a reasonable opportunity to respond over the licensee's facilities.

(b) The provisions of paragraph (a) of this section shall not be applicable (i) to attacks on foreign groups or foreign public figures; (ii) to personal attacks which are made by legally qualified candidates, their authorized spokesmen, or those associated with them in the campaign, on other such candidates, their authorized spokesmen, or persons associated with the candidates in the campaign; and (iii) to bona fide newscasts, bona fide news interviews, and on-the-spot coverage of a bona fide news event (including commentary or analysis contained in the foregoing programs, but the provisions of paragraph (a) shall be applicable to editorials of the licensee).

NOTE: The fairness doctrine is applicable to situations coming within (iii), above, and, in a specific factual situation, may be applicable in the general area of political broadcasts (ii), above. See Section 315(a) of the Act, 47 U.S.C. 315(a); Public Notice: Applicability of the Fairness Doctrine in the Handling of Controversial Issues of Public Importance. 29 Fed.Reg. 10415. The categories listed in (iii) are the same as those specified in Section 315(a) of the Act.

(c) Where a licensee, in an editorial, (i) endorses or (ii) opposes a legally qualified candidate or candidates, the licensee shall, within 24 hours after the editorial, transmit to respectively (i) the other qualified candidate or candidates for the same office or (ii) the candidate opposed in the editorial (1) notification of the date and the time of the editorial; (2) a script or tape of the editorial; and (3) an offer of a reasonable opportunity for a candidate or a spokesman of the candidate to respond over the licensee's facilities. *Provided, however*, that where such editorials are broadcast within 72 hours prior to the day of the election, the licensee shall comply with the provisions of this subsection sufficiently far in advance of the broadcast to enable the candidate or candidates to have a reasonable opportunity to prepare a response and to present it in a timely fashion." 47 CFR 73.123, 73.300, 73.598, 73.679 (all identical).

Believing that the specific application of the fairness doctrine in *Red Lion*, and the promulgation of the regulations in *RTNDA*, are both authorized by Congress and enhance rather than abridge the freedoms of speech and press protected by the First Amendment, we hold them valid and constitutional, reversing the judgment below in *RTNDA* and affirming the judgment below in *Red Lion*.

The history of the emergence of the fairness doctrine and of the related legislation shows that the commission's action in the *Red Lion* case did not exceed its authority, and that in adopting the new regulations the commission was implementing congressional policy rather than embarking on a frolic of its own.

* * *

After an extended period during which the licensee was obliged not only to cover and to cover fairly the views of others, but also to refrain from expressing his own personal views, Mayflower Broadcasting Corp., 8 FCC 333 (1941), the latter limitation on the licensee was abandoned and the doctrine developed into its present form.

There is a twofold duty laid down by the FCC's decisions and described by the 1949 Report on Editorializing by Broadcast Licensees, 13 FCC 1246 (1949). The broadcaster must give adequate coverage to public issues, United Broadcasting Co., 10 FCC 515 (1945), and coverage must be fair in that it accurately reflects the opposing views. New Broadcasting Co., 6 P & F Radio Reg. 258 (1950). This must be done at the broadcaster's own expense if sponsorship is unavailable. Cullman Broadcasting Co., 25 P & F Radio Reg. 895 (1963). Moreover, the duty must be met by programming obtained at the licensee's own initiative if available from no other source. * * *

When a personal attack has been made on a figure involved in a public issue, both the doctrine of cases such as *Red Lion* and Times-Mirror Broadcasting Co., 24 P & F Radio Reg. 404 (1962), and also the 1967 regulations at issue in *RTNDA* require that the individual attacked himself be offered an opportunity to respond. Likewise, where one candidate is endorsed in a political editorial, the other candidates must themselves be offered reply time to use personally or through a spokesman. These obligations differ from the general fairness requirement that issues be presented, and presented with coverage of competing views, in that the broadcaster does not have the option of presenting the attacked party's side himself or choosing a third party to represent that side. But insofar as there is an obligation of the broadcaster to see that both sides are presented, and insofar as that is an affirmative obligation, the personal attack doctrine and regulations do not differ from preceding fairness doctrine. The simple fact that the attacked men or unendorsed candidates may respond themselves or through agents is not a critical distinction, and indeed, it is not unreasonable for the FCC to conclude that the objective of adequate presentation of all sides may best be served by allowing those most closely affected to make the response, rather than leaving the response in the hands of the station which has attacked their candidacies, endorsed their opponents, or carried a personal attack upon them.

The statutory authority of the FCC to promulgate these regulations derives from the mandate to the "commission from time to time, as public convenience, interest, or necessity requires" to promulgate "such rules and regulations and prescribe such restrictions and conditions * * * as may be necessary to carry out the provisions of this chapter * * *." 47 U.S.C.A. § 303 and § 303(r). The commission is specifically directed to consider the demands of the public interest in the course of granting licenses, 47 U.S.C.A. §§ 307(a), 309(a); renewing them, 47 U.S.C.A. § 307; and modifying them. Ibid. Moreover, the FCC has included among the conditions of the Red Lion license itself the requirement that operation of the station be carried out in the public interest, 47 U.S.C.A. § 309(h). This mandate to the FCC to assure that broadcasters operate in the public interest is a broad one, a power "not niggardly but expansive," National Broadcasting Co. v. United States, 319 U.S. 190, 219 (1943), whose validity we have long upheld. It is broad enough to encompass these regulations.

The fairness doctrine finds specific recognition in statutory form, is in part modeled on explicit statutory provisions relating to political candidates, and is approvingly reflected in legislative history.

In 1959 the Congress amended the statutory requirement of § 315 that equal time be accorded each political candidate to except certain appearances on news programs, but added that this constituted no exception *"from the obligation imposed upon them under this act to operate in the public interest and to afford reasonable opportunity for the discussion of conflicting views on issues of public importance."* Act of September 14, 1959, § 1, 73 Stat. 557, amending 47 U.S.C.A. § 315(a) [Emphasis added]. This language makes it very plain that Congress, in 1959, announced that the phrase "public interest," which had been in the act since 1927, imposed a duty on broadcasters to discuss both sides of controversial public issues. In other words, the amendment vindicated the FCC's general view that the fairness doctrine inhered in the public interest standard. Subsequent legislation enacted into law and declaring the intent of an earlier statute is entitled to great weight in statutory construction. And here this principle is given special force by the equally venerable principle that the construction of a statute by those charged with its execution should be followed unless there are compelling indications that it is wrong, especially when Congress has refused to alter the administrative construction. Here, the Congress has not just kept its silence by refusing to overturn the administrative construction, but has ratified it with positive legislation. Thirty years of consistent administrative construction left undisturbed by Congress until 1959, when that construction was expressly accepted, reinforce the natural conclusion that the public interest language of the act authorized the commission to require licensees to use their stations for discussion of public issues, and that the FCC is free to implement this requirement by reasonable rules and regulations which fall short of abridgment of the freedom of speech and press, and of the censorship proscribed by § 326 of the act.

The objectives of § 315 themselves could readily be circumvented but for the complementary fairness doctrine ratified by § 315. The section applies only to campaign appearances by candidates, and not by family, friends, campaign managers, or other supporters. Without the fairness doctrine, then, a licensee could ban all campaign appearances by candidates themselves from the air and proceed to deliver over his station entirely to the supporters of one slate of candidates, to the exclusion of all others. In this way the broadcaster could have a far greater impact on the favored candidacy than he could by simply allowing a spot appearance by the candidate himself. It is the fairness doctrine as an aspect of the obligation to operate in the public interest, rather than § 315, which prohibits the broadcaster from taking such a step.

* * *

It is true that the personal attack aspect of the fairness doctrine was not actually adjudicated until after 1959, so that Congress then did not have those rules specifically before it. However, the obligation to offer time to reply to a personal attack was presaged by the FCC's 1949 Report on Editorializing, which the FCC views as the principal summary of its *ratio decidendi* in cases in this area.

* * * When the Congress ratified the FCC's implication of a fairness doctrine in 1959 it did not, of course, approve every past decision or pronouncement by the commission on this subject, or give it a completely free hand for the future. The statutory authority does not go so far. But we cannot say that when a station publishes a personal attack or endorses a political candidate, it is a misconstruction of the public interest standard to require the station to offer time for a response rather than to leave the response entirely within the control of the station which has attacked either the candidacies or the men who wish to reply in their own defense. When a broadcaster grants time to a political candidate, Congress itself requires that equal time be offered to his opponents. It would exceed our competence to hold that the commission is unauthorized by the statute to employ a similar device where personal attacks or political editorials are broadcast by a radio or television station.

In light of the fact that the "public interest" in broadcasting clearly encompasses the presentation of vigorous debate of controversial issues of importance and concern to the public; the fact that the FCC has rested upon that language from its very inception a doctrine that these issues must be discussed, and fairly; and the fact that Congress has acknowledged that the analogous provisions of § 315 are not preclusive in this area, and knowingly preserved the FCC's complementary efforts, we think the fairness doctrine and its component personal attack and political editorializing regulations are a legitimate exercise of congressionally delegated authority. The Communications Act is not notable for the precision of its substantive standards and in this respect the explicit provisions of § 315, and the doctrine and rules at issue here which are closely modeled upon that section, are far more explicit than the generalized "public interest" standard in which the commission ordinarily finds its sole guidance, and which we have held a broad but adequate standard before. We cannot say that the FCC's declaratory ruling in *Red Lion*, or the regulations at issue in *RTNDA*, are beyond the scope of the congressionally conferred power to assure that stations are operated by those whose possession of a license serves "the public interest."

The broadcasters challenge the fairness doctrine and its specific manifestations in the personal attack and political editorial rules on conventional First Amendment grounds, alleging that the rules abridge their freedom of speech and press. Their contention is that the First Amendment protects their desire to use their allotted frequencies continuously to broadcast whatever they choose, and to exclude whomever they choose, from ever using that frequency. No man may be prevented from saying or publishing what he thinks, or from refusing in his speech or other utterances to give equal weight to the views of his opponents. This right, they say, applies equally to broadcasters.

Although broadcasting is clearly a medium affected by a First Amendment interest, United States v. Paramount Pictures, Inc., 334 U.S. 131, 166 (1948), differences in the characteristics of new media justify differences in the First Amendment standards applied to them. Joseph Burstyn, Inc. v. Wilson, 343 U.S. 495, 503 (1952). For example, the ability of new technology to produce sounds more raucous than those of the human voice justifies restrictions on the sound level, and on the hours and places of use, of sound trucks so long as the restrictions are reasonable and applied without discrimination. Kovacs v. Cooper, 336 U.S. 77 (1949).

Just as the Government may limit the use of sound amplifying equipment potentially so noisy that it drowns out civilized private speech, so may the Government limit the use of broadcast equipment. The right of free speech of a broadcaster, the user of a sound truck, or any other individual does not embrace a right to snuff out the free speech of others. Associated Press v. United States, 326 U.S. 1, 20 (1945).

When two people converse face to face, both should not speak at once if either is to be clearly understood. But the range of the human voice is so limited that there could be meaningful communications if half the people in the United States were talking and the other half listening. Just as clearly, half the people might publish and the other half read. But the reach of radio signals is incomparably greater than the range of the human voice and the problem of interference is a massive reality. The lack of know-how and equipment may keep many from the air, but only a tiny fraction of those with resources and intelligence can hope to communicate by radio at the same time if intelligible communication is to be had, even if the entire radio spectrum is utilized in the present state of commercially acceptable technology.

It was this fact, and the chaos which ensued from permitting anyone to use any frequency at whatever power level he wished, which made necessary the enactment of the Radio Act of 1927 and the Communications Act of 1934, as the Court has noted at length before. National Broadcasting Co. v. United States, 319 U.S. 190, 210–214 (1943). It was this reality which at the very least necessitated first the division of the radio spectrum into portions reserved respectively for public broadcasting and for other important radio uses such as amateur operation, aircraft, police, defense, and navigation; and then the subdivision of each portion, and assignment of specific frequencies to individual users or groups of users. Beyond this, however, because the frequencies reserved for public broadcasting were limited in number, it was essential for the Government to tell some applicants that they could not broadcast at all because there was room for only a few.

Where there are substantially more individuals who want to broadcast than there are frequencies to allocate, it is idle to posit an unabridgeable First Amendment right to broadcast comparable to the right of every individual to speak, write, or publish. If 100 persons want broadcast licenses but there are only 10 frequencies to allocate, all of them may have the same "right" to a license; but if there is to be any effective communication by radio, only a few can be licensed and the rest must be barred from the airways. It would be strange if the First Amendment, aimed at protecting and furthering communications, prevented the government from making radio communication possible by requiring licenses to broadcast and by limiting the number of licenses so as not to overcrowd the spectrum.

This had been the consistent view of the Court. Congress unquestionably has the power to grant and deny licenses and to delete existing stations. Federal Radio Commission v. Nelson Bros. Bond & Mortgage Co., 289 U.S. 266 (1933). No one has a First Amendment right to a license or to monopolize a radio frequency; to deny a station license because "the public interest" requires it "is not a denial of free speech." National Broadcasting Co. v. U. S., 319 U.S. 190, 227 (1943).

By the same token, as far as the First Amendment is concerned those who are licensed stand no better than those to whom licenses are refused. A license permits broadcasting, but the licensee has no constitutional right to be the one who holds the license or to monopolize a radio frequency to the exclusion of his fellow citizens. There is nothing in the First Amendment which permits the government from requiring a licensee to share his frequency with others and to conduct himself as a proxy or fiduciary with obligations to present those views and voices which are representative of his community and which would otherwise, by necessity, be barred from the airwaves.

This is not to say that the First Amendment is irrelevant to public broadcasting. On the contrary, it has a major role to play as the Congress itself recognized in § 326, which forbids FCC interference with "the right of free speech by means of radio communications." Because of the scarcity of radio frequencies, the government is permitted to put restraints on licensees in favor of others whose views should be expressed on this unique medium. But the people as a whole retain their interest in free speech by radio and their collective right to have the medium function consistently with the ends and purposes of the First Amendment. *It is the right of the viewers and listeners, not the right of the broadcasters, which is paramount.* [Emphasis added.] See FCC v. Sanders Bros. Radio Station, 309 U.S. 470, 475 (1940); FCC v. Allentown Broadcasting Corp., 349 U.S. 358, 361–362 (1955); Z. Chafee, Government and Mass Communications 546 (1947). It is the purpose of the First Amendment to preserve an uninhibited marketplace of ideas in which truth will ultimately prevail, rather than to countenance monopolization of that market, whether it be by the government itself or a private licensee. * * * It is the right of the public to receive suitable access to social, political, esthetic, moral, and other ideas and experiences which is crucial here. That right may not constitutionally be abridged either by Congress or by the FCC.

Rather than confer frequency monopolies on a relatively small number of licensees, in a Nation of 200,000,000, the government could surely have decreed that each frequency should be shared among all or some of those who wish to use it, each being assigned a portion of the broadcast day or the broadcast week. The ruling and regulations at issue here do not go quite so far. They assert that under specified circumstances, a licensee must offer to make available a reasonable amount of broadcast time to those who have a view different from that which has already been expressed on his station. The expression of a political endorsement, or of a personal attack while dealing with a controversial public issue, simply triggers this time-sharing. As we have said, the First Amendment confers no right on licensees to prevent others from broadcasting on "their" frequencies and no right to an unconditional monopoly of a scarce resource which the government has denied others the right to use.

In terms of constitutional principle, and as enforced sharing of a scarce resource, the personal attack and political editorial rules are indistinguishable from the equal-time provision of § 315, a specific enactment of Congress requiring stations to set aside reply time under specified circumstances and to which the fairness doctrine and these constituent regulations are important complements. That provision, which has been part of the law since 1927, Radio Act of 1927, c. 169, § 18, 44 Stat. 1162, 1170, has been held valid by this court as an obligation of the licensee relieving him of any power in any way to prevent or censor the broadcast, and thus insulating him from liability for defamation. The constitutionality of the statute under the First Amendment was unquestioned. Farmers Educ. & Coop. Union v. WDAY, 360 U.S. 525 (1959).

Nor can we say that it is inconsistent with the First Amendment goal of producing an informed public capable of conducting its own affairs to require a broadcaster to permit answers to personal attacks occurring in the course of discussing controversial issues, or to require that the political opponents of those endorsed by the station be given a chance to communicate with the public.[18] Otherwise station owners and a few networks would have unfettered power to make time available only to the highest bidders, to communicate only their own views on public issues, people and candidates, and to permit on the air only those with whom they agreed. There is no sanctuary in the First Amendment for unlimited private censorship operating in a medium not open to all. "Freedom of the press from governmental interference under the First Amendment does not sanction repression of that freedom by private interests." Associated Press v. U. S., 326 U.S. 1, 20 (1944).

It is strenuously argued, however, that, if political editorials or personal attacks will trigger an obligation in broadcasters to afford the opportunity for expression to speakers who need not pay for time and whose views are unpalatable to the licensees, then broadcasters will be irresistibly forced to self-censorship and their coverage of controversial public issues will be eliminated or at least rendered wholly ineffective. Such a result would indeed be a serious matter, for should licensees actually eliminate their coverage of controversial issues, the purposes of the doctrine would be stifled.

At this point, however, as the Federal Communications Commission has indicated, that possibility is at best speculative. The communications industry, and in particular the networks have taken pains to present controversial issues in the past, and even now they do not assert that they intend to abandon their efforts in this regard. It would be better if the FCC's encouragement were never necessary to induce the broadcasters to meet their responsibility. And if experience with the administration of these doctrines indicates that they have the net effect of reducing rather than enhancing the volume and quality of coverage, there will be time enough to reconsider the constitutional implications. The fairness doctrine in the past has had no such overall effect.

That this will occur now seems unlikely, however, since if present licensees should suddenly prove timorous, the commission is not powerless to insist that they give adequate and fair attention to public issues. It does not violate the First Amendment to treat licensees given the privilege of using scarce radio frequencies as proxies for the entire community, obligated to give suitable time and attention to matters of great public concern. To condition the granting or renewal of licenses on a willingness to present representative community views on controversial issues is consistent with the ends and purposes of those constitutional provisions forbidding the abridgment of freedom of speech and freedom of the press. Congress need not stand idly by and permit those with licenses to ignore the problems which beset the people or to exclude from the airways anything but their own views of fundamental questions. The statute, long administrative practice, and cases are to this effect.

* * *

18. The expression of views opposing those which broadcasters permit to be aired in the first place need not be confided solely to the broadcasters themselves as proxies. "Nor is it enough that he should hear the arguments of his adversaries from his own teachers, presented as they state them, and accompanied by what they offer as refutations. That is not the way to do justice to the arguments, or bring them into real contact with his own mind. He must be able to hear them from persons who actually believe them; who defend them in earnest, and do their very utmost for them." J. S. Mill, "On Liberty" 32 ed., R. McCallum, 1947.

The litigants embellish their first amendment arguments with the contention that the regulations are so vague that their duties are impossible to discern. Of this point it is enough to say that, judging the validity of the regulations on their face as they are presented here, we cannot conclude that the FCC has been left a free hand to vindicate its own idiosyncratic conception of the public interest or of the requirements of free speech. Past adjudications by the FCC give added precision to the regulations; there was nothing vague about the FCC's specific ruling in *Red Lion* that Fred Cook should be provided an opportunity to reply. The regulations at issue in *RTNDA* could be employed in precisely the same way as the fairness doctrine was in *Red Lion*. Moreover, the FCC itself has recognized that the applicability of its regulations to situations beyond the scope of past cases may be questionable, 32 Fed.Reg. 10303, 10304 and n. 6, and will not impose sanctions in such cases without warning. We need not approve every aspect of the fairness doctrine to decide these cases, and we will not now pass upon the constitutionality of these regulations by envisioning the most extreme applications conceivable, United States v. Sullivan, 332 U.S. 689, 694 (1948), but will deal with those problems if and when they arise.

We need not and do not now ratify every past and future decision by the FCC with regard to programming. There is no question here of the commission's refusal to permit the broadcaster to carry a particular program or to publish his own views; of a discriminatory refusal to require the licensee to broadcast certain views which have been denied access to the airways; of government censorship of a particular program contrary to § 326; or of the official government view dominating public broadcasting. Such questions would raise more serious first amendment issues. But we do hold that the Congress and the commission do not violate the First Amendment when they require a radio or television station to give reply time to answer personal attacks and political editorials. * * *

In view of the prevalence of scarcity of broadcast frequencies, the government's role in allocating those frequencies, and the legitimate claims of those unable without governmental assistance to gain access to those frequencies for expression of their views, we hold the regulations and ruling at issue here are both authorized by statute and constitutional. The judgment of the court of appeals in *Red Lion* is affirmed and that in *RTNDA* reversed and the causes remanded for proceedings consistent with this opinion.

It is so ordered.

COMMENT

1. Note the Supreme Court's response to the industry position espoused by the Court in the *RTNDA* case that the fairness doctrine serves as a depressant rather than as a stimulant to debate. The end result of the fairness doctrine, under this view, is blandness rather than any offering of contentious and vigorous debate. The Court suggested that the FCC licensing process could be conditioned on the willingness of broadcast licensees to present representative community views on controversial public issues.

A particular incident where the interests of free debate were not served by a broadcaster's performance will rarely warrant denial of the broadcaster's license renewal application. How can fairness be enforced in a particular case assuming the drastic remedy of license denial at renewal time is not thought appropriate?

* * *

2. Why did the FCC in effect rule that if a person has a right of reply under the personal attack rules, the station must put him on free if he is not willing to pay? WGCB in Red Lion, Pennsylvania was a

small, independent station whose rates compared to network time were not high. Presumably the FCC reasoned that if a principle were followed of only permitting paid reply time when the personal attack rules were involved, the high cost of network time, particularly television time, would serve to make the personal attack rules a dead letter. Few could or would wish to pay for reply time under such circumstances.

Both the court of appeals and the Supreme Court in the Red Lion case cited Cullman Broadcasting Co., 40 FCC 516 (1963), for the proposition that once a fairness doctrine obligation arises, time must be provided by the licensee at his own expense if sponsorship is not available. The FCC described *Cullman* rights as follows in the *Democratic National Committee* case:

> * * * The paramount public interest, we stressed, is the right of the public to be informed. The licensee has adjudged that an issue is of importance to its area by presenting the first viewpoint; that being so, the public's right to hear the other side cannot turn on whether the licensee received money. This approach perfectly fits the public trustee concept. See, In re Democratic National Committee, Washington, D. C., Request for Declaratory Ruling Concerning Access to Time on Broadcast Stations, 25 FCC2d 216 (1970).

The *Red Lion* case marks the extension of the *Cullman* principle of a right of free response from the fairness doctrine context to the context of the personal attack rules once a licensee obligation under the personal attack rules arises.

3. Although the *Red Lion* decision professes allegiance to the scarcity rationale for broadcast regulation, does the case actually recognize a new justification for broadcast regulation? Does it add a new access-for-ideas justification for broadcast regulation which goes beyond the older rationalization of limited access to the spectrum?

4. The invalidation in Miami Herald Pub. Co. v. Tornillo, 418 U.S. 241 (1974), of a state statutory right to reply to the print media in the case of editorial attack presents a vivid contrast to the right of reply to personal attack in the broadcast media upheld in *Red Lion*. In *Miami Herald*, the Supreme Court held, in a unanimous opinion, that a Florida statute requiring a newspaper to grant a political candidate equivalent space to reply if the paper editorially attacked the candidate violated the First Amendment. (See this text, p. 584). The *Miami Herald* decision does not so much as cite the *Red Lion* case decided only five years earlier. Henry Geller, former General Counsel of the FCC, has argued that "there is a direct conflict between *Tornillo* and *Red Lion* * * *." But he argues at the same time that the conflict is understandable. See Geller, *Does Red Lion Square With Tornillo*? 29 U. of Miami L.Rev. 477 (1975).
* * *

Geller points out that even if the fairness doctrine were abolished, government regulation would still play a role in the broadcast media that it does not play in the print media:

> The point is that by eliminating the fairness doctrine, the problem of government control is not eliminated as long as regulation and licensing based on the public trust concept continues. But the public would be left wholly unprotected from licensees based on presenting only one side of an issue. I, for one, would not accept that.

In one of the opinions in the *Pensions* case, text, p. 876, Judge Tamm spoke directly to the broadcaster argument that *Red Lion* and *Tornillo* were flatly inconsistent:

> I find the decisions "flatly consistent." Arguments advanced to the contrary are only reflective of broadcasters' desires to become indistinguishable from the print media and to be freed of their obligations as public trustees. While

the relevancy of *Red Lion* was fully briefed in *Tornillo*, that decision contained no reference to *Red Lion* or to implications for the broadcast media. I read the Court's striking down a reply rule for newspapers in *Tornillo* after upholding a similar rule for broadcasters in *Red Lion* as demonstrating the Court's continuing recognition of the distinction between the two media, which is primarily manifested in the unique responsibilities of broadcasters as public trustees. See, National Broadcasting Co., Inc. v. FCC, 516 F.2d 1101 at 1193–1194 (D.C.Cir. 1974).

Do the "Fairness" Doctrine and its Related Rules Apply to Cable Television?

47 CFR § 76.209 (1981) consists of three distinct provisions, the first of which applies the "fairness doctrine" to origination cablecasting: "[A] cable television system operator engaging in origination cablecasting shall afford reasonable opportunity for the discussion of conflicting views on issues of public importance."

The second provision of § 76.209 concerns the original cablecasting of "personal attacks." The FCC requires that when an attack is made upon the "honesty, character, integrity, or like personal qualities of an identified person or group, the cable system operator shall, within a reasonable time and in no event later than one week, transmit to the person or group attacked:

1. Notification of the date, time, and identification of the cablecast;

2. a transcript or accurate summary of the attack; and

3. an offer of a reasonable opportunity to respond over the system's facilities."

The FCC exempts from the above requirements those cablecasts:

1. which personally attack foreign public figures;

2. which contain personal attacks made by a "legally qualified candidate for public office"; and

3. which occur during a *bona fide* newscast, news interview, or any on-the-spot coverage of a *bona fide* news event.

The third portion of § 76.209 concerns the cablecasting of political editorials. This provision, which is similar in nature to § 76.205, is invoked whenever a cable system publicly endorses or opposes a legally qualified candidate or candidates. Whenever a cable system engages in editorials of this nature, the operator must transmit to the candidate opposed, within twenty-four hours of the editorial, a) notice of the editorial, b) a script or tape of the editorial, and c) an offer of a reasonable opportunity for response. The FCC further requires, under part c), that where editorials are cablecast within seventy-two hours prior to the day of the election, cable system operators must comply with the procedures above sufficiently far in advance to allow for a reasonable opportunity to respond.

In short, cable operators are bound by the same fairness, political editorializing, and personal attack rules which broadcasters are bound by. The First Amendment rationale for applying the fairness doctrine to broadcasters is, according to the reasoning in *Red Lion*, the scarcity of the spectrum rationale. Is it not at least arguable that the regulations making fairness rules, et al., applicable to cable violate the First Amendment? After all, cable, unlike broadcasting, is usually described as a technology of abundance. See text, p. 998.

Cigarette Advertising in Broadcasting: From "Fairness" to Prohibition?

The BANZHAF Case

1. In December 1966, a young lawyer, John W. Banzhaf, asked WCBS-TV in New

York for reply time to respond to cigarette commercials. The request raised a familiar fairness doctrine problem: were advertisements subject to the fairness doctrine? (In the past, the FCC has said the fairness doctrine would extend to a controversy which concerned advertising. Petition of Sam Morris, 11 FCC 197 [1946].) WCBS-TV rejected the Banzhaf proposal. But on complaint to the FCC, the FCC held that time should be provided for reply to cigarette advertisements because, among other reasons, the question of whether or not cigarettes were a threat to health was a controversial issue. *WCBS-TV*, 8 FCC2d 381 (1967); affirmed Applicability of the Fairness Doctrine to Cigarette Advertising, 9 FCC2d 921 (1967).

The United States Court of Appeals, per Chief Judge Bazelon, sustained the FCC decision ordering reply time to cigarette advertising Banzhaf v. FCC, 405 F.2d 1082 (D.C.Cir. 1968).

The court made a valiant effort in *Banzhaf* to confine its decision ordering reply time to cigarette advertising alone. But is the cigarette advertising situation truly unique?

2. The court in *Banzhaf* sustained the application of the Fairness Doctrine to cigarette advertising. But the fairness doctrine was not the only ground which the court relied on for its decision. The FCC's obligation to define and enforce the public interest in broadcasting was another and independent ground for the court's decision in *Banzhaf*. The public interest in warning the public against the danger that cigarette smoking presented to health had been manifested in publications, actions, and policies of many federal government instrumentalities.

Similarly, the uniqueness of the public interest and public health factors were emphasized by Judge Bazelon for the court in *Banzhaf* in an efffort to thwart any implication that reply time to product advertisements could be ordered by the FCC under either the fairness doctrine or the public interest standard as a general proposition.

3. In *Banzhaf*, Judge Bazelon suggested that First Amendment protection may contain an affirmative dimension. The court implied that the marketplace of ideas in broadcasting may not be self-corrective. A debate between cigarette advertisers whose ads consisted of a sizable fraction of all broadcast revenues and opponents of cigarette smoking with no such "financial clout" may be no debate at all. In such circumstances the provision of free television reply time to cigarette ads appeared to the court to be entirely appropriate: "We do not think the principle of free speech stands as a barrier to required broadcasting of facts and information vital to an informed decision to smoke or not to smoke."

In summary, the court of appeals in *Banzhaf* affirmed the FCC decision ordering reply time to counter cigarette advertising on three separate grounds:

1. the fairness doctrine,

2. a definition of the public interest standard (reply time is appropriate in light of extraordinary and unique circumstances and when consistent with a demonstrably clear federal policy), and

3. the First Amendment (on a theory that governmental intervention in the form of compulsory reply time is permissible where necessary to serve as a "countervailing" force where meaningful broadcast debate would otherwise be impossible).

The latter two of these three bases of decision in *Banzhaf* were at least as important as the fairness doctrine in shaping the court's decision.

4. In its effort to make the ruling of reply time for cigarette advertisements unique and to keep it from being extended to other product advertisements, the court remarked that "the danger cigarettes may pose to health is, among others, a danger to life itself." Did this very sentence,

which was designed to confine the scope of the *Banzhaf* ruling, in fact serve to expand or contract it? See, Friends of the Earth v. FCC, 449 F.2d 1164 (D.C.Cir.1971), text, infra, p. 867.

5. The *Banzhaf* case held that cigarette advertising had to be counterbalanced by expression devoted to pointing out the hazards of cigarette smoking and affirmed the FCC ruling that the "fairness" doctrine applied to cigarette advertising. The case had stressed that cigarette smoking was a controversial issue of great gravity which demanded balanced presentation. Is the health danger of cigarette smoking any longer a controversial issue?

In the Public Health Cigarette Smoking Act of 1969 Congress banned the advertising of cigarettes (but not cigarillos!) in broadcasting. The statute, 15 U.S.C.A. § 1335 states:

> After January 1, 1971, it shall be unlawful to advertise cigarettes in any medium of electronic communication subject to the jurisdiction of the FCC.

Capital Broadcasting Co. v. Mitchell

Is a Congressional prohibition against advertisements of a particular product, no matter what the content of the ads, a violation of the First Amendment?

The issue was resolved in Capital Broadcasting Co. v. Mitchell, 333 F.Supp. 582 (D.D.C.1971), where the federal court held that enforcement of 15 U.S.C.A. § 1335 did not offend due process nor did it violate the First Amendment rights of broadcasters. The Supreme Court affirmed without opinion. Capital Broadcasting Co. v. Kleindienst, 405 U.S. 1000 (1972). The federal court sustained the statute on a number of grounds. First, product advertising is less vigorously protected by the First Amendment than other kinds of expression. Second, "[t]he unique characteristics of electronic communication make it especially subject to regulation in the public interest." Third, Congress, whether in its supervisory role over the federal administrative process or under its constitutional power to regulate interstate commerce, "has the power to prohibit the advertising of cigarettes in any media."

On the First Amendment issue, the court said that the statute did impose a loss of revenue on broadcasters but did not prohibit them from disseminating information about cigarettes.

Broadcasters contended that the cigarette advertising ban law violated due process because the print media were not prohibited from carrying cigarette ads. Only the electronic media were so restricted. Broadcasters said that such a distinction was "arbitrary and invidious." The court pointed out that the legislature can regulate one evil at a time. The test is whether there is a rational basis for regulating one medium of communication but not another. The court ruled that Congress had acted on the basis of information which indicated that such a distinction was reasonably justified:

> Substantial evidence showed that the most persuasive advertising was being conducted on radio and television, and that these broadcasts were particularly effective in reaching a very large audience of young people.
>
> * * *
>
> A pre-school or early elementary school age child can hear and understand a radio commercial or see, hear, and understand a television commercial, while at the same time be substantially unaffected by an advertisement printed in a newspaper, magazine or appearing on a billboard.

Judge Skelley Wright dissented in *Capital Broadcasting* and provided some of the background behind the controversy. As a result of the *Banzhaf* case, "exceedingly effective anti-smoking commercials" had resulted in a "sustained trend toward lesser cigarette consumption." Judge Wright said that the cigarette industry itself had asked the Congress to bar cigarette advertising:

> The *Banzhaf* ruling had clearly made electronic media advertising a losing proposition for the industry, and a voluntary withdrawal would have saved the companies approximately $250,000,000 in advertising costs, relieved political pressure for FCC action, and removed most anti-smoking messages from the air.

In Wright's view, the cigarette advertising ban law resulted in the transfer by tobacco companies of their advertising budgets to the print media "where there was no fairness doctrine to require a response." The *Banzhaf* decision had increased the information flow but, said Judge Wright, "the 1969 act cut off the flow of information altogether."

The *CBS* Case: The Broadcast Access Controversy

What has *Red Lion's* promise of suitable access to the public for ideas actually brought forth? One immediate result of the *Red Lion* decision was the release of a pent-up demand for individual and group access to television. The volume of access and fairness complaints rushing into the FCC was truly remarkable.

Symptomatic of the tremendous citizen pressure for access for political and social controversy and controversialists on television was an FCC decision which actually required a specific program to be provided for a specific point of view. See In re Complaints of the Committee for the Fair Broadcasting of Controversial Issues, 25 FCC2d 283 (1970).

In that case the FCC ordered on August 14, 1970 that, in view of the fact that Richard Nixon had given five presidential speeches in favor of American involvement in Vietnam, one prime time speech by an appropriate spokesman "for the contrasting viewpoint to that of the Administration on the Indochina war issue" was required.

Dissatisfaction with complete broadcaster control over entry to broadcasting for political groups and ideas continued unabated. In May 1970, the Democratic National Committee asked the FCC to prohibit broadcasters from refusing to sell time to groups like the Democratic National Committee for the solicitation of funds and for comment on public issues. The networks took the position that they did not sell half-hour segments of time for political and social comment. The FCC was sympathetic to the need of political parties for political spot announcements in which to solicit funds. But the FCC refused to rule that the networks were *required* to sell time to groups for the dissemination of political and social ideas. Such a rule, said the FCC, would be hostile to the broadcaster's role as trustee for the public. As between access and trusteeship, the FCC came down firmly in the *Democratic National Committee* case for licensee trusteeship, a term which the FCC defined to give broadcasters absolute discretion over programming.

Shortly thereafter, the U. S. Court of Appeals for the District of Columbia reversed and remanded the FCC's ruling. Business Executives' Move v. FCC, 450 F.2d 642 (D.C.Cir. 1971). The Supreme Court in turn reversed the court of appeals in the opinions which follow:

CBS v. DEMOCRATIC NATIONAL COMMITTEE

412 U.S. 94, 93 S.CT. 2080, 36 L.ED.2D 772 (1973).

Chief Justice BURGER delivered the opinion of the Court: * * *

* * *

In two orders announced the same day, the Federal Communications Commission ruled that a broadcaster who meets his public obligation to provide full and fair coverage of public issues is not required to accept editorial advertisements. A divided court of appeals reversed the commission, holding that a broadcaster's fixed policy of refusing editorial advertisements violates the First Amendment; the court remanded the cases to the commission to develop procedures and guidelines for administering a First Amendment right of access.

The complainants in these actions are the Democratic National Committee (DNC) and the Business Executives' Move for Vietnam Peace (BEM), a national organization of businessmen opposed to United States involvement in the Vietnam conflict. In January 1970, BEM filed a complaint with the commission charging that radio station WTOP in Washington, D. C., had refused to sell its time to broadcast a series of one-minute spot announcements expressing BEM views on Vietnam. WTOP, in common with many but not all broadcasters, followed a policy of refusing to sell time for spot announcements to individuals and groups who wished to expound their views on controversial issues. WTOP took the position that since it presented full and fair coverage of important public questions, including the Vietnam conflict, it was justified in refusing to accept editorial advertisements. WTOP also submitted evidence showing that the station had aired the views of critics of our Vietnam policy on numerous occasions. BEM challenged the fairness of WTOP's coverage of criticism of that policy, but it presented no evidence in support of that claim.

Four months later, in May 1970, the DNC filed with the commission a request for a declaratory ruling:

> That under the First Amendment to the Constitution and the Communications Act, a broadcaster may not, as a general policy, refuse to sell time to responsible entities, such as DNC, for the solicitation of funds and for comment on public issues.

DNC claimed that it intended to purchase time from radio and television stations and from the national networks in order to present the views of the Democratic Party and to solicit funds. Unlike BEM, DNC did not object to the policies of any particular broadcaster but claimed that its prior "experiences in this area make it clear that it will encounter considerable difficulty—if not total frustration of its efforts—in carrying out its plans in the event the commission should decline to issue a ruling as requested." DNC cited Red Lion Broadcasting Co. v. FCC, 395 U.S. 367 (1969) as establishing a limited constitutional right of access to the airwaves.

In two separate opinions, the commission rejected respondents' claim that "responsible" individuals and groups have a right to purchase advertising time to comment on public issues without regard to whether the broadcaster has complied with the Fairness Doctrine. The commission viewed the issue as one of major significance in administering the regulatory scheme relating to the electronic media, one going "to the heart of the system of broadcasting which has developed in this country. * * *" 25 FCC2d at 221. After reviewing the legislative history of the Communications Act, the provisions of the act itself, the commission's decisions under the act and the difficult problems inherent in administering a right of access, the commission rejected the demands of BEM and DNC.

The commission also rejected BEM's claim that WTOP had violated the Fairness Doctrine by failing to air views such as those held by members of BEM; the commission pointed out that BEM had made only a "general allegation" of unfairness in WTOP's coverage of the Vietnam conflict and that the station had adequately rebutted the charge by affidavit. The commission did, however, uphold DNC's position that the statute recognized a right of political parties to purchase broadcast time for the purpose of soliciting funds. The commission noted that Congress has accorded special consideration for access by political parties, see 47 U.S.C.A. § 315(a), and that solicitation of funds by political parties is both feasible and appropriate in the short space of time generally allotted to spot advertisements.[1]

A majority of the court of appeals reversed the commission, holding that "a flat ban on paid public issue announcements is in violation of the First Amendment, at least when other sorts of paid announcements are accepted." 450 F.2d at 646. Recognizing that the broadcast frequencies are a scarce resource inherently unavailable to all, the court nevertheless concluded that the First Amendment mandated an "abridgeable" right to present editorial advertisements. The court reasoned that a broadcaster's policy of airing commercial advertisements but not editorial advertisements constitutes unconstitutional discrimination. The court did not, however, order that either BEM's or DNC's proposed announcements must be accepted by the broadcasters; rather it remanded the cases to the commission to develop "reasonable procedures and regulations determining which and how many 'editorial advertisements' will be put on the air." Ibid.

* * *

* * * [W]e next proceed to consider whether a broadcaster's refusal to accept editorial advertisements is governmental action violative of the First Amendment.

* * * The Court has not previously considered whether the action of a broadcast licensee such as that challenged here is "governmental action" for purposes of the First Amendment. The holding under review thus presents a novel question, and one with far-reaching implications. See L. Jaffe, *The Editorial Responsibility of the Broadcaster,* 85 Harv.L.Rev. 768, 782–787 (1972).

The court of appeals held that broadcasters are instrumentalities of the government for First Amendment purposes, relying on the thesis, familiar in other contexts, that broadcast licensees are granted use of part of the public domain and are regulated as "proxies" or "fiduciaries of the people." 450 F.2d, at 652. These characterizations are not without validity for some purposes, but they do not resolve the sensitive constitutional issues inherent in deciding whether a particular licensee action is subject to First Amendment restraints.

* * * The historic aversion to censorship led Congress to enact § 326 of the act which explicitly prohibits the commission from interfering with the exercise of free speech over the broadcast frequencies. Congress pointedly refrained from divesting broadcasters of their control over the selection of voices; § 3(h) of the act stands as firm congressional statement that broadcast licensees are not to be treated as common carriers, obliged to accept whatever is tendered by members of the public. Both these provisions clearly manifest the intention of Congress to maintain a substantial measure of journalistic independence for the broadcast licensee.

* * *

The tensions inherent in such a regulatory structure emerge more clearly when we compare a private newspaper with a broadcast licensee. The power of a privately owned newspaper to advance its own political, social, and economic views is bounded by only two factors: first, the

1. The commission's rulings against BEM's Fairness Doctrine complaint and in favor of DNC's claim that political parties should be permitted to purchase airtime for solicitation of funds were not appealed to the court of appeals and are not before us here.

acceptance of a sufficient number of readers—and hence advertisers—to assure financial success; and, second, the journalistic integrity of its editors and publishers. A broadcast licensee has a large measure of journalistic freedom but not as large as that exercised by a newspaper. A licensee must balance what it might prefer to do as a private entrepreneur with what it is required to do as a "public trustee." To perform its statutory duties, the commission must oversee without censoring. This suggests something of the difficulty and delicacy of administering the Communications Act—a function calling for flexibility and the capacity to adjust and readjust the regulatory mechanism to meet changing problems and needs.

The licensee policy challenged in this case is intimately related to the journalistic role of a licensee for which it has been given initial and primary responsibility by Congress. The licensee's policy against accepting editorial advertising cannot be examined as an abstract proposition, but must be viewed in the context of its journalistic role. It does not help to press on us the idea that editorial ads are "like" commercial ads for the licensee's policy against editorial spot ads is expressly based on a journalistic judgment that 10 to 60 second spot announcements are ill suited to intelligible and intelligent treatment of public issues; the broadcaster has chosen to provide a balanced treatment of controversial questions in a more comprehensive form. Obviously the licensee's evaluation is based on its own journalistic judgment of priorities and newsworthiness.

Moreover, the commission has not fostered the licensee policy challenged here; it has simply declined to command particular action because it fell within the area of journalistic discretion. The commission explicitly emphasized that "there is of course no commission policy thwarting the sale of time to comment on public issues." 25 FCC2d, at 226. The commission's reasoning, consistent with nearly 40 years of precedent, is that so long as a licensee meets its "public trustee" obligation to provide balanced coverage of issues and events, it has broad discretion to decide how that obligation will be met. We do not reach the question whether the First Amendment or the Act can be read to preclude the commission from determining that in some situations the public interest requires licensees to re-examine their policies with respect to editorial advertisements. The commission has not yet made such a determination; it has, for the present at least, found the policy to be within the sphere of journalistic discretion which Congress has left with the licensee.

Thus, it cannot be said that the government is a "partner" to the action of broadcast licensee complained of here, nor is it engaged in a "symbiotic relationship" with the licensee, profiting from the invidious discrimination of its proxy. The First Amendment does not reach acts of private parties in every instance where the Congress or the commission has merely permitted or failed to prohibit such acts.

Our conclusion is not altered merely because the commission rejected the claims of BEM and DNC and concluded that the challenged licensee policy is not inconsistent with the public interest. * * *

Here, Congress has not established a regulatory scheme for broadcast licensees. * * * More important, as we have noted, Congress has affirmatively indicated in the Communications Act that certain journalistic decisions are for the licensee, subject only to the restrictions imposed by evaluation of its overall performance under the public interest standard. * * *

More profoundly, it would be anomalous for us to hold, in the name of promoting the constitutional guarantees of free expression, that the day-to-day editorial decisions of broadcast licensees are subject to the kind of restraints urged by respondents. To do so in the name of the

First Amendment would be a contradiction. Journalistic discretion would in many ways be lost to the rigid limitations that the Fist Amendment imposes on government. Application of such standards to broadcast licensees would be antithetical to the very ideal of vigorous, challenging debate on issues of public interest. Every licensee is already held accountable for the totality of its performance of public interest obligations.

The concept of private, independent broadcast journalism, regulated by government to assure protection of the public interest, has evolved slowly and cautiously over more than 40 years and has been nurtured by processes of adjudication. That concept of journalistic independence could not co-exist with a reading of the challenged conduct of the licensee as governmental action. Nor could it exist without administrative flexibility to meet changing needs and the swift technological developments. We therefore conclude that the policies complained of do not constitute governmental action violative of the First Amendment. * * *

There remains for consideration the question whether the "public interest" standard of the Communications Act requires broadcasters to accept editorial advertisements or, whether, assuming governmental action, broadcasters are required to do so by reason of the First Amendment. In resolving those issues, we are guided by the "venerable principle that the construction of a statute by those charged with its execution should be followed unless there are compelling indications that it is wrong. * * *" Whether there are "compelling indications" of error in this case must be answered by a careful evaluation of the commission's reasoning in light of the policies embodied by Congress in the "public interest" standard of the act. Many of those policies, as the legislative history makes clear, were drawn from the First Amendment itself; the "public interest" standard necessarily invites reference to First Amendment principles. Thus, the question before us is whether the various interests in free expression of the public, the broadcaster and the individual require broadcasters to sell commercial time to persons wishing to discuss controversial issues. * * *

At the outset we reiterate what was made clear earlier that nothing in the language of the Communications Act or its legislative history compels a conclusion different from that reached by the commission. As we have seen, Congress has time and again rejected various legislative attempts that would have mandated a variety of forms of individual access. That is not to say that Congress' rejection of such proposals must be taken to mean that Congress is opposed to private rights of access under all circumstances. Rather, the point is that Congress has chosen to leave such questions with the commission, to which it has given the flexibility to experiment with new ideas as changing conditions require. In this case, the commission has decided that on balance the undesirable effects of the right of access urged by respondents would outweigh the asserted benefits. The court of appeals failed to give due weight to the commission's judgment on these matters.

The commission was justified in concluding that the public interest in providing access to the marketplace of "ideas and experiences" would scarcely be served by a system so heavily weighted in favor of the financially affluent, or those with access to wealth. Even under a first-come-first-served system, proposed by the dissenting commissioner in these cases, the views of the affluent could well prevail over those of others, since they would have it within their power to purchase time more frequently. Moreover, there is the substantial danger, as the court of appeals acknowledged, 450 F.2d, at 664, that the time allotted for editorial advertising could be monopolized by those of one political persuasion.

These problems would not necessarily be solved by applying the Fairness Doctrine including the *Cullman* doctrine, to editorial advertising. *If broadcasters were required to provide time, free when necessary, for the discussion of the various shades of opinion on the issue discussed in the advertisement, the affluent could still determine in large part the issues to be discussed.* [Emphasis added.] Thus, the very premise of the court of appeals' holding—that a right of access is necessary to allow individuals and groups the opportunity for self-initiated speech—would have little meaning to those who could not afford to purchase time in the first instance.

If the Fairness Doctrine were applied to editorial advertising, there is also the substantial danger that the effective operation of that doctrine would be jeopardized. To minimize financial hardship and to comply fully with its public responsibilities a broadcaster might well be forced to make regular programming time available to those holding a view different from that expressed in an editorial advertisement; indeed, BEM has suggested as much in its brief. The result would be a further erosion of the journalistic discretion of broadcasters in the coverage of public issues, and a transfer of control over the treatment of public issues from the licensees who are accountable for broadcast performance to private individuals who are not. The public interest would no longer be "paramount" but rather subordinate to private whim especially since, under the court of appeals' decision, a broadcaster would be largely precluded from rejecting editorial advertisements that dealt with matters trivial or insignificant or already fairly covered by the broadcaster. * * * If the Fairness Doctrine and the *Cullman* doctrine were suspended to alleviate these problems, as respondents suggest might be appropriate, the question arises whether we would have abandoned more than we have gained. Under such a regime the congressional objective of balanced coverage of public issues would be seriously threatened.

Nor can we accept the court of appeals' view that every potential speaker is "the best judge" of what the listening public ought to hear or indeed the best judge of the merits of his or her views. All journalistic tradition and experience is to the contrary. *For better or worse, editing is what editors are for; and editing is selection and choice of material.* [Emphasis added.] That editors—newspaper or broadcast—can and do abuse this power is beyond doubt, but that is not reason to deny the discretion Congress provided. Calculated risks of abuse are taken in order to preserve higher values. The presence of these risks is nothing new; the authors of the Bill of Rights accepted the reality that these risks were evils for which there was no acceptable remedy other than a spirit of moderation and a sense of responsibility—and civility—on the part of those who exercise the guaranteed freedoms of expression.

It was reasonable for Congress to conclude that the public interest in being informed requires periodic accountability on the part of those who are entrusted with the use of broadcast frequencies, scarce as they are. In the delicate balancing historically followed in the regulation of broadcasting Congress and the commission could appropriately conclude that the allocation of journalistic priorities should be concentrated in the licensee rather than diffused among many. This policy gives the public some assurance that the broadcaster will be answerable if he fails to meet their legitimate needs. No such accountability attaches to the private individual, whose only qualifications for using the broadcast facility may be abundant funds and a point of view. To agree that debate on public issues should be "robust and wide-open" does not mean that we should exchange "public trustee" broadcasting, with all its limitations, for a system of self-appointed editorial commentators.

The court of appeals discounted those difficulties by stressing that it was merely mandating a "modest reform," requiring only that broadcasters be required to accept some editorial advertising. * * * The court suggested that broadcasters could place an "outside limit on the total amount of editorial advertising they will sell" and that the commission and the broadcasters could develop " 'reasonable regulations' designed to prevent domination by a few groups or a few viewpoints." * * * If the commission decided to apply the Fairness Doctrine to editorial advertisements and as a result broadcasters suffered financial harm, the court thought the "commission could make necessary adjustments." Thus, without providing any specific answers to the substantial objections raised by the commission and the broadcasters, other than to express repeatedly its "confidence" in the commission's ability to overcome any difficulties, the court remanded the cases to the commission for the development of regulations to implement a constitutional right of access.

By minimizing the difficult problems involved in implementing such a right of access, the court of appeals failed to come to grips with another problem of critical importance to broadcast regulation and the First Amendment—the risk of an enlargement of government control over the content of broadcast discussion of public issues. This risk is inherent in the court of appeals remand requiring regulations and procedures to sort out requests to be heard—a process involving the very editing that licensees now perform as to regular programming. Although the use of a public resource by the broadcast media permits a limited degree of government surveillance, as is not true with respect to private media, the government's power over licensees as we have noted, is by no means absolute and is carefully circumscribed by the act itself.

Under a constitutionally commanded and government supervised right-of-access system urged by respondents and mandated by the court of appeals, the commission would be required to oversee far more of the day-to-day operations of broadcasters' conduct, deciding such questions as whether a particular individual or group has had sufficient opportunity to present its viewpoint and whether a particular viewpoint has already been sufficiently aired. Regimenting broadcasters is too radical a therapy for the ailment respondents complain of.

Under the Fairness Doctrine the commission's responsibility is to judge whether a licensee's overall performance indicates a sustained good faith effort to meet the public interest in being fully and fairly informed. The commission's responsibilities under a right-of-access system would tend to draw it into a continuing case-by-case determination of who should be heard and when. Indeed, the likelihood of government involvement is so great that it has been suggested that the accepted constitutional principles against control of speech content would need to be relaxed with respect to editorial advertisements. To sacrifice First Amendment protections for so speculative a gain is not warranted, and it was well within the commission's discretion to construe the act so as to avoid such a result.[21]

The commission is also entitled to take into account the reality that in a very real sense listeners and viewers constitute a "captive audience." * * * It is no answer to say that because we tolerate per-

21. DNC has urged in this Court that we at least recognize a right of our national parties to purchase airtime for the purpose of discussing public issues. We see no principled means under the First Amendment of favoring access by organized political parties over other groups and individuals.

vasive commercial advertisement we can also live with its political counterparts.

* * *

The judgment of the court of appeals is reversed.

Justice Stewart, concurring.

* * *

Justice Blackmun, with whom Justice Powell joins, concurring.

Justice DOUGLAS.

While I join the Court in reversing the judgment below, I do so for quite different reasons.

My conclusion is that the TV and radio stand in the same protected position under the First Amendment as do newspapers and magazines. * * *

If a broadcast licensee is not engaged in governmental action for purposes of the First Amendment, I fail to see how constitutionally we can treat TV and the radio differently than we treat newspapers. It would come as a surprise to the public as well as to publishers and editors of newspapers to be informed that a newly created federal bureau would hereafter provide "guidelines" for newspapers or promulgate rules that would give a federal agency power to ride herd on the publishing business to make sure that fair comment on all current issues was made. * * *

* * *

* * * The Fairness Doctrine has no place in our First Amendment regime. It puts the head of the camel inside the tent and enables administration after administration to toy with TV or radio in order to serve its sordid or its benevolent ends. * *

* * *

Justice BRENNAN, with whom Justice Marshall concurs, dissenting. (See this text, p. 866).

* * *

COMMENT

1. Was the difficulty in securing Supreme Court acceptance for a limited right of access to editorial advertising due to the fact that Chief Justice Burger thought of the BEM and DNC requests as an effort to establish a common carrier right of entry to all broadcast programming? The Court uses the magnitude of the access problem as a reason for recognizing no First Amendment rights of access to the broadcast media. For example, the Court was extremely sensitive to the complaint that the rich would buy up all available broadcast time and that the networks would have to sell time to the highest bidder if the requests of BEM and the Democratic National Committee were granted.

2. Note the Court's regulatory history of the fairness doctrine. The Court gives great importance to the "seek out" aspect of the fairness doctrine. Under the "seek out" rule the broadcaster must seek out controversial viewpoints. He cannot merely wait for spokesmen for such views to come and ask him for time. On the basis of the cases and materials reflecting fairness doctrine considerations which you have read, has the "seek out" rule figured very significantly in the fortunes of the fairness doctrine?

3. In *CBS*, Chief Justice Burger describes the fairness doctrine as follows: "The doctrine imposes two affirmative responsibilities on the broadcaster: coverage of issues of public importance must be adequate and must fairly reflect viewpoints." Does this statement mean that there must be coverage that provides a fair reflection of controversial viewpoints of public importance generally or that the *broadcaster* must affirmatively seek out differing views the broadcaster has *chosen* to cover? What difference does it make? See Patsy Mink, 59 FCC2d 984 (1976), text, p. 873.

4. A major portion of the Court's opinion in *CBS* is devoted to the question of whether private censorship is subject to

constitutional sanction or obligation. The issue, said Chief Justice Burger, is "whether the action of a broadcast licensee such as that challenged here is 'governmental action' for purposes of the First Amendment."

When constitutional lawyers speak of the necessity that state action be present in order to invoke constitutional protection, what is meant is that constitutional limitations do not apply unless it is government which has restrained freedom. Since the First Amendment speaks to Congress and the Fourteenth Amendment speaks to the states, the argument is that if a nongovernmental source infringes freedom of expression, such an infringement does not rise to the dignity of a constitutional violation. In this respect, the fundamental issue of state action cuts across constitutional law generally. Should private power, specifically corporate power as reflected in the three corporations, CBS, NBC, and ABC, ever be constitutionalized, i.e., subject to constitutional obligation?

The Court, per Chief Justice Burger, answered this question, at least on the basis of the facts presented in the *CBS* case, in the negative. Four of the reasons given by the Court for refusing to view the broadcaster policy on editorial advertising as constituting state action are as follows:

a. Private power aggregates such as the broadcast media should not be viewed as quasipublic in order to satisfy the state action requirement.

b. As private parties, the broadcast media owe no First Amendment duties to other private parties as distinguished from the duties imposed on them by the Federal Communications Act.

c. If the state action problem can be sufficiently bridged for the broadcast media, it could be broadened for the print media as well, and this would be unthinkable.

d. Private power should not be constitutionalized because it is not all that powerful anyway.

5. The Court in *CBS* stated that the FCC neither required nor forbade the broadcaster policy of refusing to sell time for purchase of editorial advertisements; there was no state action in this case. Suppose the FCC had endorsed the position pressed on them by the Democratic National Commmittee and the BEM? Would the result have been different in the Supreme Court? On this point, the Court made the following observations:

> We do not reach the question whether the First Amendment or the act can be read to preclude the commission from determining that in some situations the public interest requires licensees to reexamine their policies with respect to editorial advertisements. The commission has not yet made such a determination; it has for the present at least, found the policy to be within the sphere of journalistic discretion which Congress has left with the licensee.

6. The Court said that neither the "public interest" standard nor the First Amendment required a right of access for editorial advertising time because such a right would mean an end to the editorial function in broadcast journalism. Using language which was very welcome to broadcast journalism, Chief Justice Burger identified the request of the petitioners in *CBS* with an assault on the editorial function.

But isn't there a difference between seeking some access to advertising time and mandating time for specific editorial advertising?

Justice Brennan in dissent made a five-pronged argument for the position that the network policy at issue did constitute state action:

1. (p)ublic "ownership" of the airwaves.

2. the direct dependence of broadcasters upon the Federal Government for their right to operate broadcast frequencies.

3. the extensive governmental control over the broadcast industry.

4. the specific governmental involvement in the broadcaster policy. There is, for example, an obvious nexus between the commission's fairness doctrine and the absolute refusal of broadcast licensees to sell any part of their airtime to groups or individuals wishing to speak out on controversial issues of public importance. Indeed in defense of this policy, the broadcaster-petitioners argue vigorously that this exclusionary policy is authorized and even compelled by the Fairness Doctrine.

5. Finally, and perhaps most important, in a case virtually identical to the one now before us, we held that a policy promulgated by a privately owned bus company, franchised by the Federal Government and regulated by the Public Utilities Commission of the District of Columbia, must be subjected to the constraints of the First Amendment. Public Utilities Commission v. Pollak, 343 U.S. 451 (1952).

Doesn't the analysis in item 4 above of the fairness doctrine rebut Chief Justice Burger's no-state-action conclusion? Justice Brennan points out that if the reason we can't have and don't need access is because we have the fairness doctrine, it should not be forgotten that the fairness doctrine manifests "specific governmental involvement" in broadcaster policy. Such involvement, in his view, constitutes state action. Thus, Justice Brennan is pointing out that although the fairness doctrine may look like a convenient weapon to club access to death, like all weapons it has its perils. It also serves to contradict the Court's conclusion that the broadcaster policy at issue here is private rather than state or governmental action.

In his dissent Justice Brennan takes the view that the Court seriously overestimates the efficacy of reliance on the fairness doctrine as an "adequate alternative to editorial advertising." He doubts the "ability—or willingness—of broadcasters to expose the public to the widest possible dissemination of information from diverse and antagonistic sources."

7. The student should contrast the *CBS* case with the print access materials in this text, p. 559. *CBS* should be evaluated with particular reference to *Miami Herald Publishing Co. v. Tornillo* where the Supreme Court invalidated the Florida right of reply to the press law.

The "Fairness" Doctrine Reconsidered— The 1974 Fairness Report

Counter-Commercials For Automobile Ads: Friends of the Earth v. FCC

1. An effort by a citizen group, relying on the *Banzhaf* case, to win time for counter-commercials in an environmental context occurred when the Friends of the Earth asked the FCC to direct WNBC–TV in New York City to make free time available for antipollution groups to reply to automobile advertisements which it had carried. The FCC refused. But the court of appeals reversed and told the FCC to reconsider the request of the Friends of the Earth for counter-commercials to point out the air pollution threat by ads for Ford's Mustang and General Motors's Impala.

Of course, the *Banzhaf* case had insisted that a grant of free time to rebut cigarette smoking advertisements was uniquely permissible in that instance only because of the public interest in reducing the threat to life itself posed by cigarette smoking. But ads for cigarette smoking are not the only advertisements extolling a product that may endanger life. Judge McGowan for the United States Court of Appeals for the District of Columbia said that pollution for the asthmatic in Manhattan is what cigarette smoking is to the lung cancer victim. See, Friends of the Earth v. FCC, 449 F.2d 1164 (D.C.Cir.1971).

2. The increased tempo of access petitions to the FCC, the uncertainty about the applicability of the fairness doctrine to access problems, and the general status and function of the fairness doctrine in the wake of the movement by groups and individuals for a right of access to television underscored for the FCC the need for rethinking the fairness doctrine. Pointing out that the fairness doctrine had been in effect for more than twenty years, since the issuance of the *Report on Editorializing By Broadcast Licensees* in 1948, the FCC announced that an overview of the fairness doctrine was in order. Therefore, on June 9, 1971, the FCC announced a "broad-ranging inquiry" into the fairness doctrine in light of the new demands for access to broadcasting. See In The Matter of the Handling of Public Issues Under the Fairness Doctrine, 30 FCC2d 25 (1971). The culmination of the FCC's reconsideration of the fairness doctrine was found in its *1974 Report.*. See In the Matter of the Handling of Public Issues Under the Fairness Doctrine and the Public Interest Standards of the Communications Act, 48 FCC2d 1 (1974). A major change made by the *1974 Fairness Report* was that the fairness doctrine would no longer be applied to normal product commercials.

3. Other aspects of the *1974 Fairness Report,* besides its ruling on product commercials, drew fire. The United States Court of Appeals for the District of Columbia consolidated three cases challenging the FCC's *1974 Report, supra*, and Reconsideration Order, 58 FCC2d 691 (1976). The court affirmed in part and reversed in part. Although the court upheld the essence of the FCC's redefinition of the fairness doctrine, the court specifically directed that the FCC reconsider two proposals which it had previously rejected.

The Committee for Open Media (COM) had suggested that a specified portion of the broadcast day be allocated for public access and the voluntary adoption of such a specific access scheme would be deemed presumptive compliance with the fairness doctrine.

Henry Geller had made a "10-issue" proposal which provided that the licensee (should be required to) list annually "the ten controversial issues of public importance, local and national, which it chose for the most coverage in the prior year."

NATIONAL CITIZENS COMMITTEE FOR BROADCASTING v. FCC

567 F.2D 1095 (D.C.CIR.1977).

MCGOWAN, Circuit Judge: These three consolidated petitions for review challenge various aspects of the Federal Communications Commission's *Fairness Report.* * * * For the reasons hereinafter appearing, we leave undisturbed the *Report* itself, including its central determination to withhold application of the fairness doctrine to broadcast communications promoting the sale of commercial products. Our remand to the FCC, however, is with directions to pursue further inquiry into two of the alternative courses of action proposed by some of the petitioners as ways by which the general objectives giving rise to the fairness doctrine can be realized. * * *

Petitioner Committee for Open Media (COM) challenges the commission's failure, on reconsideration of the *Fairness Report,* to adopt, or order further inquiry into, its access proposal as an alternative to current fairness enforcement. Intervenor Henry Geller challenges the commission's decisions to continue case-by-case consideration of fairness doctrine complaints, and its failure to consider and adopt his "10-issue" proposal relating to the fairness doctrine requirement that a broadcaster devote a reasonable amount of time to coverage of public issues.

* * *

The *Report* concludes that one type of announcement which may give rise to fairness doctrine obligations even though it is not an overt editorial is institutional advertising "designed to present a favorable public image of a particular corporation or industry rather than to sell a product." Although institutional advertising "ordinarily does not involve debate on public issues," if the advertiser "seek[s] to play an obvious and meaningful role in public debate, * * * the fairness doctrine * * applies." The commission has attempted to provide some guidance for determining whether fairness doctrine obligations apply to advertisements that are not "explicitly controversial." Licensees are advised that when the relationship of an advertisement to ongoing debate in the community is substantial and obvious the ad is likely to represent "obvious participation in public debate." In such circumstances the fairness doctrine should be applied.

We interpret the foregoing pronouncements concerning overt editorials and institutional advertising as reaffirmations of previous FCC policy in these areas. That portion of the *Report* dealing with standard product commercials, on the other hand, is an explicit departure from previous policy. The *Report* announces that advertisements for commercial products or services, such as the cigarette advertisements in *Banzhaf* and the automobile and gasoline advertisements in *Friends of the Earth,* henceforth will not give rise to fairness obligations because they "make no meaningful contribution to informing the public on any side of any issue," even though "the business, product, or service advertised is itself controversial." * * * The commission thus explicitly rejects the chain of reasoning first enunciated in *WCBS–TV:* that because promoting a product raises the issue of the desirability of its use, such promotion triggers application of the fairness doctrine if use of the product is a controversial issue of public importance.

Under the policy announced in the *Fairness Report,* promotion of controversial products will not require presentation of points of view opposing use or sale of the products. This does not mean that all product advertisements are exempt from fairness obligations, however. If in the course of promotion of a product there is "obvious and meaningful * * * discussion" on one side of a controversial issue impinging on the desirability of the product, fairness obligations attach because such advocacy qualifies as an editorial advertisement.

The *Report's* treatment of commercial advertising is vigorously challenged on both statutory and constitutional grounds. We believe that the challenges invoking the first amendment are based on a fundamental misunderstanding of the relationship between constitutional protection of commercial, or any other type of, speech and the functioning of the fairness doctrine. * * *

* * *

We reject the suggestion that any speech protected by the first amendment must, as a matter of constitutional law, trigger application of the fairness doctrine. While an ultimate function of both the first amendment and the fairness doctrine may be to encourage the dissemination of viewpoints and information, this does not mean that the two principles cover exactly the same ground. There is an obvious difference between the standard employed by the commission for determining whether the fairness doctrine applies to advertisements—that is, whether the advertisement advocates one side of a controversial public issue—and the holding in Virginia State Board, 425 U.S. 748 (1976), that advertising is protected by the first amendment because it represents dissemination of valuable information important to the functioning of a free enterprise system. Nothing in the Supreme Court's decision in Red Lion Broadcasting Co. v. FCC, 395 U.S. 367

(1969), upholding the constitutionality of the political editorializing and personal attack rules promulgated under the fairness doctrine, suggests that the obligation to present opposing points of view must be applied to all constitutionally protected speech. Indeed, in most instances in which the fairness doctrine has been held not to apply, the speech which it was contended triggered application of the obligation was clearly protected by the first amendment.

* * *

Indeed, it can be argued that the first amendment protection afforded commercial speech cuts precisely contrarily from the manner urged by petitioners. It has been contended by commentators, although viewed skeptically by the Supreme Court, that broadcasters are discouraged from presenting messages which trigger fairness doctrine obligations. If the fairness doctrine does have this chilling effect, then First Amendment protection of commercial speech would make application of the fairness doctrine to such speech less, rather than more, desirable. This was certainly the context in which the *Banzhaf* court—upholding the commission's decision to subject cigarette advertisements to the fairness doctrine—discussed the relevance of First Amendment consideration.

STATUTORY CHALLENGES TO THE NEW COMMISSION POLICY

It is alleged that * * * to withdraw standard product commercials from the purview of the fairness doctrine violates the standards of the Communications Act and was arbitrary, capricious and an abuse of discretion. * * *

The 1946 decision concerning commercial advertisements so heavily relied on by petitioners merely stated that debate over the "relative merits of one product or another" could raise "basic and important social, economic, or political issues." [48] The *WCBS–TV* approach extended upon this principle in determining that the promotion of a controversial product was an important and controversial issue. The *Fairness Report* contracts the potential scope of the principle in requiring that the controversial issue be directly and obviously raised in the debate. But neither the *WCBS–TV* approach nor the *Fairness Report* is inconsistent with the principle announced in the 1946 Commission decision. Thus, while the 1959 amendments to the Communications Act "codifi[ed] the standards of fairness," we are not convinced that the *WCBS–TV* standard was one of the standards referred to.

* * *

Nor do we believe that the commission has acted arbitrarily or that it has abused its discretion in withdrawing most commercial advertisements from application of the fairness doctrine.

* * *

We think that the commission has adequately supported its decision to exclude standard product commercials from the scope of the fairness doctrine. Three major arguments are presented by the commission. First, the commission made the judgment that the *WCBS–TV* approach to the fairness doctrine and standard product commercials at most informed the public about only one side of a controversial issue. * * *

Certainly it must be admitted that counter-commercials are of a very different genre than are the product commercials themselves. They do not simply state, "Do not buy X; it is not desirable," but rather argue one side of the issues underlying the debate over desirability. Given this fundamental asymmetry, we do not think it was unreasonable for the com-

48. Sam Morris, 11 FCC 197, 198 (1946).

mission to conclude that application of the fairness doctrine to standard product commercials does not further the objective of presenting all viewpoints on controversial issues of public importance.

The second major argument put forth by the commission is that application of the fairness doctrine to noneditorial advertisements would "divert the attention of broadcasters from their public trustee responsibilities in aiding the development of an informed public opinion." This argument is of course premised to some extent on the first. We understand the commission to be indicating that even if enforcement of fairness doctrine obligations with respect to commercial advertisements might marginally contribute to an informed public opinion, these beneifts are outweighed by the reduction in public information which results from the decreased attention that broadcasters will afford to other aspects of the fairness doctrine. Given the wide range of controversial products to which the *WCBS–TV* approach could be applied [60] and the difficulties, discussed above, in determining which issues implicitly addressed give rise to fairness obligations, it is indeed quite possible that the effort broadcasters would have to devote to enforcing the fairness doctrine with respect to commercial advertisements would contribute relatively little to the overall objectives of the doctrine. We caution, however, that it is doubtful that the new FCC policy will substantially lessen the difficulties of drawing the line between advertisements which do and those which do not incur fairness obligations. The difference between obvious and unobvious advocacy is not obvious.

Finally, the commission suggested in the *Fairness Report,* though not in its arguments to this court, that application of the fairness doctrine to commercial advertisements could undermine the economic base of commercial broadcasting. It is possible that sponsors would be discouraged from broadcasting advertisements subject to mandatory counter-commercials, and that broadcasters could suffer additional losses through operation of the *Cullman* principle, 40 FCC 576 (1963), under which they must bear the cost of presenting opposing views where paid sponsorship is not available. Yet no evidence has been presented which indicates that the *WCBS–TV* policy had an adverse effect on commercial broadcasters, though admittedly this may be due to the rather unvigorous and confused enforcement of that policy. While we do not think this economic argument is conclusive standing alone, the other two arguments put forth by the commission provide adequate and substantial support for its decision.

* * *

The commission received three major proposals designed to overcome [the] difficulties of current fairness doctrine enforcement. Petitioner COM urged that the commission adopt as an optional substitute for the current fairness doctrine a system whereby licensees devote a specified percentage of their broadcast time to what COM labeled "free speech messages" and other public issue programming. Intervenor Geller requested the commission to adopt a requirement "that the licensee list annually the ten controversial issues of public importance, local and national, which it chose for coverage in the prior year." Geller also proposed that the commission confine review of fairness doctrine complaints to the time of license renewal.

60. *See* Geller, *The Fairness Doctrine in Broadcasting: Problems and Suggested Courses of Action* 85 (Rand Corp. 1973), ("There are relatively few advertised products whose normal use does not involve some significant issue: automobiles [large or small], gasoline [leaded or unleaded], any type of medication, beer, airplanes, any product that does not have a biodegradable container, any foreign product—the list is virtually endless.")

* * * In its petition, COM proposed a specific access scheme, not presented to the commission during the fairness inquiry itself, which would be deemed presumptive compliance with the fairness doctrine. Under the scheme suggested by COM:

1. A licensee would set aside one hour per week for spot announcements and lengthier programming which would be available for presentation of messages by members of the public.

2. Half of this time would be allocated on a first-come, first-served basis on any topic whatsoever; the other half would be apportioned "on a representative spokesperson system."

3. Both parts of the allocation scheme would be "nondiscretionary as to content with the licensee."

4. However, the broadcaster would still be required to ensure that spot messages or other forms of response to "editorial advertisements" are broadcast.

The commission addressed COM's proposal in its order denying reconsideration, stating that while the proposal was "the first serious attempt to meet" what the commission deemed the essential requirements of any access scheme, "[i]t is neither perfected nor ready for adoption as a rule or policy." *Reconsideration Order* at 699. The commission also expressed the view that the COM system could be a supplement to, but not a substitute for, the current fairness doctrine requirements. * * We do not think that the commission has demonstrated in the *Fairness Report,* in the *Reconsideration Order,* or in its written and oral arguments to this court that the COM proposal retains insufficient licensee discretion. * * * COM's proposal will involve the commission even less than do present procedures in overseeing compliance with the first [fairness doctrine] obligation. At the same time, the proposal would ensure a minimum amount of coverage of public issues.

Similarly, we think that the commission cannot ignore the advantage of an access system in providing information to the public which would not be provided under even full compliance with both obligations of the fairness doctrine as currently implemented. * * *

One of the proposals submitted to the commission during the fairness inquiry seems especially promising as one step toward fuller compliance with the first fairness obligation. Intervenor Geller suggests that the licensee list annually the ten controversial issues of public importance, local and national, which it chose for the most coverage in the prior year, set out the offers for response made, and note representative programming that was presented on each issue.

* * *

* * * It does seem to us, however, that issue reports could be useful to the commission in one or more ways. For instance, the commission initially could review each annual list to determine whether its appears that the licensee fulfilled his part one obligation. * * * Alternatively the commission might take no immediate action with respect to the annual reports, but instead examine them at the time of license renewal. We leave it to the commission's further examination to consider whether these or other uses of annual reports such as those proposed by Mr. Geller would be appropriate in enforcement of the fairness doctrine. * * *

In summary, we reject the challenges to the commission's decision to exempt product commercials which do not "obviously and meaningfully address a controversial issue of public importance" from fairness doctrine obligations. * * * However we remand the orders reviewed on this appeal with instructions that the commission undertake further inquiry into petitioner COM's access proposal and intervenor Geller's "10 issue" proposal in accordance with this opinion.

It is so ordered.

COMMENT

1. How much of the *Banzhaf* case, text, p. 855, is left after the court of appeal decision in the *Fairness Report* case? If there were no statute prohibiting cigarette advertising on television, wouldn't a cigarette ad that made no mention of the smoking-health issue be outside the scope of the Fairness Doctrine?

2. In a *Notice of Inquiry,* dated March 2, 1978, FCC 78–108, the FCC announced "the initiation of an inquiry into the 'right of access' policy submitted by COM, the 'ten issue approach' to the Fairness Doctrine proposed by Geller, and as suggested by the Court, into 'other ways of achieving compliance with the Fairness Doctrine's first obligation that deserve critical consideration, either in conjunction with, or as alternatives to the procedures referred to above.'" The FCC requested comments on its "ten-issue" proposal and asked, among other questions, the following:

> Could a ten issue proposal be utilized in conjunction with an access scheme, or act itself as a substitute for or complement to present Fairness Doctrine procedures? If so, how would its application comport with the statutory mandate of Section 315(a)?

Suppose it was your task to respond to this question. What would you say?

Are there any advantages to the optional access scheme proposed by COM? One advantage of the proposal is related to the First Amendment. It will be remembered that in the *CBS* case, the Court was careful not to rule out the possibility that the FCC, if it chose, might, consistent with the First Amendment, be able to mandate a system of access. If an FCC system of *mandatory* access might be consistent with the First Amendment, then the adoption of an access scheme which is *optional* with the licensee should, by definition, be fairly well insulated from First Amendment attack.

The Duty to Cover Important Issues: Enforcing Part 1 of The "Fairness" Doctrine—WHAR

Although the *1974 Fairness Report* might be read as evidencing an FCC retreat from an expensive conception of the fairness doctrine, two years later in the *Patsy Mink* case the FCC gave new life to the first part of the broadcaster's fairness doctrine obligation.

There are two parts to a broadcaster's fairness doctrine obligation. The first part of the fairness doctrine involves the affirmative duty on the part of the broadcaster to cover important issues. The second part of the fairness doctrine involves the duty to provide balanced coverage of important issues. In Patsy Mink, 59 FCC2d 984 (1976), the FCC held for the "first time * * * that a licensee was compelled under the first part of the fairness doctrine, to offer at least some programming addressing it." 59 FCC2d 984 at 998 (1976).

Representative Patsy Mink, sponsor of an anti-strip mining bill before Congress, requested that radio station WHAR, Clarksburg, West Virginia, broadcast an eleven-minute tape regarding her anti-strip mining proposal. This tape, Mink argued, would contrast with views previously aired over WHAR on a program entitled "What's The Issue."

WHAR responded that it had not broadcast the "What's The Issue" program nor any other programming on the strip mining controversy. Mink then complained to the FCC alleging that WHAR had violated its fairness doctrine obligation to devote programming time to an issue of "extreme importance to the economy and environment of the area served by WHAR."

Mink supported her contention that strip mining was extremely controversial by pointing, among other things, to the current battle in Congress over the issue, and the fact that deep mining, an industry vital to the Appalachian economy, will be adversely affected by strip mining. Mink also noted statements by WHAR in its 1972 license renewal application that surface and deep mining were major industries and that development of new industry and air and water pollution were of great concern to its listeners.

WHAR responded to the charges with three counterarguments. First, it assured the FCC that while it had originated no local programming concerning the strip mining controversy, it had broadcast a significant number of strip mining stories that it received from the Associated Press news service.

The station further contended that "there is presently no established precedent or rule requiring a particular licensee to cover any particular issue. * * * "

Finally, WHAR denied that strip mining was of critical importance to members of its community and pointed to the absence of any request, other than from Representative Mink, that it produce any programs concerning strip mining. The FCC rejected WHAR's defenses.

In a significant opinion, the FCC emphasized the importance of licensee compliance with the first part of the fairness doctrine:

> * * * The fairness doctrine "imposes two affirmative responsibilities on the broadcaster: coverage of issues of public importance must be adequate and must fairly reflect differing viewpoints." CBS v. Democratic National Committee, 412 U.S. 94, 111 (1973). Without licensee compliance with the responsibility to cover adequately vital public issues, the obligation to present contrasting views would have little success as a means to inform the listening public. If the fairness doctrine is to have any meaningful impact, broadcasters must cover, at the very least, those topics which are of vital concern to their listeners.
>
> * * *
>
> While it is our policy to defer to licensees journalistic discretion, we must emphasize that that discretion is not absolute, *Committee for the Fair Broadcasting of Controversial Issues*, and we have previously advised licensees that "some issues are so critical or of such great public importance that it would be unreasonable for a licensee to ignore them completely." *Fairness Report.* While it would be an exceptional situation and would counter our intention to stay out of decisions concerning the selection of specific programming matter, we believe that the unreasonable exercise of this licensee discretion, i.e., failure to adequately cover a 'critical issue' in a particular community, would require appropriate remedial action on the part of the commission. Such action in those rare instances was contemplated by the Supreme Court in *Red Lion* when it declared:
>
> > "* * * if the present licensees should suddenly prove timorous, the commission is not powerless to insist that they give adequate and fair attention to public issues * * * Congress need not stand idly by and permit those with licenses to ignore the problems which beset the people." *Red Lion* at 393.
>
> These are rare instances, however, and licensees are not obligated to address each and every important issue which may be considered a controversial issue of public importance.
>
> * * *
>
> Where, as in the present case, an issue has significant and possibly unique impact on the licensee's service area, it will not be sufficient for the licensee as an indication of compliance with the fairness doctrine to show that it may have broadcast an unknown amount of news touching on a general topic related to the issue cited in a complaint. Rather it must be shown that there has been some attempt to inform the public of the nature of the controversy, not only that such a controversy exists.

> We must conclude, therefore, that WHAR has acted unreasonably in failing to cover the issue of strip mining, an issue which clearly may determine the quality of life in Clarksburg for decades to come. Given these findings, we are of the opinion that the licensee of radio station WHAR is in violation of the fairness doctrine. Considering the continuing controversial nature of the issue of strip mining, the licensee is requested to inform the commission within 20 days of the release date of this order on how it intends to meet its fairness obligations with respect to adequate coverage of the aforementioned issue.

COMMENT

1. The impact of *Patsy Mink,* of course, should not be overstated. The FCC takes pains to point out that requiring compliance with the first part of the fairness doctrine will be an exceptional occurrence. The principle of the *Patsy Mink* case will be reserved for issues that are "so critical or of such great public importance that it would be unreasonable for a licensee to ignore them completely."

2. The two proposals which the court of appeals in the *Fairness Report* case directed the FCC to reconsider—the COM specific access proposal and the Geller "ten-issues" proposal—are perhaps better evaluated in light of the *Patsy Mink* case. In *Patsy Mink,* the FCC partially based its conclusion that the first part of the fairness doctrine would be violated if the strip mining issue was not covered on the licensee's own statement of the issues which it had ascertained were important to the community. Arguably, once "ten issues" had been indicated as of importance to the community, there would be some measuring rod by which to gauge the first part of the fairness doctrine—the licensee's affirmative duty to cover important issues. The Geller "ten-issue" proposal should, under this analysis, energize enforcement of the first part of the fairness doctrine.

With respect to the specific access scheme proposed by COM, the "ten-issue" proposal has a role to play also. If the specific access time in the main fails to cover the "ten issues," then arguably the specific access scheme is simply an inadequate substitute for the fairness doctrine, particularly its first part—the affirmative duty to cover important issues.

The Scope of the "Fairness" Doctrine—Does it Apply to Entertainment, Comedy, and Documentaries?

1. Suppose a dramatic presentation on television offends a particular group? Does the "fairness" doctrine apply? An example of an effort to extend the reach of the fairness doctrine to entertainment programs arose out of the CBS television show "Maude." Two anti-abortion groups, the Diocesan Union of Holy Name Societies of Rockville Centre and the Long Island Coalition for Life, unsuccessfully filed a complaint with the FCC against WCBS–TV concerning a two-part episode of the program "Maude." Specifically, the complaint concerned Maude's discovery that she was pregnant and her decision to have an abortion. See Diocesan Union of Holy Name Societies of Rockville Centre and Long Island Coalition for Life, 41 FCC2d 497 (1973).

Citing dialogue from the "Maude" program, the groups accused CBS of presenting only the pro-abortion argument.

The anti-abortion groups invoked the fairness doctrine "on the ground that abortion is a major controversial issue" and requested that "two pro-life programs be presented on successive Tuesday evenings at 8 p.m. on the CBS network within the framework of the 'Maude' show supporting the right to life for unborn babies, or that time be made available on successive Tuesday evenings at 8 p.m. on CBS for a pro-life presentation produced by appellants herein."

The FCC rejected the fairness doctrine complaint. Even assuming that the program presented one side of a controversial issue, the FCC ruled that anti-abortion groups had failed to offer any information indicating that CBS had only presented one side of the abortion issue in its overall programming.

2. Although the "fairness" doctrine requirement of balanced presentation of controversial issues of public importance has been given new vitality by the *Red Lion* case, it should not be thought that the "fairness" doctrine restricts station licensees from declaring where they stand on issues by editorializing. Editorializing is permitted and encouraged. This was not always the case. See, Mayflower Broadcasting Co., 8 FCC 333 (1941).

At what points do the right to editorialize and the "fairness" doctrine intersect? The controversiality quotient of editorials in broadcasting is sometimes found deficient. Might this be a consequence of the intersection between editorializing and the "fairness" doctrine?

The "Fairness" Doctrine, Investigative Journalism, and the PENSIONS Case

1. On September 12, 1972, NBC broadcast a documentary examining private pension plans called, "Pensions: The Broken Promise." The program ended with the cautionary note by NBC newsman Edwin Newman that not all pension plans are bad. But, in the main, the program was a hard-hitting attack on the empty promise that pension plans had allegedly revealed themselves to be to American workers.

Accuracy in media (AIM) filed a complaint that NBC's pension show had violated the fairness doctrine, and the FCC so ruled. The sheer volume of the anti-pension statements was deemed to merit the presentation of an opposing viewpoint on pension plans. See 44 FCC2d 1027 (1973).

A panel of the United States Court of Appeals, in an opinion written by Judge Leventhal, reversed the FCC. NBC v. FCC, 516 F.2d 1101 (D.C.Cir. 1974). Judge Fahy joined in Judge Leventhal's opinion, and Judge Tamm dissented. The court of appeals stayed the FCC order so that further opportunity for reply should be granted the pro-pension plan point of view.

Leventhal's majority opinion held that the licensee had a "wide degree of discretion" in the presentation of the programming and ruled that NBC had not exceeded that discretion. The initial panel decision declared that the editorial judgment of the broadcaster, if reasonable and in good faith, will be maintained in fairness cases. In Leventhal's view, the broadcaster had reasonably concluded that the pensions program did not present a controversial issue. The fact that the FCC would have reached a different editorial judgment cannot itself justify a conclusion that the fairness doctrine was violated. The rest followed. No fairness doctrine obligation had occurred because no controversial issue of public importance had been aired.

AIM petitioned for a rehearing of the panel decision. On December 13, 1974, AIM's request for an *en banc* hearing was granted, and the panel decision authored by Judge Leventhal was voided. But after granting the petition for rehearing, a majority of the judges of the full court decided not to hear the case. The FCC filed a suggestion of mootness with the court of appeals on the ground that with the enactment of new pensions legislation, the Employment Retirement Security Act of 1974, the case had become moot. The court of appeals then vacated its own order for an *en banc* hearing (a hearing to the full court) and sent the case back to its original judicial spawning ground, the panel consisting of Leventhal, Fahy, and Tamm.

Judge Bazelon of the D.C. Federal Court of Appeals vigorously dissented from the full bench's decision to vacate its own prior order granting a rehearing before the full bench. His protests persuaded neither the full bench nor the panel. The panel of Leventhal, Tamm, and Fahy decided to remand the case to the FCC on the ground of mootness. All hope of keeping alive what started out to be a ground-breaking decision of the FCC applying the fairness doctrine to investigative journalism ended on April 19, 1976, when the Supreme Court refused to review the court of appeals order to remand to the FCC for mootness. Accuracy In Media, Inc. v. FCC, 425 U.S. 934 (1976).

Is the case precedent for anything? Since the Leventhal panel's original decision that NBC had not violated the fairness doctrine was set aside, the "Pensions" case is obviously not precedent on matters of substantive fairness doctrine law. But, nonetheless, the many opinions in the case are obviously a guide to current judicial thinking about important fairness doctrine issues. For example, if the question of fairness doctrine obligation comes to be approached as a matter of broadcaster judgment which the FCC can set aside only if that judgment is found to be unreasonable, then how much scope is left to the fairness doctrine? In the view of the majority in the initial panel decision, NBC had made a reasonable judgment that when a program addressed itself to a consideration of abuses in private "pension plans," there could be no real controversy that there were in fact such abuses. The FCC, on the other hand, viewed the program "Broken Promise" as raising a controversial issue of public importance—how well overall did the private pension system work and was there a need for governmental regulation of all private pension plans?

The fairness doctrine issue resolved around the subject matter of the pension plan show "Broken Promise." Did the show deal with the overall performance of the private pension plan system? Or was its focus on *some* abuses in *some* private pension plans?

The FCC took a different and larger estimate of the thrust and subject of the pension plan program than did NBC. In the FCC view, NBC was making a general evaluation of the overall performance of pension plans. But the court said such a subjective reassessment by the FCC should not be permitted to transform a program which the broadcaster viewed as a news documentary about some pension plans into a full-scale critical study of pension plans.

The outcome of the court's position in the pensions plan case is clear: merely because the FCC has a different idea of what a program is about than does the broadcaster who produced it does not mean that the FCC estimate of the program's content must prevail. Of course, if one wishes to diminish the necessity for wrangling over whether an issue does or does not raise a controversial issue of public importance, the simplest course is to say that the realm of investigative journalism is not covered by the fairness doctrine. The panel in the pension plan case decided not to chart so direct a course.

The court's technique of program analysis consisted of focusing only on the "handful" of specific comments concerning the "overall functioning of the pension system." The court then asked if some of the specific overall comments were favorable to the view that generally pension plans functioned well. Thus, the court concluded that there was reasonable balance.

Another approach would be to ask whether the remarks on the program favorable to pension plans were completely overshadowed when judged against the context of the entire program. In that context, Judge Tamm concluded that the program appeared to be part of an attack on the entire system. For Judge Bazelon, the technique constituted a *de facto* rejection of what had earlier been clear fairness doctrine law: In making an evaluation as to whether fairness doctrine problems attach, the implicit message of the program must be taken into account. In the majority's view of the "Broken Promise" show, analysis of express criticism of pension plans, and express criticism alone, was made the measure of fairness doctrine compliance.

In Bazelon's view, the court's conclusion that there was a reasonable balance between favorable and unfavorable comments on the issue of overall performance of pension plans was erroneous. Subdividing the issues in the program into subissues such as statements relating to the adequacy of pension plans and problems of vesting and eligibility was wrong. By pruning many of the unfavorable comments "down to a fraction" of what they might otherwise have appeared to be, the court reached a conclusion of balance on the "overall performance of the plan" which Bazelon considered unjustified.

Bazelon made the excellent point that the court perceived a "neat distinction" between a "televised presentation of a problem" or an "isolated incident" and an "overall criticism of the institution" or matter discussed. Bazelon declared: "There is no such distinction."

He perceived an implicit ultimate issue raised by the program: the overall performance of pension plans. As a result, Bazelon suggested that the court of appeals decision in the pensions plan case contained its own implicit message: "[T]he FCC may not resort to the implicit issue principle but may apply the Fairness Doctrine only to overt editorializing denominated as such."

Such a contention from Judge Bazelon was especially significant. It was Bazelon who had held for the court in the cigarette advertising case that there was an implicit issue in cigarette ads on television exploiting youth and sex; the implicit issue was the desirability or nondesirability of cigarette smoking.[5]

In Bazelon's view, the pensions plan case raised a fundamental First Amendment issue which the majority's whittling down of the implicit issues raised by the program obscured: Should the definition of a "controversial issue of public importance" be expanded "to include major legislation pending before a significant legislative body when the journalistic interest is at its height, i.e., investigative journalism?"

In dissent, Judge Tamm particularly criticized the majority's conclusion that the broadcaster's determination of whether a particular program deals with a controversial issue should prevail unless unreasonable. It was the FCC's responsibility to determine whether a program raised a controversial issue. Once the FCC made that determination, the licensee "is accorded extensive latitude and journalistic discretion in fulfilling his obligation of reasonable opportunity." If the First Amendment interests of the broadcaster are at their height in the area of presentation of news and news documentaries, then, Tamm argued, the public's First Amendment rights of access to the widest variety of conflicting viewpoints on controversial issues are similarly at their height with respect to news and news documentaries.

How fair should investigative journalism be? A perfunctory fairness is foolish as well as unconvincing. Thus, the court cited with approval David Brinkley's affidavit in the case concerning a program he narrated on highway construction: "I did not think at the time that I was obliged to recite (or find someone to recite) that not all highway construction involves corruption, that many highways are built by honorable men or the like."

5. See Banzhaf v. FCC, 405 F.2d 1082 (D.C.Cir. 1968), cert. den. 396 U.S. 842 (1969), discussed in text at p. 855.

On the other hand, if a major television network devotes itself to attacking an evil that it perceives to exist in the society, should there be no recourse for the persons who bear the brunt of the exposé? Suppose the exposé is one-sided? Suppose it unjustly ruins a whole company or throws employees out of work? It is true that investigative print journalism is not restrained by the fairness doctrine or any equivalent. But what print outlet is the equivalent of NBC television in clout?

Does the fairness doctrine apply to investigative journalism on television? By analyzing the "Broken Promise" program in a manner that made the conclusion inevitable that the program did not raise a controversial issue of public importance, a ruling that no fairness doctrine obligation attached was possible. Thus, there was no need for a square holding that the fairness doctrine did or did not apply to investigative journalism.

Should the fairness doctrine apply to investigative journalism? For Tamm, investigative journalism was especially susceptible to a "manipulated and selective presentation" which "ignores all viewpoints" other than that of investigative journalists. Judge Tamm viewed investigative journalism on television as editorializing. In this view, "Broken Promise" was an editorial against pension plans and, therefore, fairness doctrine obligations attached. The fact that the program was not presented as an editorial but as a documentary should not free the broadcaster from the duty "to present a report in which all conflicting positions and viewpoints are fairly portrayed."

Judge Tamm finally acceded to the FCC suggestion of mootness and supported the ultimate disposition of the case by the court of appeals: an order vacating the prior judgment and remanding the case to the FCC with directions to dismiss the fairness doctrine complaint. Nevertheless, in his initial opinion and in his final opinion in the case Judge Tamm insisted that NBC had violated the fairness doctrine.

Judge Tamm particularly criticized the panel's view that where the FCC determines that the broadcaster "has not discharged its fairness doctrine obligations," the court is justified in subjecting the FCC determination to a more searching scrutiny, a "hard look" as it were. This "hard look" doctrine was justified by Judge Leventhal on the ground that the fairness doctrine is "suffused with First Amendment freedoms." Judge Tamm replied that in *CBS* the Supreme Court gave at least its implicit approval to the notion that "in evaluating the First Amendment claims" of broadcasters "great weight" must be accorded to FCC decisions.[6] Judge Tamm challenged what he believed to be a single implication running throughout the court's opinion: the view that the fairness doctrine is unconstitutional. As an intermediate federal court of appeal below the Supreme Court, the federal appeals court in Washington was not free to hold the fairness doctrine unconstitutional since it had been unanimously upheld in 1969 in *Red Lion* and reaffirmed as recently as 1973 in *CBS v. DNC.* What the majority could not do directly, it tried, in Tamm's view, to do indirectly. The court tried to so limit the fairness doctrine that the broadcaster's obligations under it "would have been a dead letter."

Judge Tamm challenged some observations of veteran broadcaster Fred Friendly on the significance of the pensions plan case. The consequences of upholding the fairness doctrine in the pensions plan show were described by Friendly in the following manner:[7]

---

6. See 516 F.2d 1101 at 1188, quoting CBS v. Democratic National Committee, 412 U.S. 94, 102 (1973).

7. See 516 F.2d 1101 at 1201, quoting Friendly, *What's Fair on the Air?* N.Y. Times Magazine 11, 46 (March 30, 1975).

> * * * every assertion of wrongdoing by persons or groups would have to be balanced with an *equal* statement of their claims to innocence—however unbelievable they might be. * * * [T]he broadcasters feared a decision for the government would make it difficult to air any program that took a point of view.

Judge Tamm answered Friendly's critique of the dire consequences of applying the fairness doctrine to investigative journalism as follows:

> This is exactly what this case is not about. The commission did not substitute its judgment for the licensee's; it found the broadcaster's judgment to be unreasonable. It did *not* order equal time; it only required reasonable opportunity. The commission did not tell petitioner whom to put on the air; journalistic discretion as to format and spokesmen remains intact. The commission's decision does not preclude programming with a point of view; the fairness doctrine encourages such programming.

In discussing the *Pensions* case, Friendly emphasized the wallop the show "Broken Promise" actually packed:

> It [the show] was an example of tough investigative reporting, and its coverage did not pretend to be fastidiously fair to all concerned. Its makers were muckrakers with their eyes and hearts open, not blind disciples of the goddess of justice. One nationally recognized expert in pension plans and abuses observed, "For years there had been attempts to get pension reform through Congress, and this one program probably did more good than all the other efforts." See Friendly, *The Good Guys, The Bad Buys and The First Amendment: Free Speech vs. Fairness in Broadcasting,* 150 (1975).

After the pensions program the Congress did, in fact, pass pension reform legislation. Friendly argues that the NBC show was a powerful blow to pension plans as they then existed. Perhaps the NBC pension plan show was a major force toward stimulating legislation of pension plans reform. But can't this argument be turned around to support extension of the fairness doctrine to such programs? Precisely because of the probable impact of a network documentary with respect to influencing opinion and law, some opportunity for response may be required.

Another approach to the resolution of problems of propagandizing, imbalance, or unfairness in investigative journalism is exclusively through the license renewal process. This view received new impetus when former FCC General Counsel Henry Geller, in his *amicus curiae* brief in the *Pensions* case, argued that the FCC could not decide fairness doctrine issues on an *ad hoc* case-by-case basis. When the FCC becomes involved in specific oversight of program content, he argued, serious First Amendment objections are raised. In Geller's view, the FCC should return to the practice it had followed until 1962 when the FCC merely asked the licensee for its reaction to a fairness complaint. During that period, the FCC did not order the licensee to take steps to provide a specific response for an opposing viewpoint. Instead, the old practice was for the FCC to wait and "consider the matter definitively at renewal in connection with the overall showing of the station." Furthermore, in Geller's view, the licensee's fairness performance would be evaluated by the *New York Times v. Sullivan* standard. License renewal would only be denied if the licensee had acted with "actual malice," that is, if the licensee acted with a reckless disregard of his fairness obligations. Mere error in judgment like negligent misstatement in the law of libel would not result in sanction.

The court of appeals refused to consider the merits of the Geller position. The Geller approach is defended as doing the least violence to First Amendment standards, yet it depends on a sanction which silences an offender forever. If a right of specific response attaches to a specific issue, the broadcaster is still in business. Enforcing the fairness doctrine exclusively through the license renewal process uses the sanction the industry has for years, with good cause, called the "death penalty"—the sanction of denial of license renewal. The trouble with this sanction is that it has unnecessary overkill.

Another defect of the license renewal approach is that it may be too mild. Suppose the sanction of denial of the license renewal application for failure to observe the fairness doctrine is deemed so drastic by the FCC that it is never used? If the license renewal process is to be the only vehicle for enforcement of the fairness doctrine and that process is in fact never used to deny a licensee renewal for fairness doctrine violations, then the fairness doctrine would be a toothless command devoid of any force or importance.

Geller has suggested, impliedly at least, that investigative journalism on television should be covered by the fairness doctrine. Geller says: "[A]n investigative program [on television] can be as hardhitting and as one-sided as the broadcast journalist wishes: the only requirement is that at some time the opposing view be given the opportunity." See Geller, *The Fairness Doctrine In Broadcasting: Broadcasting Problems and Suggested Courses of Action* 39 (1973).

But this observation itself raises an issue: Must fairness in a television documentary be achieved within the confines of the documentary itself or should it be achieved through some follow-up programming? It will be recalled that the remedy afforded by the FCC in the *Pensions* case was a request that at some future time the opposing viewpoint should be given some opportunity for expression. Judge Tamm, on the other hand, who supported the FCC decision in the *Pensions* case nevertheless suggested that a balanced presentation of the controversial issue examined should be achieved within the documentary itself.

The difficulty with trying to solve fairness problems in documentaries by insisting on fairness within a particular documentary itself is that it may be a futile objective. If a news department of a network is sufficiently exercised about a social evil that it does a documentary to expose what it considers to be a social evil, should the network be obliged to portray with equal force and flair the spokesmen and views of those identified with the very "social evil" being investigated? The debate that results from such efforts is likely to be stilted and, perhaps in the end, still one-sided. In the *Pensions* case the NBC staff itself spoke of the need to include "fairness filler" on the pensions plan show. When the effort to secure balanced presentation is thought of as "fairness filler" by those who are entrusted with furnishing balance, not too much reason exists to have faith in the integrity of an effort to provide balanced presentation within the confines of a single documentary.

From a short-run point of view, the *Pensions* case was a nonevent. The issue of whether the fairness doctrine should apply to investigative journalism was not resolved. Since network journalism seems increasingly drawn to investigative journalism, the issues raised by the *Pensions* case will inevitably have to be resolved. It is, therefore, likely that the opinions in the *Pensions* case will provide a basis for reflection on the role, if any, which the fairness doctrine should play in investigative journalism on television.

"Fairness" Doctrine Procedure: Writing the Fairness Complaint

AMERICAN SECURITY COUNCIL EDUCATION FOUNDATION v. FCC

5 MED.L.RPTR. 1193 (D.C.CIR. 1979) 607 F.2D 438, CERT. DENIED 44 U.S. 1073 (1980).

Before Wright, Chief Judge, and Bazelon, McGowan, Tamm, Leventhal, Robinson,

MacKinnon, Robb and Wilkey, Circuit Judges, sitting en banc.

TAMM, Circuit Judge:

We are called upon to decide whether the American Security Council Education Foundation (ASCEF) presented prima facie evidence that CBS, Inc. (CBS) violated the fairness doctrine by giving imbalanced coverage to "national security issues" in its news programming. The Federal Communications Commission (commission) concluded that because ASCEF did not base its complaint on a particular, well-defined issue, it did not present prima facie evidence of a fairness doctrine violation. We uphold the commission's decision.

In 1972, ASCEF launched a study to analyze the national television networks' coverage of issues relating to this country's national security. ASCEF originally planned to examine the news programs of all three national networks, but later decided, "in the interests of depth and thoroughness," to examine only one. E. Lefever, TV and National Defense, An Analysis of CBS News, 1972–73 at vi (1974) (TV and National Defense). ASCEF chose CBS because CBS had the largest audience for evening news and the largest number of affiliated stations.

ASCEF examined videotapes of all CBS "Evening News" broadcasts aired during 1972. It transcribed broadcasts of all news reports that it determined were relevant to four topics: United States military and foreign affairs; Soviet Union military and foreign policy; China military and foreign policy; and Vietnam affairs. ASCEF submitted examples of the broadcasts it transcribed to the commission. * * *

ASCEF dissected the transcribed news reports into sentences and categorized each sentence into one of three basic positions on national security:

> *Viewpoint A* holds that the threat to U.S. security is more serious than perceived by the government or that the United States ought to *increase* its national security efforts;
>
> *Viewpoint B* holds that present government threat perception is essentially correct or U.S. military and foreign policy efforts are adequate[;] and
>
> *Viewpoint C* holds that the threat to U.S. security is less serious than perceived by the government or that U.S. national security efforts should be *decreased.* TV and National Defense at 78 (emphasis in original).

Using this methodology ASCEF concluded that 3.54 per cent of the sentences transcribed reflected viewpoint A, 34.63 per cent reflected viewpoint B and 61.83 per cent reflected viewpoint C. ASCEF filed a fairness doctrine complaint with the commission against CBS based upon these statistics. In its complaint, ASCEF also alleged that it reviewed CBS's news programming other than CBS Evening News for 1972, as well as CBS's news programming for 1973 and parts of 1975 and 1976, and observed the same disproportionate treatment of national security issues. On the basis of its findings, ASCEF contended that CBS had engaged in advocacy journalism on "basic national security issues." ASCEF asked the commission to find the existence of a fairness doctrine violation and order CBS to provide a reasonable opportunity for the expression of A viewpoints.

* * *

Although the Court in *Red Lion* legitimized the fairness doctrine, it recognized the argument that overly ambitious enforcement could lead broadcasters to reduce coverage of controversial public issues, or to cover those issues blandly in an attempt to avoid fairness doctrine complaints. * * * *[S]ee generally Miami Herald Publishing Co. v. Tornillo.* * * * The Court believed this danger was speculative at that time. It warned, however, that the constitutional implications could be reconsidered if the fairness doctrine, in practice, reduced rather than enhanced the volume and quality of coverage of public issues. * * *

In administering the fairness doctrine, the commission wisely attempts to avoid unnecessary risk of "chilling" presentations of controversial issues. The commission is concerned that unduly burdensome regulation will induce broadcasters to decrease vigorous and effective coverage of issues that are the subject of public debate. * * *

At center stage of the commission's regulatory scheme is its determination that broadcasters should have maximum editorial discretion in deciding how to fulfill fairness doctrine obligations. *See* Fairness Report, 48 FCC2d at 8–9, 28–31. In the course of presenting its programming, the broadcaster decides what issue has been discussed, whether an issue is a controversial issue of public importance, what views have been or should be presented on the issue, what format or which spokesmen should be used, and how much time should be allotted to discussion of various views. * * *

A viewer or listener who believes that a broadcaster is not meeting its fairness doctrine obligations must first complain to the broadcaster. *See Broadcast Procedure Manual,* 49 FCC2d 1, 5 (1974). If the broadcaster agrees to rectify the complaint or explains its position to the satisfaction of the complainant, commission intervention is unnecessary. *See id.;* Memorandum Opinion and Order on Reconsideration of the Fairness Report, 58 FCC2d at 696. A viewer or listener who remains dissatisfied may then file a complaint with the commission.

Such a complaint must present prima facie evidence of a fairness doctrine violation. Prima facie evidence consists of specific factual information which, in the absence of rebuttal, is sufficient to show that a fairness doctrine violation exists. Unless the complaint contains such evidence, the commission will not demand a response to a complaint from a broadcaster.

The prima facie evidence requirement is "part of the delicate balance allocating burdens between licensees and complainants": the complainant must produce prima facie evidence of a violation before the broadcaster will be burdened with establishing compliance with the fairness doctrine. * * * The commission explained the reasons for the prima facie evidence requirement in Allen C. Phelps, 21 FCC2d 12, 13 (1969):

> Absent detailed and specific evidence of failure to comply with the requirements of the fairness doctrine, it would be unreasonable to require licensees specifically to disprove allegations. * * The commission's policy of encouraging robust, wide-open debate on issues of public importance would in practice be defeated if, on the basis of vague and general charges of unfairness, we could impose upon licensees the burden of proving the contrary by producing recordings or transcripts of all news programs, editorials, commentaries, and discussion of public issues, many of which are treated over long periods of time. * * *

In its Fairness Primer, 40 FCC at 600, the commission set forth the information necessary to establish a prima facie case of a violation. The complainant should submit specific facts to show

> (1) the particular station involved; (2) *the particular issue of a controversial nature discussed over the air;* (3) the date and time when the program was carried; (4) the basis for the claim that the station has presented only one side of the question; and (5) whether the station had afforded, or has plans to afford, an opportunity for the presentation of contrasting viewpoints. [Emphasis added; footnote omitted.]

* * * This Court has upheld the reasonableness of these requirements. *See* Hale v. FCC, 425 F.2d 556, 558–59 (D.C.Cir. 1970) (per curiam); *see also* Democratic National Committee v. FCC, 460 F.2d at 907–08.

If the commission determines that there is prima facie evidence of a fairness doctrine violation, it will direct the broadcaster to respond to the complaint. * * * The commission finds that prima facie evidence of a violation exists in relatively few cases. During fiscal year 1973, for example, the commission received approximately 2,400 complaints and determined that only 94, or four per cent, required the filing of a response. *See Fairness Report,* 48 FCC2d at 8. When the commission does require a broadcaster to respond to a fairness doctrine complaint, it reviews the response to determine whether the broadcaster's decisions with respect to the issues raised, the views presented, the format and spokesmen used, and the time allotted were made reasonably and in good faith. * * * If the commission determines that the broadcaster acted unreasonably or in bad faith, it will advise the broadcaster to meet its fairness obligations through additional programming. * *

Our function in reviewing a decision made by the commission at any step of the fairness doctrine complaint procedure is to determine "whether the commission's order is unreasonable or in contravention of statutory purpose." Democratic National Committee v. FCC, 460 F.2d at 912 [quoting Neckritz v. FCC, 446 F.2d 501, 502–03 (9th Cir. 1971) (per curiam)]. We are mindful that the commission's task in administering the fairness doctrine is one of great delicacy and difficulty, and that the commission's experience in this matter accordingly is entitled to "great weight." Columbia Broadcasting System v. Democratic National Committee, 412 U.S. at 102.

The commission ruled that ASCEF failed to meet the prima facie evidence requirement because, *inter alia,* it did not base its complaint on a particular, well-defined issue. American Security Council Education Foundation, 63 FCC2d 366, 368 (1977). In dismissing the complaint, the commission stated:

> Although the "national security issue" is defined by the complainant as involving "the basic conflict relationship and the relative military balance between the U.S. and the U.S.S.R." in other parts of the complaint ASCEF refers to the subject of the study as "national defense and foreign policy issues," "Soviet and Chinese political and military objectives," and "domestic foreign policy." Moreover, the data collected in the accompanying study indicates that the complainant's perceived scope of the issue is much broader, encompassing subjects such as Chinese military and non-military policies, Southeast Asia and foreign relations generally.

* * * We affirm the commission's decision that ASCEF failed to base its complaint on a particular, well-defined issue because (1) the indirect relationships among the issues aggregated by ASCEF under the umbrella of "national security" do not provide a basis for determining whether the public received a reasonable balance of conflicting views, and (2), a contrary result would unduly burden broadcasters without a countervailing benefit to the public's right to be informed.

The fairness doctrine, by definition, is issue-oriented. It calls upon broadcasters to provide fair coverage on each controversial public issue discussed in their programs. * * * A fairness doctrine complaint, therefore, must focus the commission's attention on a particular, well-defined issue on which coverage was allegedly imbalanced. Presentation of such an issue is a prerequisite to a determination whether a broadcaster presented a reasonable balance of conflicting views.

ASCEF contends in this court that "national security" is a particular, well-defined issue. * * * ASCEF defines the issue, however, by aggregating under a broad umbrella concept individual issues that it determined were relevant to national security. As ASCEF stated in the material it submitted to the commission, the study which formed the basis of its allegation of imbalance "deal[t] with many U.S. foreign and defense policies" and various "national security issues facing the United States." TV AND NATIONAL DEFENSE at vi, 3. The broadcasts ASCEF studied involved issues as distinct as America's commitment to the North Atlantic Treaty Organization (NATO), detente with China, SALT, amnesty, the Vietnam war, and America's response to the Soviet Union's role in the Middle East.

The issues that ASCEF joined together may have relevance, in varying degrees, to the umbrella concept of "national security." However, their relationships to one another are tangential. The issues analyzed by ASCEF arose independently in time and were largely discussed and acted upon on an independent basis. Consideration of the issues together, rather than individually, would not provide a basis for determining whether the broadcaster presented a reasonable balance of conflicting views because views on any one issue do not support or contradict views on the others.

* * *

If ASCEF had focused on individual issues, it could have identified the actual views expressed instead of superimposing artificial A, B and C viewpoints on the broadcasts studied. The commission then could have determined which, if any, issues had been the subject of imbalanced coverage, and could have ordered a meaningful remedy in the form of additional coverage if necessary. If a broadcaster fulfills fairness obligations on the various issues relating to national security, the fairness doctrine's goal of promoting informed public opinion will be served.

Acceptance of ASCEF's contention that "national security is a particular, well-defined issue" would not only render impossible a determination of reasonable balance *vel non*, but also would place a substantial burden on the broadcaster. A broadcaster must have a clear understanding of the issue forming the basis of a complaint in order to assess its compliance with the fairness doctrine. Unless a broadcaster can recognize the issue "with precision and accuracy," American Security Council Education Foundation, 63 FCC2d at 368, proof of compliance with the fairness doctrine would require the production of "recordings or transcripts of all news programs, editorials, commentaries, and discussion of public issues, many of which are treated over long periods of time." Allen C. Phelps, 21 FCC2d at 13. The commission has wisely determined that imposition of such onerous burdens on broadcasters would, in practice, defeat the policy of "encouraging robust, wide open debate." * * *

Adoption of ASCEF's notion of the particular issue requirement would create a precedent that might well have a serious effect on daily news programming, by inducing broadcasters to forego programming on controversial issues or by disrupting the normal exercise of journalistic judgment in such programming that is aired. The broadcasting of daily news demands the exercise of enormous editorial skill. The news editor must select from the vast array of the day's fast-moving events those which, in the limited amount of broadcast time available, should be presented to the public. In attempting to comply with the fairness doctrine as interpreted by ASCEF, an editor's news judgment would be severely altered. An editor preparing an evening newscast would be required to decide whether any of the day's newsworthy events are tied, even tangentially, to events covered in the past, and whether a report on today's lead story, in some remote way, balances yesterday's, last week's or last year's. Because this requirement would not promote the public interest, the limitations on the exercise of news judgment would be unjustified.

ASCEF's blunderbuss approach to the fairness doctrine would contribute little, if anything, toward achievement of the fairness doctrine's goal while posing all the dangers associated with government administration of fairness obligations. The prima facie case requirements are designed to weed out those complaints that would burden broadcasters without sufficient likelihood that a countervailing benefit will be gained. We uphold the commission's determination that ASCEF failed to present prima facie evidence of a fairness doctrine violation. The commission's decision that no action was warranted on the complaint is therefore

Affirmed.

Wright, Chief Judge, concurring.

* * *

BAZELON, Circuit Judge, concurring:

This case vividly illustrates the substantial constitutional perils inherent in the fairness doctrine. Unlike the personal attack and political editorial components of the fairness doctrine upheld in *Red Lion,* applying the fairness doctrine to daily news coverage poses a serious threat to the independence of the broadcast press.

* * *

In view of the commission's disposition of this fairness complaint, it is unnecessary to consider whether the application of the fairness doctrine to daily news coverage, absent bad faith or deliberate distortion, could ever meet the FCC's statutory mandate or the dictates of the First Amendment. I agree completely with Judge Tamm's careful and thorough analysis of the inadequacies of petitioners' prima facie complaint. We need go no further at this time.

As Judge Tamm notes, the fairness doctrine has traditionally found its justification in the scarcity of broadcast frequencies. As that factual predicate is called into question, courts may well be required to reassess the statutory and constitutional validity of the fairness doctrine's restraints on the independence of broadcast journalism. Such a reexamination, however, must await another day.

Wilkey, Circuit Judge, with whom join MacKinnon and Robb, Circuit Judges, dissenting:

We would reverse the commission's order as an abuse of discretion.

The fairness doctrine requires that broadcasters afford a reasonable opportunity for the presentation of contrasting views on controversial issues of public importance. Although the fairness doctrine has been upheld by the Supreme Court and been given statutory recognition by Congress, "important constitutional questions continue to haunt this area of the law." We would have thought that none of these questions is presented here, for in this case we confront not the merits of ASCEF's fairness complaint, but rather the threshold question of whether ASCEF made out a *prima facie* violation. The majority, however, apparently in view of these constitutional questions, has seen fit to convert the *prima facie* evidence standard into an open-ended "prudential" doctrine allowing the commission to decline jurisdiction over hard cases. Because, unlike the majority , we find the commission's stated reason for avoiding the merits in this case wholly unsatisfying, we dissent.

* * *

The fairness doctrine is itself not directly in question in this case. The issue before us is rather more modest. As stated by the majority, the question is simply whether ASCEF's complaint presented *prima facie* evidence of a violation of the fairness doctrine sufficient to warrant an FCC inquiry to CBS. The commission, with whom the majority agrees, thought that it did not.

We cannot help but sense that something more serious than a mine run question of *prima facie* evidence has been decided today. The tone and rationale of the majority opinion suggest that the wagons are being drawn about the fairness doctrine in a fashion assured to deflect the most worrisome fairness complaints—those, like petitioner's, alleging pervasive and continuous imbalance in the coverage of controversial matters. To be sure, the measurement and remedy of chronic "unfairness" raises novel and acutely difficult constitutional questions. And we mean to intimate no view of the precise shape of this frontier. We do, however, find it most regrettable that the majority does not confront these questions, instead carving an ill-defined safe harbor into which the commission may sail when the waters are rough.

Moreover, as is evident from the majority's rationale, the *prima facie* evidence test is a rather improbable safe harbor. Not only does the majority's position run headlong into the settled application of the *prima facie* standard, but also it infuses the standard with an element of discretion, and hence vagueness, painfully at odds with the precision customarily required of regulation affecting speech. Contrary to the majority's assertion, there is simply no warrant in law for the sort of free-wheeling "balancing" of interests under cover of the *prima facie* evidence test which the court today approves, and thus from which we must dissent.

As previously understood, the *prima facie* evidence test served a limited screening function. The requirement of a *prima facie* showing places the initial burden on the complaining party. This threshold allocation of burdens is rationalized by First Amendment concerns: by preventing broadcasters from being saddled with the task of "answering idle or capricious complaints," the commission endeavors as far as possible to eschew interference with their programming discretion. * * * Assuming, as does the majority, the validity of the *Phelps* criteria, then, the only question is whether the FCC reasonably complied with its own procedural standards in dismissing ASCEF's complaint.

It is possible to distinguish in the FCC's opinion four intertwined reasons in support of its conclusion that ASCEF's complaint failed to establish a *prima facie* case. The commission argued (1) that ASCEF did not define the "controversial issue" with sufficient specificity (2) that ASCEF's evidence did not support its assertion that the programs surveyed were imbalanced; and that ASCEF failed to provide evidence of imbalance in CBS' *overall* programming, either (3) because it did not survey a broad enough spectrum of the network's news and public affairs programs or (4) because it did not continue its study for a long enough period of time. We consider these arguments in turn.

A. DEFINITION OF THE ISSUE.

* * *

The issue ASCEF posed—whether this nation should do more, less, or the same about threats to its national security—is *a specific* issue because it is singular, precisely formulated, and explicit. The issue is admittedly a *large* one, but no larger than other major issues (such as abortion, or cigarette advertising) with which the commission in fairness cases has dealt. The issue is likewise a *multi-faceted* one, but no more multi-faceted than other major issues (such as "women's liberation" or children's advertising) which the commission in fairness cases has considered. An issue's size and complexity, in any event, do not impugn its specificity or singularity, and we think that ASCEF's definition of the issue was plainly sufficient to cross the threshold of a *prima facie* statement here, * * *

We have discovered extremely few cases in which the FCC has cited non-specificity as a reason for throwing out a fairness complaint. * * *

If the position taken by the FCC and this court is sustained, it would be very difficult to make *any major issue* in American life the subject of a fairness complaint. This is shown by the majority's assertion that the relationships of the subject areas comprising the issue of national security to one another are "tangential," and that views on any one of these subject areas could not "conflict with or support" a point of view on another subject area. As indicated above, what the majority defines—ignoring the right of the viewer to define the issue on which he wishes to make a complaint—as obligatory issues are nothing but subject areas or subissues under the viewer-defined issue of national security. Each subject area or subissue is a component part of the overall issue of national security—doing more, less, or the same about perceived threats to our national security. A stated viewpoint on one of these subject areas or subissues "conflicts" with or "supports" another—in a different subject area category—*only* when all the viewpoints on the different subject areas are added up under the overall issue of national security to see what was the predominant CBS viewpoint.

The majority opinion ignores the fact that where a large amount of data is surveyed, *e.g.,* two full years of television broadcasts on the CBS "Evening News," plus additional study of limited periods of time in those and other years, the only way such a large survey can be tabulated is to analyze the defined issue in terms of its component subject areas or subissues.

* * *

There is nothing subtle or indirect about the pleadings upon whose adequacy we are asked to pass. *It is plain that the complaint on its face alleges imbalance concerning issues sufficiently narrow for the majority.* Ironically, petitioner's "inartful" pleading would apparently pass muster in any federal district court. Under the Federal Rules, only a "short and plain statement of the claim" is required, a condition obviously satisfied by petitioner's complaint. "Throwing people out of court" on overly formal pleading grounds is especially inappropriate in the fairness area, where the FCC's enforcement by its own admission depends almost entirely on "complaints received from interested citizens." Surely a complaint by laymen should not be judged by stricter standards than a court would apply to a lawyer's pleading.

While the majority affirmed the commission's dismissal of the complaint by sustaining it on the question of definition of the issue, and thus did not need to consider the other three asserted bases for the commission's dismissal, it is necessary for this dissent to do so, for in our view the other three asserted grounds were as equally devoid of merit as the first.

B. EVIDENCE OF PROGRAMMING IMBALANCE.

* * *

The FCC attacked the evidentiary basis for ASCEF's claim primarily by questioning the methodology of its viewpoint coding system. * * *

The soundness of ASCEF's methodology and the probativeness of its particular examples are questions for the merits, to be resolved on the basis of responsive submissions by the network and the complainant. They are not questions that must unanimously be answered in favor of ASCEF before an inquiry is even made to the licensee. To require that a complainant at the outset demonstrate his case beyond cavil is to transmute the requirement of a *prima facie* showing into an *ex parte* evidentiary decision on the merits. Such a transmutation would render the fairness doctrine, whose enforcement depends almost exclusively on viewer-initiated complaints, a dead letter.

* * *

* * * In this case, a host of "regular viewers" joined together not only in a "statement," but in an elaborate statistical

analysis showing that they had not heard a balanced presentation of viewpoints on national security. By so doing, they "indicated the basis for their claim" of imbalanced programming and satisfied the evidentiary requirements of a *prima facie* case. The commission acted arbitrarily in concluding otherwise.

C. SCOPE OF COMPLAINANT'S STUDY.

* * *

The requirement that a fairness complaint demonstrate, as part of his *prima facie* showing, the *absence* of contrasting viewpoints in a licensee's *overall* programming is, on its face, quite burdensome. Proving a negative proposition is never easy; it is especially difficult when the subject of which the proposition is predicated goes on 24 hours a day, 365 days a year.

* * *

Both the FCC and CBS, finally, suggest that ASCEF is to be faulted for "wait[ing] more than three years" from the time the 1972 programs were broadcast—the programs that formed the core of its study—before filing its complaint. ASCEF finished its report in October 1974 and immediately sent the results to CBS. Six months later CBS delivered its definitive response. ASCEF at once undertook to update its study (May 1975), and updated it again just before filing its complaint (May 1976). To suggest that ASCEF can be scored for dilatoriness on this record is unsupportable. Obviously, the complainant could have sent its study to the commission in 1974 without giving CBS a chance to reply. That, however, would have violated the commission's published rules of fairness doctrine procedure. Alternatively, the complainant could have omitted its recheck for the years 1975 and 1976. In that event, however, the complainant might well have anticipated a rejoinder that its findings were stale or insufficiently thorough. Having first complied with the commission rule and then made its findings thorough and up-to-date, the complainant is now faced with the charge that its complaint is untimely. This is "Kafkaesque" bureaucracy in the ultimate.

In effect, the obligation of the television licensee is the other side of the coin from the obligation of a court. The most essential part of due process for centuries has been recognized by Anglo-American jurists to be *audi alteram partem*—"hear the other side." A licensee's obligation is to permit the other side to be heard by the American public. "The essential basis for any fairness doctrine, no matter with what specificity the standards are defined, is that *the American public must not be left uninformed.*" We recognize in the courts that no justice is done if both sides are not heard; occasionally a court may reach a right result without hearing both sides, but we insist on the procedural due process of hearing both sides to validate the eventual judgment.

In regard to the exercise of free speech on the airways, the only protection under the First Amendment which those citizens not involved in the broadcast industry have is the protection of the fairness doctrine. Since television licenses cannot be granted to all, there must be a rough balance in the points of view presented over the airways. The licensee is the custodian for service to the public. Neither the licensee, nor the FCC, nor any member of the public can be the arbiter of the truth of what is broadcast. But the licensee, and then the FCC if the licensee does not perform, is the arbiter and enforcer of preserving a rough balance in the discussion of controversial issues of public importance over the facilities of each licensee.

As we stressed at the outset, so we emphasize in conclusion, that we express no views on the merits of ASCEF's complaint. Whatever flaws the study on which the complaint was based may ultimately be shown to have, the FCC did not demonstrate them in its opinion ruling on whether the complainant had made a *prima facie* case. Indeed, by the very nature of the issue and the purported exhaustive documentation, it would have been virtually impossible to have done so. We say only that, as a procedural matter, ASCEF specified "an issue" and presented sufficient evidence of imbalance in the network's overall programming on that issue to meet the threshold requirements of a *prima facie* case concerning the issue of national security. Since we anticipate the commission could hardly find the issue of national security not to be "controversial" and "of public importance," as the majority seems to agree, it should, in accordance with its own procedures, have made inquiry of CBS.

We therefore respectfully dissent.

COMMENT

1. In a footnote, in the earlier panel decision reversed by Judge Tamm's preceding *en banc* decision, Judge Wilkey pointed out that former FCC Commissioner Nicholas Johnson once suggested that the *Phelps* doctrine was itself unfair. See American Security Council Education Foundation v. FCC, 4 Med.L.Rptr. 1516, 607 F.2d 438 (D.C. Cir. 1978), cert. den. 444 U.S. 1013 (1980). Why, Commissioner Johnson asked, should the burden be on a member of the public to submit proof of something the licensee has not broadcast but should have? The theory is that less damage is done to First Amendment values if it is relatively difficult for the FCC to review the judgments of broadcast journalism. This is true if the source of First Amendment values is found in the *CBS v. DNC* decision. See text, p. 858. But does this hold true if it is argued, as Judge Wilkey does, that the appropriate source of First Amendment values is in the *Red Lion* case? See text, p. 845.

2. In his panel decision in *American Security Council,* Judge Wilkey observes that his court's reaction to the *Phelps* requirements in the past "was not exactly a ringing endorsement." See also, Democratic National Committee v. FCC, 460 F.2d 556, 559 (D.C.Cir. 1970). Judge Wilkey elaborated on this theme:

> [M]ore recently we have noted the "potential for less than full enforcement" of the fairness doctrine that inheres in [the *Phelps* requirements]. See National Citizens Committee for Broadcasting, 567 F.2d 1095, 1111 and n. 68 [*Pensions* case]. We are not required to address the propriety of the *Phelps* test here.

Is there a legal basis for a challenge to the *Phelps* requirements? Under the Federal Communications Act? On the basis of the First Amendment?

3. In its Fairness Report, 48 FCC2d 1 (1974), the FCC defended the *Phelps* rule as follows:

> [C]omplaints are not forwarded to the licensee for his comments unless they present *prima facie* evidence of a violation. * * * Thus, broadcasters are not burdened with the task of answering idle or capricious complaints. By way of illustration, the commission received some 2400 complaints in fiscal 1973, only 94 of which were forwarded to licensees for their comments.

Can it be argued that the *Phelps* rule is insulating broadcasters *too* well from effective enforcement of the fairness doctrine? Under Judge Tamm's decision in *American Security Council* are the procedural difficulties attendant on proving a fairness complaint now insurmountable as far as a complainant is concerned.

Judge Wilkey in dissent in *American Security Council* remarked in a footnote:

> We wonder if any one of these 94 complaints was better documented and more thoroughly analyzed than the complaint in the instant case. Moreover, we wonder if it can be fairly said that *all* the 94 complaints, to which a response was required, more sharply

and clearly defined the issue than was done in the instant case.

If the *American Security Council* fairness complaint failed to make out a *prima facie* case, is it possible to meet the *prima facie* rule? That question cannot be answered without also reflecting on Judge Wilkey's observation that the fairness complaint in *American Security Council* posed a fundamental challenge to network news judgment overall:

> The tone and rationale of the majority opinion suggest that the wagons are being drawn about the fairness doctrine in a fashion assured to deflect the most worrisome fairness complaints—those, like petitioner's, alleging pervasive and continuous imbalance in the coverage of controversial matters.

Would it have been better for the majority to have rejected the fairness complaint in *American Security Council,* not on the procedural basis it chose, but on the ground that complaints about "editorial slant" were outside the scope of the fairness doctrine?

4. Judge Tamm, usually an advocate of fairness doctrine enforcement (See the *Pensions* case, text, p. 876), advocated a different position in *American Security Council.* What is troubling Judge Tamm?

KENNEDY FOR PRESIDENT COMMITTEE v. FCC

6 MED.L.RPTR. 1705, 636 F.2D 432 (D.C.CIR. 1980).

[EDITORIAL NOTE
The facts of this case as well as the portion of the opinion bearing on § 312(a)(7) are reported in the text, p. 834.]
ROBINSON, Circuit Judge

III. THE FAIRNESS DOCTRINE CLAIM
Petitioner's last claim of entitlement to free broadcast time for Senator Kennedy is founded upon the well-known fairness doctrine. That label shorthands a twofold requirement that broadcasters give adequate coverage to controversial issues of public importance and fairly reflect contrasting viewpoints in that coverage. Petitioner does not impugn the networks' honesty in rejecting its free time request; indeed, it has expressly represented both to the commission and this court its belief that in doing so the networks acted in good faith. Given that, the issue before us is whether the fairness doctrine sustains petitioner's theory that Senator Kennedy was wrongly denied use of the networks' facilities for presentation of his views on the economy.

In the opinion and order affirmed by the commission, the Broadcast Bureau found three fatal flaws in petitioner's fairness complaint. One was a failure to define specifically the particular controversial issue involved. Another was the absence of any evidence indicating that the networks had neglected fairly to present contrasting viewpoints on the publicly-important aspects of the economy in the course of their overall programming. Still another was the asserted impropriety of insisting that a particular individual—Senator Kennedy—serve as a spokesman. We uphold the commission on all counts.

A complaint invoking the fairness doctrine, we have said,

> must present prima facie evidence of a fairness doctrine violation. Prima facie evidence consists of specific factual information which, in the absence of rebuttal, is sufficient to show that a fairness doctrine violation exists * *. [T]he complainant must produce prima facie evidence of a violation before the broadcaster will be burdened with establishing compliance with the fairness doctrine.[155]

---

155. American Security Council Educ. Foundation v. FCC, 607 F.2d 438 (1979) cert. denied 444 U.S. 1013 (1980).

We think the Bureau was adequately justified in concluding that petitioner fell well short of this standard.

In its opinion, the Bureau observed that petitioner "nowhere states with specificity what it believes the controversial issue really is." In its several arguments, petitioner has referred merely to such general topics as "the nation's economic crisis," "inflation, one of the most important issues in the 1980 presidential campaign," and "the economic stewardship" of the president. We agree with the Bureau that a complainant must define the proffered issue with greater particularity. In both its fairness primer and its political broadcasting primer the commission has emphasized the need to identify the issue precisely, and this court has upheld the reasonableness of such requirements.[162] Chief Judge Wright capsulized the requirement when very recently he admonished that the issue "must be * * * highly specific, one that can be defined with precision and can be addressed and responded to directly and efficiently by the broadcaster."

This is not an idle demand. As we have been careful to explain, "[a] broadcaster must have a clear understanding of the issue forming the basis of a complaint in order to assess its compliance with the fairness doctrine. Unless a broadcaster can recognize the issue 'with precision and accuracy,' * * * proof of compliance with the fairness doctrine requires the production of 'recordings or transcripts of all news programs, editorials, commentaries and discussion of public issues, many of which are treated over long periods of time.' "[164] Imprecise formulation of a controversial issue put forth thus can lead to "imposition of such onerous burdens on broadcasters [that] would, in practice, defeat the policy of 'encouraging robust, wide-open debate.' "[165] In final result, "[i]ssue ambiguity in the fairness doctrine context is a certainty to lessen the free flow of information favored by the First Amendment, and is therefore unacceptable."[166] We are not disposed to blink procedural transgressions that jeopardize realization of this lofty goal.

Even if this flaw could be excused, another is immediately perceived. The Bureau pointed out that petitioner "has not presented any evidence that the networks have failed in their overall programming to present contrasting views on the issue of the economic crisis facing America." Moreover, said the Bureau,

> [e]ven if [petitioner] believes that the controversial issue of public importance in this case is defined as which candidate for the Democratic Party's nomination has the soundest economic policies, there is no evidence presented that this issue was discussed in the broadcast. Again, we note that the networks have indicated that they have presented coverage of Senator Kennedy's economic viewpoints.

The fairness doctrine does not operate with the dissective focus of Section 315(a)'s equal-opportunity provision; it "nowhere requires equality but only reasonableness." Intelligent assessment of the nature and caliber of a broadcaster's overall programming obviously cannot be confined to one program, or even to one day's presentations, so a failure to show some fairness deficiency on the whole is necessarily fatal. Wide discretion must be accorded broadcasters in their pro-

162. See, e.g., American Security Council Educ. Foundation v. FCC, *supra*, 607 F.2d at 446–447; Hale v. FCC, 425 F.2d 556, 558–559 (1970); see also, e.g., Democratic Nat'l Comm. v. FCC, 460 F.2d at 907–908.

164. 607 F.2d at 451, first quoting American Security Council Educ. Foundation, 63 FCC2d 366, 368 (1977), and next quoting Allen C. Phelps, 21 FCC2d 12, 13 (1969).

165. 607 F.2d at 451, quoting Allen C. Phelps, 21 FCC2d 12, 13 (1969).

166. 607 F.2d at 458 (Wright, C.J., concurring).

gramming, and while short-run imbalances desirably are to be minimized, it is only in the long run that a well-founded approach to fairness consideration becomes feasible. The objectives of the fairness doctrine are thus best promoted by encouraging "the discussion and presentation of controversial issues in the various broadcast program formats * * * for it is just not practical to require equality with respect to a large number of the issues dealt with in a great variety of programs on a daily and continuing basis." So it is that compliance with the fairness doctrine is to be determined on the basis of the broadcaster's programming in its entirety. As the Bureau foresaw, the alternative would involve the agency "much too deeply in broadcast journalism; [causing it to] become virtually a part of the broadcasting 'fourth estate,' overseeing thousands of complaints that some issue had not been given 'equal treatment.' "

The commission customarily finds a fairness-doctrine violation only upon a showing that the broadcaster's decision was unreasonable or in bad faith, a review standard we have consistently endorsed. Petitioner has not attempted to refute the networks' representations that they have afforded and will continue to afford extensive coverage of all views, including Senator Kennedy's, on questions of economic policy. Particularly in this milieu, we have no cause to overturn the Bureau's holding that "[i]n order for [petitioner] to make out a prima facie case under the Fairness Doctrine, it must offer much more complete evidence than that provided in its April 4 letter [to the commission] that the networks have not balanced their coverage of controversial issues."

Addressing what it deemed to be a third deficiency in petitioner's complaint, the Bureau held that the fairness doctrine did not endow Senator Kennedy with an individual right to broadcast his views on the current economic crisis. Undoubtedly there are cases wherein a particular individual may be an appropriate spokesman for a particular position. Absent that peculiar situation, however, it is the rule that, in the Bureau's words, "under the Fairness Doctrine, no specific individual or group is entitled to present the contrasting viewpoints." Petitioner neither alleged nor endeavored to show that the Senator is uniquely and singularly qualified to represent those who dispute the President's economic leadership or strategies. Certainly with the networks' assertions that they have already presented a wide range of views on the state of the Nation's economy, the fairness doctrine does not confer an individual right on Senator Kennedy to address these issues on the air.

We thus find petitioner's fairness doctrine contentions, as well as those implicating Section 312(a)(7), to be unacceptable. The order under review is accordingly

Affirmed.

The Denial of License Renewal As a "Fairness" Doctrine Sanction: A Case History

1. On July 1, 1970, a radio station in Media, Pennsylvania won the dubious honor of being the first licensee in the history of broadcast regulation to lose its license at renewal time because of failure to comply with the fairness doctrine. Brandywine Main Line Radio, Inc., 24 FCC 2218 (1970).

The operator of the station, Brandywine Main Line Radio, Inc., was wholly owned by the Faith Theological Seminary, presided over by right-wing radio preacher, Carl McIntire.

In 1965, McIntire's group applied for transfer of control of WXUR to them from its owners. Community groups fought this application. The FCC approved the transfer only after the McIntire group pledged that they would provide opportunity for the expression of opposing viewpoints on controversial public issues.

At renewal time citizen groups in the community contended that the McIntire staff had not honored their pledge. The renewal hearing determined that Thomas Livezy, moderator of a WXUR call-in program, "Freedom of Speech," was finally removed by the station management because of his encouragement and apparent approval of the remarks of some of the program's anti-semitic callers.

Under the personal attack rules, WXUR was required to furnish the attack victims notice of the attacks, copies of the transcript, or, lacking that, tapes and summaries of an offer of an opportunity to reply. WXUR, however, had established no procedures for providing notice and response.

The result in the *Brandywine Main Line Radio* case was the product of two of the most influential communications law cases of the 1960s, Red Lion Broadcasting Co. v. FCC, 395 U.S. 367 (1969) and Office of Communications of United Church of Christ v. FCC, 359 F.2d 994 (D.C.Cir. 1960). As a result of *Red Lion,* the fairness doctrine's constitutional status at long last was resolved squarely in its favor. As a result, vigorous enforcement of the Fairness Doctrine was now possible. As a result of the *United Church of Christ* decision, citizen groups now had standing to seek and obtain a hearing before the FCC where the actual performance of the broadcasters seeking renewal could be developed. See this text, p. 938ff. No competing broadcaster was seeking WXUR's license. If citizen groups had not been conferred sufficient standing to compel a hearing, license renewal would have been *pro forma.* Citizen groups had precipitated the first denial of a broadcaster's application for license renewal on the basis of the fairness doctrine in the whole history of broadcast regulation.

Was *Brandywine Main Line Radio* a vindication of the rights of the broadcast audience? Or was WXUR silenced because of the nonconformist right-wing political and fundamentalist views advocated on it? Or was *Brandywine Main Line Radio* a group defamation case which the FCC preferred not to recognize as such? See Barron, *Freedom of the Press for Whom? The Right of Access to Mass Media* 194–208 (1973).

BRANDYWINE–MAINE LINE RADIO, INC. v. FCC

473 F.2D 16 (D.C.CIR. 1972).

TAMM, Circuit Judge * * *

The Fairness Doctrine was, in the commission's view, the central aspect of the litigation. The reason for this is axiomatic—prior to issuing Brandywine's initial license a tremendous amount of concern was expressed to the commission by numerous parties, each fearing that WXUR would fail to comply with the doctrine. Brandywine's response to these fears was clear and apparently forthright—it had promised at the time of the transfer application to fully comply with the doctrine. In point of fact, the decision of the commission had "reiterated the necessity that a licensee serve the public interest by adherence to the Fairness Doctrine, including the personal attack principle."

The commission proceeded to review the record, including fifteen days of monitored broadcasts, and concluded "that Brandywine under its new ownership did not make reasonable efforts to comply with the Fairness Doctrine during the license period." * * *

The commission closed it 23-page opinion by stating:

> We conclude upon an evaluation of all the relevant and material evidence contained in the hearing record, that renewals of the WXUR and WXUR–FM licenses should not be granted. The record demonstrates that Brandywine failed to provide reasonable opportuni-

ties for the presentation of contrasting views on controversial issues of public importance, that it ignored the personal attack principle of the Fairness Doctrine, that the applicant's representations as to the manner in which the station would be operated were not adhered to, that no adequate efforts were made to keep the station attuned to the community's or area's needs and interests, and that no showing has been made that it was, in fact so attuned. *Any one of these violations would alone be sufficient to require denying the renewals here, and the violations are rendered even more serious by the fact that we carefully drew the Seminary's attention to a licensee's responsibilities before we approved transfer of the stations to its ownership and control.*

* * *

This aspect of the case, while not the most troublesome, is clearly the most disturbing to the court. * * *

The changes which took place on WXUR within the very first days following the transfer show a common design on the part of the licensee to engage in deceit and trickery in obtaining a broadcast license. Within nine days a totally unexpected group of seven programs, each of a nature different than those on the typical program schedule, were on the air. These programs, * * * characterized as the "Hate Clubs of the Air," replaced programs which were predominantly entertainment oriented. The speed with which these changes took place can lead the court to one conclusion, and one conclusion only—Brandywine intended to place these controversial programs on the air from the first but feared to so inform the commission lest the transfer application be denied. This approach was foolish.

* * *

Journalists and broadcasters have no monopoly over concern with censorship. The courts, and indeed the American public as a whole, have a tremendous stake in a free press and an informed citizenry. Yet, how can the citizenry remain informed if broadcasters are permitted to espouse their own views only without attempting to fully inform the public? This is the issue of good faith which, unfortunately, a small number of broadcasters refuse to exercise.

* * * The commission has made no attempt to influence WXUR's programming or censor its programming in general or specifically. Had the licensee met the obligations required of it we have no reason to believe that Brandywine would have met with any difficulty. The law places requirements on licensees as fiduciaries. Failure to live up to the trust placed in the hands of the fiduciary requires that a more responsible trustee be found. This is not the public's attempt to silence the trustee—it is the trustee's attempt to silence the public. This is not the public censoring the trustee—it is the trustee censoring the public. Attempting to impose the blame on the commission for its own shortcomings can only be likened to the spoiled child's tantrum at being refused a request by an otherwise overly-benevolent parent.

* * *

In light of the extensive violations found by the commission in the areas of the fairness doctrine, the personal attack rules, and misrepresentation of program plans, the commission refused to renew Brandywine's license. * * *

* * *

Brandywine was given every opportunity to succeed in the broadcast endeavor on which it set out. The commission fulfilled its duty in granting the initial license although it may have proven more popular and expedient to bow to the protestations of Brandywine's detractors. The commission forewarned Brandywine about its fairness doctrine and its personal attack rules and made every effort to explain them. Despite the commission's sanguine outlook it was soon evident that Brandywine refused to comply with those requirements, which are designed to serve the public interest and the broadcast audience. Commission good faith was interpreted as an act of weakness.

The First Amendment was never intended to protect the few while providing them with a sacrosanct sword and shield with which they could injure the many. Censorship and press inhibition do not sit well with this court when engaged in by either the commission or by a defiant licensee. The most serious wrong in this case was the denial of an open and free airwave to the people of Philadelphia and its environs.

Consequently, the opinion of the Federal Communications Commission is

Affirmed.

Bazelon, Circuit Judge, dissenting: In this case I am faced with a *prima facie* violation of the First Amendment. The Federal Communications Commission has subjected Brandywine to the supreme penalty: it may no longer operate as a radio broadcast station. In silencing WXUR, the commission has dealt a death blow to the licensee's freedoms of speech and press. Furthermore, it has denied the listening public access to the expression of many controversial views. Yet, the commission would have us approve this action in the name of the fairness doctrine, the constitutional validity of which is premised on the argument that its enforcement will *enhance* public access to a marketplace of ideas without serious infringement of the First Amendment rights of individual broadcasters.

* * * But if we are to go after gnats with a sledgehammer like the fairness doctrine, we ought at least to look at what else is smashed beneath our blow.

* * *

We once stated that "[I]f the fairness doctrine cannot withstand First Amendment scrutiny, the reason is that to insure a *balanced* presentation of controversial issues may be to insure no presentation, or no vigorous presentation, at all." An examination of the facts of this case and the history of regulation which has brought us here raise for me serious doubts about the correctness of continuing to rely primarily on the fairness doctrine as the proper means of insuring First Amendment goals. The plain truth is that to uphold the commission's fairness ruling, not only must we bless again the road we have travelled in the past, we must go farther; for this will be the first time that the FCC has denied a license renewal because of fairness doctrine obligations.

* * *

I originally authorized issuance of the opinions of the court with my concurrence resting on the narrow ledge of Brandywine's misrepresentations under the Supreme Court's ruling in FCC v. WOKO, Inc. [329 U.S. 223 (1946)]. But it is abundantly clear that the fairness doctrine is the "central aspect" of this case which even touches the core of the applicability of *WOKO.* I have therefore concluded that the great weight of First Amendment considerations cannot rest on so narrow a ledge.

* * * Furthermore, in light of my discussion of the changing relationship between the First Amendment and broadcasting, there is some question as to what the FCC may constitutionally ask of applicants with respect to programming plans and adherence to fairness obligations. Thus the application of *WOKO* raises constitutional questions which cannot be neatly separated, as I had originally thought. * * *

I would remand the entire case to be reviewed in light of the matters discussed in this opinion.

Wright, Chief Judge, with whom Circuit Judge Tamm concurs, *responding:* Since Judge Bazelon's dissent seems to be an attack on the fairness doctrine, in fairness to the reader he should make clear at the outset of his opinion that the court's judgment in this case is not based on the fairness doctrine.

* * *

As shown in my separate opinion, I rested my concurrence in the court's judgment *solely* on the deception ground. Since Judge Tamm would affirm the commission on that ground also, that ground, and that ground alone, forms the basis of our judgment.

* * * I do not think that deception in obtaining a Government license is too narrow a ledge for voiding that license. The Supreme Court flatly so held in FCC v. WOKO, Inc., 329 U.S. 223 (1946), and there are no cases holding otherwise.

COMMENT

1. In his lone dissent, Judge Bazelon raises as many questions about fairness doctrine procedure as he does about the theoretical First Amendment justification for the fairness doctrine. He suggests, for example, that FCC requirements that a "regular procedure for previewing, monitoring, or reviewing its broadcasts" may be too costly for low budget radio stations. The FCC requirements, he suggests, may themselves raise "critical First Amendment questions." Judge Bazelon's suggestion apparently is that rules issued by a government agency which hit hardest at essentially noncommercial stations like WXUR whose reason for existence is to "propagate a viewpoint * * * not being heard in the greater Philadelphia area" may itself constitute a governmental restraint on popularly disapproved expression which is prohibited by the First Amendment.

2. Judge Bazelon makes the point that the fairness doctrine in *principle* was what was upheld in *Red Lion;* FCC applications of the fairness doctrine, on the other hand, were not necessarily upheld. This is, of course, an important and, one should have thought, an obvious distinction. Is this a distinction that gets sufficient attention in Judge Tamm's opinion for the court in *Brandywine?*

From a broader perspective, however, Judge Bazelon's dissent can also be viewed as second thoughts on the wisdom, as a First Amendment matter, of upholding the fairness doctrine even as a principle.

3. Is Judge Bazelon in *Brandywine* trying to apply the "tradition of print journalism" to broadcasting? It is in this sense, perhaps, that his dissent conflicts with the Supreme Court decision in *Red Lion.*

Judge Bazelon says in dissent that the real reason First Amendment scholars like Professor Thomas Emerson support governmental policies like the fairness doctrine is based "solely on the argument of tradition—that government is involved with radio and TV so it must be all right." Judge Bazelon says that "[w]ith all respect to Professor Emerson, this is a distinction without a difference."

Some rejoinder is perhaps in order to this criticism. First, Professor Emerson justifies broadcast regulation on the basis of the limitation of the spectrum rationale. Judge Bazelon, relying on new developments in fields like cable, belittles the significance of this argument. Second, the fact of government involvement could cause involuntary censorship to be viewed as governmental and thus subject to First Amendment obligation. Finally, doesn't the sheer impact of radio and television affect the legal approach used with regard to them as compared with the print media? NBC newsman Bill Monroe was quoted in Judge Bazelon's dissent as follows:

"Radio and television are at bottom, instantaneous, warmblooded press."

One of the implicit or unarticulated bases for broadcast regulation may well be the greater assumed impact and immediacy on the popular mind of the electronic as compared with the print media. In other words, there are other rationalizations for broadcast regulation besides either the limitation of the spectrum rationale or the access for ideas rationale, although evidence supporting those rationalizations is still sketchy.

Fairness, Group Defamation and Broadcasting

If the FCC had chosen to do so, the decision in the *Brandywine* case might well have been based on the issue of group defamation. It is by no neans clear, however, that group libel is responsive to resolution through enforcement of the fairness doctrine.

The renewal hearing in the *WXUR* case is illustrative. Offending programs on WXUR had offered time to spokesmen for the racial and religious groups attacked. But these invitations were declined because the groups involved did not wish to further reply to the libels or to dignify them with a response. The disinclination of minority groups to accept reply time as redress for group libel in broadcasting is hardly without precedent. Thus, when a California radio station sought renewal, the Anti-Defamation League of the B'nai B'rith opposed renewal on the ground that the station carried a program by a commentator, Richard Cotten, who had identified Judaism with socialism. The station had offered the ADL equal free time to respond. The ADL told the FCC that it did not want to reply. The FCC permitted the California station, KTYM, to keep its license, and the federal court of appeals affirmed. Anti-Defamation League of B'nai B'rith, Pacific Southwest Regional Office v. FCC, 403 F.2d 169 (D.C. Cir. 1968).

Judge Burger, now Chief Justice Burger, spoke for the court in the *ADL* case, and he relied heavily on the concurring opinion in the FCC decision of Commissioner Lee Loevinger. Loevinger sharply disagreed with the *ADL* position that group libel should be classified along with hard-core obscenity as unprotected speech. See Beauharnais v. Illinois, 343 U.S. 250 (1950). See text, p. 279.

Such a classification, Loevinger said, would constitute censorship. In a concurring opinion in the court of appeals, Judge Wright said that cancellation of a station's license for libeling an individual would not be censorship but that group libel was a different matter. Furthermore, Judge Wright questioned the capacity of the fairness doctrine to meet the problem of group libel.

2. Still another group defamation problem in broadcasting was the so-called *WBAI* case. In December 1968 and January 1969, WBAI–FM, a Pacifica radio station in New York City, carried two programs with anti-Semitic subject matter. The programs were symptomatic of the bitter dispute over "community control" of schools that arose in Brooklyn, New York at that time between the black community and the teachers union. The FCC declined to make any investigation. The FCC said it was satisfied that WBAI had afforded reasonable opportunity for the presentation of conflicting viewpoints. The FCC did concede, however, that there were occasions when speech was so enmeshed with "burgeoning violence" that FCC intervention would be appropriate. See In re Complaint of United Federation of Teachers, New York, N.Y., 17 FCC2d 204 (1969).

If group libel is handled as a fairness doctrine problem, the ultimate remedy for group defamation will be to require the broadcaster to make sure that group libel does not go unanswered. Unfortunately, as Judge Wright who suggested this solution in *ADL* knows all too well, such reply time is understandably regarded as unwelcome by minority groups who regard the reply as merely helping to publicize the attack and to add to the intragroup conflict which the original attack was designed to provoke.

3. On the basis of the majority opinion in *Brandywine,* it is apparent that the

group defamation practices of WXUR were a serious factor in the massive citizen group effort to persuade the FCC to deny WXUR's license renewal application. But the group defamation problem, however large it may have loomed in stimulating the movement against renewal of WXUR, does not loom very large in the formal rationalization for the result reached either by the FCC or by the court.

In fact, just a count of judicial votes at the court of appeals level shows that the real basis for decision in *Brandywine* isn't even the Fairness Doctrine but is instead the misrepresentation issue. The only theory which the two judges of the three-judge appellate panel which reviewed the FCC decision in *Brandywine* agreed upon was that deception in obtaining a broadcast license is justification for denying renewal of that license. FCC v. WOKO, Inc., 329 U.S. 223 (1946).

4. Since the personal attack rules explicitly refer to "an attack * * * made upon the honesty, character, integrity or like personal qualities of an identified person or *group*" (see text, p. 846), can the personal attack rules be used as a remedy for group defamation in broadcasting?

The Fairness Doctrine and the Personal Attack Rule: Do They Apply to Television "Comedy"?

5. The issue of whether organizations representing ethnic groups can use the personal attack rule to counteract ethnic slurs arose in Polish American Congress v. FCC, 520 F.2d 1248 (7th Cir. 1975). (See text p. 900.) The Polish American Congress filed a complaint with the FCC that a "comedy" routine on ABC's Dick Cavett show constituted a personal attack "on the character, intelligence, hygiene or appearance of members of the Polish American community, an identifiable group." The complaint contended that such defamatory attacks represented a "warped and negative point of view which has enormous influence on the viewing audience." Although the personal attack rule was held not applicable on the ground that the offending skit did not involve a controversial issue of public importance, the Broadcast Bureau of the FCC said that the personal attack rule did not apply for another reason:

> The statement of a particular view, however strongly or forcefully made, does not necessarily constitute a personal attack. The Port of New York Authority, 25 FCC2d 417 (1970). To qualify under the commission's rule, the attack must reflect upon the "honesty, character, integrity or like personal qualities" of a person or group, and not merely reflect upon ability, knowledge or like intellectual or motor skills. See In re Complaint by Polish-American Congress, 42 FCC2d 1100 (1973).

The FCC agreed with its Broadcast Bureau that the personal attack rules did not apply to the Polish jokes on the Dick Cavett show because there was no "attack on those personal qualities bearing on the moral rectitude or personal credibility of the named individual or group." 46 FCC2d 124 (1974). See In re Complaint of Thaddeus L. Kowalski, Esq., and Anti-Defamation League Commission of the Polish American Congress, Inc., 46 FCC2d 124 (1974). The court of appeals agreed with the FCC that the personal attack rule did not apply since the jokes did not involve discussion of a controversial issue of public importance.

Did the FCC take too limited an interpretation of the "personal attack" rule? The Polish National Congress contended in its complaint that the "unanswered 'Polack joke' * * * belittle[s] the Polish American in our society." While the FCC ruled that Polish jokes "perpetuating 'a dumb Polack image' " did not constitute a personal attack under the language of that rule, the FCC did not consider whether the reference to groups in the personal attack rule was intended to embrace racial or ethnic groups. Since the point was not discussed, it could be argued that by implication the FCC has accepted the view that ethnic and racial groups may invoke the personal attack rule if otherwise applicable. If this is true, a question arises as to the criteria that should be used to identify a group sufficiently representative to be permitted to request a right of reply on behalf of an ethnic group which asserts it has been attacked or defamed on television.

THE ENFORCEMENT POWERS OF THE FCC

In enforcing the Federal Communications Act and the rules, policies, and regulations issued thereunder, the FCC has tremendous discretion in terms of the range and severity of the sanctions available to it. Thus, in *FCC v. Pacifica Foundation,* text, p. 920, the Supreme Court, per Justice Stevens, quoted with apparent approval the FCC's statement of its enforcement powers in Pacifica, 56 FCC2d 94, at 96 fn. 3 (1975); "The commission noted: 'Congress has specifically empowered the FCC to (1) revoke a station's license, (2) issue a cease and desist order, or (3) impose a monetary forfeiture for a violation of Section 1464, 47 U.S.C.A. §§ 312(a), 312(b), 503(b)(1)(E). The FCC can also (4) deny license renewal or (5) grant a short term renewal, 47 U.S.C.A. §§ 307, 308.'"

Enforcement by Letter

One regulatory procedure used by the FCC is enforcement by letter. This usually takes place when a third party protests some programming decision by a licensee. The commission then dispatches a letter to the licensee stating its view of how the matter should be dealt with. There is some criticism of this method since it is very difficult to get judicial review of the course of action outlined by the FCC in a letter. These letters of reprimand, which is what they often are, constitute the so-called "raised eyebrow" technique. Do you see why such review would be difficult? [8]

Cease and Desist Orders

From a reading of the Federal Communications Act one might expect that § 312(b) would play an important role in enforcing the commission's programming standards. That provision states:

> Where any person (1) has failed to operate substantially as set forth in a license, (2) has violated or failed to observe any of the provisions of this act, * * * or (3) has violated or failed to observe any rule or regulation of the commission authorized by this act or by a treaty ratified by the United States, the commission may order such person to cease and desist from such action.

Cease and desist orders have not been granted on a widespread basis by the

8. Sometimes FCC authority is deemed to have been exercised even though formal institutional action, even that evidenced by a letter, is not present. Informal action may be said to have been taken by a new statement of policy which the FCC chairman says should be taken by the industry in the future. The industry may think the new policy is contrary to law, but its informal and undefined character may make it difficult to get a court to review it. See Writers Guild of America, West, Inc. v. FCC, 423 F.Supp. 1064 (C.D.Calif.1976) which involved the controversial family viewing policy which had been adopted by the National Association of Broadcasters (NAB). FCC Chairman Wiley was deemed by the court to have informally, through a speech and otherwise, pressured the networks and the NAB into adopting the family viewing policy. The court held that under the circumstances the Writers Guild was entitled to obtain judicial review of the First Amendment validity of the family viewing policy even though there had been no prior formal FCC proceeding adopting the policy. See Cowan, *See No Evil: The Backstage Battle Over Sex and Violence in Television* (1978).

commission. The commission nevertheless professes to be willing to use them. An example of their use in a "fairness" context is provided by Richard Sneed, 15 P. & F. Radio Reg. 158 (1967). In that case a minister, objecting to the cancellation of a religious program that had been carried by the station, asked the commission to issue a cease and desist order to restrain the licensee from dropping the program. The commission refused to issue the cease and desist order and stated that the anti-censorship provision of the Federal Communications Act (§ 326) forbade it from ordering a licensee to broadcast any particular program. But what is significant about the case is that the commission did say that it had authority to issue cease and desist orders when its programming standards had been violated.

The cease and desist order device was actually used by the FCC in Mile High Stations, Inc., 28 FCC 795, 20 P. & F. Radio Reg. 345 (1960). In that case the FCC first issued an order requiring an AM radio station licensee to show cause why its license should not be revoked because it repeatedly had carried off-color remarks. The FCC retreated from that course of action and ultimately issued a cease and desist order against any similar broadcasts in the future.

Over the years the FCC has had to struggle with a limited budget and insufficient staff. Do you think, these limitations have anything to do with the infrequent use of the cease and desist order by the commission?

Denial of the Application for License Renewal: The Death Penalty

The most severe sanction in the FCC's enforcement arsenal is the commission's power to deny an application for license renewal. The industry calls this particular sanction "the death penalty." As a sanction, it exists more as a specter than a reality since it is rarely used. The FCC, of course, may also revoke licenses under specified circumstances. See, for example, the discussion of 47 U.S.C.A. § 312(a)(7) permitting revocation of a license where there has been willful failure to provide "reasonable access" to broadcasting to a "legally qualified candidate for federal elective office." See generally, text, p. 815. A halfway house between outright denial of the application for renewal is to grant an offending party a short-term renewal for one year rather than the three-year renewal authorized under the act. See 47 U.S.C.A. § 307(d). See *Office of Communication of the United Church of Christ v. FCC,* text, p. 938.

Is denial of a petition for license renewal a meaningful sanction any longer in communications law? Longer license terms have been accorded broadcast licensees, particularly television licensees. See text, p. 769. Furthermore, relatively recently, the Supreme Court has spoken sympathetically of the licensee's legitimate renewal expectancy which was deemed to be implicit in the structure of the Federal Communications Act. See *FCC v. National Citizens Committee for Broadcasting,* text p. 959.

The case which follows is an infrequent but powerful reminder that the FCC's most severe sanction, at least in the industry's view—denial of the license renewal application—is sometimes inflicted.

RKO GENERAL, INC. V. FCC

7 MED.L.RPTR. 2313, 670 F.2D 215 (D.C.CIR. 1981).

MIKVA, Circuit Judge:

The Federal Communications Commission (FCC) denied renewal of television licenses to RKO General, Inc. (RKO) in Boston, Los Angeles, and New York City. Renewal of the Boston license was denied because of the finding that RKO lacked the requisite character to be a licensee of that station. The denial of license renewals in Los Angeles and New York City followed from the commission's earlier determination that the Boston finding would be *res judicata* in those proceedings.

RKO is a wholly owned subsidiary of General Tire & Rubber Company (General Tire). General Tire, by its own admission, has engaged in a staggering variety of corporate misconduct. During the Boston proceeding, RKO withheld evidence of General Tire's conduct from the FCC, either because RKO sought to protect its parent or because the parent withheld information from the subsidiary in order to protect itself. The commission, in turn, has disqualified RKO after years of delay in an opinion that is multifarious at best. We reject most of the grounds that the FCC used to justify its denial of RKO's license renewals. We affirm the commission's decision that RKO lacked candor, but on a quite narrow ground that cannot automatically be applied to any other proceeding. Accordingly, although we uphold denial of the Boston license renewal, the proceedings in Los Angeles and New York City must be remanded.

* * *

The need for a remand and further action by the commission is discomfiting in a fifteen-year-case, but this extended proceeding has hardly been a model for the administrative process. We admonish all parties to get on with the task.

RKO appealed from all three orders denying license renewal, and the appeals were consolidated by this court.

At the outset, we hold that the FCC has stated at least three independent grounds for its ultimate finding that RKO should be disqualified as a broadcast licensee in Boston. The decision states that RKO's reciprocal dealings "alone" require disqualification, that RKO's "willful and repeated [financial] misrepresentation warrants disqualification by itself," and that "perhaps of greatest importance, RKO has demonstrated a persistent lack of candor with the commission in these proceedings."

* * *

* * * We uphold the commission's disqualification of RKO in the Boston proceeding because we conclude that the decision's ultimate basis, RKO's lack of candor before the FCC, fully and independently supports that judgment. * * *

The record fully supports the commission's finding that RKO did not display full candor before the commission during the period from late 1975 to July 1976. * * *

* * *

* * * In spite of an SEC investigation that was rapidly gathering steam, and in spite of the fact that its qualifications as a licensee were at issue before the FCC, RKO failed to come forward with a candid statement of relevant facts. RKO did not inform the FCC that the SEC had issued a formal order of investigation in February 1976, even though this suggested the seriousness of the charges against General Tire. RKO did not advise the FCC of the SEC's preliminary findings until May 14, 1976, despite the fact that General Tire had advised its stockholders of these preliminary findings in February when it released its 1975 Annual Report. RKO did not advise the FCC until May 1976 that General Tire's own internal investigation demonstrated that many of the SEC concerns were valid, even though * * * General Tire's 10–K Report [had been submitted] the previous March. RKO never once attempted to amend or supplement its earlier pleadings with the FCC, despite a growing awareness of the facts that General Tire would later admit in its Special Report. These instances involve a lack of candor through omission. Whether or not RKO would have had an obligation to come forward with these facts under other circumstances, it could not have doubted their relevance once the filings and petitions of the intervenors put these ques-

tions before the commission. We need not decide whether RKO's pleadings were affirmatively misleading—it is enough to find that they did not state the facts.

The record suggests that RKO had ample motive for its failure to act with total candor during this period. There are numerous indications that General Tire initially decided to oppose the SEC investigation and did not begin to cooperate with that agency until sometime in the spring of 1976. Clearly, it would have been pointless for General Tire to resist the SEC inquiry at one level while RKO came forward with damaging evidence against General Tire before the commission. * * But such conjecture is not relevant, because the documents speak for themselves. It is also unnecessary to show that RKO officials had actual knowledge in early 1976 of the improprieties and illegalities to which General Tire later admitted, or that RKO officials willfully intended to misrepresent these facts to the FCC. Whether RKO sought to protect its parent, or whether the parent withheld information from the subsidiary in order to protect itself, the result is the same. We cannot improve on the language of FCC counsel: "It is obvious that where a complete disclosure of facts will militate against the interests of this organization, the commission will be deprived of that information. It is irrelevant where in the RKO-General Tire organizational structure this breakdown in candor first occurs. In the end, RKO, as the public trustee, is responsible for the reliability of the information and representations furnished by it to the commission." * * *

RKO objects to the FCC's finding on a variety of grounds. First, it contends that "there is not a shred of evidence that * * the commission was in fact 'misled'." * * Such an argument has no pertinence to this appeal, as the Supreme Court observed forty years ago:

> The fact of concealment may be more significant than the facts concealed. The willingness to deceive a regulatory body may be disclosed by immaterial and useless deceptions as well as by material and persuasive ones. We do not think it is an answer to say that the deception was unnecessary and served no purpose.

FCC v. WOKO, Inc., 329 U.S. 223, 227 * * (1946). As the commission correctly emphasizes, it must rely on the applicants who come before it for the truth of their representations; it cannot countenance willingness to mislead simply because there is no evidence that the commission was in fact misled.

Equally unpersuasive is RKO's objection that its decision not to inform the commission of the SEC investigation was made on advise of counsel. * * * In modern America, parties communicate with administrative agencies almost exclusively through lawyers, but this is all the more reason why we cannot assume that RKO did not know what its lawyers were saying—particularly when the number of pleadings and other opportunities for dissembling were as great as recounted above. It is not credible that lawyers were running the strategy of RKO and General Tire to the exclusion of all the corporate chiefs.

RKO's most persuasive objection to the FCC finding that it lacked candor is that the finding was made without giving RKO formal notice and a hearing on the charge. The FCC acknowledges a "technical failure to issue such a formal designation order," * * * and admits that "[i]n the normal case a hearing probably would have been warranted." * * * We conclude, however, that RKO's conduct has been so egregious and so conspicuous that we cannot say the FCC's decision was an abuse of its authority. No purpose would have been served in this case by extending administrative proceedings that had already moved well into their second decade. The evidence of RKO's lack of candor was obvious from the documents that RKO itself had submitted to the FCC in this proceeding, as the applicants competing with RKO had been arguing for years. The commission needed only to draw legal conclusions from "facts already known." Lakewood Broadcasting Service, Inc. v. FCC, 478 F.2d 919, 924 (D.C.Cir. 1973). In this context, the FCC was not required to designate the candor issue and reopen the proceeding for an evidentiary hearing that would have served no purpose. * * * This is especially true where RKO itself had urged that there was no need to reopen the proceeding because resolution of * * * claims "turns on inferences and legal conclusions" to be drawn from facts already before the commission. * * *

In reaching this determination, we start with the emphatic differences between a broadcast applicant before the FCC and one who faces the possibility of punishment. RKO has suffered a hardship as a result of the FCC's action, but it has not been punished; denial of a renewal application "is not a penal measure." FCC v. WOKO, Inc., 329 U.S. at 228, 67 S.Ct. at 215. As the decision explains, the FCC's purpose is not to punish licensees for past wrongs, but to ensure that these "fiduciaries of a great public resource" will "satisfy the highest standards of character commensurate with the public trust that is reposed in them." * * * A broadcast license is less a property right than a privilege, Mansfield Journal Co. v. FCC, 180 F.2d 28, 35 (D.C.Cir. 1950), and retention is not automatic but must be earned. * * *

* * * The FCC has an affirmative obligation to license more than 10,000 radio and television stations in the public interest, each required to apply for renewal every three years. * * * As a result, the commission must rely heavily on the completeness and accuracy of the submissions made to it, and its applicants in turn have an affirmative duty to inform the commission of the facts it needs in order to fulfill its statutory mandate. This duty of candor is basic, and well known. * * * The commission has said before that "no specific misrepresentation or lack of candor issues are needed to consider these matters, since the commission always has authority to deny a license or application where the record reveals such misconduct." * * *

* * *

* * * When a statute dictates that parties receive notice and a hearing, of course, the provision of those basic procedural rights is not left to be decided by administrative "flexibility" or "discretion." For that reason, RKO contends that Section 309 of the act, 47 U.S.C. § 309 (1976), requires a hearing prior to the denial of a renewal application even when there are no substantial or material questions of fact. * * * But such a literal approach to the words of the act cannot govern this case, in which RKO had already been the subject of FCC proceedings that had lasted for years. The question is not whether RKO was entitled to a hearing under Section 309, but whether during the course of agency proceedings in which this candor issue arose in the most obvious and unavoidable manner, the commission was required to call a halt to its proceedings, designate the issue formally, and begin again.

We conclude that such an approach in this case would not have promoted "the proper dispatch of business" and "the ends of justice." At some point in any administrative process, someone must determine whether the remaining issues are factual or legal, and whether hearings that have already been held must be supplemented by further proceedings. * * * In Ranger [v. FCC, 294 F.2d 240 (D.C.Cir. 1961)], we held that Section 309 requires a hearing only if, "with the required information before it," the FCC still cannot make a determination as to whether granting the application would be in the public interest. *Id.* at 242. We thereby recognized the FCC's authority to determine without an evidentiary hearing whether applicants had submitted "the required information." Cf. Guinan v. FCC, 297 F.2d 782, 785 (D.C.Cir. 1961) (FCC need not designate comparative hearing "once it has been established that one of the competing applicants is basically unqualified" because of frequency interference). The commission's discretion should also be respected in this case, in which RKO has obviously failed to supply the information required for consideration of its merit in the public interest.

* * *

* * * RKO does not for a moment contend that it has in fact been candid with the commission, nor do we see how it possibly could. No evidence remains to be introduced; no witnesses have been denied a chance to speak. There are no further issues to try. The FCC has not assumed the answers to any questions of fact, but has simply examined uncontested and uncontestable documents that are in the record at RKO's own election.

Because the commission had "so perfect a knowledge" of the RKO misconduct that was evident from the documents directly before it, we cannot say that the commission's action was erroneous. * *

Our decision to affirm the FCC's action should not be read to include situations not covered by this unique record. The commission concedes that "this case is unprecedented," * * * and we expect that successors if any will be rare. Before the FCC can take action of this sort in the future, we believe that at least three conditions must be met in order to protect the parties. First, not only must the misconduct occur directly before the agency, but it should be of such a blatant and unacceptable dimension that its existence cannot be denied. The FCC has satisfied itself that this is the case with regard to RKO, whose lack of candor "is abundantly clear." * * * Second, although formal notice may not always be necessary, it should be evident that the party has some form of actual notice of the conduct said to be at issue, and must not be prejudiced by surprise. Finally, the party must be given an "opportunity to speak in [its] own behalf in the nature of a right of allocution." Groppi v. Leslie, 404 U.S. at 504. * * * The procedure adopted by the FCC in this case satisfies these requirements, at least insofar as the Boston renewal is concerned. RKO does not contend that it was prejudiced by the lack of notice, for it undoubtedly had actual notice of the candor issue, as the pleadings filed prior to the commission's decision demonstrate. * * *

RKO does not contend that it was denied any opportunity to present for the commission's determination any matter of fact or law, or that the commission has not given all matters submitted by RKO due and full consideration. * * * RKO had a full opportunity to speak in its own behalf, and exercised it in pleadings, proffers of proof, and oral argument before the commission. We cannot say that the FCC abused its discretion by not giving RKO a formal hearing on issues arising from RKO's conduct during the initial proceeding. Section 309 was not intended by Congress to reward delay and concealment that disserves the public interest. "Congress did not intend by this section of the statute to require the formality of commission consideration of and [re]hearing on an application in which the signatory obviously fails in major material respects to abide by the regulations." Ranger v. FCC, 294 F.2d at 243. * * * The FCC's denial of the Boston license renewal must therefore be affirmed.

The narrow basis of our decision concerning RKO's Boston license illustrates why the FCC may not deny license renewals in Los Angeles and New York City simply because it happened to condition those proceedings on the Boston outcome.

RKO's lack of candor during the Boston proceeding justifies its disqualification there because the misconduct took place directly before the trier of fact and has bearing on its general character, but the same cannot be said of the Los Angeles and New York City proceedings. The latter was conditioned on the Boston outcome in order to avoid making the parties "relitigate those issues" that had already been specified with regard to Boston. * * By contrast, the former had been conditioned on the reciprocity issue only, in order to "enable the commission to proceed with the Los Angeles matter and bring it to a conclusion with no risk to the public interest." * * * The FCC could not have known, when it conditioned either of these proceedings as it did, that the Boston outcome would turn on a lack of candor issue that had not even been designated in the Boston proceeding. RKO's misconduct did not occur directly before the trier of fact in either the Los Angeles or New York City proceedings. Accordingly, these decisions must be remanded to the commission for further consideration as it deems appropriate.

This conclusion is buttressed by the commission's own discussion of what effect, if any, RKO's Boston disqualification should have on its other broadcast licenses. In an order released on November 26, 1980, the FCC designated thirteen RKO stations for hearing, but held those proceedings in abeyance until resolution of this appeal. RKO General, Inc., 82 FCC2d 291, appeal pending sub nom. New South Media Corp. v. FCC, 644 F.2d 37 (D.C.Cir. 1980). One purpose of the separate proceeding will be to allow RKO "to introduce evidence on meritorious programming with respect to the 13 other stations and any other mitigating evidence with respect to the remaining licenses."

Now that the issues in the Boston proceeding have been sorted out, the same treatment is appropriate for RKO's New York City and Los Angeles licenses. The judgment that RKO showed a lack of candor in the Boston proceeding is *res judicata,* of course, and is not subject to collateral attack in these subsequent proceedings. The commission may give that finding whatever weight it considers appropriate. Indeed, it may well be that such a finding is inconsistent with a licensee holding a license anywhere, although that decision is for the commission in the first instance. At the same time, our remand of these proceedings is more than just an empty exercise. Each of RKO's renewal applications arises in different contexts and presents different levels of complexity. For example, the Los Angeles renewal was tentatively granted in 1973 subject only to future reciprocity findings. Because we have rejected reciprocity as a legitimate basis for disqualification of RKO in Boston, the Los Angeles situation may seem quite different when that proceeding is remanded. * * * These stations are entitled to an opportunity to appear directly before the commission and to argue that they deserve different treatment than RKO's Boston station. * * *

This opinion will not close a sorry chapter in the history of American communications law. We must remand the Los Angeles and New York City proceedings because the FCC has not yet provided a principled explanation for RKO's disqualification as a licensee of those stations. The FCC's findings that RKO intentionally misrepresented financial information and engaged in unlawful reciprocal trade practices cannot stand, for one was reached without notice or hearing and the other constitutes an ex post facto application of new standards to conduct that is long past.

We affirm the FCC's decision in the Boston proceeding, however, because the commission's finding that RKO displayed an egregious lack of candor in that proceeding does not suffer from either of these infirmities. During an administrative review that had already lasted for years, the FCC suddenly was confronted by documentary evidence establishing beyond doubt that RKO had been less than candid with the commission in the very proceeding under way. The FCC could observe all material facts for itself, simply by comparing the documents that had already been submitted with those that were now before it.

The denial of a license renewal to a major licensee in a major market is of manifest moment and financial impact. The FCC's decision has not been reviewed callously, and we have tried not to lose sight of the difficult issues in this case by sweeping the reasoning of the commission under a rug of agency expertise or administrative convenience. The record presented to this court shows irrefutably that the licensee was playing the dodger to serious charges involving it and its parent company. The commission was entitled to ask whether such conduct, however convenient for corporate purposes, was consistent with the candor required of an applicant for a license to the public airwaves. We believe the commission's answer is not open to doubt. The disqualification of RKO as a licensee of WNAC in Boston is affirmed.

It is so ordered.

COMMENT

1. As should become clear from the materials in this chapter, denial of a license renewal application is an unusual event in broadcast regulation. Although licensing is not given a specific preference in the license renewal process in the Federal Communications Act, the "living law" certainly supports the view that such a preference for incumbency exists. Why does the FCC exercise such solicitude toward the applicant who has been licensed before?

If the relatively few license renewal applications which have been denied are examined, it will be seen that misrepresentation by the licensee to the FCC is apparently deemed to constitute sin of a fundamental kind. For cases where misrepresentation played a significant role in denial of a license renewal application, see *Robinson v. FCC* (arose in an obscenity context), text, p. 934 and *Brandywine-Main Line Radio, Inc. v. FCC* (arose in a fairness context). See text, p. 894. Why is "misrepresentation" a preferred ground for denial of a license renewal application compared to denial on the basis of violation of a programming standard?

2. Some highlights in the aftermath of the *RKO* decision should be of interest. On January 18, 1982, a petition for rehearing *en banc* was denied by the United States Court of Appeals. RKO then filed a motion to stay enforcement of its decision pending Supreme Court review. The motion was rejected. On June 6, 1982, FCC issued an order stating that RKO's operating authority would expire on March 3, 1982.

RKO then filed a motion with the FCC requesting that RKO should not be required to cease operation of WNAC–TV prior to the completion of *all* judicial review, i.e., Supreme Court action on RKO's petition for certiorari. RKO pleaded that the station should be kept from going dark.

The New England Television Corp. (NETV), a competitor, opposed the RKO motion for a continuance of operating authority, asserting that RKO's request was the very relief which the court of appeals had desired.

On February 25, 1982, the FCC decided the issue of RKO's continuance against it. RKO General, Inc. (WNAC–TV), 89 FCC2d 361 (1982). But the channel was not allowed to go dark. The FCC found NETV to be a qualified licensee and issued a conditional construction permit to NETV. The FCC also ruled that the public interest would best be served by authorizing RKO to operate WNAC–TV until fourteen days after NETV gave notice to the FCC that all the conditions of its construction permit were satisfied and that it was ready to commence operations. Among the conditions included in the construction permit was that the Supreme Court issue a decision either denying certiorari or affirming the FCC's decision not to renew RKO in Boston.

On April 19, 1982, the Supreme Court denied RKO's petition for writ of certiorari. RKO General, Inc. v. FCC, 456 U.S. 927 (1982). The foregoing facts illustrate that a license renewal controversy is indeed a battle *royal*. The license renewal applicant does not go gently into the dark. See generally Byrne, *RKO General: Some Lessons To Be Learned,* 27 St.Louis U.L.Rev. 145 (1983).

THE PROBLEM OF REGULATING OBSCENITY IN BROADCAST PROGRAMMING

The Basis for Regulation

1. An area of considerable obscurity in broadcast regulation has been the field of obscenity. Obscenity is a difficult problem to resolve in broadcasting because the FCC has to reconcile two statutes which appear to contradict each other: 47 U.S.C.A. § 326 of the Federal Communications Act which prohibits censorship and 18 U.S.C.A. § 1464 of the criminal code which prohibits the broadcasting of "any obscene, indecent, or profane language."

Section 326 of the Federal Communications Act states:

> Nothing in this chapter shall be understood or construed to give the commission the power of censorship over the radio communications or signals transmitted by any radio station, and no regulation or condition shall be promulgated or fixed by the commission which shall interfere with the right of free speech by means of radio communication.

The Federal Criminal Code, 18 U.S.C.A. § 1464, provides as follows:

> Whoever utters any obscene, indecent, or profane language by means of radio communication shall be fined not more than $10,000 or imprisoned not more than two years, or both.

In 1978, the Supreme Court in *FCC v. Pacifica Foundation, Inc.*, text, p. 920, set forth the legislative history of the two provisions and pointed out that 18 U.S.C.A. § 1464 and 47 U.S.C.A. § 326 had a common origin. The Court insisted that the two statutes were not in conflict:

> A single section of the 1927 (Radio) act is the source of both the anticensorship provision and the [c]ommission's authority to impose sanctions for the broadcast of indecent or obscene language. Quite plainly, Congress intended to give meaning to both provisions. Respect for that intent requires that the censorship language be read as inapplicable to the prohibition on broadcasting obscene, indecent, or profane language.

The broadcaster can be punished directly for violation of 18 U.S.C.A. § 1464 by the United States Department of Justice. Such suits are tried in the federal courts. They are more serious than complaints brought by the FCC since they carry a risk of imprisonment.

2. In the *WUHY* case, which follows, the FCC gave some attention to regulation of obscenity in broadcasting. A licensee was fined for "indecency" in broadcasting in *WUHY.* Notice that the licensee was not fined directly under 18 U.S.C.A. § 1464 but under a provision of the Federal Communications Act, 47 U.S.C.A. § 503(b)(2), which authorizes the FCC to punish infractions of 18 U.S.C.A. § 1464 by exacting forfeitures (fines) provided that a notice of apparent liability is given the offending

party. An example of such a notice is found in the opinion reported below.

In Illinois Citizens Committee for Broadcasting v. FCC, 515 F.2d 397 (D.C.Cir. 1975), more fully discussed in the text at p. 917, Judge Bazelon in a separate opinion questioned whether 47 U.S.C.A. § 503(b)(2) does in fact allow the FCC to enforce 18 U.S.C.A. § 1464:

> 47 U.S.C.A. § 503(b)(1) (1970) is not clear on the issue of whether the commission may issue a forfeiture prior to a judicial determination and its language can be read to support the position that the commission may not so act.[62] Furthermore, the FCC until 1970 and the incredible *WUHY* decision had held that it would not institute forfeiture proceedings until after a judicial determination and would instead refer all obscenity complaints to the Justice Department.

In *FCC v. Pacifica Foundation,* text, p. 920, which provided the first full Supreme Court review of the FCC's power in the area of obscenity, the point was not directly at issue since the FCC did not impose formal sanctions such as monetary forfeiture in that case. But the Supreme Court did note with apparent approval the FCC's view that it had power to impose a monetary forfeiture.[9]

In summary, the broadcaster can be punished by the FCC for infractions of 18 U.S.C.A. § 1464 since that provision is incorporated, for the purpose of levying fines against offenders, into the Federal Communications Act. See 47 U.S.C.A. § 503(b)(1)(E) and (b)(2).

3. The *WUHY* case appears to indicate a nominalistic approach to obscenity, i.e., certain words are indecent. Do you think the approach the FCC takes in *WUHY* coheres with the general structure of obscenity law in force at the time *WUHY* was decided as revealed in cases like Roth v. United States, 354 U.S. 476 (1957), reported in the text at p. 728 and Ginsberg v. State of New York, 390 U.S. 629 (1968), reported in the text at p. 913?

How does the so-called "dirty word" test of *WUHY* comport with the Supreme Court's landmark obscenity decision announced in 1973, Miller v. California, 413 U.S. 15 (1973), reported in the text at p. 753?

IN RE WUHY–FM EASTERN EDUCATION RADIO

24 FCC2D 408 (1970).

Facts: WUHY–FM, a non-commercial educational radio station, broadcasts a weekly program, CYCLE II, from 10:00 to 11:00

62. 47 U.S.C.A. § 503(b)(1)(E) (1970) speaks in terms of one who "violates" 18 U.S.C.A. § 1464 (1970) and thus may refer only to one adjudicated in violation and not one merely charged with a violation by the FCC (who can only charge a violation and not conclusively adjudicate a violation). The legislative history is similarly unclear. Originally, the FCC was given enforcement powers over obscene broadcasts. *See* Duncan v. United States, 48 F.2d 128 (9th Cir. 1931), cert. denied 283 U.S. 863. In 1948, the prohibition on obscene broadcasts was moved to Title 18 and nothing in Title 47 authorized the FCC to consider obscenity in a forfeiture proceeding. In 1960 Congress added § 503 to grant authority to the FCC to aid in the enforcement of antiquiz fraud provisions. Law 86–752, 74 Stat. 889. It was not stated whether the FCC was to have co-ordinate enforcement powers with the Department of Justice. The commission in Sonderling Broadcasting Corp., 41 FCC2d 777, 778, 781 (1973) argues that FCC v. American Broadcasting Co., 347 U.S. 284, 289–90 n. 7 * * (1954) establishes this concurrent enforcement authority. The commission misinterprets this case. The Supreme Court therein referred only to the power to enforce the general law upon licensees by revoking or failing to renew a license and expressly declined to hold in a comprehensive footnote that the FCC has forfeiture powers. The power to adjudicate violations of a criminal statute to impose a forfeiture prior to judicial review of the adjudication is a far cry from considering adjudicated illegal conduct or allegations of illegal conduct at license renewal time. *See* the perceptive discussion of this argument in Note, Broadcasting Obscene Language, 43 Ariz.St.L.J. 457, 466–70 (1974).

9. FCC v. Pacifica Foundation, 438 U.S. 726 at 730, n. 1 (1978).

P.M. On January 4, 1970, Jerry Garcia, of a musical group called *The Grateful Dead,* was interviewed by WUHY on the air from his hotel room. In the interview two of the most celebrated Anglo-Saxon four letter words were used with remarkable frequency by Garcia. The FCC investigated WUHY.

Three commissioners, Bartley, Lee and Wells, comprised the majority who notified WUHY–FM of liability for forfeiture of $100 because of indecent programming.

* * *

The issue in this case is not whether WUHY–FM may present the views of Mr. Garcia or "Crazy Max" on ecology, society, computers, and so on. Clearly that decision is a matter solely within the judgment of the licensee. See Section 326 of the Communications Act of 1934, as amended. Further, we stress, as we have before, the licensee's right to present provocative or unpopular programming which may offend some listeners. * * * Rather the narrow issue is whether the licensee may present previously taped interview or talk shows where the persons intersperse or begin their speech with expressions like, "Shit, man * * *" "* * * and shit like that," or "* * * 900 fuckin' times," "* * * right fucking out of ya," etc.

We believe that if we have the authority, we have a duty to act to prevent the widespread use on broadcast outlets of such expressions in the above circumstances. For, the speech involved has no redeeming social value, and is patently offensive by contemporary community standards, with very serious consequences to the "public interest in the larger and more effective use of radio" (Section 303(g)). * * *

* * *

This brings us to the second part of the analysis—the consequence to the public interest. * * * *And here it is crucial to bear in mind the difference between radio and other media.* Unlike a book which requires the deliberate act of purchasing and reading (or a motion picture where admission to public exhibition must be actively sought), broadcasting is disseminated generally to the public under circumstances where reception requires no activity of this nature. Thus, it comes directly into the home and frequently without any advance warning of its content. Millions daily turn the dial from station to station. While particular stations or programs are oriented to specific audiences, the fact is that by its very nature, thousands of others not within the "intended" audience may also see or hear portions of the broadcast. Further, in that audience are very large numbers of children. Were this type of programming (e.g., the WUHY interview with the above described language) to become widespread, it would drastically affect the use of radio by millions of people. * * * There are two aspects of this issue. First, there is the question of the applicability of 18 U.S.C.A. § 1464, which makes it a criminal offense to "utter any obscene, indecent, or profane language by means of radio communication." This standard, we note, is incorporated in the Communications Act. See Sections 312(a)(6) and 503(b)(1)(E), 47 U.S.C.A. § 312(a)(6); 503(b)(1)(E). The licensee urges that the broadcast was not obscene "because it did not have a dominant appeal to prurience or sexual matters." We agree, and thus find that the broadcast would not necessarily come within the standard laid down in Memoirs v. Massachusetts, 383 U.S. 413, 418 (1965); see also Jacobellis v. Ohio, 378 U.S. 184, 191 (1963). Roth v. United States, 354 U.S. 476 (1956). However, we believe that the statutory term, "indecent," should be applicable, and that, in the broadcast field, the standard for its *applicability* should be that the material broadcast is (a) patently offensive by contemporary community standards; and (b) is utterly without redeeming social value. The Court has made clear that different rules are appropriate for different media of expression in view of their varying natures. "Each method tends to present its own peculiar problems." Burstyn v. Wilson, 343 U.S. 495, 502–503 (1951). We have set forth [above], the reasons for applicability of the above standard in defining what is indecent in the broadcast field. We think that the factors set out [above] are cogent, powerful considerations for the different standard in this markedly different field.

* * *

The licensee argues that the program was not indecent, because its basic subject matters "* * * are obviously decent"; "the challenged language though not essential to the meaning of the program as a whole, reflected the personality and life style of Mr. Garcia"; and "the realistic portrayal of such an interview cannot be deemed 'indecent' because the subject incidentally used strong or salty language." We disagree with this approach in the broadcast field. * * *

The licensee itself notes that the language in question "was not essential to the presentation of the subject matter * * *" but rather was "* * * essentially gratuitous." We think that is the precise point here—namely, that the language *is* "gratuitous"—i.e., "unwarranted or [having] no reason for its existence." There is no valid basis in these circumstances for permitting its widespread use in the broadcast field, with the detrimental consequences described [above].

The matter could also be approached under the public interest standard of the Communications Act. * * * The standard for such action under the public interest criterion is the same as previously discussed—namely, that the material is patently offensive by contemporary community standards and utterly without redeeming social value. * * *

In sum, we hold that we have the authority to act here under Section 1464 (i.e., 503 (b)(1)(E)) or under the public interest standard (Section 503(b)(1)(A)(B)—for failure to operate in the public interest as set forth in the license or to observe the requirement of Section 315(a) to operate in the public interest).

However, whether under Section 1464 or the public interest standard, the criteria for commission action thus remains the same, in our view—namely, that the material be patently offensive and utterly without redeeming value. Finally, as we stressed before in sensitive areas like this [Report and Order on Personal Attack Rules, 8 FCC2d 721, 725 (1968)], the commission can appropriately act only in clear-cut, flagrant cases; doubtful or close cases are clearly to be resolved in the licensee's favor.

* * * In view of the foregoing, little further discussion is needed on this aspect. We believe that the presentation of the Garcia material quoted [above] falls clearly within the two above criteria, and hence may be the subject of a forfeiture under Section 503(b)(1)(A)(B) and (E). We further find that the presentation was "willful" (503(b)(1)(A)(B)). We note that the material was taped. Further the station employees could have cautioned Mr. Garcia either at the outset or after the first few expressions to avoid using these "gratuitous" expressions; they did not do so. That the material was presented without obtaining the station manager's approval—contrary to station policy—does not absolve the licensee of responsibility. * * Indeed, in light of the facts here, there would appear to have been gross negligence on the part of the licensee with respect to its supervisory duties.

* * * [T]he issue in this case is whether to impose a forfeiture (since one of the reasons for the forfeiture provision is that it can be imposed for the isolated occurrence, such as an isolated lottery, etc.). On this issue, we note that, in view of the fact that this is largely a case of first impression, particularly as to the Sec-

tion 1464 aspect, we could appropriately forego the forfeiture and simply act prospectively in this field.

* * * However, were we to do so, we would prevent any review of our action and in this sensitive field we have always sought to insure such reviewability. * * * Thus, while we think that our action is fully consistent with the law, there should clearly be the avenue of court review in a case of this nature (see Section 504(a)). * * *

In view of the foregoing, we determine that, pursuant to Section 503(b)(1)(A), (B), (E) of the Communications Act of 1934, as amended, Eastern Education Radio has incurred an apparent liability of one hundred dollars ($100).

* * *

COMMENT

1. In the *WUHY* case, the FCC ignored the concept of obscenity around which a whole body of constitutional adjudication was clustered. See Chapter VIII.

Did the FCC choose "indecency" as the actionable term precisely because it had not received a detailed and limiting construction by the courts but "obscenity" had? Did the FCC think that making "indecency" the key term would give itself more room to deal with the different kinds of obscenity problems presented by the broadcast media as compared with the print media?

2. The FCC definition of "indecency" differed materially from the Supreme Court's pre-*Miller v. California* definition of obscenity. The FCC defined "indecency" in *WUHY* as follows:

> * * * we believe that the statutory term, "indecent" should be applicable, and that in the broadcast field, the standard for its applicability should be that the material broadcast is (a) patently offensive by contemporary community standards, and (b) is utterly without redeeming social value.

3. The FCC identified certain words in *WUHY* as without social value. In the FCC's judgment, these words furthered no debate and served no social purpose. In A Book Named *John Cleland's Memoirs of a Woman of Pleasure* v. Attorney General of Massachusetts, 383 U.S. 413 (1966), the Supreme Court defined obscenity as it had evolved from the starting point in *Roth:*

> Under the Roth definition of obscenity, as elaborated in subsequent cases, three elements must coalesce: it must be established that (a) the dominant theme of the material taken as a whole appeals to a prurient interest in sex; (b) the material is patently offensive because it affronts contemporary community standards relating to the description or representation of sexual matters; and (c) the material is utterly without redeeming social value.

The FCC's definition of "indecency" omits any necessity to make a finding that the "dominant theme of the material taken as a whole appeals to a prurient interest in sex." Obviously, if a case of "indecency" is made out by pointing out that a broadcast used a "verboten" word, the "dominant theme" requirement must be dropped.

But the function of *Roth's* "dominant theme" requirement was to give maximum protection to expression, to prevent one objectionable word or a few words from being used to ban an entire book, play, or movie. Is there any reason why the most susceptible member of the audience and the single offensive word should be the touchstone of "indecency" when for the print media the "average reader" and the "dominant theme" requirements suffice?

4. It should be noted that the Supreme Court's new and revised definition of obscenity retains the inquiry into "(w)hether 'the average person, applying contemporary community standards' would find that the work, taken as a whole, appeals to the prurient interest." See *Miller v. California*, text, p. 753.

Are there compelling reasons for a more restricted latitude for expression in broadcasting? Is it demonstrably clear that the shock effect or impact of a single word is immeasurably greater on radio than it might be in a textbook? In the case of the radio broadcast it is difficult to make assumptions about or to establish controls for the ultimate composition of the broadcast audience. But are there not alternatives to making the most impressionable or susceptible viewer or listener the arbiter for what is tolerable in broadcasting?

5. One alternative to a rigid list of "verboten" words could be a variable obscenity approach to broadcast programming problems. The variable obscenity idea was outlined and developed in Lockhart and McClure, *Censorship of Obscenity: The Developing Constitutional Standards*, 45 Minn.L.Rev. 5 (1960). Under this approach, the same material which would be proscribed if sold to children is perfectly permissible if sold to adults. The key is how the material is treated by the primary audience for whom it is intended. Ginsberg v. New York, 390 U.S. 629 (1968), was a high watermark for the variable obscenity idea. There, a prosecution was upheld involving the sale of magazines to children although the sale of the same magazines to adults would have been permissible. See this text p. 740.

Is the variable obscenity idea transferable to broadcasting? Obviously, one difficulty is that the broadcaster, unlike the cashier in the corner drugstore, has no way of selecting those who receive his wares?

But the variable obscenity approach is by definition an elastic and flexible concept. Indeed, in *WUHY*, the broadcaster's defense against the charge of "indecent" programming was, in essence, a variable obscenity defense. The broadcaster said the program was not "indecent" because of three factors: 1) the time of the broadcast, 2) the unlikelihood that children were in the audience, and 3) the necessity of continuing announcements to listeners in advance of disagreeable programming.

6. The public interest standard the FCC used in *WUHY* is "patent offensiveness to contemporary standards." Does this standard consist of a list of shock words that cannot be used in broadcasting? Certainly it is at least that. Or is it more? It should be noted that the FCC's "patent offensiveness" standard leaves out the inquiry into whether the material in question makes an "appeal to the prurient interest."

Broadcast law would have been much richer if *WUHY–FM* had declined to pay the fine and appealed the case to the courts. Unfortunately, *WUHY* chose to pay its $100 fine. Therefore, there was no appeal.

Eight years were to elapse before the issues raised in *WUHY* were resolved.

In *WUHY–FM* the FCC decided that the reference to "indecent" utterance in 18 U.S.C.A. § 1464 permitted the FCC to expand its regulatory authority to prohibit programming which was allegedly patently offensive but which did not otherwise meet the constitutional test for obscenity. Such a policy clearly ran a risk of judicial reversal since the whole point of putting a separate and distinct meaning in the reference to "indecent" utterance in 18 U.S.C.A. § 1464 appeared to be designed to escape the rigors of the constitutional definition of obscenity. In the 1978 Supreme Court decision in FCC v. Pacifica Foundation, 438 U.S. 726, (1978), see text, p. 920, the FCC's gamble in trying to create a new category of prohibited programming on broadcasting—"indecent" programming—succeeded. In a decision which surprised broadcasters and disappointed civil libertarians, the Supreme Court agreed that the FCC's authority to regulate "indecent" programming was not limited by the constitutional requirements associated with its authority to regulate "obscene" programming. In the *Pacifica* case, the Supreme Court specifically cited *WUHY–FM* along with other FCC cases for the point that the FCC "has long interpreted § 1464 as encompassing more than the obscene." The *WUHY* case marked a first step in a new development which expanded the scope of FCC regulation of broadcast programming.

7. In Miller v. California, 413 U.S. 15, text, *supra,* at p. 753, the Supreme Court denied that "there are, or should or can be, fixed, uniform national standards of precisely what appeals to the 'prurient interest' or is 'patently offensive.'" As a result of *Miller v. California*, one element in defining obscenity is whether "the work depicts or describes, in a patently offensive way, sexual conduct specifically defined by the applicable state law."

At present, as we have seen, obscenity-type problems in broadcasting are resolved by focusing on either a public interest standard or by making the operative statutory term some term other than obscenity such as "indecency." This strategy is presumably employed to avoid making the problems of broadcasting susceptible to the general law of obscenity.

As a result of *Miller v. California*, obscenity law is now a far more relative matter than it was in the reign of *Roth*. What is obscene in Maine may now not necessarily be so in California.

Should (must) broadcast regulation take account of the cultural or geographical relativity the Supreme Court has fed into the definition of obscenity in constitutional law? Should a New York City FM radio station, for example, be given greater latitude in expression than an Iowa AM radio station? If such distinctions are required by *Miller*, is it feasible to have such determinations made by the FCC? It is one thing for state and federal courts in different parts of the country to ascertain what is "patently offensive" for their part of the country. But how can the FCC in Washington make such a determination?

SONDERLING BROADCASTING CORP., WGLD–FM

41 FCC2D 777 (1973).

This letter constitutes a Notice of Apparent Liability for forfeiture issued under Section 503(b)(2) of the Communications Act of 1934, as amended, 47 U.S.C.A. 503(b)(2), pursuant to Section 503(b)(1)(E) of the Act, 47 U.S.C.A. 503(b)(1)(E).

The Facts Station WGLD–FM, Oak Park, Illinois, licensed to Sonderling Broadcasting Corporation, is one of a number of broadcast stations which have been using a format sometimes called "topless radio," in which an announcer takes calls from the audience and discusses largely sexual topics. The program on WGLD–FM is called "Femme Forum" and runs five hours a day, from 10 a.m. to 3 p.m., Monday through Friday, moderated by Mr. Morgan Moore. On February 23, 1973, the topic was "oral sex." The program consisted of very explicit exchanges in which the female callers spoke of their oral sex experiences.

Discussion It is the commission's conclusion that broadcasts of this nature—and these particular broadcasts—call for imposition of a forfeiture under Section 503(b)(1)(E) of the Communications Act.

* * *

First, it is most important to make clear what we are not holding. We are emphatically *not* saying that sex *per se* is a forbidden subject on the broadcast medium. * * * Second, we note that we are not dealing with works of dramatic or literary art as we were in *Pacifica*. We are rather confronted with the talk or interview show where clearly the interviewer can readily moderate his handling of the subject matter so as to conform to the basic statutory standards—standards which, as we point out, allow much leeway for provocative material.[2]

* * *

We shall apply here the * * * *Roth* test and guidelines such as in Ginzburg v. U. S., 383 U.S. 463 (1966).

* * * It is important to note that these criteria are being applied in the broadcast field. The Supreme Court has made clear that different approaches are appropriate for different media of expression in view of their varying natures. * * * That *caveat* applies with particular force to broadcasting. This is peculiarly a medium designed to be received and sampled by millions in their homes, cars, on outings, or even as they walk the streets with transistor radio to the ear, without regard to age, background or degree of sophistication. A person will listen to some musical piece or portion of a talk show, and decide to turn the dial to try something else. While many have loyalty to a particular station or stations, many others engage in this electronic smorgasbord sampling. That, together with its free access to the home, is a unique quality of radio, wholly unlike other media such as print or motion pictures. It takes a deliberate act to purchase and read a book, or seek admission to the theater.[3] * * *

We also repeat what we said at the outset. The foregoing does not mean that the only material that can be broadcast is what must be suitable for children or will never offend any significant portion of a polyglot audience. But it does mean that in determining whether broadcast material meets the statutory test, the special quality of this medium must be taken appropriately into account. The consequences of not doing so would be disastrous to "the larger and more effective use of radio in the public interest." (Section 303(g) of the act.) For there is a Gresham's Law at work here. If broadcasters can engage in commercial exploitation of obscene or indecent material of the nature described above, an increasing number will do so for competitive reasons, with spiralling adverse effects upon millions of listeners.

* * *

Application of the Roth criteria to this case. First, we note the applicability of some elements of *Ginzburg* to this case. There is here "commercial exploitation," an effort at pandering. Formats like Femme Forum, aptly called "topless radio," are designed to garner large audiences through titillating sexual discussions. The announcer actively solicits the titillating response. We shall not treat this aspect further, because in any event, all this is background to the crucial consideration: Were the *Roth* criteria met by the material here broadcast?

We believe that they were. We have no doubt that the explicit material set out above is patently offensive to contemporary community standards for broadcast matter. * * * If discussions in this titillating and pandering fashion of coating the penis to facilitate oral sex, swallowing the semen at climax, overcoming fears of the penis being bitten off, etc., do not constitute broadcast obscenity within the meaning of 18 U.S.C.A. 1464, we do not perceive what does or could. We also believe that the dominant theme here is clearly an appeal to prurient interest. The announcer coaxed responses that were designed to titillate—to arouse sexual feelings. Indeed, again in this very program, one caller stated that as a result of what she had heard on the program, she was going to try

2. In order to assure compliance with the law and their own programming policies, many licensees interpose a "tape delay" in telephone interview programs, enabling the licensee to delete certain material before it is broadcast.

3. In that sense, a broadcast or cable pay-TV operation (or any "locked-key" cable operation) may well stand on a different footing.

oral sex that night. Finally, from what has been discussed, we do not believe that there is redeeming social value here. This is not a serious discussion of sexual matters, but rather titillating, pandering exploitation of sexual materials. Further, we think that not only can we examine the program in its "commercial exploitation" context but also in sections or parts. These are five-hour talk shows; some parts are of necessity not obscene—are, for example, nothing more than banal "filler". It would make no sense to say that a broadcaster can escape the proscription against obscenity if he schedules a three, four or five-hour talk program, and simply intersperses the obscenity—so critical for the ratings—with other, non-obscene material.

Our conclusions here are based on the pervasive and intrusive nature of broadcast radio, even if children were left completely out of the picture. However, the presence of children in the broadcast audience makes this an *a fortiori* matter. There are significant numbers of children in the audience during these afternoon hours—and not all of a pre-school age. Thus, there is always a significant percentage of school age children out of school on any given day. Many listen to radio; indeed it is almost the constant companion of the teenager. * * *

There is evidence that this program is not intended solely for adults. On the February 6, 1973 program on "Do you always achieve orgasm?", the announcer moved from a discussion of orgasm to a comment aimed in large part at the 16–20 year old audience.

* * *

[T]here is an alternative ground for action in this case. In *WUHY* we set out at some length our construction that the term "indecent," as used in 18 U.S.C.A. 1464, constituted a different standard from "obscene" in the broadcast field. * * * We therefore find, as an alternative ground, that the material, even if it were not found to appeal to a prurient interest, warrants the assessment of a forfeiture because it is within the statutory prohibition against the broadcast of indecent matter.

* * * [W]e recognize that we are not the final arbiters in this sensitive First Amendment field. Therefore, we welcome and urge judicial consideration of our action. As to the amount of the forfeiture, we believe that $2,000 is appropriate for the willful or repeated violations here involved (covering both the February 21 and 23, 1973, programs). While it is true that there has been no judicial consideration of obscenity or indecency in this specific broadcast situation we are not fashioning any new theory here.

* * *

In view of the foregoing, we determine that, pursuant to Section 503(b)(1)(E) of the Communications Act of 1934, as amended, Sonderling Broadcasting Corporation has incurred an apparent liability of two thousand dollars ($2000).

COMMENT

1. In *Sonderling* the FCC invoked both the indecency and the obscenity standards of 18 U.S.C.A. § 1464 and found that a forfeiture was warranted under both standards. *Sonderling* specifically applied the *Roth-Ginzburg* obscenity standard to broadcasting while making note that "the special quality of the medium must be taken into account." Note that the "commercial exploitation" theme of *Ginzburg v. United States*, text p. 746, was invoked.

2. Why did the FCC suddenly make the "obscenity" standard in 18 U.S.C.A. § 1464 operative? Perhaps the fact, as the FCC put it, that "the announcer actively solicits the titillating response," made the *Ginzburg* addendum to *Roth* appear an appropriate standard to apply.

The difficulty with this approach is one of providing adequate notice to the parties affected. Would it not have been reasonable for the broadcasters and broadcast lawyers reading *WUHY* to conclude that the FCC was going to avoid *Roth* and post-*Roth* elaborations on the definition of obscenity? If so, it would have been reasonable to suppose that the FCC intended to make the "indecency" standard the exclusively operative standard for 18 U.S.C.A. § 1464 enforcement purposes? Is the notice and fairness problem in *Sonderling* really overcome by saying somewhat perfunctorily that the "indecency" standard of 18 U.S.C.A. § 1464 was also violated?

3. The FCC says that on the basis of its discussion of obscenity in *Sonderling*, it is clear that the matter broadcast is "indecent" as well. Do you agree? Note that the "dirty words" test of *WUHY* does not seem to have been violated by the broadcasts in question in *Sonderling*

4. Commissioner Johnson in dissent attacked the FCC policy of enforcing both an obscenity standard and an indecency standard. His position was that since the FCC concedes that the "indecency" standard may proscribe material that does not constitute "obscenity," it is questionable whether "indecency" can be regulated. He complains further that the defense of "indecency" is constitutionally imprecise. What is imprecise about it?

Do you think the censorship problems objected to by Commissioner Johnson would be solved if the FCC were to announce that hereafter it would regulate only "obscene" material but not "indecent" or otherwise nonobscene material?

Commissioner Johnson offered the criticism that the majority did not define the community whose standards were supposed to have been violated. This duty to define the relevant community is now much more fundamental than ever in the light of the new importance given to the local community standard by Miller v. California, 413 U.S. 15 (1973), a case which had not been decided at the time of the announcement of the FCC's *Sonderling* opinion.

In the light of *Miller*, how should community be defined in a case like *Sonderling*?

5. Commissioner Johnson said that the enforcement of 18 U.S.C.A. § 1464 is better left to the Justice Department. This approach would leave the problem of defining § 1464 to the federal courts, and it is certainly arguable that federal judges are better equipped to deal with the sensitive First Amendment issues involved than is the FCC. On the other hand, the FCC in *Sonderling* was acting pursuant to 47 U.S.C.A. § 503(b)(1)(E), Federal Communications Act of 1934. It is not appropriate for the agency to declare a provision of its enabling statute unconstitutional.

6. The Sonderling Broadcasting Co. simply paid the forfeiture to the FCC and did not appeal. But the Illinois Citizens Committee for Broadcasting and the Illinois Division of the American Civil Liberties Union took up the fight and sought a petition for reconsideration of the notice of apparent liability and also sought remission of the forfeiture from the FCC. The fact that the appeal was taken by citizen groups rather than the affected licensee raised a standing question. See text, p. 944. These requests were denied by the FCC, and the ACLU and the committee petitioned the federal court of appeals for review.

In Illinois Citizens Committee for Broadcasting v. FCC, 515 F.2d 397 (D.C. Cir. 1975), the court, per Judge Leventhal, upheld the FCC determination in the *Sonderling* case: The FCC did not unconstitutionally infringe the listening alternatives of the public when it determined that a radio call-in show carrying an explicit discussion of ultimate sexual acts in a titillating context was an obscene broadcast.

The court reasoned that the station's approach in the radio call-in show in question, "Femme Forum," triggered the principles of *Ginzburg v. United States*, text, p.

746. Justice Brennan there found that commercial exploitation of interests in erotica could be decisive in the determination of obscenity. In *Ginzburg*, the "leering innuendo" was found in the modes of sales promotion. Here the "commercial exploitation" of titillation was found in the "tone" which was "set by the continuity provided by the announcer."

Perhaps most significant was Sonderling's choice of broadcast hours. "Femme Forum" was broadcast from 10 A.M. to 3 P.M. when the radio audience might include children, home from school for lunch, illness, or staggered school hours. Judge Leventhal concluded: "Given this combination of factors, we do not think that the FCC's evaluation of this material infringes upon rights protected by the First Amendment."

A problem arose in determining the obscenity standard that should be applied. The FCC found Sonderling's broadcasts obscene under the standards of *Roth v. United States*, text, p. 728, and *Memoirs v. Massachusetts*, text, p. 744. Between the FCC's resolution of the case and the present appeal, the Supreme Court decided *Miller v. California*, text, p. 753, which sets out the following guidelines for the trier of fact:

> (a) whether "the average person, applying contemporary community standards" would find that the work, taken as a whole, appeals to the prurient interest * * * (b) whether the work depicts or describes, in a patently offensive way, sexual conduct specifically defined by the applicable state law, and (c) whether the work, taken as a whole, lacks serious literary, artistic, political, or scientific value.

The court, per Judge Leventhal, rejected the contention that *Miller* required reversal of the FCC ruling in *Sonderling*:

> We conclude that, where a radio call-in show during daytime hours broadcasts explicit discussions of ultimate sexual acts in a titillating context, the commission does not unconstitutionally infringe upon the public's right to listening alternatives when it determines that the broadcast is obscene.

The petitioners then sought a rehearing *en banc* by the full court. On March 13, 1975, that request was denied. Judge Bazelon, however, disagreed with his colleagues in refusing a grant a rehearing. He questioned the conclusion of obscenity in light of the fact that *Miller* requires "local fact-finders to apply 'local community standards' of decency." Bazelon argued that the court should have required the FCC "to take evidence on 'local community standards' before reaching a decision under *Miller*." He was particularly scornful of the court's conclusion that petitioners had waived their right to challenge the lack of specificity (required by *Miller*) in the statutes enforced by the FCC:

> Surely petitioners did not waive their right to challenge the lack of specificity of the statutes because they did not raise it in their reply brief when the FCC decision was not even based on *Miller*. And why does the court "see no point in pursuing in the abstract" a central contention that must be considered by every court considering a post-*Miller* statute and which one can assume the petitioners would vigorously assert if they knew *Miller* was in issue? And what is the relevance of titillation and exposure to juveniles to the question of specificity and the general narrowing of the test of obscenity in *Miller*?

Judge Bazelon set forth further objections to the court's reasoning:

> There is another difficulty with the court's opinion. *Miller* retains the established requirement that material allegedly obscene must be "taken as a whole" in the judgment of obscenity. Here the commission made its judgment of obscenity on a 22 minute tape which eliminated the bulk of the Sonderling (and other broadcasters') talk show programming not involving sexual discussion. By the admitted facts

> the FCC did not take the material as a whole but rather viewed the material piece meal. * * * I think this is grounds for a remand.

Bazelon argued that the specificity requirement of *Miller* was designed to provide more than fair notice to the broadcaster—it was designed to protect listeners as well: "It is also designed to prevent statutory overbreadth and the attendant chilling effect of overbroad statutes. And the extremely obvious chilling effect in this case has deprived the petitioners of programming they desired."

7. Further, Judge Bazelon complained that the FCC's separate standard of "indecency" was inconsistent with *Miller* in that it excluded from the test of obscenity the requirement that the language appeal to a prurient interest in sex. The FCC's substantive decision could not be sustained on the basis of *Roth* and *Memoirs* for four reasons:

> First the broadcasts involved no visual material. Second, there clearly was an arguable "redeeming social value" to the broadcasts and thus we would be hard pressed to hold that the broadcasters were "utterly without" redeeming social value. Third, the commission in its decision relied on several of its precedents which are inconsistent with *Memoirs* and *Roth*, most particularly the amazing *WUHY* decision. Finally, the FCC simply misunderstood the meaning of the *Ginzburg* case and adopted a view of pandering which equates all commercialization of speech with titillation. There is no significant evidence of *Ginzburg*-type pandering.

8. In Bazelon's view the condemnation of sex oriented radio shows by then FCC Chairman Burch, and the commencement by the FCC a day earlier of a closed notice of inquiry into the broadcast of obscene, indecent, or profane material made it clear that what was involved was not a "specific attack on *Sonderling* but rather a general attack on all sex-oriented talk shows." An entire class of speech has been chased off the air:

> Here the commission has effectively terminated sex-oriented talk shows without any due process for the licensees, without any consideration of the individual merits of different shows, and without any participation by the courts which are given the primary burden of defining obscenity.

9. Finally, there was a basic statutory defect in the FCC's regulation of obscenity in broadcasting as manifested by the *Sonderling* decision: Judge Bazelon questioned whether "any FCC enforcement of obscenity prohibitions prior to a judicial determination of obscenity is consistent with the broad principles of First Amendment 'due process.' " (This point is elaborated on earlier in the text, at p. 909.

10. Judge Bazelon then discussed whether the "FCC as a national administrative agency" is equipped "to make a finding of whether speech appeals to a prurient interest under contemporary community standards (*qua Memoirs-Roth*) or under a local community standard (qua *Miller*)." The court had rejected this objection on the ground that "the Supreme Court has found that jury trials are not required in obscenity decisions." But Bazelon's rejoinder to this was that it was "irrelevant to the larger question of whether a national administrative agency can be compared even to a local trial judge."

"Indecency" in Broadcasting—A Constitutional Concept

1. May the FCC regulate, consistent with the First Amendment, a radio broadcast that is "indecent" under 18 U.S.C.A. § 1464 even though it is not obscene? This issue—the question raised at the outset of this section in *WUHY*—was squarely presented to the Supreme Court in *FCC v. Pacifica Broadcasting Co.* Although the Supreme Court was literally besieged with

amicus curiae groups from the media, media organizations, citizens groups, and civil liberties organizations arguing that the Supreme Court had no authority to proscribe any list of words on broadcasting, the Court gave the FCC a new but narrow charter to regulate both, "indecency" and "obscenity" in broadcasting.

FCC v. PACIFICA FOUNDATION

3 MED.L.RPTR. 2553, 438 U.S. 726, 98 S.CT. 3026, 57 L.ED.2D 1073 (1978).

Justice STEVENS delivered the opinion of the Court (Parts I, II, III, and IV–C) and an opinion in which the Chief Justice and Justice Rehnquist joined (Parts IV–A and IV–B).

This case requires that we decide whether the Federal Communications Commission has any power to regulate a radio broadcast that is indecent but not obscene.

A satiric humorist named George Carlin recorded a 12-minute monologue entitled "Filthy Words" before a live audience in a California theater. He began by referring to his thoughts about "the words you couldn't say on the public, ah, airwaves, um, the ones you definitely wouldn't say, ever." He proceeded to list those words and repeat them over and over again in a variety of colloquialisms. * * *

At about 2 o'clock in the afternoon on Tuesday, October 30, 1973, a New York radio station owned by respondent, Pacifica Foundation, broadcast the "Filthy Words" monologue. A few weeks later a man, who stated that he had heard the broadcast while driving with his young son, wrote a letter complaining to the commission. He stated that, although he could perhaps understand the "record's being sold for private use, I certainly cannot understand the broadcast of same over the air that, supposedly, you control."

The complaint was forwarded to the station for comment. In its response, Pacifica explained that the monologue had been played during a program about contemporary society's attitude toward language and that immediately before its broadcast listeners had been advised that it included "sensitive language which might be regarded as offensive to some."

* * *

On February 21, 1975, the commission issued a declaratory order granting the complaint and holding that Pacifica "could have been the subject of administrative sanctions." 56 FCC2d 94, 99 (1975). The commission did not impose formal sanctions, but it did state that the order would be "associated with the station's license file, and in the event that subsequent complaints are received, the commission will then decide whether it should utilize any of the available sanctions it has been granted by Congress."

In its memorandum opinion the commission stated that it intended to "clarify the standards which will be utilized in considering" the growing number of complaints about indecent speech on the airwaves. Advancing several reasons for treating broadcast speech differently from other forms of expression, the commission found a power to regulate indecent broadcasting in two statutes: 18 U.S.C.A. § 1464, which forbids the use of "any obscene, indecent, or profane language by means of radio communications," and 47 U.S.C.A. § 303(g), which requires the commission to "encourage the larger and more effective use of radio in the public interest."

The commission characterized the language used in the Carlin monologue as "patently offensive," though not necessarily obscene, and expressed the opinion that it should be regulated by principles analogous to those found in the law of nuisance where the "law generally speaks to *channeling* behavior more than actually prohibiting it. * * * [T]he concept of 'indecent' is intimately connected with the exposure of children to language that describes in terms patently offensive as measured by contemporary community standards for the broadcast medium, sexual or excretory activities and organs, at times of the day when there is a reasonable risk that children may be in the audience." 56 FCC2d, at 98.

Applying these considerations to the language used in the monologue as broadcast by respondent, the commission concluded that certain words depicted sexual and excretory activities in a patently offensive manner, noted that they "were broadcast at a time when children were undoubtedly in the audience (i. e., in the early afternoon)," and that the prerecorded language, with these offensive words "repeated over and over," was "deliberately broadcast." In summary, the commission stated: "We therefore hold that the language as broadcast was indecent and prohibited by 18 U.S.C. 1464."

After the order issued, the commission was asked to clarify its opinion by ruling that the broadcast of indecent words as part of a live newscast would not be prohibited. The commission issued another opinion in which it pointed out that it "never intended to place an absolute prohibition on the broadcast of this type of language, but rather sought to channel it to times of day when children most likely would not be exposed to it." 59 FCC2d 892 (1976). The commission noted that its "declaratory order was issued in a specific factual context," and declined to comment on various hypothetical situations presented by the petition. It relied on its "long standing policy of refusing to issue interpretive rulings or advisory opinions when the critical facts are not explicitly stated or there is a possibility that subsequent events will alter them."

The United States Court of Appeals for the District of Columbia reversed, with each of the three judges on the panel writing separately.

* * *

The relevant statutory questions are whether the commission's action is forbidden "censorship" within the meaning of 47 U.S.C.A. § 326 and whether speech that concededly is not obscene may be restricted as "indecent" under the authority of 18 U.S.C.A. § 1464. The questions are not unrelated, for the two statutory provisions have a common origin. Nevertheless, we analyze them separately.

Section 29 of the Radio Act of 1927 provided:

> Nothing in this act shall be understood or construed to give the licensing authority the power of censorship over the radio communications or signals transmitted by any radio station, and no regulation or condition shall be promulgated or fixed by the licensing authority which shall interfere with the right of free speech by means of radio communications. No person within the jurisdiction of the United States shall utter any obscene, indecent or profane language by means of radio communication.

The prohibition against censorship unequivocally denies the commission any power to edit proposed broadcasts in advance and to excise material considered inappropriate for the airwaves. The prohibition, however, has never been construed to deny the commission the power to review the content of completed broadcasts in the performance of its regulatory duties.

There is nothing in the legislative history to contradict this conclusion. * * * In 1934, the anticensorship provision and the prohibition against indecent broadcasts were re-enacted in the same section, just as in the 1927 act. In 1948, when the Criminal Code was revised to include provisions that had previously been located in other titles of the United States Code, the prohibition against obscene, indecent, and profane broadcasts was removed from the Communications Act and re-enacted as § 1464 of Title 18. That rearrangement of the code cannot reasonably be interpreted as having been intended to change the meaning of the anticensorship provision.

We conclude, therefore, that § 326 does not limit the commission's authority to impose sanctions on licensees who engage in obscene, indecent, or profane broadcasting.

The only other statutory question presented by this case is whether the afternoon broadcast of the "Filthy Words" monologue was indecent within the meaning of § 1464. Even that question is narrowly confined by the arguments of the parties.

The commission identified several words that referred to excretory or sexual activities or organs, stated that the repetitive, deliberate use of those words in an afternoon broadcast when children are in the audience was patently offensive, and held that the broadcast was indecent. Pacifica takes issue with the commission's definition of indecency, but does not dispute the commission's preliminary determination that each of the components of its definition was present. Specifically, Pacifica does not quarrel with the conclusion that this afternoon broadcast was patently offensive. Pacifica's claim that the broadcast was not indecent within the meaning of the statute rests entirely on the absence of prurient appeal.

The plain language of the statute does not support Pacifica's argument. The words "obscene, indecent, or profane" are written in the disjunctive, implying that each has a separate meaning. Prurient appeal is an element of the obscene, but the normal definition of "indecent" merely refers to nonconformance with accepted standards of morality.

Pacifica argues, however, that this Court has construed the term "indecent" in related statues to mean "obscene," as that term was defined in *Miller v. California*. Pacifica relies most heavily on the construction this Court gave to 18 U.S.C.A. § 1461 in Hamling v. United States, 418 U.S. 87. *Hamling* rejected a vagueness attack on § 1461, which forbids the mailing of "obscene, lewd, lascivious, indecent, filthy or vile" material.

* * *

In *Hamling* the Court agreed with Justice Harlan that § 1461 was meant only to regulate obscenity in the mails; by reading into it the limits set by Miller v. California, 413 U.S. 15, the Court adopted a construction which assured the statute's constitutionality.

The reasons supporting *Hamling's* construction of § 1461 do not apply to § 1464. * * * The former statute deals primarily with printed matter enclosed in sealed envelopes mailed from one individual to another; the latter deals with the content of public broadcasts. It is unrealistic to assume that Congress intended to impose precisely the same limitations on the dissemination of patently offensive matter by such different means.[17]

Because neither our prior decisions nor the language or history of § 1464 supports the conclusion that prurient appeal is an essential component of indecent language, we reject Pacifica's construction of the statute. When that construction is put to one side there is no basis for disagreeing with the commission's conclusion that indecent language was used in this broadcast.

17. But it is well settled that the First Amendment has a special meaning in the broadcasting context. See, e.g., FCC v. National Citizens Committee for Broadcasting, 436 U.S. 775; Red Lion Broadcasting Co., Inc. v. FCC, 395 U.S. 367; Columbia Broadcasting System, Inc. v. Democratic Nat. Committee, 412 U.S. 94. For this reason, the presumption that Congress never intends to exceed constitutional limits, which supported Hamling's narrow reading of § 1461, does not support a comparable reading of § 1464.

Pacifica makes two constitutional attacks on the commission's order. First, it argues that the commission's construction of the statutory language broadly encompasses so much constitutionally protected speech that reversal is required even if Pacifica's broadcast of the "Filthy Words" monologue is not itself protected by the First Amendment. Second, Pacifica argues that inasmuch as the recording is not obscene, the Constitution forbids any abridgment of the right to broadcast it on the radio.

A

The first argument fails because our review is limited to the question whether the commission has the authority to proscribe this particular broadcast. As the commission itself emphasized, its order was "issued in a specific factual context." 59 FCC2d, at 893. That approach is appropriate for courts as well as the commission when regulation of indecency is at stake, for indecency is largely a function of context—it cannot be adequately judged in the abstract.

The approach is also consistent with Red Lion Broadcasting Co. Inc. v. FCC, 395 U.S. 367. In that case the Court rejected an argument that the commission's regulations defining the fairness doctrine were so vague that they would inevitably abridge the broadcasters' freedom of speech.

* * *

It is true that the commission's order may lead some broadcasters to censor themselves. At most, however, the commission's definition of indecency will deter only the broadcasting of patently offensive references to excretory and sexual organs and activities. While some of these references may be protected, they surely lie at the periphery of First Amendment concern.

* * *

B

When the issue is narrowed to the facts of this case, the question is whether the First Amendment denies government any power to restrict the public broadcast of indecent language in any circumstances. For if the government has any such power, this was an appropriate occasion for its exercise.

The words of the Carlin monologue are unquestionably "speech" within the meaning of the First Amendment. It is equally clear that the commission's objections to the broadcast were based in part on its content. The order must therefore fall if, as Pacifica argues, the First Amendment prohibits all governmental regulation that depends on the content of speech. Our past cases demonstrate, however, that no such absolute rule is mandated by the Constitution.

The classic exposition of the proposition that both the content and the context of speech are critical elements of First Amendment analysis is Justice Holmes' statement for the Court in *Schenck v. United States.* * * * Other distinctions based on content have been approved in the years since *Schenck*. The government may forbid speech calculated to provoke a fight. See Chaplinsky v. New Hampshire, 315 U.S. 568. It may pay heed to the " 'commonsense differences' between commercial speech and other varieties." *Bates v. State Bar.* It may treat libels against private citizens more severely than libels against public officials. See *Gertz v. Robert Welch, Inc.* Obscenity may be wholly prohibited. *Miller v. California.* And only two Terms ago we refused to hold that a "statutory classification is unconstitutional because it is based on the content of communication protected by the First Amendment." *Young v. American Mini Theatres.*

The question in this case is whether a broadcast of patently offensive words dealing with sex and excretion may be regulated because of its content.[20] Obscene materials have been denied the protection of the First Amendment because their content is so offensive to contemporary moral standards. *Roth v. United States.* But the fact that society may find speech offensive is not a sufficient reason for suppressing it. Indeed, if it is the speaker's opinion that gives offense, that consequence is a reason for according it constitutional protection. For it is a central tenet of the First Amendment that the government must remain neutral in the marketplace of ideas. If there were any reason to believe that the commission's characterization of the Carlin monologue as offensive could be traced to its political content—or even to the fact that it satirized contemporary attitudes about four letter words, First Amendment protection might be required. But that is simply not this case. These words offend for the same reasons that obscenity offends. * *

Although these words ordinarily lack literary, political, or scientific value, they are not entirely outside the protection of the First Amendment. * * * Nonetheless, the constitutional protection accorded to a communication containing such patently offensive sexual and excretory language need not be the same in every context. It is a characteristic of speech such as this that both its capacity to offend and its "social value," to use Justice Murphy's term, vary with the circumstances. Words that are commonplace in one setting are shocking in another.

* * *

In this case it is undisputed that the content of Pacifica's broadcast was "vulgar," "offensive," and "shocking." Because content of that character is not entitled to absolute constitutional protection under all circumstances, we must consider its context in order to determine whether the commission's action was constitutionally permissible.

C

We have long recognized that each medium of expression presents special First Amendment problems. Joseph Burstyn, Inc. v. Wilson, 343 U.S. 495, 502–503. And of all forms of communication, it is broadcasting that has received the most limited First Amendment protection. Thus, although other speakers cannot be licensed except under laws that carefully define and narrow official discretion, a broadcaster may be deprived of his license and his forum if the Commission decides that such an action would serve "the public interest, convenience, and necessity." Similarly, although the First Amendment protects newspaper publishers from being required to print the replies of those whom they criticize, *Miami Herald Publishing Co. v. Tornillo*, it affords no such protection to broadcasters; on the contrary, they must give free time to the victims of their criticism. *Red Lion Broadcasting Co., Inc. v. FCC.*

The reasons for these distinctions are complex, but two have relevance to the present case. First, the broadcast media have established a uniquely pervasive presence in the lives of all Americans. Patently offensive, indecent material presented over the airwaves confronts the citizen, not only in public, but also in the privacy of the home, where the individual's right to be let alone plainly outweighs the First Amendment rights of an intruder. Because the broadcast audience is constantly tuning in and out, prior warnings cannot completely protect the listener or viewer from unexpected program content. To say that one may avoid further offense

20. Although neither Justice Powell nor Justice Brennan directly confronts this question, both have answered it affirmatively, the latter explicitly, * * *, and the former implicitly by concurring in a judgment that could not otherwise stand.

by turning off the radio when he hears indecent language is like saying that the remedy for an assault is to run away after the first blow. One may hang up on an indecent phone call, but that option does not give the caller a constitutional immunity or avoid a harm that has already taken place.

Second, broadcasting is uniquely accessible to children, even those too young to read. * * * Other forms of offensive expression may be withheld from the young without restricting the expression at its source. Bookstores and motion pictures theaters, for example, may be prohibited from making indecent material available to children. We held in *Ginsberg v. New York*, that the government's interest in the "well being of its youth" and in supporting "parents' claim to authority in their own household" justified the regulation of otherwise protected expression. The ease with which children may obtain access to broadcast material, coupled with the concerns recognized in *Ginsberg*, amply justify special treatment of indecent broadcasting.

It is appropriate, in conclusion, to emphasize the narrowness of our holding. This case does not involve a two-way radio conversation between a cab driver and a dispatcher, or a telecast of an Elizabethan comedy. We have not decided that an occasional expletive in either setting would justify any sanction or, indeed, that this broadcast would justify a criminal prosecution. The commission's decision rested entirely on a nuisance rationale under which context is all-important. The concept requires consideration of a host of variables. The time of day was emphasized by the commission. The content of the program in which the language is used will also affect the composition of the audience, and differences between radio, television, and perhaps closed-circuit transmissions, may also be relevant. As Justice Sutherland wrote, a "nuisance may be merely a right thing in the wrong place—like a pig in the parlor instead of the barnyard." We simply hold that when the commission finds that a pig has entered the parlor, the exercise of its regulatory power does not depend on proof that the pig is obscene.

The judgment of the court of appeals is reversed.

* * *

Justice POWELL, with whom Justice Blackmun joins, concurring.

* * *

* * * Because I do not subscribe to all that is said in Part IV, however, I state my views separately.

* * *

The issue, however, is whether the commission may impose civil sanctions on a licensee radio station for broadcasting the monologue at two o'clock in the afternoon. The commission's primary concern was to prevent the broadcast from reaching the ears of unsupervised children who were likely to be in the audience at that hour. In essence, the commission sought to "channel" the monologue to hours when the fewest unsupervised children would be exposed to it. In my view, this consideration provides strong support for the commission's holding.

* * *

As the foregoing demonstrates, my views are generally in accord with what is said in Part IV(C) of Justice Stevens' opinion. I therefore join that portion of his opinion. I do not join Part IV(B), however, because I do not subscribe to the theory that the Justices of this Court are free generally to decide on the basis of its content which speech protected by the First Amendment is most "valuable" and hence deserving of the most protection, and which is less "valuable" and hence deserving of less protection. In my view the result in this case does not turn on whether Carlin's monologue, viewed as a whole, or the words that comprise it, have more or less "value" than a candidate's campaign speech. This is a judgment for each person to make, not one for the judges to impose upon him.

The result turns instead on the unique characteristics of the broadcast media, combined with society's right to protect its children from speech generally agreed to be inappropriate for their years, and with the interest of unwilling adults in not being assaulted by such offensive speech in their homes. Moreover, I doubt whether today's decision will prevent any adult who wishes to receive Carlin's message in Carlin's own words from doing so, and from making for himself a value judgment as to the merit of the message and words. (Powell, J., concurring). These are the grounds upon which I join the judgment of the Court as to Part IV.

Justice STEWART, with whom Justice Brennan, Justice White, and Justice Marshall join, dissenting.

* * * The commission held, and the Court today agrees, that "indecent" is a broader concept than "obscene" as the latter term was defined in *Miller v. California*, because language can be "indecent" although it has social, political or artistic value and lacks prurient appeal. But this construction of § 1464, while perhaps plausible, is by no means compelled. To the contrary, I think that "indecent" should properly be read as meaning no more than "obscene." Since the Carlin monologue concededly was not "obscene," I believe that the commission lacked statutory authority to ban it. Under this construction of the statute, it is unnecessary to address the difficult and important issue of the commission's constitutional power to prohibit speech that would be constitutionally protected outside the context of electronic broadcasting.

* * *

Justice BRENNAN, with whom Justice Marshall joins, dissenting.

I agree with Justice Stewart that, under *Hamling v. United States*, and United States v. 12 200-ft. Reels of Film, 413 U.S. 123 (1973), the word "indecent" in 18 U.S. C.A. § 1464 must be construed to prohibit only obscene speech. I would, therefore, normally refrain from expressing my views on any constitutional issues implicated in this case. However, I find the Court's misapplication of fundamental First Amendment principles so patent, and its attempt to impose *its* notions of propriety on the whole of the American people so misguided, that I am unable to remain silent.

* * *

* * * Yet despite the Court's refusal to create a sliding scale of First Amendment protection calibrated to this Court's perception of the worth of a communication's content, and despite our unanimous agreement that the Carlin monologue is protected speech, a majority of the Court nevertheless finds that, on the facts of this case, the FCC is not constitutionally barred from imposing sanctions on Pacifica for its airing of the Carlin monologue. This majority apparently believes that the FCC's disapproval of Pacifica's afternoon broadcast of Carlin's "Dirty Words" recording is a permissible time, place, and manner regulation. Both the opinion of my Brother Stevens and the opinion of my Brother Powell rely principally on two factors in reaching this conclusion: (1) the capacity of a radio broadcast to intrude into the unwilling listener's home, and (2) the presence of children in the listening audience. * * *

Without question, the privacy interests of an individual in his home are substantial and deserving of significant protection. In finding these interests sufficient to justify the content regulation of protected speech, however, the Court commits two errors. First, it misconceives the nature of the privacy interests involved where an individual voluntarily chooses to admit radio communications into his home. Second it ignores the constitutionally protected interests of both those who wish to transmit and those who desire to receive broadcasts that many—including the FCC and this Court—might find offensive.

* * *

Whatever the minimal discomfort suffered by a listener who inadvertently tunes into a program he finds offensive during the brief interval before he can simply extend his arm and switch stations or flick the "off" button, it is surely worth the candle to preserve the broadcaster's right to send, and the right of those interested to receive a message entitled to full First Amendment protection. To reach a contrary balance, as does the Court, is clearly, to follow Justice Stevens' reliance on animal metaphors, "to burn the house to roast the pig."

The Court's balance, of necessity, fails to accord proper weight to the interests of listeners who wish to hear broadcasts the FCC deems offensive. It permits majoritarian tastes completely to preclude a protected message from entering the homes of a receptive, unoffended minority. No decision of this Court supports such a result. Where the individuals comprising the offended majority may freely choose to reject the material being offered, we have never found their privacy interests of such moment to warrant the suppression of speech on privacy grounds. * * *

Most parents will undoubtedly find understandable as well as commendable the Court's sympathy with the FCC's desire to prevent offensive broadcasts from reaching the ears of unsupervised children. Unfortunately, the facial appeal of this justification for radio censorship masks its constitutional insufficiency.

* * * [W]e have made it abundantly clear that "under any test of obscenity as to minors * * * to be obscene 'such expression must be, in some significant way, erotic.'" Quoting Cohen v. California, 403 U.S., at 20.

Because the Carlin monologue is obviously not an erotic appeal to the prurient interests of children, the Court, for the first time, allows the government to prevent minors from gaining access to materials that are not obscene, and are therefore protected, as to them. It thus ignores our recent admonition that "[s]peech that is neither obscene as to youths nor subject to some other legitimate proscription cannot be suppressed solely to protect the young from ideas or images that a legislative body thinks unsuitable for them." [3] The Court's refusal to follow its own pronouncements is especially lamentable since it has the anomalous subsidiary effect, at least in the radio context at issue here, of making completely unavailable to adults material which may not constitutionally be kept even from children. This result violates in spades the principle of Butler v. Michigan, 352 U.S. 380 (1957). * * Speaking for the Court, (in *Butler*). Justice Frankfurter reasoned:

> "The incidence of this enactment is to reduce the adult population of Michigan to reading only what is fit for children. * * * "

* * *

3. It may be that a narrowly drawn regulation prohibiting the use of offensive language on broadcasts directed specifically at younger children constitutes one of the "other legitimate proscription[s]" alluded to in *Erznoznik*. This is so both because of the difficulties inherent in adapting the *Miller* formulation to communications received by young children, and because such children are "not possessed of that full capacity for individual choice which is the presupposition of the First Amendment guarantees." *Ginsberg v. New York.* I doubt, as my Brother Stevens suggests * * * that such a limited regulation amounts to a regulation of speech based on its content, since, by hypothesis, the only persons at whom the regulated communication is directed are incapable of evaluating its content. To the extent that such a regulation is viewed as a regulation based on content, it marks the outermost limits to which content regulation is permissible.

As demonstrated above, neither of the factors relied on by both the opinion of by Brother Powell and the opinion of my Brother Stevens—the intrusive nature of radio and the presence of children in the listening audience—can, when taken on its own terms, support the FCC's disapproval of the Carlin monologue. These two asserted justifications are further plagued by a common failing: the lack of principled limits on their use as a basis for FCC censorship. No such limits come readily to mind, and neither of the opinions comprising the Court serve to clarify the extent to which the FCC may assert the privacy and children-in-the-audience rationales as justification for expunging from the airways protected communications the commission finds offensive. * * * For my own part, even accepting that this case is limited to its facts,[7] I would place the responsibility and the right to weed worthless and offensive communications from the public airways where it belongs and where, until today, it resided: in a public free to choose those communications worthy of its attention from a marketplace unsullied by the censor's hand.

* * *

It is quite evident that I find the Court's attempt to unstitch the warp and woof of First Amendment law in an effort to reshape its fabric to cover the patently wrong result the Court reaches in this case dangerous as well as lamentable. Yet there runs throughout the opinions of my Brothers Powell and Stevens another vein I find equally disturbing: a depressing inability to appreciate that in our land of cultural pluralism, there are many who think, act, and talk differently from the members of this Court, and who do not share their fragile sensibilities. It is only an acute ethnocentric myopia that enables the Court to approve the censorship of communications solely because of the words they contain.

* * *

Today's decision will thus have its greatest impact on broadcasters desiring to reach, and listening audiences comprised of, persons who do not share the Court's view as to which words or expressions are acceptable and who, for a variety of reasons, including a conscious desire to flout majoritarian conventions, express themselves using words that may be regarded as offensive by those from different socio-economic backgrounds. In this context, the Court's decision may be seen for what, in the broader perspective, it really is: another of the dominant culture's inevitable efforts to force those groups who do not share its mores to conform to its way of thinking, acting, and speaking.

* * *

COMMENT

1. Four major themes in the Supreme Court's decision in *Pacifica* should be emphasized. First, the decision says more than that the FCC can regulate broadcast programming that is "indecent" even though it is not "obscene." The decision is a major statement of the basis for broadcast regulation. In this sense it provides a new rationale for broadcast regu-

7. Having insisted that it seeks to impose sanctions on radio communications only in the limited circumstances present here, I believe that the FCC is estopped from using either this decision or its own orders in this case, 56 FCC2d 94 (1975) and 59 FCC2d 892 (1967), as a basis for imposing sanctions on any public radio broadcast other than one aired during the daytime or early evening and containing the relentless repetition, for longer than a brief interval, of "language that describes, in terms patently offensive as measured by contemporary community standards for the broadcast medium, sexual or excretory activities and organs." 56 FCC2d, at 98. For surely broadcasters are not now on notice that the commission desires to regulate any offensive broadcast other than the type of "verbal shock treatment" condemned here, or even this "shock treatment" type of offensive broadcast during the late evening.

lation—apart from the classic scarcity of the spectrum rationale found in the *NBC* case in 1943, text, p. 770. The "uniquely pervasive presence of the broadcast media" and the fact that broadcasting is "uniquely accessible to children"—the unique nature of the broadcast media—provided a basis in itself for broadcast regulation.

Second, the anticensorship provision of the Communications Act, § 326, did not prevent after-the-fact regulation of broadcast programming.

Third, the Court stressed the narrowness of its ruling. This was perhaps the only aspect of the decision which provided any cheer to broadcasters. The validity of FCC regulation of broadcast programming on indecency or obscenity grounds was declared to be related to the context in which the complaint arose. If the allegedly patently offensive programming was broadcast late at night when no children were in the audience, the case for regulation would presumably be far weaker than if the offending program occurred during daytime hours.

Fourth, the Court virtually rang the curtain down on the hope of broadcasters that a Supreme Court decision would one day give them equivalent constitutional status to that enjoyed by the print media. Justice Stevens directly raised and rejected this possibility: "and of all forms of communication, it is broadcasting that has received the most limited First Amendment protection."

2. Then FCC Chairman Charles D. Ferris, reacting to the decision, quickly moved to reassure broadcasters that he did not view the decision as a mandate to "involve myself or the commission in program content." See *Broadcasting*, July 10, 1978, p. 21.

3. A clue that the FCC is unlikely to take an expanded view of its powers as a result of the *Pacifica* decision is found in the commission's rejection of a petition to deny the license renewal application of WGBH, an educational broadcasting station in Boston. Morality in Media of Massachusetts made the following allegations concerning WGBH's programming:

> Petitioner alleges that WGBH–TV "has failed in its responsibility to the community by consistently broadcasting offensive, vulgar and material otherwise harmful to children without adequate supervision or parental warnings."

The FCC granted WGBH's application for license renewal. In the course of its opinion reaching this conclusion, the FCC made the following remarks on its view of its powers under *Pacifica:*

> * * * The Supreme Court's decision in *FCC v. Pacifica Foundation*, affords this commission no general prerogative to intervene in any case where words similar or identical to those in *Pacifica* are broadcast over a licensed radio or television station. We intend strictly to observe the narrowness of the *Pacifica* holding. See In re Application of WGBH Educational Foundation, FCC 78–522, July 31, 1978.

4. The impact of *Pacifica* has been to keep the status quo in place rather than to change the regulatory situation vis-à-vis the treatment of obscenity-related issues by the FCC. Illustrative is a 1981 Memorandum and Order, 87 FCC2d 40 where the FCC announced, over the objection of the ACLU, its determination to continue to apply its obscenity rule to programming under the editorial control of cable operators. Reliance on the Supreme Court's decision in *Pacifica* figured significantly in the FCC's position in the matter:

> Obscenity is not protected speech under the Constitution and its distribution may therefore be restricted. * * * A commission rule which applies only to a broadcast or a cable system operator imposes no prior restraint if it merely provides for the imposition of sanctions after the fact—*i.e.*, after a determination has been made that a rule violation has occurred. FCC v. Pacifica

> Foundation, 438 U.S. 726 (1978). However, a rule which requires the cable system operator to censor programming on a channel set aside as a public forum, to which the programmer has a right of access by virtue of local, state, or federal law, would impose a system of prior restraint in violation (of the Freedman v. Maryland, 380 U.S. 51 (1965) procedural requirements). Our *Order* * * * maintains this constitutional distinction.

In its order complying with the mandate of the Supreme Court in the mandatory public access cable case, *Midwest Video Corp. v. FCC*, text, p. 991, the FCC had announced that it would continue to distinguish between access-type programming which was provided voluntarily or as a result of state or local law and programming which was under the editorial control of the cable operator. Compare American Civil Liberties Union v. FCC, 523 F.2d 1344 (C.A.D.C.1975). See Memorandum and Order, 83 FCC2d 147 (1980). In the 1980 *Memorandum and Order*, the FCC said that it would continue to apply the specific content control rules (§ 76.215) concerning obscenity only to programming which is subject to the editorial control of the cable system operator. In short, the FCC has limited its obscenity rule to cable systems which are under the editorial control of the cable operator. Isn't an argument available that *Pacifica* might have authorized the FCC to apply its obscenity rules to access-type cable programming despite *Freedman v. Maryland*?

A Note on Violence

The issue of legal control of violence in programming is far less developed than the issues of "obscenity" and "indecency" in broadcast programming. Nevertheless, there are some legal landmarks in this area. In Writers Guild of America West, Inc. v. FCC, 423 F.Supp. 1064 (C.D.Calif. 1976), the National Association of Broadcasters (NAB) sponsored an effort to segregate a segment of television prime time which would be free from alleged exploitation of sex and violence. This development, the so-called "family viewing" hour, was held to be an invalid attempt at censorship. The court said the "family viewing" hour violated the First Amendment since it emanated from an informal FCC-induced effort at censorship. This decision was vacated. See, Writer's Guild of America v. The American Broadcasting Company, 609 F.2d 355 (9th Cir.1979). See Cowan, *See No Evil: The Backstage Battle Over Sex and Violence in Television* (1978).

Congress has been interested in the problem of violence on television particularly in terms of the impact of such programming on children. In 1974, Congress directed the FCC to detail its plans "to protect children from excessive programming of violence." The FCC's reaction to the problem is found in Report on the Broadcast of Violent, Indecent and Obscene Material, 51 FCC2d 418 (1975). In the *Report*, the FCC came out against any rigid regulation of such programming and asked the industry to police itself. But see (as a possibly bolder approach), In Re Capital Communications, Inc., 54 FCC2d 1035 (1975).

Does the *Pacifica* case where the Supreme Court permitted the FCC to regulate otherwise constitutionally protected material on the basis of "indecency" suggest that the Congress may be able to endow the FCC with jurisdiction to regulate "violence"? Could some forms of violence be deemed to constitute "indecency"?

Tort Liability of Television—Impact of PACIFICA

1. Does *Pacifica* aid in the development of a legal basis for damage claims for tortious injuries which were occasioned by incitements to violence on television?

Does the *Pacifica* case help to remove the barrier to the development of such a tort theory? See Cox Broadcasting Corp. v. Cohn, 420 U.S. 469 (1972).

2. In Weirum v. RKO General, Inc., 123 Cal.Rptr. 468, 539 P.2d 36 (1975), the Supreme Court of California held that a radio station could be liable for the deaths of two motorists who were killed as the result of a promotional program sponsored by the station. The station had sponsored a contest to reward the first listener who could locate one of the station's disc jockeys. The disc jockey was driving around Los Angeles broadcasting clues about his location. Some teenagers, anxious to locate the disc jockey, forced a car off the road, killing its two occupants. The heirs of the victims sued the radio station. The California Supreme Court held that the First Amendment would not be a bar to establishing liability against the radio station since "the foreseeable results 'of the broadcast' created an undue risk of harm." The Supreme Court of California further observed: "The First Amendment does not sanction the infliction of physical injury merely because achieved by word, rather than act." Although the *Weirum* case was decided before *Pacifica*, the California Supreme Court had no difficulty in saying that the First Amendment would not be a bar to liability.

3. In other cases, however, the First Amendment has been held to be a bar for actions to establish liability against suits to recover injuries which allegedly were occasioned by television broadcasts. In Olivia N. v. NBC, 7 Med.L.Rptr. 2359, 178 Cal.Rptr. 888 (1981), an action was brought to recover damages for physical and emotional injuries inflicted upon a female minor by her assailant who had seen the television movie "Born Innocent," broadcast by NBC. The assailant had viewed and discussed an "artificial rape scene" in "Born Innocent." The plaintiff asserted that "the film allegedly caused the assailant to decide to commit a similar act on her." The trial court granted judgment for NBC, Niemi v. NBC, 2 Med.L.Rptr. 1830 (1976). That decision was reversed by the California Court of Appeal, Olivia N. v. NBC, 3 Med.L.Rptr. 1454, 141 Cal.Rptr. 511 (1977). On remand for trial, the trial court granted NBC's motion for judgment of nonsuit, and the plaintiff appealed. The California Court of Appeal affirmed the trial court's grant of the motion for nonsuit. As a result, *Olivia N.*, the female minor, was out of court. The California Court of Appeal, in *Olivia N.*, pointed out the dangers that would follow if negligence actions for harm attributable to television broadcasts were to become freely available.

> Realistically, television networks would become significantly more inhibited in the selection of controversial materials if liability were to be based on simple negligence theory. * * * The deterrent effects of subjecting the television networks to negligence liability because of their programming choices would dampen the vigor and limit the variety of public debate.

The court in *Olivia N.* considered the impact of *FCC v. Pacifica Foundation* and said that, notwithstanding the pervasive effects of the broadcast media and the unique access afforded children by them, "the effect of the imposition of liability could reduce the U.S. adult population to viewing only what is fit for children." Considerable attention was given to the question of whether or not the film had in fact advocated or encouraged violent acts which constituted "incitement" under the rule of Brandenburg v. Ohio, 395 U.S. 444 (1969). *Olivia N.* conceded that the film did not advocate or encourage violent acts and, therefore, did not constitute an "incitement." *Olivia N.* held that the television broadcast which occasioned the law suit "concededly did not fulfill the incitement requirements of *Brandenburg*." As a consequence, the broadcast was "constitutionally protected." For there to be liability for negligence as the result of alleged harm occasioned by a television broadcast, there first has to be a showing that the broadcast actually constituted an incitement to violence, as that phrase is defined in *Brandenburg v. Ohio.* If the incitement to violence can be shown, then the First Amendment barrier to allowing the action is removed because speech, as *Brandenburg* puts it, "directed to incite or produce imminently lawless action * * * likely to incite or produce such action" is not protected under the First Amendment.

The California Court of Appeal in *Olivia N.* concluded: "The trial court's determination that the First Amendment bars appellant's claim where no incitement is alleged must be upheld." Finally, the court pointed out in passing that the "narrowness of the *Pacifica* decision precludes its application here." The court also pointed out that Justice Powell, in his concurrence in *Pacifica*, had emphasized that the Court was not free to decide on the basis of content which speech protected by the First Amendment is most valuable. In addition, the court pointed out that reliance on *Pacifica Foundation* for the suit in *Olivia N.* was "misplaced" because "*Pacifica* deals with regulation of indecency, not the imposition of general tort liability." The Supreme Court of California refused to entertain the appeal.

Do you see any distinction between *Weirum* and *Olivia N.*? Was there more of an "incitement" in *Weirum*?

4. De Filippo v. NBC, 8 Med.L.Rptr. 1873, 446 A.2d 1036 (R.I.1981), involved a negligence action brought against NBC and WJAR–TV (the NBC affiliate in Providence, Rhode Island) by the parents of a boy who hanged himself while trying to imitate a stunt that he was watching on "The Tonight Show." Johnny Carson, host of "The Tonight Show," announced that a professional stuntman would "hang" him in the broadcast. Robinson said of the stunt he would perform: "[B]elive me, it's not something that you want to go and try—this is a stunt. * * *" The audience laughed, and the following conversation took place:

> Robinson: I've got to laugh—you know, you're all laughing. * * *
>
> Carson: Explain that to me.
>
> Robinson: I've seen people try things like this. I really have. I happen to know somebody who did something similar to it, just fooling around, and almost broke his neck. * * *

Justice Murray of the Rhode Island Supreme Court states the consequence of the broadcast: "Several hours after the broadcast, the De Filippos found Nicky hanging from a noose in front of the television set, which was still on and turned to WJAR–TV."

The plaintiffs, seeking $10,000,000 in damages, asserted four theories in trial court alleging

1. that the defendant broadcasters had negligently permitted the stunt to be broadcast,
2. negligently failed to warn infant plaintiff of the dangers of the program,
3. a claim in products liability, and
4. an intentional tort-trespass.

Defendant broadcasters made a motion for summary judgment which was granted by the trial judge. The judge ruled that the First Amendment barred relief. The trial judge also ruled that the defendant's broadcast was not a product. The Supreme Court of Rhode Island affirmed the ruling of the trial court, declined to rule on the trial judge's finding that the broadcast was not a product: "We hold that the First Amendment does indeed bar recovery in such actions; therefore, we do not reach plaintiffs' other contentions."

In *De Filippo* the Rhode Island Supreme Court said that they could find no basis for a conclusion that the broadcast could be construed as an "incitement":

> Under the facts of this case, we see no basis for a finding that the broadcast in

> any way could be construed as incitement. Consequently, the exception set forth in *Brandenburg v. Ohio, supra*, is inapplicable to the case at bar. In any event, the incitement exception must be applied with extreme care since the criteria underlying its application are vague, further, allowing recovery under such an exception would inevitably lead to self-censorship on the part of broadcasters, thus depriving both broadcasters and viewers of freedom and choice, for "above all else, the First Amendment means that government has no power to restrict expression because of its message, its ideas, its subject matter or its content." Police Department of Chicago v. Mosley, 408 U.S. 92, 95, 92 S.Ct. 2286, 2290, 33 L.Ed.2d 212, 216 (1972).

Accordingly, the court held that the award of summary judgment to the defendant broadcaster was proper. The appeal was denied and dismissed, and the judgment appealed from was affirmed. The court seemed to agree with the trial justice that the *Weirum* case could be distinguished in that there was an "explicit incitement" involved in *Weirum*. Is that a fair analysis of *Weirum?*

Another case that figured in the decision of the Rhode Island Supreme Court in *De Filippo* was Zamora v. CBS, 5 Med.L. Rptr. 2109, 480 F.Supp. 199 (C.D.Fla.1979). Zamora had been convicted of murder and sued three television networks for having impermissibly "stimulated, incited, and instigated" him to "duplicate the atrocities that he viewed on television." The federal district court found that the First Amendment was a bar to suit and dismissed the complaint. *Zamora* was distinguished as follows:

> The plaintiffs maintain that the holding in *Zamora* is inapposite because there the plaintiff was not referring to one specific incident but to television broadcasting in general. While plaintiffs are correct in pointing out the differences between *Zamora* and the instant case, we do not accept their characterization of that case as inapposite. In both cases the plaintiffs tried to establish negligence and recklessness by the broadcasters. We are therefore persuaded by the [d]istrict [c]ourt's holding that the First Amendment bars this type of suit.

How does one measure incitement? The *De Filippo* court said that this was a problem but pointed out that the only person who appears to have been "incited" was young De Filippo. In such circumstances, the court said it could not find that the broadcast constituted incitement. The court was especially concerned about the adverse consequences that would flow from a holding that the broadcaster could be liable.

> This self-censorship would not only violate defendants' limited right to make their own programming decisions, Writers Guild of America, West, Inc. v. Federal Communications Commission, 2 Med.L.Rptr. 1009, 423 F.Supp. 1064, 1154 (C.D.Cal.1976), vacated sub nom. Writers Guild of America v. American Broadcasting Co. 609 F.2d 355 (9th Cir. 1979), but would also violate the paramount rights of the viewers to suitable access to "social, esthetic, moral, and other ideas and experiences * * *." Columbia Broadcasting System v. Democratic National Committee, 412 U.S. 94, 102 (1973).

De Filippo referred to the *Pacifica* case and mentioned with apparent approval its ruling that the First Amendment did not provide "the broadcast media with unabridged rights, as is evidenced by the limited governmental control over the broadcast media." But *Pacifica* was not seen by the Rhode Island Supreme Court in *De Filippo* as a basis for removing the First Amendment bar sufficient to provide a basis for tort liability against the broadcasters.

The Relationship Between Obscenity in Broadcasting and the License Renewal Process

1. The license renewal process can be used as a regulatory device to control ob-

scene, indecent, or profane utterance. In Robinson v. FCC, 334 F.2d 534 (D.C.Cir. 1964), the FCC took the unusual step of refusing to renew a license in a case where, among other issues, the licensee had allocated a substantial amount of its programming to the Charlie Walker disc jockey show which featured off-color jokes and remarks. The station involved, Palmetto Broadcasting Co., WDKD, was owned by the late Hollywood actor, movie "bad man" Edward G. Robinson, Jr. See Palmetto Broadcasting Co., 33 FCC 250 (1962).

The obscenity issue in the Robinson radio case came up in the contest of the renewal process. The FCC denied Robinson's application for renewal of radio station WDKD, Kingstree, South Carolina. One of the grounds for denial listed by the FCC was that Robinson had made misrepresentations in the license renewal proceeding. (Robinson said he had never heard complaints about the objectionable disc jockey show, but numerous witnesses testified to the contrary.) The court of appeals in a per curiam opinion affirmed the decision on that ground alone. Robinson v. FCC, 334 F.2d 534 (D.C.Cir. 1964).

Judge Wilbur Miller, in a concurring opinion, believed that some of the Charlie Walker disc jockey shows constituted violations of 18 U.S.C.A. § 1464.

One of the FCC findings which the court of appeals refused to pass upon was the finding that some of the disc jockey program material was "coarse, vulgar, suggestive, and susceptible of indecent, double meaning." Judge Miller thought this and other FCC findings should have been upheld by the court of appeals. Judge Miller speculated on why the court's opinion in *Robinson v. FCC* nervously avoided the obscenity issue:

"Perhaps, the majority refrained from discussing the other issues because of a desire to avoid approving any commission action which might be called program censorship. I do not think that denying renewal of a license because of the station's broadcast of obscene, indecent or profane language—a serious criminal offense—can properly be called program censorship."

Robinson petitioned for rehearing and raised the issue once more that censorship by the FCC of program content was unconstitutional.

Do you think the per curiam opinion for the court of appeals can be read as authorizing a denial of license renewal for violation of an FCC programming standard?

It should be noted that the FCC decision in *Palmetto Broadcasting Co.* did not rely on the statutory language of 18 U.S. C.A. § 1464. The FCC took the position that since the broadcaster must perform in the public interest to secure renewal, renewal could be denied if the FCC found that the licensee had broadcast "coarse" and "vulgar" programs not in the public interest. In *Palmetto*, the FCC scored "coarseness and indecency" and did not predicate its decision on the general law of obscenity.

2. (The *Palmetto* decision was appealed under the name of *Robinson v. FCC.*) Judge Miller in his concurrence in *Robinson* relied on KFKB Broadcasting Association v. Federal Radio Commission, 47 F.2d 670 (D.C.Cir. 1931), for the proposition that making obscene, indecent, or profane language a demerit or at least a factor in a renewal proceeding was not censorship:

"There has been no attempt on the part of the commission to subject any part of appellant's broadcasting matter to scrutiny prior to its release. In considering the question whether the public interest, convenience or necessity will be served by a renewal of appellant's license, the commission has merely exercised its undoubted right to take note of appellant's past conduct which is not censorship."

3. The whole area of obscenity in broadcasting has been an area, as *WUHY* illustrates, where general constitutional standards are apparently not applied, this despite the fact that no indigenous stan-

dards have been evolved for broadcasting by either the FCC or the courts. The result is considerable ambiguity concerning the issue of obscenity in broadcasting.

4. A monetary forfeiture proceeding, authorized by § 503(b)(1)(E) of the Communications Act against broadcast licensees who violate § 1464 for "obscene" and "indecent" programming, was inflated by the FCC into a challenge to the broadcaster's license by an order that its license renewal application be set for hearing even though the application was otherwise uncontested. See In re Notice to Trustees of the University of Pennsylvania, 57 FCC2d 783 (1975).

On January 27, 1975 radio station WXPN(FM), Philadelphia, Pennsylvania, created a furor with two allegedly obscene broadcasts of a "live" call-in program called "The Vegetable Report," broadcast Monday evenings between 4:00 P.M. and 7:00 P.M. The station was licensed to the Trustees of the University of Pennsylvania but admittedly was managed solely by the students of the University. Despite corrective action by the University, the FCC found a violation of § 1464, text, p. 908, for the broadcast of indecent and obscene matter. Accordingly, under § 503(b)(1)(E) of the Communications Act, the FCC fined the licensee $2,000.

The FCC found at least four particular segments of the January 27 broadcast obscene under the test set forth in *Miller v. California*. One of the segments dealt with sexual relations between husband and wife. The other three dealt with using an on-the-air conversation with a three-year-old boy for purposes of sexual titillation. In one instance, the program announcer asked the child who had been put on the phone by his mother, "Johnny, can you say 'fuck'?"

Concerning these four segments, the FCC stated:

> The commission believes that these particular segments appear to appeal to the prurient interest, describe sexual conduct in a patently offensive way, and lack serious literary, artistic, political, or scientific value. We note that the Court in *Illinois Citizens Committee*, indicated that it would not be inappropriate for the commission to evaluate a broadcasting program that is episodic in nature with a cluster of individual and typically disconnected commentaries such as a call-in program of this type. We believe that these segments of the January 27 broadcast appear to present a pandering approach to explicit descriptions of ultimate sexual acts. Furthermore, the broadcast not only occurred at a time of the day when children might be expected to be present in the listening audience, but at one point apparently involved a three-year-old child directly in the discussion.
>
> These two broadcasts of "The Vegetable Report" also appear to have been indecent under the then prevailing standard regarding indecent language set forth in the *WUHY* case, and the subsequent standard enunciated in *WBAI*, to comply with the *Miller* decision.

In view of the FCC determination that WXPN had broadcast obscene and indecent programming, the FCC said it was unable to find that a grant of the station's renewal application would serve the public interest, convenience, and necessity. It therefore designated the application for hearing.

The FCC placed upon the licensee, the University of Pennsylvania, the burden of proving that it possessed the requisite qualifications to be a licensee and that a grant of the application would serve the public interest.

In terms of measuring the future impact of the Supreme Court's decision in *Pacifica* on all phases of broadcast obscenity regulation, it is noteworthy that in the *WPXN* case the FCC relied on its own decision in the *Pacifica* case, or as the case was styled at the FCC level, In re Citizens Complaint Against Pacifica Foundation WBAI–FM, 32 R.R.2d 1331 (1975).

The FCC stated that in *WBAI* it had relied on the *Illinois Citizens Committee* decision which "was the first judicial decision upholding the commission's conclusion that the probable presence of children in the radio audience is relevant to a determination of obscenity."

The Supreme Court *Pacifica* decision could be used to provide new impetus and new legitimacy for use of the denial of the license renewal application as a sanction in the enforcement of the regulation of "indecency" and "obscenity" in broadcasting by the FCC. But thus far this has not happened.

"Obscene, Indecent, or Profane" Utterance in Broadcasting: The Enforcement Role of the Federal Courts

1. As has been the case with the FCC, the meaning of the words "indecent or profane" in 18 U.S.C.A. § 1464 has been a source of legal controversy in the federal courts. In Tallman v. United States, 465 F.2d 282 (7th Cir. 1972), a full inquiry into the meaning of these terms was avoided. Since the petitioner, the party being prosecuted, was indicted for having broadcast "obscene" language, the petitioner was actually tried only for using obscene language. The court said that the offending broadcasts "show plain filth by any contemporary standards of obscenity," so that there was no need for the jury to determine whether they were also "indecent" or "profane."

However, the *Tallman* case took the position that the terms "profane" and "indecent" are capable of sufficiently precise definition to withstand constitutional attack. United States v. Smith, 467 F.2d 1126 (7th Cir. 1972), appears to take a similar view. There are no indications in *Tallman* on how these terms differ from the definition of "obscenity."

2. A full inquiry into the meaning of the words "obscene, indecent, or profane" in 18 U.S.C. § 1464 in the context of a criminal prosecution is found in United States v. Simpson, 561 F.2d 53 (7th Cir. 1977). A federal court of appeals was there presented with the question of whether the words "indecent" and "obscene" used in 18 U.S.C.A. § 1464, text, p. 908, had distinct meanings. The question arose not in the context of an FCC enforcement of regulation § 1464, but in the context of a criminal prosecution brought by the Department of Justice of that statute. The defendant had used a CB radio transmitter in his home "to broadcast explicit references to sexual activities, descriptions of sexual and execretory organs, and abusive epithets directed to other radio operators with whom he was communicating, all in street vernacular." The broadcasts were received not only on citizens band radio but on AM radio, television, and telephones.

The defendant was convicted for violation of § 1464 as well as on other counts. The court stated the issue before it: "The jury's determination in its guilty verdict that the broadcast was 'indecent' but not 'obscene' requires us to decide whether those two words, as used in the statute have different meanings." The court added somewhat ruefully: "We would have had no difficulty in affirming a finding that the language was obscene, but we are of course bound by the jury's contrary finding."

In the jury instructions, the district court judge defined "obscenity" in accordance with Miller v. California, 413 U.S. 15 (1973). The judge's definition of "indecency" was similar but omitted a key element of the *Miller* definition of obscenity—appeal of the material, taken as a whole, to the prurient interest in sex. Could the defendant be convicted for "indecency" under § 1464 on the basis of anything less than the full constitutional test employed for obscenity? The *Simpson* court ruled that he could not.

The court of appeals in *Simpson* relied on the fact that the words in the mailing statute in the criminal code, 18 U.S.C. § 1461 had been interpreted in Manual Enterprises, Inc. v. Day, 370 U.S. 478 at 482–484 (1962), as reaching only indecent material which as now expressed in Roth v. United States, 354 U.S. 476, at 489 (1957) 'taken as a whole appeals to the prurient interest.' ". The *Simpson* court noted that this passage from *Manual* was later quoted with approval by the Supreme Court in Hamling v. United States, 418 U.S. 87, 117 (1974). "Indecency" appeared to be constitutionally punishable if it could meet the general definition of "obscenity."

The development that the *Simpson* court felt was decisive to whether "indecent" utterance in § 1464 should be interpreted as having a distinct meaning from "obscene" utterance derived from a companion case to *Miller*, United States v. 12 200-Ft. Reels of Super 8MM. Film, 413 U.S. 123, 130 (1973). In *12 200-Ft. Reels,* the word "indecent" in 18 U.S.C.A. § 1462 (dealing with the transportation of materials in the interstate commerce) had been defined as follows: "[W]e are prepared to construe such terms as limiting regulated material to patently offensive representations or descriptions of that specific 'hard core' sexual conduct given as examples in *Miller*. * * *"

The *Simpson* court acknowledged that the Court in *12 200-Ft. Reels* had not, in defining "indecent," specifically referred to § 1464. The *Simpson* court then attempted to prophesy on how the Supreme Court would ultimately interpret the reference to "indecent" utterance in § 1464:

> [T]he constitutional doubt may be less serious with respect to radio broadcasts than it would be with respect to § 1462's application to materials transported in interstate commerce, (but) we must assume that the Court would interpret "indecent" in § 1464 as it has in § 1462.

The *Simpson* court's prophecy on whether the Supreme Court would uphold its interpretation of the words "indecent" and "obscene" as parts of a single proscription "applicable only if the challenged language appeals to the prurient interest" proved to be entirely wrong. The Supreme Court in the *Pacifica* case, on the contrary, declared that the words "obscene, indecent, or profane" in § 1464 were in the disjunctive suggesting that each of the foregoing terms had a separate meaning. Further, even though "appeal to the prurient interest" is part of the definition of what is obscene, it was not part of the definition of "indecent" which was defined as nonconformance with accepted standards of morality.

The Supreme Court declined review in the *Simpson* case. Therefore, it is not clear whether the same latitude which was permitted to the FCC by the Supreme Court in *Pacifica* to regulate "indecent" as opposed to "obscene" speech is also open to the Department of Justice in bringing criminal prosecutions for broadcasting "indecent" programming under § 1464. Certainly, when criminal sanctions such as imprisonment are at stake, the First Amendment interests of a broadcast ought to weigh more heavily than is the case in an FCC proceeding where the threatened sanction is a monetary forfeiture, a short-term renewal, or even the denial of a license renewal.

In *Simpson*, the court emphasized that its view that the words "indecent" and "obscene" were interchangeable "parts of a single proscription" was a matter of statutory interpretation. The court was thus spared the difficult question of resolving "whether the First Amendment protects, against federal criminal sanctions, a radio broadcast made in the crude sex vernacular of the street that is patently offensive but lacks prurient appeal." With the advent of the Supreme Court decision in *Pac-*

ifica, the constitutional issue that the *Simpson* court was happy not to reach is now both open and troublesome.

STANDING TO ENFORCE THE FEDERAL COMMUNICATIONS ACT

Who is the Addressee of the Public Interest?

The sanctions available to enforce the FCC's programming policies have been indicated previously. See text, p. 900. But the question remains: who is entitled to set the enforcement process in motion? If a licensee seeks renewal of a license, who can challenge that renewal application? The law is clear that the other applicants for the license may certainly challenge a renewal application. Indeed, in such a case a comparative hearing must be held in which all the applicants are joined in a single proceeding and the merits and demerits of each applicant are weighed one against the other. See Ashbacker Radio Corp. v. FCC, 326 U.S. 327 (1945).

But who beyond the competitors of a licensee may institute and intervene in FCC proceedings? Until recently, standing to challenge the programming activity of a licensee before the FCC was rather limited. The traditional view had been established by the Supreme Court's decision in FCC v. Sanders, 309 U.S. 470 (1940), where it was held that a showing of economic injury was necessary for standing before the commission. The theory behind this doctrine was that only someone who had an economically measurable interest in a proceeding could be considered to have a *bona fide* or nonmischievous stake in it. The theory proceeded on the belief that the public interest could best be defended by someone who was economically injured by the illegal behavior of a licensee since only he would have sufficient incentive to be steadily on the alert for noncompliance with the Federal Communications Act.

The difficulty with the doctrine was that it had an industry rather than a consumer orientation. The *Sanders* doctrine proceeded on the rather simplistic assumption that the competitive interests of other members of the broadcasting industry exhausted the range of values encompassed under the category of broadcasting in the "public interest." As a result, the stake of the listening audience in the social and informing function of broadcasting was largely unrepresented. An approach to standing based on economic injury reflected a quantitative rather than a qualitative approach to the problems of broadcasting. In 1966, a heavy assault was finally made on the *Sanders* doctrine.

OFFICE OF COMMUNICATION OF THE UNITED CHURCH OF CHRIST v. FCC,

359 F.2D 994 (D.C.CIR. 1966).

BURGER, Circuit Judge: This is an appeal from a decision of the Federal Communications Commission granting to the Intervenor a one-year renewal of its license to operate television station WLBT in Jackson, Mississippi. * * * The commission dismissed appellants' petition and, without a hearing, took the unusual step of granting a restricted and conditional renewal of the license. Instead of granting the usual three-year renewal, it limited the license to one year from June 1, 1965, and imposed what it characterizes here as "strict conditions" on WLBT's operations in that one-year probationary period.

The questions presented are

a. whether appellants, or any of them, have standing before the Federal Communications Commission as parties in interest under Section 309(d) of the Federal

Communications Act to contest the renewal of a broadcast license; and

b. whether the commission was required by Section 309(e) to conduct an evidentiary hearing on the claims of the appellants prior to acting on renewal of the license.

BACKGROUND

The complaints against Intervenor embrace charges of discrimination on racial and religious grounds and of excessive commercials. As the commission's order indicates, the first complaints go back to 1955 when it was claimed that WLBT had deliberately cut off a network program about race relations problems on which the General Counsel of the NAACP was appearing and had flashed on the viewers' screens a "Sorry, Cable Trouble" sign. In 1957 another complaint was made to the commission that WLBT had presented a program urging the maintenance of racial segregation and had refused requests for time to present the opposing viewpoint. Since then numerous other complaints have been made.

When WLBT sought a renewal of its license in 1958, the commission at first deferred action because of complaints of this character but eventually granted the usual three-year renewal because it found that, while there had been failures to comply with the Fairness Doctrine, the failures were isolated instances of improper behavior and did not warrant denial of WLBT's renewal application.

Shortly after the outbreak of prolonged civil disturbances centering in large part around the University of Mississippi in September 1962, the commission again received complaints that various Mississippi radio and television stations, including WLBT, had presented programs concerning racial integration in which only one viewpoint was aired. In 1963 the commission investigated and requested the stations to submit detailed factual reports on their programs dealing with racial issues. On March 3, 1964, while the commission was considering WLBT's responses, WLBT filed the license renewal application presently under review.

To block license renewal, appellants filed a petition in the commission urging denial of WLBT's application and asking to intervene in their own behalf and as representatives of "all other television viewers in the State of Mississippi." * *

The petition claimed that WLBT failed to serve the general public because it provided a disproportionate amount of commercials and entertainment and did not give a fair and balanced presentation of controversial issues, especially those concerning Negroes, who comprise almost forty-five per cent of the total population within its prime service area; it also claimed discrimination against local activities of the Catholic Church.

Appellants claim standing before the commission on the grounds that:

1. They are individuals and organizations who were denied a reasonable opportunity to answer their critics, a violation of the Fairness Doctrine.

2. These individuals and organizations represent the nearly one half of WLBT's potential listening audience who were denied an opportunity to have their side of controversial issues presented, equally a violation of the Fairness Doctrine, and who were more generally ignored and discriminated against in WLBT's programs.

3. These individuals and organizations represent the total audience, not merely one part of it, and they assert the right of all listeners, regardless of race or religion, to hear and see balanced programming on significant public questions as required by the Fairness Doctrine and also their broad interest that the station be operated in the public interest in all respects.

The commission denied the petition to intervene on the ground that standing is predicated upon the invasion of a legally protected interest or an injury which is direct and substantial and that "petitioners * * * can assert no greater interest of claim or injury than members of the general public." * * *

Upon considering Petitioners' claims and WLBT's answers to them on this basis, the commission concluded that

> serious issues are presented whether the licensee's operations have fully met the public interest standard. Indeed, it is a close question whether to designate for hearing these applications for renewal of license.

Nevertheless, the commission conducted no hearing but granted a license renewal, asserting a belief that renewal would be in the public interest since broadcast stations were in a position to make worthwhile contributions to the resolution of pressing racial problems, this contribution was "needed immediately" in the Jackson area, and WLBT, if operated properly, could make such a contribution. * * *

The one-year renewal was on conditions which plainly put WLBT on notice that the renewal was in the nature of a probationary grant. * * *

STANDING OF APPELLANTS

The commission's denial of standing to appellants was based on the theory that, absent a potential direct, substantial injury or adverse effect from the administrative action under consideration, a petitioner has no standing before the commission and that the only types of effects sufficient to support standing are economic injury and electrical interference. It asserted its traditional position that members of the listening public do not suffer any injury peculiar to them and that allowing them standing would pose great administrative burdens.

Up to this time, the courts have granted standing to intervene only to those alleging electrical interference, NBC v. FCC (KOA), 132 F.2d 545 (1942), aff'd, 319 U.S. 239, or alleging some economic injury, e.g., FCC v. Sanders Bros. Radio Station, 309 U.S. 470 (1940). * * *

* * *

We see no reason to believe, therefore, that Congress through its committees had any thought that electrical interference and economic injury were to be the exclusive grounds for standing or that it intended to limit participation of the listening public to writing letters to the Complaints Division of the commission. Instead, the Congressional reports seem to recognize that the issue of standing was to be left to the courts. * * *

* * * Since the concept of standing is a practical and functional one designed to insure that only those with a genuine and legitimate interest can participate in a proceeding, we can see no reason to exclude those with such an obvious and acute concern as the listening audience. * * *

There is nothing unusual or novel in granting the consuming public standing to challenge administrative actions.

* * *

These "consumer" cases were not decided under the Federal Communications Act, but all of them have in common with the case under review the interpretation of language granting standing to persons "affected" or "aggrieved". The commission fails to suggest how we are to distinguish these cases from those involving standing of broadcast "consumers" to oppose license renewals in the Federal Communications Commission. * * * Furthermore, assuming, we look only to the commercial economic aspects and ignore vital public interest, we cannot believe that the economic stake of the consumers of electricity or public transit riders is more significant than that of listeners who collectively have a huge aggregate investment in receiving equipment.

The argument that a broadcaster is not a public utility is beside the point. * * *

After nearly five decades of operation the broadcast industry does not seem to have grasped the simple fact that a broadcast license is a public trust subject to termination for breach of duty. * * *

Such beneficial contribution as these Appellants, or some of them, can make must not be left to the grace of the commission.

Public participation is especially important in a renewal proceeding, since the public will have been exposed for at least three years to the licensee's performance, as cannot be the case when the commission considers an initial grant, unless the applicant has a prior record as a licensee. In a renewal proceeding, furthermore, public spokesmen, such as appellants here, may be the only objectors. In a community served by only one outlet, the public interest focus is perhaps sharper and the need for airing complaints often greater than where, for example, several channels exist. * * * Even when there are multiple competing stations in a locality, various factors may operate to inhibit the other broadcasters from opposing a renewal application. An imperfect rival may be thought a desirable rival, or there may be a "gentleman's agreement" of deference to a fellow broadcaster in the hope he will reciprocate on a propitious occasion.

Thus we are brought around by analogy to the Supreme Court's reasoning in *Sanders*; unless the listeners—the broadcast consumers—can be heard, there may be no one to bring programming deficiencies or offensive overcommercialization to the the attention of the commission in an effective manner. * * * The late Edmond Cahn addressed himself to this problem in its broadest aspects when he said, "some consumers need bread; others need Shakespeare; others need their rightful place in the national society—what they all need is processors of law who will consider the people's needs more significant than administrative convenience." *Law in the Consumer Perspective*, 112 U.Pa.L.Rev. 1, 13 (1963). * * *

The responsible and representative groups eligible to intervene cannot here be enumerated or categorized specifically; such community organizations as civic associations, professional societies, unions, churches, and educational institutions or associations might well be helpful to the commission. * * *

The fears of regulatory agencies that their processes will be inundated by expansion of standing criteria are rarely borne out. Always a restraining factor is the expense of participation in the administrative process, an economic reality which will operate to limit the number of those who will seek participation; legal and related expenses of administrative proceedings are such that even those with large economic interests find the costs burdensome.

In line with this analysis, we do not now hold that all of the appellants have standing to challenge WLBT's renewal. We do not reach that question. As to these appellants we limit ourselves to holding that the commission must allow standing to one or more of them as responsible representatives to assert and prove the claims they have urged in their petition. * * *

HEARING

We hold further that in the circumstances shown by this record an evidentiary hearing was required in order to resolve the public interest issue. Under Section 309(e) the commission must set a renewal application for hearing where "a substantial and material question of fact is presented *or* the commission for any reason is unable to make the finding" that the public interest, convenience, and necessity will be served by the license renewal. [Emphasis supplied.]

The commission argues in this Court that it accepted all appellants' allegations of WLBT's misconduct and that for this reason no hearing was necessary. * * *

The commission in effect sought to justify its grant of the one-year license, in the face of accepted facts irreconcilable with a public interest finding, on the ground that as a matter of policy the immediate need warranted the risks involved, and that the "strict conditions" it imposed on the grant would improve *future* operations. However the conditions which the commission made explicit in the one-year license are implicit in every grant. * * *

Assuming *arguendo* that the commission's acceptance of appellants' allegations would satisfy one ground for dispensing with a hearing, i.e., absence of a question of fact, Section 309(e) also commands that in order to avoid a hearing the commission must make an affirmative finding that renewal will serve the public interest. Yet the only finding on this crucial factor is a qualified statement that the public interest would be served, provided WLBT thereafter complied strictly with the specified conditions. * * * The statutory public interest finding cannot be inferred from a statement of the obvious truth that a properly operated station will serve the public interest.

* * * The issues which should have been considered could be resolved only in an evidentiary hearing in which all aspects of its qualifications and performance could be explored. * * *

We hold that the grant of a renewal of WLBT's license for one year was erroneous. The commission is directed to conduct hearings on WLBT's renewal application, allowing public intervention pursuant to his holding. Since the commission has already decided that appellants are responsible representatives of the listening public of the Jackson area, we see no obstacle to a prompt determination granting standing to appellants or some of them. Whether WLBT should be able to benefit from a showing of good performance, if such is the case, since June 1965 we do not undertake to decide. The commission has had no occasion to pass on this issue and we therefore refrain from doing so.

The record is remanded to the commission for further proceedings consistent with this opinion; jurisdiction is retained in this court.

Reversed and remanded.

COMMENT

In what sense does the very nature of the "fairness" doctrine stimulate a recognition of the inadequacy of the standing rules as they existed prior to *United Church of Christ*?

What difficulties do you see in implementing the new standing approach of *United Church of Christ* in terms of relating it to programming areas other than the "fairness" doctrine? See text, p. 944.

The Court's opinion in *United Church of Christ* appears to exude a mood of displeasure with the commission's regulatory philosophy. Why is the FCC in the *WLBT* case, unlike the court, so sympathetic to the incumbent broadcaster?

United Church of Christ II: The Meaning of Standing for the Citizen Group

1. On the basis of the holding in the first *United Church of Christ* decision that listeners and viewers had standing to participate in broadcast renewal proceedings, the United Church of Christ went back to the FCC ready to show at the hearing the unfitness of WLBT for license renewal. It was a vain effort. This time the FCC granted a full term three-year renewal to WLBT.

Once again the United Church of Christ took the FCC to court. Once again, Judge Burger reversed the FCC. Office of Communication of the United Church of Christ v. FCC (United Church of Christ II), 425

F.2d 543 (D.C. Cir. 1969). But this time, Judge Burger, now Chief Justice Burger, vacated the license renewal grant to WLBT and directed the FCC to invite applicants to apply for the license.

2. In *United Church of Christ II*, the court repudiated the treatment of the citizen group by the FCC hearing examiner:

> The [e]xaminer seems to have regarded appellants as "plaintiffs" and the licensee as "defendant," with burdens of proof allocated accordingly. This tack, though possibly fostered by the commission's own action, was a grave misreading of our holding on this question. We did not intend that intervenors representing a public interest be treated as interlopers. Rather, if analogues can be useful, a "public intervenor" who is seeking no license or private right is, in this context, more nearly like a complaining witness who presents evidence to police or a prosecutor whose duty it is to conduct an affirmative and objective investigation of all the facts and to pursue his prosecutorial or regulatory function if there is probable cause to believe a violation has occurred.

The court of appeals, per Judge Burger, complained that it was inappropriate for "the examiner or the commission to sit back and simply provide a forum for the intervenors." The court observed further: "A curious neutrality-in-favor of the licensee seems to have guided the examiner in his conduct of the evidentiary hearing." The affirmative duty of the commission and the hearing examiner in the context of a situation such as *United Church of Christ* was explicitly set forth by the court of appeals:

> The commission and the examiners have an affirmative duty to assist in the development of a meaningful record which can serve as the basis for the evaluation of the licensee's performance of his duty to serve the public interest. The public intervenors, who were performing a public service under a mandate of this court, were entitled to a more hospitable reception in the performance of that function. As we view the record the examiner tended to impede the exploration of the very issues which we would reasonably expect the commission itself would have initiated; an ally was regarded as an opponent.

3. The court of appeals in *United Church of Christ II* then took the remarkable step of itself vacating the FCC's license grant to WLBT:

> We are compelled to hold, on the whole record, that the commission's conclusion is not supported by substantial evidence. For this reason the grant of a license must be vacated forthwith and the commission is directed to invite applications to be filed for the license. We do refrain, however, from holding that the licensee be declared disqualified from filing a new application; the conduct of the hearing was not primarily the licensee's responsibility, although as the applicant it had the burden of proof. Moreover, the commission necessarily did not address itself to the precise question of WLBT's qualifications to be an applicant in the new proceeding now ordered, and we hesitate to pass on this subject not considered by the commission.
>
> The commission is directed to consider a plan for interim operation pending completion of its hearings; if it finds it in the public interest to permit the present licensee to carry on interim operations that alternative is available.

The FCC had placed the burden of showing that WLBT was unqualified for renewal on the citizen group intervenors, the United Church of Christ. Judge Burger felt that the citizen groups had been treated by the FCC as intruders in the hitherto cozy world of bureaucrat and broadcaster. The FCC had adhered to the form but not the substance of the earlier decision. Burger's opinion in *United Church of Christ II* was a stinging rebuke to FCC treatment of citizen groups. The opinion also underscored the fact that the *United Church of Christ* case was no fluke: the federal court of appeals had fully intended to give a legitimate and vital place in FCC renewal proceedings to citizen groups.

4. Judge Burger believed that on the basis of *United Church of Christ I*, and the Federal Communications Act itself, the burden of proof in a renewal hearing should be on the renewal applicant rather than the citizen group. What arguments would you make to defend Judge Burger's views on burden of proof? Against? Are there any basic reasons in the structure of American broadcast regulation which lead to the kind of FCC sympathy for licensee failings and resistance to citizen group objections displayed in the *United Church of Christ* case?

Some Limits on Citizen Group Standing?

1. Nine years after *United Church of Christ I*, the steady expansion of citizen group standing in broadcast regulation was halted somewhat in Illinois Citizens Committee for Broadcasting v. FCC, 515 F.2d 397 (D.C.Cir. 1975). The factual and substantive issues in the case, arising out of a problem in the FCC's regulation of obscene and indecent programming, are set forth in this text, p. 914. After issuing a notice of apparent liability to Sonderling Broadcasting Co. on the ground that certain broadcasts carried on its station WGLD–FM, Oak Park, Illinois, featuring discussions of oral sex, warranted a $2,000 forfeiture, the FCC informed Sonderling of its statutory right to refuse payment of the forfeiture and seek judicial review. Despite its stated belief that the FCC's action was unconstitutional, Sonderling elected to pay the fine. Sonderling said that it preferred to pay a $2,000 fine rather than spend many times that amount litigating the constitutional validity of the fine.

Although Sonderling did not want to challenge the constitutional validity of the fine, a citizen group and a civil liberties group did. The Illinois Citizens Committee for Broadcasting and the Illinois Division of the American Civil Liberties Union filed an application for remission of the forfeiture and a petition for reconsideration. The two groups asserted that they were representatives of the listening public and that their members and contributors included many in the Chicago area who were being deprived, contrary to the First Amendment, of listening alternatives because of the FCC action against Sonderling. The FCC did not grant the relief sought by the two groups but agreed to clarify its intentions in order to correct any misunderstanding about its notice of apparent liability.

In the course of its opinion, the FCC expressed doubt over the standing of the two groups to obtain a remission or reconsideration of a forfeiture which had not been challenged by the licensee against whom it was directed. The court of appeals agreed with the FCC's action in the case. See text, p. 917. The portions of the court of appeals decision, per Judge Leventhal, dealing with the standing issue follow.

ILLINOIS CITIZENS COMMITTEE FOR BROADCASTING v. FCC,

515 F.2D 397 (D.C. CIR. 1975).

LEVENTHAL, Circuit Judge:

* * *

The United States urges that the public, as distinguished from the licensee, has no interest in a forfeiture proceeding.

* * * In this case, the representatives of the public allege that the right of the public to be informed has been curtailed by limitations imposed by the government, invalidly, on the broadcaster's discretion to present material.

We uphold petitioners' standing to vindicate the public's interest. That interest is underscored by the likelihood that the licensee who is directly governed by the order in the forfeiture proceeding will, as here, find the burden too great, in terms of its own interest, to warrant its undertaking the risk and expense involved in contesting the commission's action. In comparable situations we have allowed interested parties to intervene where the party that would ordinarily be expected to press the public interest has failed to appeal an initial decision. * * * The procedure used by the FCC in issuing the notice of apparent liability raises questions with regard to the rights of the licensee. First, it includes terms of conclusions, while the statute contemplates only charges.[12] If construed as the latter, then Sonderling was not provided with notice or opportunity for a hearing before its issuance, even though it seemed to go far towards the imposition of a substantial fine. This procedure seems very like that condemned by the Supreme Court in Bantam Books, Inc. v. Sullivan, 372 U.S. 58 (1963). There the Court reviewed the practices of a state commission that sent distributors of publications that had been found objectionable for sale to minors notification of that finding, accompanied by reminders of possible criminal sanctions if the distributor failed to "cooperate." The system was found to constitute an informal "scheme of * * * censorship," based on "radically deficient" procedures.

It is true that the licensee here does have an opportunity for judicial review, if it is willing to shoulder the expense. However, the Court's "insistence [in *Bantam Books*] that regulations of obscenity scrupulously embody the most rigorous procedural safeguards," 372 U.S. at 66, 83 S.Ct. at 637, and its requirement of notice and hearing before a determination of obscenity is made, cast doubt on the procedures used by the commission.

However, we do not think that the procedural safeguards prescribed in *Bantam Books*, which were found to be essential for the protection of "[t]he publisher or the distributor," can be asserted by the *public* as procedural error. The statute contemplates that the licensee will, in the first instance, ensure that First Amendment limitations are not overstepped in forfeiture action under § 503(b)(1)(E). We have no need to consider whether the public is entitled to intervene on a petition for reconsideration after the initial determination has been made when the licensee declines to press the matter further. * * * In this case a representative of the public did in fact ask the commission to reconsider its determination, and the commission responded in some detail to the concerns expressed. Finding no prejudice from the procedure,[13] we turn to the merits.

* * *

COMMENT

1. After the court of appeals decision, the Illinois Citizens Committee asked to have a rehearing en banc (a rehearing by the full court rather than just a panel of the court). The court of appeals denied the committee's request for a rehearing. Chief Judge Bazelon would have granted a rehearing *en banc*. In a long opinion explaining his vote in favor of a rehearing, Judge Bazelon challenged the majority's

12. 47 U.S.C.A. § 503(b)(2) (1970) calls for a "written notice of *apparent* liability" that contains specific information as to the act or omission with which the licensee is "charged" before forfeiture liability can be imposed. [Emphasis added.]

13. The petitioners contend that the language of § 503(b)(1)(E), which authorizes the commission to impose a forfeiture on any licensee who "violates section * * * 1464 of Title 18," contemplates that the FCC may act only after the licensee has been convicted under § 1464 in a criminal proceeding. That issue involves the rights of the licensee, rather than the rights of the public, and is appropriately raised only by the licensee. See text, p. 909.

distinction between substantive and procedural issues in the standing rights of citizen groups.

2. Judge Bazelon suggested that the court's limitation of citizen group standing in the case to substantive as opposed to procedural issues was at odds with whole course of the law since *United Church of Christ I*:

> The legality of listener standing is so well accepted that the point is never raised in present FCC litigation. * * * [L]isteners have been implicitly granted standing to challenge just about every form of FCC program regulation or of licensee programming activity.

3. Taking a contrary view, Judge Leventhal filed a supplemental opinion in order to respond to the claim of the Illinois Citizens Committee and the ACLU in their petition for rehearing that the court was "insensitive to their role as representatives of the listening public." In defense of the court, Judge Leventhal declared:

> We do contemplate that representatives of the public have a role in FCC proceedings concerning obscenity determinations—as is indicated by our recognition that they have standing to challenge the substantive grounds of commission action even where the licensee is willing to pay the forfeiture and thus acquiesces in the commission's determination. We are cited to no Supreme Court case that goes this far in a situation where the producer or distributor directly affected has acquiesced. However, we found such a requirement implicit in the contours of the statute, a procedural right that furthers the substantive rights of the public under the First Amendment.

The Petition to Deny and the Citizens Group: HALE v. FCC

1. Suppose a citizens group is dissatisfied with the job a broadcast licensee has been doing. What can it do? If another applicant applies for a license, the citizens group can enter the renewal proceeding as a result of the *United Church of Christ* decision. But if there is no hearing in which to participate, what can a citizens group do then? It can file a petition to deny with the FCC, requesting that the incumbent's license renewal application be denied. But a denial of a license renewal application will hardly be granted without a hearing, and a petition to deny does not usually lead to the grant of a hearing.

In Hale v. FCC, 425 F.2d 556 (D.C.Cir. 1970), two citizens of Salt Lake City challenged the license renewal application of an AM radio station in Salt Lake City, KSL–AM. KSL is wholly owned by the Mormon church as is one of the daily newspapers in Salt Lake City, the *Deseret News*.

The Salt Lakers seeking to defeat the license renewal application waged a tough battle for a hearing. Without a hearing, the citizens said, the testimony, both on direct and cross-examination, which would show the poor programming response by the licensee to community needs, would be difficult to obtain. Proof of the actual programming presented by KSL was made particularly difficult for the licensee because KSL did not even publish its daily program log in any Salt Lake daily newspaper.

The FCC adamantly refused to grant a hearing on the matter because the commission interprets § 309(d) and (e) of the Federal Communications Act to require a hearing only when the petition to deny reveals a substantial issue of fact requiring a resolution by hearing. Of course, the whole thing was a triumph of circular reasoning. Without a hearing the citizens group found it nearly impossible to show the material issue of fact concerning the licensee's performance which alone would produce a hearing.

The citizens took the FCC to court for its refusal to grant them a hearing. In a decision which sharply reduced the potential effectiveness of the petition to deny, the United States Court of Appeals for the District of Columbia affirmed the FCC determination not to grant a hearing. The case is an excellent illustration of the type of difficulty citizens groups experience in obtaining a hearing from the FCC through a petition to deny.

The two citizens fighting the license renewal application of KSL–AM raised two objections to the station's past performance. One objection related to whether KSL had complied with the fairness doctrine. The second objection concerned whether "KSL–AM is part of a business conglomerate so constituted as to create an undue concentration of business and broadcasting influence in the Salt Lake City area communications market." The citizens contended that both issues required the "illumination of a hearing." The court of appeals, like the FCC, did not agree.

2. On the concentration of ownership issue, the court of appeals again concluded that the allegations were insufficient to show a material issue of fact requiring a hearing:

> Appellants do assert that this particular concentration has had ill effects on the communications media in Salt Lake City, and is thus not in the public interest. But here again, to merit a hearing under Section 309(e), appellants must go beyond generalization and allege some specific instances of injury in the immediate context of the intervenor's operations, not merely that it is unwise for newspapers to be under common ownership with radio and television interests, and for both to be part of a broader business combine. In two recent opinions, involving the license renewals of WCCO–AM and KRON–FM, the commission designated the renewal applications for hearing after the parties protesting the renewals had alleged, in the case of WCCO, that the conglomerate was using the economic power of its newspaper to obtain unique sports events broadcasting rights for its television station and, in effect, to subsidize advertising for its television station; and in the case of KRON, that the conglomerate was using the economic power of its television station to subsidize the subscription campaigns of its newspaper. Appellants here have not made such specific allegations.

The court in *Hale* concluded that in view of complainants' nonspecific showing, there was no basis "for *ad hoc* action against the licensee on grounds of undue concentration of control of media of mass communications." The court added:

"Rather, any actions in this area as to a licensee such as this would be appropriate only in the context of overall rule-making proceedings. In this connection we point out the outstanding inquiry on conglomerate ownership and the specific rule-making proceeding, FCC Docket No. 18110."

3. Petitions to deny are sometimes used to pressure stations into making changes particularly in the areas of personnel practices and minority programming policies. In view of the difficulties in obtaining a hearing on a license renewal, citizen groups sometimes file petitions to deny for their *n terrorem* effect and then bargain (often very successfully) privately and directly with the stations involved. If the citizens group requests are granted, the petition to deny is withdrawn. Sometimes the citizens group bargains with the broadcaster first, usually just before renewal time, keeping the threat of filing a petition to deny in reserve for leverage. What criticisms would you make of these developments? What suggestions for corrections? See Barron, *"The Citizen Group At Work," Freedom of the Press for Whom?* 233–248 (1973).

4. The FCC has set forth standards which, within limits, generally allow broadcasters to enter into agreements with citizen groups. See In the Matter of Agreements Between Broadcast Licensees and the Public, 57 FCC2d 42 (1975). The FCC made it clear that "a licensee is not

obliged to undertake negotiations or agreements." If a licensee does enter into an agreement with citizens, the FCC stressed that "(t)he obligation to determine how to serve the public interest is personal to each licensee and may not be delegated, even if the licensee wishes to." The FCC warned that agreements should "not take responsibility for making public interest decisions out of the hands of a licensee."

PROBLEMS OF RENEWAL AND DIVERSIFICATION OF OWNERSHIP

The Multiple Ownership Rules and the One-to-a-Market Rule

1. The FCC's so-called multiple ownership rules create a conclusive presumption that nationwide ownership by a single party of more than seven AM, seven FM radio stations or seven television stations (of which no more than five may be VHF) is in itself contrary to the public interest. Moreover, the FCC prohibits the grant of a license of the same type of facility to anyone already holding such a license in a given community. In other words, if one already holds one AM radio station license in Middletown, Connecticut, one cannot acquire a license for another such AM radio station in Middletown. See 47 C.F.R. §§ 73.35, 73.240, and 73.636. See also, Multiple Ownership of AM, FM and TV Stations, 18 FCC 288 (1953), affirmed United States v. Storer Broadcasting Co., 351 U.S. 192 (1956). In September 1983, the FCC announced a proposed rule-making designed to either repeal or at least relax the so-called initial "Rule of Sevens," *ie.* the multiple-ownership rules. See *Broadcasting*, Sept. 26, 1983, p. 27.

Do you see any connection between the "balanced programming" concept, the "fairness" doctrine, and the rules designed to diversify ownership of broadcasting stations?

The multiple ownership rules have been criticized in the past for focusing on each type of electronic medium separately. Originally, under the multiple ownership rules, the same individual was permitted to own an AM station, an FM station, and a TV station—all in the same community. Do you see how this was possible? For discussion on this point and on the multiple ownership rules generally, see Note, *Diversification and the Public Interest: Administrative Responsibility of the FCC*, 66 Yale L.J. 365, 370–373 (1957).

In 1970, the FCC prohibited the "common ownership, operation, or control of more than one unlimited-time broadcast station in the same area, regardless of the type of broadcast service involved." First Report and Order, Multiple Ownership of Standard, FM & TV Broadcast Stations, 22 FCC2d 306 (1970). This rule is known popularly as the one-to-a-market rule. The rule has not done much to alter concentration of ownership in the media since the FCC specifically exempted existing AM, FM, and TV combinations because of the disruptive effects of a divestiture order. See First Report And Order, *supra*, 22 FCC2d 306 at 323 (1970).

Although no specific provision in the Federal Communications Act of 1934 deals materially with the concentration of ownership problems in broadcasting, the multiple ownership rules have been held to lie within the administrative discretion of the FCC under the broad purposes of the act. See United States v. Storer Broadcasting Co., 351 U.S. 192 (1956).

In March 1971, the FCC amended the so-called one-to-a-market rule so that the rule will apply only to combinations of VHF television stations with radio stations in the same market. The amendment to the one-to-a-market rule will permit AM and FM radio stations in the same market to be under common ownership. See In The Matter of Amendment of Sections 73.-

35, 73.240, and 73.636 of the Commission's Rules Relating to Multiple Ownership of Standard, FM and Television Broadcast Stations, 28 FCC2d 662 (1971). The FCC Memorandum Opinion order supporting the Amendment defends the Amendment on the following grounds:

> In * * * most cases existing AM–FM combinations in the same area may be economically and/or technically interdependent. * * * We therefore adopted rules permitting the assignment or transfer of combined AM–FM stations to a single party if a showing was made that established the interdependence of such stations and the impracticability of selling and operating them as separate stations. In so doing, we observed that although this would not foster our objective of increasing diversity, it would prevent the possible closing down of many FM stations, which could only decrease diversity.

2. In its decision to lift the prohibition against AM–FM radio common ownership in the same market, the FCC observed that its "official position" is that the paramount problem in securing diversification of control of mass media is that of cross-ownership of television stations and newspapers. The reasons for this doubtless is the consistency with which major markets reveal a pattern where a VHF network-affiliated television station is presently owned by a newspaper in the same market.

3. The one-to-a-market rule applies only to new common ownership situations, does not apply to existing licensees, and does not apply to newspapers. In justification the FCC pointed out in the AM–FM combination exception proceeding, 28 FCC2d 662 (1971), that the whole point of the one-to-a-market rules was to produce more diversity of programming and viewpoints over the broadcast media. The rules did not "contemplate any action with regard to cross-ownership of newspapers and broadcast facilities." But the FCC conceded that problems of divestiture and newspaper cross-ownership gave the FCC pause. The commission further conceded that perhaps it should have adopted rules on these subjects in connection with the "one-to-a-market" proceeding. The FCC then concluded:

> We considered it the better course to issue a further notice concerning them [divestiture and newspaper cross-ownership] because of the far reaching ramifications of any rules that might be adopted on these subjects and in order to develop additional information about them.

The further notice the FCC is referring to here is the announcement the FCC made simultaneous with the promulgation of the one-to-a-market rule of the initiation of a rule-making proceeding to consider whether it would be in the public interest to require divestiture by newspapers or multiple owners in a given market. See Further Notice of Proposed Rulemaking, Multiple Ownership of Standard, FM and TV Broadcast Stations, 22 FCC2d 339 (1970). This proceeding culminated in FCC v. National Citizens Committee for Broadcasting, 436 U.S. 775 (1978), text, p. 959.

MANSFIELD JOURNAL CO. v. FCC

180 F.2D 28 (D.C.CIR.1950).

WASHINGTON, Circuit Judge.

* * *

The facts are as follows: The *Mansfield Journal* is the sole newspaper in the town of Mansfield, Ohio. The only other medium of mass communication in Mansfield is radio station WMAN, which is under different ownership than the newspaper and competes with it for local advertising. The commission found that the *Mansfield Journal* used its position as sole newspaper in the community to coerce its advertisers to enter into exclusive advertising contracts with the newspaper and to refrain from utilizing station WMAN for advertising purposes. It did this by refusing to permit certain advertisers, who also use the radio to sell their products, to secure regular advertising contracts or to place any advertisements in the newspaper whatever. The commission found further that *Mansfield Journal* had demonstrated a marked hostility to station WMAN by declining to publish WMAN's program log and by failing to print any comments about the station unless unfavorable. The commission concluded that such actions were taken with the intent and for the purpose of suppressing competition and of securing a monopoly of mass advertising and news dissemination, and that such practices were likely to continue and be reenforced by the acquisition of a radio station.

* * *

The commission has determined in the instant case that it is contrary to the public interest to grant a [broadcast] license to a newspaper which has attempted to suppress competition in advertising and news dissemination. * * * Appellant argues that this amounts to enforcement of the antitrust laws. But whether appellant has been guilty of a violation of these laws is not here in issue. The fact that a policy against monopoly has been made the subject of criminal sanction by Congress as to certain activities does not preclude an administrative agency charged with furthering the public interest from holding the general policy of Congress to be applicable to questions arising in the proper discharge of its duties. Whether Mansfield's activities do or do not amount to a positive violation of law, and neither this court nor the Federal Communications Commission is determining that question, they still may impair Mansfield's ability to serve the public. Thus, whether Mansfield's competitive practices were legal or illegal, in the strict sense, is not conclusive here. Monopoly in the mass communication of news and advertising is contrary to the public interest, even if not in terms proscribed by the antitrust laws.

It may be that appellant is contending that if the commission's findings of fact were correct, then appellant has violated the antitrust laws, and that in such case the commission is without jurisdiction to consider these matters. There is no merit in such a contention. It is provided in the Federal Communications Act itself that the Federal Communications Commission may refuse a license to any person who "has been finally adjudged guilty by a Federal court of unlawfully monopolizing or attempting unlawfully to monopolize, radio communication, directly or indirectly * * * or to have been using unfair methods of competition." 47 U.S.C.A. § 311. The *Mansfield Journal* has not been convicted of any such violation. But the statute does not for that reason place the *Journal's* past conduct with regard to monopoly and the antitrust laws beyond the consideration of the commission.

* * *

* * * We hold, therefore, that it was fully within the commission's jurisdiction to hear evidence on the alleged monopolistic practices of the appellant, regardless of whether or not such practices were specifically forbidden by statute, and to deny the licenses upon its finding that such practices had in fact taken place and were likely to carry over into the operation of the radio station.

Appellant contends that to deny it a license because it has refused to carry the log of station WMAN, or because it has refused to permit certain people to advertise, is to impinge upon the freedom of the press. We think that the appellant misconceives the commission's holding. The commission did not deny the license merely because the newspaper refused to print certain items or because it refused to serve certain advertisers, but rather because the commission concluded that those practices were followed for the purpose of suppressing competition. Similarly, it would appear that Mansfield was not denied a license because it was a newspaper, but because it used its position as sole newspaper in the community to achieve a monopoly in advertising and news dissemination. Such a denial does not constitute a violation of the First Amendment.

* * *

With regard to (the case) in which the *Lorain Journal* was denied a license for an AM station [342 U.S. 143 (1951); see this text, p.——]: The denial was predicated on the grounds that there is a complete common ownership and common control of the Lorain and Mansfield Journals, and that the same control which cannot be entrusted with a radio station in Mansfield cannot be entrusted with a radio station in Lorain, as it is likely to abuse its power in either situation. While these two newspapers were separate corporations, with separate editorial staffs, and located in communities more than fifty miles apart, the record shows that one family owns all of the stock in both corporations and that the owners took a very active part in the control and policy formulation of the newspapers. We think the commission was entitled to ascertain, and base its findings upon, the true locus of control. It could properly conclude that what had occurred in Mansfield was indicative of what might occur under similar circumstances in Lorain.

This is not to disregard the fact that the two newspaper companies conduct separate businesses. It is rather to recognize that the true applicant in each of these cases is the same individual, or group of individuals, and that the commission is empowered to consider the conduct and history of the applicant before deciding to grant the benefits represented by a broadcasting license.

* * *

Upon examination of the record we find no reversible error. The decisions of the Federal Communications Commission in all three cases are therefore affirmed.

COMMENT

1. Antitrust prosecution and conviction of the defendants in the principal case did in fact, eventually occur. As a result, the FCC denied the license application of the Lorain Journal Co. Under § 313 of the Federal Communications Act the FCC is directed to refuse a license "to any person whose license has been revoked by a court." 47 U.S.C.A. § 313 (1964). Does such an explicit statutory provision argue for or against the result reached by the court in the *Mansfield Journal* case?

2. The facts of the *Mansfield Journal* case revealed the inadequacy of the multiple ownership rules. They were entirely silent as to cross-media ownership. In other words, there was nothing in them to prohibit the acquisition by the only newspaper in a community of that community's only television station. Was the reason for this omission grounded on the fact that newspapers are not licensed and are not under the jurisdiction of the FCC?

3. While the FCC can, as seen in the *Mansfield Journal* case, consider antitrust policy when it makes a determination of whether "the public interest, convenience, or necessity" is served by granting or renewing a broadcast license, it is also clear that the broadcast industry is not itself exempt from the antitrust laws as a "regulated industry." In United States v. Radio Corp. of America, 358 U.S. 334 (1959), the Court rejected the argument made by RCA and its subsidiary, NBC, that FCC approval of the exchange of an NBC-owned station in Cleveland for one in Philadelphia barred the Justice Department's antitrust attack on that exchange. The Court held that since the broadcast industry was not regulated as a common carrier or a public utility, "there [is] no pervasive regulatory

scheme, and no rate structure to throw out of balance, [so] sporadic action by federal courts can work no mischief."

For a discussion of antitrust problems as they relate to the newspaper press, see text, Chapter VIII, p. 637.

The WHDH Case

The *WHDH* case is a milestone in broadcasting law since it represents the denial by the FCC of an application for a license renewal by an established and presently operating licensee which was a party to a broadcast-newspaper combination in the same city.

IN THE MATTER OF WHDH, INC.

16 FCC2D 1 (1969).

Commissioner BARTLEY for the commission.

Our basic disagreement with the examiner's conclusions lies in the preferred status which he gave to WHDH "not because it is an applicant for renewal but because it has an operating record and its very existence as a functioning, manned station to advance against its opponents, whose promises, after all, are as yet just so much talk." Thus, the examiner decided that the traditional mode of comparing mutually exclusive applicants, "in the mechanical or point-by-point manner especially advocated by BBI" [a competitive applicant], would have been a sterile exercise. In his judgment, the cardinal probative attribute—for good or bad—of WHDH was its operating record.

* * *

With regard to WHDH's past broadcast record, Examiner Sharfman concluded ultimately that as a whole such record is favorable. The superiority of WHDH's claims to renewal against those of its competitors for initial authorization, the examiner stated, rests on a basis of achievement, theirs on promises, often glittering, but of relatively uncertain and unestablished validity.

In our judgment, the examiner's approach to this proceeding places an extraordinary and improper burden upon new applicants who wish to demonstrate that their proposals, when considered on a comparative basis, would better serve the public interest. In fairness to the examiner, it should be pointed out that he followed what he understood to be the commission's policy in proceedings of this nature, as expressed in Hearst Radio, Inc. (WBAL), 6 R.R. 994 (1951), and Wabash Valley Broadcasting Corp. (WTHI–TV), 35 FCC 677, R.R.2d 573 (1963). Thus, in *Hearst* the determining factor in the commission's decision was "the clear advantage of continuing the established and excellent service * * * [of the existing station] when compared to the risks attendant on the execution of the proposed programming of * * * [the new applicant] excellent though the proposal may be."

* * *

As noted in the *policy statement*, diversification is a factor of first significance since it constitutes a primary objective in the commission's licensing scheme. The benefits derived from diversification have been set forth in many cases decided by the courts and by the commission, and they need not be recited in detail here. When compared with Charles River and BBI, WHDH manifestly ranks a poor third because of its ownership of a powerful standard broadcast station, an FM station, and a newspaper in the city of Boston itself. While it is true that the existence of numerous other media in Boston in which WHDH has no ownership interest may not be ignored and does somewhat diminish the weight to be accorded the preferences to Charles River and BBI on local diversification, nonetheless those preferences are quite significant here. A grant to either Charles River or BBI would clearly result in a maximum diffusion of control of the media of mass communications as compared with a grant of the renewal application of WHDH. A new voice would be brought to the Boston community as compared with continuing the service of WHDH–TV. We believe that the widest possible dissemination of information from diverse and antagonistic sources is in the public interest, and this principle will be significantly advanced by a grant of either the Charles River or the BBI application.

* * *

Although conceding that is has never editorialized, WHDH contends that this is a factor which minimizes any question of concentration of control flowing from the common ownership of newspaper and broadcast interests. We disagree with this contention. Licensees have an obligation to devote a reasonable amount of their broadcast time to the presentation of programs on controversial issues of public importance to their communities. Editorializing by Broadcast Licensees, 13 FCC 1246 (1949). If anything, the failure to editorialize demonstrates the wisdom of the commission's policy in favor of a maximum diffusion of control of the media of mass communications.

* * *

Both Charles River and BBI must be preferred to WHDH under the diversification and integration criteria. In addition, a demerit attaches to the WHDH applicant because of the unauthorized transfers of control which have occurred.

* * *

Dissenting statement of Commissioner Robert E. LEE.

* * *

* * * The majority here holds in effect that the weight to be afforded the comparative factors in a renewal application is the same as a new application. I believe that the weight to be given such evidence is substantially reduced in view of the renewal applicant's existing track record. To hold otherwise would permit a new applicant to submit a "blue sky" proposal tailor-made to secure every comparative advantage while the existing licensee must reap the demerits of hand-to-hand combat in the business world, and the community it serves. * * * Vast expenditures for facilities and good will have been made (by the renewal applicant) which it would be inequitable to declare forfeited unless the licensee has operated against the public interest.

* * *

Concurring statement of Commissioner Nicholas JOHNSON.

* * * In America's eleven largest cities there is not a single network-affiliated VHF television station that is independently and locally owned. They are all owned by the networks, multiple station owners, or major local newspapers. The decision not to award Channel 5 to the *Herald-Traveler* is supported by good and sufficient reasons beyond the desire to promote diversity of media ownership in Boston. And I take no present position on the merits of continued newspaper ownership of broadcasting properties in markets where there is competing media. But I do think it is healthy to have at least *one* station among these politically powerful 33 network-affiliated properties in the major markets that is truly locally owned, and managed independently of the other major local mass media. * * * Nor is the significance of this case limited to the impact on media ownership in Boston. For the commission also speaks generally of situations in which a new competitor is seeking the right to broadcast as against a present broadcast license holder. We suggest that the standards at renewal time ought to be the same standards that would prevail if all applicants were new applicants. * * *

COMMENT

1. In the Policy Statement on Comparative Broadcast Hearings, 5 P. & F. Radio Reg. 1901 (1965), the FCC emphasized maximum diffusion of control of the media of communications as a factor in selecting among competing applicants for the same facilities. The FCC also announced in the policy statement that it would be interested in full participation in station operation by the owner and in participation in civic affairs. The court also insisted that broadcast experience would be a factor, but that broadcast experience was not the same as a past broadcast record since, otherwise, newcomers would be unduly discouraged. The commission also renewed its support for the programming criteria set out in the Report and Statement of Policy Re: Commission en banc Programming Inquiry, 20 P. & F. Radio Reg. 1901 (1960) and declared that these criteria would still apply.

The commission opinion in the *WHDH* case strongly relies on the Policy Statement on Comparative Broadcast Hearings which had emphasized that the FCC was going to award a new degree of decisiveness to diffusion of control of the mass media in awarding broadcast licenses in comparative hearings.

2. On its broadest interpretation *WHDH* could mean those holding broadcast licenses, no matter how long they have been in business and how routinely their licenses have been renewed in the past, have no special claim to renewal. It is this broad interpretation which horrified Commissioner Robert E. Lee. On a narrower interpretation of its ruling, the *WHDH* case could be read to hold that where the applicant has substantial ownership interests in other media in the same community, his license renewal application may be denied if new applicants lacking such cross-media connections are the competing applicants for the same license. The broadcast industry did not react to the uncertainties of the *WHDH* decision calmly. The industry looked to Congress for an end to the insecurity the decision posed for renewal of existing broadcast licenses.

On January 15, 1970, the FCC came in with the new 1970 Policy Statement on Renewals. Under the policy statement, where there is a hearing in which an applicant seeks the license of an incumbent licensee, the incumbent shall be preferred if he can demonstrate substantial past performance not characterized by serious deficiencies. In such circumstances the incumbent "will be preferred over the newcomer and his application for renewal will be granted." The choice of the new criterion for renewal, "substantial service to the public," rather than, say, choosing the applicant deemed most likely to render the best possible service, was justified by the FCC on the basis of "considerations of predictability and stability." It was feared that if there was no stability in the industry, if licenses were truly up for grabs every three years, it would not be possible for a station to render even substantial service. See Policy Statement On Comparative Hearings Involving Regular Renewal Applicants, 22 FCC2d 424 (1970).

If the investment of the broadcaster were not given protection, the FCC warned, there would "be an inducement to the opportunist who might seek a license and then provide the barest minimum of service which would permit short run maximization of profit, on the theory that the license might be terminated whether he rendered a good service or not."

Professor Hyman Goldin of Boston University's School of Public Communication said the crucial flaw in the 1970 policy statement was the FCC's failure to give any meaning to the "substantial service" requirement. See Goldin, *'Spare the Golden Goose'—The Aftermath of WHDH in FCC License Renewal Policy*, 83 Harvard L.Rev. 1014 (1970). What definition of "substantial service" would you suggest? What should its components be? Community involvement and quality programming for children are components suggested by Professor Goldin.

If the FCC and the broadcast industry thought the attack on automatic renewals of broadcast licenses had been outflanked by the 1970 policy statement, they were taking comfort prematurely. For one thing, the FCC's decision in the *WHDH* case was affirmed by the United States Court of Appeals for the District of Columbia on November 13, 1970. Greater Boston Television Corp. v. FCC, 444 F.2d 841 (D.C. Cir.1970). It is true that Judge Leventhal, who wrote the opinion, emphasized that the 1970 policy statement was not involved in the case since it specifically stated it did not apply to "unusual cases" like *WHDH* where the renewal applicant, for unique reasons, is treated like a new applicant. But a basic fact remained: the FCC's dramatic decision to take away a television station from an incumbent newspaper-affiliated licensee had been affirmed by the United States Court of Appeals. The *de facto* automatic renewal process had been dealt a body blow.[10]

Additionally, Judge Leventhal's opinion in *WHDH* fully approved the preference that the FCC gave to the diversification of control of media of mass communication criterion in the *WHDH* proceeding. In other words, the FCC had been authorized, in the Court's opinion, to choose a non-newspaper-affiliated applicant in a contest between it and a newspaper-affiliated incumbent. This endorsement of the diversification policy was an indication of rising judicial dissatisfaction with the FCC's automatic renewal policy, a disenchantment given vivid expression in Judge Burger's decision in *United Church of Christ II*. See text, p. 942.

WHDH argued on appeal that the *Red Lion* decision pulled the rug out from under the FCC's "pretentious policy statement justification of its 'diversity' criterion." WHDH thought that the *Red Lion* stress on the need for access had rendered diversification of control of media unnecessary. Judge Leventhal responded that the *Red Lion* doctrine and diversification of control policy both were proper means to serve the goal of diversity of viewpoint.

The Citizens Communication Center Case: The Renewal Controversy Renewed

Citizen groups, the Citizens Communication Center, and BEST (Black Efforts for Soul in Television) challenged the legality of the 1970 policy statement.

The citizen groups prevailed, and on June 11, 1970, the United States Court of Appeals for the District of Columbia directed the FCC to stop applying the policy statement. The FCC order refusing to institute rule-making proceedings was reversed. See Citizens Communication Center v. FCC, 447 F.2d 1201 (D.C.Cir.1971).

The successful citizens groups had won on a three-pronged argument. First, the *Ashbacker* rule requiring a comparative hearing for mutually exclusive applicants was violated by depriving an applicant of such a hearing if the incumbent made a showing of substantial service. See Ashbacker Radio Corp. v. FCC, 326 U.S. 327 (1945). Further, the policy statement was unlawful because it deprived a competing applicant of a hearing in violation of § 309(c) of the Federal Communications Act. Second, the policy statement was attacked on the ground that it violated the

10. As a result of the *WHDH* case, the Boston *Herald-Traveler* found it could not go it alone. As a result, the *Herald-Traveler*, which had been financially dependent upon WHDH, merged with the *Record-American*. Paradoxically, as a result of *WHDH*, Boston had one *less* daily newspaper voice. Was this cause for reconsideration of a policy aimed against cross-ownership? Indeed it had that effect, and *WHDH* would come to be considered an aberration.

Administrative Procedure Act. Thirdly, the policy statement was successfully attacked on the ground that the decision unlawfully chilled the exercise of First Amendment rights.

The tremors the *Citizens Communication Center* case sent through the broadcast industry rivaled the FCC's *WHDH* decision of January 1969. The unwritten rule of automatic renewal for the broadcast incumbent was once more under attack.

Communications lawyers in Washington read with particular care footnotes 35 and 36 of Judge Wright's decision in the *Citizens Communication Center* case. See *Broadcasting*, June 21, 1971. Footnote 35 said licensees rendering "superior service" ought to be renewed, otherwise the public will suffer. What is necessary, therefore, is to define "superior service." Wright suggested some criteria, i.e., avoidance of excessive advertising, quality programming, and whether the incumbent reinvests his profits "to the service of the viewing and listening public." Do you see any dangers in replacing a "superior service" standard with a "substantial service" standard? Isn't the key factor the FCC attitude toward the renewal process?

Footnote 36 of the decision appeared to indicate that the "public interests" requirement of the Federal Communications Act would prohibit any standard for making judgments in renewals which did not give a chance of entry to broadcasting to new interests and racial minorities. Can you formulate a standard which would do this? Is it possible that Judge Wright's preference for a "superior service" standard could be used to frustrate concern over the fact that then "only a dozen of 7500 broadcast licenses issued are owned by racial minorities?"

In the exhaustive study of the comparative hearing procedure presented by the court in the *Citizens Communication Center* case, one of the most salient points made by Wright was his observation (Footnote 28) that the FCC had in effect "abolished the comparative hearing mandated by § 309(a) and (e) and converted the comparative hearing into a petition-to-deny proceeding." Do you see why Judge Wright said this?

Although Judge Wright spoke kindly of a "superior service" standard, presently there is no such standard. As the *Citizens Communication Center* decision stands, therefore, the renewal applicant enjoys no particular advantage in the renewal process.

The issue of diversification of media ownership received considerable attention in the *Citizens Communication Center* case. This scrutiny was significant because it meant that the efforts of broadcast owners with newspaper affiliations to escape the *WHDH* ruling on the cross-newspaper ownership point were dealt a heavy blow.

The FCC decided not to seek a rehearing of the *Citizens Communication Center* case from the full nine-judge panel of the U.S. Court of Appeals. As the decision stands, the FCC is reported to believe that the *Citizens Communication Center* decision leaves the FCC with considerable discretion over the renewal process. *Broadcasting*, July 5, 1971.

The Reaction to the CCC Case

1. Since the 1970 policy statement was invalidated in the *Citizens Communication Center* case, the FCC has moved warily with regard to promulgating new guidelines for the renewal process.

2. The FCC reaction to the *CCC* case was quite analogous to the FCC reaction to *United Church of Christ I*. In Moline Television Corp., 31 FCC2d 263 (1971), the incumbent licensee was granted renewal even though the incumbent had not provided superior programming and the competing applicant offered superior program-

ming proposals and greater integration of ownership.

3. Shortly after the *CCC* case, the FCC issued a statement interpreting the significance the *CCC* case would have in the ongoing FCC proceeding regarding the implementation of policies in broadcast renewals. In the Matter of Formulation of Policies Relating to the Broadcast Renewal Applicant, Stemming from the Comparative Hearing Process, FCC 71–826, August 4, 1971. The FCC gave the following interpretation to the *CCC* decision:

> We recognize that particular labels can be misleading. Thus, we used the term "substantial service" in the sense of "strong, solid" service—substantially above the mediocre service which might just minimally warrant renewal (see 22 FCC2d at p. 425, n. 1). We believe that the Court may have read this use of "substantial" service as meaning minimal service meeting the public interest standard and therefore employed the term "superior" service to make clear that it had in mind a contrast with mediocre service—as it put it, a "lapse into mediocrity, to seek the protection of the crowd." In short, we believe that it is unnecessary to further refine the label. What rather counts are the guidelines actually adopted to indicate the "plus of major significance"—the type of service which, if achieved, is of such nature that one can "* * * reasonably expect renewal."

4. Was the FCC really saying that "superior service" and "substantial service" are the same thing? Was this consistent with the court's reaction in the *CCC* case to the substantial service criterion? The real thrust of the foregoing excerpt was to re-establish the process of virtually automatic renewal for the incumbent licensee. If superior service, as defined by Judge Wright, were to be required before an incumbent licensee would be renewed, then routine renewal for the broadcast licensee would, of course, by no means be a certainty.

The FCC did not appeal the *CCC* decision to the Supreme Court. In the light of the FCC's substantial-equals-superior pronouncement stated above, was it reasonable that the FCC decided it would rather "interpret" the *CCC* decision than appeal it and risk having the decision resoundly affirmed?

5. In Fidelity Television Inc. v. FCC, 515 F.2d 684 (D.C.Cir. 1975), cert. den. 423 U.S. 926 (1975), an incumbent licensee whose past performance was judged to be "average" (rather than the "substantial" performance needed to earn a "plus of major significance") was renewed against a challenger. While the challenger did not particularly impress the FCC either, the challenger did have a comparative advantage over the incumbent in terms of diversification of ownership interests. Nevertheless, the FCC renewed the incumbent's license, and the appeals court affirmed. The appeals court per Judge Davis declared:

> On the whole, it is fair to say that the commission found that the ultimate effect of its analysis of the record was that Fidelity and RKO were essentially equally poor contenders—or, at the best, both were minimally acceptable applicants. While the agency was under no obligation to give the license to either competitor, we cannot say that it committed legal error when, in its attitude as of the times pertinent in this case, it took the view that "minimal service is to be preferred to no service at all." * * * There is no need here to expand on "renewal expectancies." We are not faced with a situation where a superior applicant is denied a license because to give it to him would work a "forfeiture" of his opponent's investment. We merely confirm what we intimated in the *Greater Boston Television Corp.* case—that, when faced with a fairly and evenly balanced record, the [c]ommission may, on the basis of the renewal applicant's past performance, award him the license.

See also Standards For Substantial Program Service, 43 R.R.2d 278 (FCC 1978).

6. In a 1977 report and order the FCC terminated its inquiry into comparative renewal criteria to be used in determining whether a new applicant or the incumbent licensee should be chosen at renewal time. Although it said that its preference was that Congress should abolish the comparative renewal process,[11] the FCC decided that until Congress chose to act on this suggestion it would act on a case-by-case basis.[12] The past performance of the incumbent licensee would continue to be examined. "[T]he licensee's responsiveness to the ascertained problems and needs of its community, including minority * * * concerns, remains central." But the FCC emphasized that in making decisions at renewal time "there is no 'formula of general application' that can be applied to all cases."

See In the Matter of Formulation of Policies Relating to the Broadcast Renewal Applicant, Stemming from the Comparative Hearing Process, 66 FCC2d 419 (1977).

The court of appeals decision affirming the FCC's *WHDH* decision was relied on by the FCC in the broadcast renewal applicant report in a manner which revealed how little was left of any likelihood that the FCC's *WHDH* decision would lead to any real changes in the renewal process: "Where the renewal applicant has served the public interest in such a substantial fashion it will be entitled to the 'legitimate renewal expectancy' clearly 'implicit in the structure of the [Communications] act.' *Greater Boston Television Corporation v. FCC.* * * *"

The *Broadcast Renewal Applicant* proceeding was affirmed by the court of appeals in National Black Media Coalition v. FCC, 4 Med.L.Rptr. 1085, 589 F.2d 578 (D.C. Cir. 1978).

The Cross-Ownership Case

The 1978 Supreme Court decision in the cross-ownership case was the *denouement* of the long but inconsistent effort of the FCC to wrestle with the role newspaper ownership should play in choosing from among the applicants for the licenses of broadcast stations.

In 1975, the FCC set forth its new cross-ownership rules. The substance of the new rules was to prohibit the future licensing or transfer of broadcast stations to those who owned a newspaper in the same community. The new rules were designed to forbid in the future the operation of a broadcast station and a newspaper by a common ownership in the same community. The new rules, however, were not as draconian as this account might indicate. Existing cross-ownership

11. In the Broadcasting Renewal Applicant report and order, the FCC set forth the essence of its reasons for this recommendation: "In November 1976 we therefore recommended to Congress the elimination of comparative renewal hearings, stating: 'Since the earliest broadcast legislation was considered, Congress has favored a competitive, privately run broadcast system operating free of government censorship of program content. On the other hand, we have rightfully viewed broadcasters as public trustees with obligations to serve the public interest and with no vested interest in their assigned frequencies. The optimal balance between these values would produce a renewal process that encourages licensee performance with a minimum of government intrusion into the broadcaster's programming discretion. The possibility of a comparative renewal challenge has been viewed as an incentive operating to spur the broadcaster toward the best possible public service performance. In view of the fact that the comparative process has not and cannot operate effectively for this purpose and since the subjectivity inherent in this process carries with it an ever present threat of undue government intrusion into broadcaster discretion, we believe that the comparative renewal process should be abolished. [Footnotes omitted]." See Report of the Federal Communications Commission to the Subcommittee of Communications of the Committee on Interstate and Foreign Commerce [of the House of Representatives] Re the Comparative Renewal Process, at p. 41.

12. See Ascertainment of Community Problems for Broadcast by Broadcast Applicants, 57 FCC2d 418 (1976).

situations were—with the exception of sixteen communities where the only daily newspaper and the only television station in the community were under common ownership—essentially "grandfathered."

Broadcasters thought the new rules went too far, and citizens groups thought they did not go far enough. On review to the federal court of appeals in Washington, D.C., that court in a notable opinion by Judge Bazelon upheld the new FCC rules in part and reversed them in part. The court upheld the FCC's prospective ban on the future creation of cross-ownership situations in the same community. But the court held that the FCC had erred in "grandfathering" the existing cross-ownership situations. The FCC sought review in the Supreme Court. The Court agreed with the FCC and not with the court of appeals.

FCC v. NATIONAL CITIZENS COMMISSION FOR BROADCASTING

3 MED.L.RPTR. 2409, 436 U.S. 775, 98 S.CT. 2096 56 L.ED.2D 697 (1978).

Justice MARSHALL delivered the opinion of the Court.

At issue in these cases are Federal Communications Commission regulations governing the permissibility of common ownership of a radio or television broadcast station and a daily newspaper located in the same community. Second Report and Order. 50 FCC2d 1046 (1975) (hereinafter cited as Order), as amended upon reconsideration, 53 FCC2d 589 (1975), codified in 47 CFR 73.35, 73.240, 73.636 (1976). The regulations, adopted after a lengthy rulemaking proceeding, prospectively bar formation or transfer of co-located newspaper-broadcast combinations. Existing combinations are generally permitted to continue in operation. However, in communities in which there is common ownership of the only daily newspaper and the only broadcast station, or (where there is more than one broadcast station) of the only daily newspaper and the only television station, divestiture of either the newspaper or the broadcast station is required within five years, unless grounds for waiver are demonstrated.

The questions for decision are whether these regulations either exceed the commission's authority under the Communications Act of 1934, or violate the First or Fifth Amendment rights of newspaper owners; and whether the lines drawn by the commission between new and existing newspaper-broadcast combinations, and between existing combinations subject to divestiture and those allowed to continue in operation, are arbitrary or capricious within the meaning of § 10(e) of the Administrative Procedure Act. For the reasons set forth below, we sustain the regulations in their entirety.

* * *

In setting its licensing policies, the commission has long acted on the theory that diversification of mass media ownership serves the public interest by promoting diversity of program and service viewpoints, as well as by preventing undue concentration of economic power. See e.g., Multiple Ownership of Standard, FM and Television Broadcast Stations, 45 FCC 1476, 1476–1477 (1964). This perception of the public interest has been implemented over the years by a series of regulations imposing increasingly stringent restrictions on multiple ownership of broadcast stations. In the early 1940s, the commission promulgated rules prohibiting ownership or control of more than one station in the same broadcast service (AM radio, FM radio, or television) in the same community. In 1953, limitations were placed on the total number of stations in each service a person or entity may own or control. And in 1970, the commission adopted regulations prohibiting, on a prospective basis, common ownership of a

VHF television station and any radio station serving the same market.

More generally, "[d]iversification of control of the media of mass communications" has been viewed by the commission as "a factor of primary significance" in determining who, among competing applicants in a comparative proceeding, should receive the initial license for a particular broadcast facility. Policy Statement on Comparative Broadcast Hearings, 1 FCC2d 393, 394–395 (1965). Thus, prior to adoption of the regulations at issue here, the fact that an applicant for an initial license published a newspaper in the community to be served by the broadcast station was taken into account on a case-by-case basis and resulted in some instances in awards of licenses to competing applicants.

Diversification of ownership has not been the sole consideration thought relevant to the public interest, however. The commission's other, and sometimes conflicting goal has been to ensure "the best practicable service to the public." To achieve this goal, the commission has weighed factors such as the anticipated contribution of the owner to station operations, the proposed program service, and the past broadcast record of the applicant—in addition to diversification of ownership—in making initial comparative licensing decisions. Moreover, the commission has given considerable weight to a policy of avoiding undue disruption of existing service. As a result, newspaper owners in many instances have been able to acquire broadcast licenses for stations serving the same communities as their newspapers and the commission has repeatedly renewed such licenses on findings that continuation of the service offered by the common owner would serve the public interest.

Against this background, the commission began the instant rulemaking proceeding in 1970 to consider the need for a more restrictive policy toward newspaper ownership of radio and television broadcast stations. Further Notice of Proposed Rulemaking, 22 FCC2d 339 (1970). Citing studies showing the dominant role of television stations and daily newspapers as sources of local news and other information, the notice of rulemaking proposed adoption of regulations that would eliminate all newspaper-broadcast combinations serving the same market, by prospectively banning formation or transfer of such combinations and requiring dissolution of all existing combinations within five years, id., at 346. The commission suggested that the proposed regulations would serve "the purpose of promoting competition among the mass media involved, and maximizing diversification of service sources and viewpoints." At the same time, however, the commission expressed "substantial concern" about the disruption of service that might result from divestiture of existing combinations. * * The Order * * * explained that the prospective ban on creation of co-located newspaper-broadcast combinations was grounded primarily in First Amendment concerns, while the divestiture regulations were based on both First Amendment and antitrust policies. In addition, the commission rejected the suggestion that it lacked the power to order divestiture, reasoning that the statutory requirement of license renewal every three years necessarily implied authority to order divestiture over a five-year period.

After reviewing the comments and studies submitted by the various parties during the course of the proceeding, the commission then turned to an explanation of the regulations and the justifications for their adoption. The prospective rules, barring formation of new broadcast-newspaper combinations in the same market, as well as transfers of existing combinations to new owners, were adopted without change from the proposal set forth in the notice of rulemaking. While recognizing the pioneering contributions of newspaper owners to the broadcast industry, the commission concluded that changed circumstances made it possible, and necessary, for all new licensing of broadcast stations to "be expected to add to local diversity." In reaching this conclusion, the commission did not find that existing co-located newspaper-broadcast combinations had not served the public interest, or that such combinations necessarily "speak with one voice" or are harmful to competition. In the commission's view, the conflicting studies submitted by the parties concerning the effects of newspaper ownership on competition and station performance were inconclusive, and no pattern of specific abuses by existing cross-owners was demonstrated. The prospective rules were justified, instead, by reference to the commission's policy of promoting diversification of ownership: increases in diversification of ownership would possibly result in enhanced diversity of viewpoints and, given the absence of persuasive countervailing considerations, "even a small gain in diversity" was "worth pursuing."

With respect to the proposed across-the-board divestiture requirement, however, the commission concluded that "a mere hoped for gain in diversity" was not a sufficient justification. Characterizing the divestiture issues as "the most difficult" presented in the proceeding, the Order explained that the proposed rules, while correctly recognizing the central importance of diversity considerations, "may have given too little weight to the consequences which could be expected to attend a focus on the abstract goal alone." Forced dissolution would promote diversity, but it would also cause "disruption for the industry and hardship for individual owners, resulting in losses or diminution of service to the public."

The commission concluded that in light of these countervailing considerations divestiture was warranted only in "the most egregious cases," which it identified as those in which a newspaper-broadcast combination has an "effective monopoly" in the local "marketplace' of ideas as well as economically." The commission recognized that any standards for defining which combinations fell within that category would necessarily be arbitrary to some degree, but "[a] choice had to be made." It thus decided to require divestiture only where there was common ownership of the sole daily newspaper published in a community and either

1. the sole broadcast station providing that entire community with a clear signal, or

2. the sole television station encompassing the entire community with a clear signal.

The Order identified eight television-newspaper and 10 radio-newspaper combinations meeting the divestiture criteria. Waivers of the divestiture requirement were granted *sua sponte* to one television and one radio combination, leaving a total of 16 stations subject to divestiture. The commission explained that waiver requests would be entertained in the latter cases, but, absent waiver, either the newspaper or the broadcast station would have to be divested by January 1, 1980.

On petitions for reconsideration, the commission reaffirmed the rules in all material respects. Memorandum Opinion and Order, 53 FCC2d 589 (1975).

Various parties * * * petitioned for review of the regulations in the United States Court of Appeals for the District of Columbia Circuit. * * * NAB, ANPA, and the broadcast licensees subject to divestiture argued that the regulations went too far in restricting cross-ownership of newspapers and broadcast stations; NCCB and the Justice Department contended that the regulations did not go far enough and that the commission inadequately justified its decision not to order divestiture on a more widespread basis.

Agreeing substantially with NCCB and the Justice Department, the court of appeals affirmed the prospective ban on new licensing of co-located newspaper-broadcast combinations, but vacated the limited divestiture rules, and ordered the commission to adopt regulations requiring dissolution of all existing combinations that did not qualify for a waiver under the procedure outlined in the Order. 555 F.2d 938 (1977). The court held, first, that the prospective ban was a reasonable means of furthering "the highly valued goal of diversity" in the mass media, and was therefore not without a rational basis. The court concluded further that, since the commission "explained why it considers diversity to be a factor of exceptional importance," and since the commission's goal of promoting diversification of mass media ownership was strongly supported by First Amendment and antitrust policies, it was not arbitrary for the prospective rules to be "based on [the diversity] factor to the exclusion of others customarily relied on by the commission."

The court also held that the prospective rules did not exceed the commission's authority under the Communications Act. The court reasoned that the public interest standard of the act permitted, and indeed required, the commission to consider diversification of mass media ownership in making its licensing decisions, and that the commission's general rule-making authority under 47 U.S.C.A. §§ 303(r) and 154(i) allowed the commission to adopt reasonable license qualifications implementing the public interest standard. The court concluded, moreover, that since the prospective ban was designed to "increas[e] the number of media voices in the community," and not to restrict or control the content of free speech, the ban would not violate the First Amendment rights of newspaper owners.

After affirming the prospective rules, the court of appeals invalidated the limited divestiture requirement as arbitrary and capricious within the meaning of § 10(e) of the Administrative Procedure Act, 5 U.S.C.A. § 706(2)(A). The court's primary holding was that the commission lacked a rational basis for "grandfathering" most existing combinations while banning all new combinations. The court reasoned that the commission's own diversification policy, as reinforced by First Amendment policies and the commission's statutory obligation to "encourage the larger and more effective use of radio in the public interest 47 U.S.C.A. § 303(g), required the commission to adopt a "presumption" that stations owned by co-located newspapers "do not serve the public interest." The court observed that, in the absence of countervailing policies, this "presumption" would have dictated adoption of an across-the-board divestiture requirement, subject only to waiver "in those cases where the evidence clearly discloses that cross-ownership is in the public interest." The countervailing policies relied on by the commission in its decision were, in the court's view, "lesser policies" which had not been given as much weight in the past as its diversification policy. And "the record [did] not disclose the extent to which divestiture would actually threaten these [other policies]." The court concluded, therefore, that it was irrational for the commission not to give controlling weight to its diversification policy and thus to extend the divestiture requirement to all existing combinations.

The court of appeals held further that, even assuming a difference in treatment between new and existing combinations was justifiable, the commission lacked a rational basis for requiring divestiture in the 16 "egregious" cases while allowing the remainder of the existing combinations to continue in operation. The court suggested that "limiting divestiture to small markets of 'absolute monopoly' squanders the opportunity where divestiture might do the most good," since "[d]ivestiture * * * may be more useful in the larger markets." The court further observed that the record "[did] not support the conclusion that divestiture would be more harmful in the grandfathered markets than in the 16 affected markets," nor did it demonstrate that the need for divestiture was stronger in those 16 markets. On the latter point, the court noted that, "[a]lthough the affected markets contain fewer voices, the amount of diversity in communities with additional independent voices may in fact be no greater."

The commission, NAB, ANPA, and several cross-owners who had been intervenors below, and whose licenses had been grandfathered under the commission's rules but were subject to divestiture under the court of appeals' decision, petitioned this court for review. We granted certiorari. And we now affirm the judgment of the court of appeals insofar as it upholds the prospective ban and reverse the judgment insofar as it vacates the limited divestiture requirement.

Petitioners NAB and ANPA contend that the regulations promulgated by the commission exceed its statutory rulemaking authority and violate the constitutional rights of newspaper owners. We turn first to the statutory, and then to the constitutional, issues.

* * * NAB contends that, since the act confers jurisdiction on the commission only to regulate "communication by wire or radio." 47 U.S.C.A. § 152(a), it is impermissible for the commission to use its licensing authority with respect to broadcasting to promote diversity in an overall communications market which includes, but is not limited to, the broadcasting industry.

This argument undersells the commission's power to regulate broadcasting in the "public interest." In making initial licensing decisions between competing applicants, the commission has long given "primary significance" to "diversification of control of the media of mass communications," and has denied licenses to newspaper owners on the basis of this policy in appropriate cases. As we have discussed on several occasions, see e.g., the physical scarcity of broadcast frequencies, as well as problems of interference between broadcast signals, led Congress to delegate broad authority to the commission to allocate broadcast licenses in the "public interest." And "[t]he avowed aim of the Communications Act of 1934 was to secure the maximum benefits of radio to all the people of the United States." *National Broadcasting Co. v. United States.* It was not inconsistent with the statutory scheme, therefore, for the commission to conclude that the maximum benefit to the "public interest" would follow from allocation of broadcast licenses so as to promote diversification of the mass media as a whole.

Our past decisions have recognized, moreover, that the First Amendment and antitrust values underlying the commission's diversification policy may properly be considered by the commission in determining where the public interest lies. "[T]he 'public interest' standard necessarily invites reference to First Amendment principles," Columbia Broadcasting System, Inc. v. Democratic Nat. Committee, 412 U.S. 94, 122 (1973), and, in particular, to the First Amendment goal of achieving "the widest possible dissemination of information from diverse and antagonistic sources," *Associated Press v. United States.* And, while the commission does not have power to enforce the antitrust laws as such, it is permitted to take antitrust policies into account in making licensing decisions pursuant to the public interest standard.

It is thus clear that the regulations at issue are based on permissible public interest goals and, so long as the regulations are not an unreasonable means for seeking to achieve these goals, they fall within the general rulemaking authority recognized in the *Storer Broadcasting* and *National Broadcasting* cases. Petitioner ANPA contends that the prospective rules are unreasonable in two respects: first, the rulemaking record did not conclusively establish that prohibiting common ownership of co-located newspapers and broadcast stations would in fact lead to increases in the diversity of viewpoints among local communications media; and second, the regulations were based on the diversification factor to the exclusion of other service factors considered in the past by the commission in making initial licensing decisions regarding newspaper owners. With respect to the first point, we agree with the court of appeals that, notwithstanding the inconclusiveness of the rulemaking record, the commission acted rationally in finding that diversification of ownership would enhance the possibility of achieving greater diversity of viewpoints. As the court of appeals observed, "[d]iversity and its effects are * * * elusive concepts, not easily defined let alone measured without making qualitative judgments objectionable on both policy and First Amendment grounds." Moreover, evidence of specific abuses by common owners is difficult to compile; "the possible benefits of competition do not lend themselves to detailed forecast." In these circumstances, the commission was entitled to rely on its judgment, based on experience, that "it is unrealistic to expect true diversity from a commonly owned station-newspaper combination. The divergency of their viewpoints cannot be expected to be the same as if they were antagonistically run." * * *, see 555 F.2d at 962.

As to the commission's decision to give controlling weight to its diversification goal in shaping the prospective rules, the Order makes clear that this change in policy was a reasonable administrative response to changed circumstances in the broadcasting industry. The Order explained that, although newspaper owners had previously been allowed, and even encouraged, to acquire licenses for co-located broadcast stations because of the shortage of qualified license applicants, a sufficient number of qualified and experienced applicants other than newspaper owners was now available. In addition, the number of channels open for new licensing had diminished substantially. It had thus become both feasible and more urgent for the commission to take steps to increase diversification of ownership, and a change in the commission's policy toward new licensing offered the possibility of increasing diversity without causing any disruption of existing service. In light of these considerations, the commission clearly did not take an irrational view of the public interest when it decided to impose a prospective ban on new licensing of co-located newspaper-broadcast combinations.

Petitioners NAB and ANPA also argue that the regulations, though designed to further the First Amendment goal of achieving "the widest possible dissemination of information from diverse and antagonistic sources," *Associated Press v. United States,* nevertheless violate the First Amendment rights of newspaper owners. We cannot agree, for this argument ignores the fundamental proposition that there is no "unabridgeable First Amendment right to broadcast comparable to the right of every individual to speak, write, or publish." Red Lion Broadcasting Co. v. FCC, 395 U.S., at 388.

The physical limitations of the broadcast spectrum are well known. Because of problems of interference between broadcast signals, a finite number of frequencies can be used productively; this number is far exceeded by the number of persons wishing to broadcast to the public. In light of this physical scarcity, government allocation and regulation of broadcast frequencies are essential, as we have often recognized. No one here questions the need for such allocation and regulation, and, given that need, we see nothing in the First Amendment to prevent the commission from allocating licenses so as to promote the "public interest" in diversification of the mass communications media.

NAB and ANPA contend, however, that it is inconsistent with the First Amendment to promote diversification by barring a newspaper owner from owning certain broadcasting stations. In support, they point to our statement in Buckley v. Valeo, 424 U.S. 1 (1976), to the effect that "government may [not] restrict the speech of some elements of our society in order to enhance the relative voice of others." As *Buckley* also recognized, however, " 'the broadcast media pose unique and special problems not present in the traditional free speech case.' " Id., at 50 n. 55, quoting *Columbia Broadcasting System v. Democratic Nat. Committee.* Thus efforts to " 'enhanc[e] the volume and quality of coverage' of public issues" through regulation of broadcasting may be permissible where similar efforts to regulate the print media would not be. And n. 55, quoting *Red Lion Broadcasting Co. v. FCC*; compare *Miami Herald Pub. Co. v. Tornillo.* Requiring those who wish to obtain a broadcast license to demonstrate that such would serve the "public interest" does not restrict the speech of those who are denied licenses; rather, it preserves the interests of the "people as a whole * * * in free speech." *Red Lion Broadcasting Co.* As we stated in *Red Lion*, "to deny a station license because 'the public interest' requires it 'is not a denial of free speech.' " Quoting *National Broadcasting Co. v. United States.*

* * *

Finally, petitioners argue that the commission has unfairly "singled out" newspaper owners for more stringent treatment than other license applicants. But the regulations treat newspaper owners in essentially the same fashion as other owners of the major media of mass communications were already treated under the commission's multiple ownership rules; owners of radio stations, television stations, and newspapers alike are now restricted in their ability to acquire licenses for co-located broadcast stations. Grosjean v. American Press Co., 297 U.S. 233 (1936), in which this Court struck down a state tax imposed only on newspapers, is thus distinguishable in the degree to which newspapers were singled out for special treatment. In addition, the effect of the tax in *Grosjean* was "to limit the circulation of information to which the public is entitled," an effect inconsistent with the protection conferred on the press by the First Amendment.

In the instant case, far from seeking to limit the flow of information, the commission has acted, in the court of appeals' words, "to enhance the diversity of information heard by the public without on-going government surveillance of the content of speech." 555 F.2d at 954. The regulations are a reasonable means of promoting the public interest in diversified mass communications; thus they do not violate the First Amendment rights of those who will be denied broadcast licenses pursuant to them. Being forced to "choose among applicants for the same facilities," the commission has chosen on a "sensible basis," one designed to further, rather than contravene, "the system of freedom of expression." T. Emerson, *The System of Freedom of Expression* 663 (1970).

After upholding the prospective aspect of the commission's regulations, the court of appeals concluded that the commission's decision to limit divestiture to 16 "egregious cases" of "effective monopoly" was arbitrary and capricious within the meaning of the Administrative Procedure Act (APA), § 10(e), 5 U.S.C.A. § 706(2)(A).

* * *

In the view of the court of appeals, the commission lacked a rational basis, first, for treating existing newspaper-broadcast combinations more leniently than combinations that might seek licenses in the future; and, second, even assuming a distinction between existing and new combinations had been justified, for requiring divestiture in the "egregious cases" while allowing all other existing combinations to continue in operation. We believe that the limited divestiture requirement reflects a rational weighing of competing policies, and we therefore reinstate the portion of the commission's order that was invalidated by the court of appeals.

* * *

The commission was well aware that separating existing newspaper-broadcast combinations would promote diversification of ownership. It concluded, however, that ordering widespread divestiture would not result in "the best practicable service to the American public", a goal that the commission has always taken into account and that has been specifically approved by this Court, FCC v. Sanders Bros. Radio Station, 309 U.S. 470 (1940).

In particular, the commission expressed concern that divestiture would cause "disruption for the industry" and "hardship to individual owners," both of which would result in harm to the public interest. Especially in light of the fact that the number of co-located newspaper-broadcast combinations was already on the decline as a result of natural market forces, and would decline further as a result of the prospective rules, the commission decided that across-the-board divestiture was not warranted.

The Order identified several specific respects in which the public interest would or might be harmed if a sweeping divestiture requirement were imposed: the stability and continuity of meritorious service provided by the newspaper owners as a group would be lost; owners who had provided meritorious service would unfairly be denied the opportunity to continue in operation; "economic dislocations" might prevent new owners from obtaining sufficient working capital to maintain the quality of local programming; and local ownership of broadcast stations would probably decrease. We cannot say that the commission acted irrationally in concluding that these public interest harms outweighed the potential gains that would follow from increasing diversification of ownership.

In the past, the commission has consistently acted on the theory that preserving continuity of meritorious service furthers the public interest, both in its direct consequence of bringing proven broadcast service to the public, and in its indirect consequence of rewarding—and avoiding losses to—licensees who have invested the money and effort necessary to produce quality performance. Thus, although a broadcast license must be renewed every three years, and the licensee must satisfy the commission that renewal will serve the public interest, both the commission and the courts have recognized that a licensee who has given meritorious service has a "legitimate renewal expectanc[y]" that is "implicit in the structure of the Act" and should not be destroyed absent good cause. *Greater Boston Television Corp. v. FCC.* Accordingly, while diversification of ownership is a relevant factor in the context of license renewal as well as initial licensing, the commission has long considered the past performance of the incumbent as the most important factor in deciding whether to grant license renewal and thereby to allow the existing owner to continue in operation. Even where an incumbent is challenged by a competing applicant who offers greater potential in terms of diversification, the commission's general practice has been to go with the "proven product" and grant renewal if the incumbent has rendered meritorious service.

* * *

In the instant proceeding, the commission specifically noted that the existing newspaper-broadcast cross-owners as a group had a "long record of service" in the public interest; many were pioneers in the broadcasting industry and had established and continued "[t]raditions of service" from the outset. Order, at 1078. Notwithstanding the commission's diversification policy, all were granted initial licenses upon findings that the public interest would be served thereby, and those that had been in existence for more than three years had also had their licenses renewed on the ground that the public interest would be furthered. The commission noted, moreover, that its own study of existing co-located newspaper-television combinations showed that in terms of percentage of time devoted to several categories of local programming, these stations had displayed "an undramatic but nonetheless statistically significant superiority" over other television stations. An across-the-board divestiture requirement would result in loss of the services of these superior licensees, and—whether divestiture caused actual losses to existing owners, or just denial of reasonably anticipated gains—the result would be that future licensees would be discouraged from investing the resources necessary to produce quality service.

At the same time, there was no guarantee that the licensees who replaced the existing cross-owners would be able to provide the same level of service or demonstrate the same long-term commitment to broadcasting. And even if the new owners were able in the long run to provide similar or better service, the commission found that divestiture would cause serious disruption in the transition period. Thus, the commission observed that new owners "would lack the long knowledge of the community and would have to begin raw," and—because of high interest rates—might not be able to obtain sufficient working capital to maintain the quality of local programming.

The commission's fear that local ownership would decline was grounded in a rational prediction, based on its knowledge of the broadcasting industry and supported by comments in the record. That many of the existing newspaper-broadcast combinations owned by local interests would respond to the divestiture requirement by trading stations with out-of-town owners. It is undisputed that roughly 75% of the existing co-located newspaper-television combinations are locally owned, and these owners' knowledge of their local communities and concern for local affairs, built over a period of years, would be lost if they were replaced with outside interests. Local ownership in and of itself has been recognized to be a factor of some—if relatively slight—significance even in the context of initial licensing decisions. It was not unreasonable, therefore, for the commission to consider it as one of several factors militating against divestiture of combinations that have been in existence for many years.

In light of these countervailing considerations, we cannot agree with the court of appeals that it was arbitrary and capricious for the commission to "grandfather" most existing combinations, and to leave opponents of these combinations to their remedies in individual renewal proceedings. In the latter connection we note that, while individual renewal proceedings are unlikely to accomplish any "overall restructuring" of the existing ownership patterns, the Order does make clear that existing combinations will be subject to challenge by competing applicants in renewal proceedings, to the same extent as they were prior to the instant rulemaking proceedings. That is, diversification of ownership will be a relevant but somewhat secondary factor. And, even in the absence of a competing applicant, license renewal may be denied if, *inter alia,* a challenger can show that a common owner has engaged in specific economic or programming abuses.

In concluding that the commission acted unreasonably in not extending its divestiture requirement across-the-board, the court of appeals apparently placed heavy reliance on a "presumption" that existing newspaper-broadcast combinations "do not serve the public interest." The court derived this presumption primarily from the commission's own diversification policy, as "reaffirmed" by adoption of the prospective rules in this proceeding, and secondarily from "[t]he policies of the First Amendment," and the commission's statutory duty to "encourage the larger and more effective use of radio in the public interest." 47 U.S.C.A. § 303(g). As explained above, we agree that diversification of ownership furthers statutory and constitutional policies, and, as the commission recognized, separating existing newspaper-broadcast combinations would promote diversification. But the weighing of policies under the "public interest" standard is a task that Congress has delegated to the commission in the first instance, and we are unable to find anything in the Communications Act, the First Amendment, or the commission's past or present practices that would require the commission to "presume" that its diversification policy should be given controlling weight in all circumstances.

Such a "presumption" would seem to be inconsistent with the commission's longstanding and judicially approved practice of giving controlling weight in some circumstances to its more general goal of achieving "the best practicable service to the public." Certainly, as discussed above, the commission through its license renewal policy has made clear that it considers diversification of ownership to be a factor of less significance when deciding whether to allow an existing licensee to continue in operation than when evaluating applicants seeking initial licensing. Nothing in the language or the legislative history of § 303(g) indicates that Congress intended to foreclose all differences in treatment between new and existing licensees, and indeed, in amending § 307(d) of the Act in 1952, Congress appears to have lent its approval to the commission's policy of evaluating existing licensees on a somewhat different basis than new applicants. Moreover, if enactment of the prospective rules in this proceeding itself were deemed to create a "presumption" in favor of divestiture, the commission's ability to experiment with new policies would be severely hampered. * * *

The court of appeals also relied on its perception that the policies militating against divestiture were "lesser policies" to which the commission had not given as much weight in the past as its divestiture policy. This perception is subject to much the same criticism as the "presumption" that existing co-located newspaper-broadcasting combinations do not serve the public interest. The commission's past concern with avoiding disruption of existing service is amply illustrated by its license renewal policies. In addition, it is worth noting that in the past when the commission has changed its multiple ownership rules it has almost invariably tailored the changes so as to operate wholly or primarily on a prospective basis. * * *

The court of appeals apparently reasoned that the commission's concerns with respect to disruption of existing service, economic dislocations, and decreases in local ownership necessarily could not be very weighty since the commission has a practice of routinely approving voluntary transfers and assignments of licenses. But the question of whether the commission should compel proven licensees to divest their stations is a different question from whether the public interest is served by allowing transfers by licensees who no longer wish to continue in the business. As the commission's brief explains:

> [I]f the commission were to force broadcasters to stay in business against their will, the service provided under such circumstances, albeit continuous, might well not be worth preserving.

* * *

We also must conclude that the court of appeals erred in holding that it was arbitrary to order divestiture in the 16 "egregious cases" while allowing other existing combinations to continue in operation. The commission's decision was based not—as the court of appeals may have believed—on a conclusion that divestiture would be more harmful in the grandfathered markets than in the 16 affected markets, but rather on a judgment that the need for diversification was especially great in cases of local monopoly. This policy judgment was certainly not irrational, see United States v. Radio Corp. of America, 358 U.S., at 351–352, and indeed was founded on the very same assumption that underpinned the diversification policy itself and the prospective rules upheld by the court of appeals and now by this Court—that the greater the number of owners in a market, the greater the possibility of achieving diversity of program and service viewpoints.

As to the commission's criteria for determining which existing newspaper-broadcast combinations have an "effective monopoly" in the "local marketplace of ideas as well as economically," we think the standards settled upon by the commission reflect a rational legislative-type judgment. Some line had to be drawn, and it was hardly unreasonable for the commission to confine divestiture to communities in which there is common ownership of the only daily newspaper and either the only television station or the only broadcast station of any kind encompassing the entire community with a clear signal. Cf. *United States v. Radio Corp. of America.* It was not irrational, moreover, for the commission to disregard media sources other than newspapers and broadcast stations in setting its divestiture standards. The studies cited by the commission in its notice of rulemaking unanimously concluded that newspapers and television are the two most widely utilized media sources for local news and discussion of public affairs; and, as the commission noted in its Order, at 1081, "aside from the fact that [magazines and other periodicals] often had only a tiny fraction in the market, they were not given real weight since they often dealt exclusively with regional or national issues and ignored local issues." Moreover, the differences in treatment between radio and television stations were certainly justified in light of the far greater influence of television than radio as a source for local news. See Order, at 1083.

The judgment of the court of appeals is affirmed in part and reversed in part.

It is so ordered.

COMMENT

1. The Supreme Court decision in the cross-ownership case reversed the court of appeal's effort to restructure on an across-the-board basis existing cross-ownership patterns in American communities. Beyond this holding, the Supreme Court decision in the cross-ownership case gave a new sense of security to incumbent or existing licensees by declaring that past performance by the incumbent licensee rather than diversification of ownership was the "most important factor in deciding whether to grant license renewals." See *Central Florida Enterprises v. FCC,* text, p. 973.

Citing the Broadcast Applicant Renewal proceeding, text, p. 957, the Court appeared to approve the FCC's practice of making the central factor in comparative licensing decisions the past performance of the incumbent. The Court appeared to approve as well of the FCC's refusal to make diversification of ownership a conclusive factor in such decisions.

2. The decision in National Citizens Committee for Broadcasting v. FCC, 555 F.2d 938 (D.C.Cir.1977), sent a shock through the broadcasting industry because of the court's ruling that the FCC's preservation of existing cross-ownership combinations was unreasonable.

Judge Bazelon, writing for a panel which included Judge Robinson and Judge Skelly Wright, made clear that his new passion for requiring a vigorous diversification of ownership policy arose out of a concern that the continuous and supervisory role of the FCC in fairness doctrine administration menaced the First Amendment rights of broadcasters. Diversification of ownership policy, it was hoped, would secure diversity of opinion and yet at the same time avoid the unwelcome government intrusion that intense enforcement of the fairness doctrine might engender. Bazelon declared that "the prospective ban [on cross-ownership combinations] is an attempt to enhance the diversity of information heard by the public without ongoing government surveillance of the content of speech." In short, the court of appeals decision in the cross-ownership case owed much to Judge Bazelon's profound disenchantment with the fairness doctrine.

3. Even if the court of appeals decision had stood, the result would not necessarily have been to unscramble immediately existing cross-ownership combinations in communities across the country. The court of appeals expressly authorized the FCC to administer a petition-for-waiver procedure whereby a licensee would be allowed to secure exemption from the cross-ownership ban if they could show that a particular cross-ownership combination was in the public interest.

The petition-for-waiver procedure was added to the court of appeals decision, some industry lawyers reasoned, in hopes that this feature of the decision would allow it to withstand an attack upon review by the Supreme Court. Absent some provision for waiver for existing cross-ownership combinations, even combinations that were rendering "superior" service would have been broken up. But a waiver procedure also presented existing cross-ownership combinations with an opportunity for long and expensive delay.

Moreover, if the Supreme Court had upheld the court of appeals extension of the ban on cross-ownership to existing combinations, the result would not, at least on a national basis, have necessarily led to a substantial change in ownership patterns in the communications industry. A cross-ownership ban on existing combinations was bound to encourage trades. A newspaper in one city could sell its television station in that city to a newspaper in another and buy in its stead the television station in the other city. During the time period between the appeals decision and the Supreme Court decision in the cross-ownership case, the *Washington Post* sold its CBS-affiliated VHF-television station to media interests in Detroit. When the decision of the Supreme Court in the cross-ownership case came down, it was clear that the deal had been unnecessary. The *Post* was stoic and editorialized:

> That the Supreme Court might have required the Washington Post Company to sever its link with WTOP encouraged the swap of stations now under way, but the transaction stands on its own as good public policy. If the presumption about diverse sources of information has any validity—and we believe it does—the trade of stations will serve both Detroit and Washington. That, in turn, will be good for those who own the stations. Editorial, "The Newspaper-Television Link", *The Washington Post*, p. A 22, June 16, 1978.

4. Although the Supreme Court may have "grandfathered" for the moment existing cross-ownership combinations, such combinations are by no means impervious to future attack. See *Central Florida Enterprises*, text, p. 973. The Court, per Justice Marshall, was careful to say: "And even in the absence of a competing applicant, license renewal may be denied if a challenger can show that a common owner has engaged in specific economic or programming abuses."

Citizens groups interested in working to bring a larger measure of deconcentration of ownership in the broadcast industry were thus relegated to the renewal process and resort to petitions to deny individual application for renewal. In short, absence of diversification of ownership on the part of a renewal application can still be asserted as a demerit in petitions to deny and comparative hearings. In the absence of another alternative, this remedy was better than nothing, but it was hardly likely to yield much overall change in the broadcast industry.

5. The Supreme Court did not agree with the court of appeals that the FCC should have found that existing colocated newspaper-broadcast combinations were not in the public interest. Diversification of ownership should be a factor but not the dispositive factor in determining whether a colocated combination licensee should be renewed. But there were other factors relevant to such an FCC determination:

a. Would a new ownership perform as well as the old one?

b. Would losses to existing owners result from forced sales?

c. Would losses from divestiture "discourage future investment in quality programming"?

6. The FCC had announced that its cross-ownership ban was to apply prospectively and not retroactively. The FCC had ordered divestiture of only sixteen existing colocated combinations on the ground that these were "egregious" cross-ownership situations where the combination involved the community's sole daily newspaper and either the only radio or the only television station in the community. The court of appeals had held that the FCC's order requiring divestiture in only sixteen cross-ownership situations was arbitrary and capricious.

The court of appeals had sought to make divestiture the general rule and allow exemption through a petition-for-waiver device for meritorious combinations. The Supreme Court, however, found the FCC's refusal to extend the ban on cross-ownership to most existing combinations to be reasonable. The FCC justification for refusing to apply the cross-ownership ban to existing colocated combinations was essentially accepted by the Supreme Court. These justifications included

1. fear that across-the-board divestiture would result in a loss of "stability and continuity of meritorious service" provided by newspaper owners as a group,

2. concern that newspaper owners who had provided good service would unfairly be prevented from continuing to broadcast, and

3. concern that economic dislocations might prevent new owners from obtaining the capital to maintain even existing levels of quality in local programming.

7. One additional FCC point the Supreme Court put its finger on in the cross-ownership decision was a concern that an absolute ban on cross-ownership in a community might have the result of decreasing local ownership of broadcast stations. Such a rule might also have the effect of decreasing local ownership of daily newspapers as well as further accelerating the trend to chain ownership of the daily press. Further, where the broadcast property is more financially successful than the newspaper property, the loss of the station may actually terminate the life of the newspaper as happened in Boston with respect to the WHDH situation. See text, p. 955, fn. 10.

8. In its cross-ownership rules opinion, the FCC emphasized that the rules derived from First Amendment policy rather than antitrust policy. Diversification of ownership was seen by the FCC as a First Amendment goal. The Supreme Court agreed with this perspective. The First

Amendment rights of the public as previously outlined in passages in *Red Lion* and even in *CBS* were cited and quoted by the Court in the cross-ownership case with approval.

Justice Marshall rejected the argument that if a newspaper in a community could not acquire a broadcast station in its own community, its First Amendment rights were forfeited. In a perhaps unresponsive rejoinder, Marshall said that since the same newspaper could acquire a broadcast station in another community, the newspaper's First Amendment rights were not forfeited. It might be argued that the implication of this observation is that a flat ban against newspaper ownership of broadcast stations would be unconstitutional since in that event there would be a total deprivation on the right of a particular group to engage in communication by means of broadcasting.

As in the 1978 broadcast obscenity case, *Pacifica*, the Supreme Court in the cross-ownership case made clear its view that the First Amendment status of broadcasters was not equivalent to that of newspapers and other print media:

"[E]fforts to 'enhanc[e] the volume and quality of coverage' of public issues through regulation of broadcasting may be permissible where similar efforts to regulate the print media would not be."

9. Perhaps the whole philosophy of the diversification of ownership concept in broadcasting is wrongheaded. The concept assumes apparently that the more diffuse the ownership of broadcast stations, the more diverse the content of broadcast programming will be. But is this a realistic assumption?

Justice Marshall acknowledged that an FCC study of colocated newspaper-television combinations revealed that such combinations showed an " 'undramatic but nonetheless statistically significant superiority' " in the percentage of programming time devoted to some local programming. If colocated newspaper-broadcast combinations display a measurably superior performance, how can even application of a prospective ban on the formation of such combinations be justified?

Is the reason the Court sustains the prospective ban based on the principle that the formation of broadcast regulatory policy is an FCC and not a judicial responsibility? Perhaps, the FCC's decision to root the cross-ownership rules in First Amendment policy rather than antitrust policy indicates that the rules reflect a certain leap of First Amendment faith rather than any empirically or economically demonstrable policy.

10. Since the 1975 Supreme Court ruling, the FCC has affirmed its stance on the one-to-a-market rule. However, the FCC does not always adhere strictly to the letter of the rule. In Evangelistic Missionary Fellowship (EMF), 75 FCC2d 724 (1980), because of the uniqueness of broadcast operations in Alaska, the FCC granted a VHF television construction permit to EMF despite the fact that EMF would own an AM, an FM, and a television broadcast station in the same market. The waiver of the one-to-a-market rule was deemed to be warranted because of the limited economic potential and demonstrated lack of interest in operating a broadcast station in Alaska.

Under the present one-to-a-market rule, combinations involving radio and UHF television stations are treated separately from the absolute proscriptions involving UHF–TV. Note 8 to the original rules (47 U.S.C. §§ 73.240, 73.636) provides that applications involving UHF-radio combinations will be treated on a "case-by-case basis" to determine whether common ownership, operation, or control of the stations would be in the public interest.

It is apparent that in applying this case-by-case analysis, the FCC permits combination UHF-radio ownership only where such ownership will ensure or foster the development of UHF–TV. See Commercial Radio Institute, Inc., 78 FCC2d

1016 (1980); Television Corp. of Virginia, 69 FCC2d 1161 (1978). More than likely, UHF television construction permits will be granted on the condition that the licensee divest itself of either of the proscribed combinations within a short period of time. See Palmetto Radio Corp., 67 FCC2d 771 (1978); Mid-Texas Broadcasting, Inc., 71 FCC2d 1173 (1979). In Notice of Proposed Rulemaking, Multiple Ownership of AM, FM, and TV Broadcasting Stations, 44 Fed.Reg. 55,603 (1979), the FCC appears ready to eliminate the case-by-case analysis under Note 8 and treat UHF stations the same as VHF stations with regard to the one-to-a-market and regional concentration rules. This FCC move came after a notable rise in the number of UHF applications, due in part to the fact that existing UHF stations are becoming increasingly profitable.

The Central Florida Enterprises Case: New Guidepost for Weighing the Claims of the Incumbent Against the Challenger?

Does the Supreme Court's cross-ownership decision command an implicit preference for the incumbent? In a post-cross-ownership decision case, the United States Court of Appeals for the District of Columbia indicated that it didn't think so. See Central Florida Enterprises, Inc. v. FCC, 683 F.2d 503 (D.C.Cir.1982), reported below. *Central Florida* sets forth some guidelines which, if applied, would mean that the incumbent will not necessarily prevail in renewal battles.

CENTRAL FLORIDA ENTERPRISES, INC. v. FCC

683 F.2D 503 (D.C.CIR.1982).

WILKEY, Circuit Judge:

This case involves a license renewal proceeding for a television station. The appeal before us is taken from a new decision [1] by the Federal Communications Commission ("FCC" or "the commission") after our opinion in *Central Florida Enterprises v. FCC (Central Florida I)* [2] vacated the commission's earlier orders involving the present parties. The FCC had granted the renewal of incumbent's license, but we held that the commission's fact-finding and analysis on certain issues before it were inadequate, and that its method of balancing the factors for and against renewal was faulty. On remand, while the FCC has again concluded that the license should be renewed, it has also assuaged our concerns that its analysis was too cursory and has adopted a new policy for comparative renewal proceedings which meets the criteria we set out in *Central Florida I.* Accordingly, and with certain caveats, we affirm the commission's decision.

The factual background and legal issues involved in this case were discussed at length in our earlier opinion and can be summarized briefly here. Central Florida Enterprises has challenged the FCC's decision to renew Cowles Broadcasting's license to operate on Channel 2 in Daytona Beach, Florida. In reaching a renewal/nonrenewal decision, the FCC must engage in a comparative weighing of pro-renewal considerations against anti-renewal considerations. In the case here, there were four considerations potentially cutting against Cowles: its illegal move of its main studio, the involvement of several

1. Cowles Broadcasting, Inc., 86 FCC2d 993 (1981). The proceedings prior to this new decision are at 60 FCC2d 372 (1976), reconsideration denied and clarified, 62 FCC2d 953 (1977), reconsideration denied 40 Rad.Reg.2d 1627 (1977), vacated and remanded sub nom. Central Fla. Enterprises v. FCC, 598 F.2d 37 (D.C.Cir.1978), cert. dismissed 441 U.S. 957 (1979).

2. 598 F.2d 37 (D.C.Cir.1978), cert. dismissed 441 U.S. 957 (1979).

related companies in mail fraud, its ownership of other communications media, and its relative (to Central Florida) lack of management-ownership integration. On the other hand, Cowles' past performance record was "superior," i.e., "sound, favorable and substantially above a level of mediocre service which might just minimally warrant renewal."

In its decision appealed in *Central Florida I* the FCC concluded that the reasons undercutting Cowles' bid for renewal did "not outweigh the substantial service Cowles rendered to the public during the last license period." Accordingly, the license was renewed. Our reversal was rooted in a twofold finding. First, the commission had inadequately investigated and analyzed the four factors weighing against Cowles' renewal. Second, the process by which the FCC weighed these four factors against Cowles' past record was never "even vaguely described" and, indeed, "the commission's handling of the facts of this case [made] embarrassingly clear that the FCC [had] practically erected a presumption of renewal that is inconsistent with the full hearing requirement" of the Communications Act. We remand with instructions to the FCC to cure these deficiencies.

On remand the commission has followed our directives and corrected, point by point, the inadequate investigation and analysis of the four factors cutting against Cowles' requested renewal. The commission concluded that, indeed, three of the four merited an advantage for Central Florida, and on only one (the mail fraud issue) did it conclude that nothing needed to be added on the scale to Central's plan or removed from Cowles'. We cannot fault the commission's actions here.

We are left, then, with evaluating the way in which the FCC weighed Cowles' main studio move violation and Central's superior diversification and integration, on the one hand, against Cowles' substantial record of performance on the other. This is the most difficult and important issue in this case, for the new weighing process which the FCC has adopted will presumably be employed in its renewal proceedings elsewhere. We therefore feel that it is necessary to scrutinize carefully the FCC's new approach, and discuss what we understand and expect it to entail.

For some time now the FCC has had to wrestle with the problem of how it can factor in some degree of "renewal expectancy" for a broadcaster's meritorious past record, while at the same time undertaking the required comparative evaluation of the incumbent's probable future performance versus the challenger's. As we stated in *Central Florida I,* "the incumbent's past performance is some evidence, and perhaps the best evidence, of what its future performance would be." And it has been intimated—by the Supreme Court in *FCC v. National Citizens Committee for Broadcasting (NCCB)* and by this court in *Citizens Communications Center v. FCC* and *Central Florida I*—that some degree of renewal expectancy is permissible. But *Citizens* and *Central Florida I* also indicated that the FCC has in the past impermissibly raised renewal expectancy to an irrebuttable presumption in favor of the incumbent.

We believe that the formulation by the FCC in its latest decision, however, is a permissible way to incorporate some renewal expectancy while still undertaking the required comparative hearing. *The new policy, as we understand it, is simply this: renewal expectancy is to be a factor weighed with all the other factors, and the better the past record, the greater the renewal expectancy "weight."*

In our view [states the FCC], the strength of the expectancy depends on the merit of the past record. Where, as in this case, the incumbent rendered substantial but not superior service, the "expectancy" takes the form of a comparative preference weighed against [the] other factors. * * * An incumbent performing in a superior manner would receive an even stronger preference. An incumbent rendering minimal service would receive no preference. This is to be contrasted with commission's 1965 Policy Statement on Comparative Broadcast Hearings, where "[o]nly unusually good or unusually poor records have relevance."

If a stricter standard is desired by Congress, it must enact it. We cannot: the new standard is within the statute.

The reasons given by the commission for factoring in some degree of renewal expectancy are rooted in a concern that failure to do so would hurt broadcast *consumers.*

> The justification for a renewal expectancy is three-fold. (1) There is no guarantee that a challenger's paper proposals will, in fact, match the incumbent's proven performance. Thus, not only might replacing an incumbent be entirely gratuitous, but *it might even deprive the community of an acceptable service and replace it with an inferior one.* (2) Licensees should be encouraged through the likelihood of renewal to make investments *to ensure quality service. Comparative renewal proceedings cannot function as a "competitive spur" to licensees if their dedication to the community is not rewarded.* (3) Comparing incumbents and challengers as if they were both new applicants could lead to a haphazard restructuring of the broadcast industry especially considering the large number of group owners. *We cannot readily conclude that such a restructuring could serve the public interest.*

We are relying, then, on the FCC's commitment that renewal expectancy will be factored in for the benefit of the public, not for incumbent broadcasters. In subsequent cases we must judge the faithfulness of the FCC to that commitment, for, as the Supreme Court has said, "It is the right of the viewers and listeners, not the right of the broadcasters, which is paramount," citing its earlier statement that "[p]lainly it is not the purpose of the [Communications] act to protect a license against competition but to protect the public." Then Circuit Judge Burger, as a member of this court, wrote:

> A broadcaster seeks and is granted the free and exclusive use of a limited and valuable part of the public domain; when he accepts that franchise it is burdened with enforceable public obligations. * * * After nearly five decades of operation the broadcast industry does not seem to have grasped the simple fact that a broadcast license is a public trust subject to termination for breach of duty.

As we concluded in *Central Florida I,* "[t]he only legitimate fear which should move [incumbent] licensees is the fear of their own substandard performance, and that would be all to the public good."

There is a danger, of course, that the FCC's new approach could still degenerate into precisely the sort of irrebuttable presumption in favor of renewal that we have warned against. But this did not happen in the case before us today, and our reading of the commission's decision gives us hope that if the FCC applies the standard in the same way in future cases, it will not happen in them either. The standard is new, however, and much will depend on how the commission applies it and fleshes it out. Of particular importance will be the definition and level of service it assigns to "substantial"—and whether that definition is ever found to be "opaque to judicial review," "wholly unintelligible," or based purely on "administrative 'feel.' " [27]

27. *Id.* at 50 [quoting earlier proceeding, 60 FCC2d 372, 422 (1976)]. We think it would be helpful if at some point the commission defined and explained the distinctions, if any, among: substantial, meritorious, average, above average, not above average, not far above average, above mediocre, more than minimal, solid, sound, favorable, not superior, not exceptional, and unexceptional—all terms used by the parties to describe what the FCC found Cowles' level of performance to have been. We are especially interested to know what the

In this case, however, the commission was painstaking and explicit in its balancing. The commission discussed in quite specific terms, for instance, the items it found impressive in Cowles' past record. It stressed and listed numerous programs demonstrating Cowles' "local community orientation" and "responsive[ness] to community needs," discussed the percentage of Cowles' programming devoted to news, public affairs, and local topics, and said it was "impressed by [Cowles'] reputation in the community. Seven community leaders and three public officials testified that [Cowles] had made outstanding contributions to the local community. Moreover, the record shows no complaints. * * *" The commission concluded that "Cowles' record [was] more than minimal," was in fact " 'substantial,' *i.e.,* 'sound, favorable and substantially above a level of mediocre service which might just minimally warrant renewal.' "

The commission's inquiry in this case did not end with Cowles' record, but continued with a particularized analysis of what factors weighed against Cowles' record, and how much. The FCC investigated fully the mail fraud issue. It discussed the integration and diversification disadvantages of Cowles and conceded that Central had an edge on these issues—"slight" for integration, "clear" for diversification. But it reasoned that "structural factors such as [these]—of primary importance in a new license proceeding should have lesser weight compared with the preference arising from substantial past service." [31] Finally, with respect to the illegal main studio move, the FCC found that "licensee misconduct" in general

---

standard of comparison is in each case. "Average" compared to all applicants? "Mediocre" compared to all incumbents? "Favorable" with respect to the FCC's expectations? We realize that the FCC's task is a subjective one, but the use of imprecise terms needlessly compounds our difficulty in evaluating what the commission has done. We think we can discern enough to review intelligently the commission's actions today, but if the air is not cleared or, worse, becomes foggier, the FCC's decision-making may again be adjudged "opaque to judicial review."

31. *Id.* at 1015. The Supreme Court upheld a similar decision by the FCC to weigh diversification more heavily for prospective, as opposed to existing, licensees. *NCCB,* 436 U.S. at 803–809 * * *. Thus, "diversification will be a relevant but somewhat secondary factor." *Id.* at 809, 98 S.Ct. at 2119. *See also Citizens,* 447 F.2d at 1208–09 n. 23.

The FCC argues that diversification and integration should not be given "heavy weight in the comparative renewal context" since "[c]hallengers could easily structure their proposals to be superior to the incumbent's," resulting in possible "substantial restructuring of the industry with possible disruptions of service" and a loss of "incentive to provide quality programming." 86 FCC2d at 1016.

Here we have a caveat. We do not read the commission's new policy as *ignoring* integration and diversification considerations in comparative renewal hearings. In its brief at page 6 the commission states that "an incumbent's meritorious record should outweigh in the comparative renewal context a challenging applicant's advantages under the structural factors of integration and diversification." Ceteris paribus, this may be so—depending in part, of course, on how "meritorious" is defined. But where there are weights on the scales other than a meritorious record on the one hand, and integration and diversification on the other, the commission must afford the latter two *some* weight, since while they alone may not outweigh a meritorious record they may tip the balance if weighed with something else. *See Citizens,* 447 F.2d at 1208–09 n. 23.

That, of course, is precisely the situation here, since the main studio move violation must also be balanced against the meritorious record. The commission may not weigh the antirenewal factors separately against the incumbent's record, eliminating them as it goes along. It must weigh them all simultaneously. * * *. We are convinced, however, despite some ambiguous passages like the one just quoted in the preceding paragraph, that the Commission has followed the correct procedure here. *See, e.g.,* 86 FCC2d at 1018. Thus the commission's conclusion that diversification and integration are to be given "lesser weight" than renewal expectancy does not mean that they were or will be given *no* weight. The relative weight to be given these factors will vary, depending on how much or how little diversification or integration is at stake. Here, as stated in the text, the commission did consider the degree of Central's integration advantage ("slight") and diversification advantage ("clear") 86 FCC2d at 1009–10.

"may provide a more meaningful basis for preferring an untested challenger over a proven incumbent." The commission found, however, that here the "comparative significance of the violation" was diminished by the underlying facts:

> Cowles did not actually move a studio away from Daytona Beach. It maintained two studios, one of which gradually became somewhat superior to the other. Thus, while a violation of the rule technically occurred, Cowles demonstrated no tendency to flout commission rules *or disserve the community of license.*

The FCC concluded that "the risk to the public interest posed by the violation seems small when compared to the actuality of depriving Daytona Beach of Cowles' tested and acceptable performance."

Having listed the relevant factors and assigned them weights, the commission concluded that Cowles' license should be renewed. We note, however, that despite the finding that Cowles' performance was " 'substantial,' *i.e.,* 'sound, favorable and substantially above a level of mediocre service,' " the combination of Cowles' main studio rule violation and Central's diversification and integration advantages made this a "close and difficult case." Again, we trust that this is more evidence that the commission's weighing did not, and will not, amount to automatic renewal for incumbents.

We are somewhat reassured by a recent FCC decision granting, for the first time since at least 1961, on *comparative* grounds the application of the challenger for a radio station license and denying the renewal application of the incumbent licensee.[38] In that decision the commission found that the *incumbent deserved no renewal expectancy* for his past program record and that his application was inferior to the challenger's on comparative grounds. Indeed, it was the *incumbent's* preferences on the diversification and integration factors which were overcome (there, by the challenger's superior programming proposals and longer broadcast week). The commission found that the incumbent's "inadequate [past performance] reflects poorly on the *likelihood of future service in the public interest.*" Further, it found that the incumbent had no "legitimate renewal expectancy" because his past performance was neither "meritorious" nor "substantial."

We have, however, an important caveat. In the commission's weighing of factors the scale mid-mark must be neither the factors themselves, nor the interests of the broadcasting industry, nor some other secondary and artificial construct, but rather the intent of Congress, which is to say the interests of the listening public. All other doctrine is merely a means to this end, and it should not become more. If in a given case, for instance, the factual situation is such that the denial of a license renewal would not undermine renewal expectancy *in a way harmful to the public interest,* then renewal expectancy should not be invoked.[40]

Finally, we must note that we are still troubled by the fact that the record remains that an incumbent *television* licensee has *never* been denied renewal in a comparative challenge. American television viewers will be reassured, although a trifle baffled, to learn that even the worst television stations—those which are, presumably, the ones picked out as vulnera-

38. In re Applications of Simon Geller and Grandbanke Corp., FCC Docket Nos. 21104–05 (released 15 June 1982). We intimate no view at this time, of course, on the soundness of the commission's decision there; we cite it only as demonstrating that the commission's new approach may prove to be more than a paper tiger.

40. Thus, the three justifications given by the commission for renewal expectancy, *supra,* should be remembered by the FCC in future renewal proceedings and, where these justifications are in a particular case attenuated, the commission ought not to chant "renewal expectancy" and grant the license.

ble to a challenge—are so good that they never need replacing. We suspect that somewhere, sometime, somehow, some television licensee *should* fail in a comparative renewal challenge, but the FCC has never discovered such a licensee yet. As a court we cannot say that it must be Cowles here.

We hope that the standard now embraced by the FCC will result in the protection of the public, not just incumbent licensees. And in today's case we believe the FCC's application of the new standard was not inconsistent with the commission's mandate. Accordingly the commission's decision is affirmed.

COMMENT

1. An examination of the history of the *Central Florida* litigation is instructive since it provides a particularly vivid example of FCC solicitude for the incumbent applicant in a comparative renewal proceeding, even though the incumbent has other media interests and the new applicant does not. See *Cowles Florida Broadcasting, Inc.*, 60 FCC2d 372 (1976). The stated premise of the holding is that an applicant without other media interests has a preference over an applicant without such interest. But the preference is not decisive absent proof that the new applicant will render equal or superior service to that which the incumbent with other media interests is likely to render. Quality of service was said to be primary, especially where a license grant would not add to media concentration.

The incumbent licensee, WESH–TV, Daytona, Florida, owned by Cowles Florida Broadcasting, Inc. (Cowles), was in turn owned completely by Cowles Communications, Inc. (CCI). At the time of the initial hearing, CCI also owned an AM–FM–TV combination in Iowa, and another CCI subsidiary owned AM–FM stations in Tennessee. In addition, CCI owned a substantial stock interest in the New York Times Company, which published the *New York Times*, other newspapers and periodicals, and broadcast interests. Further, certain CCI stockholders have substantial mass-media involvement. Central Florida Enterprises, Inc. (Central), the competing applicant, had no mass media interests. The incumbent licensee, WESH–TV—with other mass media interests—was renewed.

On the diversification issue, the FCC minimized Cowles's other media interests because the media involved were either not controlled by Cowles or were located in a different community than WESH–TV. The FCC stated further, referring to its cross-ownership rules that even in the more compelling situation involving common ownership of a daily newspaper and broadcast stations in the same market, except in extreme cases, it would not require divestiture to break up existing concentrations.

Then FCC Chairman Wiley dissented, emphasizing that while he personally believed WESH's record warranted renewal, the present state of the law required denial of the renewal application. Central should receive a preference under the diversification criterion, and Central should also be preferred under the best practicable service criterion. These criteria had been set forth in the 1965 Policy Statement on Broadcast Comparative Hearings, 1 FCC2d 393 (1963).

Further, under Citizens Communication Center v. FCC, 447 F.2d 1201 (D.C.Cir. 1971), an incumbent licensee was entitled to a "plus of major significance" only on a showing of "superior" service. The FCC Administrative Law Judge's characterization of Cowles's performance, however, was "thoroughly acceptable." This was a phrase Wiley pointed out which "clearly does not connote superiority." Thus, Wiley concluded that Central should have been preferred under the operational comparative criteria.

At the same time, Wiley argued that a more appropriate system would be to scrap the comparative hearing procedure and renew all incumbents who "do a good and faithful job of serving their communities."

Commissioner Robinson, in dissent, also urged reform of the comparative hearing procedure. "Something has to be changed. One place to begin is with a legal recognition of the reality: a licensee has a property right in its license which is defeasible only for serious misbehavior."

The FCC approach in *Cowles*, however, was soon undone. In Central Florida Enterprises v. FCC, 4 Med.L.Rptr. 1502, 598 F.2d 37 (D.C.Cir.1978), a panel of the federal court of appeals in Washington, D.C., per Judge Wilkey, reversed the FCC in the *Cowles* case in a decision which spread almost as much fright in broadcasting circles as the *WHDH* case had nearly a decade earlier. Judge Wilkey declared that the FCC had failed to set forth any articulate rationale in the record to justify its comparative evaluation of the incumbent and the challenger:

> (T)he state of administrative practice in commission comparative renewal proceedings is unsatisfactory. Its paradoxical history reveals an ordinarily tacit presumption that the incumbent licensee is to be preferred over competing applicants. * * * The Federal Communications Act fairly precludes any preference based on incumbency *per se*. * * * Despite the apparent statutory assurance of a free-wheeling inquiry into the relative merit of challenger and incumbent licensee, the history of commission practice reveals a strong preference for renewal. Further, until fairly recently, such choices by the commission were routinely affirmed by this court. This general phenomenon has been rationalized into what we have called on occasion "a renewal expectancy." * * * The development of commission policy on comparative renewal hearings has now departed sufficiently from the established law, statutory and judicial precedent, that the commission's handling of the facts in this case make embarrassingly clear that the FCC has practically erected a presumption of renewal that is inconsistent with the full hearing requirement of Sec. 309(e).
>
> We emphasize that lawful renewal expectancies are confined to the likelihood that an incumbent will prevail in a fully comparative inquiry. "Superior" or above average past performance is, of course, highly relevant to the comparison, and might be expected to prevail absent some clear and strong showing by the challenger under the comparative factor (either affirmative bearing on the challenger's projected program performance, or negative regarding the incumbent's media ties or perhaps discovered character deficiencies) or other designated issues. But we do not see how performance that is merely average, whether "solid" or not, can warrant renewal or, in fact, be of especial relevance without some finding that the challenger's performance would likely be no more satisfactory.
>
> On remand, the commission will have occasion to reconsider its characterization of Cowles' past performance and to articulate clearly the manner in which its findings are integrated into the comparative analysis. We remand this case in light of our abiding conviction that the commission's order is unsupported by the record and the prior law on which it purported to rely. We are especially troubled by the possibility that settled principles of administrative practice may be ignored because of the commission's insecurity or unhappiness with the substance of the regulatory regime it is charged to enforce. Nothing would be more demoralizing or unsettling of expectations than for drifting administrative adjudications quietly to erode the statutory mandate of the commission and judicial precedent.
>
> *Orders vacated and case remanded for proceedings consistent with this opinion.*

With respect to Judge Wilkey's concern that the FCC has "erected a presumption of renewal" that is inconsistent with renewal, see the discussion of RKO General Inc. v. FCC, 670 F.2d 215 (D.C.Cir.1981) where FCC denial of the license renewal application of a television station was upheld, text, p. 901.

The foregoing opinion was decided before the Supreme Court decision in the cross-ownership case.

Did the cross-ownership decision influence Judge Wilkey's decision in the *Central Florida* case?

2. Judge Wilkey summarized the FCC's new approach to renewals in *Central Florida II* as follows: "We believe that the formulation by the FCC in its latest decision, however, is a permissible way to incorporate some renewal expectancy while still undertaking the required comparative hearing. *The new policy, as we understand it, is simply this: renewal expectancy is to be a factor weighed with all the other factors, and the better the past record, the greater the renewal expectancy 'weight'.*"

Under the FCC renewal policy described by Judge Wilkey in *Central Florida II*, will an incumbent television licensee which has other media affiliations be in a worse or better position in a renewal contest with a new applicant which has no media affiliations?

Is there any basis for an argument that the renewal philosophy of *Central Florida* is inconsistent with the Supreme Court's decision in *FCC v. National Citizens Committee for Broadcasting*, text, p. 959. Why?

CABLE TELEVISION

UNITED STATES v. SOUTHWESTERN CABLE CO.
MIDWEST TELEVISION, INC. v. SOUTHWESTERN CABLE CO.

392 U.S. 157, 88 S.CT. 1994, 20 L.ED.2D 1001 (1968).

Justice HARLAN delivered the opinion of the Court.

These cases stem from proceedings conducted by the Federal Communications Commission after request by Midwest Television for relief under §§ 74.1107 and 74.-1109 of the rules promulgated by the commission for the regulation of community antenna television (CATV) systems. Midwest averred that respondents' CATV systems transmitted the signals of Los Angeles broadcasting stations into the San Diego area, and thereby had, inconsistently with the public interest, adversely affected Midwest's San Diego station.[4] Midwest sought an appropriate order limiting the carriage of such signals by respondents' systems. After consideration of the petition and of various responsive pleadings, the commission restricted the expansion of respondents' service in areas in which they had not operated on February 15, 1966, pending hearings to be conducted on the merits of Midwest's complaints. 4 FCC2d 612. On petitions for review, the Court of Appeals for the Ninth Circuit held that the commission lacks authority under the Communications Act of 1934, to issue such an order. * * * For reasons that follow, we reverse.

CATV systems receive the signals of television broadcasting stations, amplify them, transmit them by cable or microwave, and ultimately distribute them by wire to the receivers of their subscribers. CATV systems characteristically do not produce their own programming, and do not recompense producers or broadcasters for use of the programming which they receive and redistribute. Unlike ordinary broadcasting stations, CATV systems commonly charge their subscribers installation and other fees.

* * *

4. Midwest asserted that respondents' importation of Los Angeles signals had fragmented the San Diego audience, that this would reduce the advertising revenues of local stations, and that the ultimate consequence would be to terminate or to curtail the services provided in the San Diego area by local broadcasting stations. Respondents' CATV systems now carry the signals of San Diego stations, but Midwest alleged that the quality of the signals, as they are carried by respondents, is materially degraded, and that this serves only to accentuate the fragmentation of the local audience.

CATV systems perform either or both of two functions. First, they may supplement broadcasting by facilitating satisfactory reception of local stations in adjacent areas in which such reception would not otherwise be possible; and second, they may transmit to subscribers the signals of distant stations entirely beyond the range of local antennae. As the number and size of CATV systems have increased, their principal function has more frequently become the importation of distant signals. * * * Thus, "while the CATV industry originated in sparsely settled areas and areas of adverse terrain * * * it is now spreading to metropolitan centers. * * * "

* * *

We must first emphasize that questions as to the validity of the specific rules promulgated by the commission for the regulation of CATV are not now before the Court. The issues in these cases are only two: whether the commission has authority under the Communications Act to regulate CATV systems, and, if it has, whether it has, in addition, authority to issue the prohibitory order here in question.

The commission's authority to regulate broadcasting and other communications is derived from the Communications Act of 1934, as amended. The act's provisions are explicitly applicable to "all interstate and foreign communication by wire or radio. * * * " 47 U.S.C.A. § 152(a). The commission's responsibilities are no more narrow: it is required to endeavor to "make available * * * to all the people of the United States a rapid, efficient, Nation-wide and world-wide wire and radio communication service. * * * " 47 U.S. C.A. § 151. The commission was expected to serve as the "single government agency" with "unified jurisdiction" and "regulatory authority over all forms of electrical communication, whether by telephone, telegraph, cable, or radio." It was for this purpose given "broad authority." As this Court emphasized in an earlier case, the act's terms, purposes, and history all indicate that Congress "formulated a unified and comprehensive regulatory system for the [broadcasting] industry." FCC v. Pottsville Broadcasting Co., 309 U.S. 134, 137.

Respondents do not suggest that CATV systems are not within the term "communication by wire or radio." Indeed, such communications are defined by the act so as to encompass "the transmission of * * signals, pictures, and sounds of all kinds," whether by radio or cable, "including all instrumentalities, facilities, apparatus, and services (among other things, the receipt, forwarding and delivery of communications) incidental to such transmission." 47 U.S.C.A. §§ 153(a), (b). These very general terms amply suffice to reach respondents' activities.

Nor can we doubt that CATV systems are engaged in interstate communication, even where, as here, the intercepted signals emanate from stations located within the same state in which the CATV system operates. We may take notice that television broadcasting consists in very large part of programming devised for, and distributed to, national audiences; respondents thus are ordinarily employed in the simultaneous retransmission of communications that have very often originated in other States. The stream of communication is essentially uninterrupted and properly indivisible.

Nonetheless, respondents urge that the Communications Act, properly understood, does not permit the regulation of CATV systems. First, they emphasize that the commission in 1959 and again in 1966 sought legislation that would have explicitly authorized such regulation, and that its efforts were unsuccessful. In the circumstances here, however, this cannot be dispositive. The commission's requests for legislation evidently reflected in each instance both its uncertainty as to the proper width of its authority and its understandable preference for more detailed policy guidance than the Communications Act now provides. We have recognized that administrative agencies, should in such situations, be encouraged to seek from Congress clarification of the pertinent statutory provisions.

* * *

Second, respondents urge that § 152(a) does not independently confer regulatory authority upon the commission, but instead merely prescribes the forms of communication to which the Act's other provisions may separately be made applicable. Respondents emphasize that the commission does not contend either that CATV systems are common carriers, and thus within Subtitle II of the act, or that they are broadcasters, and thus within Subtitle III. They conclude that CATV, with certain of the characteristics both of broadcasting and of common carriers, but with all of the characteristics of neither, eludes altogether the act's grasp.

We cannot construe the act so restrictively. Nothing in the language of § 152(a), in the surrounding language, or in the act's history or purposes limits the commission's authority to those activities and forms of communication that are specifically described by the act's other provisions. The section itself states merely that the "provisions of [the act] shall apply to all interstate and foreign communication by wire or radio. * * * " Similarly, the legislative history indicates that the commission was given "regulatory power over all forms of electrical communication. * * * " S.Rep.No.830, 73d Cong., 2d Sess., 1. Certainly Congress could not in 1934 have foreseen the development of community antenna television systems, but it seems to us that it was precisely because Congress wished "to maintain, through appropriate administrative control, a grip on the dynamic aspects of radio transmission," FCC v. Pottsville Broadcasting Co., that it conferred upon the commission a "unified jurisdiction " and "broad authority."

* * *

Moreover, the commission has reasonably concluded that regulatory authority over CATV is imperative if it is to perform with appropriate effectiveness certain of its other responsibilities. Congress has imposed upon the commission the "obligation of providing a widely dispersed radio and television service," with a "fair, efficient, and equitable distribution" of service among the "several states and communities." 47 U.S.C.A. § 307(b). The commission has, for this and other purposes, been granted authority to allocate broadcasting zones or areas, and to provide regulations "as it may deem necessary" to prevent interference among the various stations. 47 U.S.C.A. § 303(f), (h). The commission has concluded, and Congress has agreed, that these obligations require for their satisfaction the creation of a system of local broadcasting stations, such that "all communities of appreciable size [will] have at least one television station as an outlet for local self-expression." In turn, the commission has held that an appropriate system of local broadcasting may be created only if two subsidiary goals are realized. First, significantly wider use must be made of the available ultra-high frequency channels. Second, communities must be encouraged "to launch sound and adequate programs to utilize the television channels now reserved for educational purposes." These subsidiary goals have received the endorsement of Congress.

The commission has reasonably found that the achievement of each of these purposes is "placed in jeopardy by the unregulated explosive growth of CATV." H.R. Rep.No.1635, 89th Cong., 2d Sess.

Although CATV may in some circumstances make possible "the realization of some of the [commission's] most important goals," First Report and Order, 38 FCC 683, at 699, its importation of distant signals into the service areas of local stations may also "destroy or seriously degrade the service offered by a television broadcaster," id., at 700, and thus ultimately deprive the public of the various benefits of a system of local broadcasting stations. In particular, the commission feared that CATV might, by dividing the available audiences and revenues, significantly magnify the characteristically serious financial difficulties of UHF and educational television broadcasters. The commission acknowledged that it could not predict with certainty the consequences of unregulated CATV, but reasoned that its statutory responsibilities demand that it "plan in advance of foreseeable events, instead of waiting to react to them."

* * * The commission has reasonably found that the successful performance of these duties demands prompt and efficacious regulation of community antenna television systems. We have elsewhere held that we may not, "in the absence of compelling evidence that such was Congress' intention * * * prohibit administrative action imperative for the achievement of an agency's ultimate purposes." There is no such evidence here, and we therefore hold that the commission's authority over "all interstate * * * communication by wire or radio" permits the regulation of CATV systems.

There is no need here to determine in detail the limits of the commission's authority to regulate CATV. It is enough to emphasize that the authority which we recognize today under § 152(a) is restricted to that reasonably ancillary to the effective performance of the commission's various responsibilities for the regulation of television broadcasting. The commission may, for these purposes, issue "such rules and regulations and prescribe such restrictions and conditions, not inconsistent with law," as "public convenience, interest or necessity requires." 47 U.S.C.A. § 303(r). We express no views as to the commission's authority, if any, to regulate CATV under any other circumstances or for any other purposes.

We must next determine whether the commission has authority under the Communications Act to issue the particular prohibitory order in question in these proceedings. * * *

The commission, after examination of various responsive pleadings but without prior hearings, ordered that respondents generally restrict their carriage of Los Angeles signals to areas served by them on February 15, 1966, pending hearings to determine whether the carriage of such signals into San Diego contravenes the public interest. The order does not prohibit the addition of new subscribers within areas served by respondents on February 15, 1966; it does not prevent service to other subscribers who began receiving service or who submitted an "accepted subscription request" between February 15, 1966, and the date of the commission's order; and it does not preclude the carriage of San Diego and Tiajuana, Mexico, signals to subscribers in new areas of service. 4 FCC2d 612, 624–625. The order is thus designed simply to preserve the situation as it existed at the moment of its issuance.

* * *

The commission has acknowledged that, in this area of rapid and significant change, there may be situations in which its generalized regulations are inadequate, and special or additional forms of relief are imperative. It has found that the present case may prove to be such a situation, and that the public interest demands "interim relief * * * limiting further expansion," pending hearings to determine appropriate commission action. Such orders do not exceed the commission's authority. This Court has recognized that "the administrative process [must] possess sufficient flexibility to adjust itself" to the "dynamic aspects of radio transmission,"

National Broadcasting Co. v. United States, 319 U.S. at 219, and that it was precisely for that reason that Congress declined to "stereotyp[e] the powers of the commission to specific details. * * *" * * * The judgments of the court of appeals are reversed, and the cases are remanded for further proceedings consistent with this opinion. It is so ordered. Judgments reversed and cases remanded.

The Scope of FCC Jurisdiction Over Cable

1. Does the Supreme Court in *Southwestern Cable* think it sufficient to base FCC jurisdiction over cable television on the fact that cable may have an adverse effect on broadcasting? Under such a theory is there any legal limit to FCC jurisdiction?

The Court itself is quite careful to limit the scope of FCC jurisdiction over cable in *Southwestern*. As Justice Harlan put it for the Court: "It is enough to emphasize that the authority which we recognize today under § 152(a) is restricted to that reasonably ancillary to the effective performance of the commission's various responsibilities for the regulation of television broadcasting."

2. One of the concerns expressed in the *Southwestern Cable* case was that the ability of cable to make available many channels to viewers receiving the service was at odds with the emphasis the FCC had placed on local service programming. The ability of listeners to view channels far from their homes erodes the audience of the locally based channel and therefore shrinks its appeal to local advertisers. Moreover, the FCC's licensing policy favors applicants who have strong identifications with the community they wish to serve. The basis for the policy is the belief that, if applicants are familiar with the needs of the community, they will therefore be in the best position for local expression. But the problem with the local service emphasis was that it, like all programming responsibilities, was placed on the individual station licensee. But how much responsibility does the typical TV station licensee have over his programming?

Do you suppose the networks and the broadcasting industry approve or oppose FCC jurisdiction over cable television? The argument can be made that if the FCC is industry dominated, one of the best ways to stimulate change in American broadcasting is to leave new technological developments outside the reach of the FCC.

3. The promise of cable to alter and enrich broadcasting by using its multichannel capacity in ways that will make it a viable alternative to commercial VHF television is still unfulfilled. Illustrative of the legal problems that beset the development of cable is Midwest Video Corp. v. FCC, 406 U.S. 649 (1972).

On June 24, 1970, the FCC ordered all cable systems having 3,500 or more subscribers to originate their own programming. The FCC ruling was heralded as a significant step toward providing an alternative to commercial television. The hope was that the development of local television programming by cable systems in communities throughout the country might provide an alternative to network television and an opportunity for local participation in community affairs through the new technology of cable television.

The conclusion of the Eighth Circuit in *Midwest Video* that the FCC lacked jurisdiction to require cable systems to originate programming momentarily placed the future of cable in limbo, Midwest Video Corp. v. United States, 441 F.2d 1322 (8th Cir. 1971), a status which has been the hallmark of cable since its inception. The FCC has continually issued proposed rules and regulations for cable but adopted very few of them. The harsh lower federal court reaction to one of the few positive steps the FCC has taken with regard to cable—the program origination requirement—was a bitter pill for those who advocated FCC control over cable. The Supreme Court, however, reversed the lower court, sustained the program origination rule, and ushered in a theory of FCC jurisdiction over cable which was far more encompassing than that enunciated in *Southwestern.*

UNITED STATES v. MIDWEST VIDEO CORP.

406 U.S. 649, 92 S.Ct. 1860,
32 L.ED.2D 390 (1972).

Justice BRENNAN announced the judgment of the Court, and an opinion in which Justice White, Justice Marshall, and Justice Blackmun joined.

* * *

As we said in *Southwestern,* * * * CATV "[promises] for the future to provide a national communications system, in which signals from selected broadcasting centers would be transmitted to metropolitan areas throughout the country." Moreover, as the commission has noted, "the expanding multichannel capacity of cable systems could be utilized to provide a variety of new communications services to homes and businesses within a community," such as facsimile reproduction of documents, electronic mail delivery, and information retrieval. Perhaps more important, CATV systems can themselves originate programs, or "cablecast"—which means, the commission has found, that CATV can "[increase] the number of local outlets for community self-expression and [augment] the public's choice of programs and types of services, without use of broadcast spectrum. * * *"

Recognizing this potential, the commission, shortly after our decision in *Southwestern,* initiated a general inquiry "to explore the broad question of how best to obtain, consistent with the public interest standard of the Communications Act, the full benefits of developing communications technology for the public, with particular immediate reference to CATV technology. * * *" In particular, the commission tentatively concluded, as part of a more expansive program for the regulation of CATV, "that, for now and in general, CATV program origination is in the public interest," and sought comments on a proposal "to condition the carriage of television broadcast signals (local or distant) upon a requirement that the CATV system also operate to a significant extent as a local outlet by originating." As for its authority to impose such a requirement, the commission stated that its "concern with CATV carriage of broadcast signals is not just a matter of avoidance of adverse effects, but extends also to requiring CATV affirmatively to further statutory policies."

On the basis of comments received, the commission on October 24, 1969, adopted a rule providing that "no CATV system having 3,500 or more subscribers shall carry the signal of any television broadcast station unless the system also operates to a significant extent [5] as a local outlet by cablecasting [6] and has available

---

5. "By significant extent [the commission indicated] we mean something more than the origination of automated services (such as time and weather, news ticker, stock ticker, etc.) and aural services (such as music and announcements). Since one of the purposes of the origination requirement is to insure that cablecasting equipment will be available for use by others originating on common carrier channels, 'operation to a significant extent as a local outlet' in essence necessitates that the CATV operator have some kind of video cablecasting system for the production of local live and delayed programming (e.g., a camera and a video tape recorder, etc.)." First Report and Order 214.

6. "Cablecasting" was defined as "programming distributed on a CATV system which has been originated by the CATV operator or by another entity, exclusive of broadcast signals carried on the system." 47 CFR

facilities for local production and presentation of programs other than automated services." 47 CFR 74.1111(a). In a report accompanying this regulation, the commission stated that the tentative conclusions of its earlier notice of proposed rulemaking:

> recognize the great potential of the cable technology to further the achievement of long-established regulatory goals in the field of television broadcasting by increasing the number of outlets for community self-expression and augmenting the public's choice of programs and types of services. * * * They also reflect our view that a multipurpose CATV operation combining carriage of broadcast signals with program origination and common carrier services,[8] might best exploit cable channel capacity to the advantage of the public and promote the basic purpose for which this commission was created: "regulating interstate and foreign commerce in communication by wire and radio so as to make available, so far as possible, to all people of the United States a rapid, efficient, nationwide, and worldwide wire and radio communication service with adequate facilities at reasonable charges * * " (sec. 1 of the Communications Act). After full consideration of the comments filed by the parties, we adhere to the view that program origination on CATV is in the public interest.[10] First Report and Order, 20 FCC2d 201, 202 (1969).

The commission further stated:

> The use of broadcast signals has enabled CATV to finance the construction of high capacity cable facilities. In requiring in return for these uses of radio that CATV devote a portion of the facilities to providing needed origination service, we are furthering our statutory responsibility to "encourage the larger and more effective use of radio in the public interest" (§ 303(g)). The requirement will also facilitate the more effective performance of the commission's duty to provide a fair, efficient, and equitable distribution of television service to each of the several states and communities (§ 307(b)), in areas where we have been unable to accomplish this through broadcast media.

Upon the challenge of respondent Midwest Video Corp., an operator of CATV systems subject to the new cablecasting requirement, the United States Court of Appeals for the Eighth Circuit set aside the regulation on the ground that the com-

---

74.1101(j). As this definition makes clear, cablecasting may include not only programs produced by the CATV opertor, but "films and tapes produced by others, and CATV network programming." First Report and Order 214. See also id., at 203. The definition has been altered to conform to changes in the regulation, * * * and now appears at 47 CFR 76.5(w). See Report and Order on Cable Television Service 3279. Although the definition now refers to programming "subject to the exclusive control of the cable operator," this is apparently not meant to effect a change in substance or to preclude the operator from cablecasting programs produced by others. See id., at 3271.

8. Although the commission did not impose common carrier obligations on CATV systems in its 1969 report, it did note that "the origination requirement will help ensure that origination facilities are available for use by others originating on leased channels." First Report and Order 209. Public access requirements were introduced in the commission's Report and Order on Cable Television Service, although not directly under the heading of common carrier service. See Report and Order on Cable Television Service 3277.

10. In so concluding the commission rejected the contention that a prohibition on CATV originations was "necessary to prevent potential fractionalization of the audience for broadcast services and a siphoning off of program material and advertising revenue now available to the broadcast service." First Report and Order 202. "[B]roadcasters and CATV originators * * *," the commission reasoned, "stand on the same footing in acquiring the program material with which they compete." Id., at 203. Moreover, "a loss of audience or advertising revenue to a television station is not in itself a matter of moment to the public interest unless the result is a net loss of television service," ibid.—an impact that the commission found had no support in the record and that, in any event, it would undertake to prevent should the need arise. See id., at 203–204. See also Memorandum Opinion and Order 826 n. 3, 828–829.

mission "is without authority to impose" it. 441 F.2d 1322, 1328 (1971). "The commission's power [over CATV], * * * " the court explained, "must be based on the commission's right to adopt rules that are reasonably ancillary to its responsibilities in the broadcasting field,"—a standard that the court thought the commission's regulation "goes far beyond." The court's opinion may also be understood to hold the regulation invalid as not supported by substantial evidence that it would serve the public interest. * * *

The parties now before us do not dispute that in light of *Southwestern* CATV transmissions are subject to the commission's jurisdiction as "interstate * * * communication by radio or wire" within the meaning of § 2(a) even insofar as they are local cablecasts. The controversy instead centers on whether the commission's program origination rule is "reasonably ancillary to the effective performance of [its] various responsibilities for the regulation of television broadcasting." We hold that it is.

At the outset we must note that the commission's legitimate concern in the regulation of CATV is not limited to controlling the competitive impact CATV may have on broadcast services. *Southwestern* refers to the commission's "various responsibilities for the regulation of television broadcasting." These are considerably more numerous than simply assuring that broadcast stations operating in the public interest do not go out of business. Moreover, we must agree with the commission that its "concern with CATV carriage of broadcast signals is not just a matter of avoidance requiring CATV affirmatively to further statutory policies." Since the avoidance of adverse effects, itself the furtherance of statutory policies, no sensible distinction even in theory can be drawn along those lines. More important, CATV systems, no less than broadcast stations, * * * may enhance as well as impair the appropriate provision of broadcast services. Consequently, to define the commission's power in terms of the protection, as opposed to the advancement, of broadcasting objectives would artificially constrict the commission in the achievement of its statutory purposes and be inconsistent with our recognition in *Southwestern* "that it was precisely because Congress wished 'to maintain, through appropriate administrative control, a grip on the dynamic aspects of radio transmission,' * * * that it conferred upon the commission a 'unified jurisdiction' and 'broad authority.' "

The very regulations that formed the backdrop for our decision in *Southwestern* demonstrate this point. Those regulations were, of course, avowedly designed to guard broadcast services from being undermined by unregulated CATV growth. At the same time, the commission recognized that "CATV systems * * * have arisen in response to public need and demand for improved television service and perform valuable public services in this respect." Second Report and Order, 2 FCC2d 725, 745 (1966). Accordingly, the commission's express purpose was not:

"to deprive the public of these important benefits or to restrict the enriched programming selection which CATV makes available. Rather, our goal here is to integrate the CATV service into the national television structure in such a way as to promote maximum television service to all people of the United States (secs. 1 and 303(g) of the act [nn. 9 and 11, supra]), both those who are cable viewers and those dependent on off-the-air service. The new rules * * * are the minimum measures we believe to be essential to insure that CATV continues to perform its valuable supplementary role without unduly damaging or impeding the growth of television broadcast service." In implementation of this approach CATV systems were required to carry local broadcast station signals to encourage diversified programming suitable to the community's needs as well as to prevent a diversion of audiences and advertising revenues. The duplication of local station programming was also forbidden for the latter purpose, but only on the same day as the local broadcast so as "to preserve, to the extent practicable, the valuable public contribution of CATV in providing wider access to nationwide programming and a wider selection of programs on any particular day." Finally, the distant-importation rule was adopted to enable the commission to reach a public-interest determination weighing the advantages and disadvantages of the proposed service on the facts of each individual case. In short, the regulatory authority asserted by the commission in 1966 and generally sustained by this Court in *Southwestern* was authority to regulate CATV with a view not merely to protect but to promote the objectives for which the commission had been assigned jurisdiction over broadcasting.

In this light the critical question in this case is whether the commission has reasonably determined that its origination rule will "further the achievement of long-established regulatory goals in the field of television broadcasting by increasing the number of outlets for community self-expression and augmenting the public's choice of programs and types of services. * * *" We find that it has.

The goals specified are plainly within the commission's mandate for the regulation of television broadcasting. * * *

Equally plainly the broadcasting policies the commission has specified are served by the program-origination rule under review. To be sure, the cablecasts required may be transmitted without use of the broadcast spectrum. But the regulation is not the less, for that reason, reasonably ancillary to the commission's jurisdiction over broadcast services. The effect of the regulation, after all, is to assure that in the retransmission of broadcast signals viewers are provided suitably diversified programming, the same objective underlying regulations sustained in *National Broadcasting Co. v. United States,* as well as the local-carriage rule reviewed in *Southwestern* and subsequently upheld. In essence the regulation is no different from commission rules governing the technological quality of CATV broadcast carriage. In the one case, of course, the concern is with the strength of the picture and voice received by the subscriber, while in the other it is with the content of the programming offered. But in both cases the rules serve the policies of §§ 1 and 303(g) of the Communications Act on which the cablecasting regulation is specifically premised, and also, in the commission's words, "facilitate the more effective performance of [its] duty to provide a fair, efficient, and equitable distribution of television service to each of the several States and communities" under § 307(b). In sum, the regulation preserves and enhances the integrity of broadcast signals and therefore is "reasonably ancillary to the effective performance of the commission's various responsibilities for the regulation of television broadcasting."

Respondent, nevertheless, maintains that just as the commission is powerless to require the provision of television broadcast services where there are no applicants for station licenses no matter how important or desirable those services may be, so, too, it cannot require CATV operators unwillingly to engage in cablecasting. In our view, the analogy respondent thus draws between entry into broadcasting and entry into cablecasting is misconceived. The commission is not attempting to compel wire service where there has been no commitment to undertake it. CATV operators to whom the cablecasting rule applies have voluntarily engaged themselves in providing that service, and the commission seeks only to ensure that it satisfactorily meets community needs within the context of their undertaking.

For these reasons we conclude that the program-origination rule is within the commission's authority recognized in *Southwestern.*

The question remains whether the regulation is supported by substantial evidence that it will promote the public interest. We read the opinion of the court of appeals as holding that substantial evidence to that effect is lacking because the regulation creates the risk that the added burden of cablecasting will result in increased subscription rates and even the termination of CATV services. That holding is patently incorrect in light of the record.

* * *

* * * [T]he commission chose to apply the regulation to systems with 3,500 or more subscribers, effective January 1, 1971.

* * * [A]pproximately 70 percent of the systems now originating have fewer than 3,500 subscribers; indeed, about half of the systems now originating have fewer than 2,000 subscribers * * * [T]he 3,500 standard will encompass only a very small percentage of existing systems at present subscriber levels, less than 10 percent."

On petitions for reconsideration the commission observed that it had "been given no data tending to demonstrate that systems with 3,500 subscribers cannot cablecast without impairing their financial stability, raising rates or reducing the quality of service." Memorandum Opinion and Order, 23 FCC2d 825, 826 (1970). The commission repeated that "[t]he rule adopted is minimal in the light of the potentials of cablecasting," but, nonetheless, on its own motion postponed the effective date of the regulation to April 1, 1971, "to afford additional preparation time."

This was still not the commission's final effort to tailor the regulation to the financial capacity of CATV operators. In denying respondent's motion for a stay of the effective date of the rule, the commission reiterated that "there has been no showing made to support the view that compliance * * * would be an unsustainable burden." Memorandum Opinion and Order, 27 FCC2d 778, 779 (1971). On the other hand, the commission recognized that new information suggested that CATV systems of 10,000 ultimate subscribers would operate at a loss for at least four years if required to cablecast. That data, however, was based on capital expenditure and annual operating cost figures "appreciably higher" than those first projected by the commission. The commission concluded:

"While we do not consider that an adequate showing has been made to justify general change, we see no public benefit in risking injury to CATV systems in providing local origination. Accordingly, if CATV operators with fewer than 10,000 subscribers request *ad hoc* waiver of [the regulation], they will not be required to originate pending action on their waiver requests. * * * Systems of more than 10,000 subscribers may also request waivers, but they will not be excused from compliance unless the commission grants a requested waiver * * *. [The] benefit [of cablecasting] to the public would be delayed if the * * * stay [requested by respondent] is granted, and the stay would, therefore, do injury to the public's interest."

This history speaks for itself. The cablecasting requirement thus applied is plainly supported by substantial evidence that it will promote the public interest.

* * *

Reversed.

Chief Justice BURGER, concurring in the result.

* * *

Candor requires acknowledgment, for me at least, that the commission's position strains the outer limits of even the open-ended and pervasive jurisdiction that has evolved by decisions of the commission and the courts. The almost explosive development of CATV suggests the need of a comprehensive re-examination of the statutory scheme as it relates to this new development, so that the basic policies are considered by Congress and not left entirely to the commission and the courts.

I agree with the plurality's rejection of any meaningful analogy between requiring CATV operators to develop programming and the concept of commandeering someone to engage in broadcasting. Those who exploit for private commercial surface transmission by CATV—to which they make no contribution—are not exactly strangers to the stream of broadcasting. The essence of the matter is that when they interrupt the signal and put it to their own use for profit, they take on burdens, one of which is regulation by the commission.

I am not fully persuaded that the commission has made the correct decision in this case and the thoughtful opinions in the court of appeals and the dissenting opinion here reflect some of my reservations. * * * (But) I * * * conclude that until Congress acts, the commission should be allowed wide latitude and I therefore concur in the result reached by this Court.

Justice Douglas, with whom Justice Stewart, Justice Powell, and Justice Rehnquist concur, dissenting.

* * *

* * * The commission is not given *carte blanche* to initiate broadcasting stations; it cannot force people into the business. It cannot say to one who applies for a broadcast outlet in city A that the need is greater in city B and he will be licensed there. The fact that the commission has authority to regulate origination of programs if CATV decides to enter the field does not mean that it can compel CATV to originate programs. The fact that the act directs the commission to encourage the larger and more effective use of radio in the public interest, 47 U.S.C.A. § 303(g), relates to the objectives of the act and does not grant power to compel people to become broadcasters any more than it grants the power to compel broadcasters to become CATV operators.

The upshot of today's decision is to make the commission's authority over activities "ancillary" to its responsibilities greater than its authority over any broadcast licensee. Of course, the commission can regulate a CATV (station) that transmits broadcast signals. But to entrust the commission with the power to force some, a few, or all CATV operators into the broadcast business is to give it a forbidding authority. Congress may decide to do so. But the step is a legislative measure so extreme that we should not find it interstitially authorized in the vague language of the act.

I would affirm the court of appeals.

COMMENT

1. In *Midwest Video,* the Supreme Court appears to expand the scope of FCC jurisdiction over cable far beyond the more tentative basis for FCC jurisdiction outlined in *Southwestern.* In *Midwest Video*, the Supreme Court suggested that the FCC can not only regulate cable to "protect" broadcasting but can also regulate to "promote" the objectives for which the FCC had been given jurisdiction over television broadcasting. As an illustration, the goal of diversified programming is said by the Court in *Midwest Video* to be such an objective and apparently can be implemented by FCC regulation of either cablecasting or television broadcasting.

2. Isn't the Supreme Court really saying in *Midwest Video* that any public interest objective which would justify a regulatory policy or action by the FCC with regard to television broadcasting may justify such a policy or action by the FCC with regard to cable?

If this is so, then the Supreme Court has laid the groundwork of plenary or complete jurisdiction by the FCC over cable. In other words, all of cable has now become potentially subject to FCC jurisdiction. Any aspect of cable not regulated by the FCC would then be unregulated as a matter of FCC choice not because of lack of power. If the doctrine of *Midwest Video* gives the FCC plenary jurisdiction over cable, this constitutes a significant advance over the assertion in *Southwestern* that the FCC jurisdiction over cable is "restricted to that reasonably ancillary to the effective performance" of the FCC's regulatory responsibilities over television broadcasting.

The Mandatory Public Access Controversy

Despite the 1972 Supreme Court decision in *United States v. Midwest Video* (*Midwest Video I*), reversing the Eighth Circuit decision invalidating the FCC's program origination rules, the Eighth Circuit continued to be an unreceptive forum with respect to extensive regulation of cable by the FCC. In Midwest Video Corp. v. FCC, 571 F.2d 1025 (8th Cir. 1978), (*Midwest Video II*), the court, per Chief Judge Markey, struck down as beyond the FCC's jurisdiction the 1976 Cable Report, Report and Order in Docket No. 20508, 59 FCC2d 399 (1976), which required cable operators to make available four channels for public access on a first-come, nondiscriminatory basis. The Eighth Circuit's decision in *Midwest Video II* was affirmed by the Supreme Court in *FCC v. Midwest Video Corp.*

FCC v. MIDWEST VIDEO CORP.

4 MED.L.RPTR. 2345, 440 U.S. 689, 99 S.CT. 1435, 59 L.ED. 692 (1979).

Justice WHITE delivered the opinion of the Court.

In May 1976, the Federal Communications Commission promulgated rules requiring cable television systems that have 3,500 subscribers and carry broadcast signals to develop, at a minimum, a 20-channel capacity by 1986, to make available certain channels for access by third parties, and to furnish equipment and facilities for access purposes. Report and Order in Docket No. 20528, 59 FCC2d 294 (1976) (1976 Order). The issue here is whether these rules are "reasonably ancillary to the effective performance of the commission's various responsibilities for the regulation of television broadcasting," *United States v. Southwestern Cable Co.* * * *, and hence within the commission's statutory authority.

The regulations now under review had their genesis in rules prescribed by the commission in 1972 requiring all cable operators in the top 100 television markets to design their systems to include at least 20 channels and to dedicate four of those channels for public, governmental, educational, and leased access. The rules were reassessed in the course of further rule-making proceedings. As a result, the commission modified a compliance deadline, effected certain substantive changes, and extended the rules to all cable systems having 3,500 or more subscribers, 1976 Order, *supra.* In its 1976 Order, the commission reaffirmed its view that there was "a definite societal good" in preserving access channels, though it acknowledged that the "overall impact that use of these channels can have may have been exaggerated in the past." 59 FCC2d, at 296.

As ultimately adopted, the rules prescribe a series of interrelated obligations ensuring public access to cable systems of a designated size and regulate the manner in which access is to be afforded and the charges that may be levied for providing it. Under the rules, cable systems must possess a minimum capacity of 20 channels as well as the technical capability for accomplishing two-way, nonvoice communication. 47 CFR § 76.252 (1976). Moreover, to the extent of their available activated channel capacity, cable systems must allocate four separate channels for use by public, educational, local governmental, and leased access users, with one channel assigned to each. § 76.254(a). Absent demand for full-time use of each access channel, the combined demand can be accommodated with fewer than four channels but with at least one. § 76.-254(b)–(c). When demand on a particular access channel exceeds a specified limit, the cable system must provide another access channel for the same purpose, to the extent of the system's activated capacity. § 76.254(d). The rules also require cable systems to make equipment available for those utilizing public access channels. § 76.256(a).

Under the rules, cable operators are deprived of all discretion regarding who may exploit their access channels and what may be transmitted over such channels. System operators are specifically enjoined from exercising any control over the content of access programming except that they must adopt rules proscribing the transmission on most access channels of lottery information and commercial matter.[4] §§ 77.256(b), (d). The regulations also instruct cable operators to issue rules providing for first-come, nondiscriminatory access on public and leased channels. §§ 77.256(d)(1), (3).

Finally, the rules circumscribe what operators might charge for privileges of access and use of facilities and equipment. No charge may be assessed for the use of one public access channel. § 76.256(c)(2). Operators may not charge for the use of educational and governmental access for the first five years the system services such users. § 75.256(c)(1). Leased access channel users must be charged an "appropriate" fee. § 76.256(d)(3). Moreover, the rules admonish that charges for equipment, personnel, and production exacted from access users "shall be reasonable and consistent with the goal of affording users a low-cost means of television access." § 76.256(c)(3). And "[n]o charges shall be made for live public access programs not exceeding five minutes in length." *Ibid.* Lastly, a system may not charge access users for utilization of its playback equipment or the personnel required to operate such equipment when the cable's production equipment is not deployed and when tapes or film can be played without technical alteration to the system's equipment. Petition for Reconsideration in Docket No. 20508, 62 FCC2d 399, 407 (1976).

The commission's capacity and access rules were challenged on jurisdictional grounds in the course of the rulemaking proceedings. In its 1976 Order, the commission rejected such comments on the ground that the regulations further objectives that it might properly pursue in its supervision over broadcasting. Specifically, the commission maintained that its rules would promote "the achievement of longstanding communications regulatory objectives by increasing outlets for local self-expression and augmenting the public's choice of programs." 59 FCC2d, at 298. The commission did not find persuasive the contention that "the access requirements are in effect common carrier obligations which are beyond our authority to impose." * * * Additionally, the commission denied that the rules violated the First Amendment, reasoning that when broadcasting or related activity by cable systems is involved First Amendment values are served by measures facilitating an exchange of ideas.

4. Cable systems were also required to promulgate rules prohibiting the transmission of obscene and indecent material on access channels. 47 CFR § 76.256(d) (1976). The Court of Appeals for the District of Columbia Circuit stayed this aspect of the rules in an order filed in American Civil Liberties Union v. FCC, — U.S.App.D.C. —, No. 76–1695 (Aug. 26, 1977). The court below, moreover, disapproved the requirement in belief that it imposed censorship obligations on cable operators. The commission has instituted a review of the requirement, and it is not now in controversy before this Court.

On petition for review, the Eighth Circuit set aside the commission's access, channel capacity, and facilities rules as beyond the agency's jurisdiction. 571 F.2d 1025 (1978). The court was of the view that the regulations were not reasonably ancillary to the commission's jurisdiction over broadcasting, a jurisdictional condition established by past decisions of this Court. The rules amounted to an attempt to impose common-carrier obligations on cable operators, the court said, and thus ran counter to the statutory command that broadcasters themselves may not be treated as common carriers. See Communications Act of 1934, § 3(h), 47 U.S.C. § 153(h). Furthermore, the court made plain its belief that the regulations presented grave First Amendment problems. We granted certiorari, * * * and we now affirm.

The commission derives its regulatory authority from the Communications Act of 1934, 48 Stat. 1064, as amended, 47 U.S.C. § 151 *et seq.* The act preceded the advent of cable television and understandably does not expressly provide for the regulation of that medium. But it is clear that Congress meant to confer "broad authority" on the commission, H.R.Rep. No. 1850, 73d Cong., 2d Sess., 1 (1934), so as "to maintain, through appropriate administrative control, a grip on the dynamic aspects of radio transmission." *FCC v. Pottsville Broadcasting Co.* * * *. To that end, Congress subjected to regulation "all interstate and foreign communication by wire or radio." Communications Act of 1934, § 2(a), 47 U.S.C. § 152(a). * * *

The *Southwestern* litigation arose out of the commission's efforts to ameliorate the competitive impact on local broadcasting operations resulting from importation of distant signals by cable systems into the service areas of local stations. Fearing that such importation might "destroy or seriously degrade the service offered by a television broadcaster," First Report and Order, 38 FCC 683, 700 (1965), the commission promulgated rules requiring CATV systems to carry the signals of broadcast stations into whose service area they brought competing signals, to avoid duplication of local station programming on the same day such programming was broadcast, and to refrain from bringing new distant signals into the 100 largest television markets unless first demonstrating that the service would comport with the public interest. * * *

The commission's assertion of jurisdiction was based on its view that "the successful performance" of its duty to ensure "the orderly development of an appropriate system of local television broadcasting" depended upon regulation of cable operations. 392 U.S., at 177, 88 S.Ct., at 2005. Against the background of the administrative undertaking at issue, the Court construed § 2(a) of the act as granting the commission jurisdiction over cable television "reasonably ancillary to the effective performance of the commission's various responsibilities for the regulation of television broadcasting." * * *

Soon after our decision in *Southwestern*, the commission resolved "to condition the carriage of television broadcast signals * * * upon a requirement that the CATV system also operate to a significant extent as a local outlet by originating." Notice of Proposed Rulemaking and Notice of Inquiry, 15 FCC2d 417, 422 (1968). It stated that its "concern with CATV carriage of broadcast signals [was] not just a matter of avoidance of adverse effects, but extend[ed] also to requiring CATV affirmatively to further statutory policies." *Ibid.* Accordingly, the commission promulgated a rule providing that CATV systems having 3,500 or more subscribers may not carry the signal of any television broadcast station unless the system also operates to a significant extent as a local outlet by originating its own programs—or cablecasting—and maintains facilities for local production and presentation of programs other than automated services. 47 CFR § 74.1111(a) (1970). This Court, by a five-to-four vote but without an opinion for the Court, sustained the commission's jurisdiction to issue these regulations in *United States v. Midwest Video, supra.*

Four Justices, in an opinion by Justice Brennan, reaffirmed the view that the commission has jurisdiction over cable television and that such authority is delimited by its statutory responsibilities over television broadcasting. They thought that the reasonably ancillary standard announced in *Southwestern* permitted regulation of CATV "with a view not merely to protect but to promote the objectives for which the commission had been assigned jurisdiction over broadcasting." * * * The conclusion was that the "program-origination rule [was] within the commission's authority recognized in *Southwestern.*"

* * *

Because its access and capacity rules promote the long-established regulatory goals of maximization of outlets for local expression and diversification of programming—the objectives promoted by the rule sustained in *Midwest Video*—the commission maintains that it plainly had jurisdiction to promulgate them. Respondents, in opposition, view the access regulations as an intrusion on cable system operations that is qualitatively different from the impact of the rule upheld in *Midwest Video.* Specifically, it is urged that by requiring the allocation of access channels to categories of users specified by the regulations and by depriving the cable operator of the power to select individual users or to control the programming on such channels, the regulations wrest a considerable degree of editorial control from the cable operator and in effect compel the cable system to provide a kind of common-carrier service. Respondents contend, therefore, that the regulations are not only qualitatively different from those heretofore approved by the courts but also contravene statutory limitations designed to safeguard the journalistic freedom of broadcasters, particularly the command of § 3(h) of the act that "a person engaged in * * * broadcasting shall not * * * be deemed a common carrier." 47 U.S.C. § 153(h).

We agree with respondents that recognition of agency jurisdiction to promulgate the access rules would require an extension of this Court's prior decisions. Our holding in *Midwest Video* sustained the commission's authority to regulate cable television with a purpose affirmatively to promote goals pursued in the regulation of television broadcasting; and the plurality's analysis of the origination requirement stressed the requirement's nexus to such goals. But the origination rule did not abrogate the cable operators' control over the composition of their programming, as do the access rules. It compelled operators only to assume a more positive role in that regard, one comparable to that fulfilled by television broadcasters. Cable operators had become enmeshed in the field of television broadcasting, and, by requiring them to engage in the functional equivalent of broadcasting, the commission had sought "only to ensure that [they] satisfactorily [met] community needs within the context of their undertaking." * * *

With its access rules, however, the commission has transferred control of the content of access cable channels from cable operators to members of the public who wish to communicate by the cable medium. Effectively, the commission has relegated cable systems, *pro tanto,* to common-carrier status. A common-carrier service in the communications context is one that "makes a public offering to provide [communications facilities] whereby all members of the public who choose to employ such facilities may communicate or transmit intelligence of their own design and choosing. * * *" Report and Order, Industrial Radiolocation Service, Docket No. 16106, 5 FCC2d 197, 202 (1966). * * *

A common carrier does not "make individualized decisions, in particular cases, whether and on what terms to deal." National Association of Regulatory Utility Commissioners v. FCC, 525 F.2d, at 641.

The access rules plainly impose common-carrier obligations on cable operators. Under the rules, cable systems are required to hold out dedicated channels on a first-come, nondiscriminatory basis. 47 CFR §§ 76.254(a), 76.256(d) (1976). Operators are prohibited from determining or influencing the content of access programming. § 76.256(b). And the rules delimit what operators may charge for access and use of equipment. § 76.256(c). Indeed, in its early consideration of access obligations—whereby "CATV operators [would] furnish studio facilities and technical assistance [but] have no control over program content except as may be required by the commission's rules and applicable law"—the commission acknowledged that the result would be the operation of cable systems "as common carriers on some channels." First Report and Order in Docket No. 18397, 20 FCC2d 201, 207 (1969); see *id.*, at 202; Cable Television Report and Order, 36 FCC2d 143, 197 (1972). In its 1976 order, the commission did not directly deny that its access requirements compelled common carriage, and it has conceded before this Court that the rules "can be viewed as a limited form of common carriage-type obligation." Brief for United States 39. But the commission continues to insist that this characterization of the obligation imposed by the rules is immaterial to the question of its power to issue them; its authority to promulgate the rules is assured, in the commission's view, so long as the rules promote statutory objectives.

Congress, however, did not regard the character of regulatory obligations as irrelevant to the determination of whether they might permissibly be imposed in the context of broadcasting itself. The commission is directed explicitly by § 3(h) of the act not to treat persons engaged in broadcasting as common carriers. We considered the genealogy and the meaning of this provision in Columbia Broadcasting System, Inc. v. Democratic National Committee, 412 U.S. 94, * * * (1973). The issue in that case was whether a broadcast licensee's general policy of not selling advertising time to individuals or groups wishing to speak on issues important to them violated the Communications Act of 1934 or the First Amendment. Our examination of the legislative history of the Radio Act of 1927—the precursor to the Communications Act of 1934—prompted us to conclude that "in the area of discussion of public issues Congress chose to leave broad journalistic discretion with the licensee." 412 U.S. at 105. * * * We determined, in fact, that "Congress specifically dealt with—and firmly rejected—the argument that the broadcast facilities should be open on a nonselective basis to all persons wishing to talk about public issues." *Ibid.* The Court took note of a bill reported to the Senate by the Committee on Interstate Commerce providing in part that any licensee who permits " 'a broadcasting station to be used * * * for the discussion of any question affecting the public * * * shall make no discrimination as to the use of such broadcasting station, and with respect to said matters the licensee shall be deemed a common carrier in interstate commerce: Provided, that such licensee shall have no power to censor the material broadcast.' " *Id.*, at 106, * * * quoting 67 Cong.Rec. 12503 (1926). That bill was amended to eliminate the common-carrier obligation because of the perceived lack of wisdom in "put[ting] the broadcaster under the hampering control of being a common carrier" and because of problems in administering a nondiscriminatory right of access. See 67 Cong.Rec. 12502, 12504 (1926).

The Court further observed that, in enacting the 1934 act, Congress rejected still another proposal "that would have imposed a limited obligation on broadcasters to turn over their microphones to persons wishing to speak out on certain public issues." 412 U.S., at 107–108. "Instead," the Court noted, "Congress after prolonged consideration adopted § 3(h), which specifically provides that 'a person engaged in radio broadcasting shall not, insofar as such person is so engaged, be deemed a common carrier.'" *Id.*, at 108–109.

"Congress' flat refusal to impose a 'common carrier' right of access for all persons wishing to speak out on public issues," *id.*, at 110, 93 S.Ct., at 2090, was perceived as consistent with other provisions of the 1934 act evincing "a legislative desire to preserve values of private journalism." *Id.,* at 109. Notable among them was § 326 of the act, which enjoins the commission from exercising "the power of censorship over the radio communications or signals transmitted by any radio station," and commands that "no regulation shall be promulgated or fixed by the commission which shall interfere with the right of free speech by means of radio communication." *Id.*, at 110, * * * quoting 47 U.S.C. § 326.

The holding of the Court in *Columbia Broadcasting* was in accord with the view of the commission that the act itself did not require a licensee to accept paid editorial advertisements. Accordingly, we did not decide the question whether the act, though not mandating the claimed access, would nevertheless permit the commission to require broadcasters to extend a range of public access by regulations similar to those at issue here. The Court speculated that the commission might have flexibility to regulate access, *id.*, at 122, and that "[c]onceivably at some future time Congress or the commission—or the broadcasters—may devise some kind of limited right of access that is both practicable and desirable," *id.,* at 131. But this is insufficient support for the commission's position in the present case. The language of § 3(h) is unequivocal; it stipulates that broadcasters shall not be treated as common carriers. As we see it, § 3(h), consistently with the policy of the act to preserve editorial control of programming in the licensee, forecloses any discretion in the commission to impose access requirements amounting to common-carrier obligations on broadcast systems.[14] The provision's background manifests a congressional belief that the intrusion worked by such regulation on the journalistic integrity of broadcasters would overshadow any benefits associated with the resulting public access. It is difficult to deny, then, that forcing broadcasters to develop a "nondiscriminatory system for controlling access * * * is precisely what Congress intended to avoid through § 3(h) of the Act." *Id.*, at 140 n. 9 * * * (Stewart, J., concurring); see *id.*, at 152, and n. 2 * * * (Douglas, J., concurring).[15]

14. Whether less intrusive access regulation might fall within the commission's jurisdiction, or survive constitutional challenge even if within the commission's power, is not presently before this Court. Certainly, our construction of § 3(h) does not put into question the statutory authority for the fairness doctrine obligations sustained in Red Lion Broadcasting Co. v. FCC, 395 U.S. 367 * * * (1969). The fairness doctrine does not require that a broadcaster provide common carriage; it contemplates a wide range of licensee discretion. See Report on Editorializing by Broadcast Licensees, 13 FCC 1246, 1251 (1949) (in meeting fairness doctrine obligations the "licensee will in each instance be called upon to exercise his best judgment and good sense in determining what subjects should be considered, the particular format of the programs to be devoted to each subject, the different shades of opinion to be presented, and the spokesmen for each point of view.").

15. The dissent maintains that § 3(h) does not place "limits on the commission's exercise of powers otherwise within its statutory authority because a lawfully imposed requirement might be termed a 'common carrier obligation.'" *Post,* at 1447. Rather, § 3(h) means only that "every broadcast station is not to be *deemed* a common carrier, and therefore subject to common-carrier regulation under Title II of the act, simply because it is engaged in radio broadcasting." *Post,* at 1447. But Congress was plainly anxious to avoid regulation of broadcasters as common carriers under Title II, which commands *inter alia* that regulated entities

Of course, § 3(h) does not explicitly limit the regulation of cable systems. But without reference to the provisions of the act directly governing broadcasting, the commission's jurisdiction under § 2(a) would be unbounded. See, United States v. Midwest Video, 406 U.S., at 661 * * * (opinion of Justice Brennan). Though afforded wide latitude in its supervision over communication by wire, the commission was not delegated unrestrained authority. The Court regarded the commission's regulatory effort at issue in *Southwestern* as consistent with the act because it had been found necessary to ensure the achievement of the commission's statutory responsibilities. Specifically, regulation was imperative to prevent interference with the commission's work in the broadcasting area. And in *Midwest Video* the commission had endeavored to promote long-established goals of broadcasting regulation. Petitioners do not deny that statutory objectives pertinent to broadcasting bear on what the commission might require cable systems to do. Indeed, they argue that the commission's authority to promulgate the access rules derives from the relationship of those rules to the objectives discussed in *Midwest Video.* But they overlook the fact that Congress has restricted the commission's ability to advance objectives associated with public access at the expense of the journalistic freedom of persons engaged in broadcasting.

That limitation is not one having peculiar applicability to television broadcasting. Its force is not diminished by the variant technology involved in cable transmissions. Cable operators now share with broadcasters a significant amount of editorial discretion regarding what their programming will include. As the commission, itself, has observed, "both in their signal carriage decisions and in connection with their origination function, cable television systems are afforded considerable control over the content of the programming they provide." Report and Order in Docket No. 20829, 43 Fed.Reg. 53742 (1978).

In determining, then, whether the commission's assertion of jurisdiction is "reasonably ancillary to the effective performance of [its] responsibilities for the regulation of television broadcasting," *United States v. Southwestern Cable Co.*, * * * we are unable to ignore Congress' stern disapproval—evidenced in § 3(h)—of negation of the editorial discretion otherwise enjoyed by broadcasters and cable operators alike. Though the lack of congressional guidance has in the past led us to defer—albeit cautiously—to the commission's judgment regarding the scope of its authority, here there are strong indications that agency flexibility was to be sharply delimited.

The exercise of jurisdiction in *Midwest Video*, it has been said, "strain[ed] the outer limits" of commission authority. 406 U.S., at 676 (Burger, C.J., concurring). In

---

shall "furnish * * * communication service upon reasonable request therefore. [sic]" 47 U.S.C. § 201(a). Our review of the act in *Columbia Broadcasting* led us to conclude that § 3(h) embodies a substantive determination not to abrogate a broadcaster's journalistic independence for the purpose of, and as a result of, furnishing members of the public with media access:

"Congress pointedly refrained from divesting broadcasters of their control over the selection of voices; § 3(h) of the act stands as a firm congressional statement that broadcast licensees are not to be treated as common carriers, obliged to accept whatever is tendered by members of the public. [The] provision[ ] clearly manifest[s] the intention of Congress to maintain a substantial measure of journalistic independence for the broadcast licensee." Columbia Broadcasting System, Inc. v. Democratic National Committee, 412 U.S. 94, 116 * * *. We now reaffirm that view of § 3(h): the purpose of the provision and its mandatory wording preclude commission discretion to compel broadcasters to act as common carriers, even with respect to a portion of their total services. As we demonstrate in the following text, that same constraint applies to the regulation of cable television systems.

light of the hesitancy with which Congress approached the access issue in the broadcast area, and in view of its outright rejection of a broad right of public access on a common-carrier basis, we are constrained to hold that the commission exceeded those limits in promulgating its access rules. The commission may not regulate cable systems as common carriers, just as it may not impose such obligations on television broadcasters. We think authority to compel cable operators to provide common carriage of public-originated transmissions must come specifically from Congress.[19]

Affirmed.

COMMENT

1. Since its holding invalidating the public access rules was based on the lack of FCC jurisdiction to issue them, the court of appeals, per Judge Markey, declined to base its holding on constitutional grounds.

> Despite the Court's guidance in *Miami Herald*, the commission has attempted here to require cable operators, who have invested substantially to create a private electronic "publication"—a means of disseminating information—to open their "publications" to all for use as *they* wish. * * * Though we are not deciding that issue here, we have seen and heard nothing in this case to indicate a constitutional distinction between cable systems and newspapers in the context of the government's power to compel public access.

Cable *can* be described as a technology of abundance, as compared with VHF television, a technology of scarcity. Should the First Amendment model applied to cable be the same as that applied to the newspaper press? *Tornillo*, rather than *Red Lion*, governs the public access obligations of the newspaper press, should *Tornillo*, rather than *Red Lion*, provide the appropriate First Amendment model for cable?

2. The argument for applying *Tornillo* to cable is a strong one. But there is an argument the other way as well. Cable has more communicative capacity than the newspaper press. Problems of space, caused by the cost of newsprint, present difficult practical obstacles to the development of compulsory public access schemes in the daily press completely apart from the editorial autonomy First Amendment questions such issues raise (see *Miami Herald Publishing Co. v. Tornillo*, text, p. 584). Cable, unlike the daily newspaper, has the capacity to meet the demands of an access system. The practical problems found in newspapers are simply not present in today's multi-channel cable systems. Indeed, cable operators are often unable to use all this capacity at present in the first place.

3. If the scarcity rationale is deemed to be technologically inapplicable to cable, does this mean that federal legislation imposing common carrier status on cable would present First Amendment problems just as the imposition of common carrier status on cable would present an insuperable First Amendment obstacle?

For the proponents of mandatory public access for cable, the following comment of Justice White in *Midwest Video* in footnote 14 provides an encouraging response.

"Whether less intrusive access regulations might fall within the commission's

---

19. The court below suggested that the commission's rules might violate the First Amendment rights of cable operators. Because our decision rests on statutory grounds, we express no view on that question, save to acknowledge that it is not frivolous and to make clear that the asserted constitutional issue did not determine or sharply influence our construction of the statute. The court of appeals intimated, additionally, that the rules might effect an unconstitutional "taking" of property or, by exposing a cable operator to possible criminal prosecution for offensive cablecasting by access users over which the operator has no control, might affront the Due Process Clause of the Fifth Amendment. We forego comment on these issues as well.

jurisdiction, or survive constitutional challenge even if within the commission's power, is not presently before this Court. Certainly, our construction of § 3(h) does not put into question the statutory authority for the fairness doctrine obligations sustained in *Red Lion.* * * *"

4. If the Supreme Court had had to face the First Amendment issue raised by the mandatory public access rules, how do you think they would have decided the issue? See *fn. 19* in the majority opinion in *Midwest Video.*

The Home Box Office Case or Freeing Pay Cable from FCC Bondage

The FCC does not have power under the Communications Act to restrict programming by pay television cablecasters. Home Box Office, Inc. v. FCC, 567 F.2d 9 (D.C.Cir.1977); cert. den. 434 U.S. 829 (1977). In an attempt to protect the conventional broadcast media, the FCC had issued detailed regulations limiting the types of programming available to cablecasters and subscription broadcast television stations. The regulations on subscription television were based on two assumptions. First, subscription systems should serve as supplements to conventional television, and therefore distinct programming was required. The second assumption was that revenue raised from subscription operations would allow subscription operators to bid away the best programs, thus reducing the quality of conventional television. Unregulated cable television, the FCC reasoned, would allow cable operators, through revenue raised by subscriptions, to siphon off or purchase programs currently shown on conventional free television for showing on a subscription cable channel. The FCC argued that in such a situation a segment of the American people—those in areas not served by cable or those too poor to afford subscription cable—would receive delayed access to programs or no access at all.

In a decision that should radically improve the power and potential of cable television, the federal court of appeals invalidated the FCC restrictions as they applied to cable television. Relying on *Southwestern Cable,* the court said the FCC may regulate cable television but only where the objectives to be achieved were "long-established regulatory goals in the field of television broadcasting" or were "congressionally approved." Further, the FCC may regulate cable only to achieve ends for which it could also regulate broadcast television.

Did the FCC regulations restricting the pay television programming standards offered by cablecasters satisfy these standards? The court looked to the underlying rationale of the restrictive rules to answer this question:

> [The purpose of the pay cable rules] is to prevent siphoning of feature film and sports material from conventional broadcast television to pay cable. Although there is dispute over the effectiveness of the rules, it is clear that their thrust is to prevent *any* competition by pay cable entrepreneurs for film or sports material that either has been shown on conventional television or is likely to be shown there. How such an effect furthers any legitimate goal of the Communications Act is not clear. * * * First, the commission appears to take the position that it has both the obligation and the authority to regulate program format content to maintain present levels of public enjoyment. For this reason, and because the commission also seems to assert that the overall level of public enjoyment of television entertainment would be reduced if films or sports events were shown only on pay cable or shown on conventional television only after some delay, it concludes that anti-siphoning rules are both needed and authorized. Second, and closely related, is the argument pressed here by counsel for the commission that Section 1 of the Communications Act, 47 U.S.C.A. § 151

> (1970), mandates the commission to promulgate anti-siphoning rules since cable television cannot now and will not in the near future provide a nationwide communications service. * * * Before considering each of these arguments in turn, we note that we do *not* understand the commission to be asserting that subscription cable television will divide audiences and revenues available to broadcast stations in such a manner as to put the very existence of these stations in doubt.

The court next noted that the FCC has concluded, contrary to the court's decision in *WEFM,* text, p. 786, that it has no statutory authority to dictate entertainment formats in the radio broadcast context, text, p. 787. Reflecting on the FCC's stated aversion to dictating entertainment formats, the court observed:

> If the commission's own recently announced standards are applied to the rules challenged here, it seems clear that the rules cannot stand. The very essence of the feature film and sports rules is to require the permission of the commission "to commence * * * programming, including program format services, offered to the public." However, it has been the consistent position of the commission itself that cablecasters, like broadcasters, are not to be regulated as common carriers, a view sustained by a number of courts. * * We seriously doubt that the Communications Act could be construed to give the commission "regulatory tools" over cablecasting that it did not have over broadcasting. Thus, even if the siphoning rules might in some sense increase the public good, this consideration alone cannot justify the commission's regulations.

The court said that the FCC had not produced sufficient facts to demonstrate that the public interest necessitated preservation of "free" television as the primary viewing service. The court said there is not "even speculation in the record about what material would replace that which might be 'siphoned' to cable television." Without such a comparative inquiry, the court could not understand how the FCC could determine "the current level of programming as a baseline for adequate service." The court also questioned the FCC's determination that feature films are a sufficiently unique format to warrant protection. It noted that "broadcasters are increasingly substituting made-for-television movies—for which 'siphoning' is not a problem since the broadcasters own the copyrights—for feature films."

The court then stated its conclusions as follows:

> The sole purpose of undertaking this analysis is to demonstrate that the commission has, in this proceeding, seemingly backed into an area of regulation * * * . Indeed, in this very proceeding, and despite the commission's definition of current quantity and quality levels of films and sports events as the minimum level consistent with adequate television service, there is no indication that the commission is prepared to require *broadcasters* to continue to present material presently on conventional television. In the absence of this court's opinion in WEFM, these unexplained inconsistencies in agency policy would require us to set aside the commission's rules and remand the case to the agency to allow it to "supply a reasoned analysis indicating that prior policies and standards are being deliberately changed, not casually ignored." Because we understand the commission's Memorandum Opinion and Order in the format change proceeding to constitute a request to this court to reconsider its position in WEFM, see 60 FCC2d at 865–866, and because we are hesitant to approve rules which seem inconsistent with the commission's best thinking in a closely analogous area, we think we should not affirm the feature film and sports regulations on the basis of WEFM.

Before remanding, however, the court considered and rejected the FCC's second theory of jurisdiction—the contention that Section 1 of the Communications Act, 47 U.S.C.A. § 151 requires the commission to formulate antisiphoning rules to protect those viewers to which cable is not available. The court referred to National Association of Theatre Owners v. FCC, 420 F.2d 194 (1969), cert. den. 397 U.S. 922 (1970), where the FCC itself had rejected such a construction of Section 1, stating that such an interpretation could not "reasonably be made."

The court summarized its holding on the pay cable television rules:

> Although we hold today that the commission has not established its jurisdiction on the record evidence before it, we think it important to note the limits of our holding. We do not hold that the commission must find express statutory authority for its cable television regulations. Such a holding would be inconsistent with the nature of the FCC's Organic Act and the flexibility needed to regulate a rapidly changing industry. However, we do require that at a minimum the commission, in developing its cable television regulations, demonstrate that the objectives to be achieved by regulating cable television are also objectives for which the commission could legitimately regulate the broadcast media. Where the First Amendment is involved, more will be required. Further, we require that the commission state clearly the harm which its regulations seek to remedy and its reasons for supposing that this harm exists. Because our holding is so limited, it is possible that the commission will, after remand, be able to satisfy the jurisdictional prerequisites for regulating pay cable television. In order to avoid multiple remands, therefore, we will now consider other objections raised against these rules.

A further rationale for invalidating the rules was that there was no evidence in the record to support the need for regulation:

> The commission has in no way justified its position that cable television must be a supplement to, rather than an equal of, broadcast television. Such an artificial narrowing of the scope of the regulatory problem is itself arbitrary and capricious and is ground for reversal. Moreover, by narrowing its discussion in this way the commission has failed to crystallize what is in fact harmful about "siphoning."

An additional factor leading to the invalidity of the pay cable regulations was the court's analysis of the impact of the First Amendment. Important differences between cable and broadcast television, the court said, necessitated differences in the First Amendment standards applied to each.

The First Amendment theory used to validate FCC regulation of broadcasting in *National Broadcasting Co.*, text, p. 770, the court declared, "cannot be directly applied to cable television since an essential precondition of that theory—physical interference and scarcity requiring an umpiring role for government—is absent." There is no apparent scarcity of channels with cable systems. Cable has the capacity to convey more than thirty-five channels and technology is available to increase that number to eighty. It noted further that there are no barriers of physical or electrical interference or even of economic monopoly which prohibit operation of a number of cable systems in a given locality. Even if such scarcity did exist, the court, on the basis of *Miami Herald Publishing Co. v. Tornillo*, text, p. 584, ruled that scarcity resulting from economic conditions was insufficient to justify government intrusion into First Amendment rights. *Miami Herald* dealt with intrusion upon the rights of the conventional press, but the court in *Home Box Office* found no "constitutional distinction between cable television and newspapers on this point."

The inapplicability of the scarcity rationale does not mean that cable cannot be regulated. The key is the purpose for which the government regulates. The court used the test set forth in United States v. O'Brien, 391 U.S. 367 at 377 (1960), for dealing with regulations designed to effectuate a government interest "unrelated to the suppression of free expression." The court conceded that the FCC's purpose in issuing the pay cable rules was not content suppression but protection of the viewing rights of those not served by cable or too poor to pay for cable. Nevertheless, the court held that the FCC rules could not meet the standards set forth in *O'Brien* and, therefore, violated the First Amendment. Among other things, the court found no compliance with the implied requirement of *O'Brien* that a convincing showing, particularly in a rule-making context, must be made that a problem exists and that the solution offered is related to the statutory mandate of the agency.

While the court invalidated the FCC rules for cable television, it reached a different result with respect to subscription broadcast operators. In National Association of Theatre Owners (NATO) v. FCC, 420 F.2d 194 (D.C.Cir.), cert. denied 397 U.S. 922 (1970), the court of appeals had earlier affirmed the FCC's restrictions on subscription broadcast television. These restrictions had been based on an elaborate rule-making record. Since the *NATO* case, few subscription broadcast stations have begun operations on a commercial basis. As a result, the precepts of the *NATO* proceeding had not been shaken. Accordingly, the court chose not to reopen the issue of the rationality of the antisiphoning rules as they pertained to subscription broadcast television.

Perhaps cable will at last be able to emerge from the regulatory morass in which it has been trapped and will thus be able to fulfill its potential. The demise of the pay cable rules is certainly a new legal development that augurs well for the future of cable. Similarly, the copyright law limbo into which cable had been placed has now been clarified. Congress has enacted a new copyright law which specifically addresses the copyright status of cable. For a discussion of the copyright issues in cable television, see Chapter VIII, text, p. 605.

The Deregulation of Cable

In Report and Order in Docket No. 20984 and 21284, 79 FCC2d 663 (1980), the FCC abolished two of the principal regulatory limitations on the growth of cable—the restrictions on distant signal carriage and the syndicated program exclusivity rules on cable retransmission. These restrictions aided in protecting broadcasting at the expense of the growth of cable and owed their life to a large extent to the fact that cable retransmission of copyrighted broadcast programming did not constitute copyright infringement under the old 1909 Copyright Act which had governed copyright. See Fortnightly Corp. v. United Artists, Inc., 392 U.S. 390 (1968) and Teleprompter Corp. v. CBS, 415 U.S. 394 (1974), text, p. 691.

In 1976, Congress enacted a new copyright statute. See text, p. 689. With the advent of the 1976 Act, which finally confronted and attempted to resolve the cable copyright problem, the need for broadcaster protection from cable—in the light of cable's previous immunity from copyright liability vis-à-vis broadcasting—was sharply reduced. There is little doubt that the FCC repeal of both the restrictions on distant signal carriage and the syndicated program exclusivity rules was a response to the new reality.

A number of broadcasters, including the NAB and the major television networks, brought suit in the United States Court of Appeals for the Second Circuit to set aside the FCC order to deregulate cable by rescinding the rules concerning syndicated program exclusivity and distant signal carriage. In the opinion which follows, the United States Court of Appeals for the Second Circuit in Malrite TV v. FCC, 7 Med.L.Rptr. 1649, 652 F.2d 1140 (2d Cir. 1981), upheld the FCC's deregulatory orders. Judge Newman's opinion below provides the reader with an excellent account of the rise and decline of FCC regulation of cable.

MALRITE TV v. FCC

7 MED.L.RPTR. 1649, 652 F.2D 1140 (2D CIR. 1981).

NEWMAN, Circuit Judge:

In a major reversal of its regulatory policy, the Federal Communications Commission ("FCC" or "commission") has decided to deregulate cable television by rescinding rules relating to syndicated program exclusivity and distant signal carriage. Television broadcasting and programming interests have petitioned to set aside the FCC's order and to reimpose the regulations, which have been in force since 1972. On November 19, 1980 we stayed the order pending the disposition of the appeal. We now vacate the stay and deny the petition, thereby permitting the exclusivity and distant signal rules to be repealed.

The television broadcasting industry, transmitting video signals free to viewers, is dominated by the three national networks, which contract with local station affiliates to carry network programming, most of which the networks purchase from independent producers. In addition, there are unaffiliated, independent stations which obtain most of their programming in the syndication market.[1] The cable television industry consists of various local systems, which transmit broadcast video signals from a central station to individual homes by closed circuit, coaxial cable. Cable subscribers pay a monthly fee to receive a basic set of channels plus an optional fee for special channels (pay cable).

Each of the 1,000 broadcasting stations, affiliate or independent, operates along an electromagnetic frequency established by the FCC on either very high frequency (VHF) or ultra high frequency (UHF) channels. The VHF range produces a higher quality viewing signal than UHF for most viewers. Though the FCC had avidly supported the expansion of UHF channels as a means of providing increased program diversity and expression of local interests, UHF stations have been plagued with financial difficulties due to small audiences and low revenues, stemming in part from their inferior reception, and comprise the least profitable sector of the television industry. *See* R. Noll, M. Peck & J. McGowan, *Economic Aspects of Television Regulation* 79–129 (1973) [hereafter "R. Noll, *et al.*"]; *Revised TV Broadcasting Financial Data-1978,* FCC Memo No. 30037 (July 17, 1980). The networks and their affiliates, which operate primarily in the VHF range, account for the largest audience shares and the vast majority of industry revenues and profits. *See* R. Noll, *et al., supra* at 3–5, 16–18; *Revised TV Broadcasting Financial Data-1978.*

Cable television mitigates some of the disadvantages faced by UHF stations by making possible improved reception; to a cable subscriber, the reception quality of a UHF signal is indistinguishable from a VHF signal. But cable provides an additional service by increasing the number of stations available to a viewer through the importation of signals from distant geographic areas using microwave relays or orbiting communications satellites. Cable increases viewers' program choices, offering greater content and time diversity, and consequently it diverts some portion of the

---

1. Syndicated programming, supplied by independent producers, consists of either programs previously broadcast on network stations or newly produced programs. Unlike network programming, simultaneous broadcasting of syndicated programs is infrequent because the independent stations do not all purchase the same programs. *See* Besen, Manning & Mitchell, *Copyright Liability for Cable Television: Compulsory Licensing and the Coase Theorem,* 21 J.L. & Econ. 67, 77 (1978).

viewing audience away from local broadcast stations to more distant ones.

After an initial period in which the FCC declined to exercise regulatory authority over cable television on the grounds that it did not have jurisdiction under the Communications Act, see Frontier Broadcasting Co. v. Collier, 24 FCC 251 (1958), reconsideration denied in Report and Order in Docket No. 12443, 26 FCC 403, 428 (1959), the FCC began to regulate the cable industry directly in 1966.[2] See Second Report and Order in Docket Nos. 14895, 15233 and 15971, 2 FCC2d 725 (1966). The Supreme Court upheld the FCC's jurisdiction over cable in United States v. Southwestern Cable Co., 392 U.S. 157, 178 (1968), insofar as the particular regulations were "reasonably ancillary" to the commission's performance of its statutory duties. These 1966 regulations initiated close to a decade of regulation that can fairly be described as hostile to the growth of the cable industry, as the FCC sought to protect, in the name of localism and program diversity, the position of existing broadcasters, and particularly, the struggling UHF stations. *See* Besen & Crandall, *The Deregulation of Cable Television*, 44 Law & Contemp. Prob. 77 (1981); Chazen & Ross, *Federal Regulation of Cable Television: The Visible Hand,* 83 Harv.L.Rev. 1820 (1970). These rules severely restricted the expansion of cable television services by permitting cable operators in the top 100 markets to import distant signals only after showing in an evidentiary hearing that to do so would be in the public interest and not harmful to UHF broadcast services.[3] While the cable industry continued to grow in the 1960's in spite of these restrictions and other costly operating requirements, such as mandatory program origination, access, channel capacity, and other equipment regulations, it entered the 1970's as a small industry, relegated primarily to rural areas and small communities due in large part to the FCC's policies. Besen & Crandall, *supra* at 79, 93.

In late 1971, the commission began to consider relaxation of the cable television regulations. *See Commission Proposals for Regulation of Cable Television,* 31 FCC2d 115 (1971) ("Letter of Intent" to Congress). Shortly thereafter, the 1972 regulations emerged from an industry-wide Consensus Agreement negotiated by the White House and the affected industry interests—broadcasters, cable operators, and program producers (copyright owners). Cable Television Report and Order, 36 FCC2d 143 (1972). Though the 1972 rules eased the 1966 restrictions and permitted limited cable expansion, broadcasting interests were still strongly protected. The Report and Order challenged on this appeal, Report and Order in Docket Nos. 20988 and 21284, 79 FCC2d 663 (1980) [hereafter "Report and Order"], abolishes the core of the 1972 regulatory structure by

2. The commission began regulating the cable industry indirectly as early as 1962, when it denied a request for a permit by a common carrier to install microwave relays to carry signals for a cable television system. Carter Mountain Transmission Corp., 32 FCC 459 (1962), aff'd, 321 F.2d 359 (D.C.Cir.), cert. denied, 375 U.S. 951 (1963). The commission held that granting the permit, though improving the cable system's service to its subscribers, was not in the public interest because it would adversely affect the economic operation of a local broadcast station.

3. There are about 200 television markets in the United States. Eighty-six per cent of the approximately 74 million television households are located in the top 100 markets; 33 per cent are in the top 10 markets. Notice of Proposed Rule Making in Docket Nos. 20988 and 21284, 71 FCC2d 1004, 1011 (1979). About one-third of all television households have access to cable service, and about 19 per cent of all television households subscribe. *Id.* at 1013–14. The households for which a cable connection is available are located primarily outside of the major metropolitan markets. Report in Docket No. 21284, Inquiry into the Economic Relationship Between Television Broadcasting and Cable Television, 71 FCC2d 632, 664–65 (1979) [hereafter "Economic Inquiry Report"].

repealing the two main methods of broadcaster protection, the distant signal carriage and syndicated program exclusivity restrictions on cable retransmissions.

The distant signal rules, 47 C.F.R. §§ 76.59(b)–(e), 76.61(b)–(f), and 76.63 (1980), limit the number of signals from distant stations that a cable system can transmit to its subscribers, the limit varying according to market size and the number of available over-the-air signals within the market. While cable systems are required to carry all local stations (defined as within 35 miles of the cable system's community), the number of distant signals that they can carry is limited as follows: in the top 50 markets, cable systems can make available a total of 3 network stations and 3 independents; in the second 50 markets, 3 networks and 2 independents; in the smaller markets, 3 networks and 1 independent; 2 "bonus" independent signals can be carried in major markets where local signals fill the allotted cable complement. By limiting the number of distant signals, the FCC sought to lessen potential adverse impact on the audience shares of local stations, a policy which has the additional effect of lessening the attractiveness of cable to potential subscribers.

The syndicated program exclusivity rules, 47 C.F.R. §§ 76.151–76.161 (1980), authorize a local television station, which has purchased exclusive exhibition rights to a program, to demand that a local cable system delete that program from distant signals, whether or not the television station was simultaneously showing, or ever planning to show, the program. Copyright holders, in addition to broadcasters, are also protected by the rules and can require deletion of their programs from cable systems. The extent and duration of this protection varies according to market size, program type, and time of showing with the greatest protection afforded to stations located in the largest markets.[5] Cable operators are allowed to substitute other distant signals when they have to delete a program under these rules.

These 1972 rules were fashioned in the context of a continuing policy debate as to whether cable operators should face copyright liability for the programs they retransmitted to subscribers. Prior to Congress'

5. For example, in the top 50 markets, at the request of a local station, cable operators must delete all syndicated programs under exclusive exhibition contract to the requesting station regardless of when the program is scheduled for showing on the local station, and program copyright owners can request deletion for one year after the first syndicated sale of the program, even if no local station has the rights to exhibit it. In the second 50 markets, distant syndicated programs need not be deleted if broadcast in prime time unless the requesting local station is also planning to air the program in prime time, and exclusivity rights expire at specified time periods or on the occurrence of specified events, depending on the nature of the program, *e.g.*, first-run syndicated series and feature films are protected for two years while reruns of network series are protected for only one year. Only systems in the top 100 markets are subject to these rules.

Though much less comprehensive in coverage, exclusivity rules exist for network programming. Duplication of network programming is prohibited with respect to simultaneous showings. 47 C.F.R. §§ 76.92–76.99 (1980). The duration of network program protection is more limited than that for syndicated programs in part due to the different methods of distribution. Unlike network programs, which are shown at the same time on virtually all affiliates as they come over the air, with exceptions for stations in different time zones that involve program retaping, syndicated programs are shown at separately scheduled, diverse times by each purchasing independent station. Moreover, cable systems may not carry more than three network signals, which reduces the possibility of duplication of local affiliate programming, whereas they can carry several independent signals, which increases the likelihood of a syndicated program being duplicated. The network nonduplication rules, as well as rules requiring the blacking out of certain live sports programs, 47 C.F.R. § 76.67 (1980), are not altered by the Report and Order challenged on appeal, though petitioners Commissioner of Baseball, National Football League, National Basketball Association, and National Hockey League, and intervenors American Broadcasting Companies, Inc., and Jet Broadcasting Company, Inc., contend that repeal of the distant signal and syndicated exclusivity rules will decrease the effectiveness of the network and sports programming regulations.

revision of the copyright laws in 1976, the Supreme Court had consistently held that cable systems were not liable under the copyright laws for their use of copyrighted broadcast programs without the owner's consent. Teleprompter Corp. v. Columbia Broadcasting System, Inc., 415 U.S. 394 (1974); Fortnightly Corp. v. United Artists Television, Inc., 392 U.S. 390 (1968). As a result of these rulings, while the broadcasting industry spent billions of dollars to create and purchase programming, cable operators could retransmit those programs at their operating cost without making any payments to program suppliers. Losing in the courts, broadcasters sought FCC protection from what they alleged was a situation of "unfair competition" by cable systems. The FCC rules restricting cable operators' ability to carry distant signals and syndicated programs served, in effect, as proxies for the copyright liability the courts had refused to impose, by restricting cable systems in their use of copyrighted works. *See* H.R.Rep. No. 1476, 94th Cong., 2d Sess. 176–77, *reprinted in* [1976] U.S. Code Cong. & Ad. News 5659, 5792–93; Comment, *Regulatory Versus Property Rights Solutions for the Cable Television Problem,* 69 Calif.L.Rev. 527, 536–44 (1981). Indeed, the revision of the cable television rules in 1972 pursuant to the industry-wide compromise was undertaken with a view toward facilitating enactment of legislation imposing copyright liability on cable operators. See Commission Proposals for Regulation of Cable Television, *supra,* 31 FCC2d at 115–16; Geller v. FCC, 610 F.2d 973, 974–75 (D.C.Cir.1979) (*per curiam*).

The situation changed, however, in 1976, when Congress adopted a system of partial copyright liability for cable television with a compulsory licensing scheme. 17 U.S.C. § 111 (1976). Under the new Copyright Act, cable operators are expressly permitted to retransmit programs without any need to obtain the consent of, or negotiate license fees directly with, copyright owners, but in return they must pay the owners a prescribed royalty fee, based on the number of distant signals the system carries and its gross revenues. Ibid. See generally Nimmer on Copyright § 8.18[E] (1980). After Congress had resolved the copyright issue by a system of compulsory licensing, the FCC commenced an inquiry into the need for maintaining its copyright surrogates, the distant signal and syndicated exclusivity rules. Notice of Inquiry in Docket No. 20988, 61 FCC2d 746 (1976) (announcing review of desirability of syndicated exclusivity rules); Notice of Inquiry in Docket No. 21284, 65 FCC2d 9 (1977) (announcing sweeping review of economic relationship between cable and broadcast television industries).[7] These inquiries resulted in two extensive staff reports advocating elimination of the rules, Report in Docket No. 20988, Cable Television Syndicated Program Exclusivity Rules, 71 FCC2d 951 (1979), and Report in Docket No. 21284, Inquiry into the Economic Relationship Between Television Broadcasting and Cable Television, 71 FCC2d 632 (1979) [hereafter "Economic Inquiry Report"]. After considering several econometric and case studies concerning the impact of cable television on local station audiences and future cable penetration rates, the commission found that the impact on broadcasting stations from the deregulation of cable television would be negligible, and that consumers would be decidedly better off due to increased viewing options from the greater availability of expanded cable services.

In conjunction with the release of these reports, the FCC initiated an informal notice-and-comment rulemaking proceeding to eliminate the distant signal and syndicated exclusivity restrictions. Notice of Proposed Rule Making in Docket Nos. 20988 and 21284, 71 FCC2d 1004 (1979).

7. This reevaluation was further prompted by Geller v. FCC, *supra*, 610 F.2d at 980, which required the FCC to review the necessity of retaining the syndicated exclusivity rules.

After widespread public comment and administrative reevaluation, it issued the Report and Order, which adopted the proposal for repeal with three commissioners dissenting in whole or in part. The FCC also rejected a suggestion of the National Telecommunications and Information Administration (NTIA) of the United States Department of Commerce that it impose a "retransmission consent" requirement on cable systems if it eliminated the distant signal and syndicated exclusivity rules. Under that proposal, cable operators would need the consent of the originating broadcast station before they could transmit non-network programming to their subscribers.[8] Both the United States Department of Justice and the United States Copyright Office opposed the NTIA proposal as contrary to Congress's mandate of a compulsory licensing system for cable television under the new Copyright Act, and the FCC adopted their view.

Petitioners challenge the Commission's Report and Order, among other grounds, for seriously misconstruing the mandate of the 1976 Copyright Act and for being arbitrary and capricious. We conclude that a fair reading of the Copyright Act supports the FCC's position and that the FCC's action was neither arbitrary nor capricious. While the deregulation of the cable television industry raises serious policy questions, evidenced by the sharp division within the commission as to the conclusions of the Report and Order, these questions are best left to the agencies that were created, in large part, to resolve them.

FCC AUTHORITY UNDER THE COPYRIGHT ACT

Petitioners' substantive argument concerning the FCC's interpretation of its regulatory authority over cable television under the Copyright Act is two-pronged:

1. that the act's compulsory licensing system was premised on maintenance of the existing regulatory framework and

2. that the act does not prohibit adoption of a retransmission consent requirement.

These claims are based on passages in the act and its legislative history, allegedly indicating Congress's intention to leave the FCC with free rein to readjust inter-industry relations by regulation. Specifically, petitioners refer to the provision establishing the compulsory license, § 111, which premises the license upon the "carriage of signals * * * permissible under the rules, regulations, or authorizations of the Federal Communications Commission." 17 U.S.C. § 111(c)(1). Petitioners contend that this language implies both that the FCC cannot upset the existing framework restricting the amount of programming cable systems can carry, and that the commission can adopt rules conditioning cable retransmission upon receipt of broadcaster consent, as the NTIA proposed, because the compulsory license covers only signals the FCC permits cable systems to carry pursuant to commission rules. Petitioners further rely on a passage in the report of the House Judiciary Committee, which stated that the Committee did not intend to "interfere" with FCC rules or communications policy, and that the FCC should neither read the copyright legislation to touch on issues such as increased distant signal carriage, nor rely on it to enact any significant changes in the existing "delicate balance" of regulation in areas where Congress had not resolved

8. The NTIA proposal would have required consent for only new and expanding cable systems and would have grandfathered existing systems because they were built on the basis of either no or partial copyright liability. On this appeal petitioners do not seem to envision such a limited retransmission consent rule, though their arguments are not directed to the content of such a regulation but rather to the FCC's ability to impose a consent requirement in general.

the issue. H.R.Rep. No. 1476, *supra* at 89, [1976] U.S. Code Cong. & Ad. News at 5703–04. From these glimmerings of legislative intent, petitioners contend that the legislative scheme will not tolerate repeal of the distant signal or syndicated exclusivity rules, but will accept a retransmission consent requirement.

We reject both contentions. Though Congress was aware of the underlying regulations restricting cable transmissions when it adopted the compulsory licensing system, it also recognized the legitimacy within the statutory plan of FCC modifications of that regulatory structure. Congress provided that the Copyright Royalty Tribunal ("Tribunal"), the entity established to collect and distribute the royalty fees, could readjust the statutory royalty rate if the FCC altered either the distant signal or syndicated program exclusivity rules. 17 U.S.C. §§ 801(b)(2)(B) and (C) (1976). The plain import of § 801 is that the FCC, in its development of communications policy, may increase the number of distant signals that cable systems can carry and may eliminate the syndicated exclusivity rules, in which event the Tribunal is free to respond with rate increases.

The views expressed in the House Report do not call for a different construction. Though perhaps revealing concern for congressional etiquette among the several committees with overlapping jurisdiction over the regulated subject matter, the comments do not foreclose the FCC's decision to repeal the distant signal and exclusivity rules. In repealing its rules, the FCC has heeded the Committee's caution against using the 1976 copyright legislation to determine matters that Congress "did not resolve." The FCC did not base its repeal of the cable regulations solely upon the revision, but upon a careful reassessment, in light of all the evidence, of the gains and losses to the public interest from deregulation.

While the commission is not obliged by the act to preserve existing rules, it is not free to adopt a new one that would be inconsistent with a basic arrangement of the new legislation. Retransmission consents would undermine compulsory licensing because they would function no differently from full copyright liability, which Congress expressly rejected. Under the NTIA proposal cable operators would be forced to negotiate individually with numerous broadcasters and would not be guaranteed retransmission rights, a scenario Congress considered unworkable when opting for the compulsory licensing arrangement. H.R.Rep. No. 1476, *supra* at 89, [1976] U.S. Code Cong. & Ad. News at 5704; *see* Comment, *Regulatory Versus Property Rights Solutions for the Cable Television Problem, supra* at 550. A rule imposing a retransmission consent requirement would also directly alter the statutory royalty formula by precipitating an increase in the level of payments of cable operators to obtain consent for program use. Such a rule would be inconsistent with the legislative scheme for both the specific compensatory formula and the appropriate forum for its adjustment. In an era of compulsory copyright licensing,[10] we find it difficult to imagine that Congress intended its formula for royalty fees to be only a minimum subject to FCC alteration, since it delegated broad discretionary authority to the Tribunal, and not the FCC, to readjust the rates if regulatory action so required. Congress did not specifically set the royalty rate for other types of compulsory licenses established under the new act. *See* 17 U.S.C. § 118 (1976) (public broadcasting royalty rates set by Tribunal). To hold that the compulsory license formula sets only a minimum, and not a maximum rate (subject to Tribunal adjust-

10. The 1976 Copyright Act provided for blanket licensing in several contexts in addition to cable television. *See* 17 U.S.C. § 116 (1976) (juke boxes); *id.* § 115 (mechanical royalties); *id.* § 118 (public broadcasting).

ment), would undermine the carefully established legislative arrangement.[11]

REVIEW OF THE FCC'S RULEMAKING PROCESS

Apart from arguments based on the Copyright Act, petitioners contend that the FCC's determination to repeal the cable television regulations should be set aside as arbitrary and capricious. 5 U.S.C. § 706(2)(A) (1976). The scope of judicial review of informal rulemaking under the Administrative Procedure Act is circumscribed. Though a reviewing court is to be "searching and careful" in its inquiry to ensure that the agency has articulated a "rational connection between the facts found and the choice made," Burlington Truck Lines, Inc. v. United States, 371 U.S. 156, 168 (1962), it cannot substitute its judgment for that of the agency. Citizens to Protect Overton Park v. Volpe, 401 U.S. 402, 416 (1971).

The report and order repealing the cable television regulations followed several years of thorough study by FCC staff and extensive public commentary, both before and after reports of findings were issued in 1979. Numerous econometric studies, as well as case studies of existing markets where cable systems had been less strictly regulated because of "grandfathering" provisions in the FCC regulations,[12] were carefully evaluated in reaching the administrative decision. Petitioners challenge the FCC's use of the vast material compiled in the proceeding as biased and irrational, contending that the FCC's conclusion that broadcasting stations would not be injured from cable deregulation was unfounded, and that the FCC failed to consider fully, or impartially, data projecting its decision's adverse economic impact on station finances and program supply. For example, the professional sports leagues claim the commission did not consider the effect of deregulation on sports programming; the independent television stations charge it with viewing the industry as a whole, thereby ignoring the adverse impact on independents; and American Broadcasting Companies, Inc. ("ABC") contends that the FCC failed to consider the effects of deregulation upon different groups of viewers.

The FCC specifically responded to petitioners' factual and theoretical assertions in the Report and Order, articulating clear reasons when it rejected, or did not fully use, the economic predictions in industry studies due to erroneous assumptions or modeling flaws. E.g., Economic Inquiry Report, *supra,* 71 FCC2d at 677–78 (rejecting certain results of Wharton Econometric Forecasting Associates study for National Association of Broadcasters because it used a formula that biased results toward smaller independent stations), reasserted in Report and Order, *supra,* 79 FCC2d at 696. It commissioned an outside economist to reanalyze the data in his study, one on which the FCC's 1979 reports relied, after incorporating industry criticisms of his techniques; his results were unchanged. Appendix B, Report and Order, *supra,* 79 FCC2d at 827 (Rand Note, prepared for FCC by R. Park). The Report and Order thus reasserted the 1979 reports' conclusion that unregulated cable television would divert less than ten per cent of local station audiences, a result that would have only a slight effect on broadcasting industry revenues and the

11. Because we find that the FCC's rejection of a transmission consent requirement was based on a proper construction of the Copyright Act, we do not reach petitioners' further contentions that such a requirement, if not prohibited by the Copyright Act, would be permissible under the Communications Act, 47 U.S.C. § 151 *et seq.* (1976).

12. Under 47 C.F.R. §§ 76.65 and 76.99 (1980), the regulations regarding distant signal and syndicated exclusivity, respectively, were made inapplicable to signals being transmitted by cable systems prior to March 31, 1972.

supply of programming. We cannot conclude that this finding was arbitrary or capricious. The commission offered a rational explanation for its policy founded on a predictive judgment well within its authority. See FCC v. WNCN Listeners Guild, 450 U.S. 582, 49 U.S.L.W. 4306 (Mar. 24, 1981).

Nor do we think the FCC assigned too little significance to, or overlooked, any of the contentions by any of the pertinent segments of the industry. While independent stations are less profitable than network affiliates, there were data indicating that local affiliates were subject to greater audience diversion than independents, *e.g.,* R. Noll, *et al., supra* at 162–69, that UHF stations, most of which are independent, benefited from cable television in terms of improved viewing quality, *E.g., id.* at 166, and that independent stations in the grandfathered markets prospered, Economic Inquiry Report, *supra,* 71 FCC2d at 698–701. Though in the past the FCC has accorded special treatment to UHF stations, it is not required to do so when in its judgment the public interest would be disserved; the FCC's statutory directives are to promote a "rapid, efficient" nationwide communications service and to encourage its use in the "public interest," 47 U.S.C. §§ 151, 303 (1976), neither of which commands a specific industry structure or protection of any particular stations from financial difficulty or even failure. Moreover, the FCC reviewed the circumstances of broadcast stations that filed comments alleging current or potential injury from cable television and found that cable had not adversely affected those stations. Economic Inquiry Report, *supra,* 71 FCC2d at 711. The concerns of independent broadcasters were adequately considered by the FCC and did not require retention of either set of rules.

The independent stations further maintain that the FCC should have grandfathered existing syndicated program exclusivity contracts. The FCC was not required to take such action upon elimination of the exclusivity rules. The property of regulated industries is subject to such limitations as may reasonably be imposed in the public interest, and consequently, as numerous courts have recognized, regulations may be adopted that abolish or modify preexisting interests. For example, in General Telephone Company of the Southwest v. United States, 499 F.2d 846, 863–64 (5th Cir. 1971), FCC rules were upheld requiring telephone companies to divest their interests in cable television systems; in rejecting a grandfathering claim, the Court stated that the FCC should not be limited to building on the status quo when seeking to impose a regulatory policy. Moreover, in deciding not to grandfather existing exclusivity rights, the commission considered evidence indicating that these exclusivity rights were rarely asserted.

The sports programming issue was not as thoroughly reviewed by the commission in the preliminary stages of the rulemaking process as other issues, such as the effect on independent stations, because no change in the primary means of sports program protection, the home broadcast black-out rules, 47 CFR § 76.67 (1980), was ever contemplated. However, the commission did respond to the sports leagues' comments in the report and order. The leagues contend that cable television, by making available more broadcasts of games from distant cities when a club is playing at home, will decrease gate receipts, threaten the league concept by hurting weaker franchises, and ultimately lead to less sports programming. But the leagues did not produce any evidence that the number of sports broadcasts by home clubs has been reduced in the existing areas of high cable penetration, or would be reduced in the future. Further, as the FCC noted, many variables besides the availability of sports programming on television influence gate attendance, such as the weather and the caliber of the home and visiting teams. It was not arbitrary for the FCC to conclude that sports programming requires no special protection after the repeal of the distant signal rules.

Finally, the FCC's action is not deficient, as ABC contends, for lack of precise assessment of the impact of repeal on discrete groups of viewers. While the FCC did not conduct detailed demographic studies of cable and noncable television audiences, this fact does not lessen the validity of its conclusion that deregulation is in the public interest. Though lower-income families benefit more from a system of free television than from cable television, *see* R. Noll, *et al., supra* at 25–26, the expansion of cable services was reasonably found not to threaten the basic nature of free television. Given current and estimated cable penetration rates and the profitability of the broadcasting industry, we do not doubt the reasonableness of the FCC's conclusion that programming on free television will not substantially change or diminish after deregulation.[13] If free television retains its existing programming, then there is an increase in overall consumer welfare and no significant inequity among groups of viewers from the FCC's decision: those who do not purchase cable are substantially unaffected in their viewing patterns, while those who do, being able to pay for programming, some of which does not generate sufficient mass appeal to be aired on free television, receive a service more responsive to their viewing preferences. *See id.* at 136.[14]

Ultimately, the task in adopting rules to achieve the appropriate mix between broadcast and cable services requires determining a desired tradeoff between the inefficiency of the pricing system of cable television and the inadequacy of programming under free television. Since the marginal cost of programs for an extra viewer is zero, any price paid by a cable subscriber for receiving television signals is inefficient. Though free television is price efficient, because advertisers and not viewers pay for programming, the pricing does not reflect the intensity with which viewers prefer to see certain types of shows. *See* Spence & Owen, *Television Programming, Monopolistic Competition and Welfare,* 91 Q.J.Econ. 103 (1977). Free television consequently limits program diversity by its concentration on mass audience shows, which make advertising worthwhile. In shifting its policy toward a more favorable regulatory climate for the cable industry, the FCC has chosen a balance of television services that should increase program diversity, a valid FCC regulatory goal, see FCC v. National Citizens Committee for Broadcasting, 436 U.S. 775, 795–97 (1978); United States v. Midwest Video Corp., 406 U.S. 649, 669 (1972) (plurality opinion). While there will undoubtedly be more of the same type of mass audience programming now populating the national networks on cable channels as well, the unlimited number of cable channels holds out the best possibility for special interest programming. As the market shares for mass audiences are divided up among the several stations, programming will be purchased to capture the next largest share, selective audiences, *see* R. Noll *et al., supra* at 151; Spence & Owen, *supra*, and programs will be supplied when revenues exceed cost and not only when a specified

13. As in Home Box Office, Inc. v. FCC, 567 F.2d 9 (D.C.Cir.) (per curiam), cert. denied 434 U.S. 829 (1977) (vacating FCC rules restricting pay cable showing of certain feature film and sports programming), there was no significant evidence presented of program siphoning.

14. Although in a system of only pay television (whereby the viewer pays per program or per channel, and not simply a cable subscription and installation fee) the distributional effect would be to shift income from consumers to the television industry, under a cable system consumers gain, and it is the broadcasting network segment that loses due to increased competition from independent stations. R. Noll, *et al., supra* at 135, 173–74, 182.

audience size is attained, as under the advertiser-supported system.

The commission's repeal of the distant signal and syndicated exclusivity rules, after widespread participation of all industry segments and comprehensive evaluation of technical data, reflects the "rational weighing of competing policies" Congress intended to be exercised by the agency and to be sustained by a reviewing court. See FCC v. National Citizens Committee for Broadcasting, *supra,* 436 U.S. at 803.

BURDEN OF PROOF IN THE PROCEEDINGS

Petitioners raise one further contention that merits attention. They argue that the FCC impermissibly shifted the burden of proof in its rulemaking proceeding to those parties seeking retention of the regulations. We disagree. After an extended inquiry into the effect of the existing regulations and the state of the industry that encompassed several years of investigation, and thorough consideration of the vast material compiled, the FCC concluded that the existing regulations should be repealed. Only after receiving that evidence did the FCC ask members of the public who disagreed with its findings to produce data showing how they would be injured by deregulation since it had not found any evidence to that effect. Such action did not reverse the burden of proof because the FCC had already produced an overwhelming mass of evidence supporting elimination of the rules. Rather, its request for data, evincing a desire for widespread participation from all interested segments of the public who might be aware of information that the agency's intensive inquiry did not uncover, reflects the proper exercise of reasoned decision-making.

The petition to set aside the Report and Order is denied.

COMMENT

1. The Supreme Court refused to review the second circuit's decision in the *Malrite* case. See National Association of Broadcasters v. FCC, 454 U.S. 1143 (1982). Broadcasters feel that the copyright compensation provided to them by the 1976 act is still not sufficient to justify the new opportunities for cable to exploit broadcasting made possible by the FCC's cable deregulation orders reversed in *Malrite.*

Broadcasters have striven to change the *Malrite* decision by statute. In September 1982, H.R. 5949 was passed by the House. Among other matters the bill would, with some changes, reinstitute the pre-*Malrite* syndicated exclusivity rules. The bill's provisions, however, would exempt most of the existing cable industry from coverage.

2. In response to the change in the exclusivity rules and the repeal of the restriction on importing distant signals, the Copyright Tribunal Office has adjusted the rates imposed for the new programming made available to cable operators. See CRT Deregulation Adjustment, 47 Fed.Reg. 52146, 52155. It has been contended that the cable copyright structure was built upon the assumption that the FCC-imposed restrictions on cable would remain basically intact, although there might be minor changes.

3. Perhaps it could be argued that the distant carriage and syndicated exclusivity restrictions imposed by the FCC made sense prior to the enactment of the 1976 copyright law. The FCC was protecting the owners of copyrighted broadcast programming until the Congress had an opportunity to resolve the issue. The 1976 act, however, with its Copyright Royalties Tribunal procedures, did resolve the matter. Thus, arguably, there is no longer a need for the FCC to stretch its regulatory authority to provide a degree of protection the Congress, in enacting the 1976 act, has not found necessary.

FCC Regulation of Cable System Franchising

Presently, there is a multitiered system accepted for the regulation of CATV (cable) systems in the United States. State or local government agencies have the authority to issue franchises to locally selected cable system operators. But this system of local regulation operates subject to certain FCC standards. Cable operators, therefore, unlike broadcasters, have two systems of regulation to cope with, state or local and federal. With regard to the establishment of franchise fees, the FCC requires that franchise fees for cable systems serving 1,000 or more subscribers be no more than 3 percent of the franchisee's gross revenues from that system per annum. A franchise fee in the range of 3–5 percent of such revenues will be approved by the commission upon a showing that the fee is appropriate in light of the planned local regulatory program and that it will not interfere with the effectuation of federal regulatory goals.

The FCC recommends, but does not require, that as part of the franchising process the local franchising authority should

1. hold public selection proceedings which consider the legal, character, financial, technical, and other qualifications of each candidate,

2. limit the duration of franchise periods to fifteen years and require a public proceeding prior to any decision to renew,

3. require that the franchisee make significant efforts to complete the construction of the cable system within one year after FCC certification,

4. implement a policy of construction which would optimally require the complete wiring of the franchise area,

5. specify procedures to be adopted by the franchising authority and the franchisee for the continued administration of the cable system and the investigation and resolution of all subscriber complaints.

See FCC Regulation of Cable System Franchising, 47 CFR §§ 76.30–31 (1981).

Mandatory Carriage of "Local" Television Broadcast Signals

The provisions of 47 CFR §§ 76.57, 76.59 and 76.61 (1981) require that, upon request, cable systems must carry the broadcast signals of what normally would be considered the "local" television stations of the franchise area. These provisions thus vary according to the size of the television market—the cable system's community.

> § 76.57 requires cable systems operating in communities outside of all major and smaller television markets to carry the signals of—
>
> 1. TV stations within whose Grade B contours the cable systems operate;
>
> 2. noncommercial educational TV within whose specified zone the cable system operates; and
>
> 3. significantly viewed TV broadcast stations (see note on § 76.54)
>
> § 76.59 requires those systems operating in a community in whole or in part within a small TV market to carry the signals of:
>
> 1. TV broadcasts if within specified zone;
>
> 2. noncommercial educational TV if within Grade B contours;
>
> 3. commercial TV stations of other smaller TV markets if within Grade B contour;
>
> 4. commercial TV broadcasts that are significantly viewed in the community of the cable system.
>
> § 76.61 requires those systems operating in major television markets to carry the signals of:
>
> 1. TV stations (* * * in which the community of cable system franchise is wholly or partly) within its specified zone, except that there is no require-

ment to carry the signals of a TV station licensed to a designated community in another major television market unless the designated community is located *wholly* within the specified zone of the station;

2. noncommercial educational television broadcast stations if cable system operates in whole or in part within its Grade B contours;

3. TV broadcast stations licensed to obtain designated communities of the same major television market;

4. commercial television broadcast stations that are significantly viewed in the community of the cable system.

In addition to the mandatory carriage provisions above, the FCC permits cable systems to carry any additional "distant" signals. Also, pursuant to § 76.64, the provisions of §§ 76.57, 76.59, and 76.61 do not operate to require the carriage of any subscription television broadcast program.

What is the regulatory philosophy behind the mandatory carriage provisions? Is it to prevent the fragmentation of the viewing audience of the "local" television station? Should the FCC regulate to prevent the growth of a new technology?

Nonduplication Protection of Network Programming

Pursuant to 47 CFR § 76.92 (1981), the FCC requires that cable systems carrying the same "network programming" as a local commercial television broadcasting station or a noncommercial educational television broadcasting station shall, upon the request of the station licensee, *delete* the duplicating network programming of lower priority signals. (What is the purpose of the nonduplication rules?) Specifically, § 76.92 pertains to those cable systems operating in a community located in whole or in part within the thirty-five-mile specified zone of any television station or within the secondary zone, which extends twenty miles beyond the specified zone, of smaller market television stations. The FCC assigns the highest order of nonduplicating priority to those stations within whose specified zone the cable systems operate and a second priority to those smaller market stations within whose secondary zones the cable systems operate.

There are two exceptions under § 76.92 to their system of nonduplication protection:

1. any cable system operating within the secondary zone of a smaller market station is not required to delete the duplicating network program of any major market television programming whose reference point of broadcast is also within fifty-five miles of the cable system

2. a cable system is not required to delete any duplicating broadcast which is significantly viewed in the cable television community.

Pursuant to § 76.54, those signals that are significantly viewed in a specific community are listed in appendix A of the Memorandum Opinion and Order on Reconsideration of Cable Television Report and Order, FCC 72–530, 36 FCC2d 326 (1972). Any signal not encompassed by the surveys used in appendix B of that survey may be demonstrated as significantly viewed by independent audience surveys.

Exceptions to the Nonduplication Provisions

Section 76.94 provides for some exceptions to the nonduplication protections afforded broadcast stations in § 76.92: First, § 76.-94 provides that cable systems need only refrain from simultaneously broadcasting protected network programming where the cable systems operator has received timely notification by the broadcasting stations of the date and time of the programming to be protected. Second, where the cable system is required to afford same-day protection either pursuant to FCC order or pending FCC action, the cable system need not 1) delete reception of any network program which would leave available for reception by subscribers, at any time, less than the programs of two networks; or 2) delete reception of a network program scheduled by the network between the hours of 6:00 and 11:00 P.M., but is to be broadcast by the station requesting the deletion outside the hours of what is normally considered prime time in the zone involved.

Section 76.95 provides three further exceptions to § 76.92: 1) A cable system need not delete any program which would be carried on the cable unit in color, but is to be broadcast in black and white by the station requesting deletion; 2) the mandatory deletion requirements of § 76.92 do not apply to cable systems with fewer than 1,000 subscribers; 3) cable systems need not extend network nonduplication protection beyond one hour after the scheduled time of completion of a live sports event.

The Boulder Case and Local Regulation of Cable

Are there limits to local regulation of cable? In Community Communications Co., Inc. v. City of Boulder, Colorado, 455 U.S. 40, (1982),—see p. 658—the Supreme Court ruled that Boulder had violated the antitrust provisions of the Sherman Act, 15 U.S.C. § 1, by enacting an ordinance which prohibited the assignee of a cable television permit from expanding its cable operations for a period of three months. The decision has been heralded by cablecasters as the end of restrictive municipal regulation of the cable industry.

Boulder is a "home rule" municipality under the Colorado Constitution and is entitled to exercise "the full right of self-government in both local and municipal matters." In the late 1970s, the City Council of Boulder sought to revise its cable television policy to take advantage of new developments in technology and to lure new entrants into the Boulder cable market. While the City Council was drafting its proposed "model cable television ordinance," it enacted an "emergency" (moratorium) ordinance which prohibited the plaintiff, *Community Communications Co.,* from expanding its business into other areas of the city for a period of three months.

Plaintiff sought a preliminary injunction in the federal district court to prevent the city's emergency ordinance from taking effect. Plaintiff alleged that, in enacting the ordinance, the City Council had violated § 1 of the Sherman Act which provides, in applicable part, that "Every contract, combination * * *, or conspiracy, in restraint of trade or commerce among the several States * * * is declared to be illegal." The city, in response, claimed antitrust immunity under the "state action" exemption set forth in Parker v. Brown, 317 U.S. 341 (1943). The district court rejected the city's contention, finding *Parker* to be wholly inapplicable to the present case, 485 F.Supp. 1035 (1980). On appeal, the Tenth Circuit reversed the district court's ruling and found the *Parker* doctrine applicable. 630 F.2d 704 (1980).

The Supreme Court's majority opinion, written by Justice Brennan, analyzed the "state action" issue and set forth the following two-part standard for review. "Our precedents thus reveal that Boulder's moratorium ordinance cannot be exempt from antitrust scrutiny unless it constitutes the action of the State of Colorado itself in its sovereign capacity, see *Parker,* or unless it constitutes municipal action in furtherance or implementation of a clearly articulated and affirmatively expressed state policy."

Under the first test of the proffered standard, Justice Brennan had little difficulty dismissing Boulder's contention that its emergency ordinance was an act of government performed by the city acting as a state. This was based on his finding that: "[T]he *Parker* state action exemption reflects Congress' intention to embody in the Sherman Act the federalism principles that the state possesses a significant measure of sovereignty under our Constitution. But this principle contains its own limitation: Ours is a 'dual system of government' * * * which has no place for sovereign cities." Accordingly, Boulder's emergency ordinance could fall within the state action exemption only if it was enacted pursuant to a clearly articulated and affirmatively expressed state policy.

That claim was also dismissed by Justice Brennan for the majority: "(T)he requirement of 'clear articulation and affirmative expression' is not satisfied when the state's position is one of mere neutrality respecting the municipal actions challenged as anticompetitive. A state that allows its municipalities to do as they please can hardly be said to have 'contemplated' the specific anticompetitive actions for which municipal liability is sought."

Justice Rehnquist, joined by Chief Justice Burger and Justice O'Connor, in dissent, asserted that the majority had incorrectly framed the issue in the case by focusing on "exemption" analysis rather than on principles of federal preemption under the Supremacy Clause. Justice Rehnquist claimed that the *Parker* decision was not a "state action" exemption to the Sherman Act but reflected a congressional determination that, under certain circumstances, state regulation of the economy is not *preempted* by federal law. There is one important result of classifying *Parker* as Justice Rehnquist does. Under exemption theory, where a state or municipal ordinance is not saved by the *Parker* doctrine, the state may be found to have actually *violated* the Sherman Act. Under Justice Rehnquist's approach, the statute would simply be unenforceable because it is preempted. The preemption approach thus saves municipalities from Sherman Act liability and the threat of treble damages.

Does the *Boulder* design signal the end of municipal regulation of the cable television industry? See Marticorena, *Municipal Cable Television Regulation—Is There Life After Boulder?*, 9 Western St.U.L.Rev. 113 (1982). This commentator argues that *Boulder* will not end local regulation of cable. *Boulder* does, however, impose new responsibilities on local governments to be aware of local competitive conditions which will be affected by local regulation of cable since such post-*Boulder* regulation is likely to be the subject of increased antitrust litigation.

The Supreme Court in *Boulder* rejected the claim of the *City of Boulder* that its "home rule" status automatically exempted it from antitrust liability under the "state action" exemption announced in Parker v. Brown, 317 U.S. 341 (1942).

Boulder raises important public policy concerns since it subjects municipalities with limited budgets to the threat of expensive antitrust litigation and the possibility of treble damage awards. Although the *Boulder* court recognized the negative implications of its decision, the Court felt bound by the principles of statutory construction. The public policy arguments were more appropriate for congressional debate.

Taking issue with Justice Rehnquist, Marticorena states that it is clear from the majority opinion in *Boulder* that a finding of no antitrust immunity cannot be regarded as a *per se* finding of Sherman Act liability. In the face of a *Boulder*-type decision, municipalities may still protect the integrity of their ordinances by demonstrating the reasonableness and social importance of the economic regulation.

After *Boulder*, it is clear that municipalities may restrict local competition in the cable television industry without violating the Sherman Act only where such action is somehow authorized by the state.

The future applicability of the "state action" exemption is thus entirely dependent upon the regulatory schemes of the individual states.

Marticorena points out that the regulatory schemes of the fifty states generally can be divided into three categories. First, there are those states, including Colorado, which have no statutes regulating cable television. As the *Boulder* decision makes clear, municipalities in these states cannot claim antitrust immunity as their respective states maintain a position of mere neutrality on the issue of anticompetitive cable regulation.

Falling within a second category of state regulatory schemes would be those states which either structure the cable system as a public utility or take direct responsibility for the franchising and regulation of cable operators. This centralized system should be safe from antitrust liability since any anticompetitive regulation would proceed directly from a state governmental unit.

The final category includes those states which delegate broad franchising authority to counties and municipalities and which specifically allow for local regulation of cable franchises. Marticorena asserts that municipalities acting pursuant to this type of regulatory scheme should be afforded immunity where the state has articulated a policy to displace competition in the cable market with regulation or monopoly public service.

THE RISE OF PUBLIC BROADCASTING

The Public Broadcasting Act of 1967

1. A significant development in the life of American radio and television was the Public Broadcasting Act of 1967, 47 U.S.C.A. §§ 390–401. In January 1967 the Carnegie Foundation under the chairmanship of Dr. James R. Killian, Jr. of M.I.T. recommended the development of a nonprofit corporation to encourage the development of noncommercial television. The Carnegie Report was a seminal document, and the Public Broadcasting Act of 1967 owes much to the Report. See *Public Television, A Program for Action,* The Report and Recommendations of the Carnegie Commission on Educational Television (New York, Harper & Row, 1967). See also, Carnegie II (1979), which suggests substantial changes in the present governing mechanisms and funding of public broadcasting.

The scheme for selecting the board of directors of the Corporation for Public Broadcasting, (CPB) now calls for a total of ten members, appointed by the president with the advice and consent of the Senate. Only six members of the Board appointed by the president may be members of the same political party. The act directs that members should be selected from among those eminent in educational, cultural, and artistic affairs, including radio and television; from among various regions of the nation, professions, and occupations; and from among various kinds of talent and expertise. One member of the board should be selected from among those who represent public radio stations and another from those who represent public television stations. Members should serve a term of five years but not more than two consecutive terms. See Public Broadcasting Amendments Act of 1981, 95 Stat. 725–736.

One of the broad purposes of the Public Broadcasting Act is to assist through matching grants in the construction of noncommercial educational television or radio broadcasting facilities. 47 U.S.C.A. § 391. But the truly novel aspect of the act is the provision for the creation of the Corporation for Public Broadcasting. Great Britain has had long experience with a public network run by an independent board—the much praised BBC, the British Broadcasting Corporation. Similarly, CBC, the Canadian Broadcasting Corporation, which is sponsored by the federal parliament of Canada, is an integral part of Canadian life. But an American effort in the direction of government-sponsored broadcasting is a relatively recent development in American broadcasting. Indeed, whether the federal government can finance an instrument which will influence the opinion-making process is itself an unresolved First Amendment question. For these reasons the act is in some respects necessarily unclear.

Public Broadcasting and the First Amendment

The question of the future of public broadcasting has been debated almost solely by the executive and legislative branches of government. Rarely have courts had the opportunity to consider the matter. But Justice Douglas, in a separate concurring opinion in the *CBS v. DNC* case, see text, p. 858, took the opportunity to consider public broadcasting's role as part of the "press" and to raise a doubt as to the constitutionality of public broadcasting:

> Public broadcasting, of course, raises quite different problems from those tendered by the TV outlets involved in this litigation.
>
> * * * [The Corporation for Public Broadcasting] is a nonprofit organization and by the terms of 396(b) [of the Public Broadcasting Act of 1967] is said not to be "an agency or establishment of the United States Government." Yet, since it is a creature of Congress whose management is in the hands of a [b]oard named by the [p]resident and approved by the Senate, it is difficult to see why it is not a federal agency engaged in operating a "press" as that word is used in the First Amendment. If these cases involved that [c]orporation, we would have a situation comparable to that in which the United States owns and manages a prestigious newspaper like the *New York Times.* * * * The government as owner and manager would not, as I see it, be free to pick and choose such news items as it desired. For by the First Amendment it may not censor or enact or enforce any other "law" abridging freedom of the press. Politics, ideological slants, rightist or leftist tendencies could play no part in its design of programs. * * More specifically, the programs tendered by the respondents in the present cases could not then be turned down.
>
> Governmental action may be evidenced by various forms of supervision or control of private activities. * * * I have expressed the view that the activities of licensees of the government operating in the public domain are governmental actions, so far as constitutional rights and responsibilities are concerned. * * * But that view has not been accepted. If a TV or radio licensee were a federal agency, * * * [as] a licensee of the [f]ederal [g]overnment [it] would be in precisely the situation of the Corporation for Public Broadcasting. A licensee, like an agency of the government, would within limits of its time be bound to disseminate all views. For being an arm of the government it would be unable by reason of the First Amendment to "abridge" some sectors of thought in favor of others. The Court does not, however, decide whether a broadcast licensee is a federal agency within the context of this case. Columbia Broadcasting System, Inc. v. Democratic National Committee, 412 U.S. 94 (1973).

Justice Douglas asserted that a public station could not refuse the programs offered by the DNC and the spot announcements of BEM (Business Executives' Move for Vietnam Peace). Would public television serve as a solution to the access problem? If the only difference between private commercial stations and the public, noncommercial ones, particularly if CPB control is diminished, turns out to be that public stations receive federal grants that match their private contributions, while private stations must rely on advertising revenue, is that enough justification to treat the two media differently under the First Amendment?

"Objectivity" and "Balance" in Public Broadcasting

The Corporation for Public Broadcasting is supposed to facilitate the development of programming of high quality for educational broadcasting with "strict adherence to objectivity and balance in all programs or series of programs of a controversial nature." See 47 U.S.C.A. § 396(g)(1)(A).

Is the requirement that public broadcasting must be "balanced" and "objective" enforceable? This issue was presented for decision in Accuracy In Media, Inc. v. FCC, 521 F.2d 288 (D.C.Cir. 1975).

Accuracy In Media (AIM), a feisty conservative citizens organization and a professional thorn in many a media side, filed a complaint against the Public Broadcasting System (PBS) before the FCC, charging that two programs distributed by PBS to member stations did not provide a balanced or objective presentation of the subject presented. In its complaint, AIM charged that PBS had violated the law in two respects. First, AIM charged that the PBS programs violated the fairness doctrine. (The FCC rejected this contention.) AIM's other contention involved a little-known provision of the Public Broadcasting Act of 1967, which required the Corporation for Public Broadcasting (CPB) to adhere to a standard of objectivity or balance in programming of a controversial nature.[13] AIM contended that the two offending programs (one dealing with sex education and the other dealing with the American system of criminal justice) violated the balance and objectivity requirement of the Public Broadcasting Act.

The provision of the Public Broadcasting Act which required "balance" and "objectivity" authorizes CPB to "facilitate the full development of educational television." CPB's mandate is to obtain programs of "high quality * * * from diverse sources" and to make them available to noncommercial broadcasters. This provision of the act concludes that these responsibilities are to be accomplished "with strict adherence to objectivity and balance in all programs or series of programs of a controversial nature."

AIM contended that since the PBS programs it objected to were funded by CPB, pursuant to the authorization just described, the programs were subject to the requirement of "strict adherence to objectivity and balance"—a requirement which AIM contended was "more stringent than the standard of balance and fairness in overall programming contained in the fairness doctrine."

If CPB programming must be balanced and objective, how does such a requirement differ from the fairness doctrine? AIM argued that the balance and objectivity requirement differed from the fairness doctrine in two ways. With respect to the "balance" requirement of the programming standard, AIM argued that broadcasters must achieve a balanced presentation of the issues with respect to each program. Balanced discussion in a broadcaster's overall programming would not suffice as suggested by fairness doctrine law. With respect to "objectivity" requirements, AIM contended that the FCC would have to conduct a "more searching inquiry into alleged factual inaccuracies than contemplated by the fairness doctrine."

The FCC refused to rule on the correctness of AIM's interpretation of the "balance and objectivity" standard in the Public Broadcasting Act because in its view it had no jurisdiction to enforce the Act. AIM then sought review in the federal

13. 47 U.S.C.A. § 396(g)(1)(A) (1970).

court of appeals. The federal court, per Judge Bazelon, spokesman for the new liberal unease with the fairness doctrine, agreed with the FCC and not AIM.

The court of appeals' conclusion that the FCC had no jurisdiction to enforce the "balance and objectivity" standard was based on § 398 of the Public Broadcasting Act which provides that no "agency * * of the United States" should have authority to supervise or control CPB. The court reasoned that since the FCC was an "agency of the United States," *ergo,* the FCC could not "supervise" the Corporation for Public Broadcasting. Nevertheless, as Judge Bazelon conceded, the matter was hardly free from doubt. A provision of the Public Broadcasting Act of 1967, § 399, mandates "supervision" of noncommercial licenses and contemplates FCC supervision.

The court of appeals, per Judge Bazelon, however, made it clear that there was nothing in § 398 of the Federal Communications Act which served to limit FCC authority—"including the Fairness Doctrine"—over local noncommercial licensees. "While § 398 prohibits FCC jurisdiction over CPB and its program-related activities, i.e., production, funding or distribution, the commission retains its authority concerning the broadcasting of programs, whether funded by CPB or not." Noncommercial licensees, therefore, were subject to FCC jurisdiction including programming policies like the Fairness Doctrine. But the FCC could not enforce the "objectivity" and "balance" requirement imposed on CPB by the Public Broadcasting Act.

The implication from the legislative history materials gathered by Judge Bazelon in his decision for the federal court of appeals is that permitting FCC supervision of the programming product of PBS would result in precisely that governmental supervision which Congress had desired to prevent.

If the FCC had no jurisdiction or authority to enforce the balance and objectivity requirements of the Public Broadcasting Act, who did? AIM argued that if the FCC was removed from enforcing the standard, then the specific statutory directive of the Congress was rendered meaningless. Judge Bazelon disagreed. The congressional appropriations process was the means designed to safeguard against "partisan abuse." As Bazelon put it: "Ultimately, Congress may show its disapproval of any activity of the Corporation [for Public Broadcasting] through the appropriations process."

AIM lost its effort to secure a judicial ruling that the FCC had a duty to enforce the objectivity and balance requirement of the Public Broadcasting Act. The court not only held that the FCC did not have jurisdiction to enforce the obligation found in the Public Broadcasting Act requiring the Corporation for Public Broadcasting to adhere strictly to objectivity and balance in its programming, but the court went beyond the FCC's determination of no jurisdiction to enforce the objectivity and balance provisions. The federal court of appeals in effect repealed the specific congressional directive that there be objectivity and balance in CPB programming. "The corporation is not required to provide programs with 'strict adherence to objectivity and balance' but rather to 'facilitate the full development of educational broadcasting in which programs * * * will be made available * * *.' We leave the interpretation of this hortatory language to the directors of the corporation and to Congress in its supervisory capacity."

May Public Broadcasters Editorialize?

As you will remember from the *Red Lion* case, p. 845, broadcast licensees are permitted to editorialize. Is there any justification for making a distinction with regard to noncommercial educational broadcasting?

In League of Women Voters v. FCC, 8 Med.L.Rptr. 2081, 547 F.Supp. 379 (C.D.Cal. 1982), the constitutionality of the no-editorializing rule for public broadcasting set forth in 47 U.S.C. § 399 was successfully challenged. The version of § 399 considered by the federal district court in *League of Women Voters* differed significantly from the original language of § 399. On August 13, 1981, the Public Broadcasting Amendments Act of 1981, Pub.L. No. 97–35, 95 Stat. 725–36 (1981) became law.

The challenge filed by the plaintiffs to § 399 was directed solely to the statutory ban on editorializing by public broadcasters receiving federal grants from CPB. No challenge was made to the provision in § 399 prohibiting public broadcast stations from either endorsing or opposing political candidates.

There were three plaintiffs in *League of Women Voters,* the League of Women Voters of California, Congressman Henry Waxman, and Pacifica Foundation, which operates public broadcast stations receiving grants from CPB. Although equal protection objections to the statute were asserted, the contention that § 399's ban on editorializing violated the First Amendment was the determinative issue in the case.

The court said, however, that even though § 399 is being construed narrowly, the no-editorializing rule still limits participation in public issues by public broadcasters and, therefore, raises a serious First Amendment question. Statutes on First Amendment grounds can "withstand scrutiny under the First Amendment only if they serve a compelling state interest and are narrowly tailored to that end." Should less stringent standards be applied where the broadcast media are concerned? The court said, "No." The special factors present in *FCC v. Pacifica Foundation,* text, p. 920, were deemed not relevant.

What compelling state interests might be served by § 399? The defendant relied on two related justifications: 1. funded noncommercial broadcasters should "not become propaganda organs for the government"; and 2. government funding should not interfere "with the balanced presentation of opinion on funded noncommercial stations."

The court rejected these concerns as sufficient to justify a compelling state interest sufficient to save the statute from attack under the First Amendment. "The modest level of government funding, the protective insulation of the CPB, and the restrictions of the fairness doctrine all work to ensure that funded noncommercial broadcasters will not be vulnerable to attempts to use them as propaganda organs for the government. Nor will funded noncommercial broadcasters be influenced to take particular editorial positions in order to curry favor with the government. Both the 'stick' and the 'carrot' of federal funding have been effectively eliminated."

The court concluded that the government had failed to carry the burden that the ban on editorializing in § 399 was tailored with sufficient precision to meet the compelling state interest standard of review. "The fear that funded noncommercial broadcasters will become propaganda organs for the government is too speculative to provide such a compelling interest. The desire to ensure the balanced presentation of opinion by funded noncommercial broadcasters, even if it had been a motivating factor in the passage of § 399, also fails to provide a sufficiently compelling interest to justify the ban on editorializing imposed by that statute." Accordingly, the court held that § 399 violates the First Amendment "insofar as it prohibits funded noncommercial broadcasters from editorializing."

On February 28, 1983, the Supreme Court in FCC v. League of Women Voters, — U.S. —, 103 S.Ct. 1249 (1983), decided to review the constitutionality of the ban in revised § 399 of the Public Broadcasting Act prohibiting editorializing by public broadcasting stations which receive federal funds from the Corporation for Public Broadcasting. The government, in its jurisdictional statement seeking review, contended that the no-editorializing ban should be reviewed by a balancing test rather than by use of the strict scrutiny standard of review. The strict scrutiny standard would permit validation of the statute only if the rigors of the compelling state interest would be met.

If editorializing by public broadcasters is to be encouraged, should some due process protection attach? Writing before the decisions in *AIM* and *League of Women Voters*, Professor (now Judge) Canby thoughtfully delineated the problems endemic to monitoring a standard of "objectivity" and fairness when multiple decision makers—CPB, Public Broadcasting System (PBS), and the individual stations—are involved and concluded that the editorial function must be protected even in the case of publicly sponsored communication facilities. He cautioned against abandonment of content controls and an open access approach. But he stressed the need for identifying lines of editorial authority in public broadcasting and then adhering to them:

"[I]t is important that stations take the salutary step of clearly delineating where within their hierarchies the editorial responsibility lies. Protection of that editorial function will also be facilitated if some attempt is made to defer to expertise in its allocation and if professional standards for its exercise are developed and observed. * * * The prospect of enforcement of imprecise first amendment standards in a new medium of communication may give courts pause and cause stations and network officials to fear the bonds of judicial oversight. Nevertheless, some sort of procedural due process standards should be evolved for editorial decision making by stations supported by the state or receiving substantial government funding." Canby, *The First Amendment And the State as Editor: Implications for Public Broadcasting,* 52 Tex.L.Rev. 1123 at 1164–1165 (1974). The problems raised by the next subsection are illustrative.

The State in the Editor's Chair: Problems of Access in Public Broadcasting

Muir v. Alabama Educational Television Commission, 688 F.2d 1033 (5th Cir. 1982), presented the access issue in the context of public broadcasting. Alabama Educational Television Commission (AETC), a network of nine noncommercial educational television stations, is funded from state legislative appropriations, matching federal grants through the Corporation for Public Broadcasting (CPB), and private contributions. AETC is a member of the Public Broadcasting Service (PBS) and of the Station Program Corporation (SPC), a program-funding and acquisition mechanism operated by PBS. Members of SPC select and fund national public television programs distributed by PBS. Members agreeing to contribute are free to broadcast or not to broadcast programs. PBS's "Station Users Agreement" gives licensees the absolute right to decide what to broadcast and what not to broadcast.

AETC was scheduled to program "Death of a Princess," a dramatization of the public execution for adultery in 1977 of a Saudi Arabian princess and her lover, on May 12, 1980, at 8:00 P.M. There were protests about the planned showing of "Death of a Princess" for fear that its showing would jeopardize the physical security of Alabamians working in the Middle East. Two days prior to the planned broadcast, AETC announced that it would not broadcast the film.

Residents of Alabama who had planned to watch the show filed suit in the federal district court under 42 U.S.C.

§ 1983 and the First and Fourteenth Amendments to compel AETC to broadcast the film and to enjoin it from making "political" program decisions. The district court refused to order AETC to broadcast the program and granted summary judgment for AETC. A panel of the United States Court of Appeals for the Fifth Circuit affirmed the decision of the district court.

In Texas, a federal district court reacted affirmatively to a viewer's request that a noncommercial broadcast station, KUHT–TV, owned and operated by the University of Houston, which had scheduled "Death of a Princess" but then canceled it, be compelled to show it. The federal district court held that KUHT–TV was a "public forum" and that the station could not deny access to speakers without meeting the strict standing by which prior restraints are traditionally reversed. See Barnstone v. University of Houston, 487 F.Supp. 1347 (S.D.Tex.1980).

In the Houston case the district judge said that the decision to cancel "Death of a Princess" was made by Patrick Nicholson, Vice President of University Relations for the University of Houston: "It was the government, the University of Houston, which decided not to program 'The Death of a Princess.' When the government gets involved in broadcasting, it has an obligation, at a minimum, to establish procedures that assure that programming decisions are not based on the political beliefs of its programmers and are not made arbitrarily and without due process of law."

In Barnstone v. Houston, 7 Med.L.Rptr. 2185, 660 F.2d 137 (5th Cir. 1981), cert. den. 103 S.Ct. 1274 (1983), a panel of the Fifth Circuit Court of Appeals reversed the federal district court on the basis of the panel decision in Muir v. Alabama Educational Television Commission, 7 Med.L.Rptr. 1933, 656 F.2d 1012 (5th Cir. 1981).

The Fifth Circuit directed that both panel decisions in *Muir* and *Barnstone* be consolidated and reheard *en banc.* The U.S. Court of Appeals for the Fifth Circuit in its *en banc* decision affirmed the judgment of the District Court for the Northern District of Alabama in *Muir* and reversed the decision of the Southern District Court of Texas in *Barnstone.*

Do individual members of the public have a First Amendment right to compel public television stations "to broadcast a previously scheduled program which the licensees have decided to cancel"? In its *en banc* opinion, the United States Court of Appeals for the Fifth Circuit in Muir v. Alabama Educational Television Commission, 8 Med.L.Rptr. 2305, 688 F.2d 1033 (5th Cir. 1982), cert. den. 103 S.Ct. 1274 (1983), answered "No" to this question. The First Amendment protects private rather than government expression: "To find that the government is without First Amendment protection is not to find that the government is prohibited from speaking or that private individuals have the right to limit or control the expression of government."

The Fifth Circuit decision in *Muir* may serve as a kind of *magna carta* of the rights of public broadcasting: "Under the existing statutes public licensees such as AETC and the University of Houston possess the same rights and obligations to make free programming decisions as their private counterparts; however, as state instrumentalities, these public licensees are without the protection of the First Amendment. This lack of constitutional protection implies only that government could possibly impose restrictions on these licensees which it could not impose on private licensees. The lack of First Amendment protection does not result in the lessening of any of the statutory rights and duties held by the public licensees. It also does not result in individual viewers gaining any greater right to influence the programming discretion of the public licensees."

An issue that continually arose in the "Death of a Princess" litigation was whether public television stations were "public forums." If public television stations were public forums, then, presumably, individual viewers could appropriately argue that they had a right of access to compel the broadcast of a program which had been scheduled and then canceled. In the *Barnstone* case, for example, the district court did find that the public television station there, KUHT–TV, was a public forum since it was operated "by the government for public communication of views on issues of political and social significance." The theory was that a public forum could not deny access to speakers unless the constitutional norms that were usually applied to governmentally imposed prior restraints were complied with.

The plaintiffs in *Muir*, unlike the district court in *Barnstone*, however, made a different argument based on the public forum theory. They contended that public television stations could not make programming decisions which were "motivated by hostility to the communicative impact of a program's message and stemming from a specific viewpoint of the broadcaster." In the *en banc* decision in *Muir*, Judge Hill said for the Fifth Circuit that the court of appeals disagreed with both the public forum theory of the district court in *Barnstone*, as well as the public forum theory of the plaintiffs who argued before the Fifth Circuit. The reasons which the *en banc* decision of the court in *Muir* offered for its conclusion that public television stations are *not* public forums is set forth below:

> In the cases in which a public facility has been deemed a public forum the speakers have been found to have a right of access because they were attempting to use the facility in a manner fully consistent with the "pattern of usual activity" and "the general invitation extended." The pattern of usual activity for public television stations is the statutorily mandated practice of the broadcast licensee exercising sole programming authority. The invitation extended to the public is not to schedule programs, but to watch or decline to watch what is offered. It is thus clear that the public television stations involved in the cases before us are not public forums. The plaintiffs have no right of access to compel the broadcast of any particular program.

The court of appeals in *Muir* also specifically rejected the public access argument of the plaintiffs. According to this argument, even if a public right of access were denied on the theory that public television stations were not public forums, the action of the public television stations in the "Death of a Princess" litigation was impermissible on the ground that public television stations could not "make programming decisions based on the communicative impact of a program".

"We find this contention to be untenable. It is the right of public access which is the essential characteristic of a public forum and the basis which allows a speaker to challenge the state's regulation of the forum. The gravamen of a speaker's public forum complaint is the invalid and discriminatory denial of his right of access to the forum. If a speaker does not have a right of access to a facility, that facility by definition is not a 'public forum' and the speaker is without grounds for challenge under the public forum doctrine."

Another issue which was resolved by the *en banc* decision of the Fifth Circuit Court of Appeals in *Muir* was whether the decision to cancel "Death of a Princess" by the public television stations should be deemed to constitute government censorship. The view was rejected that the decision to cancel "Death of a Princess" constituted governmental censorship. A distinction was drawn between state regulation of private expression and "the exercise of editorial discretion by state officials responsible for the operation of public television stations":

> When state officials operate a public television station they must necessarily

make discriminating choices. As the Supreme Court pointed out in *CBS*, 412 U.S. at 124, 93 S.Ct. at 2097, "[f]or better or worse, editing is what editors are for; and editing is selection and choice of material." In exercising their editorial discretion state officials will unavoidably make programming decisions which can be characterized as "politically motivated." All television broadcast licensees are required, under the public interest standard, to cover political events and to provide news and public affairs programs dealing with the political, social, economic and other issues which concern their community. The licensees are thus required to make the inherently subjective determination that their programming decisions are responsive to the needs, problems and interests of the residents of the area they serve. A general proscription against political programming decisions would clearly be contrary to the licensees' statutory obligations, and would render virtually every programming decision subject to judicial challenge.

The plaintiffs seek to draw a distinction between a decision not to show a program and a decision to cancel a previously scheduled program. They suggest that while it is a proper exercise of editorial discretion for a licensee initially to decide not to schedule a program, it is constitutionally improper for the licensee to decide to cancel a scheduled program because of its political content. In support of their view the plaintiffs cited decisions holding that school officials may be free initially to decide which books to place in their school libraries but that a decision to remove any particular book may be subject to constitutional challenge. We are not persuaded, however, that the distinction urged upon us is valid or that the school library cases are applicable.

The decision to cancel a scheduled program is no less editorial in nature than an initial decision to schedule the program. Both decisions require the licensee to determine what will best serve the public interest, and, as we noted earlier, such a determination is inherently subjective and involves judgments which could be termed "political."

Judge Hill, for the court in *Muir*, summarized the *en banc* court's reasons for concluding that the decision to cancel "Death of a Princess" could not properly be characterized as impermissible government censorship as follows: "Had the states of Alabama and Texas sought to prohibit the exhibition of the film by another party then indeed a question of censorship would have arisen. Such is not the case before us. The states have not sought to forbid or curtail the right of any person to show or view the film. In fact plaintiff Barnstone has already viewed the film at an exhibition at Rice University in Houston. The state officials in charge of AETC and KUHT–TV have simply exercised their statutorily mandated discretion and decided not to show a particular program at a particular time. There is a clear distinction between a state's exercise of editorial discretion over its own expression, and a state's prohibition or suppression of the speech of another."

Judge Rubin concurred, joined by three other judges who participated in the *en banc* review of *Muir* by the Fifth Circuit, pointing out that the government was involved in the publication of a variety of informational media. Content neutrality was not necessarily required in the operation of these media.

> The function of a state agency operating an informational medium is significant in determining first amendment restrictions on its actions. State agencies publish alumni bulletins, newsletters devoted to better farming practices, and law reviews; they operate or subsidize art museums and theater companies and student newspapers. The federal government operates the Voice of America and Radio Free Europe and Radio Liberty, publishes "journals, magazines, periodicals, and similar publications" that are "necessary in the transaction of the public business," including newspapers for branches of the Armed Forces, and

> pays the salaries of many federal officials who, like the president's press secretary, communicate with the public through the media. The first amendment does not dictate that what will be said or performed or published or broadcast in these activities will be entirely content-neutral. In those activities that, like television broadcasting to the general public, depend in part on audience interest, appraisal of audience interest and suitability for publication or broadcast inevitably involves judgment of content.

Judge Frank Johnson, joined by four other judges, dissented from the *en banc* decision of the Fifth Circuit in *Muir*. The question as he saw it was this: can executive officers of a state-operated public television station cancel a previously scheduled program because it presents a point of view disagreeable to the religious and political regime of a foreign country? Judge Johnson's answer was in the negative. He took particular issue with the majority's reliance on FCC regulation to deal with abuses in programming decisions: "* * * [T]he majority has granted state broadcasters immunity from constitutional scrutiny. * * * To rely on FCC regulation is to create a substantial gap in the protection of First Amendment interests. Because the FCC does not distinguish between private and public broadcasters in its regulation of the airwaves, it provides no protection from the kind of state censorship alleged in these cases." Drawing on support from the Supreme Court decision in the school libraries cases, Judge Johnson said that both the plurality and Justice Blackmun agreed that school officials could " 'not remove books for the *purpose* of restricting access to the political ideas or social perspectives discussed in them, when that action is motivated simply by the officials' disapproval of the ideas involved.' " See Board of Education v. Pico, 457 U.S. 853, 102 S.Ct. 2799 (1982). In Johnson's view, allegations of censorship in public television were "entitled to much greater scrutiny than similar allegations involving school board regulation of students' reading material." Judge Johnson advocated a local standard of review for programming decisions such as those involved in the "Death of a Princess": "Once the plaintiff demonstrates that the government has silenced a message because of its substantive content, the government's decision becomes presumptively unconstitutional. The government should then be allowed to demonstrate that it would have taken the same action on the basis of legitimate reasons. Finally, the plaintiff should be given a full opportunity to refuse the government's assertion."

In a separate dissent, Judge Reavley insisted that the First Amendment required neutrality by the state with respect to "relaying messages into the idea marketplace." On the other hand, Judge Reavley resisted Judge Johnson's view that if a state's decision not to show a program was based on the substantive content of the program, the decision was presumptively unconstitutional.

In a perceptive concurrence, Judge Garwood made a distinction between an "open forum" and a "conventional" public broadcasting station:

> First, plaintiffs are not attacking governmental "public" broadcasting as such. Nor do they seek to require its operation to be on a pure "open forum" basis—like an empty stage available to all comers—where each citizen can cause the broadcast of his or her program of choice, with the inevitable selectivity determined by completely content neutral factors such as lot, or first come first served or the like. Rather, plaintiffs seek to become a part of governmental "public" broadcasting essentially as it is, except they want it to broadcast this particular program of their choice. However, there is simply no way for them—together with all others who might wish to assert similar rights for their favorite "dramatization" —to become a part of such "conventional" (as distinguished from pure

> "open forum") governmental broadcasting except on the basis of governmental selection of the individual programs.
>
> * * *
>
> In the second place, plaintiffs do not assert that the stations in question have, on the basis of their agreement or disagreement with the different points of view involved or for similar "political" type reasons, structured their programming so that it constitutes a one-sided or slanted presentation of any matter of public concern, importance or controversy, whether relevant to the "message" of plaintiffs' desired program or otherwise. So far as any such matters are concerned, plaintiffs' complaint is made essentially in a vacuum—they claim that merely because on one particular occasion a "political" type decision was made not to air one specific program plaintiffs wished to see, they therefore have a right to a court order directing these conventionally operated governmental stations to promptly air this precise program. We have rejected this claim. This is not to say, however, that no private citizen has a right to question the programming of governmental "public" television stations under any circumstances, or that the remedy of complaint to the FCC will always be adequate.

COMMENT

1. Are *Muir* and *Barnstone* equivalent situations? In *Muir,* the editorial judgment of broadcast journalists was the source of the decision to cancel. Broadcast journalists were the decision makers in *Muir,* and their exercise of editorial judgment was upheld. But the decision to cancel in *Barnstone* was a governmental and politically inspired judgment made by a university official not a journalist.

2. The "Death of a Princess" case was seen by the Fifth Circuit as a case of First Amendment rights in conflict—freedom of the press versus freedom of speech and the derivative right to hear. The plaintiffs contended that the decision to cancel could not be viewed the same way as a decision to cancel a program by a private broadcaster. The presence of the state government as a sponsor and as a source of funds in part for AETC was said to have transformed the programming decisions of AETC into "governmental action" and "governmental censorship." Judge Markey, author of the Fifth Circuit panel decision in *Muir,* disagreed. See Muir v. Alabama Educational Television Commission, 7 Med.L.Rptr. 1933, 656 F.2d 1012 (5th Cir. 1981). "The application of constitutional principles cannot, however, be controlled by the bare and barren fact that government plays some role."

Judge Markey appeared to be unimpressed with the argument that government funding of public broadcasting should serve to provide the public with greater rights of participation in editorial decision making: "Hence, if government ownership and partial funding alone be synonymous with government censorship of program content, government ownership and funding would doubtless have to cease. * * * If initial rejection of some programs were considered a form of constitutionally forbidden censorship, every public television station would violate the Constitution with virtually every choice it made. * * * It would demean the First Amendment to find that it required a public referendum on every programming decision made every day by every public television station solely because the station is 'owned' and partially funded by a state government." No difference was seen between a decision canceling a scheduled broadcast and the initial scheduling decision as far as judicial oversight is concerned. Both suffered from the same infirmity. The use of court injunctions in either situation would destroy editorial freedom as well as involve excessive government entanglement in the editorial process.

Allowing government to be an editor there is a risk government might attempt to propagandize the public through public television. But there was no evidence to show that the government of Alabama had anything to do with the decision to cancel the show. What if there had been proof that government sought to propagandize? Would the First Amendment rights of the viewers then have overridden the editorial rights of a public television station? That issue was not before the court, and quite properly, Judge Markey does not answer these questions. The implication in the panel decision in *Muir* is, however, that evidence of government intent to propagandize in editorial decision making would have made a difference and would have been declared impermissible. Here then is a difference in the editorial freedom of a public broadcaster as compared to that of a private broadcaster. If private broadcasters cancel a television show out of a desire to propagandize, presumably the First Amendment is not violated although arguably some aspect of FCC law may have been violated. But if a public broadcaster cancels a show out of a desire to propagandize, then presumably the First Amendment is violated. Government cannot mandate a point of view. This would be impermissible "compelled speech." See Wooley v. Maynard, 430 U.S. 705 (1977), text, p. 177.

3. In Note, *Editorial Discretion of State Public Broadcasting Licensees,* 82 Colum. L.Rev. 1161 (1982), two possible models through which the problem of editorial discretion in public broadcasting can be analyzed are suggested. The first model sees the selection of material by public broadcasters as involving "Government-speech." Government speech presents dangers: "It may indoctrinate, distort judgment, perpetuate the current regime, drown out private media, and require taxpayers to support points of view they consider objectionable." Perhaps for these reasons, the *Columbia Note* argues, courts should extend a less deferential standard of review to the editorial discretion of public broadcasters.

The second analytical model is the so-called "Government-facility" model. This model raises the question of whether the government as facility provider may constitutionally regulate access to the facility.

What kind of "facility" *is* the public broadcasting station? Like the *en banc* decision of the Fifth Circuit in *Muir,* the *Columbia Note* argues that the public broadcasting station is neither a "traditional public forum" nor a "state created public forum". "[T]he historical role of the public broadcaster is that of public servant, using independent editorial discretion to program in specific ways for the benefit of the public as audience. * * * [G]uaranteed access—common carrier status—would be incompatible with the licensee's operation."

But must the television audience for First Amendment purposes be looked at as entirely passive? Should the only actor to be accorded First Amendment status be the public broadcaster? To recognize audience rights in public broadcasting is not necessarily the same thing as transforming public broadcasters into common carriers.

As a procedural tool to safeguard expressive access from the "prior restraint" risks inherent in the public broadcaster's editorial decision making, the *Note* concludes by asking that the initial burden be on the "speaker" or "audience member" to establish a *prima facie* case for abuse of discretion. Once the challenger has made out the *prima facie* case, the public broadcaster's decision would be presumed unconstitutional. The public broadcaster would then have to bear the burden of proving that it would have taken the same action on the basis of legitimate reasons. In the Fifth Circuit's *en banc* decision in *Muir v. Alabama Educational Television Commission,* the majority chose not to apply this approach. But it did win the approval of five judges in a dissenting opinion written by Judge Johnson.

State Regulation of Public Broadcasting: The McGlynn Case

State as well as federal law governs state-owned public television stations. This sometimes may produce divergent results. Illustrative is McGlynn v. New Jersey Public Broadcasting Authority, 7 Med.L.Rptr. 2446, 439 A.2d 54 (N.J.1981). The New Jersey Supreme Court ruled that under applicable state law, state public television networks are not required to provide equal air time to all gubernatorial candidates so long as such programming is presented with "balance, fairness and equity." This ruling opens up the New Jersey court system as an alternative forum to the FCC for aggrieved gubernatorial candidates seeking access to public television.

The *McGlynn* controversy arose out of a May 25, 1981 decision of New Jersey Public Broadcasting Authority (Authority), which excluded candidate McGlynn as well as ten other gubernatorial candidates from a series of broadcasts that focused on the leading candidates in the 1981 gubernatorial election. Specifically, the decision to exclude certain candidates came after it became apparent to the executive producer of the series that there was insufficient time available to air the taped interviews of each of the twenty-one candidates. Accordingly, the decision was made on the basis of "professional news judgment" to limit the program to a select group of leading candidates.

On May 25, 1981, the Authority announced its intention to broadcast the previously selected interviews on a program entitled "A Closer Look." The following day, plaintiff McGlynn filed a complaint with the New Jersey Superior Court, Chancery Division, alleging that his exclusion from "A Closer Look" had violated his rights under the Federal Communications Act (FCA), the Campaign Expenditures and Reporting Act, N.J.Stat.Ann. § 19:44A–39, the Public Broadcasting Authority Act, N.J.Stat.Ann. § 48:23–1 *et seq.*, and the First and Fourteenth Amendments. Plaintiff's action was transferred to the appellate division which issued an order on May 27, 1981, requiring that the taped interviews of the excluded candidates be broadcast at approximately the same hour as the original telecasts on "A Closer Look." The appellate division order was summarily affirmed by the New Jersey Supreme Court following an appeal by the Authority. 434 A.2d 1056 (N.J.1981). After the primary election was held, the New Jersey Supreme Court granted the Authority's petition for rehearing in order to clarify its previous ruling.

On rehearing, the *McGlynn* court ruled first that the Federal Communications Act did not preempt state law and second, that the First Amendment did not preclude state limitation on the editorial discretion of the state-owned/operated television authority. The New Jersey Supreme Court took notice of the equal opportunity provisions of 47 U.S.C. § 315, particularly its provisions which eliminate bona fide newscasts, interviews, news documentaries, and on-the-spot coverage of bona fide news events from all equal time constraints. The court noted that Congress, in enacting these "news" exemptions, recognized that an all-inclusive equal time requirement would inhibit campaign coverage and would actually be more detrimental to the public than preferential treatment of candidates. Further, the *McGlynn* court noted that it was FCC policy to accord individual broadcasters a great deal of deference in determining what telecasts are exempt under the enumerated "news" exemptions. See text, p. 805.

The New Jersey Supreme Court did not agree with the New Jersey Public Broadcasting Authority's assertion that 47 U.S.C. § 315 preempted state provisions which imposed greater "equal-opportunity" obligations on broadcasters. The issue was whether New Jersey's Campaign and Expenditures and Reporting Act, N.J.Stat.

Ann. § 19:44A–39, which placed an affirmative duty on public broadcasters to cover the gubernatorial campaign, actually conflicted with 47 U.S.C. § 315.

In answering this important question, the New Jersey Supreme Court found it dispositive that the Authority was owned and operated as an instrumentality of the State of New Jersey. New Jersey, in this situation, was acting as a broadcast proprietor rather than as a government regulator of private business. Consequently, using logic analogous to that of the Supreme Court in Hughes v. Alexandria Scrap Corp., 426 U.S. 794 (1976), the court ruled that New Jersey has the same freedoms as a private citizen in determining the degree to which the equal opportunity provisions of 47 U.S.C. § 315 apply. "It follows, in this context, that N.J.S.A. § 19:44A–39 is not a governmental restraint upon a broadcast medium. Rather, it constitutes an exercise of discretion on the part of the State in its capacity as a Federal licensee under the FCA. Thus, since the statutes in question were passed *pursuant* to, rather than in conflict with, the FCA, the statutes are not preempted by the FCA."

The *McGlynn* court also rejected any claim that the First Amendment barred the New Jersey Legislature from imposing on the Authority the requirements of subsection 7(h) of the Authority Act, N.J.Stat. Ann. 48:23–7(h) that: "[p]rograms or series of programs of a controversial nature shall be presented with balance, fairness and equity."

The court held that:

> The First Amendment limits governmental restraints on *private* participation in the marketplace of ideas. However, it does not prevent government itself from participating, Community-Service Broadcasting v. FCC, 593 F.2d 1102, 1110 n. 14 (D.C.Cir.1978); L. Tribe, *American Constitutional Law,* 588–90 (1978), and when the state exercises its freedom to speak, it may express its own viewpoint * * * as it may neutrally relay the messages of others. The goal of the New Jersey statutory scheme is to use the state television network to neutrally relay the messages of the candidates for governor of New Jersey.

Thus, as no private speech had been abridged, the court affirmed the constitutionality of subsection 7(h).

Though the New Jersey Supreme Court had ruled in favor of plaintiff McGlynn on the jurisdictional and constitutional issues, the court reversed its previous ruling that had guaranteed gubernatorial candidates equal access under New Jersey law. This holding was based primarily upon its interpretation of the 1981 Amendment to the Campaign Expenditures and Reporting Act. Act of April 2, 1981, ch. 107, § 1, 1981, N.J.Sess. Law Serv. 265 (codified at N.J.Stat.Ann. § 19:44A–39 (1981). That amendment eliminated the rigid equal time requirements previously contained in the act and replaced them with a "general obligation to promote full discussion by the candidates in accordance with Federal Law." The court said that this amended provision, when read with the relevant provisions of the Authority Act, subsection 7(h), imposed an affirmative duty on the Authority to "promote full discussions by the gubernatorial candidates in a balanced, fair, and equitable fashion." It did not confer a general right of access to gubernatorial candidates. Rather, it required only that the Authority provide a fair distribution of air time.

The New Jersey Supreme Court also rejected the assertion that the New Jersey statutory scheme, as construed in the majority's holding, converted the Authority into a "public-forum" to which *all* citizens have a right of access. Justice Pashman for the court noted that the public forum concept has been strictly limited to those facilities in which tradition mandates a right of access. Citing Muir v. Alabama Television Commission, 7 Med.L.Rptr. 1933, 656 F.2d 1012 (5th Cir. 1981), he further noted that the broadcast media, which lack the requisite tradition of public access, may be converted into a public forum only when it has been "dedicated to public use." Any right of access arising under New Jersey statutes, the majority claimed, was not created for public use. It extends only to "legally qualified candidates, in only one election, which occurs only once every four years." Thus, in the holding of the majority, no public forum has or may have been created.

In Note, *Political Broadcasting—New Jersey Public Broadcasting Authority Mandated to Cover Gubernatorial Elections with Balance,* 13 Seton Hall L.Rev. 153 (1982), it is pointed out that the *McGlynn* decision authorizes the use of two standards of review *vis-à-vis* New Jersey public broadcasters, the "fairness" standard applied by the FCC pursuant to 47 U.S.C. § 315, and the amorphous "balance, fairness, and equity" standard to be applied by state courts pursuant to N.J. Stat.Ann. § 19:44A–39 (West's, 1982) and N.J.Stat.Ann. § 48:23–7(h) (West's, 1982). The advent of the new state standard is likely to create confusion. In New Jersey this confusion was particularly troublesome since local news reports of state-owned public television stations are the primary source of gubernatorial election coverage. The New Jersey electorate must therefore rely on a public broadcasting system whose editorial discretion is presently subject to an uncertain set of standards. Campaign coverage in New Jersey now depends on the ability of the Authority to skillfully carry out the New Jersey fairness mandate.

Does the *McGlynn* decision threaten the Authority's editorial function? Though the decision stopped short of assigning the Authority to be a common carrier of campaign information, the decision could deleteriously restrict a reporter's ability and freedom to serve the public by inhibiting news coverage in delicate circumstances.

Will candidates for office now seek to find in public broadcasting a coverage denied them on commercial broadcasting? Will *McGlynn* encourage state legislatures to draft New Jersey-type fairness statutes to govern their public broadcasting authorities?

The Constitution of the United States

PREAMBLE

We the People of the United States, in Order to form a more perfect Union, establish Justice, insure domestic Tranquility, provide for the common defence, promote the general Welfare, and secure the Blessings of Liberty to ourselves and our Posterity, do ordain and establish this Constitution for the United States of America.

ARTICLE I

Section 1. All legislative Powers herein granted shall be vested in a Congress of the United States, which shall consist of a Senate and House of Representatives.

Section 2. [1] The House of Representatives shall be composed of Members chosen every second Year by the People of the several States, and the Electors in each State shall have the Qualifications requisite for Electors of the most numerous Branch of the State Legislature.

[2] No Person shall be a Representative who shall not have attained to the Age of twenty five Years, and been seven Years a Citizen of the United States, and who shall not, when elected, be an Inhabitant of that State in which he shall be chosen.

[3] Representatives and direct Taxes shall be apportioned among the several States which may be included within this Union, according to their respective Numbers, which shall be determined by adding to the whole Number of free Persons, including those bound to Service for a Term of Years, and excluding Indians not taxed, three fifths of all other Persons. The actual Enumeration shall be made within three Years after the first Meeting of the Congress of the United States, and within every subsequent Term of ten Years, in such Manner as they shall by Law direct. The Number of Representatives shall not exceed one for every thirty Thousand, but each State shall have at Least one Representative; and until such enumeration shall be made, the State of New Hampshire shall be entitled to chuse three, Massachusetts eight, Rhode Island and Providence Plantations one, Connecticut five, New York six, New Jersey four, Pennsylvania eight, Delaware one, Maryland six, Virginia ten, North Carolina five, South Carolina five, and Georgia three.

[4] When vacancies happen in the Representation from any State, the Executive Authority thereof shall issue Writs of Election to fill such Vacancies.

[5] The House of Representatives shall chuse their Speaker and other Officers; and shall have the sole Power of Impeachment.

Section 3. [1] The Senate of the United States shall be composed of two Senators from each State, chosen by the Legislature thereof, for six Years; and each Senator shall have one Vote.

[2] Immediately after they shall be assembled in Consequence of the first Election, they shall be divided as equally as may be into three Classes. The Seats of the Senators of the first Class shall be vacated at the Expiration of the Second Year, of the second Class at the Expiration of the fourth Year, and of the third Class at the Expiration of the sixth Year, so that one third may be chosen every second Year; and if Vacancies happen by Resignation, or otherwise, during the Recess of the Legislature of any State, the Executive thereof may make temporary Appointments until the next Meeting of the Legislature, which shall then fill such Vacancies.

[3] No Person shall be a Senator who shall not have attained to the Age of thirty Years, and been nine Years a Citizen of the United States, and who shall not, when elected, be an Inhabitant of that State for which he shall be chosen.

[4] The Vice President of the United States shall be President of the Senate, but shall have no Vote, unless they be equally divided.

[5] The Senate shall chuse their other Officers, and also a President pro tempore, in the Absence of the Vice President, or when he

shall exercise the Office of President of the United States.

[6] The Senate shall have the sole Power to try all Impeachments. When sitting for that Purpose, they shall be on Oath or Affirmation. When the President of the United States is tried, the Chief Justice shall preside: And no Person shall be convicted without the Concurrence of two thirds of the Members present.

[7] Judgment in Cases of Impeachment shall not extend further than to removal from Office, and disqualification to hold and enjoy any Office of honor, Trust, or Profit under the United States: but the Party convicted shall nevertheless be liable and subject to Indictment, Trial, Judgment, and Punishment, according to Law.

Section 4. [1] The Times, Places and Manner of holding Elections for Senators and Representatives, shall be prescribed in each State by the Legislature thereof; but the Congress may at any time by Law make or alter such Regulations, except as to the Places of chusing Senators.

[2] The Congress shall assemble at least once in every Year, and such Meeting shall be on the first Monday in December, unless they shall by Law appoint a different Day.

Section 5. [1] Each House shall be the Judge of the Elections, Returns, and Qualifications of its own Members, and a Majority of each shall constitute a Quorum to do Business; but a smaller Number may adjourn from day to day, and may be authorized to compel the Attendance of absent Members, in such Manner, and under such Penalties as each House may provide.

[2] Each House may determine the Rules of its Proceedings, punish its Members for disorderly Behavior, and, with the Concurrence of two thirds, expel a Member.

[3] Each House shall keep a Journal of its Proceedings, and from time to time publish the same, excepting such Parts as may in their Judgment require Secrecy; and the Yeas and Nays of the Members of either House on any question shall, at the Desire of one fifth of those Present, be entered on the Journal.

[4] Neither House, during the Session of Congress, shall, without the Consent of the other, adjourn for more than three days, nor to any other Place than that in which the two Houses shall be sitting.

Section 6. [1] The Senators and Representatives shall receive a Compensation for their Services, to be ascertained by Law, and paid out of the Treasury of the United States. They shall in all Cases, except Treason, Felony and Breach of the Peace, be privileged from Arrest during their Attendance at the Session of their respective Houses, and in going to and returning from the same; and for any Speech or Debate in either House, they shall not be questioned in any other Place.

[2] No Senator or Representative shall, during the Time for which he was elected, be appointed to any civil Office under the Authority of the United States, which shall have been created, or the Emoluments whereof shall have been increased during such time; and no Person holding any Office under the United States, shall be a Member of either House during his Continuance in Office.

Section 7. [1] All Bills for raising Revenue shall originate in the House of Representatives; but the Senate may propose or concur with Amendments as on other Bills.

[2] Every Bill which shall have passed the House of Representatives and the Senate, shall, before it becomes a Law, be presented to the President of the United States; If he approve he shall sign it, but if not he shall return it, with his Objections to the House in which it shall have originated, who shall enter the Objections at large on their Journal, and proceed to reconsider it. If after such Reconsideration two thirds of that House shall agree to pass the Bill, it shall be sent together with the Objections, to the other House, by which it shall likewise be reconsidered, and if approved by two thirds of that House, it shall become a Law. But in all such Cases the Votes of both Houses shall be determined by yeas and Nays, and the Names of the Persons voting for and against the Bill shall be entered on the Journal of each House respectively. If any Bill shall not be returned by the President within ten Days (Sundays excepted) after it shall have been presented to him, the Same shall be a Law, in like Manner as if he had signed it, unless the Congress by

their Adjournment prevent its Return in which Case it shall not be a Law.

[3] Every Order, Resolution, or Vote, to Which the Concurrence of the Senate and House of Representatives may be necessary (except on a question of Adjournment) shall be presented to the President of the United States; and before the Same shall take Effect, shall be approved by him, or being disapproved by him, shall be repassed by two thirds of the Senate and House of Representatives, according to the Rules and Limitations prescribed in the Case of a Bill.

Section 8. [1] The Congress shall have Power To lay and collect Taxes, Duties, Imposts and Excises, to pay the Debts and provide for the common Defence and general Welfare of the United States; but all Duties, Imposts and Excises shall be uniform throughout the United States;

[2] To borrow money on the credit of the United States;

[3] To regulate Commerce with foreign Nations, and among the several States, and with the Indian Tribes;

[4] To establish an uniform Rule of Naturalization, and uniform Laws on the subject of Bankruptcies throughout the United States;

[5] To coin Money, regulate the Value thereof, and of foreign Coin, and fix the Standard of Weights and Measures;

[6] To provide for the Punishment of counterfeiting the Securities and current Coin of the United States;

[7] To Establish Post Offices and Post Roads;

[8] To promote the Progress of Science and useful Arts, by securing for limited Times to Authors and Inventors the exclusive Right to their respective Writings and Discoveries;

[9] To constitute Tribunals inferior to the supreme Court;

[10] To define and punish Piracies and Felonies committed on the high Seas, and Offenses against the Law of Nations;

[11] To declare War, grant Letters of Marque and Reprisal, and make Rules concerning Captures on Land and Water;

[12] To raise and support Armies, but no Appropriation of Money to that Use shall be for a longer Term than two Years;

[13] To provide and maintain a Navy;

[14] To make Rules for the Government and Regulation of the land and naval Forces;

[15] To provide for calling forth the Militia to execute the Laws of the Union, suppress Insurrections and repel Invasions;

[16] To provide for organizing, arming, and disciplining, the Militia, and for governing such Part of them as may be employed in the Service of the United States, reserving to the States respectively, the Appointment of the Officers, and the Authority of training the Militia according to the discipline prescribed by Congress;

[17] To exercise exclusive Legislation in all Cases whatsoever, over such District (not exceeding ten Miles square) as may, by Cession of particular States, and the Acceptance of Congress, become the Seat of the Government of the United States, and to exercise like Authority over all Places purchased by the Consent of the Legislature of the State in which the Same shall be, for the Erection of Forts, Magazines, Arsenals, dock-Yards, and other needful Buildings;—And

[18] To make all Laws which shall be necessary and proper for carrying into Execution the foregoing Powers, and all other Powers vested by this Constitution in the Government of the United States, or in any Department or Officer thereof.

Section 9. [1] The Migration or Importation of Such Persons as any of the States now existing shall think proper to admit, shall not be prohibited by the Congress prior to the Year one thousand eight hundred and eight, but a Tax or duty may be imposed on such Importation, not exceeding ten dollars for each Person.

[2] The privilege of the Writ of Habeas Corpus shall not be suspended, unless when in Cases of Rebellion or Invasion the public Safety may require it.

[3] No Bill of Attainder or ex post facto Law shall be passed.

[4] No Capitation, or other direct, Tax shall be laid, unless in Proportion to the Census or Enumeration herein before directed to be taken.

[5] No Tax or Duty shall be laid on Articles exported from any State.

[6] No Preference shall be given by any Regulation of Commerce or Revenue to the Ports of one State over those of another: nor shall Vessels bound to, or from, one State be obliged to enter, clear, or pay Duties in another.

[7] No money shall be drawn from the Treasury, but in Consequence of Appropriations made by Law; and a regular Statement and Account of the Receipts and Expenditures of all public Money shall be published from time to time.

[8] No Title of Nobility shall be granted by the United States: And no Person holding any Office of Profit or Trust under them, shall, without the Consent of the Congress, accept of any present, Emolument, Office, or Title, of any kind whatever, from any King, Prince, or foreign State.

Section 10. [1] No State shall enter into any Treaty, Alliance, or Confederation; grant Letters of Marque and Reprisal; coin Money; emit Bills of Credit; make any Thing but gold and silver Coin a Tender in Payment of Debts; pass any Bill of Attainder, ex post facto Law, or Law impairing the Obligation of Contracts, or grant any Title of Nobility.

[2] No State shall, without the Consent of the Congress, lay any Imposts or Duties on Imports or Exports, except what may be absolutely necessary for executing it's inspection Laws: and the net Produce of all Duties and Imposts, laid by any State on Imports or Exports, shall be for the Use of the Treasury of the United States; and all such Laws shall be subject to the Revision and Controul of the Congress.

[3] No State shall, without the Consent of Congress, lay any Duty of Tonnage, keep Troops, or Ships of War in time of Peace, enter into any Agreement or Compact with another State, or with a foreign Power, or engage in War, unless actually invaded, or in such imminent Danger as will not admit of delay.

ARTICLE II

Section 1. [1] The executive Power shall be vested in a President of the United States of America. He shall hold his Office during the Term of four Years, and, together with the Vice President, chosen for the same Term, be elected, as follows:

[2] Each State shall appoint, in such Manner as the Legislature thereof may direct, a Number of Electors, equal to the whole Number of Senators and Representatives to which the State may be entitled in the Congress; but no Senator or Representative, or Person holding an Office of Trust or Profit under the United States, shall be appointed an Elector.

[3] The Electors shall meet in their respective States, and vote by Ballot for two Persons, of whom one at least shall not be an Inhabitant of the same State with themselves. And they shall make a List of all the Persons voted for, and of the Number of Votes for each; which List they shall sign and certify, and transmit sealed to the Seat of the Government of the United States, directed to the President of the Senate. The President of the Senate shall, in the Presence of the Senate and House of Representatives, open all the Certificates, and the Votes shall then be counted. The Person having the greatest Number of Votes shall be the President, if such Number be a Majority of the whole Number of Electors appointed; and if there be more than one who have such Majority, and have an equal Number of Votes, then the House of Representatives shall immediately chuse by Ballot one of them for President; and if no Person have a Majority, then from the five highest on the List the said House shall in like Manner chuse the President. But in chusing the President, the Votes shall be taken by States the Representation from each State having one Vote; A quorum for this Purpose shall consist of a Member or Members from two thirds of the States, and a Majority of all the States shall be necessary to a Choice. In every Case, after the Choice of the President, the Person having the greater Number of Votes of the Electors shall be the Vice President. But if there should remain two or more who have equal Votes, the Senate shall chuse from them by Ballot the Vice President.

[4] The Congress may determine the Time of chusing the Electors, and the Day on which they shall give their Votes; which Day shall be the same throughout the United States.

[5] No person except a natural born Citizen, or a Citizen of the United States, at the time of the Adoption of this Constitution, shall be eligible to the Office of President; neither shall any Person be eligible to that Office who shall not have attained to the Age of thirty-five Years, and been fourteen Years a Resident within the United States.

[6] In case of the removal of the President from Office, or of his Death, Resignation or Inability to discharge the Powers and Duties of the said Office, the Same shall devolve on the Vice President, and the Congress may by Law provide for the Case of Removal, Death, Resignation or Inability, both of the President and Vice President, declaring what Officer shall then act as President, and such Officer shall act accordingly, until the Disability be removed, or a President shall be elected.

[7] The President shall, at stated Times, receive for his Services, a Compensation, which shall neither be increased nor diminished during the Period for which he shall have been elected, and he shall not receive within that Period any other Emolument from the United States, or any of them.

[8] Before he enter on the Execution of his Office, he shall take the following Oath or Affirmation: "I do solemnly swear (or affirm) that I will faithfully execute the Office of President of the United States, and will to the best of my Ability, preserve, protect and defend the Constitution of the United States."

Section 2. [1] The President shall be Commander in Chief of the Army and Navy of the United States, and of the militia of the several States, when called into the actual Service of the United States; he may require the Opinion, in writing, of the principal Officer in each of the Executive Departments, upon any Subject relating to the Duties of their respective Offices, and he shall have Power to grant Reprieves and Pardons for Offenses against the United States, except in Cases of Impeachment.

[2] He shall have Power, by and with the Advice and Consent of the Senate to make Treaties, provided two thirds of the Senators present concur; and he shall nominate, and by and with the Advice and Consent of the Senate, shall appoint Ambassadors, other public Ministers and Consuls, Judges of the supreme Court, and all other Officers of the United States, whose Appointments are not herein otherwise provided for, and which shall be established by Law; but the Congress may by Law vest the Appointment of such inferior Officers, as they think proper, in the President alone, in the Courts of Law, or in the Heads of Departments.

[3] The President shall have Power to fill up all Vacancies that may happen during the Recess of the Senate, by granting Commissions which shall expire at the End of their next Session.

Section 3. He shall from time to time give to the Congress Information of the State of the Union, and recommend to their Consideration such Measures as he shall judge necessary and expedient; he may, on extraordinary Occasions, convene both Houses, or either of them, and in Case of Disagreement between them, with Respect to the Time of Adjournment, he may adjourn them to such Time as he shall think proper; he shall receive Ambassadors and other public Ministers; he shall take Care that the Laws be faithfully executed, and shall Commission all the Officers of the United States.

Section 4. The President, Vice President and all civil Officers of the United States, shall be removed from Office on Impeachment for, and Conviction of, Treason, Bribery, or other high Crimes and Misdemeanors.

ARTICLE III

Section 1. The judicial Power of the United States, shall be vested in one supreme Court, and in such inferior Courts as the Congress may from time to time ordain and establish. The Judges, both of the supreme and inferior Courts, shall hold their Offices during good Behaviour, and shall, at stated Times, receive for their Services a Compensation, which shall not be diminished during their Continuance in Office.

Section 2. [1] The judicial Power shall extend to all Cases, in Law and Equity, arising under this Constitution, the Laws of the United

States, and Treaties made, or which shall be made, under their Authority;—to all Cases affecting Ambassadors, other public Ministers and Consuls;—to all Cases of admiralty and maritime Jurisdiction;—to Controversies to which the United States shall be a Party;—to Controversies between two or more States;—between a State and Citizens of another State;—between Citizens of different States;—between Citizens of the same State claiming Lands under the Grants of different States, and between a State, or the Citizens thereof, and foreign States, Citizens or Subjects.

[2] In all Cases affecting Ambassadors, other public Ministers and Consuls, and those in which a State shall be a Party, the supreme Court shall have original Jurisdiction. In all the other Cases before mentioned, the supreme Court shall have appellate Jurisdiction, both as to Law and Fact, with such Exceptions, and under such Regulations as the Congress shall make.

[3] The trial of all Crimes, except in Cases of Impeachment, shall be by Jury; and such Trial shall be held in the State where the said Crimes shall have been committed; but when not committed within any State, the Trial shall be at such Place or Places as the Congress may by Law have directed.

Section 3. [1] Treason against the United States, shall consist only in levying War against them, or, in adhering to their Enemies, giving them Aid and Comfort. No Person shall be convicted of Treason unless on the Testimony of two Witnesses to the same overt Act, or on Confession in open Court.

[2] The Congress shall have Power to declare the Punishment of Treason, but no Attainder of Treason shall work Corruption of Blood, or Forfeiture except during the Life of the Person attainted.

ARTICLE IV

Section 1. Full Faith and Credit shall be given in each State to the public Acts, Records, and judicial Proceedings of every other State. And the Congress may by general Laws prescribe the Manner in which such Acts, Records and Proceedings shall be proved, and the Effect thereof.

Section 2. [1] The Citizens of each State shall be entitled to all Privileges and Immunities of Citizens in the several States.

[2] A Person charged in any State with Treason, Felony, or other Crime, who shall flee from Justice, and be found in another State, shall on demand of the executive Authority of the State from which he fled, be delivered up, to be removed to the State having Jurisdiction of the Crime.

[3] No Person held to Service or Labour in one State, under the Laws thereof, escaping into another, shall, in Consequence of any Law or Regulation therein, be discharged from such Service or Labour, but shall be delivered up on Claim of the Party to whom such Service or Labour may be due.

Section 3. [1] New States may be admitted by the Congress into this Union; but no new State shall be formed or erected within the Jurisdiction of any other State; nor any State be formed by the Junction of two or more States, or Parts of States, without the Consent of the Legislatures of the States concerned as well as of the Congress.

[2] The Congress shall have Power to dispose of and make all needful Rules and Regulations respecting the Territory or other Property belonging to the United States; and nothing in this Constitution shall be so construed as to Prejudice any Claims of the United States, or of any particular State.

Section 4. The United States shall guarantee to every State in this Union a Republican Form of Government, and shall protect each of them against Invasion; and on Application of the Legislature, or of the Executive (when the Legislature cannot be convened) against domestic Violence.

ARTICLE V

The Congress, whenever two thirds of both Houses shall deem it necessary, shall propose Amendments to this Constitution, or, on the Application of the Legislatures of two thirds of the several States, shall call a Convention for proposing Amendments, which, in either Case, shall be valid to all Intents and Purposes, as part of this Constitution, when ratified by the Legislatures of three fourths of the several States, or by Conventions in three fourths thereof, as the one or the other Mode of Ratification may be proposed by the Congress; Provided that no Amendment which may be made prior to the Year One thousand eight hundred and eight shall in any Manner affect the first and fourth Clauses in the Ninth Section of the first Article; and that no State, without its Consent, shall be deprived of its equal Suffrage in the Senate.

ARTICLE VI

[1] All Debts contracted and Engagements entered into, before the Adoption of this Constitution shall be as valid against the United States under this Constitution, as under the Confederation.

[2] This Constitution, and the Laws of the United States which shall be made in Pursuance thereof; and all Treaties made, or which shall be made, under the Authority of the United States, shall be the supreme Law of the Land; and the Judges in every State shall be bound thereby, any Thing in the Constitution or Laws of any State to the Contrary notwithstanding.

[3] The Senators and Representatives before mentioned, and the Members of the several State Legislatures, and all executive and judicial Officers, both of the United States and of the several States, shall be bound by Oath or Affirmation, to support this Constitution; but no religious Test shall ever be required as a Qualification to any Office or public Trust under the United States.

ARTICLE VII

The Ratification of the Conventions of nine States shall be sufficient for the Establishment of this Constitution between the States so ratifying the Same.

AMENDMENT I [1791]

Congress shall make no law respecting an establishment of religion, or prohibiting the free exercise thereof; or abridging the freedom of speech, or of the press; or the right of the people peaceably to assemble, and to petition the Government for a redress of grievances.

AMENDMENT II [1791]

A well regulated Militia, being necessary to the security of a free State, the right of the people to keep and bear Arms, shall not be infringed.

AMENDMENT III [1791]

No Soldier shall, in time of peace be quartered in any house, without the consent of the Owner, nor in time of war, but in a manner to be prescribed by law.

AMENDMENT IV [1791]

The right of the people to be secure in their persons, houses, papers, and effects, against unreasonable searches and seizures, shall not be violated, and no Warrants shall issue, but upon probable cause, supported by Oath or affirmation, and particularly describing the place to be searched, and the persons or things to be seized.

AMENDMENT V [1791]

No person shall be held to answer for a capital, or otherwise infamous crime, unless on a presentment or indictment of a Grand Jury, except in cases arising in the land or naval forces, or in the Militia, when in actual service in time of War or public danger; nor shall any person be subject for the same offence to be twice put in jeopardy of life or limb; nor shall be compelled in any criminal case to be a witness against himself, nor be deprived of life, liberty, or property, without due process of law; nor shall private property be taken for public use, without just compensation.

AMENDMENT VI [1791]

In all criminal prosecutions, the accused shall enjoy the right to a speedy and public trial, by an impartial jury of the State and district wherein the crime shall have been committed, which district shall have been previously ascertained by law, and to be informed of the nature and cause of the accusation; to be confronted with the witnesses against him; to have compulsory process for obtaining witnesses in his favor, and to have the Assistance of Counsel for his defence.

AMENDMENT VII [1791]

In Suits at common law, where the value in controversy shall exceed twenty dollars, the right of trial by jury shall be preserved, and no fact tried by jury, shall be otherwise re-examined in any Court of the United States, than according to the rules of the common law.

Amendment VIII [1791]

Excessive bail shall not be required, nor excessive fines imposed, nor cruel and unusual punishments inflicted.

Amendment IX [1791]

The enumeration in the Constitution, of certain rights, shall not be construed to deny or disparage others retained by the people.

Amendment X [1791]

The powers not delegated to the United States by the Constitution, nor prohibited by it to the States, are reserved to the States respectively, or to the people.

Amendment XI [1798]

The Judicial power of the United States shall not be construed to extend to any suit in law or equity, commenced or prosecuted against one of the United States by Citizens of another State, or by Citizens or Subjects of any Foreign State.

Amendment XII [1804]

The Electors shall meet in their respective states and vote by ballot for President and Vice-President, one of whom, at least, shall not be an inhabitant of the same state with themselves; they shall name in their ballots the person voted for as President, and in distinct ballots the person voted for as Vice-President, and they shall make distinct lists of all persons voted for as President, and of all persons voted for as Vice-President, and of the number of votes for each, which lists they shall sign and certify, and transmit sealed to the seat of the government of the United States, directed to the President of the Senate;—The President of the Senate shall, in the presence of the Senate and House of Representatives, open all the certificates and the votes shall then be counted;—The person having the greatest number of votes for President, shall be the President, if such number be a majority of the whole number of Electors appointed; and if no person have such majority, then from the persons having the highest numbers not exceeding three on the list of those voted for as President, the House of Representatives shall choose immediately, by ballot, the President. But in choosing the President, the votes shall be taken by states, the representation from each state having one vote; a quorum for this purpose shall consist of a member or members from two-thirds of the states, and a majority of all states shall be necessary to a choice. And if the House of Representatives shall not choose a President whenever the right of choice shall devolve upon them before the fourth day of March next following, then the Vice-President shall act as President, as in the case of the death or other constitutional disability of the President.—The person having the greatest number of votes as Vice-President, shall be the Vice-President, if such number be a majority of the whole number of Electors appointed, and if no person have a majority, then from the two highest numbers on the list, the Senate shall choose the Vice-President; a quorum for the purpose shall consist of two-thirds of the whole number of Senators, and a majority of the whole number shall be necessary to a choice. But no person constitutionally ineligible to the office of President shall be eligible to that of Vice-President of the United States.

Amendment XIII [1865]

Section 1. Neither slavery nor involuntary servitude, except as a punishment for crime whereof the party shall have been duly convicted, shall exist within the United States, or any place subject to their jurisdiction.

Section 2. Congress shall have power to enforce this article by appropriate legislation.

Amendment XIV [1868]

Section 1. All persons born or naturalized in the United States, and subject to the jurisdiction thereof, are citizens of the United States and of the State wherein they reside. No State shall make or enforce any law which shall abridge the privileges or immunities of citizens of the United States; nor shall any State deprive any person of life, liberty, or property, without due process of law; nor deny to any person within its jurisdiction the equal protection of the laws.

Section 2. Representatives shall be apportioned among the several States according to their respective numbers, counting the whole number of persons in each State, excluding Indians not taxed. But when the right to vote at any election for the choice of electors for President and Vice President of the United States, Representatives in Congress, the Executive and Judicial officers of a State, or the members of the Legislature thereof, is denied to any of the male inhabitants of such State, being twenty-one years of age, and citizens of the United States, or in any way abridged, except for participation in rebellion, or other crime, the basis of representation therein shall be reduced in the proportion which the number of such male citizens shall bear to the whole number of male citizens twenty-one years of age in such State.

Section 3. No person shall be a Senator or Representative in Congress, or elector of President and Vice President, or hold any office, civil or military, under the United States, or under any State, who having previously taken an oath, as a member of Congress, or as an officer of the United States, or as a member of any State legislature, or as an executive or judicial officer of any State, to support the Constitution of the United States, shall have engaged in insurrection or rebellion against the same, or given aid or comfort to the enemies thereof. But Congress may by a vote of two-thirds of each House, remove such disability.

Section 4. The validity of the public debt of the United States, authorized by law, including debts incurred for payment of pensions and bounties for services in suppressing insurrection or rebellion, shall not be questioned. But neither the United States nor any State shall assume or pay any debt or obligation incurred in aid of insurrection or rebellion against the United States, or any claim for the loss or emancipation of any slave; but all such debts, obligations and claims shall be held illegal and void.

Section 5. The Congress shall have power to enforce, by appropriate legislation, the provisions of this article.

Amendment XV [1870]

Section 1. The right of citizens of the United States to vote shall not be denied or abridged by the United States or by any State on account of race, color, or previous condition of servitude.

Section 2. The Congress shall have power to enforce this article by appropriate legislation.

Amendment XVI [1913]

The Congress shall have power to lay and collect taxes on incomes, from whatever source derived, without apportionment among the several States, and without regard to any census or enumeration.

Amendment XVII [1913]

[1] The Senate of the United States shall be composed of two Senators from each State, elected by the people thereof, for six years; and each Senator shall have one vote. The electors in each State shall have the qualifications requisite for electors of the most numerous branch of the State legislatures.

[2] When vacancies happen in the representation of any State in the Senate, the executive authority of such State shall issue writs of election to fill such vacancies: *Provided*, That the legislature of any State may empower the executive thereof to make temporary appointments until the people fill the vacancies by election as the legislature may direct.

[3] This amendment shall not be so construed as to affect the election or term of any Senator chosen before it becomes valid as part of the Constitution.

Amendment XVIII [1919]

Section 1. After one year from the ratification of this article the manufacture, sale, or transportation of intoxicating liquors within, the importation thereof into, or the exportation thereof from the United States and all territory subject to the jurisdiction thereof for beverage purposes is hereby prohibited.

Section 2. The Congress and the several States shall have concurrent power to enforce this article by appropriate legislation.

Section 3. This article shall be inoperative unless it shall have been ratified as an amendment to the Constitution by the legislatures of the several States, as provided in the Constitution, within seven years from the date of the submission hereof to the States by the Congress.

Amendment XIX [1920]

[1] The right of citizens of the United States to vote shall not be denied or abridged by the United States or by any State on account of sex.

[2] Congress shall have power to enforce this article by appropriate legislation.

Amendment XX [1933]

Section 1. The terms of the President and Vice President shall end at noon on the 20th day of January, and the terms of Senators and Representatives at noon on the 3d day of January, of the years in which such terms would have ended if this article had not been ratified; and the terms of their successors shall then begin.

Section 2. The Congress shall assemble at least once in every year, and such meeting shall begin at noon on the 3d day of January, unless they shall by law appoint a different day.

Section 3. If, at the time fixed for the beginning of the term of the President, the President elect shall have died, the Vice President elect shall become President. If the President shall not have been chosen before the time fixed for the beginning of his term, or if the President elect shall have failed to qualify, then the Vice President elect shall act as President until a President shall have qualified; and the Congress may by law provide for the case wherein neither a President elect nor a Vice President elect shall have qualified, declaring who shall then act as President, or the manner in which one who is to act shall be selected, and such person shall act accordingly until a President or Vice President shall have qualified.

Section 4. The Congress may by law provide for the case of the death of any of the persons from whom the House of Representatives may choose a President whenever the right of choice shall have devolved upon them, and for the case of the death of any of the persons from whom the Senate may choose a Vice President whenever the right of choice shall have devolved upon them.

Section 5. Sections 1 and 2 shall take effect on the 15th day of October following the ratification of this article.

Section 6. This article shall be inoperative unless it shall have been ratified as an amendment to the Constitution by the legislatures of three-fourths of the several States within seven years from the date of its submission.

Amendment XXI [1933]

Section 1. The eighteenth article of amendment to the Constitution of the United States is hereby repealed.

Section 2. The transportation or importation into any State, Territory, or possession of the United States for delivery or use therein of intoxicating liquors, in violation of the laws thereof, is hereby prohibited.

Section 3. This article shall be inoperative unless it shall have been ratified as an amendment to the Constitution by conventions in the several States, as provided in the Constitution, within seven years from the date of the submission hereof to the States by the Congress.

Amendment XXII [1951]

Section 1. No person shall be elected to the office of the President more than twice, and no person who has held the office of President, or acted as President, for more than two years of a term to which some other person was elected President shall be elected to the office of President more than once. But this Article shall not apply to any person holding the office of President when this Article was proposed by the Congress, and shall not prevent any person who may be holding the office of President, or acting as President, during the term within which this Article becomes operative from holding the office of President or acting as President during the remainder of such term.

Section 2. This article shall be inoperative unless it shall have been ratified as an amendment to the Constitution by the legislatures of three-fourths of the several States within seven years from the date of its submission to the States by the Congress.

AMENDMENT XXIII [1961]

Section 1. The District constituting the seat of Government of the United States shall appoint in such manner as the Congress may direct:

A number of electors of President and Vice President equal to the whole number of Senators and Representatives in Congress to which the District would be entitled if it were a State, but in no event more than the least populous state; they shall be in addition to those appointed by the states, but they shall be considered, for the purposes of the election of President and Vice President, to be electors appointed by a state; and they shall meet in the District and perform such duties as provided by the twelfth article of amendment.

Section 2. The Congress shall have power to enforce this article by appropriate legislation.

AMENDMENT XXIV [1964]

Section 1. The right of citizens of the United States to vote in any primary or other election for President or Vice President, for electors for President or Vice President, or for Senator or Representative in Congress, shall not be denied or abridged by the United States or any State by reason of failure to pay any poll tax or other tax.

Section 2. The Congress shall have power to enforce this article by appropriate legislation.

AMENDMENT XXV [1967]

Section 1. In case of the removal of the President from office or of his death or resignation, the Vice President shall become President.

Section 2. Whenever there is a vacancy in the office of the Vice President, the President shall nominate a Vice President who shall take office upon confirmation by a majority vote of both Houses of Congress.

Section 3. Whenever the President transmits to the President pro tempore of the Senate and the Speaker of the House of Representatives his written declaration that he is unable to discharge the powers and duties of his office, and until he transmits to them a written declaration to the contrary, such powers and duties shall be discharged by the Vice President as Acting President.

Section 4. Whenever the Vice President and a majority of either the principal officers of the executive departments or of such other body as Congress may by law provide, transmit to the President pro tempore of the Senate and the Speaker of the House of Representatives their written declaration that the President is unable to discharge the powers and duties of his office, the Vice President shall immediately assume the powers and duties of the office as Acting President.

Thereafter, when the President transmits to the President pro tempore of the Senate and the Speaker of the House of Representatives his written declaration that no inability exists, he shall resume the powers and duties of his office unless the Vice President and a majority of either the principal officers of the executive department or of such other body as Congress may by law provide, transmit within four days to the President pro tempore of the Senate and the Speaker of the House of Representatives their written declaration and the President is unable to discharge the powers and duties of his office. Thereupon Congress shall decide the issue, assembling within forty-eight hours for that purpose if not in session. If the Congress, within twenty-one days after receipt of the latter written declaration, or, if Congress is not in session, within twenty-one days after Congress is required to assemble, determines by two-thirds vote of both Houses that the President is unable to discharge the powers and duties of his office, the Vice President shall continue to discharge the same as Acting President; otherwise, the President shall resume the powers and duties of his office.

AMENDMENT XXVI [1971]

Section 1. The right of citizens of the United States, who are eighteen years of age or older, to vote shall not be denied or abridged by the United States or by any State on account of age.

Section 2. The Congress shall have power to enforce this article by appropriate legislation.

Glossary

A

Actionable. Providing legal reasons for a lawsuit.

Affidavit. The sworn written statement of a party or a witness in a suit. The person who makes the statement is called an *affiant.*

Affirmed. Signifies that the appellate court agreed with the lower court's decision and has decided to let it stand after review, thus "affirming" it.

A fortiori. It follows unavoidably, as, for example, the next step in an argument.

Amicus Curiae. A friend of the court. Usually refers to legal briefs submitted to a court by persons or groups, not parties of record to an action. Briefs amici curiae are submitted to courts to help the court reach its decision and to bring to the attention of the court factors and problems raised by a case which the parties to the action may not bring to the court's attention.

Appellant. The party who appeals a lower court decision rendered against him to a higher court is the appellant.

Appellee. The party who opposes an appeal, and who is usually content with the lower court decision is the appellee. Courts sometimes use terms like "plaintiff-appellee" or "defendant-appellant" to indicate that the defendant lost at trial and now appeals, and plaintiff won below and now opposes the appeal.

A priori. From cause to effect. Inferring specific facts from general principles.

Arguendo. Assume something true for the sake of argument.

B

Balance of Interests Doctrine. This is an approach often used by courts in cases involving First Amendment issues. The stated mission of the doctrine or test is to weigh the state's interest in effecting a restraint on freedom of expression as distilled in a particular statute against the claim that the statute offends freedom of speech or press.

Bill of Attainder. A legislative act pronouncing a person guilty of a crime without a trial.

Barratry. Provoking a lawsuit intentionally, e.g., a lawyer for profit.

Bill of Rights. First 10 Amendments to the Constitution of the United States.

Black Letter Law. Legal principles accepted by the judiciary in most jurisdictions.

Brief. The written legal arguments which are presented to the court by a party to a lawsuit. A brief is generally partisan. The brief states the facts and the relevant legal authorities on which a party relies for the result which it thinks should obtain.

C

Canon Law. The law of the Church. During the Middle Ages, the ecclesiastical or church courts had considerable control over family and other matters. The law thus developed has influenced the common law.

Certiorari. A writ by which review of a case is sought in the United States Supreme Court. Technically, when the writ is granted, the Court will order the lower court to send the record of the case, a transcript of the proceedings below, up to the Supreme Court for it to review. The Supreme Court has discretion over which petitions for certiorari (cert.) it will or will not grant, and can thus retain control over what cases it will review. This practice should be contrasted with obtaining review by way of appeal, where, theoretically at least, if the statutory requirements for appeal are met, the Court is supposed to be obliged to review the lower court decision. The dismissal of an appeal is considered to be a disposition on the merits of a case, but the denial of a petition for a writ of certiorari is held to be no statement on the merits of the case itself. The situations in which review should be sought by way of appeal and certiorari are precisely set forth in the U.S. Judicial Code.

Civil Action. A lawsuit brought to enforce a right or redress a wrong.

Civil Law. Law based on codes originating with the Romans.

Clear and Convincing Proof (or evidence). A standard of proof in civil litigation more stringent than the normal requirement that the successful party be favored by the preponderance of the evidence. The standard is, yet, less stringent than the standard of proof used in criminal litigation which is that the evidence must show guilt beyond a reasonable doubt.

Collateral Estoppel. Prohibition of making a claim that has been disproved in a prior court.

Collusion. When two or more parties agree to maintain a suit even though there is no real adversity between them, it is termed collusion. When a suit is brought under these circumstances it is called a "collusive suit" and is constitutionally proscribed since the U.S. Constitution, Art. III, limits federal courts to deciding actual "cases or controversies". Also, when two parties agree to practice a fraud upon the court or a third party.

Common Law. The legal system of the United States and Great Britain and other countries whose formative legal institutions derive in some measure from England. A common law system is distinguished from the *civil law* systems of Europe since the former is based upon general rules and principles found in judicial decisions, as opposed to the codification of those rules and principles in statutory law. Common law is judge made law as opposed to law made by legislatures, or statutory law. The historic understanding of American law as common law is no longer apt since, increasingly, "law" in the United States is statutory law.

Complainant. The person who brings a lawsuit. It can also refer to the "complaining witness" or the person who has asked the state to bring criminal charges against the defendant. Often used as a synonym for plaintiff.

Concurring Opinion. When a court, consisting of more than one judge, reaches its decision, one or more of the judges on the court comprising the majority may agree with the decision reached, but for different reasons than those found in the court's opinion. Such judges may decide to state their separate reasons for joining in the result reached by the majority of the court in a concurring opinion. A concurring opinion is often used by a judge to emphasize or de-emphasize a particular portion of a majority opinion or to argue with a dissent (an opinion filed by a judge who disagrees with the court's decision and wishes to make the reasons explicit.)

Constitutional Law. Law based on the basic principles of the constitution as to structure, rights, and functions of government.

Contempt of Court. Any act which is deemed by a court to embarrass, hinder, or obstruct the court in the administration of justice or calculated to lessen its authority or its dignity. *Direct* contempt is committed in the presence of the court, or very near thereto, and can be punished summarily, without a jury trial. *Constructive* or indirect contempt refers to actions outside of court which hinder the administration of justice, as when a court order is not obeyed.

Contra. Against.

Counterclaim. A claim brought by the defendant *against* the plaintiff. A counterclaim may be similar to the plaintiff's claim against the defendant, or it might be totally unrelated to the plaintiff's claim.

D

Damages. Money that a person receives as compensation, as the result of a court order, for injury to her person, property, or rights because of the act, omission, or negligence of another.

Declaratory Judgment. A judicial decision that sets out the rights and obligations of the parties to a dispute and expresses an opinion on a question of law, but which does not necessarily order any coercive relief such as an injunction or damages.

Defeasance. A collateral deed made at the same time as another conveyance of property, containing certain conditions upon the performance of which the estate then created may be defeated, or totally undone.

Defendant. The party against whom a suit is brought. The defendant must answer the plaintiff's complaint and defend against his allegations. In criminal cases, the defendant is the party accused of crime by the state.

De jure. A matter of law whether or not consistent with fact.

De minimis. The law does not concern itself with trifles.

De novo. Means anew or fresh. A new trial of a case is a "trial de novo." A new trial can be granted by the trial judge or ordered by an appellate court.

Deposition. A sworn, recorded, oral statement made by a party or a witness out of court, either in the form of a narrative, or as answers to questions posed by an attorney. The party whose deposition is taken is called the deponent. The deposition is a device often used to obtain testimony in advance of a trial, or to secure the testimony of a person unable to come into court. A deposition can be used at trial to contradict a deponent's testimony at trial or it can be used in the event of the deponent's unavailability.

Dicta. See *Obiter dictum.*

Directed Verdict. The trial judge decides that as a matter of law reasonable men cannot differ concerning the proper verdict in a case, and directs the jurors to reach that verdict. The judge, in effect, makes the jury's decision for them; he takes it out of their hands.

Discovery. A period of information exchange between the parties in a lawsuit accomplished by interrogatories and deposition.

Disparagement. An untrue or misleading statement about a competitor's goods that is intended to influence, or tends to influence the public not to buy the goods. Trade disparagement is distinguished from libel in that it is directed toward the goods rather than the personal integrity of the merchant.

Diversity Action. An action brought in a federal court between parties who are citizens of different states. Such an action is based on the provision in the U.S. Constitution, Article III, granting jurisdiction to federal courts in diversity cases. Congress has enacted legislation, under this authority, granting the federal courts such jurisdiction. The action is in federal court *only* because the parties are from different states. The federal court, in this situation, is supposed to apply the substantive law of the state in which it sits.

Doctrine of Judicial Restraint. A doctrine associated in twentieth century American constitutional law with Supreme Court Justices Frankfurter and Harlan as well as many other jurists. Under this view, courts should only rarely exercise their power to invalidate legislation on constitutional grounds. This doctrine holds that as long as the legislation in controversy is reasonable and has some constitutional authorization it should be given a presumption of validity. The doctrine holds that in a democratic society nonelected judges should be reluctant to invalidate legislation enacted by the elected representatives of the people.

Doctrine of Preferred Freedoms. In constitutional litigation, a statute is normally presumed to be constitutional until it is shown to be otherwise. The doctrine of preferred freedoms states that when considering statutes that limit the individual rights guaranteed by the Bill of Rights and the fourteenth amendment, the normal presumption of constitutionality should not operate. When a statute seeks to limit a preferred freedom such as the freedom of expression, those who seek to uphold the statute must prove that it is constitutional, instead of making those who attack the statute prove that it is unconstitutional. The usual presumption of validity attaching to legislation attacked on constitutional grounds is thus reversed.

Duces tecum. A subpoena commanding a person to appear in court with documentary evidence; a subpoena *ad testificandum* commands a person to appear in court to give testimony.

Due Process. A complex of rights guaranteed by the fifth and fourteenth amendments to the U.S. Constitution, as interpreted by the Supreme Court. There are two kinds of due process. Procedural due process is offended when the fair procedures of the judicial process have not been complied with such as right to notice of the charges against one and a fair hearing concerning those charges. Substantive due process is offended by legislative action abridging substantive rights guaranteed by the due process clause of the fourteenth amendment such as freedom of speech, freedom of religion, freedom of assembly, etc.

E

Equity. As distinguished from common law, equity means to be flexible where the common law is rigid. Equity fashions remedies where the law is inadequate in order to do substantial justice. Also, refers to the separate equity court system developed in England and to the remedies fashioned by those courts. Many of these remedies have now been adopted by American courts. Thus courts have the broad power to order the equitable remedy of an injunction when money damages (the legal remedy) are inadequate.

Estoppel. An estoppel works a preclusion on the basis of a party's own act, or acceptance of facts, relied upon by another party. Thus, when a party makes a promise on which another relies, such a party may later be precluded from denying such a promise or refusing to accept its consequences.

Ex parte. Something done by, for, or on the application of *one party only.* An example of an ex parte proceeding is a hearing on a temporary restraining order. Such an order can be granted to a party in the absence of the party sought to be restrained.

Ex rel. Legal proceedings which are instituted by the attorney general in the name of and in behalf of the state, but on the information and at the instigation of an individual who has a private interest in the matter.

F

Federalism. The complex interaction between federal and state governments.

Felony. A serious crime, in contrast to a misdemeanor.

G

Gloss. An annotation, explanation, or comment on any passage in the text of a work for purposes of elucidation or amplification.

Grand Jury. A jury whose responsibility it is to decide whether probable cause exists to warrant the trial of an accused for a serious crime. A finding of probable cause is not equivalent to a finding of guilt. If the grand jury believes sufficient evidence exists to establish probable cause, it issues an indictment. The grand jury is termed a "grand jury" because it has more members than the trial or "petit" jury.

H

Habeas Corpus. "You have the body." Often called the "Great Writ" because it has been considered basic to liberty in American law. Typically, a writ of habeas corpus issues to order a warden or jailer to bring a prisoner before the court so that the court can determine whether the prisoner is lawfully confined. The writ can be used to secure review of a criminal conviction in the hope that the court will release the prisoner if it decides the prisoner is unlawfully confined.

Haec Verba. In these exact words.

Holding. The essential core of a judge's holding or a court's decision.

I

In camera. In a judge's chambers, or in a courtroom with the public excluded.

Indefeasible. A right that cannot be taken away or defeated.

Indictment. A written accusation made by a grand jury charging that the person named therein is accused of committing a crime. An indictment should be distinguished from an information (see below). Most jurisdictions require a grand jury indictment as the basis for charges of the most serious crimes.

Inducement. The benefit or advantage that the promisor is going to receive from a contract is the inducement for making it.

Information. The *information* is an alternate method by which a criminal prosecution can be commenced. In states which allow a prosecutor to proceed by information as an alternative to a grand jury indictment, a preliminary hearing is first held before a magistrate to determine if there is "probable cause" to believe that a crime has been committed. If the magistrate determines that, on the evidence presented by the state prosecutor, probable cause exists, the accused is bound over for trial and the prosecutor files an information which states the crime with which the accused is charged, serving substantially the same function as a grand jury indictment.

Infra. Refers to something printed later in the text. Used in the sense of "see below."

Injunction. A court-issued writ ordering a party either to refrain from doing something or to perform a specific act. When a court issues an injunction against a party, it *enjoins* that party. This equitable remedy is issued at the request of a litigant. An injunction may be granted temporarily to preserve the *status quo* while the issue in controversy is still pending before a court. This is called a preliminary injunction. A permanent injunction is granted only after a hearing on the merits.

In limine. On or at the threshold; at the very beginning; preliminarily.

Instanter. Immediately.

Inter alia. Literally "among other things"; Reference to only a part of something.

Interlocutory Appeal. An appeal of a judicial order in a case rendered by a court prior to final decision of that case. An order which is not final, or which is not dispositive of the entire suit, is interlocutory in nature. Interlocutory appeals, except for a few statutory exceptions, are not permissible in federal practice. But this rule is sometimes circumvented by application to appellate courts for prerogative writs such as writs of mandamus which in effect do subject interlocutory orders to appeal.

Interrogatories. Written questions submitted by one party to the opposing party before the trial. The opposing party is then required under oath to provide specific written answers to the interrogatories of the other party. Interrogatories are part of the discovery process used by counsel prior to the actual trial to inform each other of the basic facts and issues in the case. The interrogatories are usually written and answered by counsel after consultation with the client.

Ipse Dixit. To rely on one's own *ipse dixit* is to say something which rests not on independent evidence but solely on the say-so of the speaker.

J

Judgment. The final decision of the court defining the rights and duties of the parties to a law suit. A judgment should be distinguished from a verdict (see below) which is the name given to the decision of a jury rather than of a court.

Judgment n. o. v. (non obstante veredicto). A judgment notwithstanding the verdict occurs when the court renders a judgment in favor of one party after the jury has returned with a verdict in favor of the other party. When a motion for a judgment *n. o. v.* is granted, the judge in effect overrules the jury's verdict. The motion is usually granted on the grounds that the jury's verdict was clearly unreasonable and not supported by the evidence. This decision by the judge can be the basis for an appeal.

Judicial Activist. A judicial activist is the opposite of an exponent of judicial restraint. See this glossary. A judicial activist believes the judiciary may, in some circumstances, serve as a fulcrum for social change. The majority of the Supreme Court under the leadership of Chief Justice Warren, the so-called Warren Court, was often charged by its critics with judicial activism. The Warren Court, through the process of constitutional interpretation, imposed new rules and duties in the areas of reapportionment, racial equality, and criminal procedure. Defenders of these examples of judicial activism say that they illustrate the democratic character of judicial review.

Judicial Review. The invalidation or validation by courts of governmental action on the ground that that action is inconsistent or consistent with the Constitution.

Jurisprudence. The philosophy of law. Sometimes used as a synonym for law itself.

L

Long-arm Statute. A state law allowing its courts jurisdiction outside the state.

M

Malfeasance. Usually refers to wrongdoing by a public official.

Mandamus. A writ ordering a lower court judge or other public official to perform a legal duty as to which he has no discretion.

Memorandum Decision. A court ruling without written opinion or reasons given.

Misprision. A word used to describe a misdemeanor which does not possess a specific name. More specifically a contempt against the government or the courts, all forms of sedition or disloyal conduct; or maladministration of high public office; or failure of a citizen to endeavor to prevent the commission of a crime, or, having knowledge of its commission, to reveal it to the proper authorities.

Mistrial. A trial interrupted and concluded for a major procedural defect.

Model Acts. Laws proposed by the National Conference of Commissioners on Uniform State Laws.

Movant (Movent). One who makes a motion before a court; the applicant for a rule or order.

Moving Papers. Such papers as are made the basis of some motion in court proceedings.

N

Nolle Prosequi (nol. pros.). When the prosecuting attorney in a criminal suit decides that he will "prosecute the case no further", a *nol. pros.* is entered into the court records. The use of a *nol. pros.* usually terminates the lawsuit. Unless a *nol. pros.* is obtained with leave of court, the case will not be reopened at a later date; a *nol. pros.* usually signifies that the matter has been dropped altogether.

N.O.V. *Non obstante veredicto.* Notwithstanding the verdict of a jury the judge gives judgment to the other side.

Non-feasance. Usually failure of a public official to perform an assigned public duty.

Nunc pro tunc. Retroactive.

O

Obiter Dictum, or Dicta. Statements made in a judge's opinion that strictly speaking are not necessary to the decision of the court. These "statements by the way" are often responsive to some suggestion that is made by the case's facts or its legal issue, but are not themselves part of the court's holding. To characterize a statement in a judicial decision as "dicta" means that the statement does not have the precedential value of a statement which recites the holding of the decision.

Original Jurisdiction. Authority to try a case.

P

Per Curiam. When the opinion of a court of more than one judge is styled *per curiam,* what is meant is that the opinion is issued by and for the entire court, rather than by one judge writing for the court.

Peremptory. Conclusive, even if arbitrary, and requiring no explanation, e.g., peremptory challenges of prospective jurors.

Petitioner. The most common way of seeking review of a lower court decision in the United States Supreme Court is by petitioning for a writ of certiorari. The person who files the petition seeking review is called by the Court the petitioner. A person who petitions for any judicial relief such as a party who seeks other writs, such as mandamus is also called a petitioner.

Plaintiff. The party who brings the lawsuit. The party who complains.

Pleading. The written statements of the parties containing their respective allegations, denials, and defenses. The plaintiff's complaint and the defendant's answer are examples of pleadings.

Police Blotter. At the police station, the book in which a record is first made of the arrest of an accused person and the charges filed against her. Often used as a source for the journalist's report on the facts of the arrest.

Positive Law. Law enacted by a legislature.

Precedent. A judicial decision that is said to be authority for or to furnish a rule of law binding on the disposition of a current case. A precedent will involve similar facts or raise similar questions of law to the case at bar.

Preliminary Hearing. A hearing before a judge to determine if there is enough evidence to show that there is probable cause to justify bringing a person accused of crime to trial. In some jurisdictions, if probable cause is shown to exist at the preliminary hearing, the accused will be bound over to the grand jury.

Preponderance of Evidence. The standard of proof in civil as distinguished from criminal litigation. The greater weight of evidence, *i.e.,* that evidence which is more credible and convincing to the mind, and therefore entitled to be given probative value (to be believed as proven true) in a civil law suit.

Prima facie. On the face of it, e.g., a *prima facie* or presumptively winning case.

Public Law. Law defining the relationship between government and persons, and the operations of government, e.g., constitutional, administrative, and criminal law.

R

Ratio decidendi. The crux of a judge's decision.

Recusation. Process of disqualifying a judge for prejudice or a special interest in a lawsuit.

Remand. A remand is an order of a higher court directing the lower court to conform its decision to the mandates of the higher court.

Remittitur. When the jury awards the plaintiff excessive damages, the court may, in lieu of awarding the defendant a new trial, remit what it considers to be the excess, and award the remaining damages to the plaintiff. The judge gives the plaintiff the option of accepting the damages the court believes authorized by the evidence in the form of reduction of damages by a remittitur or else facing a new trial.

Replevin. A lawsuit instituted to reclaim private property held by another.

Res Judicata. Literally, the "thing judicially acted upon." This doctrine states the rule that a party cannot bring the same suit on the same facts against the same parties after these matters have already been decided once by a court. A party has only one "day in court" and once a case has been finally decided, he cannot bring the same suit again.

Respondeat Superior. The legal doctrine whereby the employer can be held liable for the torts of his employee committed in the scope of his employment. Thus, in a media setting, the publisher may be required to respond in damages for defamation perpetrated in his newspaper by a journalist in his employ.

Respondent. The term used to identify the party opposed to granting a petition. The party petitioning for judicial relief is the petitioner, her opponent is the respondent.

Respondent Superior. Legal rule making an employer responsible for actions of an employee while employed.

Restatement of Torts. A publication of the American Law Institute which attempts to state in a comprehensive way the modern common law of torts on the basis of both a study of the judicial decisions and what it believes to be sound policy. The ALI also publishes restatements on other areas of the common law, such as contracts or conflicts of law.

Reversed. This term found at the end of an appellate decision simply means that an appeals court has reversed or overturned the judgment of a lower court.

Reversible Error. A judicial error in law or procedures substantial enough to warrant an appeal.

S

Scienter. Guilty Knowledge. In some criminal prosecution, an allegation of scienter, or guilty knowledge, concerning the act or omission complained of, is a prerequisite to prosecution. Proof of scienter has often been an issue in obscenity prosecutions.

Sealed Records. The records of certain cases may be sealed, and closed from public view, by order of the court. Cases involving trade secrets, or juveniles, are examples of what a court might order sealed.

Sequester. To put aside, e.g., to lock up a jury.

Slip Opinion. A copy of a court opinion printed and distributed immediately after it is delivered.

Stare Decisis. Literally, to hold the decision. A doctrine intended to provide continuity in the common law system. The doctrine requires that when a court has developed a principle of law and has applied it to a certain set of facts, it will apply the same principle in future cases where the facts are substantially the same. The doctrine does not operate inexorably and in contemporary American law, particularly constitutional law, has not been the barrier to legal, and thus to social change as may have been the case in the past.

State Action. The necessity that there be governmental involvement in a matter in order for the standards of the Fourteenth Amendment to be operative.

Sua Sponte. To do something on one's own initiative. A term used when a court makes a ruling on its own even though the ruling has not been requested by counsel for either side.

Sub nom. When used in case citations, this abbreviation means that the same case as the previous case is being noted, but that it was decided on appeal under a *different name.*

Substantive Law. The basic law of rights and duties.

Sui generis. One of a kind.

Summary Judgment. A motion for summary judgment is a pretrial motion which will be granted when the pleadings, affidavits and discovery materials disclose that there is no issue of material fact in controversy between the parties. In that event, the only issues left to resolve are questions of law which can be decided by the court. Summary judgment, therefore, is a pretrial device which if appropriate for rendition will result in judgment to the successful party without the necessity of going through a trial.

Summons. A notice delivered by a sheriff or other official (or sometimes a private individual) to a person to inform him that he has been named as a defendant in a civil suit and must come to court on a certain day and answer the complaint against him.

Supra. Refers to something printed earlier in the text in the sense of "see above."

T

Tort. A civil wrong not based on contract. A tort may be accomplished with or without force, against the person or property of another. Typical torts include trespass, assault, libel, slander, invasion of privacy, or negligence. The same word used to identify a tort may also be used to identify a crime, but the two meanings will often be quite different. Relief is usually sought through a suit seeking money damages.

Tortfeasor. One who commits a tort. A wrongdoer.

Trover (Trover and Conversion). An action for the recovery of damages against a person who has found another's goods and has wrongfully converted them to his own use.

U

Ultra Vires. Acts beyond the scope of the powers of a corporation, as defined by its charter or act of incorporation.

V

Vel Non. (Latin for "or not"), *i.e.,* the issue is the validity *vel non* of this statute. (The issue is the validity or invalidity of the statute.)

Venireman. A member of a panel of jurors.

Verdict. The decision of the trial or "petit" jury. The jury reaches its verdict on the basis of the instructions given by the trial judge. The verdict may be a general verdict of "guilty" in a criminal case or a general verdict for either the defendant or the plaintiff in a civil case.

A special verdict consists of answers in the affirmative or negative to specific questions posed by the judge.

Viva voce. Orally rather than in writing.

Void. Without legal effect.

W

Writ. A judge's order requiring or authorizing something to be done outside the courtroom.

Writ of Prohibition. An extraordinary judicial writ from a court of superior jurisdiction directed to an inferior court or tribunal to prevent the latter from usurping a jurisdiction with which it is not lawfully vested, or from assuming or exercising jurisdiction over matters beyond its cognizance or in excess of its jurisdiction.

Index

LICENSE RENEWAL

LOBBYING

LOTTERIES

MAIL

MALICE (ACTUAL)

MASS MEDIA

MEETINGS AND RECORDS

†